W.L.

A NEW LANDLORD

A NEW LANDLORD
AND TENANT

PETER SPARKES, LL.B.,
The University of Southampton

HART PUBLISHING
OXFORD AND PORTLAND, OREGON
2001

Hart Publishing
Oxford and Portland, Oregon

Published in North America (US and Canada) by
Hart Publishing c/o
International Specialized Book Services
5804 NE Hassalo Street
Portland, Oregon
97213-3644
USA

Distributed in the Netherlands, Belgium and Luxembourg by
Intersentia, Churchillaan 108
B2900 Schoten
Antwerpen
Belgium

Hart Publishing is a specialist legal publisher based in Oxford, England.
To order further copies of this book or to request a list of other
publications please write to:

Hart Publishing Ltd, Salter's Boatyard,
Folly Bridge, Abingdon Road, Oxford OX1 4LB
Telephone: +44 (0)1865 245533 or Fax: +44 (0)1865 794882
e-mail: mail@hartpub.co.uk
WEBSITE: http//www.hartpub.co.uk

British Library Cataloguing in Publication Data
Data Available
ISBN 1–84113–022–2 (hardback)
ISBN 1–84113–023–0 (paperback)

Typeset by Hope Services (Abingdon) Ltd.
Printed and bound in Great Britain on acid-free paper by
Biddles Ltd, www.biddles.co.uk

CONTENTS

COMMERCIAL LEASES

TERMS OF COMMERCIAL LEASES

PREFACE

What on earth would Montaigne have made of our current law that governs the relationship of landlord and tenant? More than 400 years ago he stated his ideal as follows:[1]

> "The most obvious laws are those that are fewest, simplest, and most general; and I even think that it would be better to be without them altogether than to have them in such numbers as we have at present."

Our security of tenure codes create a system which is the exact reverse of his paradigm—hair-splitting, complex and multitudinous—so the question is how to make the subject at once accessible and precise.

This book continues the attempt begun in *A New Land Law*[2] to introduce more workaday terminology to property law. The traditional "ees" and "ors" are a severe impediment to accessibility to students approaching property law afresh, and how much more this must be true of landlords and tenants lacking formal legal training. Good law is law tailored to the needs of people who actually use it, and although modernisation of language alone cannot make the law reach out to its customers, it does help. Except in direct quotations from older sources, this book contains no lessors and no lessees, no demises, and most emphatically no chattels real. The glossary is provided primarily to assist new students, but it should also prove valuable to lawyers with conventional learning. Otherwise the conventions follow *A New Land Law*—gender neutral terminology (if "he" is accepted to stand for "he or she") and mortgage-lender in place of a mortgagee.

If there is one central truth of this book it is the fundamental distinction between long and short leases. Someone who wants to live in central London may have to pay more than £1 million to buy a lease of a flat and having done so he does not then regard himself as a tenant. His credit rating will be high and he will receive short shrift at the local social security office. So he needs to be treated as an owner, and terminology must be designed to mark out the difference between his position and that of a student renting a bed-sit for a few terms. This book places this distinction right at its centre in two ways. In structural terms the chapters are divided into sections on short residential letting, longer residential ownership leases, and commercial sector letting, of which more shortly. It also marks out the divide linguistically. A short residential letting is described throughout as a tenancy, the parties being a landlord and a tenant. The word "lease" is reserved for longer-term arrangements, and in particular for residential ownership arrangements where the term exceeds 21 years, the parties to such an arrangement being described as a ground-landlord and a leaseholder. One cannot take 21 years as an

---

[1] *Essays*, "On Experience", (Penguin Books 1958, ed. J.M. Cohen) 345.
[2] (Hart, 1999).

absolutely watertight division of the long and short sectors—since, for example, seven years is the crunch point for repairing obligations—but nevertheless 21 years is the most fundamental division. Above it the tenant has enfranchisement rights—that is the right to buy the freehold of a house or to take an extended lease of a flat. Below it, a private sector tenant has no rights to get at the freehold but has to be content with residential security of tenure (full or limited). Coherence would be greatly assisted if this existing schism were marked even more clearly by aligning other statutory regimes with a single cut–off point shorter than the present 21 years.

Commercial sector leases form an intermediate group, where the traditional flexibility of term is more marked: some are very long and some very short. Nevertheless most commercial leases are formal in character, and they are described throughout this book as leases—generally renewable business leases or agricultural leases—in defiance of Parliamentary Counsel's inappropriate choice of "tenancy" to describe this case. This reflects the formality and stability which are the usual characteristics of commercial lettings. In this book the parties are described as landlord and tenant. In both the residential and business sections I have separated out the chapters dealing with the basic structural nature of the term—that is the length of time for which it continues—from the chapters dealing with terms on which the land is held—rent, repairs, and restrictions on dealings. Security of tenure regimes are thus introduced at a much earlier stage than is conventional in most texts, since in my opinion they lie at the very core of the modern subject of landlord and tenant law. At first it seems logical to treat a lease chronologically—commencement, terms, and termination—but this appearance is skin deep; commencement, termination and security are intimately bound up with each other. My structure puts repossession where it should be as a reflection of the forfeiture of commercial leases. Both are means of terminating a lease for breach of its term.

Most treatments of tenant law lack a coherent skeleton because of the difficulty of knitting together the common law principles which developed up to the beginning of the twentieth century with the statutory regimes that have characterised the twentieth century. Practitioners texts which predate the twentieth century—such as *Woodfall* and *Hill and Redman*—inevitably take the common law principles first and bolt on the statutory regimes. The results are ideally suited to the need of specialists, who already have a good idea where to look for the answers to the questions of detail which interest them. Most of the dozens of shorter landlord and tenant texts adopt some variation on this theme—a general part with common law principles followed by analysis of statutory schemes. The author is not convinced that this approach is helpful to the innocent making a start in the subject. After all, the so–called "common law" principles are largely statutory—the Statute of Marlborough 1267 dealt with repair, the Grantees of Reversion Act 1540 with the running of covenants; modern forfeiture was largely a creation of the eighteenth century Acts and so too was the law of distress; compared to these early Acts the nineteenth century was a period of Victorian tinkering. A less egocentric and broader historical perspective requires us to see ourselves in the middle of a continuous process of statutory development of a single subject. All security of tenure regimes concentrate primarily on extending the duration of a lease—sometimes with superadded rent controls—so it is most appropriate to treat them along with the common law principles.

It follows from what has just been said that this book departs from the mainstream of landlord and tenant books by integrating its general part into the three basic types of tenancy—short residential, longer residential, and commercial—in the hope that this will reveal functions more clearly. It will be objected, and it is in a small part true, that this involves some duplication, but in fact the repetition is much less than one would imagine before the attempt is made. In relation to rent, to take one clear example, the rent regulation schemes have been allocated to the domestic sector, with forfeiture, distress, and rent review all allocated to the commercial—leaving a surprisingly trivial common core of principles. Repair shows even more clearly the domestic/commercial divide since statutory rules allocate to the landlord the cost of major structural work to a rented dwelling, leaving most of the case law on repairing covenants to be discussed in the commercial chapters. The domestic/commercial divide is greatly assisted by the modern perception that forfeiture is primarily an operative consideration in the commercial and longer residential leases, with only passing reference required in the early chapters on short residential tenancies.

A stroke of great good fortune has facilitated this reworking. It is a remarkable feature of the year 2000 that there is virtually no divergence of policy between the main political parties about the appropriate treatment of tenants. Potential authors have rarely had the luxury of reflection on a settled structure, without the need to respond to the latest legislative onslaught. This is not, coincidentally, a book about housing policy—it is hoped that the author's preconceptions have been buried to a sufficient depth to allow an objective examination of the law as it stands. Where reform is discussed it is of the technical kind rather than the political. This unexpected calm has encouraged me to integrate the existing statutory schemes in the private sector. Parliament has inexorably increased the number of schemes and sub-schemes, because the rights of existing tenants cannot easily be reduced. As the regimes have multiplied (and paradoxically at the same time divided) a serious problem of comprehension has developed. One can now enumerate a long list of types of tenancy before one even reaches the agricultural worker in his tied cottage—assured, protected, regulated, secure, assured shorthold, protected shorthold, and introductory. The provisions in the Housing Act 1996 about the last category are a particularly bad example of the legislative technique; 20 complete sections are devoted to the creation of a completely new regime for tenants in the public sector who are on probation for their first year. Surely all that was needed was one or two deft insertions in the public sector secure tenancies scheme? Add to all this the wide variety of tenancies at large in the social sector, and one ends up with more schemes than any one person can reasonably manage. Often a tenant does not know if he is an assured tenant or a regulated tenant. What he may know is that he is having trouble paying his rent. It is like a botanical classification that starts the search for a dandelion by asking whether it is a monocotyledon or a dicotyledon rather than from the point that one has a yellow flower spreading all over the lawn.

Coherence requires that we learn—to take one simple example—of the effect of non-payment of rent, as one simple whole rather than in 10 or 12 parts liberally sprinkled around the text. Even if the details of the grounds for repossession differ between the different regimes, the case law on one may impact upon the others, so that it all needs to be drawn together in one place. Hence this book is based on function rather than upon the operative residential regime. It cannot be said that every issue has fitted comfortably into the structure adopted in this book. No humanly devised system could reduce the law as it stands to order. But is it megalomania to believe, where the law does not fit this book, that it ought to do so? Reform is desperately needed so that simple answers can be given to simple questions.[3] Montaigne had it all summed up four and a half centuries ago when he wrote:

> "What have our legislators gained by picking out a hundred thousand particular cases and deeds, and attaching to them a hundred thousand laws? This number bears no relation to the infinite diversity of human actions. The multiplication of our imaginary cases will never equal the variety of actual examples."[4]

We deserve a code, and we need it to be simple.

I have attempted to state the law as it stands in the summer of 2000. Reference is made to reform proposals, especially on leasehold enfranchisement, termination of tenancies and commonhold, and the Green Paper published by new Labour. I have gritted my teeth and taken on the challenge of the Woolf reforms of civil justice, have torn up my chapter on licences to incorporate *Bruton* v. *London & Quadrant Housing Association Ltd.*[5] and another on agricultural leases to adapt to *Barrett* v. *Morgan*.[6] I have become immune to shock. Fortunately most cases have slotted in more easily—happy examples being *Southwark L.B.C.* v. *Mills*[7] on soundproofing flats, *de Rotschild* v. *Bell*[8] on the continuation of long tenancies, and *Metropolitan Police District Commissioners* v. *Palacegate Properties Ltd.*[9] on the exclusion of business security.

Very late on in the production of this book the Government published a White Paper setting out its proposals for commonhold and leasehold reform,[10] and even later on the Commonhold and Leasehold Reform Bill 2000 was introduced into the House of Lords on 22 December 2000. The chapters on long residential leases (Chapters 14 to 17) have been completely rewritten, and it has also been possible to slip in a reference to the homelessness changes in the Homes Bill 2000 and to the House of Lords decision on the rent capping order.[11] It remains to be seen whether the reforms will be enacted before the general election expected in May this year. The remainder of the book incorporates material available in Autumn 2000. It has not proved possible to incorporate all the current crop of human rights cases.

---

[3] The problem is acknowledged in the Housing Green Paper, *Quality and Choice: A Decent Home for All* (D.E.T.R., April 2000) para.5.7. A move towards a single tenure for public and social sectors (both described confusingly as "social" in the Green Paper) has been proposed by the Chartered Institute of Housing and is being considered by the Government: paras. 9.66–9.72.

[4] n. 1 above at 345.

[5] [1999] 3 All E.R. 481 H.L.

[6] [2000] 1 All E.R. 481 H.L.

[7] [1999] 4 All E.R. 449 H.L.

[8] [2000] Q.B. 33 C.A.

[9] [2000] 13 E.G. 187 C.A.

[10] *Commonhold and Leasehold Reform—Draft Bill and C.P.* (Cm 4843, August 2000).

[11] See below at p. 233.

The result of all this labour is dedicated to Helen, who has put up with far more than it is reasonable to ask during the making of this book.

New Forest
January 2001

GLOSSARY

Agricultural holding	A lease of agricultural land granted before September 1995 and protected under the A.H.A. 1986
Agriculture	Farming and similar activities; these exclude business protection
Assignment	A transfer of an existing lease; contrast a grant
Assured tenancy	A private sector residential tenancy granted since early 1989 under a market rent regime
Block	A building containing a number of flats
Business	Shops, offices, factories etc, but not agriculture
Charter	A guarantee issued by the Housing Corporation of the rights of a social sector tenant
Commercial	Non-residential; business or agriculture
Common parts	Parts of a block of flats used communally by a number of tenants
Commonhold	A proposed system of flat ownership which will allow flat owners to hold their individual flats freehold whilst regulating the management of the block and common parts
Control	A system of rent control for early residential tenancies where rents were a fixed multiple of the rateable value
Domestic	A synonym for residential
Dwelling-house	A building or part of a building which forms a separate home i.e. a house, flat or maisonette but not a caravan or houseboat.
Early 1989	15 January 1989 when the Housing Act 1988 came into force, and assured tenancies replaced Rent Act tenancies
Enfranchisement	The right for a long residential tenant of a house to acquire the freehold ownership, or of a flat to a long extension of his lease.
Fair rent	A rent adjusted to remove scarcity value
Farm business tenancy	A lease of agricultural land granted since September 1995 and protected under the A.T.A. 1995
Flat	A part of a block used as a home and marked out by horizontal divisions as well as vertical ones.
Fresh tenancy	A tenancy granted to a tenant which does not follow a tenancy granted to the same tenant
Full security	Life long security of tenure
Fully assured	An assured tenancy with life long security of tenure

Grant	The procedure by which a landowner grants lesser interest in his land e.g. a freeholder grants a lease; contrast a transfer
Ground landlord	A person who grants a long residential lease; his main right is usually to claim a ground rent.
Ground rent	A low rent charged under a long lease, the main value of the property having been taken by a premium when the lease is granted
Home	Where a tenant lives, including a dwelling-house, a caravan and a houseboat.
House	A part of a building used as a home marked out by vertical divisions
Housing association	A charity formed to provide low cost housing; most are registered social landlords
Landlord	A person who grants a short tenancy or lease (see also ground landlord); the person entitled to demand rent for the premises
Landlord condition	Defines public sector landlords, mainly local authorities
Lease	Not a tenancy; a longer term arrangement
Leaseholder	A tenant under a long residential lease whose rights equate to ownership e.g. the owner of a leasehold flat
Limited security	Less than lifelong security of tenure
Long residential lease	A lease initially granted for more than 21 years; when it expires the tenant can continue to occupy as an assured tenant; he may also have the right to enfranchise
Market rent	A rent fixed at the level demanded in an open market
Premium	A capital sum paid at the start of a lease to "buy" the use of the land
Pretence	A written document which does not reflect accurately the agreement between the parties to it
Private sector	Grants by landlords not satisfying the landlord condition
Protected tenancy	A Rent Act tenancy
Public sector	Grants by landlords satisfying the landlord condition, mainly local authorities
Rack rent	Where the full economic value of the land is charged as rent i.e. there is no premium
Rateable value	A value attached to an individual property for the purposes of imposing a rate; it was based on the letting value of the land. This now applies to commercial property only, but in the past rateable values were used to determine entitlement to residential security
Registered social landlord	Housing associations and other landlords registered with the Housing Corporation and qualified to receive social housing grants for building new homes

Regulated tenancy	A Rent Act tenancy during a contractual phase
Renewable business lease	A lease of premises occupied for business; when it ends the tenant has the right to a renewal under L.T.A. 1954 part II
Rent Act tenancy	Strictly a protected tenancy; a tenancy under the Rent Act 1977 usually with life long security and subject to fair rents. They were granted in the private sector until early 1989
Residential	A lease of a home
Reversion	The interest of a landlord
Right to buy	The right for a public sector tenant to buy the ownership of his home at a discounted price; social sector tenants may have a right to acquire
Service charge	A sum payable by a tenant of communally managed property (e.g. a flat in a block) for maintenance
Service occupancy	A home occupied by an employee as part of his duties
Social sector	Tenancies granted by housing associations and other registered social landlords
Statutory tenancy	A tenancy created by security of tenure legislation, particularly the Rent Act 1977
Successor tenancy	A tenancy granted to a tenant to replace an existing lease held by him
Surrender	The process by which a tenant gives up his lease to his landlord with the landlord's agreement, so ending the lease
Tenancy	A short lease, especially one granted to a short residential tenant. In this book the term is not used for business leases, though the legislation does refer to "business tenancies"
Tenant	A person who holds a lease; in the case of a long residential lease this is described as a leaseholder.
Tied	Accommodation provided by an employer
Transfer	The process by which a land owner (freehold or leasehold) passes his entire interest to a new owner; in the case of a lease this is generally described as an assignment

ABBREVIATIONS

A.H.A.	Agricultural Holdings Act
A.T.A.	Agricultural Tenancies Act
B.S.	Building Society
C.C.R.	County Court Rules (pre-Woolf)
C.Ct.	County Court
C.O.A.	Charging Orders Act
C.P.Am.R.	Civil Procedure (Amendment) Rules
C.P.R.	Civil Procedure Rules
C.P.R. sch.1 R.S.C.	Rules of the Supreme Court (post-Woolf)
C.P.R. sch.2 C.C.R.	County Court Rules (post-Woolf)
cond.	Condition
Div.Ct.	Divisional Court
F.L.A.	Family Law Act
H.A.	Housing Act
H.Ass.	Housing Association
H.C.C.C.J.O.	High Court and County Courts Jurisdiction Order
H.R.A.	Human Rights Act
I.A.	Insolvency Act
L.C.A.	Land Charges Act
L.G.H.A.	Local Government and Housing Act
L.P. (M.P.) A.	Law of Property (Miscellaneous Provisions) Act
L.P.A.	Law of Property Act
L.R.A.	Land Registration Act
L.R.H.U.D.A.	Leasehold Reform, Housing and Urban Development Act
L.R.R.	Land Registration Rules
L.Ref.A.	Leasehold Reform Act
L.T.A.	Landlord and Tenant Act
L.Tr.	Lands Tribunal
Law Com.	Law Commission
	C.P. = Consultation Paper
	W.P. = Working Paper
M.C.A.	Matrimonial Causes Act
M.H.A.	Matrimonial Homes Act
P.D.	Practice Direction attached to the C.P.R.
P.E.A.	Protection from Eviction Act

R.(Agriculture) A.	Rent (Agriculture) Act
R.A.	Rent Act
R.A.C.	Rent Assessement Committee
R.A.P.	Rent Assessment Panel
R.O.	Rent Officer
R.S.C.	Rules of the Supreme Court (pre-Woolf)
Reg.	Regulations
s.	section
S.	Settlement(s)
S.C.S.	Standard Conditions of Sale (3rd ed.)
S.S.	Secretary of State
subs.	subsection
T.	Trust(s)
T.L.A.T.A.	Trusts of Land and Appointment of Trustees Act

BOOKS FREQUENTLY REFERRED TO

Places of publication are in England unless otherwise stated.

Aldridge	T. Aldridge, *Leasehold Law* (Sweet & Maxwell, looseleaf)
Blackstone's Commentaries	Sir W.E. Blackstone, *Commentaries on the Laws of England* (chapters refer to any edition)
Bright & Gilbert	S. Bright & G. Gilbert, *Landlord and Tenant Law* (Clarendon, 1995)
Cheshire & Burn	G.C. Cheshire and E.B. Burn, *The Modern Law of Real Property* (Butterworths, 15th ed., 1994)
Coke on Littleton	Sir E. Coke, *Commentaries on Littleton's Tenures* (references are to any edition)
Davey	M. Davey, *Landlord and Tenant* (Sweet & Maxwell, 1998)
Dewar & Bright	J. Dewar and S. Bright, *Land Law—Themes and Perspectives* (Oxford, 1998)
Encyclopædia F.P.	Sir Peter Millett (ed.), *Encyclopædia of Forms and Precedents* (Butterworths, 5th ed., 1993 and reissues)
Evans & Smith	P.F. Smith, *The Land of Landlord & Tenant* (Butterworths, 5th ed. 1997)
Garner	S. Garner, *A Practical Approach to Landlord and Tenant Law* (Blackstone, 2nd ed., 1998)
Gray Elements	K. Gray, *Elements of Land Law* (Butterworths, 2nd ed., 1993)
Hayton, Registered Land	D.J. Hayton, *Registered Land* (Sweet & Maxwell, 3rd ed., 1981)
Holdsworth	W.S. Holdsworth, *History of English Law* (Methuen, 4th ed. in 15 vols, 1936)
Litteton's Tenures	Litteton's *Tenures* (paras. refer to any edition)
Megarry & Wade	Sir R.E. Megarry & Sir H.W.R. Wade, *The Law of Real Property* (Stevens, 5th ed., 1984)
Ruoff & Roper	T.B.F. Ruoff and R.B. Roper, *The Law of Registered Conveyancing* (Sweet & Maxwell, 6th ed., 1996)

Snell's Equity	E.H.T. Snell, *Equity* (Sweet & Maxwell, 29th ed. by P.V. Baker and P. St.J. Langan, 1990)
Sparkes, *N.L.L.*	P. Sparkes, *A New Land Law* (Hart, 1999)
Wolstenholme & Cherry	Wolstenholme & Cherry's *Conveyancing Statutes* (12th ed Stevens, eds B.L. Cherry, D.H. Parry & J.R.P. Maxwell, 1932); (13th ed., Oyez, ed. J.T. Farrand, 1972)
Woodfall	*Landlord and Tenant* (Sweet & Maxwell, eds K. Lewison et al., looseleaf).

TABLE OF CASES

Leading cases are given in **bold** type

COURT RULES

TABLE OF STATUTES

TABLE OF STATUTORY INSTRUMENTS

(excluding commencement orders)

1

RENTING

Housing tenure. Long and short leases. Full private sector security: controlled tenancies. Rent Act tenancies. Assured tenancies. Limited private sector security, Shortholds, Private landlords. Public housing, Public landlords. The social sector. Residential accommodation.

A. HOUSING TENURE

Three out of every ten dwellings are rented: of the 24 million dwellings in England and Wales in the year 2000 there are 17 million owner-occupiers, a term embracing both freeholders and long leaseholders, but this still leaves 7 million or so rented properties. Ireland and Spain have a substantially higher proportion of owners, but there are proportionately more tenants in other parts of Europe such as France and Germany. This is particularly true of the private rented sector.[1] Ownership in England and Wales has increased, from 10 per cent at the end of the First World War to 70 per cent at the end of the twentieth century, leaving the rented sector still accounting for 30 per cent of homes. A residue of households will never buy, either because they do not wish for the commitment involved or because they will be never be able to afford to buy—the pool of potential renters is estimated at 30 per cent of the total of households. If this is a fair guess, it seems to suggest that there is currently an equilibrium between owners and renters.

Renting is divided between three sectors, according to the type of landlord making the accommodation available. Legislative controls developed first for the private sector (1915), were extended successively as a replacement for council tenancies in the public sector (1980) and to registered social landlords (present scheme 1996).

Until the First World War 90 per cent of homes were rented from private landlords, but the proportion of property rented in this way declined markedly throughout the twentieth century.[2] Local authorities held a negligible role before that War (less than 1 per cent) but the promise to those returning from the trenches of the Western Front that they would have "homes fit for heroes" was largely met by public sector provision, the dominant position of councils being reinforced by the building programme before and after the Second World War. Public tenure is concentrated, predictably enough, in the urban areas of London, Yorkshire, Manchester and Merseyside, the West Midlands, the

---

[1] *Quality and Choice: A Decent Home for All; The Housing Green Paper* (D.E.T.R., April 2000) para.5.2.
[2] Bright & Gilbert chs.1–2; Davey 189–205; D. Englander, *Landlord & Tenant in Urban Britain 1838–1918* (Clarendon, 1983); J. Burnett, *A Social History of Housing* (Methuen, 2nd ed. 1985).

North East and South Wales. A period of public sector provision of new homes drew to a close in 1980 as the catastrophic social effects of 1960s estates and tower blocks became apparent and as a result of the Government's economic policies. Enactment of the right to buy in 1980 resulted in the removal of 1.5 million of the best homes from the public sector during the last 20 years of the twentieth century.

Housing associations were first formed in the 1860s, but they had a small role in the English housing market until 1980 or so, when the government decided to stimulate the social sector in a deliberate attempt to curtail local authority power by reducing the role of councils as the providers of public housing. Between 1991 and 1996 the social sector grew by 65 per cent. Housing associations still predominate, but legislation in 1996 allowed grants for the provision of social housing to be made to other corporate land-lords, so that the social sector now consists of lettings by registered social landlords.

Figure 1 Table of housing tenure[3]

Housing stock tenure % of landlords by category						
	1914	1957	1971	1981	1991	1996
Owner-occupiers	10	31	52	58	68	69
Public	0.2	17	29	28	19	17
Social				2	3	5
Private rented	90	52	19	11	10	9

This table conceals the scandalous fact that almost 4% of all homes lie empty.[4]

B. SHORT AND LONG LEASES

Residential leases are either long or short. The basic characteristic of the short residen-tial sector is that the tenant is renting, usually paying the full value of the land monthly or weekly, and the landlord is an investor exploiting a house that he does not require for his own occupation to realise its market letting value. The parties to such an arrange-ment are called in this book the landlord and the tenant and their agreement is described as a tenancy.

Long residential leases are totally distinct in function, since the lease is a form of own-ership much more akin to a freehold than to renting; the "tenant" pays a substantial capital sum to buy the lease and only a minimal rent (a "ground rent") to retain his own-ership. Indeed, this form of tenure is under attack and is gradually being converted to freehold ownership through statutory rights of enfranchisement and the introduction of commonhold tenure, though the process may take centuries to complete. In this book

---

[3] English House Condition Survey (D.E.T.R., 1996) ch.1.
[4] para 1.13.

the parties to such an arrangement (called a lease) are referred to as the *ground landlord* and the *leaseholder*. This is intended to differentiate them from a *tenant* who is renting from a *landlord*. The two sectors are formally distinguished by the length of the initial contractual grant; a long lease is one for a term exceeding 21 years or for life; the precise definition is considered in later chapters of this book.[5]

C. FULL PRIVATE SECTOR SECURITY

Security of tenure implies protection against contractual termination of an existing tenancy. The landlord must serve notice to quit, take court proceedings and prove a ground for possession.[6] Full security implies that a tenant who pays the rent punctually and otherwise behaves himself will usually be entitled to stay indefinitely.

1. Control and decontrol

In order to curb the tendency towards inflation during war-time, rent controls were introduced as an emergency measure by the first "Rent Act"—the Increase of Rent and Mortgage Interest (War Restrictions) Act 1915. Peacetime saw the development of rent controls twinned with security of tenure—the now familiar statutory tenancy was devised by the Increase of Rent and Mortgage Interest (Restrictions) Act 1920. Controls were reduced successively in 1923 and 1933, but a new system of control was extended to most unfurnished lettings in 1938. In the period after the Second World War, Labour governments saw the retention or strengthening of control, while decontrol took place during Conservative governments, notably in 1957. No new controlled tenancies were allowed after 1965 when the more modern system of regulated Rent Act tenancies was introduced. Controls were bitterly opposed by landlords because the rent, set as a multiplier of the Rateable Value of the property, was very restrictive, and to their collective delight controlled tenancies were finally abolished in 1980.[7] These pre-modern Rent Acts bequeathed to us the basic structure of the modern residential tenancy legislation—including the restriction to self-contained residential accommodation and the concept of the statutory tenancy to step in when the landlord terminates the contractual arrangement—as well as much of the basic case law. These old Rent Acts presided over a period in which the proportion of homes rented from private landlords declined from 90 per cent to 30 per cent. It would not be fair to conclude from that statistic alone that the legislation was misconceived, since the main operative factors were the rise of owner-occupation and the provision of superior council accommodation. However, what the rent restriction legislation did was to reduce the economic return to the landlord to such an extent that it ceased to be worthwhile to make property available to rent.

2. Rent Act tenancies

The modern scheme of regulated tenancies based on fair rents was introduced by the Rent Act 1965, the subsequent legislative history including a consolidation in 1968, the

---

[5] See below Chapters 14 and 15.
[6] See below Chapter 13.
[7] H.A. 1980 s.64. The terms of converted controlled tenancies are regulated by R.A. 1977 s.18A, sch.17.

inclusion of furnished tenancies balanced by the exemption of resident landlord tenancies in 1974, and the present consolidation in 1977. The Crown Estate and Duchies were moved into control in 1980.[8]

A Rent Act tenancy is one granted by a private sector landlord before early 1989[9] and operating as a protected tenancy under the Rent Act 1977.[10] During the contractual period it is called a regulated tenancy; after termination of contractual protection it becomes a statutory tenancy; both classes together are described as protected tenancies. In this book the description "Rent Act tenancy" is used. A protected tenant enjoys "lifelong" security of tenure and succession rights. Most Rent Act tenants are now elderly, because new protected tenancies are not permitted after the Housing Act 1988.[11] The shift to assured tenancy in early 1989 made little difference to the security of tenure available, but it had a fundamental impact on the rent regime: a Rent Act tenant can insist on registration of a fair rent, a procedure which imposes a cap on the recoverable rent. At first, market rents under the new assured system were dramatically higher, but Rent Act fair rents have gradually increased since early 1989 so that the gap has narrowed.[12] "Full" security of tenure under the two schemes was broadly comparable, though there is an increasing likelihood that a grant will only be for a short hold.[13]

Succession rights sometimes allow a surviving spouse or other family member to take over the tenancy on the death of the previous tenant. Two schemes apply, according to the date on which the tenancy was granted, with the tenant's rights being reduced in early 1989.[14]

3. Fully assured tenancies

Given the century long game of tug of war played out between the two main political parties over housing policy, it is a remarkable fact that there is no longer any significant difference in the housing policy of the two potential parties of government. The fundamental tenets are straightforward. Private sector tenancies are short-term rental arrangements (shortholds) with no security of tenure beyond that agreed contractually between the parties. Rents are fixed by the market, the only intervention with free market economics being to prevent excessive claims to housing benefit. However, when this Thatcherite settlement was reached by the Housing Act 1988[15] it was on the basis that pre-existing security would remain unaffected. Hence the vital significance of the watershed when that Act came into force on January 15th 1989—throughout this book referred to as "early 1989". Only if a fresh contractual grant was made after that date will

---

[8] H.A. 1980 s.73, sch.8, as from November 28th 1980.
[9] See below p. 4 n. 14–p. 5 n. 17.
[10] Woodfall ch.23; Davey 249–286; Evans & Smith (5th) ch.17; Garner (2nd) ch.13.
[11] H.A. 1988 s.35; Woodfall 24.080–24.087.
[12] See below pp. 227–234.
[13] See below Chapter 3.
[14] H.A. 1988 s.141(3); see below at pp. 115–123.
[15] H.A. 1988 ss.1(1), 34, sch.1 para.1; D. Hoath [1989] *J.S.W.L.* 339; [1990] *J.S.W.L.* 18; M. Davey (1989) 52 *M.L.R.* 6611; C.P. Rodgers [1988] *Conv.* 122; W. Hickman [1993] *N.L.J.* 1271.

a tenant fall, reluctantly, into the assured tenancy[16] regime;[17] he is then subject to a market rent regime. If it is fully assured (as opposed to a shorthold), the tenant will enjoy "lifelong" security of tenure, broadly comparable to that under the Rent Acts, though succession rights are markedly inferior for post-1989 tenancies.[18]

4. Successor tenancies

Human rights principles prevent retrospective interference with property rights, so that new legislative schemes have left existing tenants to enjoy their existing security rights.[19] If tenancy 1 was Rent Act protected, so are replacement tenancies 2, 3 and 4,[20] so that contractual renewals do not affect security regimes provided that they all involve the same landlord, the same tenant and the same property.[21] It is necessary to trace the tenancy back to the date of the original grant in order to discover which security of tenure regime applies.

A break in the chain is possible if the tenant gives up his tenancy to his landlord by agreement (in technical terms a surrender of the existing tenancy) where this is followed by a regrant of a new tenancy. In this way a Rent Act tenancy could be replaced by an assured tenancy either a fully assured or an assured shorthold. Tenants are protected against harassment and threats used to secure an agreement to give up a tenancy,[22] but only fraud can invalidate a completed transaction by which a tenant has signed away his right to full security. Failure to give a warning is not fraud. Figures suggest a decline in Rent Act protected tenancies from 1 million in 1988 to just over 300,000 in 1994–5, with a 40 per cent drop in the first year alone.[23] So it is clear that many tenants did indeed surrender existing security rights.

D. LIMITED PRIVATE SECTOR SECURITY

1. Shortholds

The long period of Conservative government between 1979 and 1997 saw a progressive reduction in security of residential tenure, so that it is now abnormal for a tenant in the private sector to enjoy life-long security.[24] In 1980 it became possible to limit the security of a private sector tenant to a fixed contractual period of one year—a form of tenancy called a protected shorthold—and this became increasingly popular in the years from 1980 to early 1989.[25] At that date, a new scheme of assured shortholds was

---

[16] An old model of assured tenancies introduced in 1980 for purpose built properties or purpose built conversions by approved landlords. Very few were created, and any that were have been converted to assured tenancies of the new model: H.A. 1988 ss.1(3), 37.

[17] Woodfall ch.24; Bright & Gilbert 233–257; Davey 206–248; Evans & Smith (5th) ch.18; Garner (2nd) ch.18.

[18] H.A. 1988 s.141(3).

[19] J. Driscoll [1991] 36 *L.S.G.* 17.

[20] *Thalmann* v. *Evans* [1996] 2 C.L.Y. 3788.

[21] H.A. 1988 s.34(1)(b) (grants after early 1989 to existing Rent Act tenants); s.34(1)(c) (where alternative accommodation ordered by court). The categories are exclusive: sch.1 para.13.

[22] See below Chapter 12.

[23] J. Driscoll [1996] *N.L.J.* 1699, 1700, citing Green, Thomas, Iles and Dawn, *Housing in England 1994/95* (H.M.S.O., 1996).

[24] J. Morgan [1996] *J.S.W.F.L.* 445.

[25] See below Chapter 3.

introduced. These confer security for a short fixed period of at least six months but no long-term security. As from early 1997 a landlord has to elect positively to create anything other than a shorthold by giving notice.[26] It is unlikely that a private sector landlord will do so. Security is limited to any contractually agreed term of occupation, with a minimum of six months, and rents are charged at market rents.

2.   Limited residential security

Full security follows only when a tenant has exclusive rights to self-contained accommodation. Without that occupiers have strictly limited security of tenure, including people sharing accommodation, and people whose accommodation is serviced or supported by nursing and welfare staff: these are licensees like hotel guests or residents in hostels. Some tenants also have limited rights including students in halls of resident or people renting holiday accommodation. So too do occupiers of caravans, houseboats and shacks that do not form a part of a building.[27]

E.   PRIVATE LANDLORDS

The assured tenancy scheme introduced in early 1989 is based on limited private sector security and market rents. Has it been a success? It is submitted that it can be given only qualified approval.

Clearly one basic objective was to make renting more attractive to private landlords, and in that it has indubitably succeeded. The fair rent regime and long term security of the Rent Acts severely depressed the capital value of rented properties and so acted as a disincentive to invest in houses to rent. After all, a landlord sees any tenanted property primarily as a source of income, and if the returns are improved then more will choose to make property available for letting. For one thing the assured tenancy regime has stimulated the creation of a flourishing sub-sector for lettings of premium quality accommodation. For another it seems to have encouraged investors to come into the normal letting market. When the Rent Act 1977 gave way to the Housing Act 1988, one survey[28] found that the majority (63 per cent) of private landlords were individuals not resident themselves at the property they were renting out, one tenth were property companies (9 per cent), a small percentage were individuals who were letting out part of their own house (though other surveys give much higher percentages), and 21 per cent were employers. A similar survey today would find a much larger group of commercial and institutional investors. Their presence is essential to revitalise the market and establish a healthy market in the long term,[29] and for this reason the new Labour Government is committed to the retention of the assured tenancy regime it inherited from the Conservatives, aiming to improve the incentives for institutional investment.[30] During

---

[26]   H.A. 1988 s.19A, sch.2A.

[27]   See below Chapter 6.

[28]   Rauta & Pickering, *Private Renting in England 1990* (H.M.S.O., 1992).

[29]   According to the Green Paper, *Quality and Choice: A Decent Home for All* (D.E.T.R., April 2000) para.5.9, roughly half of landlords own seven houses or less and a quarter have only one; many people become landlords by inheritance or other accident.

[30]   The Green Paper, *Quality and Choice: A Decent Home for All* (D.E.T.R., April 2000) paras.5.18–5.22.

the early 1990s Business Expansion Schemes provided an input of investment to the sector.

Buying property to let suddenly became cool in the later 1990s, because when interest rates settled at an historically low level it became realistic to borrow money to buy a house which could then be let out at a rent that exceeded the instalments needed to repay the mortgage. The Association of Residential Letting Agents scheme launched in 1996 identified a panel of lenders prepared to lend on the same terms to landlords as to owner-occupiers and the number of lenders prepared to lend on these terms has increased considerably since then. There is a government sponsored arbitration scheme to resolve disputes between landlords and their letting agents.[31] It is said that in 1999, the average gross yield (that is the aggregate rents) was 8–9 per cent of the cost of the house, even in a static rental market, with a net yield 2 per cent lower. Clearly the returns fluctuate from time to time. Rental yields might be 1.3 times the monthly mortgage instalments. From this margin has to be deducted income tax and capital gains tax, and the cost of maintenance to the standard that is required by the market. Letting agents reduce the risks by conducting credit checks on tenants, dealing with maintenance, and keeping close control of void periods when the property is not let. The fee for these services is typically 10–15 per cent of the gross rent. Buying to let is a dangerous short-term investment, but in the medium term a landlord who has chosen a property wisely may expect to see the property increase in value along with the general inflation in house prices. Any increase will be subject to capital gains tax when it is realised.

For a short time in 1999 it seems that tenants were in the driver's seat, since the influx of property on to the market through buy to let schemes had created an excess of supply, especially as many potential tenants took advantage of the low interest rates to buy. However, booming house prices throughout 1999–2000 seem likely to lead to a further distortion to the market, since the returns from renting will be much reduced if the capital value of the property increases, and it will be easy to evict insecure shorthold tenants in order to sell. In short the market rent regime has bonded the private rental sector even more tightly to fluctuations in the housing market. It provides high quality flats at high rents, but is not a sustainable way to provide affordable housing to those who are unable to buy. The assured tenancy regime may prove to be only a short-term fix for the problems of the private rented sector.

The Government is considering whether tax changes could stimulate the private rented sector further.[32]

F.   PUBLIC LANDLORDS

1.   Public provision

The Housing of the Working Classes Act 1890 gave power to local authorities to build houses for renting, but in the absence of financial assistance from the government few had been built by the outbreak of the First World War in 1914: there were only 28,000 public homes. Large-scale building occurred between the Wars (900,000) with a further

---

[31] National Approved Letting Scheme launched by the Minister, Hilary Armstrong, in January 1999.
[32] The Green Paper, *Quality and Choice: A Decent Home for All* (D.E.T.R., April 2000) paras.5.23–5.25.

massive expansion after the Second World War. In 1979 some 32 per cent of all English[33] homes were in local authority ownership. Unfortunately many of these were on shoddy estates or in system built blocks of flats. Large estates have failed as basic units of social organisation. It has become apparent that much cheap housing had been thrown up without consideration of its habitability, and many estates have had to be knocked down; Glasgow is just one authority straining under the debts incurred in building homes which are no longer standing. Local authority ownership declined through the period of Conservative government which stretched from Mrs Thatcher's rise to power in 1979 to 1997. Partly this was the result of restrictions on capital spending which limited new building. Problems were exacerbated by the fact that the "Right to Buy"[34]— however valuable to those tenants who have acquired their homes under it—has stripped the public sector of all its desirable homes since 1980, leaving behind properties that are unsaleable and unlettable.

The Housing Green Paper gives us a snapshot of the position in early 2000.[35] Of those living in social housing (including tenants of public sector council landlords) it shows that only 23 per cent are in full time employment, the majority being retired (38 per cent), unemployed (8 per cent) or otherwise economically inactive.[36] One million fewer people now live in social housing than in 1977 as a result of the depletion of the stock by the right to buy.[37] So it has now become a tenure of last resort.[38]

2.   Secure tenancies and the "landlord condition"

Until recently local authorities had enormous power by virtue of their position as monopoly providers of low cost housing, which was free of any judicial intervention, for example in the removal of tenants. This supreme power has been broken: controls have been introduced over the initial allocation of public housing,[39] and administrative law has been developed to allow judicial review of almost any step taken by a housing authority. However termination of a lease or a licence[40] is a private law decision not susceptible to public law control.

Private and public sectors are distinguished by the landlord condition,[41] which apportions grants of rented accommodation between two discrete sectors. Within it, public sector landlords grant secure tenancies under the Housing Act 1985 that confer "life-long" security of tenure, whilst outside it lie private landlords who grant assured shorthold tenancies and social landlords.[42] This provision of security of tenure has caused a marked shift in power towards tenants.

---

[33] Scotland has a much higher proportion of public housing: H.W. Wilkinson [1980] *Conv.* 302.

[34] See below Chapter 18.

[35] *Quality and Choice: A Decent Home for All; The Housing Green Paper* (D.E.T.R., April 2000) paras.6.1–6.11.

[36] para.6.2.

[37] para.6.5.

[38] para.6.12

[39] See below Chapter 4.

[40] *Tower Hamlets L.B.C.* v. *Abdi* (1992) 25 H.L.R. 80 C.A.; *R.* v. *Westminster C.C. ex parte Parkins* (1995) 68 P. & C.R. 253 C.A.

[41] ss.80, 114; Woodfall ch.25; Bright & Gilbert 257–269; Davey 307–333; Evans & Smith (5th) ch.19; Garner (2nd) ch.19.

[42] R.A. 1977 s.14; H.A. 1988 sch.1 para.12.

Legislation in 1980[43] first created the concept of the secure tenancy, which applied to all new grants by public sector landlords and also tenancies which existed when the legislation was introduced,[44] though excluding any tenancy that had been terminated contractually on the commencement date of the new legislation.[45] Clearly it was felt that the courts provided the proper forum for decisions about the loss of housing.[46] The current consolidation of the secure tenancy scheme is in part IV of the Housing Act 1985.[47]

Most housing authorities are district councils or London borough councils.[48] They have a general oversight of housing standards and power to take action against unfit, overcrowded, and substandard housing. They also have powers to build new housing stock[49]—widely and unwisely exercised in the past, but rarely exercised at all today because capital spending restrictions make it difficult for authorities to find the funds for building. However, the primary focus of this book is on the role of authorities as providers and allocators of housing.[50] Authorities select their own tenants, granting secure tenancies from their own housing stock, and they also nominate tenants to social landlords. If a grant is originally in the private sector, it will switch to become a public sector secure tenancy if events occur which mean that the immediate landlord fulfils the landlord condition, for example where a private landlord is himself a tenant and he surrenders his lease to a local authority as the head landlord.[51]

Three special solutions to particular housing problems also fall within the public sector as defined by the landlord condition. New Town Corporations are set up to build such communities as Milton Keynes and remain large-scale owners of public housing provision.[52] Urban development corporations control areas of towns and cities designated for large-scale urban renewal, current ones are in London Docklands, Merseyside, the Black Country, Teeside, Trafford Park, Manchester, Tyne & Wear, Sheffield, Cardiff Bay, Birmingham Heartlands and Plymouth.[53] Housing Action Trusts (H.A.T.s) are established by ministerial order[54] to take over ownership of the public housing stock[55] and the role of public sector landlords in run down areas[56]—the object being to secure the repair and management of the housing stock, and the improvement of living conditions of the tenants;[57] planning, public health, and highway functions are often

[43] H.A. 1980 part I ch.2.

[44] *Kingston on Thames L.B.C.* v. *Prince* (1999) 31 H.L.R. 794 C.A. (letting in 1979 became secure in 1980).

[45] *Harrison* v. *Hammersmith & Fulham L.B.C.* [1981] 1 W.L.R. 650; P.H. Kenny [1981] *Conv.* 89.

[46] At 666, Waller J.

[47] Law Com. No.144 (1985) (consolidation); Woodfall ch.25.

[48] H.A. 1985 s.1.

[49] s.9. The council may build houses out of its own district, though overspill from London requires ministerial approval: s.16.

[50] A further separation of the authorities' wider strategic role and their role as public sector landlords is proposed by the Green Paper, *Quality and Choice: A Decent Home for All* (D.E.T.R., April 2000) paras.3.1–3.6. It envisages the creation of management companies operating at arm's length from the local authority with power to borrow, more borrowing by local authorities, and the continuation of the private funding initiative.

[51] s.109A; *Basingstoke & Deane B.C.* v. *Paice* (1995) 27 H.L.R. 433 C.A.

[52] New Towns Acts 1946, 1959, 1981.

[53] Local Government, Planning & Land Act 1980 pt.XVI.

[54] H.A. 1988 part III ss.63–86.

[55] ss.74–79.

[56] The local authority itself controls housing action areas, general improvement areas, slum clearance areas (H.A. 1985 parts VIII–IX) and renewal areas (L.G.H.A. 1989 part VII).

[57] H.A. 1988 s.63.

transferred to the H.A.T.[58] They have not proved to be popular. Tenants of housing co-operatives will fall back into the public sector if the landlord ceases to be registered as a social landlord.[59]

3.   Right to buy

Public sector tenants have the right to buy their homes at a discount. The right was first given in 1980, and now appears in the 1985 consolidation of the housing legislation.[60] The right to buy has proved a great boon to tenants living in desirable housing who are both qualified and able to afford to buy: more than 1.6 million homes were sold at knockdown prices, raising £7 billion for the Treasury.[61] However, its tendency has been to concentrate single parents and the poor in residual unsaleable accommodation,[62] and local authorities have not benefited from the capital raised.

4.   Introductory tenancy

The Housing Act 1996 made a number of changes of detail to the public sector scheme, and one that is more fundamental. Local authorities may choose to adopt the introductory tenancy scheme for their area, and if they do so new tenants are effectively put on probation for one year. During that time the local authority may decide the tenant is unsuitable and if it does the court is bound to order his eviction, though there are administrative procedures to challenge such a decision.[63]

G. SOCIAL SECTOR

Registered social landlords currently control property assets worth £22 billion and have 1.3 million tenants.[64] They will never be able to take over all responsibility for the provision of cheap housing, but their role is ever increasing. Public grants are provided for new building and conversion of existing housing, but the Government also envisages large-scale transfers of derelict estates to the social sector.

1.   Housing associations

These are the most common form of social landlord. Some associations were formed in the mid nineteenth century, but their collective significance as a sub-sector of the letting market developed when housing association rents were controlled in 1972 and statutory definition soon followed.[65] A few large professionally organised housing associations (8 per cent) control large numbers of properties (75 per cent), but there are innumerable small associations with fewer than 25 units.

---

[58] ss.66–69.

[59] H.A. 1985 s.80(1), (3), (4).

[60] See below Chapter 18; tenants of registered social landlords may have a right of acquisition.

[61] The Green Paper, *Quality and Choice: A Decent Home for All* (D.E.T.R., April 2000) paras.4.34–4.36, gives the figure of 1.3 million sales in England and Wales; it says that the cost to the state was roughly £10,000 for each property.

[62] The pace of sales has slackened now that most of the desirable homes have gone.

[63] H.A. 1985 ss.127–128; *Manchester C.C.* v. *Cochrane* (1999) 31 H.L.R. 810 C.A.; see below p. 319.

[64] *Regulating a Diverse Sector* (Housing Corporation, October 1999) para. 2.2.

[65] H. Finance A. 1972; H.A. 1974 s.1; Bright & Gilbert 40–47.

A housing association must be a corporate body or a body of trustees with the object of providing, constructing, improving or managing housing accommodation.[66] It must not trade for profit, and registration as a social landlord will only be allowed to a body already registered as a charity.[67] Many housing associations are fully mutual, so that membership is restricted to tenants, and any person wishing to become a tenant must first become a member of the association. Co-operative housing associations (a category including many self build societies) are also registered as industrial and provident societies.[68] Registered social landlords are entitled to seek state assistance with the cost of providing housing.

2. Other social landlords

Individuals are not eligible to receive social housing grants, but the Housing Act 1996[69] extends the social sector beyond housing associations and industrial and provident societies; now included for the first time are charitable corporations, so that they may qualify for social housing grants and this is intended to facilitate the provision of new build social housing.

A problem currently exercising the Housing Corporation as regulator is how to ensure that activities do not become too diverse.[70] The core functions of any registered social landlord should be provision of low-cost housing, including general needs housing, use of short life property for the homeless, the management of local authority housing stock, community regeneration, running residential care homes or social care services, or providing low cost home ownership. Other activities are accepted if they do not exceed 5 per cent, but beyond that threshold of diversity the Housing Corporation will wish to ensure a business strategy is in place to regulate additional functions. Regulations[71] prescribe the activities that are permitted which include the provision of loans to people wishing to buy,[72] and now also the provision of services and amenities to non-residents as well as residents.[73]

3. Registered social landlords

Social landlords are registered by the Housing Corporation.[74] In Wales, the corresponding function has been transferred from Housing for Wales to the housing "minister" of the Welsh Assembly.[75] Registration is a necessary precursor to applications for

[66] H. Associations A. 1985 ss.1, 2; H.A. 1996 s.230; J. Driscoll (1996) 140 *S.J.* 1224; J. Alder (1997) 1 *J.H.L.* 35.

[67] H.A. 1996 s.2(1)(a).

[68] Industrial and Provident Societies Act 1965; J. Alder [1988] *Conv.* 187, 254. This is no longer essential; H.A. 1996 s.57.

[69] ss.2(1)(b)–(c), 57; conditions are set out in s.2(2)–(3).

[70] *Regulating a Diverse Sector* (Housing Corporation, October 1999).

[71] H.A. 1996 s.2(4); S.Is. 1996/592, 1996/2256; *Halifax B.S.* v. *Chamberlain Martin Spurgeon* (1995) 27 H.L.R. 123, Arden J.

[72] S.I. 1999/985; C. Handy & J. Alder [1998] 1 *J.H.L.* 133; the S.I. reverses *Sutton L.B.C.* v. *Morgan Grenfell & Co. Ltd.* (1997) 29 H.L.R. 608 C.A.

[73] S.I. 1999/1206.

[74] H.A. 1996 ss.1–5, sch.1; this replaces H. Associations A. 1985 part II. See also R.A. 1977 ss.13–16, s.5A; H.A. 1988 sch. 1 paras.11–13.

[75] Government of Wales Act 1998 s.143; S.I. 1999/61; H.A. 1988 s.46 (old law).

social housing grant.[76] Something like 50 per cent of the cost of social housing is provided by the Government. Funding is conditional upon some degree of public control over the housing stock provided with it and in particular the local authority has nomination rights over the allocation of 50 per cent of new tenants.[77] Current rules prevent the payment of benefits and the provision of accommodation to board members, employees, and their relatives.[78] However, it is arguable that the current rules are too strict, and consultation is under way on a possible relaxation to allow board members and relatives to be given homes—provided that they meet the letting criteria and do not participate in the allocation decision, and that no suitable alternative accommodation is available.[79] The Housing Corporation has a general supervisory power over the constitution of registered social landlords, their accounts, audit procedures, and insolvency,[80] as well as power to conduct special inquiries.[81] There are disclosure requirements, league tables,[82] controls, and ministerial guidance.[83]

4.   Housing association tenancies (1974 to early 1989)

Housing association tenants never enjoyed full Rent Act security of tenure,[84] but the Housing Finance Act 1972 imposed fair rent controls.[85] In 1980 this was supplemented by full public sector security of tenure, since housing associations were public landlords and their tenants became secure tenants. Tenancies remain secure if originally granted before 1989 even if there is a contractual regrant; such tenants also enjoy rights under the Secure Tenant's Charter.[86] In early 1989 future grants of housing association tenancies were prohibited[87] at which time there were ½ million fair rent units held from 2,672 housing associations. Many have now been regranted in the social sector.

5.   Grants by social landlords since early 1989

For the purposes of security of tenure, housing associations were shifted from the public to the private sector early in 1989.[88] Fresh tenancies granted by social landlords after 1989 are assured, but with additional rights under the Assured Tenant's Charter. This is because the "landlord condition"[89]—which defines the public sector—now excludes any tenancy held from a registered social landlord, though the fact that this condition is applied continuously makes it possible for a tenant to move back into the public sector when a co-operative housing association ceases to be registered, or otherwise into the purely private sector. The Housing Corporation dictates the tenure, the rents, and other

---

[76] H.A. 1996 ss.18–21, 27–28.
[77] See below p. 66.
[78] s.7 and sch.1 part I; ss.56–64 (definitions).
[79] Consultation Document (Housing Corporation, August 1999).
[80] H.A. 1996 ss.39–50.
[81] ss.3–6 and sch.1 parts II–IV.
[82] ss.30–35.
[83] ss.36–38, 52–55.
[84] R.A. 1977 s.15.
[85] Now R.A. 1977 part VI; Davey 195, 299–301.
[86] Housing Corporation, 1998.
[87] H.A. 1988 s.35; some successor tenancies are also secure.
[88] H.A. 1988 s.140(2) sch.18; Housing White Paper Cm 214 (1987) para.4.6.
[89] H.A. 1985 s.80 as amended by H.A. 1988 s.83 and S.I. 1996/2325.

rights of social tenants, and in particular insists that registered social landlords should grant tenancies with a full assurance, that is full security of tenure.[90] Assured shortholds are acceptable in short life property only where a person is being assessed for suitability for a long-term grant[91] and licences only for serviced accommodation where a private landlord could legitimately make such a grant. The theoretical market rent regime[92] is moderated by the expectation that social landlords should charge "affordable" rents— roughly 20 per cent below market rents—so as to be accessible to people on low income including those in low paid employment,[93] but with the rider that social landlords must balance costs. A voluntary ombudsman scheme (H.A.T.O.) to deal with complaints has now been made statutory.[94]

6. Large scale voluntary transfers

Not even the homeless will live on some of the worst public sector estates. The best solution is often to transfer the estate out of the public sector to a housing association, possibly formed for the purpose, which is then encouraged to renovate the estate with social grants. New Labour is pressing authorities to accelerate the speed at which failing estates are hived off,[95] and the rate of transfers is increasing.[96]

7. Right to acquire

Removal of housing association tenancies from the public sector early in 1989 did not affect the right of existing tenants, who remain secure tenants and have the right to buy their homes.[97] When homes are removed from the public sector under a voluntary stock transfer, rights to buy are preserved.[98] There is also a right of acquisition conferred on a social tenant occupying a home newly built, bought or converted in or after April 1997.[99]

H. RESIDENTIAL AND COMMERCIAL LEASES

1. Commercial sectors

Residential tenancies need to be distinguished from commercial leases, and the two sub-sectors—business and agricultural. A particular lease falls into one or other of these three groups.[100] Although some businesses own freehold property from which they trade, it is the usual practice to lease premises for use as offices, shops, or for industrial

---

[90] *Housing Applicant's Charter* (Housing Corporation, 1998) Section 4.

[91] *Code of Practice on Tenure* (Housing Corporation, October 1999) para.4.1.

[92] H.A. 1985 s.81(1) as amended by H.A. 1988 s.83.

[93] *Assured Tenant's Charter* (Housing Corporation, 1998) Section 3.

[94] H.A. 1996 s.51, sch.2; also the Charters e.g. *Assured Tenant's Charter* (Housing Corporation, 1998) Section 10; *Grammer* v. *Lane* [2000] 2 All E.R. 245 C.A.

[95] *Guardian*, November 10th 1999.

[96] R. Brown [1999] 06 *L.G.C. Supp.* 4–5. The Green Paper, *Quality and Choice: A Decent Home for All* (D.E.T.R., April 2000) paras.7.11–7.34, proposes improvements in the process and stamp duty relief, and sets a target of 200,000 transfers each year.

[97] H.A. 1985 part V; *Secure Tenant's Charter* (Housing Corporation, 1998) Section 8.

[98] A preserved right to buy; *Assured Tenant's Charter* (Housing Corporation, 1998) Section 8.

[99] A right of acquisition: H.A. 1996 ss.16–17; *Assured Tenant's Charter* (Housing Corporation, 1998) Section 8.

[100] See below Chapters 20 and 22.

uses. Business tenants have much less protection than is given to residential tenants, but the one important protection is the right to a renewal at the market rental when their lease expires. This ensures that landlords cannot exploit the value attached to trading from a particular business address, that is the goodwill built up by a business. Trevor Aldridge calls such a lease a "renewable business lease"[101] and that terminology is adopted in this book. A lease of a shop is clearly commercial, but the chapters on business leases also include discussion[102] of the problems that arise from mixed lettings: is a lease of a shop with a flat above residential or commercial? Also considered in that context are leases of domestic property used for commercial ends, such as a lease of an entire block of flats for commercial exploitation by the tenant by renting out single flats to individual tenants.

Agricultural leases are distinct from residential. Leases of farms, grazing land, orchards and market gardens are clearly agricultural, but again there is an area of mixed letting where a house is let with a small paddock or orchard; these problems are discussed in the context of agricultural leases.[103] There are also highly technical provisions about tied cottages let to former agricultural workers.[104]

2.   Residential tenancies

The residential category embraces shortholds, public sector secure tenancies, full security in the private sector, as well as arrangements with restricted security such as licences, the common characteristic being that the property is used as the tenant's home. But if a lease is commercial in character, the tenant will be excluded from residential security; his lease will be a renewable business lease, an agricultural holding, or a farm business tenancy. There are many gaps, so that a particular tenancy may fall between all stools, and in the absence of security of tenure legislation the tenancy is left to terminate under common law principles. Thus if a householder rents a garage near his house in which to park a private car, the lease is neither residential nor commercial.

There is no neat definition of the residential sector. One boundary is put in place by the requirement that the lease should affect a dwelling house.[105] Another factor is the purpose of letting, since the property must be *let as* a dwelling,[106] though residential protection may accrue where the use becomes residential with the authorisation of the landlord. In addition, there is the requirement that the tenant must maintain residential occupation.[107] Dispute is particularly likely where a property is used for a mixed purpose that includes both residential and commercial elements, for example a lease of a shop and flat above, or a cottage set on farmland. Broadly, the schemes for residential and commercial letting are exclusive and in this book the allocation of mixed lettings is considered in the commercial context.[108]

---

[101] *Leasehold Law* (Oyez, 1989).
[102] See below pp. 549–551.
[103] See below Chapter 7.
[104] See below Chapter 7.
[105] R.A. 1977 s.1; H.A. 1985 s.112; H.A. 1988 s.1(1).
[106] R.A. 1977 s.1 etc, as above.
[107] R.A. 1977 s.2; H.A. 1985 s.81; H.A. 1988 s.1(1)(b); see below pp. 104–109.
[108] See below pp. 549–551.

3. Lettings of multiple units

A lease of a block of flats or a terrace of houses is obviously commercial in character. It is not intended that the tenant should occupy them all as his home, but rather that he should exploit the property let to him by renting out individual units to residential sub-tenants. In general, therefore, a lease of property consisting of multiple dwellings does not attract residential security, but falls within the business lease scheme. Thus if a head landlord lets a whole block of flats, the tenant enjoys no security. When he begins to divide the block by sub-letting individual flats, then the residential security legislation may bite, since security is afforded to a tenant who rents an individual residential unit, though full protection for the sub-tenant will depend upon the division being authorised by the head lease.[109] There could be no policy justification for protecting a lease of a group of houses or of a block of flats which does not form the tenant's home but is a form of investment vehicle, and such a lease is commercial in character.[110] Exclusion from the residential scheme is a result of the requirement that a residential lease must involve a lease of *a separate* dwelling. Thus the tenancy should be intended to provide one (and only one) unit of habitation.[111] Identification of the unit should take place as at the date of the tenancy, so that a lease of a whole building divided into multiple units will not attract statutory protection, whereas a lease of one house that is later divided may do so.[112]

[109] See below Chapter 11.
[110] See below pp. 549–551.
[111] *St Catherine's College Cambridge* v. *Dorling* [1980] 1 W.L.R. 66 C.A. (no protection for furnished house divided to provide separate accommodation for 5 undergraduates); *Grosvenor (Mayfair) Estates* v. *Amberton* [1983] 1 E.G.L.R. 96 C.A. (letting of 2 flats, one occupied by 3 licensees; not let as a single dwelling.)
[112] *Regalian Securities Ltd.* v. *Ramsden* [1981] 1 W.L.R. 611, 614, Lord Russell.

2

CONTRACTUAL DURATION

Fixed term tenancies. Periodic tenancies. Informal short-term tenancies. Longer formal tenancies. Proprietary status. Overriding interests. Surrender.

According to Lord Hoffmann, leases and other interests in land are four dimensional. This chapter explores the fourth dimension—time.[1]

A. FIXED TERM CONTRACTUAL SECURITY

1. Long leases and leases for life

The short residential sector is demarcated by the short term of the initial grant. If it exceeds 21 years, a legal lease is registrable[2] and a residential tenant may enjoy enfranchisement rights,[3] whereas shorter tenancies fall into the various regimes for residential security of tenure. Any lease granted for life or determinable with life or until marriage is converted by statute into a 90-year term and hence falls into the long residential sector.[4]

2. Fixed terms

Tenants are commonly given rights to their home for a fixed initial period—perhaps a month, six months, one academic year, or several years. During this time the tenant does not need to rely on security of tenure, since his right to retain occupation of the home is based on his contract with his landlord.[5] Of course, the same holds good in reverse: a tenant is bound to pay rent for the duration of the contractually agreed term.

English law is remarkable for the flexibility it allows in the creation of a lease. Provided only that a maximum duration is specified, the law imposes no limit on how long it may be. Or how short. The "term of years absolute" includes a

"term for less than a year or for a . . . fraction of a year . . .".[6]

---

[1] *Newlon H.T. v. Alsulaimen* [1999] 1 A.C. 313, 317C, Lord Hoffmann.
[2] See below pp. 382–385.
[3] See below Chapter 15.
[4] L.P.A. 1925 s.149(6).
[5] Bright & Gilbert 122–126; Davey 17–21.
[6] L.P.A. 1925 s.205(1)(xxvii).

The fraction could be a few months, or weeks, a holiday letting for a week,[7] or even a timeshare for one week each year,[8] and why not a lease for one day to watch a Royal procession or a concert?[9]

3. The commencement date

Short residential tenancies are usually worded to start on the day on which the tenant is to take occupation, though commercial leases commonly run from an earlier date.[10] Residential codes of security will generally take as their basis of calculation the actual length of the tenant's enjoyment of the land.[11]

4. Shortholds

Many private sector tenancies created since early 1989 have been assured shortholds.[12] Statutory protection is provided for a fixed period of six months from the date of the initial grant, a period which the landlord is not able to break during the good behaviour of the tenant. But this short period runs only once and it is not renewed by a contractual regrant. Additional security can be negotiated by an agreement to grant a fixed term exceeding the six months or by a renewal of an existing term. Until 1997 a landlord could only take advantage of the guaranteed right of repossession at the end of a shorthold if he granted an initial contractual term of at least six months, but this requirement is now removed for a section 19A shorthold[13] so that under current law an assured shorthold can be for one month, or three months, or even weekly or monthly. For the first six months the contractual rights of the tenant are supplemented by his right to a short hold. Any fixed term security in the public sector has to be negotiated with the landlord—since there is no concept of a shorthold—but most tenancies in the public sector are periodic.

5. Certainty

Legal status is reserved by section 1(1) of the Law of Property Act 1925 for leases creating a term of years absolute. The force of the word "absolute" is to require that the *maximum* duration of a tenancy (like any other lease) must be fixed in time. The end might be a fixed date or fixed by reference to an event which is certain in the sense that the latest date on which the event can take place is known when the lease is to take effect in possession. Thus:

To T for 2 years; or

To T until the next General Election.

If statute provides for a General Election every five years, this last has a maximum term, though the tenancy may well not last for the full five years. However, any tenancy is

---

[7] In this case the tenant will not have any additional security; see below pp. 167–168.

[8] *Cottage Holiday Associates* v. *Customs & Excise Commissioners* [1983] Q.B. 735; M. Haley (1995) 24 *Anglo-American* 236.

[9] Licences have generally been used: *Krell* v. *Henry* [1903] 2 Q.B. 740 C.A.

[10] See below pp. 517–518.

[11] *Roberts* v. *Church Commissioners for England* [1972] 1 Q.B. 278 C.A. (enfranchisement tests).

[12] For details see below Chapter 3.

[13] H.A. 1988 s.19A, inserted by H.A. 1996 s.96; see below pp. 45–46.

invalid if the term is not marked out with certainty. Both prospective and retrospective certainty may create problems. The former is the greater vice. It must be clear in advance when a lease is granted how long the lease is to last, so that English law does not accept a grant for undefined periods of time, such as:

To T until England achieves world domination at football;
or (more likely in practice)
To T (a builder) until he has been paid for renovation work.[14]

Lace v. *Chantler* concerned a tenancy "furnished for duration"—that is for the duration of the Second World War—which was held to be uncertain and void.[15] When it was granted, say in 1940, no one could know for how many years the war would last. The House of Lords has now unanimously approved this same test in *Prudential Assurance Co. Ltd.* v. *London Residuary Body,* in which a lease to continue until land was required for widening Walworth Road in South London was held to be uncertain and void.[16] The rule is discussed at length in the commercial context.[17]

B. TERMINATION OF FIXED CONTRACTUAL SECURITY

A valid fixed term tenancy is created if the *maximum* duration of the lease is stated and, provided that this is so, legal status is not removed simply because the term may be cut short. A term of years is absolute despite being:

> "liable to determination by notice, re-entry, operation of law, or by a provision for cesser on redemption, or in any other event (other than the dropping of a life or the determination of a determinable life interest) . . .".[18]

Few leases are so "certain" that the term is fixed rigidly in advance, and almost all residential tenancies allow early termination in stated circumstances.

1. Break clauses

Landlords may reserve the right to terminate a fixed contractual term by notice, but such provisions are rare and of limited value in residential tenancies, since a break merely brings into play the tenant's security of tenure. However, there may be a value in allowing a break where the landlord will have a ground for possession, for example if he intends to reconstruct a property let on an assured tenancy.[19] Most modern residential tenancies are assured shortholds, with a guaranteed holding for six months, and a break would not be allowed within the first six months. There is more sense in allowing a *tenant* to break a long fixed term, especially one who has no right to transfer his tenancy, since he could then end his liability to rent by notice, and the landlord could relet. Break

---

[14] *Canadian Imperial Bank of Commerce* v. *Bello* (1991) 24 H.L.R. 155 C.A. (holding this term to be valid) was overruled in *Prudential Assurance* below.

[15] [1944] K.B. 368 C.A.; (1944) 60 *L.Q.R.* 219.

[16] [1992] 2 A.C. 386 H.L.; P. Sparkes (1993) 109 *L.Q.R.* 93; P.F. Smith [1993] *Conv.* 461; S. Bridge [1993] *C.L.J.* 26; S. Bright (1993) 13 *L.S.* 38; D. Wilde (1994) 57 *M.L.R.* 117; M. Biles [1994] *N.L.J.* 156; M. Haley (1995) 24 *Anglo-American* 236.

[17] See below pp. 512–517.

[18] L.P.A. 1925 s.205(1)(xxvii). For leases for life see below pp. 363–365.

[19] See below p. 351.

clauses are much more common in commercial leases and are considered in that context.[20]

2.   Termination for misconduct by the tenant

Where a tenant is given a contractual grant for a fixed period it is important to include a provision that the tenancy can be ended if the terms of the agreement are not observed—this will certainly include non-payment of rent and service charge, annoyance of neighbours, failure to observe restrictions on use, and unauthorised sub-letting and dealings. It is also common to provide for the landlord to be able to recover possession on the tenant's bankruptcy—and this seems to be effective as a termination event despite the inconvenient effects on the residential bankruptcy code.[21] Hostile termination of a commercial fixed term lease requires a forfeiture,[22] but with a residential tenancy forfeiture is rarely a useful description of the act of terminating a lease for breach of a covenant, and is often positively inaccurate. A distinction has to be drawn between Rent Act tenancies and assured tenancies. A fixed term **Rent Act** tenancy must contain a provision for it to be ended on breach of the particular covenant—so a contractual termination event is essential. Termination can occur by proceedings,[23] in the course of which a ground for possession is proved and a reason is shown why the court should exercise its discretion to order possession. Contrast the process of forfeiture under which the landlord shows a breach of a forfeiture clause, obtains an order for possession, and the court then has a discretionary power to grant relief to the tenant. So with the Rent Acts, the procedure is essential for residential repossession, but this may be laid over an underlying forfeiture, so that in some circumstances a tenant may have two defences to a repossession: he may be able to claim a stay of forfeiture proceedings or (if he loses that) have the right to stay in his home under a suspended possession order because it is not reasonable to make an outright order.[24]

During a fixed term of an **assured tenancy**, termination can only occur if the lease provides for termination on the particular event,[25] but if so the procedure followed is that for residential repossession, and it is not a forfeiture.[26] Special provision is made for the forfeiture in the public sector of a **fixed term secure tenancy**: an order for forfeiture becomes an order for termination which brings to an end the fixed term and gives rise to a periodic tenancy;[27] the landlord would then have to prove a ground of possession. These more modern schemes described in this paragraph are more satisfactory than what went before.

---

[20] See below pp. 582–583.
[21] *Halliard Property Co. Ltd.* v. *Jack Segal Ltd.* [1978] 1 W.L.R. 377; *Paterson* v. *Aggio* [1987] 2 E.G.L.R. 127 C.A.; *Cadogan Estates Ltd.* v. *McMahon* [1999] 1 W.L.R. 1689 C.A. [2000] Times 1 November H.L.
[22] See below pp. 113–115
[23] P.E.A. 1977 s.2.
[24] See below pp. 330–331, 815–829.
[25] H.A. 1988 s.5(1); termination must be by court order: s.5(2). No periodic tenancy arises if the tenant has some other contractual right, such as an option for renewal: s.5(4).
[26] *Artesian Residential Developments Ltd.* v. *Beck* [1999] 3 All E.R. 113 C.A.
[27] H.A. 1985 s.82(3).

3.   Effluxion of time and holding over

If a tenancy of a home is not cut short and so continues until the period of years reserved by the lease has run out, it ends by effluxion of time,[28] but this will merely trigger the statutory security of tenure.[29]

C.   PERIODIC TENANCIES

1.   Express creation

Many residential leases are periodic tenancies. The term of years absolute is defined[30] so that it "includes a term . . . from year to year". A yearly tenancy is initially granted for one year, but on the basis that the tenancy can continue to grow by one year at a time, indefinitely,[31] subject always to the possibility that it can be brought to an end by a proper notice. Older authorities took one year as the archetypal period, no doubt because that was normal for agricultural tenancies, but monthly or weekly tenancies are usual in the residential sector and any longer or shorter period could be used. Negotiation might lead to an expressly created period of a calendar month or periods of 28 or 30 days, or indeed some random time such as 47 days. If the period is stated expressly it is not relevant to consider how the rent is calculated. Oral creation of the tenancy is allowed provided the initial period of the lease is for less than three years.[32] It is also common to combine a fixed contractual period with a periodic successor so that, for example, a tenancy

for a year and so on from year to year

is for a minimum duration of two years—the one year of the fixed term followed by the first year of an annual tenancy.

2.   Implied creation

Periodic tenancies are most often implied from the fact that rent is paid and accepted while a tenant is allowed possession of land to the exclusion of the landlord without any other arrangement. While the holding is against the wishes of the landlord, the tenancy is at sufferance—that is it is a tolerated trespass—but acceptance of the tenant by the landlord converts the tenancy to one at will. According to Littleton:[33]

> "Tenant at will is where lands or tenements are let by one man to another, to have to hold to him at the will of the lessor, by force of which lease the lessee is in possession . . . the lessee is called a tenant at will because he hath no certain or sure estate, for the lessor may put him out at what time it pleaseth him."

---

[28]   Woodfall 17.002–17.007; *Newlon H.T.* v. *Alsulaimen* [1999] 1 A.C. 313, 317E, Lord Hoffmann.

[29]   See below pp. 109–113.

[30]   L.P.A. 1925 s.205(1)(xxvii); *Hammersmith & Fulham L.B.C.* v. *Monk* [1992] 1 A.C. 478, 483–484, Lord Bridge.

[31]   Hence the odd rule that a yearly tenant can create a sub-lease for 99 years: *Pennell* v. *Payne* [1995] Q.B. 192 C.A.; query whether this is logical, given that the tenancy is only for a single year when looked at prospectively.

[32]   L.P.A. 1925 s.54(2); longer periods call for a deed; see below pp. 33–34.

[33]   Littleton, *Tenures,* book I, ch. VIII.

Without a contractually agreed term, the tenant is always vulnerable, as indeed the name of the tenancy at will suggests, to a change in the whim of the landlord. It seems that a tenancy at will may enjoy residential protection from eviction.[34]

Even if tenancies at will may be created expressly,[35] they much more commonly arise after a prospective tenant has been let into occupation without any formal arrangement or while negotiations for a full lease proceed. Modern case law suggests that a commercial tenancy may continue to be at will even after the tenant has offered rent and the landlord has accepted it,[36] but whether residential security of tenure can be avoided during negotiations in this way is more doubtful; it seems likely that a tenancy at will is itself a form of tenancy protected by the Rent Act and the more modern residential codes.[37]

Normally at least, the consequence of the payment of rent[38] would be to create a periodic tenancy when the money was accepted by the landlord, acting deliberately,[39] and this will ensure that a tenant who did not hitherto enjoy security of tenure will do so in future. Contracts to evade security of tenure are prohibited.[40] Creation of a tenancy may be inferred from a demand for rent or the payment and acceptance of rent by reference to a particular period, where the payment has no other explanation. A tenant holds for four years if he enters the property let to him and begins to pay rent calculated quarterly as prescribed by his lease but, if no particular term had been agreed, payment of rent in this way would lead to the implication of a quarterly tenancy. Periodic tenancies also arise where a person is allowed exclusive occupation of land with no fixed term, where a lease fails because of want of formality, or after a grant for an uncertain fixed term.[41]

What period is implied if none is expressly agreed? Early authorities suggested that it was always a yearly tenancy, but this doctrine has now been refined so that, today, the period implied follows the method by which the rent is calculated. In *Ladies' Hosiery & Underwear Ltd.* v. *Parker* the example was given, *obiter*, of a tenant holding over at the expiration of a three-year term at rent of £2 per week, which, in Maugham J.'s opinion, led to a weekly tenancy.[42] Conversely *Prudential Assurance Co. Ltd.* v. *London Residuary Body*[43] was calculated at the yearly rate of £30, payable quarterly, an arrangement which led to the creation of a yearly tenancy.

---

[34] P.E.A. 1977 s.5 (which requires 28 days' notice to quit a dwelling) does not apply: *Crane* v. *Morris* [1965] 1 W.L.R. 1104 C.A.

[35] *Wheeler* v. *Mercer* [1957] A.C. 416 H.L.; pretences can be ignored or reformed: *British Railways Board* v. *Bodywright* (1971) 220 E.G. 651.

[36] See below pp. 173–174.

[37] See below pp. 109–113.

[38] Isolated payments may be ignored: *Thompsons (Funeral Furnishers) Ltd.* v. *Phillips* [1945] 2 All E.R. 49 C.A.

[39] Not if rent is accepted by mistake: *Maconchie Bros. Ltd.* v. *Brand* [1946] 2 All E.R. 778; *Sector Properties Ltd.* v. *Meah* (1973) 229 E.G. 1097 C.A. Nor from a computer generated demand issued in error: *Dreamgate Property Ltd.* v. *Amot* (1998) 76 P. & C.R. 25 C.A.

[40] *Re Land and Premises at Liss, Hants* [1971] Ch. 986.

[41] *Prudential Assurance Co. Ltd.* v. *London Residuary Body* [1992] 2 A.C. 386 H.L.; Blackstone's *Commentaries* (1st ed., 1766) vol.2, 147; *Dossee* v. *Doe d. East India Co.* (1859) 1 L.T. 345 P.C.; *Meye* v. *Electric Transmission* [1942] Ch. 290.

[42] [1930] 1 Ch. 304, 325 (a tedious and complex case despite its promising name); the point was left open on appeal.

[43] [1992] 2 A.C. 386 H.L.

3.   Certainty of periodic tenancies

Uncertainty is inherent in the very nature of a periodic tenancy. Initially for only one period, it will roll on from period to period until one or other of the parties takes action to bring it to an end by notice. Looked at in retrospect a monthly tenancy may have lasted for 50 years, but for the future it is for one month only.[44] Nevertheless an element of certainty can be discovered in the fact that the maximum commitment of either party can be fixed at any moment by the service of notice. As Professor Gray has said:

> "each occupational unit of time, as it is added to the preceding unit of time, is itself of strictly defined duration."[45]

Hence a periodic tenancy was perfectly valid at common law and continues to be so in modern law.

D.   TERMINATION OF PERIODIC TENANCIES

1.   Nature of notice to quit

A periodic tenancy has no set length when it is created, since it can be allowed to run on indefinitely, the parties being content to start on the basis that either of them may end the tenancy by notice at any time in the future. Every periodic tenancy must be terminable by notice.[46] The effect of giving notice is that when the period of notice ends the tenancy ends with it by effluxion of time, since this is the end of the time for which both parties are prepared to continue it; the notice is not dispositive.[47]

The nature of a notice to quit has recently been considered in *Barrett* v. *Morgan,* a case which requires detailed consideration in the context of agricultural leases and also in the context of notices to quit head tenancies and their effect on sub-tenants.[48] Lord Millett said[49] that:

> "A periodic tenancy comes to an end on the expiration of a notice to quit served by the landlord on the tenant or by the tenant on the landlord. [I]t comes to an end by effluxion of time. In each case the tenancy is determined in accordance with its terms. [T]he parties have agreed at the outset on the manner of its determination. The parties and their successors in title, including those who derive title under them, are bound by their agreement."

The House of Lords drew a sharp distinction between a notice to quit which is non-consensual and a surrender which is. This is because a notice to quit operates under the terms of the original tenancy agreement and does not require the agreement of the other party.

If the landlord gives notice it is called a **notice to quit**. Sometimes the landlord genuinely wants possession, but at other times the notice to quit is simply a vehicle to secure

---

[44] *Re Midland Railway Co.'s Agreement* [1971] Ch. 725, 732F–G.

[45] *Elements of Land Law* (1987) 437; *Hammersmith and Fulham L.B.C.* v. *Monk* [1992] 1 A.C. 478, 484E, Lord Bridge; *Bacon's Abridgment* (7th ed.) vol.4, 839.

[46] Woodfall 17.196–17.269; Davey 127–134; Evans & Smith (5th) 232–236.

[47] *Newlon H.T.* v. *Alsulaimen* [1999] 1 A.C. 313, 317E, Lord Hoffmann.

[48] [2000] 1 All E.R. 481 H.L.; see below at pp. 298–301, 618–620.

[49] At 484j–485a.

a rent increase or a variation in the terms, so there is no objection to a notice to quit containing an offer of a new tenancy.[50] In theory a notice by the landlord ends the tenancy at the time set out in the notice, but very frequently a landlord's notice will not be effective to give him a right to possession because its only effect will be to trigger statutory security of tenure. Service of a notice to quit by the landlord is a binding election to terminate, rather like a decision to forfeit, and the notice cannot be withdrawn unilaterally.[51] If the tenant wishes to leave, he may give a **notice of his intention to quit.**

2. Restrictions on notice to quit: repugnancy and uncertainty

Some periodic tenancies provide that the landlord may not serve notice until a particular condition is satisfied. Such a clause gives rise to twin concerns of repugnancy and uncertainty.

A particular term may be rejected because of an inconsistency with the nature of the periodic tenancy of which the term forms a part (that is **repugnancy**), whether the term is express or implied. At first no term could relate to a time after the end of the very first period of the tenancy. Thus a yearly tenancy could not include a covenant to paint every three years,[52] or to give two years' notice to quit,[53] or to do substantial repairs.[54] Modern law takes this view only in prospect, when looking forward at the beginning of the periodic tenancy. After the lease has lasted for a number of years, terms can be enforced if they apply to the time when the tenant has actually been in occupation, including all terms at the end of the tenancy.[55] Notice provisions are forward looking, so that logically it should not be possible to require a longer period of notice than the period of the tenancy.[56] But *Breams Property Investment Co. Ltd.* v. *Stroulger*,[57] allowed a provision restricting service of notice for a fixed term of three years even though this was longer than the basic period of the lease, and this novelty is now confirmed by the Court of Appeal[58] and by Lord Templeman in the House of Lords.[59] The result is convenient, but a clause still becomes repugnant if the landlord can never terminate the lease.[60]

However any fetter has to be for a fixed period of weeks, months or years. *Prudential Assurance*[61] swept away any doubts expressed in *Re Midland Railway Co.'s Agreement*[62] and reasserted the need for **certainty** of a periodic term. The decision to the reverse in the *Midland Railway* case has since been overruled. Prospective certainty was,[63]

---

[50] *Ahearn* v. *Bellman* (1879) 4 Ex.D. 201 C.A.

[51] *Lower* v. *Sorrell* [1963] 1 Q.B. 959 C.A.; R.E. Megarry (1963) 79 *L.Q.R.* 178; D.G. Barnsley (1963) 27 *Conv. (N.S.)* 335; A. Dowling [1994] *Conv.* 437 (prefers the Irish view which permits withdrawal).

[52] *Tooker* v. *Smith* (1857) 1 H. & N. 732, 156 E.R. 1396.

[53] *Pinero* v. *Judson* (1829) 6 Bing. 206, 130 E.R. 1259.

[54] *Doe d. Thomson* v. *Amey* (1840) 12 Ad. & El. 476, 479, 113 E.R. 892.

[55] *Pistor* v. *Cater* (1842) 9 M. & W. 315, 152 E.R. 134; *Adams* v. *Clutterbuck* (1883) 10 Q.B.D. 403, 406.

[56] *Tooker* v. *Smith* (1857) 1 H. & N. 732, 156 E.R. 1396.

[57] [1948] 2 K.B. 1; D.C. Potter (1948) 11 *M.L.R.* 342.

[58] *Re Midland Railway Co.'s Agreement* [1971] Ch. 725 C.A.

[59] *Prudential Assurance Co. Ltd.* v. *London Residuary Body* [1992] 2 A.C. 386, 395A.

[60] *Centaploy* v. *Matlodge* [1974] Ch 1, Whitford J.; *Midland Railway* [1971] Ch. 725, 733F, Russell L.J.

[61] [1992] 2 A.C. 386, 395G, Lord Templeman.

[62] [1971] Ch. 725 C.A.; D. Macintyre [1971] *C.L.J.* 198; (1973) 89 *L.Q.R.* 457.

[63] *Browne* v. *Warner* (1808) 14 Ves. 156, 158, 33 E.R. 480, Lord Eldon; *Doe d. Warner* v. *Browne* (1807) 8 East. 165, 103 E.R. 305; *Cheshire Lines Committee* v. *Lewis & Co.* (1880) 50 L.J.Q.B. 121, 138, Brett L.J.

is,[64] and always will be, a requirement for periodic tenancies. Thus in *Prudential Assurance Co. Ltd.* v. *London Residuary Body* a single term was held to be uncertain because it was to endure until land was required for road widening. A tenant who entered under that void tenancy, paid rent yearly, and had this rent accepted became a yearly tenant. This was terminable by notice in the normal way because, as the Lords held, it was not permissible to imply an uncertain provision restraining termination until the land was required for the purposes of road widening.[65] Rather the implied yearly tenancy could be terminated by a half year's notice[66] at the end of *any* period of the tenancy.

3. Length of notice to quit

The period of notice to quit required is determined, first, from any **express agreement**, that is from any provision in the tenancy agreement stating what period is required. The notice need not be of the same length as the period of the tenancy. That it may be shorter is demonstrated by *Re Midland Railway Co.'s Agreement* which accepted the validity of a six-monthly tenancy terminable by three months' notice.[67] Express agreement can also require a longer period of notice, despite theoretical problems with repugnancy, so long as the period of notice is of certain duration. Thus a quarterly tenancy may provide for three years' notice of termination—the effect being to give a rolling period of contractual security for three years.[68]

Failing an express agreement, the length of notice required to terminate a periodic tenancy is determined by **implication from the tenancy's period**. A yearly tenancy can be terminated by half a year's notice that must expire on an anniversary date of the commencement of the tenancy.[69] A yearly tenancy arising by implication from payment of rent on October 10th could be terminated at the end of October 9th in any subsequent year providing that the notice is given on or before 9 April in the year of termination.[70] If the decision to terminate was taken at the worst moment in the cycle, termination may be delayed for up to 18 months, better than the period of two years which would be the maximum if the law had insisted upon a full year's notice.

With periods other than a full year, the length of notice required is one full period of the tenancy. Although it is possible to contract out of this rule,[71] notice must normally terminate at the end of a full period of the tenancy. Where the creation date of the tenancy is unknown, the term date may be assumed to be the date on which rent is paid. Thus a whole month's notice is needed to terminate a monthly tenancy:[72] a tenancy

---

[64] *Prudential Assurance* [1992] 2 A.C. 386, 394F, Lord Templeman; *Onyx (U.K.) Ltd.* v. *Beard* [1996] E.G.C.S. 55 Ch.D.

[65] [1992] 1 E.G.L.R. 47 C.A., reversed by H.L. [1992] 2 A.C. 386, 394H.

[66] See below p. 515.

[67] [1971] Ch. 725 C.A.

[68] *Breams Property Investments Ltd.* v. *Stroulger* [1948] 2 K.B. 1 C.A.; D.C. Potter (1948) 11 *M.L.R.* 342; approved in *Prudential Assurance Co. Ltd.* v. *London Residuary Body* [1992] 2 A.C. 386 H.L.

[69] *Bennett Properties Ltd.* v. *H. & S. Engineering Ltd.* [1998] 2 C.L.Y. 3683 Q.B.D.

[70] If the tenancy was created on a traditional quarter day (December 25th, March 25th, June 24th and September 29th) two quarters' notice is required, but otherwise the corresponding date rule is applied; see below p. 581.

[71] *Harler* v. *Calder* [1989] 1 E.G.L.R. 88 C.A.

[72] But see E. Cooke [1992] *Conv.* 263.

created on July 15th could be terminated by notice expiring on the 14th of August, September, October, or any subsequent month. The corresponding date rule ensures that a calendar month runs from any given date to the same day in subsequent months, and the same rule applies to years; this is discussed in detail in the commercial section.[73] For a weekly tenancy the period of notice required is one week. However, a residential occupier of a dwelling has additional rights to protection from eviction (explained immediately below): he is entitled to receive 28 clear days' notice, a period running from the date of the notice and unrelated to the period of the tenancy.

In commercial leases there is a developing principle that notices should not be served too long in advance,[74] and it would seem to be beneficial to develop the law of residential tenancies in the same direction.

4.   Protection from eviction

The Protection from Eviction Act 1977[75] regulates residential notices to quit. It applies to leases[76] and also to periodic licences,[77] but not to excluded tenancies granted after early 1989 nor to excluded licences[78] wherever granted. **Duration** is governed by the rule that notice relating to an inhabited house must be of at least 28 days or four weeks, but time runs immediately from the date of the notice and is independent of the period of the tenancy.[79] This rule applies whichever side gives the notice: a tenant who wishes to quit his accommodation is liable for four weeks' rent.[80] So far as the **form of notice** is concerned, notice to quit a dwelling[81] must contain prescribed information,[82] warning the tenant of his rights. Essential elements are a statement of the need for due process of law and reference to listed people who can advise tenants, such as solicitors and citizens' advice bureaux. The current form was prescribed in 1988[83] though an out of date form which carries the same information may be accepted as valid.[84] This information is irrelevant in the case of an agricultural lease.[85]

5.   Errors in notices

It is surprisingly difficult to draft an accurate notice stating the correct period of notice and terminating at the end of a period of the lease. Until recently many notices to quit

---

[73] See below p. 581.

[74] See below p. 585.

[75] P.E.A. 1977 s.5, as amended by H.A. 1988 s.32.

[76] Excluding attornment clauses in mortgages: *Alliance B.S.* v. *Pinwill* [1958] Ch. 788; *Peckham Mutual B.S.* v. *Registe* (1981) 42 P. & C.R. 186, Vinelott J.

[77] P.E.A. 1977 s.5(1A). The single period from employment to termination of employment is not a periodic licence: *Norris* v. *Checksfield* [1991] 1 W.L.R. 1241 C.A. (4 weeks' notice not required); on earlier legislation see *Crane* v. *Morris* [1965] 1 W.L.R. 1104 C.A.

[78] P.E.A. 1977 s.1(1)(1A).

[79] s.5.

[80] *Hounslow L.B.C.* v. *Pilling* [1993] 1 W.L.R. 1242 C.A. In the case of Rent Act statutory tenant, notice must be a contractual period or, if none, 3 months: R.A. 1977 s.3(3).

[81] Including a public sector tenancy: *Lambeth L.B.C.* v. *Udechuka* (1980) 41 P. & C.R. 200 C.A. (even though S.I. did not cover the public sector).

[82] P.E.A. 1977 s.5(1).

[83] Notices to Quit etc (Prescribed Information) Regs. 1988, S.I. 1988/2201.

[84] *Swansea C.C.* v. *Hearn* (1991) 23 H.L.R. 284 C.A.

[85] *National Trust* v. *Knipe* [1998] 1 W.L.R. 230 C.A.; C. Rodgers [1998] *J.H.L.* 123, 138.

were defective and invalid, though very often defects are waived—whether by ignorance or design. There are also numerous cases of defective shorthold notices.[86] In *Mannai Investments Co. Ltd.* v. *Eagle Star Life Assurance Co. Ltd.*[87] the House of Lords decided by a bare majority to allow more flexibility in the interpretation of commercial break clauses. The basis of the decision is to introduce the concept of the reasonable recipient. Goulding J. expressed the test in this way in *Carradine Properties Ltd.* v. *Aslam:*[88]

> "Is the notice quite clear to a reasonable tenant reading it? Is it plain that he cannot be misled by it?"

Where a notice contains an error but it would be obvious to a reasonable person receiving it what was intended by it, the defect is overlooked and the obvious meaning is applied. If the flaw in a notice is such that there is a genuine ambiguity it is still destructive of the validity of the notice.

The young life of the *Mannai* principle has already yielded a large crop of cases on defects in commercial break clauses.[89] Cases on residential shorthold notices reveal examples both of evident errors[90] and also of major ambiguity.[91] The issue with shortholds is not quite the same as with break clauses, since a relaxation designed to aid tenants seeking to break a burdensome lease works against a shorthold tenant facing eviction; *Mannai* removes one of the few defences available. This is also the case with a common law notice to quit, though again here the *Mannai* principle applies. A notice designed to end the lease must communicate this intention unambiguously and indicate the right of determination being exercised, whether given by the landlord or the tenant.[92] Similar principles apply to other types of warning notice, and the courts are also taking a more relaxed view of the use of out of date forms.[93]

6. Form and parties

The **form** of a notice must follow any contractual term[94] and must be in writing;[95] unfortunately this last requirement only applies to notices relating to a document about property, and no form is laid down for notices to end a periodic tenancy where the term about the length of the notice to quit is merely implied from the payment and acceptance of rent.[96] A landlord has a common law **duty of honesty**, so that if a landlord is

---

[86] See below pp. 47–48.

[87] [1997] A.C. 749 H.L.; see below pp. 579–581.

[88] [1976] 1 W.L.R. 442, 444, Goulding J.; approved in *Germax Securities Ltd.* v. *Spiegal* (1978) 37 P. & C.R. 204, 206 C.A.; *Morrow* v. *Nadeem* [1986] 1 W.L.R. 1381 C.A.

[89] See below pp. 579–581.

[90] *Panayi* v. *Roberts* (1993) 25 H.L.R. 421, 425, Mann L.J.; *York* v. *Casey* [1998] 2 E.G.L.R. 25 C.A.; *Andrews* v. *Brewer* (1998) 30 H.L.R. 203 C.A.

[91] *Clickex Ltd.* v. *McCann* [1999] 2 E.G.L.R. 63 C.A.

[92] *Mannai* [1997] A.C. 749,768F–H, Lord Steyn.

[93] *Tadema Holdings Ltd.* v. *Ferguson* [1999] *Times*, November 25th, Peter Gibson L.J.

[94] *Mannai Investment Co. Ltd.* v. *Eagle Star Life Assurance Co. Ltd.* [1997] A.C. 749, 776B, Lord Hoffmann.

[95] L.P.A. 1925 s.196(1); *New Hart Builders Ltd.* v. *Brindley* [1975] Ch. 342, Goulding J.; L.T.A. 1927 s.23(1).

[96] *Wandsworth L.B.C.* v. *Atwell* [1995] 1 W.L.R. 95 C.A.; J.E. Adams [1995] *Conv.* 186; J. Montgomerie (1952) 16 *Conv. (N.S.)* 98, 107.

required to state particular facts in his notice—for example that rent is in arrears—the notice is void if the landlord knows that his statements are false.[97]

Parties are also important: validity of a notice depends upon service by the correct landlord on the correct tenant. In *Hammersmith & Fulham L.B.C. v. Monk*[98] the House of Lords held that a joint periodic tenancy held by two or more **joint tenants** may be determined at common law by notice given by any one of them without the concurrence of the others. The implications and subsequent case law must be considered later.

7. Service

Service is the delivery of a document to a particular person.[99] Notices relating to property are regulated by section 196 of the Law of Property Act 1925,[100] where the notice is required by that Act or by any post-1925 document affecting property, though again there is an unfortunate gap where a tenancy has no express term about the length of a notice to quit.[101] Rent Act tenants may give notice to the landlord's agent or any other person receiving rent.[102]

Postal service of notices by registered post or recorded delivery is most common and most convenient[103] though ordinary post will not do.[104] Rules about the service of court proceedings are considered elsewhere.[105]

E. STATUTORY PROTECTION

In *Hammersmith & Fulham L.B.C. v. Monk* Lord Bridge said that:[106]

> "For a large part of this century there have been many categories of tenancies of property occupied for agricultural residential and commercial purposes, where the legislature has intervened to confer upon tenants extra-contractual rights entitling the tenant to continue in occupation without the consent of the landlord, either after the expiration of a contractual lease for a fixed term or after a notice to quit given by the landlord to determine a contractual periodic tenancy."

So security of tenure is essentially a lengthening of the contractual duration of a lease. Unfortunately slightly different techniques are adopted by each of the main residential codes.

---

[97] *Rous* v. *Mitchell* [1991] 1 W.L.R. 469 C.A.; *Lazarus Estates Ltd.* v. *Beasley* [1956] 1 Q.B. 702 C.A.; see below p. 622.

[98] [1992] 1 A.C. 478 H.L.; see below pp. 124–130.

[99] *Tadema Holdings Ltd.* v. *Ferguson*, [1999] *Times*, November 25th, Peter Gibson L.J. The case shows that a mental patient can be served in the same way as any other person.

[100] For more detail, see below pp. 591–593.

[101] *Wandsworth L.B.C.* v. *Atwell* [1995] 1 W.L.R. 95 C.A.; J.E. Adams [1995] *Conv.* 186; J. Montgomerie (1952) 16 *Conv. (N.S.)* 98, 107.

[102] R.A. 1977 s.151.

[103] L.P.A. 1925 s.196(4); Recorded Delivery Service Act 1962 s.1.

[104] *Holwell Securities Ltd.* v. *Hughes* [1973] 1 W.L.R. 757, Templeman J.

[105] See below pp 593–594.

[106] [1992] 1 A.C. 478, 483–484.

1. Holding over

When a commercial fixed term tenancy ends, a periodic renewal may be implied from the payment and acceptance of rent,[107] and it is also possible that there may be a tenancy at will during negotiations.[108] The position of a residential tenant is complicated by the impact of the security of tenure legislation since a residential tenant with security of tenure is entitled to a statutory continuation of his tenancy.[109] The landlord has no choice but to accept the rent so acceptance of rent continues the old tenancy rather than creates a contractual novation.[110]

2. Contractual periodic tenancy

Many residential tenancies will be periodic tenancies. In the past private sector tenants generally had an initial fixed period of at least six months (the assured shorthold) following which the tenant could hold over as a periodic tenant, but since early 1997 it has been possible to grant a shorthold which is periodic throughout.[111] Public sector tenancies are usually periodic, either by initial grant or because an initial fixed term has run out.[112] A Rent Act tenancy was usually periodic, either in its initial form or from holding over after a fixed term. Notice to quit is required. This will remove contractual security (that is the protected tenancy) and will lead to statutory protection (that is a statutory tenancy).[113] No notice to quit is required during a statutory phase.[114]

So long as the tenancy remains in its contractual phase, it is necessary to terminate this periodic tenancy before proceedings can be taken for possession. Notice to quit is required.[115] Landlords are obliged to give notice of the correct duration and in the correct form, though subject to waiver by the tenant.[116]

3. Statutory phase

Contractual protection is removed if the tenancy has been converted into a statutory tenancy; usually by a notice to quit. Protection depends entirely upon the appropriate regime of residential security, and no notice to quit will be needed.[117] Conversion from a contractual to a statutory phase usually arises from a notice to quit, though also possibly from some rent agreements.[118] After a long period of occupation, it is reasonable to assume that a tenancy is statutory and that contractual protection has ended.[119]

---

[107] See below pp. 173–174.
[108] A residential tenancy at will would be protected; see below p. 144.
[109] See below pp. 109–113.
[110] Woodfall 23.044.
[111] See above p. 43.
[112] H.A. 1985 s.86.
[113] R.A. 1977 s.2(1)(a).
[114] S.3(4).
[115] As to joint tenancies see below pp. 124–130.
[116] *Elsden* v. *Pick* [1980] 1 W.L.R. 98 C.A.
[117] R.A. 1977 s.3(4); H.A. 1988 ss.5(3)(e), 8(4); H.A. 1985 s.83(5).
[118] See below pp. 236–237.
[119] *White* v. *Wareing* [1992] 1 E.G.L.R. 271 C.A. (Rent Act tenancy).

4.   Warning notices

Both the assured and the secure schemes[120] require a warning notice before a landlord takes repossession proceedings. If the tenancy is periodic this will meet the period needed to end the periodic tenancy and also the 28-day period needed by the protection from eviction legislation.

F.   INFORMAL SHORT-TERM TENANCIES

Leases are generally "void for the purpose of conveying or creating a legal estate" unless made by deed.[121] Short leases of actual land[122] have been exempted from the need for full formality in creation since 1677,[123] but the exemption now appears in section 54(2) of the Law of Property Act 1925 after some amendments of detail in these terms:

> "Nothing in the foregoing provisions of this part of this Act[124] shall affect the creation by parol of leases (1) taking effect in possession (2) for a term not exceeding three years (whether or not the lessee is given power to extend the term) (3) at the best rent which can reasonably be obtained without taking a fine."

Excepted short leases can be created purely orally[125] though full formality is required for a transfer of any existing lease.[126] It is important to note that oral leases suffer some disadvantages, most notably that the accelerated procedure for repossession is not available to a landlord against an assured shorthold tenant[127] and there are obvious advantages in having the terms of any agreement recorded in writing.

1.   Best rent

The 1677 original required the lease to be at a rent at least two thirds of the full improved value.[128] Its modern equivalent is that the tenancy should reserve the best rent, so that a deed is required to create any lease reserving a fine.[129]

2.   Term not exceeding three years

The test for informal creation of a fixed term tenancy is whether the term exceeds three years. Hence a legal lease for three years certain can be written or oral, but a legal lease for three years and one week certain must be by deed.[130] A fixed term is valid only if the

---

[120] See below pp. 318–319. This is not necessary for Rent Act tenancies.
[121] L.P.A. 1925 s.52(1); see below p. 37.
[122] Megarry & Wade (6th ed.) 770 n.84; *Duke of Somerset* v. *Fogwell* (1826) 5 B. & C. 875, 108 E.R. 325.
[123] Statute of Frauds 1677 s.2.
[124] i.e. ss.40 to 54(1); the last mentioned subs. specifies that a lease not in writing is to be a tenancy at will only. The numbering in the text is supplied by the author.
[125] P. Sparkes [1992] *Conv.* 252, 337; Bright & Gilbert 212–222; Davey 22–32; Evans & Smith (5th) ch.4; Garner (2nd) ch.3.
[126] *Botting* v. *Martin* (1808) 1 Camp. 317, 170 E.R. 970; *Crago* v. *Julian* [1992] 1 W.L.R. 372 C.A.; see below pp. 293–294.
[127] See below at pp. 56–62.
[128] *Wood* v. *Beard* (1876) 2 Ex.D. 30.
[129] *City Permanent B.S.* v. *Miller* [1952] Ch. 840, 846 (similar wording of the original form of L.R.A. 1925 s.70(1)(k)).
[130] At 848.

maximum duration is fixed, and that is the duration which should be taken for formality purposes,[131] though one ignores the possibility of forfeiture, extension of the term by the tenant by exercise of an option,[132] or its curtailment by the exercise of a break clause whether by the tenant[133] or the landlord.[134] The test is applied to the natural length of the lease assuming that it is not broken.

Periodic tenancies qualify for informal creation if they are yearly, monthly,[135] or weekly, and also where there is some restriction on the service of notice for a fixed period that does not exceed three years.[136] Even in the public sector it is possible to create a secure tenancy orally. [137] The court which heard *Hammond* v. *Farrow*[138] decided without much difficulty that a tenancy from week to week determinable by a week's notice by either side was for a "term not exceeding three months" under the terms of the rating legislation, and so it would obviously also qualify for informal creation. A legal tenancy from leap year to leap year (with a period of four years) would equally clearly require full formalities. That many yearly periodic tenancies outlast three years, and that every one of them could potentially last for ever, does not remove the possibility of informality in creation. Formality tests have to be applied as if each party had served notice at the earliest possible moment, the duration being the longest time that the tenancy can last in those circumstances. Unfortunately *Ex parte Voisey*[139] decided upon a different test. It concerned a tenancy arising under an attornment clause in a mortgage that was to arise on default by the borrower, a manure manufacturer, and then to continue from month to month unless terminated by the lender. Money was lent over 14 years and the actual default occurred after six years, but still informal creation was allowed![140] Sir George Jessel M.R. said[141] that this was not obnoxious to the Statute of Frauds

"because we do not know how long it may last, because it may not last for three years or for one year."

This dictum states authoritatively that the shortest possible duration can be taken. The flaw is obvious, since if a lease is not definitely limited so as not to exceed three years it ought to fall within the main provision requiring a deed. In *Kushner* Lord Goddard C.J. explained *Voisey* in this way:

[131] Not the minimum period: *Hammond* v. *Farrow* [1904] 2 K.B. 332, 335, Wills J., as explained in *Kushner* v. *Law Society* [1952] 1 K.B. 264, 273, Goddard L.C.J.

[132] L.P.A. 1925 s.54(2); *Hand* v. *Hall* (1877) 2 Ex. D. 355; *Gray* v. *Spyer* [1922] 2 Ch. 22, 38–39; *Rollason* v. *Leon* (1861) 7 H. & N. 73, 158 E.R. 398.

[133] *Kushner* v. *Law Society* [1952] 1 K.B. 264 C.A. (lease for 14 years terminable by the tenant at the end of any year had to be made by deed); earlier cases explained are: *Ex parte Voisey* (1882) 21 Ch. D. 442, 456, 459, 464; *Hammond* v. *Farrow* [1904] 2 K.B. 332, 335, Lord Alverstone C.J.

[134] *Kushner* at 266, 274, Lord Goddard; this despite *Hammond* v. *Farrow* [1904] 2 K.B. 332, 335, Lord Alverstone C.J.

[135] Including a tenancy of indefinite duration terminable by either party by a month's notice: *Doe d. Lansdell* v. *Gower* (1851) 17 Q.B. 589, 117 E.R. 1406.

[136] *Breams Property Co. Ltd.* v. *Stroulger* [1948] 2 K.B. 1, 7, Scott L.J. (landlord restricted for exactly 3 years).

[137] H.A. 1985 s.91(3)(c); *Westminster C.C.* v. *Peart* (1991) 24 H.L.R. 389 C.A.

[138] [1904] 2 K.B. 332, 335, Wills J.; *Duncan* v. *Paki* [1976] 2 N.Z.L.R. 563, 565; Megarry & Wade (6th ed.) 771.

[139] (1882) 21 Ch. D. 442.

[140] The lender (landlord) had not executed the mortgage deed.

[141] At 456, 458, Brett L.J., 464, Cotton L.J.

"The fact that [a monthly or weekly or yearly] tenancy may go on for a great number of years does not make the tenancy one which becomes invalid if it is not in writing, nor, because it has lasted for more than three years, must it be by way of deed."[142]

Otherwise, as counsel said,[143] one reaches conclusions "contrary to all the experience and practice of conveyancing". *Voisey* is now limited to periodic tenancies, even though this inevitably creates anomalies and dubious characterisations in borderline cases. It should be overruled.

A lease for life is uncertain in duration, and, although anyone might die within three years, it is axiomatic that a lease for life required a deed at common law.[144] Most leases for life are now converted to terms of ninety years by statute,[145] and it is assumed that a deed is still required.

3. Taking effect in possession

An important change in the law occurred in 1925. Until then the rule was that a lease required a deed unless the term was limited to "three years from the making thereof",[146] time being counted from the date of the grant. So a term to start in one year's time and then to last for one year could be oral. *Foster* v. *Reeves* [147] demonstrates the need for full formality for a lease granted in May for three years from June 24th following. Section 54(2) of the Law of Property Act 1925 introduced a new requirement for tenancies granted after 1925—that the term should be in possession. In consequence a term for one month arising in one year's time,[148] or on a contingency,[149] cannot be legal without a deed.[150] Between 1925 and 1989 an oral lease that failed at law (because it was not in possession) might also fail as a contract for a lease (because not evidenced in writing).[151] *Long* v. *Tower Hamlets L.B.C.*[152] concerned a claim to adverse possession, which would be defeated if the former tenant's lease was created in writing,[153] but which succeeded if his lease was oral. The crux was a letter written on September 4th 1975. In it the land-lord's agent confirmed that his client was prepared to grant him a quarterly tenancy to commence on September 29th 1975, and indeed he did move in on this date and began to pay rent for a few years, but later he remained for 18 years without paying any rent. He sought a declaration of his squatter's title. Since the grant was made on the 4th to take effect on the 29th of one particular month, the letter did not grant a tenancy in

---

[142] At 274.

[143] [1952] 1 K.B. 265, 270, Cumming-Bruce L.J.

[144] *Doe d. Warner* v. *Browne* (1807) 8 East 165, 166, 103 E.R. 305; *Warner* v. *Browne* (1808) 14 Ves. 156, 158, 33 E.R. 480, Lord Eldon L.C.; *Re King's Leasehold Estates* (1873) L.R. 16 Eq. 521; *Zimbler* v. *Abrahams* [1903] 1 K.B. 577, 581, Vaughan Williams L.J.; *Mardell* v. *Curtis* [1899] W.N. 93.

[145] L.P.A. 1925 s.149(6).

[146] Statute of Frauds 1677 s.2; *Wood* v. *Beard* (1876) 2 Ex.D. 30, 34.

[147] [1892] 2 Q.B. 255 C.A.; query the dictum of Cotton L.J. in *Ex parte Voisey* (1882) 21 Ch.D. 442, 464.

[148] *Bowes* v. *East London Waterworks Co.* (1821) Jacob 324, 330, 37 E.R. 873, Lord Eldon (lease on 20th to take effect on 25th is in reversion).

[149] *Ex parte Voisey* is not legal today.

[150] *Bush Transport Ltd.* v. *Nelson* [1987] 1 E.G.L.R. 71, 73; the impact of contracts was not considered.

[151] L.P.A. 1925 s.40; however taking of possession by the tenant was a part performance which would usually make the contract enforceable.

[152] [1998] Ch. 197, 210–219, James Munby Q.C.; J. Perkins (1997) 113 *L.Q.R.* 394.

[153] Limitation Act 1980 sch.1 para.5(1).

possession,[154] could not operate at law, and did not prejudice his adverse possession claim, so he was given his declaration. Susan Bright[155] was right to say that the decision flies in the face of the accepted understanding, but it is also unquestionably correct.

Changes in the contract formalities made by the Law of Property (Miscellaneous Provisions) Act 1989[156] removed the need for writing for a contract for a short lease. A short lease that fails as a legal lease, because not in possession, may now operate as an informal contract for the creation of a legal lease without the need for any writing.[157] For security purposes an equitable tenancy under a specifically performable contract is just as good as a legal tenancy that does not require specific performance. Hence a distinction has to be drawn between three closely similar tenancies:

(1) A lease from today for three years and two weeks requires a deed at law.
(2) A lease from two weeks' time for a term of three years requires a deed to operate at law; but it might operate as a contract for a short lease even without writing; it is a contract for a term which will come into possession, and when possession is taken the term will not exceed three years.
(3) A contract to execute a lease in one week's time to take effect in possession one week later for a term of three years. Here the contract does not fall within the short lease exception because the lease when created will not be in possession. A deed is required for a valid legal lease, and writing for a valid contract. The present law creates wide scope for future burdens of an indeterminate category and the pre-1926 law was altogether more satisfactory.

G. FORMAL RESIDENTIAL TENANCIES

The preceding discussion demonstrates that three years is a crucial cut off point, with longer leases requiring a deed[158] before they are able to operate at law. Until recently almost all residential leases were for less than three years since Rent Act tenancies had to be at a rack rental given the prohibition of premiums. Until early 1989 there was only one exception to this principle: since the Crown was allowed to charge a premium for short residential leases, it was possible to create a lease for (say) 15 years, charging a premium and a reduced rent. Introduction of the assured tenancy scheme in early 1989 led to an increased use of longer residential terms.[159] This is because it is now possible to reserve a premium on the grant of an assured tenancy, so it becomes feasible to grant a tenancy in the private sector for a fixed term with a down payment and a lower rental payment. From the point of view of the tenant it is vitally important to ensure that this form of tenancy is assignable so that the tenant is able to realise his economic outlay. It is also important to appreciate the significance of the seven year cut off point: where the initial grant is for less than seven years, the landlord carries the obligation to maintain

---

[154] P. Sparkes [1992] *Conv.* 337, 340–341.

[155] [1998] *Conv.* 229, 235.

[156] s.2(5)(a).

[157] The distinction is of particularly little consequence if the landlord's title is registered since an equitable tenant acquires an overriding interest by taking actual occupation: L.R.A. 1925 s.70(1)(g).

[158] L.P.(M.P.) A. 1989 s.1, in force July 31st, 1990; Sparkes, *N.L.L.* 216–222.

[159] *Artesian Residential Developments Ltd.* v. *Beck* [1999] 3 All E.R. 113 C.A. (10 year term).

the structure of the dwelling-house and the installations within it.[160] So if the landlord makes an initial contractual grant for seven years or any longer fixed term, liability for these expensive items can be transferred by covenant to the tenant. From the point of view of the landlord it is important to include provisions in any fixed term tenancy that enable him to end the contractual term if there is a breach of covenant. This is similar to a forfeiture, though if there is an assured tenancy (that is if the tenant is in residential occupation) the procedure is a residential repossession rather than a forfeiture.[161]

A deed is necessary to create a legal tenancy exceeding three years. However it may not matter much if the legal formalities are overlooked provided that there is a sufficient written contract. An equitable tenancy can be created under the doctrine of *Walsh* v. *Lonsdale*[162] using contract formalities.[163] Today all the terms expressly agreed must be reduced to writing and signed by both parties, either on a single document or in contractual parts which are exchanged. Equitable rights generally prevail over legal rights provided that they have priority. Hence in *Walsh* v. *Lonsdale* itself, Lonsdale had a lease for seven years under the terms of his contract rather than a yearly periodic tenancy that was the extent of his common law entitlement. Equitable leases are discussed in the context of commercial leases[164] where they are more common, but all residential security regimes accept equitable rights as sufficient to attract security of tenure. So in *R.* v. *Tower Hamlets L.B.C. ex parte Von Goetz*[165] a 10-year shorthold created by a tenancy agreement in writing gave rise to a sufficient interest in the land to qualify the tenant to apply for an improvement grant. Equitable interests remain vulnerable on a sale of the reversion unless there is a protective registration.[166]

Tightening of the contract formalities in 1989 increased the likelihood that an agreement for a tenancy may fail to qualify as a land contract. Ultimately resort may be required to the doctrine of proprietary estoppel. All estoppels are based on an expectation in the mind of the putative tenant that he will be entitled to a tenancy created (that is, induced) by the putative landlord. Leasehold creation requires a proprietary estoppel, so that the tenant must establish a detriment incurred in reliance on the landlord's promise.[167] Many cases show that estoppel is a perfectly viable method of creating valid tenancies, both in commercial cases[168] and especially also when considering the impact of residential security of tenure.

---

[160] L.T.A. 1985 ss.11–16; see below pp. 243–251.
[161] See below p. 359.
[162] (1882) 21 Ch.D. 9 C.A.
[163] L.P.(M.P.) A. 1989 s.2, replacing Statute of Frauds 1677 s.4 (writing) and Real Property Act 1845 s.3 (upgrade to deed).
[164] See below pp. 521–524.
[165] [1999] Q.B. 1019 C.A.
[166] See below p. 520.
[167] Sparkes *N.L.L.* ch. 11.
[168] *Orgee* v. *Orgee* [1997] E.G.C.S. 152 C.A.; M. Pawlowski (1998) 114 *L.Q.R.* 351; *Pridean Ltd.* v. *Forest Taverns Ltd.* (1998) 75 P. & C.R. 447 C.A.

H. PROPRIETARY STATUS

When a tenant is seeking to enforce his rights against his original landlord it is not necessary to show that his tenancy has proprietary status.[169] But if the landlord's interest is sold, the tenant will have rights he can assert against the purchaser only if he can show that he has a property right, and one with priority over the new landlord.

1. Unregistered reversion

A short residential tenancy qualifies as a term of years absolute[170] and hence for legal status.[171] Whether or not a buyer of the land has notice of the tenancy is irrelevant since legal rights bind the world. Where a tenancy is continued in force by the security of tenure legislation this extension, if not strictly a legal estate under all residential codes, is at least sufficiently legal to be capable of binding the land irrespective of notice. The results can be capricious. A tenant given an oral weekly tenancy may in some circumstances attract full life-long security of tenure—if the landlord is in the public sector, if a social sector landlord chooses to allow it, or if a private sector grant was first made before early 1989—and his tenure will bind the land and anyone who buys it indefinitely. Most residential tenants occupy the dwelling—and qualifying occupation is often necessary to preserve security of tenure[172] so that a purchaser has an informal "notice", but security may in certain circumstances continue through periods of non-occupation, and if so the tenancy nevertheless retains its binding status. Equitable tenancies based on contractual rights will require a protective land charges registration, and tenancies created by estoppel depend for their proprietary force on notice doctrine.[173]

2. Registered reversion

The original scheme for leases of registered land was confused and fragmentary[174] so that the greater coherence introduced by the Land Registration Act 1986[175] was badly needed. Even so the law remains unsatisfactory. It would be neither practicable nor desirable to keep a complete register of all residential tenants, since they come and go, and any register would inevitably fall out of date. For this reason most short leases and tenancies are treated as being overriding so that they take effect and bind purchasers off the register. The **paragraph (k)**[176] **overriding interest** is constituted by

"leases granted for a term not exceeding 21 years".

This embraces almost all leases that are not substantively registrable. However, the force of the word "granted" needs careful appreciation since it is not immediately apparent that this restricts paragraph (k) to legal leases. *City Permanent B.S.* v. *Miller*[177]

---

[169] *Bruton* v. *London & Quadrant Housing Trust* [2000] A.C. 406 H.L.
[170] L.P.A. 1925 s.205(1)(xxvii).
[171] s.1(1)(b).
[172] See below pp. 104–109.
[173] Sparkes *N.L.L.* ch. 11.
[174] Hayton's *Registered Land* (Sweet & Maxwell, 3rd ed., 1981) ch.3.
[175] In force January 1st 1987, following Law Com. No.125 (1983).
[176] L.R.A. 1925 s.70(1)(k), as amended.
[177] [1952] Ch. 840 C.A.

concerned an oral agreement to create a lease for three years and then from week to week (that is for a minimum term of three years and one week) which was not a legal lease and so was held not to be a paragraph (k) overriding interest. It seems to follow from the course of discussion in *Miller* that had the tenancy been one week shorter and so qualified for informal legal creation[178] it would have fallen within paragraph (k). It now makes no difference whether the lease is at a rack rent, reserves a fine, or is purely gratuitous.[179] Protection adheres without any requirement that the tenant be in occupation, so that a short-term tenancy may be a totally undiscoverable incumbrance.[180] For example in *Prince* v. *Robinson*[181] it was recognised in an obiter discussion that a Rent Act tenancy could be an overriding interest that would bind a purchaser of the reversion even though the flat to which the tenancy had attached had been completely reconstructed and no longer existed in its original form. Existence of paragraph (k) protection is dependent upon the existence of the lease at the date of registration of a later dealing with the reversionary title.[182] The grant of a paragraph (k) tenancy is deemed to be by way of registered disposition,[183] so that a short lease defeats unprotected minor interests, and the tenant is bound exclusively by register entries and pre-existing overriding interests.[184]

A tenant who fails to secure protection under paragraph (k) may still fall back on an overriding interest under paragraph (g) by virtue of actual occupation or through receipt of net rents where a sub-tenant is in occupation.[185] This may also provide a second layer of protection for a paragraph (k) tenant, giving fortuitous protection to options and also to future leases held by a person who happens to be in occupation under some other right. Protection is lost, of course, under the express terms of paragraph (g) if enquiry is made of the occupier and the lease is not disclosed, and also if the tenant is not in occupation at the time of the completion of some later transaction.[186]

Some leases may be protected against the landlord's title by a protective entry, in which case the lease is a minor interest and the proprietary force is dependent upon that entry.[187] Protection by notice requires either the consent of the landlord or a court order, but a caution may be used for non-consensual entries.[188] The land registry will refuse to make an entry if the lease is substantively registered or if it is both overriding and obvious.[189] This means that protective notice is left to apply to a limited range of leases:

---

[178] L.P.A. 1925 s.54(2).
[179] Amendments by L.R.A. 1986 s.4.
[180] The same is of course true of a legal lease of unregistered land.
[181] (1999) 31 H.L.R. 89 C.A.
[182] *Pourdanay* v. *Barclays Bank plc* [1997] Ch. 321 Ch.D. (also known as *Zaroovabli*).
[183] L.R.A. 1925 s.19(2).
[184] *Freer* v. *Unwins Ltd.* [1976] Ch. 288.
[185] L.R.A. 1925 s.70(1)(g).
[186] *Abbey National B.S.* v. *Cann* [1991] 1 A.C. 56 H.L.; P. Sparkes [1986] *Conv.* 309.
[187] L.R.A. 1925 s.48(1).
[188] A restriction is another possibility: J.E. Adams [1994] *Conv.* 200.
[189] L.R.A. 1925 ss.19(2)(a), 22(2)(a); L.R.R. 1925 r.199.

(1) certain pre-1987 leases: leases for 21 years or less at a fine; leases for 21 years or less without any rent; and any lease made before 1986[190] with an absolute prohibition on assignment;
(2) agreements for leases;[191] and
(3) future leases.

Longer leases with 21 years remaining unexpired at the time of a dealing require substantive registration.

I.   SURRENDER

Many residential tenancies end by surrender.[192] The tenant offers to give up his lease to the landlord, and the landlord accepts it.[193] The very essence of a surrender is the consent of both parties, based on an intention to surrender.[194] The tenant's right to occupy ends, he is no longer liable for rent, the landlord is free to relet the property, and the overriding interest affecting a registered reversion is removed.[195] The landlord will be entitled to a possession order.[196] Lord Millett's speech in a recent House of Lords case about agricultural notices to quit, *Barrett* v. *Morgan,*[197] contains valuable observations about the nature of a surrender:

> "A surrender is simply an assurance by which a lesser estate is yielded up to the greater, and the term is usually applied to the giving up a lease or tenancy before its expiration. If a tenant surrenders his tenancy to an immediate landlord, who accepts the surrender, the tenancy is absorbed by the landlord's conversion and is extinguished by operation of law."

In Coke on *Littleton*[198] it is described graphically as a case where the estate:

> "may drowne by mutual agreement between them."

Surrender brings a tenancy to an end prematurely in a way not provided for by the terms the tenancy agreement (in stark contrast to a notice to quit) so that a surrender requires the landlord's agreement and is consensual in the fullest sense of the term.

1.   Formal surrender

A deed is required to effect a legal surrender of the most informal tenancy,[199] but it is most unlikely that the parties to a residential tenancy will bother with this. Even an equitable surrender is now unlikely; a contract to surrender is effective in equity, but it is necessary to use full contract formalities—requiring that the terms are reduced to

---

[190] L.R.A. 1986 s.3; Law Com. No.125 (1983).
[191] *Clark* v. *Chief Land Register* [1994] Ch. 370 C.A.; *Chancery plc* v. *Ketteringham* (1995) 69 P. & C.R. 426 Ch.D.; A.K.R. Kiralfy (1952) 16 *Conv. (N.S.)* 38; J.E. Adams [1994] *Conv.* 265.
[192] Woodfall 17.008–17.048, Davey 123–126, Evans & Smith (5th) 236–239.
[193] If the reversion is mortgaged the concurrence of the lender is required: L.P.A. 1925 s.100.
[194] *R.* v. *Croydon L.B.C. ex parte Toth* (1988) 20 H.L.R. 576 C.A.
[195] It is rarely necessary to give effect to a surrender of an informal tenancy on the register.
[196] *Brent L.B.C.* v. *Sharma* (1992) 25 H.L.R. 257 C.A. (public sector).
[197] [2000] 1 All E.R. 481, 485b.
[198] Coke on *Littleton*, 337b.
[199] L.P.A. 1925 s.52.

writing and signed by both parties.[200] In the past many tenancies were ended by part performance; an informal contract relating to land became enforceable (under the old law of contract formality) after (but not before[201])an unequivocal act in performance of the contract which proved its existence.[202] Under modern contract formality almost all surrenders of residential tenancies will take place on estoppel principles and it is the utility of estoppel doctrine as a means of ending a lease which is now considered.

Surrender of an existing lease may be implied where landlord and tenant conduct themselves in a manner inconsistent with continuation of the lease. This long established principle[203] is based on an estoppel,[204] requiring some change of circumstances or detriment,[205] and sometimes operating unjustly and contrary to the subjective intentions of the parties.[206]

2.   Reletting to the tenant

When a surrender is implied it is almost always because of a grant of a new lease[207] of the property. The new lease sits in place of old one,[208] which is impliedly ended[209] even if it is shorter.[210] This doctrine can work arbitrarily, but the court should not invent a new lease simply to promote a just solution.[211] An oral lease is able to bring about a surrender of a formal lease[212]—however illogical this may be, given that an oral agreement to surrender is ineffective.

Matters considered in the commercial context[213] are variations of an existing lease, agreed rent increases,[214] and changes in the physical identity of the property let. Also considered in that context are invalid regrants, where the new lease is not finalised, informal, void, voidable, or conditional. Usually a regrant of this kind will not make much of a material difference to the tenant's security because security dates from the initial grant to a particular tenant; but the effect might be to lengthen the tenant's contractual security, possibly to shorten it, or to increase the rent.

3.   Lease to another party

If the tenant gives up his home, the landlord accepts it back, and then relets it to a stranger, the former tenancy is ended. It is necessary to show that the existing tenant

---

[200] L.P.(M.P.)A. 1989 s.2; Sparkes, *N.L.L.*, ch.9.

[201] *Take Harvest Ltd.* v. *Liu* [1993] A.C. 552 P.C. (the facts are given below at pp. 597–598); *Barakat* v. *Ealing L.B.C.* [1996] 36 R.V.R. 138 Brooke J. (letter spelling out the terms of a surrender is not a surrender).

[202] *Camden L.B.C.* v. *Alexandrou (No.2)* (1998) 30 H.L.R. 534 C.A.; the facts are given below at p. 597.

[203] *Wrotesley* v. *Adams* (1560) 1 Plowd. 189, 75 E.R. 290; and many later cases.

[204] *Camden L.B.C.* v. *Alexandrou (No.2)* (1998) 30 H.L.R. 534, 540, Aldous L.J.

[205] *Jenkin R. Lewis & Son Ltd.* v. *Kerman* [1971] Ch. 477, 496, Russell L.J.; *Foster* v. *Robinson* [1951] 1 K.B. 149 C.A.

[206] *Lyon* v. *Reed* (1844) 13 M. & W. 285, 153 E.R. 118.

[207] As opposed to a contractual renewal: *Pole-Carew* v. *Western Counties & General Manure Co. Ltd.* [1920] 2 Ch. 97, 122, Warrington L.J.

[208] Another possibility is two leases to sit side by side: *J.W. Childers Trustees* v. *Anker* [1996] 1 E.G.L.R. 1 C.A.

[209] *Foster* v. *Robinson* [1951] 1 K.B. 149 C.A.; *Corpus Christi College* v. *Rogers* (1879) 49 L.J.Q.B. 4 C.A.

[210] *Ive's case* (1597) 5 Co. Rep. 11a, 77 E.R. 64; *Belfield* v. *Adams* (1615) 3 Bulst. 80, 81 E.R. 69.

[211] *Sidebotham* v. *Holland* [1895] 1 Q.B. 378.

[212] *Fenner* v. *Blake* [1900] 1 Q.B. 426.

[213] See below Chapter 21.

[214] *Donellan* v. *Read* (1832) 3 B. & Ad. 899, 110 E.R. 330.

gives up possession or agrees in some other way.[215] This same surrender principle may also work on informal assignment. Suppose a tenant wishes to transfer his tenancy to a friend and then move out. Residential tenants will rarely be allowed to transfer their tenancies freely, and, even if they have power, a deed is required. The same result is best achieved informally. The existing tenant arranges to give up his tenancy to the landlord who agrees to accept the friend as a tenant and to grant a new tenancy to him. The new tenant must take possession.[216] In *E.S. Schwab & Co. Ltd.* v. *McCarthy*[217] an agreement to return the keys followed by reletting to a weekly tenant was held to create an equitable surrender. More risky, but just as effective, is the same procedure without the involvement of the landlord. The original tenant must move out; this is essential—no new tenancy is created if a tenant proffers a cheque drawn on the bank account of a parent or friend. If he moves out leaving behind a friend in occupation of the dwelling, a new tenancy may be created if the friend tenders rent in his own name and the landlord accepts it, the periodic tenancy implied from payment and acceptance of rent implicitly acting to terminate the previous tenancy. Of course the friend is vulnerable to eviction until the landlord accepts his tender of rent, but often a landlord accepts the *fait accompli*, whereupon this reasoning validates the informal transfer.[218] If an assignee enters during negotiations about the terms of an assignment and pays rent, the acceptance of rent by the landlord is not necessarily inconsistent with the continuation of the old lease and is not alone proof of a surrender of it.[219]

4. Other acts

Surrenders are based on mutual agreement. Unilateral acts by the tenant are irrelevant. Acts held not to surrender have included abandonment of the lease,[220] moving out,[221] vacating a property after fire damage,[222] and handing back the keys without their being accepted by the landlord.[223] Receipt by the landlord of notice that the tenant will leave is also ineffective to end the lease. Inactivity will not cause a surrender.[224] Unilateral acts by the landlord are also irrelevant at a time when the tenant has not given up possession.[225]

Mutual acts falling short of reletting may form a surrender, provided that the change of possession is clearly accepted. Examples of actions by the landlord are accepting the tenant's letter of surrender of an agreement for a lease,[226] attempting to relet,

---

[215] *Wallis* v. *Hands* [1893] 2 Ch. 75; *Metcalfe* v. *Boyce* [1927] 1 K.B. 758 Div.Ct.

[216] *Tower Hamlets L.B.C.* v. *Ayinde* (1994) 26 H.L.R. 631 C.A.

[217] (1975) 31 P. & C.R. 196, Oliver J.

[218] *Westminster C.C.* v. *Peart* (1992) 24 H.L.R. 389 C.A.

[219] *Mattey Securities Ltd.* v. *Ervin* [1998] 2 E.G.L.R. 66 C.A.; the court applied *Lyon* v. *Read* (1844) 13 M. & W. 285, 153 E.R. 118.

[220] *McDougalls Catering Foods Ltd.* v. *B.S.E. Trading Ltd.* [1997] 2 E.G.L.R. 65 C.A. For older commercial sector cases see below pp. 598–601.

[221] *Preston B.C.* v. *Fairclough* (1983) 8 H.L.R. 70; *Chamberlain* v. *Scalley* (1994) 26 H.L.R. 26 C.A. (possessions left).

[222] *Bhogal* v. *Cheema* [1998] 2 E.G.L.R. 50, Vinelott J.

[223] *Proudreed Ltd.* v. *Microgen Holdings plc.* [1996] 1 E.G.L.R. 89 C.A.; *Oastler* v. *Henderson* (1877) 2 Q.B.D. 575 C.A.

[224] *Westminster C.C.* v. *Basson* (1990) 23 H.L.R. 225.

[225] *Zionmor* v. *Islington L.B.C.* (1998) 30 H.L.R. 822 C.A.

[226] *Inntrepreneur Pub Co. (C.P.C.) Ltd.* v. *Deans* [1999] B.P.I.R. 361, David Steel J.

advertising for a new tenant,[227] taking possession at the tenant's request,[228] accepting the tenant's return of the key,[229] or taking back possession and carrying out major repair work.[230] Very unusual circumstances arose in *Lansdowne Tutors Ltd.* v. *Younger*,[231] since both landlord and tenant were companies controlled by the same individual; it was held that a surrender had occurred when the landlord sued for possession, the tenant admitted the claim, and rent payments had stopped.

A surrender requires a complete delivery of possession. In *Hoggett* v. *Hoggett*[232] a husband who was a weekly tenant purported to surrender the tenancy of the matrimonial home while his wife was in hospital and asked the landlord to grant a new lease to his girlfriend, Miss Wallis. The surrender was not a sham, because the landlord was not a party to the deceit. But, the court held, the lease had not been surrendered because possession had not been delivered so long as the wife of the old tenant retained occupation. Since the old lease continued, the wife was able to claim a matrimonial home right. This case must be contrasted with *Sanctuary Housing Association* v. *Campbell*[233] in which a woman left a secure weekly tenancy because of her husband's violence and returned the keys, which the authority accepted as terminating her rent liability. Her husband moved back in and changed the locks so that the landlord did not secure possession; it was held that a surrender had occurred between the wife and the landlord, and this prevented the husband claming a matrimonial home right. On these facts, and in the case of a secure tenancy, a surrender had occurred without a delivery of possession. The last case distorts conventional doctrine to promote a just solution and must be suspect in property law terms.

5. Security schemes

All legislative schemes allow a consensual surrender, for example to allow the termination of a public sector secure tenancy,[234] or to allow a private sector tenant to be shifted from one security scheme to another.[235] In order to avoid the provisions about successor tenancies it is generally necessary for the tenant to vacate the property for a short period, but 24 hours is sufficient.[236] In *Bolnore Properties Ltd.* v. *Cobb*[237] Wing Commander Cobb had a tenancy with full security on which substantial rent arrears built up. The landlord agreed not to enforce a warrant for possession if the arrears were

---

[227] *Oastler* v. *Henderson* (1877) 2 Q.B.D. 575.
[228] *Relvok* v. *Dixon* (1972) 25 P. & C.R. 1; *Re Edward's W.T.* [1982] Ch. 30 C.A.; *R.* v. *Croydon L.B.C. ex parte Toth* (1988) 20 H.L.R. 576 C.A. However not from taking possession to keep the property safe from squatters: *McDougall's Catering Foods Ltd.* v. *B.S.E. Trading Ltd.* [1997] 2 E.G.L.R. 65 C.A.
[229] *Brent L.B.C.* v. *Sharma* (1992) 25 H.L.R. 257 C.A.; *Barakat* v. *Ealing L.B.C.* [1996] E.G.C.S. 67 Brooke J.; *Filering Ltd.* v. *Taylor Commercial Ltd.* [1996] E.G.C.S. 95 C.A.
[230] *Smith* v. *Roberts* (1892) 9 T.L.R. 77 C.A.
[231] [2000] 04 L.S.G. 34 C.A.
[232] (1979) 39 P. & C.R. 121; *Old Gate Estates Ltd.* v. *Alexander* [1950] 1 K.B. 311 C.A.; *Middleton* v. *Baldock* [1950] 1 K.B. 657 C.A.
[233] [1999] 3 All E.R. 460 C.A.; *Bolnore Properties Ltd.* v. *Cobb* (1997) 29 H.L.R. 202 C.A.
[234] *R.* v. *Croydon L.B.C. ex parte Toth* (1988) 20 H.L.R. 576 C.A.
[235] *Brown* v. *Draper* [1944] K.B. 309, 312; *Foster* v. *Robinson* [1951] 1 K.B. 149 C.A.; *Collins* v. *Claughton* [1959] 1 W.L.R. 145 C.A.; *Laimond Properties Ltd.* v. *Al-Shakarchi* (1998) 30 H.L.R. 1099, 1104, Roch L.J.
[236] At 1105, Roch L.J.; *Dibbs* v. *Campbell* (1988) 20 H.L.R. 374 C.A.
[237] (1997) 29 H.L.R. 202 C.A.

paid, the couple surrendered their Rent Act tenancy and vacated the property for 24 hours, and accepted as a substitute a shorthold tenancy. A valid surrender was followed one day later by a valid shorthold grant. Problems created by surrenders of part and the effect of a surrender of a head lease on residential sub-tenants are considered below.[238]

What is not allowed is an agreement to surrender[239]—that is an arrangement by which a tenant promises in advance to give up a tenancy at some future time. There is nothing illegal in agreeing to give up possession of rented property for payment, but an agreement to give up a Rent Act tenancy cannot be specifically performed.[240]

---

[238] See below pp. 298–301.
[239] R.A. 1977 s.98; L.T.A. 1927 s.17; *Re Hennesey's Agreement* [1975] Ch. 252.
[240] *R. v. Bloomsbury & Marylebone C.C. ex parte Blackburne* [1985] 2 E.G.L.R. 157 C.A.; S. Bridge [1989] *Conv.* 98.

3

SHORTHOLDS

The short "hold". Exclusions. Shorthold notices. Replacement tenancies. (Very limited) rent control. Other rights. Termination by the tenant. Repossession of assured shortholds. Warning notices. Accelerated procedures. Termination of protected shortholds.

A. THE SHORT "HOLD"

Shorthold tenancies now dominate the private sector residential letting market. They offer the assurance to the tenant of a right to occupy for a short fixed term, but after that short "hold" the landlord has a guarantee that he will be able to recover possession. According to the date on which the tenancy was originally granted,[1] a shorthold may fall into one of the three categories described below.

1. Section 19A assured shortholds

This is a tenancy created since the commencement of the Housing Act 1996.[2] Statute guarantees that the tenant will be entitled to remain for a minimum period of six months. However, it is no longer necessary to make a contractual grant for any fixed period. So the shorthold might be for an initial fixed term, or a periodic tenancy arising when the tenant holds over after the end of a section 19A fixed term,[3] or an initial grant of an open-ended periodic tenancy.[4] Whatever the form of the initial grant, the landlord will be prevented from terminating the lease during the initial six month period. Until 1997 formalities were a feature of the creation of shortholds, but almost all formalities have now been stripped away, so that any short residential lease granted by a private sector landlord will be a shorthold unless there is some special reason to exclude a particular grant.[5]

2. Old style assured shortholds

Assured shorthold tenancies were originally created by the Housing Act 1988.[6] Use grew from 15 per cent in 1990 to 40 per cent by 1994.[7] By the time of the major changes in

---

[1] Replacement tenancies are considered below at pp. 49–52.
[2] H.A. 1988 s.19A inserted by H.A. 1996 s.96, applying to tenancies granted on or after February 28th 1997: S.I. 1997/225. See Woodfall 24.028–24.032; Davey 238–247.
[3] H.A. 1988 s.5.
[4] An R.I.C.S. model is recommended: [1997] 11 *Comm. Leases* 1; N. Redman [1999] 3 *L.T. Rev.* 102 (precedent).
[5] For the public sector see below pp. 165–166.
[6] s.20 operating by s.141(3) from January 15th 1989; D. Clarke [1989] *N.L.J.* 74; C.P. Rodgers [1989] 12 *L.S.G.* 34; R. Cottrell (1991) 135 *S.J.* 1265; R. Smith [1994] 05 *E.G.* 144.
[7] Green, Thomas, Iles and Down *Housing in England 1994/95* (H.M.S.O., 1996).

1997 described above assured shortholds covered 90 per cent of all private sector tenancies, amounting to more than 1 million shortholds. The requirement was an initial grant for a fixed term of at least six months and the giving of a preparatory shorthold notice.[8] When a landlord granted accommodation before early 1997 it was vital to include an initial term certain of not less than six months,[9] and it was also important to ensure that the landlord had no power to terminate the tenancy within that six months[10] for any reason other than breach of covenant.[11] An unduly generous decision in favour of landlords was reached in *Bedding* v. *McCarthy*.[12] Here the fixed term ran from December 18th for exactly six months, but the shorthold notice was not given to the tenant until that same morning—the first day of the term—and it was not until later that day that the tenancy agreement was signed. The tenant enjoyed occupation rights for nine or 10 hours less than six months, but despite this shortfall it was held nevertheless to have been a valid shorthold grant. Landlord and tenant legislation was said to deal with days, and not with hours, minutes, and seconds.[13]

3.   Protected shorthold tenancies

The *assured* shorthold was a remodelling of the *protected* shorthold, a creature of the Housing Act 1980[14]—which was Conservative legislation designed to provide a way out of the full protection enjoyed by private sector residential tenants under the Rent Act 1977. They were first allowed in late 1980:[15] and continued to be granted until the assured shorthold was introduced early in 1989.[16]

In its 1980 conception, the shorthold took the form of a term certain of between one and five years,[17] though it was permissible to include an option for the extension of this fixed term. Termination by the landlord was not permitted before the expiration of the fixed contractual term, except that is through forfeiture for non-payment of rent or breach of some other covenant,[18] including bankruptcy.[19] The tenant (but not the landlord) had an opportunity to break the fixed term by notice.[20] If a fixed term shorthold was allowed to run on as a periodic tenancy, the tenancy was a protected shorthold tenancy until the end of the term certain and so, although the continuation was probably not

---

[8] See below pp. 46–47.

[9] *Mundy* v. *Hook* [1997] E.G.L.R. 119 C.A. (5 months was fully assured). There was no means of avoiding this minimum assurance: H.A. 1988 s.55; A. Jack [1995] *N.L.J.* 925; J.E. Martin [1995] *N.L.J.* 1024; J.E. Martin [1995] *N.L.J.* 1084; S. Bridge [1995] *N.L.J.* 1307.

[10] H.A. 1988 s.20(1), now as amended by H.A. 1996 sch.8 para.2(3).

[11] A right of forfeiture will not prevent a tenancy being an assured shorthold: s.45(5); really this is not a forfeiture.

[12] (1995) 27 H.L.R. 103 C.A.

[13] At 106, Nolan L.J.

[14] H.A. 1980 s.52; Woodfall 23.071–23.075; P.F. Smith [1982] *Conv.* 29; G.N. Prentice (1982) 126 *S.J.* 3, 24, 41; A. Arden [1980] 11 *L.A.G. Bull.* 26.

[15] November 28th 1980: S.I. 1980/1706.

[16] H.A. 1988 s.34 prohibited new protected tenancies on or after January 15th 1989.

[17] H.A. 1980 s.52(1).

[18] para.(a).

[19] *Paterson* v. *Aggio* (1987) 19 H.L.R. 551 C.A.; J.E. Martin [1987] *Conv.* 448.

[20] Duration: (1) 1 month (if the term was for 2 years or less); or (2) 3 months (if the term was for more than 2 years). Any contrary provision is void: H.A. 1980 s.53.

strictly a shorthold, possession could still be ordered on the shorthold ground.[21] Cases can still arise today if a fixed term was granted in, say, 1982 and has been left to run on.

B. EXCLUSIONS

Although the shorthold scheme has vastly improved the position of landlords, even the minimal guarantee of holding for six months is sometimes too much. In numerous cases a tenant is denied full residential security, and these same exceptions operate to remove the guarantee of the short fixed term hold.[22] In essence the exclusions break down into four categories:

1. Failure to grant exclusive possession of self-contained residential accommodation

So if a holiday-maker books into an hotel for a two week holiday, he does not hold a lease and cannot claim to hold for a minimum of six months.[23] This may be very important in the common situation in which a number of strangers share a flat together, an arrangement which creates a number of licences rather than one shorthold tenancy.[24]

2. Non-occupation

Statutory protection of a residential tenant is dependent upon continuing residential occupation,[25] so that a shorthold tenant can lose protection by sub-letting the entire property.[26]

3. Special circumstances

Many residential grants do not qualify for full security of tenure for a variety of reasons, examples being luxury properties, student accommodation, low rent lettings, and property with a resident landlord. These circumstances also justify withholding the guarantee of a six month short hold.

4. Other security regime

A grant cannot be a shorthold if it falls within the public residential, business, or agricultural sectors.

C. SHORTHOLD NOTICE

1. Abolition of the warning

Until early 1997 it was necessary to give the tenant a shorthold notice before creating a shorthold, though this rule was then reversed by statute.[27] The present position is that

---

[21] H.A. 1980 s.52(5); *Gent* v. *De La Mare* (1988) 20 H.L.R. 199; J.E. Martin [1988] *Conv.* 197.

[22] H.A. 1988 sch.19A, 20, 51, sch.1A; H.A. 1980 s.52, R.A. 1977 ss.4–16A.

[23] See below pp. 149–162.

[24] See below Chapter 6.

[25] Under the assured scheme this is required both during a contractual and a statutory phase: see below pp. 104–109.

[26] *Ujima H.Ass.* v. *Ansah* (1998) 30 H.L.R. 831 C.A.

[27] H.A. 1988 s.19A inserted by H.A. 1996 s.96; S. Gold [1997] *N.L.J.* 847.

a tenancy takes effect automatically as a section 19A shorthold unless steps are taken to confer full security of tenure. Full security arises under a notice to that effect given before the creation of the tenancy, by subsequent notice, or by contractual provision.[28] A shorthold notice provided a useful warning to the tenant that he would not enjoy full security of tenure, but this function is now lost. "Reform" was driven primarily by the difficulty that landlords (including, according to modern legal mythology, at least one judge!) had in coping with the technical requirements of the old law.[29] Much of the substance has been removed from the description of the shorthold as "assured".

Today shortholds may even be oral. Tenants have the limited protection of entitlement to demand from the landlord a statement of the terms of the tenancy,[30] including the date of commencement, the length of any fixed term, the amount of the rent, the rent days, and any rent review provision. Failure to provide information is an offence unless no variation has occurred since he last provided details. Though helpful in establishing rights under the tenancy, the shorthold statement is not, of course, conclusive of what has been agreed as against the tenant.[31] Removal of the requirement for a shorthold notice in 1997 represented an important change in the law, since there is no longer any requirement for the main terms of the tenancy to be evidenced in writing.[32] The impact of the change is less significant than it seems for a simple reason: accelerated repossession orders can be made to end an assured shorthold, but this procedure is withdrawn unless the shorthold (or at least the first in a chain of tenancies) is in writing.[33] This provides an overwhelming incentive for landlords to ensure that the terms of shortholds are recorded in writing.

2.   Assured shorthold notices

If a landlord wished to create an assured shorthold before early 1997, it was essential for him—the landlord[34]—to give a notice on the tenant before the tenancy was entered into stating that it was to be a shorthold tenancy.[35] Some leeway was allowed in *Bedding* v. *McCarthy*[36] since a term running from December 18th was held to be a shorthold even though notice was not given until the morning of the 18th—before the grant of the tenancy but after the start of the six months term. The form was prescribed.[37]

Wise landlords took steps to ensure that the tenant understood the warning that his security would be limited, perhaps by allowing a gap of a day before the tenancy was entered into, or by requiring the tenant to sign a copy of the notice confirming that he

[28] H.A. 1988 sch.2A paras.1–3 introduced by H.A. 1996 sch.7. If the tenant is already fully assured, a shorthold can be created by the service of a shorthold notice under sch.2A para.7.

[29] J. Driscoll [1996] 04 *L.S.G.* 22, [1996] *N.L.J.* 1699.

[30] H.A. 1988 s.20A; H.A. 1996 s.97; any one of the tenants can insist against any one of the landlords. Social sector tenants have a Charter right to a written tenancy agreement: *Shorthold Tenant's Charter* (Housing Corporation, 1998) section 3.

[31] H.A. 1988 s.20A(5).

[32] s.19A; H.A. 1996 s.96.

[33] See below pp. 57–61.

[34] Or one of them: H.A. 1988 s.20(6). However a notice served in the name of an agent was held valid in *Campbell* v. *Chu* [1999] 06 C.L. 416 C.Ct.

[35] H.A. 1988 s.20(1), now as amended by H.A. 1996 sch.8 para.2(3).

[36] (1995) 27 H.L.R. 103 C.A.

[37] S.I. 1988/2203 form 7; as amended by S.Is. 1990/1532, 1993/654. This form is now redundant: S.I. 1997/194.

had read it. It was important for the correct landlord to give notice to the actual tenant.[38] Without a notice the tenancy was not an assured shorthold, since there was no power to dispense with notice for tenancies created between early 1989 and early 1997.[39]

However innumerable defective notices were given, so many that separate discussion is required immediately below. Possession on the assured shorthold basis required a valid shorthold notice. The key is the word valid. A partial way round this was to seek possession on Ground 1,[40] namely that the landlord required the property for his own residence. It was best to reserve the future availability of Ground 1 by serving a warning notice in advance of the grant of the tenancy, but there is a residual and exceptional power to allow possession in the absence of a notice where it is just and equitable to do so.[41] So if a tenancy was granted without any prior warning notice between early 1989 and early 1997, it may still be possible to recover possession on the basis that the dwelling is required for the landlord.

3. Defective assured shorthold notices

Innumerable shorthold notices are reaching the courts that have technical defects in them. Some landlords failed to observe the correct prescribed form[42]—for example by using out of date forms which fail to give up to date warnings to the tenant.[43] The vital importance of including the statutory warnings emerges from *Manel* v. *Memon*.[44] In this case the landlord's section 20 notice omitted the prescribed[45] advice to the tenant; these "bullet points" advised the tenant of the wisdom of obtaining legal advice, pointed out that he was not committed before signing the tenancy agreement and advised him to keep the notice in a safe place. These bullet points were part of the substance of the notice, which was neither in the proper form nor a form "substantially to the like effect".[46] The particular case showed that the landlord was not entitled to use the accelerated procedure for obtaining possession, but it also followed that the tenant had a full ("life-long") assurance.

In most cases dates have been muddled. Substantial compliance with the prescribed form is essential since major errors invalidate the notice and the consequence of an error was (before early 1997) to confer life-long security on the tenant through a full assurance. A major misstatement of the length of the term means that the notice will not have been effective to secure shorthold status for the tenancy. Thus a notice stating that the term is for six months cannot protect a written tenancy document providing for a 12 month term.[47]

---

[38] *Demetriou* v. *Panayi* [1998] C.L.Y. 3597.

[39] *Marath* v. *MacGillivray* (1996) 28 H.L.R. 484 C.A.; *Clickex Ltd.* v. *McCann* [1999] 2 E.G.L.R. 63 C.A.; *R.* v. *Sefton Housing Benefit Review Board ex parte Brennan* (1997) 29 H.L.R. 735, 741 Dyson J.

[40] H.A. 1988 sch.2; see below p. 348.

[41] *Mustafa* v. *Ruddock* (1998) 30 H.L.R. 495 C.A. (estate agent's error and was just and equitable); S. & J. Murdoch [1997] 35 *E.G.* 93.

[42] S.I. 1988/2203 form 7 as amended; see immediately above.

[43] *Andrews* v. *Brewer* (1998) 30 H.L.R. 203 C.A. (notice valid on facts).

[44] [2000] Times April 5th C.A.

[45] S.I. 1988/2203 as amended by S.I. 1997/194.

[46] *Tegerdine* v. *Brooks* (1977) 36 P. & C.R. 261, 267; *Gill* v. *Cremodez* [2000] 09 C.L. 470 (agent).

[47] *Panayi* v. *Roberts* (1993) 25 H.L.R. 421 C.A.; P.F. Smith [1993] *Conv.* 301; *Mundy* v. *Hook* (1998) 30 H.L.R. 551 C.A. (notice said 5 months when 6 months was intended).

However many courts have ignored technical defects, taking the view that what matters is the substance of the warning given to the tenant that his security will be limited. The current crop of cases has coincided with the decision in *Mannai Investments Co. Ltd. v. Eagle Star Life Assurance Co. Ltd.*[48] to allow more flexibility in the interpretation of commercial break clauses, and arguably the case for flexibility is even greater where ordinary landlords are dealing with lettings without legal advice. The principle does apply to a common law notice to quit[49] and also to a statutory notice[50] and shorthold notices.[51] Evident errors are ignored where, for example, 1793 is written for 1993.[52] Also disregarded is any error which is so obvious that a reasonable reader would have no doubts about the intended meaning if the notice were to be placed side by side with the tenancy agreement. In *Andrews* v. *Brewer*[53] the shorthold notice misstated the final year of the tenancy but the notice was held to be substantially to the same effect as the statutory notice so that shorthold termination was permitted. *York* v. *Casey*[54] is the leading case; in it a notice correctly stated that the term was for six months from September 28th 1996 at £500 a month, but incorrectly stated that the term ended that same September. This error was obvious, it would be reasonably clear to any tenant that the term date was March 27th 1997, and so the notice was valid.

Clickex Ltd. v. *McCann*[55] shows the limits to the more sympathetic approach to bad drafting, since the case accepts[56] the application of *Mannai*[57] but decides that the particular notice was not clear when read in the context of the tenancy agreement and that a reasonable recipient would be left in doubt about the true termination date. It had originally been intended to grant a tenancy of a room in Hounslow from December 21st 1995. A notice was given that same day specifying December 21st as the start date and June 23rd the next year as the termination date. However the previous tenant was slow to move out and the room was not actually available until January 8th 1996. On that date the tenancy agreement was altered by someone acting for the landlord to show January 8th 1996 as the start date and July 23rd as the term date. Unfortunately the shorthold notice was not amended and reissued. Holman J., sitting in the Court of Appeal, held[58] that the confusion was such that the notice was ineffective and hence the tenant was fully assured. Possession was refused since the landlord had not proved a ground for removing the tenant's full security of tenure.

4.   Protected shortholds

Shortholds were first introduced in 1980 as an exception to the full residential security normal at that time under the Rent Act 1977, but continued to be granted until early

[48] [1997] A.C. 749 H.L.; see below pp. 579–581.
[49] See above pp. 26–27.
[50] *Germax Securities Ltd.* v. *Spiegal* (1978) 37 P. & C.R. 204 C.A.
[51] *York* v. *Casey* [1998] 2 E.G.L.R. 25 C.A.
[52] *Panayi* at 425, Mann L.J.
[53] (1998) 30 H.L.R. 203 C.A.
[54] [1998] 2 E.G.L.R. 25 C.A.
[55] [1999] 2 E.G.L.R. 63 C.A.
[56] At 65L, Holman J.
[57] [1997] A.C. 749H.
[58] At 66C.

1989 when they were superseded by the assured shortholds discussed above. To claim the advantages of the shorthold, it was necessary for the landlord to give the tenant a shorthold notice in advance.[59] A form was prescribed[60] and it was essential to follow it since major errors removed the tenancy from the category of the protected shorthold, as also was the case if no notice at all was given.[61]

Courts do have power to dispense with the requirement of a prior shorthold notice, so that a tenancy can be treated as a *protected* shorthold where the court is later of the opinion that it is just and equitable to make an order for possession.[62] As has already been explained, this power is not available for grants after early 1989 under the assured scheme. The case does not need to be exceptional. In *R.J. Dunnell Property Investments Ltd.* v. *Thorpe*[63] one factor was that most of the house was already let to the tenant under another shorthold tenancy, the new lease merely adding two extra rooms. Also there was a clear oral agreement for a shorthold, equal bargaining power, and a freely negotiated rent. Obviously an important factor is whether the tenant had been given an oral warning that there was to be no more than a shorthold. *Boyle* v. *Verrall*[64] discusses a related situation of a claim by a landlord that he requires the house as his own residence (ground 1)[65] where the question is whether that dispensation from full security should be available where no oral warning had been given in advance. In *Boyle* the tenant (who was an out of work housing officer married to an out of work solicitor) clearly knew what was intended, so the case could be equated to an oral warning where the only omission was to reduce the warning to writing. However dicta and decisions suggest that the absence of a warning is not alone decisive and that a tenancy might be treated as a protected shorthold even without an oral warning.[66] The last point may be dubious since it would surely be a strong thing to deprive a tenant of Rent Act security which was the natural concomitant of a residential letting when the intention to do so remained unexpressed in the landlord's mind, and the widest dicta and decisions may not survive if there is ever an appeal to the Lords.

D. REPLACEMENT TENANCIES

1. Assured shortholds (after early 1989)

Similar provisions apply to all assured tenancies—whether granted under section 19A or earlier—which ensure that the six-month period of statutory protection runs once and is not triggered again by a renewal of the lease. Continuation is ended by any gap between lets, any change of parties or alteration of the property, so that a new six-month period of assurance runs in these circumstances.

[59] H.A. 1980 ss.52(1)(b), s.52(3).
[60] S.I. 1987/265, replacing S.Is. 1980/1707, 1981/1579.
[61] *Dibbs* v. *Campbell* (1988) 20 H.L.R. 374 C.A.; *Thalmann* v. *Evans* [1996] 2 C.L.Y. 3788.
[62] H.A. 1980 s.55(2).
[63] [1989] 2 E.G.L.R. 94 C.A.; *Arcwood* v. *Dow* [1996] 2 C.L.Y. 3787.
[64] [1997] 1 E.G.L.R. 25 C.A.; *Fernandes* v. *Parvardin* [1982] 2 E.G.L.R. 104 C.A.
[65] *Bradshaw* v. *Baldwin-Wiseman* (1985) 49 P. & C.R. 382, 388 (R.A. case 11); *Mustafa* v. *Ruddock* (1998) 30 H.L.R. 495 C.A. (assured tenancy ground 1).
[66] *Boyle* at 28B, Auld L.J.; *Mustafa* v. *Ruddock* (1998) 30 H.L.R. 495 C.A.

At the *end of any fixed term*, including a term granted by way of renewal of the initial fixed term,[67] a periodic tenancy arises by implication. This is called a statutory periodic assured shorthold,[68] and is itself a shorthold.[69] The period of the tenancy reflects the period of rent payments,[70] so the landlord is best served by ensuring that the rent is calculated monthly rather than yearly, thus shortening the period required for termination. Other terms of the periodic tenancy are carried forward from the fixed term, with the exception of any provisions about termination,[71] but there is an outright bar on assignment without consent.[72]

A *replacement section 19A tenancy* arises where an initial grant made after early 1997 ends and is replaced by a new tenancy, the new agreement between the same parties automatically qualifying as a shorthold. However, the assurance of six months' security of tenure operates only once, so security under the successor tenancy depends upon the contractual negotiation of a fixed term renewal. All successor tenancies which follow on immediately from an earlier section 19A shorthold are "replacement tenancies" while the landlord and tenant remain the same provided that the premises let also remain substantially the same.[73] A break in the chain of tenancies will cause a new six month period of assurance to run if, for example, there is a gap between two tenancies, a change of parties, or a substantial change in the scope of the property let.

Replacements for assured shortholds initially granted *before early 1997* operate under broadly similar principles, though with different legislative authorities. If tenancy 1 is shorthold, any successor tenancy 2 is also shorthold.[74] In *Lower Street Properties Ltd.* v. *Jones*[75] a shorthold notice given in 1989 still protected the landlord in 1994 despite several renewals and the death of the original tenant in the interim. This case therefore demonstrates that a shorthold notice was only required before the initial grant and then continues to operate through any number of replacement tenancies. Roll over continues so long as the premises are substantially the same, the parties are the same and the tenancy follows on from its predecessor immediately, unless, that is, the landlord chooses to confer full security of tenure by giving the tenant a notice switching to a fully assured tenancy.[76]

2.   Succession on death of a shorthold tenant

When a shorthold tenant dies, the tenancy will pass by succession to his spouse who is living with him at the time.[77] This includes a heterosexual cohabitee[78] such as the

---

[67] *Lower Street Properties Ltd.* v. *Jones* [1996] 2 E.G.L.R. 67 C.A. (the fact are given below); M. James [1996] *N.L.J.* 1517.

[68] H.A. 1988 s.5.

[69] s.19A(b); H.A. 1996 s.96.

[70] See above pp. 25–26.

[71] H.A. 1988 s.5(2)

[72] s.5(3) disapplies L.T.A. 1927 s.19 which usually implies that consent is not to be unreasonably refused.

[73] H.A. 1988 s.21(5)–(7) inserted by H.A. 1996 s.99; this is instead of the regime described in the next para.: s.20(5A).

[74] H.A. 1988 s.20(4).

[75] [1996] 2 E.G.L.R. 67 C.A.

[76] H.A. 1988 s.20(5).

[77] s.39(7).

[78] s.17(4).

defendant in *Lower Street Properties Ltd.* v. *Jones* who had succeeded when the tenant of the flat, Mr von Praag died.[79] Succession to a shorthold tenancy is as a shorthold.

3. Protected shortholds (before early 1989)

After an initial grant of a protected shorthold tenancy, successor tenancies will continue to be protected shorthold tenancies.[80] There is no difficulty about shifting from protected shorthold to assured shorthold basis.[81]

4. Converting from a fully assured tenancy (post 1989) to an assured shorthold

Until 1997, if tenancy 1 conferred full security of tenure, so did its replacement, tenancy 2.[82] However the landlord can now make tenancy 2 into a section 19A assured shorthold by the simple expedient of serving a prescribed notice proposing a shorthold to replace the existing tenancy with full security.[83] The tenant could refuse and stand on his existing security of tenure. Full security could be lost by surrender of the old tenancy or by leaving a gap between new and old.[84] Full security operates when the fixed term of an old style assured tenancy ends,[85] on succession on the death of a tenant with full security,[86] when a public sector secure tenancy has been privatised,[87] or when a long residential tenancy expires.[88]

5. Converting from a Rent Act tenancy (before early 1989) to a protected shorthold

A protected shorthold could not be granted so as to follow immediately after a tenancy with full security. This rule was designed to protect the full security of Rent Act tenants when the landlord regranted the lease. However this rule was easily avoided by getting the tenant to surrender his existing tenancy, which left the way clear for a later grant of a protected shorthold to the same tenant. A short gap in occupation was necessary between surrender and regrant, but 24 hours was sufficient.[89] In *Bolnore Properties Ltd.* v. *Cobb*[90] Wing Commander Cobb had a tenancy with full security on which substantial rent arrears built up. The landlord agreed not to enforce a warrant for possession if the arrears were paid, the couple surrendered their Rent Act tenancy and vacated the property for 24 hours, and accepted as a substitute a shorthold tenancy. A valid surrender was followed one day later by a valid shorthold grant.

---

[79] [1996] 2 E.G.L.R. 67 C.A.
[80] H.A. 1980 s.62(5) is limited to the end of the term certain but thereafter there is a statutory periodic tenancy to which the mandatory repossession grant applies.
[81] H.A. 1988 s.34(3) as amended by H.A. 1996 sch.8 para.2.
[82] H.A. 1988 s.20(3), no longer in force as a result of subs.(5A).
[83] H.A. 1988 sch.2A (inserted in 1996) paras.7 (assured shortholds), 9 (assured agricultural occupancies); S.I. 1997/194 (form).
[84] H.A. 1988 sch.2A paras.1–3.
[85] para.8.
[86] para.4.
[87] para.5. Registered social landlords (housing associations) must use a shorthold when housing the homeless: H.A. 1996 s.209.
[88] H.A. 1988 sch.2A para.6.
[89] *Dibbs* v. *Campbell* (1988) 20 H.L.R. 374 C.A.
[90] (1997) 29 H.L.R. 202 C.A.

A surrender is also needed if a landlord wishes to move from the protected scheme (until early 1989) to an assured shorthold (after that date).

E.   (VERY LIMITED) RENT CONTROL

1.   Assured shortholds

The fundamental assumption of the assured tenancy regime operating since early 1989 is that rents should be left to market forces. However a tenant has a minor protection during the original fixed term period, that is the period for which he is locked into the tenancy, since during that time the rent can be referred to a rent assessment committee. Assuming that there are sufficient comparables in the area to make a determination, the committee fixes the rent that might reasonably be expected for an assured shorthold.[91] Reference can occur only once, in the case of an older style assured shorthold during the initial fixed period, and in the case of a section 19A shorthold tenancy during the first six months.[92] The power is little used[93] and can be disapplied in its entirety.[94] Market forces operate once the initial fixed period has passed since a shorthold can be terminated and regranted at a higher rent.[95]

2.   Protected shortholds (created before early 1989)

When shortholds were first introduced in 1980, it was against a backcloth of Rent Act tenants who had a right to register a fair rent, though of course many were unregistered. Landlords were allowed to opt out of full security of tenure only if the rent was registered either before the tenancy was granted or immediately afterwards. This requirement was progressively dropped,[96] and in any event the court has jurisdiction to relieve against failure to register a rent.[97] Protected shorthold tenants retain the right to have a fair rent assessed by a rent assessment committee,[98] but they are unlikely to take the initiative since asking for a registration may be equivalent to serving one's own notice to quit! Most registrations are instigated by social security officials, the object being to limit housing benefit payments.

F.   OTHER RIGHTS OF SHORTHOLD TENANTS

In the **private sector**, shortholds confer all the normal rights of a residential tenant so long as they last, and in particular the right to insist that the structure and exterior is

---

[91] H.A. 1988 s.22(5A).

[92] s.22, and as amended by H.A. 1996 s.100 for s.19A tenancies.

[93] Only 1,600 referrals or so are made each year: Hansard H.L. (1996) vol.574 col.327. Presumably most are instigated by housing benefit officers. Pending applications continue even after the tenancy ceases to be assured or an assured shorthold.

[94] H.A. 1988 s.23.

[95] See below Chapter 7.

[96] H.A. 1980 s.52(1)(c) was applied: (1) everywhere, from November 28th 1980 to November 30th 1981; (2) in London, only from December 1st 1981 to May 3rd 1987: S.I. 1981/1578; and (3) nowhere, from May 4th 1987 onwards: S.I. 1987/ 265.

[97] *Dibbs* v. *Campbell* (1988) 20 H.L.R. 374 C.A.; *R.J. Dunnell Property Investments Ltd.* v. *Thorpe* [1989] 2 E.G.L.R. 94 C.A.; J.E. Martin [1990] *Conv.* 496.

[98] Rent Act 1977 part IV; see below Chapter 9.

maintained by the landlord and the right to live peacefully in his property.[99] Of course, the practical value of these rights is greatly diminished by the insecurity of the shorthold tenure. Shorthold tenants in the **social sector** may enjoy additional rights under the *Shorthold Tenant's Charter*.[100] Rights include the right to a written tenancy agreement, and to agree changes, the right of access, the right to live peacefully, the right to be treated fairly and rights to information. They also have the right to advice about securing alternative accommodation if they have not broken the terms of their tenancy. The *Charter* reiterates normal rights to challenge rents and service charges[101] and restates the landlord's statutory repairing obligations, as well as giving the right to a responsive repairs service and rights to be consulted about major work.[102] More generally, social tenants have rights to be consulted and to get involved in the management of their homes.[103] The *Charter* makes clear that these rights are insecure. Thus "having a shorthold tenancy means that you may rent your home until your landlord gives notice for you to leave",[104] and substantive rights are limited to the duration of the tenancy.[105] However social tenants may have some substantive protection not available in the private sector since

> "Your landlord should make every effort to help you stay in your home, applying for repossession or an eviction order only when there is no reasonable alternative."[106]

Private sector landlords can choose to end a shorthold whenever they wish.

G. TERMINATION BY THE TENANT

Very often a tenant wishes to move, either to a new area or because he has found better accommodation in the same locality. The landlord is entitled to charge rent until the tenancy is ended. If a fixed term was granted the landlord can insist on charging rent until that time has expired, unless there is a provision for the tenant to serve notice to end it. A tenant may have an argument that the landlord has a duty to mitigate his loss of rent by attempting to relet the property, though the authority for this is equivocal to say the least.[107]

At the exact moment that a fixed term ends, the tenant is entitled to quit. However many shortholds are periodic—either by way of initial grant or when a tenant holds over after the expiration of a fixed term.[108] Termination is by notice, which must be timed to expire at the end of a period of the tenancy, and the notice must be at least four weeks,[109] though these restrictions can be avoided if the landlord agrees to accept a surrender.

---

[99] See below Chapters 10 and 12.
[100] Housing Corporation (1998).
[101] Section 4.
[102] Section 5.
[103] Section 6.
[104] Section 1.
[105] Section 3.
[106] Section 3, p.6.
[107] See below pp. 221–222.
[108] H.A. 1988 s.5.
[109] P.E.A. 1977 s.5. Rules about the form of notices (in writing) and about service are considered elsewhere; see below pp. 588–594.

H. NOTICE WARNING OF REPOSSESSION

The landlord brings an assured shorthold to an end by giving a statutory warning notice and following that by a court application for a mandatory possession order under the accelerated procedure.[110]

1. Form of warning notice

The tenant must be given a warning that the landlord[111] will require possession. Notice must be in writing,[112] and must comply with the Protection from Eviction Act 1977[113] but otherwise the form is not prescribed. It must be of at least two months in duration,[114] and must expire after the statutory six-month period of assurance.

Clearly the legislation is intended to give the shorthold tenant a breathing space of two months before proceedings are instituted, and in order to be safe, the landlord should allow the notice to expire before taking action. In *Lower Street Properties Ltd.* v. *Jones*,[115] proceedings were commenced one day early, still within the two-month warning period. Both Lords Justice who heard the appeal considered that the particular proceedings were premature. Schiemann L.J.[116] thought that the Act excluded the right to take proceedings during the currency of the notice, but Kennedy L.J.'s opinion was that a notice *could* reserve the right to take action within the two-month limit by appropriate wording.[117] The former view is to be preferred.

2. Warning notice given within the fixed contractual term

A shorthold is terminable at the end of any fixed contractual period, though this is of course subject to the statutory minimum assurance of six months. Notice can be served requiring possession at the expiration of the fixed term, but also in the two months leading up to the term date,[118] so that a correctly timed notice can leave the landlord ready to proceed the instant that the fixed term runs out. The periodic tenancy that is implied to cover the gap between the expiration of the notice and the case for possession reaching the courts will in no way inhibit repossession.[119]

Provided that the minimum six-month period of assurance has expired, the landlord may be able to terminate a shorthold tenancy by exercise of a break clause, if one was agreed in advance and incorporated into the lease. Thus in *Aylward* v. *Fawaz*[120] an assured shorthold was granted for one year, subject to termination by the landlord by

[110] C.P. Rodgers (1991) 135 *S.J.* 728.
[111] Or any one of joint landlords: H.A. 1988 s.21(1)(a).
[112] H.A. 1988 s.21(1)(b), (4)(a) as amended by H.A. 1996 s.98. This corrects the initially defective legislation. The landlord may be estopped from relying on the notice: *Mundy* v. *Hook* [1997] 2 C.L.Y. 3247 C.Ct. (on appeal (1998) 30 H.L.R. 551 C.A.).
[113] *Ujima H.Ass.* v. *Ansah* (1998) 30 H.L.R. 831 C.A.
[114] H.A. 1988 s.21(1).
[115] [1996] 2 E.G.L.R. 67 C.A.
[116] At 883–884.
[117] At 883. On this view the two month limit regulated the earliest permissible date for a possession order to take effect.
[118] H.A. 1988 s.21(1).
[119] s.21(3).
[120] (1997) 29 H.L.R. 408 C.A.

one month's prior notice at any time after the initial six months. The break clause was perfectly valid. After the end of the six month period of assurance the landlord gave a notice warning of his requirement for possession, and it was held that this statutory notice was also effective to exercise the break clause and to end the contractual term. There was no need for a second document.

3. Termination within a period of contractual security

The landlord[121] cannot generally recover possession of the property during the initial fixed term of the shorthold, except by the agreement of the tenant to surrender the term, or, as just explained, under the operation of a break clause.[122]

Most landlords will be content to wait until the end of the relatively short fixed term security provided by a shorthold tenancy, but if there has been a lengthy fixed grant it should be made terminable on breach of any term of the lease. Some of the statutory grounds for possession are available within the contractual term, provided that the lease defines them as termination events. The grounds available[123] are:

> Mandatory: Ground 8 (3 months arrears of rent at date of hearing); and Discretionary: Grounds 10 (rent arrears), 11 (persistent arrears of rent), 12 (breach of other obligation), 13 (waste, neglect or default), 14 (nuisance, illegal or immoral use), and 15 (damage to furniture).

It is also possible to rescind a tenancy for mistake if the tenant applied for the tenancy on a particular basis and it turns out that he misstated his position.[124] Any discretion exercised by the judge is based on the terms of the statutory ground for possession. Termination of a shorthold is not technically a forfeiture since no relief is available. Two months' notice of proceedings is usually required, though there is provision to dispense with the notice requirement where it is just and equitable to do so.[125]

Mortgage lenders may use the mandatory Ground 2 where the shorthold has been created in breach of the terms of the mortgage, in which case the period of notice of proceedings is reduced to two weeks.

4. Warning notice during a periodic phase

Termination of a shorthold will almost always occur while the tenancy is periodic. Where the shorthold was granted before early 1997, there had to be an initial fixed term of at least six months, so that a periodic tenancy arises by implication when that fixed term expires.[126] Termination usually occurs while the tenancy is periodic, unless the landlord serves notice within the last two months of the fixed term. A section 19A shorthold (granted after early 1997) may be for a fixed term exceeding six months, for six months exactly, or for a shorter term, or it may be periodic from the outset, though in all cases the statutory assurance will operate for the first six months.

---

[121] Or one of joint landlords: H.A. 1988 s.21(2).
[122] See above text to n. 120.
[123] See below Chapter 13.
[124] *Nutt* v. *Read* [1999] Times December 3rd C.A.; see below pp. 347–348.
[125] H.A. 1988 s.8; *Kelsey H.Ass.* v. *King* (1996) 28 H.L.R. 270 C.A.
[126] H.A. 1988 s.5.

A statutory periodic tenancy can be brought to an end by a notice to quit, being of at least two months' duration (or longer if the period is longer)[127] ending on the last day of a period of the tenancy. These rules could be a trap if the period day is wrongly identified. However, flexibility has been demonstrated by those courts which have accepted that a properly worded notice may be valid if the two months of the notice more than spans the period of a tenancy. Thus in *Lower Street Properties Ltd.* v. *Jones*[128] notice requiring possession was issued when the fixed term had ended and the shorthold had become periodic in character. The June 1994 notice did not specify a date for possession, but rather it asked for possession "at the end of the period of your tenancy, which will end after 2 months from service of this notice". This date could easily be checked and was long enough to give the statutory period of notice. Usually a specific date is stated and, if so, it must be at the end of a period of a tenancy. The effect of minor defects in the statement of the dates in a section 21 notice was considered at first instance in *Clickex Ltd.* v. *McCann*,[129] though this ceased to be relevant on appeal and, as Holman J. pointed out in the Court of Appeal, any defect is easily cured. The court is bound to order possession after a valid application, the court order operating to terminate any periodic tenancy.[130]

I.   ACCELERATED REPOSSESSION PROCEDURES

These offer a landlord a speedy means of evicting a shorthold tenant after the two month warning period given by the notice requiring possession. An order is usually made on the basis of written evidence without a hearing, though possession should only be ordered in this peremptory fashion where the landlord's right to possession is clear-cut. Many cases fail to meet the technical requirements of the accelerated procedure and are then transferred to the normal repossession procedure.

1.   Venue

County courts have jurisdiction over all actions affecting assured tenants,[131] and in the case of the accelerated repossession this is exclusive,[132] so that the claim must be made in the court for the district in which the land is situated.[133]

2.   Rules structure

The fast track to repossession was first introduced for protected shorthold tenancies in 1981, and these tenancies retain distinct legislative authorities[134] apparently outside the

---

[127] s.21(4)(a)(b). But this is "without prejudice to s.21(1) above", which suggests that a straight 2 months may be sufficient: N. Madge [1998] 03 *L.S.G.* 27.

[128] [1996] 2 E.G.L.R. 67 C.A.; *Ujima H.Ass.* v. *Richardson* [1996] 2 C.L.Y. 3771, Graham J. (period ended Monday; notice valid though ended on Thursday).

[129] [1999] 2 E.G.L.R. 63, 64F–G.

[130] H.A. 1988 s.21(3).

[131] H.A. 1988 s.40; H.C.C.C.J.O. 1991 art 2(1).

[132] C.P.R. sch.2 C.C.R. Order 49 r.6A.

[133] C.P.R. sch.2 C.C.R. Order 49 r.6A(5); P.D. 8.B7.

[134] See below pp. 325–327 (but now repealed).

Woolf reforms. Attention is here confined to the accelerated procedure against assured shorthold tenants first made available in 1993.[135]

Woolf day was April 26th 1999, the day on which the Civil Procedure Rules 1998 and associated Practice Directions came into force. The main features of the reforms are described in the chapter on domestic repossession,[136] but their impact on accelerated repossession procedures is minimal. Shorthold tenants[137] face a distinctive procedure under the terms of the old County Court Rules, which have been re-enacted with only minimal modifications in schedule 2 of the Civil Procedure Rules.[138] Part 8 procedure applies where there is no specific provision, for example in relation to service.[139]

3.   Forms

Accelerated repossession proceedings are taken yet further from the mainstream by the Part 4 Practice Direction that retains the old N forms rather than the usual Part 8 claim form—including form N5A for assured shortholds,[140] the familiar "plaintiff" becoming a "claimant", though defendants emerge from the reforms unscathed.[141] Form N5B is treated as a claim form [142] and it appears that this form may legitimately be amended to refer to the landlord as a claimant.[143] Forms used in later stages of accelerated repossession proceedings are forms N11B for the tenant's reply, N206A to issue the application with a written request for possession, and N26A as the form of order for possession. One of the fundamental objectives of the Woolf reforms is to replace the diverse methods of commencing actions with a unified claim form.

4.   Section 19A tenancies

Section 19A tenancies have been created since early 1997 and create valid shortholds without any prior shorthold notice and without the need for any fixed term grant. The procedural rules were amended at that time[144] to apply accelerated repossession procedures subject to the following conditions:

the tenancy was granted after early 1989;[145]
there is a claim to recovery of possession of a dwelling, and no other claim (for example for arrears of rent);
there was initially a grant of an assured shorthold term;[146]
the tenancy is subject to a written agreement,[147] so that initial oral grants are outside the procedure; as explained below special provisions are made for chains of shortholds so that it is the initial grant which had to be in writing; and finally

[135] C.C.R. Order 49 r.6A, introduced by S.I. 1993/2175 and amended to reflect the H.A. 1996 by S.I. 1997/1837.
[136] See below Chapter 13.
[137] N. Madge [1999] 05 *Legal Action* 16.
[138] C.P.R. 50.
[139] See below pp. 593–594.
[140] P.D. 4 Table 1; Atkins *Court Forms* (2nd ed., Butterworths) 1999 annual supplement 67–74.
[141] C.P.R. 2.3.
[142] P.D. 4.
[143] J. Frenckel [1999] 18 *L.S.G.* 36.
[144] S.I. 1997/1837 r.7(1).
[145] Thus requiring full proceedings for protected shortholds.
[146] There are additional requirements where the present tenancy is a successor; see below pp. 59–61.
[147] C.P.R. sch.2 C.C.R. Order 49 r.6A(3)(c)(i).

a notice warning that the landlord required possession was given and has expired.

The claim form (N5B) has therefore to include the following statements:

identification of the dwelling-house;

that the dwelling-house was not let to the current tenant (whether by the landlord or any predecessor) before early 1989;

that possession is required on the expiry of an assured shorthold and giving sufficient particulars to substantiate the claim to possession;

details of the notice warning of the landlord's requirement for possession under section 21;

confirmation that after the expiration of any fixed term there is no new assured tenancy other than an assured periodic tenancy; and

confirmation that no notice has been served conferring a full assurance on the tenant.[148]

The district judge will rely on the papers to judge whether a possession order should be made, so it is essential to attach to the application, and to verify on oath,[149] the following documents:

a copy of the first and current (most recent) written tenancy agreement;

a copy of the section 21 warning notice; and

any other documents necessary to prove the claim.

5.   Tenancies requiring a shorthold notice

Additional requirements apply to grants of assured shortholds made between early 1989 and early 1997, since at that time creation of a valid assured shorthold depended upon service of a valid shorthold notice before the grant,[150] and upon an initial fixed term grant for six months. These matters must be proved at the stage of repossession as an element of the entitlement to take back the land. The accelerated procedure will apply only if the recipient of the notice is also the current tenant against whom repossession is being sought.[151] Where the current tenancy is the original grant to the tenant, proof of the above matters is proof that there is a shorthold tenancy and repossession must be ordered.[152]

The N5B claim form must include all the statements specified for section 19A tenancies above *and* in addition the following statements:

that a written shorthold notice was served on the tenant;[153] where the tenancy is a successor of the original tenancy the notice must have been given before the first assured tenancy of the premises, and—if advantage is to be taken of the accelerated procedure—it must have been given to the current tenant;

---

[148] H.A. 1988 s.20(5).
[149] See below pp. 322–323.
[150] H.A. 1988 s.20; defective notices are discussed above at pp. 47–48.
[151] C.P.R. sch.2 C.C.R. Order 49 r.6A(3)(d).
[152] r.6A (3)–(8).
[153] H.A. 1988 s.20(2).

a statement confirming that the landlord had no power to determine the tenancy earlier than six months.[154]

In addition to the copy documents indicated above for section 19A tenancies, the application must also have attached to it:

a copy of the shorthold notice.

As with the other documents this must be verified on oath.

The accelerated repossession claim form (Form N5B) requires it to be sworn in accordance with the court rules governing accelerated repossession that prescribe the form[155] and require that the requisite statements and documents attached to the application "shall be verified by the claimant on oath".[156] A Practice Direction now makes clear that the statement of truth generally required in Woolf statements of case[157] is not acceptable in accelerated repossessions.[158] Retention of the requirement for an oath is surely understandable where a tenant is being evicted summarily from his home without the protection of any judicial hearing.

6. Derivative tenancies

Additional requirements exist in the case of derivative tenancies—that is where the current tenant is a successor to the original grant—because if tenancy 1 gave full security of tenure (under either the Rent Act 1977 or a full assurance), tenancy 2 will also give full security. True a valid surrender may be proved, which would enable tenancy 2 to be granted as a shorthold, but only in full repossession proceedings. Therefore, to take advantage of the accelerated procedure, it is necessary to prove that all previous tenancies were assured shortholds,[159] and that this is clearly and indisputably so. Suppose T was given a fixed term of one year and that when it expires a regrant is negotiated (tenancy 2) for a further year at an increased rent; the accelerated procedure will then apply. However, a requirement for its application to replacement tenancies, the requirement of an initial written grant, must be proved. A break occurs on a change of parties, or of the property, or on any gap between the lettings.

Rules permitting accelerated repossession differentiate cases in which an original fixed term tenancy has expired (paragraph (3)) from ones in which the current tenancy is a regrant after an earlier assured shorthold (paragraph (9)). The distinction was originally drawn before the Housing Act 1996 when the distinction was more comprehensible. Even then there were three possibilities with only two clearly allocated—termination at the exact expiration of a fixed term is placed within paragraph (3) and renewal of a fixed term is placed within paragraph (9). By far the commonest case was one in which the initial fixed term expired and the tenancy was allowed to run on

---

[154] C.P.R. sch.2 C.C.R. Order 49 r.6A(6)(g); literally this requirement also applies to a s.19A (after early 1997) grant but this is surely a mistake.

[155] r.6A(5).

[156] r.6A(8).

[157] C.P.R. 22; P.D. 22.

[158] P.D. 22.1.6; S. Gerlis (1999) 34 *L.S.G.* 38. This point caused considerable confusion immediately after Woolf day.

[159] C.P.R. sch.2 C.C.R. Order 49 r.6A(9)–(10).

without being terminated, the continuation being as a statutory periodic tenancy. This case was probably intended to fall within paragraph (3)[160]—at least if the rent has not been increased—but unfortunately also literally falls within the wording of paragraph (9). If this commonest case is excluded paragraph (3) is left with virtually no content, but if a case does fall within the wording of paragraph (9) this should apply to the exclusion of all others. The borderline between the two procedures is even more obscure with section 19A tenancies since there is no longer any requirement for an initial fixed term. A tenancy is presumably a successor (paragraph (9)) where the initial periodic tenancy is surrendered by agreement and a new one regranted after a rent increase has been negotiated, but it is also possible on modern theory to increase the rent without ending the existing tenancy in which case paragraph (3) can continue to operate after a rent increase.[161]

All of the above conditions for the operation of the accelerated procedure apply, including those for section 19A tenancies and (where the grant was before early 1997) the requirement for a shorthold notice and fixed six month period of assurance. However there are two distinctive requirements for successor tenancies.

> One: the current tenancy must not follow immediately after an assured tenancy which was not an assured shorthold, since in that case the tenant will enjoy "life-long" security;[162] and
>
> Two: there must be written evidence of the terms of the tenancy. Thus it may be that the successor is itself in writing, or that the previous agreement was in writing and that the current successor is on the same terms except as to rent, or that it relates to the same premises and is on the same terms as a previous tenancy (apart form rent and duration).[163]

In terms of statements in the N5B claim form these look very similar to those already described. All are listed for completeness, but only those italicised are distinctive for successor tenancies.

> Identification of the dwelling-house;
> *Either that the tenancy agreement is written, or (if it is oral or periodic) that it is on same terms as a previous periodic or fixed term tenancy (apart from length and term date);*
> A statement that the dwelling-house was not let to the current tenant (*whether by the landlord or any predecessor*) before early 1989;
> A statement that possession is required on the expiry of an assured shorthold and sufficient particulars to substantiate the claim to possession;
> That a written shorthold notice was served on the tenant before the first assured tenancy of the premises on the current tenant;
> Details of the notice warning of the landlord's requirement for possession under section 21;

---

[160] r.6A(6)(f).
[161] See below Chapter 9.
[162] r.6A(9)(c)(ii).
[163] r.6A(9)(c)(ii) subparas.(aa)–(ac).

If a fixed term expired, a statement that apart from an assured periodic tenancy there is no other assured tenancy in existence; and

A statement confirming that the landlord had no power to determine the tenancy earlier than six months;[164]

A statement that no notice has been served conferring a full assurance on the tenant;[165] and

A statement of the current rent payable under the tenancy.

7. Accelerated repossession orders

The sworn claim form (N5B) and the copy documents as indicated above must be issued in court. The court effects service, by sending the documents and a reply form to the defendant by first class post at the address stated in the application.[166]

A defendant who wishes to oppose the repossession has 14 days from service to complete and deliver to the court a form of reply.[167] After that date the case will not go to the district judge until the landlord applies for the possession order, and the defendant can in practice enter a defence at any time until the landlord makes that application. In any event, the court always has a residual discretion to extend time limits.[168] The case will be referred to the district judge immediately a reply is received. He considers the case only on the basis of the papers—the application, attached documents, and any reply. If there is any doubt about the clear right to possession he lists the case for hearing. Otherwise the district judge is required to make a possession order without delay.[169] A tenant may apply to set aside a possession order within 14 days.[170]

8. Hearing under normal repossession procedure

Specific cases mentioned in the rule are where the right to an accelerated repossession order is not established, no shorthold notice was given where this was required, that there was no notice warning of the landlord's requirement for possession, or that service of the proceedings was faulty, or more generally that the landlord has not established his right to possession under section 21.[171] All went wrong for the landlord in *Manel* v. *Memon*,[172] after the tenant took the point that the landlord's section 20 notice omitted the prescribed[173] "bullet points" of advice to the tenant.[174] The solicitor who was

---

[164] r.6A(6)(g); literally this requirement applies equally to a s.19A tenancy (granted after early 1997) but this is surely a mistake.

[165] H.A. 1988 s.20(5).

[166] C.P.R. sch.2 C.C.R. Order 49 r.6A(11). If the claim form is returned, the court gives notice to the landlord, who may request bailiff service; this is done by posting through the letter box of the property, by delivery to a person at the property appearing to be 16 or over, or to the tenant in person: C.P.R. sch.2 C.C.R. Order 25 r.3(3A)–(3D), inserted by C.P.Am.R. 2000 r.32.

[167] r.6A(12).

[168] C.P.R. 3.8–3.10.

[169] C.P.R. sch.2 C.C.R. order 49 r.6A(17). There is power to extend the time for possession (to a maximum of six weeks) on the grounds of exceptional hardship to the tenant; if this is argued the case must be listed for hearing: S. Gold [2000] *N.L.J.* 1369.

[170] r.6A(19).

[171] *Aylward* v. *Fawaz* (1997) 29 H.L.R. 408 C.A. (defence that tenant's son had sickle cell disease led to full hearing, though landlord won at trial).

[172] [2000] Times April 5th C.A.

[173] S.I. 1988/2203 as amended by S.I. 1997/194.

[174] See above p. 47.

advising the tenant had applied for emergency legal aid to defend and had written a letter to the court outlining his objections to the form of notice given. A possession order was made by the district judge under the accelerated procedure, but the Court of Appeal held that this was not an appropriate case to use the procedure where an issue had been raised which, if true, gave an arguable defence, as otherwise the onus would be wrongly shifted to tenant. Hence it was wrong to make an order on the papers and the judge should have fixed a day for a hearing. In this particular case it was not merely a shift to a slower procedure, since the absence of a shorthold notice prevented the creation of a shorthold before early 1997, and so it followed that the tenant had a full ("life-long") assurance.

In this and similar cases the district judge will list the case for a private[175] hearing by a judge,[176] giving any appropriate directions. The landlord has failed to obtain an accelerated possession order—some 50 per cent of cases fail[177]—but is transferred to the normal repossession proceedings and may or may not be able to establish grounds for possession. Here the failed accelerated case joins any normal repossession proceedings started against assured shorthold tenants—for example if the original grant was oral.[178] Defended cases begun before Woolf day—April 26th 1999—will fall into the net of the new procedures in relation to procedural steps taken after that date.[179]

J.   TERMINATION OF PROTECTED SHORTHOLDS

Protected shortholds were created in 1980 as a means of avoiding full Rent Act 1977 security. At the end of the fixed term and any contractual extension, the landlord may recover possession under Case 19, which was added to the Rent Act 1977 in 1980.[180] This provision is different from, and more complex than, the corresponding rules for assured shortholds.

1.   Warning notice

The landlord must give an appropriate notice to the tenant. The notice should be in writing and should state that proceedings under Case 19 may be brought when it expires. The notice must be served[181] in the correct window before the contractual term date, that is in the three month period leading up to the expiration of the fixed term, and it must be of at least three months' duration.[182] If the correct date for termination is missed in one year the protected shorthold can be terminated in the window opened in any later year.

---

[175] P.D. 39.1.4A–39.1.5; J. Frenkel [1999] 19 *L.S.G.* 31.
[176] C.P.R. 8.9(c) (District Judge may not hear case for recovery of land); S. Gold [1999] *N.L.J.* 718.
[177] N. Madge [1998] *N.L.J.* 546.
[178] See below pp. 320–325.
[179] C.P.R. 51.2; P.D. 51; M. Walker [1999] 14 *L.S.G.* 32. Dormant cases will be struck out if no step is taken before April 26th 2000. This does not affect execution: P.D. 51.19.
[180] R.A. 1977 sch.15 part II.
[181] *Henry Smith's Charity Trustees* v. *Kyriakou* [1989] 2 E.G.L.R. 110 C.A. (methods of service).
[182] Or longer if necessary to terminate a periodic tenancy under which the tenant is holding over.

2. Prompt issue of proceedings

Action is required promptly after the end of a valid notice period: proceedings must be commenced within three months of the expiry of the notice. This is a fundamental pre-condition to the existence of jurisdiction to make a possession order, so that tardy commencement of proceedings loses the right to possession, and the notice procedure must be restarted in a later year.[183] After an inappropriate notice, the defect can be remedied immediately by giving a proper notice. But if a notice is proper and simply runs out, service of a fresh notice is blocked for three months. In practice this condemns the landlord to wait until the next year's cycle.

> **Example.** A shorthold tenancy was granted on July 10th 1987 for a fixed term of five years. The contractual term expired on July 9th 1992 and has not been renewed. The landlord could then terminate the tenancy by notice and proceedings taken around that date. The notice warning the tenant of Case 19 proceedings could be served in the three months ending on July 9th 1992, that is in the period beginning on April 9th 1992. This creates the window within which notice must be served. The window April 9th to July 9th will be the period within which notice has to be served in that and every succeeding year.
>
> Suppose notice was served on June 9th 1992. The duration of the warning given to the tenant had to be at least three months. Suppose notice was served then and to give five months' warning; it would expire on November 9th 1992. Case 19 is then available to the landlord provided proceedings are instituted within three months, that is before February 9th 1993. If the landlord fails to meet this deadline he can start again by notice served in the period April 9th to July 9th in any later year.

Unnecessarily complex surely? These rules compare unfavourably with the neater rules for assured shorthold tenancies, and could now be repealed, after a period of warning has been given to sitting tenants.

3. Right to a short possession order

Once the landlord has proved that the occupier's security is limited or that there is a mandatory ground for possession, the court must make a possession order and powers of suspension are very strictly controlled. Possession should not generally be postponed for more than 14 days, though if exceptional hardship is demonstrated this could be extended to six weeks.[184]

4. Accelerated repossession procedure

Accelerated procedures were first introduced in 1981[185] to provide speedy repossession procedures where possession was sought under the mandatory grounds of the Rent Act.[186] Proceedings are commenced by originating application to the County Court of

---

[183] *Ridehalgh* v. *Horsefield* (1992) 24 H.L.R. 453 C.A.; S. Bridge [1993] *Conv.* 238.
[184] H.A. 1980 s.89.
[185] S.I. 1981/139.
[186] R.A. Cases 11, 12, 20 if notice (form A); 13–18 (form B); 19 if protected shorthold (form C).

the district where the land is situated, with no action for possession being required. Forms of application and affidavit in support are prescribed. Service must usually be 14 clear days.[187] The district judge can grant a possession order in private, though if there is any doubt about entitlement to the mandatory ground claimed the case will be listed for full hearing. The procedures survive Woolf and operate outside his reforms.

---

[187] Reduced to 7 days under Cases 11, 12, 20.

4

ALLOCATION AND HOMELESSNESS

Choice of regime: allocation transfers and exchanges, homelessness. Towards permanent housing: inquiries; homelessness; accommodation pending a review. Housing preference: allocation, homelessness, priority need, charter rights of social applicants. Family grouping. Intentionality. Suitability of accommodation. Reviews. Local connection. Overseas applicants. Asylum seekers. Reform proposals.

A. CHOICE OF REGIME

Few tenants today are lucky enough to enjoy long-term security of tenure, and most of those who do are the tenants of public or social sector landlords. So public housing is a valuable prize, always in scarce supply, which calls for fair allocation and requires procedural checks to ensure that the tenants who are chosen are those with most need. Three interlocking regimes provide respectively for the allocation of housing, the transfer or exchange of existing accommodation, and for the homeless, and the object of this introductory section is to identify which regime applies to which applicants.

1. Allocation

This is the process by which people who have applied to a housing authority are chosen to receive a public sector tenancy for the first time. After entry on the housing register the applicant has to wait until the authority is able to make an offer of accommodation and, even if it is no longer sound to talk of a "waiting list", this is in practice what a housing register is. The authority is required to enter on its register all those people who have applied to it and who appear to qualify for housing,[1] and allocation controls affect the selection from it of new secure tenants. Some authorities operate an introductory tenancy scheme by which new tenants are on probation for one year[2]—in which case it is the initial selection of the introductory tenant that counts as the allocation, whereas the decision made one year later not to evict the tenant and so to allow full security to accrue is not an allocation decision.[3] If a homeless person is given temporary accommodation and it is later decided to offer that same accommodation to him permanently, notification of that decision is an allocation.

Many tenants today live in accommodation provided by housing associations, which are social landlords who grant fully assured tenancies. Indeed some local housing

---

[1] For non-qualification see below pp. 92–99.
[2] See below pp. 165–166.
[3] ss.159(2)(a), 160(3).

authorities have transferred their entire housing stock to housing associations, leaving them with no formal powers of allocation, so that they can do no more than nominate tenants from their housing register to the housing association. Any authority may request co-operation from a registered social landlord[4] but many authorities have formal nomination arrangements that bind the housing association to take the authority's choice. Grant aid for the construction of new dwellings in the social sector is often dependent upon the acceptance of some such nomination arrangement. Allocation controls apply to the decision by a local authority to nominate a particular person from its register.[5]

2.   Transfers and exchanges

A secure tenant holding existing accommodation from a public sector landlord[6] may wish to transfer to better accommodation provided by the same landlord or may wish to move to the district of another public landlord. A specialised form of transfer is an *exchange*, that is a swap between two public sector tenants, a system designed to make it easier for public sector tenants to move. Allocation controls do not apply to successions on death, exchanges, and transfers to comply with matrimonial orders[7] nor where an existing secure tenant becomes a joint tenant with someone else.

Applications by existing tenants are treated as transfers[8] rather than as cases of homelessness,[9] a principle that is presumed to apply whenever an applicant to a housing authority is already a secure tenant. However a homelessness application is a possibility where the existing accommodation is so unsatisfactory that it is not reasonable to expect the applicant (considered with his family grouping) to continue to live there. One such case was *R. v. Islington L.B.C. ex parte B.*[10] where problems arose after B had acted as a witness in a murder investigation, so that the police supported his transfer request. The court held, obiter, that this should have been treated as a Part III (homelessness) application rather than a part II (transfer) application.

3.   Homelessness

A local housing authority has a duty to help any applicant who is homeless or whom it has reason to believe is homeless,[11] whether homelessness is actual or merely threatened within 28 days. At the very least the authority will then be under a duty to conduct inquiries to establish eligibility. Homelessness leads to an offer of settled accommodation only if the applicant overcomes other hurdles by showing that he has a priority need for housing and that his homelessness is unintentional. In a literal sense, a person is homeless if he has nowhere to sleep or, more commonly, in a legal sense where the only accommodation open to him is inadequate for his needs. Suitability is therefore a

---

[4] s.170.
[5] s.159(2)(b), (c).
[6] Including those with equivalent security in Scotland or Northern Ireland: S.I. 2000/702 reg.3 (England).
[7] H.A. 1985 s.160(1), (2).
[8] See below pp. 286–287.
[9] *R. v. Lambeth L.B.C. ex parte Pattinson* (1996) 28 H.L.R. 214, 217, Louis Blom-Cooper Q.C.
[10] (1998) 30 H.L.R. 706.
[11] s.183.

crucial concept,[12] which is defined by reference to the needs of the applicant's family grouping. A person is threatened with homelessness if he is likely to lose his existing accommodation within 28 days.[13]

B. TOWARDS PERMANENT HOUSING

This section charts the painfully slow progress from homeless applicant to fully secure tenant.

1. Inquiries into homelessness and interim accommodation

All housing authorities must make arrangements to receive applications from the homeless,[14] and duties are triggered if an applicant is homeless or threatened with homelessness. A person is homeless if he has nowhere to sleep, or, more commonly, in a legal sense where the only accommodation open to him is inadequate for his needs. A threat of homelessness if a person is likely to lose his existing accommodation within 28 days; in this case the duties are extended to include a requirement on the local authority to seek to procure as a first step that the existing accommodation remains available to him.[15] Once a person is threatened, for example by the making of a court order for possession, the local authority may not remain inactive; if it is obvious that homelessness will ensue, steps have to be taken to prepare for it.[16]

The fact which triggers the obligation to act on an application is that the authority has reason to believe that the person is homeless or threatened with homelessness.[17] Inquiries are required to establish eligibility and to ascertain what duty is owed,[18] and to ensure that a conclusion is reached reasonably promptly.[19]

The local authority comes under a duty to provide interim accommodation while it conducts inquiries to establish housing entitlement if the applicant satisfies the technical requirements for the existence of a priority need.[20] If so the local authority must act, since it is not entitled to restrict accommodation to exceptional cases only,[21] and must provide interim accommodation that is suitable.[22] Housing is provided by way of tenancy but without security of tenure.[23] The duty to provide interim accommodation lasts throughout the inquiry phase until the outcome is notified[24]—though it may terminate if other accommodation is offered, if the applicant ceases to be eligible, or if he becomes

---

[12] See below pp. 80–85.

[13] H.A. 1996 ss.195 (unintentional), 196 (intentional).

[14] s.183.

[15] ss.195 (unintentional), 196 (intentional); *R. v. Westminster C.C. ex parte Ali* (1997) 29 H.L.R. 580.

[16] *R. v. Newham L.B.C. ex parte Khan* [2000] Times May 9th, Collins J.

[17] s.183.

[18] e.g. as to suitability *R. v. Kensington & Chelsea R.L.B.C. ex parte Silchenstedt* (1997) 29 H.L.R. 728, Tucker J.

[19] *R. v. Brent L.B.C. ex parte Miyanger* (1997) 29 H.L.R. 628; *R. v. Merton L.B.C. ex parte Sembi,* (2000) 32 H.L.R. 439, Jowitt J.

[20] s.188.

[21] *R. v. Camden L.B.C. ex parte Mohammed* (1998) 30 H.L.R. 315, Latham J.

[22] *R. v. Lambeth L.B.C. ex parte Ekpo-Wedderman* (1999) 31 H.L.R. 498; see below p. 85.

[23] *Eastleigh B.C. v. Walsh* [1985] 1 W.L.R. 525 H.L.; H.A. 1985 s.79 and sch.1 para.4 as amended by H.A. 1996 sch.17.

[24] s.188(3); interim accommodation pending a local connection dispute is governed by s.200; see below pp. 90–92.

homeless intentionally by leaving the accommodation. The authority's discretion is wide and public law challenges to a refusal to to continue interim accommodation rarely succeed.[25]

2.   The full homelessness duty

Help provided to the homeless is strictly limited unless the applicant can establish that a full duty is owed, the three key components of a successful claim being: (1) homelessness, (2) priority need, and (3) unintentionality.[26] If these hurdles can be overcome, the full duty must be met by securing that accommodation is available for occupation by the applicant for the minimum period of two years.[27] In *R. v. Merton L.B.C. ex parte Sembi*[28] Jowitt J. held that there is no time limit within which a council had to satisfy the duty to provide stable accommodation, that this is bound to take time, and that the council had not broken its duty on facts, but these observations were treated as obiter by Collins J. in *R. v. Newham L.B.C. ex parte Begum*[29] who thought that the duty to house the homeless was unqualified and immediate. On the view taken by Collins J., it is no defence for a council to say that it is doing all it can.

Accommodation must be made available for a minimum period of two years. It may be offered by the authority itself, by arrangement with a social landlord (such as a housing association), through nominating the homeless applicant to it, or by placement with a private sector landlord; in this last case the duty can be met by the grant of a shorthold for a minimum period of two years.[30] If suitable accommodation exists in the district, the local authority may meet its obligations by offering advice and assistance.[31] Hence the Housing Act 1996 ensures that there is never an absolute entitlement to permanent housing via the homelessness route.

After the initial two years are up, the authority may provide continuing accommodation,[32] though it is not obliged to do so, may only make grants for two years at a time, and should act only if it is satisfied that there is no other suitable accommodation in the district, and only after conducting a review to establish continuing eligibility.[33] A drift into permanent housing is not allowed except through the mechanism of the allocation procedure. This draconian rule, introduced in 1996,[34] means that an authority is prohibited from offering accommodation from its own housing stock (apart from rooms in hostels) for more than two years in any period of three years. People have to be moved after two years simply to maintain the purity of concept that the housing register should be the only route into permanent public housing. A person removed from accommo-

---

[25] *R. v. Brighton & Hove B.C. ex parte Nacia* (1999) 31 H.L.R. 1095 C.A.; *R. v. Barnet L.B.C. ex parte Foran* (1999) 31 H.L.R. 708 (authority acted reasonably on facts).

[26] H.A. 1996 s.193. Roughly 100,000 families become unintentionally homeless each year: *Quality and Choice: A Decent Home for All; The Housing Green Paper* (D.E.T.R., April 2000) para.2.14.

[27] ss.205–209.

[28] [1999] Times June 9th, Jowitt J.; he relied on *R. v. Southwark L.B.C. ex parte Anderson* (2000) 32 H.L.R. 96, Moses J.

[29] [2000] 2 All E.R. 1.

[30] S.I. 1996/3204 inserted by S.I. 1997/1741.

[31] s.197.

[32] s.193(6), (7).

[33] s.194.

[34] s.207.

dation for this reason can simply make a new homelessness application. Rights end if the applicant ceases to be eligible, becomes homeless intentionally, accepts an offer of accommodation, refuses an offer of suitable accommodation, or ceases to occupy his temporary accommodation as his main residence; anyone asked to leave is entitled to receive 28 days notice.[35]

Between 1977, when the homelessness legislation was introduced, and 1996 it was believed that the duty imposed on the housing authority was to provide settled housing in the long term under a fully secure tenancy in council housing stock or by nomination of the homeless applicant tenant to a fully assured tenancy from a housing association, or, more rarely, by a private sector grant with full security of tenure. However, just before the introduction of the new 1996 statutory scheme, the House of Lords discovered in *Awua* (1996) that there was no requirement that accommodation should be settled and no connotation of permanence.[36] Given the growth of private sector shortholds, it was unrealistic to house all homeless persons with full security in a deplenished public housing stock, a problem which would have been exacerbated by the greater freedom to create shortholds in 1996 had not corresponding action been taken to reduce the protection of the homeless. Hence the current statutory compromise by which homelessness is met by temporary housing for two-year periods during which time the person is registered to wait for a permanent allocation. An applicant to whom a full duty is owed should be entered on the housing list and may be entitled to a reasonable preference,[37] but permanent housing can only follow from an allocation decision.

Lesser duties apply to a person without a priority need[38] or who is penalised because he has become homeless intentionally.[39] Such applicants have no gateway to the provision of stable housing.

3. Accommodation pending a review

In *Ali* v. *Westminster C.C.*[40] Otton L.J. identified two basic phases of a homelessness application. The first runs from the initial application through the inquiry period to the issue of the decision—and during this period there may be a duty to provide interim accommodation.[41] When the local authority makes its decision and informs the applicant of it, any interim duty ends.[42] Thereafter the second phase covers any internal review and the possibility of an appeal to the county court on a point of law.[43] Continued accommodation may be provided but it is in the discretion of the local authority and it will be difficult to succeed with a public law challenge since any duty is limited to wholly exceptional circumstances.[44] The Court of Appeal that decided *Ali*

---

[35] S.I. 2000/701 reg.5 (in Wales S.I. 2000/1079).

[36] *R. v. Brent L.B.C. ex parte Awua* [1996] A.C. 55, 70B–D, Lord Hoffmann; *R. v. Wandsworth L.B.C. ex parte Mansoor* [1997] Q.B. 953 C.A.; *R. v. Newham L.B.C. ex parte Hassan* (1997) 29 H.L.R. 378.

[37] See below pp. 72–73.

[38] See below pp. 73–74.

[39] See below pp. 77–80.

[40] [1999] 1 All E.R. 450; A. Underwood & K. Rutledge (1997) 141 *S.J.* 1206; N. Grundy (1998) 142 *S.J.* 104.

[41] H.A. 1996 s.188(1); see above p. 89.

[42] s.188(3).

[43] See below pp. 87–88.

[44] *R. v. Hammersmith & Fulham L.B.C. ex parte Fleck* (1998) 30 H.L.R. 679, Sedley J.; *R. v. Camden L.B.C. ex parte Mohammed* (1998) 30 H.L.R. 315, Latham J.; *Williams* v. *Tower Hamlets L.B.C.* [2000] 08 C.L. 387 C.A.

quashed a mandatory injunction issued by a county court requiring the provision of accommodation pending an appeal.[45] One successful case was *R. v. Newham L.B.C. ex parte Ojuri (No.5)*[46] after a decision to end interim accommodation had been taken by an internal review that was conducted overnight; this excessive expedition was ruled to be procedurally irregular, and the court decided that the interim accommodation should be continued for 28 days.

4. Secure tenancies

Authorities may choose to apply to their areas an introductory tenancy scheme and, if they do so, tenants selected for housing will be on probation for one year. The initial choice of the introductory tenant is the housing allocation, which needs to follow the part VI procedure,[47] leaving the subsequent upgrading to a fully secure tenancy largely uncontrolled. Should the authority decide to withdraw the tenancy because of the tenant's misconduct during his probationary period, the tenant may demand a review.[48]

A person who is allocated housing after enlisting on the housing register will be rewarded with a secure tenancy, either immediately or after the introductory first year. Thereafter this will give "life-long" security of tenure, so long as he continues his residential qualification, and provided he avoids the occurrence of any events giving rise to a right to repossession—such as large rent arrears or anti-social behaviour. So far as there ever is a home for life this is "permanent" housing.

C. HOUSING PREFERENCE

Once upon a time, allocation policies adopted by councils were almost completely free from control,[49] but this abdication of responsibility broke down in the face of the growth of public law control of administrative actions, including the requirements to act with procedural fairness, to give reasons and to abstain from acting unreasonably.[50] Legislation in 1985 introduced timid controls over the operation of waiting lists,[51] though it did usefully allow public sector tenants to transfer or exchange their homes with the landlord's consent as a contribution to the national interest in securing mobility of labour. Comprehensive legislation was enacted in the Housing Act 1996. By diluting the obligation of local authorities to homeless persons—who now have at most an entitlement to housing for a renewable period of two years—this places correspondingly greater emphasis on the allocation of housing as the sole gateway to permanent housing, both for those who are homeless in the technical sense and for others who register to wait for public accommodation.

---

[45] H.A. 1996 s.204; *Ali* v. *Westminster C.C.* [1999] 1 All E.R. 450; A. Underwood & K. Rutledge (1997) 141 *S.J.* 1206; N. Grundy (1998) 142 *S.J.* 104; N. Madge [1998] 03 *L.S.G.* 27.

[46] (1999) 31 H.L.R. 631; see also *(No.3)* (1999) 31 H.L.R. 452.

[47] See above pp. 65–66.

[48] H.A. 1996 ss.124–143; S.I. 1997/72; see below p. 165.

[49] *Shelley* v. *London C.C.* [1948] 2 All E.R. 898, 900.

[50] *Associated Provincial Picture Houses Ltd.* v. *Wednesbury Corporation* [1948] 1 K.B. 223, 228–230, Lord Greene M.R.; *R. v. S.S. for the Environment ex parte Nottinghamshire C.C.* [1986] A.C. 240, 249, Lord Scarman.

[51] H.A. 1985 s.22; this was open to challenge in court: *R. v. Canterbury C.C. ex parte Gillsepie* (1987) 19 H.L.R. 7.

1. Allocation schemes

A housing authority may allocate housing accommodation in any manner which it considers appropriate,[52] within a framework of legal controls. Each authority must establish an allocation scheme, covering priorities and procedure,[53] must publicise it,[54] and
must follow ministerial guidance.[55] Housing may only be allocated in accordance with
the scheme.[56] A qualification principle is used to exclude many overseas applicants and
asylum seekers,[57] who must not be entered on the register, or must be removed when an
error is discovered.

Each authority's housing register must include each person who has applied to the
authority, detailing his name and address, the date of his entry on the register, details of
any amendments, the number of persons in the applicant's household, as well as containing particulars of anyone who is under 10, expecting a child, or over 60.[58] Other
information may be included at the discretion of the authority.[59] They also have a discretion to decide what other circumstances will lead to removal from the register but
removal against the wishes of the applicant himself may occur only after he has been
given notice and notified of his right to require a review.[60] Privacy must be observed,
except that the applicant himself is entitled to receive details of his entry on request.[61]

Every local housing authority is free to develop its own allocation policy, provided
that it reflects the statutory preferences to be discussed below,[62] and consults first with
any social landlords affected.[63] Policies can easily fall foul of administrative law control,
for example because of the use of a points based system,[64] inflexibility,[65] the application
of blanket bans,[66] or discrimination.[67] However, the weight to be given to particular factors is a matter for the housing authority.[68] Any authority is likely to decide upon some
test of local connection, and there is (at least as yet) no judicial control of how this is
determined[69]: councils might decide upon policies which left some individuals to fall
between all stools, but the ministerial opinion is that any individual should have the
right to apply somewhere. Other matters that are obviously relevant are a person's age
and marital status and numerous cases show that the housing authority may consider

---

[52] H.A. 1996 s.159(3).
[53] s.167; S.Is. 2000/702 reg.7 (England).
[54] H.A. 1996 ss.168–169.
[55] s.169.
[56] s.167(8).
[57] s.161; S.I. 2000/702; see below pp. 92–99.
[58] s.162; S.I. 2000/702 reg.7 (England).
[59] s.162(5).
[60] ss.163(5)–(7), 164.
[61] s.166.
[62] See below p. 72.
[63] s.167(6).
[64] *R.* v. *Islington L.B.C. ex parte Reilly* (1999) 31 H.L.R. 651, Richards J.
[65] *R.* v. *Gateshead M.B.C. ex parte Lauder* (1997) 29 H.L.R. 360; *R.* v. *Lambeth L.B.C. ex parte Ashley* (1997) 29
H.L.R. 385.
[66] *R.* v. *Canterbury C.C. ex parte Gillespie* (1986) 19 H.L.R. 7.
[67] Sex Discrimination Act 1975 s.30(1); Race Relations Act 1976 s.21(1).
[68] *R.* v. *Southwark L.B.C. ex parte Melak* (1997) 29 H.L.R. 223.
[69] *R.* v. *Wolverhampton M.B.C. ex parte Watters* (1997) 28 H.L.R. 931 C.A.; also *R.* v. *Canterbury C.C. ex parte
Gillespie* (1986) 19 H.L.R. 7.

any record of anti-social behaviour, a history of rent arrears,[70] as well, presumably, as late payment of council tax.[71]

2. Allocation to preferred applicants

A housing authority must give a reasonable preference to those with special housing needs, that is people who fall into the following statutory classes:[72]

   (a) people whose accommodation is insanitary, overcrowded,[73] or unsatisfactory;
   (b) those with temporary or insecure housing;
   (c) families with dependent children;
   (d) households including a person expecting a child;
   (e) those with a particular need for settled accommodation on medical or welfare grounds,[74] with an additional preference extended to those in this category who cannot be expected to find accommodation acting alone[75]; and
   (f) those whose social or economic circumstances make it difficult for them to secure settled accommodation.

These classes can be varied by regulations,[76] a power which, as is explained immediately below, has been used by the Labour government elected in 1997 to restore some degree of preference for the homeless.[77] The preference suggested by these categories could be displaced by other factors such as substantial rent arrears.[78] However, there is a substantial danger that authorities may be motivated by risk rather than housing need when considering applications from paedophiles or members of other unpopular groups.[79]

3. Homelessness: priority need

Duties are owed by a local authority to all applicants to it who are homeless, including those who are threatened with homelessness. This is a prerequisite. A person who is housed secures no advantage whatsoever by demonstrating a priority need; thus the applicant in *R. v. Bristol C.C. ex parte Johns* had severe problems caused by multiple sclerosis, but since he (Johns) was already an owner occupier of a house he had no right to apply for rehousing as if he were homeless.[80] The only conceptual escape from this

---

[70] *R. v. Newham L.B.C. ex parte Miah* (1995) 28 H.L.R. 279, Carnwath J.; *R. v. Lambeth L.B.C. ex parte Njomo* (1996) 28 H.L.R. 737.

[71] The record of payment of community charge (poll tax) could not be considered because there was a duty to be even-handed between all citizens: *R. v. Forest Heath D.C. ex parte West* (1991) 24 H.L.R. 85 C.A. But this may not apply to council tax, which is housing specific.

[72] H.A. 1996 s.167(2); preference originated in H.A. 1935 s.51. A local authority must consider all the factors before deciding what accommodation to offer: *R. v. Westminster C.C. ex parte Al'Khorsan* [2000] Times Janaury 21st, Latham J.

[73] *R. v. Gateshead M.B.C. ex parte Lauder* (1997) 29 H.L.R. 360 Q.B.D.

[74] *R. v. Newham L.B.C. ex parte Watkins* (1993) 26 H.L.R. 434; *R. v. Southwark L.B.C. ex parte Mason* [1999] 4 C.L. 354 (mental health problems).

[75] H.A. 1996 s.167(2) is amended in detail by S.I. 1997/1902 reg.3.

[76] H.A. 1996 s.167(3)–(4); S.I. 2000/702 (England).

[77] S.I. 1996/2753, as amended by S.Is. 1997/631, 1997/1962, 1997/2046.

[78] *R. v. Wolverhampton M.B.C. ex parte Watters* (1997) 28 H.L.R. 931 C.A.; *R. v. Lambeth L.B.C. ex parte Njomo* (1996) 28 H.L.R. 737, 742, Sedley J., was doubted.

[79] D. Cowan (1999) 29 *J.L.S.* 403.

[80] (1992) 25 H.L.R. 249, Otton J.

statutory noose is to adopt the argument—already adumbrated and expanded fully below[81]—that the existing accommodation is so unsatisfactory judged in the context of the applicant's family grouping that it would not be reasonable for the applicant to continue to live there.

Assuming that an applicant is indeed homeless, demonstration of a priority need is a vital step on the road to establishing a full homelessness duty, though standing alone it is of little value unless it can also be shown that the homelessness is unintentional. By statute[82] those with a priority need for housing are:

(1) a pregnant woman; a right to housing arises as soon as a woman becomes pregnant, though there is no duty at that stage to consider the position of an expected child;[83]

(2) a person with whom dependent children reside;[84] an authority may be under additional duties towards the child under the Children Act 1989,[85] but these fall within the budget of the social work department;

(3) a person with a special vulnerability; factors specifically listed are old age (meaning past the retirement age), mental illness,[86] handicap, or physical disability.[87] There is also a sweeper up for any other special reason, which is not constricted by the earlier classes. Lack of finance is not alone enough, but a refugee with no money and no earning capacity could properly be regarded as vulnerable.[88] Drug use is a common cause of vulnerability, but it does not necessarily help the user towards housing unless he is rendered vulnerable by his dependency so as to have special difficulty with housing.[89] Domestic violence is not specifically mentioned, though no doubt it ought to be;

(4) a person homeless as a result of flood, fire or other disaster.[90]

This list can be altered by statutory instrument.[91]

4. Homelessness: duties where no priority need

An authority is not required to do any more than to provide advice and assistance to a person who is homeless if he has no priority need, and even that trivial duty is removed

[81] See below p. 82.

[82] H.A. 1996 s.189, re-enacting H.A. 1985 s.59.

[83] R. v. Newham L.B.C. ex parte Dada [1996] Q.B. 507 C.A.; R. v. Brent L.B.C. ex parte Yusuf (1997) 29 H.L.R. 48, Turner J.

[84] R. v. Westminster C.C. ex parte Bishop (1997) 29 H.L.R. 546. This includes any children who may reasonably be expected to live with the applicant: Crawley B.C. v. B. [2000] Times March 28th C.A.

[85] s.20; R. v. Tower Hamlets L.B.C. ex parte Bradford (1997) 29 H.L.R. 756, Kay J.

[86] R. v. Greenwich L.B.C. ex parte Dukic (1997) 29 H.L.R. 87 Q.B.D.

[87] e.g. epilepsy: R. v. Reigate & Banstead B.C. ex parte Di Domenico (1988) 20 H.L.R. 153 Q.B.D.; R. v. Sheffield C.C. ex parte Leek (1994) 26 H.L.R. 669 C.A.

[88] R. v. Kensington & Chelsea R.L.B.C. ex parte Kihara (1996) 29 H.L.R. 147 C.A. (under appeal to the H.L.).

[89] Ortiz v. Westminster C.C. (1995) 27 H.L.R. 364 C.A.; R. v. Camden L.B.C. ex parte Pereira (No.2) (1999) 31 H.L.R. 317 C.A. (Hobhouse L.J. doubted the test suggested by Simon L.J. in Ortiz); R. v. Hammersmith & Fulham L.B.C. ex parte Fleck (1998) 30 H.L.R. 679, Sedley J.

[90] Not from a demolition order: Noble v. South Herefordshire D.C. (1983) 17 H.L.R. 80 C.A.; nor from eviction by the landlord: R. v. Bristol C.C. ex parte Bradic (1995) 27 H.L.R. 584 C.A.

[91] H.A. 1996 s.189(2)–(4).

if the applicant's homelessness is intentional.[92] Since the duty is so empty of content it is difficult to see why intentionality needs to be penalised in this case.

5. Allocation to homeless persons

Only the full homelessness duty is of practical help, since it opens the way to the provision of accommodation for renewable periods of two years, permits a claim to that authority for entry on the housing register[93] and provides some degree of preference once entered. The legislative twists which led to the re-establishment of this last point call for some explanation.

Homelessness legislation was introduced in 1977[94] and later consolidated in 1985.[95] The form of this legislation eventually led to a distortion of the public housing sector since a full homelessness duty obliged the housing authority to make an offer of permanent accommodation from scarce resources.[96] Some 80 per cent of homes in central London were allotted to homeless persons, making it almost impossible to secure council housing without first being designated technically homeless.

This obligation was greatly watered down by the Housing Act 1996,[97] which removed the duty to provide permanent housing and replaced it with a duty to provide temporary accommodation for renewable two year periods, and which required the homeless to seek an allocation of permanent housing through the council register along with other applicants.[98] Preferential classes listed in the 1996 Act (and above) include some people who are homeless but also others who are not in the technical sense "homeless", meaning that the match between priority need under the homelessness legislation and the preferential classes for housing allocation purposes is less than perfect. The largest category of the homeless was people living with parents or relatives who were no longer willing to accommodate them. Removal of the automatic preference for the homeless gave hope to many equally worthy applicants in desperate need of housing who were not in the technical sense "homeless", a legitimate policy given the similarity in the profiles of the people allocated housing from the housing list and those given preference through homelessness.

Labour amendments[99] have again altered the slant of the legislation, since a reasonable preference is restored to the homeless, who stand alongside other classes of people who are able to demonstrate special housing needs. Preference is again given to those owed a full duty under the new homeless legislation, including for the past people owed a duty under the 1985 Act, and for the future people to whom the local authority is continuing to provide accommodation after the initial two years have passed. It also

[92] ss.190, 210. The crucial date is the date of decision: *R. v. Brent L.B.C. ex parte Sadiq* [2000] Times July 27th, Moses J.

[93] S.I. 2000/702 reg.5.

[94] Housing (Homeless Persons) Act 1977.

[95] H.A. 1985 ss.58–78.

[96] This was commonly understood to require the grant of a secure tenancy with life-long security of tenure; however this duty was watered down by the decision in *Re Awua* [1996] A.C. 55 H.L.

[97] H.A. 1996 part VII ss.175–218; in force January 20th 1997: S.I. 1996/295.

[98] Consultation Paper on Access to Local Authority and Housing Association Tenancies (January 1994); D. Cowan & J. Fionda, "Housing C.P." (1994) 57 *M.L.R.* 610; *Our Future Homes*, White Paper (H.M.S.O., June 1995) ch.6; Standing Committee, Hansard H.C. (1996) vol.273 cols.588–621.

[99] S.I. 1997/1902 reg.2; now S.I. 2000/702 reg.5.

includes people provided with advice on the ground that there is an adequate supply of housing in the area.[100] So a homeless person to whom a full duty is owed (having a priority need and being unintentionally homeless) can claim accommodation for renewable periods of two years, will seek entry on the housing register, and once there will have some degree of preference (but no longer a pre-eminence) when permanent housing becomes available for allocation.

6.   Charter rights of social sector applicants

Registered social landlords must accept the rules of the Housing Corporation if they wish to receive social housing grants for the purchase or construction of new housing. Rights for social sector tenants are currently set out in the *Housing Applicant's Charter*.[101] This requires a registered social landlord to give residents the most secure form of contract appropriate to their particular circumstances, normally a fully assured tenancy. However the charter recognises the concept of a starter tenancy—that is a shorthold for one year initially, but which will mature into one with a full assurance if there is no misconduct by the tenant in the first year—a concept that corresponds to an introductory tenancy in the public sector. Applicants to social landlords should be treated the same whether they apply via local authority nomination, or direct to the social landlord, or by transfer. They have the right to be treated fairly in accordance with the law and the landlord's rules, and to equal opportunities. Preference should be given to those of the greatest need, and priority to those requiring accommodation on medical or welfare grounds. Registered social landlords are required to have a letting policy, which should be disclosed to applicants; and information should also be given about the length of the expected waiting for accommodation.

D.   FAMILY GROUPING

1.   The family unit

Homelessness tests are applied to the family unit,[102] consisting of the applicant, any carer, all people normally living with the applicant (whether or not it is reasonable for them to live together) and all people who might reasonably be expected to live with the applicant.[103] A complete list of all relevant names must be included in the homelessness application, since duties are limited to those disclosed.[104] If a pregnant woman is not already living with the father, it would normally be reasonable to expect him to live with her in future.[105] The unit commonly consists of a couple and their dependent children, but it might also be people who have not yet lived together.[106] One example is provided by *Re Islam*,[107] in which Islam's wife and four children flew in from Bangladesh to join

---

[100] See below pp. 83–84.
[101] Housing Corporation (1998).
[102] H.A. 1996 ss.176, 177 (what is reasonable to continue to occupy).
[103] What is reasonable is a matter for the housing authority to decide, subject to public law grounds of challenge.
[104] *R. v. Southwark L.B.C. ex parte Ryder* (1996) 28 H.L.R. 56, Dyson J.
[105] *R. v. Peterborough C.C. ex parte Carr* (1990) 22 H.L.R. 206, Hutchison J. (boyfriend).
[106] D.C. Hoath [1987] *J.S.W.L.* 15.
[107] *R. v. Hillingdon L.B.C. ex parte Islam* [1983] 1 A.C. 688 H.L.

him here, an arrival that led to his eviction from a shared room. It was reasonable to expect the whole family to live together, so Islam was homeless. There is a temptation for the local authority to reduce artificially the size of the grouping requiring rehousing, which makes it much easier to find suitable accommodation, for example by taking into account immaterial considerations such as the future possibility of the applicant's wife being detained under the mental health legislation.[108]

In *R. v. Hackney L.B.C. ex parte Tonnicodi*[109] the applicant suffered from a disease which made him lethargic. In order to cope he lived with a friend (P) who was not a sexual partner, but who provided support and practical help with shopping and so on. The Council applied the wrong test in asking whether the applicant required a live-in carer, since the question it should have asked was whether P was a person with whom the applicant could reasonably be expected to live [110] and so the decision had to be remitted for reconsideration applying this correct test. However, a decision may be allowed to stand if the correct decision is reached using an incorrect test. [111]

2.   Children

A minor who has left home and is living independently may be homeless.[112] Where one person is dependent on another, the responsible person who must seek housing, using the other's dependency as a ground for establishing a priority need for housing. A child has no right to apply on his own account, even though it is possible for a child to become a public sector tenant in his own right by succession on the death of a parent.[113] The basic rule is demonstrated by the decision of the House of Lords in *Ex parte Garlick*[114] to deny the right for dependent children to claim public housing, the reason being that Parliament permits their parents to have a priority right to housing. If for some reason the person with parental responsibility does not seek adequate housing—probably because he is intentionally homeless—there are other jurisdictions in play to protect any dependent children.[115] In *Ex parte Smith*[116] the House of Lords held that intentionality by the parent negated all housing duties towards dependent children, even if social services had decided that the interests of the children dictated that housing should be made available.[117]

Very often a local authority social security department will have duties to a child under the Children Act 1989 quite independent of any obligation to house his parents.

---

    [108]   *R. v. Newham L.B.C. ex parte Arab Miah* (1998) 30 H.L.R. 691 Q.B.D.

    [109]   (1998) 30 H.L.R. 916.

    [110]   *Code of Guidance for Local Authorities on the Allocation of Accommodation and Homelessness* (D.E.T.R., 1998) para.5.3.

    [111]   *R. v. Oxford C.C. ex parte Doyle* (1998) 30 H.L.R. 506, Tucker J.

    [112]   *Kelly v. Monklands D.C.* [1986] S.L.T. (O.H.) 165.

    [113]   *Kingston upon Thames L.B.C. v. Prince* (1999) 31 H.L.R. 794 C.A.; D. Cowan & N. Dearden [1999] *J.H.L.* 19.

    [114]   *R. v. Oldham M.B.C. ex parte Garlick* [1993] A.C. 509 H.L.; D. Cowan & J. Fionda (1994) 6 *J.C.L.* 62; R. Thornton (1994) 110 *L.Q.R.* 18.

    [115]   *R. v. Barnet L.B.C. ex parte Foran* (1999) 31 H.L.R. 708.

    [116]   *R. v. Northavon D.C. ex parte Smith* [1994] 2 A.C. 402 H.L.; *R. v. Brent L.B.C. ex parte S.* [1994] 1 F.L.R. 203 C.A.; *R. v. Camden L.B.C. ex parte Mersi* [2000] Times October 11th.

    [117]   Hence the cost fell on Avon C.C. (the social services department) rather than Northavon D.C. (the housing authority). On the problems facing unitary authorities see J. Henderson [1998] *J.H.L.* 119.

In *R. v. Hammersmith & Fulham L.B.C. ex parte Damoah*[118] a woman left Sweden after suffering domestic violence and brought her children to England. The local authority was not obliged to house her given that she was not habitually resident in this country. It decided that she should be compelled to return to Sweden, where she could get social security benefits for her children, but this decision was quashed, it being an improper exercise of discretion to refuse all aid to children in need.

3. Mentally incapable persons.

Parliament surely did not intend persons with severe mental impairment to be able to secure independent housing, since there are other powers for their protection, and a majority of the House of Lords decided just this in *Ex parte B*.[119] Permanent accommodation need not be made available to a person so gravely disabled that he has no capacity to make an application for housing.

E. INTENTIONALITY

Homelessness should lead to a preference in rehousing only if the applicant is not at fault. Intentionality is the means of denying assistance to those who have brought things on themselves. After all a person who gives up perfectly adequate accommodation simply to move elsewhere has no call on public assistance, and neither does a person who loses his home because he cannot be bothered to pay the rent. That basic rationale is often undermined by the iniquitous conduct of local housing authorities, which commonly seek to evade housing obligations by determining that an applicant has acted intentionally, which finesses away the obligation to provide housing almost to nothing. Although the onus of proof lies with the authority,[120] there is far too great an incentive for some authorities to reach insupportable conclusions. The essential elements of intentionality are:

1. a loss of accommodation;
2. a deliberate act or omission which has led to that result;
3. a causal link between the conduct and the loss of accommodation; and
4. conduct which continues to prejudice the applicant.

1. A loss of accommodation

Intentionality can never be in play in the case of a person (if any such exists) who has never have had any accommodation at all at any time in the past.[121] This is because the disqualification from further assistance arises only from conduct that leads to the *loss* of a home, perhaps by giving notice to quit or failing to act to make temporary accommodation permanent. Failure to take up an offer of accommodation has a similar effect

---

[118] (1999) 31 H.L.R. 786, Kay J.

[119] Reported with *Ex parte Garlick* [1993] A.C. 509 H.L., Lord Slynn dissenting; D. Cowan (1995) 58 *M.L.R.* 256; R. Thornton (1994) 110 *L.Q.R.* 18.

[120] *R. v. Wandsworth L.B.C. ex parte Dodia* (1998) 30 H.L.R. 562, Jowitt J.

[121] *R. v. Wimbourne D.C. ex parte Curtis* (1985) 18 H.L.R. 79, Mann J.; *R. v. Westminster C.C. ex parte De Souza* (1997) 29 H.L.R. 649, Popplewell J.

since the full homelessness duties terminate if an offer is not taken up or if advice to find accommodation in the private or social sectors is not followed: future applications will result in a finding of intentionality.[122]

Din[123] held that quitting a property before being asked to leave was intentional homelessness. However, if the standard of the accommodation vacated is really poor, the applicant can counter the charge of misconduct by showing that it would not have been reasonable for him (along with the rest of his family grouping) to occupy that accommodation:[124] where accommodation is uninhabitable or overcrowded, the applicant may be homeless if he stays, and unintentionally homeless if he leaves. In one case parents with five dependent children were justified in leaving a flat with only two tiny rooms[125] and this homelessness was unintentional.

2.   Deliberate act

A person is denied housing only as a result of an act or omission that is deliberate, and no prejudice accrues from something done in good faith and in ignorance of any relevant fact.[126] For example in one case a woman was held to have acted honestly when she believed that housing benefit would cover her full rent.[127] Each applicant is considered separately. If, for example, a male partner becomes ineligible for assistance by failing to pay the mortgage, his female partner may apply herself; however, any conduct in which she has acquiesced will be held against her in assessing intentionality,[128] and it is very common for the same event to disqualify both partners. However, a wife who discovers arrears only after her husband has built up a large backlog will not necessarily be found to have acted intentionally when losing the home.

Intentionality most often arises from housing debt, that is a build up of rent or mortgage arrears,[129] a fact which is held against a person on a future application for help with rehousing if he had sufficient resources to keep his previous accommodation on foot. All depends therefore upon the reasons for non-payment.[130] Inquiries must be made by the housing officer to determine what resources were available to the applicant to pay rent. Prescribed lists indicate what costs are allowed and what resources are to be treated as being available to meet them.[131] Priority must be given to paying for housing. For example, in *Re Awua*[132] the tenant had spent money on a university course, car maintenance, and nursery fees, while allowing rent arrears to build up, and her eviction was held to lead to intentional homelessness. Inability to feed the family could be a valid rea-

---

[122] s.191(4).

[123] [1983] 1 A.C. 657 H.L.

[124] H.A. 1996 s.191, re-enacting H.A. 1985 s.60; N. Dobson [1992] *N.L.J.* 1680.

[125] *R.* v. *Westminster C.C. ex parte Ali* (1983) 11 H.L.R. 85 Div.Ct.

[126] H.A. 1996 s.191(2); *R.* v. *Westminster C.C. ex parte N'Dormadingar* [1997] Times November 20th.

[127] *R.* v. *Westminster C.C. ex parte Obeid* (1996) 29 H.L.R. 389, Carnwath J.

[128] *R.* v. *North Devon C.C. ex parte Lewis* [1981] 1 W.L.R. 328, Woolf J.

[129] I. Loveland [1993] *J.S.W.L.* 113, 185; S. O'Hare (1993) 157 *L.G.R.* 121; *Crawley B.C.* v. *B.* [2000] Times March 28th C.A.

[130] *R.* v. *Wandsworth L.B.C. ex parte Hawthorne* [1995] 2 All E.R. 331 C.A.; *R.* v. *Kensington & Chelsea R.L.B.C. ex parte Kihara* (1997) 29 H.L.R. 147 C.A.; *R.* v. *Camden L.B.C. ex parte Cosmo* (1998) 30 H.L.R. 817 Div.Ct.

[131] See below p. 83.

[132] [1996] A.C. 55 H.L.; R. Thornton [1996] *C.L.J.* 18; *Minchin* v. *Sheffield C.C.* [2000] Times April 26th C.A. (intentionality after imprisonment).

son to leave.[133] When housing is provided, it is subject to the obligation on the applicant to pay reasonable charges for any accommodation provided.[134] Misconduct of other sorts also causes an eviction to be intentional, a frequent cause for eviction being anti-social behaviour towards neighbours.[135]

3. A causal link

A person is only prejudiced by conduct "in consequence of which" he suffers the loss of his accommodation, a wording from which the courts have deduced the existence of a causation principle.[136] In *R. v. Hackney L.B.C. ex parte Ajayi*,[137] to take one typical example, a woman left settled accommodation Nigeria for unsettled accommodation here and then became pregnant. The real or effective cause of her homelessness was held to be her leaving Nigeria—which was intentional—rather than her pregnancy which was not intended, at least not in the housing sense. Any voluntary departure from accommodation will cause that person's homelessness application to fail for intentionality.[138] Many people formerly became homeless when forced out by relatives. Conservative legislators perceived, rightly or wrongly, that friendly evictions by relatives were often arranged in order to secure qualification for housing. Such cases now count as intentional homelessness[139] if the prior arrangement can be proved, since intentionality is triggered by any arrangement entered into in order to secure accommodation. Very often the cause of homelessness is relationship breakdown, but a person who moves out is not likely to be able to obtain housing through that homelessness—for example violent conduct which leads to a person's exclusion from a property by the terms of an occupation order will amount to intentional conduct.[140]

4. Breaking the chain of causation

Intentionality continues so long as homelessness continues to be "in consequence of" an earlier act,[141] but the causal chain is broken and the housing slate wiped clean by moving to settled accommodation, a principle first stated in *Dyson*.[142] Matters were complicated by the introduction of insecure shortholds as the basic form of private sector accommodation, but a series of cases has held that a shorthold tenancy is indeed sufficiently settled to wipe clean the effects of earlier intentional behaviour.[143] Future

---

[133] *R. v. Islington L.B.C. ex parte Bibi* (1997) 29 H.L.R. 498 Q.B.D.; *Saunders v. Hammersmith & Fulham L.B.C.* [1999] 06 C.L. 347 C.Ct.

[134] *R. v. Havant B.C. ex parte Marten* (1996) 28 H.L.R. 68 Q.B.D.

[135] *R. v. Nottingham C.C. ex parte Edwards* (1999) 31 H.L.R. 33, Sullivan J.

[136] H.A. 1996 s.191(1); *Din v. Wandsworth L.B.C.* [1983] 1 A.C. 657 H.L. (3:2 for intentionality); D.C. Hoath (1982) 45 *M.L.R.* 577.

[137] (1998) 30 H.L.R. 473, Dyson J.; *Robinson v. Brent L.B.C.* (1999) 31 H.L.R. 1015 C.A. (Jamaica).

[138] *R. v. Brent L.B.C. ex parte Barise* (1999) 31 H.L.R. 50 C.A.

[139] H.A. 1996 s.191(3).

[140] *R. v. Islington L.B.C. ex parte Hinds* (1995) 27 H.L.R. 65 Q.B.D.; R. Thornton [1989] *J.S.W.L.* 67.

[141] *Din v. Wandsworth L.B.C.* [1983] 1 A.C. 657 H.L. (3:2 for intentionality); D.C. Hoath (1982) 45 *M.L.R.* 577.

[142] *Dyson v. Kerrier D.C.* [1980] 1 W.L.R. 1205 C.A.; *Din v. Wandsworth L.B.C.* [1983] 1 A.C. 657 H.L. (3:2 for intentionality); *Awua* [1996] A.C. 55, 69, Lord Hoffmann; C. Hunter & J. Miles (1997) 19 *J.S.W.F.L.* 267.

[143] *R. v. Croydon L.B.C. ex parte Jarvis* (1994) 26 H.L.R. 194; *R. v. Wandsworth L.B.C. ex parte Crooks* (1995) 27 H.L.R. 660; *Ex parte Awua* (1994) 26 H.L.R. 539 C.A.; *R. v. Westminster C.C. ex parte Obeid* (1997) 29 H.L.R. 389; *R. v. Newham L.B.C. ex parte Ojuri (No.1)* [1998] 2 C.L.Y. 3004 Q.B.D.; L. Challen [1999] *J.H.L.* 3.

homelessness applications are not prejudiced by the pre-shorthold history, and leaving accommodation at the end of a shorthold is not intentional homelessness.[144]

Lord Hoffmann indicated in an aside in *Awua*[145] that other acts (apart, that is, from regaining settled accommodation) may possibly break the chain of causation. This means that a local authority cannot sit back and refuse to reinvestigate simply because a person who it has once held to have been intentional has never regained a settled home, as did the local authority in *R. v. Harrow L.B.C. ex parte Fahia.*[146] Fahia had left an assured shorthold under a possession order granted because of rent arrears, leaving him intentionally homeless. The issue was whether this finding of intentionality still prejudiced him after a year or more spent in unsettled bed and breakfast accommodation. At first his rent was paid for by the local authority and later from housing benefit, but when his housing benefit was reduced he was asked to leave, so that he was threatened once again with homelessness. Fahia's changed circumstances necessitated new inquiries by the authority, though it is left to us to guess what decision the authority arrived at! A more direct decision in favour of an applicant was reached in *R. v. Camden L.B.C. ex parte Aranda.*[147] Camden had given Aranda a grant to go to Colombia with her male partner (H) in order to settle there and buy a house, but, unfortunately, he was insincere and soon left her there. She returned to England and applied for housing. H's conduct was held to have broken the chain of causation so that Aranda was not now intentionally homeless and Henry L.J. observed[148] that generally marital breakdown might break the causal chain.

5. Penalising intentional conduct

Intentionality is severely penalised by the homelessness legislation. Even where the applicant has a priority need, the housing authority may restrict its offer of accommodation to such a period as is reasonable for him to secure accommodation in the private sector, with the benefit of their advice and assistance.[149] Without a priority need, the effect of intentional conduct by the applicant is to remove all duties; the authority is not even required to provide advice and assistance.[150]

F.   HOMELESSNESS: SUITABILITY OF ACCOMMODATION

Suitability of accommodation is of critical importance in the work of homeless persons units.[151] It is used to determine initially whether a person is homeless so as to qualify for public assistance with housing, since a person with existing accommodation is never-

---

[144] *R. v. Newham L.B.C. ex parte Ugbo* (1994) 26 H.L.R. 263; *R. v. Croydon L.B.C. ex parte Graham* (1994) 26 H.L.R. 286 C.A.

[145] *Awua* [1996] A.C. 55, 69D, Lord Hoffmann; *R. v. Harrow L.B.C. ex parte Fahia* (1997) 29 H.L.R. 94 C.A. Hospitalisation of the friend who had offered accommodation did not break the causal chain in *R. v. Brighton & Hove B.C. ex parte Harvey* (1998) 30 H.L.R. 670 Div.Ct.

[146] [1998] 1 W.L.R. 396 H.L.

[147] (1998) 30 H.L.R. 76 C.A.

[148] At 87.

[149] H.A. 1996 s.190; common practice is to offer 28 days, but an inflexible policy may be unlawful.

[150] s.190; ss.210–211 impose a duty to protect the property of the homeless.

[151] D. Cowan with J. Fionda (1998) 27 *Anglo-American* 66.

theless homeless if what he is occupying is wholly unsuitable for continued occupation. This same test of suitability is used later to determine whether an applicant who is offered accommodation is obliged to accept it in satisfaction of a homelessness duty owed to him. Even interim accommodation must be suitable.

1. Homelessness

Homelessness is the vital prerequisite for the existence of any duty. A person with a pressing priority need nevertheless has no right to public assistance with rehousing if the person in need is already supplied with adequate accommodation.[152] A person is clearly homeless if he has no accommodation at all available to him, statutory examples being a person squatting against the wishes of the owner,[153] a person occupying a caravan but without a pitch, or living in a houseboat with no legal mooring.[154] Nor is accommodation available if the lawful occupier is barred from it, for example by illegal eviction or by the threat of violence.[155]

A person cannot be said to be homeless while he has suitable accommodation available that he might occupy. Availability is very widely defined to encompass an interest under a tenancy, a licence, rights under a court order, a matrimonial home right, or other occupation right protected by any rule of law or enactment.[156] Accommodation overseas can be considered just as much as any here, the 1996 Act[157] here confirming the conclusion already reached by the House of Lords in *Re Islam* that accommodation available in Bangladesh did prevent homelessness in this country.[158] In *Begum* v. *Tower Hamlets L.B.C.*[159] the Court of Appeal indicated, obiter, that accommodation in Bangladesh would not be accessible to an applicant who could not afford to travel to it.

Short-term accommodation prevents homelessness while it continues to be available, a principle which follows from *Ex parte Awua*.[160] The Court of Appeal has subsequently rejected the argument that the House of Lords acted *per incuriam* by overlooking relevant statutory provisions.[161] There is no requirement of permanence.[162] A person in very precarious accommodation such as a women's refuge[163] or night shelter[164] should continue to be homeless as they certainly were before *Awua*.

---

[152] *R.* v. *Bristol C.C. ex parte Johns* (1992) 25 H.L.R. 249, Otton J. (owner occupier with multiple sclerosis).

[153] The wording is derived from P.E.A. 1977 s.1(1).

[154] H.A. 1996 s.175(2)(a), (b); *R.* v. *Chiltern D.C. ex parte Roberts* (1990) 23 H.L.R. 387 Q.B.D. (travelling showmen not homeless).

[155] H.A. 1996 s.177.

[156] Wording derived from P.E.A. 1977 s.1(1).

[157] H.A. 1996 s.175(1).

[158] [1983] 1 A.C. 688 H.L.; D.C. Hoath (1982) 45 *M.L.R.* 577; *R.* v. *Hillingdon L.B.C. ex parte Streeting* [1980] 1 W.L.R. 1425 Div.Ct.; *R.* v. *Islington L.B.C. ex parte Bibi* (1997) 29 H.L.R. 498; *R.* v. *Barking & Dagenham L.B.C. ex parte Okuneye* (1996) 28 H.L.R. 174 Q.B.D.; *Robinson* v. *Brent L.B.C.* (1999) 31 H.L.R. 1015 C.A.

[159] [1999] Times November 9th C.A.; but inability to afford the fare did not mean that the applicant was unable to secure entry to the home under s.175(2).

[160] [1996] A.C. 55 H.L.; R. Thornton [1996] *C.L.J.* 18.

[161] *R.* v. *Wandsworth L.B.C. ex parte Wingrove* [1996] 3 All E.R. 913 C.A.; *R.* v. *Sedgemoor D.C. ex parte McCarthy* (1996) 28 H.L.R. 607 Q.B.D.

[162] *Begum v. Tower Hamlets L.B.C.* [1999] Times November 9th C.A.

[163] *Williams* v. *Cynon Valley D.C.* [1980] 01 L.A.G. Bulletin 16; *R.* v. *Ealing L.B.C. ex parte Sidhu* (1982) 2 H.L.R. 45, Hodgson J.

[164] *R.* v. *Waveney D.C. ex parte Bower* [1983] Q.B. 238 C.A.

2.   Homelessness where existing accommodation unsuitable

In the original 1977 form of the homelessness legislation (and also its 1985 reincarnation) almost any accommodation, however grim, could remove a person from the category of the homeless—unless it was so dreadful that it could not be fairly described as accommodation,[165] or it was not habitable.[166] People were forced to continue occupying desperately poor housing. In *R. v. South Herefordshire C.C. ex parte Miles*[167] a hut with only two small rooms, an infestation of rats, and no services, was held to become unacceptable only when the couple gave birth to a third child. This outrageous rule was set in stone by *Puhlhofer v. Hillingdon L.B.C.*[168] in which a couple were not homeless while they were living with their two children in a single room in a guest house without cooking facilities. Parliamentary reversal of these decisions in 1986[169] form the basis of the current law.[170] Thus homelessness now exists where the accommodation is substandard to such an extent that it is not reasonable for an applicant to continue to occupy it with his family grouping.

Thus the standard of accommodation has to be assessed in the context of the applicant's whole family grouping including all those who can reasonably be expected to live with him. One specific instance[171] is where the applicant can show that it is not reasonable to continue to live in the accommodation because of the general housing state of the area but, more generally,[172] the reason might relate to the legal conditions attached to a tenancy, employment conditions, or financial circumstances. Most cases have been based on the state of the accommodation itself, particularly the argument that it is too small for the family intended to occupy it, that the services were grossly below standard, or that conditions make it uninhabitable. Non-compliance with fire regulations[173] or statutory overcrowding are not by themselves sufficient reasons.

Domestic violence is also a ground for deciding that a person is homeless if it makes it unreasonable for him to continue in accommodation, whether the violence is actual or threatened, and whether it is directed towards the applicant or any other member of the family unit.[174] Violence is taken into account when the instigator is associated with the victim, for example by marriage, former marriage, engagement, cohabitation, former cohabitation, sharing of a common household, or by family relationship. Children are also protected against the threat of violence from their natural parents, adopters, and those with parental responsibility towards them.[175]

---

[165] At 461, Lord Hoffmann.

[166] *City of Gloucester v. Miles* (1985) 17 H.L.R. 292 C.A.

[167] (1983) 17 H.L.R. 82.

[168] [1986] A.C. 484 H.L.

[169] Housing and Planning Act 1986 s.14; D.C. Hoath (1988) 7 *J.S.W.L.* 39; A. Jessup (1987) 137 *N.L.J.* 1045; C. Hunter & S. McGrath [1993] 05 *Legal Action* 19; D.S. Cowan [1993] *J.S.W.L.* 236; *Awua* [1996] A.C. 55, 67E, Lord Hoffmann.

[170] s.175(3).

[171] s.177(2); others are prescribed: ss.(3); S.I. 1996/3204.

[172] *R. v. Hammersmith & Fulham L.B.C. ex parte Duro-Roma* (1983) 9 H.L.R. 71 Q.B.D.

[173] *R. v. Kensington & Chelsea R.L.B.C. ex parte Ben-el-Mabrouk* (1995) 27 H.L.R. 564 C.A.

[174] As defined by H.A. 1996 s.177(1); see above p. 75; the legislative provision is new.

[175] Violence by other persons may render it unreasonable to continue to occupy accommodation under the next heading.

3. Financial suitability

Affordability is relevant when considering whether it is reasonable to continue to occupy a dwelling and also whether an offer of accommodation is one that it is reasonable to expect the applicant to accept. Regulations[176] prescribe how affordability is to be determined according to a list of factors such as income, outgoings and savings, and in particular list those expenses that are to count as part of the cost of the accommodation. Case law illustrates the application of these principles.[177] The applicant must have time to end his existing accommodation arrangements before being required to move.[178]

If suitable accommodation is offered and refused—either a homelessness offer or an allocation—duties cease provided that the local authority gave a warning of the consequences.[179] The applicant may be able to make a further application.[180]

4. Suitability of condition

Any accommodation offered by a housing authority must be judged suitable, in terms of the condition of the property offered,[181] particularly if it is affected by slum clearance or overcrowding or fails to meet the standards set for H.M.O.s.[182] However, this aspect of suitability is best judged by the authority itself, leaving a very limited scope for a public law challenge. Suitability also involves a subjective question, that is appropriateness to a particular family, a point on which it is much easier to challenge a council's decision.[183] So far as practicable accommodation should be made available within the authority's own area,[184] so that it will not be suitable to offer accommodation outside the borough to a family with children of school age.[185] A home on an estate might reasonably be refused if the tenant is terrified of living there,[186] or medical evidence shows that an inner city estate is inappropriate.[187] Other challenges have been based on a failure to comprehend the effect of high-rise accommodation on young children[188] or the impact of severe physical handicap.[189] However, since the authority is the decision maker, it is almost bound to conclude that a refusal of accommodation is unreasonable. Many public law challenges have foundered on the fact that potentially relevant information about the circumstances of the applicant and his family grouping was not

[176] Homelessness (Suitability of Accommodation) O. 1996, S.I. 1996/3204.

[177] R. v. Brent L.B.C. ex parte Grossett (1996) 28 H.L.R. 9 C.A.; Odunsi v. Brent L.B.C. [1999] 06 C.L. 348; Watson v. Lambeth L.B.C. [2000] 06 C.L. 388.

[178] H.A. 1996 s.193(8).

[179] s.193(5) and (7) respectively; R. v. Westminster C.C. ex parte Chambers (1982) 6 H.L.R. 24 Q.B.D.; R. v. Newham L.B.C. ex parte Dada [1996] Q.B. 507 C.A.

[180] s.193(9).

[181] R. v. Camden L.B.C. ex parte Jibril (1997) 29 H.L.R. 785 (family not entitled to insist on provision of two toilets).

[182] For a refusal on safety grounds see R. v. Newham L.B.C. ex parte Larwood (1997) 29 H.L.R. 670 Q.B.D.

[183] R. v. Islington L.B.C. ex parte Thomas (1998) 30 H.L.R. 111 Q.B.D.

[184] H.A. 1996 s.208.

[185] R. v. Newham L.B.C. ex parte Ojuri (No.2) (1999) 31 H.L.R. 631, Collins J.

[186] R. v. Haringey L.B.C. ex parte Karaman (1997) 29 H.L.R. 366, Brooke J. (old law).

[187] R. v. Islington L.B.C. ex parte Thomas (1998) 30 H.L.R. 111.

[188] R. v. Islington L.B.C. ex parte Degnan (1998) 30 H.L.R. 723 C.A.

[189] R. v. Lambeth L.B.C. ex parte A1 and A2 (1998) 30 H.L.R. 933 Div.Ct. (cerebral palsy); R. v. Southwark L.B.C. ex parte Campisi (1999) 31 H.L.R. 560 C.A. (polio; need to be near friends).

made available to the authority during its inquiries; new information provided after a decision has been reached is not a ground for a court challenge.[190] As with so much public law, many successful cases have homed in on procedural defects such as failure to give reasons for ignoring particular representations,[191] failure to consider relevant factors such as medical evidence relating to pregnancy,[192] or the consideration of immaterial factors such as the future possibility of the applicant's wife being detained under the mental health legislation.[193]

5. Location

Many London authorities adopted the policy of housing homeless people in bed and breakfast accommodation at seaside resorts, where accommodation was cheaper than in London. A local authority is entitled to consider housing resources, but not to that extent. In *R. v. Sacupima ex parte Newham L.B.C.*[194] judicial review was granted, since it was unreasonable to provide accommodation a long distance from the applicant's home area, given the effect on their children's education and employment prospects. There is a minimum standard below which provision should not fall.

6. One offer policies

Duties of a local authority towards an applicant cease if he does not take reasonable steps to secure accommodation, taking into account his personal circumstances and the state of the housing market.[195] An applicant must be warned of the consequences of a refusal to accept and if he persists the authority's duties cease.[196] Many local authorities have a one-offer policy—which is lawful way to meet the full homelessness duty provided that a warning is given[197] and there is some flexibility.[198] However, many authorities offer woefully inadequate housing stock, forcing the disappointed applicant to mount a public law challenge to the quality of the accommodation on offer. Most cases fail because suitability is determined by the authority, and procedural defects are often the only ground for undermining the decision which has been made.

It is lawful to require a person to move in as a condition of being allowed to pursue a review provided that there is some degree of flexibility.[199] An applicant whose life is in danger after a conviction for paedophilia requires sympathetic treatment, but even in such extreme cases the council may be able to insist that the applicant move in.[200]

---

[190] *R. v. Newham L.B.C. ex parte Chowdhury* (1999) 31 H.L.R. 383 (woman pregnant and found it hard to climb the stairs); *R. v. South Holland D.C. ex parte Baxter* (1998) 30 H.L.R. 1069 (problem with son's education).
[191] *R. v. Islington L.B.C. ex parte Okocha* (1998) 30 H.L.R. 191.
[192] *R. v. Haringey L.B.C. ex parte Sampaio* (1999) 31 H.L.R. 1.
[193] *R. v. Newham L.B.C. ex parte Arab Miah* (1998) 30 H.L.R. 691 Q.B.D.
[194] [2000] Times January 12th Dyson J.
[195] H.A. 1996 s.197.
[196] s.193(7).
[197] *R. v. Westminster C.C. ex parte Chambers* (1982) 6 H.L.R. 24 Q.B.D.
[198] *R. v. Westminster C.C. ex parte Hussain* (1999) 31 H.L.R. 645, Turner J.
[199] *R. v. Newham L.B.C. ex parte Dada* [1996] Q.B. 507 C.A.
[200] *R. v. Newham L.B.C. ex parte Larwood* (1998) 30 H.L.R. 716 C.A.

7.   Suitability of interim accommodation

In *R. v. Ealing L.B.C. ex parte Surdonja*,[201] Scott Baker J. resolved an uncertainty about whether accommodation provided at an interim stage during the inquiry phase must be suitable to the applicant's needs. Ealing had split a husband and his wife and three young daughters between a triple room in a hostel in Ealing and a double room in another hostel in Southall, but this was held not to be a lawful discharge of the duty to provide interim accommodation, the judge drawing comfort from a Code of Guidance and a previous judicial decision.[202] Hence an offer will be quashed if the authority has neglected to consider whether the accommodation offered as an interim measure is suitable for the purposes of the applicant's family grouping.[203]

G.   REVIEW

1.   Inquiries

Housing authorities must make arrangements to receive applications from the homeless.[204] Delegation to outside agencies is not allowed. Duties are triggered where the authority has reason to believe that the applicant is either homeless or threatened with homelessness. In the latter case the first step is to seek to procure that the existing accommodation remains available to him.[205] Inquiries are required to establish eligibility and to ascertain what duty is owed,[206] and a conclusion must be reached reasonably promptly.[207] In *R. v. Gravesham B.C. ex parte Winchester*[208] it was said that:

> "The burden lies upon the local authority to make appropriate inquiries . . . in a caring and sympathetic way. . . . These enquiries should be pursued rigorously and fairly albeit the authority are not under a duty to conduct detailed C.I.D. type enquiries. . . . The applicant must be given an opportunity to explain matters which the local authority is minded to regard as weighing substantially against him . . .".

These might for example consider how to deal with the problems of a child split between divorcing parents.[209] A local authority has the right to reconsider (or "revisit") an application and decide against the applicant on a new ground. The first decision in one reported case that the applicant had no priority need because she had no dependent children living with her did not hold water because they could reasonably be expected to live with her, but the authority could validly proceed to make a second decision that her homelessness was intentional on the ground of rent arrears.[210] If a previous decision is being reconsidered, it is appropriate to assume that that prior decision was correct and

---

[201] (1999) 31 H.L.R. 686.
[202] *R. v. Newham L.B.C. ex parte Ojuri (No.2)* (1999) 31 H.L.R. 631, Collins J.
[203] *R. v. Lambeth L.B.C. ex parte Ekpo-Wedderman* (1999) 31 H.L.R. 498.
[204] H.A. 1996 s.183.
[205] ss.195, 196; *R. v. Westminster C.C. ex parte Ali* (1997) 29 H.L.R. 580.
[206] e.g. as to suitability *R. v. Kensington & Chelsea R.L.B.C. ex parte Silchenstedt* (1997) 29 H.L.R. 728, Tucker J.
[207] *R. v. Brent L.B.C. ex parte Miyanger* (1997) 29 H.L.R. 628.
[208] (1986) 18 H.L.R. 207, 214–215.
[209] *R. v. Oxford C.C. ex parte Crowder* (1999) 31 H.L.R. 485 Q.B.D.
[210] *Crawley B.C. v. B.* [2000] Times March 28th C.A.

merely to see whether subsequent changes in circumstances require any change in the decision.[211]

2. Allocation reviews

Until the Housing Act 1996 challenges to housing allocations were restricted to cases of obvious impropriety, as where a councillor has sought to influence allocations or where there is a desire to help a councillor fight an election.[212] Rules now preclude a councillor from sitting in an allocation decision affecting his own ward,[213] so that decisions reached in such circumstances remain illegal. However, the Housing Act 1996 has defined the duty of make housing allocations and defined excluded and preferred classes, so greatly increasing the scope for judicial challenges to the actual allocation of houses. Notice must be given before a person is removed from the housing register[214] and reasons must also be given for adverse allocation decisions,[215] a fact which by itself greatly increases the chances of sustaining an objection.

Unsuccessful applicants (or those successful but dissatisfied[216]) can demand an administrative review[217] in accordance with the procedures laid down by the Allocation of Housing and Homelessness (Review Procedures) Regulations 1999.[218] A review of a decision to allocate or to withhold housing must be conducted by a officer different from the one involved in the original decision. The applicant must be given notice of his right to make representations and of the procedure to be adopted, and any representations must be considered.[219] Any review must be completed within eight weeks unless otherwise agreed.[220]

3. Judicial review of allocation decisions

Decisions made by an authority to allocate or withhold housing can be challenged on public law grounds in judicial review proceedings. This would include a challenge to an entire transfer policy, but a public law challenge could only succeed in the rare cases where a policy is shown to be irrational.[221]

4. Homelessness reviews

A refusal to assist a homeless applicant can be challenged in public law since an authority has duties towards a person who it has reason to believe is homeless or threatened with homelessness.[222] These will certainly include a requirement to make inquiries as to

---

[211] *R.* v. *Southwark L.B.C. ex parte Campisi* (1999) 31 H.L.R. 560 C.A.

[212] *R.* v. *Port Talbot B.C. ex parte Jones* [1988] 2 All E.R. 267, Nolan J.; *R.* v. *Tower Hamlets L.B.C. ex parte Spencer* (1997) 29 H.L.R. 64 Q.B.D.; *Porter* v. *Magill* (1999) 31 H.L.R. 823 C.A.

[213] S.I. 1997/483, S.I. 1997/72 (Wales).

[214] S.I. 2000/702 reg.8 (England); *R.* v. *Westminster C.C. ex parte Hussain* (1999) 31 H.L.R. 645, Turner J.

[215] H.A. 1996 s.164(1) (inclusion on or removal from the register).

[216] *R.* v. *Kensington and Chelsea R.L.B.C. ex parte Byfield* (1999) 31 H.L.R. 913, Moses J. (not lawful to provide that offer lapsed if the applicant asked for a review).

[217] ss.164 (21 days from notification), 165.

[218] S.I. 1999/71; this replaces S.Is. 1996/3122 and 1997/631.

[219] part II, regs. 2–5.

[220] reg. 5.

[221] *R.* v. *Tower Hamlets L.B.C. ex parte Uddin* (2000) 32 H.L.R. 391, Keene J.

[222] s.183.

eligibility, to ascertain what duty is owed,[223] to reach a conclusion reasonably promptly,[224] and to give a reasoned decision in writing.[225] Numerous cases are based on public law challenges to the thoroughness of the enquiries made.

Administrative challenges are now regulated by the Allocation and Housing and Homelessness (Review Procedures) Regulations 1999.[226] These may relate to homelessness decisions or local connection referrals. An internal review may be requested of any decision to provide or to withhold housing. It must be conducted by an officer who was not involved in the original decision, and can only occur after notification has been made to the applicant of his right to make representations and of the procedure to be adopted, and taking into account any representations made.[227] A reviewing officer may decide to confirm the original decision despite procedural defects, but if so the reasons must be explained and oral representations allowed and considered.[228] Review procedures should be completed within eight weeks unless otherwise agreed,[229] but excessive expedition may arouse suspicion.[230] Reviews should take account of any new material available up to the date of the review.[231] In *Driver* v. *Purbeck D.C.*[232] a council review confirmed the earlier decision that a hostel did provide suitable accommodation for a single parent who had responsibility for six children and a history of violence and nervous troubles. The review was inadequate because of failure to consider social and medical evidence, failure to take into account all evidence at the date of the review, consideration of irrelevant nuisances caused by the children, and failure to give adequate reasons. This may set the trend for challenges to administrative reviews.

Any further review is in the discretion of the local authority and so not open to judicial review.[233]

5. County court appeals against homelessness decisions

Much local authority decision-making is illegal.[234] In the past a challenge had to be by way of judicial review[235] in the High Court, a procedure that tended to clog the Queen's Bench Division with inappropriate applications. Lord Woolf recommended[236] a change to a statutory appeal to a country court against any homelessness decision. The width of the jurisdiction was stressed in *Warsame* v. *Hounslow L.B.C.*[237] where it was made clear that the county court had power to hear an appeal against any decision on homelessness,

---

[223] e.g. as to suitability: *R.* v. *Kensington & Chelsea R.L.B.C. ex parte Silchenstedt* (1997) 29 H.L.R. 728, Tucker J.

[224] *R.* v. *Brent L.B.C. ex parte Miyanger* (1997) 29 H.L.R. 628.

[225] H.A. 1996 s.184(3).

[226] s.202; S.I. 1999/71; G. Robson [1990] *N.L.J.* 712.

[227] S.I. 1999/71 part III regs.6–8; *R.* v. *Newham L.B.C. ex parte Ojuri (No.3)* (1999) 31 H.L.R. 452 (no prejudice on facts).

[228] reg.8; *R.* v. *Westminster C.C. ex parte Hussain* (1999) 31 H.L.R. 645, Turner J. (social services assessment not followed).

[229] regs.5, 9.

[230] *R.* v. *Newham L.B.C. ex parte Ojuri (No.5)* (1999) 31 H.L.R. 631 (review overnight).

[231] *Greenaway* v. *Newport B.C.* [1999] 7 C.L. 263 C.Ct.

[232] [1999] 10 C.L. 407.

[233] *R.* v. *Westminster C.C. ex parte Elioua* (1999) 31 H.L.R. 440.

[234] D. Cowan with J. Fionda (1998) 27 *Anglo-American* 66, 169.

[235] *Cocks* v. *Thanet D.C.* [1983] 2 A.C. 286 H.L.; M. Sunkin (1983) 46 *M.L.R.* 650.

[236] *Access to Justice* (H.M.S.O., July 1996) ch.16 paras. 73–76.

[237] (2000) 32 H.L.R. 335 C.A.

including a decision that the authority no longer owed a homelessness duty. So the county court has full public law powers.[238] Implementation of this change in 1996[239] has led mainly to a change of forum. Conventional judicial review is excluded[240] but the intention of the Woolf Committee was to decide any appeal on judicial review principles, and it seems that this is the practical effect of an appeal on a point of law. Jowitt J. accepted this principle in *R. v. Merton L.B.C. ex parte Sembi*[241] and so did the Court of Appeal which heard *Begum* v. *Tower Hamlets L.B.C.*[242] Hence the powers of the county court are the same as in the High Court on a judicial review, including for example a review of *Wednesbury* unreasonableness.[243] They will in future include human rights issues. There is a strict 21-day time limit.[244]

Procedure is by a request for entry of an appeal after which the court should fix a return day allowing at least 21 days from service.[245] Many cases will be urgent in which case expedition of the hearing should be considered.[246]

6.   Public law grounds for an appeal

Applicants have a legitimate expectation that authorities will ensure the proper operation of the statutory procedures.[247] Examples of procedural irregularity in the decision making process given in *Council of the Civil Service Union* v. *Minister for the Civil Service*[248] include:

considering irrelevant materials;
failing to consider relevant materials;
failing to give reasons; and
inflexibility in the policy or in its application.

However, a local authority can only act on the basis of information supplied to it during the inquiry phase and is not required to consider fresh evidence adduced in court on an appeal.[249] Since the local authority is the body charged by statute with making the decision and allotting the weight to the various relevant factors, an appeal against the actual decision can only occur if it is shown to be *Wednesbury*[250] unreasonable—mean-

---

[238] The decision should *not* be made by a district judge: *Crawley B.C.* v. *B.* [2000] Times March 28th C.A.; a Practice Direction is to be issued to make this clear.

[239] H.A. 1996 s.204; A. Underwood & K. Rutledge (1997) 141 *S.J.* 1206; D. Cowan & C. Hunter (1997) 1 *J.H.L.* 43; J. Holbrook (2000) 144 *S.J.* 242.

[240] *R.* v. *Merton L.B.C. ex parte Sembi* (2000) 32 H.L.R. 439, Jowitt J.; *R.* v. *Westminster C.C. ex parte Elioua* (1999) 31 H.L.R. 440 C.A.; *R.* v. *Brent L.B.C. ex parte O'Connor* (1999) 31 H.L.R. 923, Tucker J.; *R.* v. *Kensington & Chelsea R.L.B.C. ex parte Byfield* (1999) 31 H.L.R. 913, Moses J.

[241] (2000) H.L.R. 439, Jowitt J. This supports N. Grundy [1998] *J.H.L.* 92.

[242] [1999] Times November 9th C.A.

[243] *Driver* v. *Purbeck D.C.* [1999] 10 C.L. 407.

[244] *Demetri* v. *Westminster C.C.* (2000) 32 H.L.R. 470 C.A.; *R.* v. *Brent L.B.C. ex parte O'Connor* (1999) 31 H.L.R. 923, Tucker J.

[245] N. Madge [1999] *N.L.J.* 1408, 1411. Appeals against order made on or after May 2nd 2000 are regulated by C.P.R. 52, inserted by C.P.Am.R. sch.5.

[246] C.P.R. 3.1(2)(b).

[247] *R.* v. *Poole B.C. ex parte Cooper* (1995) 27 H.L.R. 605.

[248] [1985] 2 A.C. 377, 410–411 Lord Diplock.

[249] *R.* v. *South Holland D.C. ex parte Baxter* (1998) 30 H.L.R. 1069.

[250] *Associated Provincial Picture Houses Ltd.* v. *Wednesbury Corporation* [1948] 1 K.B. 223 C.A.

ing that the decision is so perverse that no authority acting properly could have come to it.[251] Human rights principles will greatly widen the scope for challenges.

The court may confirm the decision, quash or vary it. However, as the House of Lords decided in the case of *O'Rourke* v. *Camden L.B.C.* in the particular context of the withdrawal of interim accommodation, there is no right to damages.[252] Judicial review in the High Court remains the appropriate vehicle for challenges by pressure groups to the legality of the global policy of a housing authority.

7.   Accommodation pending a review

Otton L.J. identified two basic phases of a homelessness application in *Ali* v. *Westminster C.C.*[253] The first phase comprehends the initial application, the inquiry period, and the issue of the decision, during which period there may be a duty to provide interim accommodation.[254] Any interim duty ends when the local authority makes its decision and informs the applicant of it.[255] Thereafter the second phase covers any internal review and the possibility of an appeal to the county court on a point of law. At either stage there is power for the local authority to continue to provide interim accommodation, but it is in the discretion of the local authority and a refusal can only be challenged by judicial review. Needless to say, it will be difficult to succeed in such a challenge since a duty to provide accommodation pending a review is limited to wholly exceptional circumstances.[256] Thus it was decided in *Ali* that there is no power for a county court that is considering an appeal to issue a mandatory injunction so as to require the provision of accommodation pending that appeal.[257]

8.   Access to records

An important aspect of a review is gaining access to information held by the landlord. The Data Protection Act 1999 strengthens the previous data protection legislation and extends it to data held in any relevant filing system, including for the first time manual records as well as computer databases. Although the Act comes into force on March 1st 2000, manual data is only included on October 23rd 2001. Any data must be used in accordance with the Act's data protection principles[258]; it must be obtained and processed fairly and lawfully, kept up to date where necessary, discarded when appropriate, with proper security maintained. Part II gives rights to data subjects—that is people about whom data is held. This includes the right of access to personal data, the right to prevent processing causing damage or distress, restrictions on direct marketing

---

[251] M. Partington [1994] *J.S.W.L.* 47; M. Sunkin (1987) 50 *M.L.R.* 432; R. v. *City of Westminster ex parte Ermakov* (1996) 28 H.L.R. 819 C.A.; *Driver* v. *Purbeck D.C.* [1999] 10 CL. 407.

[252] [1998] A.C. 188 H.L.; R. v. *Ealing L.B.C. ex parte Parkinson* (1997) 29 H.L.R. 179 Q.B.D.

[253] [1999] 1 All E.R. 450; A. Underwood & K. Rutledge (1997) 141 *S.J.* 1206; N. Grundy (1998) 142 *S.J.* 104; R. Duddridge [1999] *J.H.L.* 53.

[254] See above pp. 69–70.

[255] H.A. 1996 s.188(3).

[256] *R.* v. *Hammersmith & Fulham L.B.C. ex parte Fleck* (1998) 30 H.L.R. 679, Sedley J.; *R.* v. *Camden L.B.C. ex parte Mohammed* (1998) 30 H.L.R. 315, Latham J.

[257] H.A. 1996 s.204; *Ali* v. *Westminster C.C.* [1999] 1 All E.R. 450; A. Underwood & K. Rutledge (1997) 141 *S.J.* 1206; N. Grundy (1998) 142 *S.J.* 104; N. Madge [1998] 03 *L.S.G.* 27.

[258] s.4, sch.1.

and automatic decision making, and rights to require rectification, blocking, erasure, destruction. Data controllers must register under the provisions of Part III. Part V confers enforcement powers on the Data Protection Commissioner, reconstituted and renamed by Part VI.

Housing records are governed by statutory disclosure rules in the Housing Act 1985. In data protection terms these are treated as accessible public records—that is information made available to the public by any enactment[259]—and in particular this includes any information held by a local authority under the Housing Act 1985 for the purpose of any of the authority's tenancies.[260] These will now be brought within the data protection legislation, but with different transitional rules so that the Act only bites on October 23rd 2001. These records are exempt from many of the most important of the data protection principles and rights, such as data subject access requests, non-disclosure, the requirement to keep records accurate and up to date, and the right to rectification, blocking erasure or destruction if inaccurate.

H. LOCAL CONNECTION

A test of local connection is applied to homeless applicants in order to determine which local authority is obliged to provide housing. A local authority that decides that a full homelessness duty is owed to an applicant may be able to pass on the application to another authority. This is so if there is no local connection with the notifying authority, but there is with the notified authority,[261] and a referral may also be made if the notified authority has provided accommodation on a homelessness application within the past five years.[262]

Local connection may be derived from residence, employment, family association or other special reasons,[263] and from any member of the applicant's family grouping. Residence over a period of time is probably the most common source of local connection,[264] though authorities with large army camps in their areas will welcome the rule that service in the armed forces does not give a local connection. Many authorities applied an informal six-month residence qualification, but this is not necessarily a strict legal test. In *R. v. Southwark L.B.C. ex parte Hughes*[265] a Frenchwoman moved to Southwark one September intending to live with her boyfriend and soon found herself pregnant, but she was forced to leave him that same November after suffering domestic violence. Judicial review was awarded on the basis that this brief residence could be sufficient to establish a local connection, given that her intention was to set up a permanent home in the area. Any place where the applicant is at risk of domestic violence is

---

[259] Data Protection Act 1999 ss.34, 68.

[260] sch.12 paras.2–3.

[261] s.198.

[262] s.198(4)(b); S.I. 2000/701 reg.6 (in Wales S.I. 2000/1079).

[263] *R. v. Westminster C.C. ex parte Kamal* (1997) 29 H.L.R. 230 C.A.

[264] *R. v. Slough B.C. ex parte Ealing L.B.C.* [1981] Q.B. 801 C.A.; *R. v. Newham L.B.C. ex parte Smith* (1997) 29 H.L.R. 213.

[265] (1998) 30 H.L.R. 1082, Turner J.

ignored.[266] Employment (even if voluntary work[267]) is a natural source of local connection since a person needs housing accommodation close to his work, and a local connection may be established simply by finding work.[268] However, in the leading case, *Eastleigh B.C. v. Betts*,[269] a woman had moved from Leicester to Southampton to follow her partner's work, but this was held not to give her any local connection in Hampshire. Family association need not necessarily derive from a blood relationship,[270] though a link through a cousin once removed is too remote.[271]

Applicants have a right to a reasoned decision about local connection and to challenge the decision made.[272]

Homeless people often apply to multiple authorities in an attempt to secure a favourable decision. The applicants involved in *R. v. Slough B.C. ex parte Ealing L.B.C.*[273] had lived in Slough over a long period but their local council held that they had all become homeless intentionally. Ealing, however, decided that their homelessness was unintentional, a finding that imposed a duty to find interim and permanent accommodation.[274] Referral is allowed where an applicant has no local connection with the authority to which he has applied, but does have a local connection elsewhere,[275] In the *Slough* case, Ealing L.B.C. was able to refer the case back to Slough, the council with which the applicant had the closest local connection, and since Slough was bound by Ealing's decision about intentionality they owed a full homelessness duty. At the time of the case (before the 1996 reforms) this meant that Slough were bound to provide permanent accommodation.

The more attractive parts of the country may face an influx of applicants, leading some councils to experience great difficulty in differentiating legitimate and illegitimate claims to housing. One example is *R. v. East Devon D.C. ex parte Robb*,[276] where the applicant, having been advised by her doctor in Aberdeen to move somewhere warmer, chose a caravan in Devon but found herself left homeless when the park closed for the winter. The council refused her housing after challenging her medical evidence, but was found on the facts to have committed a procedural irregularity in failing to give her an adequate warning of this challenge. Special rules are designed to prevent an influx of homeless people on the Scilly Isles.[277]

Referral is a means of passing costs from the referring authority to the receiving authority, for whom there is a strong financial incentive to challenge the decision.[278]

---

[266] H.A. 1996 s.199.

[267] *R. v. Ealing L.B.C. ex parte Fox* [1998] Times March 9th.

[268] *Wyness v. Poole B.C.* [1979] 07 L.A.G. Bull. 166.

[269] [1983] 2 A.C. 613 H.L.

[270] *Munting v. Hammersmith & Fulham R.L.B.C.* [1998] 2 C.L.Y. 3017.

[271] *R. v. Hammersmith & Fulham L.B.C. ex parte Avdic* (1998) 30 H.L.R. 1 C.A.

[272] s.184(4), (5). The relevant date is the date of the decision or (if there is review) of the review: *Ealing L.B.C. v. Surdonja* [2000] 2 All E.R. 597 C.A.

[273] [1981] Q.B. 801 C.A.

[274] H.A. 1996 s.200.

[275] H.A. 1996 s.198.

[276] (1998) 30 H.L.R. 922.

[277] S.I. 1997/797.

[278] *R. v. Newham ex parte Tower Hamlets L.B.C.* (1990) 23 H.L.R. 62 C.A.; D.S. Cowan (1993) 56 *M.L.R.* 218; R. Thornton [1994] *J.S.W.L.* 19.

Squabbles like that in the *Slough* case are now resolved by an arbitrator appointed from a panel maintained by the Local Government Association.[279]

I.   OVERSEAS APPLICANTS

The government has naturally been concerned to deter benefit tourists, that is people who come to this country from abroad to take advantage of superior welfare benefits. Any country is bound to have some defences to prevent itself being swamped by unmanageable numbers of immigrants, but then again everyone is entitled to humane and fair treatment.

Public housing may only be provided to qualifying applicants: restrictions apply to allocations, grants to non-qualifying people as joint tenants with qualifying applicants, and homelessness duties.[280] Qualification rules are used to exclude from entitlement any person who is subject to immigration control[281] a concept defined by the Asylum and Immigration Act 1996,[282] though this basic premise requires considerable amplification and explication.[283]

1.   British citizens

The Immigration Act 1971 confers on British citizens a right of abode in the United Kingdom, including the right to live here and to come and go to and from without let or hindrance.[284] Specialist immigration texts explain the full complexity of the definition of British citizenship in the British Nationality Act 1981,[285] here it is sufficient to note that methods of acquisition of citizenship include birth in the United Kingdom to a citizen, adoption by a British citizen, birth overseas to a parent who is a British citizen by birth, by registration while a minor, by the marriage of a woman whose husband is a British citizen, and by naturalisation. All citizens qualify for the provision of public sector housing, either through allocation from a housing register or through homelessness,[286] but any non-qualifying member of his family grouping must be excluded from consideration when assessing the suitability of an offer of accommodation.

2.   Habitual residence in the United Kingdom

A non-British citizen who is subject to immigration control is excluded from housing[287] but he may qualify through habitual residence in the United Kingdom, (though the reg-

---

[279] S.I. 1998/1578, replacing S.I. 1978/69.

[280] H.A. 1996 ss.161, 185; this is shortly to be replaced by Immigration and Asylum Act 1999 s.118.

[281] s.161(2); S. Rahilly (1998) 20 *J.S.W.F.L.* 237.

[282] Earlier rules in S.I. 1996/1982 as amended (most recently by S.I. 1999/3057 to adapt to the new national reception scheme) were not retrospective: *R. v. Hackney L.B.C. ex parte K.* (1998) 30 H.L.R. 760 C.A. These regulations are now replaced by S.I. 2000/706.

[283] *Code of Guidance to Local Authorities on the Allocation of Accommodation and Homelessness* (D.E.T.R., 1998) sch.20 and annexes 8–15.

[284] s.1(1).

[285] ss.1–13.

[286] They need first to establish habitual residence here: (1) allocation: S.I. 2000/702 reg.6 (re-enacting S.I. 1996/2753 reg.6); (2) homelessness: S.I. 2000/701 reg.4 (not following S.I. 1996/2754 reg.4); in Wales S.I. 2000/1079.

[287] S.Is. 2000/702 reg.6 (allocation in England), 2000/701 reg.4 (homelessness in England).

ulations are defined in terms of the Common Travel Area, a wider geographical area). For *allocation* purposes, the prescribed classes[288] are:

Class C   A person who is habitually resident in the Common Travel Area and has current leave to enter. However, this class excludes a person whose leave was granted on the terms that a sponsor has agreed to be responsible for his maintenance, the exclusion lasting for a period of five years or until the death of his sponsor.

Class E   A person habitually resident within the Common Travel Area who is a national of a European state with reciprocal social security arrangements.

In terms of *homelessness*, the prescribed classes[289] are:

Class C   A person who is habitually resident in the Common Travel Area (including Ireland along with the United Kingdom) and has current leave to enter. Again this class excludes a person whose leave was granted on the terms that a sponsor has agreed to be responsible for his maintenance for a period of five years or until the death of his sponsor.

Class E   A person habitually resident within the Common Travel Area who is a national of a European state with reciprocal social security arrangements.

A good example of a person who had not established habitual residence here, and so was disqualified, was the applicant in *R. v. Hammersmith & Fulham L.B.C. ex parte Damoah*.[290] A mother brought her children to this country to escape domestic violence in Sweden. She was not habitually resident here and had no entitlement to seek public assistance in this country with housing, though the ultimate given by the council that she return to Sweden or receive no further help was too dogmatic given that her children might qualify for care.

How to establish habitual residence was the issue considered in the context of entitlement to income support in *Nessa v. Chief Adjudication Officer*.[291] Mrs Joybun Nessa travelled from Bangladesh where she had lived all her life to the United Kingdom where she had a right of abode in 1994. Entitlement to income support was dependent upon her being habitually resident in this country. A short period of residence may be sufficient,[292] but on the facts of *Nessa* it was held to be insufficient to intend to settle here on arrival in the United Kingdom. Residence in fact is required for a period which shows that the residence has become habitual, and probably also that it is likely to continue to be habitual.[293] The same test will be applied to homeless arrivals.

3.   Habitual residence in other parts of the Common Travel Area

No entry checks are made on the arrival in the United Kingdom (England, Wales, Scotland and Northern Ireland) of a person resident in another part of the British Isles,

---

[288] S.I. 2000/702 reg.4 (England).
[289] S.I. 2000/701 reg.3 (England); S.I. 2000/1079 (Wales).
[290] (1999) 31 H.L.R. 786, Kay J.
[291] [1999] 4 All E.R. 677 H.L.
[292] *Re S* [1998] A.C. 750, 763, Lord Slynn.
[293] *Nessa* at 682h–j, Lord Slynn.

and the Common Travel Area also includes the Channel Islands, the Isle of Man, and the Republic of Ireland. Citizens of these countries can in practice come and go without hindrance[294] and if they are habitually resident there they will fall into the exceptional classes discussed immediately above. Irish nationals often also qualify as workers under the European rules described immediately below. Class E covers people who are nationals of other countries with reciprocal social security arrangements, normally excluded[295] from public assistance, who are let into the qualifying classes above by their habitual residence within the Common Travel Area.

4. Europe

Membership of the European Union entails opening one's borders to workers from other Member States so that work can migrate freely within a single employment market. The Immigration Act 1988[296] ensures that people who arrive in the United Kingdom in pursuance of a right of free movement between Member States of the European Union are exempt from the need for leave, though as a result of the vacillations of the Conservative Government of the day this was not brought into force until 1994.[297] Such a person now qualifies to seek a housing allocation[298] and for homelessness duties.[299] Thus in *R. v. Westminster C.C. ex parte Castelli*[300] housing had to be provided (under the old homelessness legislation) to Castelli, an Italian national who had entered the country as a worker from within the E.U. intending to set up a plastics recycling business but then suffered a business failure, and who had become unable to work through HIV infection. People are prevented from giving up adequate housing in Europe and moving here as homeless persons because their homelessness will be intentional, though no doubt such people may seek to be put on the housing register to wait for an allocation.

  European applicants from outside the Common Travel Area may not seek an allocation of housing unless they fall within the prescribed Class I,[301] that is a person who can seek housing as an aspect of the European freedom of movement of persons:

workers currently employed—Council Regulation (EEC) No.1612/68;
people formerly employed here—Council Regulation (EEC) No.1251/70;
members of the family of workers—Council Directive 68/360/EEC (the family member
     need not be a national of an E.U. state); and
self employed people—Council Directive 73/148/EEC.

The same people are qualified as homelessness applicants.[302] Students are notably absent from this list of potential claimants. A person seeking work and allowed income-

---

[294] Immigration Act 1971 s.1(3).
[295] S.Is. 2000/702 (allocation), 2000/701 and S.I. 2000/1074 (homelessness).
[296] s.7.
[297] July 20th 1994: S.I. 1994/1923.
[298] H.A. 1996 s.161(2).
[299] s.185(2).
[300] (1996) 28 H.L.R. 616 C.A.; D.S. Cowan (1995) 17 *J.S.W.F.L.* 43.
[301] S.I. 2000/702 reg.6 (England).
[302] S.I. 2000/701 reg.4 (England); S.I. 2000/1079 (Wales).

based jobseekers allowance may make a homelessness claim[303] but is not at that stage qualified for an allocation.

5. Commonwealth countries

A very limited class of citizens of British Dependent Territories also have the right to come here. There is a rather more extensive class of Commonwealth citizens, and of these anyone who had the right of abode in the United Kingdom before the British Nationality Act 1981 still retains it today. Special provision has been made for those forced out of the island of Montserrat by volcanic activity.[304] However most Commonwealth citizens are subject to the same immigration controls as arrivals from other overseas countries, described immediately below.

6. People subject to immigration control

A person subject to immigration control is defined by the Asylum and Immigration Act 1996[305] as any person who requires leave to enter or remain in the United Kingdom under the terms of the Immigration Act 1971. The concept of leave to enter and to remain is now clarified by Immigration and Asylum Act 1999.[306] The discussion at this point deals with the residue of people not in the categories already considered above.

The Asylum and Immigration Act 1996 reduced the economic incentives for illegal immigration: housing may not be allocated to a person subject to immigration control,[307] such a person cannot apply as being homeless,[308] and the position of such a person is ignored when assessing the homelessness of others within his family grouping.[309] Exceptional classes are prescribed, both for allocation and homelessness purposes, where housing may be provided despite the fact that a person is not habitually resident in the Common Travel Area[310] and is subject to normal immigration control. Of these the most important is the one lettered Class B for allocation[311] and homelessness[312] purposes:

> a person granted exceptional leave to remain outside immigration control unless leave was conditional on his not seeking assistance from public funds.

Other classes relate to refugees and are enumerated below.[313]

[303] S.I. 2000/701 reg.3 Class I (England; in Wales S.I. 2000/1079); excluded are those with a limited leave to enter and those receiving benefit after a temporary disruption of funds from abroad. However, all people subject to immigration control will be excluded from this benefit: Immigration and Asylum Act 1999 s.115.

[304] S.I. 2000/701 reg.3 Class D (homelessness in England); S.I. 2000/1079 (Wales); S.I. 2000/702 reg.4 Class D (allocation in England).

[305] s.13(2).

[306] ss.1–3; ss.9–15 deal with removal from the U.K., and ss.16–17 with the controversial provisions for taking a deposit from visitors from the Indian sub-Continent.

[307] s.9(1); H.A. 1996 s.161; see now Immigration and Asylum Act 1999 s.118.

[308] s.9(1); H.A. 1996 s.185; Immigration and Asylum Act 1999 s.118.

[309] s.9(2); s.8 imposes restriction on employment and s.10 on child benefit; H.A. 1996 s.185; Immigration and Asylum Act 1999 s.115 (exclusion from income based job seekers allowances).

[310] H.A. 1996 s.161(3); S.I. 2000/702 reg.6 (allocation in England); S.I. 2000/701 reg.3 (homelessness in England); S.I. 2000/1079 (Wales).

[311] S.I. 2000/702 reg.4.

[312] S.I. 2000/701 reg.3 (England); S.I. 2000/1079 (Wales).

[313] See below pp. 96–97.

Applicants must be residing in this country legally, so that no duty is owed to a person who enters as an illegal immigrant,[314] a person who obtains entry by deception[315] or an illegal overstayer who entered legally—perhaps as a tourist or a student or with a temporary work permit—but whose rights later terminated.[316] Any allocation is void.[317]

J. ASYLUM SEEKERS

1. Law up to 2000

Claims to asylum are made under the Asylum and Immigration Appeals Act 1993 on the basis that it would be contrary to the Geneva Convention of the Status of Refugees 1957 to remove a person from the United Kingdom.[318] Immigration rules are suspended while this claim is considered and the person is protected from deportation for the duration.[319] In 1998 there were 65,000 people seeking asylum in London alone,[320] but only some 5 per cent of claims for asylum are accepted, so that there is a large class of asylum seekers who will not in the end be allowed to stay. Asylum seekers requiring public assistance must identify themselves as such at the port of entry[321] and may then be allowed in to this country while the claim is considered.

Many asylum seekers have no accommodation, and will qualify for assistance as being homeless[322] provided they do identify themselves at the port of entry.[323] *Lismane* v. *Hammersmith & Fulham L.B.C.*[324] established that a full homelessness duty could also be owed to an asylum seeker in unsuitable accommodation. In that case a Latvian woman arrived with her young child and made a claim at the port of entry to asylum from persecution in her own country. She joined her husband who had arrived earlier but who had not claimed asylum on arrival and who had a shorthold tenancy of a small room. The three members of this family lived together in the room, 11 feet by 9, in conditions that were overcrowded, cold, and hazardous on fire safety grounds. Nourse L.J. held that Mrs Lismane could be homeless if it was not reasonable to continue to occupy the accommodation with other members of her family grouping, including her husband and all her children.

Exceptional classes of people qualifying for *allocation*[325] include:

Class A   A person recorded officially as a refugee.

---

[314] *R.* v. *Westminster C.C. ex parte Castelli* (1996) 28 H.L.R. 616 C.A.; *R.* v. *S.S. for the Environment ex parte Tower Hamlets L.B.C* [1993] Q.B. 632 C.A.

[315] *R.* v. *Westminster L.B.C. ex parte Jaafer* (1998) 30 H.L.R. 698, Scott Baker J.

[316] *R.* v. *Hillingdon L.B.C. ex parte Streeting* [1980] 1 W.L.R. 1425, 1434.

[317] *Akinbolu* v. *Hackney L.B.C.* (1997) 29 H.L.R. 259 C.A. (old law).

[318] s.1.

[319] ss.2, 6.

[320] D. Carter [1998] J.H.L. 77.

[321] Asylum and Immigration Appeals Act 1993.

[322] D.E.T.R. *Code of Guidance to Local Authorities on the Allocation of Accommodation and Homelessness* (D.E.T.R., 1998) ch.20; *Guidelines for Registered Social Landlords on the Provision of Housing and Support Services for Asylum Seekers* (Housing Corporation, 1998).

[323] H.A. 1996 s.186; *R.* v. *Kensington & Chelsea R.L.B.C. ex parte Korneva* (1997) 29 H.L.R. 709 C.A. (homelessness duty additional to asylum).

[324] (1999) 31 H.L.R. 427 C.A.

[325] S.I. 2000/702 reg.4 (England).

This stage is reached only when the Secretary of State has accepted the claim to asylum and only at that stage can permanent accommodation be allocated. Exceptional classes of people qualifying to apply as being homeless[326] are:

Class A   A refugee officially recorded as such
Class F   A person who has made a claim for asylum on his arrival in the U.K. before April 3rd 2000, when entitlement continues until his asylum claim is determined or abandoned.
Class G   A person who became an asylum seeker before April 3rd 2000 because of official acceptance of changed circumstances after his arrival.
Class H   A person who claimed asylum before February 4th 1996.[327]

Claims made after April 2nd 2000 will fall within the national Asylum Support Scheme, which is described below.

A large class of people potentially entitled to seek asylum arrive as tourists and so do not identify themselves at their port of entry as potential asylum seekers. Such a person may seek subsequently to be recorded officially as an asylum seeker on the basis of a change of conditions since entry into the United Kingdom, and entitlement to public housing dates from the time that this is officially accepted. Status as an asylum seeker lasts from the date the claim is the recorded to the date it is determined or abandoned.[328]

2. National assistance

A safety net provided under the National Assistance Act 1948[329] enables accommodation to be provided to people who would not otherwise qualify. Asylum seekers are included even if they fail to register as such at their port of entry to the United Kingdom according to the decision in *R. v. Westminster C.C. ex parte A.*,[330] though this point is currently under appeal to the Lords. It is difficult to see how the discretion could be properly exercised against a destitute asylum seeker.[331] The safety net is also available to illegal overstayers, any illegality being overridden by humanitarian concerns. In *R. v. Brent L.B.C. ex parte D.*[332] a single Brazilian man with H.I.V. had entered with a six months' visitor's visa but had failed to leave at the end of that time, so becoming an illegal overstayer, but this consideration was overridden by the requirement to safeguard this man's life and health[333]: accommodation must be provided if a deportation would cause a risk to life or of serious injury.

The formal trigger for this safety net is an assessment of the need for a person to receive community care services under the National Health Service and Community

---

[326] S.I. 2000/701 (England); S.I. 2000/1079 (Wales).

[327] See regs.3(1), (2). Former rules in Asylum and Immigration Appeals Act 1993 ss.4, 5 and sch.1 are repealed by H.A. 1996 sch.19; *R. v. Hackney L.B.C. ex parte K.* (1998) 30 H.L.R. 760 C.A.

[328] s.186; Asylum and Immigration Appeals Act 1993 ss.8–9 (appeal); asylum appeals are now dealt with by the Immigration and Asylum Act 1999 Part IV (ss.69–70).

[329] s.21.

[330] (1997) 1 C.C.L.R. 85 C.A.

[331] *R. v. Kensington & Chelsea L.B.C. ex parte Kujtim* [1999] 4 All E.R. 161 C.A.

[332] (1998) 1 C.C.L.R. 234, Moses J.; *R. v. Wandsworth L.B.C. ex parte O.* [2000] Times July 18th C.A.

[333] *D. v. U.K.* (1997) 24 E.H.R.R. 423. A person unable to leave because he is in prison is not an illegal overstayer and may be entitled to claim: *R. v. Lambeth L.B.C. ex parte Sarhangi* (1999) 31 H.L.R. 1022, Kay J.

Care Act 1990.[334] Local authorities may provide residential accommodation for adult persons who are in need of care and attention by reason of age, illness, disability, or other circumstances, if such care would not otherwise be available to them.[335] Grounds to provide accommodation include mental or physical disability, but not just because of shortage of money or absence of social security entitlement[336]: destitution is not the test, but rather whether an applicant is in desperate need of care and attention or is at risk of some damage to his health. One example was a Chinese man suffering from psoriasis, who could not realistically be expected both to find work and to walk to soup kitchens.[337]

The Court of Appeal that decided *R. v. Kensington and Chelsea R.L.B.C. ex parte Kujtim*[338] identified a two-stage process. At first the authority was under a public law duty to conduct an assessment and so was susceptible to judicial review if the decision maker acted unreasonably. Having conducted the assessment, the second stage was a discretionary assessment by the authority of what accommodation to provide, a stage normally outside the scope of a public law challenge. Once accommodation has been provided, there is a duty to continue it so long as the need continues. However, any duty is predicated on the willingness of the applicant to accept the helping hand offered, and so accommodation may be withdrawn after conduct that amounts to a persistent flouting of reasonable management requirements. A final warning letter is desirable and the applicant must have a chance to his put case, but C.I.D. type investigations are not required.

Government circulars advise that accommodation should only be provided *in specie*, and the legality of this direction was upheld in *R. v. Secretary of State for Health ex parte Hammersmith & Fulham L.B.C.*[339] Hence it is not lawful to provide meal vouchers, food without accommodation,[340] or bed and breakfast alone.[341] Newham once had a policy of carting asylum seekers off to cheaper bed and breakfast accommodation in Eastbourne, arguing that this was the only way to provide board as well as a bed, but this was held to be a misinterpretation of the legislation in *R. v. Newham L.B.C ex parte Medical Foundation of the Care of Victims of Torture*[342]: applicants should not be removed from the borough providing the accommodation.

3. National Asylum Support

Part VI of the Immigration and Asylum Act 1999[343] sets up a new national system to provide for asylum seekers[344] and their dependants[345] in the interval between them

[334] s.47.

[335] s.21(1); *R. v. Sefton M.B..C. ex parte Help the Aged* [1997] 4 All E.R. 532 C.A.

[336] *R. v. Newham L.B.C. ex parte Plastin* (1998) 30 H.L.R. 261.

[337] *R. v. Southwark L.B.C. ex parte Hong Cui* (1999) 31 H.L.R. 639.

[338] [1999] 4 All E.R. 161 C.A.; *R. v. Wigan M.B.C. ex parte Tammadge* [1998] 1 C.C.L.R. 581, Forbes J.

[339] (1999) 31 H.L.R. 475 C.A.; see also *R. v. S.S. for the Environment ex parte Shelter* [1997] 2 C.L.Y. 2654, Carnwath J.; *R. v. Hammersmith & Fulham L.B.C. ex parte M.* (1998) 30 H.L.R. 10 C.A.; *R. v. Southwark L.B.C. ex parte Bediako* (1998) 30 H.L.R. 22.

[340] *R. v. Newham L.B.C. ex parte Gorenkin* (1998) 30 H.L.R. 278, Carnwath J.

[341] *R. v. Newham L.B.C. ex parte C.* (1999) 31 H.L.R. 567.

[342] (1998) 30 H.L.R. 955, Moses J.

[343] ss.94–127; [2000] 41 *L.S.G.* 42.

[344] As defined above, see pp. 96–97.

[345] Including spouse, a child under 18 who is dependent, and additional prescribed categories.

making a claim for asylum and the Home Secretary notifying them a result of their claim. A new Home Office agency called the National Asylum Support Service takes over this onerous burden from local authorities.

The Home Secretary will have power to provide support for any asylum seeker or dependant who appears to be destitute or appears likely to become destitute—because he lacks either adequate accommodation or the resources to meet other essential living needs.[346] Regulations will define the factors to be considered in deciding whether accommodation is adequate, but these will include lack of legal entitlement to the accommodation, any requirement to share housing, and whether it is permanent or temporary, and its location. Support may take the form of the provision of accommodation, the provision for living needs, or payment of legal expenses, but cash payments may only be made if the circumstances are wholly exceptional. Accommodation must be adequate[347] but it must only be temporary until the claim for asylum is determined,[348] and no secure or assumed tenancy will arise.[349] Regulations will detail the conditions on which accommodation will be held, and the conduct requirements.[350] Asylum seekers will no longer be concentrated in London, Dover and the other ports, but will be dispersed across the country to areas where there is a ready supply of accommodation, with reception zones provided.[351] Local authorities will no longer be responsible for supplying accommodation although the Home Secretary will have powers to request accommodation from local authorities and registered social landlords.

Support for asylum seekers under the 1999 Act will replace any other claim for national assistance.[352] A discretionary scheme run by local authorities has operated from December 1999,[353] although the press reported[354] that only 4,000 places had been found against a requirement of 40,000. The Home Office took over the scheme on April 1st 2000.

K. REFORM PROPOSALS

The Homes Bill 2000 will implement the proposals of the Housing Green Paper,[355] so as to meet the manifesto commitment of the new Labour Government to increase protection and choice for those seeking public housing.

1. Altering priorities

Public housing[356] should be available to those unintentionally without accommodation or who are living in conditions which it is not reasonable to tolerate, or where a family

---

[346] s.95.
[347] s.95.
[348] s.97.
[349] sch.14 amends H.A. 1985 sch.1 and H.A. 1988 sch.1.
[350] sch.8.
[351] s.103.
[352] s.116.
[353] sch.9; S.I. 1999/3126; S. Willman [2000] 20 L.S.G. 26.
[354] *Independent* January 28th 2000.
[355] Homes Bill 2000 Part II, ss.16–29; *Quality and Choice: A Decent Home for All* (D.E.T.R., April 2000) ch.9.
[356] The Green Paper uses the term "social" to include both public and social sectors.

demonstrates a pressing need to move.[357] Allocations will no longer be made from a housing register, since these are abolished[358]; rather the authority may allocate housing to any eligible person[359] who applies to it, including everyone on the housing register when the new proposals are implemented.[360]

Allocations will be based on a new system of housing preference.[361] Reasonable preference must be given to any person who is homeless, including those to whom a full duty is owed and those housed temporarily by another authority. Also included, apparently, are those without a priority need and those intentionally homeless, though surely these last two categories are not intended? Preference must also be given, as at present, to people in insanitary, overcrowded or unsatisfactory accommodation. It also includes people who need to move on medical or welfare needs or with a need to move to a particular district to avoid hardship; this category will in future be restricted to those needing to move since any person without a home will have the homelessness preference indicated above. Additional preference may also be given to people outside those statutory categories but with urgent housing needs: the Green Paper suggested a move away from a points-based system to one based on a tripartite division into cases showing urgent need, non-urgent need, or no need—this last where a person is able to find alternative accommodation in the private sector.[362] Priorities will have to be determined, considering amongst other things, the applicant's financial resources, any local connection, and the behaviour of the applicant and his family[363]: anti-social behaviour will necessarily lead to temporary exclusion, but there should be no permanent exclusions.[364] In the final analysis, cases will have to be prioritised according to waiting time.[365] Authorities in areas of high demand might require a more refined system with a large number of bands.

Categories of priority need under the *homelessness* legislation will be widened, though this will be done by regulations rather than primary legislation. Vulnerable people requiring this additional protection include children leaving care, those with institutional backgrounds, victims of domestic violence, and those aged between 16 and 17.[366] Very often prisoners lose their housing while in prison, and when they emerge back into society therefore lack the stable background which would discourage them from re-offending. Similar support may be needed for unmarried ex-servicemen. Local authorities will retain a discretion to refuse priority to those whom they believe might disrupt the stability of the community. Qualification rules will be reformed to ensure that it will no longer be possible to engineer priority deliberately.[367] A homeless person provided

[357] Green Paper para.9.16.
[358] Homes Bill 2000 cl.25 repealing H.A. 1996 ss.161–165
[359] H.A. 1996 new s.160A excluding (as at present) people subject to immigration control unless in prescribed classes. Instead allocations will be based on application to the authority (cl.26 amending H.A. 1996 s.166) including all those on the housing register at the commencement of the Homes Bill.
[360] Homes Bill 2000 cl.26 amending H.A. 1996 s.166.
[361] Homes Bill 2000 cl.27 substituting H.A. 1996 s.167(2).
[362] Green Paper para.9.18.
[363] H.A. 1996 s.167(2A).
[364] Green Paper paras.9.13–9.15.
[365] para.9.20.
[366] paras.9.55–9.56.
[367] para.9.14.

with temporary accommodation will retain his priority need while waiting for a permanent allocation.[368] Action is to be taken to tackle the 2,000 or so most vulnerable people who sleep rough.[369]

2. Improving choice

Customer-centred choice should be available to new applicants, to existing tenants seeking to move and to homeless applicants. Choice should be free, as wide as possible, and well-informed,[370] access systems should be simple and the views of customers should be taken into account.[371] Allocation policies and notices relating to homelessness inquiries will be required to include a statement of the authority's views about choice and expression of housing preference.[372] Even homeless people will be given a period of freedom of choice for a fixed period before the local authority will be allowed to impose a one-offer policy[373]; an indefinite period will be allowed in areas where pressure on the housing stock is low.[374]

3. Providing accommodation to the homeless

Substantial reform is proposed of the Conservative-inspired principle that housing for the homeless should be in temporary accommodation. The local authority should be allowed to use its own stock for longer than the present two-year period.[375] Indeed, where stock is available it will be permissible for the authority to provide temporary accommodation to those not having a priority need.[376] Changes are also to be made to the circumstances in which the full homelessness duty is satisfied and so ends: these will now include an offer of non-public home with full assurance[377] or a decision to take a non-public shorthold (though a homeless person will remain free to refuse an *offer* of a shorthold) and also the refusal of a final offer of permanent public-sector accommodation after a warning about the consequences of refusal.[378]

4. Homelessness reviews and strategy

Housing authorities will be required to conduct periodic homelessness reviews—the first within 12 months of the new legislation and thereafter at least every five years. From this the authority will formulate and publish a homelessness strategy designed to prevent homelessness and to secure accommodation and support for those who are homeless.[379]

---

[368] Homes Bill 2000 cl.24 amending H.A. 1996 s.159(5)–(6).

[369] Green Paper ch.10.

[370] paras.9.28–9.36.

[371] para.9.17.

[372] Homes Bill 2000 cl.27 amending H.A. 1996 s.167.

[373] Homes Bill 2000 cl.24 amending H.A. 1996 s.159(5)–(6); Green Paper paras.9.47–9.53.

[374] Green Paper para.9.52.

[375] Homes Bill 2000 cl.21 amending H.A. 1996 s.193 and repealing s.194; Green Paper para.9.53.

[376] Homes Bill 2000 cl.20 amending H.A. 1996 s.192; Green Paper paras.9.57–9.59. A similar amendment is made to the duty under s.195 where a person is threatened with homelessness.

[377] Full assurance will not normally arise for the first year: Homes Bill 2000 sch.2 amending H.A. 996 s.209.

[378] Homes Bill 2000 cl.22 amending H.A. 1996 s.193(6)–(8); s.197 (duty to provide help where other accommodation in the authority's region) will be revoked by cl.23. In each case the accommodation must be suitable.

[379] Homes Bill 2000 cls.16–19.

5

FULL RESIDENTIAL SECURITY

Tenants with full security. Residential occupation. "Life long" security. Bankruptcy. Succession. Relationship breakdown. Sole tenancies. Joint periodic tenancies. Occupation orders. Transfer orders. Position of landlord on relationship breakdown.

A. TENANTS WITH FULL SECURITY

It may be as well to restate briefly the conclusions reached in Chapter 1 and to anticipate some of the conclusions of Chapter 6 about the sorts of tenants who enjoy full residential security of tenure.

1. Rent Act tenants

A Rent Act tenancy is one that was granted by a private sector landlord before early 1989 and operating as a protected tenancy under the Rent Act 1977.[1] During the contractual period it is called a regulated tenancy; after termination of contractual protection it becomes a statutory tenancy; both classes together are described as protected tenancies. A protected tenant enjoys "lifelong" security of tenure and succession rights. However, by far the greatest impact of this legislative scheme was the restriction of rents to fair rents. Most Rent Act tenants are now elderly—or at least middle aged—because new protected tenancies are not permitted after early 1989.[2] However existing tenancies run on indefinitely, and replacements for Rent Act tenancies continue to be protected, though nothing prevents an agreed surrender.

2. Fully assured tenants

An assured tenancy is a private sector tenancy granted from early 1989 onwards under the Housing Act 1988.[3] If it is fully assured (as opposed to an assured shorthold), the tenant will enjoy lifelong security of tenure. In fact the security of tenure under the two main regimes is broadly comparable.[4] The long period of Conservative government between 1979 and 1997 saw a progressive reduction in security of residential tenure, so that it is now abnormal for a tenant in the private sector to enjoy life-long security, since shorthold tenancies now predominate in the private sector, and as from early 1997 a

---

[1] Woodfall ch.23.

[2] H.A. 1988 s.35.

[3] H.A. 1988 ss.1(1), 34, sch.1 para.1; Woodfall ch.24; D. Hoath [1989] *J.S.W.L.* 339; [1990] *J.S.W.L.* 18; M. Davey (1989) 52 *M.L.R.* 6611; C.P. Rodgers [1988] *Conv.* 122; W. Hickman [1993] *N.L.J.* 1271.

[4] Hence a fully assured tenancy may be a suitable alternative to a protected tenancy; see below pp. 352–353.

landlord has to elect positively to create anything other than a shorthold by giving notice.[5] The shift to assured tenancies in early 1989 had a fundamental impact on the applicable rent regimes, since rents under assured tenancies are regulated only by the market in rented accommodation and the power to prevent rents from being increased above market levels.[6]

3. Social tenants

Most tenants with a full assurance are tenants of a registered social landlord, a category consisting of housing associations, and similar charitable organisations. In early 1989 housing associations were shifted to the private sector,[7] where they now grant assured tenancies.[8] Social tenants have additional Charter rights and these ensure that most grants by registered social landlords will confer a full assurance.[9]

4. Public sector secure tenants

Landlords falling within the public sector are local authorities, New Town Corporations, Housing Action Trusts, urban development corporations, the Housing Corporation, the relevant "Minister" of the Welsh Assembly, and Housing Action Trusts. The *landlord condition*[10] identifies the public sector in rented accommodation where secure tenancies are granted under the Housing Act 1985[11] which confer life-long security of tenure. The Housing Act 1996 permits councils to adopt an introductory tenancy scheme that puts new tenants on probation for a year.[12] Public sector tenants also have the *right to buy* their homes at a discount.

5. Accommodation providing full security

Assuming that a tenancy is one that basically attracts full security—as opposed to being a shorthold—it is necessary also to find that the tenant has exclusive possession of self-contained residential accommodation. This is clear with a house, self-contained flat, or maisonette, but calls for more discussion in the case of a bed sit, a room in a hostel, or similar shared accommodation. So much so that the whole of the next chapter is devoted to this topic. Even if the accommodation is self-contained there are many factors (also discussed in Chapter 6) that limit or remove security, for example where the letting is for a holiday or is by a college to a student. Full security is also qualified by some of the mandatory grounds for possession which qualify the right to full security.

B. RESIDENTIAL OCCUPATION

Residential security of tenure is dependent upon continued residential occupation of the dwelling. If an existing tenant no longer needs a home, his housing accommodation

---

[5] H.A. 1988 s.19A; see above p. 46.
[6] See below pp. 225–227.
[7] H.A. 1988 s.140(2) sch.18 operating from January 15th 1989.
[8] s.81(1) as amended by H.A. 1988 s.83.
[9] *Code of Practice on Tenure* (Housing Corporation, 1999) para.4.1.
[10] ss.80, 114.
[11] Woodfall ch.25.
[12] H.A. 1996 ss.127–128; *Manchester C.C.* v. *Cochrane* (1999) 31 H.L.R. 810 C.A.; see below p. 165.

should be recycled and made available to other applicants. Phraseology varies between the security regimes, though the actual test is similar in all cases. The Rent Act 1977 refers to occupation "as a residence",[13] which however is interpreted as a requirement of residence "as a home".[14] This last test appears explicitly in the statutory regimes for assured[15] and public sector[16] tenancies, but the change of vocabulary enshrines no change of principle,[17] despite dicta in one case that the new test is stricter. Similar tests are also applied when determining qualification for leasehold enfranchisement[18] and the public sector right to buy,[19] though a landlord is favoured by a more liberal test when determining whether he is resident in the same building.[20]

1.   Contractual and statutory phases

Residential qualification was first developed by the judges,[21] but the statutory implementation of the rule has been slightly different for each of the security regimes. Under the *Rent Act 1977* residential qualification is not a requirement so long as the tenant has a contractual tenancy, the rule having an impact only when the contractual tenancy is terminated and the tenancy has passed to a statutory phase, so that it is solely dependent upon the Rent Act for its existence. In *Colin Smith Music Ltd.* v. *Ridge*[22] a tenant lost protection when, after having lived with a woman with whom he had children, he left her and moved out of the flat. Giving up occupation lost him statutory protection. Special provisions are required to avoid loss of security on relationship breakdown, since very often the contractual tenant moves out leaving his former partner in occupation, and it is necessary to deem that this occupation is that of the contractual tenant; as explained below[23] this deemed transfer of occupation is more satisfactory between spouses than cohabitees.

A statutory tenancy may be destroyed by physical destruction of the building containing it,[24] but the recent case of *Prince* v. *Robinson*[25] shows that a tenant can continue his statutory rights by continuing to assert his intention to return. In the particular case, the tenant of a flat in London had already moved out and moved to Devon two years before the building containing his flat was burnt to the ground. Afterwards he moved to Portugal and had not visited it between February 1991 and March 1998. When it was reconstructed it was rebuilt in such a way that the original flat had ceased to exist, the

---

[13] R.A. 1977 s.2(1)(a); Woodfall 23.047–23.051.

[14] *Hampstead Way Investments Ltd.* v. *Lewis-Weare* [1985] 1 W.L.R. 164, 169B, Lord Brandon; *Crawley L.B.C.* v. *Sawyer* (1988) 20 H.L.R. 98, 101, Parker L.J. Note also *Caradon D.C.* v. *Paton* [2000] Times May 17th C.A. (holiday lettings infringed covenant against use other than as a private dwelling; had to be used as a home).

[15] H.A. 1988 s.1(1)(b).

[16] H.A. 1985 s.81 ("the tenant condition").

[17] *Ujima H.Ass.* v. *Ansah* (1998) 30 H.L.R. 831 C.A.

[18] See below pp. 396–398.

[19] See below pp. 495–496.

[20] This excludes security; see below pp. 162–163.

[21] *Hicks* v. *Scarsdale Brewery Co.* [1924] W.N. 189 Div.Ct.; *Skinner* v. *Geary* [1931] 2 K.B. 546 C.A.; R.E. Megarry (1951) 67 *L.Q.R.* 505.

[22] [1975] 1 W.L.R. 463 C.A.

[23] See below pp. 131–134.

[24] *Morley's (Birmingham) Ltd.* v. *Slater* [1950] 1 All E.R. 335 C.A.; R.E. Megarry (1950) 66 *L.Q.R.* 162.

[25] (1999) 31 H.L.R. 89 C.A.

space it once occupied now being part of an open plan kitchen and dining area. Prince was held to have lost his statutory tenancy but only because of his decision to move and not as an inevitable result of the fire. On the facts, Prince had lost his tenancy before the landlord had sold the reconstructed block and so Prince had no interest capable of being an overriding interest. A tenant succeeded in *Viking Property Co. Ltd.* v. *Rawlinson*[26] where she was forced out of a property by water penetration in 1987 but was still in residential occupation in 1998, the symbol of that being the presence of her furniture; throughout her enforced move next door she intended to return when the property was in repair.

Assured tenancies (granted after early 1989) are defined to continue if, and so long as, the tenant occupies the dwelling-house as his only or principal home,[27] and *public sector secure tenancies* operate in the same way.[28] Residence need not be lawful, so that an immigrant who overstays his permission to be in the country may still enjoy a secure tenancy.[29] Under these modern schemes, continued occupation is required from the beginning of the tenancy: so, for example, the power to fix the rent under an assured tenancy is removed if the tenant moves out. Once the agreed contractual period ends, a non-resident tenant can be ejected immediately,[30] for example where an assured tenant admits in the course of proceedings that he has another house.[31]

2.   Joint tenants

It is not necessary that *all* joint tenants share their residence together on the premises. Occupation by any one is enough. In *Lloyd* v. *Sadler*[32] a flat was leased to two young women, one of whom left to get married and had no intention of returning, but the single woman who stayed on was successful in her claim for security of tenure. Statutory regimes for assured[33] and public sector secure tenancies[34] state the same rule expressly: several individuals may qualify for security as joint tenants provided that one of them has qualifying occupation.

3.   Non-personal residence

Vicarious residence is possible, for example through members of the tenant's family,[35] or a friend, since leaving someone in occupation of one's home shows that it has not been surrendered: the right to buy continues even if the local authority takes it upon itself to change the locks and to end the tenant's rent account.[36]

---

[26] [1999] 08 C.L. 440.
[27] H.A. 1988 s.1(1).
[28] H.A. 1985 s.81; *Hussey* v. *Camden L.B.C.* (1995) 27 H.L.R. 5 C.A.
[29] *Akinbolu* v. *Hackney L.B.C.* (1997) 29 H.L.R. 259 C.A.; see above p. 96.
[30] *Croydon L.B.C.* v. *Buston* (1991) 24 H.L.R. 36 C.A.
[31] *Bruce* v. *Worthing B.C.* (1993) 26 H.L.R. 223 C.A.
[32] [1978] Q.B. 774 C.A.; no reference was made to *Foreman* v. *Beagley* [1969] 1 W.L.R. 1387 C.A.; P.V. Baker (1970) 86 *L.Q.R.* 16
[33] H.A. 1988 s.1(1).
[34] H.A. 1985 s.81.
[35] *Skinner* v. *Geary* [1931] 2 K.B. 546 (sea captain).
[36] *Zionmor* v. *Islington L.B.C.* (1998) 30 H.L.R. 822.

On the other hand residence by a tenant cannot continue through the person of a sub-tenant, so that statutory protection of the tenant ends the moment that the entire dwelling is sub-let,[37] and the sub-tenant will also be vulnerable to eviction by the head landlord. This is obviously right, since it is appropriate to end protection of a residential tenant who decides upon commercial exploitation of his tenancy. In *Ujima Housing Association* v. *Ansah*[38] a housing association tenant granted an assured shorthold to a sub-tenant, and this caused the loss of residential qualification and the end of the tenant's security. Sub-letting of a *part* may not destroy the tenant's security provided that he has occupation of the remainder as his home and has an intention to resume possession of the whole at some time in the future.[39]

4. Continued residence through temporary absences

Occupation need not be continuous.[40] Tenants need to go shopping and go to work. Longer absences may occur during holidays, renovations, the confinement of a pregnant woman in hospital, or as a result of domestic violence. A tenant should not lose Rent Act protection while prevented from occupying his home by a temporary ouster order (usually the result of violence towards a cohabitee). Indeed this is the law, provided there is a real prospect of his return.[41] One tenant vacated his rented property for an entire winter while his wife was pregnant,[42] and long absences have also been accepted where the tenant is caring for a dying parent.[43] The tenant has the onus of showing continued residence[44] by demonstrating (1) an intention to return, supported by (2) some physical symbol of that intention.

Without an *intention to return*, a tenant who gives up occupation loses statutory protection. In *Duke* v. *Porter*[45] a tenant of long standing moved to live elsewhere in 1975, visiting the rented house twice daily to feed his cats and chickens. Proceedings taken in 1982 to remove the tenant failed because the judge found at that stage that the tenant intended to return. Next year, a sub-tenant was evicted and the house was redecorated, but the tenant did not return before, in 1985, fresh proceedings were instituted. These were successful, even though the tenant *had* moved back into the house by the time the case came to court, because the judge found as a fact that the tenant did not intend to return in the period between 1982 and 1985. Retention of protection throughout a temporary move elsewhere requires the tenant to show that he intends to return in the

[37] *Hussey* v. *Camden L.B.C.* (1995) 27 H.L.R. 5 C.A. (obiter on facts).

[38] (1998) 30 H.L.R. 831 C.A.; S. Murdoch [1999] 17 *E.G.* 126. Roch L.J. made use of a variety of analogies: *Brown* v. *Brash* [1948] 2 K.B. 247 C.A. (Rent Act); *Poland* v. *Cadogan* [1980] 3 All E.R. 544 C.A. (leasehold enfranchisement); and *Jackson* v. *Pekic* [1989] 2 E.G.L.R. 104 C.A. (resident landlords).

[39] *Regalian Securities Ltd.* v. *Ramsden* [1981] 1 W.L.R. 611 H.L.

[40] A.H.R. Brierley [1991] *Conv.* 345, 432.

[41] *Tickner* v. *Hearn* [1960] 1 W.L.R. 1406, 1410; *Osei-Bonsu* v. *Wandsworth L.B.C.* [1999] 1 All E.R. 265, 271, Simon Brown L.J.

[42] *Atyeo* v. *Fardoe* (1978) 37 P. & C.R. 494 C.A.

[43] *Richards* v. *Green* [1983] 2 E.G.L.R. 104; J.E. Martin [1984] *Conv.* 151.

[44] *Brown* v. *Brash* [1948] 2 K.B. 247 C.A. (obiter; contingent hope only on the facts); *Ujima H.Ass.* v. *Ansah* (1998) 30 H.L.R. 831 C.A.

[45] (1987) 19 H.L.R. 1 C.A.; *Robert Thackray's Estate* v. *Kaye* [1989] 1 E.G.L.R. 127 C.A. (statutory tenant of flat 6 moved, during work on the original flat, to flat 5 which he liked more. Failure to move back on completion of the work led to the loss of protection); S. Bridge [1989] *Conv.* 450.

future,[46] but, provided that this is so, long periods have been allowed for a resumption of possession. For example, in *Gofor Investments Ltd.* v. *Roberts*,[47] a tax exile had already been abroad for five years at the time of the hearing and did not intend to return for another 10 years, at which time her children's education would be complete. Despite all this she was still held to be in possession, and entitled to protection, however much this decision was contrary to the obvious social policy of the legislation.

A tenant's subjective intention to return must be accompanied by an *outward and visible sign* of that intention—also described as "any deliberate symbol of continued occupation"[48]—sufficient tokens being a resident caretaker, relatives, or furniture.[49]

5.   Second homes

Security regimes again diverge.

The *Rent Act 1977* requires residence as a home, with emphasis on the singular "a", leaving open the possibility that the continued residence test might be satisfied by a home that is one of two.[50] Tenants seeking security of tenure in a second home protected by the Rent Act 1977 must satisfy two requirements. (1) The home must be a *residence*. A brother of a newsagent failed in his claim for security in *Hampstead Way Investments Ltd.* v. *Lewis-Weare*.[51] The brother helped out in the shop at unsociable hours and so used a flat above the shop to catch up on his sleep during the daytime, but he owned a house only half a mile away and it was there that he conducted the remainder of his life. His claim to security was rejected since the flat was not a residence. Another similar claim went against a tenant who studied and slept in one set of rooms but who spent the rest of his time in adjoining rooms and so a claim to protection for the property containing his bedroom and study was rejected.[52] (2) *Occupation by the tenant* is another requirement, which is satisfied in relation to a second home only if there is a "reasonably substantial number of occupation visits". Right at the extreme limit is *Bevington* v. *Crawford*[53] in which the tenant ran a golf course in Cannes, deigning to visit his London flat for two or three months each year. His unmeritorious claim to security was allowed. Two homes cases always involve a question of fact,[54] but it was never the intention to cover holiday housing,[55] and *Bevington* now looks isolated and out of line.[56] Even more offensive was the decision in *Gofor Investments Ltd.* v. *Roberts*[57] to allow security to a

---

[46] *Camden L.B.C.* v. *Goldenberg* (1996) 28 H.L.R. 727 C.A.

[47] (1975) 29 P. & C.R. 366 C.A.; *Prince* v. *Robinson* (1999) 31 H.L.R. 89, 95, Walker L.J.; *Brickfield Properties Ltd.* v. *Hughes* (1988) 20 H.L.R. 108 C.A. (sufficient intention to return to rented flat in London despite inheriting a home in Lancashire); S. Bridge [1988] *Conv.* 300.

[48] *Brown* v. *Brash* [1948] 2 K.B. 247 C.A.; R.E. Megarry (1948) 63 *L.Q.R.* 452.

[49] *Leslie & Co.* v. *Cumming* [1926] 2 K.B. 417; *Wigley* v. *Leigh* [1950] 2 K.B. 305; *Tickner* v. *Hearn* [1960] 1 W.L.R. 1406; *Viking Property Co. Ltd.* v. *Rawlinson* [1999] 08 C.L. 440.

[50] *Langford Properties Co. Ltd.* v. *Tureman* [1949] 1 K.B. 29 C.A.; *Hampstead Way Investments Ltd.* v. *Lewis-Weare* [1985] 1 W.L.R. 164, 169F, Lord Brandon.

[51] [1985] 1 W.L.R. 164 H.L.

[52] *Kavanagh* v. *Lyroudias* [1985] 1 All E.R. 560 C.A.; but see above pp. 143–148.

[53] (1974) 232 E.G. 191 C.A.

[54] *Regalian Securities Ltd.* v. *Ramsden* [1981] 1 W.L.R. 611, 621, Lord Roskill; *Hampstead Way* [1985] 1 W.L.R. 104, 169F.

[55] *Walker* v. *Ogilvy* (1974) 28 P. & C.R. 288.

[56] *D.J. Crocker Securities (Portsmouth) Ltd.* v. *Johal* [1989] 2 E.G.L.R. 102, 104G, Mann L.J.

[57] (1975) 29 P. & C.R. 366 C.A.

woman in tax exile abroad who used her flat in England for only a few days each year, with no intention of returning permanently during the 15 years that it would take to complete her children's education. Her protection flouted the obvious Parliamentary intention. An understandable reaction has set in, prompting a thorough review of second home cases in *Regalian Securities Ltd.* v. *Scheuer.*[58] Possession was ordered in that case against a man who moved out of his rented accommodation to live with his wife and children in a house that she had bought. How could he have two homes within a mile of each other? In another similar case a barrister working in Malaysia could not be said to retain a home in Britain.[59] In short, the Rent Act 1977 looks flabby, since the justification for interfering with the landlord's ownership is to preserve people in their homes, and there is no legitimate reason to protect second homes.

The legislation for *assured* tenancies is framed in a more coherent form to take this point on board, since the requirement is residence as the tenant's *only or principal* home.[60] Policy in the *public sector* is stated even more clearly, since every public sector tenant given a home is merely one from a pool of countless other deserving applicants, and so it is quite right to insist that a tenant should be required to occupy as his only or principal residence in order to preserve his security.[61] Leniency was nevertheless displayed in *Crawley B.C.* v. *Sawyer.*[62] A tenant had moved out of his public sector home to live with his girlfriend for 14 months, during which time the gas and electricity to his previous house were disconnected, and it was only after their relationship had ended that he returned to his original home; this was nevertheless held to have remained his principal home throughout. True, he had showed an intention to return throughout, but even so the decision in his favour was surely unduly lax.

C. "LIFE-LONG" SECURITY

Residential security regimes operate by permitting a tenant to remain in his home until his tenancy is terminated by a court order, and by restricting the grounds on which the court is able to make a possession order. The precise value of the right depends upon the width of the available grounds for possession, but the learning on that subject is so extensive that it requires a complete chapter to itself.[63] The right to long-term accommodation is extremely valuable.[64] Unfortunately the exact mechanism by which security is conferred differs between each of the residential schemes.

1. The Rent Act 1977

Protected tenancies are private sector residential tenancies granted before early 1989 which, during a *contractual phase*, are called regulated tenancies.[65] Security of tenure at

---

[58] [1982] 2 E.G.L.R. 96 C.A.
[59] *D.J. Crocker Securities (Portsmouth) Ltd.* v. *Johal* [1989] 2 E.G.L.R. 102 C.A.
[60] H.A. 1988 s.1(1)(b).
[61] H.A. 1985 s.81.
[62] (1988) 20 H.L.R. 98 C.A.
[63] See below Chapter 13.
[64] *Murray* v. *Lloyd* [1989] 1 W.L.R. 1060 (£115,000, the same as the depreciation in value of the freehold reversion); J.E. Martin [1990] *Conv.* 446.
[65] R.A. 1977 s.1.

that stage is dependent on the contractual right to review. Rent regulation is the most important aspect of the Rent Act 1977 during the contractual phase: since residential qualification is not required *at this stage* it follows that a tenant can seek a rent registration even if he is not in occupation.[66]

Security of tenure comes into play when the contractual tenancy ceases to exist. A fixed term may expire or the landlord may serve notice to quit on the tenant. At the end of the contractual period, a statutory tenancy arises, providing the tenant is in residential occupation.[67] The landlord will not be able to terminate the statutory tenancy except by proving grounds for possession, such as serious rent arrears, so that a tenant who keeps up his occupation, pays rent and who behaves himself may enjoy security quite literally for life. However the scope of residential security is delimited by the available grounds for possession, and some of the statutory grounds are available even against a well-behaved tenant.[68] Although the tenant cannot contract out of his security in advance, there is nothing to prevent landlord and tenant reaching an agreement for a surrender and so to terminate all protection.

Security becomes an issue where the landlord wishes to end the lease against the wishes of the tenant. If the tenant holds for a fixed term,[69] he has contractual security until that term runs out, unless the lease is open to forfeiture. When it expires, the tenant can continue in occupation through the mechanism of a statutory tenancy. Most houses and flats are let on monthly or weekly periodic tenancies which, apart from the residential security of tenure legislation, could be terminated by the landlord if he chose to serve a notice to quit. A notice to increase the rent may also convert from a contractual to a statutory phase.[70] The duration of a notice must be a full period of the tenancy and it must expire at the end of a period of the tenancy[71] and, as a separate rule, it must be at least 28 days in duration.[72] However, when the contractual tenancy is ended, a statutory tenancy will normally spring into its place, which explains why landlords do not generally bother to terminate the contractual periodic tenancy so long as the tenant is in occupation. Contractual termination is worthwhile when it gives an outright entitlement to possession, for example if the whole property has been sub-let, so that the tenant has no residential qualification and is unable to claim possession.

Statutory tenancies arise under the Rent Act 1977 on termination of the contractual tenancy in the person who, immediately before that termination, was the protected tenant of the dwelling-house "if and so long as he occupies the dwelling-house as his residence".[73] Corresponding rights can arise by estoppel where a landlord leads the tenant to believe that he will be treated as a statutory tenant, even if one of the vital ingredients

---

[66] See below pp. 234–237.

[67] *John Lyon's Free Grammar School Governors* v. *James* [1995] 4 All E.R. 740, 743g–h.

[68] See below Chapter 13.

[69] If it is for a long term (over 21 years) at a low rent a different regime applies; see below pp. 389–396.

[70] *Thomas Pocklington's Gift Trustees* v. *Hill* (1979) 21 H.L.R. 391 C.A.; J.E. Martin [1989] *Conv.* 287.

[71] Half a year's notice if the tenancy was yearly; see above pp. 21–22.

[72] P.E.A. 1977 s.5; this period is unrelated to the period of tenancy.

[73] R.A. 1977 s.2(1)(a); allocation between multiple claimants occurs under sch.1 part I.

of a statutory tenancy is missing.[74] A statutory tenancy is not an estate.[75] Given the negative form of the definition of its content, it confers no more than a personal right to be free from disturbance by his landlord unless and until a court makes an order for possession.[76] Rights cannot be assigned or sold, and it is an offence to ask for or to receive payment for giving up possession.[77] Its personal character is most clearly demonstrated when there would normally be a transmission on death or bankruptcy: a contractual tenancy was a form of property which could pass to a trustee in bankruptcy and which the tenant could disclaim,[78] whereas a statutory tenancy cannot pass. Proprietary characteristics that are included are the right to sue in trespass, power to sub-let parts,[79] entitlement to compensation after compulsory purchase of the home, and endurability against purchasers and lenders. Nevertheless the tenant's "status of irremovability"[80] cannot properly be classified even as "quasi-property".[81]

A statutory tenant holds on the same terms as his original contractual tenancy so far as consistent with the Rent Act.[82] However a right for the landlord to terminate the tenancy is inconsistent with the character of the statutory tenancy, so that hostile termination is confined to cases where the landlord obtains a court order, and to do this the landlord must be able to show a ground for possession.[83] It is, of course, possible for a statutory tenant to surrender his rights by agreement with the landlord.

2. "Life-long" security for fully assured tenants

Assured tenancies are private sector tenancies created after early 1989, which attract "life long" security unless the tenancy is a shorthold.[84]

Contractual security is provided during any fixed term so that the basic method for a tenant to secure a home for a fixed period is through contractual negotiation with the landlord. An agreed period of contractual security could be ended by an agreed surrender or by exercise of a break clause, but it could also be extended by a negotiated extension or through inclusion of an option for renewal.[85] Hostile termination within a contractual term can only occur for breach of covenant—a process which is not technically a forfeiture but which requires a term in the contractual tenancy for termination and a court order for possession on a statutory ground.[86]

---

[74] *Daejean Properties Ltd.* v. *Mahoney* [1995] 1 E.G.L.R. 75 C.A. (landlord's managing agents regarded daughter as joint tenant with her mother for whom she was caring).

[75] *Johnson* v. *Felton* (1995) 27 H.L.R. 265 C.A. (not a "tenant" in closing order legislation).

[76] *Remon* v. *City of London Real Property Co.* [1921] 1 K.B. 49 C.A.; *American Economic Laundry Ltd.* v. *Little* [1951] 1 K.B. 400 C.A.

[77] R.A. 1977 sch.1 part II para.12.

[78] *Sutton* v. *Dorf* [1932] 2 K.B. 304, Acton J.; *Smalley* v. *Quarrier* [1975] 1 W.L.R. 938 C.A.; but for the current law see below at p. 115.

[79] *Roe* v. *Russell* [1928] 2 K.B. 117 C.A.

[80] *Jessamine Investment Co. Ltd.* v. *Schwartz* [1978] Q.B. 264, 272, Sir John Pennycuick.

[81] *Keeves* v. *Dean* [1924] 1 K.B. 685, 694, Scrutton L.J.; *Marcroft Wagons Ltd.* v. *Smith* [1951] 2 K.B. 496, 500, Evershed M.R.; *Jessamine Investment Co. Ltd.* v. *Schwartz* [1978] Q.B. 264 C.A.; C. Hand [1980] *Conv.* 351.

[82] R.A. 1977 s.3.

[83] A tenant must (if the landlord so insists) give contractual notice (or 3 months if no other period is specified) R.A. 1977 s.3(3); no payment may be demanded for giving up possession.

[84] See above Chapter 3.

[85] H.A. 1988 s.5.

[86] s.5; see below p. 339.

When the contractual period ends, it is followed by a *statutory periodic tenancy*, which entitles the tenant to remain in possession of the dwelling-house which is let by the assured tenancy. His right to do so is dependent upon "a periodic tenancy arising by virtue of this section" (that is section 5).[87] Hostile termination requires a court order. So, in marked contrast to the position under the Rent Act, an assured tenant holds an estate in the land, a difference illustrated by the possibility of making a gift by will of an assured tenancy during its statutory phase.[88] Contractual terms are rolled forward, with the exception of any which relate to termination of the tenancy, whether by the landlord or the tenant.[89] During the first year of the statutory phase either party can serve a notice on the other party proposing different terms, with any disputes about what terms might reasonably be expected being resolved by a rent assessment committee.[90] The procedure for increasing the rent is considered elsewhere.[91]

Protection throughout the life of an assured tenancy—during both contractual and statutory phases—is dependent upon continued occupation as the main home of the tenant. Loss of residential qualification[92] by moving out leads to the loss of assured status, after which the landlord is free to terminate the tenancy at common law.

3.   Social sector

Tenants have a full assurance coupled with Charter rights.[93] However there is a concept of a "starter" tenancy which allows a year's probation to a new tenant.[94]

4.   Introductory tenants in the public sector

Since 1996 local authorities have had power, if they choose to exercise it, to set up an introductory tenancy scheme.[95] After an introductory period lasting 12 months,[96] the tenancy becomes secure. However during that probationary period, the local authority may terminate the tenancy by notice if it forms the opinion that the tenant is unsuitable. Reasons for the authority's decision must be given, and the removal of security can be challenged on review.[97]

5.   Public sector secure tenants

Public sector tenants were first given security of tenure in 1980,[98] and the legislative structure that was created at that time is now reproduced, more or less, in the Housing Act 1985. "Life-long" security is similar in its practical effect to that enjoyed in the private sector, and public sector tenants are indeed the most numerous category of tenants

---

[87] s.5(2); the name is given by subs.(7).
[88] *N. & D. London Ltd.* v. *Gadsdon* [1992] 1 E.G.L.R. 112, 116, Auld J.
[89] H.A. 1988 ss.5(3), 66.
[90] s.6(2), (3); S.I. 1997/194 (forms); also subs.(6), (7) (agreement between landlord and tenant).
[91] See below p. 212.
[92] See above p. 23.
[93] See above p. 12.
[94] See below p. 165.
[95] H.A. 1996 s.124; N.J. Smith & G.A. George (1997) 19 *J.S.W.F.L.* 307.
[96] s.125; S.I. 1997/72.
[97] ss.127–130.
[98] It applied to existing tenants, but not to tenancies already terminated at the statutory commencement: *Harrison* v. *Hammersmith & Fulham L.B.C.* [1981] 1 W.L.R. 650 C.A.

enjoying real security of tenure, given that shortholds now dominate the private sector market.

Contractual security is provided during any fixed term subject to termination by a process akin to "forfeiture".[99] At the end of the contractual term, a periodic tenancy arises automatically unless the contractual tenancy is renewed. Security of tenure provisions therefore apply to initial grants of periodic tenancies and to periodic tenancies implied at the end of fixed terms. Until then, it has been held in the context of bankruptcy, the tenancy creates a non-assignable and personal right of occupation,[100] though the public sector legislation is less explicit than the Rent Act 1977. The terms of the contractual fixed term are carried forward into its periodic continuation in the usual way, unless there is any incompatibility[101] with specific provisions to allow variation of the rent[102] and with rights of re-entry or forfeiture excluded. This continuation tenancy is secure[103] and can only be terminated by court order,[104] so that a public sector tenant enjoys a security of tenure delineated as usual by the tight statutory limits on the grounds on which possession may be ordered. The value of "life-long" security is therefore inversely correlated to the width of the grounds on which the court will order repossession, in relation to which the law is so extensive that it requires treatment in a full chapter.[105]

Public sector tenancies are subject to the peculiar rule that they terminate automatically on the breach of the terms of a suspended possession order, with consequences that require full explanation elsewhere.[106]

D. BANKRUPTCY

Broadly speaking bankruptcy will pass control of the tenancy to the trustee in bankruptcy, who can decide to terminate the bankrupt's occupation if he chooses to do so.

1.   The trustee in bankruptcy

Assets of a bankrupt vest in the trustee, who has power to sell them in order to raise money to put towards the debts which brought about the insolvency. All property rights pass,[107] but particularly those which have monetary value. Thus on the insolvency of an owner-tenant holding a long lease of a flat, the flat vests in the trustee and it will have to be sold. This same principle formerly applied to many short residential leases, at least during the contractual phase, but amendments to the insolvency code in 1988 created a uniform system.[108] Under the new law most short residential tenancies are unaffected by an insolvency. Automatic vesting is left in place only if a tenancy has some intrinsic

---

[99] H.A. 1985 s.82(3), (4).
[100] *City of London Corp.* v. *Bown* (1990) 60 P. & C.R. 42 C.A.; J.E. Martin [1990] *Conv.* 61; see below pp. 113–115.
[101] H.A. 1985 s.80(2). *R.* v. *Brent L.B.C. ex parte Blatt* (1991) 24 H.L.R. 319 Div.Ct.
[102] ss.102, 103; see below pp. 234–237.
[103] J. Alder [1982] *Conv.* 298; D. Yates & A.J. Hawkins [1982] *Conv.* 301; J. Alder [1982] *Conv.* 304.
[104] H.A. 1985 s.82(1).
[105] See below Chapter 13.
[106] See below pp. 333–334.
[107] I.A. 1986 s.283.
[108] ss.283(3A), 308A, inserted by H.A. 1988 s.117.

realisable value, that is—an assured tenancy which permits dealings, those rare cases where a premium can be demanded on the transfer of a Rent Act 1977 tenancy,[109] and fixed term grants in the public sector made before late 1982 when assignment was allowed.[110] If such tenancies have value the trustee in bankruptcy is obliged to realise it for the benefit of the unpaid creditors of the tenant by sale. If the tenancy happens to be onerous the trustee in bankruptcy should end it by disclaimer.

Tenancies with no realisable value can be controlled by the trustee in bankruptcy, but he has to make the choice that he should do so. Most residential tenancies are defined by the 1988 amendments[111] to be excluded property, meaning an asset that will not vest automatically in the trustee in bankruptcy. This includes all assured tenancies, Rent Act protected tenancies whose terms inhibit assignment,[112] and almost all public sector secure tenancies. The trustee in bankruptcy has power to give a notice that will cause the tenancy to vest (retrospectively) in him.[113] A trustee in bankruptcy who gives such a notice is enabled to reap any realisable profit on behalf of the creditors to whom money is owed, perhaps by sub-letting. Opting to vest the tenancy is also a necessary first step if the trustee decides to disclaim the lease,[114] and so to end it. A trustee in bankruptcy can, and usually will, decide upon a disclaimer so as to end the drain of rent from the assets of the bankrupt. A short residential tenancy almost automatically falls within the definition of onerous property, since it is unsaleable and incurs the continuing liability to shell out rent.[115] The bankrupt necessarily loses statutory security of tenure[116] since a disclaimer ends the existence of the lease.[117] All people affected must be given a chance to object, including sub-tenants and secured lenders[118] and notice must also be given to every person in occupation of a dwelling-house and every person known to be claiming a right to occupation.[119]

2.   Repossession by the landlord

Even if the trustee in bankruptcy does not take action on the tenant's bankruptcy, the landlord will usually be able to recover possession, since the bankrupt will not be able to claim a statutory tenancy: the lease is vested in the trustee and *he* does not have the residential qualification for statutory protection.[120] If a periodic tenancy remains contractual at the onset of the bankruptcy, the landlord can serve notice to quit and so bring about the loss of statutory protection.

Many tenancies will contain a provision for termination in the event of a tenant's bankruptcy. This is not strictly a forfeiture in the case of a residential tenant, but the

---

[109] See below p. 214.

[110] Grants before November 5th 1982.

[111] I.A. 1986 s.308A.

[112] Whether absolute or subject to a fine or a prior offer to surrender: R.A. 1977 s.127(5).

[113] I.A. 1986 ss.308A, 309 (time limit).

[114] s.315.

[115] s.315(2); *Eyre* v. *Hall* [1986] 2 E.G.L.R. 95 C.A.

[116] *Fletcher* v. *Davies* [1981] 1 E.G.L.R. 77 C.A.

[117] I.A. 1986 s.315(3).

[118] s.317.

[119] s.318.

[120] *Smalley* v. *Quarrier* [1975] 1 W.L.R. 938 C.A.; *Eyre* v. *Hall* [1986] 2 E.G.L.R. 95 C.A.; J.E. Martin [1987] *Conv.* 205.

effect is similar. In *Cadogan Estates Ltd.* v. *McMahon*,[121] a case concerning a Rent Act protected tenancy, it was held that a term for re-entry if the tenant became bankrupt was incorporated into the statutory tenancy when the contractual tenancy ended, which became an obligation of the subsequent statutory tenancy, so that a breach occasioned by the bankruptcy was a ground for possession.[122] Despite a paucity of authority[123] Lord Hoffman wished to avoid divergences between the contractual and statutory tenancies. Lord Millett's dissent is more convincing: he felt that a provision for termination of a tenancy could have no relevance once it had ended.

3. Old law for statutory Rent Act and all public sector tenancies

Statutory tenancies are personal in character and so (under the old law as it applied before 1988) were not "property" and did not vest in the trustee in bankruptcy. This was always true of the Rent Act 1977,[124] though the assured tenancy scheme was drafted so as to avoid this result.[125] More ambiguous and between these two schemes was the legislation affecting secure tenancies[126] which was reviewed in *London City Council* v. *Bown*.[127] Marked differences in language suggested that Parliament intended to differentiate the old private sector scheme from that operating in the public sector[128] but nevertheless Dillon L.J. concluded that the Rent Act rule did indeed apply on the bankruptcy of a public sector tenant. Bown was granted a tenancy of a flat for three years, but he held over afterwards as a periodic tenant, and it was while he was continuing to do so that he became bankrupt. His trustee in bankruptcy was not allowed to disclaim the tenancy. A secure periodic tenancy was not assignable, was personal in character, was not a realisable asset, and so it could not pass for the benefit of creditors.[129] The decision in *Bown* was slightly surprising in view of section 85 of the Housing Act 1985, but in any event its practical effect has been nullified by the amendments to the insolvency legislation already discussed.

E. SUCCESSION

When a residential tenant dies, the tenancy may pass by succession to a family member, provided that the successor is qualified by residence at the family home in the period leading up to the death. Most often the home will pass to a spouse or cohabitee. Recent legislation has imposed severe restrictions on the number and destination of successions, at the same time increasing the law's complexity.

---

[121] [1999] 1 W.L.R. 1689 C.A.; approved [2000] Times November 1st H.L.
[122] R.A. 1977 sch.15 case 1.
[123] *Paterson* v. *Aggio* [1987] 2 E.G.L.R. 127 C.A.; *Halliard Property Co. Ltd.* v. *Jack Segal Ltd.* [1978] 1 W.L.R. 377, Goulding J.; *R.M.R. Housing Society Ltd.* v. *Combs* [1951] 1 K.B. 486, 493.
[124] *Sutton* v. *Dorf* [1932] 2 K.B. 304, Acton J.
[125] H.A. 1988 s.5(2) provides for a statutory periodic tenancy as opposed to a statutory right of occupation.
[126] H.A. 1985 ss.85, 86(1)-(2), 91.
[127] (1990) 60 P. & C.R. 42 C.A.
[128] At 44, Dillon L.J.
[129] At 48, Dillon L.J.

1. Private and public sector regimes

Assured tenancies have the most restrictive rules introduced in early 1989—only one succession is allowed and that only to a spouse, a term wide enough to include heterosexual cohabitees.[130]

Conversely the *Rent Act* gives the most extensive succession rights.[131] On deaths before early 1989[132] two successions were allowed, meaning that the landlord could end up parting with his house for up to three generations.[133] Qualification rules have been tightened, but even so the permitted successions to Rent Act tenancies remain the most extensive. Under the current rules[134] a first succession can occur to a surviving spouse, in which case a second succession is permitted on the spouse's death to another spouse or family member. If the original tenant leaves no qualified spouse, there is at most a single succession to a family member.

In the *public sector* the same rules apply to secure tenancies[135] and introductory tenancies;[136] these allow a single succession to pass the tenancy, the destination being either a spouse of the original tenant or another family member. On a second death the tenancy ceases to be secure. Special rules protect the landlord's right to allocate public sector housing according to need; this is done by a very wide definition of a "succession" so that the one permitted succession is used up whatever legal form is taken by the devolution of the tenancy on death. A fixed term tenancy will pass on death to the personal representatives of the deceased secure tenants who will pass it under his will or on his intestacy or under a family provision order. It continues to be a secure tenancy if it is vested in a person entitled to succeed or if it passes under a matrimonial order. On the other hand, it will cease to be secure if it passes to an unqualified person,[137] or technically at the moment when it is known that it will not be secure. Since this new tenant has no security, a new tenancy will arise if the landlord accepts him as a tenant, even inadvertently, perhaps by demanding rent or accepting a tender of rent.[138] For the future this is beneficial to the later family of the new tenant because, the chain of successions having been broken, the slate is wiped clean and counting of the one permitted succession starts again.

Special rules operate for successions to *tied cottages*.[139]

---

[130] H.A. 1988 s.17. A fixed term can be left by will, but there is a ground for possession if the tenancy is periodic at the time of the tenant's death: sch.1 Ground 7; *Shepping* v. *Osada* [2000] Times March 23rd C.A. (proceedings must be commenced within one year).

[131] It makes no difference whether the deceased was a statutory or contractual tenant, as under earlier legislation: *Moodie* v. *Hosegood* [1952] A.C. 61 H.L.

[132] R.A. 1977 s.2(1), sch.1 part I; Woodfall 23.057–23.065.

[133] (1) parent to child; (2) child to grandchild.

[134] H.A. 1988 s.39, sch.4 (death after early 1989); A. Samuels (1990) 134 *S.J.* 530.

[135] H.A. 1985 s.87; Woodfall 25.054–25.061; *Peabody Donation Fund Governors* v. *Grant* [1982] 2 E.G.L.R. 37 C.A.; J.E. Martin [1987] *Conv.* 205.

[136] H.A. 1996 s.131.

[137] s.90.

[138] *General Management Ltd.* v. *Locke* [1980] 2 E.G.L.R. 83 C.A.

[139] R.(Agriculture) A. 1976 s.4 (agricultural occupancies) as amended by H.A. 1988 sch.4 part II (deaths after early 1989); H.A. 1988 ss.24, 17 (assured agricultural occupancies); see below Chapter 7.

2. Spouses

All security regimes permit a first succession to the spouse of the deceased tenant,[140] provided that he or she is resident at the time of the tenant's death.[141] If the marriage broke down before the death, the spouse will usually have lost qualification by ceasing residential occupation of the property for which succession is claimed; however he or she may be assisted by the matrimonial homes legislation if the dwelling was a matrimonial home,[142] by the matrimonial legislation which enables a tenancy to be transferred on divorce,[143] or by the inheritance legislation which provides for claims by dependents who are inadequately provided for on death.[144]

3. Cohabitees

Early legislation conceded succession rights only to those who had gone through a formal marriage,[145] but this moral penalty has given way in the face of the modern reality of widespread and stable cohabitation; the less secure inheritance rights of cohabitees greatly increases their need for housing rights. In all sectors, private[146] and public,[147] the concept of a "spouse" now includes a person with whom the original tenant was living as husband or wife.

The fact that a partner must have lived with the original tenant as his wife or her husband[148] has been held to exclude *homosexual partners* from succession rights. *Harrogate B.C.* v. *Simpson*[149] excluded gay men and lesbian women from public sector succession. Ward and Roch L.JJ., who formed a majority of the Court of Appeal in *Fitzpatrick* v. *Sterling Housing Association Ltd.,*[150] felt bound to follow the earlier case and this has been approved in the Lords.[151] *Fitzpatrick* concerned a stable homosexual relationship between the protected tenant of a flat in Hammersmith, West London, (John Thompson) and Martin Fitzpatrick that lasted for almost 20 years; for the last eight years of his life Thompson was paralysed by a stroke and nursed by Fitzpatrick. When Thompson died in 1994, Fitzpatrick failed in his most beneficial claim, to succeed as a "spouse" of Thompson. Had he won on that ground he would have succeeded to a Rent Act protected tenancy at a fair rent. To do so, he had to show that he was a spouse living with the tenant "as his or her wife or husband". All five of the Lords who heard the case thought that this was not the case. The last qualifying phrase extended succession rights

---

[140] R.A. 1977 sch.1 para.2 (protected); H.A. 1988 s.17 (assured); H.A. 1985 s.87 (secure).

[141] *Hulme* v. *Langford* (1985) 50 P. & C.R. 199 C.A.; J.E. Martin [1986] *Conv.* 272

[142] F.L.A. 1996 ss.30–32 replacing M.H.A. 1983; *Hall* v. *King* (1987) 19 H.L.R. 440 C.A. (house bought after the separation was not a matrimonial home).

[143] H.A. 1985 s.89(3).

[144] Inheritance (Provision for Family & Dependents) Act 1975.

[145] R.A. 1977 sch.1 para.2; cohabitees often qualified as family members, as explained below at p. 118.

[146] H.A. 1988 s.17(4) (assured); H.A. 1988 sch.4 para.1 (Rent Act 1977 tenancy where death after early 1989).

[147] H.A. 1985 ss.87(a), 113(a).

[148] R.A. 1977 sch.1 para.2(2) as inserted by H.A. 1988 sch.4 para.2 (private sector); H.A. 1985 s.113 (public sector); [1994] 4 All E.R. 705, 708b–d, Lord Slynn.

[149] (1987) 17 H.L.R. 205 C.A.; J.E. Martin [1985] *Conv.* 355; approved *Fitzpatrick* v. *Sterling Housing Association Ltd.* [1999] 4 All E.R. 705 H.L.

[150] [1998] Ch. 304 C.A.; N. Dearden [1998] *J.H.L.* 51; N. Wikeley (1998) 10 *C.F.L.Q.* 191.

[151] [1999] 4 All E.R. 705 H.L.; M.P. Thompson [2000] *Conv.* 153; M. Pawlowski [2000] *J.H.L.* 21.

to heterosexual cohabitees but Parliament obviously intended to rule out succession to a same sex partner.

Ward L.J.'s dissent in the Court of Appeal was based on his perception that the word "as" in the phrase "as husband and wife" implied a functional test based on social organisation rather than the character of the constituent members. Although this is not the law, it is true, of course, that the vulnerability of a surviving homosexual partner is just as great as that of a heterosexual partner, so the case for Parliamentary reform is pressing.[152]

4. Family members in the public sector

Calls on public sector housing are limited by a restrictive definition of family membership. Qualification to succeed extends to a parent, grandparent, child,[153] stepchild, grandchild, brother, sister, uncle, aunt, nephew, or niece. Relationship may be by whole blood, by half blood, or by marriage, and there is no differentiation of births in or out of marriage.[154] Wide as it is, this definition precludes claims by homosexual partners as family members.[155] In addition, residential qualification will be required.

5. Family members in the private sector

Family members cannot succeed to *assured* tenancies granted in the private sector since early 1989, so the only issue that requires discussion is the position under the *Rent Act 1977*. A *first* succession can pass the tenancy to a member of the deceased's family if there is no spouse entitled to succeed. However, on a death after early 1989[156] the *second* succession is now to an *assured* tenancy[157] which means that the second successor must pay a market rent.[158] Further, this second succession is only allowed at all if the first succession was to a spouse.[159] The second successor must have been a member of the original tenant's family immediately before his death and also a member of the successor spouse's family, and must also qualify by residence with the spouse for the two years leading up to the second death.[160]

The Rent Act 1977 gives no precise test,[161] contenting itself with limiting succession to a person who is a "member of the original tenant's family". Case law has developed a test of family nexus, in the absence of a statutory test, which is whether an ordinary person would regard the applicant as a member of the tenant's family.[162] It should include blood relatives, relations by marriage and informally adopted children. Changes in family structures have created great problems of interpretation beyond those obvious cases.

---

[152] It is believed that 4/5ths of London local authorities allow equal rights and Ministers have urged that such rights be granted universally.

[153] *Bassetlaw D.C.* v. *Renshaw* [1992] 1 All E.R. 925 C.A. (son); *Hereford C.C.* v. *O'Callaghan* [1996] 2 C.L.Y. 3831 (foster child could not succeed).

[154] i.e. relationship may be through a reputed father.

[155] *Harrogate B.C.* v. *Simpson* (1987) 17 H.L.R. 205 C.A.; J.E. Martin [1985] *Conv.* 355.

[156] Previous law: R.A. 1977 sch.1 paras.5–6; *Sefton Holdings Ltd.* v. *Cairns* (1988) 20 H.L.R. 124 C.A.

[157] paras.5–6 as amended by H.A. 1988 sch.4 para.6.

[158] *Daejean Properties Ltd.* v. *Mahoney* [1995] 1 E.G.L.R. 675 C.A. (result avoided on facts).

[159] H.A. 1988 sch.4 para.4.

[160] sch.4 para.6.

[161] *Carega Properties S.A.* v. *Sharratt* [1979] 1 W.L.R. 928, 931, Lord Diplock.

[162] *Brock* v. *Wollams* [1949] 2 K.B. 388, 395, Cohen L.J.

Stretching of the statutory concepts first took place in the context of heterosexual cohabitees, though this case law is now superseded by the statutory decision to include a heterosexual cohabitee within the category of a "spouse". The couple involved in *Dyson
Holdings Ltd.* v. *Fox*[163] had lived together for 21 years, albeit without having children,
facts which led to the decision that the female cohabitee was a member of her partner's
family—and a similar decision was reached in another case of cohabitation for 20
years.[164] In another case cohabitation for three years sufficed where the couple had
become engaged to be married.[165] Clearly the strength of the relationship and the conduct of both parties are important factors.

The courts have been naturally reluctant to lumber landlords with successors of more
disparate classes, such as cronies of the same sex, servants, lodgers and those within a
platonic relationship.[166] In *Sefton Holdings Ltd.* v. *Cairns*[167] a woman aged 70 lost her
claim to succeed to the tenancy of a family with whom she had lived since she was 23
after her parents and boyfriend died in war. Taken in as a stranger, she was a member of
the household but not a member of the family.

Homosexual cohabitees present a more difficult problem of statutory interpretation.
They cannot succeed as a spouse or cohabitee,[168] nor as a family member of a public sec-
tor tenant.[169] However in the private sector there remains the possibility of redirecting
a homosexual partner's claim into the category of family member. A majority of the
House of Lords allowed succession to occur on the facts of *Fitzpatrick* v. *Sterling Housing
Association Ltd.*[170] John Thompson was the protected tenant of a flat in Hammersmith,
West London. In 1976 he formed a stable homosexual relationship with Martin
Fitzpatrick, but in 1986 Thompson suffered a stroke that left him paralysed, and
Fitzpatrick nursed him until his death in 1994. The housing association[171] wanted to
move him to smaller accommodation, but the House of Lords ultimately held that he
was entitled to succeed to the tenancy, though only as a family member; this meant that
his succession was to an assured tenancy and the rent could be increased to a market
level.

Lord Slynn led the majority (with Lords Nicholls and Clyde) who felt that a homosexual partner could succeed as a family member. The concept of a family could vary
between a person's children and all of his relatives, so the context was all important. The
courts had held over the years that a Rent Act family was not restricted to legal or blood
relationship, but depended upon a degree of mutual inter-dependence, of the sharing of
lives, or caring, love, commitment and support. Transient relationships are not enough.
If sufficient commitment was proved a same sex partner could now establish the

---

[163] [1976] Q.B. 503 C.A.; A.A.S. Zuckerman (1980) 96 *L.Q.R.* 248, 264–271; D.C. Bradley (1976) 39 *M.L.R.* 222.
[164] *Watson* v. *Lucas* [1980] 1 W.L.R. 1493 C.A.; A Sydenham [1981] *Conv.* 78.
[165] *Chios Property Investment Co. Ltd.* v. *Lopez* (1988) 20 H.L.R. 120 C.A.; J.E. Martin [1988] *Conv.* 197.
[166] *Helby* v. *Rafferty* [1979] 1 W.L.R. 13 C.A. (80 year old woman with 20 year man; no succession); C.H. Sherrin
(1980) 43 *M.L.R.* 77; *Carega Properties S.A.* v. *Sharratt* [1979] 1 W.L.R. 928 H.L.; P. Tennant [1980] *C.L.J.* 31.
[167] (1988) 20 H.L.R. 124 C.A.; *Ross* v. *Collins* [1964] 1 W.L.R. 425 C.A.
[168] See above pp. 117–118.
[169] *Harrogate B.C.* v. *Simpson* (1987) 17 H.L.R. 205 C.A.; J.E. Martin [1985] *Conv.* 355.
[170] [1999] 4 All E.R. 705 H.L.; M.P. Thompson [2000] *Conv.* 153; M. Pawlowski [2000] *J.H.L.* 21; the H.L.
reversed [1998] Ch. 304 C.A.; N. Dearden [1998] *J.H.L.* 51; C. Hunter [2000] *J.H.L.* 53.
[171] The case concerns the private sector since the housing association involved was unregistered.

necessary familial link. Fitzpatrick's case was clear in these terms. The decision pushed English law ahead of human rights law.[172]

Lords Hutton and Hobhouse dissented. If same sex partners were to have Rent Act succession rights at all, they fell most naturally into the category of spouses, because the essence of the claim was that they shared the same relationship with the tenant as that shared by a husband and wife or a heterosexual couple. Parliament had excluded homosexuals by providing that cohabitees had to be as if husband and wife, and this must have been intended to exclude them from the category of family members. As a purely technical exercise in interpretation of what Parliament intended in 1988, Lord Hutton was surely right, and there is also merit in the view that this issue is precisely one which should be decided through the democratic process rather than in court. Yet the greater liberality of Lord Slynn's conclusion is unarguably more just on the facts of the case, and more in tune with modern social thinking.

6.   Residential qualification of family members

Family members are qualified to succeed a tenant only if they satisfy a residence qualification,[173] a rule designed to prevent claims to security by people who move in only shortly before the tenant's death. Residence must be shown for a qualifying period and in a qualifying dwelling and of sufficient quality to count as residence. The qualifying *period of residence* is 12 months in the public sector[174] and two years in the private sector.[175] Rules about the *property* vary between the regimes. In the private sector, residence qualification must now be *in the* dwelling house[176] to which succession rights are claimed.[177] Hence the private and public sectors diverge. Succession to a secure tenancy is allowed if the claimant "*has resided with the tenant*" throughout the 12 months leading up to his death.[178] *Waltham Forest L.B.C.* v. *Thomas*[179] demonstrates the greater latitude allowed by this rule. Guy Thomas had lived with his brother, Webster, for two and a half years, but they moved to new accommodation only 10 days before Webster died, and Guy's succession rights were recognised. As this decision by the House of Lords shows, it is not essential that residence should have occurred in the same house as that in which succession rights are being asserted.

Residence must also pass a *qualitative test.* Rent Act succession rights depend upon occupation by the successor of the dwelling-house as his residence and assured and secure tenants have to meet the requirement of occupation as his only or principal home.[180] Different wordings create identical tests.[181] Residence is not construed too

---

[172]   At 716e–f, Lord Slynn.

[173]   J. Hill [1987] *Conv.* 349.

[174]   H.A. 1985 s.87(b); *Peabody Donation Fund Governors* v. *Grant* [1982] 2 E.G.L.R. 37 C.A.

[175]   R.A. 1977 sch.1 para.7 (6 months if death before early January 1989, with transitional provisions for 2 years afterwards); H.A. 1988 sch.4 para.3(b) (increase to 2 years).

[176]   *Edmunds* v. *Jones* (1952) 213 L.T. 62 C.A.; *Collier* v. *Stoneman* [1957] 1 W.L.R. 1108 C.A. (rooms in the same building).

[177]   H.A. 1988 sch.4 para.3; contrast the original R.A. 1977 sch.1 para.7.

[178]   H.A. 1985 s.87(b).

[179]   [1992] 2 A.C. 198 H.L.; J.E. Martin [1993] *Conv.* 152; S. Jones [1993] *N.L.J.* 1689. The H.L. doubted *South Northants D.C.* v. *Power* [1987] 1 W.L.R. 1433 C.A.; J.E. Martin [1988] *Conv.* 197.

[180]   H.A. 1985 s.87 (secure); H.A. 1988 s.17(1) (assured).

[181]   See above pp. 104–109.

strictly, since otherwise temporary absences would destroy succession rights—whether by the dying tenant or the caring claimant. In *Hedgedale Ltd.* v. *Hards*[182] temporary absence by the original tenant while recovering from an accident did not prejudice his putative successor. Similarly in *Camden L.B.C.* v. *Goldenberg*[183] a temporary move to other accommodation by the potential successor did not exclude him from claiming to succeed, since he left his possessions at the property, retained it as his postal address, and (according to a majority of the Court of Appeal) intended to return. It is only to be expected that the courts are less sympathetic to a person with two homes who claims the right to succeed to the tenancy of one of them. Thus in *Swanbrae* v. *Elliott*[184] a daughter had left the parental home, which was the house in which she was claiming succession rights, at the time of her marriage in order to live with her husband two miles away. Although she moved back into her mother's house to nurse her during her final illness, the daughter did not have a residential qualification to succeed, since her intention was to care for her mother rather than to live with her as part of her household. However, a converse decision was reached in *Hildebrand* v. *Moon* where the carer stayed rather than just visiting.[185]

A tenancy by succession is a statutory tenancy, which must be preserved by continuing residential occupation.[186]

7. Succession by a minor

A minor (aged under 18) can succeed to a secure tenancy. In *Kingston upon Thames R.L.B.C.* v. *Prince*[187] the successful claimant, Marie, was the 13-year-old daughter of Peter Prince. Peter's adult daughter (Wendy) had only been in residence for six months at the time of his death and so was not qualified to succeed. The 13-year-old daughter (Marie) had three years' qualification, and so the family defeated a possession action by the council by joining her as a party and asserting her rights of succession. Clearly she could not hold a legal estate[188] but in housing law a minor could hold an equitable tenancy of any property including a council house,[189] and there was nothing to prevent her equitable tenancy being secure. Apparently succession is also allowed to a Rent Act statutory tenancy since that Act does not create an interest in land and a minor did have sufficient capacity to contract for lodgings.[190] This case supports the Housing Corporation's *Code of Practice on Tenure*[191] which recognises that minors could be appropriate grantees in some circumstances. Housing is a necessary, which means that the contract is binding during the minority though it can repudiated when majority is attained.

---

[182] [1991] 1 E.G.L.R. 118 C.A.; *Foreman* v. *Beagley* [1969] 1 W.L.R. 1387 C.A. (both Rent Acts cases).
[183] (1996) 28 H.L.R. 727 C.A. (public sector).
[184] (1987) 19 H.L.R 86 C.A.
[185] [1989] 2 E.G.L.R. 100 C.A.
[186] R.A. 1977 s.2(3) and sch.1 paras. 2–7.
[187] (1999) 31 H.L.R. 794 C.A.
[188] L.P.A. 1925 s.1(6).
[189] At 801, Hale J.
[190] *Portman Registrars* v. *Latif* [1987] C.L.Y. 2239.
[191] (October 1999) paras.3.13–3.15.

8.   Allocation between successors

Only one person can qualify to succeed to any tenancy. Spouses are always preferred to other family members. If there is no spouse, there may be several claimants of equal rank, for example several children each of whom has cared for a dying parent. Allocation between private sector successors should be by agreement, but any dispute is adjudicated by a county court.[192] Public sector allocation is also by agreement, but the default power to resolve disputes lies with the landlord.[193] Succession is always limited to a single person, even if the landlord accepts a joint application—though the justice of the decision on this last point is open to doubt. In *Newham L.B.C.* v. *Phillips*[194] three sisters were living with their mother when she died. All agreed that one of them (A) should be the successor. However another (B) asked to be joined and was accepted by the council so that there appeared to be a joint tenancy between A and B. On the particular facts, B was included on the basis that this was not to affect A's position as successor, so no expectation arose and there was no estoppel.

9.   Restriction on number of successions

Successions are limited, usually to one. Enforcement of this policy depends upon a wide definition of a succession to ensure that the slate is not wiped clean when a tenancy is passed on death. Otherwise the landlord would be bound to allow another succession when the new tenant dies. The most exhaustive legislative provisions relate to public sector tenancies[195]: successors encompass any person who has received a tenancy under the automatic vesting[196] of the succession provisions for periodic tenancies, a survivor of joint tenants,[197] a person who takes under matrimonial reallocation powers, or by vesting on death in a person entitled to succeed.[198] A tenancy ceases to be secure, after a fixed term has vested in personal representatives, if it becomes clear that the beneficiary entitled to receive it will not be a qualified successor.[199] Surrender of the tenancy existing up to the tenant's death and regrant of a new tenancy creates a break in the chain, even if the surrender is informal,[200] and such a regrant is particularly likely to occur after acceptance of rent from a family member who stays in the home but without any formal succession rights.[201]

---

[192]   R.A. 1977 sch.1 para.7 (Rent Act before early January 1989); H.A. 1988 s.17(5) (assured); H.A. 1988 sch.4 paras.1, 6 (Rent Act from early 1989).

[193]   H.A. 1985 s.89(2).

[194]   (1998) 30 H.L.R. 859 C.A.

[195]   H.A. 1985 s.88 (secure); H.A. 1996 s.132 (introductory). In the private sector: H.A. 1988 s.17 (assured); R.A. 1977 sch.1 para.10 (regulated tenancy where succession or grant after August 27th 1972.)

[196]   H.A. 1985 s.89 (secure); H.A. 1996 s.133 (introductory).

[197]   Also a tenant by assignment except one taking under a matrimonial order.

[198]   *Peabody Donation Fund Governors* v. *Higgins* [1983] 1 W.L.R. 1091 C.A. (daughter qualified to succeed); J.E. Martin [1985] *Conv.* 129.

[199]   H.A. 1985 s.90.

[200]   *Epping Forest D.C.* v. *Pomphrett* [1990] 2 E.G.L.R. 46 C.A.; *Bassetlaw D.C.* v. *Renshaw* [1992] 1 All E.R. 925 C.A.

[201]   *General Management Ltd.* v. *Locke* [1980] 2 E.G.L.R. 83 C.A.

10. Succession after a possession order

In the private sector where a possession order is made against the tenant a succession can occur, though the successor will be subject to the terms of the possession order made against the tenant.[202] But in the public sector it is provided that the tenancy terminates on breach of a possession order, so that if there is a breach at the time of the death, no succession can occur: a right to appeal against a possession order is not an interest in land.[203]

F. RELATIONSHIP BREAKDOWN: SOLE TENANCIES

Accommodation occupied by a couple together is very often held in the sole name of one person as tenant. Difficulties with security of tenure arise if the relationship between the occupiers breaks down,[204] particularly where it is the legal tenant who moves out, leaving his former partner in occupation. This is illustrated by the possession action brought by the landlord against the tenant's wife in *Crago* v. *Julian*[205] in respect of a flat rented in 1966 in the sole name of her husband as contractual tenant.[206] She stayed in the flat after they divorced, but when, five years later, she asked the managing agents to change the rent book from the name of her former husband to her own, the landlord declined and sued for possession. He succeeded. Mrs Julian's former husband had ended the tenancy and in any event had lost residential qualification,[207] whereas she was not a tenant and her continued occupation *after* the finalisation of their divorce did not entitle her to residential protection. So there is a risk that the tenant who leaves and his partner who stays will both be left without any statutory security of tenure.

One solution is for the departing spouse to agree to transfer the tenancy to the other spouse who is left behind, but this is fraught with difficulty, unless the landlord knows of it and acknowledges the new tenant. Almost all short residential leases will prohibit dealings. Particularly stringent restrictions apply in the public sector, in which case permitted assignees must qualify both by family membership and by residence for 12 months before the transfer.[208] Private sector tenancies invariably impose an absolute bar on dealings. Assignment is possible if a *contractual* tenancy contains nothing to forbid it, but not during the statutory phase of a Rent Act tenancy.[209]

Where an assignment is possible, the parties are required to use a deed in order to effect a legal assignment,[210] a formality requirement which is wholly inappropriate for a short term tenancy and which is frequently overlooked, even by the courts.[211] An

[202] *Church Commissioners for England* v. *Al Emarah* [1997] Fam. 34 C.A.
[203] *Brent L.B.C.* v. *Knightley* (1997) 29 H.L.R. 857 C.A.
[204] *Relationship Breakdown—A Guide for Social Landlords* (Housing Corporation, May 1999).
[205] [1992] 1 W.L.R. 372 C.A.; P. Sparkes [1992] *Conv.* 375.
[206] At 374A.
[207] *Metropolitan Properties Co. Ltd.* v. *Cronan* (1982) 44 P. & C.R. 1; J.E. Martin [1982] *Conv.* 384; *Croydon L.B.C.* v. *Buston* (1991) 24 H.L.R. 36 C.A.
[208] See below pp. 285–288.
[209] *Thomas Pocklington Trustees* v. *Hill* (1989) 21 H.L.R. 391 C.A.
[210] L.P.A. 1925 s.52(1); *Crago* v. *Julian* [1992] 1 W.L.R. 372 C.A.; *Camden L.B.C.* v. *Alexandrou (No.2)* (1998) 30 H.L.R. 534 C.A.
[211] *Thomas Pocklington* as above.

equitable assignment should also be sufficient, as Parker L.J. recognised in *Croydon L.B.C.* v. *Buston*.[212] A secure tenant of a council flat remarried and moved out of the flat, thus losing protection, but afterwards his son claimed protection as an assignee.[213] Given the absence of a written assignment, the son claimed that there had been an oral assignment in 1987 (under the pre-1989 contract formalities) supported by acts of part performance. Parker L.J. said that that would be a good claim if it could be proved, though on the facts there was actually no agreement to assign.[214] *Crago* v. *Julian* looked only at the position of an assignee of a Rent Act protected tenancy at common law and may be open to question in equity.[215]

A surrender requires the participation and consent of the landlord, and so it can be effected by an informal letter. Very often the practical effect is an informal transfer. For example, in *Camden L.B.C.* v. *Alexandrou (No.2)*[216] the marriage of a secure tenant broke down in 1982, whereupon he wrote to say that he was no longer able to pay rent but he had no objection to his wife remaining behind and paying rent. This letter could not be an assignment given the absence of a deed, but it was held to be a valid surrender. The former wife had paid rent from 1982 to 1984 and so become tenant, a fact confirmed by a contractual grant in 1984. The former husband moved back in at a later stage and it was held that his ex-wife was entitled to end his right of occupation by giving a notice to quit, since it was she who was now the contractual tenant by surrender and regrant.

G. RELATIONSHIP BREAKDOWN: JOINT PERIODIC TENANCIES

1. General

Statute now confirms earlier case law prohibiting joint *succession* to a Rent Act tenancy,[217] and it is also possible that the status of irremovability of the statutory tenant must belong to a single person.[218] However, nothing prevents the possibility of there being a grant to more than one joint contractual tenant. After all most residential lettings are made to families and one would expect both spouses (or cohabitees) to be involved in holding the family home as tenants, and it is also very common for groups of students to take a house collectively for the duration of an academic year. That a joint tenancy could exist has been assumed in the Court of Appeal[219] and more recently in the House of Lords in flat sharing cases.[220] Two or more people taking a grant jointly can certainly attract security collectively under an express grant, and there is also the possibility of creation by estoppel—in one reported case between a daughter and her mother[221]—if the landlord induces an expectation that both of them will be treated as tenants.

---

[212] (1991) 24 H.L.R. 36 C.A.
[213] The son was a permitted assignee since he was qualified to succeed.
[214] At 38.
[215] P. Sparkes [1992] *Conv.* 375.
[216] (1998) 30 H.L.R. 534 C.A.
[217] R.A. 1977 sch.1 paras.3, 7 (amendments by the H.A. 1988 sch.4 do not affect this point); see above p. 122.
[218] *Dealex Properties Ltd.* v. *Brooks* [1966] 1 Q.B. 542, 550–551, Harman L.J.
[219] *Lloyd* v. *Sadler* [1978] Q.B. 774 C.A.
[220] *Antoniades* v. *Villiers,* reported with *AG Securities* v. *Vaughan* [1990] 1 A.C. 417 H.L.
[221] *Daejean Properties Ltd.* v. *Mahoney* (1996) 28 H.L.R. 498, 510, Hoffmann L.J.

Specific provision is made for joint tenants in private sector lettings made under the *assured tenancy* scheme since early 1989. Tenancies qualify to be assured or assured shortholds if "the tenant or . . . each of the joint tenants is an individual",[222] the "tenant" including all persons who together constitute the tenant.[223] On the termination of a jointly held fixed term, the statutory periodic tenancy which follows is itself a joint entitlement. Survivorship will occur on the death of any one of the individual tenants so that the tenancy ultimately passes to he who lives longest.[224] A *secure tenancy* can be granted to a number of individuals as joint tenants even if only one satisfies the residence condition,[225] but any succession on death will be restricted to a single person.[226]

It was assumed in *AG Securities* v. *Vaughan*[227] that co-ownership of a tenancy had to take the form of a beneficial joint tenancy (as opposed to a tenancy in common). That case concerned a Rent Act arrangement, but the assumption is general. A furnished flat consisted of four bedrooms with a sitting room and bathroom, accommodation that was shared by four men, who each signed a separate "licence", who arrived at various dates, and who made various monthly payments. The House of Lords agreed with the Court of Appeal that it was necessary for the four unities to be present, but considered that on the facts unity of time, title and interest were missing.[228] If the rights of occupation were initially several, "I do not understand by what legal alchemy they could ever become joint".[229]

Co-ownership provisions of the Law of Property Act 1925 limit the creation of tenancies in common to cases where land is "expressed to be conveyed" in undivided shares, which probably includes any lease in writing,[230] but certainly excludes any purely oral lease.[231] So a tenancy in common is not possible if a short lease is not reduced to writing. However it is submitted that section 34 should not be interpreted literally in relation to informal tenancies, given the lax interpretation allowed when considering tenancies in common arising from informal contributions,[232] the general relaxation of strict property law needed to make sense of the codes of residential security of tenure,[233] and the artificiality of any trust analysis.[234] It would be for the best if the courts could find a way to override section 34(1) of the Law of Property Act 1925 and allow a direct *legal* tenancy in common of an informal short lease.[235]

---

[222] H.A. 1988 ss.1(1), 17(3)(b); *Regalgrand Ltd.* v. *Dickerson* (1997) 29 H.L.R. 620 C.A.

[223] s.45(3).

[224] s.17(2)(b).

[225] H.A. 1985 s.81.

[226] See above p. 122.

[227] [1990] 1 A.C. 417 H.L.; P.V. Baker (1988) 104 *L.Q.R.* 173, 174–175.

[228] At 472B, Lord Oliver, agreeing with Sir George Waller in the C.A. at 433.

[229] At 454A, Lord Bridge.

[230] *Borman* v. *Griffith* [1930] 1 Ch. 493, 498–499 (L.P.A. 1925 s.62.)

[231] *Rye* v. *Rye* [1962] A.C. 496 H.L.

[232] *Bull* v. *Bull* [1954] 1 Q.B. 234 C.A.; *Williams & Glyn's Bank Ltd.* v. *Boland* [1981] A.C. 487 H.L.; *City of London B.S.* v. *Flegg* [1988] A.C. 54, 77D–78A, Lord Oliver.

[233] *Lloyd* v. *Sadler* [1978] Q.B. 774, 788G, Lawton L.J. ("The Rent Acts are not *in pari materia* with the Act of 1925").

[234] *Savage* v. *Dunningham* [1974] Ch. 181, 185, Plowman J.

[235] P. Sparkes (1989) 18 *Anglo-American* 159.

Collective action is required of joint tenants, who must all join together in any act affecting the tenancy, for example the giving of notices or the making of an application to the Rent Tribunal though, as explained below, service of a notice to quit is an exception where the notice is allowed to be unilateral.[236] Over-literal insistence on joint acts often rubs up against the spirit of the legislation which requires that one tenant should be able to claim protection acting alone, so a mischief-based approach to interpretation departing from the formal logic of the joint tenancy is often fairer. In *Lloyd* v. *Sadler*[237] one of two contractual tenants had left the flat to get married, but it was held that the remaining contractual tenant was entitled to claim a statutory tenancy alone. Conventional co-ownership theory would not, as Sir Robert Megarry observed,[238] treat departure as equivalent to death, so that the result must be attributable to a novelty of the security of tenure legislation. However, there is no immutable rule that a statutory reference to "the tenant" is invariably to be taken as a reference to all the joint tenants.[239] Jill Martin has pointed out[240] the existence of an alternative strand of authority which requires co-tenancies to be analysed on traditional property law lines. This has now become the dominant judicial opinion.[241] In a much praised judgment in *Newman* v. *Keedwell*,[242] Fox J. held that a counter-notice claiming the protection of the Agricultural Holdings legislation had to be given by all of the existing agricultural tenants. Tenants must act jointly in claiming statutory protection, in rent regulation matters,[243] and when carrying out any act supported by the legal estate where one owner alone holds no legal interest.[244]

2.   Unilateral notices to quit joint periodic tenancies

Hammersmith & Fulham L.B.C. v. *Monk*[245] concerned a very common fact situation. Mr Monk was the joint tenant of council property with Mrs Powell, but after they had fallen out, she left the property and sought to be rehoused. The housing authority offered to rehouse her on condition that she agreed to terminate her existing tenancy freeing their shared accommodation for other public sector housing applicants. Mrs Powell did as she was told and served a notice of sufficient duration to end the periodic tenancy, the single question for the House of Lords to decide being whether the unilateral notice to quit was effective: if a tenancy is vested in T1 and T2, can T1 give a notice to L which

---

[236] See below pp. 126–128.
[237] [1978] Q.B. 774. *Howson* v. *Buxton* (1928) 97 L.J.K.B. 749 (one of two agricultural tenants allowed to claim compensation for disturbance); *Woodward* v. *Dudley* [1954] Ch. 283; H.W.R. Wade [1954] *C.L.J.* 194.
[238] *The Rent Acts* (Stevens, 11th ed., 1988) 230.
[239] *Featherstone* v. *Staples* [1986] 2 All E.R. 461, 472g, Slade L.J.; C.P. Rodgers (1985) 48 *M.L.R.* 460; C.P. Rodgers [1986] *Conv.* 429.
[240] [1978] *Conv.* 436, 446–448.
[241] C.P. Rodgers [1986] *Conv.* 429, 430–431; *R.* v. *Plymouth C.C. ex parte Freeman* [1988] R.V.R. 89, 95, Neill L.J.
[242] (1978) 35 P. & C.R. 393, 398; *Featherstone* v. *Staples* [1986] 2 All E.R. 461 C.A.; *Jacobs* v. *Chaudhuri* [1968] 2 Q.B. 470 (similar on business tenancies).
[243] *Turley* v. *Panton* (1975) 29 P. & C.R. 397; *R.* v. *R.O. for Camden L.B. ex parte Felix* [1988] 2 E.G.L.R. 132, Hutchison J.
[244] J. Driscoll (1993) 136 *S.J.* 294.
[245] [1992] 1 A.C. 478 H.L.; J. Dewar (1992) 108 *L.Q.R.* 375; L. Tee [1992] *C.L.J.* 218.

effectively removes T2's occupation rights? Yes, according to the House of Lords, such a notice is valid.

At first sight both sides of the appeal were arguable. On the one hand a joint legal tenancy requires a joint act for termination,[246] which suggests that a woman could not unilaterally terminate the tenancy of a joint home but would have to apply to the court for an order forcing her partner to serve notice.[247] On the other, the reasoning adopted by Lord Bridge, in the leading speech, was that a periodic tenancy created an estate in the land for one period at a time, which continued only if all parties intend that it should. Blackstone observed that a yearly tenancy continues during the will of both parties, and nineteenth[248] and twentieth[249] century opinions agree, since otherwise a tenant would be inconvenienced by being held liable for life by a tenancy he no longer wants. The tenancy agreement may negate the *Monk* rule, and perhaps tenancy agreements should indeed be drafted so as to exclude it.

Unilateral *Monk* notices must be of sufficient duration to end the tenancy at common law, that is of a full period's duration expiring at the end of a period of the tenancy, and also meeting the statutory minimum period of 28 straight days.[250] A short notice by one joint tenant has no effect on the rights of the other joint tenant, a point which a local authority demonstrated at great cost to its council tax payers in *Osei-Bonsu* v. *Wandsworth L.B.C.*[251] A wife left a jointly held property for bed and breakfast accommodation after alleged violence from her husband, but when she subsequently gave notice to quit the tenancy of the joint home, it was to quit in 14 days as opposed to the 28 days which statute required. The husband was barred from access to the property by a court order, during which time the local authority repossessed the property, but after this ouster order was discharged he claimed the right to take back possession and obtained from the court a declaration that he remained a joint tenant of the property as a result of the wife's failure to give the 28 days required to quit a dwelling-house. True, his rights could be terminated by a second notice of full duration but, in the meantime, he had been wrongfully evicted by the local authority landlord and was entitled to damages of £30,000 in tort. So it is vitally important that a unilateral notice is of sufficient duration, especially since a hostile, one-sided, termination of a joint tenancy cannot be interpreted as a surrender of the tenancy. Thus in *Hounslow L.B.C.* v. *Pilling*[252] a letter by Miss Doubtfire written on Friday to terminate a weekly tenancy the next Monday was invalid,[253] since the period allowed was too short to act as a notice of intention to quit and a unilateral letter could not act as a valid surrender of a joint tenancy.

---

[246] *Wax* v. *Chelsea* [1996] 2 E.G.L.R. 80; see above p. 126.

[247] *Cork* v. *Cork* [1997] 1 E.G.L.R. 5, Knox J. But see now *Crawley B.C.* v. *Ure* [1996] Q.B. 13 C.A.; see below pp. 128–130.

[248] *Doe d. Aslin* v. *Summersett* (1830) 1 B. & Ad. 135, 109 E.R. 738; *Doe d. Kindersley* v. *Hughes* (1840) 7 M. & W. 139, 151 E.R. 711; *Alford* v. *Vickery* (1842) Car. & M. 280, 174 E.R. 507.

[249] *Leek and Moorlands B.S.* v. *Clark* [1952] 2 Q.B. 788 C.A.; *Greenwich L.B.C.* v. *McGrady* (1982) 46 P. & C.R. 223 C.A.; F. Webb [1983] *Conv.* 194; J.T. Farrand [1984] *Conv.* 166; *Smith* v. *Grayton Estates Ltd.* [1960] S.C. 349.

[250] See above p. 26.

[251] [1999] 1 W.L.R. 1011 C.A.

[252] [1993] 1 W.L.R. 1242 C.A.

[253] P.E.A. 1977 s.5 required 28 days' notice.

Is *Monk* just? Local authorities have used it to break joint tenancies after allegations of domestic violence in order to relet the property to the victimised partner. If violence has indeed occurred that is obviously the correct outcome. Surely, however, any such transfer should be preceded by a judicial determination that violence had occurred and an investigation of what arrangement was in the best interests of the children? Why should councils usurp this judicial function? In other cases the *Monk* principle can work most unfairly. What is to stop a party who deserts the home serving a notice to quit as a simple matter of spite and forcing the former partner out of their shared home? Much the same happened in *Bater* v. *Bater*[254] where a husband who had been left in the property was negotiating to exercise the right to buy his home, but had not yet completed the purchase. After his wife had moved out, she served a notice to end the joint periodic tenancy with the intention of extinguishing the right to buy, and she was held to have succeeded in her scheme. She successfully exploited the substantial period of vulnerability during the right to buy process when the tenant must keep on foot both his tenancy and his residential qualification.[255] A notice can also be used to prejudice the succession rights of the tenant who is left in the family home, since notice ends the contractual tenancy which is the prerequisite for the existence of succession rights.[256]

Almost all the *Monk* cases have arisen in the public sector, in which case the effect of the decision is destructive of all security of tenure, given that a statutory periodic tenancy only arises at the end of a fixed term tenancy and not where a contractual tenancy is ended by act of the tenant.[257] The same unmerited bonus accrues to a private sector landlord, who is not under any duty whatsoever to rehouse either party. Surely reform of the residential tenancy schemes is required to ensure that the tenant who wishes to remain in occupation can claim security if he is able to afford the whole rent. It would obviously be wrong that a person should be bound to continue paying rent indefinitely simply because his co-tenant refuses to agree to terminate the arrangement,[258] but this difficulty could be overcome by allowing a unilateral release of the interest of one joint tenant to the other.[259]

3.   Preventing unilateral termination

What should a person do if he wishes to prevent a *Monk* style unilateral termination? A number of solutions have been attempted, but most have failed to get off the ground. One is to take action for breach of trust, a solution rejected by the courts in *Crawley B.C.* v. *Ure*[260] because giving notice is not a positive act which amounts to a breach of trust. Surely this is questionable? In any event the usefulness of trust actions is limited given that there will rarely be a statutory trust of an informal tenancy.[261] A second attempted solution in the shape of a non-molestation order was also tried and found to fail in

---

[254] [1999] 4 All E.R. 944 C.A.
[255] See below pp. 503–504.
[256] *Newham L.B.C.* v. *Phillips* (1998) 30 H.L.R. 859 C.A.
[257] H.A. 1985 s.86.
[258] *Monk* [1992] 1 A.C. 478, 483C–D, Lord Bridge.
[259] See below p. 286.
[260] [1996] Q.B. 13 C.A.; K. Shorrock [1995] *Conv.* 424.
[261] See above p. 126.

Harrow L.B.C. v. *Johnstone.*[262] When the wife left a public sector home held on a joint secure tenancy in 1994, her husband obtained a non-molestation order, that is a county court injunction[263] ordering her to take no step which would hamper his occupation of the home. On the wording of the particular injunction, at least according to the House of Lords, she was not in breach of injunction, and the council which had advised her to serve notice had not encouraged a contempt of court. The decision is alarming, but not nearly so much as Lord Hoffmann's opinion[264] that there would have been no contempt even if the wording of the injunction had expressly prohibited service of a notice to quit. Surely not?

If no action is taken, the partner left in the property remains very vulnerable to hostile termination by the joint tenant who has left, a vulnerability increased by judicial exposition of the law. This is because the power aimed at preventing the dissipation of matrimonial assets[265] has been narrowed where it is used retrospectively, after a damaging transaction has occurred. The Court of Appeal in *Newlon Housing Trust* v. *Alsulaimen,*[266] did indeed set aside a notice to quit which had actually been served by a wife at the instance of her husband to enable him to apply for a transfer of the tenancy, but Lord Hoffmann in *Harrow L.B.C.* v. *Johnstone*[267] thought that the *Newlon* case turned on an inappropriate concession that a notice to quit was a potentially reviewable transaction,[268] and, when *Newlon Housing Trust* v. *Alsulaimen*[269] reached the Lords, Lord Hoffmann held to his earlier opinion that there was no power to unravel a notice to quit after it had been served.

Section 37 of the Matrimonial Causes Act 1973 is limited to upsetting a "reviewable disposition", that is a "disposition of any property or any other dealing with any property",[270] which excludes a notice to quit. In *Alsulaimen* a husband and wife held a joint assured weekly tenancy but, after the wife had left and commenced divorce proceedings, she gave notice to quit and so terminated the tenancy. The landlords sought possession after the expiration of the wife's notice to quit and only then, in response to the landlord's request for possession, did the husband seek an order transferring the tenancy to himself. This was too late. The notice to quit had terminated the tenancy and so there was nothing to transfer. Matters moved to paragraph (b)[271] under which the only power was to undo a "disposition" of property, a phrase inapt in Lord Hoffmann's view to describe a notice to quit, which destroys a property right rather than transferring one. The narrow interpretation is surprising, given the wide statement of the Parliamentary intention within section 37 itself—that is to counteract any transaction intended to prevent or reduce an award of financial relief or intended to frustrate or impede the

---

[262] [1997] 1 W.L.R. 459 H.L.; M.P. Thompson [1997] *Conv.* 288.
[263] It was obtained unilaterally (*ex parte*) and was not followed, as it should have been, by *inter partes* proceedings.
[264] At 471, Lord Hoffmann.
[265] M.C.A. 1973 s.37.
[266] [1997] 1 F.L.R. 914 C.A.
[267] [1997] 1 W.L.R. 459 H.L.
[268] At 471, Lord Hoffmann, 470G, Lord Mustill.
[269] [1999] A.C. 313 H.L.
[270] s.37(2)(a).
[271] s.37(2)(b).

enforcement of any order including not only those actually made but also those that might have been made.[272] Immediate intervention is required to restore the obvious legislative intention.

The best solution is to seek an order transferring the tenancy to the partner left in the property under the jurisdictions discussed later in this chapter,[273] the question whether to order a transfer being decided by a family court on family law principles. As soon as a separation occurs a joint tenant should take pre-emptive action to prevent the service of a notice to quit, since the paragraph (a) power to deal with matters prospectively is wide enough to stop any attempt "otherwise to deal with any property".[274] According to Thorpe L.J. in *Bater* v. *Bater*[275] the court could issue an order to prevent termination of the tenancy either under the power to prevent transactions which dissipate matrimonial assets after the issue of a divorce petition[276] or under the inherent jurisdiction of a family court over molestation and harassment after service of a divorce petition. A cheaper alternative is to obtain from the other joint tenant an undertaking not to give notice to quit and to hand a copy of that undertaking to the landlord.

4. Consensual termination

Surrenders[277] and other consensual terminations of a joint tenancy require joint action. A unilateral release was held to be ineffective in *Burton* v. *Camden L.B.C.*,[278] a case discussion in detail below.[279]

H. OCCUPATION ORDERS

1. Matrimonial home right

Part of the Family Law Act 1996[280] derives from the Matrimonial Homes Act 1967 as re-enacted in 1983. It provides important protection in the shape of a statutory matrimonial home right to cover the gap between the separation of a married couple and the subsequent divorce. Of its limitations, the first and most important is that the matrimonial home right applies only to a matrimonial home: a spouse is protected when the couple cease to live together as man and wife but a partner who cohabited without marrying must rely on an occupation order.[281] Pre-1996 coverage of matrimonial homes[282]

---

[272] s.37(1).

[273] s.53, sch.7; see below pp. 135–141.

[274] s.37(2)(a).

[275] [1999] 4 All E.R. 944, 952g–953b C.A. Roch L.J. and Lord Lloyd (at 953h) offered no opinion on these points. See K. Jenrick [1999] *Fam. Law* 815; K. Jenrick & K. Bretherton [2000] *J.H.L.* 8; L. Fox [2000] *Conv* 208.

[276] M.C.A. 1973 s.37(2)(a).

[277] *Hounslow L.B.C.* v. *Pilling* [1993] 1 W.L.R. 861 C.A.; *Osei-Bonsu* v. *Wandsworth L.B.C.* [1999] 1 W.L.R. 1011 C.A.; see above pp. 37–41.

[278] [2000] 2 W.L.R. 427 H.L.; [1998] 1 F.L.R. 681 C.A. reversed.

[279] See below p. 286.

[280] ss.30, 31, sch.4; the operative date was October 1st 1997: S.I. 1997/1892; Sparkes, *N.L.L.* ch.13 ; A. Barlow [1998] *J.H.L.* 72.

[281] See below p. 134.

[282] *Collins* v. *Collins* (1973) 4 Fam. Law 133 C.A.; *Whittingham* v. *Whittingham* [1979] Fam. 9, 16B; *Kemmis* v. *Kemmis* [1988] 1 W.L.R. 1307, 1321A.

is now extended to include dwellings *intended* for use as a home by a married couple,[283] but it continues to be the case that a home occupied by one spouse alone is unprotected.[284] Use as a matrimonial home must occur before the commencement of any bankruptcy.[285] Dwelling houses are protected, but not mobile homes or caravans.[286] Rented homes are included whatever the form of the tenancy, the matrimonial home right being defined to exist wherever entitlement to occupy arises under any beneficial estate or interest and also any contract that confers a right to remain in occupation.[287] This includes all forms of contractual tenancies and contractual licences. A spouse also has a matrimonial home right if the other spouse has a statutory right to remain in the home, perhaps under a Rent Act statutory tenancy, a Housing Act 1988 assured tenancy, or a public sector secure tenancy.[288]

The old law was that an abandoned wife could not assert residence through her husband if he had left her and had no intention of returning,[289] so in order to make the safety net sufficient it was necessary for the matrimonial homes legislation to strengthen a spouse's right against the landlord. The spouse of a residential tenant is empowered to tender rent, which the landlord must accept as if made by the tenant.[290] Occupation by the spouse counts as occupation by the actual tenant for the purposes of obtaining security of tenure under the Rent Act 1977 or the more modern security of tenure schemes.[291] Like the matrimonial home right itself, the rent payment right and the deemed transfer of residential occupation presumably end on divorce, so that if a divorce occurs without a judicial transfer of the tenancy the court should be asked to order an extension of these rights; apparently a landlord is bound by such an application only if it is made before the termination of the contractual tenancy.[292] This protection is of fundamental importance to a spouse and, as explained below, the failure to provide corresponding protection if the couple are unmarried is a major handicap to a separated cohabitee.

More generally, all matrimonial home rights end on divorce[293] so that it is essential to obtain a transfer order vesting any residential tenancy in the party who is to live in the rented accommodation after the divorce before the decree is made absolute. An alternative is an order made before the decree absolute prolonging the rights,[294] but it is only in exceptional cases that this should be preferred to a transfer order. Under the old law

---

[283] F.L.A. 1996 sch.4 para. 2; Law Com. No.207 (1992) paras.4.4, 7.9; this reverses *Syed* v. *Syed* (1980) 1 F.L.R. 129.

[284] *Nanda* v. *Nanda* [1968] P. 351; *Hall* v. *King* (1987) 19 H.L.R. 440 C.A.; J.E. Martin [1987] *Conv.* 448.

[285] I.A. 1986 s.336(1).

[286] F.L.A. 1996 s.63(1), (4), re-enacting M.H.A. 1983 s.10(1).

[287] F.L.A. 1996 s.30(1) re-enacting M.H.A. 1983 s.1(1).

[288] *Tarr* v. *Tarr* [1973] A.C. 254 H.L.; *Richards* v. *Richards* [1984] A.C. 174 H.L.

[289] *Heath Estates Ltd.* v. *Burchell* [1979] 2 E.G.L.R. 81 C.A.

[290] F.L.A. 1996 s.30(3) re-enacting M.H.A. 1983 s.1(5).

[291] F.L.A. 1996 s.30(4) re-enacting M.H.A. 1983 s.1(6). The results can be capricious: *Hall* v. *King* (1987) 19 H.L.R. 440 C.A. See also *Hoggett* v. *Hoggett* (1980) 39 P. & C.R. 121; *Griffiths* v. *Renfree* (1989) 21 H.L.R. 338 C.A.; J.E. Martin [1990] *Conv.* 58.

[292] *Sopwith* v. *Stutchbury* (1985) 17 H.L.R. 50 C.A. (husband had left Rent Act tenancy and given notice to quit).

[293] The rights of occupation may also be terminated by a court order and may be defeated by a protected purchaser if unregistered.

[294] F.L.A. 1996 s.31(8) re-enacting M.H.A. 1983 s.2(4).

a divorce ended the powers of the court to issue an ouster injunction,[295] a lacuna filled by the modern law, but if any occupation order is made it will be for renewable periods of six months.[296]

Potential inadequacies of the matrimonial home right are highlighted by the decision in *Sanctuary Housing Association* v. *Campbell*.[297] A woman was the secure tenant of a housing association maisonette that she left as a result of her husband's violence, but while she attempted to surrender the tenancy, he changed the locks and prevented her from removing her belongings. The Court of Appeal decided against her entitlement to a matrimonial home right. Thorpe L.J. showed that the legislation regulated the contractual relationship between husband and wife, but it did not prevent the tenant terminating her contractual relationship with the landlord. A surrender had in fact occurred,[298] and her husband was obliged to yield up possession to the landlord. It goes without saying that a spouse needs protection against termination of the tenancy by a spiteful "ex" more than he or she does protection against possession proceedings brought by the landlord, and the decision has rendered matrimonial home rights almost nugatory as a means of protecting the spouse of the tenant of a rented home. Of course if a spouse is proved to have been violent that is a good reason for exercising the discretion to exclude him from the home and leaving the victimised spouse free to surrender the tenancy, but Thorpe L.J. was satisfied that the legislation did indeed allow the spouse who has left to terminate her contractual relationship with the landlord without judicial intervention.[299] A surrender could only be prevented by advance protection of the charge created by the matrimonial home right, the form of protection being by class F land charge or entry of a land registry notice[300] and, since the husband had failed to do this before the surrender it was held that the landlord was a purchaser for value, the terms of the surrender constituting sufficient value.[301] The registration system is wholly inappropriate to deal with rented property. Nevertheless the decision chimes with the refusal in *Thompson* v. *Elmbridge B.C.*[302] to join a husband in possession proceedings brought by a local authority against his wife after she had left the home. A suspended possession order had been made against the wife and she had subsequently breached the repayment terms laid down in that suspension, so that her public sector secure tenancy ended at the time of the first breach of the suspended possession order.[303] Hence when a warrant was issued for possession there was no longer a tenancy in existence and it was too late for the husband to try to challenge the landlord's title to possession.

---

[295] *O'Malley* v. *O'Malley* [1982] 1 W.L.R. 244 C.A. (statute); *Brent* v. *Brent* [1975] Fam. 1, 7, Dunn J. (common law right).

[296] F.L.A. 1996 s.35.

[297] [1999] 3 All E.R. 460 C.A.

[298] At 463, Thorpe L.J., where he rejected the analogy of Rent Act cases which suggested that occupation had to be delivered: *Old Gate Estates Ltd.* v. *Alexander* [1950] 1 K.B. 311; *Middleton* v. *Baldock* [1950] 1 K.B. 657 C.A.; *Hoggett* v. *Hoggett* (1979) 39 P. & C.R. 121.

[299] At 464g.

[300] This is recognised as a good protection at 465. It seems to reverse the principle of *Hoggett* v. *Hoggett* (1980) 39 P. & C.R. 121, 128, that registration is *not* essential as between the spouses.

[301] F.L.A. 1996 s.31(9) (re-enacting M.H.A. 1983 s.2(6)) makes this reasoning hard to accept.

[302] [1987] 1 W.L.R. 1425 C.A.

[303] See below pp. 333–335.

2. Occupation orders: spouses

The best way to stop a tenant who has left the matrimonial home from serving notice to quit or surrendering the tenancy is to obtain an occupation order. Once an order has been made it will stabilise the position of the matrimonial home while consideration is given to the possibility of obtaining a transfer order. Usually a bundle of applications will be considered together.[304] Part IV of the Family Law Act 1996[305] replaces those parts of the Matrimonial Homes Act which are concerned with the exercise of the discretion to regulate occupation of the matrimonial home, at the same time making substantial changes to the factors to be considered and the orders which can be made. The occupation order itself will aim to stabilise the occupation of the matrimonial home after the relationship between the spouses breaks down while consideration is given to the possibility of ordering a transfer of the tenancy. Orders can be used to enforce the applicant's right to occupation against the respondent, to require the admission of the applicant to the home, and to regulate occupation by one or both parties.[306] A respondent may be prohibited from occupying, ordered to leave, or excluded from a defined area of the house.[307] Presumably there is power to prohibit the service of a notice to quit or voluntary surrender if the home is rented. Orders can be made to pay for repairs and maintenance, to discharge outgoings, or to make compensatory payments, as well as regulating the use of furniture and keeping the property secure.[308] *Non-molestation orders* are used in cases of violence, threatened violence, or other harassment,[309] to prohibit specific acts or general molestation directed at a person who is associated with the aggressor or any relevant child, whenever this order is required to secure the health, safety and well being of the victim. A *power of arrest* should be attached to an occupation order or non-molestation order if violence has been threatened or used against the applicant or a relevant child.[310] Orders can be made *ex parte* if it is just and convenient to do so,[311] weighing for example the risk of significant harm to the applicant or any relevant child.[312] All orders are subject to *variation and discharge*.[313]

The court *must* make an order where harm is likely to be suffered by the applicant or a relevant child living with him which outweighs the harm likely to be suffered by the respondent and children living with him.[314] If the balance of harm does not require an order, the court has a discretion in weighing listed factors which include[315]: (1) the housing needs and resources of each party including relevant children, (2) the financial resources of each party, (3) the likely effect on the health, safety, wellbeing of the parties and any relevant child, and (4) conduct in relation to each other and generally.

---

[304] F.L.A. 1996 s.39(2).
[305] s.33(3) replacing M.H.A. 1983 s.1(2). The court may instead accept an undertaking: s.46.
[306] s.33(3)(a)–(c).
[307] s.33(3)(d)–(g).
[308] s.40, considering e.g. financial needs and resources.
[309] A. Barlow [1998] *J.H.L.* 72, 85.
[310] F.L.A. 1996 s.47.
[311] s.45(1).
[312] s.45(2)(a); other factors are stated in paras.(b)–(c).
[313] s.49.
[314] F.L.A. 1996 s.33(7).
[315] s.33(6).

Duration may be unlimited in time, for a limited period, or until further order.[316] Marriage is favoured under the scheme of the 1996 Act since orders may be indefinite, that is to last until death[317] or variation.[318] Divorce usually ends an occupation order, since the court will consider whether to transfer the tenancy before authorising the divorce, but there is power to order that the right should survive death and/or divorce, a power which can be exercised whenever it is just and equitable to do so[319] provided that the application is made during the existence of the marriage. If a party completes a divorce without adequate provision the court has power to make temporary (but renewable) orders in favour of a former spouse,[320] though only while both spouses remain alive. Temporary renewable orders are also available where the matrimonial home is held under a bare licence.[321]

3. Occupation orders on cohabitation breakdown

A person who has cohabited in accommodation rented in the name of the other cohabitee is, in the terms of the Family Law Act 1996, a "non-entitled cohabitee", that is a person with no right to stay in the property at law or in equity. Powers to make occupation orders under this head are limited to a couple who have lived together as man and wife,[322] a phraseology which excludes a homosexual partner who is not a joint tenant. Factors to be weighed against all other circumstances include the length of the relationship, the degree of commitment,[323] the interests of any children, and the length of time since the relationship terminated.[324] A moral penalty is imposed on cohabitation so as to favour those who choose to marry: orders are time limited to six months with at most one renewal,[325] and it is more difficult to obtain the exclusion of a cohabitee in the absence of any statutory presumption that the balance of convenience favours making such an order.

4. Where a possession order is in force

Many public sector tenants have possession orders in force, which are suspended while payments towards rent arrears are made. All too often at this stage, the parties separate. The partner who has been left in the property needs to be able to take the benefit of this provision for payment by instalments and to intervene in future court proceedings as if affected by any adjournment, stay, suspension, or postponement. Specific provision is needed to guard against the difficulty that the lease is terminated if the terms of the suspension are breached—as is very likely to occur if a couple in financial difficulties separate. A spouse can claim the benefit of a matrimonial home right as if the tenancy had

---

[316] s.33(10).
[317] s.33(9)(b).
[318] s.47.
[319] s.33(5), (8).
[320] s.35. Factors include the length of time since the marriage breakdown and the divorce, and whether other proceedings are pending.
[321] s.37; factors are listed in subss.(6)–(7), but the possible orders are similar.
[322] s.62.
[323] s.41.
[324] s.36(6).
[325] s.36(10).

not been terminated, and the same is true between cohabitees where an occupation order is in force.[326]

5. Occupation orders between joint tenants

In the terms of the Family Law Act 1996, an entitled applicant is a person entitled to occupy a family home as a beneficial co-owner or joint tenant, or a person with a joint entitlement to statutory security of tenure. Orders may relate to a current home, a former home or an intended home. Orders can be made to regulate the occupation of a home if the applicant and the respondent are associated,[327] a vital concept and one defined at length.[328] Categories are:

> people married;
> those formerly married;
> people who had agreed to marry[329];
> cohabitants or former cohabitants[330];
> people who have lived in one household under a non-commercial arrangement[331];
> relatives, a concept widely defined[332];
> a child to a parent or person with parental responsibility[333]; and
> parties to the same family proceedings.

It was initially proposed to extend protection to all those who had ever enjoyed—or indeed not enjoyed—sexual relations, a proposal dropped because of the difficulty of proof (!) but even so the Act retains a wide net, including unmarried cohabitees, homosexual partners, elderly relatives and house sharers who are not "an item". The powers of the court, the factors it is required to consider, and the orders it is permitted to make are very similar to those between spouses.[334]

I.   TRANSFER ORDERS

1.   Transfer orders between spouses

Tenancies can be transferred on the divorce of married tenants or in some similar matrimonial proceedings. The power made available by the Family Law Act 1996 consolidates the earlier provisions made by the Matrimonial Homes Act 1983.[335] A transfer order will usually be made before a decree is made absolute but if the divorce has been finalised and the need to deal with the tenancy of the matrimonial home has been overlooked, there is a power to backdate the application in order to deal with it.

---

[326] H.A. 1985 s.85(5), (5A).
[327] F.L.A. 1996 s.33(1)(a)–(b).
[328] s.62.
[329] If: (1) there is written evidence, a gift of an engagement ring, or a ceremony of engagement: s.44; and (2) proceedings are brought within 3 years of breaking off the engagement: s.33(2).
[330] Meaning a man and a woman: s.62(1).
[331] i.e. not as employee, tenant, lodger or boarder.
[332] s.63(1).
[333] A child may apply personally if of sufficient understanding or otherwise by a representative: ss.40, 59–60, 64.
[334] See above pp. 133–134.
[335] sch.1.

Unfortunately it appears that the 1983 legislation which introduced this power was not retrospective, so that the current transfer powers are not available for divorces finalised before early 1983,[336] the reason that the wife failed in *Crago* v. *Julian*.[337] Most residential tenancies can be made the subject of a transfer order including Rent Act tenancies, public sector secure tenancies, assured tenancies and occupation agreements for tied cottages.[338] Some residential tenancies will also count as forms of "property"[339] so as to fall with the more general powers to make property adjustment orders on divorce, such cases overlapping with the specialised transfer powers[340] and similar principles applying. Tenancies with a contractual existence are Rent Act tenancies during contractual phases,[341] assured tenancies throughout their existence, council tenancies,[342] and their modern equivalent—public sector secure tenancies. Purely statutory confections such as Rent Act tenancies after the ending of the contractual phase rely on the deemed transfer of occupation to keep them on foot,[343] and can only be dealt with under the specialised transfer provisions.

Transfers under the Family Law Act 1996 must relate to the property in which the spouses lived together, that is the home which has at some time been a matrimonial home.[344] Usually an order will be made on divorce. If a divorce has been completed, a retrospective application is allowed, with any order being dated back to the decree absolute.[345] No power exists if a couple separate without either divorcing or seeking a judicial separation, a problem illustrated by the unusual facts of *Vuong* v. *Hoang*.[346] A couple had married in China in a ceremony before ancestral stones before emigrating to Britain. They were joint secure tenants at the time of the separation in 1997, but the husband served a *Monk* notice to quit, thus ending the rights of the wife who remained in occupation. Transfer of the tenancy was impossible given that there was no decree nisi, so the wife was driven to argue that the customary marriage was invalid, that she was in fact a cohabitee, and that transfer was therefore allowed as from their separation. However, the court applied the presumption that a foreign marriage is valid and so ruled that there was no power to transfer the tenancy.

Application for a vesting order must be made before termination of the contractual tenancy, so that in the position of a Mrs Julian, it will be too late to seek a transfer. *Lewis* v. *Lewis* decides that the matrimonial homes transfer of a statutory tenancy "presup-

---

[336] *Lewis* v. *Lewis* [1984] Fam. 79, 87–91 (left open [1985] A.C. 828, 834E–G); the exact date is February 14th, 1983.

[337] [1992] 1 W.L.R. 372 C.A.

[338] F.L.A. 1996 sch.7 para.1 and part III (forms of orders). The reach of the provisions has been gradually extended: M.H.A. 1967 s.7; N.E. Hickman (1979) 129 *N.L.J.* 52; M.H. and Property Act 1981 s.6 and sch.2; M.H.A. 1983 s.7 and sch.1; H.A. 1988 sch.17 para.33.

[339] *Hale* v. *Hale* [1975] 1 W.L.R. 931, 937D, Stephenson L.J.

[340] F.L.A. 1996 sch.7 para.2.

[341] *Hale* v. *Hale* [1975] 1 W.L.R. 931 C.A.

[342] *Thompson* v. *Thompson* [1976] Fam. 25 C.A.; doubting *Brent* v. *Brent* [1975] Fam. 1, Dunn J.

[343] F.L.A. 1996 s.30(4)(spouses).

[344] F.L.A. 1996 sch.7 para.3.

[345] M.C.A. 1973 s.24; *Hale* v. *Hale* [1975] 1 W.L.R. 931 C.A.; M.H.A. 1983 sch.1 para 6; *Lewis* v. *Lewis* [1985] A.C. 828; J.E. Martin [1985] *Conv.* 127; *Thompson* v. *Thompson* [1976] Fam. 25; *Regan* v. *Regan* [1977] 1 W.L.R. 84; *Rodewald* v. *Rodewald* [1977] 2 All E.R. 609.

[346] [1999] 05 C.L. 384.

poses the existence of a statutory tenancy at the date when application is made for a transfer".[347] The same must apply to the jurisdiction to transfer a contractual tenancy following divorce. It is therefore possible to fall into an unfortunate gap, not being protected by rent payments and occupation because of a divorce, and unable to apply for a transfer of the tenancy after its termination. Section 37 of the Matrimonial Causes Act 1973 aims to prevent the dissipation of matrimonial assets to circumvent the court's powers to order property adjustment or to award financial relief. However the previous discussion of *Newlon Housing Trust* v. *Alsulaimen*[348] demonstrates the inadequacy of this provision against a unilateral notice to quit that has already been served.

Discretionary exercise of the Family Law Act transfer jurisdiction must be based on a list of statutory factors that have to be taken into account. As between *spouses* these are[349]:

the circumstances in which the tenancy was granted;
the housing resources and needs of the parties and any children;
the financial resources of the parties;
the likely effect of the order on the health, safety or well being of any child; and
the suitability of both parties as tenants.

No mention is made of conduct, not even as a residual factor (!), though it might come into the overall discretion of the court. Clearly it should do. In *Jones* v. *Jones*[350] husband and wife were secure tenants. When she applied for a judicial separation, her husband had been living in the property for 20 years and with a disability. Exercise of the discretion in favour of the wife was inappropriate since she could rehouse and her husband had demonstrated a special need.[351] If property adjustment is possible (that is if there is a contractual tenancy) the full range of divorce factors has to be taken into account, including for example the clean break provision,[352] so it is therefore theoretically possible to reach a position under which transfer would be ordered under one jurisdiction but not under the other.

2. Transfer between cohabitees

The Family Law Act 1996[353] confers power on the family court to order the transfer of a tenancy on the separation of cohabitees, an extension of the earlier legislation made on the recommendation of the Law Commission.[354] It must be shown that it was the family home of the cohabitees who lived in it together as man and wife,[355] the power being exercisable when they cease to live together as such. Tenancies which may be transferred include Rent Act tenancies, public sector secure tenancies, assured tenancies and

---

[347] [1985] A.C. 828, 833H, Lord Bridge.
[348] [1999] 1 A.C. 313 H.L.; see above pp. 129–130.
[349] F.L.A. 1996 s.33(6).
[350] [1997] Fam. 59 C.A.
[351] *Thompson* v. *Thompson* [1976] Fam. 25 C.A. applied.
[352] M.C.A. 1973 s.25A.
[353] sch.7 para.3.
[354] Law Com. No.207 (1992) paras.6.1–6.12.
[355] F.L.A. 1996 sch.7 para.3; this excludes homosexual partners.

occupation agreements for tied cottages. Statutory factors to be taken into account between cohabitees are[356]:

the housing needs and resources of the parties and any children;
the likely effect of the order on the health, safety or wellbeing of any relevant child;
the suitability of both parties as tenants;
the conduct of the parties in relation to each other and otherwise;
the nature of the parties' relationship, the length of their cohabitation, and the length of time since it ceased;
the interests of children for whom the parties have parental responsibility; and
the existence of proceedings for financial relief against the parent of a child.

Defects in this legislation were exposed ruthlessly in *Gay* v. *Sheeran*.[357] John Sheeran was a secure tenant[358] of a flat owned by Enfield in 1992 into which Josephine Gay moved and where they lived together for six months until, in April 1996, Sheeran moved out. Enfield became aware of Ms Gay's existence 18 months later when she claimed housing benefit. Ms Gay was refused a transfer order by the court because when Sheeran moved out the tenancy ceased to be secure and therefore, since April 1996, there had been no secure tenancy and nothing to transfer. Had the couple been married this would have been of small consequence, because the matrimonial homes legislation would have deemed her occupation that of her deserting spouse so as to support the existence of a statutory tenancy. Between unmarried cohabitees, there was no deemed transfer of occupation unless a cohabitee had first obtained an occupation order.[359] So Sheeran was a contractual tenant without qualifying occupation and Ms Gay was an occupier without any tenancy. Parliament had used[360] language of present entitlement to occupy under a secure tenancy, meaning that all requirement for the existence of a public sector security must be satisfied at the time of the transfer.[361] All rights can be lost, much too easily, by termination of the secure tenancy.

A transfer order is possible if a concurrent application is made for an occupation order. Enfield argued that an order should be refused where its sole purpose is to found a transfer application. This implied that it was necessary to prove violence or some other genuine reason to protect the woman, but the court held on the particular facts that there was some practical purpose in the order to guard against the possibility that Sheeran might even now return. Peter Gibson L.J. thought that there was no objection to using an occupation order simply as a foundation for a transfer order, whereas Chadwick L.J. thought that an order was void if this was its sole purpose.[362]

---

[356] s.36(6).
[357] [1999] 3 All E.R. 795 C.A.
[358] In fact he was a joint tenant with a former cohabitee.
[359] F.L.A. 1996 s.36 (3), (4).
[360] F.L.A. 1996 sch.7 para.3(1).
[361] The C.A. did not decide between the date of application or the date of the hearing, though Peter Gibson L.J. favoured the latter.
[362] At 807h–808a, 815g–h.

3. General provisions about transfers

Powers of transfer apply not only where a tenancy in the sole name of one person is to be transferred to the other (A to B) but also where a tenancy in joint names is to be transferred to the name of one person alone (A and B to B).[363] The order can require the tenancy (or as appropriate any interest in it) to be transferred or vested from any date specified, and no further assurance is required. The transfer can also transfer liabilities, including existing liabilities, or can require an indemnity to be given against liabilities or require a balancing payment; the financial loss and financial position of the parties need to be taken into account when deciding what order to make.[364] In *Church Commissioners for England* v. *Al Emarah*[365] a joint tenancy of a public sector flat was already subject to a suspended possession order that required arrears of rent to be paid off by instalments when the tenants divorced. The tenancy was transferred subject to the terms of the possession order and the existing arrears. If there is no provision in the transfer order for arrears to transfer, the new tenant is not liable for the previous tenant's defaults.[366]

Rules of the court require the court to give the landlord an opportunity to be heard.[367]

4. Property adjustment on behalf of children

Property adjustment orders can be made in favour of children, and this could theoretically include an order to transfer a tenancy if it was of the kind which did constitute "property", though not for purely statutory arrangements such as statutory Rent Act tenancies. There are two powers, first in proceedings ancillary to *divorce*,[368] and secondly under the *Children Act 1989*[369] on the application of a parent or other person with a residence order regulating the housing of the child. Orders can only be made against a parent if the child is under 18,[370] and usually terminate when the child reaches his majority or ends his full time education.[371] Commonly an unmarried mother will seek the order against the father of the child—for example to transfer the father's interest as joint tenant in a council house,[372] or to oust a violent father[373]—though it is not available against a man who has cohabited with the mother but who is not the father of the child.[374] However it is assumed that orders will be rare now that it is permissible to transfer the tenancy directly to an unmarried cohabitee. It is inappropriate to evict an

[363] F.L.A. 1996 sch.7 paras.2(1), 3(1). Unfortunately this does not include a case where a third person is a joint tenant: *Gay* v. *Sheeran* [1999] 3 All E.R. 795 C.A. (Sheeran and Gunn to Gay).

[364] paras.7, 10, 11; if the transferor is a successor so is the transferee.

[365] [1997] Fam. 34 C.A.

[366] *Notting Hill Housing Trust* v. *Rakey Jones* [1999] L. & T.R. 397 C.A.

[367] F.L.A. 1996 sch.7 para.14; S.I. 1991/1247 r.3.8(12) as substituted by S.I. 1997/1893.

[368] M.C.A. 1973 s.24.

[369] Children Act 1989 s.15, sch. 1 para.1(2)(c)–(e); Sparkes *N.L.L.* 367–369.

[370] Children Act 1989 sch.1 para.1.

[371] *H.* v. *P.* [1993] Fam. Law 515; *A.* v. *A.* [1994] 1 F.L.R. 657 (6 months after 18 or termination of full time education); *T.* v. *S.* [1994] 2 F.L.R. 883 (where the order lasted until 21 rather than 18, but query whether this was correct except where the child was in full time education)

[372] *K.* v. *K.* [1992] 1 W.L.R. 530 C.A.; *J.* v. *J.* [1993] 2 F.L.R. 56, Eastham J.

[373] *Pearson* v. *Franklin* [1994] 1 W.L.R. 370 C.A. (ouster cannot be obtained under Children Act 1989 by a non-owning mother without a property adjustment order in favour of the child).

[374] *J.* v. *J.* [1993] 2 F.L.R. 56, Eastham J. This would have been possible if the couple had married.

unmarried mother without first considering the entitlement to a transfer of the tenancy on behalf of her child. [375]

J.   RELATIONSHIP BREAKDOWN: POSITION OF LANDLORD

1.   Domestic violence—grounds for possession

In *Davis* v. *Johnson*[376] the House of Lords envisaged that the council would terminate the aggressor's tenancy and grant a new one to the victimised woman. An ironic result of the increased security of tenure for public sector tenants is that it became more difficult to achieve this result.[377] Hence the need for provisions permitting the transfer of tenancies between co-habitees and the fact that violence by a tenant to his spouse or cohabitee is a ground for possession in the public and social sectors[378]: a warning notice is required and must be served on the victim as well as the aggressor, but no period of notice is required.[379]

2.   Objection to property transfer

Rules of the court require the court to give the landlord an opportunity to be heard.[380] The landlord needs to exercise this right to ensure that the new tenant is financially satisfactory, and that arrears are dealt with adequately—if a transfer order is made without reference to the arrears, the landlord is left to chase the partner who has disappeared for the arrears.

Where a transfer order affects a *private sector* lease the consent of the landlord[381] must be obtained before an order can be made. However in relation to rented accommodation the power is to order transfer of a contractual tenancy or to transfer security of tenure rights.[382]

In the *public sector*, housing allocation controls do not apply to transfers ordered on relationship breakdown.[383] Family proceedings often lead to an order that a secure tenancy should be transferred, for example if the couple divorce and the court orders the transfer to the parent who remains in the home looking after the children. The landlord must respect any order and allow the transfer.[384] The old law in the public sector was that the council had to consent.[385] Thus it is no longer true as it once was that consent of the local authority is the single most important factor and that no transfer order should be made against an unwilling authority.[386]

[375] *R.* v. *Hammersmith & Fulham L.B.C. ex parte Quigley* [1999] 06 C.L. 354.
[376] [1979] A.C. 264 H.L.
[377] A. Arden [1982] *Conv.* 334; A. Samuels (1993) 157 *L.G.R.* 301.
[378] Public sector ground 2A introduced by H.A. 1996 s.145; private sector assured ground 14A introduced by H.A. 1996 s.149; in force February 12th and 28th 1997 respectively; see below p. 344.
[379] H.A. 1985 s.83A as substituted.
[380] F.L.A. 1996 sch.7 para.14; S.I. 1999/1247 rr.3.8–3.12, as substituted by S.I. 1997/1893.
[381] *J.* v. *J.* [1980] 1 All E.R. 156.
[382] M.C.A. 1973 s.24(1)(a); *Thompson* v. *Thompson* [1976] Fam. 25 C.A. (obiter); F.L.A. 1996 s.53 and sch.7 (replacing M.H.A. 1983 s.7, sch.1); *Church Commissioners for England* v. *Al Emarah* [1997] Fam. 34 C.A.
[383] H.A. 1996 s.160(1), (2).
[384] s.91(3)(a)–(b).
[385] *Regan* v. *Regan* [1977] 1 W.L.R. 84; D. Yates (1977) 41 *Conv. (N.S.)* 309.
[386] *Thompson* v. *Thompson* [1976] Fam. 25, 31.

The landlord should exercise his right to be heard before a transfer is ordered, particularly if there are objections to the behaviour of the partner to whom the tenancy is being transferred, outstanding arrears, or a subsisting suspended possession order.[387]

---

[387] *Church Commissioners for England* v. *Alemarah* [1997] Fam. 34 C.A. (transfer subject to terms of the possession order); but see *Thompson* v. *Elmbridge B.C.* [1987] 1 W.L.R. 1425 C.A. (breach of terms of suspended possession order ended tenancy and too late for spouse to apply to be joined in possession proceedings to seek a transfer).

6

LIMITED RESIDENTIAL SECURITY

Sectors. Self-contained accommodation. Shared accommodation. The end of a long lease. Exclusive possession. Joint occupation. Serviced accommodation. Resident landlord tenancies. Short-term tenancies. Other exempt leases. Exclusive licences. Caravans and houseboats.

A. A LEASE OF SELF-CONTAINED ACCOMMODATION

Since protection applies only to a dwelling which "is let", security is restricted to a tenant who occupies under a lease. Licensees are excluded from lifelong security and even from the minimal assurance available to a shorthold tenant.

1. Private sector

Lease/licence litigation took off against the backdrop of the Rent Acts. In order to qualify for a protected tenancy under the Rent Act 1977, an occupier had to show "a tenancy" under which self-contained residential accommodation "is let"[1] to him. This wording excluded licences. It was vitally important to differentiate between leases and licences when the Rent Act provided three very valuable rights—security of tenure, the right to a fair rent registration, and succession rights—in stark contrast to the minimal protection of licensees. Landlords stood to profit substantially if they succeeded in fobbing off an occupier with a licence rather than a lease. However, evasion of the security regime was prevented by judicial development of exclusive possession as a touchstone, the presence of which meant that a lease was created.[2] This rule, which is described in detail in this chapter, ensures that a landlord cannot avoid security simply by renaming an arrangement that conferred exclusive occupation as a licence. Landlords and tenants cannot contract out of the Rent Acts.[3]

Introduction of the assured tenancy scheme in early 1989 made no change to the security of tenure and other rights enjoyed by existing Rent Act protected tenants.[4] Protected shortholds were possible, theoretically at any time after 1980 though in practice the restrictive rules surrounding them meant that they were a minority of new lettings.[5]

---

[1] R.A. 1977 s.1(1).

[2] *Street* v. *Mountford* [1985] A.C. 809 H.L.; see below pp. 152–155.

[3] *Artizans Labourers and General Dwellings Co.* v. *Whitaker* [1919] 2 K.B. 301; *AG Securities* v. *Vaughan* [1990] 1 A.C. 417, 458D, Lord Templeman; *Laimond Properties Ltd.* v. *Al-Shakarchi* (1998) 30 H.L.R. 1099, 1104, Roch L.J.

[4] H.A. 1988 sch.1 paras.1, 13(1).

[5] H.A. 1980 s.21; see above pp. 44–45.

Existing licenses, on the other hand, could be terminated[6] and replaced by a shorthold. Older cases continue to reach the courts, though the stream is now drying up.[7]

Since early 1989, the Housing Act 1988[8] has operated to created assured tenancies, now at a market rent but with lifelong security of tenure left in place. Licensees are again totally unprotected.[9] However the pressure driving lease/licence litigation has been released, since full security can be avoided by the simple expedient of granting an assured shorthold. Since the Housing Act 1996[10] a grant in the private sector is presumed to be a shorthold unless the contrary is agreed, so that a form of holding which has been common since early 1989 is now almost universal in the private sector. It is only social landlords who commonly decide to opt into "life-long" security. Statute provides a maximum assurance of security for the first six months against hostile termination. Creation of a licence will avoid this assurance, but this is no longer a really substantial benefit and few landlords think it worthwhile to engage in deliberate evasion of the assured shorthold regime. Exclusive possession of self-contained accommodation remains the crucial stepping-stone in order to reach the residential tenancy legislation, but this test has a severely diminished practical function.

It does not much matter what particular form of lease is created provided that *some* contractual arrangement is in place. Certainly most residential tenancies are short term periodic tenancies created informally at law,[11] but a legal grant is not essential. For example the Rent Act 1977 may operate on the equitable interest,[12] where the base tenancy is a *Walsh* v. *Lonsdale*[13] agreement for a lease, where protection is claimed by a beneficiary under an express trust, or where an infant incapable of holding a legal estate holds over as a statutory tenant.[14] "Provided the tenancy is one under which the tenant is entitled to possession, it is always assumed to be immaterial whether it is legal or equitable."[15] In *Bruton* v. *London & Quadrant Housing Trust*[16] the House of Lords has recently held that security can be attracted between a sub-landlord and sub-tenant even if the sub-tenancy is not binding on the head landlord.

To summarise, the private sector provides security for all tenants, and the landlord cannot evade this rule by granting a licence instead because the test of exclusive occupation is applied to determine the existence of a lease. Licences are permitted, and security is excluded, if the occupation given is shared or limited or if the accommodation is not self-contained or in the rare cases of exclusive licences discussed later in this chapter.

---

[6] Subject only to the very limited security of tenure enjoyed by those entitled to a restricted contract; see below pp. 164–165.

[7] *Stribling* v. *Wickham* [1989] 2 E.G.L.R. 35 C.A.; *Aslan* v. *Murphy* (*Nos.1 and 2*) and *Wynne* v. *Duke* [1990] 1 W.L.R. 766 C.A.

[8] January 15th 1989: H.A. 1988 s.141(2).

[9] s.1(1).

[10] H.A. 1988 s.19A.

[11] L.P.A. 1925 s.54(2); see above p. 34.

[12] P. Sparkes (1989) 18 *Anglo-American* 151, 157–159.

[13] (1882) 21 Ch.D. 9 C.A.

[14] *The Rent Acts* (Stevens, 11th ed., 1988) 229, citing *Halford's Executors* v. *Boden* [1953] E.G.D. 329 C.Ct.

[15] R.E. Megarry (1946) 62 *L.Q.R.* 323, 324; *Lawrance* v. *Hartwell* [1946] K.B. 553 C.A.; *Halford's Executors* v. *Boden* [1953] E.G.D. 329 C.Ct.; *Davies* v. *Benyon-Harris* (1931) 47 T.L.R. 424.

[16] [2000] A.C. 406 H.L.; S. Bright (2000) 116 *L.Q.R.* 7; M. Dixon [2000] *C.L.J.* 25; see below pp. 170–179.

2. Public sector

The term "secure tenancy" is used to describe a grant in the public sector that attracts "life-long" security, a term that embraces both leases and exclusive licences.[17] Despite this difference in the statutory framework there is actually very little difference between the two sectors, the only difference being the statutory reaffirmation that there is no point in trying to evade the creation of a secure tenancy by the grant of a licence to a person who has exclusive use of public sector self-contained accommodation.[18] There were initially some dicta which suggested that public sector security was attracted to accommodation which is non-exclusive[19] but *Westminster City Council* v. *Clarke*[20] decides that no security is possible in this case and that the public and private systems are the same.

3. A dwelling-house

To take the Rent Act 1977 as the progenitor of other modern legislation, a protected tenancy is a tenancy under which

"a dwelling house (which may be a house or part of a house) is let as a separate dwelling."[21]

This same definition applies to all other security regimes[22] and requires that a tenant should hold exclusive rights in one unit of self-contained residential accommodation.[23] Within this basic scope there are numerous exceptions—lettings to employees, student lettings and holiday lets and many others discussed in this chapter—where security may either be limited or removed completely.

In a simple case, a landlord lets a complete detached, semi-detached or terraced house[24] to a tenant who occupies it as his home. However the inclusion within the common definition of a tenancy of a *part* of a house ensures that protection extends to any tenant who has exclusive use of a self-contained part of a building—such as a flat, a maisonette, or a single room.[25] A series of disconnected rooms may be a dwelling-house if contained within a single building[26] but will not literally fall within the statutory definition if spread over several buildings, as for example at Sissinghurst Castle; this exclusion from protection is artificial and one hopes that the courts would be able to discover sufficient flexibility to overcome this drafting defect. Since 1974, there has been no

---

[17] s.79(3).

[18] s.79(1), replacing H.A. 1980 s.1.

[19] *Family H.Ass.* v. *Jones* [1990] 1 W.L.R. 779, 790, Balcombe L.J.; J. Warburton [1990] *Conv.* 397; also doubtful is *Swansea C.C.* v. *Hearn* (1991) 23 H.L.R. 284.

[20] [1992] 2 A.C. 288 H.L.; D.S. Cowan [1992] *Conv.* 285; *Bruton* v. *London & Quadrant H. Trust* [2000] A.C. 406, 413G, Lord Hoffmann.

[21] R.A. 1977 s.1(1).

[22] H.A. 1988 s.1(1) (assured tenancies); H.A. 1988 s.20 (assured shortholds); H.A. 1980 s.52 (protected shortholds); H.A. 1985 s.79 replacing H.A. 1980 s.1 (public sector secure).

[23] Security is removed where a tenant has self-contained accommodation but the landlord is resident in the same building; see below pp. 149–155.

[24] H.A. 1985 s.112 (secure tenancies); H.A. 1985 s.45(1) (assured tenancies including assured shortholds); the term is not defined in R.A. 1977.

[25] *Curl* v. *Angelo* [1948] 2 All E.R. 189; *Mohamed* v. *Manek* (1995) 27 H.L.R. 439 C.A.; *Uratemp Ventures Ltd.* v. *Collins* [1999] Times December 10th, Peter Gibson L.J.

[26] *Wimbush* v. *Cibulia* [1949] 2 K.B. 564 C.A.

difference between furnished and unfurnished property.[27] As explained below, the use of the word dwelling-*house* imports a requirement of a home with some degree of structural stability, and therefore excludes shacks, caravans, other mobile homes, and houseboats.[28]

4.   Self-contained accommodation

Residential accommodation must be self-contained in order to attract full security since the statutory rule is that a house (or part of one) must be let as a *separate* dwelling.[29] This test must be applied as things stood when the lease was granted, ignoring subsequent unauthorised alterations. It works well enough in a simple case in which there is a discrete package containing the essential living accommodation, including cooking facilities, living rooms, toilet, bathroom, and sleeping accommodation. According to the date and form of the letting the lease will either be a shorthold or a tenancy with full security.

Until recently there was some uncertainty about what accommodation had to be included in a dwelling-house, but illumination is provided by *Uratemp Ventures Ltd.* v. *Collins*.[30] Cooking facilities were held to be an essential attribute of a dwelling, and so there was no assured tenancy of Room 403, Viscount Hotel, Kensington, on the facts of the case, since there was neither a cooker nor any expectation that the tenant would provide one. Peter Gibson L.J. relied on the authoritative obiter statement in *Westminster C.C.* v. *Clarke*[31] that all essential living rooms necessary for sleeping and cooking must be included, though the bathroom and laundry facilities could be elsewhere. It may be questionable whether the absence of cooking facilities is a sensible criterion given the proliferation of fast food outlets.

Taken literally the statutory definition would preclude protection in any case where facilities for cooking, living or ablution were shared, and so destroy all the security enjoyed by many tenants, for example ones occupying self-contained bedsits but sharing a toilet or bathroom. However, special provision is made to protect some tenants in this position, permitting residential security despite the sharing of essential living accommodation as *between the tenants* themselves, though almost all protection is removed if any facilities are shared *with the landlord*.[32]

Again, taken literally, the statutory definition would remove protection where a self-contained unit of living accommodation is held by one tenant from a single landlord under two separate leases, since the requirement is that the unit is let as a separate dwelling, that is by one lease.[33] Landlords could exploit such a rule artificially, but the courts have avoided such an injustice by reading together multiple leases that are interdependent so that they are treated as forming a single lease.[34]

---

[27] R.A. 1974 s.1, in force August 14th 1974.

[28] See below pp. 179–183.

[29] R.A. 1977 s.1(1); H.A. 1988 s.1(1) (assured tenancies); H.A. 1988 s.20 (assured shortholds); H.A. 1980 s.52 (protected shortholds); H.A. 1985 s.79 replacing H.A. 1980 s.1 (public sector secure).

[30] [1999] Times, December 10th C.A. Mance L.J. dissenting thought that cooking facilities were relevant but not decisive.

[31] [1992] 2 A.C. 288, 298, Lord Templeman; *Parkins* v. *Westminster C.C.* [1998] 1 E.G.L.R. 22, Chadwick L.J.

[32] See below p. 147.

[33] *Kavanagh* v. *Lyroudias* [1985] 1 All E.R. 560 C.A.

[34] *Hampstead Way Investments Ltd.* v. *Lewis-Weare* [1985] 1 W.L.R. 164, 171, Lord Brandon.

5. Sharing facilities with the landlord

Any requirement to share living accommodation with the landlord will prevent any security (including even the minimum entitlement to a short hold) attaching to those rooms that are occupied exclusively. For example in *Mortgage Corporation Ltd.* v. *Ubah*[35] a tenant of a whole house agreed to move into a part of it, allowing the owner to live in the other part, on the basis of joint use of the kitchen. So the tenant's new accommodation was not self-contained and the tenant, who was formerly protected in his occupation of the whole, afterwards enjoyed no security in any part. Indeed the same is true whenever the landlord is resident in the same house.[36] Historically, a restricted contract arose where a person occupied on terms that he would use some living accommodation in common with the landlord (with or without others), but even that minimal protection[37] is absent where the occupation was first granted after early 1989. However, the most recent case, *Miller* v. *Eyo,*[38] emphasises that if the landlord wishes to reserve any right of entry it has to be very clear. An assured tenant had exclusive use of a bedroom, with a shared living room, kitchen and bathroom, and also exclusive rights to another bedroom, but the problem was that the landlady herself moved into this extra bedroom. It was held that the landlady had unlawfully evicted the tenant; to find that the occupier was protected from eviction involved finding that she was indeed a tenant, and that in turn involved a decision that she had exclusive use of the accommodation to the exclusion of the landlady. This was because the landlady had not explicitly reserved rights to herself.

6. Sharing facilities with other tenants

Careful consideration is required in any case in which any accommodation is shared since, taken literally, the requirement that it must form a separate dwelling would preclude protection whenever *any* rooms were shared.[39] Clearly no prejudice accrues to a tenant from joint use of a staircase or front door. Problems start when a person is given exclusive occupation of some living accommodation on the basis that he will share other facilities, for example a bathroom and/or kitchen, with other occupants. Each private sector code of protection gives some leeway where non-essential accommodation is shared. Suppose that a tenant occupies some separate accommodation (a bedroom and kitchen) but on terms that that other accommodation (a kitchen) must be shared, and suppose further that the only reason for removing that tenant's security of tenure is that sharing. The separate accommodation is deemed in such a case to be self-contained,[40] a deeming provision that has the effect of restoring full security or allowing the shorthold assurance. This provision should be applied where the tenant was required to share with any person nominated by the landlord, unless it is clear that the landlord is specifically

---

[35] (1997) 29 H.L.R. 489 C.A.
[36] See below pp. 162–165.
[37] R.A. 1977 s.21; *Gray* v. *Brown* [1993] 1 E.G.L.R. 119 C.A. (grant 1978); see below pp. 164–165.
[38] (1999) 31 H.L.R. 306 C.A.
[39] *Baker* v. *Turner* [1950] A.C. 401 H.L.; R.E. Megarry (1950) 66 *L.Q.R.* 446; *Central Y.M.C.A. H.Ass.* v. *Saunders* (1990) 23 H.L.R. 212 C.A.
[40] R.A. 1977 s.22(1); H.A. 1988 s.3 (assured and assured shorthold).

included as a potential sharer.[41] Use of the shared accommodation is also protected since there is a separate legislative provision to the effect that the right to it cannot be terminated independently by any subsequent agreement[42] or by court order,[43] though the tenant is compelled to observe his contractual promise to share with other tenants.[44] Where a head landlord grants self-contained accommodation to a tenant and the tenant grants a sub-tenancy of part, the tenant retains his security as against the head landlord even if he is sharing some accommodation with the sub-tenant. The sub-tenant does not acquire security under this provision and presumably occupation by the tenant will usually mean that the sub-tenant has a resident landlord.[45]

In the *public sector* accommodation must be truly self-contained or there is no "lifelong" security.[46]

B. SELF-CONTAINED ACCOMMODATION AT THE END OF A LONG LEASE

A long lease is one granted for a term exceeding 21 years. At the end of a long lease at a low rent, the tenant will not lose his home, since the lease will be continued automatically by part I of the Landlord and Tenant Act 1954. In the past the tenant may have been protected by the Rent Act 1977 but where the term date falls after 1999 he may acquire a fully assured tenancy.[47] Naturally the rent will rise. However the tenant has a continuing home and a continuing right to enfranchise (that is to buy the freehold).[48] The statutory continuation of the lease extends only to that part of the property contained in the lease that is occupied for residential purposes, a rule which may limit the enfranchisable unit.

Continuing residential security is dependent upon the tenant meeting the requirements for protection under the appropriate short residential code, that is formerly the Rent Act 1977 and now the assured tenancy scheme.[49] One requirement is personal residence.[50] The accommodation must also fulfil the requirements for protection. The physical extent of the new lease is determined by the extent of the property occupied for residential purposes.[51] If part is sub-let, this will be excluded from the land to which security attaches.[52] However in many cases the courts have avoided unfair results by relying on the relaxed view of Rent Act occupation: if the tenant intends to reoccupy the

---

[41] *Stanley* v. *Crompton* [1951] 1 All E.R. 859 C.A.; *Gray* v. *Brown* [1993] 1 E.G.L.R. 119 C.A.; *Miller* v. *Eyo* (1999) 31 H.L.R. 306 C.A.

[42] R.A. 1977 s.22(3), (8); H.A. 1988 s.3(3).

[43] R.A. 1977 s.22(5); H.A. 1988 s.3(1).

[44] R.A. 1977 s.22(4)–(8); H.A. 1988 s.3(4).

[45] R.A. 1977 s.23; H.A. 1988 s.4; *Baker* v. *Turner* [1950] A.C. 401 H.L.

[46] H.A. 1985 s.79.

[47] See below pp. 393–394.

[48] L.Ref.A. 1967 s.16 (house); L.R.H.U.D.A. 1993 s.59 (flat—further renewal but no security of tenure after grant of new lease); *Galinski* v. *McHugh* [1989] 1 E.G.L.R. 109 C.A.

[49] L.T.A. 1954 s.2(1).

[50] s.2(2).

[51] *Baron* v. *Phillips* [1978] 2 E.G.L.R. 59 C.A.

[52] *Regalian Securities Ltd.* v. *Ramsden* [1981] 1 W.L.R. 611 H.L. (parts sub-let for residential purposes are included).

part presently sub-let he may have sufficient residential qualification to claim protection for the whole unit including both what he actually occupies and also what he has sub-let.[53]

Whatever unit is isolated by the residence test must satisfy two restrictive conditions: (1) it must form self-contained accommodation when the long lease expires; and (2) it must have been let as separate residential accommodation. However the short residential codes are modified to ensure that the second test is applied when the long lease *ends* and not when it was *originally granted*. Otherwise the normal rule that these are assessed at the date of the grant would be a real trap in the case of a long lease: sub-lettings and divisions are only to be expected during the course of a long period of ownership, tenants quite reasonably seek to recoup some of the value of the premium paid to buy the lease by dealings with parts, and so the unit occupied at the term date is very often different from that let at the outset. Any potential unfairness is alleviated by statute[54]: in determining whether the property is self-contained and how it was let, the nature of the property or part at the time of the creation is presumed to be the same as at the time that the question arises. Hence in the case of a long lease one should look at the unit *remaining at the end of the lease* and see whether it is self-contained and whether it is in the occupation of the tenant. Thus if a tenant takes a house on two floors, and sub-lets the upper floor, the *sub-tenant* can acquire security if the upper floor is self contained, and so may the *tenant* if what he retains is also self-contained.[55]

One trap can produce incredibly unfair results. This is where a tenant divides the unit not by subletting but by an assignment of part. In *Grosvenor Estates Belgravia* v. *Cochran*[56] a house was let on a long lease, but 39 days before the end of the headlease the basement was sub-let for a period of three years. Because the term of the sub-lease exceeded the term remaining, this acted not as a true sub-lease but as an assignment of that part.[57] The tenant of the basement claimed security at the end of the long lease, but this claim failed. The basement had been let with the whole of the rest of the house and not as a separate dwelling. Although the Court of Appeal was bound by authority[58] to take this narrow view of the statutory wording,[59] the legislative intention was surely to apply a much simpler test: whether accommodation is self-contained ought to be determined at the end of a long lease.

C. EXCLUSIVE POSSESSION

Security of tenure legislation operates where there is a grant of the right to exclusive use of self-contained residential accommodation. *Street* v. *Mountford*[60] creates a complementary rule that the acid test for the existence of a tenancy is the presence of a grant of

[53] *Haines* v. *Herbert* [1963] 1 W.L.R. 1401 C.A.
[54] L.T.A. 1954 s.22(3).
[55] *Regalian Securities Ltd.* v. *Ramsden* [1981] 1 W.L.R. 611 H.L.
[56] [1991] 2 E.G.L.R. 83 C.A.; P.F. Smith [1991] *Conv.* 393.
[57] See below p. 294.
[58] *Crown Lodge (Surbiton) Investments Ltd.* v. *Nalecz* [1967] 1 W.L.R. 647, 652, Winn L.J., followed in *Cochran* at 86.
[59] L.T.A. 1954 s.22(3).
[60] [1985] A.C. 809 H.L.

exclusive possession.[61] However this is not quite a litmus test, because there are some categories of exclusive licences where the circumstances show that only a licence is intended despite a grant of exclusive possession.[62] Without it the occupier is merely a licensee. Landlords are prevented from granting rights to self-contained residential accommodation with one hand and, with the other, denying the occupier his rights as a residential tenant though the principle was more useful to occupiers in the past when it was the gate which guarded access to "life-long" security, than it is now that the only issue is the right to a six month short hold. When *Street* v. *Mountford* reached the House of Lords, Lord Templeman reaffirmed three essential *indicia* of a tenancy,[63] that is

(1) a grant of exclusive possession
(2) for a term
(3) at a rent.

Most fundamental is the first of these tests since a lease must confer the right to exclude all others from the property.

1.   The leading case

Street v. *Mountford* decided that a tenant could not contract out of the security of the Rent Act 1977. A series of earlier Court of Appeal decisions had attached importance to the intention of the parties, thus appearing to allow landlords to evade the Rent Acts merely by expressing an intention to do so. But in *Street* v. *Mountford*,[64] Lord Templeman reasserted orthodox doctrine in forceful terms, resulting in the single most important statement of the lease/licence distinction, and one that has attracted much comment.[65]

Street, a landlord and a solicitor in Bournemouth, entered into an agreement with a Mrs Mountford which gave her the right to occupy two furnished rooms in Boscombe for £37 a week. This accommodation was self-contained, so that Mrs Mountford did have a right to exclusive possession of the flat. Mrs Mountford was not obliged to share the room with any one else. *Street* v. *Mountford* was, therefore, an unpromising case for argument on behalf of the landlord, since the occupier undoubtedly did enjoy exclusive possession, a point conceded in the Lords. Superficially Mrs Mountford's agreement displayed the three *indicia* of a tenancy, since she had a weekly term, paid a rent, and had exclusive use of self-contained residential accommodation. Protection under the Rent Act 1977 ensued and, as the House of Lords held, Mrs Mountford was entitled to seek registration of a fair rent.[66] Such a lease granted after early 1989 would create an assured tenancy and after early 1997 an assured shorthold. Two related arguments were advanced on behalf of the landlord, Mr Street. The document stated that "this personal

---

[61] Woodfall 1.020–1.033; Bright & Gilbert 126–154; Davey 1–12; Evans & Smith (5th.) ch.3; Garner (2nd) ch.2.

[62] See below pp. 170–179.

[63] At 816G. Older cases are collected in *Baker* v. *Turner* [1950] A.C. 401, 414, Lord Porter; see *Parkins* v. *Westminster C.C.* (1998) 30 H.L.R. 894 C.A.

[64] [1985] A.C. 809 H.L.

[65] S. Anderson (1985) 48 *M.L.R.* 712; S. Tromans [1983] *C.L.J.* 351; R. Street [1985] *Conv.* 328 H.L.; S. Bridge [1986] *Conv.* 344 H.L.; A.J. Waite (1987) 50 *M.L.R.* 226.

[66] See below pp. 227–237.

licence is not assignable" showing that the landlord's intention was to create only a licence. Again Mrs Mountford signed a statement that she recognised that her licence was not to have Rent Act protection. These boil down to one common argument, that the parties are free to contract to grant exclusive possession and yet to agree that it shall be given only by way of licence. Previous Court of Appeal decisions had made both arguments tenable, since otherwise *Street* v. *Mountford* could not have reached the Lords,[67] yet both arguments were crushed. Of course parties to all other forms of dealings with property are free to make them personal simply by expressing the intention to do so,[68] but it is a time-honoured principle that the test for exclusive possession under a tenancy agreement is substantive. *Street* v. *Mountford* was therefore an easy case, decided unanimously in favour of Mrs Mountford. The clear and simple conceptual test for the existence of a lease may be difficult to apply to variant facts.

In almost all cases of single occupation, *Street* v. *Mountford* requires that a residential occupier should be either a tenant or a lodger[69] depending only on the presence or absence of exclusive possession.[70] However in *Brooker Settled Estates Ltd.* v. *Ayers*[71] the Court of Appeal said that the true touchstone is exclusive possession, rather than characterisation of the agreement as either for lodging or for a tenancy, a result apparently accepted by Lord Templeman for cases involving multiple occupiers.[72] So the true position is that the category of licensee includes both lodgers and also some other non-exclusive occupiers.

2. Exclusive possession based on rights

Exclusive possession is the right to exclude all others from the property, and this must include the landlord. Usually it takes the form of exclusive occupation by the tenant personally to the exclusion of all others. A sub-letting is tested in the same way to see whether there has been a grant of exclusive possession to a sub-tenant,[73] but even if there has been and the right to occupation has been conceded to a sub-tenant the sub-landlord retains exclusive possession consisting of the right to receive rents and profits from the land.[74] Nor would a sub-licence detract from the tenant's right to exclusive possession, as demonstrated by Mrs Mountford's understandable decision to share occupation of her home with her husband.[75] Exclusive possession is determined by legal right, that is by construction of the contract between owner and occupier. Legal entitlement to exclude all others marks out the occupier as a tenant,[76] it being the *right* to do so which is decisive, rather than the factual operation of the agreement. A person may

---

[67] The litigation cost £40,000: (1985) 129 *S.J.* 852.

[68] J. Hill (1996) 16 *L.S.* 200.

[69] *Monmouth B.C.* v. *Marlog* (1994) 27 H.L.R. 30 C.A.

[70] [1985] A.C. 809, 817H–818A.

[71] (1987) 54 P. & C.R. 165 C.A.

[72] [1990] 1 A.C. 417, 459G–460A; *Aslan* v. *Murphy (No.1)* [1990] 1 W.L.R. 766, 770F–G, Lord Donaldson M.R.

[73] *Brent L.B.C.* v. *Cronin* (1997) 30 H.L.R. 43 C.A. However if two people share the use of a house this is to be seen as house sharing rather than as a sub-letting: *Monmouth B.C.* v. *Marlog* (1994) 27 H.L.R. 30 C.A.

[74] *AG Securities* v. *Vaughan* [1990] A.C. 417, 455, Lord Templeman; *Camden L.B.C.* v. *Shortlife Community Housing* (1992) 25 H.L.R. 330, 347, Millett J.

[75] (1985) 49 P. & C.R. 324, 326.

[76] *Heslop* v. *Burns* [1974] 1 W.L.R. 1241, 1251G, Scarman L.J.; this is confirmed by *Street*.

be in undisturbed occupation for a number of years, and yet have no right to insist that it should continue. For example in *Shell-Mex & B.P. Ltd.* v. *Manchester Garages Ltd.*,[77] a company's undisturbed occupation of a filling station for four years was quite consistent with the owner's right to interrupt that occupation, and the same principle applies to residential property. However, as explained immediately below, artificial terms and pretences are excluded in determining what agreement has been reached.

Leases usually contain reservations by the landlord of limited *rights of access* to the property for specific purposes—perhaps to enter to view the state of repair of the property, or to carry out repairs, or to show prospective buyers round the property. This does not affect the tenant's exclusive possession. Thus in *Street* v. *Mountford* the landlord reserved the right to inspect the condition of the rooms,[78] as landlords often do, but this merely served to emphasise the fact that he did not have any general right of access to Mrs Mountford's flat. If the landlord could come in anyway, why did he need to reserve a right of access to view the state of condition? Rights to re-enter the property by terminating the lease for breach of covenant obviously do not remove the tenant's entitlement to exclusive possession while the lease continues.[79] Special consideration is required of cases where access is given to allow for cleaning or the provision of other services.[80]

3.   Pretences

The parties' description of their transaction is not conclusive, a point repeated many times in the case law. A bald description of a written occupation agreement as a "licence" does not dictate a judicial construction of it as a licence. It may be mislabelled.[81] After all a document which reflects precisely the true agreement between the parties may nevertheless be misleading in its language, suggesting that it falls into one legal category (a licence) when properly analysed it falls into another category (a lease).[82] Lord Templeman said in *Street* v. *Mountford* that a five-pronged digging implement is a fork, even if its manufacturer calls it a spade.[83] The substance of the arrangement must be tested. In *Facchini* v. *Bryson*,[84] to take one random example, a service tenancy granted by an employer to his employee displayed all the features of a tenancy, apart from the last clause of the document which said that nothing was to be construed so as to create a tenancy, but this obvious drafting device was ignored by the court so that the arrangement did indeed create a tenancy. Similarly in *Street* v. *Mountford*[85] the House of Lords ignored the statement that "this personal licence is not assignable" as well as the "coda" by which Mrs Mountford recognised that a licence in that form was not to have Rent Act protection.

---

[77] [1971] 1 W.L.R. 612 C.A.

[78] Cl. 3.

[79] *Southampton Community Health Services N.H.S. Trust* v. *Crown Estate Commissioners* [1997] E.G.C.S. 155 Ch.D.

[80] See below pp. 158–162.

[81] *Aslan* v. *Murphy* [1990] 1 W.L.R. 766, 770D, Lord Donaldson.

[82] *Hadjiloucas* v. *Crean* [1988] 1 W.L.R. 1006, 1019F, Mustill L.J.

[83] [1985] A.C. 809, 819F; [1990] 1 W.L.R. 766, 770F–G, Lord Donaldson M.R. However the writer uses garden forks with four tines!

[84] [1952] 1 T.L.R. 1386 C.A.

[85] [1985] A.C. 809 H.L.; see above p. 150.

A pretence is a term that misstates the real agreement reached between the parties. Many landlords were tempted to insert artificial provisions in occupation agreements in order to exclude the right to exclusive possession, and so to preclude Rent Act protection. However, in order to determine the correct meaning of the agreement it is first necessary to exclude any provisions which are artificial before construing the genuine terms which are left.[86] Artificiality may undermine an entire agreement or some of the clauses in an otherwise unobjectionable agreement, two possibilities which should be considered separately.[87] "Pretence" has proved to be a better test that "sham", since Diplock L.J. restricted the second term in *Snook* v. *London & West Riding Investments Ltd.*[88] to tax avoidance schemes involving a *mutual* intention to deceive by both parties to the agreement.[89] In residential letting practice the intention to deceive is the landlord's,[90] so that there is rarely a "sham"—one rare exception being *Bhopal* v. *Walia*[91] in which case the tenant went along with his landlord's attempted deception of a lender. Unilateral "pretences" are very frequent.[92] The best examples are the sharing arrangements in *Somma* v. *Hazelhurst* and *Antoniades* v. *Villiers* discussed below[93] but there are a number of more recent illustrations.[94]

The parol evidence rule, which ensures that any contract that has been reduced to writing consists only of its written terms, is often strengthened by an express term that the document contains the entire contract between the parties. This stacks the dice in favour of the landlord. However the rule is riddled with exceptions and considerable help is at hand for occupiers. It may, for example, be possible to argue that the real relationship between the parties was created by an oral grant[95] that predated the written document, for example where a flat was advertised in a newspaper as "To let".[96]

4.   Factors to determine whether an agreement is genuine

Landlords frequently adopt *standard form* licence agreements. For example, the form of agreement in the *AG Securities* case was settled by counsel for use at a number of properties. Unthinking adoption of a standard form leaves the owner vulnerable to the charge that the document did not reflect a real agreement,[97] especially if the *pro forma* agreement does not fit the particular property.[98] More generally, the *language* of a

---

[86]   *Street* v. *Mountford* [1985] A.C. 809, 825C, Lord Templeman; *Hadjiloucas* v. *Crean* [1988] 1 W.L.R. 1006, 1013–1014, Purchas L.J.; *Antoniades* v. *Villiers* [1990] 1 A.C. 437, 445G, Bingham L.J. in C.A.

[87]   *Aslan* v. *Murphy (No.1)* [1990] 1 W.L.R 766 C.A.; J.E. Martin [1990] *Conv.* 60.

[88]   [1967] 2 Q.B. 786, 802D; A. Nichol (1981) 44 *M.L.R.* 21.

[89]   *Antoniades* v. *Villiers* [1990] 1 A.C. 437, 444G Bingham L.J. in C.A.; *Sturolson & Co.* v. *Weniz* [1984] 2 E.G.L.R. 121, 122J, Eveleigh L.J.; *Hoggett* v. *Hoggett* (1979) 39 P. & C.R. 121.

[90]   *Aslan* v. *Murphy (No.1)* [1990] 1 W.L.R. 766, 770H, Lord Donaldson M.R. ("pressure on both parties to pretend, albeit for different reasons").

[91]   (2000) 32 H.L.R. 302 C.A.

[92]   *AG Securities* v. *Vaughan* [1990] 1 A.C. 417, 462H, Lord Templeman; *Stribling* v. *Wickham* [1989] 2 E.G.L.R. 35 C.A.; *Aslan* v. *Murphy (No.1)* [1990] 1 W.L.R. 766 C.A.

[93]   See below pp. 155–158.

[94]   *Nicholaou* v. *Pitt* [1989] 1 E.G.L.R. 84 C.A. (sharing); *Skipton B.S.* v. *Clayton* (1993) 66 P. & C.R. 223 C.A. (licence for life).

[95]   L.P.A. 1925 s.54(2).

[96]   *O'Malley* v. *Seymour* [1979] 1 E.G.L.R. 116 C.A.

[97]   *Hadjiloucas* v. *Crean* [1988] 1 W.L.R. 1006, 1023D.

[98]   *Demuren* v. *Seal Estates Ltd.* [1979] 1 E.G.L.R. 102 C.A. (inappropriate room number).

document may lead to a decision that it is mislabelled as a licence.[99] Internal inconsistency may exist between the description of the document, the rights of occupancy, and the description of the parties.[100] Over-egging the pudding, by excessive insistence on the fact of personal licences, may arouse suspicion.[101] However, "marking" drafting for consistency[102] has fallen from favour because, although it catches poorly drafted licence agreements well enough, better-drafted but more iniquitous agreements are left to slip through the net.

The reality of a lease may displace the language of a licence, where evidence of the *negotiations* and other conduct of the parties before signature of the agreements shows that the written agreements are a pretence. In *Antoniades*, for example, the occupiers made clear before taking the flat that they wished to use a double bed, demonstrating clearly that they were "an item".[103] Written agreements can also be broken if it can be shown that the landlord represented to the occupants that particular provisions of the written agreement would not be enforced, or were mere technicalities.[104] In contrast with prior negotiations, the courts have diminished the significance of *later conduct*[105] and "the actual mode of accommodation".[106] Common sense suggests that the real intentions are best found by looking at the working out of the agreement in practice, in the period before a dispute arose, and later conduct may be relevant in ascertaining whether a particular provision is artificial.[107] Thus a term that the occupier should vacate each day between 10.30 a.m. and noon, *with his belongings*, just might be genuine, but the course of events is highly likely to display its artificiality.[108] Failure by the landlord to maximise his income is inevitably suspicious.[109] Consideration of actual conduct is the only method of revealing a pretence that is latent in the intentions of the landlord.[110] *Relationships* between the parties are obviously relevant. Married couples and cohabitees should be viewed jointly as tenants of the property. Sharing between strangers gave more scope for avoidance of the old security of tenure legislation, a fact recognised in *AG Securities*.[111] Between these extremes lie cases where friends share, an arrangement that is consistent with a joint tenancy[112] or with separate licences.

---

[99] T.M. Aldridge (1974) 118 *S.J.* 3; J.E. Adams (1976) 120 *S.J.* 125.

[100] The "sharer": *Sturolson & Co.* v. *Weniz* [1984] 2 E.G.L.R. 121 C.A., a case now overruled.

[101] *Somma* v. *Hazelhurst* [1978] 1 W.L.R. 1014, 1022.

[102] A. Waite (1980) 130 *N.L.J.* 939, 959.

[103] [1990] 1 A.C. 417, 463D, Lord Templeman; *Aslan* v. *Murphy* [1990] 1 W.L.R. 766, 770F, Lord Donaldson M.R.

[104] *Gisborne* v. *Burton* [1989] Q.B. 390 C.A.

[105] *Walsh* v. *Griffiths-Jones* [1978] 2 All E.R. 1002; *Sturolson & Co.* v. *Weniz* [1984] 2 E.G.L.R. 121 C.A., a case rejected at [1985] A.C. 809, 826A. However, a right is not lost simply because it is not enforced.

[106] *Stribling* v. *Wickham* [1989] 2 E.G.L.R. 35, 36H, Parker L.J.

[107] At 36H.

[108] *Markou* v. *Da Silvaesa* (1986) 52 P. & C.R. 204; *Aslan* v. *Murphy (No.1)* [1990] 1 W.L.R. 766 C.A. Licensees in the social sector must have access to their homes for 24 hours each day; see e.g. the Charter for Residents in Temporary Housing (Housing Corporation, 1998), section 3.

[109] [1990] 1 A.C. 417, 463G, Lord Templeman, 469E, Lord Oliver.

[110] *Wang* v. *Wei* (1976), cited by A. Waite (1980) 130 *N.L.J.* 939, 941.

[111] [1990] 1 A.C. 417, 454C, Lord Templeman.

[112] *Hadjiloucas* v. *Crean* [1988] 1 W.L.R. 1006 C.A. disapproved at [1990] 1 A.C. 417, 465, Lord Templeman.

Although a joint approach is important evidence,[113] it may in some cases be consistent with genuinely severable occupation rights.[114]

When determining whether parties have recorded a genuine agreement, the terms must be checked against the *physical scope of the accommodation* to be shared. In *Somma v. Hazelhurst*[115] an unmarried couple occupied a bed sitting room 22 feet by 18 feet containing two single beds, so that the introduction of a third occupant was unrealistic, and no one could imagine that any woman would agree to share such accommodation with an unknown man.[116] The addition of a small sitting room made no difference in *Antoniades v. Villiers.*[117] A contract that requires overcrowding should not be upheld as a genuine term.[118]

D. JOINT OCCUPATION: LEASE OR LICENCE?

When a self-contained house or flat is provided for occupation by a group of people— perhaps a cohabiting couple or a group of students—there are broadly three possibilities: they may collectively form a single tenant or they may form a group of individual licensees sharing with each other, or they may be tenants of individual parts of the whole. Differentiation of these cases depends upon the test of exclusive possession as determined from the contractual rights of the parties. This leaves considerable scope for drafting which aims to secure that occupation is shared between the occupiers or between the occupiers and the landlord and, since any genuine contractual provision for sharing will prevent the creation of a lease, attention is necessarily directed towards the identification of those agreements or terms of agreements which are pretences.

1. Strangers sharing

Residential sharing arrangements led to a mass of inconsistent Court of Appeal decisions,[119] now clarified by the House of Lords in two combined appeals.[120] In *Antoniades v. Villiers* a couple took a self-contained flat, intending to co-habit, and they were held to be joint tenants. The landlord's attempt to create two separate residential licences was

---

[113] [1990] 1 A.C. 417, 475C, Lord Jauncey.

[114] *Stribling* v. *Wickham* [1989] 2 E.G.L.R. 35 C.A.

[115] [1978] 1 W.L.R. 1014 C.A.; *Mikeover Ltd.* v. *Brady* [1989] 3 All E.R. 618, 622e, Slade L.J.

[116] [1985] A.C. 809, 825G, Lord Templeman; P. Robson & P.Q. Watchman [1980] *Conv.* 27, 39–45. Even more surprising was the term in *Aslan* v. *Murphy* [1990] 1 W.L.R. 766 C.A. requiring sharing of a room measuring 4ft. 3 ins. by 12ft 6ins.

[117] [1990] 1 A.C. 417, 464, Lord Templeman.

[118] An argument based on overcrowding was rejected in *Somma* v. *Hazelhurst* [1978] 1 W.L.R. 1014, 1028G–1029B, but the general decision in that case is now overruled.

[119] *Somma* v. *Hazelhurst* [1978] 1 W.L.R. 1014; *Demuren* v. *Seal Estates Ltd.* [1979] 1 E.G.L.R. 102 C.A.; *Walsh* v. *Griffith-Jones* [1978] 2 All E.R. 1002; K. Gray [1979] *C.L.J.* 38; *Aldrington Garages Ltd.* v. *Fielder* (1978) 37 P. & C.R. 461; *Sturolson & Co.* v. *Weniz* [1984] 2 E.G.L.R. 121 C.A.; *Markou* v. *Da Silvaesa* (1987) 52 P. & C.R. 204; *Crancour Ltd.* v. *Da Silvaesa* (1987) 52 P. & C.R. 204; *Brooker Settled Estates Ltd.* v. *Ayers* (1987) 54 P. & C.R. 165 C.A.; *Hadjiloucas* v. *Crean* [1988] 1 W.L.R. 1006; *Antoniades* v. *Villiers* [1990] 1 A.C. 437 C.A.; P.V. Baker (1988) 104 *L.Q.R.* 511; P.F. Smith [1988] *Conv.* 305; *AG Securities* v. *Vaughan* [1990] 1 A.C. 419 C.A.; P.V. Baker (1988) 104 *L.Q.R.* 173; Woodfall 3.002–3.004.

[120] *AG Securities* v. *Vaughan* and *Antoniades* v. *Villiers* [1990] 1 A.C. 417 H.L.; P.V. Baker (1989) 105 *L.Q.R.* 165; S. Bright (1991) 11 *O.J.L.S.* 136; C. Harpum [1989] *C.L.J.* 19; J. Hill (1989) 52 *M.L.R.* 408; H. Wallace (1990) 41 *N.I.L.Q.* 143; P. Sparkes [1989] *J.S.W.L.* 293; P.V. Baker (1989) 105 *L.Q.R.* 165.

a pretence, which was ignored by the House. However, there is still scope for sharing arrangements to create genuine licences, as shown by the other co-joined appeal, *AG Securities* v. *Vaughan*. Four occupants of a shared flat who each moved in on a different day, paid a different rent, and were strangers before moving in, were held by the House to be licensees.[121] No individual occupier had a right to exclusive occupation of the whole flat,[122] so that each held a licence.

Where one person is allowed into occupation of a twin bed-sit—meaning a single room with two single beds—the owner can legitimately and genuinely impose terms that the occupier will be required to share when another occupant is introduced. This was precisely the position in *AG Securities* after the first of four flat sharers had moved in. Since at that time that first arrival had exclusive occupation of the whole house, but no right to retain exclusivity, that is no exclusive possession.[123] So it was too in *Parkins* v. *Westminster C.C.*[124] in which case two schoolteachers each had a licence to occupy one bedroom in a three-bedroomed flat, sharing a living room, kitchen, bathroom and lavatory. When Parkins was sacked in 1992 it was held that he could also be evicted from the flat, since his shared right to it created no more than a licence.

2. Couples sharing

Artificially splitting the totality of possession between two joint occupiers could yield rich dividends for landlords, as illustrated by the success of the landlord in *Somma* v. *Hazelhurst*,[125] but the authority of that case has been terminated by the dual attack of *Street* and *Antoniades*. In *Somma* v. *Hazelhurst* the owner entered into two separate agreements one with a Mr Hazelhurst and the other with his girlfriend—Miss Savelli—for use of a double bed-sitting room for 12 weeks for £120 each. Each was given the right to share the room with each other (which was all right), but also with the landlord Somma or another person nominated by him (which was decidedly dubious). The room, it should be said, measured 22 feet by 18 feet and contained two single beds. If these provisions were to be taken at face value, neither occupier had exclusive occupation since, to take just the least objectionable provision, they were required to share occupation with each other. The Court of Appeal accepted that view. Each occupier understood the agreement that he or she was signing, had agreed to forego exclusive possession, and as such there were two licences rather than one joint lease. On the face of the agreements this was unquestionably correct: total exclusivity was removed by the provision that Hazelhurst had to share with Savelli, and she with him, so that neither had that exclusive possession which was the essential hallmark of any tenancy.

---

[121] *Hadjiloucas* v. *Crean* [1988] 1 W.L.R. 1006 C.A.; as decided in *AG Securities* [1990] 1 A.C. 417, 465E–F, Lord Templeman.
[122] There was no exclusive occupation of any particular bedroom because of the genuine arrangement that the owner could reallocate the rooms when any individual occupier left: [1990] 1 A.C. 417, 460E, Lord Templeman; *Hadjiloucas* v. *Crean* [1988] 1 W.L.R. 1006, 1023A–B, Mustill L.J.; also *Brennan* v. *Lambeth L.B.C.* (1998) 30 H.L.R. 481 C.A. (Tooting Bec Hostel). A case where this was successfully argued is *Gray* v. *Brown* [1993] 1 E.G.L.R. 119 C.A.
[123] [1990] 1 A.C. 417, 470G, Lord Oliver.
[124] (1998) 30 H.L.R. 894 C.A.
[125] [1978] 1 W.L.R. 1014 C.A.; M. Partington (1979) 42 *M.L.R.* 331; K. Gray (1979) 38 *C.L.J.* 38.

But the decision was absurd. Were it to be true, any landlord could have avoided the Rent Act by sharp drafting. The flaw in the appellate court's reasoning was the assumption that the documentation correctly reflected the legal arrangement between the couple, when it patently did not. Lord Templeman observed in *Street*[126] that the whole purpose was that Hazelhurst and Miss Savelli might live together "in undisturbed quasi-connubial bliss"—that is jointly—so it was quite wrong to accept as genuine a licence which gave two partial rights to occupy one room. As a result of *Street* we now know that the arrangement in *Somma* should have been construed as a single grant of exclusive possession to the couple as joint tenants. A later Court of Appeal in *Antoniades* reverted to the *Somma* heresy and asserted the validity of a clause requiring sharing of a flat containing a bedroom and a small lounge, arguing that a third occupier could be introduced into the lounge, which drew the response from the occupiers that the room "was not big enough to put the goldfish bowl in". At the time of the letting, the landlord and the couple discussed whether they were to have two single beds or a double bed, and by opting for a double bed they could not have expressed more clearly their intention to take jointly. A second burst of fire from the House of Lords, which reversed the Court of Appeal ruling in Antoniades and decided that the couple were joint tenants, ensures that for the future any *Somma* clause allowing the landlord to nominate another sharer is suspicious,[127] especially if the accommodation is small.

3. Splitting the rent

If joint occupiers are all jointly liable to pay a single rent, the strong presumption must be that they are jointly taking the entire accommodation as tenants. On the other hand, separate agreements are indicated by separate occupation rights for a shifting population with each occupier paying a genuinely separate rent.[128] What about letting jointly but splitting the rent, so that (say) each of two occupiers pays a half of the total rent? In *Mikeover Ltd.* v. *Brady*[129] an unmarried couple rented a two-room flat, the layout making it clear that they took it as a couple. By two separate licence agreements each promised to share with the other and each agreed to pay a separate rent of £86.66 monthly which the Court of Appeal regarded as genuinely separate rents, like those in *AG Securities* and which therefore pointed to separate licences. However since the Court of Appeal reformed the agreements to find joint occupation in *Mikeover* surely they should have reformed the rent agreement as well? As the case was actually decided it provides an unwarranted escape route from joint letting arrangements, but one suspects that it stands as an authority only because the occupiers did not appeal to the Lords.

4. Sharing with the landlord or his nominee

Somma,[130] *Antoniades*, and *Mikeover* all concerned licence agreements that included a provision that the occupiers should share with the landlord or (more realistically) with

---

[126] [1985] A.C. 809, 825G. Two cases were disapproved: *Aldrington Garages Ltd.* v. *Fielder* (1978) 37 P. & C.R. 461; *Sturolson & Co.* v. *Weniz* [1984] 2 E.G.L.R. 121.

[127] An example is *Mikeover*, discussed immediately below.

[128] *AG Securities* v. *Vaughan* [1990] 1 A.C. 417 H.L.; *Stribling* v. *Wickham* [1989] 2 E.G.L.R. 35 C.A.

[129] [1989] 3 All E.R. 618 C.A.; J.L. Barton (1990) 106 *L.Q.R.* 215.

[130] [1978] 1 W.L.R. 1014 C.A.

a person nominated by the landlord. Indeed *Somma* made this a standard term of many licences. This clause may be perfectly valid where strangers share a twin bedsit,[131] so that one occupier leaves independently of the other, but it is quite unrealistic where a couple share a bedsit or more particularly a bed. By overruling *Somma*[132] and rejecting this clause in *Antoniades*,[133] the House of Lords has shown that this clause will often be treated as a pretence. Validity of a sharing provision depends upon finding a real intention that the original occupiers should share with future strangers.

There are a number of subsequent cases. In *Duke* v. *Wynne*[134] Lord Donaldson differentiated between cases where a person is entitled to exclusive possession unless and until required to share and a case where the only right is to share. In the particular case, which concerned a three-bedroomed house let by owner while deciding whether to sell it, the Court of Appeal decided that exclusive possession had been granted and the tenant had Rent Act protection. Conversely *Monmouth B.C.* v. *Marlog*[135] concerned a house sharing arrangement between two strangers of a house in Abergavenny. A public sector tenant retained the use of one bedroom, the woman sharer making use of the other two bedrooms herself and for her two daughters. All shared the kitchen, bathroom and living accommodation. On the facts the woman was a lodger. Even though she had the exclusive rights to two bedrooms, the tenant could enter if he wished to do so, and in general it was true to say that if two people moved in and shared premises there was a house sharing arrangement rather than a sub-tenancy. Payments of "rent" really only amounted to contributions to living expenses.

E.   SERVICED ACCOMMODATION

1.   Reservation of access to provide services

As Lord Templeman has said a residential occupier is a licensee if "the landlord provides attendance or services which require the landlord or his servants to exercise unrestricted access to and use of the premises".[136] The extremes are quite clear, but between lies what Lord Donaldson M.R. has described as a "spectrum of exclusivity".[137] A person allowed sole occupation of a whole house or a self-contained flat is clearly a tenant if the landlord promises to leave him alone. But a guest in a hotel taking a room for a week or so is a licensee, since the management reserves the right of access to the room at all times, provides services, and can terminate the arrangement after the week's stay.

In *Brillouet* v. *Landless*[138] the landlord decided upon forcible eviction when he discovered that the occupier of a hotel room was homeless and unable to pay the £100 a day charges. The property was operated as a normal hotel with rooms cleaned by a chambermaid and fresh linen supplied by the management. An occupier of a hotel room for

---

[131] *AG Securities* (four strangers sharing a four-bedroomed flat).
[132] [1985] A.C. 809, 825G.
[133] [1990] 1 A.C. 417, 465A–H; *Mikeover Ltd.* v. *Brady* [1989] 3 All E.R. 618 C.A.
[134] [1990] 1 W.L.R. 766 C.A.
[135] (1994) 27 H.L.R. 30 C.A.
[136] *Street* v. *Mountford* [1985] A.C. 809, 818. This test is less helpful in flat sharing cases; see immediately below.
[137] *Aslan* v. *Murphy* [1990] 1 W.L.R. 766, 770F–G.
[138] (1996) 28 H.L.R. 836 C.A.; *Carroll* v. *Manek* (2000) 79 P. & C.R. 173 Ch.D.

an indefinite period still has no exclusive possession, no tenancy, and no protection from eviction. Similar is *Mehta* v. *Royal Bank of Scotland plc.*[139] a clear case on the facts even if some of the sweeping dicta on *Street* v. *Mountford* require careful use. A purchaser from the landlord's lender gave one day's notice that he had bought the property to the occupier of one of the rooms in an hotel. Mehta, for it was he, had been given exclusive use of room 418 by the receiver acting with the consent of the bank and occupied it over a substantial period making monthly payments. Both parties agreed that any cleaning was minimal but Mehta was held nevertheless to be a contractual licensee with an interest incapable of binding a purchaser of the hotel, even one with notice,[140] though even so he was entitled to more than one day's notice.

If a landlord needs access to a property to provide genuine services, the occupier does not have a lease. In *Huwyler* v. *Ruddy*[141] the rent genuinely included "Service— Laundry—Cleaning" and, since this could not be done without access to the rooms, the occupier could not have a Rent Act tenancy. Another undisputed example is provided by the letting of rooms in the "Emperors Gate Hotel" discussed in *Appah* v. *Parncliffe.*[142] Of course a hotel guest is a lodger, and not entitled to claim security of tenure in his room. This particular hotel was much more like a set of residential apartments than a commercial hotel, being split into 17 different rooms, each with a Yale lock. The management provided daily cleaning, could ask occupants to vacate without notice, and insisted that visitors leave by 10.30 at night. Occupants were held to be licensees. By way of contrast, *Luganda* v. *Service Hotels Ltd.,*[143] also concerned a large house in multiple occupation described as a hotel, with a number of rooms each having its own key and gas rings. A student at the Bar was given two days' notice to quit after he had been in occupation for three years when he objected to a rent increase. Held to be a protected tenant, he was able to secure a mandatory injunction to require his reinstatement even after the room had been relet. In *Marchant* v. *Charters*[144] "bachelors" occupying service apartments which were cleaned daily by a housekeeper and provided with clean linen weekly were held to be licensees, though that decision may have been weakened by *Street* v. *Mountford.*[145] More certain, because the decision was specifically approved by Lord Templeman is *Abbeyfield (Harpenden) Society* v. *Woods*[146] holding that residents of an old people's home with sole use of a room were licensees, given that the management provided cleaning, meals, heating, and the services of a housekeeper. The most recent lease/licence case follows these two decisions. *Nelson Developments Ltd.* v. *Toboada*[147] concerned one room in a house of 23 bedsits in London S.W.3. all of which were provided with a number of services—daily cleaning, a full weekly laundry, refuse removal,

---

[139] [1999] *Times,* January 25th Q.B.D.; *Carroll* v. *Marek* (2000) 79 P. & C.R. 173 Ch.D
[140] Sparkes, *N.L.L.* 384–388.
[141] (1996) 28 H.L.R. 550 C.A.
[142] [1964] 1 W.L.R. 1064 C.A. (liability of the owners in negligence).
[143] [1969] 2 Ch. 209 C.A.
[144] [1977] 1 W.L.R. 1181 C.A.; also in the commercial context *Vandersteen* v. *Agius* (1992) 65 P. & C.R. 266 C.A. (exclusive possession of rooms used for osteopathy practice, even though landlady was paid separately to clean the rooms); *Brillouet* v. *Landless* (1996) 28 H.L.R. 836 C.A.
[145] The reasoning though not necessarily the result was criticised by Lord Templeman at [1985] A.C. 809, 825C.
[146] [1968] 1 W.L.R. 374; see [1985] A.C. 809, 824B, Lord Templeman.
[147] [1992] 2 E.G.L.R. 107 C.A.

domestic hot water, window cleaning, lighting and heating, a non-residential house-keeper, and a pay phone. Of the registered rent of £38, £15.51 was attributed to services. Services accounted for a substantial proportion of the rent and so possession was ordered.

2. Genuine rights of access

Provision of attendance by the landlord will only reduce the occupier's status to that of a lodger if it is necessary while providing that service to require that the owner should have unrestricted access to the premises.[148] Residential protection will not apply. Simple examples are the provision of breakfast or porterage. Retention of keys by the management is a fact often used to found an argument that the occupiers are licensees, but in fact such provisions are not decisive given that the really significant issue is the underlying agreement: are the keys required by the management for the provision of services?[149] If not, as in *Duke* v. *Wynne*[150] a provision that keys must be handed in will be treated as a pretence.

What is important, more generally, is the *right* to a particular facility as opposed to its actual provision. Hence an obligation to provide a continental breakfast will amount to board, even if not taken up.[151] Only genuine rights prejudice an occupier. An agreement to provide a particular service that is not actually available provides a ready defence to the action, whatever the legal theory about the irrelevance of later conduct when construing the contract. Indeed a term of a licence which refers to fictional services may itself cast doubt on the validity of the entire written licence agreement,[152] and open up the argument that the whole licence should be struck down as a pretence.[153]

3. Removal from Rent Act protection

Assured tenancies granted in the private sector after early 1989 are based on market rents, taking account of the services provided, though very often all assurance will be removed by the fact that the occupier does not enjoy exclusive possession of serviced accommodation. Provision of services had a more fundamental effect on the scheme of rent regulation applying to Rent Act tenants, since the scheme envisaged that the rent had to be capable of registration in such a way that it could be limited to a fair rent. This is impossible to calculate if the rent includes payment for services. Hence the rule that an occupation agreement will not create a protected (Rent Act) tenancy if it is "bona fide let at a rent which includes payments in respect of board or attendance",[154] provided that the term is not designed to remove Rent Act protection.[155]

---

[148] *Markou* v. *Da Silvaesa* (1986) 52 P. & C.R. 204.
[149] *Aslan* v. *Murphy (No.1)* [1990] 1 W.L.R. 766, 773E, Lord Donaldson M.R.; *Family H.Ass.* v. *Jones* [1990] 1 W.L.R. 779, 789C–D, Balcombe L.J.
[150] [1990] 1 W.L.R. 733, 776A–B, Lord Donaldson M.R.
[151] *Markou* v. *Da Silvaesa* (1986) 52 P. & C.R. 204.
[152] *Otter* v. *Norman* [1989] A.C. 129, 146C, Lord Bridge.
[153] See above pp. 153–154.
[154] R.A. 1977 s 7(1).
[155] R.A. 1977 s.7; *Palser* v. *Grinling* [1984] A.C. 291, 310, Viscount Simon; *Otter* v. *Norman* [1989] A.C. 129, 142F, Lord Bridge; *Huwyler* v. *Ruddy* (1996) 28 H.L.R. 550 C.A. (was genuine).

Rent Act protection is excluded by the provision of *board*. Guesthouses provide full or half board and this is the correct sense of "board"—the provision of food and drink. The element of the rent attributable to board need not be a substantial,[156] provided that it is genuine. In the leading case, *Otter* v. *Norman*,[157] the landlord of a 36-room house in Egerton Terrace S.W.3 provided a continental breakfast[158]—consisting of rolls, marmalade and tea or coffee—and if the residents provided their own cornflakes, milk was available to go with them. The House of Lords held that this was more than a minimum provision of board, and that it removed Rent Act protection. There is no necessity to provide a main meal in addition to breakfast. Although board is not defined, it clearly applies to a boarding house that provides either full board or bed and breakfast. Provision of an early morning cup of tea would not suffice. The onus is on the landlord to demonstrate that protection is lost for this reason, and that any allocation of rent made by the lease is genuine.[159]

Rent Act protection was also excluded by the provision of *attendance*, provided it is *substantial*. Viscount Simon L.C. defined "attendance"[160] in *Palser* v. *Grinling* to be a "service personal to the tenant performed by an attendant provided by landlord for the convenience of an individual tenant in his enjoyment of demised premises"[161] including, for example, cleaning, laundry, hot water and the supply of clean linen,[162] carrying coal, delivering letters, and removing refuse. Impersonal services which do not strip away security of tenure include the provision of a lift, supplying hot water,[163] cleaning common parts, and porterage.

Once upon a time, furnished lettings were exempt from protection, so that even a trivial payment for linoleum removed statutory security of tenure.[164] Hence the statutes had to be amended to introduce a requirement that payments for furniture had to form a substantial part of the rent.[165] When all furnished lettings were brought into protection in 1974,[166] the requirement of substantiality survived as a basis for assessing whether attendance is sufficiently significant to remove Rent Act protection. A rough test is whether attendance accounts for more[167] or less[168] than 10 per cent of the rent. In *Nelson Developments Ltd.* v. *Toboada*[169] the services provided were daily cleaning, full weekly laundry, refuse removal, domestic hot water, window cleaning, lighting and

---

[156] Contrast attendance below.

[157] [1989] A.C. 129 H.L.; P. Watchman [1988] *J.S.W.L.* 147; C.P. Rodgers (1988) 51 *M.L.R.* 642 C.A.

[158] *Holiday Flat Co. Ltd.* v. *Kuczera* [1978] S.L.T. 47 (Sheriff Ct.)

[159] *Palser* v. *Grinling* [1948] A.C. 291 H.L.; R.E. Megarry (1947) 63 *L.Q.R.* 157; L.C.B. Gower (1947) 10 *M.L.R.* 63 (in C.A.); *Baldock* v. *Murray* [1981] 1 E.G.L.R. 70 C.A.

[160] R.A. 1977 s.7(1).

[161] [1948] A.C. 291, 310.

[162] *Marchant* v. *Charters* [1977] 1 W.L.R. 1181 (linen).

[163] On earlier legislation see *Asher* v. *Seaford Court Estates Ltd.* [1950] A.C 508 H.L.; R.E. Megarry (1950) 66 *L.Q.R.* 19.

[164] *Wilkes* v. *Goodwin* [1923] 2 K.B. 86 C.A.

[165] *Otter* v. *Norman* [1989] A.C. 129, 143–145, Lord Bridge. On furnished lettings: *Mann* v. *Cornella* [1980] 1 E.G.L.R. 73 C.A.; *Woodward* v. *Docherty* [1974] 1 W.L.R. 966 C.A.; R.E. Megarry (1946) 62 *L.Q.R.* 123.

[166] R.A. 1974 s.1.

[167] *Nelson Developments Ltd.* v. *Toboada* [1992] 2 E.G.L.R. 107 C.A. (£15 out of a total rent of £50 was substantial); *Marchant* v. *Charters* [1977] 1 W.L.R. 1181.

[168] *Palser* v. *Grinling* [1948] A.C. 291 H.L. (£4 out of £175 not substantial).

[169] [1992] 2 E.G.L.R. 107 C.A.

heating, non-residential housekeeper, and a pay-phone. Of the £38 registered for rent, £15.51 was attributable to services, a substantial proportion judged against the informal benchmark of 10–20 per cent of the rent. This fact precluded the recognition of Rent Act security.

4.   Former protection as restricted contracts

Restricted contracts are a dying category since protection was removed for grants after early 1989,[170] though pre-existing contracts could continue to reach the courts for many years.[171] They include exclusive licences and tenancies that include payments for services or attendance, and those with a small element of board. The limited protection is explained below.[172]

5.   Supported housing

Many social landlords provide supported housing, for example wardened accommodation for the elderly, in which case the residents are licensees, but they have Charter rights.[173]

F.   RESIDENT LANDLORD EXEMPTION

Social embarrassment could arise out of close proximity between a landlord and tenant, where for example a landlord rented out a room in his own house. According to Scarman L.J. in *Bardrick* v. *Haycock*,[174] this is why statutory protection is removed from any tenant whose landlord resides on the same premises. Exemption began for Rent Act tenancies in 1974,[175] so that when new Rent Act grants were shut down in early 1989, 6 per cent of all Rent Act lettings fell into this category, but it continues to be available to landlords letting under the present assured tenancy scheme.[176] The former protection that resident landlord tenancies enjoyed as restricted contracts[177] was withdrawn for grants made after early 1989[178] so that there is now no protection at all.

1.   Landlord must be resident

A landlord claiming exemption must prove that he[179] is resident, at the time of the grant and throughout the life of the tenancy, though too close a temporal analysis will not be pursued, so that if both parties move out temporarily during renovations, the resident

---

[170] H.A. 1988 s.36 in force January 15th 1989.

[171] *Gray* v. *Brown* [1993] 1 E.G.L.R. 119 C.A. (grant 1978, litigation 1991).

[172] See below pp. 164–165.

[173] *Charter for Licence Holders Living in Supported Housing* (Housing Corporation, 1998).

[174] (1976) 31 P. & C.R. 420, 424, Scarman L.J.

[175] R.A. 1977 s.12 applying from August 14th, 1974.

[176] R.A. 1977 s.12, sch.2; H.A. 1988 sch.1 para.10 and sch.1 pt.III.

[177] *Bryant* v. *Best* [1987] 2 E.G.L.R. 113 C.A. (postponement of possession for post 1980 tenant limited to 3 months); *Gray* v. *Brown* [1993] 1 E.G.L.R. 119 C.A. (interest created in 1973 litigated in 1993; full protection on the facts); see below pp. 164–165.

[178] H.A. 1988 s.36 (grants on or after January 15th 1989).

[179] Only one of joint landlords needs to be resident: *Tilling* v. *Whiteman* [1980] A.C. 1 H.L.; *Cooper* v. *Tait* (1984) 48 P. & C.R. 460 C.A.; J.E. Martin [1985] *Conv.* 127.

landlord exemption may be applied to the replacement house.[180] Residence has a relaxed definition in the Rent Act,[181] the normal rule that so often works to the advantage of tenants here working in favour of landlords so that, to take just one example, a landlord may qualify as a resident of a block by occupying one room during the daytime while continuing to sleep elsewhere.[182] Personal occupation is not considered essential[183] and residence can survive temporary absences: in one extreme case a landlord was held to be resident in Hull during a time when her main home was in America.[184] Abandonment may eventually occur once the landlord has ceased both use and physical occupation, in one case after an absence for four years during which the flat was unfurnished.[185]

2. Same building

A landlord wishing to avoid giving security to a tenant must show that the tenant's dwelling forms part of the same building as that in which the landlord resides. An adjacent terraced house would obviously not be sufficient, but if the case is less clear the judge must decide as a matter of fact whether there is one building or two.[186] A single building may consist of a central house with extensions on either wing to which there were no internal connections,[187] or a large subdivided Victorian house with a modern structure added outside it,[188] or a house with an extension in course of conversion to separate letting units,[189] and even buildings physically separated by an alleyway.[190] Exemption cannot be claimed where both landlord and tenant have flats both of which are within a purpose-built block,[191] meaning any building constructed so as to include two or more flats.[192]

3. Landlord by purchase

A landlord by purchase cannot limit the security of his tenants, since he knows the score when he buys the property, a principle which operated in one case to exclude a landlord who purchased the house at its market value under an option in his employer's will.[193]

---

[180] *Barnett* v. *O'Sullivan* [1994] 1 W.L.R. 1667 C.A.
[181] R.A. 1977 sch.2 para.5; see above pp. 104–109.
[182] *Palmer* v. *McNamara* [1991] 1 E.G.L.R. 121; J.E. Martin [1991] *Conv.* 289.
[183] *Lyons* v. *Caffery* [1983] 1 E.G.L.R. 102 C.A. (wife); contrast *Markou* v. *Da Silvaesa* (1986) 52 P. & C.R. 204 (not by a resident housekeeper).
[184] *Wolff* v. *Waddington* [1989] 2 E.G.L.R. 108 C.A. (13 months in Hull).
[185] *Jackson* v. *Pekic* [1989] 2 E.G.L.R. 104 C.A.
[186] *Lewis-Graham* v. *Conacher* [1992] 1 E.G.L.R. 111 C.A.; J.E. Martin [1993] *Conv.* 157.
[187] *Griffiths* v. *English* [1982] 1 E.G.L.R. 96 C.A.
[188] *Barnes* v. *Gorsuch* (1982) 43 P. & C.R. 294 C.A.
[189] *Lewis-Graham*; *Bardrick* v. *Haydock* (1976) 31 P. & C.R. 420 C.A.
[190] *Wolff* v. *Waddington* [1989] 2 E.G.L.R. 108 C.A.
[191] Though it can for a flat within a flat: R.A. 1977 s.12(1)(a).
[192] R.A. 1977 sch.4 para.5 and sch.2 para.4; H.A. 1988 sch.1 paras.10, 22; J.T. Farrand [1983] *Conv.* 341; A. Samuels [1983] *Conv.* 343; illustrations are *Barnes* and *Griffiths* as above.
[193] *Amaddio* v. *Dalton* (1991) 23 H.L.R. 332 C.A.

4.   Death of a resident landlord

The right to evict a tenant continues following the death of a resident landlord, both for the Rent Act scheme[194] and for assured tenancies.[195] Trustees and personal representatives[196] are protected for two years. This is more ample than the one year previously allowed,[197] and properly so, since there was a risk under the earlier more restrictive law that the executor's year might be taken up by securing a grant or that the (now redundant) power to suspend possession notices for restricted contracts might interfere.[198] After the property is vested in[199] a subsequent landlord who is entitled as successor on the death of the first landlord, that second landlord (as beneficiary) has 28 days to occupy the property—or to give notice of his intention to occupy within six months— and so to secure the status of a resident landlord.[200]

5.   Restricted contracts (before early 1989)

Restricted contracts are a dying breed since protection was removed for grants after the Housing Act 1988,[201] though the death is painfully protracted and pre-existing contracts could continue to reach the courts for many years.[202] The following discussion assumes that a grant was made before early 1989. Categorisation of such a grant as a restricted contract provides a limited protection for those lacking full protection as Rent Act tenants, the main target being the private sector,[203] though bizarrely the definition caught local authorities (as opposed to other public sector landlords) before the introduction of the secure tenancies scheme in 1980.[204]

Resident landlord tenancies were the largest category of restricted contracts,[205] though it also includes grants of accommodation to be shared with the landlord[206] and serviced accommodation[207] and pre-1974 furnished lettings.[208] Completely excluded were non-exclusive licences (those that did not give rights to any separate accommodation), luxury lettings, holiday lettings, and lettings with substantial board.[209] *Protection from eviction* is a right enjoyed by all exclusive licensees, including any person who occupies under a restricted contract.[210] Very limited *security* was conferred on a

---

[194] R.A. 1977 sch.2 paras.1, 2, 2A.

[195] H.A. 1988 sch.1 para.17.

[196] *Landau* v. *Sloane* [1982] A.C. 490 H.L.; A. Sydenham [1981] *Conv.* 225.

[197] H.A. 1980 s.65; *Caldwell* v. *McAteer* [1984] 1 E.G.L.R. 89 C.A. (not retrospective).

[198] *Williams* v. *Mate* (1983) 46 P. & C.R. 43 C.A.

[199] *Beebe* v. *Mason* [1980] 1 E.G.L.R. 81 C.A. (brother who occupied as sole beneficiary and executor for 10 months without an assent held to be a resident landlord).

[200] R.A. 1977 sch.2 para.1; H.A. 1988 sch.1 para.17.

[201] H.A. 1988 s.36; in force January 15th 1989.

[202] *Gray* v. *Brown* [1993] I E.G.L.R. 119 C.A. (grant 1978, litigation 1991).

[203] R.A. 1977 s.19; Davey, 301–304.

[204] *Lambeth L.B.C.* v. *Udechuka* (1980) 41 P. & C.R. 200 C.A.

[205] R.A. 1977 s.20.

[206] s.21; *Gray* v. *Brown* [1993] 1 E.G.L.R. 119 C.A.

[207] See above pp. 152–158.

[208] R.A. 1977 s.19.

[209] s.19(4).

[210] P.E.A. 1977 as extended by H.A. 1980; *Alexander* v. *Springate* [1951] 1 All E.R. 351; R.E. Megarry (1951) 67 *L.Q.R.* 166, 290 (1946 legislation); see below pp. 310–312.

restricted contract granted *before late 1980*, in the sense that the Rent Tribunal could postpone operation of the notice to quit for renewable periods of up to six months[211]; however if the grant was made *between late 1980 and early 1989*, postponement powers were limited to a maximum of three months. [212] Either party may apply to the rent tribunal for a reasonable rent to be fixed, which may be reconsidered after two years.[213]

G. SHORT TERM TENANCIES

1. Shorthold tenancies

It is now abnormal for a tenant in the private sector to enjoy life-long security.[214] Shorthold tenancies predominate, and they confer security for a short fixed period of at least six months but no long-term security. As from early 1997[215] a landlord has to elect positively to create anything other than a shorthold by giving notice[216]; few do so.

2. Introductory tenants in the public sector

Local authorities have had power since 1996, if they choose to exercise it, to set up an introductory tenancy scheme.[217] Tenancies become secure after a probationary period lasting 12 months,[218] but during that probationary period, the local authority may terminate the tenancy by notice if it forms the opinion that the tenant is unsuitable. Reasons for the authority's decision must be given, and the removal of security can be challenged on review.[219] In *Manchester C.C.* v. *Cochrane*[220] a grant was made to Cochrane in April 1997 but the authority made an application for possession in March 1998. The Court of Appeal confirmed the possession order. Sir John Knox said that an introductory tenancy was a right to possession until the court made an order for possession and a county court was obliged to order possession. There was no appeal though there is an internal review procedure[221] and the only possible challenge in court was through judicial review. If the tenants or their visitors caused a nuisance the local authority was entitled to apply for a possession order and proceedings could not be defended on the basis of a denial of the allegations in the notice requiring possession. An appeal has been lodged with the House of Lords, but the statutory wording is so tight that it is difficult to see that there is any room for judicial manoeuvre.

---

[211] R.A. 1977 ss.103–106; s.102A removes this protection as from November 28th 1980. Owner occupiers who had warned in advance that they might require possession were given an overriding right to possession: R.A. 1977 s.105.

[212] R.A. 1977 s.106A(3) (after November 28th 1980 but before January 15th 1989); *Bryant* v. *Best* [1987] 2 E.G.L.R. 113 C.A. (no postponement beyond 3 months). There was no owner occupier exemption.

[213] See below p. 238.

[214] J. Morgan [1996] *J.S.W.F.L.* 445.

[215] H.A. 1988 s.19A operating from February 28th 1997: S.I. 1997/225.

[216] H.A. 1988 sch.2A.

[217] H.A. 1996 s.124; N.J. Smith & G.A. George (1997) 19 *J.S.W.F.L.* 307.

[218] s.125; S.I. 1997/72.

[219] ss.127–130.

[220] (1999) 31 H.L.R. 810 C.A.

[221] Introductory Tenants (Review) Regs S.I. 1997/72.

3.   Charter rights of social sector applicants

Registered social landlords must accept the rules of the Housing Corporation if they wish to receive social housing grants for the purchase or construction of new housing. The *Housing Applicant's Charter*[222] requires that tenancies are normally fully assured, but the Charter recognises the concept of a starter tenancy—that is a shorthold for one year initially, but which will mature into one with a full assurance if there is no misconduct by the tenant in the first year. This is the social sector equivalent of the introductory tenancy in the public sector.

H.   OTHER EXEMPT LEASES

1.   Low rent leases

These are excluded from all security of tenure regimes. The criterion originally adopted was to compare the rent with the rateable value[223] leases being excluded if the rent was less than two thirds of the appropriate Rateable Value. But with the abolition of domestic rating, fixed rent limits were introduced for new lettings in 1990. These limits will be explained in the context of long leases.[224] Their effect is to remove lifelong security in the private sector and entitlement to a minimum short hold,[225] but the rules introduce three particular problems.

Long leases are excluded. All public sector long leases are excluded from security,[226] but the private sector legislation is more intricate. When rent regulation existed for short residential tenancies, it was essential to distinguish between long and short leases. If a tenant had bought a 99-year lease of a house for £100,000 and pays a £10 a year ground rent it would have been grossly unfair to allow the landlord to increase the rent to a market rent (assured) or even to a fair rent (Rent Act). Hence tenants benefited from the exclusion of leases at a low rent from rent regulation, though coincidentally this exclusion also removed normal residential security. During the contractual term the tenant does not really need security, but at the end of a long lease (for a term longer than 21 years) residential security can attach to the lease at that stage. The low ground rent will rise at that stage. For ten years after the switch to assured tenancies (that is until early 1999) the long lease was followed by a Rent Act tenancy allowing the rent to be increased to a fair rent, whereas if the long lease expires now it is an assured tenancy at a market rent. Security of tenure and rent regulation are removed until the end of the contractual term of a long lease. This security is described in the context of long leases, where it is also explained how the qualification to enfranchise requires that a lease of a house was initially at a low rent.[227]

---

[222] Housing Corporation (1998).

[223] Increase of the rateable value above the limit will end protection if the lease is in a contractual phase but not once it has moved to a statutory phase: *J. & F. Stone Lighting and Radio Ltd.* v. *Levitt* [1947] A.C. 209 H.L.

[224] £1,000 a year in London; £250 elsewhere; see below pp. 390–392.

[225] R.A. 1977 s.5; H.A. 1988 sch.1 para.3; H.A. 1988 s.1(2)–(2A) (variable rateable value limits).

[226] H.A. 1985 sch.1 para.1.

[227] See below pp. 390–392.

Agricultural tied cottages also receive special treatment, since low rents would normally remove protection from many agricultural workers living in tied cottages.[228] Difficulties remain for employees in other industries where rent is deducted from wages—the deduction is treated as a monetary rent if a fixed sum on account of rent is deducted from wages[229] but not if rent-free occupation is allowed on top of normal occupation.[230]

2. Rent-free occupation

Rent was one of Lord Templeman's three *indicia* of a lease, but in fact it is not essential provided only that exclusive possession is yielded to the tenant.[231] It would be more accurate to say that the absence of a rent is a reason for removing the protection of the residential security of tenure legislation. Rent-free arrangements are often familial or charitable in character, but even if there is no charitable explanation they will still fall outside all protection. In *Bostock* v. *Bryant*[232] an arrangement to take exclusive possession of the larger part of a house, rent-free but sharing expenses of gas and electricity, was outside the Rent Act since those payments were not rent. Payments of household bills or donations to a third party look very similar but do not count as a monetary rent,[233] but such arrangements are readily found to be a pretence, and hence vulnerable to reform so as to create a money-based letting.[234] These types of arrangement also avoid public sector security.[235]

Other obligations that are not quantifiable in money, or at least are not in fact quantified, remove Rent Act protection, examples being cleaning and shopping. Rent regulation machinery was not an appropriate method of quantifying in monetary terms the worth of such services. In *Barnes* v. *Barrett*[236] an arrangement whereby a person was allowed to occupy three rooms in return for providing cleaning, cooking, and shopping was outside the Rent Act. (Today there would not even be a shorthold tenancy). The agreement was framed as a lease, using the words "rent" and "tenant", but the head landlords succeeded in obtaining possession against an occupier who was merely a licensee. Rent-free occupation under a non-assignable agreement counted against its recognition as a lease, as did the provision of services.

3. Holiday lettings

Some short leases obviously do fall outside the scope of the residential security regimes. Holiday lettings create tenancies, but ones without security of tenure, that is where the purpose is to confer on the tenant the right to occupy a dwelling-house "for a

---

[228] See below Chapter 7.
[229] *Montague* v. *Browning* [1954] 1 W.L.R. 1039, 1044.
[230] *Scrimgeour* v. *Waller* [1981] 1 E.G.L.R. 68 C.A.
[231] *Ashburn Anstalt* v. *Arnold* [1989] Ch. 1, 10B, Fox L.J.
[232] [1990] 2 E.G.L.R. 101; R. Lee [1991] *Conv.* 270.
[233] *Michel* v. *Volpe* (1967) 202 E.G. 213 (donations to 'the Vanguard').
[234] *Scrimgeour* v. *Waller* [1981] 1 E.G.L.R. 68 C.A. Payments are taxable as rent: *Jeffries* v. *Stevens* [1982] S.T.C. 639, 651.
[235] *West Wiltshire D.C.* v. *Snelgrove* (1998) 30 H.L.R. 57 (payments for services and food).
[236] [1970] 2 Q.B. 657 C.A. The agreement provided for sharing of a bathroom with the owner; similar is *Hornsby* v. *Maynard* [1925] 1 K.B. 514, 523 (accommodation for landlord).

holiday".[237] No precise definition is provided, but essentially a holiday is a break from routine, possibly including a working holiday.[238] The courts can reject a sham holiday letting, since any label attached to a tenancy is irrelevant if the substance is misrepresented.[239] However, in *Buchmann* v. *May*,[240] a false label of holiday let could not be challenged on the grounds of inequality of bargaining power nor the tenant's failure to apprehend the legal significance of the express term. A mandatory ground for repossession is provided at the end of an off-season let.[241]

4.   Student accommodation

Lettings of accommodation made to students by authorised[242] educational institutions[243] do not provide security of tenure. A mandatory ground for possession prevents long-term security of tenure arising for vacation lettings.[244]

5.   Luxury property

Only residential tenants with limited means should benefit from rent regulation, so luxury lettings are excluded. *Rent limits* now apply. For assured tenancies granted since the abolition of domestic rates (in spring 1990), a luxury letting is one at a rent exceeding £25,000 a year.[245] In *R.* v. *London Rent Assessment Panel ex parte Cadogan Estates Ltd.*[246] the Estate acquired the reversion on a property in London and promptly served notice to increase the rent to £40,000 a year, thus taking it outside the assured tenancy scheme by making it a luxury letting. An error in the regulations converting the legislation from its reliance on rating apparently created a Catch 22: power to review the rent was given only while there continued to be an assured tenancy, so that if the increase was so great as to create a luxury letting which was no longer assured there seemed to be no power to increase the rent. Kay J. sidestepped this problem and took a common sense view. If the assessment of the rent took the tenancy into the luxury category, the rent assessment panel was required to assess the rent at the real figure and by doing so to end protection as an assured tenancy.

Rateable value limits were used to differentiate between protected tenancies and luxury property, and the same rule applied to assured tenancies granted in the short period

---

[237] R.A. 1977 s.9 (Rent Act); H.A. 1988 sch.1 para.9 (assured); this exemption is unnecessary in the public sector; in the past there was not even a restricted contract: R.A. 1977 s.19.

[238] *Francke* v. *Hakmi* [1984] C.L.Y. 1906; *McHale* v. *Daneham* [1979] 1 E.G.L.R. 119 C.Ct. Contrast *Caradon D.C.* v. *Paton* [2000] Times May 17th C.A. (holiday lettings infringed covenant against use other than as a private dwelling; the property had to be used as a home, even if only for a short period).

[239] *R.* v *R.O. of Camden ex parte Plant* [1981] 1 E.G.L.R. 73 Q.B.D. (letting to student nurses; not genuine holiday letting).

[240] [1978] 2 All E.R. 993, 998.

[241] R.A. 1977 sch.15 case 13; H.A. 1988 sch.2 ground 3; *Killick* v. *Roberts* [1991] 4 All E.R. 289 C.A. (no advance notice, so case 13 not applied). Rent Act lettings are within the provision for rent control while they last.

[242] As defined by S.I. 1998/1967; the most recent additions are by S.Is. 1999/1803 and 1999/2268.

[243] R.A. 1977 s.8 (Rent Act); H.A. 1988 sch.1 para.8 (assured); H.A. 1985 sch.1 para.10 (secure where notice given in advance); S.I. 1980/1407.

[244] R.A. 1977 sch.15 case 14; H.A. 1988 sch.2 ground 4.

[245] H.A. 1988 sch.1 para.2 (part II explains Rateable Values) as amended by S.I. 1990/434 i.e. on or after April 1st 1990; until that date the same limits applied as for protected Rent Act tenancies.

[246] [1998] Q.B. 398, Kay J.

between their introduction (early 1989) and the abolition of domestic rating (spring 1990). For lettings after April 1973 the rateable value limit was £1,500 in Greater London (or half that figure elsewhere) and dwellings with higher rateable values were excluded from protection.[247] Luxury is relative, since the rateable value limits were high enough to allow protection for a handsome period country house in *Hill* v. *Rochard*.[248]

6. Property without residential use

Tenants qualify for protection only by meeting the requirement of residential occupation.[249] Modern legislation requires that the tenant qualify from the outset and throughout, though the older Rent Act requires occupation only when the tenancy reaches a statutory phase. No protection whatsoever attaches to a lease of residential accommodation to an investor who intends to relet it. Nor, usually, can a tenant claim any protection for a house he is using as a second home. Occupation is a continuing requirement, so that a lease that at the time of its original grant has some protection will lose that status if the tenant gives up his residence.

7. Company lets

Residential security of tenure requires personal occupation as a home so security is easily avoided by the simple device of granting the tenancy to a company. *Rent Act tenancies* are clearly protected during a contractual phase when there is no requirement that the tenant occupy the property as his home at that stage. Thus a letting to X Co. Ltd. before early 1989 for occupation by a director X is a protected tenancy. But when the contractual tenancy is ended no statutory tenancy can arise, because its existence is dependent upon residential occupation by the tenant. Since a company cannot have a residence and its occupation lacks the vital element of domesticity, it can never become a statutory tenant.[250] Landlords could easily exploit this sure-fire method of avoiding full residential security simply by refusing to let unless the tenant was a company. Protection is also lost on an assignment to a company.[251] In *Estavest Investments Ltd.* v. *Commercial Express Travel Ltd.*[252] a lease was taken by a company, because the landlord had expressed itself to be unready to grant a Rent Act protected tenancy. Throughout the term of the lease Mrs Sachak, who was a director of the tenant company, occupied the premises but the rent and all other liabilities were met solely by the company. There was said to be overwhelming evidence that this was genuine, and the same decision was reached in *Hilton* v. *Plustitle Ltd.*[253] where the company had been purchased off-the-shelf specifically with the intention of avoiding the Rent Act 1977. Security is

---

[247] R.A. 1977 s.4 (which also states the rules for tenancies granted earlier) defines rateable value and the appropriate day for applying the test; *Guestheath* v. *Mirza* (1990) 22 H.L.R. 399 (effect of reduction in rateable value); J.E. Martin [1990] *Conv.* 446; H.A. 1988 sch.1.para.2 (assured). The exemption is not relevant in the public sector.

[248] [1983] 1 W.L.R. 478.

[249] See above pp. 104–109.

[250] *Hiller* v. *United Dairies (London) Ltd.* [1934] 1 K.B. 57 C.A.; *Carter* v. *S.U. Carburetter Co.* [1942] 2 K.B. 288 C.A.; *Firstcross Ltd.* v. *East West (Export/Import) Ltd.* (1981) 41 P. & C.R. 145, 151, Stephenson L.J.

[251] *Murray* v. *Lloyd* [1989] 1 W.L.R. 1060; J.E. Martin [1990] *Conv.* 446.

[252] [1988] 2 E.G.L.R. 91 C.A.

[253] *Hilton* v. *Plustitle Ltd.* [1989] 1 W.L.R 149 C.A.; P. Sparkes (1989) 52 *M.L.R.* 557; S. Bright (1991) 11 *O.J.L.S.* 136; P.V. Baker (1989) 105 *L.Q.R.* 167; T. Radevsky [1990] *N.L.J.* 620; G. Webber [1990] *N.L.J.* 1205.

determined according to the real rights of the parties, ignoring any pretence,[254] and at least in theory a company letting which could be characterised as a pretence should be open to review.[255] However, if the letting in *Hilton* v. *Plustitle Ltd.* was genuine, how can a company letting ever be reopened?

For *assured tenancies* granted after 1989 protection continues only "if and so long as the tenant or, as the case may be, each of the joint tenants is an individual".[256] This ensures the exclusion of company lets. Provided that the company letting is genuine, this suggests a cast-iron method of contracting out of security. Of course the removal of life-long security from all tenants and its replacement with an assurance of a short hold has removed much of the need for company lets.

8. Crown immunity

No security arises where the landlord is the Crown or a Government department,[257] but otherwise (!) the Rent Act applied to the Crown and lettings by the Crown Estates Commissioners.[258] As an exception to the general rule, the Crown was allowed to charge a premium for the grant of a tenancy.[259] All Crown lettings are excluded from the assured tenancies scheme[260] and also fall outside the public sector.[261]

I.   EXCLUSIVE LICENCES: CATEGORISATION

1.   Private sector

Grants of exclusive possession of self-contained residential accommodation generally confer a lease,[262] but there are many cases where the surrounding circumstances make clear that the occupation is to be short-term or temporary. Statutory exclusions considered in the last section and exceptions recognised by case law showing that exclusive possession is for once consistent with a licence act as mutual buttresses. Denning L.J. identified some exceptional categories in *Errington* v. *Errington*,[263] their existence was confirmed by Lord Templeman in *Street* v. *Mountford*,[264] and Millett L.J. adopted the resultant three-fold classification when he considered the most recent case, *Bruton* v. *London & Quadrant Housing Trust,* in the Court of Appeal.[265] They are:

---

[254] *AG Securities* v. *Vaughan* [1990] 1 A.C. 417, 462B, Lord Templeman; *Jones* v. *Lipman* [1962] 1 W.L.R. 832, 836, Russell L.J. (corporate veil pierced to permit specific performance of a contract); see above pp. 152–153.

[255] *S.L. Dando Ltd.* v. *Hitchcock* [1954] 2 Q.B. 317, 322, Denning L.J.; *Firstcross Ltd.* v. *East West (Export/Import) Ltd.* (1981) 41 P. & C.R. 145, 158, Stephenson L.J. (obiter in view of the concession); J.E. Martin [1982] *Conv.* 151, 153; P. Sparkes (1989) 52 *M.L.R.* 357.

[256] H.A. 1988 s.1(1)(a).

[257] R.A. 1977 s.3.

[258] *London County Territorial and Auxillary Forces Association* v. *Nichols* [1949] 1 K.B. 35 C.A.; D.P. Derham (1963) 79 *L.Q.R.* 54. (long leases in Regents Park; no rights because of variability of rent).

[259] See below p. 241.

[260] H.A. 1988 sch.1 para.11.

[261] H.A. 1985 s.80.

[262] *Street* v. *Mountford* [1985] A.C. 809 H.L.; see above p. 150.

[263] [1952] 1 K.B. 290, 296–298.

[264] *Street* at 823D, Lord Templeman.

[265] [1998] Q.B. 834, 843B–D.

(1) where the circumstances negative any intention to create legal relations at all;
(2) where the possession is referable to some other legal relationship, such as buyer and seller or employer and employee—possibly the only true exception[266]; and
(3) where the grantor has no power to create a tenancy.

It was this third category that figured in *Bruton,* but the reversal of that decision by the Lords[267] casts particular doubt on the third category, and in any event Lord Templeman was not attempting an exhaustive categorisation. This book adopts a longer and more specific list.

2. Public sector

Separate treatment is required of exclusive licences in the public sector because of the impact of the special statutory rule that an exclusive licence is to create a secure tenancy.[268] In fact its effect is decidedly lacking in drama. It was first enacted at a time when it was arguable that private sector security could be excluded by the grant of an exclusive licence simply by expressing the intention to use a licence. Since an exclusive licence in the public sector is a secure tenancy, it is not necessary to go through the private sector rigmarole of labelling a transaction as a pretence and so reworking a licence agreement as a tenancy. After *Street* the practical effect of the two systems is very closely similar.

After earlier doubts,[269] it is now clear that the two systems work in tandem and that full security can only be conferred on a licensee who enjoys exclusive possession of a dwelling. The need for exclusive possession was held to be of overriding significance by the House of Lords in *Westminster City Council* v. *Clarke.*[270] Licences were granted to homeless men to occupy a hostel owned by the council on terms which reserved to the management the right to allocate a particular person to a particular room each night, and so, since Clarke lacked exclusive occupation of any particular accommodation, he was not a secure tenant but only a licensee. Numerous other cases confirm that men in hostels are licensees[271] particularly where the occupants can be moved from room to room.[272] So too in *Parkins* v. *Westminster C.C.*[273] a school teacher given a licence to use one bedroom in a three bed-roomed flat sharing with other teachers was held to have a licence and not a secure tenancy.

Special provisions[274] are required to exempt from "life-long" security arrangements in the public sector that are clearly intended to be temporary in character. These are:

---

[266] At 843C–D; *Camden L.B.C.* v. *Shortlife Community Housing* (1992) 25 H.L.R. 330, 340–341, Millett J.

[267] [2000] A.C. 206 H.L.

[268] H.A. 1985 s.79(3).

[269] *Family H.Ass.* v. *Jones* [1990] 1 W.L.R. 779, 790, Balcombe L.J.

[270] [1992] 2 A.C. 288 H.L.; D.S. Cowan [1992] *Conv.* 285; *Bruton* v. *London & Quadrant H. Trust* [1998] Q.B. 834, 841–2, Sir Brian Neill, [1999] 3 All E.R. 481, 486, Lord Hoffmann.

[271] *Kensington & Chelsea R.L.B.C.* v. *Hayden* (1984) 17 H.L.R. 114 C.A.; *Tower Hamlets L.B.C.* v. *Miah* (1992) 24 H.L.R. 199 C.A.; *Central Y.M.C.A. H.Ass.* v. *Goodman* (1991) 24 H.L.R. 98 C.A.; *Central Y.M.C.A. H.Ass.* v. *Saunders* (1991) 23 H.L.R. 212 C.A.

[272] *Brennan* v. *Lambeth L.B.C.* (1998) 30 H.L.R. 481 C.A.

[273] (1998) 30 H.L.R. 894 C.A.

[274] H.A. 1985 sch.1 paras.2–7, 12.

Premises occupied in connection with employment;
Land acquired for development;
Accommodation for homeless people or asylum seekers;[275]
Temporary accommodation for persons taking up employment;
Short-term arrangements;
Temporary accommodation during works; and
Almshouses.

Many of these categories are considered in more detail below.

No security arises where a public sector landlord allows a temporary exemption from repossession, for example after the end of a periodic tenancy,[276] after discovery of an illegal assignment,[277] or where a squatter is allowed to stay rent-free,[278] since the circumstances make clear that occupation is under an insecure licence.

3.   Social sector

Normal private sector principles are often supplemented by Charter rights.[279]

J.   EXCLUSIVE LICENCES: SPECIFIC CATEGORIES

1.   Family relationship or charity

That it would be unfair to impose security in family relationships is illustrated by a case in which the owner of a house allowed his brother to occupy rent-free, a kindness to which the brother ungenerously responded by claiming security of tenure. This outrageous claim was rejected.[280] However, the most enduring authority is *Errington* v. *Errington*[281] itself. A father bought a house for his son and daughter-in-law with the aid of a building society mortgage, taking legal title in his own name, but promising the couple that if they paid off all the mortgage instalments he would transfer the house to them. The couple occupied as (contractual[282]) licensees rather than tenants at will. A licence arose in another case from a loose family arrangement that a mother should make monthly payments for accommodation.[283] Family relationship is not decisive if there is overriding evidence of a quasi-commercial letting at a market rent.[284] *Booker* v.

---

[275] Accommodation provided under Part VI of the Immigration and Asylum Act 1999 is not secure: H.A. 1985 sch.1 paras.4A, 12A.

[276] *Harrison* v. *Hammersmith & Fulham L.B.C.* [1981] 1 W.L.R. 650 C.A.; P.F. Smith [1982] *Conv.* 218.

[277] *Westminster C.C.* v. *Basson* (1990) 23 H.L.R. 225 C.A. (illegal transferee allowed possession from 1985 to 1987 and given rent book still licensee); surely this case was close to the line?

[278] H.A. 1985 s.79(4); *Southwark L.B.C.* v. *Logan* (1997) 19 H.L.R. 40 C.A.

[279] *Charter for Licence Holders Living in Supported Housing* and *Charter for Residents in Temporary Housing* (Housing Corporation, 1998).

[280] *Cobb* v. *Lane* [1952] 1 All E.R. 1199 C.A.

[281] [1952] 1 K.B. 290 C.A.

[282] Contractual licences do not bind purchasers, so this may be better classified as an estoppel licence: *Camden L.B.C.* v. *Shortlife Community Housing* (1992) 25 H.L.R. 330, 340–341; Sparkes *N.L.L.* ch.15.

[283] *Hardwick* v. *Johnson* [1978] 1 W.L.R. 683 C.A.; also a licence granted by an employer to a retired employee for life: *Foster* v. *Robinson* [1951] 1 K.B. 149 C.A.

[284] *Nunn* v. *Dalrymple* (1989) 21 H.L.R. 569 C.A. (parents-in-law); *Ward* v. *Warnke* (1990) 22 H.L.R. 496 C.A. (daughter); R. Lee [1991] *Conv.* 270.

Palmer[285] involved a similar moral problem, this time in the context of a wartime evacuee from London rather than a relative, and again the claim to security foundered. Rent-free accommodation was provided in *Heslop* v. *Burns*[286] through the straightforward generosity of an office manager towards his office cleaner and her husband, to help them move out of an unsatisfactory attic. Since no arrangement was reached as to the terms of their accommodation, the man visited them every day to take his meals at the cottage, and had free access to the property at all times, the couple were held to be bare licensees with no right to remain after the death of their benefactor. Legal relations were not intended when no terms had been agreed.

2. During negotiations

Residential security requires a basal letting of the property. What happens if a landlord allows a person to take exclusive *occupation* of land while they continue to negotiate for a lease? Is this the same as granting exclusive *possession*? Traditional theory was that exclusive occupation indicated a tenancy, which marked out the arrangement as either a tenancy at will if the landlord assents to the occupation, or a tenancy at sufferance if he expresses neither approval nor disapproval. Each case carries a significant risk that residential security will attach since the legislative schemes include both a tenancy at will[287] and one at sufferance.[288] However the courts have sought to evade this result, believing it unfair to catch landlords while matters are still in negotiation.

Technical analysis necessarily varies between residential and commercial property, because in the latter case the business renewal provisions do not apply to a tenancy at will, whether it is express[289] or implied,[290] provided only that it is genuine.[291] A tenancy at will is usually implied where a person holds pending negotiations.[292]

Direct translation of this case law to *residential property* is unhelpful given that tenants *at will* are protected, so to allow a potential tenant to take occupation of residential accommodation on a trial basis during negotiations it has been necessary to allow a diversion into *licence doctrine*. Parties negotiating for a new residential lease *may* fall into the *Errington* classes of exclusive licences. Surely extreme was *Southwark L.B.C.* v. *Logan*[293] in which a tenant had been moved to temporary accommodation during work on his home but had taken a fancy to the new accommodation and had stayed there paying rent from 1985 to 1994. Since the local authority had made clear that his occupation was unauthorised throughout, no tenancy had been created. *V.G. Fraulo & Co. Ltd.* v.

---

[285] [1942] 2 All E.R. 674 C.A.; *Minister of Health* v. *Bellotti* [1944] K.B. 298 C.A. (a requisitioning authority allowing possession at a weekly rent).

[286] [1974] 1 W.L.R. 1241 C.A.

[287] *Francis Jackson Developments Ltd.* v. *Stemp* [1943] 2 All E.R. 601 (if express); contrast *Dunthorne and Shore* v. *Wiggins* [1943] 2 All E.R. 678. See Woodfall 6.062–6.072.

[288] *Artisans Labourers & General Dwellings Co. Ltd.* v. *Whitaker* [1919] 2 K.B. 301.

[289] *Hagee (London) Ltd.* v. *A B Erikson & Larson* [1976] Q.B. 209 C.A.; *British Railways Board* v. *Bodywright* (1971) 220 E.G. 651.

[290] *Wheeler* v. *Mercer* [1957] A.C. 416 H.L.

[291] *Hagee* case at 217, Scarman L.J.

[292] *Hagee* case at 217, Scarman L.J.; *Cardiothoracic Institute* v. *Shrewdcrest Ltd.* [1986] 1 W.L.R. 368; *London & Associated Investment Trust plc.* v. *Calow* (1987) 53 P. & C.R. 340; *Javad* v. *Aqil* 1991] 1 All E.R. 243 C.A.; *Brent L.B.C.* v. *O'Bryan* [1993] 1 E.G.L.R. 59 C.A.; *Mattey Securities Ltd.* v. *Ervin* [1998] 2 E.G.L.R. 66 C.A.

[293] (1997) 29 H.L.R. 40 C.A.

Papa[294] concerned negotiations for the grant of a tenancy after publicly funded reconstruction work on the property had been completed. Miss Papa was recommended to
the landlord by the local authority from the housing register and moved in while negotiations continued for the grant of a shorthold tenancy, but she admitted in the witness
box that more had to be done before she was confirmed as tenant. Possession was
ordered in the absence of proof of any concluded agreement. Allowing occupation during negotiations for a tenancy remains hazardous because of the possibility that the
court will find that a periodic tenancy has been created informally, and also because of
the risk that an estoppel may create a legal relationship in advance of a formal conclusion of negotiations where the landlord leads the occupier to believe that he will be
treated as a tenant, though many cases fail[295] for want of detriment or on the balance of
equities.[296]

Holding over at the end of a tenancy raises similar problems. When an existing tenancy expires, it will normally be replaced by a periodic tenancy, implied from the payment and acceptance of rent. However the circumstances may negative an intention to
grant a lease, where the owner is considering his position or negotiating to see whether
terms can be agreed for a new tenancy, an area in which commercial cases[297] are aligned
with the domestic. Thus in *Marcroft Wagons Ltd.* v. *Smith*,[298] after a sitting tenant had
died, the landlords—rather than proceed to an immediate eviction of the daughter who
had lived with her—accepted rent from her for a short period while they considered
their position. A licence was the result. In *Vaughan-Armatrading* v. *Sarsah*[299] a student
at South Bank Polytechnic was allowed to stay on for nine weeks to prepare for a resit
examination, but it was made clear that the extension was limited in time and that no
tenancy was being created. Continued occupation was at the sufferance of the landlord
and could legitimately be terminated simply by changing the locks. Payments had been
made but these were not in any technical sense rent payments.

3.   Purchasers allowed possession before completion

A seller will often allow his buyer to take possession of the land he is buying before completion, especially if redecoration and adaption work is required. A licence is permitted
and no security of tenure accrues.[300] This is despite the nineteenth century learning that
a purchaser who took occupation did so as a tenant at will,[301] perhaps because these
were all contracts that provided for possession from the time of exchange. Modern cases
consider the position under an open contract where the assumption is that possession
will be taken only on completion, so that there has to be some vehicle found to cover
occupation in the interim period. Denning L.J. sought to avoid the danger of accidental

---

[294] [1993] 2 E.G.L.R. 99 C.A.

[295] *A.G. of Hong Kong* v. *Humphreys Estate (Queen's Gardens) Ltd.* [1987] A.C. 114 P.C.

[296] *Southwark L.B.C.* v. *Logan* (1997) 29 H.L.R. 40 C.A.

[297] *Longrigg Burrough & Trounson* v. *Smith* [1979] 2 E.G.L.R. 42; *Canterbury Cathedral Dean* v. *Whitbread plc.*
[1995] 1 E.G.L.R. 82 Ch.D.

[298] [1951] 2 K.B. 496.

[299] (1995) 27 H.L.R. 631 C.A.

[300] P. Sparkes [1987] *Conv.* 278; Woodfall 6.085–6.088.

[301] *Howard* v. *Shaw* (1841) 8 M. & W. 118, 151 E.R. 973; *Ball* v. *Cullimore* (1835) 2 Cr. M. & R. 120, 150 E.R. 51;
Doe d. Tomes v. *Chamberlaine* (1839) 5 M. & W. 14, 151 E.R. 7.

residential security in *Errington* v. *Errington*[302] by deciding that a purchaser in possession is in fact a licensee rather than a tenant at will. Restatement of this opinion in *Wheeler* v. *Mercer*[303] led to the customary crushing rebuttal by Viscount Simonds L.C.,[304] but Lord Templeman said in *Street* v. *Mountford*[305] that occupancy under a contract for the sale of land was such that it "*would* or *might* negative the grant of an estate or interest in the land".

Most modern contracts apply the Standard Conditions of Sale, so that where the purchaser takes possession early by permission of the seller occupation is by way of a licence[306] that is revocable.[307] The effectiveness of these conditions is accepted by the courts in precluding security both in their current form[308] and in their previous incarnations.[309] Care is needed to impose an express licence in those cases in which the Standard Conditions do not work, such as occupation of alternative property,[310] entry for repair, and prospective purchasers who have not yet contracted,[311] and also to avoid express terms which can be argued to negate the ordinary revocability of the licence under the Standard Conditions.[312]

Occasionally a contract may provide for the purchaser to take possession in advance of the completion date. The common law perception that there was a tenancy at will[313] is trumped by the equitable view that possession is held under the equitable interest created by the contract,[314] so that according to Somervell L.J. in *Errington* v. *Errington*[315] a purchaser is safe from eviction unless and until the vendor is able to rescind the contract.[316] On the particular facts of that case the couple had a right to occupy so long as they chose to continue paying the interest on the mortgage taken out by the father, but they were in fact treated as contractual licensees since they were not obliged to pay the mortgage interest,[317] even if Lord Templeman explained *Errington* in *Street* v. *Mountford*[318] as a case of seller and buyer.

---

[302] [1952] 1 K.B. 290, 296–298, Denning L.J.; his reliance on *Howard* v. *Shaw* (1841) 8 M. & W. 118, 151 E.R. 973 is unconvincing.

[303] [1956] 1 Q.B. 274, 284.

[304] [1957] A.C. 416, 425, and also at 435, Lord Somervell.

[305] [1985] A.C. 809, 827.

[306] (3rd ed.) cond.5(2); earlier general conditions can be traced back to 1953: B. Hoggett (1972) 36 *Conv. (N.S.)* 325, 330.

[307] *Hyde* v. *Pearce* [1982] 1 All E.R. 1029 C.A.; *Crisp* v. *Fox* (1967) 201 E.G. 769 (right to mesne profits as if purchaser is trespasser).

[308] *Belabel* v. *Mehmet* [1990] 1 E.G.L.R. 220 C.A.

[309] *Hyde* v. *Pearce* as above; *Walters* v. *Roberts* (1981) 41 P. & C.R. 210; *Sparkes* v. *Smart* [1990] 2 E.G.L.R. 245 C.A.

[310] *Chamberlain* v. *Farr* [1942] 2 All E.R. 567.

[311] *Bretherton* v. *Paton* [1986] 1 E.G.L.R. 172 C.A.; though query how this case can be reconciled with *Isaac* v. *Hotel De Paris Ltd.* [1960 1 W.L.R. 239.

[312] *Hyde* v. *Pearce*, above; *Chamberlain* v. *Farr*, above; *Joel* v. *Montgomery & Taylor* [1967] Ch. 272.

[313] *Right d. Lewis* v. *Beard* (1811) 13 East. 210, 104 E.R. 350; *Doe d. Newby* v. *Jackson* (1823) 1 B.& C. 448, 107 E.R. 166; *Saunders* v. *Musgrave* (1827) 6 B. & Cr. 524, 108 E.R. 545.

[314] *Ball* v. *Cullimore* (1835) 2 Cr. M & R. 120, 150 E.R. 51; *Doe d. Tomes* v. *Chamberlaine* (1839) 5 M. & W. 14, 151 E.R. 7; *Howard* v. *Shaw* (1841) 8 M. & W. 118, 151 E.R. 973. *Crockford* v. *Alexander* (1808) 15 Ves. 138, 138, 33 E.R. 707; *Williams* v. *Greatrex* [1957] 1 W.L.R. 31, 40, Hodson L.J.; *Industrial Properties (Barton Hill) Ltd.* v. *Associated Electrical Industries Ltd.* [1977] Q.B. 580 C.A.

[315] [1952] 1 K.B. 290, 293.

[316] *Lakshmijit* v. *Faiz Sherani* [1974] A.C. 605 P.C.; *Allen* v. *I.R.C.* [1914] 2 K.B. 327, 332, Cozens-Hardy M.R.

[317] At 294, Somervell L.J., 296, Denning L.J., 301, Hodson L.J.

[318] [1985] A.C. 809, 821.

A purchaser is most often entitled to possession under an *instalment purchase* contract,[319] that is where a person occupies a house under an arrangement by which he will
acquire ownership of the house over a period of time paying the purchase price by regular instalments. In the interim, the practical position was exactly as if he were a tenant
without any security, leaving him in a position of extreme vulnerability if he missed one
or two monthly payments. This uncertainty and insecurity led Parliament to intervene
to provide protection for the purchaser under an instalment purchase arrangement, a
protection that is roughly equivalent to statutory security of tenure.[320]

4.   Beneficiaries

Trustees of land are normally obliged to allow their beneficiaries to occupy under the
terms of the statutory right of occupation[321] or under the express terms of their trust.
When (before 1925) co-ownership existed at common law, a co-owner allowed exclusive use of the property by permission of the others was viewed as a tenant at will,[322] but
modern law imposes an implied trust and occupation is by virtue of the beneficial interest so that the position is more like that of a licensee.[323] *Gray* v. *Taylor*[324] considered a
person housed by a trust in an almshouse on the terms that he was only to have a personal privilege of occupation and not an assured tenancy. Vexatious behaviour by the
alms person led to his eviction since there was no security. A specific statutory provision
prevents a secure tenancy arising in a publicly owned almshouse.[325]

5.   Temporary accommodation for the homeless

Housing authorities often make available to a homeless person temporary accommodation for the interim period while the authority is making inquiries to decide whether he
is entitled to more permanent housing. Often non-exclusive bed and breakfast or hostel style accommodation is provided, in which case *Westminster C.C.* v. *Clarke*[326] makes
clear that the occupation is by way of licence.

The contentious issue is whether there is a lease or licence where exclusive rights are
given to self-contained accommodation. The relevant phase of a homelessness application is the interim phase where a person is allowed temporary accommodation pending
inquiries. If it is decided that the applicant does not have a priority need or was homeless intentionally the authority is no longer obliged to provide housing, but it is possible
that they will not take steps to remove the applicant from the temporary accommodation provided.

This matter is now covered by express legislative provisions, which were already
favourable to landlords when they were relaxed even further in 1996. In the public sector, landlords were formerly allowed 12 months from the date of the notification of the

---

[319] B. Hoggett (1972) 36 *Conv. (N.S.)* 325, 331–332 (fusion), 328–330 (pretences).
[320] H.A. 1980 s.88 (not affected by the 1985 housing consolidation); by s.89 powers of postponement are long
term and so not limited to 14 days.
[321] T.L.A.T.A. 1996 s.12.
[322] *Geanes* v. *Portman* (1594) Cro. Eliz. 314, 78 E.R. 565.
[323] *Harrison* v. *Wing* [1988] 2 E.G.L.R. 4 C.A.
[324] [1998] 1 W.L.R. 1093 C.A.; *Stanley* v. *Compton* [1951] 1 All E.R. 859 C.A.
[325] H.A. 1985 sch.1 para.12.
[326] [1992] 2 A.C. 288 H.L.

outcome of homelessness inquiries to decide to seek to terminate the tenancy,[327] after which time full security was attracted. The Housing Act 1996 has significantly worsened the position of homeless applicants since temporary accommodation granted to a homeless person is not a secure tenancy unless and until the authority has notified him that it is to be secure.[328] Many homeless applicants are found temporary accommodation with private sector landlords. Formerly they also had 12 months from the conclusion of inquiries to ask the homeless person to leave.[329] Since 1996 any temporary housing provided by a private or social landlord would be by way of a shorthold.[330]

In *Eastleigh B.C.* v. *Walsh*[331] a homeless person was given temporary accommodation pending inquiries in July 1982. His wife left with the children, so that he no longer had a priority need, and the authority decided to evict. Proceedings were started on the basis that he was a licensee in February 1983. The authority still had several months in which it could have treated him as a tenant but one without long-term security, but it missed the chance to do so. The House of Lords dismissed the possession proceedings against Walsh as a licensee.

The decision that Walsh was a tenant is susceptible of explanation in two ways. One is that any temporary accommodation offered to a homeless person creates a tenancy. This can be tested by a case in which the occupation agreement is described as a licence, that is against *Family Housing Association Ltd.* v. *Jones*.[332] A housing association was given a licence to use a property to provide accommodation for homeless people referred to it by a local authority. A self-contained flat was given to Jones, who refused to move out of it when alternative accommodation was offered elsewhere. He was held to have a secure tenancy (at the time housing associations were in the public sector). This was his right because he was held to be a tenant; indeed it is very difficult to give accommodation without creating a tenancy.[333]

Another tenable view is that *Walsh* created a tenancy because of the express agreement to give more than the public law entitlement to temporary housing during homelessness inquiries.[334] Lord Bridge had indeed stressed the unequivocal wording of the particular tenancy agreement.[335] This argument was adopted in *Ogwr B.C.* v. *Dykes*,[336] which said that it is permissible to create a licence where occupation is for 13 weeks or some other very short term.[337] However the decision assumed that a clearly stated intention to create a licence is effective, a principle inconsistent with the doctrine earlier laid down in

---

[327] H.A. 1985 sch.1 para.4 in its pre-1996 form.
[328] H.A. 1985 sch.1 para.4 as amended by H.A. 1996 s.216.
[329] H.A. 1988 s.1(6).
[330] H.A. 1996 s.209(3).
[331] [1985] 1 W.L.R. 525 H.L.; J.E. Martin [1985] *Conv.* 217. *Eastleigh* must be taken to cast doubt on *Restormel B.C.* v. *Buscombe* (1982) 14 H.L.R. 91 C.A. Also doubtful is *South Holland D.C.* v. *Keyle* (1985) 19 H.L.R. 97 C.A. where the Lords' decision was not cited.
[332] [1990] 1 W.L.R. 779 C.A.
[333] *Family H.Ass Ltd.* v. *Jones* [1990] 1 W.L.R. 779, 794B, Slade L.J.
[334] *Mohamed* v. *Manek* (1995) 27 H.L.R. 439, 448, Auld L.J., 451, Nourse L.J.
[335] [1985] 1 W.L.R. 525, 530G.
[336] [1989] 1 W.L.R. 295 C.A.
[337] *West Wiltshire D.C.* v. *Snelgrove* (1998) 30 H.L.R. 57 (casual arrangement for 2 weeks); similar is *Northern Ireland Housing Executive* v. *McCann* [1979] N.I. 39; G. McCormack [1987] *Conv.* 56.

the House of Lords,[338] and it seemed to have been destroyed in the *Family Housing Association* case.[339] However, its authority has been reinstated by *Mohamed* v. *Manek*,[340] another case in which accommodation had been made available as a temporary measure to a man who was homeless. He was given exclusive use of a room in a private sector bed and breakfast establishment with shared access to a kitchen. Ultimately it was decided that he did not have a priority need and he was asked to move to a Salvation Army hostel. Manek was not entitled to an injunction protecting him against eviction. Nourse L.J. ruled[341] that accommodation made available for a very short period as a result of homelessness inquiries cannot in general be premises let as a dwelling under a tenancy. So it seems once again to be possible to explain *Walsh* as a case in which the general rule of a licence had been displaced by the specific terms agreed between the parties.

6.   Redevelopment and short-life property

Local authorities often acquire property for redevelopment and then decide to use it to provide very temporary accommodation to the homeless until demolition actually occurs. Security is removed if a local authority itself grants a residential tenancy of accommodation pending its imminent demolition[342] or any tenancy of land acquired specifically for development.[343]

Unfortunately there is no express provision to cover the much more common grants in the private sector. Usually what happens is that a council acquires land and then licenses it to a social landlord—a housing association or trust—on the terms that sub-licences will be granted to individuals who are homeless. This is a sensible and socially desirable use of short-life property, which depends for its viability on the ability of the local authority to recover vacant possession of the land when redevelopment is about to commence. In fact grants of tenancies require the consent of the Secretary of State and, except in the rare cases where this is granted, no lease can be created; the right of the freeholder to retake possession is clear.

The House of Lords in *Bruton* v. *London & Quadrant Housing Trust* finally settled the position as between the housing trust that provides temporary accommodation and the individual who takes it.[344] Lambeth L.B.C. granted a licence of Oval House in Brixton to the Trust, which granted exclusive possession of Flat 2 to Bruton. As explained elsewhere,[345] the fact that London & Quadrant Housing Trust lacked title to grant sub-tenancies did not affect the creation of a valid tenancy as between the trust and Bruton. The circumstances of the grant were a temporary occupation of a flat in a property ear-

---

[338] *AG Securities* was cited in the C.A. before its reversal in the H.L. [1990] 1 A.C. 417 H.L.

[339] [1990] 1 W.L.R. 779, 789G–790A, Balcombe L.J., 793G–794A, Slade L.J.

[340] (1995) 27 H.L.R. 439 C.A.

[341] At 451.

[342] H.A. 1985 sch.1 para.6.

[343] H.A. 1985 sch.1 para.3; *Attley* v. *Cherwell D.C.* (1989) 21 H.L.R. 613 C.A. (10 year lease included); *Hyde H.Ass. Ltd.* v. *Harrison* (1990) 23 H.L.R. 57 C.A. (house on site of proposed road); *Brent L.B.C.* v. *O'Bryan* [1993] 1 E.G.L.R. 59 C.A. (rent free occupation by squatter). The tenancy becomes secure when development is no longer pending: *Lilleshall Road Housing Co-operative* v. *Brennan* (1991) 24 H.L.R. 195 C.A.

[344] [2000] A.C. 406 H.L.; S. Murdoch [1999] 30 *E.G.* 90; S. Jones [1998] 7 *P.L.J.* 3; D. Rook [1999] *Conv.* 517; S. Bright (2000) 116 *L.Q.R.* 7; M. Dixon [2000] *C.L.J.* 25.

[345] See below pp. 301–303.

marked for redevelopment granted to a person who clearly understood that his occupation was temporary. Was this a case for an exclusive occupational licence under the
Errington exceptions? When assessing the sharp division of judicial opinion caused by
this simple question, it must be remembered that the proposals had long since been
dropped and that Bruton had been forced to live in inadequate conditions for six years
before he was advised to commence proceedings.

A similar situation had arisen in *Camden L.B.C.* v. *Shortlife Community Housing
Ltd.*[346] where Millett J. held that a short life housing organisation granted only licences
to its occupiers, rather than tenancies, given the purposes of the arrangement, the flu-
idity of the occupation rights, the reference to licence fees, and the need for access.
When *Bruton* reached the Court of Appeal, Millett L.J. held to his earlier view that there
was no more than a licence,[347] though (because of the authorities discussed below) now
basing himself on the lack of capacity to create a tenancy. There was however substantial authority for the proposition that exclusive possession is decisive even in this case:
Slade L.J. considered in *Family Housing Association* v. *Jones*[348] that the intention to make
use of short life accommodation is not sufficient to justify the creation of an exclusive
licence, and this view has been approved several time in the Lords.[349] So a grant of exclusive possession creates a tenancy under *Street* v. *Mountford* even where the landlord is a
trust performing socially valuable functions, has agreed not to grant tenancies, has no
estate out of which to grant them and the occupier has agreed that he is not to have a
tenancy.

7.   Employees

Service occupancies are considered in the next chapter.

K.   MOBILE HOMES

1.   Chalets

Normal security (whether "life-long" or for a shorthold) requires entitlement to accommodation in a dwelling-house, meaning simply a dwelling which forms part of a house.
The added ingredient is a structure with some degree of permanence—whether a building, a part of a building, or even a cave[350]—but not houseboats or caravans. A line has
to be drawn somewhere between buildings and mobile homes, with chalets falling into
the grey area. The leading case, *Elitestone Ltd.* v. *Morris*,[351] concerned a property developer who was prevented from clearing a chalet park near Swansea for redevelopment
since the occupiers were held to have full residential security under the Rent Act 1977.

---

[346] (1992) 25 H.L.R. 330, Millett J.; D.S. Cowan [1993] *Conv.* 157; *Shepherds Bush H.A. Ltd.* v. *Hats Co-operative*
(1991) 24 H.L.R. 176 C.A.
[347] [1998] Q.B. 834; also Kennedy L.J.; S. Bright (1998) 114 *L.Q.R.* 345; J. Morgan [1999] *Conv.* 493 (fallacious).
[348] [1990] 1 W.L.R. 779, 794B.
[349] *Westminster C.C.* v. *Clarke* [1992] 2 A.C. 288, 300–302, Lord Templeman; *Bruton* [2000] A.C. 406, 414E–F,
Lord Hoffmann.
[350] *Horsford* v. *Carnill* (1957) 157 E.G. 243, (1957) 158 E.G. 287.
[351] [1997] 1 W.L.R. 687 H.L.; Sparkes *N.L.L.* ch.20; *Nutt* v. *Read* [1999] Times December 3rd C.A. (innocent
misrepresentation that a chalet was a chattel).

The chalets were not like Portakabins or caravans but had been built *in situ* many years ago in such a way that they could not be moved without total destruction. Full security attached even though the cabins rested on their own weight on concrete pillars and were not physically attached to the land. The circumstances showed that they had become part of the land, a classification to be adopted as more precise than the familiar class of fixtures. Attachment of fixed services such as electricity and water is not decisive either way. The principle of the case does not apply to a houseboat.[352]

2.   Caravans on licensed sites

Where a caravan does not attract full security,[353] it may nevertheless fall into a special regime for mobile homes. The availability of this second tier of protection is dependent upon there being a "caravan"[354] or, which is the same thing,[355] a "mobile home". This is a structure designed or adapted to live in, but capable of being moved from one place to another. Rolling stock on a working railway line is excluded. A park home, consisting of four prefabricated sections delivered to the site by a lorry and bolted together, is not a caravan if it is immovable.[356] The *Mobile Homes Act 1983*[357] provides security of tenure where a person owns a mobile home and rents a pitch from a site-owner on a licensed site. Additional protection provided by this Act has led to a boom in park homes, especially in those bought for retirement, which must now be considered.

Pitch fees are based on express agreement as to the amount, rent periods and terms for review.[358] In *Jones* v. *Gospel*[359] it was held that an agreement had been properly terminated for non-payment of pitch fees, and it followed that the management was then entitled to remove the structure and store it. Prices for resale of gas and electricity are fixed on private sites. Services on site and payments for them depend upon express terms. Tenants of mobile homes remain vulnerable to site owners who exploit the monopoly position in the supply of essential services. *Howard* v. *Kinvena Homes Ltd.*[360] shows for example that the site owner was entitled to treat profits from the sale of bottled gas to fuel tenants' central heating systems as an important source of income. When a tenant decided to buy more cheaply elsewhere, the pitch fee could legitimately be increased to cover the loss of profit. Loss of profits on gas sales was a relevant factor applicable to the operation of the park under the written agreement. In *Crittenden (Warren Park) Ltd.* v. *Elliott*[361] the agreement provided for "such communal facilities as

---

[352] See below pp. 182–183.

[353] *Makins* v. *Elson* [1977] W.L.R. 221, 223H, Foster J.; *R.* v. *Nottingham R.O. ex parte Allen* (1986) 52 P. & C.R. 41, Farquharson J.; J.E. Martin [1985] *Conv.* 353 (easily movable caravan not within Rent Act 1977).

[354] Caravan Sites and Control of Development Act 1960 s.29(1) including twin unit caravans; Caravan Sites Act 1968 s.13.

[355] Mobile Homes Act 1983 s.5(1). Query whether there is a gap between mobile homes and full security chalets where all protection fails.

[356] *Carter* v. *S.S. for the Environment* [1994] 1 W.L.R. 1212 C.A.; *Tyler* v. *Woodspring D.C.* [1991] J.P.L. 727 (definition of caravan in planning permission).

[357] The Act came into force on May 20th 1983 to replace the Mobile Homes Act 1975; K. Hodkinson [1982] *Conv.* 364; Bright & Gilbert 581–587.

[358] A. Pool [1994] 08 *E.G.* 102.

[359] [1998] E.G.C.S. 108.

[360] [1999] 25 L.S.G. 30 C.A.; P.H. Kenny [1999] *Conv.* 374.

[361] (1998) 75 P. & C.R. 20 C.A.

may be provided", a term which entitled the owner to provide and control car parking. Where services such as tree felling are provided, the management may set whatever price is fair, for example index linking increases unless this gave a charge that was wholly out of proportion. Consultation is not required.[362]

Tenants of mobile homes have the right to receive from the site-owner a *written statement* of the terms of the tenancy.[363] It includes their names and addresses, the date of the agreement (after which date the notice must be given within three months)[364] any planning restriction which limits the time from which the site can be used, other prescribed information, and details of any express or implied terms. Other terms will relate to quiet enjoyment, the provision of services, preservation of site amenity, repair and maintenance of the site by its owner, repair and maintenance of the home by the resident, and access to the pitch. There are also likely to be restrictions on use. Resiting can occur, but only be under an express term, and only to a comparable site and with all costs borne by the site-owner.[365] Terms can be varied by agreement.[366]

Residential occupiers of caravans have enjoyed *protection from eviction* and harassment since 1968[367] whether they have a licence to station their own caravan on a pitch or to occupy a caravan already on site.[368] Notice to quit a residential caravan or pitch must be of four weeks' duration (on either side)[369] and there is power to suspend the site owner's right to possession for extendible periods of 12 months.[370] *Security* against termination is dependent upon use of the mobile home as an only or main residence[371] and ends where use as a residence has ceased at the date of the court hearing.[372] Hence there is no security for second or holiday homes—not even protection from eviction.[373] If the tenant is resident occupation rights are indefinite unless terminated.[374] A resident must be given four weeks' notice,[375] and only has to give possession under a court order.[376] Grounds are specified, which are much like the grounds for residential repossession,[377] but with the particular addition of these:

deleterious effect on site (this ground can be used every five years)[378];
breach by the resident of the terms of his agreement (after notification and allowance of a reasonable time to rectify the breach)[379]; and

---

[362] *Walker* v. *Badcock* [1997] 2 E.G.L.R. 163 C.A.
[363] Mobile Homes Act 1983 ss.1, 2 and sch.1.
[364] If late, the notice is still valid, but is subject to variation by the court: *Barton* v. *Care* (1992) 24 H.L.R. 684 C.A.
[365] Mobile Homes Act 1983 sch.1 para.10.
[366] There is a right to challenge the stated terms within 6 months; disputes are resolved by arbitration or in court.
[367] Caravan Sites Act 1968 s.3 (both private and public sectors); C.P.R. sch.2 C.C.R. Order 49 r.13.
[368] s.1.
[369] s.2.
[370] s.4.
[371] Mobile Homes Act 1983 sch.1 part I para.5. A holiday caravan is protected only by the terms of the contract: *Brookes* v. *Iddon* [1999] 04 C.L. 431.
[372] *Omar Parks Ltd.* v. *Elkington* [1992] 1 W.L.R. 1270 C.A. (not date of landlord's application).
[373] Not even protection from eviction: Caravan Sites etc. Act 1960 s.1(2)
[374] Mobile Homes Act 1983 sch.1 para.1.
[375] Caravan Sites Act 1968 s.2.
[376] Mobile Homes Act 1983 sch.1 paras.4–6; C.P.R. sch.2 C.C.R. Order 49 r.13.
[377] There is no protection for a person employed as site manager: *Ford* v. *Morrison* [1997] 2 C.L.Y. 4245.
[378] Mobile Homes Act 1983 sch.1 para.6.
[379] para.4.

a need for occupation of the site of the pitch to carry out work.[380]

If the landlord holds a leasehold site or if there are conditions attached to his planning permission or site licence, the rights of the occupiers are limited correspondingly.[381]

Owners of park homes have a right of *sale* but it is heavily qualified: sale is subject to the approval of the buyer by the site owner, which is not to be unreasonably withheld. An appeal lies to a court or (better) to an arbitrator[382] but the procedural protections that require prompt attention to applications for consents relating to fixed dwellings do not apply.[383] The site owner is entitled to charge a 10 per cent commission [384] and also to reserve a right of first refusal. There is a right to make a gift of the home or a gift by will to a resident member of the family, [385] but a non-resident member of the family can only be given the right to sell it and to inherit the value of it.

3.   Caravans on unlicensed sites

Caravans are subject to special control, to prevent sites encroaching all over areas of natural beauty. Protection from eviction applies in the private sector only to licensed sites.[386] The Mobile Homes Act 1983 applies to private licensed sites and local authority sites, but not to sites provided for gypsies,[387] or unlicensed sites.[388] A licence can only be obtained for a site that has planning permission, though some sites for agricultural workers are exempt.[389] Strangely therefore the site owner who has not bothered to apply for a licence and planning permission is in a better position than one who has complied with the law: the occupiers of an unlicensed site do not enjoy protection from eviction.[390] If a planning permission is time-limited, this will naturally impose time limits on all security arrangements on the site.[391]

4.   Houseboats

Licences to moor houseboats are rare, so that most of the estimated 8,000 houseboats have unofficial moorings. This does not affect liability to council tax.[392] Along with the little security, the fees for most moorings are renewable annually, and there is no protection against increases. Inherent difficulties are mooring fees, the difficulty of finding a suitable boat (whether or not it is boat-shaped![393]), the cost of maintenance, problems of financing the acquisition of the boat, and the expense of insurance.

---

[380]   *Tapsell* v. *Cemery* (1995) 27 H.L.R. 114 C.A. (sea wall).
[381]   Mobile Homes Act 1983 sch.1 para.2.
[382]   para.8.
[383]   *Berkeley Leisure Group Ltd.* v. *Lee* (1997) 29 H.L.R. 663 C.A.
[384]   S.I. 1983/748.
[385]   Mobile Homes Act 1983 sch.1 para.9.
[386]   Caravan Sites and Control of Development Act 1960; s.24 provides for local authority sites.
[387]   Mobile Homes Act 1983 s.5(1); *Greenwich L.B.C.* v. *Powell* [1989] A.C. 995 H.L.; successors are bound by s.3.
[388]   *Adams* v.*Brown* [1989] C.L.Y. 2295.
[389]   Caravan Sites etc. Act 1960 sch.1 para.7; *Vale of White Horse D.C.* v. *Mirmalek-Sani* (1993) 25 H.L.R. 387 Div.Ct.
[390]   *Adams* v. *Watkins* [1990] 2 E.G.L.R. 185 C.A.; *Hooper* v. *Eaglestone* (1977) 34 P. & C.R. 311 Div.Ct.; *Balthazar* v. *Mullane* [1985] 2 E.G.L.R. 260 C.A.
[391]   Caravan Sites etc. Act 1960 s.1(2); Mobile Homes Act 1983 sch.1 para.1.
[392]   *Nicholls* v. *Wimbledon V.O.* [1995] R.V.R. 171.
[393]   *Sussex Investments Ltd.* v. *S.S. for the Environment* [1997] Times, December 29th C.A.

A brave attempt to extend the principle of *Elitestone Ltd.* v. *Morris* [394] to a houseboat failed in *Chelsea Yacht and Boat Club Ltd.* v. *Pope*.[395] It concerned a converted D.Day landing craft, moored at Chelsea in such a way that it was afloat for six houses and aground for the next six. The intention to create a lease was clear since the document regulating occupation described the parties as landlord and tenant and was in a form appropriate to a letting. The problem was the spurious extent of the physical annexation to the land. The boat was connected by hoses to water, gas, electricity, telephone and vacuum drainage, and it was attached to pontoons, to rings in the embankment and to an anchor in the river bed, but this did not make the boat part of the land since all could be undone readily enough. Rating cases which indicated that a houseboat could be a rateable hereditament were not thought to be relevant.[396] Without annexation, the purpose of fixing the thing was irrelevant. A boat used as a home is not of the same genus as "real property"—that is land, and the boat remained a mere chattel. The tenant could not qualify for an assured tenancy since the Housing Act 1988 applied only to lettings of land.

---

[394] [1997] 1 W.L.R. 687 H.L.; see above p. 179.
[395] [2000] Times June 7th C.A.
[396] *Cory* v. *Bristow* [1877] 2 A.C. 262 H.L.; *Forrest* v. *Greenwich Overseers* (1858) 8 E. & B. 890, 120 E.R. 332; *Westminster C.C.* v. *Woodbury* [1991] 2 E.G.L.R. 173 C.A.; *Stubbs* v. *Hartnell* (1977) 74 P. & C.R. D36 (poll tax).

7

TIED ACCOMMODATION

Employees. Agricultural tied cottages. Rights and security in tied cottages.

A. EMPLOYEES

1. Private sector

Private sector employers often provide accommodation for employees. Some grant normal residential tenancies—especially now that it is so easy to create a shorthold. Another possibility is a service occupancy (a form of licence[1]) which arises where residential accommodation is provided because occupation of it is necessary for the better performance of the job. This is one of the exceptional cases, discussed in the previous chapter,[2] in which exclusive occupation is consistent with a licence. Expressed in the older terminology of master and servant:

> "the test is whether the servant requires the premises he occupies in order the better to perform his duties as a servant."[3]

In *Norris* v. *Checksfield*[4] a coach driver was allowed to live in a bungalow to ensure that he was near his place of work and was available to do urgent driving work at short notice. Disqualification as a driver led to his dismissal from his employment, and also, sadly, to termination of his service licence of the bungalow. No security was available.[5] A caretaker given a flat in the building that he is employed to guard has only a licence,[6] which is coterminous with his employment contract, but a caretaker given an independent house elsewhere will usually be a tenant.[7]

Even where a lease is created, mandatory grounds for possession are available for employers letting in some industries, such as ministers of religion[8] and farming.[9]

---

[1] *Street* v. *Mountford* [1985] A.C. 809, 827, Lord Templeman.

[2] See above pp. 170–172.

[3] *Smith* v. *Seghill Overseers* (1875) L.R. 10 Q.B. 422, 428, Mellor J.

[4] [1991] 1 W.L.R. 1241 C.A.

[5] However redundancy does not automatically terminate the occupation agreement, so accepting rent will not automatically create a new lease: *Brent L.B.C.* v. *Charles* (1997) 29 H.L.R. 876 C.A.

[6] *Methodist Secondary Schools Trustees* v. *O'Leary* [1993] 1 E.G.L.R. 105 C.A.

[7] *Facchini* v. *Bryson* [1952] 1 T.L.R. 1386; *Scrimgeour* v. *Waller* [1981] 1 E.G.L.R. 68 C.A. (gardener was tenant on the facts); *Royal Philanthropic Society* v. *County* [1985] 2 E.G.L.R. 109 C.A.; P.F. Smith [1986] *Conv.* 215 (care worker was service occupant of previous flat but tenant of new one).

[8] R.A. 1977 sch.15 case 15; H.A. 1988 sch.2 ground 5.

[9] R.A. 1977 sch.15 cases 16–18; H.A. 1988 sch.2 ground 16; *Springfield Investments Ltd.* v. *Bell* (1990) 22 H.L.R. 441 C.A.; *Braithwaite* v. *Elliott* [1947] K.B. 177; R.E. Megarry (1947) 63 *L.Q.R.* 419; *Fowler* v. *Minchin* (1987) 19 H.L.R. 224 C.A.; S. Bridge [1987] *Conv.* 457.

However occupiers of agricultural tied cottages have special protection after their retirement from farming even if they pay a low rent or share facilities with the farmer.[10]

2.   Impact of the minimum wage

Where accommodation is provided for an employee, the minimum wage is currently £3.10 an hour,[11] and there are detailed regulations about how to take account of the value of living accommodation.[12] There is so far no reported case on what is likely to be a very contentious issue, though a settlement between a cleaner, Mrs Diane Pool, and the Immanuel Church, Southsea, was widely reported in the national press.[13]

3.   Public sector

Special legislation applies in the public sector to remove from secure status a tenancy (including an exclusive licence) held by an employee of the landlord if "his contract of employment requires him to occupy the dwelling-house for the better performance of his duties".[14] The scope of this exclusion was explored by the House of Lords in *Hughes* v. *Greenwich L.B.C.*[15] The headmaster of a boarding school and his wife were offered the use of a house in the grounds of the school near Haywards Heath on his appointment in 1961. When he retired he sought to buy the property under the right to buy provisions as a secure tenant of the house. He was indeed held to be a secure tenant. This was because his contract of employment did not require occupation of the property for the purposes of carrying out his job, since a headmaster could live miles away and commute in, the house being conducive to carrying out his functions but not essential. The converse decision was reached in *Surrey C.C.* v. *Lamond*[16] in the case of a council-employed caretaker who occupied a house 162 metres away from his school and was held not to be entitled to any security of tenure. He was required to live on site for the better performance of his duties. The white-collar headmaster could live elsewhere, but the blue-collar worker had to be on hand. It should be noted that a finding that the accommodation is inessential is only of assistance to an employee who occupies exclusive accommodation, since any sharing is necessarily indicative of a licence. In *Parkins* v. *Westminster C.C.*[17] a schoolteacher had only a licence because he shared a flat with other teachers, and so his dismissal from his teaching job was followed by his eviction from the flat.

B.   AGRICULTURAL TIED COTTAGES

1.   Cottages forming part of an agricultural lease

Sometimes a farmer will house an employee in a cottage which has so much land attached to it that the tenancy of land and cottage combined will form an agricultural

---

[10] See below pp. 187–190.
[11] S.I. 1999/584 reg.9.
[12] regs.36–37.
[13] April 12th 2000.
[14] H.A. 1985 sch.1 para.2(1); subparas (2)–(3) deal with police officers and firefighters and para.5 with a person taking up temporary accommodation in order to take up an offer of employment.
[15] [1994] 1 A.C. 170 H.L.
[16] [1999] 1 E.G.L.R. 32 C.A.; S. Murdoch [1999] 12 *E.G.* 164.
[17] (1998) 30 H.L.R. 894 C.A.

lease, that is (according to its commencement date) either an agricultural holding or a farm business tenancy. Protection attaches as an agricultural tenant, and not as a tenant of tied cottage.[18]

On other occasions the position is that the farmer is a tenant under an agricultural lease, and he grants a sub-tenancy of a cottage to an employee. The employee may have residential security. This is despite the decision in *Maunsell* v. *Olins*[19] by a majority of the House of Lords that a sub-tenant could have Rent Act security only if the property comprised in the head lease was a residence. That decision was so inconvenient that it had to be reversed by Parliament.[20] So, today, the fact that the employer is himself an *agricultural* tenant does not prevent his employee having *residential* security in his tied cottage.[21]

2. Assured shortholds

Since early 1989, it has been open to an agricultural employer to grant his employee an assured shorthold tenancy, and in such a case the employee is not treated as a tenant of a tied cottage[22]: he has an assurance for the duration of any fixed contractual period and for a short hold of six months, but no right to long term security. Normally[23] a shorthold cannot be created at a low rent, but this rule is overridden, so that security in a tied cottage can be limited to a short hold even if the agricultural employee is paying a low rent.[24] This will be because his wages are reduced to reflect the fact that accommodation has been provided. If his employment ends, a mandatory ground for possession is available.[25]

Even after the legislative changes of early 1997, a prior warning notice was necessary for the creation of a shorthold in the case of an occupier of a tied cottage: so long as the agricultural worker condition is fulfilled,[26] an assured tenancy cannot be a shorthold unless notice was given in advance.[27] And a tenant of a tied cottage enjoying full protection cannot be fobbed off with a shorthold on renewal.[28] The only difference made by the Housing Act 1996 is that it will no longer be necessary to grant an initial six-month fixed term.

3. Occupancies of tied cottages

Workers on farms often swap higher wages for tied accommodation. This leaves them vulnerable to exploitation, particularly when their employment ends, they retire, or die

---

[18] R.A. 1977 s.10 (as amended by A.T.A. 1995 sch. para.27); R. (Agriculture) A. 1976 sch.2 paras.2–3; H.A. 1988 ss.24(2)(b), 24(2A) (inserted by H.A. 1996 s.103).

[19] [1975] A.C. 373 H.L.; but see the analysis in *Wellcome Trust Ltd.* v. *Hamad* [1998] Q.B. 638 C.A.

[20] See below pp. 300–301.

[21] Unless the employee controls the farming on the holding.

[22] H.A. 1988 s.24(2)(a).

[23] sch.1 para.3.

[24] s.24(2)(b).

[25] s.21.

[26] See below pp. 188–189.

[27] H.A. 1988 sch.2A para.9(2) inserted by H.A. 1996 sch.7; S.Is. 1988/2203, 1997/640 (form); the changes came into force on February 28th 1997. A periodic tenancy which follows the end of a fixed term for which notice was given will also be shorthold.

[28] As above para.9(3).

leaving a spouse who requires housing: so special protection is provided in these cases.[29] Many agricultural workers share some accommodation, occupy subsidised accommodation, or have their meals provided. Normally these factors would make them licensees, so precluding residential security, but special protection is provided for employees engaged in agriculture. Features of this scheme are security of tenure, succession rights and regulation of rents. As with ordinary residential tenants, there are two schemes according to the date of creation of the occupation arrangement:

Protected agricultural occupancies—Rent (Agriculture) Act 1976: if a tied cottage was first occupied at a time when the Rent Act applied to residential leases (that is before early 1989), it was possible to grant full security by granting a lease at a full rent of self-contained residential accommodation. But if this was not done[30] an agricultural occupancy arose under the Rent (Agriculture) Act 1976.[31] Protected licences include those existing when the legislation was first introduced,[32] and those granted up to the start of the assured scheme. This is the scheme most beneficial to the employee.

Assured agricultural occupancies—Housing Act 1988: early 1989[33] saw the introduction of the assured agricultural occupancy, by which full protection was watered down. On termination of the employment, the occupation is converted to what is effectively a full assured tenancy, at a market rent. Protection is afforded to any worker with a tenancy, including one at a low rent which otherwise qualifies for a full assurance. Also included are leases of cottages on land forming part of an agricultural lease[34] and exclusive licences. However, as already explained,[35] the employer always has the option of creating an assured shorthold by giving a warning notice that security will be limited.

4.   Tied workers

Occupants of tied cottages must satisfy similar conditions for qualification under both the 1976 and the 1988 schemes. (1) The landlord: protection accrues to a tenant while the cottage is in qualifying ownership, which means that the landlord must be the employer or a person providing accommodation by arrangement with the employer.[36] Only the Crown and local authorities escape.[37] (2) The worker: protection for tied cottages is defined in terms of the occupier, who must be a qualifying worker in agriculture or forestry,[38] including farm workers and also a person working as a mechanic servicing agricultural machinery.[39] The qualification period is full time agricultural employment

---

[29] Woodfall 23.226–23.255, 24.072–24.079.
[30] See below p. 189.
[31] L.M. Clements (1978) 42 *Conv. (N.S.)* 259. The Act is free-standing: *Durman* v. *Bell* (1988) 20 H.L.R. 340 C.A.
[32] *Skinner* v. *Cooper* [1979] 1 W.L.R. 666 C.A.
[33] H.A. 1988 ss.22–25; the start date was January 15th 1989: s.34.
[34] Unless the tenant controls the farming on the holding.
[35] See above p. 187.
[36] R.(Agriculture) A. 1976 s.2, sch.3 para.3; H.A. 1988 sch.3 para.2(a).
[37] R.(Agriculture) A. 1976 s.5; H.A. 1988 sch.1 paras.11, 12.
[38] R.(Agriculture) A. 1976 sch.3; H.A. 1988 sch.3 is similar but with more extensive provision for joint tenants. Gamekeepers are not protected: *Normanton* v. *Giles* [1980] 1 W.L.R. 28 H.L.; *Glendyne* v. *Rapley* [1978] 1 W.L.R. 601 C.A.
[39] *McPhail* v. *Greensmith* [1993] 2 E.G.L.R. 228 C.A.; R. *Body* [1994] 19 *L.S.G.* 26; also fruit packers: *Re Prior* (1927) 43 T.L.R. 784.

for 91 weeks out of the last 104.[40] Once qualification has accrued it will continue so long as the tied cottage is occupied as his residence,[41] and protection may roll over into replacement accommodation.[42] Those swept into the net include a former employee who has been dismissed, an employee who has retired, and a former employee who is now incapable of full-time work because of some qualifying injury or disease.

5. Self-contained accommodation—1976 (protected) scheme

Until early 1989 it was possible for a farmer to grant full Rent Act protection to his farm worker, but this would only follow from a grant of exclusive possession of self-contained residential accommodation at a rent which is not low. Otherwise the case falls within the Rent (Agriculture) Act 1976—with the grounds for possession further limited.[43] Some relaxations of the normal security scheme are designed to favour agricultural employees. *Firstly*, exclusive licences are treated as tenancies: this is important because service occupiers granted accommodation for the better performance of their duties will be licensees rather than tenants.[44] *Secondly*, an agricultural worker who enjoys exclusive possession of *some* accommodation will attract security, even if some other accommodation is shared with another person (apart that is from the landlord), and rights in what is shared cannot be terminated independently.[45] *Thirdly*, the low rent test is omitted: most agricultural workers have subsidised accommodation and pay a low rent, but they will have security in their cottage if their employment ceases, though the rent can be increased.[46] *Fourthly*, although protection is avoided by a substantial provision of board or attendance, agricultural workers are protected if meals are provided by the employer or if attendance is non-substantial.[47] To the extent of these four relaxations, agricultural employees have better security than ordinary residential tenants. However other factors which limit normal residential security also act as *exclusions from the 1976 scheme*. One example would be a luxury let.[48] Sharing any accommodation with the landlord is fatal to a claim to protection. There is also an exemption from all 1976 scheme security where the worker had the use of a single room in a building in which four or more rooms are let.

6. Self-contained accommodation—1988 (assured) scheme

Protection is not available if there is a valid shorthold,[49] but full security applies to all assured tenancies and exclusive occupation licences.[50] Agricultural workers are better protected than ordinary tenants because low rent leases are protected.[51] However, other

---

[40] Allowance is made for injuries, holidays, etc.
[41] R.(Agriculture) A. 1976 s.4; H.A. 1988 s.25.
[42] R.(Agriculture) A. 1976 s.2(3).
[43] sch.2 para.2.
[44] See above pp. 185–186.
[45] R.(Agriculture) A. 1976 s.23.
[46] See below p. 190.
[47] R.(Agriculture) A. 1976 sch.2 para.3(2).
[48] sch.2 paras.1, 2.
[49] See above p. 187.
[50] H.A. 1988 s.24(2); subs.(3) treats it as if it were a tenancy.
[51] sch.1 paras.3–3B (see S.I. 1990/434 sch. paras.29–30); also sch.1 para.7.

exemptions remove both normal residential security and protection in tied cottages; examples are resident landlords, student lets and holiday lets.[52]

C. RIGHTS OF AGRICULTURAL WORKERS

1. Succession rights

Under *the 1976 scheme*, succession rights apply to surviving spouses and family members;[53] where a death occurs after early 1989 residence for two years is required and succession is to an assured tenancy. Under the *1988 scheme*, only surviving spouses[54] are qualified to succeed.

2. Rent

Under the *1976 (protected) scheme* contractual protection is lost when the worker loses his employment.[55] At this stage the rent can be increased by agreement or the landlord can seek an increase by notice.[56] Alternatively, a rent can be registered by either party.[57] The maximum permitted is what is registered as a fair rent,[58] or a figure derived from applying a fixed multiplier to the rateable value.[59] Excess rent payments can be recovered.

Rents can also be increased under the *1988 (assured) scheme* on the termination of the employment: a tenant of a tied cottage faces an increase to a market rental.[60] If there was previously no rent, it will now be payable monthly.[61]

3. Fitness for habitation

Whenever residential accommodation is let to an agricultural employee, it is an implied term that the accommodation will be kept fit for human habitation.[62]

D. SECURITY OF TENURE

1. Full Rent Act protection

A worker who qualifies for a full Rent Act tenancy—because he occupies self-contained residential accommodation at a full rent—has security in the sense that the landlord must show a ground for possession. Termination of employment is not a ground, and

---

[52] H.A. 1988 sch.1.

[53] R.(Agriculture) A. 1976 s.3; also s.4. Family members other than spouses need to have been resident for 6 months before the death.

[54] H.A. 1988 s.17 (including people living together).

[55] *Burgoyne* v. *Griffiths* [1991] 1 E.G.L.R. 14 C.A.

[56] R.(Agriculture) A. 1976 ss.11, 12.

[57] ss.13, 14 (increase up to the registered level by notice).

[58] s.13 applying R.A. 1977 part IV.

[59] If there was a rateable value on March 31st 1990, it is fixed at 1.5 × the Rateable Value: R. (Agriculture) A. 1976 s.12(9)(a); otherwise it is set according to s.12(9)(c) (as amended by S.I. 1990/434 reg.2 sch. paras.1–13) according to an estimate of what the rateable value would be.

[60] H.A. 1988 s.25 applying ss.13, 14 with modifications; S.Is. 1997/194, 1998/2203 (forms).

[61] H.A. 1988 s.25(1)(b).

[62] L.T.A. 1985 ss.9, 10.

only the discretionary grounds are available,[63] though coupled with a more extensive provision for cases where the tied worker is offered alternative accommodation.[64]

2.   Rent (Agriculture) Act 1976

A farm worker who was granted a licence (rather than a tenancy) before early 1989 is called a protected occupier and has security under the Rent (Agriculture) Act 1976, as well as an enhanced protection from eviction.[65] Security is dependent upon continued residential occupation.[66] As usual the statutory technique is to limit the grounds for possession.[67] If the landlord takes on a new worker who needs the accommodation, the landlord may move his former employee by offering suitable alternative accommodation, either personally or through the local authority.[68] Possession is discretionary in this case,[69] as it is with most others, including particularly those based on misconduct by the tenant[70] such as arrears of rent,[71] or abuse of the security legislation.[72] Thus in *Durman* v. *Bell*[73] a tenant who was clearly in breach of use covenants by starting up business as a small time jobbing builder escaped eviction since the breach had been waived, and anyway it was not reasonable to order possession. Landlords may be able to recover possession for their personal occupation on the discretionary ground.[74] Overcrowding is a mandatory ground.[75]

3.   1988 (assured) scheme

Since early 1989 most agricultural workers have been granted shortholds. However the worker falls within full protection if no shorthold notice was served before the grant and he satisfies the agricultural worker condition; in this case an assured agricultural occupancy arises when occupation is under a periodic tenancy.[76] Protection survives the termination of his employment, since a notice to terminate the employment is not a notice to quit the tenancy.[77] Security is provided by the requirement that a court order be obtained before repossession.[78] Most of the assured tenancy grounds for

---

[63]   R.A. 1977 s.99, sch.15 part I; case 8 (dismissal of an employee) is not available.

[64]   s.99, sch.16 cases 1 and 2.

[65]   Protection from Eviction Act 1977 s.4 as amended by H.A. 1988 s.30(3).

[66]   *Durman* v. *Bell* (1988) 20 H.L.R. 340 C.A.

[67]   R.(Agriculture) A. 1976 s.6, sch.4; notice to quit is not required: s.6(2).

[68]   R.(Agriculture) A. 1976 ss.27–29, sch.4 (cases 1 and 2); *R.* v. *Agricultural Dwelling-houses Advisory Committee ex parte Brough* (1987) 19 H.L.R. 367, Hodgson J.; *R.* v. *East Hertfordshire D.C. ex parte Dallhold Resources Management (U.K.) Pty Ltd.* (1990) 22 H.L.R. 77, Pill J.

[69]   s.7.

[70]   sch.4 case III (rent or other breaches); IV (nuisance, annoyance, illegal or immoral use); Case V (deterioration through waste neglect or default); Case VI (deterioration of furniture).

[71]   *Burgoyne* v. *Griffiths* [1991] 1 E.G.L.R. 14 C.A. (arrears of £1,500 after conversion to a fair rent; was reasonable to order possession).

[72]   Case VII (Tenant's notice to quit and landlord has contracted to sell); Case VIII (unauthorised sub-letting or assignment); case X (sub-letting at an excessive rent).

[73]   (1988) 20 H.L.R. 340 C.A.

[74]   Case IX.

[75]   Case XIII.

[76]   H.A. 1988 s.25, sch.3.

[77]   s.25(4), (5).

[78]   A warning notice is required: H.A. 1988 s.8; S.Is. 1997/194, 1998/265 (form).

repossession are available,[79] the obvious exception being Ground 16 where employment has ceased.

---

[79] H.A. 1988 s.25.

8

DOMESTIC PROTECTION

Express terms. Implied terms. Domestic sector legislation. Standardisation of terms. Reform. Unfair terms. Fundamental rights. Alternative dispute resolution. Small claims.

The subject of this chapter is the distinctive protection provided for residential tenants against abuse by landlords of their dominant negotiating position. It will be shown that these are both well developed and currently inadequate.

A. TERMS OF RESIDENTIAL TENANCIES

1. Termination

Many residential tenancies are periodic—that is made on an indefinite basis on the terms that the tenant can cut it short by notice; however the landlord is circumscribed by the requirements of security of tenure legislation, which prevents immediate termination. In the case of a shorthold, termination is restricted during the first six months, and afterwards the landlord will have to follow a statutory notice procedure and obtain a possession order. Where a tenant has full security of tenure the landlord will not generally be able to obtain possession at all during the good behaviour of the tenant. The history of the security of tenure legislation, its over complexity and proposals for its reform, have all been explained in previous chapters.[1]

2. Common form of a short residential tenancy

Residential tenants tend to be offered similar terms. The tenancy will state the initial rent and how it is paid. Rents are always subject to statutory regulation (if only to prevent excessive housing benefit claims) and most landlords leave rent increases to the statutory notice procedures. The tenant will be required to maintain the property internally (the structure and installations being allocated to the landlord by statute) and should be put under an absolute prohibition on making any alteration or improvement. It is most important for a residential landlord to impose an absolute prohibition on all dealings—to prevent the introduction of an unsatisfactory new tenant and to prevent sub-lettings that might attract independent security. The bar will not affect statutory succession on death and transfers ordered by a family court after a relationship breakdown. The tenancy should provide for its termination during any fixed contractual period if the

[1] See above Chapters 1 and 5.

tenant breaks any term of the tenancy, though actual repossession will be subject to the grounds for possession laid down by the relevant security regime. Reference should be made to the succeeding chapters, each of which has a title that should be self-explanatory.

3.   Written statement of the express terms

Tenancy agreements contain detailed terms regulating the interrelationship of landlord and tenant. Theoretically, perhaps, a residential tenancy is just one more type of contract,[2] but if so it is inevitably a lop-sided affair. Landlords lay down terms, imposing numerous obligations on tenants but few on themselves, and a tenant seeking a home is rarely free to negotiate terms. Short residential tenancies are generally informal, this making no difference to the enforceability of the terms, but it is an inconvenience that a tenancy can be created orally.[3] One right that every residential tenant should have is to a written statement of the terms of his tenancy. The various Charters for social tenants include: "Your Right to a Written Tenancy Agreement", as well as a right to agree changes.[4] Shorthold tenancies no longer need to be in writing, though the withdrawal of the accelerated procedure for repossession unless there is a tenancy in writing is a significant incentive to provide a written agreement, and tenants do have the right to a written statement of terms.[5] Weekly residential tenants have the right to a rent book,[6] and all tenants can insist on receiving notification of an address for complaints before any rent falls due.[7] If these titbits add up to a significant protection, they also fall far short of a satisfactory right to a written statement of the terms of the tenancy.

4.   Implied obligation of quiet enjoyment

The landlord's promise that the tenant will be left to live peacefully in his property is the most important obligation that is implied on the landlord's side.[8]

5.   Implication in leases—business efficacy

Contractual rules for the implication of terms are based on the principle that a clause can only be introduced on the basis that a necessity for it is shown. Arguably this test is too restrictive, since terms cannot be implied simply because it would be reasonable to do so. This results in an exhaustive style of drafting but, the more that an attempt is made to spell out a provision for every contingency, the more likely it becomes that there will be hidden gaps.

   The court can imply terms only if they are necessary to give business efficacy to the lease. In *Liverpool City Council* v. *Irwin*[9] the House of Lords highlighted both the possi-

---

   [2] *Hammersmith & Fulham L.B.C.* v. *Monk* [1992] 1 A.C. 478, 483B–C, Lord Bridge; *Bruton* v. *London & Quadrant Housing Trust* [2000] A.C. 406 H.L.
   [3] L.P.A. 1925 s.54(2); see above pp. 34–38.
   [4] e.g. the *Assured Tenant's Charter* (Housing Corporation, 1998) section 3. There is a *Secure Tenant's Charter* (D.E.T.R., 1998) but this does little more than to confirm a public sector tenant's statutory rights.
   [5] See above pp. 52–53.
   [6] See below p. 181.
   [7] See below p. 223.
   [8] See below p. 223.
   [9] [1977] A.C. 239 H.L.; D. McIntyre [1977] *C.L.J.* 15.

bility of implying terms relating to common parts of a building outside the control of individual tenants, and the possible inadequacy of those terms. The case concerned the Piggeries, a notorious block of high-rise flats in Liverpool. Tenants signed tenancy agreements relating to individual flats, which imposed obligations on the tenants but not on landlords, so that there was scope for implying terms against the landlords. They provided communal lifts and garbage disposal units. Since the tenancy agreements made no reference to any communal facilities, it was necessary to imply rights in the nature of easements to make use of them, a necessity not contested in view of the height of the tower blocks. Realistically the flats were not habitable if the tenants had to use the stairs. More pressing was the question whether the landlord was under an obligation to maintain the facilities. A duty was implied, but it was limited to doing what was reasonable in the circumstances. Since damage to the lifts was attributable to repeated vandalism, which was beyond the control of the council landlords, there was no breach of duty on the facts of the case. The flats remained useless, and ultimately it became necessary to blow up the block. The result would have been radically different if a full repairing covenant could have been implied, since in that case the landlord would have been obliged to keep the lifts in working order irrespective of the reason for the disrepair.

Numerous other cases on repair[10] and insurance[11] demonstrate the very restricted scope of contractual implication.

6. Implication in contracts—usual covenants

This subject is discussed in the commercial context in which it usually arises.[12]

B. STATUTORY SCOPE OF DOMESTIC PROTECTION

Quite apart from security of tenure, legislation treats short residential tenants with a tenderness not displayed to commercial tenants. Distinctive protection is confined to a small legislative compass, but its practical effect is far-reaching. One very significant area is the guarantee of peaceful habitation provided by the Protection from Eviction Act 1977.[13] A second crucial intervention is in repairing covenants, the major burdens relating to structure and installations being placed on the landlord.[14] A third element is the rights to information.[15] One might also add the right to buy enjoyed by public sector tenants, though that is considered in this book in the context of enfranchisement.[16]

---

[10] *Sleafer* v. *Lambeth M.B.C.* [1960] 1 Q.B. 43 C.A.; J.C. Hall [1960] *C.L.J.* 40; *Barrett* v. *Lounova (1982) Ltd.* [1990] 1 Q.B. 348 C.A.; *Duke of Westminster* v. *Guild* [1985] Q.B. 668 C.A.; *Hafton Properties Ltd.* v. *Camp* [1994] 1 E.G.L.R. 67; *Southwark L.B.C.* v. *Camacho* [2000] 06 C.L. 468.

[11] See below pp. 685–690.

[12] See below pp. 632–633.

[13] See below pp. 309–315.

[14] L.T.A. 1985 ss.11–17; L.T.A. 1927 s.18 restricts damages for anything left within the tenant's sphere; see below pp. 243–246.

[15] L.T.A. 1985 ss.1–3 (general), 4–7 (rent books), L.T.A. 1987 Part VI (rent and service charge notices); see below p. 223.

[16] See below Chapter 18.

In addition there is an important group of rights, primarily targeted at long residential tenant owners, which may assist some renters, including the right to refer service charges to a Leasehold Valuation Tribunal[17] and the right of first refusal when the owner of a block sells his freehold.[18] Tenants in blocks and on estates also have rights of participation in communal management.[19]

C. LAW COMMISSION REFORM

According to Professor Kenny, the state of the landlord and tenant legislation is sufficient to puzzle and amaze a future archaeologist stepping out of his starship.[20] The Law Commission was formed "for the purpose of promoting the reform of the law"[21] and it was no surprise to find that the First Programme of Reform included the "Codification of the Law of Landlord and Tenant".[22] Calls for reform have continued. Standardisation of residential leases was identified as a priority by the Royal Commission on Legal Services,[23] and since it reported in 1979 this has become even more pressing given the wide divergence of statutory regimes for residential security of tenure.[24] Lord Woolf's report on *Access to Justice*[25] observes that reform of the substantive law would do more than anything else to assist tenants.

1.   Consolidation

The Commission has been most successful in facilitating the consolidation of the security of tenure schemes.

Law Com. Report	Topic consolidated or amended	Result
81 (1977)	Rent Bill	R.A. 1977
144 (1985)	Housing Acts	H.A. 1985 etc.

Despite this work the security of tenure codes are in desperate need of comprehensive consolidation—even codification. Since the basic structure of the law is for the moment politically uncontentious, however surprising this may seem, this is work that the Commission could usefully be asked to undertake. Surely a single code for all residential sectors is achievable?

2.   Substantive reform

Work has been equally impressive on substantive reforms, but the enacted reforms fall far short of expectations as the following table shows.

[17] L.T.A. 1985 ss.18–30 as amended by L.T.A. 1987 part V and H.A. 1996.
[18] See below pp. 426–432.
[19] See below pp. 279–283.
[20] P.H. Kenny [1999] *Conv.* 281.
[21] Law Commissions Act 1965 s.1.
[22] Law Com. No.1 (1966) Item VIII.
[23] Cmnd. 7648 (1979) annex 21.1 para.13.
[24] A. Tunkel [1991] *N.L.J.* 1567.
[25] (H.M.S.O., July 1996) ch.16 paras.2(b), 7–8.

Tabulation of Law Commission work on business property
(excluding security of tenure)

Law Com No.	Law Com W.P./C.P.	Topic	Implementation
67 (1975)	W.P. 8 (1967)	Obligations of landlord and tenant	
141 (1985)	W.P. 25 (1970)	Restrictions on Dispositions, Alterations and Change of Use	L.T.A. 1988
162 (1987)		Reform of the law	
238 (1996)	W.P. 123 (1992)	Responsibility for the State and Condition of Property	

Statutory obligations and overriding terms (such as quiet enjoyment and non-derogation from grant) were envisaged. Contracting out would have been severely restricted in the domestic sector, creating an irreducible core of obligations, and a wide gulf from commercial leases where most standard terms would simply be defaults.[26] A later report added the suggestion of key words, which would trigger the implication of standard term.[27] Standardisation of residential leases was identified as a priority by the Royal Commission on Legal Services.[28]

3. Plain English

No one could accuse the English legislation on landlord and tenant of comprehensibility. Any author on the subject will testify to the hours of patient research required to untangle the most basic points. Perhaps the intelligibility requirement of the regulations on unfair contract terms[29] should be applied to the legislators themselves. It would help lawyers if the terminology were clarified and simplified, and a single code laid down for all renting arrangements. Even more important is that terms of the tenancies—both rights and responsibilities—should be spelled out in terms comprehensible to the people who will need to refer to them. Most people will honour reasonable terms which they know of and understand. In this respect the *Charters for Social Tenants*[30] are a model, and quite properly carry the Plain Language Commission Clear English Standard.

4. Progress poor

However, there is no sign of any consensus about what reform is desirable in relation to repairing covenants or the general terms of commercial leases and no Consultation

---

[26] Law Com. No.67 (1975).
[27] Law Com. No.162 (1987) paras.3.14–3.18.
[28] Cmnd. 7648 (1979) annex 21.1 para.13.
[29] S.I. 1999/2083 reg.7; see below pp. 199–200.
[30] (Housing Corporation, 1998).

Paper has been published since 1992. Work on fitness standards has been subsumed into a wider review of housing law,[31] and no progress is imminent. The innate restriction of the Commission to non-contentious reform makes it an unsuitable vehicle to tackle the landlords' lobby, and one must turn hopefully towards the D.E.T.R. whose Green Paper[32] adopts a call from the Chartered Institute of Housing for a move to a unified tenure for the public and social sectors; but why stop there—why not reform the private sector at the same time. A political impetus is required if the ultimate goal of a thorough codification of the entire law of landlord and tenant is ever to be achieved.

D. UNFAIR TERMS

The Unfair Contract Terms Act 1977 does not apply to land,[33] but it appears that the Unfair Terms in Consumer Contracts Regulations may apply, especially since the 1994 model[34] was re-enacted in 1999[35] in order to reflect more closely the wording of the European Directive that they were intended implement.[36]

1. Parties

The regulations apply to unfair terms in any contract concluded between a "seller or supplier" on the one hand and a "consumer", defined to include any natural person acting otherwise than for his trade, business or profession.[37] There is no longer any specific need for a sale of goods or a supply of services: a "seller or supplier" is any natural or legal person who enters into a contract for purposes relating to trade, business, or profession (which may be public or private).[38] Even before that change, it was probably possible to see the grant of a tenancy as a supply of services, both under V.A.T. rules and probably under the text of the European Directive that the regulations are designed to implement.[39] According to Professor Adams, "residential leases are clearly in the firing line".[40] Assuming that leases may be caught in the net, the 1999 Regulations apply only to a lease made to a tenant who is a consumer, defined as a natural person who is acting for purposes which are outside his business. Leases to companies and all other commercial leases fall outside this ambit.

---

[31] 33rd Annual Report Law Com. No. 258 (1999) paras.1.20–1.21; Law Com. 7th Programme Law Com. No. 259 (1999) para.1.4.

[32] *Quality and Choice: A Decent Home for All* (D.E.T.R., April 2000) paras.5.9, 9.66–9.72.

[33] sch.1 para.1(6); *Electricity Supply Nominees Ltd.* v. *I.A.F. Group plc.* [1993] 1 W.L.R. 1059; *Havenridge* v. *Boston Dyers Ltd.* [1994] 2 E.G.L.R. 73 C.A.; *Star Rider Ltd.* v. *Inntrepreneur Pub Co. Ltd.* [1998] 1 E.G.L.R. 53.

[34] S.I. 1994/3159 in force July 1st 1995; S. Bright & C. Bright (1995) 111 *L.Q.R.* 655; J.E. Adams [1995] *Conv.* 10; J.E. Adams [1999] *Conv.* 8; H.W. Wilkinson [1999] *N.L.J.* 773.

[35] S.I. 1999/2083 as from October 1st 1999; J. Holbrook [1999] 09 *Legal Action* 26.

[36] Directive 93/13, [1993] O.J. L95/29.

[37] reg.3.

[38] reg.3.

[39] sch.1 excludes contracts relating to employment, succession rights, family law rights, and the incorporation of companies.

[40] J.E. Adams [1995] *Conv.* 10.

2. Main terms

The regulations catch terms which have not been individually negotiated. Review cannot alter the main body of the agreement, that is the terms which define the main subject matter of the contract and the price (that is any premium and the rent). Intelligibility is required,[41] but otherwise there is no assessment of the fairness of these main terms.[42]

3. Unfair terms

Terms are open to review if they are not individually negotiated.[43] A lease will inevitably contain some terms which are subject to specific agreement, so that it will be necessary to make an overall assessment that the lease forms a pre-formulated standard contract.[44] Unfair terms are not binding on the tenant,[45] though the remainder of the lease would continue in force.[46] The Director General of Fair Trading could take action to secure an injunction against a landlord using unfair standard terms.[47]

An unfair term is defined as any term which causes a significant imbalance in the parties' rights and obligations under the contract to the detriment of the consumer, contrary to the requirement of good faith.[48] Assessment of whether there is an imbalance is to take into account the nature of the services (that is the tenancy), to refer to all circumstances attending the conclusion of the contract, and to the whole contractual package, including any related contract. Factors requiring consideration are the relative bargaining positions, special inducements given for agreement to a particular term, any special order, and the extent to which the landlord has dealt fairly with the tenant.[49] An indicative list of dubious terms is provided: examples are terms limiting rights against the landlord or tenant's remedies, terms precluding a set off, terms with which the tenant has not had an opportunity to become familiar, terms permitting unilateral alteration, terms permitting termination without reasonable notice, and those limiting liability for misrepresentations by agents.[50]

4. Intelligibility

The landlord is required to ensure that any written term of a contract is expressed in plain intelligible language, and any doubt is resolved in favour of the consumer.[51]

---

[41] reg.7(2).
[42] reg.6(2).
[43] reg.5(1), including any drafted in advance: reg.5(2).
[44] reg.5(3), (4) (onus on the landlord).
[45] reg.8(1).
[46] reg.8(2).
[47] regs.10–12.
[48] reg.5(1).
[49] reg.5(3).
[50] sch.2.
[51] reg.7.

E. FUNDAMENTAL RIGHTS

The Human Rights Act 1998 came into force on October 2nd 2000,[52] and from that day onwards it has been possible to raise arguments in the English courts based directly on the European Convention for the Protection of Human Rights and Fundamental freedoms. Although academic opinions vary,[53] it must be anticipated that, sooner or later, the incorporation of these rights will have a profound and seismic effect on the law affecting landlords and tenants in this country, and in particular on domestic tenants. At the very least, many new arguments have become available to those pursuing housing cases through the courts. Substantive rights and freedoms are considered first, and there follows a review of the new procedural mechanisms by which Convention rights are made available in the English courts.

1. Fundamental and human rights

This distinction needs clear and sharp delineation, given that the main substantive right affecting property lawyers—the right to property under Article 1 of Protocol 1[54]—is available to "every natural or legal person", so that companies and building societies[55] may seek protection just as much as any individual. So this is best described as a fundamental right. Perhaps it is most likely to be tenants who seek to take advantage of this right, but the leading challenge to the enfranchisement laws—*James* v. *U.K.*[56]—shows that landlords may just as much challenge interference with their reversionary rights. Other rights are likely to be of use mainly to tenants, such as the right to a family home—which is strictly a human right. Ancillary and procedural protections are also important.

2. Fundamental rights to property

Mellacher v. *Austria*[57] established that Article 1 of Protocol 1 to the Convention[58] contains two rights: (1) a right to peaceful enjoyment; (2) freedom from deprivation. These are qualified by a third element of the article, (3) the public interest justification. But the case also shows that the three principles are interconnected.[59] The text of the basic *rights of property* is as follows:

> *First,* "Every natural or legal person is entitled to the peaceful enjoyment of his possession". And *second* "No one shall be deprived of his possessions . . .".

---

[52] s.22; a commencement order was made in July 2000.

[53] A. Arden & C. Baker [1998] 03 *Legal Action* 8; J. Howell [1999] *Conv.* 287; J. Alder [1999] *J.H.L.* 67; R. Buxton (2000) 116 *L.Q.R.* 48; M. Davies [2000] 27 *L.S.G.* 30, [2000] 37 *L.S.G.* 31; J. Luba [2000] 09 *Legal Action* 27.

[54] H.R.A. 1998 sch.1; the Protocol was agreed at Paris on March 20th 1952.

[55] *National & Provincial B.S.* v. *U.K.* (1998) 25 E.H.R.R. 127.

[56] (1986) 8 E.H.R.R. 123; *Immobiliare Saffi* v. *Italy* (1999) 7 B.H.R.C. 256.

[57] (1990) 12 E.H.R.R. 391, 408.

[58] H.R.A. 1998 sch.1.

[59] *Mellacher* v. *Austria* at 408; *Lithgow* v. *U.K.* (1986) 8 E.H.R.R. 329 (compulsory acquisition of shares in aircraft companies).

Both are targeted at "possessions", which clearly includes land and personal property,[60] but also intangible things like a right to receive a fair rent[61] and a right of restitution.[62] The French text uses the words "*biens*" (goods) which makes explicit that the intended scope is wider than just property. The first limb guarantees peaceful enjoyment of property, so that it might be infringed by loss of the use of the property; examples are planning blight,[63] creation of a nature reserve,[64] compulsory transfer of hunting rights,[65] modification of restrictive covenants,[66] or failure to enforce a landlord's right to possession.[67] A guarantee against actual loss of the property itself is relegated to the second limb, this providing a guarantee against arbitrary confiscation.[68]

European rights are not directly in play unless the state acquires the right.[69] However, if a state enacts legislation (or leaves in force case-law rules) that operates to allow one property owner to expropriate the property of another, a claim based on that type of interference is potentially within Article 1 of Protocol 1.[70] A crucial issue is whether the Human Rights Act 1998 will have a "horizontal" as well as a "vertical" effect. The latter arises where a person's property is taken by the government or other public body, and the action is taken against that public body for violation of the property owner's Convention rights. That is straightforward and clearly within the scope of the Act. A horizontal action is taken between two private property owners, the one complaining that the other has violated his human rights in reliance on legislation or property ownership rules laid down by a public body, and there might be even more scope for horizontal defences. In *James* v. *United Kingdom*[71] a ground landlord took action against the government arguing that enfranchisement rights violated his right to his property. At the time of the case the "vertical" action against the Government in Strasbourg was the only action available, though on the merits it failed. Suppose that a leaseholder now seeks to enfranchise and the ground landlord (with a stronger case on the merits) seeks to defend the case arguing that the enfranchisement legislation contravenes the Convention. If a court is a public body whose judgments must comply with the Convention, can an individual leaseholder obtain a judgment authorising him to enfranchise in contravention of the rights of his ground landlord? If not, and the vertical effect is conceded, the Act could turn out to have a very radical and far-reaching effect.

---

[60] *Vasilescu* v. *Romania* [1999] 28 E.H.R.R. 241.

[61] *R.* v. *S.S. for E.T.R. ex parte Spath holme Ltd.* [2000] 1 All E.R. 884, 905b, Lord Bingham M.R.

[62] *National & Provincial B.S.* v. *U.K.* (1998) 25 E.H.R.R. 127.

[63] *Sporrong* v. *Sweden* (1983) 5 E.H.R.R. 35 (use of land blocked for 23 years).

[64] *Matos e Silva Lda.* v. *Portugal* (1996) 24 E.H.R.R. 673, 590–593.

[65] *Chassagnou* v. *France* (1999) 7 B.H.R.C. 151.

[66] *Scott* v. *U.K.*, App. No. 10741/84, 41 *Decisions of Commission* 226; N. Dawson [1986] *Conv.* 124.

[67] *Immobiliare Saffi* v. *Italy* (1999) 7 B.H.R.C. 256; *Iatridis* v. *Greece* [2000] 30 E.H.R.R. 97.

[68] *Powell* v. *U.K.* (1987) 9 E.H.R.R. 241 (unsuccessful case based on noise disturbance from Heathrow).

[69] App. No. 1194/86—claim that forfeiture infringed rights was inadmissible. See also *Adam* v. *Czech Republic* (1997) 1 B.H.R.C. 451; I. Loveland [2000] *N.L.J.* 1595.

[70] *James* v. *U.K.* (1986) 8 E.C.H.R. 123; *Arrondale* v. *U.K.* [1983] 5 E.H.R.R. 118 (noise from Gatwick); *Immobiliare Saffi* v. *Italy* (1999) 7 B.H.R.C. 256.

[71] (1986) 8 E.C.H.R. 123.

3.   Qualifications to the convention right to property

There are three major limitations on Article 1 of Protocol 1. *One* permits the deprivation of possessions,

> "in the public interest and subject to the conditions provided for by the law and by the general
> principles of international law."

Two permits laws to control the use of property, since the right to property,

> "shall not . . . in any way impair the right of a State to enforce such laws as it deems necessary
> to control the use of property in accordance with the general interest."

And *three* permits laws,

> "to secure the payment of taxes or other contributions or penalties."[72]

Since it is usually clear that a complaint does involve an interference with the right to
property of the person complaining, states very often invoke these limitations when
seeking to defend property legislation by showing that the interference is justified. Case
law principles developed by the human rights judges at Strasbourg will now be applied
in the interpretation of English case law and statutes.[73]

Any interference with property rights must be lawful, a point which has been clear in
most reported cases. More debatable is the requirement that the interference should
seek to achieve a legitimate purpose. Finally the rule must be necessary in a democratic
society. However a margin of appreciation is allowed to the state, by which an area of
discretion is left to the state to determine whether particular legislation is useful.[74]
Proportionality is the principle, typical of common law systems if unfamiliar to common lawyers, that the court must assess an interference with property rights in the light
of the social problem requiring the interference; a legislative remedy must be reasonably
commensurate with the problem being tackled,[75] or in other words there must be a fair
balance between the right to property and the social needs of the community. Rent regulation schemes and security of tenure legislation have generally survived attacks in
Strasbourg in principle, though the detail of the legislation requires separate scrutiny
and in extreme cases it may be held that the landlord's human rights have been contra-
vened.[76]

The most important human rights challenge to landlord and tenant legislation
involves our own enfranchisement scheme, which withstood a strong attack by the Duke
of Westminster in *James v. U.K.*[77] The Leasehold Reform Act 1967 was intended to
enable long leaseholders to acquire the freehold reversion in their homes at a price below
the full market value. Underlying the legislation was the motivating philosophy that

---

[72] *National & Provincial B.S. v. U.K.* (1998) 25 E.H.R.R. 127; *Gasus Dosier und Fördertechnik GmbH v.
Netherlands* (1995) 20 E.H.R.R. 403.

[73] s.2.

[74] *Mellacher v. Austria* (1990) 12 E.H.R.R. 391; A. Arden & C. Baker [1998] 03 *Legal Action* 8. Temporary suspensions of evictions might fall within this margin: *Immobiliare Saffi v. Italy* (1999) 7 B.H.R.C. 256.

[75] *Mellacher* (Austrian rent control legislation not a breach).

[76] *Scollo v. Italy* (1996) 22 E.H.R.R. 514 (Italian security of tenure regime beyond margin of appreciation).

[77] (1986) 8 E.C.H.R. 123; S. Bright [1994] *Conv.* 211.

leaseholders under long leases had the moral right to the bricks and mortar for which they had paid when acquiring the lease and that ground landlords should only have the moral right to the undeveloped site. That this legislation involved expropriation was indisputable. The human rights issue was whether leasehold reform legislation satisfied the Convention's public interest exception.

Objective justification is required of legislation, which demonstrates a need for the legislation and also shows that it is appropriate and proportionate. It was held that the English legislation was justified in *James* v. *United Kingdom*. James was one of the trustees of the Duke of Westminster's Grosvenor estate in Central London with 2,000 houses, which faced claims by 80 tenants in four years in the early 1980s. Estimates of the profit to individual tenants from enfranchising ranged between £32,000 and £182,000, and this also measured the loss to the landlord estate. Legislation to remove social injustice could satisfy the public interest test, even if its effect was to transfer private rights from one individual to another rather than to achieve direct public ownership. Enfranchisement legislation was fair, since occupying leaseholders are morally entitled to ownership, ground landlords collectively having exploited a monopoly to create a form of tenure which was disadvantageous to leaseholders. Sales of houses on long leases should be based on the value of the land itself rather than the market value of the land carrying the house. In equity the leaseholder should not be required to buy again what he has already bought, and unjust enrichment of landlords should be reversed. The 1967 Act was appropriate to this end and not disproportionate. Given that this overtly socialist legislation passed muster, what prospect is there of a successful challenge to the basic tenets of any tenant protection scheme that is likely to be enacted?

Anomalies in the legislation require separate justification, as they tend to discriminate between different property owners,[78] but the court accepted in *James* that objective reasons were available to justify the form of the Leasehold Reform Act 1967.

4.   Right to a home

Human rights affecting property are most likely to involve the peripheral impact of other rights. Most directly relevant is Article 8 which guarantees respect for an individual's family life and home in these terms:

> "1. Everyone has the right to respect for his private and family life, his home and his correspondence."

Family property disputes may well involve the right to marry and to found a family.[79] These are strictly "human" rights. Curiously the jurisprudence of the European Court of Human Rights does not include any recognition of the rights of gay men and women, the Strasbourg Court not yet having evolved to the view that a stable homosexual relationship constitutes a family.[80] Curious this certainly is, for who would expect to find our House of Lords leading on the human rights lawyers?

---

[78] Contrary to Art. 14.

[79] Art. 12. This is not just restricted to family life within marriage: *X, Y, Z* v. *U.K.* (1997) 24 E.H.R.R. 143.

[80] *Fitzpatrick* v. *Sterling H.Ass Ltd.* [1999] 4 All E.R. 705, 716e–f, Lord Slynn; P.J. Kirby [2000] *N.L.J.* 550; H. Conway [2000] *N.L.J.* 506; see also *A.G. for Ontario* v. *M.* (1999) 7 B.H.R.C. 489.

The potentiality of Article 8 was demonstrated in *Albany Home Loans Ltd.* v. *Massey*[81] where a lender's repossession action was challenged on the grounds that it infringed the human right of the borrower to his home. Schiemann L.J. decided the case on domestic legislation, but clearly considered that the convention rights were relevant in this sphere. Similarly, in *Buckley* v. *U.K.*,[82] domestic planning law was challenged by a gypsy who was unable to get planning permission to live in a caravan on land in South Cambridgeshire which she owned. The fact that the case was admitted to argument before the Strasbourg Court shows that the home protected by Article 8 need not be a lawful home.[83] Article 8 was relevant in that her home was threatened.

Paragraph 2 of Article 8 provides the public interest justification, in these terms:

"There shall be no interference by a public authority with the exercise of this right except such as in accordance with the law and is necessary in a democratic society in the interests of national security, public safety, or the economic well being of the country, for the prevention of disorder or crime, for the protection of health or morals or for the protection of the rights and freedoms of others."

No violation occurs if the interference with the home is (1) in accordance with the law, (2) for a legitimate aim, and (3) necessary in a democratic society.[84] In *Buckley,* as in most cases, it could not be argued that the intervention was contrary to law, and the aim of conservation was clearly legitimate. Dispute focused on the third issue, which divided the court, though the enforcement proceedings against Buckley only survived by six votes to three.[85]

Incorporation of this Convention right may therefore have an immediate and dramatic effect on housing law.[86]

5.   Procedural and subsidiary rights

A number of Convention rights that are procedural or ancillary to the substantive rights are likely to provide the main focus for challenges to property law.

Article 14 guarantees freedom from discrimination in the enjoyment of these rights.[87] This is much argued in human rights, since legislation that differentiates between two classes of property owners requires objective justification. This is demonstrated perfectly by *Larkos* v. *Cyprus.*[88] A civil servant was allocated rented accommodation by the government under the terms of an administrative order but when he retired they evicted him, arguing that his right to accommodation ended with his employment. It was held that this was discriminatory treatment without any reasonable or objective justification given that the tenancy agreement was silent as to the consequences of his retirement.

---

[81] [1997] 2 All E.R. 609, 612g–h; *Larkos* v. *Cyprus* (1999) 7 B.H.R.C. 244.

[82] (1996) 23 E.H.R.R. 101. In *Lopez-Osta* v. *Spain* (1995) 20 E.H.R.R. 277 air pollution was challenged as a threat to the applicant's family life.

[83] At 124–125.

[84] *Howard* v. *U.K.* (1987) 9 E.H.R.R. 116. The test is just interference.

[85] Enforcement procedures also survived scrutiny in *Bryan* v. *U.K.* (1995) 21 E.H.R.R. 342.

[86] C. Baker & E. Saunders (1997) 141 *S.J.* 886.

[87] *Mellacher* v. *Austria* (1990) 12 E.H.R.R. 391, 413; *National Provincial B.S.* v. *U.K.* (1998) 25 E.H.R.R. 127, 173–175.

[88] (1999) 7 B.H.R.C. 244 (art 14 in conjunction with art.8); also *Chassagnou* v. *France* (1999) 7 B.H.R.C. 151 (large and small landowners treated differently).

Article 6 guarantees due process for the resolution of civil claims, that is the right to a fair and public hearing, prompt resolution, and an independent and impartial tribunal.[89] The basic complaint is that the state has failed to provide an adequate court.[90] S. Gerlis[91] suggests as possible areas of attack the need for a public hearing, fees, "equality of arms" between litigants, sanctions, fast track procedures, without notice hearings, and the appointment of judges,[92] and one might add a failure to enforce orders adequately.[93] Self help procedures like forfeiture by peaceable re-entry and distress are also suspect, though this is mainly an issue in the commercial context.[94] However, points should be made responsibly. It will be interesting to see whether history supports the view of Lord Woolf M.R. that his reforms of civil procedure meet the requirements of the Convention so that case management issues should not be argued on human rights principles.[95]

One certain area for attack is *retroactivity* in legislation. Very often property owners will argue that removing existing rights will be a deprivation of property rights, and one for which the state is responsible. Taken to extremes this could almost paralyse the process of reforming property law and certainly the process of simplifying property law. The legislators of 1925 were able to make transitional provisions that swept away obsolete law and we do not want to lose the freedom. A recent attack on U.K. tax legislation on the ground of retroactivity failed in *National & Provincial Building Society* v. *United Kingdom*.[96] The Strasbourg challenge followed the success of the Woolwich Equitable B.S. in reclaiming tax demanded from it by the Inland Revenue when it was not due under existing tax legislation. Before other societies could act, the government amended the law to prevent further repayments. Claims that this infringed the fundamental rights of a number of other societies failed. No discrimination arose because the Woolwich Society, having litigated and won, was in a different position from other societies that had not sued. And expropriation could be justified because the amending legislation merely restored the original Parliamentary intention that tax should in fact be paid. So the amending legislation did fall within the margin of state appreciation.

Coherent development of the law requires simplification, and this necessarily involves trivial changes to existing rights to fit them into the reformed scheme. It is hoped that the *National & Provincial* case will provide a precedent for allowing retroactive legislation to this small extent. It should not, for example, prevent the consolidation of the existing residential tenancy codes into a single, simple, structure.

---

[89] *Scollo* v. *Italy* (1996) 22 E.H.R.R. 514, 530–532; *National & Provincial B.S.* (1998) 25 E.H.R.R. 127, 175–183; *Terra Woningen* v. *Netherlands* (1997) 24 E.H.R.R. 456; *Vacher* v. *France* (1997) 24 E.H.R.R. 482; *R.* v. *S.S. for Wales ex parte Emery* [1996] 4 All E.R. 1 (unsuccessful invocation in relation to a public inquiry for a path diversion), on appeal [1998] 4 All E.R. 367 C.A.

[90] *Locobail U.K. Ltd.* v. *Waldorf Investment Corp.* [2000] Times June 13th, Evans-Lombe J.

[91] [2000] 23 *L.S.G.* 51.

[92] *Clancy* v. *Caird* [2000] Times May 9th C.S. I.H. (temporary judges); *McGonnell* v. *U.K.* [2000] 13 L.S.G. 40 (independent arbiters).

[93] *Immobiliare Saffi* v. *Italy* (1999) 7 B.H.R.C. 256.

[94] See below pp. 650–654 and Chapter 29.

[95] *Daniels* v. *Walker* [2000] Times May 17th C.A.

[96] (1998) 25 E.H.R.R. 127.

6.   Defences

Miscellaneous defences are provided, including a safeguard for existing human rights—that is a person's reliance on convention rights should not infringe any other right or freedom—for freedom of expression, and for freedom of thought, conscience and religion.[97]

F.   INFRINGEMENTS OF FUNDAMENTAL RIGHTS

It was surely wise to end the system by which a victim of an abuse of human rights had to litigate through the domestic courts before being allowed to complain to the European Court of Human Rights in Strasbourg. Those Convention rights to which the United Kingdom subscribes[98] are now guaranteed directly in British domestic law, a form of incorporation which should reduce the number of cases that it will be necessary to take to Strasbourg in future. Apart from the residual challenge in Strasbourg,[99] there are four main strands to the incorporation of human rights into English law.

1.   Primary legislation

Parliament retains its sovereignty and the capacity, if it chooses to do so, to legislate expressly in a way that is incompatible with the human rights of its citizens. However a number of provisions of the Human Rights Act 1998 make it much less likely that future legislators will indeed act to derogate from fundamental rights. Existing tenets of interpretation allowed consideration of human rights issues only in cases of ambiguity,[100] a rule so restrictive that Hunt identified only four cases in which the Article 1 of Protocol 1 right to property had been cited in English courts up to 1998.[101] This technique will be modified[102] so that all legislation will be construed so far as is possible, and given effect to in a way which is compatible with the Convention.[103] Interpretative techniques will be modified to take account of existing human rights jurisprudence, including particularly judgments of the Strasbourg Court,[104] and this will surely tilt the balance even further towards purposive construction. If a potential breach is shown, the Government can be joined in the action to argue in favour of the validity of the legislation.[105] Where a clear incompatibility exists between the Convention rights and a statute,[106] the court

---

[97]   Respectively H.R.A. 1998 ss.11, 12, 13; see also *Chassagnou* v. *France* (1999) 7 B.H.R.C. 151 (article 11).

[98]   H.R.A. 1998 sch.1.

[99]   In general no stay should be granted pending a decision of the European Court of Human Rights, since the remedy against the Government is damages for failing to observe the Convention rights: *Locobail U.K. Ltd.* v. *Waldorf Investment Corp.* [2000] Times June 13th, Evans-Lombe J.

[100]   *R.* v. *S.S. for the Home Department ex parte Brind* [1991] 1 A.C. 696 H.L.; *Hughes* v. *S.S. for the Environment* (1996) 71 P. & C.R. 168.

[101]   M. Hunt, *Using Human Rights Law in English Courts* (Hart, 1997) app. 1.

[102]   As defined by s.21.

[103]   s.3(1).

[104]   s.2.

[105]   s.5.

[106]   s.3(2)(b); or more accurately it is primary legislation as defined by s.21. Secondary legislation will be set aside directly, unless primary legislation precludes the removal of any incompatibility. The Welsh Assembly is limited to acting within the Convention.

will not be able to strike down the legislation, but will only be able to make a formal declaration of incompatibility.[107] Presumably the court should make a declaration after such a finding. This will not change the law but it should prompt the government to change the law. A fast track procedure will be available in Parliament to enable existing Acts to be changed by Ministerial Order after approval by both Houses of Parliament, including consequential amendments required to other statutory provisions.[108] It is unlikely that Parliament would decline to act since this would leave open the possibility of a claim to damages in Strasbourg. New Bills that are introduced into Parliament will require a declaration that the proposals will comply with the Convention.[109]

2. Judicial review

Judicial control of administrative actions will be greatly strengthened. This includes quashing secondary legislation and challenges to the actions of any public authority. It will be unlawful for any public authority to act (or fail to act[110]) in a way which is incompatible with any Convention right,[111] unless, that is, the act is in accordance with incompatible primary legislation.[112] This will provide a new head for judicial review of administrative actions, since it will be open to any litigant to claim that any action of a public authority or any exercise of executive discretion occurred in breach of the Convention.[113] It is likely that the principles, outlined above, on which infringements of the Convention rights are judged will be more limiting than existing grounds for judicial review. Authorities subject to control will include the central government, executive agencies, local government, and privatised utilities, as well as any person with any function of a private nature.[114] An important issue is whether a local authority is a public body when acting as a landlord in the public sector. The issue was aired in *Pemberton* v. *Southwark L.B.C.*[115] though the discussion was necessarily inconclusive before the implementation date of the 1998 Act. The case concerned a tolerated trespasser holding a public sector flat under a suspended possession order, who made a nuisance claim based on a cockroach infestation. At least one Lord Justice considered that a claim based on Convention rights might succeed.

Locus standi will depend upon showing that one is a victim according to existing human rights case law.[116] This requires one to show that one is directly and intimately affected by the contravention, though a risk of being affected is sufficient and pressure groups may be able to take action in relation to campaigning issues.

---

[107] s.4.

[108] s.10.

[109] s.19.

[110] s.6(8).

[111] s.6(1).

[112] As defined in s.21.

[113] ss.6, 7.

[114] s.6(3)–(7); Parliament is excluded; on courts and tribunals see below p. 208.

[115] [2000] 21 E.G. 135 C.A. M. Davies [2000] 27 *L.S.G.* 30, 31 takes the view that a local authority is clearly a public authority under the Act.

[116] s.7(1), (3), (6); E.C.H.R. Art.34; *Bryan* v. *U.K.* (1995) 21 E.H.R.R. 342; *Agrotexim* v. *Greece* (1996) 21 E.H.R.R. 250 (shareholders in land-owning company had no *locus standi* to bring complaint).

The court may grant such relief or remedy as is just and appropriate. No doubt in judicial review proceedings it will be usual simply to quash an illegal act or to declare that it is illegal. But the court will also have power to award damages or compensation, provided that it is within the jurisdiction of the particular court,[117] and it is necessary to afford just satisfaction to the recipient.[118] Damages will be awarded against the Crown and a special procedure must be followed which gives the Crown power to intervene in the proceedings.[119]

3. Case law

Attacks on common law and equitable principles will be allowed if it can be shown that the law developed by precedents infringes Convention rights. The public authorities obliged to observe Convention rights include the House of Lords as a judicial body, the Supreme Court, lower courts and tribunals.[120] A litigant will be able to plead in any court at any level that his fundamental rights are infringed by the state of the law, and pursue adverse decisions through the court system by way of an appeal.[121] Incorporation will be of use primarily in launching an attack on a case law principle, either common law or equity—as opposed to statutory rules. Case law built up by the European Court of Human Rights will be useful as authority, though of persuasive authority rather than being binding, along with human rights principles such as proportionality and non-retroactivity.[122]

4. Direct actions

New causes of action may arise, because a claimant will be able to base an action on the fact that his Convention rights have been infringed.[123] Thus it will be possible to take direct action in which the cause of action is a breach of one of the Convention rights, though the claimant will have to show that he is so directly affected by the breach that he is a victim.[124] For example a decision to confiscate all houses worth over £1 million without compensation would normally be a breach of the convention rights, but a person could sue directly only if he owned one of the properties to be taken. This might preclude action by a person affected by uncertainty over the future route of a motorway since such a person may not yet be a victim.[125] Incorporation is likely to benefit the wealthy more than the poor and companies more than individuals.

---

[117] s.8(2).

[118] s.8(3).

[119] s.9. For a discussion of the possible "horizontal" effect of the Act, see above p. 201.

[120] s.6(3)(a), (4). Power for tribunals to award damages are given by s.8(5). Damages for judicial acts in good faith are limited by s.9.

[121] s.9.

[122] s.2, including judgments of the European Court of Human Rights, opinions and decisions of the Commission, and decisions of the Committee of Ministers.

[123] s.7(1)(b).

[124] Damages will be limited by the Convention principle of just satisfaction: s.8 depending upon Art.50.

[125] App. No. 10390/83 X. v. U.K. [1986] 8 E.H.R.R. 39.

G. COMPLAINTS PROCEDURES

1. Alternative dispute resolution

Courts are not a suitable forum for the resolution of minor disputes about the condition of housing, and alternative dispute resolution is both appropriate and actively encouraged. Demands for payments of service charge can be challenged at a leasehold valuation tribunal[126] and there is also a move towards independent ombudsmen. When Lord Woolf reported in 1996,[127] 37 per cent of the work of the Local Government Ombudsman consisted of housing cases, with one in ten cases involving disrepair. Repairs were achieved more quickly than through litigation and at no cost to the complainant. In 1996 the existing social sector scheme was made statutory so that tenants may now seek the help of the Housing Association Tenants' Ombudsman[128]; it would be desirable if, as Lord Woolf suggested, the courts had power to transfer a case to this scheme. Surely there should be one comprehensive administrative scheme covering service charge and all other complaints and all security codes?

2. Small claims

Most landlord and tenant disputes will be heard in the county court[129] and in the small claims track.[130] Disrepair falls within the scheme if specific performance is claimed, the work will cost no more than £1,000, and associated claims to damages are no more than £1,000; these facts should be stated in the claim form to facilitate correct allocation.[131] Claims to damages without specific performance are allocated to the small claims track to the figure of £5,000, unless the case is of abnormal complexity.

Part 7 procedure is used for all claims, which should be brought on a Part 7 claim form supported by a statement of truth[132]—it is usual to include the particulars of the claim. The defendant must file notice of his intention to defend, followed within 28 days of service of the claim by a defence supported by a statement of truth[133] or face the risk of a default judgment.[134] Woolf requires a more complete statement of the grounds of defence, so that the issue is narrowed at an earlier stage. Cases are subject to active case management by the court.[135] The court will allocate the case to a track as a response to the filing of the defence and allocation questionnaire. The £80 allocation fee is now dropped for small claims. This provides a streamlined procedure for small money claims, now heard in public and with a shift away from arbitral procedure. Standard

---

[126] See below Chapter 14.

[127] *Access to Justice* (H.M.S.O., July 1996), ch.16 paras.81–90.

[128] H.A. 1996 s.51, sch.2; *Assured Tenant's Charter*, Section 10; *Secure Tenant's Charter*, Section 10; *Shorthold Tenant's Charter*, Section 7 (all Housing Corporation, 1998).

[129] H.C.C.C.J.O. 1991 art. 2. Money actions may not be begun in the High Court unless the money in dispute is at least £15,000 (£50,000 in personal injury cases).

[130] C.P.R. 26.8.

[131] C.P.R. 16.3(4); C.P.R. 26.6; P.D. 7.3.9.; N. Madge [1999] *N.L.J.* 1408, 1409.

[132] Form N1; including particulars of claim or soon after and a statement of truth.

[133] C.P.R. 15.

[134] C.P.R. 9, 12, 13. C.P.R. 12.3 is amended by C.P.Am.R. 2000 r.6.

[135] C.P.R. 3, 26–29.

directions are provided in actions for the return of a tenant's deposit[136] and for a land-lord to recover the cost of damage done by the tenant. Many disrepair cases will require an expert; the Woolf procedure for a single expert[137] gives the expert an important role in determining facts. Given this it is strange that a local authority may use one of its own employees as an expert in a housing disrepair case.[138] Lord Woolf[139] considered that fur-ther research was needed before further changes to small claims procedures to deal with the problems of complexity of law, multiplicity of experts, heavy documentation, and complexity of the history of many disputed repair cases. The fast track applies to money claims up to £15,000 with a target of 30 weeks to the hearing and restrictions on costs.[140]

3.   Proposals for a pre-action protocol

Another proposal made by Lord Woolf[141] is to provide a protocol for the procedure to be followed before a tenant brings a claim for disrepair. This will focus on ensuring that the landlord (especially in the public or social sector) has been notified before proceed-ings and that there has been an expert assessment of the problem, preferably by an agreed expert. Cases should then be adequately documented when they reach court. Landlords wanted to restrict experts' reports to matters already notified by the tenant, but Lord Woolf regarded this proposal as unrealistic.

---

[136]   P.D. 27 App. A Form D.
[137]   C.P.R. 27.2(1). If one party is unhappy with the report, the court should usually allow another: *Daniels* v. *Walker* [2000] Times May 17th C.A.
[138]   *Field* v. *Leeds C.C.* [1999] All E.R. (D) 140 C.A.
[139]   *Access to Justice* (H.M.S.O. July 1996) ch.16 paras.9–15.
[140]   C.P.R. 26.6(4)–(5). Appeals fall within C.P.R. 52.
[141]   Lord Woolf, *Access to Justice* (H.M.S.O. July 1996) ch.16 paras.59–72.

9

RESIDENTIAL RENTS

Rent obligation: nature, express and implied obligations. Service charges.
Council tax. Other rates and taxes. Remedies. Defences. Residential rents.
Low rent exclusions. Secure tenancy rents. Social sector rents. Private assured
rents. Rent Act fair rents. The Rent Act registration machinery. Public con-
trols. Social security benefits. Premiums. Deposits.

A. THE RENT OBLIGATION

A rent is a periodical payment for the use of land.[1] According to Lord Diplock in *United*
Scientific Holdings Ltd. v. Burnley B.C.,[2]

"The old concept of rent as service rendered by the tenant to the landlord has been displaced
by a payment which a tenant is bound by his contract to pay to the landlord for the use of his
land."

Short leases tend to reserve a rack rent that is a rent reflecting the full periodic value of
the land.[3]

1. Payment of rent

Rent is presumed to be payable annually,[4] but since a residential landlord generally
requires weekly or monthly payments it is necessary to state expressly the rent days on
which payment is to be made. The exact date is important for the method of giving
notice to quit.[5] Unless the lease provides otherwise, rent is payable in arrears, early payment being inadvisable.[6] This common law principle is most inconvenient to landlords,
who not unreasonably want to see the colour of a tenant's money before allowing him
possession. Almost all residential tenancies, like all other leases, require rent to be paid
in advance, that is at the start of the period for which rent is paid. It will be necessary to
effect an apportionment if the lease is terminated by an agreed surrender,[7] though liability for arrears naturally continues.[8]

---

[1] Woodfall chs.7, 10; Bright & Gilbert 417–489; Davey 189–205; Evans & Smith (5th) ch.8; Garner (2nd ed.)
60–66.
[2] [1978] A.C. 904, 953B.
[3] As to residential leases with premiums see below p. 241.
[4] *Turner* v. *Allday* (1836) Tyr. & Cr. 819.
[5] Beware quarterly tenancies created on traditional quarter days; see above pp. 25–26.
[6] See below p. 774.
[7] Apportionment Act 1870; *William Hill (Football) Ltd.* v. *Willen Key & Hardware Ltd.* (1964) 108 S.J. 482.
[8] *Shaw* v. *Lomas* (1888) 59 L.T. 477.

2.   Provisions required in fixed contractual terms

Residential tenancies are commonly short periodic tenancies, perhaps monthly or weekly, in which case it is unnecessary for the landlord to take advance precautions to enable him to increase the rent. If he decides that it ought to be increased he can serve notice to quit on the tenant, there being no difference in legal form between a notice genuinely intended to end the tenancy and one which is an invitation to accept a new tenancy at an increased rent. Indeed, it is perfectly possible to include a provision for the landlord to increase the rent by notice without termination, since the rent is certain provided its amount is known when the time comes for payment; such a provision was once widely used in tenancies of council houses.[9] Modern tenancy agreements invariably rely on the statutory machineries for rent increases: if the tenant has full residential security it will not be possible to terminate the tenancy, but the notice will convert the tenancy to a statutory phase and bring into play the statutory powers to increase rents by notice.[10]

Longer fixed term tenancies call for the inclusion of provisions to facilitate rent increases and also provisions to enable the contractual security to be broken if the rent is not paid. Suppose that an assured tenancy is granted for a fixed period of 10 years at a rent of £500 a month: this rent is likely to become unrealistic over a ten-year term, and if hyper inflation ever returns this form of lease could be disastrous to a landlord, so a rent review provision may be needed.[11] If no provision is made for review of the rent under an assured tenancy it will still be possible to give a statutory notice of increase.[12] Commercial leases will also provide for forfeiture in the event of non-payment of rent, which enables the landlord to terminate the lease if the rent is unpaid, and this term is implied if the lease is equitable.[13] Residential tenancies require a corresponding provision to enable the holding to be ended if rent arrears build up—though the technical nature of the procedure used for termination is a residential repossession rather than that for a commercial forfeiture.

3.   Express and implied covenants

Until the later part of the nineteenth century the law used to differentiate rent payable under a lease by deed from other forms of rent, with different forms of action required, but any differences have disappeared with the Judicature Act leaving the single modern action for rent—whether the obligation is imposed by deed or in an informal short legal lease or under a *Walsh* v. *Lonsdale* contract.[14]

A tenant may hold property with the permission of the owner without having reached any agreement about the quantum of rent, and if so there is an obligation to pay reasonable compensation for his use and occupation. In the absence of any agreement this is a restitutionary remedy (originally in quasi-contract[15]) to reverse the unjust enrich-

---

[9] *Greater London C.* v. *Connolly* [1970] 2 Q.B. 100 C.A.
[10] See below pp. 224–227.
[11] See below pp. 656–667.
[12] See below p. 224.
[13] See below Chapter 29.
[14] (1882) 21 Ch.D. 9 C.A.; see below pp. 521–564.
[15] *Thetford* v. *Tyler* (1845) 8 Q.B. 95, 1020, 115 E.R. 810.

ment the tenant obtains by using the land rent free. This may be assessed on the letting value but any agreement about the rent may be used as evidence.[16] A tenant may also be liable where a sub-tenant retains occupation,[17] though not where the sub-tenant has security of tenure.[18] If rent-free occupation is intended, this should be stated clearly in the lease.

4.   End of liability to rent

The contractual liability to pay rent ends with the termination of the lease. Of course a tenant cannot cut short his liability to pay rent simply by moving out and not even by dying: rent continues until the personal representatives give notice to quit.[19] If he wishes to stop paying rent a tenant must move out but also end the contractual arrangement, if he is able to do so, perhaps by waiting for a fixed term to expire, giving notice to quit a periodic tenancy, exercising a break clause or by agreed surrender.[20] Many cases of alleged surrender are bitterly disputed because the landlord wishes to continue charging rent.

Ending the lease will not end the obligation to pay rent unless the tenant also vacates the property. If he continues in occupation after his right to do so a correlative obligation arises to pay for use and occupation of the premises. If the land was already let at a rack rental—as is normal with short residential lettings—the mesne profits will be the same in quantum as the previous rent, but if the rent was below market levels (because a premium had been paid) the mesne profits will be set at the market level. This could be seen as a restitutionary remedy where the contract has ended but the tenant obtains an unjust enrichment by retaining the use of the landlord's property.

In fact an additional penalty was enacted by the Distress for Rent Act 1737.[21] If a former tenant continues in occupation after hostile termination of his lease, for example by forfeiture or after a notice to quit has expired, he is liable for double rent, that is double the rent or sum which he would otherwise have paid to continue for the whole time that he continues in possession. This provision is aimed at holding over hostile to the interest of the landlord, so the rent is not doubled where the tenant gives a break notice but continues in occupation because the landlord disputes the validity of the break. Just this happened in *Oliver Ashworth (Holdings) Ltd.* v. *Ballard (Kent) Ltd.*[22] where the landlord at first held the break notice technically defective, later had to concede its validity after the *Mannai* decision was reported, and uncharitably responded by claiming double rent on the basis of the tenant's involuntary holding over. The 1737 Act was concerned only with a case where the landlord treated his ex-tenant as a trespasser, that is where the

---

[16] Woodfall ch.10; *Canterbury Cathedral Dean & Chapter* v. *Whitbread plc.* [1995] 1 E.G.L.R. 82; for other commercial cases see below p. 641.

[17] *Ibbs* v. *Richardson* (1839) 9 Ad. & El. 849, 112 E.R. 1436.

[18] *Watson* v. *Saunders-Roe Ltd.* [1947] K.B. 437 C.A.

[19] *Youngmin* v. *Heath* [1974] 1 W.L.R. 135 C.A.

[20] Note there are special rules which continue business tenancies until statutory notices have been served; see below Chapter 21.

[21] s.18.

[22] [2000] Ch. 12 C.A.; S. Murdoch [1999] 23 *E.G.* 142. The point was first put by Laws L.J. in argument and on this basis the decision at [1998] 3 E.G.L.R. 60 Ch.D. was reversed. See Woodfall 19.011–19.029; Evans & Smith (5th) 261–264.

tenant was wilfully holding over, perhaps having given notice to quit which had expired. Ballards had not treated their tenant as a trespasser and so they were entitled only to normal rent. According to the preamble to the section, the target was tenants who determined their tenancies and refused to deliver them up when promised to another, but Laws L.J. was not prepared to restrict the section to cases of reletting, describing this as the thrust of the section but not its necessary focus.[23]

B. SERVICE CHARGES

Many communal living arrangements depend upon a service charge to maintain the building in which a particular dwelling is situated, for example to cover the structure and common parts of a block of flat. Long residential leases and commercial leases commonly reserve these sums as rent, a device that allows a distress and opens up for the landlord the possibility of the rent only procedure for forfeiture[24]; however, this has less point if the lease is residential since it does no more than to shift a case from the breach of covenant ground for possession to the arrears of rent ground. Special provisions are made under some of the residential codes[25] and social tenants have special Charter rights about service charges.[26] However the most valuable right is the right to challenge residential service charges before the Leasehold Valuation Tribunal, a matter discussed as an aspect of communal living arrangements.[27]

C. COUNCIL TAX.

Council tax was introduced on April 1st 1993[28] and is generally payable by tenants.[29]

1.   Unit of charge

The taxable unit is the chargeable dwelling[30] meaning any unit of residential accommodation that is not exempted. "Dwelling" is defined by reference to the rateable hereditaments in use under the General Rate Act 1967:[31]

> "property which is or may become liable to a rate, being a unit of such property which is, or would fall to be, shown as a separate item in the valuation list."

Some adjustments are made splitting multiple units and combining multiple hereditaments to ensure that the result is a single residential unit of occupation.[32]

---

[23] At 39A.
[24] See below pp. 795–796.
[25] See below pp. 233–234, 281.
[26] e.g. the *Assured Tenant's Charter* (Housing Corporation, 1998) section 4.
[27] See below Chapter 16.
[28] Local Government Finance Act 1992 s.100.
[29] P. Sparkes [1992] *B.T.R.* 305; Woodfall 12.008–12.016.
[30] Local Government Finance Act 1992 s.1(1), 3.
[31] s.115.
[32] S.I. 1992/549 as amended by S.I. 1997/656 regs.3–4; for the presumption of non-exemption see S.I. 1992/613 regs 7–12.

The legislation provides for a daily basis of charge,[33] despite the clear merits in an annual or monthly basis of charge that would make the analysis of residence much simpler.[34] Special provision is made for liability on death, which proved to be a very sensitive aspect of the old poll tax on individuals.[35]

2. Exempt dwellings

Regulations provide exemptions for properties[36] that are unoccupied. The most significant exemption (Class C) is for any property unoccupied and substantially unfurnished for any period of six months.[37] Other important exemptions are unlimited in time; this is so for property occupied only by students (Class K), and property occupied only by people under 18 (Class R). There is also an indefinite exemption (Class W) for "granny flats"—that is a flat attached to another home occupied by a relative who is dependent upon the carer. Another exemption relates to property unoccupied for up to six months during and after relevant alterations (Class A). There are numerous other exemptions. In each case reference must be made to the regulations to establish the exact terms of the exemption.

The regulations[38] also take out of charge halls of residence, students' term-time accommodation and barracks (classes M to P).

3. The domestic sector

Commercial property (including holiday cottages[39]) is subject to non-domestic rating rather than council tax. Property that is partly domestic and partly non-domestic is called a "composite hereditament" and is liable to council tax on the domestic element.[40] For example a shop with a flat above is likely to be treated as two completely distinct units for local taxation, but if it is listed as a single hereditament, it will be apportioned into domestic and commercial parts and be banded only on the value of the residential part.

4. Capital value

Domestic rates were based on the letting value of the house, but the council tax switches to a system based on the capital value of the house in 1992,[41] divided into the following bands[42]:

---

[33] Local Government Finance Act 1992 s.2(1); subs.(2) requires the assumption that affairs at the end of day operate throughout the day.

[34] D.O.E. Consultation Paper, para.2.39.

[35] Local Government Finance Act 1992 s.18; S.I. 1992/613 reg.18.

[36] S.I. 1992/558, reg.3. The regulations have been amended on numerous occasions, most recently by S.I. 2000/424.

[37] Class C; details of how the periods are computed appear in the regulations.

[38] S.I. 1992/558, as amended on numerous occasions, reg.3.

[39] Local Government Finance Act 1992 s.3(2)(b).

[40] s.3(3).

[41] D.O.E. Consultation Paper paras 2.12–2.17.

[42] Local Government Finance Act 1992 s.5; see subs. (2) for England and subs.(3) for Wales.

Values	Band	Proportion
Not exceeding £40,000	A	6
£52,000	B	7
£68,000	C	8
£88,000	D	9
£120,000	E	11
£160,000	F	13
£320,000	G	15
Exceeding £320,000	H	18

There has been no revaluation (at least up to 2000), and when there is there may be serious dislocation given the changes in house values that have occurred.

5. Liability of residents

The first five categories of potential taxpayers[43] apply to an adult who has his sole or main residence in the dwelling[44]; if such a person is liable so too is his spouse or cohabitee.[45] The categories are:

(a) a resident with a freehold interest in the whole or any part of the dwelling;
(b) a resident with a leasehold interest in the whole or any part which is not inferior to another such interest held by another resident;
(c) a resident who is a statutory, secure or introductory tenant of the whole or any part;
(d) a resident with a contractual licence to occupy the whole or any part;
(e) a resident;

The taxpayer is the first person[46] encountered in descending this list: liability does not pass down the chain if the person primarily liable fails to pay.

A freehold owner who is resident must pay, recovering contributions by contract from those he allows to share. If the property is let and the freehold owner is not there the tenant is taxpayer (if resident). If the property is sub-let it is the sub-tenant who is liable. This all works reasonably well if the whole property is let, and the occupier establishes a main residence in the property. If the main residence is elsewhere the result can be very confusing. The council tax is payable on a dwelling,[47] and the legislation is concerned to direct liability to one person or another. Suppose that the owner of a house in the provinces moves to London to work, returning to the provinces at weekends. He takes in a lodger who occupies the whole throughout the week. The lodger becomes liable to the entire council tax. This might not be obvious when making the arrangement, so that the lodger would not be able to tell of the need for contractual provision. In any event a non-lawyer would be unlikely to contract to meet such a counter-

[43] s.6.
[44] s.6(4).
[45] s.9.
[46] s.6(3
[47] Local Government Finance Act 1992 s.1(1).

intuitive contingency. The provisions relating to leaseholders are also odd, in that the sub-tenant of part attracts liability rather than the head-tenant of the whole.

6.   Liability of owners if no resident

If there is no resident liable to pay council tax, liability passes to a sixth category,[48] that is:

(f) the owner,

This means the person entitled to possession of the dwelling or any part.[49]

7.   Liability of owner in communal and institutional homes

In some cases, the council may decide to transfer liability to pay council tax to the owner of the property.[50] The most important class is of Houses in Multiple Occupation (Class C).[51] Hence the occupant of a single bed sit will probably not be liable for tax directly to the council; rather the landlord pays and he has to reach a contractual arrangement with the individual occupier either to charge an inclusive rent which takes account of the tax or to charge an exclusive rent and an additional payment to cover council tax. Other classes cover residential care homes, religious communities, dwellings with resident staff, and dwellings of ministers of religion.

8.   Discounts

The provisions for discounts water down the pure conception as a tax on property, but retain some linkage between the quantum of charge and the number of adults consuming local services. Tax is reduced for properties occupied by fewer than two adult residents, but no extra charge is levied on the relatively small number of larger households.[52] The charge is reduced by 25 per cent[53] if the property is occupied by a single adult resident. A double discount (50 per cent)[54] is allowed where there is no resident, more or less recreating the old rating position. For holiday homes this charge might seem too generous. Special provision is made for holiday homes in Wales, since the council may decide that specified classes of unoccupied dwellings may (after the first six months) be charged at either 75 per cent or 100 per cent of the full tax.[55]

A further class of residents is excluded when calculating the number of residents.[56] If the number of residents is reduced to one or none this gives rise to a discount, called a "status discount". Those disregarded are: persons in detention, severely mentally

---

[48] s.6.

[49] s.6(5).

[50] Local Government Finance Act 1992 s.8; S.I. 1992/551 (as amended) reg.2

[51] For control of H.M.O.s see below pp. 272–274.

[52] D.O.E. Consultation Paper para 2.3 only 10% of properties have 3 adult residents and only 3% have 4 or more.

[53] Local Government Finance Act 1992 s.11; regulations may alter this percentage: s.11(3).

[54] Two discounts of 25%; the minister can alter the 25% discount figure: s.11(3).

[55] Local Government Finance Act 1992 s.12; S.I. 1992/3023 as amended by S.I. 1998/105. The wording "disregarded for the purposes of discount" is decidedly odd, but it means that this person is treated as not being resident, and thus the property may qualify for a discount when it would not otherwise do.

[56] Local Government Finance Act 1992 sch.1; S.Is. 1992/548, 1992/552, as copiously amended; see also the administration and enforcement regulations S.I. 1992/613 regs.13–16.

impaired, persons for whom child benefit is payable, students,[57] student nurses, apprentices, youth training trainees, hospital patients, patients in nursing homes, care workers, and residents of hostels and night shelters.[58] In each case reference to the legislation is needed to flesh out the details of the disregards.

D. RATES AND TAXES

1.   Taxation of rent

Stamp duty is not payable on the grant of a short residential lease unless the term exceeds seven years,[59] though if there is a premium the lease must be certified as being below the stamp duty threshold. Rent will be subject to *income tax,* or corporation tax in the case of a corporate landlord. New rules for calculating income were introduced in 1994.[60] If the landlord is an overseas company, tax must be deducted and handed over to the revenue, so the tenant must be careful to make only a net payment to the landlord.[61] There is no *value added tax* on domestic rents.

2.   Rates

Statutes impose numerous charges on occupiers of land, which means that, as between landlord and tenant, most have to be paid by the tenant. Clear language is required if the terms of the lease are to reverse the primary statutory responsibility.[62] Apart from council tax, domestic tenants are most concerned with water and sewerage charges. Innumerable cases[63] consider the meaning of particular words such as rates, taxes, assessments, duties, and burdens. Protection for the landlord is required in the form of a covenant by the tenant to pay these statutory charges, and to reimburse the landlord if he is called upon. However, there is no doubt that if the landlord is forced to make a payment for which the tenant is primarily liable there will in any event be a liability to make restitution.[64]

3.   Charges for services

Services provided by public undertakers include electricity and gas—in each case the tenant will be liable as tariff consumer[65] unless there is any contract to vary this position; the charging structure for each of these services is determined by the undertaker under a system of centralised supervision.[66] Tenants are also liable to pay for water and

---

[57] Properties occupied only by students are exempted, as are halls of residence: S.I. 1992/558 reg. 3 (classes M, N).

[58] Also members of certain international organisations, religious communities, and school leavers: S.I. 1992/552 reg.3.

[59] Stamp Act 1891 sch.1 Lease or Tack (3).

[60] Finance Act 1995 s.39.

[61] Income and Corporation Taxes Act 1988 s.42A, inserted by Finance Act 1995 s.40; *Tenbry Investments Ltd.* v. *Peugeot Talbot Motor Co. Ltd.* [1992] S.T.C. 791 Ch.D.

[62] *Stockdale* v. *Ascherberg* [1904] 1 K.B. 447 C.A.

[63] Woodfall ch.12.

[64] *R.* v. *Bristol C.C. ex parte* Jacobs [1999] Times November 16th, Owen J.; A. Burrows, *The Law of Restitution* (Butterworths, 1993) 205–230.

[65] Electricity Act 1989 s.22; Gas Act 1986 s.14.

[66] Gas Act 1986 ss.12–14; Electricity Act 1989 ss.16, 18, 22, sch.7 (meters).

sewerage unless there is some other contractual arrangement.[67] Significant changes have been made by the Water Industry Act 1999. Disconnections of domestic supplies are no longer allowed and limiting devices are also outlawed.[68] Tenants have a specific right to elect to have their supply metered irrespective of the terms of their tenancy agreement.[69] The original plan to switch all consumers from rating to metered charging in 2000 has been dropped.[70]

4. Recovery of overpayments

Mistake of law is no longer a defence to a claim for restitution.[71] So *prima facie* a tenant who pays an excessive rent demand will be able to recover the overpayment. This basic principle was fully recognised by Neuberger J. in *Nurdin & Peacock plc. v. D.B. Ramsden & Co. Ltd. (No.2)*[72] although the quarterly rent was £51,000, the tenants made several payments of £66,000. They did so after mistaken advice from their legal advisers that they would be able to recover any overpayments. This was a mistake of law, but for which they would not have made the payment. It was possible that there had to be a direct connection between the mistake and the payment, but even if this was a requirement it was satisfied on the facts. A common sense approach was required. The landlord was therefore unjustly enriched to the amount of the overpayment and would be required to make restitution to the tenant. Possible defences are change of position after receipt of the overpayment and proof that the payment was a genuine compromise of a dispute about the correct amount.

E. REMEDIES FOR NON-PAYMENT

1. Personal actions

Arrears of rent can be pursued as a debt through a personal action through the courts, almost invariably today in the County Courts since they have unlimited jurisdiction,[73] with enforcement by the court bailiff.[74] The lease remains in place for the future, with the inconvenience that the tenant may again fail to pay the rent, a fact that explains why most landlords seek repossession instead.

2. Repossession

A tenant who fails to pay his rent exposes himself to an action for repossession of the property. This can be used as a lever to secure payment of arrears, since if the tenant is

---

[67] Water Industry Act 1991 ss.142–145, 148–149; new ss.143A, 144A-B are inserted by Water Industry Act 1999 ss.5–7.

[68] Water Industry Act 1991 ss.61(1A), 63A, 142A, sch.4A (which includes dwellings, caravans and houseboats); these are inserted by Water Industry Act 1999 ss.1–3.

[69] Water Industry Act 1991 s.209A.

[70] Water Industry Act 1991 s.145, repealed by Water Industry Act 1999 s.8.

[71] *Kleinwort Benson Ltd.* v. *Lincoln C.C.* [1999] A.C. 349 H.L.

[72] [1999] 1 E.G.L.R. 15, Neuberger J.; A. Bruce [1999] *N.L.J.* 1053; W. Miller & J. Pickston [1998] 51 *E.G.* 76; C. Lamont [1999] 3 *L.T.Rev.* 12.

[73] H.C.C.C.J.O. 1991, S.I. 1991/724, para.7. Actions valued at up to £25,000 should be commenced in the county court and above £50,000 in the High Court.

[74] In the High Court, the sheriff.

in arrears the court will make an order for possession of the property but suspend it on terms that payments are made to clear off the arrears. It is also a means of removing a tenant who has not met his financial commitments, though courts very often exercise their discretion to allow the tenant to remain, unless a private sector landlord is able to prove a mandatory ground for possession—persistent defaults or large arrears by an assured tenant. Repossession for rent arrears is common and has attracted an enormous case law which requires separate treatment.[75]

3. Rent diversion notices

If the rent of a tenant is in arrears the head landlord may divert the rent payable by a sub-tenant or lodger, the mechanism being a notice requiring future payments of rent to be made direct to the head landlord.[76] *Rhodes* v. *Allied Dunbar Pension Services Ltd.*[77]—a commercial case concerning a floating charge[78]—shows that if the head tenant has mortgaged his lease before the head landlord serves notice, it is the lender who will be entitled to receive the rents.

4. Distress

It is over 30 years since the Law Commission first considered the abolition of this arcane remedy. At that time its description of distress[79] was the process of seizing goods belonging to a debtor as a means of securing satisfaction of a demand, commonly a claim to rent due from a tenant[80] under a lease. The process of seizure is called a distraint. Distress is most commonly used against residential tenants to recover arrears of local taxation[81] and duties.[82] Rent is rarely recovered in this way because permission is required from the court before distress is levied for rent against most residential tenants,[83] permission which is rarely sought and still less often given. Courts have to consider as a matter of discretion whether a tenant should be allowed time to pay. It is better to seek repossession or to sue for the rent and to ask the court bailiffs to enforce the judgment. Execution[84] is the process of enforcing a court judgment, one method being to ask an officer of the court[85] to seize and sell the debtor's goods, but this is only one from a whole range of available methods, including obtaining money from the debtor's bank account or attaching his earnings. A wide-ranging review of enforcement and distress is currently (2000) under way under the auspices of the Lord Chancellor's Department.

---

[75] See below pp. 335–340.

[76] Law of Distress Amendment Act 1908 s.6; *Lawrence Chemicals Co. Ltd.* v. *Rubinstein* [1982] 1 W.L.R. 284 C.A. (notice may be signed by the landlord's solicitors).

[77] [1989] 1 W.L.R. 800 C.A.; F. Oditah [1990] *J.B.L.* 431; J.E. Adams [1993] *Conv.* 11.

[78] See below p. 649.

[79] Law Com. No.5 (1966) para.3.

[80] The goods of a licensee are not liable to distress: *Rendell* v. *Roman* (1839) 9 T.L.R. 192.

[81] Rules for rent do not necessarily apply: *Potts* v. *Hickman* [1941] A.C. 212, 241, Lord Wright; *Quinlan* v. *Hammersmith & Fulham L.B.C.* [1989] R.A. 43 C.A.

[82] S.I. 1997/1431.

[83] H.A. 1988 s.19 (assured); R.A. 1977 s.147 (Rent Act protected tenants); R.(Ag.)A. 1976 s.8 (tied cottages). There is no public sector provision.

[84] A. Hill-Smith [1983] *Conv.* 444.

[85] The sheriff in the High Court or the bailiffs in a County Court.

5. Deduction from payments due to the tenant

Just as a tenant can claim to set off damages for disrepair against rent payments, so the landlord can deduct arrears of rent owing to him from any payment that he makes to the tenant. Thus in *Khan* v. *Islington L.B.C.*[86] a council paid one of its tenants a home loss payment of £1,500 only after deducting £77.64 due for rent. These two debts arose from the same landlord and tenant relationship so the basic condition for a set-off was established,[87] though, as was emphasised, the right would only be exercisable by the landlord if it was fair and just to allow it.

F.   DEFENCES

1.   Tender

A tenant is naturally entitled to defend an action for rent or a rent-based repossession by showing that rent is not owing, for example that the rent has been paid, that a proper tender of the rent has been rejected, or that the lease has ended. An important statutory addition is the failure by the landlord to give an address for service of notices relating to rent and service charge.[88] Technically, perhaps, rent must be offered in legal tender but an agreement to accept a cheque is often implied.[89] Landlords commonly require a tenant to pay by a bank standing order, and if so the tenancy agreement should include this requirement. People other than the tenant have no right to preserve the lease by tendering the rent[90] except a spouse covered by the terms of the matrimonial homes legislation[91] or a cohabitee who has obtained an occupation order from the court.[92]

2.   Set off

The tenant may defend a rent action or repossession by showing some set off or counterclaim which reduces or extinguishes liability for unpaid rent.[93]

3.   Duty to mitigate

If the tenant quits the property, can he stop future rent accruing by insisting that the landlord mitigate his loss by seeking to relet the property? No, it appears.[94] English law asserts the absolute character of the rent action so that mitigation is not required. However in Australia a duty to mitigate is recognised,[95] which means that the landlord cannot claim rent after he should have relet. Courts are shifting markedly towards a

---

[86] [1999] E.G.C.S. 87 C.A.
[87] Woodfall 7.097–7.118; see also below pp. 256–258.
[88] See below p. 223.
[89] See below p. 644.
[90] *Presson Plus plc.* v. *Lancaster* [1997] E.G.C.S. 42 C.A. (cohabitee).
[91] F.L.A. 1996 s.30(3), replacing M.H.A. 1983 s.1(5).
[92] See above pp. 133–134.
[93] See below pp. 256–258.
[94] *Bhogal* v. *Cheema* [1998] 2 E.G.L.R. 50.
[95] *Vickers* v. *Stichtenoth Investments Pty. Ltd.* (1989) 52 S.A.S.R. 90, Bollen J.; *Progressive Mailing House Pty* v. *Tabali Pty* (1985) 157 C.L.R. 17, Mason J.; *Highway Properties Ltd.* v. *Kelly Douglas & Co. Ltd.* (1971) 17 D.L.R. (3d) 710.

contractual analysis of the landlord–tenant relationship[96] and if so it seems logical to allow a mitigation principle to develop. This is an area in which it would be useful to differentiate between commercial and domestic leases.

4. Limitation

Action is limited to arrears accruing within the six years before the start of an action.[97]

5. Suspension of rent

If the property is wholly destroyed by fire, the tenant must continue to pay the rent throughout the lease. This is the case even if reconstruction of the property is prevented by planning restrictions or by building restrictions. The same applies where a hostile bomb destroys the property, or indeed one that is friendly. A short periodic tenant can simply end the lease by notice to quit. Unfairness can arise with a longer term, but it can be avoided by providing for a suspension of rent while the property is unfit for use or by enabling the tenant to break the lease by notice.[98] It is important to deal with insurance premiums and service charge separately if these are also to be suspended, since this is not implied.[99] Rent also continues on requisition,[100] the tenant being obliged to seek compensation from the military authorities.

Rent is suspended after *eviction* either by title paramount or by the landlord. It is a fundamental term of a lease that the landlord should allow the tenant to take possession so that any interference with his possession stops the landlord's right to rent, but if the exception is obvious its case law source is less so. This is not a frustration but rather a temporary suspension of liability until the eviction is lifted.

6. Frustration

Legal interference with the property rights of a tenant may cause the lease to end by frustration. Contract cases identify the outbreak of war, government interference, and supervening illegality as frustrating events. Frustration will not be triggered by requisition[101] or by destruction by a hostile bomb.[102] However a building lease might be ended by building restrictions, or by dedication of the land as an open space,[103] and a lease of a holiday cottage by restrictions on the use of second homes.[104] There is no convincing illustration of the frustration of a short residential lease, and no need for one since a short-term tenant will normally be content to terminate his lease and so end his liability for rent for the future.

---

[96] See esp. below p. 691.

[97] Limitation Act 1980 s.19.

[98] Woodfall 7.138–7.149.

[99] *P. & O. Property Holdings Ltd.* v. *International Computers Ltd.* [1999] 2 E.G.L.R. 17, Neuberger J.; J.E. Adams [1999] *Conv.* 284.

[100] *Crown Lands Commissioners* v. *Page* [1960] 2 Q.B. 274 C.A.; H.W.R. Wade [1961] *C.L.J.* 34; *Matthey* v. *Curling* [1922] 2 A.C. 180 H.L.; *Eyre* v. *Johnson* [1946] K.B. 481.

[101] *Whitehall Court Ltd.* v. *Ettlinger* [1920] 1 K.B. 680; tenants receive statutory compensation.

[102] *Denman* v. *Brise* [1949] 1 K.B. 22 C.A.

[103] *Cricklewood Property & Investment Trust Ltd.* v. *Leighton Investment Trust Ltd.* [1945] A.C. 221, 229, Viscount Simon L.C.

[104] *Swift* v. *Macbean* [1942] 1 K.B. 375, Birkett J.; *Cricklewood* [1943] K.B. 493, Asquith J. at first instance.

G. INFORMATION TO RESIDENTIAL TENANTS

A residential landlord is under a duty to supply a *rent book* to a weekly tenant, unless board[105] is a substantial element of the rent. Contents are prescribed.[106] Sanctions are criminal, but failure to provide a rent book does not affect the recoverability of the rent.[107] Where a tenant has full Rent Act security (under a private sector residential tenancy granted before early 1989), it is an offence to make an entry in a rent book showing any irrecoverable rent,[108] and if a court determines what rent is payable there is power to call for the rent book so that it can be rectified.[109]

Residential tenants also have the right to the *disclosure of details of their landlord*, the test being that the property is occupied as a dwelling. If so, a written request can be made to the landlord's agent or rent collector for disclosure of the name and address of the immediate landlord,[110] as well as further details of a corporate landlord.[111] This same information should be included in rent demands.[112] Any transfer of the landlord's interest in a dwelling triggers a duty to inform the tenant of the details of the new landlord, information that must be provided not later than the next rent day.[113] The previous landlord should ensure that this information is given so as to end his liability under the covenants.[114] If the landlord has sold the reversion in a block of flats it will have been sold without first giving the tenants an opportunity to acquire the reversion themselves by exercising their right of first refusal[115] and if so the notice must alert the tenants to their collective right to acquire the property.[116]

Tenants of social landlords have additional *Charter Rights*, including the right to information about the rent, variations, and rights of challenge[117]; these include the right to know what the initial rent is, to be notified of changes to the rent, and the right to information, as well as the statutory right of appeal to a Rent Assessment Committee.

H. LOW RENT

No residential protection attaches to low rent arrangements.[118]

---

[105] As defined above at p. 161.

[106] s.5; S.I. 1982/1474 as amended; Woodfall 20.030–20.034.

[107] *Shaw* v. *Groom* [1970] 2 Q.B. 504 C.A.

[108] R.A. 1977 s.57(4)

[109] s.58

[110] L.T.A. 1985 s.1.

[111] s.2.

[112] L.T.A. 1987 part VI ss.46–49. This crucially important provision is considered below at p. 367. No rent accrues due until it is complied with.

[113] s.3 as amended L.T.A. 1987 s.50.

[114] subs.(3A), (3B).

[115] L.T.A. 1987 part I, see below pp. 426–432.

[116] L.T.A. 1985 s.3A; as amended by H.A. 1996 s.93 in force September 24th 1996.

[117] See e.g. *Assured Tenant's Charter* (Housing Corporation, 1998) section 4.

[118] R.A. 1977 s.5; H.A. 1988 s.1, sch.1 paras.3–3B; see above p. 166.

I.   RENTS FOR RECENT RESIDENTIAL GRANTS

1.   Secure tenants

Councils and other public sector landlords[119] are free to fix the rents charged to their tenants. Reasonable charges should be made for rent, licence fees, and heating charges,[120] and then reviewed periodically.[121] Public sector rents are supposed to be "affordable", The pricing structure adopted by a housing authority should maintain a differential between different types of property similar to that current in the private sector,[122] though at a more affordable level. Personal circumstances of tenants should no longer[123] be taken into account—since the housing benefit system is available to deal with genuine difficulties in paying rent. However, rents should not be too low; rents must be put into a housing revenue account and this must be kept in credit.[124] Legislation now gives the government considerable leverage through the grant settlements.[125] Public law challenges can be made to unreasonable increases, either in judicial review proceedings or as a defence to a rent action or repossession,[126] but most administrative challenges have been unsuccessful.[127]

Long tenancies may contain a contractual provision for alteration of rent, in the nature of a rent review provision,[128] which should be operated disregarding the existence of any right to buy.[129] Most public sector tenancies are short, commonly periodic. If so many will contain a contractual provision permitting the landlord to increase the rent by notice, a term validated in *Greater London Council* v. *Connolly*[130] and recognised under the modern secure tenancy regime.[131] If the express clause is omitted, statute supplies a variation procedure. Rent can be increased prospectively[132] by notice[133] and decreases are also a theoretical possibility. The period of notice must be at least four weeks, or a full rental period if longer,[134] and the tenant must be given an opportunity to quit rather than paying the increase proposed.[135] A variation of the actual terms of the tenancy (as opposed to the rent level) can occur only after a preliminary notice has

---

[119] See above pp. 7–10.

[120] H.A. 1985 s.108.

[121] s.24; Woodfall 25.062–25.065.

[122] s.24(3).

[123] Contrast on earlier legislation: *Leeds Corporation* v. *Jenkinson* [1935] 1 K.B. 168 C.A.; and *Luby* v. *Newcastle under Lyme* [1965] 1 Q.B. 214 C.A.

[124] Local Government and Housing Act 1989 ss.74–77; *Asher* v. *S.S. for the Environment* [1974] Ch. 208.

[125] Bright & Gilbert 424–430. Rents should not be subsidised from the rates: Local Government and Housing Act 1989 Parts IV, VI.

[126] *Wandsworth L.B.C.* v. *Winder* [1985] A.C. 461 H.L.

[127] *Belcher* v. *Reading Corp.* [1950] Ch. 380, Romer J.; *Summerfield* v. *Hampstead B.C.* [1957] 1 W.L.R. 167, Harman J.

[128] H.A. 1985 s.102(1).

[129] *Dickinson* v. *Enfield L.B.C.* [1996] 2 E.G.L.R. 88 C.A. (20 year term with 5 year review).

[130] [1970] 2 Q.B. 100 C.A.

[131] H.A. 1985 s.102; because of the security of tenure first introduced in 1980 it is no longer possible to terminate the tenancy and regrant it as in *Bathavon R.D.C.* v. *Carlile* [1958] 1 Q.B. 461 C.A.

[132] *Havant & Waterlooville B.C.* v. *Norum* [1958] 1 W.L.R. 721 C.A.

[133] H.A. 1985 ss.102, 103.

[134] H.A. 1985 s.103(4).

[135] s.103(6).

given the tenant an opportunity to make observations.[136] If the tenant is not secure (because the tenant lacks occupation) the authority can increase the rent by four weeks' notice.[137]

Public sector tenants have a right to improve their properties at the expense of the landlord,[138] but only after obtaining the landlord's consent. If the council chooses not to pay for an alteration but allows the tenant to proceed with it, the rent should not be increased so as to charge the tenant again for the value of that improvement.[139]

2. Social landlords

Since early 1989, housing associations have created assured tenancies operating in the private sector under a market rent regime. However, most housing associations rely on government funding, which is provided in the expectation that rents charged will be affordable and on the basis that the resulting properties will be subject to ministerial guidance about rents.[140] Housing action trusts create tenancies in the public sector, for which they can impose reasonable charges, but with provision for the charges to be increased if the tenancy is transferred to a private sector landlord.[141] Thus, for example, the *Assured Tenant's Charter* provides that[142]:

> "Registered social landlords should try to set rents which are affordable to people in low-paid employment and which, in general needs housing, are less than rents for similar, privately rented, properties in the area."

The fair rent structure of the Rent Act 1977 applies to pre-1989 tenancies created by housing associations as explained below.[143]

The Housing Green Paper[144] considers the case for a fairer scheme for social rents. It reveals that in 1999 the average rent for private sector assured tenancies was £75 a week, in the public sector it was £44 a week and for tenants of registered social landlords it was £52 a week. The Government proposes to move to a single system for public and social rents, with affordable rents close to the present level of local authority rents, though it is recognised that convergence might take 10 years to achieve.[145]

3. Private sector assured tenancies and assured shortholds

Again the vital watershed was early in 1989 when the Housing Act 1988 superseded the Rent Act 1977.[146] Residential tenancies granted after that date operate as assured tenancies, with a regime of market rents determined by the open market in lettings with minimal state intervention. The lease itself fixes the rent for the duration of any contractual

---

[136] s.102(2)–(3).
[137] s.25.
[138] ss.99A–99B (inserted by L.R.H.U.D.A. 1993 s.122), s.100.
[139] s.101.
[140] H.A. 1996 s.219.
[141] H.A. 1988 ss.85–86.
[142] (Housing Corporation, 1998) section 4.
[143] At p. 234.
[144] *Quality and Choice: A Decent Home for All* (D.E.T.R., April 2000) ch.10 and appendix.
[145] para.10.44.
[146] January 15th 1989.

period,[147] meaning that the initial rent is fixed by a free negotiation between landlord and tenant. Fixed terms often include a rent review provision,[148] but otherwise the notice procedure described below allows rent increases. At the end of the contractual term, the contractual rent will be carried forward and continues in force until an increase occurs.

Rent increases may occur by *notice* given by the landlord unless otherwise agreed between landlord and tenant.[149] Notice is allowed during any statutory period—when any agreed contractual period has ended—and also during any contractual period for which there is no rent review provision.[150] A form is prescribed.[151] The rent proposed becomes the new rent for the tenancy at the end of the notice period, which varies according to the period of the tenancy: notice must be of six months if the tenancy is yearly, of one month if less than monthly, and otherwise of one full period of the tenancy.[152] Rents are fixed for 12 months at a time, measured at first from the initial creation of the tenancy and at later stages from the date of the most recent rent increase.

Life long security of tenure is enjoyed by some assured tenants—mainly housing association tenants but also those in the private sector who do not have a shorthold[153]— but it could be undermined if the landlord was allowed to demand extortionate rent increases. Hence there is a procedure providing for adjudication of rent increases to ensure that the rent is not increased above the level of an open market rental. Within the currency of the landlord's notice, the tenancy is able to apply[154] to a *Rent Assessment Committee*. This committee determines whether the rent is significantly higher than the landlord might reasonably be expected to obtain, taking a comparison from other assured tenancies, and fixing the market rent for a letting on the same terms by a willing landlord under an assured tenancy.[155] There are some disregards,[156] while council tax[157] and service charges[158] are considered separately. If the rent proposed in the landlord's notice is significantly out of line, the Committee will cap the rent at market levels.

Luxury properties are not assured, the borderline being a rent which exceeds £25,000 a year. It is possible therefore for a tenancy to be assured before a proposed increase but to be removed from all protection by the effect of the increase itself. Just this happened in *R. v. London R.A.P. ex parte Cadogan Estates Ltd.*[159] Kay J. held that in these circumstances the Rent Assessment Panel was required to take on the case and reassess the rent

---

[147] H.A. 1988 s.13; Woodfall 24.039–24.046.

[148] See above p. 224.

[149] s.13(5).

[150] s.13(1).

[151] S.I. 1997/194 form 5; *Tadema Holdings Ltd.* v. *Ferguson* [1999] Times November 25th C.A. (rent increase notice giving the agent's address was sufficient; a notice can be valid as against a mental patient who cannot understand it).

[152] H.A. 1988 s.13(2).

[153] See above Chapter 5.

[154] H.A. 1988 s.13(4)–(5); S.I. 1997/194 forms 6B (assured), 8 (shorthold).

[155] s.14(1).

[156] (1) the effect of the grant to a sitting tenant, (2) relevant improvements while let as an assured tenancy during the last 21 years, and (3) any reduction in value caused by the tenant's failure to honour his obligations: H.A. 1988 s.14(2), (3).

[157] H.A. 1988 ss.14A, 14B; S.I. 1993/651.

[158] H.A. 1988 ss.14(4)–(5), 41A.

[159] [1998] Q.B. 398, Kay J.

but, if their determination fixed the market rent above the £25,000 ceiling, the effect of the determination was to remove all protection from the tenancy for the future.

Most leases are now assured shortholds under which the tenant has no more guarantee than of a six-month short hold,[160] so use of this procedure by a shorthold tenant will almost certainly precipitate his eviction. Housing benefit authorities often insist on adjudication of the rent before agreeing to make social security payments, and indeed the greatest use of a Rent Assessment Committee is for this purpose.

Ministers have *reserve powers* to regulate the rents of new or existing lettings, though these powers have not been exercised in relation to assured tenants.[161]

J. RENT ACT 1977 FAIR RENTS

Rents under private sector grants made before early 1989 continue to be regulated by the Rent Act 1977,[162] as do some related forms of grant.[163] Rent Act tenants have the right to insist on registration of a fair rent, which becomes the maximum recoverable rent. Although the basis of a fair rent is the open market rent, fair rents were much fairer to tenants than to landlords, because of the statutory method laid down for quantification of the rent, which required the market level to be reduced by a discount to reflect the scarcity of accommodation. Historically this may have benefited the tenant to the extent of a 40 per cent saving in the rent. However, since assured tenancies were introduced rents have rocketed, partly because there are more market rents with which to make comparisons and partly because stimulation of the rental market has removed the previous scarcity of accommodation to rent. Capping had to be introduced in 1999 to limit rent increases.

It is a curiosity that the Rent Act 1977 does not define a fair rent, but relies instead on a provision that shows how to determine it.[164] What has to be registered is "what is or would be a fair rent". Regard must be paid to all the circumstances", specific mention being made of the age, character, and locality, the state of repair and the condition of any furniture.[165] There are some specific regards and disregards. Personal circumstances of the tenant must be ignored,[166] including his security of tenure.[167] However by far the most important consideration is that any increase in the rent arising from a scarcity of accommodation in the area must be eliminated in fixing the fair rent.[168] As Lord Kilbrandon said in *Mason* v. *Skilling*,[169] determination of a fair rent requires a skilled estimate of a hypothetical figure, that is the rent which a landlord would demand and that a tenant would be prepared to pay if the market were roughly in a state of equilibrium without any serious shortage or surplus of subjects available for letting.

[160] H.A. 1988 s.22.
[161] L.T.A. 1985 s.31.
[162] Woodfall 23.086–23.113; Davey 288–297.
[163] Woodfall 23.148–23.187; see also below p. 234.
[164] *Curtis* v. *London R.A.C.* [1999] Q.B. 92, 95H, Auld L.J.
[165] R.A. 1977 s.70(1).
[166] s.70(1).
[167] *Mason* v. *Skilling* [1974] 1 W.L.R. 1437 H.L.
[168] s.70(2).
[169] [1974] 1 W.L.R. 1437, 1443B.

1. Older methods of determination

When the House of Lords heard *Mason* v. *Skilling*[170] Lord Reid recognised that it was permissible for the rent officer or rent assessment committee to adopt any method or methods of ascertaining fair rents which was neither unlawful nor unreasonable. As it happens the two cases to reach the Lords both involved fair rents based on the capital value of the property from which an attempt was made to work out a fair rate of return to a landlord. This was the only method feasible in the early days of a fair rent regime.[171] *Mason* itself allows the calculation to be based on either the capital value with vacant possession or with a sitting tenant—provided that the valuer recognises that the sitting tenant value is lower precisely because it takes account of a market scarcity. *Western Heritable Co Ltd.* v. *Husband*[172] upheld a fair rent fixed using 80 fair rent comparables which were themselves based on a notional return of 6 per cent on the capital value of the houses with vacant possession, from which a 40 per cent deduction was afterwards made for scarcity value.

Until recently a more popular method was to base fair rents on similar fair rent registration but fair rents are poor comparables unless it is possible to assess what discount was allowed at the time of the earlier registration for scarcity. Inflation-based increases of previous registrations are not generally acceptable.[173] The correct procedure was explained in *Northumberland & Durham Property Trust Ltd.* v. *London R.A.C.*[174] One has to work out what scarcity discount was applied, gross up the fair rents to determine the market rent at the time, adjust it for increases in market rents since the time of the last registration, and then apply the discount appropriate to the degree of scarcity existing at the time of the current determination. This process is riddled with imponderables. Keene J. ruled that the use of fair rent comparables would be surprising where comparables based on assured tenancies were available.

2. Market rent comparables

The move to market rents pioneered by the Housing Act 1988 for assured tenancies has made it easier to establish a true market rent, and cases decided during the 1990s have emphasised that the correct methodology is to start from a market rent[175] and then to adjust this for the statutory disregards and any scarcity factor. In *Spath Holme Ltd.* v. *Greater Manchester & Lancashire R.A.C.*[176] the Court of Appeal had to decide the correct way to fix a fair rent for flats in an apartment block in Didsbury, South Manchester. It held that a market rent for an assured tenancy was the same as the market rent used as a basis for the assessment of fair rents, the only difference being the scarcity discount

---

[170] At 1440A.

[171] At 1439H.

[172] [1983] 2 A.C. 849 H.L.

[173] *Kovats* v. *Trinity House Corporation* [1982] 1 E.G.L.R. 103, Forbes J.; R.G. Lee (1983) 4 O.J.L.S. 287; *White* v. *Wareing* [1992] 1 E.G.L.R. 271 C.A.

[174] [1998] 3 E.G.L.R. 85, Keene J.

[175] At 84C; *Mountview Court Properties Ltd.* v. *Devlin* (1970) 21 P. & C.R. 689 C.A.; *Tormes Property Co. Ltd.* v. *Landau* [1971] 1 Q.B. 261 C.A.; *Metropolitan Property Holdings Ltd.* v. *Finegold* [1975] 1 W.L.R. 349, 352, Lord Widgery C.J.; *B.T.E. Ltd.* v. *Merseyside & Cheshire R.A.C.* (1991) 24 H.L.R. 514, Hutchison J.

[176] [1995] 2 E.G.L.R. 80 C.A.; see [1999] Q.B. 92, 96H, Auld L.J. and [2000] 1 All E.R. 884, 887f, Stuart Smith L.J.

applied to the former when reaching the latter figure. Before 1989 all residential rents were regulated and so few market rents were available, but the growth of assured tenancies has provided far more comparables for use by a rent officer and on appeal a rent assessment committee. Morritt L.J. ruled in *Spath Holme* that available market rents should be used as a starting point in preference to fair rent comparables. This ruling had a dramatic impact and created a sudden surge in rents.[177] McCulloch J. expressed clearly the benefit to landlords when he said that:

> "experience since 1989 has increasingly shown that fair rents have fallen too far behind market rents (allowing for an element of scarcity in the latter). As the years progress this disparity may be expected to diminish and ideally should be eliminated."[178]

Fair rent registrations have tended to be set at much higher levels than the ones which they replace.

Morritt L.J.'s dicta in *Spath Holme* were not unambiguously clear since he also paid lip service to the freedom of choice allowed to a rent officer or rent assessment committee in the choice of methodology, and it was in any event arguable that this exegesis was obiter. However it was treated as ratio—or at least flowing directly from his ratio—confirmed, and bolstered by Auld L.J. in *Curtis* v. *London R.A.C.*[179] If there were lots of market comparables from assured tenancies in the same block, the method which should be adopted is to find the market rental and adjust it; in such circumstances it would be positively wrong and a ground for judicial review to work from Rent Act fair rent registrations. Indeed the instruction to ignore scarcity in section 70(2) presupposes that subsection (1) is based on a market rent and every route to a fair rent should have that starting point.[180]

3. The state of repair

Lord Widgery C.J. observed in *Metropolitan Property Holdings Ltd.* v. *Finegold*[181] that the Parliamentary intention was that the inherent amenities or disadvantages of the property should be reflected in the rent, and so the statute[182] requires consideration of the state of repair both of the property[183] and of any furniture, as well as its age and general character. Personal circumstances of the tenant such as receipt of improvement grants must be ignored.[184] Statutory disregards aim to ensure that current parties do not profit from their own sins, but that the sins of earlier tenants are not visited on the current occupant. Structural repair is the responsibility of the landlord,[185] so the repair attributable to the tenant is internal work, but any such attributable to the tenant or any predecessor[186] is ignored, thus increasing the rent to what it would be if the tenant had

---

[177] N.P. Gravells [1998] *J.H.L.* 67.
[178] [1999] Q.B. 92, 106A.
[179] At 99; first instance decisions are reviewed at 109–112.
[180] At 115B, Auld L.J.
[181] [1975] 1 W.L.R. 349 C.A.; see further below p. 230.
[182] R.A. 1977 s.70(1), (2).
[183] *Sturloson & Co.* v. *Mauroux* (1988) 20 H.L.R. 332 C.A.
[184] R.A. 1977 s.70(1); *Royal British Legion H.Ass.* v. *East Midlands R.A.P.* [1989] 1 E.G.L.R. 131, Schiemann J.
[185] See below pp. 243–246.
[186] But disrepair owing to earlier tenants does count against the landlord: *N. & D. (London) Ltd.* v. *Gadson* (1991) 24 H.L.R. 64, Auld J.; J.E. Martin [1992] *Conv.* 271.

carried out his obligations. Non-contractual improvements carried out by the tenant will not increase his rent.[187] Unfortunately the rent might increase in the unlikely event of the tenant carrying out repairs properly within the landlord's responsibility.[188]

Very often the rent of a property which is out of repair has to be based on the rent of a comparable refurbished property, or vice versa. In *B.T.E. Ltd.* v. *Merseyside and Cheshire R.A.C.*[189] the committee had disregarded evidence of new lettings in the market on the basis that these concerned refurbished properties which were not genuinely comparable to the tenancies of dilapidated properties held by the sitting Rent Act tenants who were seeking to register their rents. Hutchison J. ruled that this approach was impermissible and that the correct procedure would have been to take the assured tenancies as comparables but with an adjustment to reflect the different standard of repair of the various properties.

Unfit properties present a problem. Superficially the rent for a house should be nil if it cannot be inhabited, but ironically a nil registration might itself operate to remove the tenant's Rent Act protection and so facilitate eviction.[190] From the tenant's point of view, it may be better to register a substantial rent, and rely on the principle that the landlord probably cannot enforce the rent after a closing order has been made.[191]

4.   Locality

Lord Widgery C.J. observed in *Metropolitan Property Holdings Ltd.* v. *Finegold*[192] how all sorts of factors tend to push rents up or down in the market, such as whether the property is older or more modern, its character and that of the locality. Parliament intended that inherent amenities or disadvantages of a property should be reflected in the rent, including[193] the character of the locality. According to Lord Widgery C.J.[194] Parliament was seeking to deprive a landlord of a wholly unmeritorious increase in rent which came about simply because there was a shortage of houses to rent in the district and thus an excess of demand over supply. When determining scarcity is crucial the first issue is the identification of the base area. Local distortions may create a shortage in a small area even though no scarcity exists on a wider scale. In *Finegold* the Court of Appeal had to consider the impact of an American school which greatly increased the demand for apartments from American families in a small part of St John's Wood, London. This did work to increase the rent. Lord Widgery C.J. allowed a reduction to reflect the much broader overall general scarcity affecting a really substantial area[195]—here meaning London—but on this wider canvas the scarcity was at a much lower level. Richards J. followed this case and again applied a broad brush approach in *Queensway Housing*

---

[187] R.A. 1977 s.70(3); *Morcom* v. *Campbell-Johnson* [1956] 1 Q.B. 106 C.A.; D. MacIntyre [1956] *C.L.J.* 32; *Henry Smith Charity Trustees* v. *Hemmings* [1981] 2 E.G.L.R. 90 C.A.

[188] J.T. Farrand [1983] *Conv.* 411.

[189] (1991) 24 H.L.R. 514, Hutchison J.

[190] J.T. Farrand [1981] *Conv.* 325.

[191] *Williams* v. *Khan* (1982) 43 P. & C.R. 1 C.A.; J.T. Farrand [1980] *Conv.* 182, 389.

[192] [1975] 1 W.L.R. 349 C.A.

[193] R.A. 1977 s.70(1)(d).

[194] At 352D–E.

[195] At 352; *Crown Estate Commissioners* v. *Connor* (1986) 19 H.L.R. 35, McCowan J. (London, not just Regent's Park).

Association Ltd. v. *Chiltern Thames & Eastern R.A.C.*[196] Rents in a high amenity area were necessarily increased by the fact that the immediate locality was a favoured residential district, but no scarcity of accommodation was discernible in a wider area. Richards J. said that one had to look at the wider area where the tenant could reasonably be expected to live, that is to consider what reasonable alternatives were available to the tenant of the subject property.

5.   Scarcity

Fair rents are assessed making the assumption that there is an even balance between the number of prospective tenants and the number of properties to let.[197] Historically fair rents were far below market rents because they were discounted for scarcity value.[198] There had been a shortage of dwelling-houses available to let unfurnished ever since 1920.[199] As it happens the two cases to reach the Lords both came from Scotland, and each case accepted that an historical figure for scarcity of 40 per cent was not so far out of line as to be quashed.[200] Rents were reduced proportionately so as to eliminate that factor.[201] Landlords felt aggrieved both because of the diminution of their income and because the capital value of any house with a sitting tenant was reduced correspondingly.[202]

During the 1990s the supply of rented accommodation increased dramatically,[203] reducing the scarcity factor, and consequently increasing the fair rent to be registered. Some scarcity factor may still exist, but it is now at a much lower level than its historical high.[204] In *Spath Holme*[205] there was no scarcity in Greater Manchester because the poor market in houses for sale had encouraged many owner-occupiers to let out temporarily unsaleable homes. By the time of *Curtis* v. *London R.A.C.*[206] estate agents gave evidence that there was no shortage in London because the assured tenancy regime had stimulated the letting market and created an adequate flow of houses and flats on to the market. If this is so, and there is in fact an ample supply of accommodation, fair rents should

---

[196] (1999) 31 H.L.R. 945, 959–964, Richards J.

[197] *Dennis* v. *McDonald* [1982] Fam. 63, 81H–82D, Arnold P.; query whether it was appropriate to use fair rents as between tenants in common of freehold land.

[198] s.70(2); *Mountview Court Properties Ltd.* v. *Devlin* (1970) 21 P. & C.R. 689, 691, Parker C.J.; *Tomes Property Co. Ltd.* v. *Landau* [1971] 1 Q.B. 261, 267, Parker C.J.; *Crown Estate Commissioners* v. *Connor* (1986) 19 H.L.R. 35, McCowan J. (London, not just Regent's Park); *R.* v. *S.S. for E.T.R. ex parte Spath Holme Ltd.* [2000] 1 All E.R. 884, 888f, Stuart Smith L.J.

[199] *Mason* v. *Skilling* [1974] 1 W.L.R. 1437, 1440E, Lord Reid.

[200] *Mason* as above; *Western Heritable Investment Co. Ltd.* v. *Husband* [1983] 2 A.C. 849 H.L.; P.Q. Watchman [1985] *Conv.* 199; also *Apsley Hall Estates Ltd.* v. *Nottinghamshire R.O.* [1992] 2 E.G.L.R. 187.

[201] *Metropolitan Property Holdings Ltd.* v. *Finegold* [1975] 1 W.L.R. 349, 352, Lord Widgery C.J.; *Spath Holme Ltd.* v. *Greater Manchester & Lancashire R.A.C.* [1995] 2 E.G.L.R. 80, 85F, Morritt L.J.

[202] *Mason* at 1440C, Lord Reid, 1444E, Lord Kilbrandon.

[203] *R.* v. *S.S. for E.T.R. ex parte Spath Holme Ltd.* [2000] 1 All E.R. 884, 888d, Stuart Smith L.J.

[204] *Northumberland & Durham Property Trust Ltd.* v. *London R.A.C.* [1998] 3 E.G.L.R. 85, Keene J. (15% too low, 50% too high).

[205] [1995] 2 E.G.L.R. 80 C.A.

[206] [1999] Q.B. 92 C.A.; *Queensway H.Ass. Ltd.* v. *Chiltern Thames & Eastern R.A.C.* (1999) 31 H.L.R. 945, Richards J. The local authority housing register provides some evidence of scarcity: *Forebury Estates Ltd.* v. *Chiltern Thames & Eastern R.A.P.* [2000] 27 L.S.G. 38, Keene J.

be equal to market rents.[207] There is power to end all regulation when supply equals demand.[208]

6. The introduction of assured tenancies in 1989

Superficially, introduction of a market rent regime for assured tenancies created after early 1989 left the system for existing Rent Act tenancies unchanged. Indeed the value of Rent Act security was greatly enhanced, since a sitting tenant who wished to move would have to pay much more for accommodation elsewhere. The landlord could profit from removing the existing tenant and reletting at a market rent, though tough new controls on harassment[209] were supposed to be a sufficient protection for existing tenants. In fact however they often proved to be little protection against really ruthless landlords. There was, and is, nothing to stop a tenant surrendering his existing tenancy and accepting a regrant of an assured tenancy, whether acting deliberately or (more likely) in ignorance of the law.

In the event fair rents have increased substantially since 1989. Assessment of market rents became easier once there was a genuine market in assured tenancies. *Spath Holme Ltd.* v. *Greater Manchester & Lancashire R.A.C.* ruled that market rents charged under assured tenancies[210] were suitable comparables to use when assessing the market rent element of a fair rent. *Curtis* v. *London R.A.C.*[211] went much further by holding that assured tenancies are the *best* comparables and that existing registrations of fair rents should be disregarded when fixing other fair rents. Further the availability of higher returns for landlords might be expected to lead to the appearance on the market of more accommodation to rent, and so to reduce the scarcity of accommodation,[212] causing even larger increases in fair rents.

Fair rents have indeed risen as predicted. Government figures record rent increases exceeding 10 per cent or more in each year between 1988 and 1994, with a corresponding surge in housing benefit claims. Capital values of properties with sitting tenants have also increased, from an historical low of 35–50 per cent to a figure now nearer 80 per cent. Good news for landlords, but terribly hard on many elderly tenants. Little substance remains in the "fair" aspect of the Rent Act rent regime.

7. Fair rent capping

The Rent Acts (Maximum Fair Rent) Order 1999[213] attempts to deal with the surge in fair rents by limiting increases for all tenants within the Rent Act scheme of regulation—including occupiers of agricultural tied cottages and longer standing housing associa-

---

[207] *B.T.E. Ltd.* v. *Merseyside and Cheshire R.A.C.* (1991) 24 H.L.R. 514, 517 Hutchison J.; M. Davey [1992] J.S.W.L. 497; J.E. Martin [1992] *Conv.* 271; H. Lewis [1992] *N.L.J.* 729; A. Prichard [1992] *N.L.J.* 965; *District Estates Ltd.* v. *Merseyside & Cheshire R.A.C.* [1997] 2 C.L.Y. 3316 Q.B.D.

[208] R.A. 1977 s.143.

[209] See below pp. 314–315.

[210] [1995] 2 E.G.L.R. 80, 85E, Morritt L.J.

[211] [1999] Q.B. 92 C.A.

[212] *Apsley Hall Estates Ltd.* v. *Nottinghamshire R.O.* [1992] 2 E.G.L.R. 187 (scarcity reduced to 10%); *Curtis* as above; *Queensway H.Ass. Ltd.* v. *Chiltern Thames & Eastern R.A.C.* (1999) 31 H.L.R. 945, 964–967, Richards J. (appeals allowed against rents with 10–15% scarcity deduction in the Home Counties).

[213] S.I. 1999/6; made under the reserve power in L.T.A. 1985 s.31.

tion tenants. Increases in registered rents are restricted by a mathematical formula linked to the rate of inflation since the last registration.

> The existing registered rent (referred to as LR) can be increased by the rate of inflation revealed by the increase in the Retail Prices Index between the month before the determination and the month of the first registration, and also by a factor P, which is 7.5 per cent on a first application and 5 per cent for a second or subsequent application. Results known as the maximum fair rent (MFR) are rounded to the nearest 50p. Variable sums are ignored for the purposes of this calculation, and the cap ceases to operate if there is a change of the condition of the property or of common parts exceeding 15 per cent.

Government research indicated that if this order had been in force in mid 1997 86 per cent of increases would have been capped. [214] However the rule applies only to applications made after early 1999 [215] and it is arguable that the cap was applied too late to save most tenants[216]; landlords were given six months' warning during which time they could apply for an uncapped increase. What is really required is an amendment of the formula for assessing a fair rent.[217]

An apparently devastating blow was dealt to the Order by the Court of Appeal in *R. v. Secretary of State for the Environment, Transport & the Regions ex parte Spath Holme Ltd*,[218] since it was held that the legislation employed by the government[219] could only be used to counter inflation.[220] The order was void since it sought to achieve the extraneous purpose of alleviating the perceived hardship on a small group of tenants of recent decisions about how to calculate fair rents. However, the House of Lords has now reversed this decision and has upheld the validity of the capping order.[221]

8. Variable rents

Rents may be *variable*[222] because they include council tax, water rates, or separate sums payable by the tenant for furniture[223] or services. These may be noted separately on the register. Where the rent includes variable sums in respect of services, depreciations,[224]

---

[214] C.P. Rodgers [1999] *Conv.* 201, 226; P.H. Kenny [1999] *Conv.* 169; J. McGeough [1998] 14 *P.L.J.* 19; S. Chahal [1998] 7 *Legal Action* 23.

[215] February 1st 1999.

[216] N.P. Gravells [1998] *J.H.L.* 67.

[217] C.P. Rodgers [1999] *Conv.* 201, 226.

[218] [2000] 1 All E.R. 884 C.A. The Registration of Fair Rents Bill 2000 is a private member's bill intended to reverse the result of this case.

[219] L.T.A. 1985 s.31.

[220] Counter Inflation Act 1973 s.11, re-enacted as Housing Rents & Subsidies Act 1975 s.11.

[221] [2000] N.L.J. 1855 H.L.

[222] R.A. 1977 ss.67A, 70(3A), 72A.

[223] Even if the furniture is removed: *R. v. London R.A.P. ex parte Mota* (1988) 20 H.L.R. 159; J.T. Farrand [1981] *Conv.* 9.

[224] *Perseus Property Co. Ltd. v. Burberry* [1985] 1 E.G.L.R. 114, Nolan J. (lifts).

and repairs, the rent can (and must[225]) be registered as a single variable rent.[226] The variable element has to be removed before the rent capping formula just described is operated.

K. RENT ACT 1977 FAIR RENT LIMITS AND REGISTRATIONS

1. Scope

The "constrained world of fair rents"[227] applies to three kinds of residential tenant. (1) Private sector tenancies created before early 1989 operated as *protected tenancies* under the Rent Act 1977 with life-long security of tenure and a regime of rent regulation which continues to apply so long as the tenancy continues. (2) Between 1915 and 1980 there was a category of *controlled tenancies* which derived from earlier rent restriction legislation. Until 1980 rents were even more tightly controlled, the landlord being entitled to a fixed multiple of the rateable value.[228] However, to the delight of all landlords these were converted to ordinary Rent Act tenancies in 1980, at the expense of a fair rent registration.[229] (3) Longstanding tenants of *housing associations* may also fall within the mesh of the fair rent scheme. Since early 1989, housing associations have created assured tenancies operating in the private sector under a market rent regime and between 1985 and 1989 they were in the public sector (secure tenancies). Rent Act 1977 fair rents[230] may still apply to longer standing housing association tenancies. Comparables used when fixing the rent should ideally be other housing association rents.[231] Registration creates a rent limit,[232] which continues in force on a reletting, until a higher rent is registered,[233] and overpayments are recoverable.[234] Rent under a periodic tenancy can be increased by notice, but only up to the rent limit.[235]

Some tenants with *limited security* are excluded from the fair rent regime. Thus a tenancy with a resident landlord is excluded from the rent regulation—until 1988 this was the classic example of a restricted contract—and it is only if the landlord moves out that a fair rent registration becomes possible.[236] This depends upon the grant of a tenancy since licensees have no rent registration rights, but many tenancies fall into exclusions.

---

[225] *Firstcross Ltd.* v. *Teasdale* [1983] 1 E.G.L.R. 87, McNeill J.; *Wigglesworth* v. *Property Holding & Investment Trust* [1984] 1 E.G.L.R. 93, McCullough J.

[226] R.A. 1977 s.71(4); J.T. Farrand [1983] *Conv.* 90; *Betts* v. *Vivamat Properties Ltd.* [1984] 1 E.G.L.R. 95, Hodgson J.; the rent officer must be satisfied that the terms are reasonable: R.A. 1977 s.71. Service charges paid voluntarily (as opposed to under an obligation of the tenancy) should not be registered: *Eaton Square Properties Ltd.* v. *Ogilvie* [2000] 16 E.G. 143.

[227] *Ellis & Son Fourth Amalgamated Properties Ltd.* v. *Southern R.A.P.* [1984] 1 E.G.L.R. 91, 92K, Mann J.

[228] R.A. 1977 part VIII; *Regis Property Co. Ltd.* v. *Dudley* [1959] A.C. 370 H.L.; P.V. Baker (1959) 75 *L.Q.R.* 25; *Wellcome Trust Ltd.* v. *Hammad* [1998] Q.B. 638, 648C–D, Leggatt L.J.

[229] R.A. 1977 s.18A and sch.17; also s.116 inserted by H.A. 1980 sch.25.

[230] R.A. 1977 ss.87–96, sch.14.

[231] *Re Leeds Federated H.Ass.* [1981] 2 E.G.L.R. 93 Q.B.D.

[232] R.A. 1977 s.88.

[233] ss.88(4), 95 (particulars required of previous rents).

[234] s.94.

[235] s.93.

[236] sch.2 para.6.

For example a holiday letting is not a protected tenancy and no fair rent registration possible whereas an off-season holiday letting does allow a fair rent registration during the limited period of security enjoyed by the tenant. This is usually a difference without a difference since anyone applying for a fair rent registration would almost certainly be met by a termination of his limited occupation rights, though a tenant is able to bequeath to his successors a binding registration.

2. Former rent limits on the grant of new tenancies

If *no rent was registered* there was no limit for a new tenancy, and so the rent was whatever was fixed by contractual negotiation between landlord and tenant, though the tenant could impose a limit subsequently by applying for a registration.

Where the *rent was registered* at the time of the grant of the tenancy, the registered rent sets a limit for what was recoverable,[237] though it was obviously open to a benevolent landlord to ask for less! It was once thought that an existing rent registration could be ignored if it had been invalidated by major improvements or changes in the character of the tenancy,[238] but decisions to this effect are now known to be wrong, and it is in fact necessary to implement the machinery which governs the alteration of a registered rent to allow for changes in the conditions affecting the tenancy.[239] *Rakhit* v. *Carty*[240] applies the correct modern law: a registration dating from 1974 at £550 *a year* for an unfurnished dwelling would continue to apply to a furnished letting made in 1987. Registration of the rent at any time past continues to set a limit on the recoverable rent until the structure is so altered that there is a new dwelling[241] or there is a new registration.

After a property had remained free of a Rent Act letting for two years, the landlord could apply unilaterally to *cancel* the existing registration.[242] If, on the other hand, the landlord relet the property, it was open to him to enter into a rent agreement with a prospective tenant, which will result in an increase in the rent registered.[243]

None of this affects landlords after early 1989 since they can now grant assured tenancies at market rents.

3. Rent during the continuation of the tenancy

Before the rent is first registered, the contractual rent continues to operate during the contractual phase of the tenancy and during any statutory continuation of the tenancy.[244]

---

[237] R.A. 1977 s.44. The machinery is explained in *R.* v. *S.S. for E.T.R. ex parte Spath Holme Ltd.* [2000] 1 All E.R. 884, 889j–891b, Stuart Smith L.J.

[238] *Kent* v. *Millmead Properties Ltd.* (1982) 44 P. & C.R. 353 C.A.; J.T. Farrand [1983] *Conv.* 412; J.E. Martin [1983] *Conv.* 145; *Cheniston Investments Ltd.* v. *Waddock* [1988] 2 E.G.L.R. 136 C.A.

[239] R.A. 1977 s.67(3).

[240] [1990] 2 Q.B. 315 C.A.

[241] R.A. 1977 s.44(1).

[242] s.73(2); S.I.1980/1698 (procedure and forms).

[243] s.51.

[244] As varied for changes in rates, services etc., ss.46, 47.

Registration of the rent has the effect of setting a maximum limit for the recoverable rent,[245] though any lower contractually agreed rent takes precedence while the contractual period continues. Registration takes effect on the date that the rent is decided or confirmed, either by the rent officer or on appeal by the rent assessment committee.[246] During a statutory period the higher rent is recoverable immediately.[247] However, during a contractual period,[248] registration does not by itself increase a contractual rent, nor does it convert the tenancy to a statutory one,[249] so that a registration has to be followed by a formal notice of increase.[250]

The landlord can give *notice to increase the rent* after it has been registered for two years, any increase operating from the date of re-registration,[251] though it was common to make an anticipatory application during the last three months to take effect as soon as the two years are up.[252] The tenant cannot protect his existing rent level by re-registering the same rent.[253] Unilateral application by the landlord within the two years is permitted only where there is a material change, such as reconstruction, of such an extent that the rent shown on the register is no longer a fair rent.[254] Inclusive rents can always be altered to reflect changes in rates, service charges and charges for furniture, through the mechanism of a formal notice of increase.[255]

Landlord and tenant can agree to increase the rent under an existing tenancy on a renewal,[256] but only by a *formal rent agreement* signed by both parties. An informal agreement is ineffective and the increase is irrecoverable,[257] though recovery is subject to a time limit of one year.[258] If the rent is not already registered, the agreement must contain a prominent statement of the tenant's rights.[259] This last precaution is unnecessary if the rent is already registered, since the rent agreement will operate only after joint application for cancellation of the existing registration, and then only after the registration has been in force for two years.[260] The rent officer must scrutinise the rent agreement in order to satisfy himself that the new rent does not exceed a fair rent, that it will operate for at least 12 months, and that any terms about services are reasonable. The

---

[245] ss.44 (contractual), 45 (statutory).

[246] s.72(1), (2).

[247] s.45(1).

[248] See above pp. 109–111.

[249] *Thomas Pocklington's Gift Trustees* v. *Hill* (1989) 21 H.L.R. 391 C.A. (a phased notice of increase does so); J.E. Martin [1989] *Conv.* 287.

[250] R.A. 1977 ss.45(2)(b), 49; S.I. 1980/1697 (prescribed form); genuine errors can be corrected by a county court: s.49(5)–(7).

[251] R.A. 1977 s.72(4), (5).

[252] s.72(3).

[253] *R.* v. *R.O. of Kensington & Chelsea R.L.B.C. ex parte Moberly* (1986) 18 H.L.R. 189 C.A.; J.E. Martin [1986] *Conv.* 272

[254] R.A. 1977 s.67(3), (4); *Gluchowska* v. *Tottenham B.S.* [1954] 1 Q.B. 439 C.A.; *London Housing & Commercial Properties Ltd.* v. *Cowan* [1977] Q.B. 148.

[255] R.A. 1977 ss.46, 47; S.I. 1980/1697. Fraud invalidates a notice: *Lazarus Estates Ltd.* v. *Beasley* [1956] 1 Q.B. 702 C.A.; H.W.R. Wade [1956] *C.L.J.* 143.

[256] R.A. 1977 s.51; *Sopwith* v. *Stutchbury* (1985) 17 H.L.R. 50 C.A. (only tenants with existing Rent Act security).

[257] Informal increases are of no effect: *Aristocrat Property Investments Ltd.* v. *Harounoff* (1982) 43 P. & C.R. 284 C.A.

[258] ss.54, 57.

[259] s.51(3), (4).

[260] R.A. 1977 s.73(1), (4), (5); S.I.1980/1698 (prescribed form of application).

new rent operates from the date of the agreement, but is subject to re-registration at any later time.[261]

L. PUBLIC CONTROL OF RESIDENTIAL RENTS

1. Assured tenancies and assured shortholds

Rents under *fully assured tenancies* are fixed at market levels, but when the contractual period ends the tenant attains life-long security of tenure. Imposing an excessive rent increase could undermine this security very easily. Hence the corollary of granting security is a mechanism to keep rent increases to market levels. The landlord initiates a rent increase by serving a notice to increase the rent.[262] If the rent cannot be agreed, the tenant may, within the currency of a notice to increase the rent,[263] refer the notice to a Rent Assessment Committee.[264] Its function is to determine whether the rent is significantly higher than the market rent, after obtaining necessary information from the parties[265] and drawing a comparison from other assured tenancies.[266] Rates and service charge are considered separately.[267]

Excessive rents under *assured shortholds* can also be referred to the rent assessment committee.[268] A tenant is unlikely to exercise this right in view of the very limited security enjoyed by shorthold tenants. But housing benefit authorities may insist on reference of the rent before agreeing to make social security payments.

2. Rent Act tenancies

Fair rents are determined for Rent Act tenancies by rent officers.[269] Until recently the system was organised by county and London borough,[270] but it has now been reconstituted as a national service.[271] Clearly business is declining as the number of protected tenancies reduces. Usually tenants apply to register rents[272] and landlords to cancel them.[273] The application on a prescribed form[274] must propose a specific rent.[275] The rent officer carries out the initial assessment, records the dwelling, the tenancy, and the rent,[276] and maintains this information in a public register of fair rents.[277]

[261] s.73(6), (7).

[262] H.A. 1988 s.13.

[263] The duration is six months if the tenancy is yearly, one month if monthly and otherwise follows the period of the tenancy: s.13(3).

[264] H.A. 1988 s.13(4), (5); S.Is. 1993/653 (procedure), 1997/194 (form).

[265] s.41(2).

[266] s.42 (demand for information about and register of rents); S.I. 1988/2199 as amended.

[267] subss.(4), (5).

[268] S.I. 1997/194 (form 6B).

[269] Subject to judicial review: *R. v. R.O. of Camden L.B.C. ex parte Ebiri* [1981] 1 W.L.R. 881; J.T. Farrand [1983] *Conv.* 401.

[270] R.A. 1977 ss.62–64A, 67 and sch.11 (procedure); S.I. 1980/1696.

[271] Administration of the Rent Officer Service (England) O. 1999, S.I. 1999/2403.

[272] *R. v. R.O. of Camden L.B.C. ex parte Felix* [1988] 2 E.G.L.R. 132, Hutchison J. (where application signed by some only of joint tenants.)

[273] S.I. 1980/1698 (cancellation procedure).

[274] S.I. 1980/1697 as amended (form 5).

[275] R.A. 1977 s.67; S.I. 1980/1696 (procedure).

[276] S.I. 1980/1697 sch.2 as amended.

[277] R.A. 1977 s.66; S.I. 1980/1697, as amended, forms 8 (certificate of fair rent), 9 (registration).

Appeal against the rent officer's determination of a fair rent is made on the prescribed form[278] to the *Rent Assessment Committee.*[279] There is nothing to prevent a successful landlord from appealing to seek a yet higher increase or to challenge the reasoning of the Rent Officer.[280] Procedure is informal[281] and the committee can rely on its own expert knowledge.[282] Reasons are required, probably supported by a calculation.[283] The committees[284] saw a decline in business as the number of Rent Act tenancies reduced, but have been reconstituted as Leasehold Valuation Tribunals to take on new business in relation to enfranchisement and service charges.[285]

A minor degree of rent control applied to *restricted contracts* (such as licences and resident landlord lettings) created before 1980,[286] but the volume of applications is now minimal. Rents could be referred to a rent tribunal[287] (that is a rent assessment committee constituted in a different guise) to determine a *reasonable* rent.[288]

3.   Control of housing benefit claims by rent officers

Much rent is paid, indirectly, by the social security fund, in the form of housing benefit. If no controls were in place, it would be possible for landlords to inflate the rents which they charged, knowing that tenants were in no position to argue and leaving the social security fund to pick up the tab. This is prevented by what are obliquely described as the "additional functions" of rent officers. Proper charges have to be determined for particular accommodation, including single rooms,[289] and if the rent demanded is found to be excessive or the accommodation exceeds the needs of the applicant, housing benefit will be withheld. Some 40 per cent of referrals lead to a reduction, the average being 20 per cent.

4.   Public law control

The decisions of rent officers and rent assessment committees can be challenged on public law grounds, including unreasonableness in the *Wednesbury* sense.[290] Central to the ability to challenge a decision is the right to obtain a written statement of the reasoning of a committee, a right conferred by the Tribunal and Inquiries Act 1992 and statutory

---

[278]   S.I. 1980/1700 r.3, as amended.

[279]   R.A. 1977 sch.11 para.7; S.I. 1971/1065; *Tingey* v. *Sutton* [1984] 1 W.L.R. 1154 C.A. (a County Court has no jurisdiction).

[280]   *Curtis* v. *London R.A.C.* [1999] Q.B. 92 C.A.

[281]   C. Yates [1980] *Conv.* 136.

[282]   P.Q. Watchman [1979] *Conv.* 205.

[283]   *Curtis* v. *London R.A.C.* [1997] 4 All E.R. 842, 865–868, Auld L.J.; *District Estates Ltd.* v. *Merseyside & Cheshire R.A.C.* [1997] 2 C.L.Y. 3316, Owen J.

[284]   R.A. 1977 sch.10 and numerous S.Is.

[285]   A.M. Prichard [1991] *Conv.* 447, [1991] *N.L.J* 973.

[286]   See above pp. 104–105.

[287]   R.A. 1977 ss.77–82; S.I. 1980/1700 as amended by S.I. 1981/1493; J.T. Farrand [1980] *Conv.* 319; Woodfall 23.188–23.207; Davey 301–304.

[288]   R.A. 1977 s.78. Premiums were also prohibited: s.122.

[289]   H.A. 1988 s.121; S.I. 1997/1984; S.I. 2000/1; for the national reorganisation of the rent officer service see above n. 271.

[290]   *R.* v. *London R.A.P. ex parte Wells* (1996) 71 P. & C.R. D4, Turner J. (perverse to fix a fair rent above that sought by the landlord).

instruments[291] and fully recognised by cases such as *Spath Holme Ltd.* v. *Greater Manchester & Cheshire R.A.C.*[292] Inadequate reasoning is a ground for quashing a decision[293] or, as Auld L.J. described it in *Curtis* v. *London R.A.C.*,[294] some working through based on some arithmetical markers or some guide figures. Proper, intelligible, and adequate reasons must be stated if assured comparables are ignored.[295]

5. Human rights challenges

Rent regulation involves a political decision to interfere with the returns that a landlord could recover in a free market in the interests of social justice.[296] Provided that the social objective is legitimate, rent control legislation will not infringe the landlords' human rights.[297] Now that the Human Rights Act 1998 is in force new grounds have become available for challenges to administrative decisions.[298]

M. SOCIAL SECURITY BENEFITS TO HELP WITH HOUSING COSTS

Social security benefits provide assistance with housing costs. Benefits are paid under the Social Security Contributions and Benefits Act 1992 and its subordinate regulations, which are subject to annual upratings and frequent changes in poverty thresholds, details, and indeed fundamental principles.[299]

Housing benefit covers payments of rent, some service charges,[300] water rates,[301] and council tax by those with a low income. Local housing authorities administer the benefit, though with subsidy from state funds and according to national rules. Housing benefit is income-related—means testing is carried out by reference to a poverty threshold—but it is non-contributory, that is it is not necessary to have a record of national insurance contribution. Housing benefit is often paid direct to a landlord.[302] Local authorities can call on rent officers to determine whether the rent is significantly high or exceptionally high in relation to local reference rents[303] as well as determining whether the accommodation is reasonable for a particular applicant to occupy. If children spend equal time with their father and mother but the mother is allowed housing benefit, the Rent Officer is entitled to disregard the children when determining what size

---

[291] s.10 and sch. 1; also S.I. 1971/1065 reg.10A.

[292] See above pp. 228–232.

[293] [1995] 2 E.G.L.R. 80, 86, Morritt L.J.; he cited *Guppys Properties Ltd.* v. *Knott (No.3)* [1981] 1 E.G.L.R. 85; *Midanbury Properties (Southampton) Ltd.* v. *Houghton T. Clark & Son Ltd.* [1981] 2 E.G.L.R. 88, Woolf J.; *Metropolitan Properties Co. (F.G.C.) Ltd.* v. *Good* [1981] 2 E.G.L.R. 88, Woolf J.; [1982] *Conv.* 8.

[294] [1999] Q.B. 92, 117–121; *Queensway H.Ass. Ltd.* v. *Chiltern Thames & Eastern R.A.C.* (1999) 31 H.L.R. 945, 964–967, Richards J.

[295] At 118H, Auld L.J.

[296] M.J. Barnett [1971] *C.L.J.* 321; R.G. Lee (1992) 12 *O.J.L.S.* 543.

[297] *Mellacher* v. *Austria* [1990] 1 E.H.R.R. 391.

[298] See above pp. 200–208.

[299] Ogus, Barendt & Wikely, *The Law of Social Security* (Butterworths, 4th ed., 1995); practical up-to-date advice is best secured from a series of leaflets issued by the Department of Social Security and available in libraries.

[300] *R.* v. *Swansea C.C. ex parte Littler* [1998] Times September 9th C.A.

[301] Only if paid by the landlord so that the tenant is liable to make a reimbursement in restitution: *R.* v. *Bristol C.C. ex parte Jacobs* [1999] Times November 16th, Owen J.

[302] H.A. 1996 s.120.

[303] H.A. 1996 s.122; S.I. 1997/1984.

of accommodation is required by the father.[304] Benefits may be reduced as a result of these decisions. People receiving income support will be entitled to housing benefit on their rent and their entire council tax liability will be covered. Other people with income just above the income support level may be entitled to housing benefit, although they are likely to be receiving some other benefit, and they will be means tested.

Two particular problems require mention. One is that many local authorities fail to process housing benefit applications promptly, causing a claimant to fall into arrears with his rent; the potential defence in this case is considered as an aspect of residential repossession.[305] A converse problem arises if the landlord is forced to repay housing benefit to the local authority because the tenant has been allowed too much benefit.[306] *Jones* v. *Waveney D.C.*[307] shows that a council must follow a prescribed procedure for correcting overpayments[308] and if they fail to do so, the landlord may sue for the housing benefit withheld.

The Government Green Paper on Housing[309] reveals that housing benefit is paid to 4.5 million households, including 41 per cent of those aged 60 or over and 60 per cent of those in council accommodation, at a total cost in 1999 of £11 billion.[310] It is proposed to improve customer service by the introduction of information technology to help cope with the complexity of the system and to improve work incentives.[311] Widespread fraud and exploitation of the system by landlords have to be tackled.[312] The Paper also considers the possibility of making housing benefit payments conditional on the satisfactory standard of the property being let or at least of preventing direct payments to landlords of unsatisfactory premises.[313] Problems are identified with the system of making payments direct to a tenant.[314]

Income support and family credit are benefits designed to help those of low income who are not in full time work with general living expenses, the scheme being administered by the Department of Social Security. There are also a number of allowances for disabled people. Only one member of a household can claim a particular benefit,[315] *means testing* being applied to the family unit consisting of the applicant for benefit and also his household.

Aggregation of income and capital resources applies to married couples who are living together, unmarried couples living together,[316] and children.[317]

---

[304] *R.* v. *Swale B.C. ex parte Merchant* [1999] 1 F.L.R. 1087, Kay J.

[305] See below pp. 338–339.

[306] *R.* v. *Greenwich L.B.C. ex parte Deely* (1999) 31 H.L.R. 446; N. Hickman [1996] *N.L.J.* 1620.

[307] [1999] 48 L.S.G. 40 C.A.; *Warwick D.C.* v. *Freeman* (1994) 27 H.L.R. 616.

[308] S.I. 1987/1971.

[309] *Quality and Choice: A Decent Home for All* (D.E.T.R., April 2000).

[310] para.11.1.

[311] paras.11.7, 11.12–11.49.

[312] para. 11.4.

[313] paras.5.39–5.48.

[314] paras.11.77–11.79.

[315] Social Security Contributions and Benefits Act 1992 s.134(3).

[316] The cohabitation rule: *R.* v. *Penwith D.C. ex parte Menear* (1992) 24 H.L.R. 114; *Crake* v. *Supplementary Benefits Commission* [1982] 1 All E.R. 498. Relationships taken into account include sexual, financial, and general.

[317] Social Security Contributions and Benefits Act 1992 s.137(2).

Contributory benefits are available to those with a record of national insurance contributions, including particularly unemployment benefit. Money received from this source can be used to help with rent.

N. PREMIUMS AND DEPOSITS

1. Prohibition of premiums

Premiums were illegal on the grant of a Rent Act tenancy,[318] and remain illegal when an existing one is assigned.[319] Indirect and disguised[320] premiums are also caught. Receipt of an illegal premium is an offence, and the tenant can demand restitution.[321] A deposit may be taken to a maximum of two months' rent, provided that it is reasonable in relation to the potential liability,[322] and it is also legitimate to recover sums for improvements.[323] It is also an offence for a statutory Rent Act tenant to demand or receive a sum for giving up possession.[324] By way of exception to the general rule, the Crown Estates Commissioners were entitled to levy a premium, a course which led to a corresponding reduction in the fair rent.[325] A premium may also have been paid if the tenancy was unprotected when it was created and has only been brought into protection at some time after it was created, in which case the tenant is allowed to reimburse himself by demanding a premium when he assigns the lease to a new tenant.[326] There is no restriction on premiums if the tenancy is a more modern grant operating under the assured tenancy scheme.

2. Deposit protection

As indicated immediately above, deposits have always been permissible on the grant of residential accommodation, and these are left by the assured tenancy scheme to market negotiation. It is estimated that deposits amount to £¼ billion a year, with a grand total of £1 billion. All too often tenants find that landlords refuse to return deposits when the tenancy ends. Probably one half of tenants lose their deposits and in one half of these cases the deposit is unfairly withheld. There is presently a voluntary Code of Management Practice prepared by the National Federation of Residential Landlords and Association of Residential Letting Agents,[327] but the Government is considering[328] primary legislation to require deposits to be held in a client account of a managing agent

---

[318] s.119; Woodfall 23.208–23.222, 20.040–20.042; *Farrell* v. *Alexander* [1977] A.C. 59 H.L.; A.S. Owen (1977) 40 *M.L.R.* 216.

[319] s.120; *Nock* v. *Muck* [1982] 2 E.G.L.R. 100 (£40,000 for a luxury flat in Westminster); *Saleh* v. *Robinson* [1988] 2 E.G.L.R. 126 C.A. (a bung of £2,000 stuck in the pocket of the agent!)

[320] s.123 (excessive charges for furniture); also *Elmdene Estates Ltd.* v. *White* [1960] A.C. 528 H.L.; R.E. Megarry (1960) 76 *L.Q.R.* 179.

[321] ss.124, 125.

[322] s.126; H.W. Wilkinson [1992] *Conv.* 308.

[323] *Adair* v. *Murrell* [1982] 2 E.G.L.R. 77, Skinner J.; *Steele* v. *McMahon* [1990] 2 E.G.L.R. 114 C.A. (part lawful, part unlawful).

[324] R.A. 1977 sch.1 para.12; *Prince* v. *Robinson* (1999) 31 H.L.R. 89 C.A. (close to agreement at £20,000).

[325] *Crown Estate Commissioners* v. *Connor* (1986) 19 H.L.R. 35, McCowan J.; J.E. Martin [1987] *Conv.* 205.

[326] R.A. 1977 s.127, sch.18; H.A. 1988 s.115.

[327] P.H. Kenny [1999] *Conv.* 1.

[328] D.E.T.R., December 1998; a pilot is to be run until 2002.

with a rent deposit bond, and dispute resolution by an ombudsman. Tenants are currently forced to make a small claim; cases are so numerous that there are standard directions prepared for deposit cases, but only 54 per cent are successful.

3.   Accommodation agencies

The provision of private sector housing has little control apart from the Accommodation Agencies Act 1953. Lists of accommodation must be supplied free of charge, and no payment of money is allowed for registering a person who is seeking a residential tenancy.[329] Charges can be made after a person has been placed in accommodation successfully.[330] Fees can, of course, be taken from the landlord, and shops and newspapers can charge for wanted advertisements. It is an offence to advertise property to let without the authority of the owner.

[329] *McInnes* v. *Clarke* [1955] 1 W.L.R. 102.
[330] *Saunders* v. *Soper* [1975] A.C. 239 H.L., overruling *Crouch & Lees* v. *Haridas* [1972] 1 Q.B. 158.

10

CONDITION OF RENTED PROPERTY

Landlord's obligation to repair dwellings. Fitness for habitation. Furnishings and appliances. Notice and access to repair. Non-financial remedies. Damages. Tenant's responsibilities. Public and social sector repair. Alterations. Administrative enforcement. H.M.Os. Renovation grants. Reform. Communal management of public and social sector estates. Service charges on rented estates. Rights of leaseholders also available to renting tenants.

A. LANDLORD'S OBLIGATION TO REPAIR DWELLINGS

1. Short leases of dwellings

Repairs to a dwelling can be enormously expensive. Much of the benefit of repair works will accrue to the landlord of rented property, since the value of his reversion will be enhanced, while a short-term residential tenant secures a much more ephemeral benefit for the short time that he has the right to occupy. Business tenants can be left to negotiate the best deal that market conditions allow them.[1] Tenants of residential accommodation may be less aware of the potential problems, and could be compelled to accept harsh terms if there is a shortage of accommodation to rent. This explains why statute has intervened to ensure that it is the landlord who must carry out major structural repairs to a dwelling house.[2] The current legislation in the Landlord and Tenant Act 1985[3] replaces the Housing Act 1961[4] and affects leases granted after late 1961.[5] *Barrett* v. *Lounova (1982) Ltd.*[6] involved a grant in 1941, but the court was able to imply a similar term that the landlord is to repair the structure in order to give business efficacy to the tenancy.

The statute only bites if there has been an initial grant of a tenancy. The claimant in *Bruton* v. *London & Quadrant Housing Trust*[7] occupied a flat in a block held by a voluntary homelessness trust under a licence granted by a local authority. He complained that the flat was in disrepair and sought to make the Trust liable under section 11 of the

---

[1] L.T.A. 1985 s.11 excludes business tenancies (s.32(2)), agricultural leases and mortgage terms.

[2] s.16.

[3] ss. 11–17; Woodfall ch.13; Bright & Gilbert 313–385; Davey 45–76; Evans & Smith (5th) ch.9; Garner (2nd) ch.8.

[4] ss.32–33; D.G. Valentine (1962) 25 *M.L.R.* 343; W.A. West (1962) 26 *Conv. (N.S.)* 132, 187; J. Reynolds (1974) 37 *M.L.R.* 377.

[5] On or after October 24th 1961.

[6] [1990] Q.B. 348 C.A.; P.F. Smith [1988] *Conv.* 448.

[7] [2000] A.C. 406 H.L.; see above pp. 176–179.

Landlord and Tenant Act 1987. The Trust had granted exclusive possession to Bruton, creating a tenancy that was binding between themselves, and which was sufficient to entitle Bruton to enforce the statutory repairing covenant. This was so despite the fragility of Bruton's tenure as against the local authority as freeholder. Had Bruton been a licensee, as a majority of the Court of Appeal thought,[8] the Trust would not have been obliged to repair.

What is a short lease? The statutory cut-off point is seven years. Leases for less than seven years are caught,[9] but freedom of contract operates for a lease of exactly seven years,[10] or any longer period, or for life.[11] A lease is treated as continuing until it can first be terminated by the landlord—meaning that a lease for 99 years terminable by notice by the landlord after five years is caught[12]—and conversely an option to renew can take the lease out of the grasp of the legislation. Only periods during which there is an actual entitlement to possession are considered when measuring the seven years, so that any part of the term before the grant of the lease is ignored; hence a lease granted in 2000 for 10 years from 1995 is for five years and is caught by the Act.[13] A renewal of a lease outside the Act is again excluded.[14] However, liability under a lease that is technically outside the legislation can arise by estoppel where the landlord charges an increased rent on the basis that he is liable to repair.[15]

If a tenant enjoys full residential security he will be able to occupy the property indefinitely, but his tenancy will still be viewed as "short", so that the landlord is nevertheless liable to repair. There may be a temptation for a landlord to try to force the tenant out by making the property uninhabitable, but even if the tenant is forced out he will still be entitled to insist upon his security of tenure, the enforced absence being ignored when considering whether the tenant retains qualifying occupation.[16]

2. Public sector landlords

These were removed from the ambit of the legislation in 1980,[17] and are able to obtain a county court declaration that a tenancy is not affected.[18] Administrative procedures are the best weapons against dilatory councils.[19] Public sector tenants may still be protected by the express terms of a tenancy agreement or if the initial grant was made before 1980.[20] Very many public sector properties are subject to the terms of suspended possession orders, usually because of rent arrears, meaning that the tenancy ends automatically on the first failure to keep up to date with the instalments required by the

---

[8] [1998] Q.B. 834 C.A.

[9] L.T.A. 1985 s.13; "lease" is widely defined by s.16.

[10] *Brikom Investments Ltd.* v. *Seaford* [1981] 1 W.L.R. 863 C.A.

[11] *Parker* v. *O'Connor* [1974] 1 W.L.R. 1160 C.A. (death of landlord).

[12] L.T.A. 1985 s.13(1)(b).

[13] s.13(1)(a)

[14] s.14.

[15] *Brikom Investments Ltd.* v. *Seaford* [1981] 1 W.L.R. 863 C.A.

[16] *Viking Property Co. Ltd.* v. *Rawlinson* [1999] 08 C.L. 440.

[17] L.T.A. 1985 s.14(4); *Wainwright* v. *Leeds C.C.* [1984] 1 E.G.L.R. 67 C.A.; *Department of Transport* v. *Egoroff* [1986] 1 E.G.L.R. 89 C.A.

[18] s.15.

[19] See below pp. 266–272.

[20] Social sector tenants are covered; e.g. *Assured Tenant's Charter* (Housing Corporation, 1998) Section 5.

suspended possession order.[21] However the court has power to overlook trivial defaults if there has been substantial compliance with the possession order, by varying its terms to postpone the date for possession, a course which revives the disrepair claim.[22]

3. Work affected

Structural work is within the landlord's implied covenant[23] to repair the structure and exterior of the house. This includes all the most expensive work, but allows freedom of contract to operate in relation to internal decoration and similar less expensive items. Structural disrepair existing at the outset must be put right.[24] Regard is had to the age, character, and prospective life of the dwelling in fixing the particular standard of repair required,[25] but the onus of proving a breach rests on the tenant.[26]

The structure and exterior includes all drains, gutters, and external pipes, and also included by judicial decision are the internal plasterwork,[27] ceilings,[28] and external doors,[29] as well as the windows, sashes, cords and frames which define the essential appearance, stability and shape of the dwelling.[30] Outside it can include steps leading to the back door,[31] but neither the back-yard[32] nor a rear footpath.[33]

There was formerly a difficulty with blocks of flats. Originally, only the individual flat[34] was treated as part of the structure of the dwelling-house, but an amendment to the legislation has now made clear that the landlord's duties extend to the structure of the entire block and not just to the structure of individual flat units[35]; an individual tenant can only enforce the covenant in relation to defects outside his flat to the extent that his enjoyment of the dwelling-house or of any common parts is affected.

The landlord must maintain *installations*, so as to keep them in repair and proper working order, including all installations in the dwelling-house for the supply of water (such as basins, sinks, and baths),[36] electricity, gas,[37] and sanitation (including toilets).

---

[21] See below pp. 333–334.

[22] *Southwark L.B.C.* v. *Edem* [1999] 07 C.L. 264 C.Ct.; see also *Lambeth L.B.C.* v. *Rogers* [2000] 03 E.G. 127.

[23] Whoever is entitled to the immediate reversion: L.T.A. 1985 s.16.

[24] The covenant is to keep in repair; see below p. ***.

[25] The rule in *Proudfoot* v. *Hart* (1890) 25 Q.B.D. 42 C.A.; see below p. 676.

[26] *Foster* v. *Day* (1968) 208 E.G. 495 C.A.

[27] *Staves* v. *Leeds C.C.* (1990) 23 H.L.R. 107 C.A.

[28] *Hussein* v. *Mehlman* [1992] 2 E.G.L.R. 87, Stephen Sedley Q.C.

[29] *Morris* v. *Liverpool C.C.* [1988] 1 E.G.L.R. 47.

[30] *Irvine* v. *Moran* (1991) 24 H.L.R. 1, 5, Thayne Forbes Q.C.

[31] *Brown* v. *Liverpool Corporation* [1969] 3 All E.R. 1345 C.A.; F.J. Odgers (1976) 92 *L.Q.R.* 327.

[32] *Hopwood* v. *Cannock Chase D.C.* [1975] 1 All E.R. 796 C.A.; *McAuley* v. *Bristol C.C.* [1992] Q.B. 134 C.A.; J.E. Martin [1992] *Conv.* 346; *Irvine* v. *Moran* (1991) 24 H.L.R. 1 (gates, driveway, gardens and garage excluded).

[33] *King* v. *South Northants D.C.* [1992] 1 E.G.L.R. 53 C.A. (obligation implied, but not statutory); J.E. Martin [1982] *Conv.* 346.

[34] *Campden Hill Towers Ltd.* v. *Gardener* [1977] Q.B. 823 C.A. (exterior walls adjoining flat included, but not other walls or roof); *Douglas-Scott* v. *Scorgie* [1984] 1 All E.R. 1086; J.E. Martin [1984] *Conv.* 229 (includes roof in case of top floor flat); *Sheldon* v. *West Bromwich Corporation* (1973) 25 P. & C.R. 360 C.A. (cold water tank).

[35] L.T.A. 1985 s.11(1A), inserted by H.A. 1988 s.16(1)–(4) for leases made on or after January 15th 1989 but excluding those made under an earlier contract; see also *Peters* v. *Prince of Wales Theatre (Birmingham) Ltd.* [1943] K.B. 73 C.A.; see also below Chapter 16.

[36] *Sheldon* v. *West Bromwich Corporation* (1973) 25 P.& C.R. 360 C.A. (cold water tank); *Wycombe H.A.* v. *Barnett* [1982] 2 E.G.L.R. 35 C.A. (not lagging of pipes).

[37] See below p. 252.

Space heaters and water heaters must also be maintained, but other appliances for making use of the services are excluded.[38] Installations must be kept in good working order. This is not the same as a duty to ensure that they are in fact functioning: a radiator which is in excellent working order will be cold if no hot water is supplied to the central heating system.[39] Defects of design and structure are not covered; but toilets that flood the floor whenever they are flushed cannot be said to be in proper working order.[40]

A landlord must *make good* all damage caused during repair work and to effect consequential redecoration.[41]

4. Fire damage

Rebuilding or reinstatement after a fire is excluded from the landlord's statutory responsibilities, but this cannot be shifted to the tenant.[42] Piecemeal repair must be both possible and appropriate.[43] Short-life property is excluded, so landlords are not compelled to carry out very expensive work that would be wasteful and useless.[44] A landlord insures under a short lease because he has most to lose, but usually the tenancy agreement says nothing.[45] A residential tenant holding for a short time should not be required to insure,[46] though there is no statutory rule to prevent this.

5. Exclusion and tenant's responsibilities

These matters are considered below.[47]

B. FITNESS FOR HABITATION

1. Unfitness

A property is fit for human habitation only if it is reasonable for a person to continue to live there. Unfitness could arise from lack of safety, lack of ventilation[48] or the disrepair of a flight of stone access steps,[49] even if a tenant is required to tolerate the occasional intrusion of rats.[50] Properties should be checked against the following statutory checklist of relevant factors[51]:

[38] L.T.A. 1985 s.11(1)(b)–(c); *Hussein* v. *Mehlman* [1992] 2 E.G.L.R. 87 (gas heaters).

[39] *Campden Hill Towers Ltd.* v. *Gardner* [1977] Q.B. 823 C.A.

[40] *Liverpool C.C.* v. *Irwin* [1977] A.C. 239, 257E–F, Lord Wilberforce, 264C–D, Lord Salmon, 269H–270A, Lord Edmund Davies, 270E, Lord Fraser; the C.A. [1976] Q.B. 319 thought these were design faults.

[41] *Bradley* v. *Chorley B.C.* (1985) 17 H.L.R. 305 C.A.; *McGreal* v. *Wake* [1984] 1 E.G.L.R. 42 C.A.; J.E. Martin [1984] *Conv.* 229.

[42] L.T.A. 1985 s.11(4).

[43] *Murray* v. *Birmingham C.C.* [1987] 2 E.G.L.R. 53; *Dame Margaret Hungerford Charity Trustees* v. *Beazeley* [1993] 2 E.G.L.R. 143 C.A. (repair to grade 1 listed building would cost £100,000 against annual income of charity landlord of £2,500); J. Morgan [1994] *Conv.* 145.

[44] *Newham L.B.C.* v. *Patel* (1978) 12 H.L.R. 77 C.A.; *Kenny* v. *Kingston-upon-Thames R.L.B.C.* [1985] 1 E.G.L.R. 26 C.A.

[45] Bright & Gilbert 395–398.

[46] For commercial insurance see pp. 685–690.

[47] See pp. 261–264.

[48] *Hall* v. *Manchester Corporation* (1915) 84 L.J.Ch. 732 H.L.; *Belcher* v. *M'Intosh* (1839) 2 Moo. & R. 186, 174 E.R. 257; *Summers* v. *Salford Corporation* [1943] A.C. 283 H.L.

[49] *McCarrick* v. *Liverpool Corporation* [1947] A.C. 219 H.L.

[50] *Stanton* v. *Southwick* [1920] 2 K.B. 642.

[51] L.T.A. 1985 s.10, adopting the definition in H.A. 1985 s.604(2).

repair; stability; freedom from damp; internal arrangement; natural lighting; ventilation; water supply; drainage and sanitary convenience; facilities for the preparation
and cooking of food and the disposal of waste water.

It should be noted that this list excludes soundproofing, and there is no proposal to
amend it to include this item.[52] Each factor is considered only to the extent that the
defect makes the dwelling unsuitable for reasonable occupation. By these standards 5
per cent of all homes are unfit, but this rises to at least 20 per cent of those in the private
rented sector.[53]

Fitness for habitation is a concept distinct from repair.[54] A property that is out of
repair may or may not be fit for habitation, depending upon how far the defect inter-
feres with safe occupation of the property.[55] Equally a property that is in repair may be
rendered quite unsuitable as a house by matters such as condensation.[56]

2.   Absence of duty to ensure fitness

Although landlords have a duty to repair dwellings let on short residential leases, they
have no further obligation to ensure that the dwelling is fit for habitation. There is no
implied contract, still less any implied condition in a letting of land.[57] This at any rate is
the general rule, though admittedly subject to a number of exceptions that require enu-
meration below. Proposals emanating from the Law Commission to impose a requirement to ensure and maintain fitness are discussed below.[58]

The point has recently been re-emphasised in the House of Lords in *Southwark L.B.C.*
v. *Mills.*[59] The House of Lords decided that a landlord was not liable to provide residential accommodation that was fully soundproofed against the activities of neighbours. As
a headline in the Estates Gazette reported "Sound proofing decision saves councils mil-
lions".[60] The appellants were local authority tenants occupying flats in purpose built
blocks. Due to inadequate soundproofing the appellants could hear all the everyday
activities of the tenants in neighbouring flats, their televisions, their babies crying, their
comings and goings, their quarrels and their lovemaking.[61] The actions against the landlords were intended to require the councils to remedy the position, two based on the
landlord's failure to ensure quiet enjoyment and one[62] framed in nuisance. All failed for
reasons explained elsewhere.[63] In essence all the actions involved the suggestion that
the landlord should be held liable on a warranty that the property is fit to live in.

---

[52] *Southwark L.B.C.* v. *Mills* [1999] 4 All E.R. 449, 453e–f, 461e.
[53] D.O.E. *House Condition Survey* (1993).
[54] P.F. Smith [1998] *Conv.* 189.
[55] *Edwards* v. *Etherington* (1825) Ry. & M. 268, 171 E.R. 1016 (walls unsafe).
[56] *Quick* v. *Taff Ely B.C.* [1986] Q.B. 809, 817F, Dillon L.J., 821H, Lawton L.J.
[57] *Hart* v. *Windsor* (1843) 12 M. & W. 68, 87, 152 E.R. 1114, Parke B; *Edler* v. *Auerbach* [1950] 1 K.B. 359, 374,
Devlin J.
[58] See below pp. 277–278.
[59] [1999] 4 All E.R. 449 H.L.; S. Murdoch [1999] 46 *E.G.* 186; N. Madge [2000] 02 *L.S.G.* 37; D. Rook
[2000] *Conv.* 161.
[60] [1999] 43 *E.G.* 151.
[61] At 452d, Lord Hoffmann.
[62] *Baxter* v. *Camden L.B.C.*, reported with *Mills; Southwark L.B.C.* v. *Camacho* [2000] 06 C.L. 468 C.Ct.
[63] See below pp. 719–721.

Lord Hoffmann refused to recognise such a warranty, relying on earlier authorities,[64] and observing that repair was limited to the restoration of the property to its previous good condition.[65]

3. Inherent defects

Landlord's statutory obligations are limited to repair, that is making good damage caused by the natural effects of time and renewal of subsidiary parts. As Lord Hoffmann said in *Southwark L.B.C. v. Mills*[66]:

> "Keeping in repair means remedying disrepair. The landlord is obliged only to restore the house to its previous good condition. He does not have to make it a better house than it originally was."

So the covenant to repair does not extend to reconstruction of the property nor to remedying inherent defects. Martin B. said in *Carstairs v. Taylor*[67] that

> "One who takes a floor in a house must be held to take the premises as they are, and cannot complain that the house was not constructed differently."

In the absence of statutory intervention the parties are free to let and take a lease of poorly constructed premises and to allocate the cost of putting them in order between themselves as they see fit.[68]

In a commercial context it is the tenant who is generally responsible for all structural work to business premises, so the exclusion of work to remedy inherent defects removes what would otherwise be a very unfair burden on tenants.[69] Dwellings stand on a different footing since it is the landlord who is responsible for the most expensive work to the structure. Exclusion of inherent defects from the concept of a repair here provides an unmerited defence to a landlord, who can refuse to correct defects in the house that he has rented out on the basis that the property is not in disrepair. Our existing law does not require a residential landlord to improve the condition of the property he has rented out even if it is unsuitable as a home, a defective conceptual framework that condemns many tenants to accept inadequate conditions. Thus in *Quick v. Taff Ely B.C.*[70] houses were uninhabitable[71] as a result of design defects that led to excessive condensation. Alleviation would have required the replacement of the metal windows (an improvement) since the existing windows and lintels were sound. A thing is not in disrepair simply because it provides unsatisfactory living conditions and so the council were not liable to repair these defects. Another tenant failed in *McDougall v. Easington D.C.*[72] because the work needed to rectify an inherent design defect, and so prevent water

---

[64] *Hart v. Windsor* (1843) 12 M. & W. 68, 87, 152 E.R. 1114, Parke B.; *Edler v. Auerbach* [1950] 1 K.B. 359, 374, Devlin J.

[65] At 453a.

[66] [1999] 4 All E.R. 449, 453a.

[67] (1871) L.R. 6 Exch. 217, 222; *Kiddle v. City Business Properties Ltd.* [1942] 1 K.B. 269, 274–275, Lord Goddard C.J.

[68] [1999] 4 All E.R. 449, 461j–462a, Lord Millett.

[69] See below pp. 679–680.

[70] [1986] Q.B. 809 C.A.; *Palmer v. Sandwell M.B.C.* [1987] 2 E.G.L.R. 79 C.A.

[71] At 323H, Dillon L.J.

[72] (1989) 58 P. & C.R. 201 C.A.; P.F. Smith [1990] *Conv.* 335.

penetration, involved such major work—replacement of the front and rear elevations, a new roof and new windows—that it exceeded a mere repair.

However, some element of repair may be included in the work necessary to cure a disrepair.[73] *Elmcroft Developments Ltd.* v. *Tankersley-Sawyer*[74] involved a defective damp course in a Victorian mansion block which consisted of a layer of slates below ground level, it being uncertain whether the defects arose from poor design, construction faults or poor workmanship. Curing the resultant rising damp was held to fall within the landlord's repairing covenant.[75] Similarly in *Stent* v. *Monmouth D.C.*[76] the council was required to stop water running in under the front door of a house, a problem caused by the absence of a sill to stop rain seeping in. Since the original door had rotted and had to be repaired, work to fit special aluminium, self-sealing, doors was a repair. Here it was cheaper to do the job properly. Very extensive work would not count as a repair.

The principles just discussed put at risk the whole scheme of protective legislation in sections 11 to 17 of the Landlord and Tenant Act 1985: although a landlord cannot impose liability for remedial work to structural defects or reconstruction after fire on a residential tenant, the Act does not legislate against covenants to reconstruct or to remedy defects in construction! Tenants can certainly overcome this problem, if they are aware of it, by contractual negotiation, and a clause imposing liability may be held to be an unfair term. Some public sector secure tenancy agreements provide for the property to be kept in good condition, a term which implies more than repair; it focuses on the end result of producing a dwelling suitable to live in rather than on the process by which the dwelling has become unfit for occupation. In one such case a tenant secured a remedy for the fact that his house was streaming with condensation even though no structural damage had been caused.[77] Another partial solution is to negotiate a term suspending rent if the property becomes unusable,[78] or to allow termination in these circumstances. However free market negotiation is rare in the private rented sector and it must be concluded that the present law is inadequate. Tenants are not interested in why their home is uninhabitable, they simply want it made habitable.

4. Obsolete statutory liability to ensure fitness

Early housing legislation remedied the defective common law by imposing a statutory obligation on the landlord of a dwelling to ensure that it was, and remained, fit for habitation.[79] A tenancy of a house[80] was subject to obligations to ensure that it was fit for human habitation at the time of the grant and that any defect of which notice had been

---

[73] Commercial cases are discussed below at p. 678.

[74] [1984] 1 E.G.L.R. 47, 48G, Ackner L.J., approving *Ravenseft.*

[75] On d.p.c.s contrast *Pembery* v. *Lamdin* [1940] 2 All E.R. 434; and *Sotheby* v. *Grundy* [1947] 2 All E.R. 761; also *Wainwright* v. *Leeds C.C.* [1984] 1 E.G.L.R. 67 C.A. *Eyre* v. *McCracken* (2000) 8OP & C.R. 220 C.A.

[76] [1987] 1 E.G.L.R. 59 C.A.; H.W. Wilkinson (1988) 138 *N.L.J.* 161, 186.

[77] *Welsh* v. *Greenwich L.B.C.* [2000] 27 L.S.G. 40 C.A.

[78] *Smedley* v. *Chumley & Hawke Ltd.* (1982) 44 P.& C.R. 50.

[79] L.T.A. 1985 s.10 (the standard is not same as under H.A. 1985 s.604 as amended by L.G.H.A. 1989 sch.9 para.83). Housing of the Working Classes Act 1885 s.12; Housing Act 1957 s.6; W.A. West (1962) 26 *Conv. (N.S.)* 132.

[80] L.T.A. 1985 s.10(6); *Dunster* v. *Hollis* [1918] 2 K.B. 795 (not a common flight of stairs).

given[81] should be remedied for the future. Since this was an implied condition the tenant had a right to repudiate the lease for breach of this term, a remedy additional to the right to sue for damages.[82] Inherent defects had to be remedied, for example a design defect leading to condensation so severe that the dwelling became unfit to live in.[83] Soundproofing was not required.[84] The duty was limited to cases where the home was capable of being rendered fit at reasonable expense,[85] and otherwise it was necessary to approach the local authority to ask for the issue of a repairs notice.[86] Leases for a term exceeding three years were excluded if the basis was that the tenant should put the property into a reasonable condition.[87]

The last paragraph is written in the past tense because, unfortunately, the statutory provision has been allowed to become a dead letter. Today[88] the rent limit for any contract of letting dated after mid 1957 remains at £80 *a year* or less in Inner London and £52 elsewhere[89]—limits that are iniquitous enough even before one adds that these figures are gross figures with no deduction allowed where rates or council tax are included in the rent.[90] In *Southwark L.B.C.* v. *Mills*[91] Lord Hoffmann traced this provision back to its legislative origin in 1885, and noted that the financial limits had been increased until 1957, when inflation-based increases had ceased, leaving very few lettings in London to which it could apply. Had the legislation kept pace with inflation in rentals, inherent defects in dwellings would never have become a serious problem.[92] Lord Hoffmann agreed with earlier observations in the Court of Appeal[93] to the effect that this was a matter for Parliament and that judicial creativity should not tread where Parliament had refused to walk. Reform is under consideration.[94]

5. No liability for unfitness of unfurnished property

In *Cavalier* v. *Pope*[95] the House of Lords held that the landlord of an unfurnished house owed no duty to maintain it, precluding any tort action based on unfitness for habitation. For example, in *McNerny* v. *Lambeth L.B.C.*,[96] condensation in a 1940s council block gave rise to no action, since the property was not in disrepair. This rule, based on

[81] See below pp. 252–254.

[82] *Walker* v. *Hobbs & Co.* (1889) 23 Q.B.D. 458.

[83] *Quick* v. *Taff Ely B.C.* [1986] Q.B. 809 C.A.; *Stent* v. *Monmouth B.C.* [1987] 1 E.G.L.R. 59 C.A.; J.E. Martin [1988] *Conv.* 138.

[84] *Southwark L.B.C.* v. *Mills* [1999] 4 All E.R. 449, 453, Lord Hoffmann.

[85] *Buswell* v. *Goodwin* [1971] 1 W.L.R. 92, 96H–97B, Widgery L.J. (closing order); D. Morgan (1979) 43 *Conv.* (N.S.) 414.

[86] *Hillbank Properties Ltd.* v. *Hackney L.B.C.* [1978] Q.B. 998 C.A.

[87] L.T.A. 1985 s.10(5); E.O. Walford (1944) 8 *Conv.* (N.S.) 219 (long building leases are included!).

[88] L.T.A. 1985 ss.8, 9 (agricultural licences).

[89] s.8(4). The figures were doubled at that time.

[90] *Jones* v. *Nelson* [1938] 2 All E.R. 171; *Rousou* v. *Photi* [1940] 2 K.B. 379 C.A.

[91] [1999] 4 All E.R. 449, 453b–g, also 461e, Lord Millett.

[92] *Quick* v. *Taff Ely B.C.* [1986] Q.B. 809, 821D, Lawton L.J.

[93] *McNerny* v. *Lambeth L.B.C.* (1988) 21 H.L.R. 188, 194, Dillon L.J., 195–196, Taylor L.J.

[94] See below pp. 277–278.

[95] [1906] A.C. 428 H.L.; *Robbins* v. *Jones* (1863) 15 C.B.N.S. 221, 143 E.R. 768 (person killed falling down grate in street); *Bartram* v. *Aldous* (1886) 2 T.L.R. 237; *Lane* v. *Cox* [1897] 1 Q.B. 415 C.A.

[96] (1988) 21 H.L.R. 188 C.A.; P.F. Smith [1989] *Conv.* 216; N. Nichol [1998] *J.H.L.* 103.

the old law of misrepresentation,[97] has been left looking like an isolated and unjust outpost by advances in contract law. The Court of Appeal is free to narrow the principle, for example to exclude its application to licences,[98] but May L.J. declined in *Boldack* v. *East Lindesy D.C.*[99] to take the "flamboyant" step of reversing the rule, a task which the courts must now leave to Parliament.[100] The landlord's duty in tort is restricted by the scope of the contractual[101] and statutory repairing duties, and beyond that there is no obligation to make a dwelling habitable.[102] Liability to pay rent continues for an unfit house.[103] The house must be taken as it stands.[104]

A builder who grants a long lease may be liable to the tenant for defects in construction,[105] but a builder employed by the landlord is not liable to the tenant.[106] Building regulations impose administrative controls over the standards of new buildings.[107]

6. Furnished property

Property let *furnished* is subject to an implied condition that it is reasonably fit for habitation.[108] A woman who took a furnished house for the season in Brighton only to find it infested with bugs was entitled to repudiate the lease, and quit without notice.[109] A landlord must disclose if a previous occupant suffered an infectious disease,[110] though there is curiously no converse duty on the tenant to tell his landlord that he has been ill.[111] It is possible that this is a condition in the strict sense that operates only at the outset to allow repudiation of the tenancy,[112] but it is better to treat it as a continuing duty given that defects in the accommodation have been allowed as a defence to a rent action.[113]

---

[97] *Keates* v. *Cadogan* (1851) 10 C.B. 591, 138 E.R. 234.

[98] *Greene* v. *Chelsea B.C.* [1954] 2 Q.B. 127, 138, Denning L.J.

[99] (1999) 31 H.L.R. 41, 49, May L.J.

[100] *McNerny* v. *Lambeth L.B.C.* (1988) 21 H.L.R. 188, 193, Dillon L.J.

[101] *De Lassalle* v. *Guildford* [1901] 2 K.B. 215 C.A.

[102] *Hart* v. *Windsor* (1844) 12 M. & W. 68, 152 E.R. 1114; *Bartram* v. *Aldous* (1886) 2 T.L.R. 237; *Arden* v. *Pullen* (1842) 10 M. & W. 321, 152 E.R. 492.

[103] *Bunn* v. *Harrison* (1886) 3 T.L.R. 146 C.A.

[104] *Chappell* v. *Gregory* (1863) 34 Beav. 250, 55 E.R. 631.

[105] *Rimmer* v. *Webster* [1902] 2 Ch. 163; *Perry* v. *Sharon Development Co. Ltd.* [1937] 4 All E.R. 390 C.A.; *Targett* v. *Torfaen B.C.* [1992] 1 E.G.L.R. 275 C.A.

[106] *Strathford East Kilbride Ltd.* v. *Film Design Ltd.* [1997] Times December 1st (Scottish law follows English).

[107] *Southwark L.B.C.* v. *Mills* [1999] 4 All E.R. 449, 453j–454d, Lord Hoffmann, 461b, Lord Millett.

[108] *Sutton* v. *Temple* (1843) 12 M. & W. 52, 152 E.R. 1108; *Chester* v. *Powell* (1885) 52 L.T. 722 C.A. (partly furnished).

[109] *Smith* v. *Marrable* (1843) 11 M. & W. 5, 152 E.R. 693; *Wilson* v. *Finch-Hatton* (1877) 2 Ex.D. 336 (deposit of "filth and foecal substance" in drains). *Collins* v. *Barrow* (1831) 1 M. & Rob. 112, 174 E.R. 38; *Hart* v. *Windsor* (1844) 12 M. & W. 68, 152 E.R. 1114.

[110] *Collins* v. *Hopkins* [1923] 2 K.B. 617 (tuberculosis), distinguishing *Sarson* v. *Roberts* [1895] 2 Q.B. 395 C.A.

[111] *Humphreys* v. *Miller* [1917] 2 K.B. 122 C.A.

[112] *Sarson* v. *Roberts* [1895] 2 Q.B. 395 C.A.

[113] *Campbell* v. *Wenlock* (1866) 4 F & F. 716, 176 E.R. 760; *Harrison* v. *Malet* (1886) 3 T.L.R. 58; *Edwards* v. *Etherington* (1825) Ry. & M. 268, 171 E.R. 1016; *Salisbury* v. *Marshal* (1829) 4 Car. & P. 65, 172 E.R. 609.

C. FURNISHINGS AND APPLIANCES

Statutory regulations require regular checks of the safety of gas appliances.[114] There have been a number of prosecutions for manslaughter for failure to ensure that gas installations were safe.[115]

Another important duty is imposed on landlords by the Furniture & Furnishing (Fire)(Safety)(Amendment) Regulations 1993,[116] which require that all furniture and furnishings should meet fire retardant standards. The regulations came into force for new lettings from March 1993 and were extended to pre-existing lettings at the beginning of 1997. Items manufactured before 1950 are allowed, and there are a number of other exemptions, including temporary lettings of the landlord's own home. Letting agents are safe from prosecution unless they themselves are suppliers.[117] Many landlords exploit loopholes, for example by selling infringing items to the tenant for a nominal sum, and there is nothing to stop the landlord from storing unsafe furniture in a locked room even though the fire hazard is just as great. Statutory rules govern fire precautions.[118]

There are new rules in relation to disabled access.[119]

D. NOTICE AND ACCESS TO REPAIR

1. Notice to repair

A landlord's duty to repair arises only when the tenant has given notice of the need for repair and the landlord has been allowed access to carry out the work. This is so whether the repairing duty arises under an express covenant,[120] under the statutory duty to make a house fit for habitation,[121] or under the modern statutory obligation to maintain the structure and installations in a dwelling.[122]

There is no particular form for a notice, and so it is often a problem to know whether notice has been given. A letter promising further details may not be a notice,[123] but a letter sent in relation to another matter may act as a complaint about the disrepair.[124]

In one sense the notice rule is logical since the tenant has exclusive possession and thus the right to exclude the landlord, and even if the tenancy agreement gives the landlord the right of access to inspect the state of repair, one cannot expect landlords to

---

[114] S.Is. 1994/1886, 1996/254, 1996/2541; R. Critchley & S. Greenan [1997] 01 *Legal Action* 15; imprisonment is a possible penalty.

[115] *R. v. D.P.P. ex parte Jones* [1996] Independent June 12th. Div.Ct.; *R. v. Singh* [1999] Times April 17th C.A.

[116] S.I. 1993/207; N. Wheeler & S. Lawrie [1995] 33 *E.G.* 78; T. Corbitt (2000) 164 *J.P.* 719.

[117] As defined by Consumer Protection Act 1987 s.46.

[118] R.A. 1977 s.140, sch.20; H.A. 1980 ss.81–82 replacing L.T.A. 1927 s.19(2).

[119] See below p. 619.

[120] *Makin v. Watkinson* (1870) L.R. 6 Ex. 25; *Torrens v. Walker* [1906] 2 Ch. 166, Warrington J.; *Hugall v. M'Lean* (1885) 53 L.T. 94 C.A.

[121] *Hall v. Manchester Corporation* (1915) 84 L.J.Ch. 732 H.L.; *Summers v. Salford Corporation* [1943] A.C. 283 H.L.; *McCarrick v. Liverpool Corporation* [1947] A.C. 219 H.L.

[122] *O'Brien v. Robinson* [1973] A.C. 912 H.L.

[123] *Al Hassani v. Merrigan* [1988] 1 E.G.L.R. 93 C.A.

[124] *Dinefwr B.C. v. Jones* [1987] 2 E.G.L.R. 58 C.A.; J.E. Martin [1988] *Conv.* 138 (officer of local authority acting in another capacity); *Hall v. Howard* [1988] 2 E.G.L.R. 75 C.A. (survey for proposed sale).

patrol their estates all day.[125] In another sense, however, it can work very unfairly in allowing the landlord to escape contractual liability for injuries caused to a tenant because of the failure to give notice. Absurdity is reached when the defect requiring repair was unknown to the tenant, and possibly undiscoverable, so that he was unable to give notice. In the leading case, *O'Brien* v. *Robinson,*[126] the bedroom ceiling collapsed on tenants while they were in bed, due to an inherent defect that was not apparent from inspection. For the future, the tenants were able to ensure that the ceiling was put right, but they were not able to recover for their injuries, since they had failed to give the landlord prior notice of the need for repair. A tenant who decides to embark on a rent strike must first give notice of the defective state of his home, since until he does so there is no potential liability for disrepair to set off against the rent. [127]

Landlords are not in breach until a reasonable time has elapsed after notice,[128] so that the landlord may not be liable for an injury that occurs before or shortly after notice is given.[129] If the case does not require notice, the landlord's duty arises immediately.[130] If the defect lay wholly outside the control of the landlord, then, perhaps, a reasonable time must be allowed.

2. Property under the control of the landlord

No notice is required where the property is under the control of the landlord,[131] including defects in a common part or in a part let to another tenant. *British Telecommunications plc.* v. *Sun Life Assurance Society plc.*[132] concerned a bulge in the external cladding of an office block in Croydon that appeared at 5th floor level, one floor below the tenant company's office suite. Notice was not required from the tenant, since the defect was in a part of the building under the landlord's control. Another illustration is *Passley* v. *Wandsworth L.B.C.*[133] in which pipes burst in a part of a block under the local authority's control, the resulting flood causing damage to the plaintiff's top floor flat. The principle exempting the tenant from giving notice is the same where vandals cause damage to a sewage stack.[134] However, notice is required where a defect is in a part of a

---

[125] *Summers* v. *Salford Corporation* [1943] A.C. 283 H.L. Its importance was stressed by Lord Woolf's report on *Access to Justice* (H.M.S.O., July 1996) ch.16 para.58.

[126] [1973] A.C. 912 H.L.; *Hussein* v. *Mehlman* [1992] 2 E.G.L.R. 87, 91L–M, Stephen Sedley Q.C. On earlier legislation see: *Morgan* v. *Liverpool Corporation* [1927] 2 K.B. 131 C.A.; *McCarrick* v. *Liverpool Corporation* [1947] A.C. 219 H.L.

[127] *Andrews* v. *Brewer* (1998) 30 H.L.R. 203 C.A.

[128] *Morris* v. *Liverpool C.C.* [1988] 1 E.G.L.R. 47; *Calabar Properties Ltd.* v. *Stitcher* [1984] 1 W.L.R. 287, 298, Griffiths L.J.

[129] *Griffin* v. *Pillet* [1926] 1 K.B. 17.

[130] *British Telecommunications plc.* v. *Sun Life Assurance Society plc.* [1995] 4 All E.R. 44 C.A.; J. Morgan [1995] *J.B.L.* 264; H.W. Wilkinson [1995] *N.L.J.* 1793; J.E. Adams [1996] *Conv.* 408; P.F. Smith [1997] *Conv.* 59.

[131] *Murphy* v. *Hurly* [1922] 1 A.C. 369, 389 (sea wall on neighbouring property); *Bishop* v. *Consolidated London Properties Ltd.* (1933) 102 L.J. K.B. 257 (roof under landlord's control); *Melles & Co.* v. *Holme* [1918] 2 K.B. 100 Div.Ct.; *Ladsky* v. *T.S.B. Bank plc.* (1997) 74 P. & C.R. 372 C.A. (simple disrepair was breach of mortgage).

[132] [1995] 4 All E.R. 44 C.A.; P.F. Smith [1997] *Conv.* 59 (query whether notice is required where the covenant is "to repair" as opposed to "to keep in repair").

[133] (1998) 30 H.L.R. 165 C.A.

[134] *Bavage* v. *Southwark L.B.C.* [1998] 2 C.L.Y. 3623.

block within the exclusive control of the tenant, even if it existed at the time that the lease was granted so that the landlord had power to discover it at that time.[135]

3. Damages for occupiers other than the tenant

If the tenant has not given notice of the need for repair, he will nevertheless usually be able to take action in tort under section 4 of the Defective Premises Act 1972[136] where premises are let under a tenancy[137] on the terms that the landlord is under an obligation to maintain or repair the property. Usually the tenant is required to have notified the landlord of the defect, but the position of the tenant is greatly assisted by the provision[138] that the landlord is also caught if he knows of the defect, if he ought to have known, or if he has a right to enter to inspect the state of repair and such inspection would have revealed the defect.[139] A duty is imposed to take such care as is reasonable in all the circumstances to see that occupiers are reasonably safe from personal injury or damage to their property caused by a relevant defect, meaning any defect existing as a result of an act or omission that constitutes a failure to carry out material obligation of the tenancy.[140] Unfortunately the liability is restricted to disrepair, and damages must be reduced to exclude liability for defects such as mould and condensation that are attributable to inherent defects in the construction of the property.[141] The landlord also escapes for matters that are not aspects of repair, such as the requirement to remove a paving slab after work done by a previous tenant.[142]

4. Negligence liability after notice

Even if a landlord is not under a duty to repair, some obligations may arise in negligence once notice of a defect is given. Thus if a council landlord is warned that pipes are frozen, there is a duty on the council to do all that is reasonable in the circumstances: not perhaps to turn the water off, but at least to tell the tenant the location of the stop cock.[143]

5. Access to repair

Repairing covenants that impose duties on the landlord usually include an express right to enter to carry out the work[144] and if this is omitted—perhaps for example in a weekly tenancy—such a right may be implied.[145] Where structural work is required under the statutory repairing covenant, the tenant must allow the landlord access to view the state of property and to carry out works,[146] and it is a defence to show that

---

[135] *Uniproducts (Manchester) Ltd.* v. *Rose Furnishers Ltd.* [1956] 1 W.L.R. 45.

[136] Law Com. No. 40 (1970).

[137] This includes any tenancy or sub-tenancy, a tenancy at will or sufferance, and a statutory tenancy: s.6.

[138] s.4(2).

[139] s.4(4); *Mint* v. *Good* [1951] 1 K.B. 517 C.A..

[140] s.4(3).

[141] *Alinus* v. *Tower Hamlets L.B.C.* [1998] 2 C.L.Y. 2987

[142] *Boldack* v. *East Lindsey D.C.* (1999) 31 H.L.R. 41 C.A.

[143] *Stockley* v. *Knowsley M.B.C.* [1986] 2 E.G.L.R. 141. Contrast *Deadman* v. *Southwark L.B.C.* [1999] 1 C.L. 281 (no duty to board up premises to protect tenant's belongings).

[144] *Saner* v. *Bilton* (1878) 7 Ch.D. 815, Fry J.

[145] *Mint* v. *Good* [1951] 1 K.B. 517 C.A.; *McAuley* v. *Bristol C.C.* [1992] Q.B. 134 C.A.; also under R.A. 1977 s.148; Social Tenant's Charter (Housing Corporation, 1998) Section 5.

[146] L.T.A. 1985 s.11(6).

the landlord does not have the right to carry out the work and is unable after reasonable endeavours to secure the right.[147] In *McAuley* v. *Bristol C.C.*[148] the Court of Appeal implied a right to enter in order to remedy defects that might render the landlord liable to an outsider in tort. Refusal to allow work may expose the tenant to loss of his security of tenure, since this is a breach of covenant and hence a ground for possession, and in these circumstances it then becomes reasonable to order possession.[149] The leading modern case, *Jervis* v. *Harris*,[150] concerns the application of section 1 of the Leasehold Property Repairs Act 1938 to a commercial lease and is considered in that context.

E. NON-FINANCIAL REMEDIES FOR DISREPAIR

Negotiations for a pre-action protocol in housing cases are currently stalled,[151] so tenants have to have resort to legal remedies if unaided negotiations founder.

1. Specific performance

This is the most efficacious remedy since it compels a landlord to carry out the works of repair, avoiding the need for tenants to have to cope with the cost and organisational problems involved in major work.[152] Historically Lord Eldon's speech in *Hill* v. *Barclay* (1810)[153] appeared to impose a bar on the issue of orders to carry out repairs, the reason being that a court should not make an order requiring constant supervision. It has taken a long time to overcome this unfortunate decision.

Residential tenants have most need for specific performance, and it is no surprise to find a statutory jurisdiction in relation to *dwellings*. Since 1974[154] the court has had power to order specific performance of landlord's repairing obligations[155] in favour of a tenant or statutory tenant[156] of a dwelling. Lack of mutuality and similar equitable bars are no longer any impediment. The jurisdiction is much used, for example in county court trials[157] and also where a district judge sits as a small claims arbitrator.[158] There seems to be no reason to use it with caution or as a last resort,[159] and certainly lack of funds is no defence.[160] An even wider discretion is proposed.[161]

---

[147] s.11(3A) inserted by H.A. 1988 s.116; *McDougall* v. *Easington D.C.* (1989) 58 P. & C.R. 201, 205, Mustill L.J.
[148] [1992] Q.B. 134 C.A.
[149] *Campell* v. *Daramola* [1975] 2 E.G.L.R. 65 C.A.
[150] [1996] Ch. 195 C.A.
[151] Woolf, *Access to Justice* (H.M.S.O., July 1996) ch.16 paras.53–72; [1999] 21 L.S.G. 4.
[152] Woodfall 13.099–13.100.
[153] (1810) 16 Ves. 402, 33 E.R. 1037, Lord Eldon L.C.
[154] L.T.A. 1985 s.17, re-enacting H.A. 1974 s.125.
[155] Including any successor who is bound by the covenant: s.17(2).
[156] s.17(2).
[157] *Quick* v. *Taff Ely B.C.* [1986] Q.B. 809 C.A.
[158] *Joyce* v. *Liverpool C.C.* [1996] Q.B. 252 C.A.
[159] Despite *Rainbow Estates Ltd.* v. *Tokenhold* [1998] 2 E.G.L.R. 34, 37G, Lawrence Collins Q.C.
[160] *Francis* v. *Cowlcliff Ltd.* [1976] 2 E.G.L.R. 54 Ch.D.; *Alexander* v. *Lambeth L.B.C.* [2000] 02 C.L. 386.
[161] See below p. 278.

Common parts of a dwelling[162] fall within the decision in *Jeune* v. *Queen's Cross Properties Ltd.*[163] where Pennycuick V.C.[164] allowed specific performance of a covenant to repair if the case fell within three requirements stated by *Snell*.[165] First, there must be a sufficient definition of the work, in order to overcome the difficulty of supervision of unspecified work. Second, the tenant must show a substantial interest in the performance of the covenant, for example because the value of the tenant's flat depends upon proper repair of the common parts. Third, the landlord must be in possession of the land affected, a rule that precludes specific performance in relation to the land let to the tenant, but which permits a decree in relation to common parts retained by the landlord. An alternative remedy is to seek a mandatory injunction requiring the landlord to carry out work within his repairing obligation, one advantage being the possibility of adding a penal notice making it a contempt of court to fail to carry out the work.[166]

Claims should usually be started in the county court[167] and allocated to the small claims track—this is appropriate for any claim by a tenant of residential premises for repairs estimated to cost not more than £1,000, provided that any associated claim for damages does not exceed £1,000.[168] There is considerable scope for the development of the existing methods of Alternative Dispute Resolution.

2. Rent strikes

Is a tenant entitled to go on *"rent-strike"* until the property is put into repair? In general, no.[169] Covenants are absolute, so that the obligation on the tenant to pay rent is not related to the performance by the landlord of his side of the bargain. Use of self-help is strictly controlled, for otherwise rent collection would become a nightmare. Stopping rent is only legitimate if there is a right to recoupment at common law or to a set off in equity.

A tenant may carry out necessary repairs and deduct the cost from the rent. It is essential that the repairs in question fall within the landlord's obligation, and this means that if the work relates to the property under the exclusive control of the tenant he must have given notice to the landlord of the need for repair and given an opportunity for the repairs to be completed.[170] Estimates on the cost of the work to be undertaken should be given to the landlord so that he has an opportunity to challenge the cost of what is proposed. *Common law recoupment* is subject to stringent restrictions: the tenant must have carried out repairs for which the landlord is liable[171] so that the tenant is recovering by stopping from the rent an amount which he has already paid out. Although

---

[162] L.T.A. 1985 s.17(1).

[163] [1974] Ch. 97 Ch.D., applied in *Francis* v. *Cowlcliff* as above.

[164] At 99–100.

[165] Snell's *Equity* (Sweet & Maxwell, 30th ed. by J. McGhee, 2000) 658–659.

[166] *R.* v. *Wandsworth C.Ct. ex parte Munn* (1994) 26 H.L.R. 697, Sedley J.; *Hackney L.B.C.* v. *Mullen* (1997) 29 H.L.R. 592 C.A.

[167] H.C.C.J.O. 1991 arts.4–5; C.P.R. 16.3(6).

[168] C.P.R. 27.1(2); see above Chapter 8.

[169] *Camden Nominees* v. *Forcey* [1940] Ch. 352; *R.* v. *Parnell* (1831) 14 Cox. C.C. 508.

[170] *Andrews* v. *Brewer* (1998) 30 H.L.R. 203 C.A.; A.J. Waite [1981] *Conv.* 199, 203–205; he postulates emergencies and disappeared landlords as exceptions.

[171] This can be used to accumulate a sum to use to pay arrears: *Asco Developments Ltd.* v. *Lowes Lewis & Gordon* [1978] 2 E.G.L.R. 41, Megarry V.C.

ancient in origin,[172] the right was lost sight of until Goff J.'s decision in *Lee-Parker* v. *Izzet*[173] re-established the possibility of recoupment. The common law right is restricted to cases where there was an ascertained liability, that is that the repair work had been carried out and a fixed sum was being deducted from the rent,[174] though it is clear that no distinction is to be drawn between future rent as it accrues and existing arrears.[175] It may[176] also be a requirement that the sum should be indisputable. In *British Anzani (Felixstowe) Ltd.* v. *International Marine Management (U.K.) Ltd.*[177] claims to a common law deduction failed because the sums were uncertain. No matter, since equity allows a set off in wider circumstances.

Equitable set-off is permitted to any defendant who faces a claim by action or distress,[178] so that the claim he faces is reduced by the amount of the counterclaim, leaving only the net balance owing.[179] If the tenant's claims for damages for disrepair exceed the landlord's claim for rent, the set-off is a complete defence to the rent action. An example of a successful defence was the *British Anzani* case[180] in which the claim was for arrears of rent owing on two warehouses built on land reclaimed from the sea, the freeholder being Trinity College Cambridge, but involving an attempt by their tenant, acting as sub-landlord, to forfeit sub-leases of the two warehouses. The sub-tenants withheld rent because serious defects existed in the floors which fell within the repairing responsibilities of the sub-landlord, and which gave rise to claims for damages amounting to £1 million. These claims were unquantified since the court had not yet made an award that assessed the monetary worth of the claims, but a set-off is allowed in these circumstances,[181] and on the particular facts it was clear that the damages would be more than double the unpaid rent. Forbes J. held the set-off to be a complete defence.[182]

A counterclaim can only be considered if it is so intimately connected as to go to the foundation of the plaintiff's claim. Clearly this condition will be satisfied by a claim to rent and a counterclaim to enforce a repairing covenant in the same lease. *British Anzani* took this a step further because there the claim to damages arose from a free-standing covenant to remedy the defective floors, and although this covenant was made by a collateral deed outside the lease these two claims were sufficiently integrated to give rise to a set-off. All that is required is a common subject matter.[183]

---

[172] *Taylor* v. *Beal* (1591) Cro.Eliz. 222, 78 E.R. 478; *Waters* v. *Weighall* (1591) 2 Anst. 575, 145 E.R. 971; A.E. Hughes (1901) 17 *L.Q.R.* 26.

[173] [1971] 1 W.L.R. 1688, Goff J.; P.M. Rank (1976) 40 *Conv. (N.S.)* 196; A.J. Waite [1981] *Conv.* 199; *Hanak* v. *Green* [1958] 2 Q.B. 9 C.A.; *Melville* v. *Grapelodge Developments Ltd.* (1979) 39 P. & C.R. 179, Neill J.

[174] At 1693; *Asco* as above (properly explained as a set-off).

[175] *Asco* as above; A.J. Waite at 205.

[176] But see A.J. Waite at 205–207.

[177] [1980] Q.B. 137, Forbes J.

[178] *Lee-Parker* v. *Izzet* (1971) 1 W.L.R. 1688, 1692–1693, Goff J.

[179] Supreme Court Act 1981 s.49(2).

[180] [1980] Q.B. 137, Forbes J.; A.J. Waite [1983] *Conv.* 373.

[181] *Gilbert Ash (Northern) Ltd.* v. *Modern Engineering (Bristol) Ltd.* [1974] A.C. 689 H.L.; I.N. Duncan Wallace (1974) 90 *L.Q.R.* 21.

[182] *Bankes* v. *Jarvis* [1903] 1 K.B. 549 applied; *Televantos* v. *McCulloch* [1991] 1 E.G.L.R. 123 C.A.

[183] *British Anzani* [1980] Q.B. 137, 154H, Forbes J.; *Courage Ltd.* v. *Crehan* [1999] 2 E.G.L.R. 145 C.A. (refusal of commercial set off).

A clause that rent is to be paid *without deduction* does not affect a recoupment[184] since the money spent on repairs is indeed a rent payment. However it might prevent a set-off and a better-drafted clause might be effective in a commercial lease to prevent even a common law deduction. That said, in a domestic lease such a clause is vulnerable to attack as an unfair term under European inspired regulations,[185] even if such an attack has failed in relation to commercial leases.[186]

3. Termination and repudiation

Residential tenants with short-term tenancies can simply terminate the tenancy by notice to quit and walk away.

If the contractual tie is longer it is also possible to terminate the lease and so end the liability to rent if the condition of the property is unacceptably poor by a form of contractual repudiation.[187] The matter has to be very serious to justify such a step, repudiation, amounting to a breach by the landlord of a fundamental term of the lease.[188] In *Hussein* v. *Mehlman*[189] a tenant held a shorthold for a three-year term, but returned the keys with 18 months remaining when it became apparent that the landlord would not maintain the property. A serious breach of covenant by the landlord led to the collapse of the ceiling, which was itself sufficient to vitiate the tenancy agreement. Stephen Sedley Q.C. relied on nineteenth century authorities[190] and treated an adverse Court of Appeal decision[191] as impliedly overruled by recent developments in frustration law. The brilliant reasoning of this judgment represents a further step towards recognition of a contractual basis to leasehold law and is now fully accepted.[192] The claim is even more likely in relation to commercial lettings and there are already signs that the landlord's right to forfeit for a breach by a tenant is now matched by an equally powerful remedy of termination by the tenant for the landlord's breach.[193] Cases have been successful[194] and unsuccessful.[195]

---

[184] A.J. Waite [1981] *Conv.* 199, 210–211.

[185] Unfair Terms in Consumer Contracts Regs. 1999, S.I. 1999/2083; see above p. 199.

[186] See below p. 638.

[187] Evans & Smith (5th) 229–231; P.F. Smith, "Termination of Tenancies by Tenants: A Just Cause" in *The Reform of Property Law*, eds. P. Jackson & D.C. Wilde (Ashgate Dartmouth, 1997) ch.6.

[188] *Nynehead*, discussed in detail below.

[189] [1992] 2 E.G.L.R. 87, Stephen Sedley Q.C.; C. Harpum [1993] *C.L.J.* 212; S. Bright [1992] *Conv.* 71; M. Pawlowski [1985] *Conv.* 374; J.W. Carter [1985] *Conv.* 289; J.W. Carter & J. Hill [1986] *Conv.* 262.

[190] *Edwards* v. *Etherington* (1825) Ry. & M. 268, 171 E.R. 1016; *Collins* v. *Barrow* (1831) 1 M. & Rob. 112, 174 E.R. 38; *Izon* v. *Gorton* (1839) 5 Bing. (N.C.) 501, 132 E.R. 1193; *Arden* v. *Pullen* (1842) 10 M. & W. 321, 152 E.R. 92; *Smith* v. *Marrable* (1843) 11 M. & W. 5, 152 E.R. 693; *Wilson* v. *Finch-Hatton* (1877) 2 Ex.D. 336.

[191] *Total Oil Great Britain Ltd.* v. *Thompson Garages (Biggin Hill) Ltd.* [1972] 1 Q.B. 318 C.A.

[192] *Re Olympia & York Canary Wharf Ltd. (No.2)* [1993] B.C.C. 159, 166; *Kingston on Thames R.L.B.C.* v. *Marlow* [1996] 1 E.G.L.R. 101, 102K–L.

[193] S. Murdoch [1999] 09 *E.G.* 174.

[194] *Chartered Trust plc.* v. *Davies* [1997] 2 E.G.L.R. 83 C.A.

[195] *Nynehead Developments Ltd.* v. *R.H. Fibreboard Containers Ltd.* [1999] 1 E.G.L.R. 7; M. Pawlowski & J. Brown [1999] *Conv.* 150; S. Murdoch [1999] 09 *E.G.* 174.

F.   DAMAGES FOR DISREPAIR

1.   Procedure

Claims to damages will commonly fall under the small claims limit—that is, the case will be allocated to the fast track—thus removing entitlement to legal aid.[196]

2.   Measure of damages

The object of damages is not to punish a landlord but rather to put the tenant in the position that he would have been in if there had been no breach.[197] It is necessary therefore to see what damage the tenant has suffered—comparing the property as it would be in full repair and how it was out of repair—and to see how this loss may be compensated in money.[198] An award of damages should put the tenant[199] in the position that he would have been in if there had been no breach of covenant. This involves a comparison of the property as it was during the period of breach with the property as it ought to have been if there had been no breach.[200]

A landlord cannot evade his responsibility to repair by offering alternative accommodation.[201]

If the tenant does not obtain specific performance and pays for work himself, he will be entitled to the cost. In addition to the cost of any work done by the tenant, he should also be awarded the diminution in value of the property to the tenant for the relevant period. The cost of renting alternative accommodation is allowed if the property is rendered uninhabitable.[202]

A tenant who remains in the property is entitled to the loss of comfort and convenience arising from living in a property in disrepair, which could be expressed either as diminution in value or discomfort, this could be expressed as a notional reduction in the rent, and in any event should at least be cross-checked against the amount of the rent for the period of breach.[203] Nic Madge detected an unofficial tariff of between £1,000 and £3,000 a year for inconvenience,[204] and this may have particular significance in the

---

[196] C.P.R. 27.1(2); N. Madge [1998] *N.L.J.* 238. See generally Woodfall 13.075–13.094.

[197] *Calabar Properties Ltd.* v. *Stitcher* [1984] 1 W.L.R. 287, 297F, Griffiths L.J.; *Wallace* v. *Manchester C.C.* [1998] 3 E.G.L.R. 38, 42B, Morritt L.J.

[198] *Wallace* at 42B, Morritt L.J.

[199] A lender may be entitled to claim. However, if there is negative equity on the first mortgage, a second lender is not entitled to damages for disrepair since he would not have been paid in any event: *Castle Phillips Finance Co. Ltd.* v. *Raja* [1996] 2 C.L.Y. 3720 C.A.

[200] *Calabar Properties Ltd.* v. *Stitcher* [1984] 1 W.L.R. 287 C.A.; J.E. Martin [1984] *Conv.* 229.

[201] *Alexander* v. *Lambeth L.B.C.* [2000] 02 C.L. 386.

[202] *Lubren* v. *Lambeth L.B.C.* (1988) 20 H.L.R. 165 C.A.; *Bradely* v. *Chorley B.C.* (1985) 17 H.L.R. 305 C.A.; *McGreal* v. *Wake* (1984) 13 H.L.R. 107 C.A. An alternative claim is for the loss of rents from sub-letting or for a reduced premium obtained on assignment.

[203] *Wallace* v. *Manchester C.C.* [1998] 3 E.G.L.R. 38 C.A.; *Southwark L.B.C.* v. *Bente* [1998] 2 C.L.Y. 2986; also the commercial case *Electricity Supply Nominees* v. *National Magazine Co. Ltd.* [1999] 32 E.G. 84.

[204] At 1643–1644; *Chiodi* v. *De Marney* [1988] 2 E.G.L.R. 64 C.A. (rent £8 a week; damages £30 a week; top end but not reduced); *Davies* v. *Peterson* [1989] 1 E.G.L.R. 121 C.A. (nominal award of £250 increased on appeal to £1000); *Taylor* v. *Knowsley B.C.* (1985) 17 H.L.R. 376 C.A. (disrepair less serious); *Milligan* v. *Halton B.C.* [1999] 12 C.L. 326 (£1750 a year).

public and social sectors where rents do not reflect the market value of the home.[205] Factors held to be relevant include the receipt of housing benefit, refusal of a suitable alternative accommodation,[206] and an allowance for disrepair by reduction of a registered fair rent.[207]

Special damage can be claimed for any injuries caused by disrepair and for damage to the tenant's belongings or furnishings where, for example, his possessions are damaged by damp leaking through the ceiling or where disrepair leaves the property open to burglary.[208] The tenant is entitled to the cost of redecoration even if in the usual way the tenant is liable for the internal state of the property.[209] All tenants are likely to suffer ill health, discomfort, anxiety and inconvenience,[210] though recovery is limited to the injuries that are a foreseeable consequence of the disrepair.[211]

3. Damages for occupiers other than the tenant

Contractual liability extends to the tenant alone. Members of the family may, for example, have no action even if gas poisoning kills the tenant.[212] They should therefore rely on the tort duty[213] under the Defective Premises Act 1972[214] which imposes a duty to take such care as is reasonable in all the circumstances to keep occupiers reasonably safe from personal injury or damage to their property caused by a relevant defect (that is a disrepair which is a breach of the terms of the tenancy agreement).[215] The landlord's duty is owed to all reasonably expected to be affected by defects in the state of the premises.

4. Tort duties to outsiders

These lie beyond the scope of this work.[216]

---

[205] *Brent L.B.C.* v. *Carmel* (1996) 28 H.L.R. 203 C.A.

[206] *Lubren* v. *Lambeth L.B.C.* (1988) 20 H.L.R. 165 C.A.

[207] *Sturloson & Co.* v. *Mauroux* (1988) 20 H.L.R. 332 C.A.

[208] *Marshall* v. *Rubypoint Ltd.* [1997] 1 E.G.L.R. 69 C.A.

[209] *Bradely* v. *Chorley B.C.* (1985) 17 H.L.R. 305 C.A. *McGreal* v. *Wake* (1984) 13 H.L.R. 107 C.A.

[210] *Taylor* v. *Knowsley B.C.* (1985) 17 H.L.R. 376 C.A.; *McCoy & Co.* v. *Clark* (1982) 13 H.L.R. 87 C.A.; *Chiodi* v. *De Marney* [1988] 2 E.G.L.R. 64 C.A.; *Davies* v. *Peterson* [1989] 1 E.G.L.R. 121 C.A.; *Hussein* v. *Mehlman* [1992] 2 E.G.L.R. 87, 92–93, Stephen Sedley Q.C.; *Lloyd* v. *Rees* [1996] 2 C.L.Y. 3725 (£100 a month); *Holmes* v. *Lambeth L.B.C.* [1997] 2 C.L.Y. 2643; *Brent L.B.C.* v. *Carmel* (1996) 28 H.L.R. 203 C.A. (£350,000 damages); *Arnold* v. *Greenwich L.B.C.* [1998] 2 C.L.Y. 3618.

[211] *Berryman* v. *Hounslow L.B.C.* (1998) 30 H.L.R. 567 (slipped disk from carrying bags up stairs when lift not working; not foreseeable).

[212] *Bottomley* v. *Bannister* [1932] 1 K.B. 458; *Davis* v. *Foots* [1940] 1 K.B. 116 C.A. (husband killed on marriage night); *Travers* v. *Gloucester Corporation* [1946] 2 All E.R. 506, Lewis J.

[213] *Middleton* v. *Hall* (1913) 108 L.T. 804 (wife); *Ryall* v. *Kidwell & Son* [1914] 3 K.B. 135 (daughter). This may be available even after the tenant has obtained damages for disrepair: *Chin* v. *Hackney L.B.C.* (1996) 28 H.L.R. 423 C.A.

[214] s.4.

[215] s.4(3).

[216] Woodfall ch.15; Evans & Smith (5th) ch.10; Garner (2nd) ch.8.

G. TENANT'S RESPONSIBILITY FOR DWELLINGS

1. Express covenants to redecorate etc.

The landlord has a statutory duty to maintain the structure, exterior and main installations in a dwelling, a statutory covenant that negates and overrides any express covenant by the tenant,[217] eliminating, for example, any duty to paint the exterior.[218] Contracting out of the landlord's responsibility is most unusual since the consent of a county court is required.[219] The parties remain free to reach their own agreement about the liability for matters that fall outside the area of the landlord's statutory responsibility, including such matters as internal decorative repairs[220] and the maintenance of fixtures.[221] These matters are frequent sources of friction, because of course from the point of view of a landlord many tenants are nightmares and no tenant uses a rented property as carefully as one he owns. Rented property is almost invariably returned with damages to surfaces, chipped paint, and scuffed carpets. Careful selection of potential tenants is the only defence. Landlords invariably demand a deposit against damage, and when tenants leave retention of the deposit is a frequent source of dispute.[222] Very minor work may be excluded, however, since the principle is that a tenant is not obliged to rectify fair wear and tear.[223]

2. Obligation to use in a tenant-like manner

Injury *caused by the tenant* must be put right by him. Denning L.J. thought it obvious that a tenant must not damage the house that he has rented.[224] Historically tenants were liable automatically for voluntary waste,[225] a concept embracing damage arising from the tenant's own acts,[226] without any express mention of that liability in the lease.[227] Case law provides numerous examples of deliberate damage which has to be reinstated, including broken glass,[228] removal of walls, doors, windows, or fixtures,[229] removal of a shelf,[230] and—with a suitable period flavour—destruction of a dovecote.[231] Damage also has to be reinstated if it is caused by that tenant's negligence. It is not, however, negligent to leave the house for a few days in freezing weather without draining the cold

---

[217] L.T.A. 1985 s.11(4), (5).

[218] *Irvine* v. *Moran* (1991) 24 H.L.R. 1, 5, Thayne Forbes Q.C.

[219] L.T.A. 1985 s.12.

[220] *Irvine*, as above. Social sector tenants are entitled to a precise written definition of any obligations in relation to internal repairs: e.g. The Assured Tenant's Charter (Housing Corporation, 1998) Section 5.

[221] *Mancetter Developments Ltd.* v. *Garmanson Ltd.* [1986] Q.B. 1212, 1221, Sir George Waller.

[222] See above pp. 241–242.

[223] See below p. 264.

[224] *Warren* v. *Keen* [1954] 1 Q.B. 15, 20.

[225] *Edge* v. *Pemberton* (1843) 12 M. & W. 187, 152 E.R. 1164.

[226] *Mancetter*, as above at 1218, Dillon L.J.

[227] *Walgrave* v. *Somerset* (1587) Goulds. 72, 75 E.R. 1002; *Gibson* v. *Wells* (1805) B. & P. (N.R.) 290, 127 E.R. 473 (tenant at will).

[228] *Irvine* v. *Moran* (1991) 24 H.L.R. 1.

[229] *Marsden* v. *Edward Heyes Ltd.* [1927] 2 K.B. 1 C.A.

[230] *Pyot* v. *St John* (1613) Cro. Jac. 329, 79 E.R. 281.

[231] *Kimpton* v. *Eve* (1813) 2 Ves. & B. 349, 35 E.R. 352, Eldon L.C.

water, and so damage caused by frozen pipes is not down to the tenant.[232] This duty not
to cause damage to the property let to the tenant was distinct from repair,[233] since voluntary waste did not arise from omissions[234] nor from proper use of the property.[235]

Small jobs have to be carried out by all tenants—whether holding for a fixed term,
yearly, or under a tenancy of some other period[236]—since the principle is that all tenants have an obligation to use the property let to them in a *tenant-like manner*. Denning
L.J. expressed what was required in *Warren v. Keen*[237]:

> "The tenant must take proper care of the property. He must, if he is going away for the win-
> ter, turn off the water and empty the boiler. He must clean the chimneys, when necessary, and
> also the windows. He must mend the electric light when it fuses. He must unstop the kitchen
> sink when it is blocked by waste. In short he must do all of the little jobs about the place which
> a reasonable tenant would do."

Replacement of tap washers and similar minor jobs fall to the tenant.

The obligation to use in a tenant-like manner qualifies the landlord's duties in relation both to the structure and to the installations,[238] the latter being most significant in
practice. However, the landlord remains liable if it is unreasonable to expect the tenant
to carry out particular work.[239]

3. Waste

Leases that lack a covenant to repair bring into play the archaic[240] law of waste. Any spoil
or destruction or injury to the reversion amounts to waste.[241] Permissive waste equates
to disrepair since it arises where the tenant allows the condition of the property to
worsen, that is he permits the property to fall into disrepair.[242]

Liability for waste was attached by the medieval common law only to estates created
by operation of law, but it was extended by the Statute of Marlborough 1267[243] to "fermors"—a term later interpreted by Lush J.[244] as meaning all who held by a lease for *lives*
or for *years*,[245] whether or not the lease was made by deed. In *Dayani v. Bromley
L.B.C.*[246] a local authority took three houses to house homeless people each for a term
of three years, and was held liable on vacating for allowing the state of the properties to

---

[232] *Wycombe Health Authority v. Barnett* [1982] 2 E.G.L.R. 35 C.A.
[233] *Regis Property Co. Ltd. v. Dudley* [1959] A.C. 370 H.L.; *Haskell v. Marlow* [1928] 2 K.B. 45, Talbot J.
[234] *Mancetter Developments*, as above.
[235] *Saner v. Bilton* (1878) 7 Ch.D. 815.
[236] *Marsden v. Edward Heyes Ltd.* [1927] 2 K.B. 1 C.A. Earlier cases are: *Powley v. Walker* (1793) 5 T.R. 373, 101
E.R. 208; *Ferguson v. Anon* (1797) 2 Esp. 590, 170 E.R. 465; *Horsefall v. Mather* (1815) Holt. 7, 171 E.R. 141. *Auworth
v. Johnson* (1832) 5 C. & P. 241, 172 E.R. 955; *Torriano v. Young* (1833) 6 C. & P. 8, 172 E.R. 1123.
[237] [1954] 1 Q.B. 15, 20.
[238] L.T.A. 1985 s.11(2)(b).
[239] *Sturloson & Co. v. Mauroux* (1988) 20 H.L.R. 332, 338, Glidewell L.J. (tenant's wife blind; no failure to mitigate).
[240] *Mancetter Developments Ltd. v. Garmanson Ltd.* [1986] Q.B. 1212, 1223D, Kerr L.J.
[241] At 1218, Dillon L.J.
[242] *Davis v. Davies* (1888) 38 Ch.D. 499, 504.
[243] 52 Hen.3 c.23 (still in force).
[244] *Woodhouse v. Walker* (1880) 5 Q.B.D. 404, 406, Lush J.; *Davies v. Davies* (1888) 38 Ch.D. 499, Kekewich J.
[245] *Harnett v. Maitland* (1847) 16 M. & W. 257, 153 E.R. 1184; *Greene v. Cole* (1672) 2 Wms. Saunds. 252, n.7,
85 E.R. 1037; *Yellowly v. Gower* (1855) 11 Exch. 274, 156 E.R. 833.
[246] [1999] 3 E.G.L.R. 144 Q.B.D.

decline. On modern construction techniques it was arguable that fixed terms were not covered by the Statute of Marlborough 1267[247] but old statues should be interpreted as they were understood at the time. So if land is let for a period of years the tenant is liable for permissive waste, though the standard required is limited to the condition of the property at the time of the lease.[248]

A tenant *from year to year* fell outside the Statute of Marlborough and so was not liable for waste.[249] Coleridge J. once observed that the absence of authority for imposing liability on landlord was conclusive against it. Hence neither landlord nor tenant is liable to repair,[250] though it is possible that the tenant is obliged to keep a building wind and water tight.[251]

Actions on express repairing covenants lie in contract,[252] but if the lease omits an express covenant and reliance has to be placed on the law of waste, the action is in tort.[253]

4. Shorter periods

In *Warren* v. *Keen*[254] the local authority required a landlord to repair the roof of a tenanted property, and the landlord then sought to pass on the cost to his weekly tenant. He failed. It would be absurd if a tenant with such a short term interest should be landed with an obligation to repair.[255] His only duty was to use the property in a tenant-like manner, and it was not expected that a short term tenant would keep the property wind and watertight.[256] By extension, no liability for waste attaches to a person who initially enters as a tenant at will.[257]

Where a tenant holds over at the end of a contractual term, whether as a tenant at will or under a periodic tenancy implied from the payment and acceptance of rent, the old terms of the tenancy may be extended to cover the period of holding over.[258]

---

[247] Woodfall 13.124.

[248] *Pomfret* v. *Ricroft* (1671) 1 Wms. Saunds. 321, 323, 85 E.R. 462, note (7); unless the property was ruinous at the time of the lease: Coke on *Littleton* 54b.

[249] The statement to the contrary in Coke on *Littleton*, 54b, was not followed in *Horsefall* v. *Mather* (1815) Holt 7, 171 E.R. 141; see also *Auworth* v. *Johnson* (1832) 5 C. & P. 239, 172 E.R. 955; *Torriano* v. *Young* (1833) 6 C. & P. 8, 172 E.R. 1123; *Martin* v. *Gilham* (1837) 7 Ad. & El. 540, 112 E.R. 574; *Pomfret* v. *Ricroft* as above nn. (7) and (x).

[250] *Gott* v. *Gany* (1853) 2 E. & B. 845, 118 E.R. 984.

[251] *Leach* v. *Thomas* (1835) 7 C. & P. 327, 173 E.R. 125; *Wedd* v. *Porter* [1916] 2 K.B. 91 C.A.

[252] *Yellowly* v. *Gower* (1855) 11 Exch. 274, 156 E.R. 833; *Jones* v. *Hill* (1817) Taunt. 392, 129 E.R. 156 (assumpsit not case).

[253] *Pomfret* v. *Ricroft* (1671) 1 Wms. Saunds. 321, 323, 85 E.R. 462 note 7; *Greene* v. *Cole* (1672) 2 Wms. Saunds 252, 85 E.R. 1037, 1037–1038 note (7) (damages only but superior procedure); *Mancetter Developments Ltd.* v. *Garmanson Ltd.* [1986] Q.B. 1212 C.A.; Woodfall 13.108–13.130; see below pp. 672–673.

[254] [1954] 1 Q.B. 15 C.A.; R.E. Megarry (1954) 70 *L.Q.R.* 9; H.W.R. Wade [1954] *C.L.J.* 71; J.D.B. Mitchell (1954) 17 *M.L.R.* 81.

[255] At 18, Somervell L.J. Of course this would now fall within the landlord's statutory obligation.

[256] At 18, Somervell L.J., 20, Denning L.J., 21, Romer L.J.; *Wedd* v. *Porter* [1916] 2 K.B. 91, 100, Swinfen Eady L.J.

[257] *Shrewsbury's case* (1600) 5 Co. Rep. 13b, 77 E.R. 68; *Gibson* v. *Wells* (1805) B. & P. (N.R.) 290, 127 E.R. 473; *Harnett* v. *Maitland* (1847) 16 M. & W. 257, 153 E.R. 1184; *Blackmore* v. *White* [1899] 1 Q.B. 293, 299–300.

[258] *Wedd* v. *Porter* [1916] 2 K.B. 91 C.A. (tenant for year to year); *Burchell* v. *Hornsby* (1808) 1 Camp. 360, 170 E.R. 985; *Beale* v. *Sanders* (1837) 3 Bing. N.C. 850, 132 E.R. 638 (void lease); *Torriano* v. *Young* (1833) 6 C. & P. 8, 172 E.R. 1123 (tenant at will).

5. Fair wear and tear excepted

The Statute of Marlborough 1267 excluded liability for inevitable accident,[259] a principle reproduced in modern repairing obligations by the exclusion of liability for fair wear and tear.[260] In *Regis Property Co. Ltd.* v. *Dudley*[261] the House of Lords had to determine the rent for a residential letting, the rent being determined according to the extent of the tenant's obligations to repair the interior, from which fair wear and tear and fire were excepted. The rent fixed[262] shows that the House regarded the exemption as relatively minor, and that the tenant was left with an onerous repairing obligation. Fair wear and tear excuses damage to minor things that wear out in the course of time, following reasonable use by the tenant under the ordinary operation of natural forces. Grubby decorations can be left.[263] Even if the damage itself is covered by the fair wear and tear exception, the tenant may be liable for consequential damage.[264]

H. PUBLIC AND SOCIAL SECTOR REPAIR

1. Charter rights

Social sector tenants have additional Charter rights. All *tenants* have rights in similar terms[265]: the statutory responsibility of the landlord is restated, they have the right to carry out repairs at the landlord's expense, and the right to be consulted about major work. The major addition to common law and statutory rights is the right to responsive repairs service: emergency repairs should be carried out within 24 hours, urgent repairs within seven calendar days and routine repairs within one calendar month, these times running from when a problem is reported! Assured and secure tenants[266] also have the following rights if they are required to move out during work: the right to home loss payments, the right to consultation about maintenance and improvements, and to information about their rights. Rather lesser rights in relation to repair are given to licence holders and those in supported housing or temporary housing.[267]

2. Right to repair

Special rights are given to public sector tenants to overcome the perception that it is often difficult to ensure that proper repairs are carried out to public sector properties.

---

[259] *Paradine* v. *Jane* (1647) Aleyn 26, 82 E.R. 897; *Carstairs* v. *Taylor* (1871) L.R. 6 Ex. 217 (rat eating water pipe could not be guarded against).

[260] L.A. Blundell (1937) 2 *Conv.* (*N.S.*) 1; *Brown* v. *Davies* [1958] 1 Q.B. 117 C.A.; R.E. Megarry (1958) 74 *L.Q.R.* 33. The onus lies on the tenant: *Haskell* v. *Marlow* [1928] 2 K.B. 45.

[261] [1959] A.C. 370 H.L.; A.L. Diamond (1959) 22 *M.L.R.* 323.

[262] 5/3rds of Rateable Value, where 4/3rds was appropriate if the tenant was liable for *all* repairs.

[263] *Citron* v. *Cohen* (1920) 36 T.L.R. 560 (tenant not liable for bursting of frozen pipe); *Terrell* v. *Murray* (1901) 17 T.L.R. 570 Div.Ct. (tenant not liable for repointing, painting outside, and the repair of a kitchen floor with dry rot).

[264] *Regis Property Co. Ltd.* v. *Dudley* [1959] A.C. 370, 393–394 approving *Haskell* v. *Marlow* [1928] 2 K.B. 45, Talbot J., in preference to *Taylor* v. *Webb* [1937] 2 K.B. 283 C.A.

[265] *Assured Tenant's Charter*, *Secured Tenant's Charter*, and *Shorthold Tenant's Charter* (Housing Corporation, 1998), in each case Section 5.

[266] Section 6.

[267] Section 5 of their respective Charters.

Similar rights are given in the social sector under the terms of the Tenant's Guarantee.[268] The rights are largely symbolic, the most important aspect being a written reporting procedure which ensures that complaints are logged. There is a right to call on a listed contractor to carry out repairs. Times for work to be completed are laid down, with compensation for any delay, though this can be set off against rent arrears. Tenants have a right to go ahead with a repair within the landlord's statutory obligation and to deduct the cost from future rent payments.[269] Tenant's repairs require written consent,[270] the maximum cost is £200, the contractor can be nominated by the landlord, and the landlord has rights to ensure that work is satisfactory, and can decline to allow deduction if access to check the work is refused.

I. ALTERATIONS

1. Private sector

Landlords naturally wish to control changes to their property, so that any private lease of a dwelling will include an absolute obligation not to alter the property, or at the very least an obligation to obtain the landlord's consent before making any change. The law of waste [271] guards against harmful changes, but it is inadequate as a defence for a landlord against a short term residential tenant, and landlords should insist upon an absolute veto over any alteration, good or bad.[272]

2. Public and social sector right to improve

Secure tenants[273] and social tenants[274] must not make improvements without the consent of their landlord, so the council should first be asked to agree in writing and consent may not be withheld unreasonably.[275] Improvements that are approved and which add materially to the price or rental value attract compensation rights on the termination of the tenancy; payments are in the discretion of the landlord and should not exceed the cost of the improvement.[276] If the council chooses not to pay for an alteration but allows the tenant to proceed with it, the rent should not be increased so as to charge the tenant again for the value of that improvement.[277] Social sector tenants enjoying full security (that is assured and secure tenants)[278] have a similar right to improve their homes, the right to compensation for improvements, rights if they are required to move

---

[268] e.g. *Assured Tenant's Charter* (Housing Corporation, 1998) Section 5.

[269] H.A. 1996 s.96 as amended by L.R.H.U.D.A. 1993 s.121 (secure); H.A. 1996 s.137 (introductory); S.I. 1994/133 as amended; J. Driscoll (1994) 57 *M.L.R.* 788; G. Envis [1994] 07 *Legal Action* 16, (1994) 138 *S.J.* 504. The scheme is extended by S.I. 1999/2766.

[270] ss.97–98 (not to be unreasonably withheld).

[271] See above pp. 262–263.

[272] Woodfall 11.254–11.263; Bright & Gilbert 385–390; Garner (2nd) 70–72.

[273] s.97(1); improvements are defined by subs.(2).

[274] *Tenant's Guarantee* (Housing Corporation, 1998) C6(d).

[275] ss.97(3)–(4), 98; consents may be conditional: s.99.

[276] ss.99A–B (inserted by L.R.H.U.D.A. 1993); S.I. 1994/613; J. Driscoll (1994) 57 *M.L.R.* 788; H.A. 1985 s.100(1) (earlier scheme for improvements after 1980).

[277] H.A. 1985 s.101.

[278] *Assured Tenant's Charter* and *Secure Tenant's Charter* (Housing Corporation, 1998) Section 6.

out during work, the right to home loss payments, the right to consultation about maintenance and improvements, and to information about their rights.

J. ADMINISTRATIVE ENFORCEMENT OF REPAIRS

1. Repair standard

The standard of the nation's housing stock as recorded by the English House Condition Survey 1996[279] is appalling, and it is the rental sector that suffers most. Matters have neither improved nor worsened in the five years since the previous survey; half a million homes had been made fit for habitation in that time, but another half a million had become unfit. The highest proportion of unfit homes is in the private rental sector (18 per cent)—though there is a small sub-sector of high quality rentals—whereas only 7 per cent of local authority homes are unfit and the proportion is lower still of homes rented from registered social landlords. Of the nine factors that make for unfitness under the statutory criteria, the most common faults are food preparation facilities, disrepair or dampness. Problems can be tackled either as a statutory nuisance or through the powers of local authorities to require work to houses that are unfit or unsatisfactory.[280]

2. Statutory nuisances

In *Pearshouse* v. *Birmingham C.C.*,[281] Bingham L.C.J. said that the Environmental Protection Act 1990 is intended to deal with any statutory nuisance of any one of various kinds itemised in section 79(1), which may relate to:

> "the state of the premises or the emission of fumes or gases, or dust, steam, smells or other effluvia arising on premises or the accumulation of deposits or the keeping of an animal or noise or anything else declared by statute to be a statutory nuisance."

One form of statutory nuisance occurs where premises are in such a state as to be prejudicial to health or a nuisance.[282] A classic example is a physical layout of rooms which places a toilet adjacent to a kitchen.[283] *Cunningham* v. *Birmingham C.C.* held that an objective test is used to decide what is "prejudicial to health" so that a landlord is not required to take account of the health problems of a particular tenant.[284] This may be proved by evidence of qualified environmental health officers without additional medical evidence.[285] The statutory definition is targeted at premises which create a risk of disease or illness,[286] and therefore excludes premises which merely create a risk of acci-

---

[279] D.E.T.R., 1998.

[280] Woodfall 13.182–13.223; Davey 72–76.

[281] (1999) 31 H.L.R. 756, 768.

[282] Environmental Protection Act 1990 s.79(1)(a), re-enacting Public Health Act 1936 s.91(1)(a).

[283] *Birmingham C.C.* v. *Oakley* (1999) 31 H.L.R. 1070 C.A.

[284] (1998) 30 H.L.R. 158 Q.B.D.

[285] *O'Toole* v. *Knowsley M.B.C.* (2000) 32 H.L.R. 420, Dyson J.; *Southwark L.B.C.* v. *Simpson* (1999) 31 H.L.R. 725 Div.Ct.

[286] The 1990 Act must be interpreted in the light of earlier decisions: *Great Western Rly* v. *Bishop* (1872) L.R. 7 Q.B. 550; *Coventry C.C.* v. *Cartwright* [1975] 1 W.L.R. 845 Div.Ct.

dent or physical injury; it was held in *R. v. Bristol C.C. ex parte Everett*[287] an internal staircase which was so steep as to create a risk of injury was not a statutory nuisance.

A second form of statutory nuisance arises where there is a nuisance (again judged objectively), whether it is one recognised at common law[288] or one that falls within the wide statutory expansion of the common law definition. Matters caught include defects in blocks of flats and common parts,[289] dangerous walls,[290] a dangerous rock face behind cottages,[291] insect infestations,[292] damp,[293] and houses unfit for habitation.[294] Interference with the comfort of the occupier—for example the removal of doors and window sashes[295]—is sufficient without the need for a state of affairs that constitutes a nuisance in the technical sense.

The 1990 Act incorporates the procedure for serving an abatement notice relating to *noise*,[296] but this does not cover problems caused by traffic noise[297] or inadequate soundproofing of flats.[298] A notice is adequate if it is "to cease the playing of amplified music at levels which cause a nuisance at neighbouring premises".[299]

3.   Action by the local authority against statutory nuisances

Local authorities are required to survey their areas and to investigate complaints from residents within it.[300] If a nuisance is discovered the authority has a discretion[301] to serve an abatement notice on the owner—a concept widely defined to mean a person entitled to receive the rack rent from the property, but including in this strange statutory definition both a beneficial receipt and receipt of rent as an agent.[302] However *Camden L.B.C. v. Gunby*[303] holds that a notice cannot be served on a chartered surveyor who was acting as the landlord's managing agent.

An appeal procedure is provided,[304] and so any challenge to the validity of a notice must go to the magistrates court within 21 days; judicial review is excluded by this specific appellate jurisdiction. If a notice takes effect without any successful appeal, it is an

---

[287] [1999] 2 All E.R. 193 C.A.; H.W. Wilkinson [1999] *N.L.J.* 443.

[288] *R. v. Dudley Magistrates Court ex parte Hollis* [1998] 1 All E.R. 759, Moses J.

[289] *Birmingham D.C. v. McMahon* (1987) 19 H.L.R. 452 Div.Ct.; D. Hoath [1988] *Conv.* 377.

[290] *Turley v. King* [1944] 2 All E.R. 489 Div.Ct.

[291] *Kirklees M.B.C. v. Field* (1998) 30 H.L.R. 869 Div.Ct.

[292] *McGuigan v. Southwark L.B.C.* [1996] 2 C.L.Y. 3721 (cockroaches); *Habinteg H.Ass. v. James* (1994) 27 H.L.R. 299 C.A. (not if source of infestation outside control of landlord).

[293] *Botross v. Hammersmith & Fulham L.B.C.* (1995) 27 H.L.R. 179 Q.B.D.

[294] *Carr v. Hackney L.B.C.* (1996) 28 H.L.R. 747 Q.B.D.; *R. v. Southwark L.B.C. ex parte Cordwell* (1995) 27 H.L.R. 594 C.A.

[295] *Betts v. Penge U.D.C.* [1942] 2 K.B. 154 Div.Ct.

[296] *Network H.Ass. v. Westminster C.C.* (1995) 27 H.L.R. 189 Q.B.D.; *Butuyuyu v. Hammersmith & Fulham L.B.C.* (1997) 29 H.L.R. 584 Div.Ct; *Lambie v. Thanet D.C.* [2000] 32 L.S.G. 39.

[297] *Haringey L.B.C. v. Jowett* (2000) 32 H.L.R. 308 Div.Ct. (s.79(1)(ga) limited by s.79(6A)).

[298] *Southwark L.B.C. v. Mills* [1999] 4 All E.R. 449 H.L.

[299] *S.F.I. Group plc. v. Gosport B.C.* [1999] Times April 5th C.A.; *Budd v. Colchester B.C.* [1999] Times April 14th C.A. (barking greyhounds); *Camden L.B.C. v. London Underground Ltd.* [2000] 01 L.S.G. 25 Div.Ct.

[300] Environmental Protection Act 1990 s.79(1).

[301] J. Pointing [2000] *N.L.J.* 340.

[302] s.80(2). There is a more restrictive definition of those "owners" who can be required to pay the cost of remedial work in s.81A(9).

[303] [1999] 44 E.G. 147 C.A., reversing [1999] 4 All E.R. 602 Div.Ct.

[304] Environmental Protection Act 1990 s.80(3); sch.3; S.I. 1995/2644.

offence to fail to comply with the notice[305] subject to defences that the best practicable means were taken to counteract the nuisance,[306] of reasonable excuse,[307] and refusal of access.[308] The duty could also be enforced by injunction.[309] In *Vale of White Horse D.C. v. Allen & Partners*,[310] a case concerning the abatement of smells from a pig farmer's slurry units, it was held that it was not necessary when obtaining an injunction to show that the defendant was deliberately or flagrantly flouting the criminal law. An injunction could be granted even if the defendant was following steps agreed in connection with an earlier abatement notice if in fact the smells persisted, but the local authority must first decide that a prosecution is an inadequate remedy, and since they had failed to consider this question no injunction was possible. Theoretically it is also open to a local authority to enter the property and carry out the necessary work at the owners' expense.[311]

4. Complaint against statutory nuisance by the person affected

Any person affected by a nuisance may also apply direct to the magistrates court for an abatement order.[312] This procedure is available to a private sector tenant as a short cut in preference to action on the statutory covenant for repair, an alternative that is available even if the tenant has obtained legal aid to pursue a civil action.[313] The tenant may be awarded compensation,[314] but this short cut should not be used as a means of compensating a tenant for personal injuries such as illness caused by mould.[315] Since public sector landlords are exempted from the statutory duties to maintain the structure and exterior of a dwelling,[316] many public sector tenants are forced to proceed against their landlords for statutory nuisance.[317]

Just before the enactment of the Environmental Protection Act 1990 the House of Lords decided that its 1936 predecessor did not require any warning to the owner of what work was required before the commencement of proceedings.[318] As a direct response to that decision this defect in the procedure was rectified by the 1990 Act, so that it is now necessary to initiate a complaint by a notice of intention to apply to the

---

[305] s.80(4).

[306] s.80(7).

[307] *Butuyuyu* v. *Hammersmith & Fulham L.B.C.* (1997) 29 H.L.R. 584 Div.Ct.

[308] *Carr* v. *Hackney L.B.C.* (1996) 28 H.L.R. 747 Div.Ct.

[309] Environmental Protection Act 1990 s.81(5).

[310] [1997] Env. L.R. 212, Bell J.

[311] s.81(3), sch.3. There is a restrictive definition of "owner" in this context.

[312] s.82; J. Matthews (1989) 153 *L.G.R.* 547; J. Luba [1991] 02 *Legal Action* 18.

[313] *R.* v. *Highbury Corner Magistrates Court ex parte Edwards* [1995] Crim. L.R. 65 Div.Ct.; *Botross* v. *Hammersmith & Fulham L.B.C.* (1995) 27 H.L.R. 179 Div.Ct.

[314] s.82(6); *R.* v. *Liverpool Crown Court ex parte Cooke* [1997] 1 W.L.R. 700 Div.Ct. (only runs from date notice expires); *Davenport* v. *Walsall M.B.C.* (1996) 28 H.L.R. 754 Div.Ct. (only simple cases).

[315] *Issa* v. *Hackney L.B.C.* (1997) 29 H.L.R. 640 C.A.; C. Hunter (1997) 1 *J.H.L.* 27.

[316] See above pp. 244–245.

[317] Recent examples are: *R.* v. *Liverpool Crown Court ex parte Cooke* as above; *O'Toole* v. *Knowsley M.B.C.* (2000) 32 H.L.R. 420, Dyson J.; *Southwark L.B.C.* v. *Simpson* (1999) 31 H.L.R. 725 Div.Ct.; *R.* v. *Bristol C.C. ex parte Everett* [1999] 2 All E.R. 193 C.A. However the "limbo" during the suspension of a possession order may create problems; see below pp. 333–334.

[318] *Sandwell M.B.C.* v. *Bujok* [1990] 1 W.L.R. 1350 H.L.

magistrates court.[319] The notice may require abatement, prevention of a recurrence, or the execution of remedial works.[320]

There is considerable case law about how explicit the notice needs to be. *Kirklees M.B.C.* v. *Field*[321] decides that the work required must now be specified in the notice, and otherwise the authority will not succeed in recovering its costs, to which *East Staffordshire B.C.* v. *Fairless*[322] adds that the notice need not be over-technical: a letter with an attached surveyor's report was adequate despite its failure to particularise the remedial work needed to remedy the defects and its omission to mention the capacity in which the addressee received the notice. The 1990 statute does not prescribe the form of notice nor require an exact specification of the remedial work precisely because members of the public should not be deterred from complaining about a nuisance by technical requirements. Since the object is to provide a simple procedure for a private citizen to obtain redress when he has suffered a statutory nuisance, the notice need do no more than alert a person served to the matters complained of.[323] There is no requirement to consult the party who is required to abate the nuisance before serving a notice on him, even if this is often a sensible step.[324] However the leading discussion is that of Bingham L.C.J. in *Pearshouse* v. *Birmingham C.C.*,[325] who after observing that section 82 of the 1990 Act is intended to provide a simple procedure for a private citizen to obtain redress when he or she suffers a statutory nuisance, added that:

> "It would frustrate the clear intention of Parliament if the procedure provided by s.82 were to become bogged down in unnecessary technicality or undue literalism. It is important that the system should be operable by people who may be neither sophisticated nor very articulate and who may not . . . . have the benefit of specialised and high quality advice."

The test is what would reasonably alert the recipient to the matters of which the aggrieved person is complaining.[326] An indication that the problem was damp would suffice, but a reference to some undefined statutory nuisance would not.

Notices to local authorities must technically be served on the secretary or clerk of the authority; although some cases require strict compliance[327] there are others (surely right?) that take a more liberal view.[328] Costs must be awarded to the tenant if there was a nuisance at the time of the notice of intention to complain, even if the defect is remedied at the time of the subsequent hearing.[329] Under the 1990 Act, the nuisance is

---

[319] H.A. 1985 s.82(6).

[320] s.90; where the defect is of a structural character see s.80(2).

[321] (1998) 30 H.L.R. 869 Div.Ct.; *Camden L.B.C.* v. *London Underground Ltd.* [2000] 01 L.S.G. 25 Div.Ct. (reasonable recipient principle applied).

[322] (1999) 31 H.L.R. 677 Div.Ct.

[323] *Hall* v. *Kingston upon Hull C.C.* [1999] 2 All E.R. 609 Div.Ct.; *Birmingham C.C.* v. *Ireland* (1999) 31 H.L.R. 1078 Div.Ct.

[324] *R.* v. *Falmouth & Truro Port Health Authority ex parte S.W. Water Services Ltd.* [2000] 3 All E.R. 306 C.A.

[325] (1999) 31 H.L.R. 756, 768.

[326] At 769, approving the test suggested by Sullivan J. in *Fairless*.

[327] *Leeds* v. *Islington L.B.C.* [1998] Env. L.R. 655 C.A. (notice served on Senior Estate Manager ineffective; notice relating to rent under L.T.A. 1987 s.48 not effective to determine address for service of abatement notice).

[328] *Hall* v. *Kingston upon Hull C.C.* [1999] 2 All E.R. 609 Div.Ct.; *Hewins* v. *McLean Homes East Anglia Ltd.* [2000] Times August 31st Rafferty J.

[329] *R.* v. *Dudley Magistrates Court ex parte Hollis* [1998] 1 All E.R. 759, Moses J.

assessed as at the date of service of the notice[330] so that costs of a proper[331] notice are allowed even if has been abated by the time that the case reaches court.[332] A Divisional Court has favoured a broad-brush approach to costs, reducing the award to a complaining tenant who misses site meetings intended to resolve the problem.[333] It would be a defence to show that a tenant had acted unreasonably in refusing to move to allow work to be carried out.[334]

5.   Repairs notice

Local authorities have powers[335] to deal with a house[336] which is unfit for human habitation, a principle defined by the statutory definition of unfitness as interpreted under government guidance.[337] If they decide that the house is unfit they are obliged to do something. In *Taggart* (discussed below) four options were enumerated; they could issue a repairs notice, or close the property (making it unlawful to occupy it), order its demolition (provided that the property is not listed[338]), or issue a deferred action notice pending consideration of grant aid.[339] A further option is to accept an undertaking by the owner to remedy the situation.[340] There is also a discretionary power to serve a repairs notice if it is not technically unfit but where substantial repairs are required to bring it up to a reasonable condition.[341]

Procedural safeguards are provided for a landlord whose property might be affected—even demolished—as a result of the decision made by the local authority. At first sight one would expect landlords to be arguing for repairs rather than closure or demolition, but in fact *Taggart* v. *Leeds C.C.*[342] is just one example of many where the owner argued in favour of a closing order. The tenant was a Rent Act tenant who insisted on renovation of the property so that he could stay in the property. The local authority actually made a closing order, which required much less outlay on the part of the landlord, a decision that would inevitably lead to the eviction of the tenant since it became unlawful to inhabit the property.[343] In circumstances like those in *Taggart*, the housing authority has a discretion that can only be exercised after it has considered what would be the most satisfactory course of action. Ministerial Guidance[344] requires a cost and

---

[330] *S.F.I. Group plc.* v. *Gosport B.C.* [1999] Times April 5th C.A. (noise); contrast *Coventry C.C.* v. *Doyle* [1981] 1 W.L.R. 1325 (old law).

[331] *East Staffordshire B.C.* v. *Fairless* (1999) 31 H.L.R. 677 Div.Ct.

[332] *R.* v. *Dudley Magistrates Court ex parte Hollis* [1998] 1 All E.R. 759, Moses J.; *Hughes* v. *Kingston upon Hull C.C.* (1999) 31 H.L.R. 779 Div.Ct.

[333] *Taylor* v. *Walsall & District Property Investment Co. Ltd.* (1998) 30 H.L.R. 1062 Div.Ct.

[334] *Quigley* v. *Liverpool H.T.* [1999] E.G.C.S. 94, Sedley J.

[335] H.A. 1985 s.189; this derives from H.A. 1957 ss.10–11; Law Com. No.144 (1985) para.30.

[336] Including an H.M.O.: *Camden L.B.C.* v. *Marshall* [1996] 1 W.L.R. 1345 Div.Ct.; see below pp. 273–274.

[337] ss.604–604A.

[338] *R.* v. *Woking B.C. ex parte Adams* (1995) 28 H.L.R. 513 C.A.

[339] Respectively H.A. 1985 ss.189, 264, 265, Housing Grants, Construction and Regeneration Act 1996 s.81.

[340] *Johnson* v. *Leicester Corporation* [1934] 1 K.B. 638; *Leslie Maurice & Co. Ltd.* v. *Willesden Corporation* [1953] 2 Q.B. 1 C.A.; *R.* v. *Woking B.C. ex parte Adams* (1995) 28 H.L.R. 513 C.A.

[341] H.A. 1985 s.190; *Hillbank Properties Ltd.* v. *Hackney L.B.C.* [1978] Q.B. 998 (not internal decorative repairs).

[342] (1999) 31 H.L.R. 693, Richards J.

[343] See below p. 271.

[344] H.A. 1985 s.604; D.O.E. Circular 17/96 Annex B. This replaces the old law which required the service of a repairs notice where property was unfit unless it was incapable of being rendered fit at reasonable expense.

economic appraisal and also a consideration of socio-economic factors. Repairs would
be disproportionately expensive. Work costing £30,000 would leave a house with a tenanted value of no more than £17,000. The cost of making a closing order was trivial and
this was what the owner wanted. Social factors had also to be considered in the second
appraisal, and here the local authority had to consider the interests of the tenant as well.
The local authority had made a proper economic appraisal and the question what action
to take was a matter for their discretion.

A similar approach was adopted by the local authority in *R. v. Southwark L.B.C. ex
parte Cordwell*.[345] Too much work was required to repair the property and so, since the
cost exceeded the reasonable expense, closure was ordered. Future use must be considered in all cases, but it was reasonable for the authority to assume that making a closing
order would lead to early repair. This was the economically favoured decision, and the
socio-environmental assessment was neutral, even taking into account the distress and
disturbance caused to the tenant. Figures suggest[346] a trend away from closure and
demolition towards repair.

Notice must be in a prescribed form,[347] served on the person having control of the
property[348] with a copy to the occupier.[349] Specification of the work should be quite
detailed.[350] The notice becomes operative if no appeal is made to a county court within
21 days,[351] after which failure to comply is a summary offence. An oddity is that the
right to challenge the notice is limited to a tenant with an interest exceeding three years,
thus excluding from the statutory appeal process any short-term residential tenant
including any Rent Act protected tenant. This seems harsh, given that the effect of a
closure order is that the landlord can evict the tenant. Judicial review is allowed in exceptional circumstances,[352] though the leading case failed on the facts when it appeared
that the local authority had acted on counsel's advice.[353]

Actions on leasehold repairing covenants are unaffected,[354] and indeed it is perfectly
possible for the authority to issue a notice against a landlord when it is in fact the tenant who is responsible for repair.[355] The local authority has power to execute the work,
with powers of entry, and powers to recover the cost from the person having control.[356]

---

[345] (1995) 27 H.L.R. 594 C.A.

[346] Bright & Gilbert 382.

[347] S.I. 1990/1730.

[348] Any person in receipt of rent or who would be entitled to receive it if there was a rent: H.A. 1985 s.207;
Pollway Nominees Ltd. v. Croydon L.B.C. [1987] A.C. 79 H.L.

[349] Separate provision is now made for houses, flats and H.M.Os. by ss.189–190, in each case respectively
subs.(1), (1A), and (1B).

[350] *Cohen* v. *West Ham Corporation* [1933] Ch. 814 C.A.; *Bacon* v. *Grimsby Corporation* [1950] 1 K.B. 272 (no
need for detailed estimates).

[351] H.A.1985 s.191; *Ryall* v. *Cubitt Heath* [1922] 1 K.B. 275 (as at date of hearing); *Melhuish* v. *Adam* [1995]
C.L.Y. 3076 C.A. (public law challenge).

[352] *R. v. Mansfield D.C. ex parte Ashfield Nominees Ltd.* (1999) 31 H.L.R. 805, Harrison J.; *R. v. Northavon D.C.
ex parte Ashman* [1993] C.L.Y. 2116, Potts J.

[353] *R. v. Woking B.C. ex parte Adams* (1995) 28 H.L.R. 513 C.A.

[354] H.A. 1985 s.203.

[355] *Rawlance* v. *Croydon Corporation* [1952] 2 Q.B. 803; *Constantinou* v. *Enfield L.B.C.* [1997] 2 C.L.Y. 2640.

[356] H.A. 1985 ss.193–199A; *Pollway Nominees* as above.

6. Reform of enforcement procedures

Synchronisation of the enforcement procedures for statutory nuisances and repairs notices may be desirable.[357]

K. HOUSES IN MULTIPLE OCCUPATION

1. Definition

A house in multiple occupation (H.M.O.) is defined[358] as a house occupied by persons who do not form a single household.[359] In 1996 there were around 550,000 of them housing 1.5 million people.[360] This figure excludes student halls of residence, but students and the young are typical occupiers. Many H.M.O.s are common lodging houses—that is hostels accommodating people by the night.[361] Others are hostels,[362] houses divided into bedsits, conversions into self-contained flats,[363] children's homes,[364] or hotels providing bed and breakfast accommodation to the homeless.[365] Many are run as businesses, but the point is that the accommodation provided is residential.[366] The test for occupation is one of fact rather than legal entitlement.[367]

What is a household? Slightly surprisingly the answer given, in *Barnes* v. *Sheffield C.C.*, was that a group of students living in a house, Young Ones style, form a single household, preventing the house being classed as in multiple occupation.[368] It had previously been thought that a household could be limited to six people, given that this is the maximum size stated in the Planning Use Class[369] as a household but a recent appeal in relation to a property in Bournemouth suggests that the maximum is flexible provided that the property is not overcrowded and that eight students in a single house could be a "household".[370] *Barnes* was distinguished in *Rogers* v. *Islington L.B.C.*[371] a case in which rooms in a house with shared facilities were let out to young adults starting work in the professions. Since the occupants were found by newspaper advertisement and they had no family relationship, common employment or long-standing friendship, they were held not to form a single household. University students were distinguishable if they came to the house as a pre-formed group from the same university to share for

---

[357] *Housing Fitness Standard* (D.E.T.R. C.P., February 17th 1998).

[358] H.A. 1985 part XI, as amended by L.G.H.A. 1989 and H.A. 1996 ss.65–79; S.Is. 1997/872, 1997/1903, 1997/227 (enforcement); N.J. Smith [1997] *Conv.* 206. The first legislation dates from 1958.

[359] *Simmons* v. *Pizzey* [1979] A.C. 37 H.L.; *Hackney L.B.C.* v. *Ezedinna* [1981] 3 All E.R. 438 Div.Ct.

[360] *English House Condition Survey* (D.E.T.R., 1996) ch.1.

[361] A special scheme in H.A. 1985 part XII was repealed by H.A. 1996 s.80.

[362] *R.* v. *Southwark L.B.C. ex parte Levy* (1983) 8 H.L.R. 1; *R.* v. *Camden L.B.C. ex parte Rowton (Camden Town) Ltd.* (1983) 10 H.L.R. 28.

[363] Even if owner-occupied: *Norwich C.C.* v. *Billings* (1997) 29 H.L.R. 679 C.A.

[364] *Reed* v. *Hastings Corp.* (1964) 62 L.G.R. 588.

[365] *R.* v. *Hackney L.B.C. ex parte Evenbray* (1987) 19 H.L.R. 557.

[366] *Living Waters Christian Centres Ltd.* v. *Conwy B.C.* [1999] 3 E.G.L.R. 1 C.A.

[367] *Thrasyvoulou* v. *Hackney L.B.C.* (1986) 18 H.L.R. 370.

[368] (1995) 27 H.L.R. 719 C.A.; N.J. Smith [1997] *Conv.* 395.

[369] S.I. 1987/764 sch, Use Class C3.

[370] [1999] 27 *E.G.* 119.

[371] [1999] 37 E.G. 178 C.A.

the predefined period of an academic year, even if they were not known to each other in advance and paid rent individually.

Controls extend to houses that may be made suitable for occupation.[372]

2. Registration

Local authorities may choose to apply a registration scheme to their area either covering the whole of the district, or a particular area or type of property,[373] and there is the choice of applying a more rigorous scheme enacted in 1996 if the authority chooses to do so.[374] An owner whose house is designated by the local authority has a right of appeal to a county court in order to try to escape H.M.O. control.[375] The Government is currently consulting about whether to make licensing schemes compulsory.[376]

3. Control over management

H.M.Os. are subject to stringent control.[377] The local authority must ensure they are safe and prosecute offences.[378] Matters controlled include fitness for habitation,[379] provision of fire escapes,[380] and standards of management, as well as overcrowding[381]: H.M.Os. must be fit for the number of occupants.[382] Occupiers can be limited by a notice registered as a land charge and so become a binding incumbrance on the property.[383]

A person having control of an H.M.O. may be ordered to carry out work,[384] with the possibility of a penal notice being attached.[385] The notice continues so long as work remains undone.[386] If work has to be carried out by the authority, it can recover the cost from the owner.[387] A local authority officer who wrongly advises the owner that work is required to comply with regulations may expose his employer to liability in negligence.[388] A repairs notice may also be issued in relation to work required at an H.M.O.[389]

---

[372] *Tsao* v. *S.S. for the Environment* (1996) 28 H.L.R. 259 Q.B.D.

[373] H.A. 1985 ss.346–351; S.Is. 1997/229, 1997/230 as amended (fees), 1991/982 (charges).

[374] H.A. 1996 ss.65–70 (power to refuse to register substandard H.M.O.s); S.I. 1998/1812 (registration scheme). Compulsory schemes are proposed by the Green Paper: *Quality and Choice: A Decent Home for All* (D.E.T.R., April 2000) para.5.30.

[375] *Nolan* v. *Leeds C.C.* (1990) 23 H.L.R. 135 C.A.; *Burke* v. *S.S. for the Environment* (1994) 26 H.L.R. 10 (effect of an erroneous date).

[376] *Licensing Houses in Multiple Occupation* (D.E.T.R. C.P., April 9th 1999).

[377] H.A. 1985 ss.346–379; S.I. 1990/830; S.I. 1990/1730 (forms); N.J. Smith [1997] *Conv.* 206.

[378] H.A. 1996 part III; in force March 3rd 1997: S.I. 1997/350.

[379] H.A. 1985 ss.352–357.

[380] H.A. 1985 ss.365–368; S.I. 1981/1576; S.I. 1997/230.

[381] H.A. 1985 ss.358–364; H.A. 1996 s.73.

[382] H.A. 1996 s.73. in force March 3rd 1997: S.I. 1997/350.

[383] H.A. 1985 s.354.

[384] ss.375–378.

[385] *Desmond* v. *Bromley L.B.C.* (1996) 28 H.L.R. 518 Q.B.D.

[386] *Camden L.B.C.* v. *Marshall* [1996] 1 W.L.R. 1345 Div.Ct.

[387] H.A. 1985 s.352; S.Is. 1997/228, 1997/872.

[388] *Berg* v. *Trafford B.C.* (1988) 20 H.L.R. 47 C.A.; *Welton* v. *North Cornwall D.C.* [1997] 1 W.L.R. 570 C.A.

[389] *Camden L.B.C.* v. *Marshall* [1996] 1 W.L.R. 1345 Div.Ct.; *Stafford* v. *Charnwood B.C.* (2000) 32 H.L.R. 289.

Controls may be tightened even further as a result of the current D.E.T.R. consultation exercise.[390]

4.   Repair standard

It is estimated that four out of every 10 H.M.O.s in England and Wales are unfit. Local authorities have considerable powers to deal with unfitness.[391] The fitness standard is set by legislation taking five factors into account (which are not the same as for dwellings)[392]:

> food preparation,
> toilets,
> baths,
> fire escapes,[393] and
> other fire precautions.

These standards are applied to require the H.M.O. to be kept fit for the number of occupiers.[394]

5.   Control order

The local authority has power to make a control order,[395] by which the owner of the property is displaced by the local authority as its manager, or the authority has power to make a compulsory purchase order. A decision as to which course of action to pursue must be made within a time limit of eight weeks.

L.   RENOVATION GRANTS

Local housing authorities[396] may make grants for work to private houses under the Housing Grants, Construction and Regeneration Act 1996.[397]

1.   Disabled facilities grants

These[398] cover works of adaption to any buildings (whether more or less than 10 years old[399]) which are occupied by a disabled person and intended to benefit that person as occupier.[400] Some disabled facilities grants are mandatory, that is where the work is to provide access to the disabled person or ensure his safety.[401] In relation to these grants, the authority has no right to take into account its own resources since the grants are

---

[390] *Licensing Houses in Multiple Occupation* (D.E.T.R., April 9th 1999).
[391] H.A. 1985 ss.352–357.
[392] s.604 as amended.
[393] ss.365–368; S.I. 1981/1576; S.I. 1997/230.
[394] s.353A.
[395] ss.379–394; S.I. 1990/830; *Jacques* v. *Liverpool C.C.* (1997) 29 H.L.R. 82 Q.B.D.
[396] District councils or London borough councils.
[397] In 1995 there were 95,000 grants, averaging £7,500.
[398] ss.1(4), 19–24; N.M. Clement [1999] 4 *E.C.A.* 8.
[399] s.4(1)(a).
[400] ss.20 (disabled occupant), 100 (disabled person).
[401] s.23(1); other purposes can be specified.

mandatory.[402] The housing authority retains a discretion to make grants for any other work that is intended to make the accommodation suitable for the disabled occupant.[403] However, all work must be necessary, appropriate, reasonable, and practicable.[404]

Grants will usually be paid to an owner occupier, but they are also available to a tenant of a dwelling having at least five years remaining[405] or a tenant with a short term interest who is required to carry out the work by the terms of his lease.

2. Renovation grants

Grants may be made towards the cost of renovation works on dwellings,[406] consisting of the improvement or repair of existing dwellings. The property may be a house or flat, but it must be at least 10 years old.[407] Renovation grants are always discretionary.[408] Purposes for which grants may be made are[409]:

—to comply with a repair notice served on the occupier[410];
—to provide thermal insulation, space heating, or fire precautions;
—to provide satisfactory internal arrangements, standards of construction, standards of physical condition or adequate services and amenities.[411]

If the dwelling is not fit for human habitation,[412] the grant-aided work must bring it up to that standard[413]; such a grant is mandatory.[414]

3. Other grants

The following discretionary grants are available:

Conversion grants to provide new dwellings or units in H.M.O.s by conversion.[415]
Common parts grants provide for work to the common parts of a block containing two or more flats, where the work is needed to make it suitable for occupation by a number of occupiers. Qualifying work is listed.[416] Application must be made by the

---

[402] *R. v. Birmingham C.C. ex parte Taj Mohammed* (1999) 31 H.L.R. 392.

[403] s.23(2).

[404] s.24(3).

[405] s.19(1) with detail in subs.(2)–(5).

[406] ss.7–13 replacing H.A. 1985 part XV and Local Government and Housing Act 1989 ss.101–138. Under the 1989 Act some grants were mandatory: *R. v. Greenwich L.B.C. ex parte Glen International Ltd.* [2000] Times March 29th C.A.

[407] s.4, except for disabled facilities grants and the creation of a new H.M.O. by conversion.

[408] s.13(1). This enables grants to be targeted at specific run down areas. The council can determine its allocation policy without giving reasons: *R. v. Bristol C.C. ex parte Bailey* (1995) 27 H.L.R. 307, Hidden J.

[409] s.12; if the defective dwelling scheme applies, aid must be sought under that scheme first: s.6. It is illegal to make grants in other circumstances: *R. v. Sunderland C.C. ex parte Rendezvous Ltd.* (1995) 27 H.L.R. 477, Judge J. (on old legislation).

[410] H.A. 1985 ss.189 (unfit), 190 (fit but requiring substantial work).

[411] Others may be added: s.12.

[412] s.97 adopts the definition in H.A. 1985 s.604.

[413] s.13(4), (5), (6); regard must be had to the expected life.

[414] *Denis Rye Pension Fund Trustees* v. *Sheffield C.C.* [1998] 1 W.L.R. 840 C.A. (sue in debt since judicial review is disproportionate).

[415] ss.12(2), 27(2). In the latter case, the building may be less than 10 years old: s.4(1)(b).

[416] The list in s.17 is similar to that for renovation grants; when the work is complete the building must satisfy the standards in H.A. 1985 s.604(2)(a)–(e).

freeholder, but he is required to certify that ¾s of flats are occupied by qualifying residential tenants who have their only or main residence there.[417] The grant is discretionary, regard being had to the expected life of the finished building.[418]

H.M.O. grants are available,[419] in the discretion of the local authority,[420] for works of improvement[421] to houses in multiple occupation, that is to dwellings not occupied by a single household. The owner applies, but must certify that he intends to continue to make the property available for residential accommodation.[422] Grants may also be made to provide a separate water supply to a dwelling.[423]

4. Applicants and conditions

Most grants are paid to *owner occupiers*, but they are subject to a number of restrictive conditions. Generally grants are available to an adult with an "owner's interest", meaning the freehold or a lease with at least five years remaining,[424] including an equitable *Walsh* v. *Lonsdale* lease.[425] A tenant with a shorter leasehold interest qualifies for grant aid (for renovation though not for conversion) if he is required to carry out the works by the terms of his tenancy agreement.[426] Applicants for some grants must have owned and lived in the property for the three years leading up to the grant application,[427] though there are limited succession rights. Grants are means-tested.[428]

A certificate has to be signed when applying for the grant that the applicant intends to continue residential occupation for five years after completion of the work.[429] This will be a condition of the grant payment,[430] and part of the grant has to be repaid if a relevant disposal[431] occurs within five years.[432] This possibility that the grant will be repayable is called a grant condition[433] and will be a local land charge affecting a purchaser of the land if registered. Grant aid is also available to a private[434] *landlord* of property who intends to make the dwelling available for letting. Availability for letting will be a condition of grant aid.[435] Restrictions on disposal apply for five years.

---

[417] ss.14, 15, 16; S.I. 1999/68 (entitlement for tenants under 5-year leases).

[418] s.18(1), (5).

[419] ss.25–28.

[420] s.28(1).

[421] Specified in s.27. The list is very similar to that for renovation grants; the work must make the property fit for habitation: s.28(5).

[422] ss.25, 26.

[423] H.A. 1985 s.523.

[424] Housing Grants Construction and Regeneration Act 1996 s.6.

[425] *R.* v. *Tower Hamlets L.B.C. ex parte Von Goetz* [1999] Q.B. 1019 C.A.

[426] s.6.

[427] Not renewal grants, grants to provide disabled facilities, and home repair grants.

[428] s.30; this was first introduced by the Local Government & Housing Act 1989.

[429] s.8.

[430] s.48.

[431] ss.53 (relevant disposal), 54 (exempt disposals); definitions are based on the right to buy though with no discount for completed years.

[432] Grant condition period, 5 years from the date the certified work was finished.

[433] ss.44–55.

[434] s.3(2). The Local Government Act 1988 s.24 gives a power to provide financial assistance for privately let housing accommodation.

[435] s.49.

A person qualifying for grant aid must make an *application* to the local housing authority in the correct form.[436] The proposed work should be described, and two estimates provided, but the details can be amended when the grant is allocated. It is vitally important that application for grant aid is made before work is begun.[437] Detailed rules regulate procedure and payment.[438] Grants can be limited, with the housing authority having no discretion to exceed the government prescribed maxima, except in the case of disabled facilities grants.[439] Grant aid may be withdrawn if the work is not completed within 12 months.[440]

5. Home repair assistance

This is available to an owner occupier on social security benefits to provide assistance for home repair, either by monetary grant or through the provision of materials[441]; amounts are limited.

6. Miscellaneous

There are a number of schemes where a local authority can regenerate an area. Examples are enveloping (where the structure and exterior of a group of dwellings are repaired leaving intact the interiors),[442] provision of a single regeneration budget for an area,[443] and grant aid for relocation after slum clearance.[444]

M. REFORM

The Law Commission has a current report on the *Responsibility for the State and Condition of Property*.[445] It proposes to leave the general concept of repair to case-law development. The statutory covenant relating to short residential leases would not be changed, and but otherwise the parties would remain free to settle the liability for repair by negotiation. However, the landlord would be responsible for repairs under a new implied covenant unless some other arrangement was made.[446] A second implied covenant would relate to what the report describes as "associated premises", that is common parts, which the landlord would be obliged to keep in repair unless there was some other agreement.[447] The most important innovation is the proposal to supplement the repairing obligation in a residential lease up to seven years in length with an implied obligation on the landlord to ensure that premises are fit for human habitation at the

---

[436] s.2.

[437] ss.12, 29.

[438] ss.34 (decision and notification), 35–43 (payment).

[439] s.33.

[440] *R. v. Newham L.B.C. ex parte Trendgrove Properties Ltd.* [1999] 22 L.S.G. 36, Dyson J. (on the 1989 Act).

[441] ss.76, 78 (houseboats and mobile homes); S.I. 1999/2766, 1999/3084 (Wales).

[442] ss.60–75.

[443] part IV.

[444] ss.131–140; S.I. 1999/1541.

[445] Law Com. No.238 (1996); S. Bridge [1996] *Conv.* 342; Law Com. C.P. No.123 (1992); P.F. Smith [1994] *Conv.* 186. Earlier proposals: Law Com. No.67 (1975) paras.108–157; D. Hughes [1984] *J.S.W.L.* 137.

[446] Law Com. No.238 (1996) para.7.10; draft Bill cls.1, 2.

[447] paras.7.26–7.29; draft Bill cls.1(2)–(5), 2(2)–(5).

outset and to keep them fit afterwards,[448] applying the housing law standard of fitness for habitation.[449] The obligation would apply to tied cottages, but not to agricultural leases nor temporary public-sector housing. All of these proposals would only apply to new tenancies after the implementation of the new legislation.

The law of waste and the duty to use in a tenant-like manner would be abolished, to be replaced by an obligation to take proper care of property, avoiding negligence, wilful damage and unauthorised alterations.[450] The Commission also proposes improvements to the legislation governing specific performance of covenants relating to repairs and similar obligations.[451] The remedy should be made generally available to either party, though the court would retain a discretion whether to make an order in a particular case. All these improvements in the law are welcome, and the Labour Lord Chancellor proposed further work on this Report in 1998, but the financial implications remain to be considered and primary legislation will be needed.[452]

Even when these reforms are enacted the fundamental problem remains that landlords must be made to meet their existing obligations, probably as a result of more direct administrative intervention in housing law. Perhaps there should be an MOH test—rather like the car MOT—before a house is let and periodically thereafter.[453]

Reforms are also proposed by the Housing Green Paper.[454] The poor standard of much housing in the private sector needs to be tackled,[455] as does the £10 billion backlog of work needed to local authority housing.[456] It is proposed to replace the current pass/fail fitness test with a graded health and safety rating.[457] The Law Commission proposals (just discussed) to impose a duty on a landlord to ensure the fitness for habitation of a dwelling he is letting will be refined to reflect this rating system.[458] Another administrative control under discussion is the power to withhold housing benefit from landlords of inadequate properties.[459] The standard of private sector housing should be improved by voluntary accreditation of landlords,[460] letting schemes, and best practice guidance. However local authorities will be given a new power to tackle the poor condition of private rented homes in particular areas by imposing compulsory licensing,[461] and a scheme for licensing H.M.Os. will be imposed universally.[462]

---

[448] paras.8.35–8.59; draft Bill cls.5–8; *Southwark L.B.C.* v. *Mills* [1999] 4 All E.R. 449, 453e–g, Lord Hoffmann, 461e–f, Lord Millett.

[449] H.A. 1985 s.604; see above pp. 246–247.

[450] Law Com. No.238 (1996) paras.10.35–10.37; draft Bill cls.9–11; the parties would be free to modify the terms implied.

[451] paras.9.32–9.33; draft bill cl.13; no changes are proposed to damages.

[452] *Housing Fitness Standard* (D.E.T.R., February 1998) paras.5.49–5.50; Law Com. No.258 (1999) para.1.20.

[453] A. Tunkel [1991] *N.L.J.* 453.

[454] *Quality and Choice: A Decent Home for All* (D.E.T.R., April 2000).

[455] para.2.8.

[456] para.2.9

[457] para.5.28.

[458] para.5.29.

[459] paras.5.41–5.45.

[460] paras.5.11–5.17.

[461] paras.5.32–5.35.

[462] para.5.30.

N. MANAGEMENT OF PUBLIC AND SOCIAL SECTOR ESTATES

1. Management of public estates

Although local housing authorities have full powers over their housing stock,[463] these are hedged around by consultation requirements[464] and public law controls aimed at ensuring that the tenants on their estates have a real say in how they are run. All authorities are required to adopt and publicise a management plan[465] and to follow a Code of Management Practice.[466] It is not up to the court to decide what scheme should be adopted.[467] The local plan does not vary the terms of the tenancy,[468] but it may confer additional rights on tenants. Landlords are required to provide explanations and to provide information at least once a year.[469]

2. Consultation about management

Tenants' associations which meet statutory criteria must be recognised by the authority,[470] a duty which can be enforced by judicial review where necessary.[471] Provision is made for entry into management agreements with such organisations,[472] giving a so-called "right to manage".[473] Otherwise tenants have the right to consultation on housing management,[474] for example before the council decides to knock down the estate.[475] Consultation might take the form of meetings advertised in the local library[476] or through public meetings and questionnaires.[477]

3. Tenant participation compacts

Tenants should now have a much wider role in forming and shaping decisions taken by the council over housing issues. A *National Framework for Tenant Participation Compacts*[478] lays down a framework about how councils are to involve tenants in decision-making as part of the "best value" programme—the new Labour initiative designed to replace compulsory competitive tendering[479] which was gradually phased in during 1999 and 2000. Section 3(1) of the Local Government Act 1999 looks forward to continuous improvements in the economy, efficiency, and effectiveness, of local

---

[463] H.A. 1985 ss.23, 27; Woodfall 25.066–25.072.

[464] H.A. 1985 s.27A.

[465] L.R.H.U.D.A. 1993 ss.69–75, 87.

[466] S.I. 1998/106.

[467] H.A. 1985 s.105; *R. v. Brent L.B.C. ex parte Morris* (1998) 30 H.L.R. 324 C.A.

[468] H.A. 1985 ss.102, 103; *Palmer* v. *Sandwell M.B.C.* (1988) 20 H.L.R. 74; N.J. Wikeley (1988) 51 *M.L.R.* 517.

[469] H.A. 1985 s.104; L.R.H.U.D.A. 1993 s.123; H.A. 1996 ss.136–137 (introductory tenancies).

[470] L.T.A. 1985 s.29.

[471] *R. v. London R.A.P. ex parte Henry Smith's Charity Trustees* [1988] 1 E.G.L.R. 34; C.P. Rodgers [1988] *Conv.* 363. *R. v. S.S. for the Environment ex parte Harrow L.B.C.* (1997) 29 H.L.R. 1, Judge J.

[472] H.A. 1985 ss.7A, 7B; L.R.H.U.D.A. 1993 s.132.

[473] H.A. 1985 s.27AB (inserted by L.R.H.U.D.A. 1993 s.152); S.I. 1994/627.

[474] H.A. 1985 s.105; more extensive provisions were repealed by H.A. 1996 sch.19 pt.X.

[475] *R. v. Gateshead M.B.C. ex parte Smith* (1999) 31 H.L.R. 97, Collins J.

[476] *R. v. Brent L.B.C. ex parte Morris* (1998) 30 H.L.R. 324 C.A.

[477] *R. v. Gateshead M.B.C. ex parte Smith* (1999) 31 H.L.R. 97, Collins J.

[478] (D.E.T.R., June 1999); A. Selman [2000] J.H.L. 13.

[479] L.R.H.U.D.A. 1993 s.131.

government. Key elements are wide consultation, performance indicators, best value performance plans, internal audit, and inspections by the audit commission. In the specific context of housing it aims to improve housing services, to monitor and report on performance, to ensure that remedial action is taken as needed. Policy will be informed by the tenants' view, and they should also be involved in the planning and delivery of services.

Tenant participation is encouraged (though no one is compelled to become involved) at two levels—the strategic level is council wide, and the local decision-making level is based on each neighbourhood. Tenants should be involved in decision-making, setting policy agendas, checking how compacts operate, and in dispute procedures. Tenant empowerment grants will be available to provide money for training tenants. Compacts are aimed primarily at council tenants—such as secure tenants, introductory tenants, or those in sheltered or temporary accommodation—but the council should also seek to involve other stakeholders such as social tenants. A registered social landlord which takes over an estate under a large-scale voluntary transfer is not affected, but the rules governing transfer should ensure that tenants have a say via the governing bodies of each estate transferred.

By April 1st 2000, each council should have stated its intention to enter into a compact, with a joint statement of expected outcomes and a joint action plan. Standards are provided for a wide range of housing issues—services, policy, budget, improvements, allocation of tenancies, policy on anti-social behaviour, management of services, repairs, rent collection and voids, the conditions on which tenancies are granted, advice on housing benefit, service charges, monitoring of standards, and equality policies. Other benchmarks will test the level of government support, meetings, information, and the constitution and management of tenant groups. The whole operation will require monitoring and an annual budget to cover costs.

4. Tenants' choice

Local authorities must consult before disposal to private sector landlords.[480] Flaws in the consultation process may provide a basis for judicial review if they are sufficiently serious.[481] If there are several suitable organisations bidding to take over the estate, the tenants may choose between them—Tenant's Choice.[482] This has been largely symbolic.

5. Charter rights of social tenants

The *Council Tenant's Charter*[483] confirms the right of secure tenants to be consulted about management and to become involved in management through the tenants' organisation, and also the rights to receive good service and information from the landlord. In the public sector this restates basic legal entitlement. Social sector tenants, for example those holding from a housing association, have much improved rights under

---

[480] H.A. 1985 s.106A.

[481] *R. v. S.S. for the Environment ex parte Walters* [1997] Times September 2nd C.A.; *R. v. Brent L.B.C. ex parte O'Malley* (1998) 30 H.L.R. 328 C.A.

[482] ss.133–136; J. Driscoll (1994) 57 *M.L.R.* 788, 791–793.

[483] D.E.T.R., 1998. It is proposed to apply the best value regime: Green Paper, *Quality & Choice: A Decent Home for All* (D.E.T.R., April 2000) paras.7.45–7.50.

the Housing Act 1996—for example the right to ask the Housing Corporation to appoint a manager of a flat scheme which is insolvent. These statutory rights are supplemented by tenants' charters giving basic guarantees similar to the rights in the public sector. And disputes can be referred to an independent Housing Ombudsman.[484] The main charters for social tenants confirm the right to be consulted and opportunities to get involved in the management of the tenant's home, and as well as information about these rights. There is also the right to consultation about any changes to the tenancy agreement.[485]

O. SERVICE CHARGES ON RENTED ESTATES

1. Work covered

Full service charges[486] are rarely appropriate for rented blocks because the structural repairing obligations necessarily fall on the landlord,[487] but service charges may be needed to finance communal facilities and the maintenance of common parts of a development. Short residential lettings of one unit in a block will commonly anticipate that the tenant will be entitled to make use of communal facilities, but otherwise the right to use lifts and garbage disposal units can be implied.[488] Where tenants have rights over common parts, there is no objection to imposing a charge to pay for the provision of those facilities. The *Assured Tenant's Charter*[489] refers in Section 4 to the provision of communal heating, cleaning, lighting in shared areas, gardening and caretaking, and this probably gives a good idea of the matters included in service charges affecting rented properties.

2. Service charges and the short residential codes

Under the Rent Act 1977, which applied to private sector leases before early 1989, the rent could be registered as variable, to cover for example charges made for the provision of hot water.[490] The assured scheme in operation for fresh grants since early 1989 contains no restrictions, so that a service charge could be imposed in addition to rent, though not to pay for structural repairs. A service charge could also become incorporated in a residential letting where a tenant holds a long lease which expires, the liability to pay service charge being incorporated in the statutory tenancy which follows.[491] Social tenants may have certain additional charter rights, including the right to know about service charge, the right to be told about changes and be given one month's notice of the change, and the right to information.[492]

---

[484] H.A. 1996 s.51 (replaces earlier schemes from April 1997).

[485] *Assured Tenant's Charter*, Section 9; *Secure Tenant's Charter*, Section 9; *Shorthold Tenant's Charter*, Section 6 (all Housing Corporation, 1998).

[486] Woodfall 7.162–7.231; Davey 345–353; Evans & Smith (5th) 416–422; Garner (2nd) ch.17.

[487] See above pp. 243–246.

[488] *Liverpool City Council* v. *Irwin* [1977] A.C. 239 H.L.; see above pp. 194–195.

[489] (Housing Corporation, 1998).

[490] *Asher* v. *Seaford Court Estates Ltd.* [1950] A.C. 508 H.L.; R.E. Megarry (1950) 66 *L.Q.R.* 19.

[491] *Blatherwick (Services) Ltd.* v. *King* [1991] Ch. 218 C.A. (on L.T.A. 1954 s.10).

[492] The *Assured Tenant's Charter*, the *Secure Tenant's Charter*, the *Shorthold Tenant's Charter* (Housing Corporation, 1998), Section 4.

3. Challenges to service charges

This is discussed below.[493]

P. RIGHTS OF LEASEHOLDERS ALSO PROTECTING SHORT
RESIDENTIAL TENANTS

The Landlord and Tenant Acts 1985 and 1987 confer a number of valuable protections on residential long leaseholders. In this section we consider which of them is available to a tenant renting his home.

1. Right of pre-emption

Only leaseholders owning long leases are entitled to enfranchise or to participate in collective enfranchisement of a block; these rights are not available to short residential tenants.[494] The owners of flats in a block can also club together to assert a right of pre-emption, that is they have the right to prevent the landlord selling the reversion to an outside investor, by insisting that the landlord should sell to them at the same price.[495] There is no right to initiate an acquisition, and so all depends upon the landlord choosing to sell. This right is not available to those renting in the public sector nor to private sector tenants renting under assured tenancies (created since early 1989).[496] However the group of qualifying tenants is defined to include Rent Act tenants with full security.[497] Perhaps this will be of most value in a mixed block where most tenants hold long leases, but in theory it enables a group of Rent Act tenants to secure their homes.[498] The cost of buying a block of investment property is likely to be prohibitive. At least tenants have the right to notice of the landlord's intention to sell,[499] and to participate collectively in a purchase if they are able to do so. The rights are much more commonly exercised by tenants holding long leases, and procedure will be explained in that context.[500]

The government has announced[501] its intention to *reform* the right of first refusal by extending it to houses and by amending the definition of a qualifying tenant to include assured tenants who have a long-term interest in the building, though assured shorthold tenants will continue to be excluded. Many tenants of registered social landlords have a full assurance, so this extension could be very significant.

---

[493] See below p. 283.

[494] The cut-off point is a grant for 21 years, except that a shorter lease granted under the right to buy counts as a long lease.

[495] L.T.A. 1987 part I.

[496] ss.1(4), 58(1).

[497] Excluding protected shorthold tenants, service occupiers, and tenants of resident landlords.

[498] But see *Belvedere Court Management Ltd.* v. *Frogmore Developments Ltd.* [1996] 1 All E.R. 312 C.A.

[499] L.T.A. 1987 s.2.

[500] See below pp. 426–432.

[501] *Leasehold Reform: The Way Forward* (D.E.T.R., December 1999) para.14.

2. Information

Tennants on rented estates have rights to information about sales of the landlord's interest, statute spells out the details required in a rent demand before any rent or service charge can fall due.[502]

3. Service charge

The right to challenge service charge demands before a Leasehold Valuation Tribunal and restrictions on forfeiture for non-payment of service charge apply to short residential tenants.[503] Recognised tenants' associations have the right to be consulted about the appointment of managing agents.[504] There are as yet no professional qualifications required of managing agents, though reform is anticipated.[505] Ministerial approval can be given to a code of management practice for residential property,[506] which is helpful when proving what standard of work is reasonable. Certain reforms are proposed.[507]

4. Appointment of manager

If tenants are dissatisfied with the standard of management provided by the landlord, they may apply to a Leasehold Valuation Tribunal for a new manager to be appointed.[508] It seems likely that the proposed no fault right to manage will also apply.[509]

5. Insurance

Where a landlord is insuring a block at the tenants' expense, residential tenants have a right to challenge the landlord's choice of insurer and the reasonableness of demands for premiums before a Leasehold Valuation Tribunal.[510]

6. Rights restricted to long leaseholders

Certain rights enjoyed by long leaseholders are not available to renters; these include the right to a management audit,[511] the power for a Leasehold Valuation Tribunal to order compulsory acquisition of the landlord's interest, and the Tribunal's power to vary leases.[512]

---

[502] See above p. 223.
[503] L.T.A. 1985 ss.18–30 as amended by L.T.A. 1987 ss.41–42; H.A. 1996 ss.81–82, 83–84; *Williams* v. *Southwark L.B.C.* [2000] Times April 5th, Lightman J. Changes are proposed by the Commonhold and Leasehold Reform Bill 2000, see below pp. 462–464; see also pp. 439–440 for proposed changes to L.V.T.s.
[504] L.T.A. 1985 s.30B; *R.* v. *London R.A.P. ex parte Henry Smith's Charity Trustees* [1988] 1 E.G.L.R. 34; C.P. Rodgers [1988] *Conv.* 363.
[505] See below p. 454.
[506] L.R.H.U.D.A. 1993 s.87; S.Is. 1996/2839, 1998/106.
[507] See below pp. 462–464.
[508] L.T.A. 1987 ss.21–24; H.A. 1996 ss.85–88.
[509] See below pp. 444–452.
[510] H.A. 1996 s.83(2).
[511] L.R.H.U.D.A. 1993 ss.76–84.
[512] L.T.A. 1987 ss.25–34, 35–37.

11

RESIDENTIAL ASSIGNMENT AND SUB-LETTING

Public sector controls. Private sector controls. Social sector controls. Absolute prohibitions. Qualified rights to deal. Assignment formality. Running of covenants. Authorised sub-tenancies and their preservation. Unauthorised sub-tenancies. Dealings with the landlord's reversion. Tenancies unauthorised by the landlord's mortgage.

Broadly speaking, there are three transactions which can effect a change in the position of a residential tenant—he may assign (or transfer) his lease to a new tenant, sub-let it to a sub-tenant, or take in a lodger.[1] Landlords generally control dispositions, partly to make sure that they have a responsible tenant who will pay the rent, but also to guard against the creation of unwonted security of tenure. So there is an important distinction between transactions with permission and those without—residential security tenure is generally dependent upon authorised dealings from an authorised base. A landlord who has not authorised a transaction retains a title paramount enabling him to evict the new tenant or sub-tenant. This chapter looks at the balance between what transactions a person is allowed to carry out and those that are unauthorised in each of three main sectors—public, private, and social—followed by a consideration of transfers and sub-tenancies. The chapter concludes with a consideration of dealings with the reversion and the title paramount of a mortgage-lender.

A. PUBLIC SECTOR DEALINGS

The rules about assignment are most fully developed in the public sector, because it is necessary to ensure that allocation of public housing is fair. There would be no logic in limiting the original allocation of public housing but allowing free transfer—and in fact all dealings are strictly controlled.

1. Prohibition on assignment and sub-letting

As a general principle, public sector secure tenancies are personal to the tenant and this is also true of equivalent tenancies where the tenant is not in residence.[2] Assignment is

---

[1] Woodfall 11.113–11.178; Bright & Gilbert 490–529; Davey 96–98; Evans & Smith (5th) 115–126.
[2] H.A. 1985 s.95; Woodfall 25.024–25.029,25.054–25.061; Davey 334–335.

prohibited in the case of any periodic tenancy and any fixed term tenancy granted after late 1982,[3] irrespective of the terms of the tenancy agreement. In *Burton* v. *Camden L.B.C.*[4] it was held that a joint tenancy which was affected by the statutory prohibition on assignment of public sector tenancies could not be turned into a sole secure tenancy by execution of a release. In simple terms the tenancy bore a label not transferable. Assignment connoted any transfer of a lease from one person to another. Thus a transaction which resulted in the transfer of the tenancy from T1 and T2 to T1 alone was an assignment, whatever its precise form.

2.   Lodgers and sub-tenants

All tenants have an implied right to share occupation with members of their family, such as a step-daughter and her boyfriend.[5] In addition, it is an implied term of every secure tenancy agreement that the tenant may take in lodgers.[6] Sub-letting of part may occur[7] but it requires the written consent (prospective or retrospective) of the landlord; consent is not to be unreasonably withheld, reasons must be given in writing, and the onus to show cause against allowing the transaction is cast onto the landlord.[8] Legitimate reasons would be overcrowding or work proposed by landlord. The tenancy will cease to be secure if the tenant parts with possession of the whole property.[9]

3.   Transfers

An existing tenant of a public sector landlord may wish to move to better accommodation still within the public sector—within England and Wales or (under regulations) to and from Scotland and Northern Ireland.[10]

A person who is already a secure tenant is not usually homeless,[11] unless, that is, his existing accommodation is so unsatisfactory that it is not reasonable to expect him to continue to live there. As usual this is judged in the context of the applicant's family grouping. One such case was *R.* v. *Islington L.B.C. ex parte B.*[12] where B had acted as a witness in a murder investigation and then suffered threats to such an extent that the police supported his request for a transfer. Although his application should have been treated as a Part III (homelessness) application rather than a Part II (transfer) application, judicial review was refused since this erroneous procedure had not had an adverse effect on the actual decision.

Local authorities are required to act under a housing management agreement,[13] but are largely left to develop their own policies after consultation, being free for example to

---

[3]   H.A. 1985 s.91; the exact date is November 5th 1982; *Peabody Donation Fund Governors* v. *Higgins* [1983] 1 W.L.R. 1091 C.A.; *Burton* v. *Camden L.B.C.* [2000] 1 All E.R. 943 H.L.

[4]   [2000] 1 All E.R. 943 H.L., Lord Millett dissenting; S. Bridge [2000] *Conv* 474.

[5]   *Blanway Investments Ltd.* v. *Lynch* (1993) 25 H.L.R. 378 C.A.

[6]   H.A. 1985 s.93(1)(a).

[7]   s.93(1)(b).

[8]   s.94.

[9]   s.93(2); *Hussey* v. *Camden L.B.C.* (1995) 27 H.L.R. 5 C.A. (sub-letting not proved).

[10]   S.I. 1996/2753 reg.3.

[11]   *R.* v. *Lambeth L.B.C. ex parte Pattinson* (1996) 28 H.L.R. 214, 217, Louis Blom-Cooper Q.C.; *R.* v. *Sefton M.B.C. ex parte Healiss* (1995) 27 H.L.R. 34 Q.B.D.

[12]   (1998) 30 H.L.R. 706; *R.* v. *Lambeth L.B.C. ex parte Woodburne* (1997) 29 H.L.R. 836.

[13]   H.A. 1985 s.27.

require rent arrears to be cleared before allowing a transfer.[14] However transfer policy is subject to public law control, so that reasons must be stated and a policy may be unlawful if it is too inflexible.[15] For example it is unlawful to adopt a rigid policy of downgrading an applicant after one refusal of an offer of accommodation irrespective of the circumstances.[16] Housing policies should be published, but care is needed because publication of a housing policy may raise a legitimate expectation that a particular decision will be made. For example a spouse left in a home after a matrimonial breakdown may acquire a legitimate expectation of becoming the sole tenant if the housing department applies for transfer of the tenancy to his sole name, and an eviction ignoring this legitimate expectation would be quashed.[17] A published policy will benefit any applicant and not just existing authorised residents.

4. Exchanges

This is a specialised form of transfer where homes are swapped between two public sector tenants. Exchanges are permitted with the written consent of the landlord,[18] the procedures being introduced to reduce the difficulty experienced by public sector tenants seeking to move. There remain the practical difficulties of finding a tenant willing to exchange and securing the consent of both landlords. Grounds for refusing consent[19] include there being grounds for repossession, that the accommodation is excessive when related to the proposed tenant's needs or because either property has been specially adapted. The observations above about transfer policies apply equally to exchanges.[20]

5. Matrimonial transfers and assignments to qualified successor

Special principles apply to death and divorce. Family proceedings often lead to an order that a secure tenancy should be transferred, for example if the couple divorce and the court orders the transfer of the tenancy to the parent who remains with the children; the landlord must respect any such order and allow a transfer.[21] Before the death of a tenant, there is no objection to an assignment of the secure tenancy to a person who will be qualified to succeed on the death of the existing tenant. Thus in *Peabody Donation Fund Governors* v. *Higgins,*[22] an assignment by father to daughter was not a ground for possession because the daughter was a qualified successor of the father.[23] Such an

---

[14] *R* v. *Islington L.B.C. ex parte Aldabbagh* (1995) 27 H.L.R. 271.

[15] At 276, Harrison J. (medical status should have been considered); *R.* v. *Lambeth L.B.C. ex parte Woodburne* (1997) 29 H.L.R. 836.

[16] *R.* v. *Wandsworth L.B.C. ex parte Lawrie* (1998) 30 H.L.R. 153.

[17] *R.* v. *Lambeth L.B.C. ex parte Trabi* (1998) 30 H.L.R. 975.

[18] H.A. 1985 s.92; refusal must occur within 42 days of a request for consent. The landlord may require arrears of rent and other breaches of covenant are made good, but other conditions are invalid.

[19] H.A. 1985 s.92, sch.3.

[20] *Ex parte Aldabbagh* as above.

[21] H.A. 1985 s.91(3)(a), (b).

[22] [1983] 1 W.L.R. 1091 C.A.; J.E. Martin [1985] *Conv.* 129.

[23] Action could be taken for the father's breach of covenant.

assignment uses up the one permitted succession.[24] But if the recipient is not qualified as a successor by residence the assignment is a ground for possession.[25]

B. PRIVATE SECTOR CONTROLS

Security of tenure requires both an authorised base—in the shape of a valid contractual letting—and authorised dealings from that base. Tenancies almost always restrict dealings, and thus leave the landlord with title paramount free to eject any occupier whom he has not authorised.[26] Existing rights to security cannot usually be passed to a later tenant chosen by the current one. The identity and character of the occupier are of vital importance to the landlord, who is fully entitled to keep control of dealings. Slight variations exist between the various legislative schemes and between the contractual and statutory phases of a tenancy.

1. Shortholds

A tenant holding a shorthold has strictly limited security: his entitlement is to occupy for an initial period of six months, after which he is vulnerable to eviction at any time with only a short warning period. Any transfer of a shorthold passes on these strictly limited rights,[27] but it would be rare for a shorthold tenant to have any right whatsoever to assign his tenancy.

2. Assured tenancies with a capital value

During a contractual period of an assured tenancy, free market theory applies. It is open to the landlord to demand a substantial premium when granting an assured tenancy, and if he does so, the tenancy will have a capital value, albeit one that wastes away throughout the term of the lease. The tenant must ensure that he is free to recoup his outlay by sale of his leasehold interest.[28] The most likely compromise will be that the tenant has a right to assign, but only with the consent of his landlord. Such a lease will operate much like a business lease—statute will imply a proviso that the consent of the landlord must not be unreasonably withheld, and procedural safeguards are imposed to ensure that the landlord acts promptly.[29]

3. Normal assured tenancies

Most assured tenancies are relatively short-term affairs, which are essentially personal in character, with the landlord retaining rigid control over sale and sub-letting. During a statutory continuation following the ending of the contractual term of an assured tenancy, a statutory periodic tenancy arises. The express prohibition is usually carried for-

[24] See above p. 116.
[25] *Croydon L.B.C.* v. *Buston* (1991) 24 H.L.R. 36 C.A. (mother left to live with new husband and assigned tenancy to daughter; possession ordered).
[26] J.E. Martin (1977) 41 *Conv. (N.S.)* 96; Woodfall 23.138–23.147, 24.036–24.038; Davey 257–258, 286.
[27] S. Bridge [1998] *Fam. Law* 26. Social sector tenants have no special rights: *Shorthold Tenant's Charter* (Housing Corporation, 1998).
[28] The restrictions outlined below will not apply: H.A. 1988 s.15(2).
[29] L.T.A. 1927 s.19; L.T.A 1988; see below pp. 291–293.

ward, but it will always be an implied term that consent is obtained from the landlord before any dealing, comprehending any assignment, sub-letting or parting with possession, and covering both the whole and parts. There is no requirement that the landlord should act reasonably.[30]

4.   Rent Act tenancies

Tenancies first granted before early 1989 continue to operate under the Rent Act, and it is also vital to know whether the arrangement is statutory or contractual. During a contractual phase the tenant holds a lease, which he can assign. Thus in *Thomas Pocklington's Gift Trustees* v. *Hill*[31] having decided that the tenancy remained contractual, the right to security was passed by an informal arrangement to assign, although many assignments fail because of the failure to reduce the arrangement to writing. *Crago* v. *Julian*[32] decides that strict legal formalities are necessary to transfer Rent Act protected tenancies or public sector secure tenancies,[33] a point overlooked in *Pocklington*.[34] Landlords generally ensured that onward transmissions of security were prevented by the inclusion of an absolute prohibition on assignments and sub-lettings. If so, any transfer of a short residential tenancy is unauthorised, if the landlord has not consented to it, and he can recover possession from the new tenant by virtue of his paramount title.[35]

Transfer of a Rent Act tenancy is not permitted during a statutory phase, since the tenant has no estate in the land but rather only a personal "status of irremovability" which is incapable of supporting a transfer. Statute allows[36] a transfer with the consent of the landlord and of any superior landlord. It is almost always unlawful to require a premium.[37]

5.   Private sector authorised dealings

Dealings may become authorised because permission for them is given in advance. Some tenancies may omit to impose restrictions on dealings, or they may permit dealings with the consent of the landlord, so that security of tenure can be transferred to a new tenant. Where permission is required, it may be given by the tenancy agreement or for a specific transaction.

Even though a dealing is initially unauthorised, the landlord may subsequently accept the new tenant or sub-tenant. While the lease remains contractual, this is equivalent to a waiver of a breach of covenant consisting of the unauthorised dealing so as to remove the threat of repossession. During the statutory phase of a Rent Act tenancy there is no lease and so no possibility of waiver, and given the seriousness of granting security to the

---

[30] H.A. 1988 s.15(1); L.T.A. 1927 s.19 (requiring reasonable grounds) is disapplied.

[31] (1989) 21 H.L.R. 391 C.A.; J.E. Martin [1989] *Conv.* 287.

[32] [1992] 1 W.L.R. 372 C.A.

[33] *Burton* v. *Camden L.B.C.* (1998) 30 H.L.R. 991 C.A., on appeal [2000] 1 All E.R. 943 H.L.

[34] *Crago* [1992] 1 W.L.R. 372, 378, Nicholls V.C.

[35] [1992] 1 W.L.R. 372, 378.

[36] R.A. 1977 sch.1 para.13; *Daejean Properties Ltd.* v. *Mahoney* (1996) 28 H.L.R. 498 C.A. (writing; agreement of commencement date; can be overcome by estoppel).

[37] R.A. 1977 s.120; but the landlord can recover the cost of structural alterations: *Steele* v. *McMahon* [1990] 2 E.G.L.R. 114 C.A.

sub-tenant, the courts require clear proof that the landlord has consented.[38] A landlord only becomes bound by an act which is a genuine recognition of the legitimacy of a transfer or sub-tenancy so that, for example, mistaken issue of a rent demand to a Rent Act tenant will not amount to a waiver of an unlawful sub-letting.[39]

C. SOCIAL SECTOR DEALINGS

Section 7 of the *Assured Tenant's Charter*[40] gives rights to a social tenant in relation to "Sharing or Passing on Your Home". These include the right to invite other people to move in without payment, provided that the property does not become overcrowded as a result; the landlord may only object with good reason. There is also the right to take on a lodger—that is a paying guest—to live in the home; again the landlord should not object without good reason. There is no charter right to sub-let, but most social tenants will have the rights of assured tenants that have already been discussed.[41] A social tenant who dies has the usual right of a private sector assured tenant to pass on the tenancy to his spouse or partner. There is also the right to exchange his home with another tenant of the same landlord, of another registered social landlord, or of a public sector landlord; all parties must agree and so must both landlords, though permission can only be refused with good reason.[42]

D. EXPRESS ABSOLUTE RESTRICTIONS

An absolute prohibition imposes a total bar on dealings by the tenant,[43] and this is normal in short tenancies of residential property.[44] Express restriction is needed, if not in the tenancy agreement then possibly in a rent book.[45] The apparent severity of total prohibition is tempered by the fact that the landlord may waive the restriction, so that an absolute bar on dealings really operates as a covenant not to deal without obtaining the landlord's permission to the particular dealing. But there is an enormous difference between a tenant who has a *right* to transfer, and one who has to go cap in hand to the landlord to beg for permission.[46] Apart from the statutory prohibition of sexually and racially discriminatory covenants,[47] there is no Parliamentary intervention in absolute covenants, so the landlord can act in his own interest without being required to act reasonably and there is nothing to compel procedural efficiency.[48]

---

[38] *Oak Property Co. Ltd.* v. *Chapman* [1947] K.B. 886; *Metropolitan Properties Co. Ltd.* v. *Cordery* (1979) 39 P. & C.R. 10 C.A. (porters warned to look out for new occupants so landlord bound); *Chrisdell Ltd.* v. *Johnson* [1987] 2 E.G.L.R. 123 C.A. (failure to evict for 10 years not waiver).

[39] *Henry Smith's Charity Trustees* v. *Willson* [1983] Q.B. 316 C.A.; J.E. Martin [1983] *Conv.* 248.

[40] (Housing Corporation, 1998) Section 7.

[41] See above pp. 288–289.

[42] Section 8.

[43] Woodfall 11.113–11.178; Bright & Gilbert 417–489; Davey 79–95; Evans & Smith (5th) 115–126; Garner 72–77.

[44] See below p. 730.

[45] *R. C. Glaze Properties Ltd.* v. *Alabdinboni* (1992) 25 H.L.R. 150 C.A.

[46] *F.W. Woolworth & Co. Ltd.* v. *Lambert* [1937] Ch. 37, 58–59, Romer L.J.

[47] See below p. 730.

[48] L.T.A. 1988 s.1(1)(b).

Residential landlords need comprehensive restrictions to cover all possible forms of transaction—assigning, sub-letting, and parting with possession of the premises comprised in the tenancy.[49] This last overcomes the problem that a covenant against assignment prevents only those assignments which are valid at law since it includes equitable dealings.[50] It is perfectly proper to impose absolute restrictions on physical division by sub-letting parts, given the substantial risk that a sub-tenant might acquire independent security of tenure.

E. QUALIFIED RIGHTS TO DEAL

Some residential tenants may be subject to a qualified restriction on dealings or, to put it another way, may have a qualified right to deal.[51] With an assured tenancy, there is nothing to prevent a landlord from demanding a substantial premium when granting an assured tenancy. If he does so, the tenancy will have a capital value that wastes away gradually throughout the term of the lease. The tenant must ensure that he is free to recoup his outlay by sale of his leasehold interest.[52] The most likely compromise will be the tenant has a right to assign,[53] but only with the consent of his landlord, the same balance that is reached in most business leases. It is a good balance because the landlord has scope to object to a buyer on the basis of his unsatisfactory financial status, while the tenant is free to sell his lease if he needs to do so. The tenant has some substantive and procedural protections.

1. Consents should not be a source of profit

Unless a tenancy agreement expressly provides to the contrary the landlord is not entitled to any premium for granting consent to an assignment, though he may charge his reasonable legal expenses.[54]

2. Implied obligation to act reasonably

Any tenancy, agreement or sub-tenancy[55] containing a qualified covenant against dealings has implied into it, by section 19(1) of the Landlord and Tenant Act 1927, a proviso that the landlord's consent is not to be unreasonably withheld. In fact this is usually anticipated by express provision. The qualification is of enormous practical significance in the commercial context and it may be as well to anticipate one of two points of the discussion contained below.[56]

The landlord may object on any of four broad grounds: undesirability of the proposed new tenant, control over changes of use, potential damage to the landlord's reversion, and the interests of estate management. Landlords are properly concerned to

---

[49] L.T.A. 1988 s.1(1)(a) (procedure); L.T.A. 1927 s.19 is similar.

[50] *Gentle* v. *Faulkner* [1900] 2 Q.B. 267 C.A.

[51] Woodfall 11.113–11.178; Bright & Gilbert 417–489; Davey 79–95; Evans & Smith (5th) 115–126; Garner 72–77.

[52] The restrictions outlined below will not apply: H.A. 1988 s.15(2).

[53] There may well be absolute prohibitions on other acts such as mortgaging or dividing the property.

[54] L.P.A. 1925 s.144.

[55] L.T.A. 1927 s.25(1).

[56] See below pp. 731–742.

ensure that a new tenant will pay the rent and service charges, and financial doubts are probably the most common ground for refusals. Awkwardness is not the same as undesirability.[57] Overwhelmingly the most important consideration for a landlord is to ensure that a dealing does not attract unwelcome security of tenure or new rights of enfranchisement[58] for the incoming tenant. These may reduce the value of the reversion, though the courts have given up the attempt to differentiate between "normal" and "abnormal" dealings.[59] The landlord can also object to transactions which confer new residential security of tenure directly[60] or indirectly,[61] or which may do so.[62] A company (which cannot enjoy statutory protection) may be prevented from transferring a tenancy to an individual director who could,[63] and the landlord is also entitled to prevent a transfer of staff accommodation from employees to outsiders.[64] Refusals on grounds of sex are prohibited by statute.[65] Race is another improper factor to consider, though the legislation[66] exempts a landlord of small premises if he or a near relative is sharing any accommodation.

The parties to a residential lease may require the landlord to allow transactions of a particular type, but they cannot impose tighter restrictions on the tenant since the statutory requirement to act reasonably applies "notwithstanding anything to the contrary" in the lease.[67] This prevents the landlord insisting upon an offer of a surrender of the tenancy before being allowed to transfer it.[68]

3. Procedural fairness

Delay in securing approval to a transaction often damns a tenant as much as an outright refusal. The Landlord and Tenant Act 1988[69] set out to remedy this defect in the machinery of qualified restrictions on dealings,[70] statutory and express.[71] Landlords are required to act promptly and to give reasons. In order to bring into play these duties, the tenant must serve a written request for permission to assign.[72] Otherwise the new

---

[57] A. Samuels [1982] *Conv.* 6.

[58] See below pp. 387–419.

[59] *West Layton Ltd.* v. *Ford* [1979] Q.B. 593 C.A.; *Brann* v. *Westminster Anglo-Continental Investment Co. Ltd.* [1976] 2 E.G.L.R. 72 C.A.

[60] *West Layton Ltd.* v. *Ford* [1979] Q.B. 593, 605, Roskill L.J.

[61] *Brann* v. *Westminster Anglo-Continental Investment Co. Ltd.* [1976] 2 E.G.L.R. 72, 74, Cairns L.J.

[62] *Pimms Ltd.* v. *Tallow Chandlers Co.* [1964] 2 Q.B. 547; *Bickel* v. *Duke of Westminster* [1977] Q.B. 517, 528F, Waller L.J.

[63] *Lee* v. *K. Carter Ltd.* [1949] 1 K.B. 85 C.A.; R.E. Megarry (1948) 63 *L.Q.R.* 453; *Swanson* v. *Forton* [1949] Ch. 143 C.A.

[64] *West Layton Ltd.* v. *Ford* [1979] Q.B. 593 C.A.

[65] Sex Discrimination Act 1975 s.31.

[66] Race Relations Act 1976 s.24.

[67] L.T.A. 1927 s.19(1).

[68] *Re Smith's Lease* [1951] 1 All E.R. 346, Roxburgh J.; E.O. Walford (1950) 14 *Conv. (N.S.)* 303; *Bocardo S.A.* v. *S. & M. Hotels Ltd.* [1980] 1 W.L.R. 17 C.A.; R. Sheldon & M. Friend (1982) 98 *L.Q.R.* 14; C.G. Blake [1980] *Conv.* 14.

[69] Law Com. No.141 (1985); see below pp. 731–742.

[70] "Covenant" includes condition or agreement: s.5(1); "lease" is also widely defined by s.5, though secure (public sector residential) tenancies are excluded.

[71] L.T.A. 1927 s.19. The 1988 Act (but not the 1927 one) applies to a term granting the head landlord control over the dealings of his sub-tenant.

[72] L.T.A. 1988 s.1(3).

tenant will be unauthorised, and the landlord will have the right to repossess the property for breach of the terms of the tenancy.

After a tenant serves a written application for consent, the landlord owes a duty to the tenant to serve[73] a written notice of decision on the tenant within a reasonable time.[74] In a dispute it is up to the landlord to show that he dealt with matters within a reasonable time. A written notice of decision must be given to the tenant, it must be given promptly, and it must contain reasons.[75] The landlord is under a duty to give consent unless it is reasonable not to do so,[76] and once more the onus rests on the landlord.

It is very important for the tenant to appreciate that delay by the landlord in giving his decision is *not* a deemed consent to a dealing. Rather he should seek an injunction or make a claim to damages.[77] If the landlord refuses consent unreasonably *after being asked for permission* the tenant may proceed anyway, since the transaction is not a breach of the tenancy agreement, though it would be very risky for a buyer to accept a lease on this basis; only if the money involved is small should the new tenant take upon himself this risk.

F. FORMALITY OF ASSIGNMENT

1. Formal

Even if a tenancy is created informally, formality is required for its assignment. In *Crago* v. *Julian*[78] an ex-wife stayed in a flat which had been rented in the sole name of her husband as contractual tenant.[79] Most unusually the tenancy allowed assignment, but unfortunately the assignment contemplated by the divorce agreement was never completed. The landlord succeeded in a repossession against her, since she was not a tenant and she had no matrimonial home right *after* the finalisation of their divorce. An assignment requires the use of a deed in order to effect a legal assignment,[80] a formality requirement wholly inappropriate for a short-term tenancy and one which is frequently overlooked—even by the courts.[81]

2. Informal

An equitable assignment should also be sufficient, as Parker L.J. recognised in *Croydon L.B.C.* v. *Buston*.[82] A secure tenant of a council flat remarried and moved out of the flat, thus losing protection, but afterwards his son claimed protection as an assignee.[83] Given

---

[73] s.5(2), using methods provided by the tenancy or by L.T.A. 1927 s.2.
[74] L.T.A. 1988 s.1(3); the duty is imposed by subs.(2) on the landlord, any superior landlord or mortgage-lender, those included in the s.5 definition, and also the Crown (s.6).
[75] s.1(3)(b).
[76] s.1(3)(a).
[77] s.4.
[78] [1992] 1 W.L.R. 372 C.A.; P. Sparkes [1992] *Conv.* 375.
[79] At 374A.
[80] L.P.A. 1925 s.52(1); *Crago* v. *Julian* [1992] 1 W.L.R. 372 C.A.; *Camden L.B.C.* v. *Alexandrou (No.2)* (1998) 30 H.L.R. 534 C.A.
[81] *Thomas Pocklington's Gift Trustees* v. *Hill* (1989) 21 H.L.R. 391 C.A.
[82] (1991) 24 H.L.R. 36 C.A.
[83] The son was a permitted assignee since he was qualified to succeed.

the absence of a written assignment, the son claimed that there had been an oral assignment in 1987 (under the pre-1989 contract formalities) supported by acts of part performance. Parker L.J. said that that would be a good claim if it could be proved, though
on the facts there was actually no agreement to assign.[84] *Crago* v. *Julian* looked only at
the position of an assignee of a Rent Act protected tenancy at common law and may be
open to question in equity.[85]

A surrender requires the participation and consent of the landlord and so it can be
effected by an informal letter. Very often the practical effect is an informal transfer. For
example, in *Camden L.B.C.* v. *Alexandrou (No.2)*[86] the marriage of a secure tenant broke
down in 1982, whereupon he wrote to say that he was no longer able to pay rent but he
had no objection to his wife remaining behind and paying rent. This was not a legal
assignment, but it was an offer to surrender, which was completed by regrant to the former wife.

3.   Sub-tenancy which disposes of entire term

A sub-tenancy must leave a reversion for the sub-landlord—that is some time when the
sub-tenancy will end and the sub-landlord will become entitled to possession of the
property as tenant under the head lease. This is not the case where an attempt is made
to sub-let land for longer than the remaining term of the head lease, and therefore such
a transaction is treated as intended to effect an assignment of the head term. The two
leading cases discussed in the commercial context[87] are *Milmo* v. *Carreras*[88] and *Parc
(Battersea) Ltd.* v. *Hutchinson.*[89] The latter case confirms that a short oral sub-tenancy
may be effective as a legal assignment without a deed.

G.   RUNNING OF COVENANTS BETWEEN TENANTS

A standard terminology is adopted throughout this book:

This indicates that the current landlord (LC) is seeking to enforce the terms of a residential tenancy against the current tenant (TC) who has acquired the tenancy via the
original tenant (T0) and various intermediate tenants (T1 etc). As one would expect,
after a tenant has taken a transfer of a lease, he is required for the future to pay the rent
for the use of the land and to carry out the other covenants in the lease.

---

[84] At 38.
[85] P. Sparkes [1992] *Conv.* 375.
[86] (1998) 30 H.L.R. 534 C.A.
[87] See below p. 725.
[88] [1946] K.B. 306 C.A.; (1946) 62 *L.Q.R.* 212.
[89] [1999] 2 E.G.L.R. 33, 36–37, Moore-Bick J.; S. Murdoch [1999] 24 *E.G.* 154; *Stretch* v. *West Dorset D.C.* [1998]
3 E.G.L.R. 62 C.A.

1. New tenancies

The Landlord and Tenant (Covenants) Act 1995[90] applies to "new tenancies" freshly granted after the Act came into force on January 1st 1996, here described as post-1995 tenancies. It applies to informal tenancies in just the same way as formal leases, and whether assignments are formal or informal. Both the benefit and the burden of the obligations in the lease are made to run by the Act, so that the current tenant pays the rent, and the current landlord collects it.[91] This liability of TC applies to all terms of the tenancy for the duration of his ownership, but when the tenancy is passed on this passes the benefit and burden of all covenants to the new tenant, binding him immediately.[92] A fundamental reform in 1995 was to apply the law to *all* terms of new tenancies as a single package, though excluding terms expressed to be personal and options void for non-registration.

Authorised assignments are ones permitted, either by the terms of the lease or by a consent given by the landlord in the particular case. The effect is to release the former tenant from liability for all covenants, including any that are personal. Releases operate prospectively from the date of the sale, leaving existing arrears and defaults unaffected.[93] A transfer of residential premises will often constitute an "excluded assignment",[94] either because it is a transmission by operation of law or because the assignment is in breach of the terms of the tenancy. In these cases liability is attached to the new tenant but there is no release until the next properly authorised transfer; both will be freed, prospectively,[95] after the next non-excluded assignment.[96]

Commercial leases may require that the assigning tenant should guarantee the performance of the terms until the next sale, but there is no means for a landlord of residential premises to insist on such an authorised guarantee agreement.[97]

2. Old privity of estate

"Old tenancies" are tenancies created before 1996 and also any granted after 1995 under pre-Act contracts or options[98] to which the old law of the running of covenants will continue to apply.[99] Legislative provisions do not apply to the passage of obligations between tenants, but *Spencer's case*[100] ensures that an action can be taken against the current tenant. Liability for privity of estate depends, as its name suggests, upon holding the legal estate. It was restricted by analogy by the Grantees of Reversion Act 1540 (which passed covenants between landlords as opposed to tenants) to legal leases. The suggestion of an even tighter restriction to leases by deed was surely incorrect—if this

---

[90] Discussed in full in the commercial context: see below Chapter 28.
[91] L.T. (Covenants) A. 1995 ss.1–2.
[92] s.3(2); a personal waiver or release is disregarded: s.3(4).
[93] s.24(1).
[94] s.11(1); the "or" should read "and".
[95] s.24(3).
[96] s.11(2).
[97] See below pp. 779–780.
[98] s.1 (contracts, court orders and options).
[99] Woodfall 11.048A–11.075; Evans & Smith (5th) 77–88; Garner (2nd) 112–129.
[100] (1585) 5 Co. Rep. 16a, 77 E.R. 72.

was the case there was nothing to make a new tenant liable on the terms of an informally created tenancy. A previous tenant can get out of the landlord's way by an assignment—even one in breach of covenant.[101] The old law was restricted to core covenants—those that touch and concern the land—but this matters little since all terms of residential tenancy agreements are likely to form part of that core.[102] It might also be possible for the current landlord (LC) to take action against the original tenant (T0) on privity of contract, though intermediate tenants are not liable.[103]

H. AUTHORISED SUB-TENANCIES

1. Security of tenure

All security regimes define the scope of the leases protected so as to encompass sub-leases.[104] So security of tenure is attracted if the sub-letting is lawful.[105] If it is of part, it is essential to show that the sub-tenant has exclusive rights to self-contained accommodation.[106] When sub-letting part, the *tenant* needs to be careful to ensure that his security is not threatened by ceasing to occupy self-contained accommodation. However this is made less likely by a special dispensation: provided the tenant retains some exclusive accommodation, his security is allowed to continue even though he is sharing some accommodation with his sub-tenant.[107]

2. Nature

A grant of a head lease arises where a freehold owner creates a lease of his land when it is devoid of any letting. A sub-lease[108] is created, using normal leasehold formalities,[109] where the person granting the lease is a leasehold estate owner rather than a freeholder. Assuming that exclusive possession of the land (or any part of it) has been given, and that the sub-landlord retains a reversion, there is a sub-tenancy.[110] Two separate leasehold relationships are created: the person creating the lease can be seen to occupy a dual position, as tenant under the head lease and as landlord under the sub-lease,[111] the freeholder being referred to as a head landlord, and the ultimate tenant as the sub-tenant.[112] Thus:

---

[101] *Paul* v. *Nurse* (1828) 8 B. & C. 486, 108 E.R. 1123. This would render the lease liable to forfeiture.
[102] See below pp. 765–772.
[103] See below pp. 760–761.
[104] R.A. 1977 s.152 (Rent Act); H.A. 1988 ss.18, 45 (assured); H.A. 1985 s.621 (secure).
[105] *Roe* v. *Russell* [1928] 2 K.B. 117, 131, Sargant J.
[106] *Fredco Estates Ltd.* v. *Bryant* [1961] 1 All E.R. 34 C.A.
[107] R.A. 1977 s.22(3); *Regalian Securities Ltd.* v. *Ramsden* [1981] 1 W.L.R. 611 H.L.; *Herbert* v. *Byrne* [1964] 1 W.L.R. 519 C.A.
[108] Woodfall 16.081–16.087.
[109] See above Chapter 2.
[110] *Brent L.B.C.* v. *Cronin* (1998) 30 H.L.R. 43 C.A.
[111] i.e. as head tenant and sub-landlord.
[112] The older terminology was head-lessor, head-lessee, sub-lessor and sub-lessee respectively.

HL

|

HT/SL

|

ST

Sub-letting can be repeated to create chains of three[113] or more leases, and the process is theoretically infinite, but there are practical restraints on the manageable number of relationships.

3. Sub-tenants—running of covenants

Since two tenancies are created, there is no direct relationship between the head landlord and the sub-tenant, so that the one cannot sue the other for rent. This was true of the old law—there was no privity of estate[114]—and is also true of the new law under the Landlord and Tenant (Covenants) Act 1995.[115] This does not mean that a sub-tenant can flout the terms affecting the head lease.[116] A sub-tenant can be made liable to pay rent by a rent diversion notice.[117] If no such notice has been served a sub-tenant must be wary of paying rent to the head landlord, since the rent under the two leases are different debts, and there will usually be no restitutionary reimbursement.[118]

4. Control of private sector sub-letting

Security can be created by a sub-letting during a contractual phase of a Rent Act tenancy or throughout an assured tenancy.[119] It is vital that the landlord asserts and maintains control over the identity of the occupier to prevent this happening, either by prohibiting all sub-leases[120] or by imposing tight restrictions on what form of sub-letting is permitted.[121] Any authorised sub-letting will not attract security.[122] Sub-tenancies of part are almost always unauthorised, but it is necessary to state this explicitly since a covenant against sub-letting the whole may not operate on parts.[123]

---

[113] The ultimate tenant is described in this book as a sub-under-tenant.

[114] *Hall* v. *Ewin* (1887) 37 Ch.D. 74 C.A.; *South of England Dairies Ltd.* v. *Baker* [1906] 2 Ch. 631, Joyce J.

[115] s.3 applies to *assignments*.

[116] See below pp. 762–763.

[117] See above p. 220.

[118] See below pp. 788–790.

[119] The tenant holds no estate in the land during a statutory phase, and so is incapable of creating a sub-lease: *Leith Properties Ltd.* v. *Byrne* [1983] Q.B. 433 C.A.; J.E. Martin [1983] *Conv.* 155.

[120] *R.C. Glaze Properties Ltd.* v. *Alabdinboni* (1992) 25 H.L.R. 150 C.A. (term of rent book).

[121] Covenant only to allow high class furnished sub-letting; held to be unauthorised: *Patoner Ltd.* v. *Alexandrakis* [1984] 2 E.G.L.R. 124 C.A.; *Patoner Ltd.* v. *Lowe* [1985] 2 E.G.L.R. 155.

[122] R.A. 1977 s.137(2); *Henry Smith's Charity Trustees* v. *Willson* [1983] Q.B. 316 C.A.; J.E. Martin [1983] *Conv.* 248. At the end of a long tenancy: see subs.(5); and in relation to furniture and services see s.138.

[123] *Esdaile* v. *Lewis* [1956] 1 W.L.R. 709 C.A.; R.E. Megarry (1956) 72 *L.Q.R.* 35.

5.   Public sector sub-letting

A tenancy ceases to be secure if the tenant parts with possession of the whole property.[124] The sub-tenancy will usually be unauthorised so that the sub-tenant could also be evicted. Sub-letting of part may occur[125] but only with the written consent (prospective or retrospective) of the landlord; consent is not to be unreasonably withheld, reasons must be given in writing, and the onus to show cause against allowing the transaction is cast onto the landlord.[126] Legitimate reasons would be overcrowding or interference with work proposed by landlord. Public sector tenants have rights to share with partners and family members and to take in paying lodgers.

6.   Extraction of commercial value from the land

One problem for a head landlord is that a sub-tenancy may extract commercial value from the land—when a tenant grants a sub-lease at a premium or when he later agrees to commute (that is reduce) the rent in return for a capital payment. Tenants should be prohibited from sub-letting on these terms, and the covenant also needs to cover payments for accepting a surrender.[127]

Under an assured tenancy it is necessary to control sub-letting by covenants in the lease, as otherwise security will attach to a sub-tenant. But under the Rent Act an additional discretionary ground for possession is available under Case 6 even though the sub-lease is authorised.[128] It applies [129] "where, without the consent of the landlord, the tenant has . . . assigned or sublet the whole of the dwelling-house . . .".[130] Case 6 is probably designed to prevent commercial exploitation of the Rent Act[131]—operating only when an excessive rent is charged on a sub-lease so draining economic value from the landlord's reversion, but it is arguable that it is also available more generally to safeguard the landlord's right to choose the next tenant.[132]

I.   PRESERVATION OF SUB-TENANCIES

An authorised sub-tenancy for residential[133] purposes survives the termination of the head tenancy.

---

[124]   H.A. 1985 s.93(2); *Hussey* v. *Camden L.B.C.* (1995) 27 H.L.R. 5 C.A. (sub-letting not proved).

[125]   s.93(1)(b).

[126]   s.94.

[127]   *Associated Newspaper Properties Ltd.* v. *Drapers Co.* [1997] 1 E.G.L.R. 88 C.A.

[128]   If the sub-tenancy is unauthorised the landlord will be able to seek repossession on the breach of other obligation ground.

[129]   R.A. 1977 sch.15; R.E. Megarry, *Rent Acts* (Stevens, 11th ed., 1988) 412–416.

[130]   Case 6, like its predecessors, applies even though there is no covenant against assignment: *Regional Properties Co. Ltd.* v. *Franskenschwerth* [1951] 1 K.B. 631; *Hyde* v. *Pimley* [1952] 2 Q.B. 506; *Pazgate Ltd.* v. *McGrath* (1984) 17 H.L.R. 127.

[131]   R.E. Megarry's *Rent Acts* (11th ed. as above) 415.

[132]   *Pazgate Ltd.* v. *McGrath* (1984) 17 H.L.R. 127, 134, Fox L.J.; J.E. Martin [1985] *Conv.* 353.

[133]   Contrast the rules for commercial leases discussed in *Barrett* v. *Morgan* [2000] 1 All E.R. 481 H.L. and below at pp. 618–621. In that context a distinction is drawn between surrenders (on which sub-leases are preserved) and hostile termination by notice to quit (which can destroy a sub-lease).

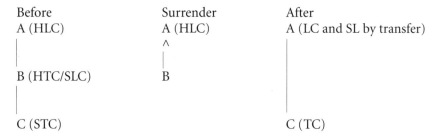

Before	Surrender	After
A (HLC)	A (HLC)	A (LC and SL by transfer)
B (HTC/SLC)	B	
C (STC)		C (TC)

1. Surrender

Statute has long ago adopted Coke's view[134] that a sub-tenancy is preserved on a surrender.[135] All parties with derivative interests are put in the same position as if no surrender had occurred,[136] so a surrender has to be treated as a transfer.[137] With a sub-tenancy the next interest moves up to form the reversion.[138] This facilitates contractual extensions, rent reviews, variations of terms, and regrants,[139] and it may also create new public sector residential security of tenure.[140] Problems may arise if the sub-tenancy is only of part.

2. Assured tenancies

In the case of a sub-tenancy operating under the assured regime (after early 1989) the assurance will continue on termination of the head-lease, the former sub-tenant holding directly from the new superior landlord.[141] An assured tenancy cannot be broken by the grant of a reversionary lease, that is a lease placed between the original landlord and the original assured tenant.[142]

3. Rent Act tenancies

The statutory provisions relating to Rent Act sub-tenancies are similar in effect if less neat in execution.[143] Security of tenure for a *lawful* sub-tenant survives termination of the head lease, subject to any mandatory ground for possession. After the end of the head lease the sub-tenant holds directly from the landlord, either a contractual or

---

[134] Coke on *Littleton* 338.

[135] L.T.A. 1730 s.6; now L.P.A. 1925 s.150; *Ecclesiastical Commissioners for England* v. *Treemer* [1893] 1 Ch. 166, 172, Chitty J.

[136] *Doe d. Palk* v. *Marchetti* (1831) 1 B. & Ad. 715, 109 E.R. 953.

[137] N. Hopkins [1996] *Conv.* 284.

[138] Real Property Act 1845 s.9; now L.P.A. 1925 s.139; *London Regional Transport* v. *Brandt* (1997) 29 H.L.R. 193 C.A.; *Barrett* v. *Morgan* [2000] 1 All E.R. 481, 485h, Lord Millett.

[139] *Pleasant d. Hayton* v. *Benson* (1811) 14 East. 234, 104 E.R. 590 (notice had to be in the tenant's name!); *Doe d. Beadon* v. *Pyke* (1816) 5 M. & S. 146, 105 E.R. 1005; *Mellor* v. *Watkins* (1874) L.R. 9 Q.B. 400; *Parker* v. *Jones* [1910] 2 K.B. 32 (even if sub-tenancy unlawful).

[140] *Basingstoke & Deane B.C.* v. *Paice* [1995] 2 E.G.L.R. 9 C.A.

[141] H.A. 1988 s.18(1), unless the new landlord is outside the assured tenancy scheme (e.g. the Crown).

[142] s.18(3), (4).

[143] R.A. 1977 s.137.

statutory tenancy according to the nature of his sub-tenancy.[144] The sub-tenant is required to notify the head landlord of the onset of protection.[145]

4.   Rent Act sub-tenancies of part of commercial premises

Suppose that there is a lease of a shop and flat together granted to a *business* tenant, who then sub-lets the self-contained flat to a *residential* occupier. Residential security cannot accrue if the sub-tenant qualifies for a renewable business lease, so here[146] we are concerned solely with sub-leases of residential parts. When the lease of the shop is surrendered can the sub-tenant stay on? Clearly the answer should be yes if the sub-tenancy was authorised, and otherwise it should be no, but the law has become horribly complicated as a result of case-law explication.

Tremendous problems were created in the past about how to bring together the principles applying on a surrender with the basic rule that residential security required a property "let as a separate dwelling".[147] In *Cow* v. *Casey*[148] the Court of Appeal laid down that a residential sub-tenant could not be protected unless the head tenant was also protected. In that case the rent was such that the head tenancy was a luxury letting, and this fact also destroyed the security of the sub-tenant. A formidable body of case law derives from this, particularly the decision of the majority of the House of Lords in *Maunsell* v. *Olins*. Lord Wilberforce said[149] that a sub-tenant was only protected if the premises contained in the head lease formed a dwelling; hence a residential sub-tenant lost protection because his landlord was an agricultural tenant. This led the Court of Appeal in *Pittalis* v. *Grant*[150] to refuse protection to a sub-tenant of a flat above a shop simply because the head lease included commercial premises. Similarly, in *Bromley Park Garden Estates Ltd.* v. *George*,[151] it was held that a residential sub-tenant was not protected on a surrender of the commercial head lease. Finally in *London Regional Transport* v. *Brandt*[152] a flat was sub-let to Brandt, but his tenancy had no residential security because he was renting from Medici, a business tenant. After surrender of the business tenancy, he was left without any protection.

The inconvenience and injustice of these decisions is obvious, and in fact Parliament has reversed them. The leading case, *Maunsell* v. *Olins*, was overruled by legislation geared directly to farmhouses sub-let on agricultural holdings.[153] However it now appears that there has been a much more general reversal, so that any sub-letting of a

---

[144] s.137(2); *John Lyon's Free Grammar School Governors* v. *James* [1995] 4 All E.R. 740 C.A. (the defendant is given as *Jordan* at (1995) 27 H.L.R. 727 C.A.); s.138 applies where the head lease is unfurnished and the sub-lease is furnished.

[145] s.139 (14 days' notice).

[146] See below Chapter 27.

[147] R.A. 1977 s.1(1) and earlier versions.

[148] [1949] 1 K.B. 474 C.A.; R.E. Megarry (1949) 65 *L.Q.R.* 166; *Knightsbridge Estates Trust Ltd.* v. *Deeley* [1950] 2 K.B. 228; *Cadogan* v. *Henthorne* [1957] 1 W.L.R. 1.

[149] [1975] A.C. 373, 388–389; (1975) 91 L.Q.R. 163; The law has now been changed.

[150] [1989] Q.B. 605 C.A.; C.P. Rodgers [1990] *Conv.* 204; J.E. Martin [1989] *N.L.J.* 1260. The C.A. decided that L.P.A. 1925 s.139 had not been overlooked in *Cow*.

[151] [1991] 2 E.G.L.R. 95 C.A.; P.F. Smith [1991] *Conv.* 393; *London Regional Transport* v. *Brandt* (1997) 29 H.L.R. 193 C.A.

[152] (1997) 29 H.L.R. 193 C.A.

[153] A.H.A. 1986 sch.14; *Pennell* v. *Payne* [1995] Q.B. 192 C.A.

residential unit is protected, even if the premises in the head lease were commercial or non-protected for some other reason. *Wellcome Trust Ltd.* v. *Hamad*[154] concerned the simple facts outlined above: a sub-tenancy of a flat above a shop. The Court of Appeal recognised that a Rent Act sub-tenant has security against eviction on the termination of a commercial head lease. It is treated as if there were separate leases of the business part and of the dwelling contained in the sub-lease.[155] When the business lease is ended, the residential sub-tenancy is continued and acts as a direct lease from the original land-lord. Security of tenure is available if there was exclusive occupation of self-contained accommodation and no other special factor (such as a holiday letting) to limit security. This is the simple and natural interpretation of the Rent Act provisions applied in the *Wellcome Trust* case. When Leggatt L.J. refused to follow *Pittalis* it was because the ear-lier case did not explore inconsistent case law on the principles underlying Lord Wilberforce's opinion in *Maunsell*[156] and because of a failure to explore the history of the statutory precursors of the modern Rent Act[157] and also because of the failure to consider the proviso to the current provision.[158] *Wellcome* has been reinforced by *Laimond Properties Ltd.* v. *Al-Shakarchi*.[159] In that case the head tenancy was an assured tenancy whereas the sub-tenancy was granted before early 1989; the fact that the head tenancy was outside the Rent Act scheme was held, in an obiter discussion, to have no adverse effect on the Rent Act protection of the sub-tenant. The flat comprised in the sub-tenancy must be let as a separate dwelling, but if so the protection of section 137(3) is a stand-alone provision.

Technically there may be two inconsistent lines of Court of Appeal authority, and the point is anyway open in the Lords, but the decision in *Wellcome* is well named and it must be hoped that it will now be followed.

J.   UNAUTHORISED SUB-TENANCIES

1.   Absolute restrictions

An absolute prohibition on dealing is normal in short tenancies of residential premises.[160] Any restriction needs to be express, for example in the tenancy agreement or possibly in the rent book.[161] It should cover sub-letting,[162] physical divisions by deal-ings with part of the land, charging, and also parting with possession of the dwelling (to catch licences[163]). Any apparent severity is tempered by the fact that the landlord may

---

[154] [1998] Q.B. 638 C.A.; A. Cafferkey [1999] *Conv.* 232; T. Blackburn [1998] 6 *P.L.J.* 8; three cases were reported together, the others being *Ebied* v. *Hopkins* and *Church Commissioners for England* v. *Baines.*

[155] R.A. 1977 s.137(3); *Boston Capital Ltd.* v. *Chee-a-Tow* [2000] 09 C.L. 472.

[156] At 649–653; *Epsom Grand Stand Association Ltd.* v. *Clarke* (1919) 35 T.L.R. 525; *Hicks* v. *Snooks* (1928) 27 L.G.R. 175; *Vickery* v. *Martin* [1944] K.B. 679; *Wolfe* v. *Hogan* [1949] 2 K.B. 194; *Feyereisel* v. *Turnridge* [1952] 2 Q.B. 29; *Whiteley* v. *Wilson* [1953] 1 Q.B. 77; *Cheryl Investments Ltd.* v. *Saldanha* [1978] 1 W.L.R. 1327, 1331–1332.

[157] At 656; Increase of Rent and Mortgage Interest (Restrictions) Act 1920 s.15(3); H. Repairs and Rents Act 1954 s.41; R.A. 1977 s.137(3).

[158] At 657A–B; R.A. 1977 s.24(3) proviso.

[159] (1998) 30 H.L.R. 1099; J. Martin [1999] *Conv.* 248; S. Murdoch [1999] 14 *E.G.* 148.

[160] See above pp. 290–291.

[161] *R. C. Glaze Properties Ltd.* v. *Alabdinboni* (1992) 25 H.L.R. 150 C.A.

[162] For case law on whether this is covered by a restriction on assignment see below p. 726.

[163] D.G. Barnsley (1963) 27 *Conv. (N.S.)* 159, 170–175.

waive the restriction, so that an absolute prohibition on dealings really operates as a promise not to deal without obtaining the landlord's permission to the particular dealing. Sexually and racially discriminatory covenants are barred, but otherwise there is no Parliamentary intervention in absolute covenants, so the landlord can act in his own interest, and is not required to act reasonably.[164] There is no requirement of procedural efficiency.[165]

2.   The position of the head landlord

A residential tenancy provides no protection against a title paramount, that is a person who is entitled to say that the tenancy should not have been granted. Apart from lenders (considered in a later section[166]) others with paramount titles may be head landlords objecting to a sub-tenant or true owners objecting to the grant of a tenancy by an interloper. These two categories blur into one as a result of the conflation achieved in *Bruton v. London & Quadrant Housing Trust.*[167] A local authority acquired a block of flats in Brixton under compulsory powers with a view to redevelopment. Statutory rules operated to prevent the creation of any tenancies by the authority, any attempt to do so being null and void.[168] Instead the authority granted a licence to use the block for housing homeless people to a charitable housing trust in order that they could provide short-term accommodation. One person who secured exclusive use of a flat on a weekly basis in this way was Bruton. The case concerns the position as between him and the Trust, his immediate landlord, but the predominance of the local authority's title and its right to evict Bruton was recognised by Millett L.J. in the Court of Appeal,[169] and also by implication when the case reached the Lords.[170]

3.   The position between sub-landlord and sub-tenant

What actually happened in *Bruton* was that the redevelopment proposals were dropped and Bruton ended up living in unsatisfactory conditions for more than six years. Eventually he argued that the Trust that had rented him a room in Oval house was in breach of its statutory repairing obligation,[171] an argument which could succeed only if he could show that he was a tenant of the property. Lord Hoffmann held that a tenancy had been created between the trust (the sub-landlord) and Bruton (the sub-tenant) since he had been granted exclusive possession of land.[172] However in the coda to his speech, Lord Hoffmann turned to address Millett L.J.'s judgment based on the existence of a tenancy by estoppel.

---

[164] *Property & Bloodstock Ltd.* v. *Emerton* [1968] Ch. 94, 119G–120A Danckwerts L.J. has not been followed: *Bocardo S.A.* v. *S. & M. Hotels Ltd.* [1980] 1 W.L.R. 17, 22, Megaw L.J., 26G, Browne L.J.; *Guardian Assurance Co. Ltd.* v. *Gants Hill Holdings Ltd.* [1983] 2 E.G.L.R. 36, 37B, Mervyn Davies J.; *Vaux Group Ltd.* v. *Lilley* [1991] 1 E.G.L.R. 60, Knox J.

[165] L.T.A. 1988 s.1(1)(b).

[166] See below pp. 306–307.

[167] [2000] A.C. 406 H.L.; S. Murdoch [1999] 30 *E.G.* 90; S. Jones [1998] 2 *P.L.J.* 3; S. Bright (2000) 116 *L.Q.R.* 7.

[168] H.A. 1985 s.32(3); disposals of land acquired for redevelopment required the consent of the Secretary of State; see also Stretch v. *West Dorset D.C.* [1998] 3 E.G.L.R. 62 C.A. (no power to grant option for renewal).

[169] [1998] Q.B. 834, 846D.

[170] [2000] A.C. 406 H.L.

[171] L.T.A. 1985 s.11; see above pp. 243–246.

[172] *Street* v. *Mountford* [1985] A.C. 809 H.L.; see above Chapter 6.

A landlord may have sufficient factual control to be able to grant away undisturbed occupation of land that he does not own. Such a grant cannot create an estate in the land because one cannot give what one does not hold; *nemo dat quod non habet*. Nevertheless it operates as a valid grant of a tenancy as between the parties to it. A tenant is not permitted to dispute that his landlord is indeed his landlord and has title to make a grant, and a similar principle binds the landlord.[173] If the lease is by deed, this is a true estoppel but otherwise there is a corresponding implied rule of law. Usually tenancies by estoppel arise in relation to commercial premises where they are discussed more fully.[174] It had long been thought that a tenancy by estoppel was within the private sector security legislation[175] and *Bruton* confirms just that.

Millett L.J.[176] held that a lease must be a legal estate in the land that binds the whole world unless there is a tenancy by estoppel. No estoppel arose in his view unless the grantor purported to grant a lease,[177] whereas what the defendant Trust had actually purported to do was to grant a licence. Lord Hoffmann demolished this argument. He used the term tenancy to describe a relationship between two parties who are designated landlord and tenant, it being immaterial whether it creates an estate or proprietary interest which may be binding on a third party. The fact that an agreement is characterised as a lease is what creates a proprietary interest when the landlord does have a sufficient estate to support a grant.[178] Tenancy by estoppel describes an agreement not otherwise a lease or tenancy that is, however, treated as one by virtue of the estoppel. Lord Hoffmann cited the example of *Morton* v. *Woods*[179] in which an estoppel arose against a borrower who attorned tenant to a second mortgage-lender, where the legal estate was outstanding in the hands of a first mortgage lender but the estoppel made it irrelevant that he held no legal estate. *Bruton* was a case of an agreement that did create a tenancy and one which is properly called a tenancy even if the landlord lacked the legal estate. In any event, Lord Hoffmann thought that there was an inconsistency between what the trust purported to do and its denial of the tenancy, so that there was indeed a true estoppel.

K. DEALINGS WITH THE LANDLORD'S REVERSION

1. Transfer (assignment of the reversion)

Where the landlord's interest is sold subject to a lease, it is traditional to refer to an "assignment" of the reversion[180] though in this book it is referred to as a transfer (or a sale) of the reversion. A deed is required for a legal transfer,[181] as well as land

---

[173] *E.H. Lewis & Son Ltd.* v. *Morelli* [1948] 2 All E.R. 1021, 1024–1025 Harman J. in C.A.

[174] *Harrison* v. *Wells* [1967] 1 Q.B. 263 C.A.; *Industrial Properties (Barton Hill) Ltd.* v. *Associated Electrical Industries Ltd.* [1977] Q.B. 580 C.A.; *National Westminster Bank Ltd.* v. *Hart* [1983] Q.B. 773 C.A.; *Bell* v. *General Accident Fire & Life Assurance Corporation Ltd.* [1998] 1 E.G.L.R. 69 C.A.; see below pp. 565–566.

[175] *Stratford* v. *Syrett* [1958] 1 Q.B. 107 C.A.

[176] [1998] Q.B. 834, 845; S. Bright (1998) 114 *L.Q.R.* 345.

[177] *Lewisham B.C.* v. *Roberts* [1949] 2 K.B. 608, 622, Denning L.J. (requisition).

[178] [2000] A.C. 406, 415B–H; *Family H.Ass.* v. *Jones* [1990] 1 W.L.R. 779 C.A. approved.

[179] (1869) L.R. 4 Q.B. 293 Ex.Ch.

[180] Woodfall 16.037–16.040; parties are the assignor (seller) and assignee (buyer).

[181] *Brawley* v. *Wade* (1824) M'Clel. 664, 148 E.R. 278, Hullock B.

registration formalities where appropriate; if title is unregistered a transfer will often trigger first registration.[182] The tenant cannot generally control the identity of his landlord (except in the case of the right of pre-emption for tenants of a residential block of flats[183]) but the landlord who is selling needs to implement the statutory procedure described below to free himself of liability on the covenants after the sale has been completed.[184] The buyer also needs to ensure that he gives notice of his identity before he can collect rent.[185]

2. Collecting the rent

It is the current landlord who is able to enforce the covenants in a tenancy agreement. Action may be brought by the person who can show title to the immediate reversionary estate—for example by transfer,[186] under an Act,[187] or by estoppel.[188]

Statutory provisions[189] pass the right to collect rent and the benefit of the tenant's covenants to the current landlord, and these apply to formal leases, informal tenancies and to equitable leases. The old law passed existing arrears of rent, but these will not pass automatically under the new law, but require separate assignment.[190]

3. Burdens

If the tenant wishes to enforce the landlord's obligations for quiet enjoyment or repair, he will be able to sue the current landlord.[191] Under old tenancies it was possible to sue the original landlord (L0) at any time during the term, but this liability is abolished for new tenancies; instead (under the new law) the previous reversioner remains liable unless he applies to be released.[192]

4. Transfer of part

Landlords have a simple method of splitting the reversion so as to create two separate leases, which occurs if part of the land is sold.[193] A transfer to a nominee for himself also works. The covenants run to benefit each part. Section 140 of the Law of Property Act

---

[182] That is if the reversion is freehold or a legal lease with 21 years outstanding.
[183] See below pp. 426–432.
[184] See below pp. 748–749.
[185] See above p. 243.
[186] *Davis* v. *James* (1884) 26 Ch.D. 778; *Pledge & Sons* v. *Pomfret* (1905) 74 L.J.Ch. 357; *Harris* v. *Beavan* (1828) 4 Bing. 646, 130 E.R. 918.
[187] *Sutherland Orphan Asylum* v. *River Wear Commissioners* [1912] 1 Ch. 191; *Halifax* v. *Coal Commissioners* [1945] Ch. 253.
[188] *Cuthbertson* v. *Irving* (1860) 6 H. & N. 135, 158 E.R. 56.
[189] L.P.A. 1925 s.141 (old law); L.T. (Covenants) A. 1995 ss.1–2 (post-1995 tenancies).
[190] L.P.A. 1925 s.141 and case law discussed below at pp. 753–754; L.T. (Covenants) A. 1995 s.23(2).
[191] L.P.A. 1925 s.142; L.T. (Covenants) A. 1995 ss.3(3), 24.
[192] L.T. (Covenants) A. 1995 ss.6–8; S.I. 1995/2964 forms 3–6; notice is also required by L.T.A. 1985 s.3(3A).
[193] L.P.A. 1925 s.140(3).

1925 permits the severance of a holding into its several parts, each part being treated as if originally comprised in a separate tenancy, meaning that a notice to quit can be served affecting each individual part. A commercial landlord is able to sever off parts of the property which will not in isolation attract security of tenure and shave these off the tenant's protected holding.[194] However, the position with residential property is complicated by the fact that land "let together" with a dwelling-house is treated as part of the house so that the whole unit attracted residential security irrespective of section 140.[195] Tenants may also be protected by estoppel.[196] A tenant left with an *unusable or undesirable part* of the original holding has the right, exercisable within one month of the partial termination, to demand that the landlord also accept the termination of the remainder.[197]

5. Lease of the reversion

A landlord may create a lease that sits between the reversion and the existing lease,[198] using a deed if the period exceeds three years, but if it is for three years or less even an oral lease suffices.[199] This is called a concurrent lease or a lease of the reversion. It could be longer or shorter than the existing lease.[200] For its contractual duration it separates the pre-existing lease and the pre-existing reversion, giving the right to collect rent from the original tenant.[201]

Before	A (LC)	After	A (HLC)
			X (HTC/SLC)
	B (TC)		B (STC)

6. Enforcement by a lender secured by a mortgage of the reversion

Lenders secured by a mortgage of the landlord's reversion are entitled to collect the rent, but only after taking possession of the land (or in other words of the rents).[202]

[194] See below pp. 701–702.

[195] *Jelley* v. *Buckman* 1974] Q.B. 488 C.A.; *Neville Long & Co. (Boards) Ltd.* v. *Firemanaich* (1984) P. & C.R. 59 C.A.; *Dodson Bull Carpet Co.* v. *City of London Corporation* [1975] 1 W.L.R. 781, Goff J.

[196] *John* v. *George* [1996] 1 E.G.L.R. 7 C.A.

[197] L.P.A. 1925 s.140(2); *Liddy* v. *Kennedy* (1871) L.R. 5 H.L. 134 H.L. (Irish Act).

[198] *London & County (A. & D.) Ltd.* v. *Wilfred Sportsman Ltd.* [1971] Ch. 764 C.A.; *Neale* v. *Mackenzie* (1836) 1 M. & W. 747, 150 E.R. 635.

[199] *Plummer & John* v. *David* [1920] 1 K.B. 326, Lush J. But note that L.P.A. 1925 s.54(2) allows informality only if the lease is in possession, which should surely be construed narrowly in this context.

[200] *Horn* v. *Beard* [1912] 3 K.B. 181; *Cole* v. *Kelly* [1920] 2 K.B. 106.

[201] *Cole* v. *Kelly* [1920] 2 K.B. 106; contrast *Lewis* v. *Baker* [1905] 1 Ch. 46.

[202] L.P.A. 1925 s.141(2); *Re Ind Coope & Co. Ltd.* [1911] 2 Ch. 223.

L.   LEASES UNAUTHORISED BY THE LANDLORD'S MORTGAGE

1.   Where lender has title paramount

A residential tenant's status of irremovability[203] provides no protection against a title paramount. Very often, the landlord's property is mortgaged at the time that the lease is made, and mortgages will invariably contain a prohibition on the borrower entering into leases.[204] If title is registered, that exclusion should be noted on the register.[205] So in a conflict between an earlier mortgage and a later residential tenant, the lender is bound to win. Precedence was first accorded to the title paramount of a lender in *Dudley & District B.S.* v. *Emerson*.[206] A house in Walsall was bought with the aid of a mortgage which barred all letting, and so the Society succeeded in a claim for possession against Goodlad, who had been let into possession by the borrower, and who remained a contractual tenant. Lenders stood outside the category of "landlords" and so were not restricted from obtaining possession.[207] Although Lord Evershed M.R. left open the position of a tenant during a statutory phase,[208] *Britannia B.S.* v. *Earl*[209] makes clear that the same rule applies. Hence a lease granted in breach of a mortgage can be terminated whatever the phase of the tenant's holding. These principles were first developed for Rent Act tenancies (pre early-1989 grants) but they now also apply to modern private sector grants taking effect as assured tenancies.[210]

Lenders may today retain the right to possession even after consenting to a lease. Probably the simplest procedure is to grant a shorthold, but here the lender concedes possession for six months. Additional protection is secured by service of a notice before the grant of the lease reserving the right to sell the property, thus conserving the right to possession in order to enforce the mortgage.[211]

2.   Residential tenancies granted by borrowers but binding lenders

Lenders may become bound by residential tenants in a number of ways. Very rarely money may be lent secured on a mortgage but without excluding the borrower's power to grant leases. More commonly a lease is unauthorised—because the borrower has granted it without the lender's consent—but when he discovers it the lender accepts the tenant.

The lender can no longer complain if he accepts the tenant. In *Nijar* v. *Mann*[212] a person brought a large freehold house with the aid of a bank loan which prohibited lettings

---

[203] *Jessamine Investment Co. Ltd.* v. *Schwartz* [1978] Q.B. 264, 272H–273A, Sir John Pennycuick; Woodfall 2.160–2.189, 6.075–6.078.

[204] L.P.A. 1925 s.99.

[205] M. Robinson (1997) 113 *L.Q.R.* 390, (1998) 114 *L.Q.R.* 354.

[206] [1949] Ch. 707 C.A.; *Woolwich B.S.* v. *Dickman* [1996] 3 All E.R. 204, 210j–211a, Waite L.J.

[207] Increase of Rent and Mortgage Interest (Restrictions) Act 1920 s.12(1)(f); now R.A. 1977 s.152(1). The decision was surely a dubious exercise in statutory interpretation, given that landlords included those entitled to possession apart from the lease.

[208] At 718; J.E. Martin (1977) 41 *Conv.* (*N.S.*) 96; P.F. Smith (1977) 41 *Conv.* (*N.S.*) 197; J. Hill [1987] *Conv.* 77.

[209] [1990] 1 W.L.R. 422 C.A. (leave to appeal was refused); *Quennell* v. *Maltby* [1979] 1 W.L.R. 318, 323, Templeman L.J.

[210] H.A. 1988 s.5(1) referring to a "landlord"; the definition in s.54(1) is identical to that in R.A. 1977 s.152(1).

[211] H.A. 1988 sch.2 ground 2 (assured).

[212] (2000) 32 H.L.R. 223 C.A.

by borrowers. The bank was aware that the purchaser would convert the house to letting units and in fact an assured tenancy of the basement was granted to Mann. Shortly afterwards the property was surrendered to the bank, who appointed a receiver. On the advice of the receiver, the property was sold subject to Mann's tenancy. The issue was what damages to award against the purchaser of the property who harassed Mann in an attempt to force him to leave. The purchaser argued that a prohibition against letting in a mortgage deed entitled the lender to treat the tenancy as a nullity, even if he has allowed the tenant to occupy over a long period.[213] Damages would be greatly increased if it could be said that the bank had accepted Mann as a tenant and so was bound by his tenancy. In fact this is what was decided. The test was whether the landlord had acted so as to be precluded from saying he had not consented or, in simpler terms, had the lender accepted the tenant as his own?[214] Mere appointment of a receiver does not indicate acceptance, since a receiver is an agent of the borrower (that is the true landlord).[215]

3. Residential tenancies granted before the mortgage

A lease granted before the mortgage may have priority,[216] since most short residential tenancies are automatic burdens, that will bind a later lender,[217] and in any event occupation by the tenant will secure his protection through an overriding interest.[218] Lenders therefore need to ensure that existing tenants waive their priority and submit to the mortgage, but care is needed to obtain a waiver that is effective. *Woolwich B.S.* v. *Dickman*[219] concerned a mortgage of a long residential lease of a flat which, as the lender knew, was subject to a Rent Act tenancy granted to the borrower's parents in law. The lender obtained written consents from the tenants.[220] It was held, however, that a consent form could not qualify a paragraph (g) overriding interest unless the qualification was expressed on the register. This decision is often ignored in practice.

Another possibility is illustrated by *Barclays Bank plc.* v. *Zaroovabli*[221] in which case Barclays lost priority, which it would otherwise have secured as lender, by omitting to register the mortgage. Mrs Pourdanay as tenant was therefore able to secure a paragraph (k) overriding interest, and when the mortgage was registered it was too late to affect the fact that her tenancy already bound the lender.[222] She had priority over the mortgage on property law terms.

---

[213] *Taylor* v. *Ellis* [1960] 2 All E.R. 549.

[214] *Stroud B.S.* v. *Delamont* [1960] 1 W.L.R. 431; *Chatsworth Properties Ltd.* v. *Effiom* [1971] 1 W.L.R. 144.

[215] *Stroud B.S.* as above; *Mann* v. *Nijar* as above.

[216] *Woolwich B.S.* v. *Dickman* [1996] 3 All E.R. 204, 211. So too does a lease granted by a prior lender: *Berkshire Capital Funding Ltd.* v. *Street* [1999] Times May 27th C.A.

[217] As overriding interests under L.R.A. 1925 s.70(1)(k) or as legal interests affecting unregistered land.

[218] L.R.A. 1925 s.70(1)(g).

[219] [1996] 3 All E.R. 204 C.A.; J. Morgan [1997] *Conv.* 402.

[220] The building society inaccurately assumed that the couple were beneficial co-owners, but the effectiveness of the consent was not affected by this mistake.

[221] [1997] Ch. 321, Scott V.C. (also reported as *Pourdanay* v. *Barclays Bank plc.*); M. Robinson (1997) 113 *L.Q.R.* 390.

[222] Contrast rights under para.(g): *Abbey National B.S.* v. *Cann* [1991] 1 A.C. 56 H.L.

12

PEACEFUL OCCUPATION

Due process. Illegal eviction and harassment. Damages. Offences of harassment. Notice of repossession. Administrative control of eviction.

A. INTERFERENCE BY THE LANDLORD

All tenants have what the *Social Tenants' Charter* describes as "Your right to live peacefully in your home".[1] A landlord must grant exclusive possession of property to his tenant for the duration of the term, but the lease may define circumstances in which the landlord may interfere, for example by giving rights of access to view the state of repair.[2] This section considers the remedies for unauthorised intrusions by the landlord.

1. Trespass

Physical entry by the landlord on the property which is let to the tenant without lawful authority will lead to an action in trespass. Trespass to land is available against a direct physical encroachment such as nailing up the tenant's door, and trespass to goods prevents the landlord throwing out the tenant's belongings.[3] One example of an interference with the tenant's land was *Lawson* v. *Hartley-Brown*[4]; a landlord redeveloped the property which he had let by erecting scaffolding outside the tenant's existing shop and building two stories on top of the existing building. Since the lease of the shop included the air space above it this new building was a trespass to that air space, for which the tenant obtained damages of £8,000, even though he was unable to prove any damage to his trade. A trespass is usually also a breach of the covenant for quiet enjoyment and a derogation from grant, but these additional heads of actions will not increase the recoverable damages.

2. Quiet enjoyment

The major obligation of a landlord is to allow the tenant to take physical possession of the property leased to him and to allow him to continue in undisturbed occupation.[5] This obligation to allow quiet enjoyment is implied by law[6] and is usually an express

---

[1] See e.g. *Assured Tenant's Charter* (Housing Corporation, 1998) Section 3.

[2] *Charville Estates Ltd.* v. *Unipart Group Ltd.* [1997] E.G.C.S. 36.

[3] *Drane* v. *Evangelou* [1978] 1 W.L.R. 455.

[4] (1996) 71 P. & C.R. 242 C.A.; M. Haley [1997] *Conv.* 304.

[5] *Southwark L.B.C.* v. *Mills* [1999] 4 All E.R. 449, 454j, Lord Hoffmann, 466g, Lord Millett; *Jenkins* v. *Jackson* (1888) 40 Ch.D. 71, 74, Kekewich J.

[6] *Kenny* v. *Preen* [1963] 1 Q.B. 499; R.E. Megarry (1963) 79 *L.Q.R.* 21; *Abbott* v. *Bayley* [1999] L.T.R. 267 C.A.; Woodfall 11.266–11.313; Davey 37–44; Evans & Smith (5th) 101–105, 113; Garner (2nd) ch.5 and p.66; H.W. Wilkinson [1990] *N.L.J.* 1158.

term.[7] It has a technical meaning, so it is perfectly possible to find that the landlord is not in breach of his obligations even though the tenant's flat is not quiet and the tenant is not enjoying it.[8] Legitimate uses of the obligation are to prevent the landlord from obstructing access to the tenant's property[9] or to recover damages for inconvenience after a workman's foot comes through the ceiling of a flat.[10] These examples show that the tenant may obtain damages or an injunction. Quiet enjoyment may also be used to control acts of other tenants holding from the landlord,[11] though the House of Lords decision in *Southwark L.B.C.* v. *Mills*[12] rejected its use to remedy poor sound insulation. This means that quiet enjoyment is not an appropriate vehicle for complaining about the condition of the property.[13] Quiet enjoyment is much wider than trespass because it also covers any physical use of the landlord's property which has a direct impact on the tenant's property—making it a useful means of controlling harassment. Rudeness or interference with the comfort of a residential occupier[14] is not a breach of the tenant's quiet enjoyment—these should be addressed through the statutory protection from harassment enjoyed by domestic tenants.[15]

3. Non-derogation from grant

Landlords must not derogate from their grants, an obligation which is always implied and usually expressed.[16] The basic concept is common sense. If the landlord lets property to a tenant for a particular purpose, the landlord is prevented from using his adjoining land so as to interfere with the purpose for which the premises were let to the tenant. In a residential context this seems to add little to quiet enjoyment,[17] so this is considered in the context of commercial lettings and communal living.[18]

B. PROTECTION FROM EVICTION

1. Due process

Hostile termination of a residential *tenancy* should only occur under a court order made after possession proceedings have been taken. The right to insist upon this is described as protection from eviction.[19] Each scheme of residential security of tenure includes this right,[20] but the real guarantee of the tenant's position comes from the Protection from

---

[7] *Browne* v. *Flower* [1911] 1 Ch. 219, 228, Parker J.; *Perera* v. *Vandiyar* [1953] 1 W.L.R. 672 C.A.; (1953) 69 L.Q.R. 295.

[8] At 454h, Lord Hoffman.

[9] *Owen* v. *Gadd* [1956] 2 Q.B. 99 C.A. (award of £2 damages upheld on appeal(!)).

[10] *Mira* v. *Aylmer Square Investments Ltd.* (1990) 22 H.L.R. 182 C.A.

[11] See below pp. 716–721.

[12] [1999] 4 All E.R. 449, 454g–459f, Lord Hoffman, 966f–470g, Lord Millett.

[13] *Duke of Westminster* v. *Guild* [1985] Q.B. 688 C.A.; *Baxter* v. *Camden L.B.C. (No.1)* [1999] 2 E.G.L.R. 29 C.A., *(No.2)* [1999] 1 All E.R. 237 C.A.

[14] *Kenny* v. *Preen* [1963] 1 Q.B. 499; approved in *Mills.*

[15] See below p. 315.

[16] D.W. Elliott (1964) 80 *L.Q.R.* 244.

[17] *Mills* at 467f, Lord Millett.

[18] See below pp. 716–721.

[19] Bright & Gilbert 587–641; Davey 99–116; Evans & Smith (5th) 101–105, 113; Garner (2nd ed.) ch.20.

[20] H.A. 1988 s.5 (assured); R.A. 1977 s.2(1)(a) (Rent Act), 3; H.A. 1985 s.82 (secure); *Haniff* v. *Robinson* [1993] Q.B. 419 C.A.

Eviction Act 1977. Forfeiture—that is the ending the contractual term of a lease as a response to a breach of contract—must also occur in court if the property is domestic.[21] A similar guarantee applies against forcible eviction during or at the end of a term since a court order is needed to terminate any lease where some person is lawfully residing on any part of the property.[22] It should be noted that the guarantee of due process is restricted to hostile termination by a landlord and has no impact on an agreed surrender.

Due process requirements also apply to most residential *licensees*—including those created since 1989,[23] restricted contracts created between 1980 and 1989,[24] and service occupiers.[25] However, the licence must be exclusive. Two recent cases illustrate the position where accommodation is shared or non-exclusive. In *Brennan* v. *Lambeth L.B.C.*[26] a former tenant of a pub was housed in a room in Tooting Bec Hostel. He was asked to leave after it was decided that his homelessness was intentional, and when he refused to leave he was barred physically. This particular occupier had no guarantee of due process because the terms of his occupation were that he could be moved from room to room, so the use he made of any particular room was not exclusive. In *Brillouet* v. *Landless*[27] an occupier of a room paying £100 a day for the use of two rooms was told to leave when it was found that he was reliant for funds on housing benefit and that the local authority would not in fact meet the cost of his accommodation. An injunction to restrain the eviction was refused since an occupier of hotel rooms did not enjoy any exclusive possession.

An occupier holding under an *excluded tenancy or excluded licence* can be evicted without proceedings.[28] Particular categories are[29]:

—tenancies or licences involving resident landlords, including any arrangement to share living accommodation with a member of the landlord's family[30];
—accommodation granted as a temporary expedient to a trespasser;
—holiday accommodation;
—gratuitous leases and licences[31]; and
—licences in some publicly funded hostels.[32]

Licensees in these categories have never had a guarantee of due process, but protection for *tenants* is only removed if the grant was made after early 1989.[33] Only a person who

---

[21] P.E.A. 1977 s.2.

[22] s.3(1); assured tenancies and shortholds are included by the amendments made by H.A. 1988 s.30(1). There may be problems if a possession order is voidable: *Haniff* v. *Robinson* [1993] Q.B. 419 C.A.

[23] P.E.A. 1977 s.3(2B) as amended by H.A. 1980 s.30.

[24] s.3(2A); see above pp. 164–165.

[25] s.3(2B); *Warder* v. *Cooper* [1970] Ch. 495, Stamp J.

[26] (1998) 30 H.L.R. 481 C.A.

[27] (1995) 28 H.L.R. 836 C.A.

[28] s.3A inserted by H.A. 1988 s.31.

[29] s.3A inserted by H.A. 1988 s.31; s.4 has special rules for agricultural employees.

[30] *Mohammed* v. *Manek* (1995) 27 H.L.R. 439 C.A. If the landlord wishes to reserve rights to share, they must be very explicit: *Miller* v. *Eyo* [1998] 2 C.L.Y. 3632.

[31] *West Wiltshire D.C.* v. *Snelgrove* (1998) 30 H.L.R. 57 (rent-free occupation for 2 weeks).

[32] P.E.A. 1977 s.3A(8); S.Is. 1991/1943, 1996/2325, 1999/1758; *Mohamed* v. *Manek* (1995) 27 H.L.R. 439.

[33] P.E.A. 1977 s.3(2C) introduced by H.A. 1988 s.30 from January 15th 1989.

entered as a lawful occupier has a guarantee of due process, so no protection is available to a trespasser under the 1977 Act, as at common law.[34] Similarly placed is a person whose tenancy can be avoided because of the fraudulent conduct of his agents, since a voidable tenancy attracts no residential protection.[35] Protection attaches to the property rather than to individual occupiers, so that a possession order obtained against a wife also permits the eviction of her husband without separate proceedings.[36] Eviction of an occupier out of court may lead to the commission of other torts or criminal offences,[37] so it is often safer to obtain a possession order even if this is not strictly necessary

2.   Tortious eviction

A specific tort of improper eviction was created by the Housing Act 1988.[38] Residential occupiers have a remedy in damages if they are unlawfully deprived of occupation of the whole or part of any premises. If the tenant is not actually forced out the case may be one of harassment as explained below. One defence is to show that the landlord believed that occupation had ceased, provided that there is reasonable cause for that belief,[39] and another is to show a reasonable basis for carrying out the acts.[40]

Disputes very often arise after the landlord has served a notice to quit and believes that he is now entitled to possession whereas the tenant argues that he has been improperly evicted under an invalid notice. In *Osei-Bonsu* v. *Wandsworth L.B.C.*,[41] the council evicted a husband after his wife had served a *Monk* style unilateral notice of termination of their joint tenancy. Unfortunately for the council the notice was for only 14 days, whereas statute required 28 days, the husband was improperly excluded from the property in the interim period between acceptance of the first notice and the expiration of a second proper notice some four months later. Damages of £30,000 were awarded. The only possible defence was that the council reasonably believed that the man had ceased to reside in the property,[42] which was a plea of ignorance of the civil law, but on the facts it was held not to be a reasonable belief. The occupier had claimed readmittance, and once that was so it was essential to take proceedings for a possession order or for a declaration that he was no longer entitled to occupy. A reasonable cause defence was not available where the landlord acted in the incorrect belief that the lease had ended.

The person liable to pay damages is a landlord, a concept defined to mean a person entitled to possession of the land subject to the lease. *Francis* v. *Brown*[43] held that this excluded a purchaser who benefited from the eviction. A mother who wished to sell the property to her daughter with vacant possession arranged for the eviction of the sitting

---

[34] *Delaney* v. *T.P. Smith Ltd.* [1946] 1 K.B. 393 C.A.

[35] *Ozer Properties Ltd.* v. *Ghaydi* [1988] 1 E.G.L.R. 91 (Rent Act); *Nutt* v. *Read* [1999] Times December 3rd C.A. (assured).

[36] *Thompson* v. *Elmbridge B.C.* [1987] 1 W.L.R. 1425 C.A.; J. Driscoll (1988) 51 *M.L.R.* 371. A person with an independent right to possession (for example a matrimonial home right) can apply to be joined as a party even after a possession order has been made.

[37] Criminal Law Act 1977; see below pp. 315–317.

[38] H.A. 1988 s.27 as from June 9th, 1988; N. Madge [1993] *N.L.J.* 880.

[39] s.27(8); *Regalgrand Ltd.* v. *Dickerson* (1997) 29 H.L.R. 620 C.A.

[40] H.A. 1988 s.27(8)(b).

[41] [1999] 1 W.L.R. 1011 C.A.

[42] s.27(8); this in turn mirrored the defence to a criminal charge under s.1(2); below p. 316.

[43] (1998) 30 H.L.R. 143 C.A.

tenant, but an award against the daughter was ruled out on appeal. An earlier case, *Jones v. Miah*,[44] had held that a potential purchaser of the land could be liable, but this decision must now be treated as doubtful.[45] Agents also escape having to pay damages personally,[46] though the landlord may well be liable for what the agent does. Landlords cannot be held responsible for the conduct of another residential tenant.[47]

3. Tortious harassment

Harassment is a second limb[48] of the tort created by the Housing Act 1988.[49] This form of the tort consists of conduct intended to cause the occupier to leave—a category which includes attempts, acts calculated to induce the occupier to leave, and acts calculated to interfere with the occupier's peace or comfort. A constructive eviction arises after conduct such that it is no longer reasonable to expect the tenant to live in the property.[50] Silence is not a form of harassment for these purposes.[51] It is a defence to show that the landlord believed that occupation had ceased, provided that there is reasonable cause for that belief,[52] and another defence is to show a reasonable basis for carrying out the acts.[53]

The landlord is liable in damages for his own acts and also for those of any person acting on his behalf, but not for the conduct of a short-term tenant.[54] Liability attaches only to a landlord, as statutorily defined to include any person entitled to possession of the land subject to the lease. As explained above a purchaser is not liable, nor are the landlord's managing agents.[55]

4. Housing Act damages

The main object of the Housing Act 1988 was to enhance awards of damages to tenants who have been threatened by their landlords. Occupation of a house by sitting tenants with full Rent Act protection may depress the value of the landlord's reversion by as much as 40 per cent. When a market rent regime was introduced for new lettings after early 1989, landlords stood to profit by evicting their existing Rent Act tenants and reletting at a higher rent under the assured tenancy scheme. Damages under the 1988 Act[56] are intended to strip away any profit from illegal evictions and harassment operations, since they are assessed on the amount by which the landlord's reversion is increased in

---

[44] (1992) 24 H.L.R. 578 C.A.

[45] *Sampson* v. *Wilson* [1996] Ch. 39, 49–50, Bingham M.R.; *Francis* at 148, Peter Gibson L.J.

[46] *Sampson* v. *Wilson* [1996] Ch. 39 C.A. (contrasting s.27 subss.(1)–(2) with subs.(3)).

[47] *B.* v. *M.H.A. Ltd.* [1999] 2 C.L. 372.

[48] s.27(1), (2); the tenant fell between the two stools in *Murray* v. *Aslam* (1994) 27 H.L.R. 284 C.A.

[49] H.A. 1988 s.27 as from June 9th, 1988; N. Madge [1993] *N.L.J.* 880.

[50] *Tagro* v. *Cafane* [1991] 1 W.L.R. 328; *Abbot* v. *Bayley* [1999] L.T.R. 267 C.A.

[51] *Morris* v. *Knight* [1999] 2 C.L. 373.

[52] s.27(8); *Regalgrand Ltd.* v. *Dickerson* (1997) 29 H.L.R. 620 C.A.

[53] H.A. 1988 s.27(8)(b).

[54] *B.* v. *M.H.A. Ltd.* [1999] 2 C.L. 372.

[55] *Sampson* v. *Wilson* [1996] Ch. 39 C.A. Information can be requested from a landlord's agent: P.E.A. 1977 s.7; but no offence is committed by failing to reply to the notice unless the tenant does commence proceedings: *Lewisham L.B.C.* v. *Ranaweera* [2000] 02 C.L. 385.

[56] s.28. The county courts have jurisdiction: H.C.C.J.O. 1991 art.2.

value by the eviction.[57] Very large awards of damages are commonplace[58] and there is considerable difficulty about getting the method of valuation correct.[59]

Of course, if the reversion is not enhanced in value, there are no damages under the statute.[60] A good illustration is *King* v. *Jackson*[61] in which the landlord pre-empted the effect of the tenant's notice of his intention to quit by getting in six days before the notice was due to expire and changing the locks, thus excluding the tenant. An award of £11,000 damages at first instance was manifestly wrong since the reversion could not possibly have been increased by that amount by securing possession only six days early, so the award was reduced on appeal to £1,500 for loss of quiet enjoyment for those six days. *Osei-Bonsu* v. *Wandsworth L.B.C.*[62] considered the position of a man facing a *Monk* style unilateral termination by his wife, and whose tenure was therefore precarious in the extreme. The award of £30,000 at first instance was manifestly wrong for such a flimsy tenure, and the particular claimant's conduct also called for reduction of the damages; a figure of £10,000 was substituted on appeal. If several tenants are harassed the award should be split between them,[63] but if only one of three tenants is forced out, the continued existence of the tenancy in the other two means that no statutory damages may be awarded.[64]

The landlord may reinstate the occupier to avoid paying damages, or the court may order readmission,[65] or give the tenant a choice whether to go back into the property or claim damages.[66] These are usually alternative remedies between which an election has to be made at trial,[67] but in the special circumstances of *Abbot* v. *Bayley*[68] the tenant got two awards of damages. The landlord had relet the property while the tenant was away on a three-month trip (throughout which time he paid rent), but he was readmitted on his return, only to be subjected to a campaign of threatening calls which forced him to leave after 10 weeks. Damages of £10,000 were allocated ¾ to Housing Act damages and ¼ to quiet enjoyment. Failure to observe an order to readmit the tenant is a serious contempt of court.[69] After a reletting the court cannot in practice readmit the first tenant, and so he will have to be satisfied with a declaration of his status and an award of damages.[70]

---

[57] *Jones* v. *Miah* (1992) 24 H.L.R. 578, 588–591, Dillon L.J.

[58] *Tagro* v. *Cafane* [1991] 1 W.L.R. 378 C.A. (£31,000); C.P. Rodgers [1991] *Conv.* 297; J. Bettle and S. Bright [1991] 30 *L.S.G.* 18; also N. Madge [1993] *N.L.J.* 880, [1995] *N.L.J.* 937.

[59] J. Murray [1998] *J.H.L.* 107; J. de Havilands [1998] 37 *E.G.* 158.

[60] *Melville* v. *Bruton* (1997) 27 H.L.R. 319 C.A.

[61] (1998) 30 H.L.R. 541 C.A.

[62] [1999] 1 W.L.R. 1011 C.A.

[63] *Jones* v. *Miah* (1992) 24 H.L.R. 578 C.A.; S. Bridge [1993] *Conv.* 84.

[64] *Melville* v. *Bruton* (1997) 27 H.L.R. 319 C.A.

[65] H.A. 1988 s.27(6); *Murray* v. *Aslam* (1994) 27 H.L.R. 284 C.A.

[66] *Tagro* v. *Cafane* [1991] 1 W.L.R. 378 C.A. (providing a key is not necessarily sufficient); C.P. Rodgers [1991] *Conv.* 297; J. Bettle and S. Bright [1991] 30 *L.S.G.* 18.

[67] *Osei-Bonsu* [1999] 1 W.L.R. 1011, 1024F–1025G, Simon Brown L.J.

[68] [1999] L.T.R. 267 C.A.

[69] *Saxby* v. *McKinley* (1997) 29 H.L.R. 569 C.A.

[70] *Love* v. *Herrity* (1990) 23 H.L.R. 217 C.A.

5.   Damages for other torts

Where the tort created by the Housing Act fails the tenant, many other principles of civil law may step in to help. Withdrawal of services in an attempt to force a tenant out may amount to a breach of contract.[71] Additional remedies may also be available in tort, for example for trespass, trespass to the person or goods, nuisance, intimidation, conspiracy to injure, and procuring breach of contract.

Recoverable damages in tort may be greater, and in either case an injunction may be obtained in addition to damages. Compensation cannot be awarded twice in respect of the same loss.[72] Common law damages must be set off against Housing Act damages where they cover loss of the right to occupy[73] but not where a different loss is compensated, for example for loss of quiet enjoyment.[74] Subject to the limits of *Rookes* v. *Barnard*,[75] exemplary damages may be available to punish a landlord whose conduct is particularly gross,[76] though only if a jurisdiction is first established to award ordinary damages.[77] There is no separate head of damage for compensation for injured feelings,[78] and a reduction may be made for poor conduct on the part of the tenant.[79]

Like any other person, a tenant may be able to make use of the Protection from Harassment Act 1997.[80]

C.   OFFENCES OF HARASSMENT

Criminal law was used to regulate the activities of landlords in 1964[81] as a response to the activities of the notorious racketeer Perec Rackman. After consolidation into the Rent Acts in 1965, the legislation regained its independence of the security of tenure legislation in the guise of the Protection from Eviction Act 1977.[82] Unfortunately the level of successful prosecutions for this common crime is pitifully low: Martin Davey[83] shows that prosecutions run at about 150 a year, with 50 or so convictions.

---

[71] *McCall* v. *Abelesz* [1976] Q.B. 585 C.A. (cutting off electricity and gas).

[72] H.A. 1988 s.27(4)(b), (5).

[73] *Nwokorie* v. *Mason* (1994) 26 H.L.R. 60 C.A.; S. Bridge [1994] *Conv.* 411.

[74] *Kaur* v. *Gill* [1995] Times June 15th C.A.

[75] [1964] A.C. 1129 H.L.

[76] *Drane* v. *Evangelou* [1978] 1 W.L.R. 455; D. Morgan (1979) 42 *M.L.R.* 223; *Ashgar* v. *Ahmed* (1984) 17 H.L.R. 25 C.A. (tenant evicted after injunction to readmit); *Ramdath* v. *Oswald Daley* [1993] 1 E.G.L.R. 82 C.A. (no exemplary damages); *Branchett* v. *Beaney* [1992] 3 All E.R. 910 C.A. (exemplary damages); *Harland* v. *Chadda* [1997] 2 C.L.Y. 3254.

[77] *Francis* v. *Brown* (1998) 30 H.L.R. 143 C.A.

[78] Despite *McCall* v. *Abelesz* [1976] Q.B. 585, 594G, Lord Denning M.R.; see *Branchett* v. *Beaney* [1992] 3 All E.R. 910 C.A.; *Perera* v. *Vandiyar* [1953] 1 W.L.R. 672; H. Street (1956) 16 *M.L.R.* 522 *Kenny* v. *Preen* [1963] 1 Q.B. 499; *Sampson* v. *Floyd* [1989] 2 E.G.L.R. 49 C.A.

[79] *Regalgrand Ltd.* v. *Dickerson* (1997) 29 H.L.R. 620 C.A. (rent arrears).

[80] Claims are allocated to Part 8 and proceed under the fast or multi-track: P.D. 8B.B.B1; C.P.R. 26.7(4); N. Madge [1999] *N.L.J.* 1408, 1409.

[81] P.E.A. 1964; A. Brammall (1964) 29 *Conv. (N.S.)* 6.

[82] s.1(3); amended by H.A. 1988 s.29.

[83] Davey 100; see generally Woodfall 20.027–27.029.

1. Offence of unlawful eviction

The 1977 Act makes it an offence to deprive a residential occupier of his occupation.[84] Temporary eviction might be an offence, but not if it is very transient.[85] Attempts are also criminalised. An essential ingredient of the offence is knowledge on the part of the landlord that the person evicted was a residential occupier.[86] Once that is established, the only defence is a belief, held with reasonable cause, that occupation had ceased.[87] *Mens rea* must be proved.[88] Until 1988 the guilty mind was formed by an intention to induce the residential occupier to quit,[89] but proof of the offence has been simplified. Today it is sufficient that the landlord has knowledge that the acts are likely to cause the occupier to give up occupation.[90] A counterbalance is provided in the form of a defence available if there were reasonable grounds to carry out the acts or to withhold the services.[91]

2. Offence of harassment

Physical eviction of a tenant without a court order is an offence, so that bad landlords[92] often resort to harassment in order to force tenants to leave, or ask their agents to act for them. Offences can only be committed by the owner of the premises. So a council is not in the frame when notifying a person who has been placed in temporary accommodation with a private landlord that his accommodation will not be renewed.[93]

Direct threats of violence are common, but so too are subtler forms of harassment, including the withdrawal of services, withholding keys, delaying repairs, demanding excessive repairs, or suspending work when it is unfinished. Case-law examples include stamping up and down on the floor, bolting the tenant out, assault, removing floorboards, taking all the slates from the roof, and petrol bombing the tenant's letterbox.[94] Under the 1977 Act it is an offence to do acts[95] likely[96] to interfere with the peace or comfort of a residential occupier, as is the persistent withholding of services required for residential comfort.[97] Threatening the tenant's occupation of part is enough for commission of the offence. A person who is not a residential occupier has no protection from the criminal law as was demonstrated on the facts of *West Wiltshire D.C.* v. *Snelgrove*.[98] The owner of a house moved out of his home temporarily and allowed

---

[84] P.E.A. 1977 as amended by H.A. 1988 s.29. The offence may be committed by violent and abusive behaviour by the landlord leaving the tenant to leave by fear: *Sampson* v. *Floyd* [1989] 2 E.G.L.R. 49 C.A.; J. Hill [1987] *Conv.* 265.

[85] *R.* v. *Yuthiwattana* (1985) 80 Cr.App.R. 55 C.A. (refusal to replace missing keys for 1 day and night not an offence); *Costelloe* v. *Camden L.B.C.* [1986] Crim. L.R. 249 Div.Ct.

[86] *R.* v. *Phekoo* [1981] 1 W.L.R. 1117 C.A.

[87] P.E.A. 1977 s.1(2); *R.* v. *Davidson-Acres* [1980] Crim. L.R. 50 C.A. (belief was a matter for the jury).

[88] *R.* v. *Phekoo* [1981] 1 W.L.R. 1117 C.A.; M. Wasik [1981] *Conv.* 377.

[89] *R.* v. *A.M.K. (Property Management) Ltd.* [1985] Crim. L.R. 600.

[90] P.E.A. 1977 s.1(3A), inserted by H.A. 1988 s.29.

[91] P.E.A. 1977 s.1(3B), inserted by H.A. 1988 s.29.

[92] On harassment by lenders see D.G. Barnsley [1991] *J.S.W.L.* 220.

[93] *Mohamed* v. *Manek* (1995) 27 H.L.R. 439 C.A.

[94] Case law is tracked by *Legal Action*.

[95] Failure to act (e.g. leaving repairs unfinished) is not an offence: *R.* v. *Ahmad* (1986) 18 H.L.R. 416 C.A.

[96] s.1(3); this crucial word is substituted (in place of "calculated") by H.A. 1988 s.29(1).

[97] The whole jury must be satisfied about the same specific act: *R.* v. *Mitchell* [1994] Crim.L.R. 66 C.A.

[98] (1998) 30 H.L.R. 57 C.A.

Lacey to move in for two weeks. His refusal to vacate when his time was up led to a confrontation, after which the owner (Snelgrove) was charged with an offence under section 1(3), but this charge was ultimately dismissed since Lacey was not a residential occupier and anyway Snelgrove believed that he was not.[99]

An offence is constituted by harassment that is designed to cause a residential occupier to give up occupation, or to refrain from exercising any rights or remedies.[100] Lawful acts, such as disconnecting a doorbell, may be criminalised by the intention with which the act is carried out.[101] *Mens rea* must be proved, its constituent elements being the same for harassment as for eviction.[102]

3. Offence of violent entry on residential premises

The Criminal Law Act 1977 makes it an offence to use violence to secure entry to residential premises (whether or not there is an intention to recover possession) knowing that entry is opposed by someone who is present.[103] Squatters forcing the owner out of his own property usually commit this offence, but it is equally apt to cover an owner forcing entry against the wishes of a tenant, licensee, or squatter. The owner's right to occupation does not represent lawful authority for the use of force,[104] since the principle of due process requires that possession should be recovered through the courts. However a limited exception is provided for a displaced residential occupier,[105] meaning a person who was in lawful occupation of residential premises immediately before being excluded from occupation by a person who entered as trespasser. Force may be used against the original trespasser or any later successor.[106] Clearly this latitude is not available to a landlord against his tenant.

D. TERMINATION OF CONTRACTUAL PROTECTION

Statutory protection is not needed so long as a tenant or licensee has a contractual right of occupation, but conversely ending contractual entitlement is a vital step for any landlord seeking repossession. In most cases the warning notice referred to in the next section is sufficient to terminate any contractual protection, but in the case of fixed term tenancies reference is required back to the section on hostile termination of short residential contracts.[107]

---

[99] *R.* v. *Phekoo* [1981] 1 W.L.R. 1117 C.A.

[100] *Schon* v. *Camden L.B.C.* (1987) 53 P. & C.R. 361 Div.Ct. (alternative offences, of which the correct one must be charged).

[101] *R.* v. *Burke* [1991] 1 A.C. 135, 147, Lord Griffiths; approving *R.* v. *Yuthiwattana* (1985) 80 Cr.App.R. 55 C.A. obiter.

[102] *R.* v. *Phekoo* [1981] 1 W.L.R. 1117 C.A.; M. Wasik [1981] *Conv.* 377.

[103] Criminal Law Act 1977 s.6(1).

[104] s.6(2).

[105] s.6(3).

[106] s.12(3).

[107] See above pp. 19–30.

E. NOTICE OF REPOSSESSION

Tenants are entitled to a preliminary notice warning that the landlord is about to take repossession proceedings, at least under the more recent legislation covering assured tenancies and public sector secure tenancies.[108] Curiously the Rent Act 1977 does not require any notice to quit or preliminary notice before repossession proceedings,[109] and, in this regard, the Rent Act looks antiquated when set against the newer schemes.

Assured tenants are entitled to a warning notice in a prescribed form before the court may entertain possession proceedings.[110] The duration of the notice may be nil,[111] two weeks,[112] or two months[113] depending upon the ground relied upon. It is assumed that the notice must be allowed to expire before proceedings are commenced.[114] Notice is sufficient to terminate any statutory periodic tenancy.[115] Grounds on which repossession can be ordered are limited during any fixed contractual term, and repossession is only possible at all if the ground is specified as a cause of forfeiture of the lease.[116] The court may overlook a failure to serve a prior notice where it is just and equitable to do so.[117]

Similar rules apply to *secure tenancies*. A notice in a prescribed form,[118] which must specify the ground for possession relied upon and must particularise the breach, is required before any proceedings for repossession of the dwelling-house. The minimum period of notice warning of proceedings to end a periodic tenancy is that sufficient to bring the tenancy to an end, which is usually one period of the tenancy.[119] Notices expire unless proceedings are commenced within 12 months.[120] There is no just and exceptional exception in the public sector, so that notice *must* be served before proceedings can be taken.

Common principles are as follows. The warning notice must set out the ground to be relied on, with sufficient precision to provide an explicit warning to the tenant,[121] and to enable the tenant to decide what action to take. Thus, in *Mountain* v. *Hastings*,[122] a statutory notice based on the ground that at least three months' rent is unpaid did not

---

[108] See general discussion of notices, below Chapter 19.

[109] R.A. 1977 s.3(4); R.(Agriculture) A. 1976 s.6(2).

[110] H.A. 1988 s.8 as substituted by H.A. 1996 s.151 (from February 28th 1997: S.I. 1997/194). Service by one of joint landlords is sufficient.

[111] Nuisance (ground 14): H.A. 1988 s.8(4) as substituted; *North British H.Ass. Ltd.* v. *Sheridan* (2000) 32 H.L.R. 346 C.A.

[112] H.A. 1988 s.8(4B); grounds 3 (holiday), 4 (student), 8 (mandatory ground for major rent arrears).

[113] H.A. 1988 s.8(4A); all grounds except 3, 4, 8, and 14.

[114] *Lower Street Properties Ltd.* v. *Jones* [1996] 2 E.G.L.R. 67 C.A.; P. Waller [1997] *N.L.J.* 1471.

[115] H.A. 1988 s.8(6).

[116] s.7(6); grounds 2 (mortgage), 8 (major rent arrears), 10–15 (discretionary grounds other than ground 10).

[117] s.8(1)(b); *Kelsey H.A.* v. *King* (1995) 28 H.L.R. 270 C.A. (order made). However in the case of rent arrears, the mandatory ground (ground 8) is removed by subs.(5) and action must be pursued on the discretionary ground.

[118] H.A. 1985 ss.83, 83A, as amended by H.A. 1996 s.147 as from February 12th 1987; S.I. 1987/755, as amended by S.Is. 1997/71, 1997/377 (forms).

[119] H.A. 1985 ss.83, 83A; [1998] 03 *L.S.G.* 27; see above pp. 25–26.

[120] H.A. 1985 s.83(3), (4); these provisions do not apply to a fixed term tenancy, nor to a periodic tenancy arising after a fixed term tenancy.

[121] *Slough B.C.* v. *Robbins* [1996] C.L.Y. 3832.

[122] (1993) 25 H.L.R. 427 C.A.; S. Bridge [1994] *Conv.* 74.

set out ground 8 accurately, since it was also necessary to show that rent was due at the date of the service and the date of the hearing, and was not "substantially to the like effect". In another case, a notice stated that: "The reasons for taking this action are non-payment of rent"; this was not sufficiently precise about the amount.[123] Minor errors are ignored, such as a failure to make clear that rent arrears include arrears of rates.[124] When forms keep changing, it is all to easy to use an out-of-date form. In *Tadema Holdings Ltd.* v. *Ferguson*[125] the Court of Appeal were lenient towards an out-of-date form used to effect a rent increase and the move towards accepting notices plain to a reasonable recipient may apply in the repossession context.[126] The court may allow alterations and additions to the stated grounds[127] and, at least in the public sector, this includes power to alter a party.[128] Special rules apply where proceedings are taken on the ground of domestic violence.[129]

General rules about service[130] do not apply, so adequate proof of service of the notice is required.[131]

F. ADMINISTRATIVE CONTROL

1. Public landlords

Public sector landlords are susceptible to public law control of their actions, and challenge on the grounds of perversity or *Wednesbury* unreasonableness. Judicial review is required, so that the repossession proceedings between landlord and tenant are not an appropriate forum in which to resolve such a challenge,[132] but it may be possible to suspend private proceedings until public law issues are resolved.[133] Termination of a licence is a matter of private law and the local authority's decision is not susceptible to judicial review.[134]

---

[123] *Torridge D.C.* v. *Jones* (1985) 18 H.L.R. 107 C.A. There is no need to state the arrears exactly: *Marath* v. *MacGillvray* (1996) 28 H.L.R. 484 C.A.

[124] *Dudley M.B.C.* v. *Bailey* (1990) 22 H.L.R. 424 C.A.; *City of London C.* v. *Devlin* (1997) 29 H.L.R. 58 C.A. (typed "Director of Housing" rather than signature).

[125] [1999] Times November 25th C.A.

[126] See below pp. 579–581.

[127] H.A. 1988 s.8(2); H.A. 1985 s.83; S.I. 1987/755 as amended by S.I. 1997/377; *Croydon L.B.C.* v. *Nana* [1997] C.L.Y. 2720 (not completely new grounds); *Islington L.B.C.* v. *Reeves* [1996] C.L.Y. 437 (evidence of grounds not stated in the possession notice may be relevant when exercising the discretion whether or not to end the tenancy); *City of London C.* v. *Devlin* (1997) 29 H.L.R. 58 C.A.

[128] *Camden L.B.C.* v. *Oppong* (1996) 28 H.L.R. 701 C.A.

[129] Ground 8A inserted by H.A. 1996 s.150; see below p. 364.

[130] L.P.A. 1925 s.196; see below pp. 591–593.

[131] *Wandsworth L.B.C.* v. *Attwell* [1995] 1 W.L.R. 95 C.A.

[132] *Ali* v. *Tower Hamlets L.B.* [1993] Q.B. 407 C.A.; *Hackney L.B.C.* v. *Lambourne* (1992) 25 H.L.R. 172 C.A.; *Tower Hamlets L.B.* v. *Abdi* (1992) 25 H.L.R. 80 C.A.; *R.* v. *Westminster C.C. ex p. Parkins* (1995) 68 P. & C.R. 253 C.A.

[133] *Wandsworth L.B.C.* v. *Winder* [1985] A.C. 461 H.L.; *R.* v. *Hammersmith & Fulham L.B.C. ex parte Quigly* (2000) 32 H.L.R., Ognall J.

[134] *Tower Hamlets L.B.C.* v. *Abdi* (1992) 25 H.L.R. 80 C.A.; *R.* v. *Westminster C.C. ex parte Parkins* (1995) 68 P. & C.R. 253 C.A.

2. Registered social landlords

Social sector tenants fall into the private sector, with significantly fewer rights than secure tenants of public landlords, but an attempt has been made to improve their position by Charters. One assessment is that this has been unsuccessful and that housing association tenants are left with significantly less protection.[135] To take the most important example, the *Assured Tenant's Charter*[136] confers rights to a written tenancy agreement, to agree changes to the tenancy agreement, the right to access to their home, to live peacefully there, to be treated fairly, and to see information. In terms of eviction, the tenant has the right to stay in his home, with protection from eviction unless the landlord has no other choice; the landlord should only elect to evict his social tenants if there is no reasonable alternative. If the worst comes to the worst, a tenant of good behaviour has the right to information and advice about alternative accommodation, and information about his security.

A shorthold tenant has significantly worse protection because of the legal right of the landlord to evict him after the first six months, but again there is a Charter expectation that the landlord will make every effort to enable the tenant to stay in his home, applying for repossession "only when there is no reasonable alternative".[137] Residents of temporary housing have a limited right to stay and be treated fairly, and the right of access to their home for 24 hours each day.[138] Licence holders and occupiers of supported housing also have limited security—the right to stay is modified where, for example, the person no longer needs support, though a person should be moved only after housing support agencies have been informed. Such people should have access to the home for 24 hours a day, but on the basis that staff can enter the accommodation as required.[139]

---

[135] T. Mullen, S. Scott, S. Fitzpatrick & R. Goodlad (1999) 62 *M.L.R.* 11.
[136] (Housing Corporation, 1998) Section 3.
[137] *Shorthold Tenant's Charter* (Housing Corporation, 1998) Section 3.
[138] *Charter for Residents in Temporary Housing* (Housing Corporation, 1998) Section 3.
[139] *Charter for Licence Holders Living in Supported Housing* (Housing Corporation, 1998) Section 3.

13

RESIDENTIAL REPOSSESSION

Full county court repossession proceedings. Accelerated repossession procedures. Full and limited security. Possession orders. Breach of public sector suspended possession orders. Warrants for possession. Grounds for possession. Rent arrears. Nuisance or annoyance to neighbours. Disrepair. Abuses of security of tenure. Recovery for private sector landlords. Redevelopment. Alternative accommodation. Summary of grounds for possession.

A. COUNTY COURT REPOSSESSION PROCEDURE

1. Venue

Domestic repossessions almost inevitably commence in one of the county courts—which have full jurisdiction over actions relating to land,[1] as well as over Rent Act tenancies,[2] assured tenancies, assured shortholds,[3] and public sector secure tenancies.[4] A case should be brought in the High Court only if the financial value, complexity, or importance is such that it should be heard by a High Court judge.[5] Assuming that a county court is chosen, claims must be started in the court for the district in which the land is situated.[6]

2. Fixed date claims for repossession

In 1981 a fixed date action was introduced in the county court[7] which provided a "relatively simple" procedure for repossessions:[8] the idea was to bring a case to court for a hearing without any extensive pre-trial procedure, so the court summons includes a fixed date for the hearing. The Woolf reforms have made few changes to this pre-existing structure, though they have muddied the water. The Civil Procedure Rules provide[9] for a fixed date claim procedure, which is laid down by Section B of the Part 8B Practice Direction, to which any county court action for the recovery of possession of

---

[1] County Courts Act 1984 s.21.
[2] R.A. 1977 s.141(3), (5).
[3] H.A. 1988 s.40 (including any other actions joined); H.C.C.C.J.O. 1991 S.I. 1991/724 art 2.
[4] H.A. 1985 s.110.
[5] P.D. 7.2.3–7.2.4. This will be very unusual, but see below if the High Court is chosen, p. 325.
[6] P.D. 8B.B.7.
[7] C.C.R. Order 3 r.2.
[8] *Access to Justice* (H.M.S.O., July 1996) ch.16 para.17.
[9] C.P.R. 7.9.

land is allocated.[10] This does not fit comfortably into the three-track format for money claims, so the case is allocated to the catch all multi-track.

3. Claim forms

Retention of the flavour of the old procedures is greatly assisted by the use of the old forms, in particular those for claims and for the tenant's reply. The summons and sundry other methods of starting actions under the old procedure are all replaced by a single type of claim form—so that the landlord seeking possession is now called a "claimant".[11] The landlord must prove ownership of the land, so that proceedings in the name of a managing agent are not properly commenced,[12] and special consideration is needed of proceedings brought by a corporate landlord.[13] The Practice Direction relating to forms preserves the old county court forms for the recovery of land at this stage of the Woolf reforms: including Form N5 as a form of summons for the possession of property and Form N6 in the case of a forfeiture.[14]

Particulars of Claim to repossess rented property must be in Form N119,[15] and must be attached to the claim form and served with it.[16] These particulars must identify the land and also allocate the proceedings to the correct security regime: essential details[17] are a statement of whether a dwelling is included and details of the tenancy to enable the court to identify whether the tenancy is Rent Act protected, assured or secure. If the tenant enjoys full security a statutory ground for possession must be identified. If the claim is to forfeit a lease, the particulars of claim must include the names of all people having the right to apply for relief from forfeiture, and extra copies are required for service on such persons. In any case based on rent arrears, the landlord must set out the amount due at commencement, a record of all payments missed, and the enforcement history— that is the dates of previous judgments and steps taken in enforcement. If he intends to rely on them, the landlord must set out his own financial circumstances. The landlord should also set out any relevant circumstances of the tenant that are known to him.

Any written evidence to be used by the claimant must be served with the claim form, as otherwise court permission will be required to make use of it.[18] However a schedule of rent arrears as they stand at the date of any hearing should be prepared. Amendments to which the other party will not consent require permission from the court.

The pre-existing claim form (N5) does not include a statement of truth, and it is now clear that the form should not be amended to include one: where a form has a jurat for

---

[10] P.D. 8B.B.9; J. Frenkel [2000] 20 *L.S.G.* 49.

[11] C.P.R. 2.3.

[12] *Chester's Accommodation Agency Ltd.* v. *Abebrese* [1997] Times July 18th C.A.

[13] C.P.R. 39.6(b); P.D. 39.5.3; *R.H. Tomlinssons (Trowbridge) Ltd.* v. *S.S. for the Environment* [1999] Times August 31st C.A.; M. Walker [1999] 47 *L.S.G.* 35.

[14] P.D. 4.5.2; P.D. 8B Table 3.

[15] P.D. 4.5.2.

[16] P.D. 8B.B.4.

[17] C.P.R. sch.2 C.C.R. Order 6 r.3; P.D. 8B.B.4; A. Myers [1999] 12 *E.G.* 160; P.D. 16.6 applies a similar rule in the High Court.

[18] C.P.R. 8.5–8.6. (Part 8 procedure; query whether this applies to P.D.8B.B). In the High Court a copy of any written agreement must be served with the Particulars: P.D. 16.9.3.

an affidavit, then a statement of truth is not required in addition. This applies, for example, to the form N5B used for accelerated repossessions.[19]

4. Service

Claim forms are usually served by the court by first class post, whereas later documents are usually served between the solicitors.[20] Special procedures are laid down for unoccupied land.[21]

5. Reply

The tenant is still described as a defendant. The courts are still sending out the old reply form[22]—this gives the tenant an opportunity to put forward a defence, to ask for time to pay, and to give details of any circumstances which he wishes to be taken into account. He need not serve a defence or an acknowledgement of service[23] and does not risk a default judgment by failing to do so.[24] Theoretically it might be possible to obtain a summary judgement where a case or a defence has no hope of success but this is not available against a tenant holding over under Rent Act or assured tenancy protection.[25]

6. Initial hearing

When issuing a fixed date claim for repossession a County Court fixes a date for the hearing[26] sufficiently far in advance to allow 21 days' notice to be given of the hearing calculated from the date of deemed service on the defendant.[27] Usually of course the court serves proceedings and gives notice of this hearing date, but it is open to the landlord to take responsibility for service, in which case a separate notice of the hearing date must be served with the claim form.[28] This hearing is now in private for landlord and tenant cases, but it should be before a judge—District Judges do not have power to dispose of a repossession action except with consent.[29] This hearing may be used to dispose of the case or it may turn into a case management conference in a defended case. Very often the tenant fails to appear, in which case it is likely that a possession order will be made.[30]

---

[19] P.D. 22.1.6 ; S. Gerlis (1999) 34 *L.S.G.* 38; see also J. Frenkel [1999] 18 *L.S.G.* 36; N. Madge [1999] 22 *L.S.G.* 38.

[20] See below pp. 591–594.

[21] C.P.R. sch.2 C.C.R. Order 7 r.15 (County Court); C.P.R. sch.1 R.S.C. Order 10 r.4 (High Court).

[22] Forms N11 (reply), N11R (reply—rented property); P.D. 4.5.2.

[23] P.D. 8B.12.

[24] C.P.R. 8.3.1 (defence); P.D. 8B.12 (acknowledgement); C.P.R. 15.1; however by C.P.R. 9.2 he *may* serve a defence.

[25] C.P.R. 24.3(2). An abusive claim could be struck out under C.P.R. 3.

[26] P.D. 8B.B.9.

[27] P.D. 8B.B.10.

[28] P.D. 8B.B.11.

[29] P.D. 2B.11.1(b).

[30] P.D.8B.B.13; for variation of a possession order, see below p. 332.

7. Defended cases

There may be a substantial defence to a repossession action which requires a full hearing to resolve the dispute between the parties—for example the tenant may argue that rent has been paid. Another possibility is that the tenant may have a legitimate counter-claim[31]—if for example the landlord sues for rent arrears the tenant may plead that the property is in disrepair and that he has the right to withhold rent to cover the cost of resulting damage.[32]

Active management of cases becomes a primary function of the court. The overriding objective in Part 1 of the Civil Procedure Rules comes into play with full force when exercising any power or interpreting any rule[33] though it seems that it is not relevant to the decision about what possession order to make.[34] All court procedures should be operated so as to enable the court to deal justly with cases before it. Case management should aim to keep the parties on an equal footing, to save expense, and to keep procedural steps proportionate to the value of the issue.[35] The court retains wide power to vary time limits, to vary and revoke its orders, or to set them aside and to rectify errors of procedure.[36] Delay is much more important than before but is not necessarily a knockout blow.[37]

Part 8 cases are automatically allocated to the multi-track. The hearing will be used to allocate any case that is seriously defended to a track[38] and to give case management directions.[39] It will be beneficial to agree directions and to avoid an allocation questionnaire.[40] Aspects of the claim or defence that are bound to fail may be disposed of summarily in order to save costs at trial.[41] Defended cases are tried at feeder courts as opposed to civil trial centres.[42] When the case does come to full hearing it will be in private[43] but before a County Court judge (as opposed to a District Judge).[44]

8. Dormant cases

All actions commenced now will fall within the ambit of the new rules, but so do most pre-commencement defended actions so far as concerns procedural steps taken after that date. Dormant cases were struck out if no step was taken before April 26th 2000.[45]

---

[31] C.P.R. 20 (details are amended by C.P.Am.R. 2000 r.10); permission is required from the court: P.D. 8.7.

[32] See above pp. 256–258.

[33] The old rules do not regulate the C.P.R. even if the wording is the same: *Lombard Natwest Factors Ltd.* v. *Sebastian* [1999] L.T.L. November 1st, Hart J.

[34] In relation to relief from forfeiture see below pp. 331–332.

[35] C.P.R. 1.1(2).

[36] C.P.R. 3.1, 3.6, 3.10.

[37] *Macdonald* v. *Thorp plc.* [1999] L.T.L. September 1st C.A. (setting aside judgment in default).

[38] C.P.R. 26 (allocation); P.D. 8B.B.15.

[39] P.D. 8B.B.13; C.P.R. 26.5–26.10.

[40] P.D. 26.2.4. (not needed); J. Frenkel [1999] 18 *L.S.G.* 36; N. Madge [1999] *N.L.J.* 1408, 1409.

[41] C.P.R. 24; *Swain* v. *Hillman* [1999] Times November 4th C.A. (do not conduct a mini trial).

[42] P.D. 2B.11.1; P.D. 26.10.1; M. Walker [1999] 47 *L.S.G.* 35.

[43] C.P.R. 39.2(3)(c); P.D. 39.1.5(1); P.D. 39.1.12.

[44] C.P.R. 8.9(c); S. Gold [1999] *N.L.J.* 718.

[45] C.P.R. 51.2; P.D. 51; M. Walker [1999] 14 *L.S.G.* 32. This does not affect execution.

9. High Court procedure

As already indicated[46] the High Court will rarely be the correct venue for repossessions, but any case that is taken there will require full particulars of claim following the county court procedure.[47]

B. ACCELERATED PROCEDURES

A landlord may be able to take advantage of an accelerated procedure to obtain a possession order on the basis of written evidence without a hearing, provided his right to possession is clear-cut.

1. Shorthold tenants

Accelerated procedures against both assured and protected shorthold tenants have been considered in the chapter on shortholds.[48]

2. Mandatory repossession against fully assured tenants

A very similar procedure was (until very recently) available against fully assured tenants[49] where repossession was required on the following mandatory grounds:

Ground 1—property required for landlord's occupation;
Ground 3—former holiday accommodation;
Ground 4—former student letting; and
Ground 5—occupation by minister of religion.

Any assured tenant (that is one granted a private sector tenancy after early 1989) must be given a notice warning that the landlord requires possession, and proceedings are only permitted after the stated period (which must be at least two months) has elapsed. The accelerated procedures are designed to secure swift and outright possession orders where there is a mandatory ground for possession once those formalities are completed.

Proceedings must be brought in the county court for the district in which the land is situated.[50] Accelerated repossession proceedings retain the old Form N5B as a claim form[51] though this may legitimately be amended to refer to the landlord as a claimant.[52] Forms used later in the procedure are N11A for the tenant's reply, N206A to issue the application with a written request for possession, and N26A as the form for ordering that the claimant should have possession.[53] These papers for an accelerated repossession must still be sworn.[54]

---

[46] See above p. 321*.
[47] P.D.16.6. Part 8 procedure applies: P.D.8B.A.1; see also J. Frenkel [2000] 20 *L.S.G.* 49.
[48] See above pp. 56–62.
[49] C.P.R. sch.2 C.C.R. Order 49 r.6. This procedure was repealed by C.P.Am. (No. 4) R. 2000.
[50] P.D. 8.B.7; C.P.R. sch.2 C.C.R. Order 49 r.6(5).
[51] P.D. 8B.B Table 2; P.D. 4.5.1.
[52] J. Frenckel [1999] 18 *L.S.G.* 36.
[53] P.D. 4.5.1.
[54] See above p. 57.

Accelerated procedures are restricted to clear-cut cases, that is where the following conditions are satisfied[55]:

(1) The tenancy must be an assured tenancy;
(2) Possession is sought on mandatory grounds 1, 3, 4, or 5;
(3) Written notice was given before the tenancy was granted invoking the particular mandatory ground, and the current tenant was the oringal recipient of that notice;
(4) The tenancy must be in writing. This usually means the current agreement. Accelerated repossession is allowed where a statutory tenancy[56] follows a written agreement with no variation of terms other than a rent increase—but not where the previous tenancy from which the statutory tenancy follows is oral. A third acceptable case is where an oral agreement follows a prior written agreement of substantially the same premises between the same parties and on the same terms, ignoring any rent increase;
(5) A notice warning of the requirement for possession was given.[57]

Contents of the claim form are prescribed. The statements indicated below establish in evidential terms that the conditions for use of the speedy procedure must be verified on oath; this appears to be a case where the specific provisions of the re-enacted County Court Rules override the general acceptance of a statement of truth.

(1) A statement identifying the dwelling-house.
(2) A statement that the current landlord (and any predecessor) did not let it to the tenant before early 1989.
(3) A statement identifying the nature of the tenancy—either a written agreement or a statutory tenancy or an oral regrant of a written grant.
(4) A statement of the date and method of giving the requisite notice.
(5) Identification of the ground on which repossession is sought and sufficient particulars to substantiate the claim to possession.
(6) Details of the notice under section 8 warning that the landlord requires possession, including its date, the period of notice and the method of service.
(7) The amount of rent currently payable.

Documents to be attached to the application and verified on oath are copies of[58]:

the first and the current (or most recent) written tenancy agreement;
the requisite notice; and
the section 8 warning notice.

Service is by the court by first class post.[59]

---

[55] C.P.R. sch.2 C.C.R. Order 49 r.6(3)–(4).
[56] Under H.A. 1988 s.5.
[57] H.A. 1988 s.8; C.P.R. sch.2 C.C.R. Order 49 r.6(3)(g).
[58] r.6(7).
[59] r.6(9). If the claim form is returned, the court gives notice to the landlord, who may request bailiff service; this is done by posting through the letter box of the property, by delivery to a person at the property appearing to be 16 or over, or to the tenant in person: C.P.R. sch.2 C.C.R. Order 25 r.3(3A)–(3D), inserted by C.P.Am.R. 2000 r.32.

In many cases a *possession order* is made without any hearing. After service of the claim form, the defendant has 14 days in which to oppose the making of an order.[60] The matter is referred to a district judge when the defendant replies or when the time limit runs out and the claimant applies for a possession order.[61] The district judge considers the papers and unless there is any doubt about the clear right to possession he is required to make a possession order without delay.[62] Doubtful cases must be transferred for a normal hearing before a judge.[63] Specific cases mentioned in the rule are that no mandatory ground notice was given where this was required, that there was no notice warning of the landlord's requirement for possession, or that service of the proceedings was faulty, or more generally that the landlord has not established his right to possession under section 21.[64]

3.   Rent Act mandatory grounds

Where a tenancy was created before early 1989, the Rent Act 1977 applies to the tenancy but, especially where the tenancy was created after the reforms of the Housing Act 1980, it is possible that a mandatory ground for possession exists. Accelerated procedures were first introduced in 1981[65] to provide speedy repossession procedures where possession was sought under the mandatory grounds of the Rent Act; apart from case 19 protected shortholds, these are Rent Act cases 11, 12, 20 if notice has been given (form A), and cases 13 to 18 (form B). Proceedings are commenced by originating application to the County Court of the district where the land is situated, with no other action for possession being required. Forms of application and affidavit in support are prescribed. Service must usually be 14 clear days.[66] The district judge can grant a possession order in private, though if there is any doubt about entitlement to the mandatory ground claimed the case will be listed for full hearing.

4.   Removal of trespassers

Summary procedures are available for the recovery of land from squatters and other trespassers. High Court and county court procedures are not yet integrated, but depend upon re-enacted forms of the Rules of the Supreme Court[67] and County Court Rules.[68] Potential defendants are any squatter or trespasser who entered into possession without the licence of the current owner or any of his predecessors. Full repossession proceedings are required against existing tenants, former tenants holding over after the end of a tenancy, former licensees, and mortgage borrowers.

---

[60] r.6(10).

[61] r.6(11), (12), (18).

[62] r.6(13), (15). There is power to set aside on application made within 14 days of service of the order: r.6(17).

[63] P.D.2B.11.1(b). On accelerated repossession from shorthold tenants see *Manel* v. *Memon* [2000] Times April 20th C.A.

[64] C.P.R. sch.2 C.C.R. Order 49 r.6(14); *Aylward* v. *Fawaz* (1997) 29 H.L.R. 408 C.A.

[65] S.I. 1981/139.

[66] Reduced to 7 days under cases 11, 12, 20.

[67] C.P.R. sch.1 R.S.C. Order 113.

[68] C.P.R. sch.2 C.C.R. Order 24. P.D. 8A.1.4(3) allows the use of Part 8 procedure unless there is likely to be a substantial dispute of fact.

5. Interim possession orders

This is an application to restore possession to a displaced residential occupier under the Criminal Law Act 1977.[69] Section B of the Part 8B Practice Direction regulates procedure in the county court. The specified form is N130, which is presumably a claim form.[70] Hence apply the County Court Procedure discussed above.

C. FORMS OF SECURITY

1. Full security

This is a declining commodity, but still applies to:

> *Rent Act tenants*: those holding under a private sector tenancy granted before early 1989 except a protected shorthold.
> *Fully assured tenants:* those holding a private sector tenancy granted after early 1989 with full security, either because no shorthold warning notice was served or because it was granted after early 1997 with no steps taken to given full assurance.
> *Public sector secure tenants:* tenancies granted by councils and other public landlords, except introductory tenancies.
> *Tenants of social landlords:* housing associations grant assured tenancies and tenants are usually given a full assurance.[71]
> *Instalment purchase agreements.*
> *Tenants holding over after the end of a long lease.* Here the security of tenure is particularly strong.[72]

In all these cases repossession proceedings are required, a ground for possession must be shown, and the court often has powers to refuse to order possession or to suspend a possession order on terms.[73]

2. Limited security

Security is limited for many reasons:

> Shortholds;
> Licensees who do not enjoy exclusive occupation of self-contained residential accommodation;
> Licensees where there is some special reason to limit security;
> Tenants who fall into one of the exclusions from security;
> Introductory public sector tenants.[74]

---

[69] C.P.R. sch.2 C.C.R. Order 24 part II.
[70] C.P.R. sch.2 C.C.R. Order 24 r.10.
[71] See above p. 164.
[72] See below pp. 392–396.
[73] Woodfall 19.047–19.133 (actions), 23.076–23.137 (Rent Act), 24.050–24.059, 24.247–24.2071 (assured), 25.030–25.053 (secure); Bright & Gilbert 233–269; Davey 206–286, 307–333; Evans & Smith (5th) chs.17–19; Garner (2nd) chs.13–16, 19.
[74] H.A. 1996 ss.127/128; *Manchester C.C.* v. *Cochrane* (1999) 31 H.L.R. 810 C.A. An appeal has been lodged with the H.L.

These frequently interlock with the mandatory grounds described below. For example a persons occupying accommodation for a holiday does not have a lease, whereas a person taking the accommodation out of season does have a lease, but one with limited security because it is subject to a mandatory ground for possession.

The first consideration is whether the occupier is protected against eviction, because proceedings may not be necessary at all. If they are there may an accelerated procedure or it may be necessary to take full proceedings. Where the landlord proves that security is limited, the court is obliged to make a short possession order as described below.

3. Full security tenants: mandatory grounds for possession

Each security regime has its own list of mandatory grounds, though they tend to follow a common pattern. Under the *Rent Act* they are:

Requirement for an owner occupier (case 11) or a retirement home (case 12);
Holiday dwellings let out of season (case 13);
Educational institutions letting during vacations (case 14);
Lettings of surplus tied farm cottages to persons outside agriculture (case 16)[75];
Dwellings held for occupation by a minister of religion (case 15); and
Lettings of surplus farmhouses, two grounds being made available according to whether or not an amalgamation scheme has been approved.[76]

Under the *assured* scheme they are:

Old model assured tenancies[77];
Requirement as a home (ground 1) or for sale by lender (ground 2);
Out of season holiday home (ground 3);
Institutional letting to student (ground 4);
Minister of religion (ground 5);
Reconstruction by a social landlord (ground 6); and
Requirement for sale by a personal representative (ground 7).[78]

Compensation is often payable if the landlord misrepresents the facts in order to secure possession on a mandatory ground.[79]

Repossession proceedings are required, though accelerated procedures are available under some of these grounds. If a ground is proved, the court is required to make a short possession order.

4. Short possession orders

Once the landlord has proved that there is limited security of a mandatory ground for possession, the court must make a possession order and powers of suspension are very strictly controlled. Possession should not generally be postponed for more than 14 days,

---

[75] *Fowler* v. *Minchin* (1987) 19 H.L.R. 224 C.A.
[76] Cases 17, 18
[77] H.A. 1988 sch.1 paras.11, 12.
[78] Ground 8 relating to rent arrears is discussed below.
[79] R.A. 1977 s.102 cases 8/9.

and suspensions must not exceed six weeks even in cases of exceptional hardship.[80] In a list of exceptional cases the court has wide powers of postponement; these are: lender's possession actions, forfeitures, where possession is discretionary, restricted contracts, and rental purchase agreements. The judge has a discretion to make a possession order on many of the grounds available against private sector tenants (the discretionary grounds but not the mandatory grounds) and on all of the grounds available in the public sector, so in these cases the court is not obliged to make a short possession order.

D. POSSESSION ORDERS

1. Orders

Orders for possession may be made by a named judge after a hearing or in the name of the court after documentary procedures.[81] The order is drawn up by the court[82]— unless it is a consent order[83]—and served by the court on the parties affected by it. Woolf retains the older forms for possession orders[84] and also for orders for forfeiture for non-payment of rent.[85]

2. Outright possession orders

In some cases the court will order possession on a fixed day.[86] Once the landlord has proved that there is limited security of tenure the court must make a possession order and powers of suspension are very strictly controlled, as explained immediately above. Possession *may* be ordered immediately against a tenant with full security. One example is if a defendant concedes that he has no security.[87] Another is if the court finds that a ground for possession exists *and* that it is reasonable to order possession—perhaps because of a long history of rent arrears, a large default, or gross behaviour towards neighbours.

3. Discretionary grounds—proof of the ground

Possession against a tenant with full security is by no means automatic, since the landlord has to prove some reason why possession should be ordered—that is a ground for possession. Unless the tenant consents to an order proof of a ground will normally require a hearing. Proof of the ground is usually straightforward enough: if the tenant owes arrears of rent amounting to £50, this breach of covenant establishes a ground for possession. However this is only the first small hurdle facing the landlord.

---

[80] H.A. 1980 s.89.

[81] C.P.R. 40.2.

[82] C.P.R. 40.3; minor errors can be corrected under the slip rule in C.P.R. 40.12.

[83] C.P.R. 40.6. This is unusual in the case of a full security tenant. Usually no appeal is possible, unless there was no true admission: *Hounslow L.B.C.* v. *McBride* (1999) 31 H.L.R. 143 C.A.

[84] P.D. 4.5.2; Forms N26 (possession order rented), N26A (order that claimant have possession against an assured tenant), N28 (suspended possession order, rented).

[85] Forms N27, N27(1) (possession refused against a Rent Act tenant), N27(2) (possession refused and suspended under the Rent Act).

[86] C.P.R. 2.8–2.10 (time).

[87] *Barton* v. *Finchman* [1921] 2 K.B. 291; *Syed Hussain* v. *A.M. Abdullah Sahib & Co.* [1985] 1 W.L.R. 1392 Div.Ct.

4. Discretionary grounds—the discretion

Where the ground relied upon is discretionary, possession is not automatic, since the landlord must also show that it is *reasonable* for the court to order possession. In some cases he may also need to establish an offer of suitable alternative accommodation.[88] A judge should consider all relevant circumstances at the date of the hearing in a broad common sense way.[89] It is relevant that the defendant will be left homeless, but the judge should not attempt to prejudge the result of a homelessness application.[90] Reasonableness and the weight to be given to various factors are primarily matters for the judge to consider at the initial hearing: appeals should only succeed if the judge's reasoning is demonstrably wrong. If the Court of Appeal[91] differs from the judge it usually remits the case for further consideration of the question of reasonableness, though it is open to the Court of Appeal to order possession if, for example, the question of reasonableness was not relevant on the view of the law taken by the trial judge.[92]

5. Powers of suspension

Full security arrangements[93] where the court has a discretion whether or not to order possession are an exception to the 1980 rule that possession should not usually be suspended for more than 14 days.[94] Rather the court has a wide discretion about the form of order to make, including powers to dismiss, stay, or adjourn proceedings. However the most common result is that the court orders possession but makes a suspended possession order—meaning that the landlord cannot execute the order and recover possession while the tenant meets the given conditions of the suspension. For example if there are rent arrears of £600, the court may order the tenant to pay £50 a month towards the arrears over a year and to suspend possession so long as he makes these payments. If there are any arrears of rent the judge *should* impose a condition requiring that these are cleared—unless this would cause exceptional hardship to the tenant or it is otherwise unreasonable. An order may[95] or may not include future arrears as they accrue: clearly landlords should ask for these to be included. Other conditions *may* be imposed. In order to enable the court to exercise its powers, the particulars of claim should set out the tenant's payment history and previous steps taken to recover the rent, along with known details of the circumstances of the tenant.[96] The tenant can put his point of view,

---

[88] H.A. 1985 sch.2 part I grounds 1–8 (reasonable) part II grounds 9–11 (suitable accommodation) part III grounds 12–16 (reasonable and alternative accommodation); part IV indicates what is suitable.

[89] *Cumming* v. *Danson* [1942] 2 All E.R. 653, 655, Lord Greene M.R.; J. Manning [1998] *J.H.L.* 59. For example it may be important to give a tenant convicted of an offence an opportunity to turn over a new leaf: *Greenwich L.B.C.* v. *Grogan* [2000] Times March 28th C.A.

[90] *Croydon L.B.C.* v. *Moody* (1999) 31 H.L.R. 738, 745, Evans L.J.; see also *Shrewsbury & Atcham B.C.* v. *Evans* (1998) 30 H.L.R. 123 C.A.; *Lewisham L.B.C.* v. *Akinsola* (2000) 32 H.L.R. 414 C.A.

[91] Appeals from final orders in multi-track cases continue to go to the C.A., but other appeals from county courts now go to a High Court judge: C.P.Amendment R. 2000.

[92] *Hamid* v. *Jeje* [1994] C.L.Y. 2784 C.A. The Court of Appeal may also accept new facts relevant to such issues as greater hardship: *King* v. *Taylor* [1955] 1 Q.B. 150 C.A.; R.E. Megarry (1955) 71 *L.Q.R.* 29.

[93] R.A. 1977 s.98; H.A. 1988 ss.7, 9 (assured); H.A. 1985 s.85 (secure); *Islington L.B.C.* v. *Reeves* [1997] 2 C.L.Y. 2715. C.P.R. 2.8–2.10 cover time limits.

[94] H.A. 1980 s.89; see above n. 80.

[95] *Tower Hamlets L.B.C.* v. *Azad* (1998) 30 H.L.R. 241 C.A.

[96] C.P.R. sch.2 C.C.R. Order 6 r.3.

either in the formal reply or by presenting evidence at the court hearing. Spouses are given corresponding rights to a suspension,[97] though any consent order requires the consent of the spouse who is the actual tenant.[98]

6. Undertakings

A common alternative to a suspension is to accept an undertaking by the landlord not to enforce a possession order until certain events occur; this is useful to deal with future misconduct by the tenant such as causing flooding—any future misconduct can be dealt with by lifting the undertaking and allowing the landlord to enforce his possession order.[99]

7. Variation, setting aside and suspension of possession orders

To a large extent possession orders are just like any other court orders, being open to variation in the discretion of the court, and subject to appeal. This will be clear if the tenant has not been served.[100] Very often a tenant who has received the papers will not reply or will not appear in court to put his defence. A possession order is likely to be made in these circumstances, but an application may be made to set it aside[101] or to suspend orders after they have been made,[102] or vary the conditions—including power to vary or revoke an order.[103] There is considerable case law about how to exercise these powers where the tenant did not attend court—the predominant question is why the tenant did not appear.[104] An order that is set aside ceases to have effect and cannot be executed.[105] Orders may be corrected under the slip rule, which is retroactive.[106] An unfortunate procedural defect permits a warrant for possession to be executed even if the tenant is appealing from the making of a possession order or the issue of a warrant by the District Judge.[107]

8. Outsiders

People other than tenants are often affected by a possession order, notably sub-tenants. Any person who is directly affected by a judgment or order may apply to have it set aside or varied.[108] If someone other than the defendant claims to be a tenant, then the court

---

[97] R.A. 1977 s.100; H.A. 1988 s.8; H.A. 1985 s.85(5); all are amended in their detail by F.L.A. 1996 sch.8.

[98] *Wandsworth L.B.C.* v. *Fadayomi* [1987] 1 W.L.R. 1473 C.A.; *R.* v. *Newcastle on Tyne C.C. ex parte Thompson* (1988) 20 H.L.R. 430, McNeill J. (Rent Act).

[99] *Kensington Housing Trust* v. *Oliver* (1998) 30 H.L.R. 608 C.A.

[100] C.P.R. 23.10.

[101] C.P.R. 3.6.

[102] C.P.R. 3.1; N. Madge [1995] *N.L.J.* 1852 (old law).

[103] C.P.R. 3.1(3), (7).

[104] *Shocked* v. *Goldschmidt* [1998] 1 All E.R. 372; *Lambeth L.B.C.* v. *Henry* [2000] 06 E.G. 169 C.A. (could not set aside after 9 years). On the old law see: *Haymen* v. *Rowlands* [1957] 1 All E.R. 321 C.A.; *Grimshaw* v. *Dunbar* [1953] 1 Q.B. 408 C.A.; *Tower Hamlets L.B.C.* v. *Abadie* (1990) 22 H.L.R. 264 C.A.; *Rhodes Trust* v. *Khan* [1980] 1 E.G.L.R. 64 C.A.

[105] *Peabody Donation Fund Governors* v. *Hay* (1986) 19 H.L.R. 145 C.A. But if it has been executed, damages cannot be obtained by the tenant: *Brent L.B.C.* v. *Botu* [2000] E.G.C.S. 34 C.A.

[106] *Scott-James* v. *Chehab* [1988] 2 E.G.L.R. 61 C.A. (old law).

[107] C.P.R. sch.2 C.C.R. Order 37 r.8(2). However Order 37 is revoked by C.P.Am.R. 2000 sch. 8.

[108] C.P.R. 40.9.

should set aside any possession order or warrant for possession, and add that person to the proceedings to argue for his rights.[109]

E. BREACH OF A SUSPENDED POSSESSION ORDER

1. Private sector

A tenancy ends only when the tenant gives up possession.[110] This means, for example, that a succession could occur where a possession order was made against the original tenant but he died during a suspension of that order,[111] and a tenant against whom there is a suspended possession order could sue for disrepair. The tenancy ends when the landlord obtains a warrant for possession and the tenant is physically evicted under it. Unfortunately this is not the position in the public sector.

2. Public sector secure tenancies ("tolerated trespassers")

These were considered in *Burrows* v. *Brent L.B.C.*[112] A possession order had been made against a secure tenant owing £2,500 rent, but before execution of the order she entered into an arrangement with the council, acknowledging the extent of the arrears and promising to make regular payments in future, on the basis that eviction could occur if payments ceased or were irregular. She fell behind with the agreed repayments, and the council sought to activate the possession order.[113] The Housing Act 1985[114] defines the precise moment at which a secure tenancy ends—when the tenant is to give up possession under the order—and this is held to mean that a tenancy terminates automatically when the terms of a suspended possession order are breached. This is a matter of great moment given that one third of all public sector tenants are involved in possession proceedings at any one time.[115] When the wife involved in *Thompson* v. *Elmbridge B.C.*[116] was in breach of a suspended possession order, it was too late for the husband to claim a matrimonial home right in a non-existent tenancy. If the tenant dies while in breach of a possession order there is no succession right.[117] The effect of a breach of an order is that the tenant is a tenant no more and is incapable of taking action for disrepair during the period of limbo.[118] However this draconian view should not be taken if the

---

[109] E.g. *S.S. for Transport* v. *Jenkins* (2000) 79 P. & C.R. 118 C.A. (arguable claim to business tenancies protection).

[110] *Sherrin* v. *Brand* [1956] 1 Q.B. 403; *Thompson* v. *Elmbridge B.C.* [1987] 1 W.L.R. 1425, 1430E, Russell L.J.

[111] *American Economic Laundry Ltd.* v. *Little* [1951] 1 K.B. 400 C.A.

[112] [1996] 1 W.L.R. 1448 H.L.; S. Bright (1997) 113 *L.Q.R.* 216; A. Caffereky [1998] *Conv.* 39; N. Nicol [1999] 2 *J.H.L.* 11; *Greenwich L.B.C.* v. *Regan* (1996) 28 H.L.R. 469 C.A. approved; *Hackney L.B.C.* v. *Porter* (1997) 29 H.L.R. 401 C.A.

[113] This was based on old form N28; the new form, introduced in 1993, states that the "plaintiff can ask the court to evict you".

[114] s.82(2).

[115] S. Bright (1997) 113 *L.Q.R.* 216.

[116] [1987] 1 W.L.R. 1425 C.A.

[117] *Brent L.B.C.* v. *Knightley* (1997) 29 H.L.R. 857 C.A.; ironically this works to the advantage of the new tenant's family since it means that a succession may occur on his death: *Enfield L.B.C.* v. *Devonish* (1997) 29 H.L.R. 691 C.A.

[118] *Lambeth L.B.C.* v. *Rogers* [2000] 03 E.G. 127 C.A. *Dolonay* v. *Southwark L.B.C.* [1999] 12 C.L. 414. But a nuisance claim is possible: *Pemberton* v. *Southwark L.B.C.* [2000] 21 E.G. 135 C.A. (cockroach infestation).

default in compliance with the order is trivial[119] and the bar is lifted retrospectively if the suspended possession order is discharged.[120]

Clearly the court could vary the terms of the possession order, even after it has theoretically terminated.[121] What if the *parties* agree a variation? In *Burrows* the occupier argued that the original tenancy had been terminated when the terms of a possession order were broken, and that a new arrangement for payment of the arrears had been reached between landlord and tenant so as to create a new secure tenancy. The House of Lords rejected this outrageous argument, preferring to allow the arrangement for clearing the arrears to take effect as the parties intended. Lord Browne-Wilkinson considered that the old tenancy remained in force until actual execution of the order for possession, perhaps in a state of limbo,[122] but in a state in which it was capable of revival if the court later varied the date for possession. A problem may remain where re-instatement occurs on terms different to those of the suspended possession order.[123]

F.   WARRANTS FOR POSSESSION

1.   Current law

An order for possession may only be executed by issue of a warrant for possession.[124] It is a forcible ejectment to evict a tenant physically before execution of the warrant for possession and one which creates serious problems for a landlord whose possession order turns out to have been voidable.[125] A certificate is required that the land has not been vacated and money judgments can be enforced against the tenant's goods at the same time. The tenant is safe from eviction (or should that be execution?) on Christmas Day, Sundays and Good Friday.[126] Enforcement must occur within six years of the possession order,[127] after which time fresh proceedings will be required, and a warrant requires renewal after 12 months.[128] No notice is required by the court rules before executing a warrant for possession, and this cannot be implied.[129] So, after a judgment or order for the recovery of land, possession is obtained on the landlord's certificate that the land has not been vacated, and, if an order has been made for payment of money by instalments, his certificate that instalments are unpaid.[130]

---

[119] *Southwark L.B.C.* v. *Edem* [199] 07 C.L. 264 C.Ct.

[120] *Lambeth L.B.C.* v. *Rogers* [2000] 03 E.G. 127 C.A.; A. Moore (1999) 143 *S.J.* 1188.

[121] *R.* v. *Newham L.B.C. ex parte Campbell* (1991) 26 H.L.R. 183 Q.B.D.

[122] *Lambeth L.B.C.* v. *Rogers* [2000] 03 E.G. 127 C.A.

[123] *Sackey* v. *Greenwich L.B.C.* [1996] C.L.Y. 3784 (new tenancy).

[124] C.P.R. sch.2 C.C.R. Order 26 r.17; C.P.R. 4.5.3 (Form N49); applications are governed by C.P.R. 23.

[125] *Haniff* v. *Robinson* [1993] Q.B. 419 C.A.

[126] C.P.R. sch.2 C.C.R. Order 26 (county court); C.P.R. sch.1 R.S.C. Order 46 (High Court); M. Walker [1999] 47 L.S.G. 35.

[127] C.P.R. sch.2 C.C.R. Order 26 r.5 (and not if there has been a change of circumstances such as a death). *Hackney L.B.C.* v. *White* (1996) 28 H.L.R. 219 C.A.

[128] C.P.R. sch.2 C.C.R. Order 26 r.6.

[129] *Leicester C.C.* v. *Aldwinckle* (1991) 24 H.L.R. 40 C.A. Contrast the position in the Supreme Court: C.P.R. sch.1 R.S.C. Order 45 r.3(2); Chancery Division P.D. 7.

[130] C.P.R. sch.2 C.C.R. Order 26 r.17. However the Court may overlook trivial defaults: *Southwark L.B.C.* v. *Edem* [1999] 07 C.L. 264 C.Ct.

Automatic execution of a warrant can be avoided by imposing a requirement that the landlord obtain permission from the court before executing the order.[131] An undertaking not to enforce a possession order has a similar effect, but the landlord is released from it if the tenant is in breach of the order.[132] The tenant can apply to stay the application for the warrant[133]; this might be granted, for example, where a tenant has failed to defend possession proceedings and he shows that he was traumatised and unsure what to do.[134] A new hearing is required to consider the question of reasonableness.[135] Powers of suspension end after execution of the possession order,[136] so that if the landlord has retaken possession a warrant can only be set aside for fraud, abuse of process, or oppression, or if the underlying possession order is set aside.[137] A warrant cannot in practice be reopened after the demolition of the tenant's property.[138]

2. Outsiders

A person who is not a party to the proceedings could apply to set aside a warrant in the same way that he could seek to set aside a possession order. [139]

3. Reform

An Enforcement Review has considered reform of the warrant procedure but has concluded that little can be done.[140] Landlords often complain about last minute applications for suspension, but a cut off point might work substantial injustice. It might be desirable to set a date for an eviction (perhaps 21 days hence) at the same time as making a possession order. The official view is that the current advice to tenants about eviction procedures is beyond improvement(!). Desirable reforms are the creation of a unified procedure in the High Court and the county courts and the introduction of an accelerated procedure against squatters reoccupying the property.

G. RENT ARREARS

Details vary slightly between the different schemes of protection, but the similarities are more striking than the differences: possession can always be ordered against a misbehaving tenant, but the ground is usually discretionary, so the court should only order

---

[131] This is not normal: *Exeter C.C.* v. *Palmer* [2000] 06 C.L. 467.

[132] *Kensington Housing Trust* v. *Oliver* (1998) 30 H.L.R. 608 C.A.

[133] County Courts Act 1984 s.88; C.P.R. sch.2 C.C.R. Order 26 r.17. C.P.R. 3.1. (power to vary all time limits or stay); C.P.R. 3.6 (set aside order); C.P.R. 2.8–2.10 (time); C.P.R. 23.10 (set aside if application not served); C.P.R. 23.11; P.D. 23.12.2 (where solicitor fails to attend, can relist, set aside, vary, discharge, suspend etc.).

[134] *Palmeira Properties Ltd.* v. *Bennett* [1995] C.L.Y. 3037 C.A.; but not if the tenant simply fails to comply with a court order: *Camden L.B.C.* v. *Akanni* (1997) 29 H.L.R. 845 C.A.

[135] *Hounslow L.B.C.* v. *McBride* (1999) 31 H.L.R. 143 C.A.

[136] *Tower Hamlets L.B.C.* v. *Azad* (1998) 30 H.L.R. 241 C.A.

[137] *Hammersmith & Fulham L.B.C.* v. *Hill* [1994] 2 E.G.L.R. 51 C.A. (oppression arguable on facts); *Southwark L.B.C.* v. *Sarfo* [1999] 12 C.L. 413 C.A. (failure to process housing benefit on 3 occasions; no pre-eviction letter or visits and only 1 day's notice of eviction.

[138] *Southwark L.B.C.* v. *Sarfo* as above.

[139] See above pp. 332–333.

[140] C.P. No.4 (L.C.D. January 2000).

possession if it is reasonable to do so.[141] This is just as well—something like one third of all public sector tenants are involved in possession proceedings at any one time.[142]

1.   Rent arrears as a discretionary ground

Non-payment of rent is invariably a ground for possession against a tenant, but usually one that is discretionary; only the assured tenancies scheme (discussed below) provides any mandatory ground for major arrears. Case 1 of the Rent Act provides a basis for ordering possession where "rent lawfully due has not been paid or any obligation of the tenancy has been broken". Non-payment of council tax and water charges can be seen, according to the landlord's taste, either as arrears of rent or as breach of another obligation of the tenancy.[143] Ground 11 for assured tenancies is almost identical. Public sector orders number 100,000 a year, many of which are suspended on terms. Following a repossession the authority is under no obligation whatsoever to offer alternative accommodation. Although the person evicted may be able to make an application as a homeless person practical help is limited, since most people evicted for arrears will be found to be homeless intentionally and so debarred from receiving an offer of accommodation.[144] Rent arrears may also prejudice a future application for an allocation of housing.

Assured sector secure tenants must be given prior warning of the claim to possession,[145] the notice period giving the tenant a chance to clear the arrears. It is a valid defence to proceedings that the necessary warning notice was not given before proceedings were commenced.[146] An honest error in the amount of the arrears stated does not invalidate the notice but it might weigh against the landlord when deciding how to exercise the discretion.[147] Generally the court has a discretion whether or not to order possession. Clearly the order should not be made if there is a valid counterclaim for a larger sum,[148] where the landlord has been demanding more than a registered fair rent,[149] or has refused a valid tender,[150] since in these and similar cases rent is not really "due".

Discretion takes the field where there *are* arrears, since the court has still to decide whether the default is so serious that possession should be ordered. Reasonableness is an overriding consideration when making a possession order,[151] and the issue recurs when deciding whether to allow the execution of a warrant for possession that has been

---

[141] R.A. 1977 sch.15 (Rent Act Cases); H.A. 1988 sch.2 (assured); H.A. 1985 sch.2 (public-sector secure) Woodfall 23.076–23.137, 23.047–23.071, 25.030–25.038.

[142] S. Bright (1997) 113 *L.Q.R.* 216.

[143] *Lambeth L.B.C.* v. *Thomas* (1998) 30 H.L.R. 89 C.A.; *Dudley M.B.C.* v. *Bailey* (1990) 22 H.L.R. 424 C.A. If a landlord alleges both non-payment of rent and nuisance, but the nuisance is disputed, that should be tried separately: *Hammersmith & Fulham L.B.C.* v. *Brown* [2000] 05 C.L. 350 C.Ct.

[144] *Darlington B.C* v. *Sterling* (1998) 29 H.L.R. 309 C.A.

[145] See above pp. 318–319.

[146] *Torridge D.C.* v. *Jones* (1985) 18 H.L.R. 107 C.A.

[147] *Dudley M.B.C.* v. *Bailey* (1990) 22 H.L.R. 424 C.A.

[148] *Televantos* v. *McCulloch* [1991] 1 E.G.L.R. 123 C.A.; *Haringey L.B.C.* v. *Stewart* [1991] 2 E.G.L.R. 252 C.A.; see above pp. 318–319.

[149] *Rakhit* v. *Carty* [1990] 2 Q.B. 315 C.A.

[150] *Sopwith* v. *Stutchbury* (1985) 17 H.L.R. 50 C.A.; *Bessa Plus plc* v. *Lancaster* [1997] E.G.C.S. 42 C.A. (rejection of housing benefit cheques to cohabitee). But arrears arise where an overpayment is reclaimed: *Hyde H.Ass* v. *Brown* [1999] 07 C.L. 328.

[151] *Cumming* v. *Danson* [1942] 2 All E.R. 653, Greene M.R.; *Smith* v. *McGoldrick* [1977] 1 E.G.L.R. 53 C.A.

suspended.[152] Tenants are generally allowed to remain if they clear all arrears, though there is certainly power to order possession against a tenant with a bad payment record.[153] It is common to make a possession order where some arrears remain but to suspend it on terms, giving the tenant a chance to clear the arrears by instalments.[154] The object of suspension is to give the tenant a chance to pay off the arrears. Thus there was a radical error in the exercise of judicial discretion in *Taj* v. *Ali*.[155] A tenant failed to pay rent alleging that the property was in serious disrepair but even allowing for damages of £10,000 to be set off, the tenant is still owed about £14,500. A county court judge ordered the suspension of possession on payment of the current rent and £5 a week off arrears. The Court of Appeal substituted an outright possession order. A suspended order should be for a definite time during which the arrears would be cleared and should not extend into the mists of time. The court can also take into account bad behaviour by the landlord—such as giving false evidence[156]—the consequences for the individual tenant of ordering possession, and the availability of alternative accommodation.[157] It is then for the court to decide whether it is reasonable for the court to order possession. This confers a very substantial discretion. The role of the trial judge is crucial, since it is largely a question of fact within his domain; no appeal can be pursued on this question of fact.[158]

2. Non payment of rent by assured tenants

Landlords can more easily obtain possession against assured tenants in the private sector (tenancies granted since early 1989) because the general discretionary ground for possession on the basis of arrears is supplemented by two additional grounds, one mandatory and one discretionary.

Ground 8 makes possession mandatory where there are two months (or eight weeks) of arrears of rent.[159] Considerable care is needed in drafting the section 8 notice that commences proceedings. The ground requires the stated quantum of arrears[160] *one* when the pre-action warning notice is given, *two* when proceedings are served, and *three* at the time of the hearing. A notice referring only to stage one is invalid, since it does not alert the tenant to the possibility of avoiding possession by clearing the arrears before stages 2 and 3.[161] If the ground is proved, the court has no power to suspend or delay making a possession order. One wrinkle has emerged: a landlord who relies on Ground 8 must insist on an outright possession order because if he reaches an arrangement with

---

[152] *Peachey Property Corp. Ltd.* v. *Robinson* [1967] 2 Q.B. 543 C.A.

[153] *Dellenty* v. *Pellow* [1951] 2 K.B. 858 C.A. (rent paid after summons issued); *Brown* v. *Davies* [1958] 1 Q.B. 117 C.A. (serious disrepair, even though remedied).

[154] *Woodspring D.C.* v. *Taylor* (1982) 4 H.L.R. 95 C.A. (no order where arrears £700); *Lambeth L.B.C.* v. *Thomas* (1997) 74 P. & C.R. 189 C.A. (only suspended order reasonable).

[155] [2000] 17 L.S.G. 36 C.A.

[156] *Yelland* v. *Taylor* [1957] 1 W.L.R. 459 C.A.; R.E. Megarry (1957) 73 *L.Q.R.* 156.

[157] *Battlespring Ltd.* v. *Gates* [1983] 2 E.G.L.R. 103 C.A.

[158] *Minchburn Ltd.* v. *Fernandez* (1987) 19 H.L.R. 29 C.A.

[159] H.A. 1988 sch.2 part I as amended by H.A. 1996 s.101.

[160] A notice may be valid if it does not state the precise arrears, provided they are quantifiable: *Marath* v. *MacGillvray* (1996) 28 H.L.R. 484 C.A. (statement of arrears on fixed day).

[161] *Mountain* v. *Hastings* (1993) 25 H.L.R. 427 C.A.; S. Bridge [1994] *Conv.* 74.

the tenant to accept the arrears by instalment he can only do so by abandoning the claim on the mandatory ground 8.[162] It pays to be strict.

Ground 11 is a discretionary ground available for persistent delay in paying rent. Possession may be recovered from a tenant with a bad payment record even if there are no arrears at the time of proceedings. However this ground is discretionary. It sits alongside the normal discretionary ground (ground 10) which is available where rent is in arrears.[163]

3.   Housing benefit

Very many tenants rely on housing benefit, problems and delays in the payment of housing benefit cheques being the most common cause of rent arrears. In the public sector the landlord is also the authority responsible for housing benefit payments. In the private sector the landlord is entitled to demand rent from the tenant and to refuse a housing benefit cheque tendered by a third party. In *Bessa Plus plc.* v. *Lancaster,*[164] the tenant was a single mother with four children but housing benefit was claimed in the name of her male partner (Burnham) who had moved in with her. A housing benefit cheque in his name was refused by the landlord, a decision accepted to be legitimate by the court. Arrears now amounted to more than two months giving a mandatory ground for possession against an assured tenant and entitlement to an immediate possession order. Repossession can often be avoided by making arrangements for housing benefit to be paid direct to the landlord.[165] If payments are delayed or arrangements are confused there may be grounds for possession against a private tenant[166] though no doubt the landlord could not succeed if he had contributed to the error.

In several cases, large arrears have built up under an assured tenancy as a result of local authority errors with housing benefit.[167] The problem arises in particular in the public sector, where the council as landlord should not take advantage of its own inefficiency in processing benefit claims. Obviously there is nothing to hamper repossession if the tenant is advised to seek housing benefit but fails to do so.[168] There are many case law examples of local authority incompetence.[169] The leading authority is now *Southwark L.B.C.* v. *Scarfo*[170] in which a tenant applied for housing benefit, backdated to cover arrears on no fewer than three occasions, but each time the authority failed to process the application for benefit. The court found oppressive use of the court procedure in failure to process the applications properly. This was compounded by the fact that Scarfo was evicted on only one day's notice and with no prior visit. This was done

---

[162] *Capital Prime Plus plc.* v. *Wills* (1999) 31 H.L.R. 926; N. Allen & M. Chawwner [1999] *J.H.L.* 74.

[163] Rent must be in arrears at (1) the commencement of proceedings, and (2) service of the s.8 pre-action warning notice: *Paddington Churches H.Ass. Ltd.* v. *Sharif* (1997) 29 H.L.R. 817 C.A.

[164] (1998) 30 H.L.R. 48 C.A.

[165] *Second W.R.V.S. Housing Society Ltd.* v. *Blair* (1986) 19 H.L.R. 104 C.A. (large arrears; but secure tenant with psychiatric illness); *Marath* v. *MacGillvray* (1996) 28 H.L.R. 484 C.A.

[166] *Haringey L.B.C.* v. *Powell* (1996) 28 H.L.R. 798 C.A.

[167] *Marath* v. *MacGilvray* (1996) 28 H.L.R. 484 C.A.

[168] *Camden L.B.C.* v. *Akanni* (1997) 29 H.L.R. 845 C.A.

[169] *Barking & Dagenham L.B.C.* v. *Saint* (1999) 31 H.L.R. 520; *Brent L.B.C.* v. *Marks* (1999) 31 H.L.R. 343 C.A.

[170] [1999] 12 C.L. 413 C.A.

to enable the landlord to demolish the block of flats, an event which obviously precluded the setting aside of the possession order.

4.   Repossession and forfeiture

Commercial and long residential tenancies have to be ended by forfeiture if repossession is sought for non-payment of rent or other defaults. Re-entry usually occurs by possession proceedings, based on the theory that the term for which the land is held has ended if the conditions on which it is held have not been fulfilled, though peaceable re-entry is also allowed to commercial landlords. The essential characteristic of the court procedure is that a tenant who pays up before proceedings reach court is entitled to a stay and that there is a discretionary power to allow relief even after possession has been ordered. Wide scale availability of relief substantially reduces the pressure on the tenant to pay rent punctually. The procedure applies primarily to commercial tenants and is described in that context. With a *Rent Act* tenancy, forfeiture may be used to break a fixed contractual term, though if the court orders that a forfeiture should succeed the landlord has still to establish a Rent Act ground for possession. Most Rent Act tenancies are short periodic tenancies which can be ended contractually by notice to quit, so that forfeiture is irrelevant and the only proceedings necessary are for repossession.

   Forfeiture is not relevant if the tenant falls within the protection of the *modern codes* for short residential tenancies. Once the contractual tenancy has ended and the tenant's rights are statutory, the only way to remove the tenant is to take possession proceedings and prove a ground for possession based on arrears of rent. The position was less clear during a contractual period, especially during the initial fixed period of a residential grant, since there seems to be a logic in requiring a landlord to end the fixed term by forfeiture before securing a possession order on the residential ground. Yet this is not the correct way of looking at things, as shown by *Artesian Residential Developments Ltd.* v. *Beck.*[171] It concerned an assured tenancy in Bridgnorth for a fixed term of 10 years, of which repossession was sought in year 9 on account of arrears exceeding £2,000. Proceedings for possession were based on the mandatory rent arrears ground, and a district judge duly made an immediate order for possession. All the arrears were then paid. Had the procedure been for forfeiture the tenant could now apply for discretionary relief from forfeiture,[172] but the Court of Appeal refused relief since the proceedings were not for forfeiture, ruling that the possession order that had been made did terminate the contractual grant. The provision that an order for possession *ipso facto* brings the tenancy to an end[173] impliedly excluded all other methods of hostile termination.[174]

---

[171] [1999] 3 All E.R. 113 C.A.; S. Murdoch [1999] 25 *E.G.* 184.
[172] County Courts Act 1984 s.138; the County Court judge did so.
[173] s.7.
[174] At 32, Hirst L.J.

5. Homelessness

A person evicted on the ground of rent arrears will almost always be found to be intentionally homeless and so disqualified from public assistance with rehousing. This is not
a factor to consider when exercising the discretion to order possession.[175]

6. Reform of the rent procedure

Lord Woolf's reforms of the procedure in money claims have merely highlighted the
shambles left for housing cases, though it is probably fair to say that the carpentry
needed to fit housing cases into the new procedures has temporarily made matters
worse.[176] In fact the Woolf Report on *Access to Justice*[177] contained lengthy proposals
about housing which remain to be implemented. This report considered that the existing procedure to deal with rent arrears was unsatisfactory[178] because tenants rarely
attend fixed date hearings and the procedure does not provide for payment of arrears
without a possession order. Postponements are often given to enable a tenant to have a
last chance to pay, and there are problems about working out whether suspension of a
possession order has ended. A new two-stage procedure is suggested with a paper procedure leading to a court order for payment of arrears, with a second stage hearing if the
tenant fails to comply, leading to a possession order. This would reduce costs and give a
greater threat of possession. There would be a penalty in costs in seeking a possession
order immediately without justification.

H. NUISANCE OR ANNOYANCE TO NEIGHBOURS

1. Ground for possession

Possession can be ordered on the basis of nuisance or annoyance to adjoining occupiers,
or conviction for immoral or illegal uses. Until 1996 the discretionary grounds had
proved to be an inadequate weapon against the scourge of unruly and disruptive neighbours on public sector estates.[179] Some authorities were spending a quarter of a million
pounds each year on proceedings to combat noise nuisances,[180] only to find the courts
granting excessive indulgence towards unmeritorious tenants. Badly needed legislative
tightening arrived as part of the Housing Act 1996. One aspect of it was the introductory tenancy scheme, which requires public sector tenants to serve a probationary year
before acquiring fully secure tenancies; where local authorities adopt this scheme it
often flushes out tenants who are going to create problems at the early stage.[181] The
aspect of the 1996 Act relevant to the drive against anti-social behaviour here is the

---

[175] *Shrewsbury & Atcham B.C.* v. *Evans* (1998) 30 H.L.R. 123 C.A.; contrast *Lewisham L.B.C.* v. *Akinsola* (2000)
32 H.L.R. 44 C.A.

[176] Prof. I. Scott, letter to the Times, April 26th 1999.

[177] (H.M.S.O., July 1996) ch.16. An L.C.D. C.P. in July 2000 proposed more limited reforms.

[178] paras.20–30.

[179] Lord Woolf, *Access to Justice* (H.M.S.O., July 1996) paras.38–52.

[180] [1998] 07 *L.S.G.* 6. Registered social landlords are required to have policies to deal with anti-social behaviour: *Assured Tenant's Charter* (Housing Corporation, 1998) Section 3.

[181] H.A. 1996 ss.124–143; *Manchester C.C.* v. *Cochrane* (1999) 31 H.L.R. 810 C.A.; see above p. 165.

toughening of the grounds for possession available against public sector tenants [182] and also against private sector tenants with assured tenancies,[183] though no change has been made to the old discretionary ground for possession against Rent Act tenants.[184]

A nuisance is anything that would disturb honest people.[185] In *Woking B.C.* v. *Bistram*[186] possession was ordered after complaints of loud music, slamming of car doors, and abusive language. Possession of cannabis and cohabitation[187] have to be tolerated by neighbours, but not drunkenness, abuse, noise, obstruction, and obscene language,[188] not streams of business callers,[189] and not, of course, the playing of Jim Reeves records.[190] Conviction[191] of the occupier for an arrestable offence in the neighbourhood of the dwelling is also a ground for possession,[192] a point particularly useful to deal with properties used for dealing in or taking drugs. In *West Kent Housing Association Ltd.* v. *Davies* a county court judge failed to make a possession order against a tenant guilty of racial abuse, but the Court of Appeal indicated that this was a wrong exercise of the discretion: a sanction had to be imposed after such a serious breach of the tenancy agreement.[193]

Technically possession remains discretionary even after a nuisance[194] or a conviction is proved, one consequence being that it is always essential to take proceedings and obtain a court order. For example if the council knows that the tenant has a personality disorder which makes antisocial behaviour likely, as in *Southwark L.B.C.* v. *Kennedy*,[195] this could (on other facts) raise an estoppel or be relevant when deciding the reasonableness of ordering possession.[196] Where a possession order is made but suspended, a warrant will be required to execute the possession order and a trial will have to be held if there is an application to set aside the warrant.[197] This even applies after a drugs seizure at the property, but the circumstances would have to be wholly exceptional to outweigh such a serious breach.[198] Contractual terms providing for subjective evaluation of a nuisance are likely to be ruled out as unfair contractual terms.[199]

---

[182] Ground 2 (secure): H.A. 1996 s.144 as from February 28th 1997; N. Madge [1998] 03 *L.S.G.* 27; C. Hunter [2000] *J.H.L.* 3 (research study); A. Baker [2000] *J.H.L.* 30.

[183] Ground 14 (assured); H.A. 1996 s.148 in force February 28th 1997.

[184] Case 2 (protected).

[185] *Chorley B.C.* v. *Ribble Motor Services Ltd.* (1997) 74 P. & C.R. 182, 185, Millett L.J.

[186] (1995) 27 H.L.R. 1 C.A.

[187] *Heglibiston Establishments* v. *Heyman* (1978) 36 P. & C.R. 351 C.A.

[188] *Cobstone Investments Ltd.* v. *Maxim* [1985] Q.B. 140 C.A.

[189] *Florent* v. *Horez* [1983] 2 E.G.L.R. 105 C.A.

[190] *Poole B.C.* v. *Carruthers* [1994] Independent January 20th.

[191] This overcomes the problems of proof revealed in *Fred Platts Co. Ltd.* v. *Grigor* (1950) 66 T.L.R. 859 C.A.; (1950) 66 *L.Q.R.* 288.

[192] Ground 2(b).

[193] (1999) 31 H.L.R. 415 C.A.

[194] Especially if caused by a visitor or family member: *Bryant* v. *Portsmouth C.C.* [2000] Indep. C.S. July 10th C.A.

[195] [1998] 2 C.L.Y 2988.

[196] *Croydon L.B.C.* v. *Moody* (1999) 31 H.L.R. 738 C.A.

[197] *Hounslow L.B.C.* v. *McBride* (1999) 31 H.L.R. 143 C.A.

[198] *Bristol C.C.* v. *Mousah* (1998) 30 H.L.R. 32 C.A.; contrast *Tower Hamlets L.B.C.* v. *Kellum* [2000] 06 C.L. 466 C.Ct.

[199] *Camden L.B.C.* v. *McBride* [1999] 01 C.L. 284 (but a statutory ground was made out anyway).

It was often difficult to prove that the tenant was responsible for a nuisance that appeared to emanate from his property or for acts committed by his family.[200] *Wandsworth L.B.C.* v. *Hargreaves* was a extreme example in which possession was refused even after the tenant had been present (albeit when too drunk to participate) while friends made firebombs and lobbed them out of the window of his flat causing £14,000 worth of damage.[201] The 1996 changes extend the nuisance and annoyance ground to allow repossession of secure and assured tenancies on account of the actions of family members[202] and visitors.[203] Hence possession was ordered against the parents in *Northampton B.C.* v. *Lovatt*[204] on the ground that the sons of the tenant had engaged in criminal and anti-social behaviour. The old problem of proof remains for Rent Act tenancies.

A second important aspect of the 1996 tightening up is that the geographical area in which a nuisance may legitimately provoke a complaint is widened. The Rent Act ground refers to adjoining tenants. "Adjoining" has the technical meaning of "touching", but this literal sense was never used to constrict the residential ground for possession, in which context it was interpreted simply to mean "neighbouring", including, for example, complaints from tenants on other floors of the same block of flats,[205] or indeed any other person close enough to the source of complaint to be adversely affected by it.[206] Wider it may be, but this non-literal interpretation still proved to be inadequate to stop anti-social behaviour. For example possession was refused in *Lewisham L.B.C.* v. *Simba-Tola*[207] since the threatening behaviour in issue occurred at the authority's neighbourhood office. The 1996 Act widened the protection for neighbours of public sector and assured tenants to cover the locality of the tenant's property, which is clearly a much wider area even if its outer limit has deliberately been left vague.[208] Hence in *Circle 33* v. *Watt*[209] harassment of housing association staff at an office 3/4 mile from the flat was sufficiently close to the locality of the tenant's home for possession to be ordered. Locality is a matter of fact for the judge, but it may include shops three streets away from the house in question.[210]

A pre-action notice is needed before possession proceedings are taken against disruptive neighbours. A statement that "[t]he tenant frequently disturbs neighbours" did not specify a nuisance with sufficient precision, but an amendment was allowed so that

---

[200] *Leeds C.C.* v. *Harte* [1999] 4 C.L. 470.

[201] (1995) 27 H.L.R. 142 C.A.; *R.* v. *Barnet L.B.C. ex parte Babalola* (1996) 28 H.L.R. 196 Q.B.D.; *Darlington B.C.* v. *Sterling* (1998) 29 H.L.R. 309 C.A. (fires, stones, knives, and assaults).

[202] Under the old law possession based on conduct of a teenage son was relevant only if the tenant was responsible for it: *Kensington & Chelsea R.L.B.C.* v. *Simmonds* (1996) 29 H.L.R. 507 C.A.

[203] *Camden L.B.C.* v. *Gilsenan* (1999) 31 H.L.R. 81 C.A.

[204] (1998) 30 H.L.R. 875 C.A.; *West Kent H.Ass. Ltd.* v. *Davies* (1999) 31 H.L.R. 415 C.A. (possession suspended for 2 years); *Hounslow L.B.C.* v. *McBride* (1999) 31 H.L.R. 143 C.A.

[205] *Cobstone Investments Ltd.* v. *Maxim* [1985] Q.B. 140, 147B–D, Dunn L.J.; T.J. Lyons [1985] *Conv.* 168. Contrast the wider test for public sector tenancies discussed below.

[206] *Northampton B.C.* v. *Lovatt* (1998) 30 H.L.R. 875 C.A.

[207] (1991) 24 H.L.R. 644 C.A.

[208] *Northampton B.C.* v. *Lovatt* (1998) 30 H.L.R. 875 C.A.

[209] [1999] 4 C.L. 355; *Enfield L.B.C.* v. *B.* [2000] 1 All E.R. 255 C.A. (assault in library; people working not protected; there had to be a residential nexus).

[210] *Manchester C.C.* v. *Lawler* (1999) 31 H.L.R. 119 C.A.

it did.[211] The 1996 changes short circuit the normal period of notice and allow the immediate commencement of proceedings based on a nuisance.[212]

Technically possession remains discretionary even after a nuisance or conviction is proved. For this reason it will always be essential for there to be a court order. Where a possession order is made but suspended, a warrant will be required to execute the possession order and a trial will have to be held if there is an application to set aside the warrant.[213] Circumstances would have to be wholly exceptional to outweigh serious breaches such as a drugs seizure at the property.[214] Leniency might be exercised by making a possession order but with an undertaking by the landlord not to enforce it while the tenant behaves, with a provision for the variation of that undertaking in the event of future misconduct.[215]

An additional weapon made available by the 1996 Act is an injunction against anti-social behaviour,[216] the advantage being that it can be supported by a power of arrest.[217] No undertaking in costs is required.[218] It is quite likely that a tenant who has behaved in an aggressive way towards neighbours will take violent exception to the court proceedings, and it may well be necessary to protect witnesses by contempt proceedings against the tenant. In *Manchester C.C.* v. *McCann*[219] the neighbour was no sooner back from giving evidence in court than the tenant threatened him

"I'll fucking have you, you bastard."

This conduct fell within the county court's power to punish contempts even though the threat was not actually issued in the face of the court. A further innovation introduced in 1999 is the Anti Social Behaviour Order, a community-based order akin to an injunction against any person (not necessarily a tenant) acting in an anti-social manner causing distress to people in another household.[220] After eviction for causing a nuisance, the tenant is likely to be found to be intentionally homeless[221] and so will have to re-house himself.

In future housing benefit may be cut.[222]

---

[211] *Camden L.B.C.* v. *Oppong* (1996) 28 H.L.R. 701 C.A.

[212] H.A. 1985 s.83(3) inserted by H.A. 1996 s.147; there is also power to apply without notice to the tenant to dispense with service of a s.83 notice: [1998] 03 *L.S.G.* 27.

[213] *Hounslow L.B.C.* v. *McBride* (1999) 31 H.L.R. 143 C.A.

[214] *Bristol C.C.* v. *Mousah* (1998) 30 H.L.R. 32 C.A.

[215] *Kensington H. Trust* v. *Oliver* (1998) 30 H.L.R. 608 C.A.

[216] H.A. 1996 ss.152–158; as from September 1st 1997; applications for injunctions are regulated by C.P.R. sch.2 C.C.R. Order 49 r.6B; S.I. 1997/1837 r.8; form N110A: S.I. 1997/1838; V. Sterling (1999) 163 *J.P.* 643.

[217] *Enfield L.B.C.* v. *B.* [2000] 1 All E.R. 255 C.A.

[218] *Coventry C.C.* v. *Finnie* (1997) 29 H.L.R. 658, Scott-Baker J.

[219] (1999) 31 H.L.R. 770 C.A.; *Tower Hamlets L.B.C.* v. *Long* (2000) 32 H.L.R. 219 C.A. (committal for 3 weeks for first breach of injunction).

[220] Crime and Disorder Act 1998 s.1; in force April 1st 1999; P. Plowden [1999] *N.L.J.* 479, 520.

[221] *R.* v. *Nottingham C.C. ex parte Edwards* (1999) 31 H.L.R. 33, Sullivan J.

[222] *Quality and Choice: A Decent Home for All*; the Housing Green Paper (D.E.T.R., April 2000) paras.5.46–5.48; also paras.9.13–9.15 and 12.27–12.30.

2. Injunctions for anti-social behaviour

Injunctions to stop anti-social behaviour by tenants[223] are obtained using part 8 procedure.[224] The application should be on the part 8 claim form, must state the terms of the injunction required, and must be supported by a witness statement or affidavit stating the terms of the injunction required.[225] Service on the respondent personally is required, and usually at least two days before the hearing; if this is not possible a witness statement must explain why this was not possible and the application must then be served personally without delay.[226] The hearing will generally be in public[227] and before a district judge.[228] Very often an injunction will include a power of arrest, which should be a separate term and drawn to reflect the statutory grounds for arrest.[229] The injunction should then be delivered to the police station for the locality affected and any variation or discharge must also be reported to the appropriate police station.[230]

3. Domestic violence

Violence by a tenant to his spouse or cohabitee is a ground for possession in the public and social sectors. It is not misconduct directed against the landlord, but rather a reason for removing the privilege of allocation of public housing. Before security of tenure was introduced in the public sector councils would generally terminate the aggressor's tenancy and relet to the victim, but ironically strengthening the security of tenure of public sector tenants made it more difficult to protect victims of violence in the home.[231] This difficulty has been met by providing new grounds for possession.[232] A warning notice is required and must be served on the victim as well as the aggressor, but no period of notice is required.[233] The whole question of the breakdown of family relationships is considered in more detail in the chapter on residential security of tenure.[234]

I.   DISREPAIR AND OTHER BREACHES

1.   General

It is a ground for possession that the condition of premises has deteriorated owing to acts of waste by the tenant.[235] Exterior work will usually fall within the landlord's sphere,[236] so the possession ground relates to internal decorative repair, neglect of the

---

[223] H.A. 1996 s.152.

[224] C.P.R. sch.2 C.C.R. Order 49 r.6B.

[225] r.6B(2).

[226] r.6B(3)–(4).

[227] r.6B(5).

[228] r.6B(12). This remedy does not affect repossession: *Newcastle C.C.* v. *Morrison* [2000] L.T.R. 333 C.A.

[229] H.A. 1996 ss.152(1)(a)–(c), 153(a)–(c); Form N110A; P.D. 4.5.3.

[230] C.P.R. sch.2 C.C.R. Order 49 r.6B(6)–(9).

[231] A. Samuels (1993) 157 *L.G.R.* 301.

[232] Public sector ground 2A introduced by H.A. 1996 s.145; private sector assured ground 14A introduced by H.A. 1996 s.149; in force February 12th and 28th 1997 respectively.

[233] H.A. 1985 s.83A as inserted by H.A. 1996 s.147 as from February 12th 1997.

[234] See above pp. 123–141.

[235] Case 3 (protected); ground 13 (assured); ground 3 (secure). In *Foxell* v. *Mendis*, unrep 1982, the tenants unusual ablutionary practices were held to be waste.

[236] See above Chapter 10.

garden,[237] deliberate damage, or failure to allow access.[238] Separate reference is made to damage to furniture by the tenant.[239] The discretion open to the court prevents abusive complaints by landlords requiring over-fussy compliance with decorative covenants.

In the case of other regulations,[240] the court has even more clearly to balance the reasonableness of the request for possession, but possession is likely after deliberate and repeated beaches.[241] Many public sector landlords now obtain injunctions to enforce tenancy conditions.[242]

2. Housing legislation

Private sector security of tenure does not prevail against a requirement to deliver possession of a dwelling house required under the housing legislation.[243] Closing orders are automatic grounds for possession[244] since it becomes illegal to occupy a property after a closing order has been made. However the tenant has an opportunity to intervene in the administrative procedures and argue that the housing authority should make a repairs order rather than a closing order. Properties are generally only closed if they are not capable of being rendered fit at reasonable expense.[245]

After compulsory purchase of residential accommodation, the local authority must secure that suitable[246] alternative accommodation is made available to the tenant.[247] This does not apply to a council dwelling declared unfit.[248]

Overcrowding is another automatic ground for possession.[249] It can easily arise where the number of persons sleeping in a dwelling contravenes the statutory standards.[250] The room standard is infringed if two persons of the opposite sex must sleep in the same room when they are neither married to each other nor living together (though children under 10 are ignored). The space standard checks the number of people occupying a dwelling in comparison with the number of available rooms,[251] or the aggregate floor area.[252] A landlord who permits overcrowding may be penalised,[253] and the local

---

[237] *Holloway* v. *Povey* [1984] 2 E.G.L.R. 115 C.A. (neglect of garden, but only during occupancy of current tenant); J.E. Martin [1985] *Conv.* 127.

[238] *Empson* v. *Forde* [1990] 1 E.G.L.R. 131 C.A. (refusal of access to landlord to carry out repairs not proved on facts, but was ground for possession).

[239] Case 4 (protected); ground 15 (assured); ground 4 (secure).

[240] Case 1 (protected); ground 12 (assured); ground 1 (secure).

[241] *Sheffield C.C.* v. *Jepson* (1993) 25 H.L.R. 299 C.A. (keeping dog); *Green* v. *Sheffield C.C.* (1994) 26 H.L.R. 349 C.A. (dog); *Barking & Dagenham L.B.C.* v. *Hyatt* (1992) 24 H.L.R. 406 C.A. (parking caravan).

[242] *Sutton Housing Trust* v. *Lawrence* (1987) 19 H.L.R. 520 C.A. (dog).

[243] H.A. 1985 s.612 (R.A. 1977 and assured tenancies).

[244] *Johnson* v. *Felton* (1994) 27 H.L.R. 265 C.A.; *Beaney* v. *Branchett* [1987] 2 E.G.L.R. 115 C.A.; S. Bridge [1988] *Conv.* 64; *Buswell* v. *Goodwin* [1971] 1 W.L.R. 92 C.A.; W.A. West (1971) 87 *L.Q.R.* 21, 471 (no defence that landlord failed to avert the closing order).

[245] *Aslan* v. *Murphy (No.2)* [1990] 1 W.L.R. 773 C.A.

[246] *R.* v. *Brent L.B.C. ex parte Omar* (1991) 23 H.L.R. 466.

[247] Land Compensation Act 1973 s.39 as amended; *R.* v. *Bristol Corporation ex parte Hendy* [1974] 1 W.L.R. 498, 501, Lord Denning M.R.

[248] *R.* v. *Corby D.C. ex parte McLean* [1975] 1 W.L.R. 735, 738, Lord Widgery C.J. ; *R.* v. *Cardiff C.C. ex parte Cross* (1980) 6 H.L.R. 1 C.A.

[249] *Henry Smith's Charity Trustees* v. *Bartosiak-Jentys* [1991] 2 E.G.L.R. 276 C.A.

[250] H.A. 1985 s.324.

[251] 1 room—2 persons; 2 rooms—3; 3 rooms—5; 4 rooms—7½; 5+ rooms—2 per room, children aged 1 to 10 count ½.

[252] 110 sq feet or more; this is subject to a reduction in the case of small rooms.   [253] H.A. 1985 s.331.

authority have power to serve a notice requiring overcrowding to be abated,[254] after which some of the occupiers will be required to move.

In the private sector there is no automatic right to be rehoused, though no doubt the displaced tenant will often qualify as a homeless person.

3.   Bankruptcy

Until *Cadogan Estates Ltd.* v. *McMahon*[255] there was a paucity of authority[256] about whether a proviso for re-entry on a tenant's bankruptcy was a breach of obligation. In that case the Court of Appeal decided recently that a term of a contractual Rent Act tenancy for re-entry in the event of the tenant becoming bankrupt was imported into and became a term of the subsequent statutory tenancy. Hence bankruptcy was a ground for possession. It was not repugnant to incorporate this term in the statutory tenancy and the courts would try to avoid divergences between contractual and statutory tenancies. The House of Lords upheld this decision, which is no doubt technically correct it is disruptive of the statutory scheme for the effect of bankruptcy on short residential tenancies, and is illogical as Lord Millett's dissent shows.[257]

J.   ABUSES OF SECURITY OF TENURE

Residential security of tenure is a valuable right, and it should only be made available to people qualifying, for example by continuing residential occupation. Normally if qualification ends there is a right to possession, either through a mandatory ground for possession or simply because there is no security and so no defence to a possession action. Miscellaneous grounds ensure that unfair advantage will not be taken of residential security.

1.   Unauthorised Rent Act sub-lettings

A *sub-tenant* whose grant is in breach of covenant can be evicted since no security arises where the base letting is unauthorised.[258] The Rent Acts also contain special provisions designed to punish the *tenant* and to ensure that he cannot make a profit from subletting at his landlord's expense. Case 6 arises where the tenant has assigned or sub-let the whole dwelling or has sub-let the last part. This case could only very rarely arise, since it is inherently restricted to sub-letting authorised by the lease, whereas almost all leases will preclude sub-letting. Case 10 applies where the tenant is charging more than the recoverable rent for part of the premises sub-let as a separate dwelling. These grounds are not available under the assured tenancy scheme, because the tenant is entitled to recoup his financial input to the tenancy by dealings, so that if the landlord wants to control dealings, he must insert appropriate covenants in the lease.

---

[254] s.338.
[255] [1999] 1 W.L.R. 1689 C.A., approved [2000] Times November 1st H.L.
[256] *Paterson* v. *Aggio* [1987] 2 E.G.L.R. 127 C.A.; *Halliard Property Co. Ltd.* v. *Jack Segal Ltd.* [1978] 1 W.L.R. 377.
[257] See above pp. 113–115.
[258] *Ujimah H.Ass.* v. *Ansah* (1998) 30 H.L.R. 831 C.A.

2. Unauthorised public sector exchanges

There is no reason to allow public sector housing to be exploited for commercial gain. A ground for possession arises after a tenancy has been assigned to the tenant[259] by way of exchange with any premium or similar sum paid in either direction.[260]

3. End of security of tenure

Normally if security of tenure ends, the landlord is left free to recover possession and the tenant has no security of tenure to plead as a defence. This applies, for example, where the tenant dies and there is no qualified successor. However it is easy for the landlord to lose the right to possession by mistake, and the assured tenancy scheme provides particular protection for modern private sector lettings.[261] It applies where a periodic tenancy[262] has devolved after the death of the previous tenant. The landlord may seek possession at any time up to 12 months after the death, provided that the landlord has not agreed in writing[263] to accept the new tenant.

4. Tenancy induced by misrepresentation

Before a tenancy is granted, the tenant will make statements about his need for accommodation or his proposed use of the property. In order to obtain housing in the public and social sectors, the tenant is bound to make statements to show why he should be favoured with a housing allocation, and the housing authority is bound to act upon such statements. Security should not be awarded to a tenant who lies.[264] Thus it is a ground for possession that the tenant is an initial grantee and the landlord was induced to grant the tenancy to him by a false statement, if it was made knowingly or recklessly by the tenant or another person acting at the tenant's instigation.[265] A similar result had been achieved by case-law development for Rent Act tenancies. It is not the policy to protect those who should never have had a lease in the first place, so a lease voidable for fraud is excluded. In *Killick* v. *Roberts*[266] the landlord was able to rescind the tenancy when it was induced by a fraudulent statement by the tenant that he was having a house built and the tenancy was needed until the house was complete. Rescission was allowed even after the end of the tenancy. The policy was to protect tenants, but not a person who was not entitled to be a tenant in the first place. No statutory tenancy could arise unless there was a protected tenancy from which it could spring. In *Nutt* v. *Read*[267] a shorthold

---

[259] Including any predecessor in title who is a member of his family.

[260] H.A. 1985 sch.2, Ground 6.

[261] H.A. 1988 sch.2, Ground 7; *Shepping* v. *Osada* [2000] Times March 23rd C.A.

[262] A fixed term tenancy is an asset which could vest under the will or on the intestacy of the deceased tenant without succession.

[263] Mere receipt of rent does not prevent possession.

[264] *Rushcliffe B.C.* v. *Watson* (1991) 24 H.L.R. 124 C.A. (untruthfully stated he was sharing).

[265] H.A. 1985 sch.2 Ground 5, as amended by H.A. 1996 s.146 (public sector); H.A. 1988 sch.2 Ground 17 as amended by H.A. 1996 s.102 (assured tenancy scheme).

[266] [1991] 4 All E.R. 289 C.A.; J.E. Martin [1992] *Conv.* 268; L. Tee [1992] *C.L.J.* 21; *Shrewsbury & Atcham B.C.* v. *Evans* (1998) 30 H.L.R. 123 C.A. (secure tenancy obtained when already housed).

[267] [1999] Times December 3rd C.A.; see also *Lewisham L.B.C.* v. *Akinsola* (2000) 32 H.L.R. 414 C.A.

tenancy was rescinded for an innocent mutual mistake. Legislation in 1996 creates an offence of obtaining accommodation by false statements.[268]

5. Notice to quit followed by sale

Under the Rent Act, possession can be ordered if the tenant has given notice to quit and as a consequence the landlord has contracted to sell or let the dwelling.[269] An agreement direct with the purchaser to give up possession is not enforceable.[270] Damages for eviction out of court will also be reduced.[271] There is no corresponding provision for an assured tenancy, though no doubt it will often be reasonable to order possession in these circumstances.

K. RECOVERY FOR PRIVATE-SECTOR LANDLORDS

A number of grounds for possession are provided for private sector landlords to enable them to recover possession, either for themselves or for reletting. These are obviously inappropriate in the public sector where the landlord is a local authority.

1. Mandatory assured tenancy ground

That the landlord requires the dwelling as a residence is a mandatory ground (ground 1) for possession against an assured tenant,[272] where the requirement is to provide the principal home of the landlord or his spouse. It is available where the landlord who is seeking possession occupied the dwelling-house as his only or main residence at some time before the grant of tenancy. Normally the possibility of a ground 1 repossession needed to be reserved in advance by notice stating that it is to apply, though there is power to dispense with notice where it is just and equitable to do so.[273]

2. Mandatory Rent Act case

Case 11 applies where notice is given before the grant of the tenancy that the landlord may require the property as a residence. The object is to ensure that the landlord can recover possession without any dispute,[274] but doubt is cast on the attainment of this objective by the numerous technical rules which restrict the scope of the case.[275]

Prior residence was essential: Case 11 assists a landlord[276] who occupied the dwelling as his residence as an owner-occupier before letting it on a Rent Act tenancy. A case 11 claim failed in *Ibie* v. *Trubshaw*[277] because the landlord bought a house in 1980 for occu-

---

[268] H.A. 1996 s.171.

[269] R.A. 1977 sch.15 Case 5.

[270] *Appleton* v. *Aspin* [1988] 1 W.L.R. 410 C.A.; S. Bridge [1988] *Conv.* 212; though contrast *Rajbenback* v. *Mamon* [1955] 1 Q.B. 283 (agreement by tenant to give up possession on payment of £300 valid); R.E. Megarry (1955) 71 *L.Q.R.* 327.

[271] *King* v. *Jackson* (1998) 30 H.L.R. 541 C.A. (damages small where tenant in last 6 days of a shorthold).

[272] H.A. 1988 sch.2.

[273] See above p. 47.

[274] *Tilling* v. *Whiteman* [1980] A.C. 1 H.L.

[275] *Hellings* v. *Parker Breslin Estates Ltd.* [1995] 2 E.G.L.R. 99 Ch.D. (agent negligent in failing to ensure conditions met).

[276] Or one of joint landlords: *Tilling*, as above.

[277] (1990) 22 H.L.R. 191 C.A.

pation by his girlfriend and her two children rather than for himself; visits and overnight stays ceased in 1983 when the relationship broke down, so the landlord was held not to be in residence when the protected tenancy was granted two years later. According to its literal wording, the case appears to require that the landlord had occupation immediately before the grant of the *current* tenancy. The injustice of this literalism became apparent in *Pocock v. Steel*,[278] in which case a landlord was refused possession in 1982 when he had last occupied in 1967 before the grant of a whole string of tenancies. This decision was reversed by the Rent (Amendment) Act 1985 which ensures that the landlord retains the right to use case 11 provided he was in occupation before case 11 letting began. A chain of case 11 letting is broken by any grant of a tenancy of the property with full security and case 11 only becomes available again if the landlord reoccupies before reletting.

Advance *notice* to the tenant of the potential application of case 11 is required, though there is power to dispense with the requirement of prior notice where it is just and equitable to do so.[279] Dispensation should not occur where the tenant was originally intended to enjoy full security.[280] Suitable cases are where notice was sent but not received by the tenant,[281] where oral notice had been given,[282] or where the tenant knew anyway that his security of tenure was limited.[283]

Requirement as a residence is the basis of the application of case 11.[284] The relaxed Rent Act definition of residence[285] here works in favour of landlords, allowing for example repossession for use as an occasional holiday home.[286] In analogous circumstances the requirement is for residence for any member of the landlord's family, who must have lived with the landlord when he last occupied the dwelling as his residence.[287] Also where the owner has died and the dwelling-house is intended as a home for a member of his family resident with him at the time of his death, or where the successor entitled on his death intends to live there. Case 12 applies where an owner intends to occupy a dwelling as his residence when he retires from regular employment and has in the meantime let on a Rent Act tenancy, and case 20 permits recovery after service in the regular armed forces.

There are analogous circumstances where possession is ordered to facilitate *sale*. These are where the owner has died and the successor in title intends to sell the house with vacant possession, where a mortgage-lender intends to sell it, or where an owner intends to sell it to buy a home more suitable to his needs having regard to his place of

---

[278] [1985] 1 W.L.R. 229 C.A.; *Bissessar v. Ghosn* (1986) 18 H.L.R. 486, 490, O'Connor L.J.; *Hewitt v. Lewis* [1986] 1 W.L.R. 444 C.A.

[279] R.A. 1977 sch 15 part II case 11.

[280] *Bradshaw v. Baldwin-Wiseman* (1985) 49 P. & C.R. 382 C.A.; J.E. Martin [1985] *Conv.* 353; see also pp. 46–49.

[281] *Minay v. Sentongo* (1983) 45 P. & C.R. 190 C.A.

[282] *Fernandes v. Parvardin* [1982] 2 E.G.L.R. 104 C.A.; *Davies v. Peterson* [1989] 1 E.G.L.R. 121 C.A.; [1989] *Conv.* 287.

[283] *Ibie v. Trubshaw* (1990) 22 H.L.R. 191 C.A. (licence); *White v. Jones* (1993) 26 H.L.R. 477 C.A. (oral notice irrelevant).

[284] *Tilling v. Whiteman* [1980] A.C. 1, 18H, Lord Wilberforce.

[285] See above pp. 104–105.

[286] *Davies v. Peterson* [1989] 1 E.G.L.R. 121 C.A. (case 11—3 to 5 weeks each year); J.E. Martin [1989] *Conv.* 287.

[287] *Mistry v. Isidore* [1990] 2 E.G.L.R. 97 C.A. (brother); H. Lewis [1990] *N.L.J.* 1505; *Naish v. Curzon* [1985] 1 E.G.L.R. 117 C.A.; but compare *Ibie v. Trubshaw* above.

work.[288] An owner who intends to reside in the house pending an ultimate sale may obtain possession on the residence case. If it is sold very shortly afterwards the possession order could be set aside for fraud.[289]

3.   Discretionary Rent Act case

Case 9 enables a landlord[290] to recover possession from a Rent Act tenant where the landlord requires the dwelling as a residence for himself or his family. Advance warning to the tenant is not necessary, but the balance of convenience of the landlord and tenant has to be weighed, and certain cases are excluded.

Family requirement is the basis of case 9: it must be shown that the dwelling is required by the landlord for occupation as a residence for himself or close relatives listed in the case, that is any adult[291] son or daughter,[292] or a father, mother or parent-in-law. It is necessary to show a *reasonable requirement* for residential occupation by the landlord, which enables the courts to filter out claims where, for example, the landlord intends to relet.[293] Need has to be established as of the date of the court hearing[294] and, whilst it need not be immediate, it should not be too distant.[295] A tenant may defend a case 9 repossession on the ground that *greater hardship* would be caused by granting the order than by refusing it. Possession may be refused to a landlord who simply wants the property as a holiday home,[296] who has adequate housing,[297] or who wants to evict a tenant who is financially vulnerable.[298] Successful claims[299] often demonstrate ill health,[300] difficulty in obtaining accommodation,[301] or existing accommodation that is grossly unsuitable.[302]

Becoming a landlord by purchase[303] of the dwelling-house or any interest in it excludes the use of case 9 if the purchase occurs after 1965.[304] The court may pierce a corporate veil in order to prevent abuse of this requirement.[305] A voluntary transfer of a house

---

[288] *Bissessar* v. *Ghosn* (1986) 18 H.L.R. 486 C.A. (decided to sell when tour of duty in West Indies extended from 5 to 10 years; possession ordered).

[289] *Lipton* v. *Whitworth* (1993) 26 H.L.R. 293 C.A.

[290] *Baker* v. *Lewis* [1946] K.B. 186 (or one of joint landlords); R.E. Megarry (1947) 63 *L.Q.R.* 26.

[291] *Patel* v. *Patel* [1981] 1 W.L.R. 1342 C.A.; J.E. Martin [1982] *Conv.* 443 (parents as trustees for infant children could occupy for themselves along with the beneficiaries).

[292] *Potsos* v. *Theodotou* (1991) 23 H.L.R. 356 C.A. (child of either of joint landlords); J.E. Martin [1991] *Conv.* 292; *Bostock* v. *De la Pagerie* (1987) 19 H.L.R. 358 C.A. (daughter).

[293] *Ghelani* v. *Bowie* [1988] 2 E.G.L.R. 130 C.A.

[294] *Alexander* v. *Mohamedzadeh* [1985] 2 E.G.L.R. 161 C.A.; J.E. Martin [1986] *Conv.* 272.

[295] *Kidder* v. *Birch* (1983) 46 P. & C.R. 362 C.A.; J.E. Martin [1982] *Conv.* 444.

[296] *Davies* v. *Peterson* [1989] 1 E.G.L.R. 121 C.A. (won on case 11); J.E. Martin [1989] *Conv.* 287.

[297] *Coombs* v. *Parry* (1987) 19 H.L.R. 384 C.A. (inherited agricultural estate with vacant cottage).

[298] *Bradshaw* v. *Baldwin-Wiseman* (1985) 17 H.L.R. 260 C.A.; *Baker* v. *McIver* (1990) 22 H.L.R. 328 C.A.; S. Bridge [1991] *Conv.* 152.

[299] *Fernandes* v. *Parvardin* [1982] 2 E.G.L.R. 104 C.A.; *Rakhit* v. *Carty* [1990] 2 Q.B. 315 C.A.

[300] *Lohan* v. *Hilton* [1994] E.G.C.S. 83 C.A.

[301] *Hodges* v. *Blee* (1988) 20 H.L.R. 32 C.A.

[302] *Manaton* v. *Edwards* (1985) 18 H.L.R. 116 C.A. (caravan); J.E. Martin [1986] *Conv.* 272.

[303] *Bostock* v. *De La Pagerie* (1987) 19 H.L.R. 358 C.A. (acquisition under covenant to transfer to daughter would have caused her to be landlord by purchase); J.E. Martin [1987] *Conv.* 205

[304] March 23rd 1965; relevant dates if the accommodation is furnished are March 8th 1973 and May 24th 1974.

[305] *Evans* v. *Engelson* [1980] 1 E.G.L.R. 62 C.A.

subject to a covenant to discharge the existing mortgage is a gift rather than a purchase,[306] and leaves case 9 in play.

4. Comparison of the two Rent Act cases

Case 11 is mandatory, if prior residence is shown and notice is given before the tenancy
is created. The landlord needs to show requirement for a residence, rather than that this
is reasonable, but hardship to the tenant is irrelevant. *Case 9* is available to a landlord
who has never been in residence and prior notice is not required. The ground is discretionary, hardship to the tenant being balanced against the reasonable *requirements* of the
landlord.

L. REDEVELOPMENT

This ground is not available for Rent Act 1977 tenancies. Under the assured tenancy
scheme (that is *private sector* tenancies granted after early 1989) the landlord's intention[307] to demolish or reconstruct constitutes Ground 6 for repossession. The landlord
must demonstrate that it is impossible to complete the work without possession.
Compensation may be ordered to cover removal expenses.[308] Possession is not available
on this ground to a landlord who acquires the reversion by purchase.

In the *public sector* redevelopment is not a ground for complete removal of a tenant's
home, but is rather a ground for moving a tenant out of his existing property that is to
be redeveloped and shifting him to a temporary alternative,[309] which must be suitable.
If the tenant does move, a mandatory ground[310] is available to remove the tenant from
that alternative accommodation on completion of the works to his original home.

M. ALTERNATIVE ACCOMMODATION

1. Private sector

Tenants do not have a right to security in a particular private sector house or flat; rather
they have the right to the provision of a home, either in the dwelling that was let or
another which is equally suitable. Rejection of an offer of suitable alternative accommodation is therefore a ground for possession of the property.[311] Three fundamental
issues are involved, suitability in terms of the physical size of the accommodation, suitability to the particular tenant as an alternative home, and suitability of tenure and
price.

---

[306] *Mansukhani* v. *Sharkey* (1992) 24 H.L.R. 600 C.A.; J.E. Martin [1993] *Conv.* 156. Contrast *Amaddio* v. *Dalton*
(1991) 23 H.L.R. 332 C.A. (bought from employer's son with money left by employer; was landlord by purchase);
J.E. Martin [1991] *Conv.* 291.

[307] On proof of the intention see: *Poppet's (H.)(Caterers) Ltd.* v. *Maidenhead B.C.* [1971] 1 W.L.R. 69 C.A.;
Wansbeck D.C. v. *Marley* (1988) 20 H.L.R. 247 C.A.

[308] H.A. 1988 s.11.

[309] H.A. 1985 sch.2 (ground 10); ground 10A applies where the dwelling is in a redevelopment scheme area.

[310] Ground 8 (despite any change of landlord).

[311] R.A. 1977 s.98; J. Montgomerie (1957) 21 *Conv.* (*N.S.*) 299; mandatory ground 1 for assured tenancies under
H.A. 1988 sch. 2.

Physical suitability affects matters such as the size and location of the accommodation on offer. If a local authority offers alternative housing, that authority will certify that the size and facilities are sufficient, leaving the judge to decide whether that constitutes a suitable alternative.[312] In the private sector all is a matter of fact for the judge.[313] It is possible for a part of the tenant's existing holding to be a suitable alternative,[314] for example where the part excluded has been sub-let or under-utilised, though even if the tenant is able to make do with what is left there remains an additional question of whether or not it is reasonable to order possession.[315] Where a tenant owns a house in addition to the one he is renting, the landlord may even offer the tenant's own house as a suitable alternative, though the tenant can apparently sidestep this by disposing of his second home before the action for repossession of the rented property is heard.[316]

Accommodation must also be suitable to the tenant's needs, meaning the tenant and his family, but ignoring any person who is not a part of tenant's family.[317] When considering suitability attention is focused on the physical factors, with some attention paid to the tenant's pattern of work, less emphasis is put on his social and cultural base,[318] though these matters may be relevant to the question of reasonableness.[319] In many cases the tenant does not wish to move because he likes either the present house or its locality. *Hill* v. *Rochard* [320] was a clear case, in which a tenant was forced to trade in a handsome country house with a large paddock for a detached house on a modern state in a cul-de-sac with no stabling. A tenant is entitled to take objection to being moved to a neighbourhood of much worse character. A flat on a busy road containing a fried fish shop, a hospital, cinema, and pub is a not suitable alternative to a flat in a quiet residential road with a garden.[321]

Suitability also depends upon affordability of the rent and similarity of the tenure to that of the existing accommodation. If the existing accommodation has full security, so should the alternative. Clearly a full security tenant should not be fobbed off with a shorthold replacement. It is very important to a tenant though whether a Rent Act tenancy (fair rent) can be replaced with an assured tenancy (market rent). There is certainly power for the court to order that a replacement for a Rent Act tenancy will itself operate under the Rent Act, though this power should only be exercised if the court considers that an assured tenancy would not afford the required security. This provision was

---

[312] *Jones* v. *Cook* (1990) 22 H.L.R. 319 C.A.; S. Bridge [1991] *Conv.* 152; *MacDonnell* v. *Daly* [1969] 1 W.L.R. 1482, 1487D, Edmund Davies L.J.; *Roberts* v. *Macilwraithe-Christie* [1987] 1 E.G.L.R. 224 C.A.

[313] *Dame Margaret Hungerford Charity Trustees* v. *Beazeley* [1994] 2 E.G.L.R. 143 C.A. (ancient house at Corsham, Wiltshire; judge's decision could not be upset).

[314] *Mykolyshyn* v. *Noah* [1971] 1 All E.R. 48 C.A.

[315] *Yolande Ltd.* v. *Reddington* [1982] 2 E.G.L.R. 80 C.A.; J.E. Martin [1983] *Conv.* 145.

[316] *Fennbend Ltd.* v. *Millar* (1988) 20 H.L.R. 19 C.A.

[317] *Kavanagh* v. *Lyroudias* [1985] 1 All E.R. 560, 563, Arnold P. obiter.

[318] *Siddiqi* v. *Rashid* [1980] 1 W.L.R. 1018 C.A. (Muslim with cultural base in London required to accept offer of accommodation in Luton); R.G. Lee [1980] *Conv.* 443.

[319] *Yewbright Properties Ltd.* v. *Stone* (1980) 40 P. & C.R. 402 C.A. (freelance clothes designer offered accommodation near his customer base but 2 hours' travelling time from his existing home; this was not reasonable).

[320] [1983] 1 W.L.R. 478 C.A.; P.F. Smith [1983] *Conv.* 320.

[321] *Redspring* v. *Francis* [1973] 1 W.L.R. 134; *Dawncar Investments Ltd.* v. *Plews* (1993) 25 H.L.R. 639 (flat offered in Kilburn High Road); contrast *Minchburn Ltd.* v. *Fernandez* (1987) 19 H.L.R. 29 C.A. (noisy alternative held reasonably suitable).

discussed recently by the Court of Appeal in *Laimond Properties Ltd.* v. *Al-Shakarchi*,[322] when it was decided that a full assurance is equivalent to Rent Act security so that an offer of an assured tenancy is usually sufficient.

2. Reasonableness of ordering possession

Alternative accommodation under the assured tenancies scheme (for grants in the private sector after early 1989) is a mandatory ground,[323] so the landlord does not need to show that it is reasonable to want possession.[324] For older private sector tenancies operating under the Rent Act 1977, an offer of alternative accommodation is a discretionary ground. The judge is required to ask two questions: whether the accommodation offered is reasonable and whether it is reasonable to order possession.[325] The last issue involves balancing the interests of landlord and tenant, and is always open to argument.[326] The length of time for which the tenant has lived in the particular house is an important factor.[327] So too is the nature of the proposed alternative. An Oxford college lecturer cannot be expected to move into a house in North Oxford sharing with students![328]

3. Social

Tenants of registered social landlords have the right under the *Assured Tenant's Charter*[329] to alternative accommodation (at least "normally") if the landlord wishes to carry out work to the home and it is necessary for the tenant to move out to allow it to be done; he may also be able to claim a disturbance allowance.

4. Alternative public sector accommodation

An offer of alternative accommodation is not by itself a ground for possession against a secure tenant, but there are several grounds on which the public sector landlord can insist on repossession when the existence of the ground is coupled with an offer of suitable alternative accommodation,[330] and in that case rejection of a suitable offer is a ground for possession.[331] This means that a public sector landlord cannot move its tenants simply by offering suitable alternative accommodation. An offer must be backed up with one of the grounds justifying a requirement to move, which are overcrowding (ground 9), proposed redevelopment (ground 10) or obligations affecting charitable trusts (ground 11). Others cover specially adapted property where the need of the current tenant has ended and the property is required for another such tenant; more particular examples are property for physically disabled persons, lettings with special

---

[322] (1998) 30 H.L.R. 1099 C.A.; J. Martin [1999] *Conv.* 248; S. Murdoch [1999] 14 *E.G.* 148; *Goringe* v. *Twinsectra Ltd.* [1994] 04 L.A.G. Bulletin 11.
[323] See above pp. 329–330.
[324] *Boyle* v. *Verrall* [1997] 1 E.G.L.R. 25 C.A.
[325] *Minchburn Ltd.* v. *Fernandez* (1987) 19 H.L.R. 29 C.A.
[326] *Land Law plc.* v. *Sinclair* (1991) 24 H.L.R. 57 C.A.
[327] *Battlespring Ltd.* v. *Gates* [1983] 2 E.G.L.R. 103 C.A. (elderly tenant of 35 years' standing); *Minchburn Ltd.* v. *Fernandez* (1987) 19 H.L.R. 29 C.A. (24 years).
[328] *Gladyric Ltd.* v. *Collinson* [1983] 2 E.G.L.R. 98 C.A.; J.E. Martin [1984] *Conv.* 151.
[329] (Housing Corporation, 1998) Section 6.
[330] H.A. 1985 sch.2 part.II.
[331] *Battersea Churches Housing Trust* v. *Hunte* (1997) 29 H.L.R. 346 C.A.

adaptations by social landlords and dwellings in a group with communal facilities let to tenants with special needs.[332] Ground 16 applies after a recent[333] succession on death if the dwelling is more extensive than reasonably required[334] by the successor.

Detailed rules are used to determine issues of suitability.[335] Attention is directed to the physical scope of the accommodation, its tenure, and the proximity of places of work and education, it is right to give less weight to hobbies.[336]

N. SUMMARY OF GROUNDS FOR POSSESSION

1.   Assured tenancies—mandatory grounds[337]

Ground 1.   Requirement by landlord as residence.

1. Notice was served specifying that ground 2 applied before grant of tenancy (or it is just and equitable to dispense with notice);
2. The landlord who is seeking possession occupied the dwelling-house as his only or main residence at some time before the grant of the tenancy; and
3. The landlord requires as his principal home (or for spouse).

Ground 2.   Mortgage-lender.

1. A mortgage of the property was granted before the assured tenancy;
2. The lender is entitled to exercise power of sale;
3. Vacant possession is required in order to sell; and
4. Notice was served before the grant of the tenancy (unless it is just and equitable to dispense).

Ground 3.   Out of season holiday home.

1. The term does not exceed 8 months;
2. Notice before grant of lease (there is NO just and equitable exemption); and
3. At some time in the 12 months prior to the grant of the assured tenancy the property was occupied for a holiday.

Ground 4.   Property required for institutional letting to student.

1. A fixed term tenancy not exceeding 12 months;
2. Notice was given before the grant of tenancy (there is NO just and equitable exemption); and
3. In the 12 months prior to the grant of the assured tenancy it had been let by an educational institution to a student.

---

[332] Ground 13; *Freeman* v. *Wansbeck D.C.* [1984] 2 All E.R. 746; Grounds 14,15.

[333] 6–12 months after death.

[334] Considering his age, the period of time for which the property has been his home, and the degree of financial support provided to the previous tenant.

[335] H.A. 1985 sch.2 Part IV; *Wandsworth L.B.C.* v. *Fadayomi* [1987] 1 W.L.R. 1473 C.A.

[336] *Enfield L.B.C.* v. *French* (1985) 49 P. & C.R. 223 C.A. (flat offered with no garden).

[337] H.A. 1988 sch.2 part I as amended.

Ground 5.   Minister of religion.
    1. Premises are held to be made available to a minister of religion;
    2. Notice was given before the grant of the tenancy; and
    3. The dwelling-house is required for occupation by a minister of religion.

Ground 6.   Demolition or reconstruction.
    1. The landlord intends to demolish or reconstruct;
    2. The landlord did not acquire the reversion by purchase; and
    3. It is impossible to do the work without possession.

Ground 7.   Death of tenant (periodic tenancy).
    1. The tenancy is periodic or statutory periodic;
    2. It has devolved after the death of the previous tenant;
    3. Possession is sought within 12 months of the death; and
    4. The landlord has not agreed in writing to accept the new tenant (mere receipt of rent does not prevent possession).

Ground 8.   Two months' arrears of rent.
    1. Two months arrears of rent at the time of service of notice of the possession proceedings; and
    2. Two months arrears at the time of the hearing.

2.   Assured tenancies—discretionary grounds[338]

Ground 9.   Alternative accommodation.
    Suitable alternative accommodation is available for the tenant or will be available for him when the order takes effect.

Ground 10.   Arrears of rent.
    Rent is in arrears at
    1. the commencement of proceedings; and
    2. service of the notice before proceedings.

Ground 11.   Persistent delay in paying rent.
    The tenant has persistently delayed in paying rent (whether or not any rent is due at the time of the proceedings).

Ground 12.   Breach of covenant.
    Breach of any obligation of the tenancy (other than payment of rent).

Ground 13.   Waste etc.
    1. The condition of the dwelling-house or common parts has deteriorated through waste, neglect or default; and

---

[338] H.A. 1988 sch.2 part II.

2. If the waste is by a sub-tenant etc, the tenant has not taken reasonable steps to remove the person responsible.

Ground 14.   Nuisance to neighbours.
The tenant has caused nuisance or annoyance to adjoining occupiers or has been convicted of using premises for illegal or immoral purposes.

Ground 14A Domestic violence where registered social landlord seeks possession.

Ground 15.   Deterioration of furniture.
Deterioration owing to ill-treatment by a tenant.

Ground 16.   Service tenancies.
The dwelling was let to the tenant in consequence of his employment, and that employment has ceased.

Ground 17.   Tenancy induced by a false statement.

3.   Rent Act 1977 tenancies—discretionary grounds[339]

Alternative accommodation is available to the tenant.[340] This ground is discretionary.

Case 1   Breach of covenant.
Rent lawfully due has not been paid, or any obligation of the tenancy has been broken.

Case 2   Nuisance or annoyance.
Nuisance or annoyance to adjoining occupiers, or conviction of immoral or illegal user.

Case 3   Waste.
Condition of premises has deteriorated owing to acts of waste by the tenant.

Case 4   Furniture.
The condition of any furniture provided by the landlord has deteriorated owing to ill treatment by the tenant.

Case 5   Notice to quit by tenant.
The tenant has given notice to quit and in consequence thereof the landlord has contracted to sell or let the dwelling.

Case 6   Sub-letting.
The tenant has, without the landlord's consent, assigned or sub-let the whole dwelling, or has sub-let part where the remainder was already sub-let.

---

[339] R.A. 1977 sch.15 part 1.
[340] R.A. 1977 s.98.

Case 7   [Repealed].

Case 8   Service occupants.
The landlord reasonably requires the premises for occupation as a residence for someone employed by the landlord and the premises were let to the tenant in consequence of his employment by the landlord which has since ceased.

Case 9   Landlord's occupation.
Where the dwelling is reasonably required for occupation by the landlord (not spouse), his son or daughter over 18 years, his father or mother, or his father-in-law or mother-in-law.

Case 10.   Excessive rent on sub-letting.
That the tenant is charging more than the recoverable rent for part of the premises sub-let as a separate dwelling.

4.   Rent Act tenancies—mandatory grounds for possession[341]

Case 11   Requirement for owner-occupier.
1. An owner-occupier has let his dwelling;
2. It is required for residence by the landlord;
3. Before the letting written notice was served on the tenant.

Case 12   Retirement home.
The owner intends to occupy a dwelling as his residence when he retires from regular employment. Prior notice was served.

Case 13   Holiday dwelling let out of season. Prior notice was served.

Case 14   Vacation lets by educational institutions. Prior notice was served.

Case 15   Minister of religion. Prior notice was served.

Case 16   Surplus tied farm cottages. Prior notice was served.

Case 17   Surplus farmhouses (approved amalgamation schemes).

Case 18   Surplus farmhouses (not approved amalgamation scheme).

Case 19   Protected shorthold tenancy.

Case 20   Tenancy granted by a serving member of regular armed forces.

---

[341] R.A. 1977 sch.15 part 2.

5. Public sector secure tenancies—discretionary grounds[342]

Ground 1   Rent or breach of covenant.
           Rent lawfully due from the tenant has not been paid, or an obligation of the
           tenancy has been broken or not performed.

Ground 2   Nuisance or annoyance.
           The tenant or a person residing in the dwelling house has been guilty of
           conduct which is a nuisance or annoyance to neighbours, or has been con-
           victed of using the dwelling house or allowing it to be used for immoral or
           illegal purposes.

Ground 2A   Domestic violence.

Ground 3   Condition of dwelling.
           The house or any common parts has deteriorated due to acts of waste,
           neglect or the default of the tenant or any person residing with him.

Ground 4   Furniture.
           1. Deterioration in the condition of furniture provided by the landlord,
           owing to ill treatment by the tenant or a person residing in the dwelling
           house.
           2. In the case of ill treatment by a lodger or sub-tenant, that the tenant has
           not taken reasonable steps for the removal of the lodger or sub tenant.

Ground 5   False statement inducing the grant of the tenancy.
           The landlord was induced to grant the tenancy by a false statement made
           knowingly or recklessly by the tenant or a person authorised by him.

Ground 6   Exchange for value.
           The tenancy was assigned to tenant (or a predecessor in title by a member
           of the family) by exchange and a premium was paid either way.

Ground 7   Employment.
           1. The dwelling is within the curtilage of a building held by the landlord
           mainly for non-housing purposes;
           2. It is let to a person in the employment of the landlord;
           3. The tenant or person residing in dwelling-house has been guilty of con-
           duct such that it would not be right for him to continue in occupation.

Ground 8   Temporary home during works.
           1. The dwelling-house was made available for occupation by the tenant
           while works are carried out on his principal home

---

[342] H.A.1985 s.84, sch.2 part I as amended.

2. A new tenancy was granted on understanding that the tenant would give up occupation when other house available;

3. The work has been completed.

6. Public sector secure—where alternative accommodation offered[343]

Ground 9   Overcrowding.
Overcrowding so that occupation would be an offence.

Ground 10   Demolition or reconstruction.
The landlord intends within reasonable time to demolish or reconstruct or carry out works and the work cannot reasonably be carried out without a possession order.
Ground 10 A applies where the property is within a redevelopment scheme area.

Ground 11   Charitable landlord.
The landlord is a charity and the tenant's occupation conflicts with the objects of the charity.

7. Public sector secure—discretionary grounds where alternative accommodation offered

Ground 12   Employment.
1. The property was let in consequence of employment by the landlord or another public sector employer;
2. That employment has ceased;
3. The landlord reasonably requires the dwelling as a residence of another employee.

Ground 13   Disabled property.
Property adapted for a physically disabled person, and it is no longer required for occupation by such a person.

Ground 14   Specially adapted property.
1. The landlord is a housing association or housing action trust that lets dwellings only to people whose circumstances make it specially difficult to satisfy needs;
2. The tenant no longer has that need or has offer of alternative accommodation; and
3. The property is needed for new tenant.

Ground 15   Special needs.
1. The dwelling-house is one of a group, which is let by the landlord for occupation by persons with special needs;

[343] H.A. 1985 sch.2 part II.

2. Social or special facilities are provided;
3. It is no longer needed by tenant;
4. The landlord requires it for another tenant.

Ground 16   Accommodation that is too large.
1. Accommodation is more extensive than reasonably required by the tenant;
2. The tenant succeeded to the property;
3. Possession is sought between 6 and 12 months after the death of the previous tenant.

14

LEASEHOLD HOMES

Long leases. Leases for life. Payments. Ground rents. Proposals for ground rent demands. Repairs and insurance. Residential uses. Forfeiture and protections against it. Proposals for the reform of the law of forfeiture. Sales. Stamp duty. Title and registration.

A. DURATION

Many houses are held on long leases. At the top end of the market in central London, a 50-year lease might fetch say £5 million. The tenant has to repair the home, pay the council tax, and is in most senses an "owner". For this reason this book adopts Professor Clarke's term "leaseholder" to describe a person who has paid a premium for a long lease of an apartment at a low rent.[1] But the freehold is also of substantial value since it reflects both the right to receive rent for 50 years and the right to possession in 50 years' time, so that in reality (as well as in legal theory) the totality of ownership is split. The degree to which the arrangement approximates to ownership depends primarily on the length of the lease and the extent to which the rent is nominal. Discussion is needed of leases for 999 years, those for 99 years, the 21 year cut off, and leases for life.

1. Terms of 999 years

No one has provided a convincing explanation of why terms should be granted for one year short of 1,000, but this has been standard practice for many centuries past.[2] Outside London, houses are commonly sold on 999 year leases at ground rents of say £10 a year, in which case the great majority of the value of the house attaches to the leasehold interest, and there is no practical difference between freehold and leasehold ownership. The landlord's interest consists mainly of the right to receive the ground rent, and can be valued as a multiple of the rent.[3] With a very long lease (that is for 999 years), the annual loss in value is so small that the owner need not worry about it. If the freeholder has the right to possession in 999 years' time, who cares whether it is 998, 997, or even 900 years?

2. Term of 99 years

In the 1970s and 1980s an alarming trend emerged for shorter leases in London—often

---

[1] D.N. Clarke, "Occupying Cheek by Jowl", ch.15 in Bright & Dewar, 380 n.21.
[2] D.N. Clarke, as above, 388.
[3] D.N. Clarke, as above, 389. Ground rent yield may be as high as 20% (that is the price of a ground rent is only 5 years' purchase — enabling one fifth of the cost to be recovered each year) but expenses involved in rent collection are high.

no longer than 99 years—where there is a real division of value between the holder of the reversion and the owners of the flats. Actually, the right to a reversion of possession in 99 years' time is of small value: freeholds are generally valued for enfranchisement purposes at around £1,500 per flat.[4] Conversely this means that leaseholders commonly paid almost as much for a 99-year lease as they would for a much longer term.

Leases of this curious intermediate duration seem to have become prevalent as a result of the self-centredness of lenders. In essence they are willing to lend money on the security of any lease that is long enough to provide adequate cover for repayment of their loan. If money is lent over 25 years lenders will require the security to run say 30–40 years beyond the redemption date of the mortgage. Applying these criteria from the narrow standpoint of a lender, a 99-year term looks a solid security. A potential leaseholder may be very unwise to pay a very large sum for a short lease. It is true that a person may be able to afford a home in an expensive part of London that he could not afford to buy outright. However, the value of the lease will begin to fall dramatically after a few years, especially once the outstanding term falls below 70 years or so. A buyer will pay less for a 50-year term than he will for the freehold, and still less for the five-year rump end of a long lease. This problem is particularly acute in central London, since the houses are more valuable. If £5 million has been paid for a 50-year lease, the transfer of value to the landlord as the lease runs out becomes acute. The simple fact is that short-ish leases are wasting assets. At the end of a building lease, if nothing were done, the landlord would recover back both the land which he let and the house built on it for which he did not pay. The problem is exacerbated where tenants have spent large sums on repairs or are required to incur large liabilities for dilapidations at the end of the lease.[5] It is estimated that around 150,000 leases have less than 80 years to run.

What disadvantages a leaseholder naturally benefits the ground landlord. During the remaining term, the value of his reversion is made up mainly of the right to receive the ground rent and the right to exploit the terms of the lease, for example by earning commission on placing insurance with a particular company. An important element of its value is the right to possession when the term ends, though it will be less than the vacant possession value since (as is explained in the next chapter[6]) the former leaseholder will be entitled to a statutory continuation of his tenancy. The rate of increase in value of the landlord's reversion accelerates as the term date nears. The division of value between landlord and tenant depends to some extend upon what covenants the lease contains to protect the landlord's interest.[7] There may also be a small value attached to the right to re-enter the land during the term of the lease after a forfeiture for breach of covenant; but it will generally be difficult to complete a forfeiture without the tenant claiming relief, so this element may be small. The ground landlord may also derive value from the exploitation of common parts of a block of flats or of flats let out to short-term renters and from development potential.[8]

---

[4] See below pp. 406–409
[5] *Dixon* v. *Allgood* [1987] 1 W.L.R. 1689, 1694, Lord Templeman.
[6] See below pp. 392–396
[7] D.N. Clarke, "Occupying Cheek by Jowl", ch.15 in Bright & Dewar, 380.
[8] D.N. Clarke, as above, 390–391.

3. Cut off point at 21 years

A long lease is one granted for residential purposes for a term of 21 years or more usually at a low rent. The duration is significant for three reasons. First, a lease with 21 years outstanding will require registration.[9] Second, residential security of tenure applies to short rack rental tenancies but not to a long lease at a low rent, though the former leaseholder will have a statutory right to continuation of his long lease when it expires.[10] Finally, a long lease will confer enfranchisement rights which are denied to a short residential tenant, but only if term was originally granted for a certain period exceeding 21 years.[11]

4. Start date

A maximum duration must be fixed by a lease. It is usual with an estate of houses or a block of flats to grant leases to run from a fixed term date, for example to hold[12] to the tenant for 999 years from January 1st 2000; the right to possession runs only from the later grant of the lease, but this technique ensures that all the leases expire together.[13]

B. LEASES FOR LIFE

Periods of years which could operate as legal leases were necessarily distinguished by the structure of the 1925 legislation from periods of lives which could only operate in equity behind a trust. Leases for life were common before 1926. Special provision was therefore required to fit them within the straightjacket created by section 1(1) of the Law of Property Act 1925, since they are outside the statutory concept of the term of years absolute which certainly embraces terminable leases but explicitly excludes those determinable on "the dropping of a life or the determination of a determinable life interest".[14] Without redefinition a lease for life is incapable of forming a legal lease after 1925, since no number of years is fixed in advance. Thus the following leases are not legal as they stand:

> L *to T for life*;
> L *to T for A's life*; and
> L *to T for 10 years if T so long lives.*

5. Leases for life at a rent or fine

Historically it was common to grant "commercial" leases for a life or lives (meaning here only ones that are bought and sold), and before 1926 these could be legal. Great inconveniences flowed from allowing commercial negotiation in relation to leases limited by lives. Buyers were not usually interested in taking an estate limited to the seller's life, and termination of the measuring life could leave a family homeless overnight. Thomas

---

[9] See below pp. 382–385
[10] This will be as an assured tenant; see below pp. 392–396
[11] L.Ref.A. 1967 s.3(1); L.R.H.U.D.A. 1993 s.7(1)(b); see below Chapter 18.
[12] In older terminology this is the *habendum.*
[13] See also below pp. 517–519.
[14] L.P.A. 1925 s.205(1)(xxvii).

Hardy's *The Woodlanders*[15] turns on the devastating consequences for the Winterborne family of the death of old South by whose life the tenure of their cottage was measured. It was difficult to fix a proper commercial value for a lease dependent on an uncertain event, and an unexpectedly early death might hand a large windfall to the landlord. Just as the 1925 legislation sought to prevent the creation of legal life estates, so it also prevented legal leases for life. However when the provisions relating to commercial leases for life are examined it is found that the change was largely cosmetic.

Section 149(6) of the Law of Property Act 1925 effects a statutory *conversion* of any lease for life which is at rent or fine into a term of 90 years. It applies to any lease:

> "for life or lives or for any term of years determinable with life or lives, or on the marriage of the lessee".

It is converted to:

> "a term of ninety years determinable after the death or marriage (as the case may be) of the original lessee, or of the survivor of the original lessees, by at least one month's notice in writing . . .".[16]

Detailed provisions follow about the date on which notice must be served.

A lease for life is rewritten as a lease for 90 years terminable by notice after the dropping of that same life. If the landlord chooses to exercise the power to terminate the lease by notice, the difference in actual duration of the lease is minimal. But the new term fits within the conceptual structure of the 1925 legislation. A lease *for the life of X* cannot be legal after 1925, but a term for *90 years terminable by one month's notice after the death of X* is absolute and has a certain maximum duration.[17] Section 149(6) is therefore very limited in effect. That it is also quite unnecessarily arbitrary can be appreciated by considering a series of examples.

> Example 1. *to A for life.* The lease is not a term of years absolute as it stands, but is converted to a lease of 90 years determinable by notice after the death of A. If a legal lease was granted to a tenant at 18,[18] then the tenant would have to live to more than 108 to exhaust the statutory duration, longevity which is possible but unlikely.
>
> Example 2. *to B for 99 years if she so long lives.* This is not a term of years absolute as it stands, for the time stated is terminable with the dropping of a life.[19] Statutory conversion reduces the agreed term from 99 to 90 years, though for no discernible reason. The converted lease is terminable by notice and so is a term of years absolute.
>
> Example 3. *to C for 99 years if D so long lives.* The lease is converted to a 90 year term, terminable by notice after the death of D.[20]

---

[15] chs.13–15. Hardy's father held the birthplace near Dorchester (now owned by the National Trust) on a lifehold.

[16] This applies to leases whenever created; also to sub-leases and contracts for commercial leases for life: *Blamires v. Bradford Corporation* [1964] Ch. 585.

[17] L.P.A. 1925 s.205(1)(xxvii); *Bass Holdings Ltd.* v. *Lewis* [1986] 2 E.G.L.R. 40 C.A. (14 days' notice after tenant's death).

[18] Query what happens if a lease for life is given to a minor; before 1997 it may have operated under a strict settlement and so kept out of the conversion provision, but now it seems that conversion may occur in equity.

[19] L.P.A. 1925 s.205(1)(xxvi).

[20] s.149(6) proviso (c).

Example 4. *to E for 10 years if he so long remains a bachelor.* This is apparently a term of years absolute,[21] but even so section 149(6) will convert it as a lease terminable on marriage. Again there is no good reason to extend the lease from 10 years to 90 years, terminable by notice after the marriage. The tenant may, by virtue of the increase in length of the basic term, acquire rights long after the parties had intended, and without the possibility of the landlord increasing the rent.

Termination of the converted lease can occur by written notice, possibly by either party, though it will usually be the landlord who has the greatest interest in ending the lease. As the tenant will usually be dead, provision is made for service of the notice by affixing it to the property itself if there is no person in existence entitled to the leasehold interest. The notice must be of at least one month's duration, and must expire on any subsequent quarter day.[22] Suppose that a lease at a rent was granted in 1954 *to X for life* meaning that the converted term will expire in 2044. If X died on October 28th 1999, the lease can be terminated by one month's notice to expire on December 25th 1999 or any subsequent quarter day.

6.   Trusts

Leases for life may also be created under trusts. A lease for life is purely *voluntary* if it reserves no rent and no premium and there is no other consideration such as a discount on the price of the freehold estate.[23] Such leases can be created under trusts, being overreachable by the trustees, and for most purposes effectively identical to a life interest under a trust. There is no statutory conversion. An advantage is that it is easier to impose repairing obligations. Historically (that is until 1997) they could be created under a trust for sale, but otherwise a lease for life operated as a beneficial interest under a strict settlement.[24] *Commercial leases for life* could be created *under express trusts.* Conversion to a 90-year term did not affect any lease taking effect in equity under a settlement or created out of an equitable interest under a settlement, meaning a strict settlement.[25] This was a means of creating a life interest under a trust so as to reserve a rent or to charge a premium. New strict settlements can no longer arise after 1996,[26] and so it appears that this exception is no longer available for new leases.

7.   Leases for life and enfranchisement

Special consideration is required of leases for life in the context of enfranchisement.[27]

---

[21] s.205(1)(xxvii) does not refer to marriage.

[22] The quarter days are December 25th, March 25th, June 24th, and September 29th, unless special quarter days are agreed: s.149(6)(d).

[23] *Skipton B.S.* v. *Clayton* (1993) 66 P. & C.R. 223 C.A.; *Waite* v. *Jennings* [1906] 2 K.B. 11 (on Conveyancing Act 1881).

[24] Settled Land Act 1925 s.1; *Binions* v. *Evans* [1972] Ch. 359 C.A.

[25] L.P.A. 1925 s.149(6)(a) refers to a settlement, defined by Settled Land Act 1925 s.117(1)(xxiv) to mean land held under a strict settlement.

[26] T.L.A.T.A. 1996 s. 2(1).

[27] See below p. 390.

C. PAYMENTS

1. Premium

In *Johnston* v. *Duke of Westminster* Lord Griffiths observed that[28]:

> "There are basically two ways in which a landlord can obtain moneys worth for a house that
> he wishes to let on a long lease. Either he can let the premises for the highest annual rent he
> can obtain in the market, i.e. the rack rent, or he can accept a lower rent plus the payment of
> an immediate capital sum—a premium."

This chapter explores Lord Griffiths' second method in which leasehold tenure
approaches ownership, which is used for some houses and almost all flats. At some time
in the past a landlord or developer has sold the house, taking most of the value of the
land in the form of a premium, that is a capital receipt in hand at the outset. A receipt
clause is needed in the lease to permit payment of the amount of the premium to the
landlord's solicitor.

Generally there is no restriction on charging a premium for the grant of a long residential lease at a low rent. However in the past—when the Rent Acts applied to new
renting arrangements—there were restrictions on premiums charged on the grant of
short residential tenancies, and these could also apply to a long lease if it happened to be
at a high rent. For most of the relevant time in the past, the test was whether the rent
exceeded 2/3rds of the rateable value of the house—which was very unlikely to be the
case for a property sold for more than 21 years at a premium. However it was possible
to get caught if a long lease included a provision for review of the rent. The trap was that
if the Rent Act 1977 later came to apply to the tenancy it then became illegal to recoup
the premium paid on the grant of the lease to the ground landlord by selling the lease to
a buyer. This was a rare trap. It should also be remembered that the Crown was always
allowed to charge premiums, so that the pattern of leases on Crown Estate is different.

2. Building leases

In the past it was very common for a landowner to parcel up his land and sell vacant
plots on the basis that the buyer would erect a house on it, an arrangement called a
building lease. At the end of the lease, the land reverts to the ground landlord who seems
to secure a double profit by recovering the land with a building on it for which he has
not paid.[29] It is these leases that underlay the philosophy of the earliest enfranchisement
legislation, which was that the ground landlord should be compensated for the value of
the land but not for the value of the building on it.[30]

3. Ground rent

A ground rent[31] is opposed to a rack rent. If a ground landlord has extracted some of the
value from the land by taking a premium when granting a lease he will only be able to
obtain a rent that is below the full annual value of the land. Long leases will almost

---

[28] [1986] A.C. 839, 845A.
[29] D.N. Clarke, "Occupying Cheek by Jowl", ch.15 in Bright & Dewar, 388 n.67.
[30] L.Ref.A. 1967; see below pp. 401–404.
[31] In older terminology the *reddendum* ("yielding and paying therefore")

always satisfy the low rent tests of the short residential and enfranchisement codes. In the past the test was whether the rent did not exceed 2/3rds of the letting value[32] or rateable value.[33] The abolition of the domestic rating system in mid-1990[34] led to a simple monetary test: the rent (ignoring council tax) must not exceed £1,000 a year in Greater London or £250 a year elsewhere.[35] The precise tests are considered in the next chapter.[36]

4. Information in ground rent demands etc.

A tenant of property occupied as a dwelling can make a written request to the landlord's agent or collector of rent for disclosure of the immediate landlord's name and address.[37] This information must be provided in rent demands.[38] There is a duty to inform the tenant of any assignment of the landlord's interest if a dwelling is assigned.[39]

5. Proposals to require ground rent demands

There is a problem of unscrupulous ground landlords imposing excess charges for late payments of ground rent in some cases where payment is made only one day late. Ground landlords often do not bother to ask for payments but impose additional charges when the leaseholder forgets to pay, in some cases requesting payments wholly disproportionate to the cost of a reminder letter. Penalties on late payment will be one form of "administration charge". The reasonableness of which might, under the terms of the draft Bill, be challenged before a Leasehold Valuation Tribunal.[40] But since many leaseholders may be reluctant to challenge costs before a Tribunal, the Government has decided upon a more general provision[41] that a leaseholder should be entitled to receive a demand for ground rent. Information to be included in the demand will be prescribed.[42] Additional interest charges could not be levied until a demand period of between 30 and 60 days had expired, and forfeiture would also be frozen during that period. Notice could be sent by post either to the dwelling or to another address notified by the leaseholder.

---

[32] L.Ref.A. 1967 s.4(1) proviso; L.R.H.U.D.A. 1993 s.8(1)(a); *Johnston v. Duke of Westminster* [1986] A.C. 839 H.L.; *Hembry v. Henry Smith's Charity Trustees* [1987] 2 E.G.L.R. 109 C.A.; *Crean Davidson Investments Ltd. v. Earl Cadogan* [1999] 2 E.G.L.R. 96 C.Ct.

[33] L.Ref.A. 1967 s.4(1); payments for services, repairs, etc. are ignored, as are abnormal fluctuations.

[34] For leases granted on and after April 1st 1990; leases granted after 1990 under a pre 1990 contract are assessed on the rateable value basis.

[35] L.G.H.A. 1989 sch.7; References to Rating (Housing) Regs. 1990, S.I. 1990/434 reg.2 and sch., paras.7–8.

[36] See below pp. 390–392.

[37] L.T.A. 1985 ss.1, 2 (corporate landlord); only the immediate landlord is affected.

[38] L.T.A. 1987 part VI ss.46–49.

[39] L.T.A. 1985 s.3 as amended L.T.A. 1987 s.50; the information must be provided not later than the next rent day. It is in the interests of the seller to give notice to avoid liability under the covenants: subss.(3A), (3B). Additional requirements apply to the freehold in a block of flats; see below pp. 429–430.

[40] See below pp. 464–465.

[41] Commonhold and Leasehold Reform Bill 2000 cl. 142, C.P. (Cm 4843, August 2000) Part II paras.2.2.7, 4.5.

[42] This would be additional to the existing requirements of L.T.A. 1987 s.47 to include the name and address of the landlord and (if outside England and Wales) an address in England and Wales for the service of notices, discussed below at pp. 464–467.

6. Service charge

This is used to pay for repairs, maintenance and services in blocks of flats. Payments made by individual leaseholders are almost always reserved as additional rent. Sums are often substantial—much more so than the ground rent. Service charges and the current reforms are considered at length in a later chapter.[43]

7. Other payments

Council tax, water rates, and charges for electricity, gas and telecommunications will be the responsibility of individual leaseholders, and there will commonly be a covenant to meet any demand paid by the ground landlord.

D. REPAIRS AND INSURANCE

1. Houses

Responsibility for maintaining a house naturally falls on a leaseholder as an aspect of his ownership. Statute imposes a responsibility to maintain the structure of a dwelling let for up to seven years on to the landlord,[44] but it has nothing to say about long lease-holders. A ground landlord will protect the value of his reversion by requiring the ten-ant to covenant to repair, and reserving rights in default, and even if he fails to take this natural precaution, the tenant will still be liable for waste.[45] Case law on the nature of repair is considered in the commercial context,[46] where it will be seen that some restrictions are imposed on what a leaseholder is required to do: the standard only has to be what is reasonable for the locality and quality of building, the leaseholder is only required to reach the original standing of the particular house without improvement, and no work is required to deal with inherent defects in the construction of the house.

Ground landlords cannot do much about poor repair, even if there is serious dilapi-dation, since it is unlikely to have much effect on the value of the reversion. Leaseholders should not be required to repair their property at the behest of the ground landlord. First, damages obtainable by a ground landlord are capped at the loss in value of his reversion.[47] Second, actions for damages or for forfeiture are prevented by the Leasehold Property (Repairs) Act 1938 until the last five years of the term[48]; the bar imposed by the 1938 Act is lifted only if the ground landlord can show that the value of his reversion is threatened or there is some other reason why immediate enforcement is important. This protection for a leaseholder is removed if the long lease is allowed to expire without the exercise of enfranchisement rights: at this stage the ground landlord may well be able to make large claims for damages for dilapidations, the normal measure of damages being the cost of the repairs needed.[49]

---

[43] See below pp. 456–464.

[44] L.T.A. 1985 ss.11–16.

[45] Statute of Marlborough 1267, 52 Hen.3 c.23 (still in force); *Dayani* v. *Bromley L.B.C.* [1999] 3 E.G.L.R. 144 Q.B.D.

[46] See below pp. 671–680.

[47] L.T.A. 1927 s.18(1); see below pp. 681–685.

[48] See below pp. 801–804.

[49] See below pp. 681–685.

2. Flats

Leaseholders of flats will also have to pay for the cost of maintenance and repair, but the mechanism is different. Structural elements and common parts are maintained by a flat management company which levies a service charge on the leaseholders to cover the cost. Such arrangements are discussed in a subsequent chapter.[50] Leaseholders retain direct responsibility for internal parts and decoration.

3. New homes

A new lease is often granted when a house or flat has just been constructed. In this case the lease should contain a warranty by the builder about defects and the buyer will also require a guarantee such as that provided by the National House Builders' Council.[51]

4. Insurance

Both the leaseholder's estate and the landlord's reversion lose value if the property is burnt down, or is destroyed by some other insurable risk. Adequate provisions about insurance[52] are vital to make a long lease acceptable to a lender, and insurance covenants are the most troublesome to draft. The essence of insurance is simple: an insurance company agrees to bear certain risks in return for the payment of regular premiums. Insurance obligations arise from express covenants, matters to be dealt with including:

The choice of insurance company;
The insured risks—fire and what else?
The value insured—usually the full reinstatement cost;
Provisions against increasing the cost of insurance;
Who insures?—probably the leaseholder of a house or the management company of a block of flats;
Production of proof of insurance to the other party, with default powers to insure; other leases provide for the *landlord* to effect insurance (giving control over the cover) but *at the cost of the tenant.*
Reinstatement—what form it should take;
A right to require reinstatement either under an express covenant or by statute[53]; and
Provisions for the suspension of ground rent and service charge[54] if the property becomes uninhabitable.

What happens if, ultimately, reinstatement of the house after a fire proves to be impossible? It seems most logical to treat the fund of money paid out by the insurer as a fund to be divided between leaseholder and ground landlord according to their proportionate interests in the building at the time of the fire.[55] This can certainly be

---

[50] See below Chapter 16.
[51] Barnsley's *Conveyancing Law and Practice* (Butterworths, 1996, 4th ed by M.P. Thompson) 182–183.
[52] Woodfall 11.089–11.090.
[53] Fires Prevention (Metropolis) Act 1774 s.83.
[54] *P. & O Property Holdings Ltd.* v. *International Computers plc.* [1999] 2 E.G.L.R. 17; J.E. Adams [1999] *Conv.* 284.
[55] *Re King* [1963] Ch. 459, 484–486; *Beacon Carpets Ltd.* v. *Kirby* [1985] Q.B. 755 C.A.; *Mark Rowlands Ltd.* v. *Berni Inns Ltd.* [1986] Q.B. 211 C.A.; J. Birds (1986) 6 *O.J.L.S.* 304.

achieved by express provisions, though care is needed to ensure that the arrangements will be considered to provide sufficient guarantee of a lender's security. Unfortunately, it is also possible to argue that there is an implied resulting trust to the party paying the premiums.[56]

Protection for residential leaseholders against unfair insurance rents is described below.[57]

5. Improvements

These will often require the consent of the ground landlord, who will be charged with the duty of protecting his own reversion and also the interests of neighbours. The old law of waste has been superseded by express covenants against alterations or additions.[58] What is prohibited depends upon the wording used in the covenant. For example, in *Bent* v. *High Cliff Developments Ltd.*,[59] a covenant in a 999-year lease of a penthouse apartment not to make *structural* alterations may not prevent the replacement of windows and external doors, given the careful definition of the "structure" contained in the lease.

Most covenants will be qualified so that the leaseholder's right is to make improvements only with the prior consent of the landlord. Statute implies a proviso that the consent of the landlord is not to be unreasonably withheld,[60] and the common law implies a similar proviso into a covenant to secure approval to building plans.[61] Caselaw on the reasonableness of refusing consent, remedies, and reinstatement, is considered as an aspect of commercial leases.[62]

Proposals to control "administration charges"—which will include charges for grants of consents—are described below.[63]

6. Fixtures

The rule is that a fixture becomes a part of the land when it is annexed to it. Unintended gifts to ground landlords are made much less likely by a number of principles. First, an item which is physically attached to the property may not be a fixture if the object of annexing it is so that it can be enjoyed as a chattel.[64] Secondly, ornamental and domestic fixtures belong to the tenant and can be removed by him when he moves. Admittedly there is an archaic flavour to the case-law examples of panelling,[65] chimney glasses, stoves, grates, ranges and ovens. Finally a lease may reserve the right for the leaseholder

---

[56] *Re King* at 492–494, Upjohn L.J., 498–500, Diplock L.J.

[57] See below pp. 465–466.

[58] Woodfall 11.254–11.263; caselaw is considered below at pp. 672–673, 692–696.

[59] [1999] 34 L.S.G. 35.

[60] L.T.A. 1927 s.19(2); *F.W. Woolworth & Co. Ltd.* v. *Lambert (No.1)* [1937] Ch. 37, 53, Romer L.J; L.T.A. 1954 s.83 (county courts have jurisdiction).

[61] *Cryer* v. *Scott Bros. (Sunbury) Ltd.* (1988) 55 P. & C.R. 183 C.A.; J.E. Adams [1988] *Conv.* 172.

[62] See below pp. 692–696.

[63] See below pp. 464–465.

[64] *Leigh* v. *Taylor* [1902] A.C. 157 H.L. (tapestry); Sparkes *N.L.L.* 558–560.

[65] *Spyer* v. *Phillipson* [1931] 2 Ch. 183.

to remove fixtures[66] though this will be balanced by a requirement to minimise and make good damage to the freehold.[67]

E. RESIDENTIAL USES

Leaseholders of houses and flats have enfranchisement rights—the right to acquire the freehold or to extend their leasehold—and there are statutory controls on residential service charges. Long leases are also commonly used for some types of business lease, one archetype being a head lease of an entire office block intended for exploitation by the grant of sub-leases to the tenants who will actually operate businesses there. Commercial tenants are left to fend for themselves. It is therefore essential for a long lease to include a use covenant in order to allocate a particular lease to the long residential or the commercial sphere. Allocation is based on the primary use, though many buildings have mixed uses, for example a lease of a shop with a flat above, or a block of flats with a layer of shops at ground level. Mixed blocks create problems under the legislation governing security of tenure[68] and enfranchisement.[69]

F. FORFEITURE

Forfeiture is the right of the landlord to re-enter the premises that he had let to the tenant because of the tenant's breach of covenant, and to terminate the lease on account of that breach. Forfeiture is frequently used to repossess commercial premises (and is discussed in detail in the business context).[70] The threat of forfeiture is the main weapon available against the leaseholder of a house or flat to ensure that he complies with his covenants. If the leaseholder is supposed to repair his flat but fails to do so, the ground landlord can threaten to terminate the lease, knowing that any sensible owner will choose to carry out repairs rather than lose the money invested in his leasehold estate.

Apart from the rare case of denial of title, the right of the ground landlord to re-enter the premises on account of the tenant's breach of covenant must be reserved by the terms of the lease. The clause is described as a proviso because it begins with the words "provided always that". It may operate on any breach or when particular covenants are broken. However, when drafting residential leasehold schemes it is important to ensure that rights of re-entry will be acceptable to potential lenders, since otherwise they will detract from the value of the leasehold estate created.

It is necessary to consider the various termination events in turn, since there are two main procedures and numerous sub-categories.

1. Arrears of ground rent

A lease will commonly provide for it to terminate if the ground rent is a certain number of days overdue, whether formally demanded or not, and without any requirement to

---

[66] *Poster* v. *Slough Estates Ltd.* [1968] 1 W.L.R. 1515, 1520G, 1521C.
[67] *Mancetter Developments Ltd.* v. *Garmanson Ltd.* [1986] 1 All E.R. 449 C.A.
[68] See below pp. 549–551.
[69] See below pp. 433–434.
[70] See below Chapter 29.

give any notice to the tenant. With long leases, the sums are generally small and many ground landlords are lax about collection, so it seems out of proportion to treat arrears as a termination event without any warning. In any event a long lease will hardly ever be ended for arrears of rent in the real world: leaseholders have the right to prevent forfeiture by making good the arrears—either by staying the proceedings before judgment or by seeking relief from the forfeiture afterwards.[71] It will become much more difficult to forfeit for arrears of ground rent if the proposals to require a demand are implemented.[72]

2. Service charge

Non payment of service charge is the commonest reason for forfeiting a lease of a flat. The Housing Act 1996 introduces special restrictions on forfeiture of the lease of a dwelling[73] on the ground of non-payment of service charge. Forfeiture cannot proceed until the amount payable has been agreed, admitted, settled by arbitration, or determined by a Leasehold Valuation Tribunal.[74] After adjudication 14 days must be allowed for payment before proceedings are commenced, though an appeal need not delay a forfeiture. The rent procedure will apply if service charge is reserved as rent. Otherwise it is necessary to serve a preliminary section 146 notice[75]: it is permissible to give the notice before the amount of the charge is adjudicated,[76] but the notice must be in a prescribed form warning the tenant of his rights[77] and it cannot be acted on until 14 days after the adjudication.

Escalus Properties Ltd. v. *Robinson*[78] decides that the terms of the lease are decisive when allocating a lease between the rent and the notice procedures. Four leases of houses and flats in South London were considered by the Court of Appeal in each case subject to a service charge. In two cases[79] the service charge was deemed by the lease to be additional rent, so the Court of Appeal held that the rent procedure applied. Another lease lacked this provision[80] meaning that the section 146 notice procedure applied. The later Court of Appeal which decided *Khar* v. *Delmounty Ltd.*[81] confirmed that *Escalus* was a binding decision, so that the terms of the lease are decisive: the rent procedure does not apply unless the service charge is either mentioned in the reddendum—the technical part of the lease beginning "reserving" which creates the rent—or is deemed to be recoverable as rent. A tenant whose breach is "rent-only" may be entitled to an automatic stay of the proceedings by paying what is due into court,[82] whereas relief is always discretionary under the notice procedure.

---

[71] See below pp. 815–829.

[72] See above p. 367.

[73] H.A. 1996 s.81(5); L.T.A. 1985 s.18 (definition of a "dwelling"). For proposed reforms see below p. 375.

[74] H.A. 1996 ss.81, 83; S.I. 1997/1854 (form and contents of applications).

[75] *Abbey National B.S.* v. *Maybeech* [1985] Ch. 190, Nicholls J.; *Rexhaven Ltd.* v. *Nurse* (1996) 28 H.L.R. 241, Colyer J.

[76] H.A. 1996 s.81.

[77] s.82(3), (4); the warning must be at least as conspicuous as the operative parts.

[78] [1996] Q.B. 231 C.A.

[79] *Robinson* and *Cooper-Smith*; the case of *Walsh* concerned arrears of rent exclusively.

[80] *Dennis*; this may now be subject to the H.A. 1996 just described.

[81] (1998) 75 P. & C.R. 232 C.A.

[82] See below pp. 815–818.

3.   Disrepair

A ground landlord will rarely be able to end the interest of a leaseholder for failure to repair. The vital first step is to give a section 146 notice.[83] The object of this is to indicate to the leaseholder precisely what is wrong and to give him a chance to put things right. Leaseholders will very often challenge the notice, either because the work required is unnecessary, or it is not a repair, or because the standard of internal repair required is unreasonable.[84] A landlord must allow a reasonable time for the breach to be remedied before proceeding to forfeit by taking action. Once the ground landlord obtains possession under a section 146 notice, the right to relief has ended.

The *Leasehold Property (Repairs) Act 1938* protects leaseholders since the ground landlord must obtain permission from the court before proceeding to forfeit the lease. Five grounds are set out and, if none of them can be established, the action is blocked. In essence the requirement is for the landlord to demonstrate why immediate enforcement is important, so the ground landlord has to show that the value of his reversion is under threat. The Act protects all houses until the last five years of the term.[85] The clumsy notice and counter notice procedure is explained as an aspect of commercial forfeiture.[86]

4.   Other breaches

Breaches other than arrears of rent entitle a landlord to forfeit only after service of a *notice* on the leaseholder under section 146 of the Law of Property Act 1925.[87] The three (almost) essential contents of a pre-forfeiture notice are that it must: (1) specify the particular breach complained of; (2) require the tenant to remedy the breach, assuming that it is capable of remedy; and (3) require the tenant to make compensation in money for the breach. The case law on these requirements will be considered as an aspect of commercial forfeiture,[88] but a very short period of notice may suffice where a leaseholder has allowed an *immoral stigma* to attach to the flat by allowing its use for prostitution, a breach not remedied by cessation of the prostitute's trade. However some breaches of *negative covenant* are capable of remedy.[89]

5.   Bankruptcy

A long lease of a flat is an important asset of the leaseholder. If the lease has been mortgaged before the owner of it becomes bankrupt, the lenders will seek to exercise the security of their mortgage by selling the flat. In order to protect their right to sell in these circumstances, building societies will not generally accept a lease which gives the ground landlord the right to terminate on the leaseholder's bankruptcy. If, exceptionally, a lease is granted on these terms, a lender will have a right to relief from the forfeiture.[90] If it is

[83]   L.P.A. 1925 s.146. It must be shown that the leaseholder knew of the notice: L.T.A. 1927 s.18(2).
[84]   L.P.A. 1925 s.147.
[85]   s.1(1); *Starrokate Ltd.* v. *Burry* [1983] 1 E.G.L.R. 56, 57G, May L.J.
[86]   See below pp. 801–804.
[87]   Re-enacting the Conveyancing Act 1881 s.14, as amended by Conveyancing Act 1892 s.4.
[88]   See below pp. 796–802.
[89]   *Savva* v. *Houssein* [1996] 2 E.G.L.R. 65 C.A.
[90]   See below pp. 829–831.

possible to pay off the mortgage, the trustee in bankruptcy of the leaseholder also has a chance to raise money by the sale of the lease; he must do so within *one year* of the date of the forfeiture after which the purchaser is protected indefinitely.[91] Unfortunately the year can all too easily slip by without the need to sell being appreciated.[92]

6. Reform proposals

These are considered below as an aspect of protection of leaseholders.[93]

G. PROTECTION AGAINST FORFEITURE

1. Protection of occupiers

A ground landlord cannot terminate the lease of a dwelling that is occupied simply by changing the locks. For 40 years or more, residential landlords have been required to obtain a court order before re-entering.[94] It is an offence to use force in a repossession,[95] and also an offence to forfeit against a residential occupier who is opposed to the repossession.[96] Nothing just said prevents repossession out of court once the leaseholder has abandoned the flat.[97]

2. Protection for leaseholders

Wide-scale protection is given to the owners of leasehold houses and flats against forfeiture. On one level, this is simply a belated chance to comply with their covenants; if all breaches are made good, relief will generally be granted provided that it was claimed in time. As already explained[98] the precise procedures vary for each of the kinds of termination event. On another level there is an important protection in the law of waiver—which wipes the slate clean when the ground landlord recognises the existence of the lease by accepting ground rent.[99] In addition a leaseholder has some substantial statutory protection in cases where a ground landlord is not able to insist on strict compliance with the terms of the lease. Examples considered above[100] are the protection against disrepair claims until the last five years of the lease and the need to secure an adjudication of the reasonableness of a service charge demand.

Otherwise, there is no general protection against the over-literal ground landlord. In *Betterkey* v. *Joseph*[101] a lease of a flat provided that the lease should be forfeited unless the windows were cleaned regularly. By allowing re-entry, the court handed the capital value of the flat to the ground landlord for a trivial breach of a trivial covenant. In *Dollar*

---

[91] L.P.A. 1925 s.146(10).
[92] See below p. 831.
[93] See below Chapter 29.
[94] Protection from Eviction Act 1977 s.2; *Kataria* v. *Safeland plc.* [1998] 1 E.G.L.R. 39, 41M, Brooke L.J.
[95] s.3.
[96] Criminal Law Act 1977 s.6.
[97] *Betterkey* v. *Joseph* [1991] Independent, November 1st 1991 (forfeiture because windows not cleaned); relief would now be available after a physical re-entry: see below pp. 821–823.
[98] See above pp. 371–374.
[99] See below pp. 812–815.
[100] See above p. 373.
[101] [1991] Independent November 1st.

Land (Cumbernauld) Ltd. v. *C.I.N. Properties Ltd.*[102] it was held that a landlord who had followed the Scottish procedure for forfeiting a lease was entitled to retain the lease after a breach of covenant. An action by the displaced tenant for compensation for the unjust enrichment obtained by the landlord was dismissed. There was indeed an enrichment, but the retention of this profit was not unjust. Forfeiture is almost always unfair where a lease has a capital value. In *Khar* v. *Delmounty Ltd.*[103] the parties to a lease of a flat agreed that the court should make an order for sale of the property rather than end the lease for non-payment of service charge. This enabled the ground landlord to recover the arrears of service charge while returning the net value of the flat to the leaseholders. Sale should now be developed to replace forfeiture of leases with a capital value just as judicial sale replaced the foreclosure of mortgages.

3.   Law Commission reform proposals

Law Commission proposals to reform the procedures for the termination of leases are currently stalled while the Government considers more radical reform.[104] Its provisional proposals should lead to a fairer regime. Determination of facts is to be separated from the subsequent repossession proceedings (as at present is the case for service charges); procedural safeguards will be in place before penalties or extra interest can be added to late payments of ground rent or service charges. A new procedure for the formal demand of ground rent will be introduced with the ground landlord retaining a right to a possession, but having to account for any balance left after his demands are satisfied. No draft Bill has materialised by January 2001.

4.   Government proposals to reform the law of forfeiture

The Government White Paper proposes to introduce a requirement that the existence of a breach of covenant should be determined by a Leasehold Valuation Tribunal before any proceedings for forfeiture of residential premises would be allowed.[105] This falls considerably short of the outright ban on residential forfeitures for which one might have hoped, even though the Government acknowledges the Draconian nature of the penalty imposed by the loss of a home on account of a small debt[106] or minor breach of covenant. Unscrupulous ground landlords often exploit leaseholders' fears.

Slightly different procedures will apply to different kinds of breach. The proposed requirement of a demand for *ground rent* will significantly reduce the risk of forfeitures arising from arrears of ground rent.[107] At present leaseholders are protected against forfeiture for arrears of *service charge* by the requirement that the reasonableness of the service charge should be determined by a Leasehold Valuation Tribunal before a forfeiture

---

[102] [1998] 3 E.G.L.R. 79 H.L.; *Target Home Loans Ltd.* v. *Iza Ltd.* [2000] 02 E.G. 117, C.Ct.

[103] (1998) 75 P. & C.R. 232, 239, Lord Woolf M.R.

[104] *Residential Leasehold Reform in England and Wales — a C.P.* (D.E.T.R., November 1998) para.5; *An Analysis of Responses to Residential Leasehold Reform in England and Wales — a C.P.* (D.E.T.R., December 1999) paras.54–56; *Leasehold Reform: The Way Forward Summary of Proposals* (D.E.T.R., December 1999) paras.11–12.

[105] Commonhold and Leasehold Reform Bill 2000 cl. 143; C.P. (Cm 4843, August 2000) Part II paras.2.2.8, 4.6.

[106] It is also proposed that any unreasonable "administration charge" should be open to challenge before a Leasehold Valuation Tribunal, see below pp. 464–465.

[107] See above p. 367.

notice is served,[108] but a wide extension of this principle is now proposed. No notice preparatory to forfeiture will be allowed before the fact of the breach has been determined.

Where a *sum of money*[109] is alleged to be outstanding, and this is not agreed, either the ground landlord or the leaseholder will be able to apply to a Leasehold Valuation Tribunal for determination of whether the money claimed is reasonable and is due. Once the Tribunal has determined what sum is properly due, there will be a settlement period of 14 days, during which time the leaseholder can end all his liabilities; he will be required to pay the sum as determined and the application fee to the Tribunal, but would only pay costs in those cases where the Tribunal exercised its discretion to award costs to the ground landlord. After the 14 day period, the exhausted ground landlord would finally be free to serve a section 146 forfeiture notice on the defaulting leaseholder. It might be argued that the requirement to serve a second notice is unnecessarily punitive at this stage—all it could do would be to give the leaseholder even more time to pay. Where it was some other *non-pecuniary breach*,[110] it would also be necessary for the ground landlord to substantiate the alleged breach before taking forfeiture action. The notice to the leaseholder setting out details of the alleged breach would allow 30 days for a response. The leaseholder could pay any compensation demanded within that period and end the matter. If there was no settlement within the 30-day period either party could apply to the Leasehold Valuation Tribunal to settle the dispute by determining whether or not there was a breach, what is needed to put it right, and what compensation should be paid. The leaseholder would be allowed a period of 14 days after that determination (and of any appeal) to comply, after which the ground landlord would be free to issue a section 146 notice preparatory to forfeiture proceedings. However, a post-dispute arbitration agreement will be binding.

5.   Protection for buyers

The buyer of a lease is paying for the remaining years of the term. Before parting with his money he wishes to ensure that the lease still exists. What threatens the viability of the lease is a breach of covenant which would enable the landlord to forfeit the lease. For this reason there is a vital difference between a head lease and a sub-lease. The latter is subject to two (or more) rights to forfeit. The security of the person buying the lease depends on the continued existence of all intervening leases. The seller of the lease *must* disclose if it is the case that the lease is not held direct from the freeholder.

Practice is heavily dependent upon the doctrine of waiver, a form of estoppel, which is, put simply, that the ground landlord is not entitled to blow hot and cold. Leaseholders need to know that they will not for ever be vulnerable to old claims for forfeiture and a buyer needs to know that the slate has been wiped clean. Waiver ensures that a ground landlord does not have the right to terminate the lease for a breach of covenant if, once he knows of it, he does any act to recognise the continued existence of

---

[108]   H.A. 1996 s.81.

[109]   Commonhold and L.Ref. Bill 2000 cl. 148 will apply to service charges (H.A. 1996 s. 81 rewarded) and administration charges (Sch. 10), but not to ground rent arrears (as to which see cl. 142 and p. 367 above).

[110]   Commonhold and L.Ref. Bill 2000 cls. 143–144 (L.P.A. 1928 s. 146 does not apply to rent arrears).

the lease.[111] Thus, if the ground landlord issues a receipt for ground rent he waives all breaches of covenant known to him at that date.[112] Buyers must insist upon production of a receipt for the last rent payment due. Many leases attempt to modify the doctrine of waiver by stating that demand for or acceptance of rent shall not be deemed to be a waiver, but the validity of such provisions must be doubted.[113] A buyer should also inspect the state of the property and ask his seller whether there are any breaches or complaints by the landlord.

6. Protection for lenders

Relief is available to lenders of all kinds[114] secured on a residential long lease under section 146(4) of the Law of Property Act 1925, whether the breach is non-payment of rent or any other breach.[115] Holders of derivative interests will most often need to claim relief where the tenant is disqualified by bankruptcy or where he regards the lease as onerous. Relief is given to the holder of a derivative interest (such as a mortgage-lender) by the grant of a new lease ordered by the court, a process which necessarily creates a gap between the termination of the leaseholder's rights and the court's decision to relieve his lender. This was very inconvenient on the facts of *Escalus Properties Ltd.* v. *Robinson*[116] since the landlord was entitled to mesne profits equal to the rack rental value of the land, even though the property was let on long leases at low ground rents. It was only fair to require the lender to be made to pay the relatively low ground rents that the tenant had omitted to pay. A procedural means of achieving this was discovered in *Escalus:* the lenders succeeded in bringing themselves within the extended statutory definition of "tenants" and so were able to claim retrospective relief as if the original lease had never gone away.[117]

7. Protection of sub-tenants

Sub-tenants have the same rights as lenders.[118]

H. TRANSACTIONS AND DEALINGS

1. Grant

A grant of a long lease is usually preceded by a contract, which should have a full copy of the draft lease annexed to it.[119] Stamp duty is payable on the agreement.[120] The lease must take the form of a deed,[121] with appropriate land registry trappings if the landlord's title is registered. It will set out details which would be found just as much in

---

[111] See below pp. 812–815.

[112] L.P.A. 1925 s.45; *Re Highett & Bird's C.* [1903] 1 Ch. 287 C.A. (did not apply where disrepair proved).

[113] *R.* v. *Paulson* [1921] 1 A.C. 271 P.C.

[114] See below pp. 823–827.

[115] *Belgravia Investments Co. Ltd.* v. *Meah* [1964] 1 Q.B. 436, 448, Russell L.J.; *Abbey National B.S.* v. *Maybeech Ltd.* [1985] Ch. 190, 198A, Nicholls L.J.

[116] [1996] Q.B. 231 C.A.

[117] See below pp. 825–830.

[118] L.P.A. 1925 s.146(4); see below pp. 823–827

[119] S.C.S. (3rd ed., 1995) cond.8.2.3.

[120] See below pp. 382–384.

[121] L.P.A. 1925 s.52(1).

a freehold transfer such as the date, parties, description of the property, details of any co-ownership between the tenants, stamping details and will be executed in the same way as a freehold transfer or conveyance. It will also have the distinctive features of a lease described in this chapter. Long leases are usually executed in duplicate or as an original and counterpart—in fact the Standard Conditions provide for a counterpart.[122] Usually the tenant is required by express proviso to pay the landlord's costs.[123] He cannot be prevented by contract from employing his own solicitor.[124]

2.   Right to sell a lease

Although landlords are permitted to control the sale of leases,[125] this is rarely appropriate with a long lease, where an important part of the tenant's ownership is the ability to liberate the premium he paid on its grant or the price he paid when buying the lease. Building societies often object to a clause requiring the consent of the ground landlord to the choice of a new leaseholder. Hence the only normal requirement is for a sale to be registered with the ground landlord[126] after completion. The fee payable and time-scale to be observed will be set out in the lease. A condition that an assignment be prepared by the ground landlord's solicitor becomes a requirement to register an assignment with the ground landlord's solicitor's within six months.[127] It may well be appropriate to control other transactions such as sub-letting, division, or taking in lodgers.

One particular example of this type of arrangement is a building lease, that is a lease granted for more than 40 years at a price that includes the erection or improvement of buildings. Consent to dealings is not required during most of the years of the lease, provided that the tenant gives notice in writing of the dealing to the landlord within six months.[128] Any term of the lease requiring consent is overridden. However repairing obligations are more onerous in the last seven years of the term, so a requirement to obtain consent is permitted during that last phase of the lease. Ground landlords who wish to control dealings can easily evade the statutory provisions by taking a covenant to offer a surrender of the lease before any dealing proceeds.[129]

3.   Information on sale

The information a seller of a lease must provide to the buyer is as follows[130]:

> Management company: its constitution and the seller's share certificate, accounts for the past 3 years, any additional regulations made by the company, and its officers;
> Ground landlord: his name, address, and agent;

---

[122]   S.C.S. (3rd ed., 1995) cond.8.2.7; for stamping see below n. 151.

[123]   Otherwise each party bears own costs under Cost of Leases Act 1958.

[124]   L.P.A. 1925 s.48.

[125]   In future fees for granting consents will be controlled as "administration charges"; see below pp. 464–465.

[126]   Notice may also be required, and it is important that notice is given so the landlord can notify the change to the insurers.

[127]   The fee is one guinea (£1.05). This is not VATable: [1990] 26 L.S.G. 14.

[128]   L.T.A. 1927 s.19(1)(b). Certain public landlords are excepted. The deemed consent is withdrawn for commercial leases by L.T.A. 1927 s.19(1D), which was inserted by L.T. (Covenants) A. 1995 s.22.

[129]   *Vaux Group Ltd.* v. *Lilley* [1991] 1 E.G.L.R. 60; P. Sparkes [1991] *J.B.L.* 494; J.E. Adams [1990] *Conv.* 332; see below p. 558.

[130]   Sellers Leasehold Information Form in Transaction Protocol.

Service charges: amounts, details of receipts for recent payments, challenges, and problems of collection;

Notices: those given or received; consents obtained or refused; complaints; previous claims to enfranchise;

Insurance: details of the policy;

Decoration: the state, and any complaints;

Occupiers.

4. Mortgages

Leasehold homes are sold for large sums of money, and the possibility of raising mortgage finance is a vital aspect of the utility of leasehold ownership.[131] The historical form of mortgage was unsatisfactory because it automatically required the creation of a sublease, but the invariable practice today is to use a charge by deed by way of legal mortgage. This modern form means that there is virtually no difference between a mortgage of freehold or leasehold land, and indeed land of both tenures can be mortgaged together in simple form.[132]

5. Running of covenants—post -1995 leases

Where a long lease is granted after 1995, the law on the running of covenants is very simple. The Landlord and Tenant (Covenants) Act 1995 provides for the benefit and burden of all covenants to pass immediately on the transfer of the lease or the reversion. A former ground landlord is released by a sale of his reversion so long as he gives the necessary notice and there is no objection.[133] A tenant is released by any sale, presuming that there is no restriction on assignment so the sale is authorised, though after a devolution the release will have to wait until the next sale occurs.[134] A previous tenant can never be liable, privity of contract is abolished, and with a long lease of a house there will be no possibility of compelling the leaseholder who is selling to give any guarantee. Hence there is no longer any need for indemnity covenants when a post-1995 lease is sold.

6. Running of covenants and indemnity—pre-1996 leases

The current parties to the leasehold estate are the central characters in the enforcement of covenants to a pre-1996 long lease, since liability attaches by privity of estate. As explained elsewhere, this is true only of the core covenants, and special consideration is needed of informal leases and sales.[135]

However the position is vastly complicated by the possibility of liability for privity of contract. A leaseholder who took an original grant for (say) 99 years accepted liability on the covenants in the lease for the full 99 years unless (as was wise) the lease was worded so as to restrict this liability to the duration of his personal estate ownership.

---

[131] D.N. Clarke, "Occupying Cheek by Jowl", ch.15 in Bright & Dewar, 381.

[132] L.P.A. 1925 s.87.

[133] L.T. (Covenants) A. 1995 ss.6–8; see also below pp. 748–749.

[134] ss.5, 11.

[135] See below Chapter 28.

A ground landlord could revert to taking action against the original tenant (T0) in preference to the current tenant (TC). As a result the original tenant had to protect himself by taking a covenant from the person to whom he sold (T1) to observe all the terms of the lease, and to indemnify his seller (T0) if he was made liable in future. Similarly T1 had to take an indemnity covenant when he came to sell to T2 and so on. An indemnity covenant is implied by statute when a pre-1996 lease is assigned for value,[136] but on a gift or following a devolution an express covenant is required.

7. Extension

A simple extension of a lease is ineffective, though it is commonly used. In law an existing term can only be extended by the grant of a new term.[137] The existing term is usually surrendered by implication, though there is nothing to prevent the parties granting a new lease to operate subject to the existing one. If the existing term is surrendered charges will disappear, and it is necessary to prove the consent of the mortgage lender; otherwise the title will be subject to the rights of the lender. In registered conveyancing it is necessary to apply to terminate the title or the note of the existing lease, to prove the landlord's title to grant the new lease and to demonstrate all necessary consents. The new title will contain a note of the rights of the prior lender unless his lender has consented to the registration.[138]

I.   STAMP DUTY ON LEASES

Lease duty is still just as complicated as it was before the recent re-enactment of the charging provisions.[139] Duty may be payable on grants of leases, sale, surrenders,[140] rent reviews and other variations, and any other transaction. Documents must be stamped within 30 days of execution and otherwise there is a penalty.[141]

1.   Agreement

Since 1994, the duty payable on an agreement for a lease has been the same as the duty on a lease.[142] So the date on which duty has to be paid is usually the date of the preceding agreement.[143] Stamp duty is paid only once over, so if the agreement is stamped, the amount of the duty will be set against (and should normally cancel out) the duty to be paid on the lease. In order to be properly stamped, a lease must be denoted with the amount of duty paid on the preceding agreement. It there was no preceding agreement,

---

[136] L.P.A. 1925 s.77(1)(c) (unregistered title); L.R.A. 1925 s.24(1)(b) (registered title); *Harris* v. *Boots the Cash Chemists (Southern) Ltd.* [1904] 2 Ch. 376; *Stanhope Pension Trust Ltd.* v. *Registrar of Companies* [1993] 2 E.G.L.R. 118 Ch.D.

[137] Ruoff & Roper (6th ed.) paras.21–23 to 21–24.

[138] R.L. Practice Note 21.

[139] F.A. 1999 sch.13. Further changes are expected in the 2001 Finance Bill to cope with electronic conveyancing. See M. Hutton (2000) 41 *E.G.* 44.

[140] Finance Act 2000 s.128 will make duty payable on surrenders by operation of law; S. Wheeler [2000] 33 *L.S.G.* 42.

[141] Stamp Act 1891 ss.15–15B, as amended by F.A. 1999 s.109.

[142] F.A. 1999 sch.13 para.14.

[143] F.A. 1994 s.240, substituted by F.A. 1999 sch.12 (penalties).

the lease must contain a certificate to that effect.[144] If an agreement is rescinded, the duty paid on it can be reclaimed.

2. Conveyance or transfer on sale

This head of charge applies to the price paid on the sale of a leasehold estate[145] and to the premium element paid on the grant of a lease,[146] and also to sums such as a price paid on a surrender of a lease. It also applies to transfers ordered by a family court. The *amount* of duty is *ad valorem*—that is a percentage of the price. The *rate* of duty is assessed in relation to the certified value of the transaction including any related transactions, so it is important to include a certificate if the total consideration is less than £½ million in order to claim the benefit of the lower rates. Documents executed on or after March 16th 1999 are subject to the following rates[147]:

Certified at up to £60,000	nil
Certified at up to £250,000	1%
Certified at up to £500,000	2.5%
£500,000 or more	3.5%

In the case of a building lease, the duty will be payable on the value of the plot, but not on the value of the building to be erected on it later.

3. Creation of a short furnished tenancy

A short tenancy for less than a year of a furnished dwelling-house with a rent exceeding £500 is dutiable at £5.

4. Creation of all other leases

Any premium payable for the grant of a lease will be charged as a conveyance or transfer on sale, but there will be an additional charge on the rent (including V.A.T. if this is included in the rent). The rates current for documents executed on or after October 1st 1999 are[148]:

Term less than 7 years	
Rent £500 a year or less	Nil
Rent more than £500	1%
Term 7 to 35 years	2%
More than 35 but not more than 100 years	12%
More than 100 years	24%

If the rates appear high in the last two groups, it must be remembered that ground rents are usually purely nominal in value—24 per cent of £100 is not a large sum.

---

[144] F.A. 1994 s.240A, inserted by F.A. 1999 sch.12.

[145] F.A. 1999 sch.13 para.1.

[146] para.11.

[147] para.4; para.6 provides for certificates; F.A. 1999 s.111 amending F.A. 1963 s.55. Sums are rounded up to the next £5: F.A. 1999 s.112.

[148] F.A. 1999 sch.13, replacing Stamp Act 1891 sch.1.

5. Increase of rent

A document evidencing an increase in the rent after a rent review is charged at the rates in the table immediately above on the amount of the increase.[149] A variation of a lease which does not affect the rent is not subject to *ad valorem* duty unless the length of the term is extended (when it is analysed as a surrender and regrant).

6. Fixed duties

These have been increased to £5, including any lease not in the table immediately above,[150] duplicates,[151] a conveyance or transfer not on sale,[152] and a surrender without any premium.[153]

J. TITLE AND REGISTRATION

1. Registrable leases

The Land Registration Act 1925 had a confused and fragmentary[154] scheme for leases, but greater coherence was introduced by the Land Registration Act 1986.[155] Each registered lease has its own title number, property register, proprietorship register showing the current legal tenant, and charges register. A new title will be opened for each registrable lease. Technically it is title to an estate which is registered, rather than title to the land, so that it is quite possible for one physical piece of land to be represented by a number of concurrent registered titles, perhaps the freehold, a head lease and a number of sub-leases of parts. Estates are registered independently of each other, so that a registered freehold and registered sub-lease may sandwich an unregistered intermediate lease. Registrability of the lease does not depend upon the landlord's title being registered.

Any legal lease with a term exceeding 21 years remaining unexpired at the time of registration now requires completion by substantive registration.[156] Leases are incapable of substantive registration if the grant is not by deed and so is not legal.[157] This at any rate is how the legislation is interpreted though it is a *curiousum* that section 2 refers to a lease "capable of subsisting as a legal estate" which appears literally to include any term of years absolute, whether or not it is by deed. A lease is not substantively registrable unless the outstanding term at the time of registration exceeds 21 years.[158]

---

[149] F.A. 1999 sch.13 para.20.

[150] F.A. 1999 sch.13 para.13.

[151] para.19; the duty paid on the original needs to be denoted. A counterpart (executed by the tenant but not by the landlord) is not dutiable.

[152] para.16.

[153] para.23.

[154] D.J. Hayton, *Registered Land* (3rd ed.) ch.3; F.R.R. Burford (1936) 1 *Conv.* 344; R. Graham Page (1937) 2 *Conv.* 98.

[155] In force January 1st 1987, following Law Com. No.125 (1983).

[156] L.R.A. 1925 s.8(1)(b) as amended by L.R.A. 1986 s.2.

[157] L.R.A. 1925 s.2.

[158] G. Dworkin (1961) 24 *M.L.R.* 135 suggested 14, 7 or 3 years.

2.   Leases granted by a ground landlord with unregistered title

The buyer will also wish to know that the ground landlord had title to grant the lease in the first place. It is usual practice today to produce to the buyer before contract the lease and all superior titles. Historically the practice was not to insist on any title on the grant of a lease. The original leaseholder took for granted the ground landlord's right to grant the lease in the first place.[159] The Law of Property Act 1925 preserves the legal basis for this practice, for the tenant on the contractual grant of a lease has no right to see the landlord's title.[160] When such a title is sent to the land registry, it can only be registered with a good leasehold title. This practice was extraordinarily sloppy: no one would pay for a freehold house without checking that the seller had title to sell, so why should he be trusted when he grants a lease instead? Modern lenders have insisted on reversal of the practice and expect the security offered to be a leasehold absolute title. The original leaseholder should therefore contract for deduction of the freehold title, and it is assumed when a lease is granted under the Standard Conditions of Sale that the title will be good enough to secure an absolute title.[161]

A grant of a new long lease by a ground landlord with an unregistered title calls for first registration.[162] Today all parts of the country are compulsory and trigger events which compel the registration of the title include the grant of any long legal lease.

3.   Title granted by a ground landlord with registered title

There are no special rules about title for registered land so a prospective leaseholder should contract to see his ground landlord's title[163]: if the Standard Conditions of Sale are relied upon, title should be good enough to secure an absolute title.[164] The grant of a long legal lease by an existing registered proprietor will act as a disposition.[165] Two entries are required: a note against the ground landlord's title and a new title for the lease, evidenced by the issue of a new land certificate to the tenant showing the leasehold title. The ground landlord's land certificate should be lodged to facilitate entry of a notice against the superior title but, bizarrely, the Court of Appeal decided in *Strand Securities Ltd.* v. *Caswell*[166] that this step was not essential.

4.   Sale of an unregistered lease

The buyer can insist on production of a full title to the *lease* (meaning back to a good root of title at least 15 years old as well as the lease itself), but under an open contract he cannot insist upon deduction of the superior titles.[167] He should therefore contract for

---

[159] L.P.A. 1925 ss.44(2)–(3), 45(2)–(3); *White* v. *Bijou Mansions Ltd.* [1938] Ch. 351 C.A.; Barnsley's *Law of Conveyancing* (Butterworths, 4th ed. by M.P. Thompson, 1996) 296–302.

[160] L.P.A. 1925 s.44. The tenant is not affected by notice of rights he could have discovered if he had contracted for full title. But land charges registered against the landlord's title will bind.

[161] S.C.S. (3rd ed, 1995) cond.8.2.4.

[162] L.R.A. 1925 s.123 as amended by L.R.A. 1986 s.2; the 21 years are measured from the grant, not the later date of the application for registration: s.8(1A) as inserted in 1986.

[163] Ruoff & Roper (6th ed.) para.21–02.

[164] S.C.S. (3rd ed, 1995) cond.8.2.4.

[165] *Strand Securities Ltd.* v. *Caswell* [1965] Ch. 958 C.A.

[166] [1965] Ch. 958 C.A.

[167] L.P.A. 1925 s.44(2).

a full title that will enable him to secure registration with title absolute, but of course the seller will not be able to concede to this request if he himself accepted the statutory title when he bought.

It is necessary to consider whether the title ought already to have been registered. Since 1990 all parts of the country have been compulsory areas. *Trigger events* which compel the registration of the title include the grant of any long legal lease and any dealing with an existing registrable lease. Until recently only sales of existing leases attracted a requirement to register, so that leases remained unregistered after a gift or devolution on death.[168] However since 1997[169] the triggers have been extended to include almost all dealings, second mortgages being the only common exception. Where a long lease remains unregistered and it was granted *before December 1990* (when the last parts of the country became compulsory) it is necessary to consider the old law to see whether the legal title is defective for want of registration. If the grant and the last sale occurred while the district was non-compulsory, registration has never been triggered. For grants before 1987[170] further factors come into play. If the ground landlord's title was unregistered at the time of the grant of the lease, registration of leases (both grants and assignments) was only compulsory where the term was for 40 years or more, and so was voluntary where the term was between 21 and 40 years in length.[171] Further, substantive registration was not allowed for leases containing an absolute prohibition against registration.[172]

An assignment will be required either in the unregistered form, or in the form of a transfer adapted to reflect the fact that title is not yet registered. It should include a covenant for title.[173]

First registration will be compulsory if the lease has at least 21 years of the term unexpired at the time that it passes.[174]

5. Proof of title to a registered lease

Exactly as for freehold land, title to a registered lease is shown from office copies of the register entries, supplemented by a search. The price is now included on the register.[175] Leases are an exception to the open register. When the Land Registration Act 1997 was passing through Parliament, the then Lord Chancellor rejected the suggestion that leases should be made public, but he suggested that liberal use should be made of the existing discretion to make available copies of leases to anyone who can demonstrate an interest in seeing the lease.[176] A filed copy of the lease is proof of the title. So, it remains a respon-

---

[168] L.R.A. 1925 s.123.

[169] s.123 as amended by L.R.A. 1997 s.1.

[170] L.R.A. 1986 in force January 1st 1987.

[171] L.R.A. 1925 s.13(1) as originally drafted.

[172] s.8(2) as originally drafted; this was on the theory that such leases were not traded; but in fact such leases could be sold with the consent of the ground landlord; the anomaly was removed by L.R.A. 1986 s.3 following Law Com. No.125 (1983).

[173] L.P. (M.P.) A. 1994 s.4; Sparkes *N.L.L.* 718–721.

[174] L.R.A. 1925 s.8(1) and (1A) as amended as above. Almost any dealing attracts compulsory first registration: L.R.A. 1997 s.1.

[175] L.R. (No.3) R. 1999 S.I. 1999/3462.

[176] R. Hudson [1996] *N.L.J.* 1820.

sibility of the seller to send a copy of the lease to the buyer. This is usually done before exchange of contracts to make sure that the seller has met the contractual obligation to disclose onerous covenants.[177]

6.   Transfer of lease with registered title

Where there is an existing registered title it is necessary to use the correct land registry transfer forms,[178] particularly after the overhaul of the forms for dealings with the whole[179] and dealings with part,[180] and another variable is whether the lease is within or outside the Landlord and Tenant (Covenants) Act 1995. A covenant for title should be included.[181] A problem with registered machinery remains that legal title only passes on completion of registration formalities (that is the date of a proper application to the land registry); during the registration gap the previous tenant remains legal owner of the land.[182]

---

[177] Equivalent to knowledge under S.C.S. (3rd) Cond. 8.12.

[178] L.R.R. 1925 r.115; Ruoff & Roper (6th ed.) para.21–20, also paras.15–06 to 15–06B.

[179] L.R.R. 1925 sch.1, substituted by L.R.R. 1997 S.I. 1997/3037.

[180] L.R.R. 1925 sch.2 substituted by L.R. (No.3) R. 1999 S.I. 1999/3462.

[181] L.R.A. 1925 s.38(2) as amended by L.P.(M.P.) A. 1994; new L.R.R. 1925 r.76 as amended by S.I. 1995/377.

[182] *Brown & Root Technology Ltd.* v. *Sun Alliance & London Assurance Co. Ltd.* [1997] 1 E.G.L.R. 39 C.A.; S. Kavanagh [1998] 4 *P.L.J.* 16.

15

INDIVIDUAL ENFRANCHISEMENT

Extension and enfranchisement. Long leases. Leases for life. Low rents. Statutory continuation of long residential leases. Residence qualification to enfranchise. Proposed abolition of the residence test. Enfranchisement of houses, flats, and business premises. Low cost houses. Human rights attacks. High cost houses. Flats. Proposed changes to valuation. Defences. Procedure. Absentee landlords. Estate management schemes. Proposed pre-emption rights over houses.

A recent official report[1] records that there are 900,000 leasehold houses and one million flats; half the houses are in the North West and Merseyside region, and half of all the flats in London and the South East. Large-scale adoption of leasehold tenure as a form of ownership is relatively recent, and it has proved to be fundamentally unsatisfactory especially in relation to flats.[2] A pool of disaffected leasehold owners has been created, and there is strong political pressure to extend rights to enfranchisement.

To enfranchise is to make free. The original sense of securing freedom from manorial obligations[3] was extended in the past to the conversion of copyhold land to freehold, and to the conferral of a Parliamentary vote by the conversion of a non-qualifying leasehold estate into a qualifying freehold estate. Today enfranchisement refers exclusively to the process of compulsory acquisition by a leaseholder of his ground landlord's reversionary estate. The various regimes applying to houses and flats are described at the beginning of this chapter. True enfranchisement is characterised by a compulsory[4] transfer of an estate in the land (either the freehold or a long lease) from the ground landlord to an individual leaseholder. A former leaseholder who cannot afford to enfranchise will acquire residential security by way of continuation of his lease as it expires. Most of these rights are restricted to leaseholders who hold (or at least have held in the past) a long lease at a low rent.

Individual enfranchisement refers to the rights of an individual leaseholder to strengthen his ownership of his particular home. It is to be contrasted with the collective rights of all the leaseholders in a particular block or on a particular estate, rights which are the subject of the next chapter.

---

[1] *Leasehold Reform in England & Wales* (D.E.T.R., November 1998), paras.1.2–1.3.
[2] Para.1.4.
[3] Littleton on *Tenures* s.204.
[4] *Cadogan* v. *Morris* [1999] 1 E.G.L.R. 59, 60J, Stuart Smith L.J.

Reference is made throughout this chapter to the impending reform—a White Paper containing a draft Bill was published in August 2000 and the Government introduced the Commonhold and Leasehold Reform Bill 2000 into the House of Lords on 20 December 2000; given the manifesto commitment to the reform of the law applying to leasehold homes, speedy implementation must be hoped for.[5]

A. EXTENSION AND ENFRANCHISEMENT

1. Continuation

At the worst a former leaseholder is likely to be able to claim a statutory continuation of his tenancy as a short residential tenancy with full security of tenure, though this will be at the price of a considerable hike in the rent to the level of a rack rental set at a market rate. This scheme operates under part I of the Landlord and Tenant Act 1954.[6]

2. Agreed extension

The simplest way to extend a lease is to reach an agreement with the landlord. No doubt a premium will be required to induce the ground landlord to push back the time at which he will be able to obtain vacant possession and it will be at the market rent. Recent cases[7] have become more sympathetic to the idea that a lease could be extended by a simple variation of the terms of the existing lease, using a deed of variation. However conventional theory was that an existing lease could not be altered in this way, so an extension had to be by the grant of a second lease to run from the termination of the existing lease (a future or reversionary lease), or by way of surrender of the existing shorter lease and the regrant of a new longer lease. Mortgages and other adverse interests are preserved on a surrender.[8] In registered conveyancing it is necessary to apply to terminate the title or note of the existing lease, prove the ground landlord's title to grant the new lease, and to produce all necessary consents, including the consent of any existing lender.[9]

3. Enlargement

Very long leases at very low rents can be converted to freehold ownership by unilateral execution of a deed of enlargement.[10] Requirements are: (1) an original term for 300 years or more; (2) not less than 200 years remaining; (3) no rent of any money value[11]; and (4) no third party rights in the shape of a beneficial interest under a trust of land, a right of redemption of a mortgage, or a forfeiture clause. Only very rarely will these

---

[5] *Commonhold and Leasehold Reform—Draft Bill and C.P.* (Cm 4843, August 2000) hereafter "White Paper"; see also Green Paper, *Quality and Choice: A Decent Home for All* (D.E.T.R., April 2000) para.4.17.

[6] See below pp. 392–396.

[7] See above p. 380.

[8] See below pp. 601–603.

[9] R.L. Practice Note 21.

[10] L.P.A. 1925 s.153; re-enacting Conveyancing Acts 1881 s.65 and 1882 s.11; T.P.D. Taylor (1958) 22 *Conv. (N.S.)* 101. A sub-tenancy can be enlarged provided the head tenancy qualifies.

[11] *Re Chapman & Hobbs* (1885) 29 Ch.D. 067 (1 silver penny if demanded); *Blaiberg* v. *Keeves* [1906] 2 Ch. 175 (1 shilling (5p) of no value); *Re Smith & Stott* (1883) 29 Ch.D. 1009n (3 shillings is valuable rent). Extension is permitted where the rent is less than £1 a year and has not been paid for 20 years.

conditions be satisfied.[12] Most extendible leases are artificial creations, designed to take advantage of the possibility of attaching positive covenants to freehold land and even restrictions on sale.

4. Enfranchisement of houses

Enfranchisement of houses occurs under the Leasehold Reform Act 1967[13] and usually leads to the transfer of the freehold estate. The original scheme was very favourable to leaseholders in terms of the price that has to be paid; houses within it are here described as low cost houses. Many other houses were brought within the scope of enfranchisement by later Acts, particularly the Leasehold Reform, Housing and Urban Development Act 1993, but leaseholders falling into these additional schemes must pay a market price for the reversion; these cases are here described as high cost houses. Qualification to enfranchise depends upon holding a long lease at a low rent, and there is also a requirement of residential occupation.

5. Enfranchisement of flats

At present, flats usually have leasehold titles. This traditional method of selling flats developed in order to overcome the problems of enforcing positive repairing covenants against future freehold owners. Leasehold flat schemes are described in detail in the next chapter. There are three interlocking schemes. Given that a person who wishes to buy a flat will only be able to buy a leasehold estate, the value of that estate will begin to leak away as soon as he pays for it, as explained in the previous chapter.[14] This explains why leaseholders are so anxious to avoid the wastage of the value from their home by enfranchisement. It takes two forms—individual and collective.[15] Individual flat owners can seek an extension of their leasehold estate for 90 years, a right conferred on qualifying leaseholders by the Leasehold Reform, Housing and Urban Development Act 1993. Collective rights for the leaseholders in a block of flats to club together to take over ownership and/or the control of the management of their block, are commonhold proposals and are described in the next two chapters.[16]

B. LONG LEASES

1. Long leases

Qualifying leases are residential long leases. Normally the tenant must hold a long lease (21 years or more) which is at a low rent. Additional enfranchisement rights were granted in 1996 to a super-long lease (that is of 35 years or over) regardless of the rent. Only long leases qualify the tenant to enfranchise. The lease must originally have been granted for a term certain exceeding 21 years.[17] The period counted must be both after

---

[12] An exception is *Bosomworth* v. *Faber* (1992) 69 P. & C.R. 288, 292, Dillon L.J.
[13] Woodfall ch.26; Davey 354–364; Evans & Smith (5th ed.) 422–433; Garner (2nd ed.) ch.18.
[14] See above pp. 361–363.
[15] Woodfall 29.001–29.115 (collective), 29.116–29.148A (individual).
[16] See below Chapters 16 and 17.
[17] L.Ref.A. 1967 s.3(1); L.R.H.U.D.A. 1993 s.7(1)(b).

the date of the grant [18] *and* after the onset of the right to possession.[19] Options to determine, rights of re-entry and break clauses are ignored.[20] After the original term has ended, a new tenancy which follows—whether by continuation, regrant or holding over at a low rent—continues to qualify the tenant.[21] Qualification also arises where a short lease is renewed under an option, so as to bring the total period of occupation above 21 years.[22] Also included are: (1) a perpetually renewable lease; (2) a mortgage term after the right of redemption is barred;[23] and (3) shorter leases granted to public sector tenants under the right to buy[24]—though equity shared leases are excluded.[25]

2.   Leases for life and enfranchisement

Leases for life at a rent or fine are generally converted to a term of 90 years.[26] Special consideration is required in the context of enfranchisement, since leases for life were excluded from the Leasehold Reform Act 1967 (low cost houses), including any lease determinable with a life. Needless to say this opened a most undesirable loophole, since a landlord could easily avoid giving enfranchisement rights by granting a long lease terminable on the death of the last living descendant of King George V.[27] This lacuna was plugged allowing low cost enfranchisement for leases granted after April 18th 1980[28]; earlier leases (and later ones under earlier contracts) are enfranchisable but are high cost.[29] Also caught are leases terminable by notice after the death of the tenant,[30] including in this category any "commercial" lease for life that has been converted to a 90 year term by the Law of Property Act 1925.[31] Personal, non-assignable, leases for life cannot be enfranchised.[32]

C.   LOW RENT

1.   The test

Where part of the economic value of the land is removed by way of a premium, the ground rent is usually a low rent. This is essential for low-cost enfranchisement.[33] The conditions are as follows:

---

[18] *Roberts* v. *Church Commissioners of England* [1972] 1 Q.B. 278, 284, Russell L.J.

[19] L.R.H.U.D.A. 1993 s.105(5); T. Radevsky [1994] *N.L.J.* 1130.

[20] *Eton College* v. *Bard* [1983] Ch. 321 C.A.; R. Griffith [1984] *Conv.* 136.

[21] *Austin* v. *Dick Richards Properties Ltd.* [1975] 1 W.L.R. 1033 C.A. (extension for 15 years of a fixed term of 30 years which expired in 1960); *Baron* v. *Phillips* [1978] 2 E.G.L.R. 59 (extension limited to residential part, which was not a house on the facts); *Bates* v. *Pierrepoint* [1979] 2 E.G.L.R. 69.

[22] L.Ref.A. 1967 s.3(4); L.R.H.U.D.A. 1993 s.7(4).

[23] *Re Fairview, Church St, Bromyard* [1974] 1 W.L.R. 579, Megarry J. The lender is not qualified.

[24] H.A. 1985 s.174(a); L.R.H.U.D.A. 1993 s.7(1)(c).

[25] L.Ref.A. 1967 ss.1(1A), 33A, sch.4A; (houses) L.R.H.U.D.A. 1993 s.7(7) (flats—where equity share less than 100%).

[26] L.P.A. 1925 s.149(6); see above pp. 363–365.

[27] *Proma Ltd.* v. *Curtis* [1990] 1 E.G.L.R. 117 C.A.; J.E. Adams [1990] *Conv.* 83.

[28] H.A. 1980 s.141, sch.2 para.3, amending L.Ref.A. 1967 s.3(1).

[29] See below pp. 404–406.

[30] L.Ref.A. 1967 s.3(1); L.R.H.U.D.A. 1993 s.7(1)(b) (same rules for high and low cost).

[31] L.P.A. 1925 s.149(6).

[32] L.Ref.A. 1967 s.3(1); L.R.H.U.D.A. 1993 s.7(2).

[33] *Hordern* v. *Viscount Chelsea* [1997] E.G.C.S. 25 (high rent so no enfranchisement).

Leases granted after August 1939 up to March 1963: the initial rent must not exceed 2/3rds of the letting value,[34] except building leases which were assessed on rateable value.

Leases granted April 1963—March 1990: A low rent is one below 2/3rds of the rateable value.[35] The rent is taken *at the moment of enfranchisement* and compared to the rateable value *on the appropriate day,*[36] which is March 1965 or any later day on which the property was first rated unless that is there is such a significant change in the rateable unit as to establish a later base date.[37] Detailed changes made in 1996 ensure that nil rateable values (given when a dwelling was unfit for habitation or was undergoing renovation) are ignored so that it is the first "proper" rateable value which is taken.[38] The low rent test facilitates evasion by landlords of the right to enfranchise, for a landlord has only to include a provision for review of the rent to increase it beyond the enfranchisable limit.[39]

Leases granted after mid 1990: most long leases will have been granted before the domestic rating system was abolished in 1990[40] in favour of the community charge ("poll tax") which was in turn later replaced by council tax. For those granted afterwards, low rent is defined from a simple monetary test: the rent (ignoring council tax) must not exceed £1,000 a year in Greater London or £250 a year elsewhere.[41] As will be explained below, cases falling outside these tests do allow enfranchisement but only on a high cost basis, if the lease is for at least 35 years.

2.   Continuation

At the expiration of a long lease at a low rent, the former leaseholder will have the right to continue in occupation under an assured tenancy at a rack rental.[42] In the rare cases in which a long lease is at a high rent, the lease will already be covered by whichever residential security scheme was applicable at the date of the grant.

3.   Enfranchisement—current law

In order to qualify to enfranchise, a leaseholder must hold either (1) a long lease (21 years or more) at a low rent, or (2) a super-long lease (that is of 35 years or over) regardless of the rent—the additional right in category (2) was granted in 1996[43] and in the case of a house it will lead to high cost enfranchisement.

---

[34] L.Ref.A. 1967 s.4(1) proviso; L.R.H.U.D.A. 1993 s.8(1)(a); *Johnston* v. *Duke of Westminster* [1986] A.C. 839 H.L.; *Hembry* v. *Henry Smith's Charity Trustees* [1987] 2 E.G.L.R. 109 C.A.; *Crean Davidson Investments Ltd.* v. *Earl Cadogan* [1999] 2 E.G.L.R. 96 Ct.Ct.

[35] L.Ref.A. 1967 s.4(1); payments for services, repairs, etc. are ignored, as are abnormal fluctuations.

[36] *Dixon* v. *Allgood* [1987] 1 W.L.R. 1689 H.L.

[37] *Griffiths* v. *Birmingham City D.C.* [1987] C.L.Y. 2172.

[38] L.Ref.A. 1967 ss.1(1), 4(1), 4A; L.R.H.U.D.A. 1993 s.8; both as amended by H.A. 1996 ss.105 and 114.

[39] For the legislative response see below pp. 404–405.

[40] For leases granted on and after April 1st 1990; leases granted after 1990 under a pre-1990 contract are assessed on the rateable value basis.

[41] L.G.H.A. 1989 sch.7; References to Rating (Housing) Regs. 1990, S.I. 1990/434 reg.2 and sch., paras.7–8.

[42] See below pp. 392–396.

[43] H.A. 1996 s.106, sch.9.

4. Enfranchisement—reform proposals

The Government now proposes to rationalise the law by removing the low rent test for enfranchisement of houses and flats, in line with changes also proposed to the collective enfranchisement scheme.[44] Hence leases of between 21 and 35 years at a high rent would become enfranchisable, though anyone gaining the right to enfranchise should pay an open market price including marriage value so that, in other words, the enfranchisement of a house would be high cost.[45] The low rent test will have to remain on the statute book to allocate houses between high and low cost procedures and also for the purposes of a exemption for houses in designated rural areas for leases granted before 31st March 1997. Provisions of the Commonhold and Leasehold Reform Bill 2000 will abolish the low rent test for flats[46] and amend the existing rules about low-rent flats,[47] but there is as yet no draft of the changes relating to houses.

D. STATUTORY CONTINUATION AT THE END OF A LONG LEASE

When a long residential lease reaches its term date[48] the lease will not end automatically if, as is usual, there is a tenant in occupation and entitled to claim a statutory continuation of the tenancy. Actually this Parliamentary choice of descriptor is inaccurate since a short residential tenancy is created in whoever qualifies by residence at the end of the long lease—this is not necessarily the former leaseholder where there are joint owners.[49] Continuation is important in its own right to preserve the homes of tenants whose leases have expired, and also of vital importance in reducing the price which tenants have to pay to enfranchise.[50]

1. High and low rents

Where a long lease reserved a high rent (that is at or just below market levels) full security of tenure is available. The Rent Act 1977 continues to apply to leases granted before early 1989[51] and an assured tenancy arose under the Housing Act 1988 for later grants (though these will not as yet have expired).[52] The previous scheme is more favourable to the tenant since the rent is restricted to a fair rent, whereas under the new scheme the landlord can demand a market rent.[53]

Part I of the Landlord and Tenant Act 1954 applies at the termination of a long lease at a low rent.[54] A long lease is defined to be for a term certain exceeding 21 years,

---

[44] *White Paper* Part II paras.2.2.6, 2.13–2.15, 3.III.8 and 4.4.A. As to collective enfranchisement see below pp. 434–437.

[45] See below pp. 405–408.

[46] L.R.H.U.D.A. 1993 s.39(3)(c)–(d) omitted by Commonhold and L.Ref. Bill 2000 cl. 127.

[47] Repeals to be made by Commonhold and L.Ref. Bill 2000 sch.13: (A) L.R.H.U.D.A. 1993 ss.39(3)(d), 42(3)(b)(iii), 91(2)(c), 91(7), 94(12); and (B) H.A. 1996 s.105(3) and sch.9 paras.4, 5(2), 5(3).

[48] L.T.A. 1954 ss.2(6), 3, 64; Woodfall 23.256–24.132, 24.091–24.132; Davey 345–353; Evans & Smith (5th ed.) 416–422; Garner (2nd ed.) ch.17.

[49] *de Rothschild* v. *Bell* [2000] Q.B. 33, 46–47, Buxton L.J.   [50] See below pp. 402–403.

[51] R.A. 1977 s.5 excludes security where there is a low rent as defined.

[52] Subject to the exclusions in H.A. 1988 sch.1 paras.3, 3A, 3B.

[53] See above pp. 225–227.

[54] L.T.A. 1954 s.2. The position at the end of an extended lease granted under the L.Ref.A. 1967 is discussed below at p. 401.

whether or not subsequently extended,[55] and including any continuation at a low rent.[56] Most long leases reserve a premium, and if so the rent is usually well below the market level and will count as a low rent. The precise test is the same as that used to determine the cost of enfranchisement and is considered in that context.[57]

2. Who may claim a continuation?

Essentially this is a former leaseholder who holds over at the end of a long lease at a low rent. Problems arising from relationship breakdown were discussed in *de Rothschild* v. *Bell*.[58] During the last few years of a 40-year term held in joint names, the couple divorced and the wife moved out. The contractual term ended with the husband alone in occupation. The first question was whether a single one of the original joint lease-holders could obtain a continuation tenancy under Part I of the Landlord and Tenant Act 1954. This was indeed held to be the case: the continuation tenancy arose in the single individual qualified by residential occupation at the term date. The rule for residential Rent Act tenancies[59] provided a better analogy than the rule for renewable business leases,[60] and it followed therefore that continuation is strictly inaccurate as a way of describing what occurs at the end of a long lease. An unhappy result followed on the facts, since the husband was adjudicated bankrupt. The continuation tenancy was a piece of property for insolvency purposes, but was not in the excluded list of residential tenancies,[61] and so it vested in the trustee in bankruptcy. He had disclaimed the lease, and was entitled to do so.

3. Form of security

This is determined from the term date of the tenant—that is the end of the lease. If this *occurred before January 15th 1999* (10 years after the introduction of the assured tenancies scheme) a tenancy protected under the Rent Act 1977 arose at the end of the lease, provided that the tenant met the requirements for protection under *that* Act (such as personal residence).[62] The rent is a fair rent, much higher no doubt than the ground rent under the long lease which has expired, but probably somewhat below the market rent.[63] If the terms cannot be agreed, a rent assessment committee will fix the rent[64] and a county court any other terms.[65]

[55] L.T.A. 1954 s.2(5); this would include a lease for life converted by L.P.A. 1925 s.149(6); if the lease is periodic sch.4 applies.

[56] L.T.A. 1954 s.19.

[57] s.2(1),(1A),(5),(7).

[58] [2000] Q.B. 33 C.A.; S. Murdoch [1999] 20 *E.G.* 155.

[59] *Lloyd* v. *Sadler* [1978] 1 Q.B. 774.

[60] *Jacobs* v. *Chaudhuri* [1968] 2 Q.B. 471; though see below p. 559 for the statutory reversal in the case of business partners.

[61] I.A. 1986 s.283(3A).

[62] *Herbert* v. *Byrne* [1964] 1 W.L.R. 519 C.A.; *St Ermin's Property Co. Ltd.* v. *Patel* (1998) 30 H.L.R. 462 C.A. (discussed below at p. 394).

[63] See above pp. 227–239.

[64] L.T.A. 1954 ss.6–10, schs.1, 2.

[65] ss.6–10, schs.1–2; *Blatherwick (Services) Ltd.* v. *King* [1991] Ch. 218 C.A. (service charge); *Établissement Commercial Kamira* v. *Shiazzano* [1985] Q.B. 93 C.A. (covenant against assignment, but not against sharing); *Lagens Properties Ltd.* v. *Bandino* [1965] E.G.D. 69 (no right to sub-let). The county court has jurisdiction by L.T.A. 1954 s.63.

Where the long lease expires on January 15th 1999 or afterwards, an assured tenancy arises at a market rent. Rent assessment committees continue to have jurisdiction to fix rents which are in dispute.[66] The shift from fair rents to market rents has an important impact in increasing the price to be paid on enfranchisement, since the price paid is based on the value of the landlord's reversion subject to the tenant's long lease and subject to its extension when the long lease terminates[67]: increasing the rent also increases the cost of enfranchisement.

4. Self-contained residential accommodation

One particular difficulty requires discussion. Full security accrues only if property is let as a separate dwelling, meaning that there must have been a grant of exclusive possession of self-contained accommodation. For short tenancies this test is applied *when the tenancy was first created,*[68] but it has to be applied to a 1954 Act long lease[69] *at the end of the lease* when security of tenure starts to operate. There is a statutory presumption that the state of affairs at the end of the lease existed at the beginning.[70] During the term of a long lease, it is quite likely that the property may be sub-let or divided up, so that the unit occupied at the end of the lease is often not identical to that let at the outset. The end result is to create a statutory tenancy of the part of the premises which is in the residential occupation of the tenant at the time of termination.[71]

In *St Ermins Property Co. Ltd.* v. *Patel*[72] a four-storey house let on a long lease had long ago been divided into two separately rated maisonettes. The residue of the term of each flat was acquired not long before the lease expired one September, and notices were given to fix the terms of a continuation tenancy of each flat. The judge refused, saying that there should be one notice in relation to the whole building, but the case was remitted for further consideration of the question who, if anyone, had Rent Act protection of what property. Since residential security requires residential occupation of a separate dwelling, it is reasonable to assume that the occupier of each maisonette would qualify for a separate continuation. However, the case law shows that this provision does not meet all the difficulties with which it was designed to deal, and many tenants have been unfairly denied protection.[73]

5. Opportunity to enfranchise

A statutory continuation suffers many disadvantages identified in *Cadogan Estates Ltd.* v. *Shahgholi.*[74] The contract is not assignable, the rent is high, and there is no capital appreciation. So the former leaseholder is given a chance to enfranchise.[75] The new lease

---

[66] The landlord can claim an interim rent increase: S.Is. 1997/3005, 1997/3007, 1997/3008 (forms).
[67] *Eyre Estate Trustees* v. *Shack* [1995] 1 E.G.L.R. 213 L.V.T.; *Black* v. *Eton College* [1995] 1 E.G.L.R. 223 L.V.T.
[68] R.A. 1977 s.1; H.A. 1988 s.1; see above pp. 143–149.
[69] L.T.A. 1954 s.2(2).
[70] s.22(3).
[71] s.3(3).
[72] (1998) 30 H.L.R. 462 C.A.
[73] See above pp. 148–149.
[74] [1999] 1 E.G.L.R. 189 L.Tr.
[75] L.Ref.A. 1967 s.16 (house); L.R.H.U.D.A. 1993 s.59 (flat—further renewal but no security of tenure after grant of new lease); *Galinski* v. *McHugh* [1989] 1 E.G.L.R. 109 C.A. L.T.A. 1954 s.21 and sch.5 contains provisions about who is the relevant landlord.

extends only to the property occupied for residential purposes—though including residential units which are sub-let[76]—so that the enfranchisable unit (excluding business parts) may be less than was included in the long lease.[77] A market rent will be payable after the end of the contractual term while the enfranchisement is in progress.[78] The fact that the tenant has little security or stake in the property inevitably increases the price payable on enfranchisement as compared to a leaseholder who enfranchises while he retains a long residue on his existing lease.

6. Restrictions on termination

A long lease will not automatically end when its term runs out. If the former leaseholder has rights to an assured tenancy, he can remain until a statutory notice to quit has been given by the landlord,[79] a right which cannot be excluded.[80] The procedure is complex, if similar in its broad outline to the more familiar business tenancies notice and counter-notice procedure for renewal: the landlord must give notice between six and 12 months before the intended termination date,[81] and the former leaseholder may respond to it with a counter-notice claiming security of tenure.[82]

Termination by the landlord is restricted at the end of the long lease, to ensure that the security of tenure arises.[83] Grounds for possession broadly follow those available against life-long tenants. If it is a Rent Act tenancy (that is the long lease ended before early 1999) the procedure to end the tenancy is laid down[84] and the grounds are limited to the following:

(1) Suitable alternative accommodation[85];
(2) Rent arrears, breach of covenant and other discretionary grounds[86];
(3) Requirement as residence for the landlord or his family[87]; and
(4) Intention to demolish or reconstruct.[88]

If the long lease ends after early 1999 there is an assured tenancy, but possession can be ordered on any ground available under an assured tenancy, *except* the following[89]:

---

[76] *Regalian Securities Ltd.* v. *Ramsden* [1981] 1 W.L.R. 611 H.L.

[77] *Baron* v. *Phillips* [1978] 2 E.G.L.R. 59 C.A. (enfranchisement excluded altogether, since at that time only houses could be enfranchised).

[78] H.A. 1996 sch.11 (including individual and collective enfranchisement) in force January 15th 1999.

[79] L.T.A. 1954 ss.3, 64 (interim continuation).

[80] s.17; *Re Hennessy's Agreement* [1975] Ch. 252 (agreement to surrender void).

[81] L.T.A. 1954 s.4; L.G.H.A. 1989 sch.10 para.4; S.I. 1957/1157 as amended by S.I. 1983/133.

[82] L.T.A. 1954 s.2(2); L.G.H.A. 1989 sch.10. The tenant must give notice of his claim to protection under L.T.A. 1954 s.18.

[83] L.T.A. 1954 s.4. The *tenant* can give one month's notice: s.5.

[84] ss.13 (landlord's application), 14 (decision in favour of tenant), 16 (relief from forfeiture), 55 (compensation where possession obtained by misrepresentation).

[85] L.T.A. 1954 s.12; sch.3; S.I. 1957/1157 as amended by S.I. 1983/133; H.A. 1988 sch.3, ground 9.

[86] L.T.A. 1954 sch.3; H.A. 1988 sch.2, grounds 10–15 (thus excluding ground 16—ending of employment).

[87] L.T.A. 1954 sch.3; H.A. 1988 sch.2, ground 1 (subject to a test of greater hardship); ground 1 is not available if the landlord bought after February 18th 1966.

[88] L.T.A. 1954 s. 12; H.A. 1988 sch.2, ground 6 (not if a former 1954 Act tenancy; para.(c) is omitted).

[89] H.A. 1988 s.7(5A); see above pp. 354–356.

ground   1 home for landlord;
        2 sale by lender;
        5 minister of religion;
        6 demolition and reconstruction;
      16 employment.

E.   RESIDENTIAL QUALIFICATION TO ENFRANCHISE

Enfranchisement should be available only to a leaseholder who can demonstrate that he occupies the property as his home. Residential qualification is established by showing, at the time of the application to enfranchise,[90] that the leaseholder must have occupied the property as his home for the three years before enfranchisement or for three of the previous 10 years.[91] Other residences must be disclosed and any failure to do so invalidates the notice to enfranchise.[92]

1.   Residence in a house

A house must be occupied as a main residence, a rule which prevents enfranchisement by a company.[93] Adoption of the Rent Act test of residence[94] suggests that continuous personal occupation is not required provided that there is an intention to occupy, though the onus will shift to an absent tenant. Residence might be retained through extended absences, especially if a caretaker is left in the property, and, possibly, simply by leaving it furnished.[95] Husband and wife may have separate residences.[96] It is not essential to occupy the entire house as a single residence. Enfranchisement is allowed if the leaseholder himself uses a part of the house for business purposes,[97] or if he sub-lets part to a business sub-tenant.[98] In *Harris* v. *Swick Securities Ltd.*[99] a sub-lease of all but one of the floors of a house to residential sub-tenants did not prevent enfranchisement, since the tenant retained the basement. Sub-letting of the entire property will remove qualification.[100] Occupation of a house must be in right of a long tenancy giving a right to enfranchise,[101] so the tenant must be both leasehold owner and occupier.[102] The residence period runs from acquisition of a long lease[103] or extension of a short lease.[104]

---

[90] Refusing consent to an assignment may block the acquisition of residential qualification: *Norfolk Capital Group Ltd.* v. *Kitway Ltd.* [1977] 1 Q.B. 506 C.A.; *Bickel* v. *Duke of Westminster* [1977] Q.B. 517 C.A.

[91] Houses: L.Ref.A. 1967 s.1(1)(b), s.1(2) (the period was reduced from 5 to 3 years by H.A. 1980 s.141, sch.21); flats: L.R.H.U.D.A. 1993 ss.36, 9(2)(b).

[92] *Dymond* v. *Arundel-Timms* [1991] 1 E.G.L.R. 109 C.A.

[93] L.Ref.A. 1967 s.37(5); *Duke of Westminster* v. *Oddy* (1984) 128 S.J. 316 C.A.

[94] *Poland* v. *Earl Cadogan* [1980] 3 All E.R. 544, 548h, Waller L.J.; see above pp. 104–109.

[95] *Poland* v. *Earl Cadogan* [1980] 3 All E.R. 544, 550c, Eveleigh L.J.; *Re Fairview, Church Street, Bromyard* [1974] 1 W.L.R. 579, Megarry J.

[96] *Fowell* v. *Radford* (1970) 21 P. & C.R. 99.

[97] See below p. 400.

[98] *Lake* v. *Bennett* [1970] 1 Q.B. 663 (ground floor let as a betting shop).

[99] [1969] 1 W.L.R. 1604 C.A.

[100] *Poland* v. *Earl Cadogan* [1980] 3 All E.R. 544, 550.

[101] L.Ref.A. 1967 s.1(2).

[102] *Harris* v. *Plentex Ltd* (1980) 40 P. & C.R. 483, Vinelott J.

[103] *Austin* v. *Dick Richards Properties Ltd.* [1975] 1 W.L.R. 1033 C.A.

[104] *Harris* v. *Plentex Ltd.* (1980) 40 P. & C.R. 483, Vinelott J.

Borrowers are disqualified while the lender has possession, even if they retain physical occupation.[105]

Succession occurs where a previous leaseholder occupied the house as his home when he died and the tenancy passes[106] to a successor who is a member of the deceased's family[107] who resided with him. The new leaseholder may add to his period of residence on his own account the period of residence prior to the original leaseholder's death, thus more rapidly accumulating the necessary years of qualifying occupation.[108]

2. Residence under a trust

A beneficiary can qualify to enfranchise by occupying a house[109] or flat[110] under the terms of a trust.

3. Residential qualification by flat owners

Comparable results are achieved for leaseholders seeking to extend a lease of a flat, though in a simpler form. The leaseholder must qualify through occupation of the flat as his only or principal home,[111] the periods being the same as for houses.[112] Occupation is tested factually, with no necessity for it to be in right of the long lease which provides the qualification.[113] Hence succession provisions are unnecessary.

4. Reform of residence condition—houses and flats

The residence test has proved to be a major obstacle to collective enfranchisement of a block by a group of leaseholders, because the turnover of new owners in large blocks is such that it becomes difficult to find a sufficient number of qualified and willing participants. Hence the proposal to change the collective procedure,[114] and to mirror this with matching changes to the qualification rules for individual enfranchisement.[115] Removal of the residence test will allow second homeowners and those sub-letting their flats to benefit from enfranchisement for the first time. In order to shut out speculators seeking short-term windfall gains, there will be a substitute requirement that a leaseholder must qualify by holding the long leasehold for two years before exercise of the right, though the present drafting only embraces flats.[116] The right to enfranchise will be transmissible

---

[105] *Poland* v. *Earl Cadogan* [1980] 3 All E.R. 544 (the qualification period was 5 years at the time).

[106] Succession on death is very widely defined: L.Ref.A. 1967 s.7(2)–(5); it includes inheriting by will or on intestacy, purchase by a beneficiary from personal representatives, or succeeding under a trust.

[107] L.Ref.A. 1967 s.7(7) includes spouse, children, (step, illegitimate and adopted), parents and parents-in-law, but excludes grandparents.

[108] L.Ref.A. 1967 s.7.

[109] L.Ref.A. 1967 s.6. The trustee could not: *Duke of Westminster* v. *Oddy* (1984) 128 S.J. 316 C.A.

[110] L.R.H.U.D.A. 1993 s.39 as amended by H.A. 1996 s.112 from October 1st 1996; the rules for collective enfranchisement are brought into line by H.A. 1996 s.111.

[111] Taking the "home" rule from the public-sector: H.A. 1985 s.81.

[112] L.R.H.U.D.A. 1993 s.39(2). Only one of joint leaseholders needs to qualify: s.39(6).

[113] L.R.H.U.D.A. 1993 s.39(5).

[114] See below p. 436.

[115] White Paper Part II paras.2.14–2.15, 2.2.6, 3.III.1–6, 3.III.9, and 4.4.B.

[116] L.R.H.U.D.A. 1993 s.39(2)(a) as amended by Commonhold and L.Ref. Bill 2000 cl.126(2). L.R.H.U.D.A. 1993 s.39(2)(b) and (2A) and (2B) would be omitted by Bill cl.126(3); sch.13 of the Bill would repeal L.R.H.U.D.A. 1993 s.39 subss.(2)(b), (2A), (2B), (4A), (5), and s.42 subss.(3)(b)(iii)–(iv), (4); also H.A. 1996 s.112.

on the death of a leaseholder to his personal representative,[117] though notice of exercise would have to be given within six months of receipt of a grant of representation, and the deceased would need a two-year ownership qualification at the date of his death.[118]

F. ENFRANCHISEMENT OF HOUSES, BUSINESS PROPERTY AND FLATS

Claims to enfranchise long leases may fall into one of three categories:

(1) Houses—freehold enfranchisement under either the 1967 scheme or (at greater cost) under later additions to the statutory scheme.
(2) Flats—leasehold extension at market value under the 1993 scheme.
(3) Business premises and other non-residential lettings—these are excluded.

1. Freehold and leasehold enfranchisement

Leasehold enfranchisement confers rights to freehold ownership of a house or to an extended lease of a flat, so it is important to determine whether a particular leaseholder lives in a house or a flat when matching him to the appropriate procedure. Only lease-holders of a house have the right to freehold enfranchisement under the Leasehold Reform Act 1967.[119] A house is susceptible of freehold ownership, with rights over neighbouring property adequately provided by easements, so that the ground landlord is compelled to transfer the freehold estate to his leaseholder claiming enfranchise-ment.[120] Flats are better managed through leasehold schemes because of the difficulties involved in securing proper management and maintenance. Hence collective enfran-chisement of a block of flats is available to secure the transfer of the freehold to a man-agement company[121] and individual leases of flats can be extended for 90 years at a time.[122] Exercise of enfranchisement rights will preclude a future grant for security of tenure.[123]

2. Property comprised in the lease

The starting point for identification of the unit to be enfranchised is to identify the property contained in the lease, which sets a maximum: the leaseholder cannot compel the ground landlord to transfer more than is held from him.[124] Once a house is identified as suitable for freehold enfranchisement, the property transferred to the

---

[117] L.R.H.U.D.A. 1993 s.39(2)(a) as amended by Commonhold and L.Ref. Bill 2000 cl.128(2) (flats).

[118] White Paper Part II paras.2.15 (outline), 3.III.10 (flats), 4.4.C (houses).

[119] The right to extend the term by 50 years is very rarely exercised; see below pp. 401–402.

[120] L.Ref.A. 1967; D. Macintyre [1968] *C.L.J.* 38; N. Hague (1967) 31 *Conv. (N.S.)* 187; H.W. Wilkinson (1968) 31 *M.L.R.* 193.

[121] L.R.H.U.D.A. 1993 part I chap.I.

[122] L.R.H.U.D.A. 1993 part I chap.II.

[123] L.Ref.A. 1967 s.16 (extended lease of house). L.R.H.U.D.A. 1993 s.59 (extended lease of flat); however, this point is to be changed, see below n. 154.

[124] Property held under two leases can be linked: L.Ref.A. 1967 s.3(6); *Wolf* v. *Crutchley* [1971] 1 W.L.R. 99, 101C Lord Denning M.R.; only the longest needs to exceed 21 years.

leaseholder should include all appurtenances which are part of his holding, such as a garage[125] or garden.[126]

3. Vertical division

The right to enfranchise is conferred on "a tenant of a leasehold house",[127] a unit which must be defined by strictly vertical divisions. The concern was to avoid the creation of flying freeholds.[128] If any material part of the property to be enfranchised lies above or below the adjoining property, freehold enfranchisement becomes impossible.[129]

Flats are excluded, as are maisonettes extending over several floors. Conversely, houses that are structurally detached[130] obviously qualify. Litigation tends to arise from houses which are semi-detached or terraced, where careful consideration is required to ensure that any dividing line is vertical.[131] In *Parsons* v. *Gage*[132] a mews house consisted of the whole of No. 24 and the upper floor of No. 25, the lower floor of No. 25 being occupied by the garage of the neighbouring house.[133] There was no unit which could be isolated as a house by vertical divisions, meaning that enfranchisement was refused. Similarly in *Duke of Westminster* v. *Birrane*[134] a basement[135] beneath a leasehold mews house extending beneath the rear part of an adjoining High Commission building of the Singapore Government meant that the mews building did not count as a house. In identifying the house, one should look at the physical structure and not its mode of occupation.[136]

The unit identified by vertical division must be a house *"reasonably so-called"*.[137] This provision is used to nullify some of the more bizarre results which can arise from drawing arbitrary vertical lines through buildings, and, since it is so open to subjective interpretation, it has attracted much litigation. In a normal terrace, vertical lines could isolate one, two, three or even 20 dwellings, but the only acceptable unit of enfranchisement is a single house. No one leaseholder can claim the freehold in the whole terrace, because that cannot ever be described as a house. It is different where two houses are linked internally, since the two together may reasonably thought of as a single house.[138] If a

---

[125] Not a garage in the ownership of a neighbour: *Dugan-Chapman* v. *Grosvenor Estates* [1997] 1 E.G.L.R. 96 C.Ct.

[126] See below p. 413. Not a garden held on a separate short lease: *Burr* v. *Eyre* [1999] 2 E.G.L.R. 92 C.Ct.

[127] L.Ref.A. 1967 s.1(1).

[128] *Gaidowski* v. *Gonville & Caius College, Cambridge* [1975] 1 W.L.R. 1066, 1069H, Ormrod L.J.; *Duke of Westminster* v. *Birrane* [1995] Q.B. 262, 269E, Nourse L.J.

[129] L.Ref.A. 1967 s.2(2).

[130] A phrase explained in *Parson* v. *Gage* [1974] 1 W.L.R. 435 H.L.

[131] A single house spread across several distinct buildings (like Sissinghurst Castle) is not enfranchisable: *Dugan-Chapman* v. *Grosvenor Estates* [1997] 1 E.G.L.R. 96 C.Ct.

[132] [1974] 1 W.L.R. 435 H.L.

[133] Materiality of this part was conceded. The house excluding the part over the garage was not a house properly so called.

[134] [1995] Q.B. 262 C.A.; P.F. Smith [1995] *Conv.* 166.

[135] Clearly material even though it was unused: at 268H–271D, Nourse L.J.; *Maliekshod* v. *Howard de Walden Estates Ltd.* [2000] E.G.C.S. 37 C.Ct.

[136] At 267H–268F, Nourse L.J.; he doubted *Peck* v. *Anicar Properties Ltd.* [1971] 1 All E.R. 517, 519, Lord Denning M.R.

[137] L.Ref.A. 1967 s.2(1).

[138] *Wolf* v. *Crutchley* [1971] 1 W.L.R. 99 C.A.

leaseholder occupies number 6 and stores his furniture in part of number 5, vertical division can be used to exclude the storage room and so leave number 6 as an enfranchisable unit.[139] Exclusion of this type is not possible if it removes a kitchen or some other essential living accommodation, since in such a case it would not be reasonable to call what is left a house.[140] In parts of Mayfair one will find luxury apartments spread out over two adjoining buildings to impede claims to enfranchisement.

Greatest difficulty has been caused by maisonettes above shops. If vertical division catches the whole of the living accommodation in the maisonette, the whole building (including the shop below) may qualify for enfranchisement even though access to the two parts is obtained from different streets.[141] A whole house divided internally into two maisonettes may also qualify,[142] especially if there are internal access arrangements.

4. Houses with partial business use

A house is defined as a building designed or adapted wholly or in part for living in,[143] thus encompassing purpose built houses and conversions. A property used *solely* for business cannot be enfranchised, since the leaseholder will have no residential occupation. Neither can a building where the primary use is for business; it is not possible to enfranchise ancillary living accommodation,[144] such as a caretaker's flat in a large factory.[145]

Partial business use may be consistent with a claim to enfranchise. The question is whether the unit defined by vertical divisions can reasonably be described as a house, which is a building (if not necessarily a machine!) for living in. The leading case concerned a building in which 75 per cent of the rental value was attributable to a shop, but nevertheless the house and the shop in combination qualified for enfranchisement.[146] Similarly a four-floor house can be enfranchised despite the fact that the ground floor is sub-let as a betting shop.[147] In both cases it was reasonable to call the whole building a house. In exceptional cases a leaseholder may qualify both for enfranchisement and business lease renewal,[148] in which case he must choose which course to pursue.[149]

5. Flats

The scheme for flats is much simpler, since it was introduced in one sweep in 1993 with only minor amendments to date. A flat requires rights of support over the flats below,

---

[139] *Gaidowski* v. *Gonville & Caius College, Cambridge* [1975] 1 W.L.R. 1066 C.A.

[140] *Parsons* v. *Gage* [1974] 1 W.L.R. 435 H.L.

[141] *Peck* v. *Anicar Properties Ltd.* [1971] 1 All E.R. 517 C.A. (even though the ground floor shop communicated with the next shop).

[142] *Sharpe* v. *Duke Street Securities NV* (1987) 55 P. & C.R. 331; *Malpas* v. *St Ermin's Property Co. Ltd.* [1992] 1 E.G.L.R. 109 C.A.; L.Ref.A. 1967 s.2(1).

[143] L.Ref.A. 1967 s.2(1). The last phrase implies a restriction: *Tandon* v. *Spurgeons Homes Trustees* [1982] A.C. 755, 764G, Lord Roskill.

[144] L.Ref.A. 1967 s.1(3)(a).

[145] [1982] A.C. 755, 762A Lord Fraser dissenting.

[146] *Tandon* v. *Spurgeons Homes Trustees* [1982] A.C. 755 H.L. (by a majority of 3:2); S. Tromans [1982] *Conv.* 378.

[147] *Lake* v. *Bennett* [1970] 1 Q.B. 663; *Harris* v. *Swick Securities Ltd.* [1969] 1 W.L.R. 1604.

[148] Tenants of agricultural holdings cannot enfranchise: L.Ref.A. 1967 s.1(3)(b); *Lester* v. *Ridd* [1990] 2 Q.B. 430 C.A.

[149] Care is needed if the business use is in breach of covenant. On termination of the lease by the landlord the tenant has 2 months to elect to seek to enfranchise: L.Ref.A. 1967 ss.22, 35 and sch.3 paras.1, 2, 14.

requires access over common parts of the block, and must itself support the flats above. The block requires management to regulate repairs and maintenance. So freehold enfranchisement is not feasible, given the present crude state of the law on the enforceability of positive covenants.[150] Freehold ownership of flats will have to wait for the enactment of commonhold proposals. Instead the Leasehold Reform Housing and Urban Development Act 1993 concentrates on improving the lot of flat owners as leaseholders. A flat is defined as a separate set of premises forming part of a building, constructed or adapted for use as a dwelling, but with some material part lying above or below another part of the same building.[151] Included are flats, maisonettes stretching over several floors, and some constructions that might in ordinary life—that is outside the bizarre world of enfranchisement—be regarded as houses. Collective rights over the block of flats are considered in the next chapter.[152]

G. LOW COST HOUSES

Enfranchisement of low cost houses occurs at site value under the original 1967 scheme. Topics considered here are extension of leases by 50 years, freehold enfranchisement, and the valuation of the freehold, as well as relevant reform proposals.

1. Extended lease

A leaseholder with a long lease at a low rent should always seek freehold enfranchisement if he is able to afford it. However, there is a little-used procedure to claim an extension of his lease for 50 years.[153] This is most often done where the leaseholder has a relatively short outstanding term so that the value of the reversion is large. A leaseholder who cannot afford the reversion, even on the generous basis provided for by the 1967 scheme, may benefit from an extension. At least it keeps him in his home—for a time. But there are severe disadvantages. First, there is no right to security of tenure at the end of the extended term—so the former leaseholder will not become an assured tenant but will have to give up possession.[154] Once the term date of the original (pre-extension) lease has gone by, there is no right to exercise the right to freehold enfranchisement.[155] So the main practical benefit of extension is the retention of the home for a period. The terms of extension are as follows. No premium is payable. The rent payable after the end of his existing term is increased to a modern ground rent—the full market rent of the land, but excluding the value of the house, reviewable after 25 years.[156] According

---

[150] *Gaidowski* v. *Gonville & Caius College, Cambridge* [1975] 1 W.L.R. 1066, 1069H, Ormrod L.J.; *Duke of Westminster* v. *Birrane* [1995] Q.B. 262, 269E, Nourse L.J.

[151] L.R.H.U.D.A. 1993 s.101(1).

[152] See below Chapter 16.

[153] L.Ref.A. 1967 ss.14–16. Security of tenure is excluded at the end of the 50-year extension, and the lease is subject to a re-development defence. The new lease is a separate asset for taxation purposes: *Lewis* v. *Walters* [1992] S.T.C. 97.

[154] s.16 subss.(1)(c), (1B), (1)(d)—removal of business renewal rights. Contractual renewal rights are also overridden.

[155] s.16(1)(a); nor is there any right to a further extension: s.16(1)(b).

[156] L.Ref.A. 1967 s.15(2); other terms are set out in s.15.

to Government figures, this is generally about a third of the market rent for the house.[157]

The real significance of extension is conceptual, since when determining the price at which low cost freehold enfranchisement will occur it is assumed that the right to an extension has already been exercised. This avoids the practical need to undertake two steps, and it is therefore usual for a leaseholder to proceed straight to freehold acquisition. The cost is greatly reduced as explained below in the context of enfranchisement of low cost houses.

2.   Extended lease—reform proposals

The Government White Paper issued in August 2000 proposes to remove both of the substantial hurdles in the path of a leaseholder who has extended his lease by 50 years.[158] First the right to purchase the freehold would be continued beyond the expiration date of the original lease. A sub-tenant holding a long lease would also have the right to enfranchise. These are new rights and so would be subject to high cost enfranchisement.[159] The Government also proposes to remove the provision of the Leasehold Reform Act 1967 which precludes the right to an assured tenancy at the expiration of the extended term.

3.   Low cost houses

Enfranchisement is most advantageous for a leaseholder of a house under a long lease at a low rent, provided it is not a luxury property (few are)[160] and that there was no other exclusion from the original 1967 Act scheme. The price is particularly advantageous. A leaseholder can acquire a freehold reversion well below its market value, because of the assumption that he has already exercised the little-used procedure to claim an extension of his lease for 50 years.[161] The rent payable after the end of his existing term is a ground rent for the site (that is excluding the house built on it)[162] reviewable after 25 years. If the leaseholder has, say, seven years left of his lease when enfranchising,[163] the freehold will be valued on the basis that the ground landlord will recover possession only in 57 years time, and until then will receive only a ground rent. Had the leaseholder enfranchised when 57 years remained, the landlord's interest would have been valued on the assumption that vacant possession would only be recovered in 107 years, giving a still lower price. Hence the assumption that this right has been exercised before a freehold enfranchisement greatly depresses the price that the ground landlord receives.

Freehold enfranchisement of low value houses is always beneficial if it can be afforded. The price to be paid for a low value house, ascertained at the date of an effective notice to enfranchise,[164] is the purchase price that would be obtained on the open

---

[157] White Paper Part II para.3.IV.A.1.
[158] Commonhold and L.Ref. Bill 2000 cl. 134; White Paper Part II paras.2.16–2.17, 3.IV.A–B.
[159] See below pp. 404–405.
[160] See below p. 404; at the time of the 1967 Act it was estimated that 98–99% were included: Cmnd. 2916 (1966).
[161] L.Ref.A. 1967 ss.14–16; see above p. 401.
[162] L.Ref.A. 1967 s.15(2).
[163] The right to an extended lease must be exercised during the contractual term.
[164] L.Ref.A. 1967 ss.9(1), 37(1)(a).

market by a willing seller. It is assumed that the leaseholder and members of his family are not in the market (which would increase the price),[165] and that there is no statutory right to enfranchise (which would decrease it). The interest valued is the ground land-lord's freehold reversion, subject to the leaseholder's lease, on the assumption that the right to obtain a 50-year extension has been exercised first. Any improvements made by the tenant are ignored.[166] This achieves (perhaps rather indirectly) the legislative inten-tion to allow the leaseholder to acquire the freehold by paying only the site value for the house. If the lease is very long, the value of the rent may simply be a multiplier of the ground rent, say 10 years' purchase.[167] With shorter leases, an approximation may be obtained by calculating what capital sum must be invested to give a yield of roughly 7 per cent, or by taking roughly 30 per cent of the overall value[168]; however the Court of Appeal has emphasised that each reversion must be valued on a market basis, taking par-ticular account of similar enfranchisements.[169]

4. Human rights attacks

The scheme of the Leasehold Reform Act 1967 was unquestionably expropriatory, since ground landlords lost their reversion without receiving compensation to the full market value. The European Convention on Human Rights[170] guarantees the integrity of pri-vate property rights, by ensuring peaceful enjoyment of all possessions and preventing removal of property rights without full payment. The Human Rights Act 1998 entrenches this protection in English law as from October 2nd 2000.

In human rights law, leasehold reform legislation can only be justified by showing that it satisfies the Convention's public interest exception. Objective justification is required of legislation, which must be appropriate and proportionate. It was held that the English legislation was justified in *James* v. *United Kingdom*.[171] The applicant, James, was one of the trustees of the Duke of Westminster's Grosvenor estate in Central London, an estate of 2,000 houses which faced claims by 80 leaseholders between the years 1979 and 1983, with estimated profits to individual leaseholders ranging between £32,000 and £182,000. The European Court of Human Rights ruled that legislation to remove social injustice could satisfy the public interest test, even if its effect was to trans-fer private rights from one individual to another rather than to achieve direct public ownership. Enfranchisement legislation was just since occupying leaseholders are

[165] L.Ref.A. 1967 s.9(1) as amended by H.A. 1969 s.82; A. George (1969) 33 *Conv. (N.S.)* 86.

[166] L.Ref.A. 1967 s.9(1A); *Rosen* v. *Campden Charities Trustees* [1999] 2 E.G.L.R. 213 L.Tr. (house was included because before original lease, but later improvements ignored).

[167] Ground rent—£10; freehold price—£100. See *Windsor Life Assurance Co. Ltd.* v. *Austin* [1996] 2 E.G.L.R. 169 L.T. (23 Y.P. of ground rent where 77 years remained); *Jarrett* v. *Burford Estates & Property Co. Ltd.* [1999] 1 E.G.L.R. 181 L.Tr. (review of rent was as a ground rent; hence enfranchisement of the residue of a 81-year lease for £758).

[168] *Eyre Estate Trusteees* v. *Saphir* [1999] 2 E.G.L.R. 123 L.Tr. (house with 38-year lease at ground rent of £200 enfranchised for £519,000 against a vacant possession value of £2.4m for the freehold); J. Russell & G. Porter [1995] 18 *L.S.G.* 18.

[169] *Official Custodian for Charities* v. *Goldridge* (1973) 26 P. & C.R. 191 C.A.; *Witham* v. *Collins* [1976] 2 E.G.L.R. 183 (£400–500 for reversion on 31 year lease with vacant possession value of £10,000); A. George and A.K. Dowse (1968) 32 *Conv. (N.S.)* 168.

[170] Article 1 of Protocol 1; see above pp. 200–208.

[171] (1986) 8 E.C.H.R. 123; S. Bright [1994] *Conv.* 211.

morally entitled to ownership, ground landlords collectively having exploited a monopoly to create a form of tenure which was disadvantageous to tenants. Sales of long leases
should be based on the value of the land itself rather than the market value of the land
carrying the house. Leaseholders should not be required to buy again what they have
already bought, so that it is equitable to reverse the unjust enrichment of landlords. The
1967 Act was appropriate and proportionate to these ends.

Anomalies in the legislation require separate justification, as they tend to discriminate between different property owners.[172] However the court accepted that objective
reasons were available to justify the form of the English legislation. Overall, therefore,
enfranchisement falls within the margin of appreciation allowed to a state to determine
its own policy towards property ownership. Since this case failed, it is difficult to see how
any challenge to enfranchisement legislation could succeed.

H. HIGH COST HOUSES AND FLATS

Despite the Government's win in *James*, subsequent extensions to the enfranchisement
scheme have required the leaseholder to pay the market value. This holds good both for
flats and for high cost houses, that is houses added to the statutory scheme since 1967,
particularly in 1993[173] and 1996.[174] This may have been natural for the Conservative
governments of the time, but New Labour is following the same policy; if nothing else
this should remove any political controversy (at least between the parties) from their
reforms.[175]

1. High cost houses

The high cost basis gives the ground landlord a better price on enfranchisement and the
tenant a correspondingly smaller gain. Substantial new rights were given in central
London, though Mayfair should not yet be displaced from its premier position on the
Monopoly board.[176] The main additions are:

(1) Luxury houses. Luxury houses were excluded from enfranchisement before 1993
by a high rateable value.[177] If, as was usual, the house was subject to domestic rates on
March 31st 1990, the exemption applied where the rateable value exceeded £1,000 in
Greater London or £500 elsewhere.[178] Houses built or converted after the abolition of

---

[172] Contrary to article 14.
[173] L.R.H.U.D.A. 1993 inserting L.Ref.A. 1967 s.1A.
[174] H.A. 1996.
[175] White Paper Part II para.3.IV.A.7.
[176] P. Nuki and H. Davidson, Sunday Times, November 7th 1993.
[177] L.Ref.A. 1967 s.1(1)(a), as amended by S.I. 1990/434 sch. para.5; *Parsons* v. *Gage* [1973] 1 W.L.R. 845 C.A.
[178] L.R.A.1967 s.1(1); ordinarily a change in the valuation list is not retrospective: *Rodwell* v. *Gwynne Trusts Ltd.*
[1970] 1 W.L.R. 327 H.L. However there is a procedure for the tenant to apply to reduce rateable values to exclude
the effect of leaseholder's improvements: L.Ref.A. 1967 s.9(1B); H.A. 1974 sch. 8; *Pearlman* v. *Harrow School* [1979]
Q.B. 56 C.A.; *Pollock* v. *Brook-Shepherd* (1983) 45 P. & C.R. 357 C.A.; *Macfarquhar* v. *Phillimore* [1986] 2 E.G.L.R.
89; *Rendall* v. *Duke of Westminster* (1987) 19 H.L.R. 345 C.A.; *Mayhew* v. *John Lyon Free Grammar School* (1990)
23 H.L.R. 479 C.A. Negligence claims may arise where agreement of high rateable value removes the right to enfranchise: *McIntyre* v. *Herring Son & Daw* [1988] 1 E.G.L.R. 231.

domestic rating are subjected to a complex arithmetical formula to determine whether the property is of higher value.[179]

(2) Additional low rent test. Under the 1967 Act, low rent was determined by comparing the rent at the time of the election to enfranchise with the rateable value. Enfranchisement rights could be evaded by including a rent review provision causing the rent to increase in later years. The 1993 Act compares the rent *in the initial year of the tenancy* with the rateable value at the time of first rating.[180] This brings into enfranchisement leases with rent review provisions, but at the higher cost.

(3) Leases for life. The 1967 Act excluded leases for life,[181] and when the gap was plugged in 1980,[182] the high cost basis was imposed for leases already in existence.[183]

(4) High rent houses. The Housing Act 1996[184] provides a new basis for enfranchisement where a lease fails the low rent test, but the lease is for a very long term, that is of at least 35 years.[185]

2. Proposed additions to the category of high cost houses

The additional categories proposed by the Commonhold and Leasehold Reform Bill 2000[186] are:

(5) Leaseholders under extended leases. The limits on enfranchisement after extension of the lease will be removed,[187] and there will be consequential amendments to the provisions for valuation during a lease extension,[188] but enfranchisement would be at high cost after the expiration of the original contractual term.[189]

(6) Removal of the low rent test. The Government proposes[190] to remove the low rent test for leaseholders with terms of between 21 and 35 years. Changes for collective enfranchisement require comparable changes in relation to houses. The low rent test would remain on the statute book to ensure that leaseholders benefiting form this change would pay an open market price including marriage value.

---

[179] References to Rating (Housing) Regulations 1990, S.I. 1990/434, sch. para.9; R should be less than £16,333 in the formula

$$R = \frac{P \times I}{1 - (1 + I)^{-T}}$$

where P is the premium, I is 0.06 and T is the term in years.

[180] L.R.H.U.D.A. 1993 s.65 introducing L.Ref.A. 1967 s.4A; also s.1A(2).

[181] See above p. 390.

[182] On or after April 18th 1980 except for a later lease under earlier contract.

[183] L.Ref.A. 1967 s.1B; L.R.H.U.D.A. 1993 s.64.

[184] s.106; sch.9.

[185] L.Ref.A. 1967 s.1AA; existing leases of part in designated rural areas are exempt: s.1AA(3).

[186] Commonhold and L.Ref. Bill 2000 cl.135; White Paper Part II paras.3.iv.6–7, 3.B.1–4.

[187] L.Ref.A. 1967 s.16(1)(a), (1B) will be omitted and s.16(4) amended, by Draft Commonhold and L.Ref. Bill 2000 cl.108.

[188] L.Ref.A. 1967 ss.9, 9A as amended by Draft Commonhold and L.Ref. Bill 2000 cl.106. Lost cost enfranchisement (s.9) applies where notice is given before the original term date of the tenancy and high cost enfranchisement (s.9A) afterwards.

[189] See above pp. 401–402.

[190] White Paper Part II, paras.4.4.A, 4.4.7. No legislative wording is available in January 2001.

3. Flats

The scheme for flats is much simpler than for houses, since it was introduced in one sweep in 1993 with relatively minor amendments to date. A leaseholder of a flat has the right to an extension of his current lease by 90 years[191] on payment of a market premium.[192] Of an estimated 1.5 million leasehold dwellings, the 1993 Act was aimed to help ½ to ⅔rds of leaseholders. In addition the leaseholders of a purpose-built or converted block have the right to collective enfranchisement—that is the right to club together to buy out the ground landlord's interest at the market value.[193] The price to be paid for a long leasehold extension is laid down by the 1993 Act,[194] and is essentially the market value of the interest being acquired.

I. MARKET VALUATION

1. High cost houses

Additions to enfranchisement, particularly those made by the Conservative Government between 1979 and 1993, have been made on the high cost basis, giving the ground landlord a better price on enfranchisement and the tenant a correspondingly smaller gain. When assessing the price to be paid for a high cost house in all of these cases, the lease is taken to end on its term date,[195] with no 50-year extension.[196] Security of tenure will arise at the end of the long lease, as an assured tenancy at a market rent (or a Rent Act tenancy at a fair rent if it expired before early 1999) but the market rent regime should not greatly reduce the value of the freehold reversion.[197] Marriage value is included in assessing the value of the landlord's reversion, though limited to half.[198] Where enfranchisement rights were given in 1993,[199] the leaseholder must also pay compensation to the ground landlord equal to the diminution or loss in value of the ground landlord of the value of any remaining property.[200] This current basis for valuation is broadly comparable to the basis for flats, now discussed.

---

[191] D.N. Clarke [1994] *Conv.* 223; S. Bight [1994] *Conv.* 211; A. Diamond & S. McGrath [1993] 11 *Legal Action* 17; J. Ellis [1994] *N.L.J.* 1376; M. Davey (1994) 57 *M.L.R.* 773.

[192] L.R.H.U.D.A. 1993 s.39(1).

[193] See below pp. 432–440.

[194] L.R.H.U.D.A. 1993 sch.13; T. Gordon, *The Cost of Buying Your Freehold or Extending Your Lease* (1997).

[195] L.Ref.A. 1967 s.9(1A) amended H.A. 1974 s.118(4). No express or implied liability to repair and any repairs or maintenance effected by the tenant or his predecessors are ignored. In addition it is assumed that the tenant will be in the market (which increases the price further).

[196] L.Ref.A. 1967 s.9(1A); amendment made by Housing and Planning Act 1986 s.23(1)(3) reversed the decision in *Mosley* v. *Hickman* [1986] 1 E.G.L.R. 161 C.A. Even actual extension of the lease does not reduce the price.

[197] *Eyre Estate Trustees* v. *Shack* [1995] 1 E.G.L.R. 213 L.V.T.; *Black* v. *Eton College* [1995] 1 E.G.L.R. 223 L.V.T.

[198] L.R.H.U.D.A. 1993 s.6 amending L.Ref.A. 1967 s.9; see L.R.H.U.D.A. 1993 sch.15 for the current wording; marriage value is explained below at p. 408.

[199] Categories (2), (4), (5) and (6) above p. 405.

[200] L.Ref.A. 1967 s.9(1C); L.R.H.U.D.A. 1993 s.66; Commonhold and L.Ref. Bill 2000 cl.135.

2. Flats

A leaseholder of a flat has the individual right to an extension of his current lease by 90 years[201] on payment of a market premium.[202] Similar valuation principles apply to the collective enfranchisement of a block.[203] The price to be paid for a long leasehold extension is laid down by the 1993 Act,[204] and is essentially the market price for the interest which is being acquired, with three elements: the value of the lease granted, a share of marriage value, and compensation for any loss to the landlord's remaining property.

3. Flats with over 90 years remaining

Where a leaseholder enfranchises when he already has a long term, the price is likely to be small. If the leaseholder's existing rights exceed 80 years, the average cost of enfranchisement is about £1,5000. This is because the value of the ground landlord's interest is small, and marriage value is not in play with long leases.[205]

The value of the lease acquired. This is assessed according to the open market price between a willing seller and buyer. The premium payable for individual extension is the diminution in value of the ground landlord's interest, taking the difference in the value before and after the grant of the extended lease.[206] An open market value is taken assuming willing parties, reflecting the value of any existing security of tenure[207] and of improvements.[208]

Compensation. In addition, compensation is payable for any loss in value of the ground landlord's remaining property,[209] especially the loss of rights to insurance commission.[210]

4. Flats with short remaining terms

Here the price to be paid may be very large. It will include:

Value of the lease. This will be much greater if the leaseholder waits until the fag end of his existing lease before extending, or even worse if he leaves it until after his long lease has expired when he is relying on statutory continuation.[211] The market value will be discounted to reflect the fact that the former leaseholder would have the right to

---

[201] D.N. Clarke [1994] *Conv.* 223; S. Bright [1994] *Conv.* 211; A. Diamond & S. McGrath [1993] 11 *Legal Action* 17; J. Ellis [1994] *N.L.J.* 1376; M. Davey (1994) 57 *M.L.R.* 773.

[202] L.R.H.U.D.A. 1993 s.39(1).

[203] See below pp. 437–440.

[204] L.R.H.U.D.A. 1993 sch.13; T. Gordon, *The Cost of Buying Your Freehold or Extending Your Lease* (1997).

[205] *Goldstein* v. *Cawley* [1999] 1 E.G.L.R. 95, 99D–H L.Tr

[206] L.R.H.U.D.A. 1993 sch.13 paras.2–3. Disregarded are (1) rights of enfranchisement, (2) improvements made by the tenant at his own expense, (3) bids from those already interested in the property (who may pay more than outsiders); the rules are improved by H.A. 1996 s.110.

[207] *Vignaud* v. *John Lyons Free Grammar School Governors* [1996] 2 E.G.L.R. 179 L.Tr. (business renewal rights); *Hordern* v. *Viscount Chelsea* [1997] 1 E.G.L.R. 195 L.V.T. (25% deduction for value of security of tenure).

[208] *Williams* v. *Portman Family S.E. Trustees* [1996] 1 E.G.L.R. 217.

[209] L.R.H.U.D.A. 1993 sch.13 para.5 (individual extension); *Maryland Estates Ltd.* v. *63 Perham Road Ltd.* [1997] 2 E.G.L.R. 198 L.Tr.

[210] *Blackstone Investments Ltd.* v. *Middleton-Dell Management Co. Ltd.* [1997] 1 E.G.L.R. 135 L.Tr. There may also be some development value.

[211] *Hordern* v. *Viscount Chelsea* [1997] 1 E.G.L.R. 195 L.V.T. (premium of £283,000 required when existing lease had expired).

continue as an assured tenant. In the past there was an even greater discount when continuation was as a Rent Act tenant. In one case the tenant obtained only a 15 per cent
discount from the full freehold vacant possession value to reflect his right to a 1954 Act
continuation, though 35 per cent is more normal for this factor.[212]

Compensation, as above.

A share of marriage value. Where land is subject to a shortish lease (say 20 or 30 years)
the combined value of all estates in the land is depressed because the lease is short but
the landlord's reversion is deferred. Value can be unlocked by extending the lease, transferring most of the value to the lease and causing the combined value of all interests in
the land to equate more nearly to the vacant possession value of the freehold. The extra
value which appears in this way from adding the shorter lease to the longer extension of
it is called marriage value.[213] It is computed by deducting the aggregate of the values
before the enfranchisement from the aggregate values afterwards.[214] The ground landlord is entitled to at least half[215] and possibly more, depending what would be agreed in
an open market, but 50-50 division is normal.[216] If the term extended has only a very
short time left to run at the time of enfranchisement the landlord may be entitled to
much more.[217]

5. Price—proposed reforms

The Government is proposing changes to the basis for valuation in the event of collective enfranchisement, and knock on changes will bring into line the valuation of high
cost houses[218] and flats.[219] It is proposed that marriage value should be apportioned on
a 50–50 basis[220] and that there should be a presumption that there is no marriage value
where the lease exceeds 90 years.[221] There would be a number of associated repeals.[222]

---

[212] *Cadogan Estates Ltd.* v. *Shahgholi* [1999] 1 E.G.L.R. 189 L.Tr. (£572,000 for a 90-year lease in Cadogan Place against a vacant possession value of £600,000); *Goldstein* v. *Cawley* [1999] 1 E.G.L.R. 95 L.Tr. (40% after expiry of lease of flat in Belsize Gardens); *Shina* v. *Elghanian* [1999] 48 E.G. 147 L.Tr. (10% discount where 4 years remained).

[213] *Goldstein* v. *Cawley* [1999] 1 E.G.L.R. 95 L.Tr.

[214] *Maryland Estates Ltd.* v. *63 Perham Road Ltd.* [1997] 2 E.G.L.R. 198 L.Tr.; *Goldstein* v. *Cawley* [1999] 1 E.G.L.R. 95 L.Tr.

[215] L.R.H.U.D.A. 1993 sch.13 para.4.

[216] *Black* v. *Eton College* [1995] 1 E.G.L.R. 223 L.V.T. (no deduction for security at end of long tenancy; capital-
isation at 7.5% to ground rent; marriage value at 50%); *Waitt* v. *Morris* [1994] 2 E.G.L.R. 224 L.V.T. (ground rent at 7 years' purchase + 50% marriage value); J. Ellis & N. Brown. [1995] 37 *E.G.* 166 (review of early cases); *Williams* v. *Portman Family S.E. Trustees* [1996] 1 E.G.L.R. 217.

[217] *Cadogan Estates Ltd.* v. *Shahgholi* [1999] 1 E.G.L.R. 189 L.Tr. (72.5% agreed); *Goldstein* v. *Cawley* [1999] 1 E.G.L.R. 95 L.Tr. (also 72.5%).

[218] There is no legislative wording as at January 2001. White Paper Part II para.2.2.6, 4.4.D.

[219] White Paper Part II paras.2.13–2.15, 3.III.11–3.III.12.

[220] L.R.H.U.D.A. 1993 sch.13 para.4(1) as amended by Commonhold and L.Ref. Bill 2000 cl.131.

[221] L.R.H.U.D.A. 1993 sch.13 para.4(2A), inserted by Commonhold and L.Ref. Bill 2000 cl.132.

[222] Commonhold and L.Ref. Bill 2000 sch.13 repealing and amending L.R.H.U.D.A. 1993 ss.45(5)(b), 62(4),
91(2)(c), 91(7), 99(5)(a); cls.147–150 propose procedural changes in the L.V.T.; see below pp.439–40.

6. Valuation date—current law and proposed reforms

Under the present law the value of a house is determined on the "relevant time" when the leaseholder serves his initial notice asking to enfranchise.[223] That is a sensible and logical rule. Unfortunately the value of a flat is determined on the "valuation date",[224] which is when the right to enfranchise is agreed. This is clearly unsatisfactory because a ground landlord may increase the price by delaying the enfranchisement process. The Government proposes instead that the price should be fixed on the "relevant date"— that is the date of the initial notice.[225] This will remove any incentive for delay. Other aspects of procedure for determining the price, costs, and so forth, are considered below.[226]

J. LANDLORD'S DEFENCES TO ENFRANCHISEMENT

1. Exempt ground landlords and excluded properties

The statutory right of enfranchisement does not apply to certain landlords. The Crown, meaning Crown Estate Commissioners, Duchies of Lancaster and Cornwall and Government ministries, is not bound, though it is normal practice after 1993 for the Crown to comply with the enfranchisement rights as a matter of grace.[227] Charitable housing trusts are also exempt.[228] Local authorities are bound, though with wider development defences. Other exemptions apply to cathedral precincts,[229] and certain parts of Wales.[230] Freehold enfranchisement is restricted in some areas owned by the National Trust[231] or of heritage significance.[232]

2. Other procedures

Compulsory purchase ends enfranchisement rights, which are not considered when assessing compensation.[233] Enfranchisement suspends forfeiture and other termination procedures,[234] subject to the possibility that the court may give permission to the ground landlord to proceed with his forfeiture action if enfranchisement is being used simply to forestall re-entry and is not being pursued in good faith.[235] Disrepair very often blights enfranchisement claims.

---

[223] L.Ref.A. 1967 ss.9(1), 9(1A), 37(1)(d).

[224] L.R.H.U.D.A. 1993 sch.13.

[225] L.R.H.U.D.A. 1993 sch.13 as amended by Commonhold and L.Ref. Bill 2000 cl.130; White Paper Part II paras.3.III.11–12.

[226] See below pp. 413–414.

[227] L.Ref.A. 1967 s.33; L.R.H.U.D.A. 1993 s.94(11); Hansard H.C. vol.213 (1992) written answers cols.19–20 (Sir George Young) Commonhold and L.Ref. Bill 2000 cl.129.

[228] L.R.H.U.D.A. 1993 (flats) ss.67 (houses let before 1995).

[229] L.Ref.A. 1967 s.31 (houses); L.R.H.U.D.A. 1993 s.96 (flats).

[230] S.I. 1997/685.

[231] L.Ref.A. 1967 s.32; L.R.H.U.D.A. 1993 s.95.

[232] L.Ref.A. 1967 s.32A; L.R.H.U.D.A. 1993 s.68; L.R.H.U.D.A. 1993 s.31.

[233] L.Ref.A. 1967 s.5 (6)(7); L.R.H.U.D.A. 1993 s.55; *Johnson* v. *Sheffield C.C.* (1982) 43 P. & C.R. 272; *Uddin* v. *Birmingham C.C.* (1990) 59 P. & C.R. 341; A.M. Prichard (1975) 39 *Conv. (N.S.)* 52.

[234] L.Ref.A. 1967 sch.3; L.R.H.U.D.A. 1993 sch.12 para.4.

[235] *Central Estates (Belgravia) Ltd.* v. *Woolgar* [1972] 1 Q.B. 48; *Liverpool Corporation* v. *Huson* [1972] 1 Q.B. 48.

3. Redevelopment defence

The reversioner can claim possession for redevelopment after the grant of an extended lease of a house or flat, though this is not available as a defence to *freehold* enfranchisement of a house. The application can be made up to one year before the original term date of the lease of a house or flat (when the leases ends on the term date)[236] or during the last five years of the extended term of a flat.[237] The basis is that the ground landlord intends to demolish or reconstruct the whole or a substantial part of the house and premises, a ground copying that in the legislation governing renewable business leases.[238] In order to avoid the loss of a valuable property and its redevelopment potential, the leaseholder should apply to enfranchise sufficiently far in advance to prevent the ground ever arising. Disputes are settled by notice and counter notice leading to application to the court to resolve whether the ground landlord has shown the relevant intention. If so possession is ordered, but the leaseholder will be entitled to compensation based on the open market value of his lease as extended.[239] Public landlords have greater rights to preserve future development prospects.[240]

4. Residence for ground landlord (houses)

A ground landlord may apply to the court[241] for an order entitling him to resume possession on the basis that all or part is reasonably required for occupation as his only or main residence or for an adult member of his family.[242] This defence applies to freehold enfranchisement and to extension of leases of houses. Possession is granted at the end of the existing lease.[243] The defence is not available to a ground landlord by purchase,[244] including one acquiring on the merger of a higher interest. Leaseholders can in turn contest the application of the defence on the ground of greater hardship. Compensation is payable to the tenant at the full value of his interest, that is the selling value of the lease as extended.[245]

5. Exclusion

A common feature of all these statutory procedures is that valuable rights are conferred on leaseholders. Ground landlords have a strong incentive to try to avoid rights which as a class they regard as expropriatory, especially houses subject to low cost enfranchisement from which tenants stand to profit most. An agreement is void to the extent that it purports to exclude or modify a future right to enfranchise,[246] though there is

---

[236] L.Ref.A. 1967 ss.17(1),(4),(6), 20(1); L.R.H.U.D.A. 1993 s.47.

[237] L.R.H.U.D.A. 1993 s.47; collective enfranchisement is also excluded.

[238] L.T.A. 1954 s.30(1)(f); see below pp. 509–571.

[239] L.Ref.A. 1967 s.17(2), 8(4), sch.2 para.7; L.R.H.U.D.A. 1993 s.61, sch.14.

[240] L.Ref.A. 1967 ss.28–30.

[241] L.Ref.A. 1967 ss.18(1)(2)(4), 20(1), sch.2 para.3(4).

[242] L.Ref.A. 1967 s.18(1); L.Ref.R. 1967 r.18(3). Family is defined to mean the following adults: a spouse, children or spouse's children (illegitimate, adopted, and step), children-in-law over 18, parents, and parents in law.

[243] *Gurvidi* v. *Marget* (1972) 116 S.J. 255.

[244] After February 18th 1966.

[245] L.Ref.A. 1967 sch.2 para.5.

[246] The prohibition applies to a provision for termination, any requirement to surrender, or imposing a penalty or disability when claiming the benefit of the Act: L.Ref.A. 1967 s.23(1) (houses); L.R.H.U.D.A. 1993 s.93(1) (flats and blocks).

nothing to destroy actual surrender or other transactions which have actually occurred.[247] If the leaseholder serves a claim notice, but then withdraws it, he may validly agree not to serve another for up to five years.[248] A number of illegitimate tactics designed to increase the price for enfranchisement artificially are also proscribed.[249]

K. PROCEDURE FOR INDIVIDUAL ENFRANCHISEMENT

Anyone who wishes to pursue a claim to enfranchisement will need to turn to one of the specialist texts, in order to avoid the pitfalls that await the unwary. Space permits only a rough sketch of the common elements of the procedures.

1. Notice to trigger individual enfranchisement

Procedure is initiated by a notice to enfranchise. *Enfranchisement of a house* is set off by a desire notice,[250] in a prescribed form[251] which requires the leaseholder to lay out the main facts forming the basis of his claim to the freehold.[252] Deliberate errors or omissions invalidate the notice.[253] Details required include particulars of the house, the leaseholder's lease, the rent and rateable value (to enable the lease to be identified as at a low rent), the leaseholder's residential qualification, and any succession.

The tenant's notice which triggers the procedure for *extending a lease of a flat* is similar.[254] Details required by subsection (3) are: the name of the leaseholder, identification of the flat and of the lease, proof of qualification to enfranchise, the premium proposed, and the proposed term. Stating the correct date for the extended lease is critical: this is not a case where the *Mannai* principle will assist.[255] Successive extensions are possible.[256] Notice must be given by all joint leaseholders of the leasehold estate, a rule which might create difficulty if, for example, a married couple have separated.[257]

Normally failure to serve a valid notice will not be of great moment, because the error can be rectified by giving a fresh notice. Problems may arise if, for example, the qualifying period of occupation has been lost in the interim.[258] Delay shortens the outstanding term of the lease and may therefore increase the price that has to be paid for the freehold: in one case delay for 10 years would have cost £100,000.[259]

---

[247] *Woodruff* v. *Hambro* (1991) 62 P. & C.R. 62 C.A.; *Rennie* v. *Proma Ltd.* [1990] 1 E.G.L.R. 119, 123 (transfer to trustees subject to consent of B when B intended to defeat enfranchisement); N.D.M. Parry [1991] *Conv.* 460.

[248] See below n. 263.

[249] See below p. 415.

[250] L.Ref.A. 1967 s.8(1). The notice must elect either for freehold enfranchisement or leasehold extension: *Byrnlea Property Investments Ltd.* v. *Ramsay* [1969] 2 Q.B. 253 C.A.

[251] L.Ref.A. 1967 sch.3 para.6; L.Ref. (Notices) Regs. 1997, S.I. 1997/640, Form 1.

[252] L.Ref.A. 1967 s.8; L.R.H.U.D.A. 1993 s.42(2)(b).

[253] *Dymond* v. *Arundel-Timms* [1991] 1 E.G.L.R. 109 C.A.

[254] L.R.H.U.D.A. 1993 s.42; no form is prescribed.

[255] *John Lyon's Free Grammar School* v. *Secchi* [1999] 41 E.G. 153 C.A.; *Viscount Chelsea* v. *Hirshorn* [1998] 2 E.G.L.R. 90 C.Ct.

[256] L.R.H.U.D.A. 1993 s.57.

[257] *Wax* v. *Viscount Chelsea* [1996] 2 E.G.L.R. 80 C.Ct.

[258] *Byrnlea Property Investments Ltd.* v. *Ramsay* [1969] 2 Q.B. 253 C.A. (term date before the 1967 Act came into force).

[259] *Collin* v. *Duke of Westminster* [1985] Q.B. 581 C.A.; *Snipper* v. *Enever Freeman & Co.* [1991] 2 E.G.L.R. 270, Sheen J. (damages for negligence).

The initial notice forms the basis of a contract. It therefore requires precise information of the property claimed[260] and the price. With a house the leaseholder must elect to claim either the freehold or an extended lease; alternative contracts are impossible.[261] Service of a valid claim notice puts the parties in the same position as if a contract for sale had been entered into.[262] It binds the ground landlord to sell and the tenant to pay the price, until withdrawn[263] or barred by the passage of time.[264] A deposit can be demanded at any time.[265] The enfranchisement notice should be protected as an estate contract, whether the land is registered or unregistered.[266] The benefit of a notice to enfranchise can be assigned when the house is transferred[267]; the Land Registry view is that a separate document should be used. However, it is vitally important to use proper legal formalities and to make the assignment contemporaneous with the transfer of the land.[268]

2.   Challenging the right to individual enfranchisement

Ground landlords will commonly dispute a notice to enfranchise, either because they challenge the qualification to enfranchise, or because they wish to negotiate a higher price, or because they disagree with the terms proposed by the leaseholder. The ground landlord can also claim defences, such as the intention to redevelop at this stage. A counter-notice must be served indicating the grounds of objection.[269] There is a complex timetable for the later stages.

Disputes about qualification to enfranchise or the validity of defences will be settled in court.[270] The normal (Part 7) procedure is used for most enfranchisement claims,[271] though the alternative procedure of Part 8 is used for one or two specialised claims.[272] A dispute about the terms of acquisition is settled by a Leasehold Valuation Tribunal,[273] which may award costs[274]; an appeal to the Land Tribunal is by way of a rehearing.[275]

---

[260] See below p. 413.

[261] *Byrnlea Property Investments Ltd.* v. *Ramsay* [1969] 2 Q.B. 253 C.A.

[262] L.Ref.A. 1967 s.5(3) (house); L.R.H.U.D.A. 1993 s.43 (flat).

[263] L.Ref.A. 1967 s.9(3); L.R.H.U.D.A. 1993 s.52.

[264] A specialty claim under L.Ref.A. 1967 s.8: *Collin* v. *Duke of Westminster* [1985] Q.B. 581 C.A. No abandonment can be inferred.

[265] £25 or 3 × rent (house); £250 or 10% (flat): S.Is. 1967/1879, 1993/2407.

[266] L.Ref.A. 1967 s.5(5); L.R.H.U.D.A. 1993 s.97; L.R. Practice Leaflet No.8. Cancellation: S.I. 1967/1879 part I para.11, S.I. 1993/2407.

[267] L.Ref.A. 1967 s.5(2).

[268] *Aldavon Co. Ltd.* v. *Deverill* [1999] 2 E.G.L.R. 69 C.Ct.

[269] S.I. 1997/640, form 2 (house); L.R.H.U.D.A. 1993 s. 45 (flat).

[270] L.Ref.A. 1967 s.20 (houses); L.R.H.U.D.A. 1993 ss.40, 47, 49 (flats).

[271] C.P.R. sch.2 C.C.R. Order 49 r.8 (L.Ref.A. 1967), r.9 (L.R.H.U.D.A. 1993 except as below).

[272] P.D.8B.B.1 (L.R.H.U.D.A. r.9(3) s.26(1)(2), s.50(1)(2)).

[273] L.Ref.A. 1967 s.21; S.I. 1993/2408 sch 1 form 1; S.I. 1996/2305; a new pre-trial review procedure is introduced: H.A. 1996 s.119.

[274] L.Ref.A. 1967 s.21(1) as amended by H.A. 1996 s.115(6); this reverses *Covent Garden Group* v. *Naiva* (1994) 27 H.L.R. 295 C.A. By H.A. 1996 sch.11 the landlord is entitled to compensation for a defective claim to enfranchise. Costs of an internal valuation are not allowed: *Jones* v. *Avon Estates* [1996] C.L.Y. 3738; but *Re Cressingham Properties Ltd.* [1999] 2 E.G.L.R. 117 L.Tr. (in house costs recoverable).

[275] *Swann* v. *White* [1996] 1 E.G.L.R. 99; *Re Speedwell Estates Ltd.* [1999] 2 E.G.L.R. 121 L.Tr.; *Wellcome Trust Ltd.* v. *Romines* [1999] 3 E.G.L.R. 229 L.Tr.

3. Scope of the house

What is included with the house? The leaseholder's notice claiming the right to enfranchise will state what he thinks should be included, both in terms both of the extent of the property and the scope of the rights to be granted with it,[276] though the ground landlord can object by counter notice, and may sometimes require adjustment of the property either by exclusion or inclusion.[277] Disputes are settled in court.

Enfranchisement of a house is restricted first to the property let by the lease under which the leaseholder claims enfranchisement. A garden strip let under a separate lease does not qualify for enfranchisement just because it is later vested in a qualifying tenant.[278] All of the living accommodation must fall within the house—that is the unit isolated by vertical division.[279] Also included within the scope of the enfranchisement are any premises associated with the house,[280] this includes any garages, outhouses, gardens,[281] yards and appurtenances,[282] but excludes paddocks[283] and mineral rights.[284]

A flat includes its appurtenances within the curtilage of the block of flats.[285]

4. Fixing the price

The procedure for fixing the price varies according to the nature of the property enfranchised. A leaseholder of a *house* serves a desire notice indicating that he wishes to enfranchise at a price to be suggested by the ground landlord in his counter-notice. The price is increased by the requirement that the leaseholder pay the ground landlord's reasonable costs of deducing title, considering the claim, valuation, and conveyancing fees.[286] The leaseholder has a right to withdraw within one month of the price being determined, but he is then barred from further application for three years.[287]

A leaseholder of a *flat* must include in his notice originating the enfranchisement procedure the suggested premium for the lease extension; the ground landlord can challenge the premium in his counter-notice.[288] A vital qualification to the validity of the enfranchisement notice appeared in *Cadogan* v. *Morris*.[289] The leaseholder's notice stated £100 as the premium for the extension of a lease of a flat, when a realistic figure for the value was between £100,000 and £300,000. Stuart Smith L.J.[290] gave short shrift

---

[276] L.Ref.A. 1967 s.10(1)–(3).

[277] s.2(4),(5),(7).

[278] *Gaidowski* v. *Gonville & Caius College, Cambridge* [1975] 1 W.L.R. 1066, 1071H, Ormrod L.J. The test is applied at the date of the notice of application; at p.1072F.

[279] *Wolf* v. *Crutchley* [1971] 1 W.L.R. 99 C.A.

[280] L.Ref.A. 1967 ss.1(1), 2(3).

[281] However not a garden which is included in a separate short lease: *Burr* v. *Eyre* [1999] 2 E.G.L.R. 92 C.Ct.

[282] L.Ref.A. 1967 s.2(3).

[283] *Methuen-Campbell* v. *Walters* [1979] Q.B. 525.

[284] L.Ref.A. 1967 s.2(6).

[285] *Cadogan* v. *McGirk* [1996] 4 All E.R. 643 C.A. (storeroom).

[286] L.Ref.A. 1967 s.9; L.R.H.U.D.A. 1993 ss.32, 60 the cost of application to the tribunal is excluded; the landlord has a lien for the purchase price. Payment of premium is a precondition of exercise of the right (s.56).

[287] L.Ref.A. 1967 s.9(3); L.R.H.U.D.A. 1993 s.52; *Galinski* v. *McHugh* [1989] 1 E.G.L.R. 109.

[288] L.R.H.U.D.A. 1993 ss.42(3)(c), 48.

[289] [1999] 1 E.G.L.R. 59 C.A. (on L.R.H.U.D.A. 1993 s.42).

[290] At 61B–C.

to the argument seeking to uphold the validity of the notice. The leaseholder must specify the premium he proposes to pay, and he did not do so. It must be a realistic figure, the only comfort to the leaseholder being that a counter notice by the landlord also had to be realistic. As with a house the price is increased by the requirement that the leaseholder pay the ground landlord's reasonable costs of deducing title, considering the claim, valuation, and conveyancing fees.[291] The leaseholder has a right to withdraw within one month of the price being determined, but he is then barred from further application for three years.[292]

Ground landlords will commonly dispute a notice to enfranchise, either because they challenge the qualification to enfranchise, or because they wish to negotiate a higher price, or because they disagree with the terms proposed by the leaseholder. The ground landlord can also claim defences, such as the intention to redevelop at this stage. A counter-notice must be served indicating the grounds of objection.[293] There is a complex timetable for the later stages. A dispute about the price is resolved by an application by the leaseholder to a Leasehold Valuation Tribunal,[294] which may award costs[295]; an appeal to the Land Tribunal is by way of a rehearing.[296]

5.　Completing the enfranchisement

If the claim is accepted or the court orders it to be accepted,[297] the landlord must complete the contract created by the initial notice by conveyance.[298] If it is a house, the leaseholder is entitled to a conveyance of the freehold subject to the tenancy and any incumbrances created by the leaseholder but otherwise free from incumbrances apart from restrictive covenants and easements to which the leaseholder was subject while holding under the lease.[299] A lease of a flat is completed by the grant of a new lease at a peppercorn for a term expiring 90 years after term date.[300] The new lease will be on the same terms, unless there is an agreement to vary the terms or either party shows a good reason to vary. Enfranchisement overrides any restriction on assignment.

If the reversion is mortgaged, the conveyance or transfer automatically discharges any mortgage provided that the leaseholder takes care to pay the purchase money to the

---

[291] L.Ref.A. 1967 s.9; L.R.H.U.D.A. 1993 ss.32, 60 the cost of application to the tribunal is excluded; the landlord has a lien for the purchase price. Payment of premium is a precondition of exercise of the right (s.56).

[292] L.Ref.A. 1967 s.9(3); L.R.H.U.D.A. 1993 s.52; *Galinski* v. *McHugh* [1989] 1 E.G.L.R. 109.

[293] S.I. 1997/640, form 2 (house); L.R.H.U.D.A. 1993 s. 45 (flat).

[294] L.Ref.A. 1967 s.21; S.I. 1993/2408 sch 1 form 1; S.I. 1996/2305; a new pre-trial review procedure is introduced: H.A. 1996 s.119. Procedural reforms are included in the Commonhold and L.Ref. Bill 2000 cls. 147–150 Sch.11, see below pp. 439–40.

[295] L.Ref.A. 1967 s.21(1) as amended by H.A. 1996 s.115(6); this reverses *Covent Garden Group* v. *Naiva* (1994) 27 H.L.R. 295 C.A. By H.A. 1996 sch.11 the landlord is entitled to compensation for a defective claim to enfranchise. Costs of an internal valuation are not allowed: *Jones* v. *Avon Estates* [1996] C.L.Y. 3738; but *Re Cressingham Properties Ltd.* [1999] 2 E.G.L.R. 117 L.Tr. (in house costs recoverable).

[296] *Swann* v. *White* [1996] 1 E.G.L.R. 99; *Re Speedwell Estates Ltd.* [1999] 2 E.G.L.R. 121 L.Tr.; *Wellcome Trust Ltd.* v. *Romines* [1999] 3 E.G.L.R. 229 L.Tr.

[297] Procedure to overcome delays: L.Ref.A. 1967 ss.5(3), 20; L.R.H.U.D.A. 1993 s.49.

[298] J. Tiley (1968) 32 *Conv. (N.S.)* 43, 141.

[299] L.Ref.A. 1967 s.8; *McAully* v. *Chiswich Quay Freeholds Ltd.* [1998] E.G.C.S.163 C.A.

[300] L.R.H.U.D.A. 1993 s.56.

[301] L.Ref.A. 1967 ss.11, 12; L.R.H.U.D.A. 1993 s.58. Proof will be required of the discharge of mortgages affecting the ground landlord's title. e.g. by form 53, by a receipt signed by the lender, or by payment into court.

lender.[301] It includes necessary easements.[302] Regulations deal with conveyancing details, such as the deposit, deduction of title, requisitions, rights and restrictions, completion, apportionments, preparation of the conveyance or lease, and failure to comply with covenants.[303] A limited covenant for title is given.[304] The presumption is that a flat lease is extended on the same terms as before, though with provision to vary them as justified by the circumstances.[305] The regrant acts as a surrender of the existing lease, though with existing priorities and matrimonial home rights are preserved.[306] Registration of title will be required.[307]

6.   Procedure where reversion is divided

In a simple case a leaseholder demands the freehold from his immediate ground landlord who is beneficial owner[308] of the freehold. However enfranchisement operates in just the same way if there are intervening leases. A sub-leaseholder who qualifies through residence can enfranchise.[309] The leaseholder can seek to acquire the freehold and all intervening leases. The actual process is carried out by the nearest reversioner with a sufficiently long reversion outstanding who must act for the other ground landlords.[310] Each reversionary interest is valued separately.[311] It would be much simpler if the Act required a single valuation of the reversion and then provided for the price which is determined upon to be apportioned between the various ground landlords.[312]

7.   Artificial transactions to increase price invalid

The device adopted successfully in *Wentworth Securities Ltd.* v. *Jones*[313] was extremely disadvantageous to the leaseholder. A ground landlord granted a concurrent lease of the property with a provision that any sub-lease of the property had to be granted at the market rent. This significantly increased the income to be derived from the ground landlord's interest and hence the value of the reversion,[314] but it was an artificial ruse, and the decision had to be reversed by legislation. Statute now provides that the price must not be made less favourable to a leaseholder by any transaction involving a superior interest.[315] Further a mathematical formula is provided for valuing minor superior tenancies, that is ones with low rents and short reversions.[316]

[302] L.Ref.A. 1967 s.10; *Langevad* v. *Chiswick Quay Freeholds Ltd.* (2000) 80 P. & C.R. 26 C.A.

[303] S.I. 1967/1879 sch. part I (houses); S.I. 1993/2407 r.3, sch. 2 (flats).

[304] L.P. (M.P.) A. 1994 s.1(2).   [305] L.R.H.U.D.A. 1993 s.57.

[306] s.58A inserted by H.A. 1996 s.117.

[307] L.R. Practice Leaflet No.8.

[308] For special cases see L.Ref.A. 1967 ss.25–31, (houses); L.R.H.U.D.A. 1993 ss.19, 40, sch.2 (flats & collective).

[309] He must hold a long tenancy; a sub-lease granted out of a short tenancy in breach of covenant does not qualify the sub-tenant: L.Ref.A. 1967 s.5(4).

[310] L.Ref.A. 1967 s.5(4), sch.1 (house—30-year reversion); L.R.H.U.D.A. 1993 s.40 (individual extension of flat lease—90-year reversion); L.R.H.U.D.A. 1993 s.9, sch.1 (collective).

[311] L.Ref.A. 1967 sch.1; L.R.H.U.D.A. 1993 sch.13 pt.II.

[312] *Wentworth Securities Ltd.* v. *Jones* [1980] A.C. 74, 108H, Lord Russell.

[313] [1980] A.C. 74 H.L.

[314] On the facts, £4,000 as against £250.

[315] L.Ref.A. 1979 applying to transactions after February 15th 1979 (houses); L.R.H.U.D.A. 1993 sch.13 para.3(6) (flats).

[316] Which gives an expectation of possession for less than 1 month and the rent does not exceed £5: L.Ref.A. 1967 sch.1 para.7A (houses); L.R.H.U.D.A. 1993 sch.13 part III.

L. ABSENT LANDLORDS

1. Existing procedure for houses

The High Court has jurisdiction to authorise an enfranchisement where the freeholder cannot be found or his identity cannot be ascertained.[317] The court will direct the applicant what advertisements and other enquiries should be undertaken and will satisfy itself of the applicant's qualification to enfranchise. The "appropriate sum" is a fair valuation ascertained by a surveyor selected by the President of the Lands Tribunal, with the addition of any arrears of ground rent and costs. This sum must be paid into court[318] in satisfaction of the reversionary claims, and the freehold is then transferred by court vesting order.

2. Reform of the procedure for houses

Amendments are made to the procedure where the landlord cannot be found by the Government's draft Commonhold and Leasehold Enfranchisement Bill 2000.[319] A county court replaces the High Court as the venue for deciding upon entitlement to enfranchise and a Leasehold Valuation Tribunal would determine the price payable rather than a surveyor appointed by the president of the Lands Tribunal.[320]

3. Existing procedure for flats

These proposals will, if enacted, bring the procedure for leasehold houses into line with the procedure for collective enfranchisement, and it is also broadly similar to the procedure for extension of an individual flat lease. In the latter case, a county court can make a vesting order where the landlord cannot be found or his identity is unknown, the court being required to satisfy itself of the applicant's qualification and the absence of defences.[321] The court will order what advertisements and other steps should be taken. There is also a jurisdiction for the court to dispense with the need for a notice where it is not possible to give notice, in which case notices given to any other party must alert them to the use of the dispensation procedure. A Leasehold Valuation Tribunal determines the "appropriate sum" to be paid, representing the premium, costs and arrears of rent. This sum must be paid into court, whereupon a person designated by the court will execute a new lease; this operates to surrender the existing lease and to grant a new one.

---

[317] L.Ref.A. 1967 s.27.

[318] *Re 51 Bennington Road, Aston* [1993] Times July 21st, Vinelott J.

[319] L.Ref.A. 1967 s.27 as amended by Commonhold and L.Ref. Bill 2000 cl.136. Sch.13 repeals and amends L.Ref.A. 1967 s.16.(1)(a), (1B), (2), (3), (4); White Paper Part II paras.2.17, 3.IV.C.

[320] L.Ref.A. 1967 s.27(5) as amended by Commonhold and L.Ref. Bill 2000 cl.137; s.21(1) dealing with the jurisdiction of the L.V.T. is amended accordingly.

[321] L.R.H.U.D.A. 1993 ss.50, 51.

M. ESTATE MANAGEMENT SCHEMES

1. Property law

A recent Government estimate[322] was that there were 900,000 leasehold houses, more than half of them being in the North West and Merseyside. Leasehold tenure is fundamentally unsatisfactory.[323] Leasehold tenure is only ever used on an estate of houses, but if the structural integrity of each unit is independent of every other there is no need for a scheme of communal repairs and management and no inherent reason to use a long lease rather than a freehold.

An estate of houses can get by with a scheme of easements and restrictive covenants, which is of course valid if the houses on the estate are sold freehold, and just as much so if it is sold leasehold.[324] *Easements* are commonly implied on the grant of a lease of part of the land, the more so if the property has been occupied before the lease (for example where a lease is renewed)[325] or if the property is let for a particular commercial purpose.[326] Landlords need to be cautious, since implied grants to a leaseholder are more generous than implied reservations back to the landlord. For these reasons it is desirable to have a scheme of express covenants which is fully articulated, with grants to each leaseholder matching reservations of comparable easements for the landlord and other leaseholders, and it is therefore essential for the whole development to be planned in advance.[327] Rights requiring consideration are support, access, storage, parking, pipes and wires, and waste disposal. *Restrictive covenants* regulate the use of servient land in favour of neighbouring dominant land. Freehold sales usually reserve restrictive covenants for neighbours. In case of a leasehold sale they may benefit neighbours, but the landlord's reversion is also a sufficient interest to support action on covenants. It is likely that a leasehold estate of houses will include some *positive covenants,* particularly for the maintenance of common parts of the estate, since these covenants run and are enforceable between successive leasehold owners.[328]

Leasehold titles to houses are vulnerable to enfranchisement—that is the right of the leaseholder to acquire the freehold—which will end the possibility of positive covenants running, though schemes of covenants could be preserved if the former ground landlord created a post-enfranchisement management scheme. This must now be explained.

2. Estate Management Schemes

Enfranchisement takes effect subject to the restrictive covenants reserved by the lease for the benefit of the neighbouring properties.[329] The landlord of a leasehold housing

---

[322] *Leasehold Reform in England & Wales—a C.P.* (D.E.T.R., November 1998) 13.

[323] para.1.4.

[324] L.P.A. 1925 s.1(2)(a).

[325] L.P.A. 1925 s.62 then applies if the lease is legal: *Sovmots Investments Ltd.* v. *S.S. for the Environment* [1979] A.C. 144 H.L.

[326] *Wong* v. *Beaumont Property Trust Ltd.* [1965] 1 Q.B. 173 C.A.

[327] It is also important to consider the problem of prescription.

[328] See above Chapter 26.

[329] L.Ref.A. 1967 s.8; L.R.H.U.D.A. 1993 s.57; *Langevad* v. *Chiswick Quay Freeholds Ltd.* (2000) 80 P. & C.R. 26 C.A.

scheme may wish to reserve stronger controls by securing approval of a management scheme to preserve wide controls after enfranchisement[330] or after exercise of the right to buy.[331] The aim of the scheme is to preserve the quality and appearance of the area.

The ground landlord will continue management, but should not be given excessive control[332]; it would be wrong to allow the ground landlord a right of pre-emption to reserve future rights to redevelopment.[333] There is no procedure for the leaseholders to take over control of their area, though they should have a say,[334] and in certain circumstances control can pass to the local authority.[335] Initial applications could be made under the 1967, 1993, and 1996 schemes of enfranchisement.[336] However, at present all time limits have expired, so that the ground landlord must first persuade the minister that it is desirable to set up a scheme.[337] With a ministerial certificate the landlord can apply to the court (that is to a judge[338]) for approval of the detailed drafting of the scheme.[339]

A scheme may be approved even if it is less than perfect.[340] It should cover a defined geographical area,[341] and must be registered as a local land charge.[342] The object is to secure the amenity of the area. Factors enhancing the freehold and rental values of a residential estate include the period character of the properties, the cohesive look of the estate, and a high standard of maintenance. There may be restrictive covenants to control changes of use and prevent adverse development.[343] New restrictions can be introduced.[344] Like any other restrictive covenants,[345] those imposed by an estate management scheme can be varied by application to the Lands Tribunal.[346] Communal management arrangements could extend to the maintenance of the exterior of the dwellings,[347] maintenance contributions,[348] communal insurance,[349] and membership

[330] L.Ref.A. 1967 s.19; L.R.H.U.D.A. 1993 ss.69–75; H.A. 1996 s.118; M. Vitoria (1975) 39 *Conv. (N.S.)* 398.
[331] *Re Beech's Application* (1990) 59 P. & C.R. 502.
[332] L.R.H.U.D.A. 1993 s.70.
[333] *Eton College* v. *Nassar* [1991] 2 E.G.L.R. 271, Harman J.
[334] *Re Calthorpe Estate* (1973) 26 P. & C.R. 120, Foster J.
[335] L.R.H.U.D.A 1993 s.73.
[336] H.A. 1996 s.118; *Re Dulwich Estate Trustees' Appeal* (1998) 76 P. & C.R. 484 L.Tr. (existing scheme amended to include new properties brought in by the 1993 Act).
[337] L.R.H.U.D.A. 1993 s.72.
[338] Practice Direction [1990] 1 All E.R. 255.
[339] *Re Sherwood Close* [1972] Ch. 208, 211, Goulding J.
[340] *Re Dulwich College's Application* (1973) 231 E.G. 845, Walton J.
[341] *Cadbury* v. *Woodward* (1972) 23 P. C.R. 281; *(No.2)* (1972) 24 P. C.R. 335 (Bourneville Estate, Edgbaston).
[342] L.R.H.U.D.A. 1993 s.71(13).
[343] Commonly consent for work is required from the management trustees: e.g. *Mosley* v. *Cooper* [1990] 1 E.G.L.R. 124; *Alleyn's Estate Governors* v. *Williams* (1995) 70 P.& C.R. 67, Nicholls V.C.
[344] *Re Dulwich College's Application* (1973) 231 E.G. 845, Walton J.
[345] Sparkes *N.L.L.* 616–620.
[346] H.A. 1985 s.157; H.A. 1996 s.118; *Mosley* v. *Cooper* [1990] 1 E.G.L.R. 124; *Re Milius' Application* (1995) 70 P. & C.R. 427 (application under H.A. 1985 s.157 refused because still substantial benefit).
[347] *Re Sherwood Close* [1927] Ch. 208, Goulding J.
[348] *Re Abbot's Park Estate (No.2)* [1972] 1 W.L.R. 1597. Pennycuick V.C. (charge for the cost of repairs should be postponed to first mortgages).
[349] *Re Sherwood Close* [1972] Ch. 208, Goulding J.; *Eton College* v. *Nassar* [1991] 2 E.G.L.R. 271, Harman J.

of a management company.[350] Existing estate management schemes[351] can be varied if there is a material change of circumstance.[352]

N. PROPOSALS FOR A PRE-EMPTION RIGHT OVER HOUSES

Leaseholders and short residential tenants in a block of flats benefit from a pre-emption right—that is the right to compel the ground landlord to sell to them collectively if and when he decides to sell, overriding the rights of any outside investor who makes an offer to buy. In the recent consultation exercises, there was a considerable degree of support for extending this right to houses[353]—indeed the *Analysis of Responses* showed 75 per cent support for this proposal,[354] and the intention to implement it was announced.[355] However this proposal does not feature in the Commonhold and Leasehold Reform Bill 2000.

---

[350] *Re Abbot's Park* [1972] 1 W.L.R. 598.
[351] H.A. 1996 s.118.
[352] L.R.H.U.D.A. 1993 s.70. Reforms are proposed by Commonhold and L.Ref. Bill 2000 Sch.12.
[353] *Residential Leasehold Reform in England and Wales—a C.P.* (D.E.T.R., November 1998) para.5.2.
[354] A. Brittan, *An Analysis of Responses to Residential Leasehold Reform in England and Wales—a C.P.* (D.E.T.R., December 1999) para.52.
[355] M. Pye, *Leasehold Reform: The Way Forward—a Summary of Proposals* (D.E.T.R., December 1999) para.14.

16

FLAT SCHEMES

Defects of leasehold tenure. Leasehold flat schemes. Reform proposals. Communal management. Flat schemes. Collective pre-emption (tenant's first refusal on sale). Collective enfranchisement. Qualification to enfranchise. Valuation. Corporate vehicle. Reform of collective enfranchisement. Proposal for a right to manage. Residential management controls. Reform of residential management. Service charges. Control of domestic service charges. Proposals to reform the controls. Proposed control of administration charges. Controls of insurance rents.

The Commonhold and Leasehold Reform Bill 2000 was introduced into the House of Lords on 20 December 2000 and may be expected to pass during the 2000–2001 session of Parliament unless, of course, an election intervenes. In August 2000, the Government published a draft Bill[1] and White Paper[2] to build on its previous consultation exercise.[3] Extensive reference is made to these official papers in this chapter.

There are 900,000 leasehold houses and one million flats[4] with half the houses in the North West and Merseyside region, and half of all the flats in London and the South East. The White Paper published in August 2000 suggests[5] that the residential leasehold tenure has its roots in the feudal system, but in fact large-scale adoption of leasehold tenure as a form of ownership is relatively recent. Nevertheless it is the case, as the White Paper states, that this tenure gives great powers and privileges to ground landlords and that it suffers from fundamental defects as a vehicle for home ownership.[6]

This chapter considers the existing schemes intended to redress the imbalance of power between the ground landlord and the real owners (i.e. the leaseholders) and the current proposals to improve them. The next chapter considers the longer-term solution of commonhold tenure for new flat developments. Commonhold will not cure the

---

[1] Hereafter Draft Commonhold and L.Ref. Bill 2000.

[2] *Commonhold and Leasehold Reform—Draft Bill and C.P.* (Cm 4843, September 2000), hereafter "White Paper". This and the other consultation documents are available electronically at <www.detr.gov.uk/housing>.

[3] (1) *Residential Leasehold Reform in England and Wales—a C.P.* (D.E.T.R., November 1998), hereafter "*Consultation 1998*"; see J. Driscoll [1998] *N.L.J.* 1855; D. Marcus [1998] 50 *E.G.* 78; P.H. Kenny [1999] *Conv.* 74; (2) A. Brittan, *An Analysis of Responses to Residential Leasehold Reform in England and Wales—a C.P.* (D.E.T.R., December 1999), hereafter "*Analysis*"; (3) M. Pye, *Leasehold Reform: The Way Forward—a Summary of Proposals* (D.E.T.R., December 1999), hereafter "*Way Forward*".

[4] *Consultation 1998* para.1.4.

[5] White Paper Part II para.3.II.1.1.

[6] White Paper Part II para.3.II.1.1.; *Consultation 1998* para.1.4.

problems of leaseholders on existing developments, because conversion to the new tenure will require unanimity among the leaseholders and the consent of the ground landlord. So reforms are needed for those unable or unwilling to convert.[7]

Abuses cause misery and distress to many leaseholders. A pool of disaffected owners has been created, and there is strong political pressure to extend rights to enfranchisement.

A. PROBLEMS OF LEASEHOLD FLAT TENURE

Ownership of a flat suffers from disadvantages of three sorts—the wasting character of the tenure, the freehold ownership of the ground landlord, and the problem of securing acceptable communal management. It is beyond human ingenuity to make all neighbours live happily together, but badly designed leasehold schemes can increase the drawbacks and well-designed ones can ameliorate them. Commonhold will be the best possible solution.

1.   Wastage of value from individual flats

Leasehold tenure is not markedly inferior to freehold ownership provided that the lease is very long and the ground rent is low. A serious problem of wastage of value affects shorter leasehold terms—where the outstanding term is less than 90 years. This difficulty is addressed by the individual enfranchisement scheme considered in the previous chapter.[8]

2.   Block ownership

If all the leases in a block of flats are very long, the leaseholders may not be unduly concerned by the theoretical freehold ownership of a ground landlord, but a ground landlord may become a nuisance if he exploits his ownership aggressively, for example by demanding excessive interest on arrears of ground rent or by extracting value in the shape of large commission payments on the premiums to insure the block. There are a number of ways of tackling this problem of block ownership, but all involve the transfer of the freehold to a management company controlled by the flat owners collectively. Properly organised flat schemes will be set up so that the developer transfers the freehold to a management company run by the leaseholders as soon as the development work is completed. If the scheme is not set up in this way, it may be possible to achieve the same result by agreement. Otherwise the leaseholders have to use the compulsory mechanisms to take over collective ownership of their block. Legislation extended rights in two phases—first, a right of collective pre-emption (or first refusal) was enacted in 1987 which applies where the landlord decides to sell the block and this was followed by a right to compel the landlord to sell on the initiative of the leaseholders by collective enfranchisement in 1993. The 1993 right is more important and is restricted to leaseholders. Both schemes are restrictive and over-complex, but at least the present reform proposals will make it easier for tenants to qualify, if they do not do anything to improve

---

[7] White Paper Part II paras.1.2–1.5.
[8] See above Chapter 18.

the coherence and comprehensibility of the law. Both procedures involve a compulsory[9] transfer of the freehold estate in the land from the ground landlord to a flat management company acting for a group of leaseholders. This may lead to an undesirable situation in which only some of the leaseholders participate in the ownership.

3. Communal management

Most houses are, in legal terms, more or less isolated from their neighbours in legal terms. They rest on the bare earth and communal facilities are limited to a shared garden fence, access drive or telephone line, matters which can be dealt with under the law of easements and covenants. Flats are completely different, since no one flat has any value in isolation. The structural integrity and enjoyment of each flat is intimately connected with every other one, so a scheme of reciprocal rights and covenants is essential, and these must include repairing obligations and many other positive covenants.

B. LEASEHOLD FLAT SCHEMES

1. General

One million flats, almost all held leasehold are concentrated in London and the South East.[10] Leases are used because the value of each flat is dependent upon the condition of the block and of every other flat, so positive covenants are needed to cope with repair and the payment of service charges. Covenants in leases run with the reversion and with the land, thus ensuring that the covenants are always enforceable between the current parties,[11] so that leasehold schemes provide a suitable vehicle for ensuring proper maintenance and repair of the block. Positive covenants do not run with freehold titles,[12] a fact which creates problems with the sale of freehold flats, though the difficulties can be exaggerated.

Any flat will be a part of a larger title, so it will be essential to create a scheme of easements for access and restrictive covenants for regulation of the block,[13] but much more important will be mutually enforceable obligations for the repair of the block.

Essentially a flat development involves three interest groups: (1) the owners of individual flats; (2) a management company—consisting of the owners of individual flats brought together in a corporate structure to manage a block of flats; and (3) the developer. The division of overall ownership between these groups depends upon the scheme adopted. An ideal scheme for managing a block of flats would display a number of features. Each resident must own a long-term interest in his own flat, and also has a stake in the management of the whole block, and ideally a share in the freehold ownership of the block. A scheme is needed to ensure that the block is properly maintained, with each flat owner paying a share of the overall costs through a service charge. It is invariable practice to use a flat management company.

---

[9] *Cadogan* v. *Morris* [1999] 1 E.G.L.R. 59, 60J, Stuart Smith L.J.
[10] *Consultation 1998* paras.1.3–1.4.
[11] See above pp. 397–398.
[12] *Rhone* v. *Stevens* [1994] 2 A.C. 310 H.L.; Sparkes *N.L.L.* 622-623.
[13] See below p. 426.

2.   Where a developer retains the freehold

Least satisfactory from the point of view of the owners of flats is a scheme under which the freehold reversion in the entire block is retained by the developer. Common parts and repairing obligations are passed to a management company. Hence the developer has the freehold estate in the development without burdens, subject to a long lease of the common parts and long leases of individual flats to the individual owners. Very careful schemes of covenants are required. For example, if the management company fails to repair, it cannot be implied that the freeholder will do so.[14] Freehold ownership confers the right to collect the ground rents for the future as a source of profit. Running of covenants is no problem for blocks set up since 1996, since covenants with management companies pass in the same way as covenants between landlord and tenant[15]; this is so if the covenant relates to a "relevant function", meaning a function relating to the property let as opposed to a financial guarantee. There were more problems under the pre-1996 law.[16]

Until 1993 many blocks were vested in moribund landlords, but the increased management controls introduced in that year[17] induced many old landlords to sell up to outside investors. Even if the leasehold interests are very long, income is always lost in the shape of ground rents passing to an outside investor, and the landlord may be tempted to profit from placing insurance. Leaseholders have an important right granted in 1993 to an individual extension of the lease of their flat.[18] It is often wise to break such schemes by acquiring the freehold from the landlord, either by agreement or (if the landlord proves recalcitrant) by enfranchisement or pre-emption.[19]

3.   Where a management company holds the freehold

More attractive from the point of view of purchasers is a scheme under which the freehold estate in the whole block is vested in a management company, so that it holds not only the common parts of the development, but also the reversion after the leases of the individual flats. This scheme ensures proper management, while minimising tenurial problems. Leases of each flat are granted[20] to the initial buyer, ideally for a term of 999 years. When all units are sold, the freehold is conveyed to a management company. The management company (controlled by the tenants collectively) can negotiate the extension of the leases of individual flats[21] or if there is an difficulty the right of individual extension can be invoked. There is no outside investor collecting ground rents, so that rents will be put into the same pot as service charge contributions to help pay for management of the block.

---

[14]   *Hafton Properties Ltd.* v. *Camp* [1994] 1 E.G.L.R. 67.

[15]   L.T. (Covenants) A. 1995 s.12.

[16]   See below p. 765.

[17]   L.R.H.U.D.A. 1993; see below pp. 426–432.

[18]   See above pp. 400–401.

[19]   See below pp. 426–444.

[20]   The developer grants the leases and collects the premiums during the development process before the transfer to the management company.

[21]   Even if shorter leases are used, the reversion will belong to the owners collectively through their ownership of the management company.

4. Flat management companies

A company is used to manage a block of flats. It would be hopeless to vest the freehold estate in a mass of constantly changing flat owners,[22] and instead the freehold is vested in a flat management company to secure the advantage of its existence as a separate corporate entity and its perpetual succession; no conveyancing should be needed after the initial vesting of the freehold in the company.

There is no alternative at present to use of an ordinary company, usually one whose members have limited liability,[23] but problems arise because ordinary company law is not well adapted to flat management. It is essential to keep ownership of the flats in step with the ownership of the corresponding shares in the management company. Only flat owners may be members of the management company, and they may only resign by selling their flats, with membership continuing until the buyer is registered. So each flat buyer is forced to hold the corresponding share in the management of the development. Share transfers are required as part and parcel of every sale of every flat, and default powers are needed (usually vested in the directors of the management company) to ensure that a person who sells his flat can be compelled to pass on his share with his flat.

Special provisions are required for the early stages after the first flats have been sold but when other flats remain unsold while the developer completes the construction of the development. The builder or developer needs to retain control to facilitate successful completion of the block sales. This is usually done by reserving special voting rights, giving the developer sufficient fire power to carry a special resolution on any subject.[24] This phase will continue until all flats are sold and the developer certifies that the block is complete; at that stage the management company will be handed over to the control of the flat owners.

A serious concern is the need for any company to comply with all the bureaucratic machinery designed to regulate trading companies: willing officers are needed and there are onerous accounting and filing requirements. Big developments will generate a management culture that is semi-professional, but the administrative superstructure is too heavy to deal with small conversions of house into a few flats. Many management companies default in compliance with the technical requirements of the companies legislation. *Shire Court Residents Ltd.* v. *Registrar of Companies*[25] is just one example of a flat management company being struck off the Companies Register for failure to file accounts. In that case the head lease held by the company passed to the Crown, which disclaimed it as onerous property, so the tenants were compelled to make a court application for a vesting order causing the head lease to re-vest in them. In another case a flat management company was wound up,[26] and the freeholder also went into liquidation,

---

[22] It is possible, but undesirable to use a trust where there are four or fewer units, but L.P.A. 1925 ss.1(6), 34 prohibits more than four trustees.

[23] Bureaucracy can be minimised in a simple case by the use of a company limited by guarantee, but even here certificates of ownership are usually needed. Guarantees are not flexible enough to cope with complex developments with variable voting rights within the development.

[24] An alternative is to provide for the freehold to be transferred to the management company only after the sale of all the flats.

[25] [1995] B.C.C. 821, Carnwath J.

[26] *Re Crawley Mansions Ltd.* [1994] E.G.C.S. 95.

so the tenants had to litigate to obtain an assignment of the freeholder's rights before being able to sue in the freeholder's name to enforce obligations to carry out refurbishment.[27]

5.   Mutuality of obligation

It is fundamental to the value of a flat in a block that all other parts of the block are properly maintained. Each tenant must be liable to the landlord to contribute to the cost, usually through a service charge.[28] It must be open to every other owner to secure compliance with this covenant, possibly by an arrangement giving the benefit of the covenants to other leaseholders or more probably because the landlord promises to enforce covenants against other leaseholders[29]; without this provision the leases of individual flats are likely to be unmortgageable.[30] It may be wise to create a formal letting scheme with mutual obligations[31] though a problem is that this may restrict the developer as well as the leaseholders.[32]

6.   The developer

A developer usually owns the freehold estate in a flat scheme, builds the development, grants leases of individual flat, and controls the management company during the development process. Practice has evolved common forms of documentation, the main elements being individual flat leases, a lease of common parts to the management company and a corporate constitution for the company. The professional advisers of the developer must ensure that the documentation is common for the whole estate and that it meshes properly and those advising buyers and lenders are left to check that their investment of money will be adequately protected. All needs to be put in place in advance of the first sale, and there are unfortunately many defective schemes. Some problems may be overcome by court application for variation of the leases.[33] The current law does not cater adequately for what is to happen at the end of the useful life of the block.

C. COLLECTIVE PRE-EMPTION (LEASEHOLDERS' RIGHTS OF FIRST REFUSAL)

A scheme was introduced in 1987[34] to give tenants (meaning here both leaseholders and Rent Act tenants) of private residential accommodation the right of first refusal on a proposed sale of the block, that is the right to acquire the reversion if the landlord tries

---

[27] *Saigol* v. *Cranley Mansions Ltd.* [1996] E.G.C.S. 81 C.A.

[28] See below pp. 456–465.

[29] *Britel Corporation N.V.* v. *Orbach* (1997) 27 H.L.R. 883 C.A.

[30] J.E. Martin [1984] *Conv.* 248.

[31] Sparkes *N.L.L.* 605–607.

[32] *Devonshire Reid Properties Ltd.* v. *Trenaman* [1997] 1 E.G.L.R. 45; but contrast *Hannon* v. *169 Queen's Gate Ltd.* [2000] 09 E.G. 179 Ch.D.

[33] See below pp. 455–456.

[34] L.T.A. 1987 part I; following the Nugee Committee Report, *The Management of Privately Owned Blocks of Flats* (October 1985) paras.7.9.13–7.9.15; M. Perceval (1988) 51 *M.L.R.* 97; C. Rodgers [1988] *Conv.* 122; A. Jessup & S. Burrage [1988] 11 *Legal Action* 14; P. Smith [1992] *L.S.* 42; T. Lumsden [1992] 33 *L.S.G.* 25; J. Blackburn [1998] 3 *P.L.J.* 13; Woodfall 28.001–28.036.

to sell it. First refusal (or collective pre-emption) arises where the landlord wishes to sell to somebody, the right being for the tenants or leaseholders to compel him to sell to them. The advent of collective enfranchisement[35] has reduced the significance of the right of first refusal under long leases—since this enables the leaseholders to initiate a purchase—but the right of pre-emption is a stand alone protection for Rent Act tenants.[36] The following discussion uses the terminology of long leaseholders, since it is likely to be leaseholders who are able to afford to buy. Even within its own limited ambit, the Act lacked teeth. It was fondly imagined that ground landlords would gladly sell to their sitting tenants, since the price would be the same as on a sale to an outside investor, but this legislative assumption proved to be laughably wide of the mark. Ground landlords preferred a swift sale to a single commercial investor rather than being bogged down in lengthy statutory procedures involving a ragbag of leaseholders with conflicting interests and little money. Reforms in 1996 introduce new and serious sanctions which make the scheme work.[37]

1. Blocks

Essentially the target is *residential blocks,* though this is a non-statutory description. The Act bites in the private sector, public sector landlords being excluded, as are private sector blocks with a resident landlord.[38] A first essential is a building or part of a building,[39] so that a development consisting of a number of buildings must be split for the purposes of serving notice.[40] The block must contain two or more residential flats,[41] with the floor area of the residential parts covering at least half of the total.[42] There must be at least two qualifying tenants, as defined below, and there must be qualifying tenants in at least half of the total number of flats in the building. If the block is caught, so are all appurtenances[43] judged at the time of the original disposal.[44]

2. Qualifying tenants

This defines the people entitled to receive notice of the landlord's intention to sell,[45] who are then entitled to participate in the purchase if they choose to do so and, as has already been explained, the concept is also used in defining which blocks are caught by the legislation. To qualify, tenants must be residential rather than business tenants and must fall into one of two main categories: (1) buyers of flats under long leases (leaseholders);

[35] See below pp. 432–444.
[36] See below n. 46.
[37] H.A. 1996 ss.89–92; in force October 1st 1996, S.I. 1996/2212.
[38] L.T.A. 1987 ss.1(4), 58(1).
[39] s.1(2)(a).
[40] s.5(3) as substituted by H.A. 1996 sch.6; this confirms *Kay Green* v. *Twinsectra Ltd.* [1996] 1 W.L.R. 1587 C.A.
[41] s.1(2)(b).
[42] s.1(3); common parts are excluded from the calculation; the percentage can be varied by statutory instrument. However, much depends upon what is defined as a "building": G. Murphy [1999] 23 *E.G.* 133.
[43] *Nolan* v. *Eagle Wharf Developments Ltd.* [1992] 2 E.G.L.R. 223 L.V.T. (loft space and car parking); *Denetower Ltd.* v. *Toop* [1991] 1 W.L.R. 945 C.A. (gardens and appurtenances, but not garages held on separate leases, nor unused land).
[44] *Twinsectra Ltd.* v. *Jones* [1998] 2 E.G.L.R. 129 L.Tr.
[45] s.2.

or (2) Rent Act tenants[46] with full security. Excluded are protected shorthold tenants, service tenants, tenants of resident landlords, and assured tenants under private sector grants made since early 1989. There is no residence test, but the Act excludes multiple leaseholders—defined as those holding three or more flats—who are likely to be investors.

A tenant of the common parts is excluded when carrying out the arithmetic. Unfortunately the exclusion[47] is worded loosely to exclude any lease that includes any part of the common parts—literally allowing evasion of the legislation by including a small portion of the staircases in every lease—but cases have negated the potentially devastating impact of this loophole by limiting it to tenancies with two distinct demises—a lease of residential accommodation and a separate lease of the common parts.[48]

3.   Transactions with the reversion

The Act bites on any relevant disposal of the immediate landlord's *reversion* or any estate or interest in it. A *superior* landlord is affected by the restriction on the disposal of his reversion if the *immediate* landlord has a reversion of less than seven years or one terminable within seven years. [49] This does not necessarily enable the group of leaseholders to get at the freehold. For example in *Belvedere Court Management Ltd.* v. *Frogmore Developments Ltd.* [50] the reversion in a block in Hampstead Garden Suburb was divided artificially between a 99-year lease and a term of 1992 years, so that the main value in the reversion (which lay in the longer head-lease) was freely saleable. This artificial transaction effectively destroyed the leaseholders' rights.[51]

When the ground landlord decides to sell, the leaseholders and short term tenants have the right of first refusal of the block, that is a right of pre-emption. Qualifying tenants are alerted to the need to act because the ground landlord is required to give a notice of his intention to dispose of his interest and to inform the tenants of their collective right of first refusal. The normal transaction affected is a sale and purchase, but more generally the Act prevents *any disposal* of any interest (legal or equitable) in the building or its common parts[52] including the grant of an option.[53] Leaseholders and tenants have no pre-emption rights on compulsory sales, mortgages, sales by mortgage lenders,[54] gifts,[55] or on any form of devolution.[56] Transfers between associated com-

---

[46] *Belvedere Court Management Ltd.* v. *Frogmore Developments Ltd.* [1997] Q.B. 858 C.A. In a chain of leases, it is the one closest which qualifies.

[47] L.T.A. 1987 s.3(2)(a)(ii).

[48] *Denetower Ltd.* v. *Toop* [1991] 1 W.L.R. 945 C.A.

[49] L.T.A. 1987 s.2.

[50] [1997] Q.B. 858 C.A.

[51] The taxation principle in *W.T. Ramsay Ltd.* v. *I.R.C.* [1982] A.C. 300 H.L.—which ignores artificial avoidance devices—was not applied.

[52] L.T.A. 1987 s.4.

[53] R. Frost [1999] *Conv.* 107.

[54] s.4(1A) was inserted by H.A. 1988 sch.13 para.3.

[55] But a transfer at nil value which is part of a larger series of transactions gives a right to acquire for nothing: *Woodridge Ltd.* v. *Downie* [1997] 2 E.G.L.R. 193 L.Tr.

[56] L.T.A. 1987 s.4(2) includes a disposal of a beneficial interest in settled land, incorporeal hereditaments, devolutions on bankruptcy or liquidation, property adjustment on divorce and family provision on death, gifts to members of the family or transfers, transfers between charities, and changes of trustees; also exempted are disposals to the Crown.

panies are allowed. A notorious avoidance scheme involving the grant of a lease of the reversion to a company floated for the purpose followed by sales of shares in the associated company[57]; this dodge is now blocked by limiting the exclusion to cases where companies have been associated for two years.[58] The right to compel a surrender of a lease is respected along with all other existing contractual rights, and the restrictions obviously do not prevent grants of leases of individual flats.[59]

4. Notice by the original landlord

Browne-Wilkinson V.C. described the 1987 legislation as "ill-drafted",[60] criticism which was later said by Bingham M.R. to be understated,[61] the problems arising from an exquisite blend of both excessive and inadequate drafting.[62] The Housing Act 1996 carried out a complete redrafting of the procedural requirements of the legislation,[63] and it can now be said to work much better. Before a ground landlord proceeds to sell a block to an outsider, *notice* of the intended disposal should be given to the qualifying tenants.[64] This must indicate the terms on which the ground landlord intends to sell, and offer the qualifying tenants the right to buy it on those terms.[65] In other words the qualifying tenants are offered the block at the price at which it would otherwise be sold to an outside investor.[66]

Under the original drafting of the legislation, the Court of Appeal held that the *conveyance*[67] was the relevant disposal, and that notice was not required before a *contract*. This worked to the tenants' advantage in *Mainwaring* v. *Henry Smith's Charity Trustees*,[68] since after the ground landlords had completed a sale, the time limit for the qualifying tenants to take action ran from the date of completion; had it run from the earlier contract they would already have been out of time. But the limits are now altered[69]: notice of a proposed sale has to be given at the latest when contracts are exchanged—including conditional contracts and those not specifically performable,[70] though obviously excluding an informal unenforceable arrangement. Separate provisions cover sales by auction, grants of options, and transactions which proceed direct to completion.[71]

[57] *Michaels* v. *Harley House (Marylebone) Ltd.* [2000] Ch. 104 C.A.; *Michaels* v. *Taylor Woodrow Developments Ltd.* [2000] 20 L.S.G. 47, Laddie J. (no damages).

[58] H.A. 1996 s.90 in force October 1st 1996, amending L.T.A. 1985 s.4(2).

[59] L.T.A. 1987 s.4(1)(a); this includes appurtenances.

[60] *Denetower* at 952.

[61] *Belvedere Court Management Ltd.* v. *Frogmore Developments Ltd.* [1997] Q.B. 858, 881D.

[62] At 882A, Hobhouse L.J.

[63] H.A. 1996 sch.6, replacing L.T.A. 1987 ss.5–17. References hereafter are to the amended sections.

[64] L.T.A. 1987 new s.5(1), defined here in terms of the "constituent flats"; substantial compliance (service on 90% of qualifiers) suffices: new s.5(5).

[65] The contents are prescribed by L.T.A. 1987 new ss.5A–5D.

[66] *Cousins* v. *Metropolitan Guarantee Ltd.* [1989] 2 E.G.L.R. 223 L.V.T.; *Gregory* v. *Saddiq* [1991] 1 E.G.L.R. 237 L.V.T.; *Newman* v. *Kay* [1991] 2 E.G.L.R. 237 L.V.T.; *Saga Properties Ltd.* v. *Palmeira Square Nos.2–6 Ltd.* [1995] E.G.L.R. 199 L.V.T.

[67] The date of registration was irrelevant: *Michaels* v. *Harley House (Marylebone) Ltd.* [1997] 3 All E.R. 446, Lloyd J.; on appeal [2000] Ch. 104 C.A.

[68] [1998] Q.B. 1 C.A.

[69] H.A. 1996 s.89 amends L.T.A. 1987 s.4A as from October 1st 1996.

[70] L.T.A. 1987 new s.5A.

[71] L.T.A. 1987 new ss.5B–5D; J.E. Adams [1997] *Conv.* 417; G. Murphy [1997] 35 *E.G.* 44; R. Frost [1999] *Conv.* 107.

The original Act relied on a civil duty to serve a preliminary notice and to observe subsequent time limits.[72] Bingham M.R. regarded this sanction as wholly inadequate[73] and in response Parliament has imposed serious *sanctions* for the first time: it is an offence to override the qualifying tenants' rights without a reasonable excuse, [74] though the offending disposal remains valid.

5.   Procedure after the landlord's notice

Notice should be given to the qualifying tenants, and at least two months[75] allowed for their decision.[76] Those who fail to respond will be excluded from participation in the purchase.[77] A decision to take up the offer must be made by a majority of the qualifying tenants,[78] in the form of an *acceptance notice*.[79] A further two months is allowed for the nomination of a purchaser, usually a management company formed for the purpose.[80] The ground landlord has one month in which to withdraw,[81] but otherwise is obliged to proceed under a statutory timetable towards exchange of contracts and completion.[82] Time is of the essence of any sale.[83] Qualifying tenants are protected so long as they remain within the statutory timetable or any agreed extensions,[84] and during that time the civil and criminal sanctions outlined above continue to apply.

The qualifying tenants cannot proceed if they fail to respond to the ground landlord, if the acceptance rate is insufficient, or if the list of qualifying tenants is inadequate.[85] These events leave the ground landlord free, for a period of 12 months, to proceed with the sale to his chosen purchaser on the same terms as were notified to the tenants. After that time, or in the case of any variation of the sale terms, a fresh notice to the tenants is required.[86]

6.   Enforcement against a purchaser

Before 1996 ground landlords often pressed ahead with a sale of a reversion,[87] leaving it to the purchaser[88] to serve notice to clear the title of the risk of pre-emption by the

---

[72] L.T.A. 1987 s.6.

[73] *Belvedere Court Management Ltd.* v. *Frogmore Developments Ltd.* [1997] Q.B. 858, 870B, Bingham M.R.

[74] L.T.A. 1987 s.10A introduced by H.A. 1996 s.91 (level 5 fine—currently £5,000; this can also catch officers of a corporate landlord).

[75] Running from service of the last notice: L.T.A. 1987 new s.5(4).

[76] new s.5(2)(c). All joint tenants must participate in the notice: *Wax* v. *Chelsea* [1996] 2 E.G.L.R. 80 C.Ct.

[77] *Bhatti* v. *Berkeley Court Investments Ltd.* (1991) 23 H.L.R. 6, Warner J.

[78] L.T.A. 1987 s.18A inserted by H.A. 1996 sch.6.

[79] new s.6(3).

[80] new s.6(4), (5).

[81] s.8(3); he will be unable to sell for 12 months and will have to pay costs: new ss.9A–9B.

[82] new ss.8A (private sale), 8B (auction), 8D (option etc), 8E (obligation to seek necessary consents).

[83] *Chiltern Court (Baker St.) Residents Ltd.* v. *Wallabrook Property Co. Ltd.* [1989] 2 E.G.L.R. 207 C.A.

[84] L.T.A. 1987 new ss.6(1), 6(2), 8(2) etc.; S.I. 1996/2371 (two months allowed). Under the old procedure, there was nothing to prevent one tenant from withdrawing: *Mainwaring* v. *Henry Smith's Charity Trustees (No. 1)* [1998] Q.B. 1 C.A.; (No.2) [1997] 1 E.G.L.R. 93.

[85] *El Naschie* v. *Pitt Place (Epsom) Ltd.* (1999) 31 H.L.R. 228 C.A.

[86] L.T.A. 1987 new s.7.

[87] *Cousins* v. *Metropolitan Guarantee Ltd.* [1989] 2 E.G.L.R. 223; *Wilkins* v. *Horrowitz* [1990] 2 E.G.L.R. 217 L.V.T.; *Belvedere Court Management Ltd.* v. *Frogmore Developments Ltd.* [1998] Q.B. 1 C.A.; *Mainwaring* v. *Henry Smith's Charity Trustees* [1998] Q.B. 1 C.A.

[88] L.T.A. 1987 original ss.11, 12, 16, 17; J.E. Adams [1988] *Conv.* 251. *Crumpton* v. *Unifox Properties Ltd.* [1992] 2 E.G.L.R. 82 C.A.

tenant.[89] Qualifying tenants had only 28 days to respond, and were rarely able to organise themselves effectively in time.[90] Although the original drafting imposed no obligation on the later buyer, the Court of Appeal was able to imply that he was obliged to convey to the qualifying tenants.[91] Problems of priority remained where a buyer carried out later transactions before the qualifying tenants enforced their pre-emption rights.[92]

Modern procedure under the 1996 rewrite of the legislation [93] attempts to address these problems and particularly to impose more effective sanctions on later purchasers. There is a duty to serve a notice informing the qualifying tenants that a transfer has occurred[94] which must notify them of their right to a pre-emption.[95] Tenants are also entitled to serve a notice requiring information about a sale which they discover by any other means—for example when they receive a rent demand carrying the name of an unfamiliar ground landlord.[96] They have the right to take the benefit of a contract or, if the purchase has been completed, to compel a sale of the property on the same terms as those on which the purchaser acquired the reversion[97] plus any arrears of rent.[98] Time limits have been doubled to two months.[99]

7. Disputes

If a dispute is about terms it should be directed to a Leasehold Valuation Tribunal.[100] Its powers are limited to disputes referred to in the purchase notice[101] and the court retains jurisdiction over the validity of the notice itself.[102] There is ample scope for obstructive ground landlords to dispute the validity of the qualifying tenant's purchase notice, though on the whole the courts have been supportive of the legislative intent, allowing the correction of errors in the purchase notice in order to preserve the validity of the notice itself.[103]

8. Reform

The *Consultation Paper* issued in 1998[104] proposes that the right of first refusal should be extended to houses, that rights should be extended to include tenants with a full

[89] L.T.A. 1987 s.18.

[90] s.19 (court can order default in duty to be made good after 14 days' notice).

[91] *Kay Green* v. *Twinsectra Ltd.* [1996] 1 W.L.R. 1587, 1603, Staughton L.J.

[92] *Nolan* v. *Eagle Wharf Developments Ltd.* [1992] 2 E.G.L.R. 223 L.V.T.

[93] H.A. 1996 s.92 sch.6 parts II (amending ss.11–15 on the first buyer), III (amending ss.16–17 on later buyers), IV (consequential amendments).

[94] L.T.A. 1985 new s.3.

[95] s.3A inserted by H.A. 1996 s.93(1).

[96] new s.11A.

[97] new ss.12A–12C; *Staszewski* v. *Maribella Ltd.* [1998] 1 E.G.L.R. 34 C.A.

[98] *Linkproud Ltd.* v. *Ballard* [1997] 1 E.G.L.R. 181 L.Tr.

[99] S.I. 1996/2371.

[100] That is a reconstituted Rent Assessment Committee: L.T.A. 1987 new s.13; S.I. 1993/2408; there is power to vary the terms beyond those originally proposed: *Newman* v. *Kay* [1991] 1 E.G.L.R. 237 L.V.T.

[101] *134 Shirland Road Management Co. Ltd.* v. *Lester* [1997] 2 E.G.L.R. 207 L.V.T.

[102] *Denetower Ltd.* v. *Toop* [1991] 1 W.L.R. 945 C.A.; *Saga Properties Ltd.* v. *Palmeira Square Nos.2–6 Ltd.* [1995] E.G.L.R. 199 L.V.T.

[103] *Kay Green* v. *Twinsectra Ltd.* [1996] 1 W.L.R. 1587 C.A. In *Twinsectra Ltd.* v. *Jones* [1998] 2 E.G.L.R. 129 L.Tr. (the gardens were included even though the rights to it were terminable, since pre-emption proceeds as at the date of the original disposal).

[104] para.5.2

assurance (though not shorthold tenants) and that the time limit for prosecutions should be extended to 18 months. The *Analysis of Responses* showed 75 per cent support for the first proposal,[105] and all are now adopted as the *Way Forward*,[106] but they do not appear in the Commonhold and Leasehold Reform Bill 2000.

D. COLLECTIVE ENFRANCHISEMENT: QUALIFICATION RULES

1. Object of the procedure

Collective enfranchisement is a procedure whereby the leaseholders in a block of flats club together to acquire the ground landlord's reversionary interest against his wishes.[107] The procedure is initiated by a notice given by the leaseholders, in contrast to collective pre-emption where the acquisition is made in response to the ground land-lord's decision to sell out. Short-term rack renting tenants have no right to enfranchise. The freehold and intervening leasehold interests will be transferred to a nominee pur-chaser—usually a management company intended to hold for the leaseholders collec-tively. Hence collective enfranchisement addresses the twin problems of the wasting nature of leasehold tenure and management control by outsiders. The freehold in the entire block will be transferred to the benefit of the leaseholders collectively and they will retain direct control of the common parts and block management by virtue of that ownership. Leaseholders with shortish leases will usually arrange to acquire extensions on their leases from the management company as part of the terms on which they par-ticipate. Collective enfranchisement rights are conferred by the Leasehold Reform, Housing and Urban Development Act 1993,[108] as modified in 1996.[109] Procedure is tor-tuous and many attempted acquisitions fail.[110]

2. Reform proposals

New Labour was elected in 1997 on a manifesto commitment to leasehold reform, and in particular to make it easier for leaseholders to buy the freehold of their block by reforming the over complex qualification rules.

The proposals are designed to integrate collective rights, commonhold and the right to manage.[111] Indeed the rules for qualifying to take over the management will be iden-tical to the reformed rules for collective enfranchisement.[112] The main aims are:

> to simplify the existing criteria for exercise of the right;
> to remove barriers for which there is no clear policy rationale;
> to reduce the likelihood of disputes over valuation;
> to allow all qualifying tenants an opportunity to participate in
> the enfranchisement;

---

[105] para.52.
[106] para.14.
[107] T. Aldridge (1993) 137 *S.J.* 1180; D.N. Clarke [1994] *Conv.* 223; D.N. Clarke (1995) 139 *S.J.* 314.
[108] L.R.H.U.D.A. 1993 part I chap.I; S.I. 1993/2407.
[109] By H.A. 1996 s.107 and sch.10 with effect from October 1st 1996: S.I. 1996/2212.
[110] See below pp. 440–444.
[111] White Paper Part II para.3.II.18
[112] See below pp. 444–452.

and

to provide a standardised, purpose-built company structure.

A consultation process has taken place since the election in 1997,[113] leading to a White Paper published in August 2000[114] and the Commonhold and Leasehold Reform Bill 2000.[115] Discussion of detail follows throughout the next two sections, but it may be as well to list the main proposals:

Participants would have to hold ½ the flats in the block (rather than ⅔rds);
Abolition of the residence test;
Enfranchisement would be allowed where the non-residential proportion was 25% (an increase from 10%);
The resident landlord exemption would be restricted to landlords who have carried out the conversion;
The low-rent test in relation to leases of between 21 and 35 years would be abolished;
A requirement to use a management company;
Simplification of the valuation process.[116]

3. Blocks affected

Collective enfranchisement applies loosely to a *block* of flats, including purpose built blocks, large houses converted into separate flats, and any self-contained part of a building isolated by vertical divisions.[117] Between the introduction of the scheme in 1993 and its reform in 1996, collective enfranchisement could be evaded by creating multiple freeholds within a block, particularly by creating flying freeholds within it, but this problem is now resolved, so that collective enfranchisement is available against multiple freeholders within a self-contained part of a building,[118] the leaseholders choosing to operate the procedures against one ground landlord who is then forced to act for all the others.[119]

Restriction of collective enfranchisement to *residential* blocks is achieved primarily through the definition of qualifying tenants discussed below. In addition, parts not intended for residential occupation (including for example garages) must not exceed 10 per cent of the internal floor area.[120] Once this rule is satisfied, enfranchisement can apply to ancillary property held with the block, including for example a communal car parking facility.[121]

There are a number of types of block immune from collective enfranchisement. Rent Act security is removed from leaseholders of flats in a block with a *resident landlord*[122] and this is matched by an exemption of resident ground landlords from suffering the

---

[113] *Consultation 1998* paras.2–3; *Analysis of Responses* paras.12–13; *Way Forward* paras.2–6.
[114] Part II paras.2.2.6–12; 3.II.1–95.
[115] Part II Chapter II, amending L.R.H.U.D.A. 1993 Part I Chapter I.
[116] See below pp. 437–440.
[117] L.R.H.U.D.A. 1993 s.3.
[118] s.4(3A) introduced in 1996; s.1(3) is amended and sch.10 has consequential provisions.
[119] sch.1 part 1A, inserted by H.A. 1996 sch.10.
[120] s.4(1)(b).
[121] s.1(5), but subs.(6) excludes minerals.
[122] R.A. 1977 s.12; see above pp. 162–166.

compulsory loss of his reversion[123] though only if the block is small[124] and not if it is purpose built. Leaseholders in such a block must rely on their right to individual extension of their leases. There is also a *redevelopment defence*. Ground landlords can prevent collective enfranchisement, where ⅔rds of all the long leases are to expire within five years,[125] by showing that possession is required for redevelopment. Compulsory purchase by public authorities also precludes enfranchisement.[126]

4. Proposed reform of block qualification and exemption

It is proposed to amend the *floor area test* by raising the maximum qualifying percentage of property with a non-residential use (either commercial or business) from 10 per cent to 25 per cent.[127] This would allow the enfranchisement of a block comprising shops on the ground floor if the block had four stories, in contrast to the current rule of one floor in 10. As at present, the landlord will have the option of requiring the enfranchising leaseholders to grant a 999-year lease of the non-residential part at a peppercorn rent.[128]

Changes are also proposed to the resident ground landlord exemption.[129] This special privilege is only justified if it is the ground landlord who has converted his or her own home. Very often in a small house conversion the freehold is conveyed to whichever of the leaseholders buys his flat last, so that the benefit of the exemption is a purely fortuitous by-product of his purchase. Hence the resident landlord exception would be limited to cases where the landlord (or a qualifying member of his family) owned the freehold since before the time of conversion of the premises into two or more flats or other units.[130] Resident ground landlords losing their protection under this proposal would be compensated by a right to require the enfranchising group to grant him a 999-year lease of his flat at a peppercorn rent. There would also be the right to buy into the enfranchising company after completion of the process.

There is an existing exemption for the *inalienable land* of the National Trust and it is proposed to extend this to the numerous organisations which Parliament has protected against compulsory purchase, though there is as yet no new legislative definition of the exempt ground landlords.[131]

5. Qualification of leaseholders

These are the leaseholders entitled to serve a notice to enfranchise and to participate in the collective purchase. The essential requirement, as for any enfranchisement, is to hold

---

[123] L.T.A. 1987 s.1(4) (first refusal); L.R.H.U.D.A. 1993 s.10 (collective enfranchisement).

[124] i.e. with four or fewer units: s.4(4).

[125] L.R.H.U.D.A. 1993 s.23.

[126] ss.30, 31 (heritage property).

[127] Commonhold and L.Ref. Bill 2000 cl.112, amending L.R.H.U.D.A. 1993 s.4(1); White Paper Part II paras.3.II.9, 3.II.13, 3.II.23.

[128] White Paper Part II paras.3.II.23. This was proposed by the British Property Federation to allow exploitation of commercial parts; see *Way Forward* paras.2.6–2.12.

[129] Commonhold and L.Ref. Bill 2000 cl.114, amending L.R.H.U.D.A. 1993 s.4(1); White Paper Part II paras.3.II.24–27.

[130] This condition could be satisfied by holding a beneficial interest under a trust.

[131] White Paper Part II paras.3.II.92–95.

a *long residential lease.* Any leaseholder who holds a lease[132] for "a particularly long term", meaning a term over 35 years[133] qualifies under changes made in 1996.[134] A leaseholder holding a term of between 21 and 35 years must in addition demonstrate that his lease satisfies the low rent test for individual enfranchisement in order to qualify to join in a collective enfranchisement.[135] Investors holding multiple leases are excluded.[136] The rights are valuable.[137]

A *block qualifies* for compulsory acquisition only if there are two or more flats held by qualifying leaseholders. The total number of qualifying flats (held on long leases) must be not less than one half of the total number of flats (including for example those let on short-holds). At least ⅔rds of those leaseholders who qualify must join in giving the notice, and they will be the people participating in, and paying for, the purchase. In *Crean Davidson Investments Ltd.* v. *Earl Cadogan*[138] the question was whether ⅔rds of the sub-tenants of a six-storied terraced house had joined in the process. The ground landlord succeeded in including a caretaker's flat in the arithmetic, and the non-participation of the caretaker reduced the participation below the required ⅔rds. Reform of this requirement is likely.[139]

At least half of the leaseholders giving notice must have *residential qualification*[140] by having occupied the flat as his principal home for the last 12 months, or if not then for three years out of the last 10.[141] This is designed to prevent control by an absentee majority.[142] Changes in 1996 ensure that trustees may enfranchise where a beneficiary satisfies the residence condition, thus bringing collective enfranchisement into line with the existing rules for houses.[143] The Government proposes to abolish the residence requirement.[144]

6. Proposals to reform the qualifying rules

The *low rent* test was originally designed to exclude from collective rights properties subject to rack-rental leases. However, the test no longer applies to leases over 35 years, but only acts as a filter for leases granted for a term of between 21 and 35 years, and the Government now proposes to abolish the test for all long leases. The low rent filter will be removed.[145]

---

[132] new s.5; an authorised sub-lease is included, but not one that is unauthorised; the vital lease is the lowest one which qualifies: subss.(3)–(4).

[133] s.8A.

[134] H.A. 1996 sch.9 para.3.

[135] L.R.H.U.D.A. 1993 s.5(1) (ignoring a nil rateable value: s.8 as amended in 1996); see above pp. 390–392.

[136] A leaseholder of three flats qualifies for none (counting a company and its associated companies together); joint leaseholders count as a single leaseholder: s.5(3)–(5).

[137] *Homsy* v. *Searle* (1997) 73 P. & C.R. 26 C.A.; C. Boston [1998] 14 *E.G.* 122.

[138] [1999] 2 E.G.L.R. 96 C.Ct.

[139] See below p. 436.

[140] L.R.H.U.D.A. 1993 s.13(2).

[141] s.6; residence at the time of the claim is not required; note the period is 12 months and not 3 years as for individual enfranchisement.

[142] R. Hudson [1993] *N.L.J.* 253, 932; H. Lewis [1993] *N.L.J.* 303.

[143] H.A. 1996 s.111 amending L.R.H.U.D.A. 1993 s.6(4), (5); trustees enfranchise under s.93A.

[144] See below p. 436.

[145] Commonhold and L.Ref. Bill 2000 cl.113, amending L.R.H.U.D.A. 1993 s.131; sch.13 makes consequential repeals of L.R.H.U.D.A. 1993 ss.5, 7(3), 8, 8A, 13(3)(e)(ii) and H.A. 1996 ss.105(3) and sch.9; White Paper Part II para.3.II.22.

A second important hurdle is to secure *participation of ⅔rds of qualified leaseholders*.[146] It will no longer be necessary to secure this degree of participation. Protection against control by a minority is ensured by the requirement that the participants must hold long leases of at least half the units in the building.

The *residence test* currently requires at least half of the participating tenants to have their main residence in the block, but this requirement has proved to be a major obstacle because of second home ownership, sub-letting of flats, and the high turnover of flats in some blocks: some qualified tenants will move out during the enfranchisement and others will have moved in too recently to qualify by residence. The test has encouraged artificial avoidance techniques, such as requiring leases to be vested in a company which is incapable of having a residence. So it is to be removed,[147] subject to consultation on these issues which continues until October 2000. The Government proposals should bring in some core Labour voters in the shape of second home owners and investors in leaseholds.

7.   Right to participate

Individual leaseholders may be unfairly ostracised under the current law[148] and it is possible for a management company representing a majority of the leaseholders to prove to be just as great an oppressor as the worst ground landlord. Arbitrary exclusions will not be possible if, as is proposed, all leaseholders are given the right to participate in collective enfranchisement. It will not be permissible to give notice to trigger a collective acquisition until all qualified leaseholders have been given notice inviting them to participate.[149] In principle there is no reason why leaseholders should not be allowed to join at an even later stage, and it is possible that the present drafting will be widened to provide for late decisions to participate.[150]

It may be possible to become a member for six months from the date of the initial notice, unless contracts were exchanged earlier.[151] After exchange of contracts, entry into the management company would require the agreement of the other leaseholders, though it is arguable that the purchaser of a flat from a non-participator should be put in a stronger position than a leaseholder who has himself decided not to participate.

One potential problem is that the compensation paid to the ground landlord will vary according to the value of the leaseholds held by the participators, so that late additions might alter the price payable, encouraging leaseholders to try to get the block more cheaply by leaving out until the last minute any leaseholders with relatively short

---

[146] Commonhold and L.Ref. Bill 2000 cl.115, amending L.R.H.U.D.A. 1993 s.13(2)(b); sch.13 repeals L.R.H.U.D.A. 1993 s.100 subss.(2), (3), (4A); White Paper Part II paras.3.II.28–30.

[147] Commonhold and L.Ref. Bill 2000 cl.116, amending L.R.H.U.D.A. 1993 s.13(2); sch.13 repeals L.R.H.U.D.A. 1993 ss.6, 13(3)(c)(iii) and H.A. 1996 ss.111–122; White Paper Part II Section 3.II paras.5, 9–12, 28–30.

[148] *The Way Forward* para.4.

[149] Commonhold and L.Ref. Bill 2000 cl.119; sch.13 will make consequential amendments; White Paper Part II paras.3.II.18, 3.II.59–65.

[150] White Paper Part II paras.3.II.65–70.

[151] Personal representatives of a deceased participator will have additional rights to participate beyond the six-month time limit.

remaining terms. It will also be necessary to reflect the professional costs associated with collective enfranchisement to ensure that there is no incentive to hang back and leave the hard work to others.

E. COLLECTIVE ENFRANCHISEMENT: VALUATION

1. Price for collective enfranchisement

Collective purchases under the block enfranchisement provisions will occur at the market value. The initial notice must specify the price proposed by the tenants.[152] Conclusion of the deal is left to negotiation, though a statutory timetable is provided for the negotiation.[153] Disputes are resolved by a Leasehold Valuation Tribunal,[154] with an appeal to the Lands Tribunal—which should however be slow to interfere.[155]

2. Proposal to alter the valuation date

Under the 1993 Act the purchase price is fixed on "the valuation date"[156] meaning the date on which the price is agreed or determined by the Leasehold Valuation Tribunal. If the market is rising a ground landlord has an incentive to delay the matter. This is now to be amended to refer instead to "the relevant date", that is the date of the leaseholder's notice to initiate the enfranchisement,[157] which will bring the rule into line with that for the enfranchisement of houses.[158]

A landlord's existing right to access to individual flats for valuation purposes[159] is to be extended to include any purposes reasonably required in connection with the collective enfranchisement. [160]

3. Current rules for valuing a block with very long leases

The price should reflect the value of the freehold subject to the existing leases, but ignoring enfranchisement rights,[161] and ignoring the position of the nominee purchaser, the tenants, and the owners of interests to be acquired.[162] As with individual extension the basic measure is the market value of what the landlord has lost, and there are again three elements,[163] but only two are in play with leases over say 90 years or so[164]:

---

[152] L.R.H.U.D.A. 1993 s.13(3)(d). It is no longer necessary to start with a valuation by qualified surveyor: H.A. 1996 s.108 repealing L.R.H.U.D.A. 1993 s.13(6)(7).

[153] There is a time limit for service of a counter-notice and no jurisdiction to relieve against failure to serve notice: *Willingale* v. *Global Grange Ltd.* [2000] 18 E.G. 152 C.A.

[154] L.R.H.U.D.A. 1993 ss.24, 32, sch.6 para.1; S.I. 1993/2408; H.A. 1996 s.119 (pre-trial review).

[155] *Verkan & Co. Ltd.* v. *Byland Close (Winchmore Hill) Ltd.* [1998] 2 E.G.L.R. 139 L.Tr.; *Daejean Properties Ltd.* v. *Weeks* [1998] 3 E.G.L.R. 125 L.Tr.

[156] L.R.H.U.D.A. 1993 sch.6 para.1(1).

[157] Commonhold and L.Ref. Bill 2000 cl.122, amending L.R.H.U.D.A. 1993 s.32 and sch.6; sch.13 deletes the definition of valuation date in L.R.H.U.D.A. 1993 sch.6 para.1(1); White Paper Part II paras.3.II.73–74.

[158] See above p. 409.

[159] L.R.H.U.D.A. 1993 s.17(1).

[160] Commonhold and L.Ref. Bill 2000 cl.121, amending L.R.H.U.D.A. 1993 s.17(1).

[161] L.R.H.U.D.A. 1993 sch.6 para.3.

[162] H.A. 1996 s.109.

[163] L.R.H.U.D.A. 1993 sch.6.

[164] See above p. 407.

the *market value* of the ground landlord's interest (subject to the long leases); with very long leases, almost all of the value resides with the leaseholders, marriage value has a minimal impact, [165] and it is therefore sufficient to fix the price at a multiple of the ground rent; [166] and

compensation for loss to the remaining property of the ground landlord. Landlords often claim for the loss of the right to commission an insurance premium.[167] Costs are added.[168]

Unfortunately, it is possible to defend a claim to enfranchise by levying a heavy service charge, thus weakening the leaseholders' financial position and making it more difficult for them to afford to enfranchise.

4. Current rules for enfranchisement of blocks with shorter leases

If the leases of the tenants enfranchising are for less than 90 years or so, it may not give a fair value simply to multiply the ground rent, and the prevailing method seems to be capitalisation.[169] Marriage value is also an important consideration. As explained above this is the overall growth in value of a block (taking the freehold and leaseholds together) when short leases are extended. At least half, and possibly more, is allocated to the ground landlord. Another important element may be the hope value that non-participating tenants will seek to renew their leases and offer premiums for doing so, even if on the particular facts of *Becker Properties Ltd.* v. *Garden Court NW8 Property Co. Ltd.*[170] the value of these rights was nominal.

In *Maryland Estates Ltd.* v. *Abbathure Flat Management Co. Ltd.*[171] seven rights that participating leaseholders acquire were identified: the ability to extend their own leases at no premium, to vary the terms of their leases, to extinguish the ground rent, to manage and to control management charges, to carry out repairs of their own choosing, to eliminate disputes with the ground landlord, and to grant new rights. On the particular facts a block of 20 flats was acquired by 16 participating leaseholders with 79-year unexpired terms for £23,450.

---

[165] *Sinclair Gardens Investments (Kensington) Ltd.* v. *Franks* (1998) 76 P. & C.R. 230 L.Tr.(no marriage value in a lease of 112 years).

[166] *Scarlett* v. *Halcrow Ltd.* [1995] 1 E.G.L.R. 219 L.V.T. (10 years purchase); *Groundpremium Property Management Ltd.* v. *Longmint Ltd.* [1998] 1 E.G.L.R. 131 L.V.T. (11 years purchase).

[167] *Solent Pines Residents Association Ltd.* v. *Campbell* [1996] 1 E.G.L.R. 213; *Blackstone Investments Ltd.* v. *Middleton-Dell Management Co. Ltd.* [1997] 1 E.G.L.R. 185 L.V.T.; *Moore* v. *Escalus Properties Ltd.* [1997] 1 E.G.L.R. 200 (unsuccessful); *Sinclair Gardens Investments (Kensington) Ltd.* v. *Franks* (1998) 76 P. & C.R. 230 L.Tr. (not in absence of covenant to pay premiums).

[168] L.R.H.U.D.A. 1993 s.33.

[169] *Sked* v. *Towngran Developments Ltd.* [1995] 1 E.G.L.R. 216 L.V.T. (at 13% plus 1/2 marriage value); *63 Perham Road Ltd.* v. *Manyfield Ltd.* [1995] 2 E.G.L.R. 206 (at 13%); J. Ellis & N. Brown. [1995] 37 E.G. 166 (review of early cases); *Donat* v. *Second Duke of Westminster's Trustees* [1997] 1 E.G.L.R. 203 L.V.T.; *Hordern* v. *Chelsea* [1997] 1 E.G.L.R. 195 L.V.T.

[170] [1998] 1 E.G.L.R. 121 L.Tr.

[171] [1999] 1 E.G.L.R. 100 L.Tr.

5. Proposals to reform the valuation rules

The Government accepts that a ground landlord facing a compulsory purchase of his reversion is entitled to a market price, including a share of marriage value.[172] So the proposals, matching those proposed for individual enfranchisement, are limited to reducing the scope for costly arguments.[173] There are two concrete proposals:

(1) the share of marriage value to which the landlord is entitled is fixed at 50% in all cases.[174]

(2) there will be a statutory presumption that marriage value is nil where the unexpired term of the lease exceeds 90 years; however, this presumption will apply to collective enfranchisement only if the remaining terms *of every participating member* exceeds that length on the relevant date (when the initial notice is given).[175]

Work continues to see whether the valuation process can be simplified by prescription of various elements of the valuation process.[176] Research conducted at Reading showed that the market was, in economic jargon, thin, imperfect and non-transparent. One major variable is the interest rate (also called the yield or capitalisation rate) used when determining the present value for projected future receipts from ground rents and hence in valuing a freehold reversion. It would be possible to prescribe this by finding the return sought on a risk free investment and evaluating the degree of risk in investing in leasehold reversions. A second variable is the relativity between the value of the existing unexpired leases of a particular duration and the value of a very long lease that is equivalent to freehold ownership, a figure used when determining marriage value. The researchers found considerable consistency in practice, given that central London has to be distinguished from the rest the country. Indeed if yields and relativities were prescribed the market might be improved in its theoretical operation. The Government is seeking further views on this issue.

6. Reform of Leasehold Valuation Tribunals

Consultation has revealed an overwhelming dissatisfaction with the functioning of Leasehold Valuation Tribunals, primarily because leaseholders are encountering delays of between six months to one year. Automatic appeals against decisions irrespective of the merits will be discouraged by limiting grounds to general points of law or principle and serious mistakes of fact and by permission requiring that from the Leasehold

---

[172] White Paper Part II paras.2.6–2.12, 3.II.14–15; *Consultation 1998* para.4; *Analysis* paras.21–32; *The Way Forward* paras.6–7.

[173] White Paper Part II para.3.II.5.

[174] Draft Commonhold and L.Ref. Bill 2000 cl.98, amending L.R.H.U.D.A. 1993 sch.6 para.4(1); White Paper Part II paras.3.II.14, 3.II.75.

[175] Draft Commonhold and L.Ref. Bill 2000 cl.99, inserting L.R.H.U.D.A. 1993 sch.6 para.4(2A); sch.II amends H.A. 1996 sch.10; White Paper Part II para.3.II.76. It would, apparently, be impractical to provide for marriage value from some of the leases having 90 years or more to run.

[176] White Paper Part II paras.3.II.77–80.

Valuation Tribunal or the Lands Tribunal.[177] New procedural rules will accompany a rationalisation of Leasehold Valuation Tribunals.[178]

F.   COLLECTIVE ENFRANCHISEMENT: RTE COMPANIES

1.   Nominee purchasers under the current law

At present a collective enfranchisement occurs through the mechanism of a "nominee purchaser". In practice the vehicle usually adopted is a flat management company, but the legislation is not prescriptive, preferring to leave it to potential enfranchisees to obtain advice about satisfactory arrangements between themselves.[179]

2.   Proposal for a right to enfranchise company

The Government now proposes to require the use of an RTE company in a collective enfranchisement because non-corporate vehicles have not proved to be suitable. The 1993 Act will be subjected to extensive revision to ensure that an acquisition under the collective enfranchisement provision can only be made by such a company. A number of additional sections are inserted in the 1993 Act.[180] Numerous consequential amendments are made throughout the collective enfranchisement provisions to ensure that they refer throughout to an RTE company rather than a nominee purchaser.[181] There will be a standardised, purpose-built, company structure that is adequate for the orderly and democratic conduct of the enfranchisement process and subsequent management of the building. Prescription of the corporate form will smooth the transition from the proposed right to manage and the transition to commonhold.[182]

The vehicle used will be a company limited by guarantee, with each member being required to guarantee debts to the tune of £1. Share certificates will be unnecessary since membership will pass automatically with the flat to which it attaches. Standard contents will be prescribed for the memorandum and articles of association (in place of the Companies Acts requirements) with unauthorised variations prohibited.[183] These rules are similar to those proposed for right to manage and commonhold companies. This would avoid the existing problems caused by the use of an off the shelf company with inappropriate provisions in the memorandum and articles of association. It is unclear whether there will be an exemption for small house conversions and other blocks with

---

[177]   White Paper Part II para.3.II.6.

[178]   Commonheld and L.Ref. Bill 2000 cls. 147–150, Schs. 11, 12.

[179]   White Paper Part II paras.2.6–12, 3.II.8, 3.II.31–36.

[180]   Commonhold and L.Ref. Bill 2000 cl.118 inserting L.R.H.U.D.A. 1993 ss.4A–4C; see also the amendments and repeals by sch.13 of L.R.H.U.D.A. 1993 ss.2(3), 11(6), 13(3)(e), 14–16, 18 and 28(3)–(4).

[181]   Commonhold and L.Ref. Bill 2000 cl.120 and sch.8; amendments are made to the following provisions of L.R.H.U.D.A. 1993: ss.1(2)(a), 1(5), 2(1), 11(4), 13(3), 13(11), 13(13), 17, 20, 21, 22, 23, 24, 25, 26, 27, 28, 29, 30, 31, 32, 33, 34, 35, 36, 37A, 38, 41, 54, 74, 91, 93, 93A, 97, 98, sch.1, sch.3 paras.1–7, sch.3 paras.12–16, schs.4–9.

There will also be minor amendments to the Land Compensation Act 1973 s.12A.

[182]   White Paper Part II para.3.II.18.

[183]   L.R.H.U.D.A. 1993 s.4C, to be inserted by Commonhold and L.Ref. Bill 2000 cl.118; White Paper Part II paras.3.II.41–42.

up to 4 units—since in those cases it is possible to use a direct co-ownership trust,[184] though only at the price of having to change trustees every time a flat is sold.

Only one company can qualify at any one time.

3. Membership rules for proposed right to enfranchise companies

Membership of the company will be limited and only if those limits are observed will it be an RTE company.[185] A requisite number of qualifying leaseholder must have become members (holding the leases of half the flats in the block) before the company will qualify to proceed. Once that is the case all other qualifying tenants must be given a notice containing an invitation to participate. Anyone who wished to participate would have to become a member of the company in order to do so. Where there are only two qualifying leaseholders, both must be participating members of the RTE company.[186]

Control will be needed since membership would confer part ownership of the freehold in the block and this could be extremely valuable where other flats remained unenfranchised; it will be necessary to match company membership to participation in the enfranchisement. There would be no right to resign. Where a member died during the enfranchisement process, membership would be available to his personal representative, though the representative would have 56 days to give a notice (in a prescribed form) of his withdrawal. Membership would cease automatically on disposal of the lease of the flat but the purchaser would be entitled to membership.[187] Sub-letting on a long lease would pass the entitlement to membership of the right to enfranchise company to the sub-leaseholder.

Management control would be vested in the management company, subject to the standard memorandum and articles of association, and also to the tailor made provisions. Each lease would confer the right to at least one vote, but of course it may be necessary to weight the voting to reflect, for example, the proportions in which service charge contributions had to be made or floor areas. Larger flats pay more but obtain larger voting rights. Allocation could be made on any non-discriminatory basis.[188]

4. Right to participate

There is limited evidence of a group of eligible leaseholders initiating enfranchisement and refusing to allow other leaseholders to join in.[189] A major objective will be to implement the right to participate: membership of the RTE company will be open to all qualified leaseholders who wish to participate.[190] Before any exercise of the right of collective enfranchisement, a notice of invitation to participate must be served on all qual-

---

[184] White Paper Part II paras.3.II.31–36.

[185] L.R.H.U.D.A. 1993 s.4B, to be inserted by Commonhold and L.Ref. Bill 2000 cl.118.

[186] Commonhold and L.Ref. Bill 2000 cl.117(3), adding L.R.H.U.D.A. 1993 s.13(2ZA).

[187] A person who bought a flat during the acquisition process would have to give a notice (in a prescribed form) of his participation within 14 days of the date of the assignment (including an assent or assignment by operation of law to a trustee in bankruptcy).

[188] White Paper Part II paras.3.II.43–46.

[189] White Paper Part II para.3.II.7.

[190] White Paper Part II para.3.II.37–40.

ifying tenants who are not already members of the company[191]: it will give notice that the company intends to enfranchise, provide explanations, indicate the estimated price, indicate how the price is to be paid, and invite recipients to become members of the company. The form of the notice will be prescribed. Leaseholders must have at least 14 days to consider the notice.[192]

At least 14 days would have to elapse after service of the invitation to participate before the initial notice could be given to the ground landlord. A copy of the initial notice would have to be served on all qualifying tenants who were not yet participators offering a further six months to consider participating.

Though there is nothing in the Act about this, it is the general practice for the enfranchisement company, after completion of the acquisition, to grant 999-year leases to each of the participating leaseholders without requiring any premium to be paid.[193] Participation rights could be frustrated by an improper allocation of the costs of enfranchisement, and so a regulatory framework is proposed which would prevent arbitrary apportionments between favoured and unfavoured groups; it will be necessary to adopt some fair and objective test such as floor area or council tax band.[194]

5.   Transition from the proposed right to manage

After the right to manage is introduced, the leaseholders may wish to proceed to an enfranchisement in order to resolve the issue of block ownership. It may then be necessary to alter the memorandum and articles of association if enfranchisement was not already included amongst the company's objects. On completion of the enfranchisement, non-participating leaseholders would cease to be members of the company. At the very least, the ground landlord would have to leave the company. It is also likely that some of the members attracted by the right to manage would not wish to (that is were not able to afford to) participate in the enfranchisement.[195] Although it might be possible to include participating and non-participating members in the same company, conflicts would inevitably arise. The Government proposal is that membership should be restricted to leaseholders qualifying for *and participating in* the enfranchisement, meaning that any other leaseholders would have to leave the company on completion of the transfer of the freehold, though with a limited period allowed for reconsideration.

6.   Existing procedure for collective enfranchisement

The procedure for collective enfranchisement is complex. Recalcitrant ground landlords can often shake off groups of leaseholders,[196] despite the judicial favouritism towards

---

[191] Commonhold and L.Ref. Bill 2000 cl.119(1), inserting L.R.H.U.D.A. 1993 s.12A; White Paper Part II paras.3.II.47–51.

[192] Commonhold and L.Ref. Bill 2000 cl.119(2), inserting L.R.H.U.D.A. 1993 s.13(2ZB). The White Paper reports that there was only a small response on this issue: White Paper Part II paras.3.II.7, 3.II.17.

[193] White Paper Part II para.3.II.2.

[194] White Paper Part II para.3.II.58.

[195] White Paper Part II paras.3.II.53–57.

[196] Compensation is payable for defective claims: H.A.1996 s.116 introducing L.R.H.U.D.A. 1993 sch.11.

tenants.[197] Broadly the notice and counter-notice procedure mirrors that for individual enfranchisements, but there are some special considerations.[198]

An *initial notice* is given by the management company. It must identify the leaseholders who participate in it, other leaseholders who are qualified but do not participate, and short-term residential tenants who do not qualify.[199] A nominee purchaser must be identified, usually an existing flat management company or one purpose-built.[200] Collective enfranchisement raises special problems because it is necessary to gather together enough qualifying leaseholders to serve a notice and to reach agreement between them on the basis on which collective enfranchisement is to proceed.[201]

The emphasis of the procedure is on facilitating a *negotiated enfranchisement:* it leads to entry into a contract through a strictly regulated timetable, with a dispute resolution procedure.[202] Although non-contractual, the initial notice should be protected by registration. These rights cannot be overriding.[203] *Completion provisions* are modelled closely on those for individual enfranchisement.[204]

Collective enfranchisement suspends individual enfranchisement and most other procedures such as forfeiture,[205] though changes of detail are to be made to these provisions.[206]

7. Parts not held by participating leaseholders

Under the existing law, the nominee purchaser will be required to grant leases back to local authorities who have granted secure tenancies in the block,[207] thus preserving the right of such tenants to buy. The ground landlord has the option of requiring the enfranchise leaseholders to lease back to him commercial parts on 999-year leases at a peppercorn rent, with an appropriate reduction in the enfranchisement price.[208] The same principle applies to the revised procedures, though here no RTE company will be acting.

8. Proposed changes to the initial notices

The contents[209] of the initial notice will be changed to include the name and registered office of the RTE company, and regulations will be able to prescribe other contents.

---

[197] *Cadogan* v. *McGirk* [1996] 4 All E.R. 643, 648b, Millett L.J.

[198] S.I. 1993/2407 (procedure).

[199] L.R.H.U.D.A. 1993 ss.11, 12; there are complex provisions to deal with changes in individual flat ownership; see also *Staszewski* v. *Maribella Ltd.* [1999] 1 E.G.L.R. 34 C.A.

[200] J.C. Hicks [1995] *Conv.* 46.

[201] Omission of plan invalidates a s.13 notice: *Mutual Place Property Management Ltd.* v. *Blaquiere* [1996] 2 E.G.L.R. 28 C.Ct.; *Crean Davidson Investments Ltd.* v. *Cadogan* [1998] 2 E.G.L.R. 96 C.Ct.

[202] S.I. 1993/2408.

[203] *Melbury Road Properties 1995 Ltd.* v. *Kreidi* [1999] 3 E.G.L.R. 108.

[204] L.R.H.U.D.A. 1993 ss.34–37, schs.7–10.

[205] L.R.H.U.D.A. 1993 s.54, sch.7; *Martin* v. *Maryland Estates Ltd.* [1998] 2 E.G.L.R. 81 C.A.

[206] Commonhold and L.Ref. Bill 2000 sch.13 amending and repealing L.R.H.U.D.A. 1993 sch.3 heading para.7, paras.8–9, 10(1).

[207] s.36.

[208] White Paper Part II para.3.II.4.

[209] L.R.H.U.D.A. 1993 s.13 as amended by Commonhold and L.Ref. Bill 2000 sch.8 para.6; see also the amendments and repeals by sch.13 of L.R.H.U.D.A. 1993 ss.12(1), (2), (4), (6) and 13(2), (3).

A copy must be given to each qualifying leaseholder.[210] An initial notice will not be invalidated by including a non-qualifying leaseholder, so long as there remain a sufficient number of qualifying and participating leaseholders.[211]

There will be new provisions for deemed withdrawal from an enfranchisement, where the RTE company is subject to winding up, administration, receivership, repossession under a charge, or the approval of a voluntary arrangement.[212]

9.   Absent landlords

The existing procedure where a landlord cannot be found will be amended to bring it into line with the individual enfranchisement rules.[213]

G.   PROPOSED RIGHT TO MANAGE

1.   The existing system

Control of the management, maintenance, and insurance of a block of flats often remains in the hands of the ground landlord. This monopoly is granted in defiance of the financial reality that the value of the ground landlord's interest is usually very small.[214] Leaseholders have to pay the full cost of management via the service charge mechanism, but they enjoy little control of the quality, value for money or promptness of those services, [215] matters which provoke the concern of many leaseholders.

The existing law provides a number of mechanisms to remove the ground landlord's control.[216] Any leaseholder may apply to a leasehold valuation tribunal for the appointment of a manager, but this requires proof of serious abuse by the ground landlord, and the procedure is adversarial in character. There are significant rights for any leaseholder to challenge any service charge demand and leaseholders have the right to be consulted about major work in advance. Under a collective enfranchisement, collectivisation of management is a side-product of the collective ownership, but the drawback is the cost. If it is enacted, the right to manage is not intended to override any aspect of the lease and nor will it affect ownership.[217]

2.   Nature of the right to manage

A new "right to manage" is proposed, that is the collective right to take over day-to-day control of the block of flats on behalf of the long leaseholders.[218] They would be able to take over the management of their building without having to prove shortcomings on

---

[210] L.R.H.U.D.A. 1993 s.13(5A) inserted by Commonhold and L.Ref. Bill 2000 sch.8 para.3(3).

[211] L.R.H.U.D.A. 1993 sch.3 para.16 inserted by Commonhold and L.Ref. Bill 2000 sch.8 para.36(12).

[212] L.R.H.U.D.A. 1993 s.29(4A) inserted by Commonhold and L.Ref. Bill 2000 sch.8 para.17(2). sch.13 will amend or repeal L.R.H.U.D.A. 1993 ss.29(5)(a)–(b), 29(7), 33(1).

[213] L.R.H.U.D.A. 1993 s.26(4), to be amended by Commonhold and L.Ref. Bill 2000 sch.8 para.14(6)(b); see above p. 416.

[214] White Paper Part II para.2.1.

[215] White Paper Part II para.3.I.1.

[216] White Paper Part II paras.3.I.1–4.

[217] White Paper Part II. para.3.I.11.

[218] Commonhold and L.Ref. Bill 2000 cl.68(1) and generally Part II Chapter I; White Paper Part II para.3.I.4. The right could not be excluded: cl.104.

the part of the ground landlord[219] and without any compensation.[220] This follows the wishes of leaseholder respondents to the recent consultation,[221] though ground landlords and property professionals were predictably less enthusiastic.

3. Qualifying blocks

It is intended that the qualifying conditions are the same as the revised proposals for collective enfranchisement,[222] to include only buildings where flat owners hold the predominant interest and to prevent takeovers by minorities. The first basic requirement is that there is a block of flats, though this is not a statutory expression and the definition is oblique. The premises must form a detached building or a self-contained part, though any appurtenant property will be included with the building.[223] A test is provided to determine whether part of a building is self-contained; any division must be vertical, so, that it would be possible to redevelop the property independently of the rest of the building; any fixed services must be independent, or, if shared, it must be possible to make them independent without significant interruption.[224] A building will be divided for enfranchisement and right to manage purposes if the freehold is divided into parts which are themselves self-contained parts.[225] The restriction to blocks of *flats* derives from the rules for qualifying tenants described below. Consultation took place[226] on how to treat retirement estates, and also to see whether it is possible to frame a satisfactory test of commonality to deal with large estates including several individual blocks or communally managed estates which are geographically separated.

The Bill excludes premises where a *local housing authority* is the immediate landlord of any of the qualifying tenants in the premises, in order to prevent any overlap with the public sector right to manage.[227] Tenants of charitable housing trusts[228] and other social landlords are included.[229] Two other exclusions mirror those for collective enfranchisement:[230]

Buildings with a *substantial commercial use*—that is 25% non-residential parts by floor area;[231] and

Large blocks with a *resident landlord.*[232] Large in the RTM context now means a block having four or more units, in contrast to the position for RTE.

---

[219] White Paper Part II para.3.1.

[220] White Paper Part II paras.2.1, 3.I.10.

[221] White Paper Part II para.3.I.5–9; see also *Analysis* paras.34–36; *Way Forward* paras.7–8.

[222] White Paper Part II para.2.1.3.

[223] Commonhold and L.Ref. Bill 2000 cl.69(1). Appurtenant property is defined by cl.109, and cl.74(5) provides for aggregation where there are separate leases of a flat and appurtenant property. See also sch.6, para.2.

[224] Commonhold and L.Ref. Bill 2000 cl.69(2)–(4); "relevant services" are defined by cl.69(5) to be ones provided by pipe, cable or other fixed installation.

[225] Commonhold and L.Ref. Bill 2000 cl.69(6), sch.6, para.4.

[226] White Paper Part II paras.3.I.22–24.

[227] Commonhold and L.Ref. Bill 2000 cl.69(6), sch.6; White Paper Part II paras.3.I.18–21; see below Chapter 18. The Crown will be bound by cl.105.

[228] Draft Commonhold and L.Ref. Bill 2000 cl.57(3)–(5) no longer appears.

[229] White Paper Part II paras.3.I.18–21.

[230] See above pp.432–437.

[231] Commonhold and L.Ref. Bill 2000 cl.69(6), sch.6; White Paper Part II paras.3.I.18–21.

[232] Commonhold and L.Ref. Bill 2000 sch.6 para.3; White Paper Part II paras.3.I.18–21.

4.   Qualifying leaseholders

It is intended that the qualifying conditions are the same as under the revised collective enfranchisement procedure,[233] in order to limit the right to buildings where flat owners hold the predominant interest and to prevent takeovers by minorities. "Flat" is defined in this way:

A separate set of premises (whether or not on the same floor) which forms part of a building,
constructed or adapted for use for the purposes of a dwelling, and
with a material part lies above or below some other part of the building.[234]

This definition presents some problems, since it appears to exclude a single storey annexe attached to a block but sharing common parts with it; surely the correct form of definition is to include every self-contained residential unit within a block?

A leaseholder who qualifies is one who holds a flat under a long lease,[235] with the usual definition of a long lease,[236] but excluding tenants of business leases.[237] Qualification rules are worked out by applying the following mathematical rules to the number of flat owners:

They must contain two or more flats held by qualifying leaseholders;[238]
Qualifying leaseholders must hold not less than 2/3rds of the total number of flats contained in the premises;[239] and
Participating leaseholders must hold at least half the flats.

The object of these rules is to ensure that control cannot be taken by a minority of qualifying tenants or a minority of residents.

5.   The RTM company

Management could only be exercised through an RTM company, which would be required to maintain qualification throughout, the right to manage falling as soon as qualification was lost.[240] It is intended to combine adequate participation in the process, democratic management, and a clear demarcation of rights and responsibilities.[241] Entitlement would be limited to a single company.[242] It would have to be a private company limited by guarantee,[243] having a memorandum and articles of association complying with a prescribed form rather than with Companies Act 1985 rules and with

---

[233] White Paper Part II para. 2.1.3.
[234] Commonhold and L.Ref. Bill 2000 cl.109(1).
[235] Commonhold and L.Ref. Bill 2000 cl.72(1)–(2). Cl.106 ensures that trustees may act; to participate they must treat the decision as an investment decision and obtain any necessary consents. See also White Paper Part II paras.3.I.13–17.
[236] Commonhold and L.Ref. Bill 2000 cls.71–74, 109(2)–(6); see above pp. 389–390.
[237] Commonhold and L.Ref. Bill 2000 cl.72(3). The rules for commercial floor area are discussed above n. 231. Cls. 72(4)–(7) apply to sub-leases, joint leases and multiple leases.
[238] Commonhold and L.Ref. Bill 2000 cl.69(1)(b).
[239] Commonhold and L.Ref. Bill 2000 cl.69(1)(c).
[240] Commonhold and L.Ref. Bill 2000 cl.77(5).
[241] White Paper Part II paras.3.I.25–27.
[242] Commonheld and L.Ref. Bill 2000 cl.70(3); White Paper Part II paras.3.I.28–31.
[243] White Paper Part II para.2.1.4.

some of the contents included automatically.[244] Management companies acquired off-the-shelf often have inappropriate memoranda and articles.[245] Exercise of the right to manage would have to appear in the memorandum as one of the objects.[246]

Membership of the company would be largely restricted to qualifying leaseholders of flats within the block, all of whom would have the right to join the managing body.[247] There would be no right to resign membership, which would be transferred automatically with the title to a flat, and which would be terminated automatically by the forfeiture of any lease, by death, or where a new long lease was created by sub-letting.[248]

However, in addition the ground landlord will retain an interest in a block subject to the right to manage, and so he would also be entitled to membership of the managing body and to have his interest taken into account.[249] Voting rights will be weighted (five votes for flat owners for every one for a ground landlord) to ensure that his voice remains in the minority. The real rights of the ground landlord are to seek the appointment of an independent manager if he feels that the right to manage company is acting to override his right improperly.[250]

Weighting would also be used to balance the interests of residential as against any non-residential parts. Voting rights in a mixed block will be allocated according to floor area, but with one square metre of non-residential floor space carrying three times the votes allocated to one square metre of residential floor space. This reflects the greater value of commercial parts whilst retaining control for the flat owners (since there must be three floors of flats to every one floor of shops.

6. The right to participate

All qualifying leaseholders must be given an opportunity to participate in the right to manage. A first step towards exercise of the right to manage will usually be to give a "notice of invitation to participate" in a form to be prescribed to each qualifying leaseholder giving information about what is proposed and an invitation to join in.[251] At least 14 days notice is required before a claim notice could be served (under the procedure outlined immediately below).[252] A copy of the claim notice would have to be given to all those leaseholders who were still not participators at that stage giving a further two weeks to participate. These steps could be omitted if all qualified leaseholders were already within the RTM company.

7. The claim notice and its effect

Procedure will be triggered when the RTM company gives a "claim notice" asserting the right for the company to manage the block, the claim being given to each ground

---

[244] Commonhold and L.Ref. Bill 2000 cl.71(3)–(6).
[245] Cl.71(1); White Paper Part II paras.3.I.28–31.
[246] Cl.70(2); White Paper Part II paras.3.I.28–31.
[247] Cl.71(1); White Paper Part II paras.3.I.32–40.
[248] Cl.72; White Paper Part II para.3.I.35.
[249] White Paper Part II para.2.1.3.
[250] White Paper Part II paras.2.1, 3.I.10.
[251] Commonhold and L.Ref. Bill 2000 cl.75; White Paper Part II paras.3.I.44–49.
[252] Commonhold and L.Ref. Bill 2000 cl.77(2). Cl. 76 gives rights to obtain information.

landlord at that time,[253] with a copy to each qualifying leaseholder[254] and any manager who is in post.[255] At that time the qualification and participation rules must be complied with.[256] The form of notice, which will be prescribed,[257] will require identification of:

the premises and explain why the right to manage applies to them;
the full name and address of each qualifying tenant;
the full name and address of each member of the RTM company;
the date, term, and commencement date of each lease;
the registered office of the RTM company;
a period of at least one month for service of a counter notice, and
a period of at least one month before the right to manage is activated.[258]

Inaccuracies will not invalidate the notice, provided sufficient qualifying tenants remain when any inaccurately described tenants are excluded to exceed the one-half threshold.[259]

A landlord may admit the right to manage. Alternatively a landlord may by counternotice challenge the validity of the claim notice on technical grounds,[260] in which case the management company has two months in which to apply to a Leasehold Valuation Tribunal to establish the validity of the claim notice. There would be no right to object on the merits of the leaseholders as managers. There will be a right of access as is reasonable in relation to the right to manage for the management company and its authorised agents and for any landlord.[261] Once the time for all appeals has lapsed, the decision of the tribunal process will be final.[262] A claim notice may be withdrawn, but leaseholders will be liable for costs.[263]

The management company will be liable for the reasonable costs of any landlord in dealing with an application, whether it is successful[264] or unsuccessful,[265] but not for

---

[253] Commonhold and L.Ref. Bill 2000 cl.77(1), (6). The address is that furnished under L.T.A. 1987 ss.47–48 by cl.108. Notice need not be given to an unknown or untraceable persons, but cl.82 applies where no one would otherwise receive notice; it will require advertisement and other steps ordered by the court: White Paper Part II paras.3.I.58–59.

[254] Commonhold and L.Ref. Bill 2000 cl.77(8); notice can be given at the flat or another address furnished for the purpose: cl.83(5).

[255] Commonhold and L.Ref. Bill 2000 cl.77(9).

[256] Commonhold and L.Ref. Bill 2000 cl.77(3)–(5).

[257] Commonhold and L.Ref. Bill 2000 cl.78.

[258] Commonhold and L.Ref. Bill 2000 cl.78(6); for this period no other claim notice may be served: cl.79(3).

[259] Commonhold and L.Ref. Bill 2000 cl.79(1)–(3). There does not seem to be any protection envisaged against failure to serve copies on the tenants.

[260] Commonhold and L.Ref. Bill 2000 cl.65; White Paper Part II paras.3.I.50–54. It seems likely that it will be necessary to set out the grounds for opposition in the counter notice to avoid spurious notice.

[261] Commonhold and L.Ref. Bill 2000 cl.80. Ten days' notice must be given to any flat owner.

[262] Commonhold and L.Ref. Bill 2000 cl.81(3)–(8). The notice is deemed to be withdrawn by cl.84 if no Tribunal application is made within the two months.

[263] Commonhold and L.Ref. Bill 2000 cl.83; White Paper Part II paras.3.I.55–57.

[264] Commonhold and L.Ref. Bill 2000 cl.85.

[265] Commonhold and L.Ref. Bill 2000 cls.86.

[266] White Paper Part II paras.3.I.50–54.

costs before the Leasehold Valuation Tribunal.[266]

8. Duration of the right to manage

A right to manage accrues when all challenges are out of the way—either when the time for service of a counter-notice expires, when the right to manage is conceded,[267] or on the date ordered in a Leasehold Valuation Tribunal ruling.[268] The take over should be registered.[269]

All management responsibilities pass unless it is agreed that a particular function should rest with the ground landlord. There would be a duty to hand over relevant documents, with one month allowed for compliance.[270] Money in hand for service charges that was not already committed would have to be handed over, but the ground landlord would retain the power to collect any arrears of service charge contributions.[271] A tricky problem is what effect the right to manage should have on existing management contracts. Contracts will transfer automatically as will employment contracts under T.U.P.E.,[272] but if that rule was applied generally it would be ages before the leaseholders could get effective control. There are complex provisions[273] designed to ensure that the pre-existing manager (usually the ground landlord) gives a notice of existing management contracts both to the RTM company (a contract notice) and to the person carrying out the management (a contractor notice).

9. Operation of the right to manage

The company supersedes the ground landlord[274] in the exercise of the management functions—meaning functions relating to services, repairs, maintenance, improvements, insurance and management.[275] Covenants are amended accordingly.[276] There would be no right to step outside the terms of the lease. The original ground landlord remains entitled to service charge payments to cover costs incurred before the handover date.[277]

Consequential amendments are proposed to the legislation dealing with qualified covenants, defective premises, repairing obligations in short leases, service charges, insurance, managing agents, the obligation to hold service charge contributions on

---

[266] Commonhold and L.Ref. Bill 2000 cl.87(2): the claim notice must state a case at least one month hence on which the right is to accrue: cl. 78(7).

[268] Commonhold and L.Ref. Bill 2000 cl.87(4)–(6).

[269] Commonhold and L.Ref. Bill 2000 cl.101; White Paper Part II para.3.I.66; an application will be cautionable.

[270] Commonhold and L.Ref. Bill 2000 cl.90.

[271] Commonhold and L.Ref. Bill 2000 cl.91.

[272] White Paper Part II paras.3.I.60–64, 3.I. 89–94.

[273] Commonhold and L. Ref. Bill 2000 cls. 88–89.

[274] Commonhold and L.Ref. Bill 2000 cl.93. Landlords and others may only act under an agency agreement made with the management company. The company may later give up particular functions: sch.7 para.9.

[275] Commonhold and L.Ref. Bill 2000 cl.93(2)–(4); subcl.(7) provides for the amendment of this definition by regulations; White Paper Part II paras.3.I.67–69.

[276] Commonhold and L.Ref. Bill 2000 cl.93(2)–(4). Duties owed by the management company can be enforced by a landlord; and duties owed to the landlord are owed to the company. White Paper Part II para.3.I.81.

[277] Commonhold and L.Ref. Bill 2000 cl.91.

[278] Commonhold and L.Ref. Bill 2000 cl.99, sch.7; respectively: L.T.A. 1927 s.19 and L.T.A. 1988 Defective Premises Act 1972, L.T.A. 1985 part I, L.T.A. 1985 ss.18–30, L.T.A. 1985 s.30A and sch, L.T.A. 1985 s.30B, L.T.A. 1987 s.42, L.T.A. 1987 Part VI, L.R.H.U.D.A. 1993 Part I chapter V, H.A. 1996 s.84 and L.T.A. 1987 ss.35–39; also the proposed controls of administration charges.

trust, information to tenants, the right to a management audit, the right to appoint a surveyor, and defective documentation.[278] Some special procedures relating to long leasehold management call for special comment. A right of collective pre-emption applies where the landlord chooses to sell a block of flats to an outside investor; a copy of the landlord's notice notifying them of their opportunity to exercise this right must be served on the right to manage company.[279]

The right to manage company takes over from the landlord (including any superior landlord or outside party) the right to grant approvals to tenants. However prior notice must be given to the landlord—30 days' notice in the case of a structural alteration and otherwise 14 days'—and he can prevent the grant of approval without his permission by notice to the right to manage company; a landlord's refusal can only be overridden by a Leasehold Valuation Tribunal.[280]

There will be a duty on the right to manage company to monitor the performance of the tenant's obligations and to report to the landlord any breaches (unless the landlord has waived the right to information about particular types of breach).[281] Management can be assisted by a county court order requiring any person to make good any default and/or to remedy any breach within a set time.[282]

A ground landlord is required to make good any shortfall in service charge contributions where the proportions allocated to leaseholders are less than 100 per cent of the cost of providing services; the ground landlord's share must be paid by him to the right to manage company.[283]

10. Effect of the right to manage on non-leasehold units

As presently drafted, the right to manage will extend to all units and common parts, including non-leasehold units and commercial parts let on business tenancies. However the Government wishes to adhere to the principle that the right to manage should not interfere in the relationship between the landlord and non-flat owners, and in particular it may be undesirable to displace a social landlord providing for special housing needs. Consultation is taking place until October 2000 on how to reconcile these competing interests.[284] It would be simplest to exclude from the right to manage company all responsibilities towards non-flat owners, but this would require clear demarcation of the various areas of responsibility, and would inevitably entail wasteful duplication. Another possibility is to pass responsibility for all communal areas and services, but to leave the landlord responsible to his rack-renting tenants. The statutory responsibilities for the structure and services[285] are suggested as a model, though this would need exten-

---

[279] L.T.A. 1987 s.5 as amended by Commonhold and L.Ref. Bill 2000 sch.7 para.7.
[280] Commonhold and L.Ref. Bill 2000 cl.95–96; the period of notice can be increased by regulations; White Paper Part II paras.3.I.82–86.
[281] Commonhold and L.Ref. Bill 2000 cl.98; White Paper Part II paras.3.I.76–81.
[282] Commonhold and L.Ref. Bill 2000 cl.103.
[283] Commonhold and L.Ref. Bill 2000 cl.100.
[284] White Paper Part II para.3.I.70–71.
[285] L.T.A. 1985 ss.8–17.

sion to cover hallways and gardens. Another possibility is to make the right to manage company responsible to the landlord, who would remain liable to his rack-renting tenants. The final suggestion is that the right to manage company should be confined to catering for the long leaseholders, but on terms that any landlord under a rack rental arrangement could require the company to take on his responsibilities to his tenant.[286]

11. Appointment of manager

If it turned out that the leaseholders were not running the block satisfactorily or were ignoring the interests of the ground landlord or a minority of the tenants, anyone affected would have the right to go to the Leasehold Valuation Tribunal to argue for the appointment of an independent manager.[287]

12. Transition from management to ownership

The right to manage will not address the tenurial problems of leasehold ownership, but very often collective management will be a first step to collective enfranchisement, or even towards a commonhold conversion, and the proposals are drafted to make this chain of transition as smooth as possible.[288] The right to manage will not be available where the block is already subject to collective pre-emption or collective enfranchisement.[289] This last procedure could lead to acquisition of the freehold in the block either by the RTM company or by a new RTE company; in either case the right to manage regime would cease to apply when the freehold was transferred to that other company.[290] The proposals for matching forms of corporate structure are framed to ease the transition from management to ownership.[291] Where a RTM company was used it would be necessary to amend the membership by removing the ground landlord and also any leaseholders who decided not to participate in the enfranchisement.[292] It will be wise to frame the objects of a RTM company to facilitate any future enfranchisement or commonhold conversion.

13. Withdrawal

After a number of years the composition of the leaseholder body may change to such an extent that the current owners no longer wish to manage the block themselves, and in these circumstances the leaseholders will be free to withdraw from management by agreement, reverting to the normal operation of the lease. After withdrawal, the right to

---

[286] White Paper Part II para.3.I.75

[287] L.T.A. 1987 Part II; see below pp. 452–453; Commonhold and L.Ref. Bill 2000 cl.99 sch.7 para.8—the resident landlord exemption is disapplied; White Paper Part II paras.2.1.3, 3.I.97–109. All the other controls of residential management described in this chapter would also be available. The right of compulsory acquisition of the ground landlord's reversion for poor management will be suspended: sch.7 para.9.

[288] White Paper Part II para.2.1.2.

[289] Commonhold and L.Ref. Bill 2000 cl.69(6), sch.6, para.5.

[290] Commonhold and L.Ref. Bill 2000 cl.70(3)–(6).

[291] White Paper Part II paras.3.II.28–31.

[292] White Paper Part II paras.3.I.41–43.

[293] Commonhold and L.Ref. Bill 2000 cl.54(6), sch.6, para.6; White Paper Part II paras.3.I.20, 3.I.100–101. An alternative will be to surrender particular functions: sch.7 para.8(6).

manage will be suspended for four years unless the Leasehold Valuation Tribunal rules that it would be unreasonable to prevent its resumption.[293]

14. Liquidation

The right to manage would end if an order was made for the company to be wound up or put into administration, or on the appointment of a receiver or manager, or on entry into a voluntary arrangement.

H. EXISTING CONTROLS OF RESIDENTIAL MANAGEMENT

It is a paradox of our system of managing communally owned property that the ground landlord's interest is of nominal value, yet his managing agent is given supreme power in controlling the way that a development is run.[294] The Nugee Committee on the *Management of Privately Owned Flats*[295] set out the need for legislation to redress this imbalance of power. Most of the restrictions discussed below originated in the Landlord and Tenant Act 1987, though there have already been several rewrites, and consultation is under way on a more thorough going reform.

1. Information about the identity of the manager

A leaseholder of property occupied as a dwelling can make a written request to the landlord's agent or collector of rent for disclosure of the immediate landlord's name and address.[296] This information must be provided in rent demands.[297] There is a duty to inform the leaseholder of any assignment of the landlord's interest if a dwelling is assigned,[298] and this must give a warning of the right to acquire the property.[299]

2. Appointment of a manager

Leaseholders[300] of a block of flats (that is any building containing two or more flats) have the right[301] to apply to the Leasehold Valuation Tribunal[302] for the appointment of managers of the block, a procedure which is a clear improvement on using the general

---

[294] J. Driscoll [1998] *N.L.J.* 1855.

[295] (October 1985); H.W. Wilkinson [1985] *Conv.* 162; A.J. Hawkins [1986] *Conv.* 12; Nugee followed the James Cttee of the R.I.C.S. (1983).

[296] L.T.A. 1985 ss.1, 2 (corporate landlord); only the immediate landlord is affected.

[297] L.T.A. 1987 part VI ss.46–49.

[298] L.T.A. 1985 s.3 as amended L.T.A. 1987 s.50; the information must be provided not later than the next rent day. It is in the interests of the seller to give notice to avoid liability under the covenants: subss.(3A), (3B).

[299] L.T.A. 1985 s.3A; as amended by H.A. 1996 s.93 in force September 24th 1996; i.e. that it has been sold in breach of the leaseholder's right of first refusal under L.T.A. 1987 part I, see above pp. 426–432.

[300] L.T.A. 1987 s.21(1),(2); joint applications are under subss.(4), (5).

[301] L.T.A. 1987 s.24 as amended by H.A. 1996 s.85 (see sch.5); procedure is governed by S.I.s 1997/1852, 1997/1853, 1997/1854.

[302] H.A. 1996 s.86; in force September 1st 1997: S.I. 1996/2305; M. Biles [1999] *Conv.* 472 (the last word on the subject); S. Gallagher [1999] *J.H.L.* 58, 79.

[303] *Hart* v. *Emelkirk Ltd.* [1983] 1 W.L.R. 1289, Goulding J. (no attempt to collect rents); J.E. Martin [1984] *Conv.* 229; *Daiches* v. *Bluelake Investments Ltd.* [1985] 2 E.G.L.R. 67; *Evans* v. *Clayhope Properties Ltd.* [1988] 1 All E.R. 444 C.A. (costs); J.E. Martin [1986] *Conv.* 427; C.P. Rodgers [1986] *Conv.* 427.

equitable power to appoint a receiver.[303] A receiver is restricted to collecting rent, whereas a manager can continue in business and apply the money collected in managing the block. A Leasehold Valuation Tribunal should therefore appoint a manager (who is likely to be a Chartered Surveyor) and it should also consider including the power to mortgage and to sell vacant flats.[304] This remedy is not available in the public sector, nor where the landlord is resident in the block, nor if the block forms part of the functional land of a charity.[305]

Power to make an order has been transferred to the Leasehold Valuation Tribunals. Problems are the need for assistance from the court in enforcing orders and the difficulty in compelling adherence to the time scale laid down; both points should be dealt with.[306] Grounds for the appointment are that the landlord is in breach of covenant,[307] has levied an unreasonable service charge,[308] or generally that it is just and convenient.[309] In *Howard* v. *Midrome Ltd.*[310] water was penetrating through the roof, the landlord was not prepared to fix it, and had ceased to function as a manager at all, so an interim management order was made. A preliminary notice gives the landlord a chance to remedy the problem and application is permitted only when this notice expires.[311] Appointments are likely to be temporary.[312]

The Tribunal order may confer such functions of repair, maintenance and insurance as it thinks fair.[313] Landlords should not be allowed to add the costs of opposing an order to the service charge, but they should be required to pay the remuneration of the manager appointed.[314]

3.   Management code of practice

Ministerial approval can be given to a code of management practice for residential property.[315] This is helpful in proof of the standard of work which is reasonable.

---

[304] M. Biles [1999] *Conv.* 472, 475–479.

[305] L.T.A. 1987 s.58.

[306] Biles at 474, 491.

[307] *Howard* v. *Midrome Ltd.* [1991] 1 E.G.L.R. 58, Warner J. (major water penetration); also *Blawdziewicz* v. *Diadon Establishment* [1988] 2 E.G.L.R. 52 Ch.D. The grounds are amended by H.A. 1996 s.85.

[308] H.A. 1996 s.85, sch.5.

[309] L.T.A. 1987 s.24(2)(a), (b); *Hafton Properties Ltd.* v. *Camp* [1994] 1 E.G.L.R. 67 (management company has failed to repair when the landlord is not liable); the cases on receivers mentioned above give some guidance: Biles at 485–489.

[310] [1991] 1 E.G.L.R. 58, Warner J.; Biles also discusses *Sparkle Properties Ltd.* v. *Residential Developments Ltd.* [1998] unreported.

[311] L.T.A. 1987 ss.22, 23. As to defects in the application see s.24(7) and *Howard* v. *Midrome Ltd.* [1991] 1 E.G.L.R. 58, Warner J. An appointment should be registered as if he were a receiver.

[312] Biles at 479–480.

[313] L.T.A. 1987 s.24(11).

[314] Biles at 475, 481–483, 491.

[315] L.R.H.U.D.A. 1993 s.87; S.Is. 1996/2839, 1998/106.

[316] s.58.

[317] See above pp. 432–437.

4. Compulsory acquisition of reversion

This right is restricted to the private residential sector.[316] Qualifying long leaseholders (who would qualify for collective enfranchisement[317]) may require the acquisition of the reversion by a management company, provided that two thirds of the leaseholders concur in the service of the initial notice,[318] and the Tribunal agrees to grant an acquisition order.[319] Grounds for making an order are a breach of covenant which is likely to continue, appointment of a manager (under the previous head) who has operated for two years[320] or that appointment of a manager is not an adequate remedy.[321] Terms are fixed by the Tribunal.[322]

5. Variation of defective leases

Perhaps 8 per cent of all leases are seriously defective.[323] Consensual variation of flat schemes requires the agreement of all parties interested—including the developer, the management company, each flat owner and all mortgage lenders—so that it is virtually impossible to secure all necessary consents. Part IV of the 1987 Act provides a better procedure for varying long leases of flats by court order.[324] Leases can be varied if they fail to make satisfactory provision for repair or maintenance—whether of the flat, the block, or ancillary land—for insurance,[325] for repair or maintenance of installations and services, or for the service charge.[326] Application can be made by any party[327] and the variation may also involve other tenants in the same block of flats.[328] An order should not be made so as to cause any person substantial prejudice, but minor losses can be overcome by an order for compensation; if an order is made it binds all parties.[329]

I. CONTROL OF RESIDENTIAL MANAGEMENT: REFORM PROPOSALS

Changes are proposed in the White Paper published in August 2000, but these do not figure in the Bill introduced into Parliament.

1. Control of third party managers

An overwhelming majority of consultees from all interest groups supported the impo-

---

[318] s.27 as amended by L.R.H.U.D.A. 1993 s.85.

[319] L.T.A. 1987 ss.28–29, 33 (landlord untraceable), 34 (default in completing). Minor changes of wording to s.29 will be made by Draft Commonhold and L.Ref. Bill 2000 sch.11.

[320] The period was reduced from 3 to 2 years by H.A. 1996 s.88.

[321] L.T.A. 1987 s.29(2); *Gray* v. *Standard Home & Counties Properties Ltd.* [1994] 1 E.G.L.R. 119.

[322] *Oakley* v. *Martin* [1993] 06 E.G. 113 L.Tr. (price 12 years purchase ground rent).

[323] Observer June 26th. 1994.

[324] ss.35–40; *John Lyon's Charity Trustees* v. *Haysport Properties Ltd.* [1995] E.G.C.S. 171.

[325] A similar provision operates in relation to houses: s.40.

[326] Contributions may be increased or decreased: L.R.H.U.D.A. 1993 s.86 amending L.T.A. 1987 s.35(4).

[327] L.T.A. 1987 ss.35(1), 37 (majority of those affected).

[328] s.36.

[329] ss.38–39.

[330] White Paper Part II paras.3.I.87–88; see also *Consultation 1998* paras.4.1–4.6; *Analysis* paras.37–39, 46–51; *Way Forward* paras.9–10.

[331] White Paper Part II paras.2.2.5, 4.3.

sition of additional controls on managing agents employed by landlords—including both ground landlords and those engaged in rack renting to short residential tenants.[330] This will be tackled by extending the existing power to appoint a manager to cover tripartite leases that impose management control on outside parties.[331] A licensing scheme may emerge in future.

2. Reform of the power to appoint a manager

This power will be extended in three ways. The existing exemption for blocks with a *resident landlord* will be removed. Care is needed to prevent disruption to the supply of rented accommodation, so that this would be targeted at blocks where the majority interest is held by long leaseholders, and it will not apply to a block let on short residential tenancies. In line with extended controls of service charge[332] it will be made clear that mismanagement in relation to improvements will give intervention rights; this extension will cover the power of appointment of the manager, the power to order the compulsory acquisition by long leaseholders of the ground landlord's interest, the right to a management audit, approval of codes of management practice and the right to appoint a surveyor.[333] A ground landlord who makes unreasonable administration charges may be displaced by the appointment of a manager.[334]

3. Sheltered housing

A Code of Practice governs retirement housing,[335] but legislation can be expected to introduce more substantial controls over management charges made for the elderly living in sheltered accommodation.[336]

4. Defective documentation: reform proposals

The Government is proposing to extend and clarify the grounds on which leases may be varied. Since the existing law[337] is thought to be vague one important objective would be to clarify the existing grounds and to provide a more detailed definition of what is a failure to make "satisfactory provision". In relation to repair or maintenance, the lease should define the aspects of the covenant to be considered, such as the scope of the obligation, who is responsible for work and the frequency with which work is required. An insurance provision should not be viewed as satisfactory unless a single policy is required for an entire property. In terms of the recovery of expenditure, a lease should include the cost of works of repair or maintenance, day-to-day administration, the cost of insurance premiums, the cost of loans to cover the cost of works and interest on loans.

---

[332] See below pp. 462–464.
[333] White Paper Part II para.3.V.14; respectively L.T.A. 1987 ss.24(11), 29 (via a new s.29(2A)), L.R.H.U.D.A. 1993 ss.84, 87(8), H.A. 1996 sch.4 para.4(2).
[334] White Paper Part II para.3.V.17; for the meaning of administration charges, see below pp. 464–465.
[335] S.I. 1998/106.
[336] *Analysis* para.58; *Way Forward* paras.18–19; see also H.W. Wilkinson [1987] *Conv.* 1, [1993] *Conv.* 1.
[337] White Paper Part II paras.2.2.4, 4.2.1–4.2.12.
[338] White Paper Part II paras.4.2.13–4.2.17
[339] White Paper Part II paras.2.2.4, 4.2.18.

It is also proposed to specify as additional grounds in respect of management matters, failure to provide for advance payments of service charge and failure to require interest (to a maximum prescribed interest rate) on arrears of service charge[338] The Government is also proposing to reserve the right to add further grounds by regulations. The jurisdiction is to be transferred to the Leasehold Valuation Tribunal[339] with the aim of reducing the cost of lease variations.

Precisely the same problems may arise with commonhold documentation, and so it was no surprise to find a proposal for a similar power to deal with defective drafting;[340] what is a surprise is that this provision has dropped out of the current draft of the commonhold legislation.[341]

J.   SERVICE CHARGES

1.   Flat schemes

Service charges for flats are based on the contractual arrangement accepted when the flat scheme was set up, but with substantial legislative controls.[342] These two aspects must be considered in turn. It is assumed throughout the discussion which follows that a management company controlled collectively by the leasehold owners of all the flats holds the freehold in the block of flats and is charged with providing services at the expense of the leaseholders, who each contribute a proportion of the overall costs.[343] The property might be a block of residential flats or sheltered housing for the elderly which is provided with wardening.[344]

2.   Flats and common parts

The basis of flat schemes is the division of the entire structure into flats and common parts. The latter are the aspects covered by the service charge and are generally vested in the management company itself; it may include hallways, stairs, lifts, and gardens. Generally, it also includes the structure and load-bearing walls, so that these fall within the maintenance obligations of the management company, while leaving repair or internal walls and other parts within the flat to the owner of the individual flat.[345] Rights will be required over the common parts. The estate documentation must ensure that the two

---

[340] Draft Commonhold Bill 1996 cl.42; see below Chapter 17.

[341] Commonhold and L.Ref. Bill 2000.

[342] Woodfall 7.162–7.231; Davey 345–353; Evans & Smith (5th ed.) 416–422; Garner (2nd ed.) ch.17; see below pp. 459–464.

[343] Proposals for commonhold schemes are considered below at pp. 481–484.

[344] H.W. Wilkinson [1987] *Conv.* 4, [1993] *Conv.* 1.

[345] There will be a covenant that the individual leaseholder should carry out this work to ensure that other flat owners are not affected by the poor standard of maintenance of one flat; there will probably be reserve powers of entry to effect this.

[346] *Graystone Property Investments Ltd.* v. *Margulies* [1984] 1 E.G.L.R. 27 C.A.; J.E. Adams [1984] *Conv.* 171; D. Williams [1988] 01 *L.S.G.* 14.

[347] *Devonshire Reid Properties Ltd.* v. *Trenaman* [1997] 1 E.G.L.R. 45; there are many earlier cases.

[348] *Bent* v. *High Cliff Developments Ltd.* [1999] 34 L.S.G. 35, Ch.D.; *Pearlman* v. *Harrow School Governors* [1979] Q.B 56 C.A.; *Irvine* v. *Moran* [1991] 1 E.G.L.R. 261.

[349] See above pp. 243–246.

elements—flats and common parts—mesh perfectly so that nothing is included twice and nothing is left out.[346] Definition needs to pay particular attention to walls, ceilings, and floors, ownership of the roof space,[347] and matters such as windows and doors.[348]

Maintenance of the individual flats is the responsibility of each owner, since lease-holders own flats for long terms which exceed the seven years for which structural oblig-ations are cast on to the landlord.[349] Leaseholders will covenant with the management company to maintain their parts, with reserve powers for the management company to enter and carry out necessary work at the cost of a defaulting flat owner.

3. Maintenance obligations

Maintenance of common parts is the responsibility of the flat management company, the cost being recovered through a service charge. There will be a positive duty to carry out structural repairs as these become necessary. Work which is authorised may cover repairs only, in which case it may be important to determine whether work such as installation of a new window is an improvement as opposed to a repair,[350] though repair is not restricted just to first aid.[351] This limitation is irrelevant if the service charge cov-ers work of improvement,[352] though no doubt leaseholders will insist upon some definition of the types of improvement for which they can be forced to pay. Frequently the landlord will have to produce plans of proposed work and there will be some proce-dure for leaseholders to object to over-lavish work.[353]

A less satisfactory arrangement is to leave communal facilities vested in the developer as landlord, but to provide a scheme of covenants by which the management company agrees to their maintenance and is able to impose a service charge, collect contributions and enforce other covenants against individual flat owners. No terms can be implied.[354] Care is needed in such cases to ensure that there is a mutuality of obligation, for exam-ple by imposing a scheme of development.[355]

If the service charge is limited to sums "expended", the landlord can recover money only after it has actually been spent.[356] However many leases provide for the creation of a sinking fund, that is a fund saved up to provide for future work or to cover the cost of depreciation of machinery. Tax could be levied under schedule A as income from prop-erty, though the former practice was to levy no charge where expenditure equalled

---

[350] *Mullaney* v. *Maybourne Grange (Croydon) Management Co. Ltd.* [1986] 1 E.G.L.R. 70 (new window not repair).

[351] *Manor House Drive Ltd.* v. *Shahbazian* (1965) 195 E.G. 283.

[352] *Reston Ltd.* v. *Hudson* [1990] 2 E.G.L.R. 51; *Holding & Management Ltd.* v. *Property Holding & Investment Trust plc.* [1989] 1 W.L.R. 1313 C.A.; *New England Properties plc.* v. *Portsmouth News Shops Ltd.* [1993] 1 E.G.L.R. 84.

[353] *Northway Flats Management Co. (Camden) Ltd.* v. *Wimpey Pension Trustees Ltd.* [1992] 2 E.G.L.R. 42 C.A.

[354] *Hafton Properties Ltd.* v. *Camp* [1994] 1 E.G.L.R. 67 (landlord not liable for failure of management company to maintain).

[355] Sparkes *N.L.L.* 605–607.

[356] *Capital & Counties Freehold Equity Trust Ltd.* v. *B.L. plc.* [1987] 2 E.G.L.R. 49 Ch.D.; *Finchbourne* v. *Rodrigues* [1976] 3 All E.R. 581 C.A.; *Frobisher (Second Investments) Ltd.* v. *Kiloran Trust* [1980] 1 All E.R. 488.

[357] Property Income Manual (Inland Revenue) para.5095; P. Spencer [1990] 31 *L.S.G.* 24; J. Carter [1994] 08 *E.G.* 111.

[358] Inland Revenue Tax Bulletin Issue 36 (November 1998) 2–3.

receipts over a five-year period.[357] Revenue practice is now changed to reflect the existence of the trust on service charge contributions: as from March 31st 1998, sums paid to occupier-controlled flat management companies will be received as capital, but interest received on contributions deposited at a bank or building society will be treated as trust income, and directors of companies need to declare this income under the self-assessment procedures.[358] If so, it will be the current leaseholder who is liable to contribute when charges are levied, even if the work is not done until long after the current leaseholder has sold.[359]

4. Services within the charge

Leases also commonly provide for communal services—such as porterage or lifts—and other beneficial services[360] which may or may not be included in the service charge according to the discretion of the managing agents. Costs of employing managing agents can be included but only if there is a clear contractual provision.[361] Other sums included are V.A.T.[362] and interest (the right to which is implied if not expressed[363]).

5. Certification of costs and allocation between leaseholders

The ground landlord's managing agent is required to certify the sums chargeable to the service charge that have been spent and also the proportions to be allocated to each tenant.[364] Leases generally provide that the certificate is to be conclusive.

Leases may adopt any method of allocation which is agreed, which means in practice the system laid down by the developer when the block is first sold. It might be equal division between units or set proportions for particular units, according to floor area or rateable value.[365] A certificate cannot exclude the jurisdiction of the court over errors of calculation or incorrect inclusion of items within the charge.[366]

6. Disputes

Leaseholders often complain about *excessive work*.[367] Landlords should only recover what was fair and reasonable, this being an implied limitation at common law, so the

---

[357] *S.S. for the Environment* v. *Possfund (North West) Ltd.* [1997] 2 E.G.L.R. 56 C.A. However on sale midway through a service charge period, the charge has to be apportioned: G. Sheriff [1991] *N.L.J.* 1148.

[360] This should not be used for major external repairs: *Lloyds Bank plc.* v. *Bowker Orford* [1992] 2 E.G.L.R. 44 Ch.D.

[361] *Embassy Court Residents Association Ltd.* v. *Lipman* [1984] 2 E.G.L.R. 60 C.A.; *Woodtrek Ltd.* v. *Jezek* [1982] 1 E.G.L.R. 45 (cost of rent collection).

[362] *Nell Gwynn House Maintenance Fund* v. *Commissioners of Customs & Excise* (1996) 72 P. & C.R. 522 C.A.

[363] *Skilleter* v. *Charles* [1992] 1 E.G.L.R. 73 C.A.; *Boldmark Ltd.* v. *Cohen* [1986] 1 E.G.L.R. 47 C.A.

[364] *Rexhaven Ltd.* v. *Nurse* (1996) 28 H.L.R. 241.

[365] Variable formulae are discussed in the commercial context, below p. 705.

[366] *Re Davstone Estate Ltd.'s Lease* [1969] 2 All E.R. 849; *Dean* v. *Prince* [1954] 1 All E.R. 749; *Universities Superannuation Scheme Ltd.* v. *Marks and Spencer plc.* [1999] 1 E.G.L.R. 13 C.A. (Telford town centre).

[367] *Postel Properties Ltd.* v. *Boots the Chemist Ltd.* [1996] 2 E.G.L.R. 60, Ian Kennedy J. (reasonable to repair roof before it failed).

[368] *Finchbourne Ltd.* v. *Rodrigues* [1976] 3 All E.R. 581 C.A.

[369] *Jollybird Ltd.* v. *Fairzone Ltd.* [1990] 2 E.G.L.R. 55 C.A.

[370] *Yorkbrook Investments Ltd.* v. *Batten* (1985) 18 H.L.R. 25 C.A.

[371] *Gordon* v. *Selico Co. Ltd.* [1986] 1 E.G.L.R. 71 C.A.

landlord has no power to adopt the highest possible cost.[368] Charges should be based on the actual cost of providing services, with no profit element.[369] Another problem is work of *defective quality:* a court may disallow any part that is not within the service charge provision,[370] and the leaseholder may be justified in refusing to pay a demand.[371]

7.   Other service charges

Special statutory jurisdictions apply to public sector flats bought under the *right to buy*, since the tenant is entitled to information before deciding to buy about the landlord's estimate of the annual amount of service charge and details of structural defects,[372] and the amount of service charge is restricted for the first five years to the pre-sale level adjusted for inflation.[373] Challenges to reasonableness of service charges are allowed only after completion of the right to buy conveyance.[374] *Retirement housing* is governed by a Code of Practice,[375] but legislation can be expected to introduce more substantial controls.[376] Service charges for communal facilities on estates let on short residential tenancies have already been described;[377] the controls of domestic service charges described in the remainder of this chapter will apply. When a commonhold scheme is introduced there will be a new kind of service charge called a commonhold assessment levied by a commonhold association.[378]

K.   SERVICE CHARGES: DOMESTIC CONTROLS

1.   Transfer of jurisdiction to Leasehold Valuation Tribunals

As from September 1997, a Leasehold Valuation Tribunal has jurisdiction to determine whether service charges are reasonable,[379] and to control many other aspects of block management. It is inappropriate to seek an injunction from the court to prevent the work going ahead,[380] and the court may transfer any proceedings relating to service

---

[372]   H.A. 1985 s.125 amended by H.P.A. 1986 s.4; *Sutton (Hasloe) H.Ass. Ltd.* v. *Williams* [1988] 1 E.G.L.R. 56 C.A. (replacement of windows; said improvement; but express warning of liability; so was reasonable).

[373]   S.I. 1986/2195 (previously 10 years); A. Sanders (1993) 137 *S.J.* 517 (loans).

[374]   *Sheffield C.C.* v. *Jackson* [1998] 1 W.L.R. 1591 C.A. (play areas).

[375]   S.I. 1998/106.

[376]   *Analysis* para.58; *Way Forward* paras.18–19; see also H.W. Wilkinson [1987] *Conv.* 1, [1993] *Conv.* 1.

[377]   See above p. 281.

[378]   See below pp. 481–484.

[379]   L.T.A. 1985 ss.31A, 31B, 31C, as amended by H.A. 1996 s.83(3); S.Is. 1996/2305, 1998/1768 (cases already in the court system); A. McNeil [1998] 13 *P.L.J.* 16.

[380]   *Hi-Lift Elevator Services Ltd.* v. *Temple* (1996) 28 H.L.R. 1 C.A. Contrast *Aylesbond Estates Ltd.* v. *MacMillan* (2000) 32 H.L.R. 1 C.A. (other complaints, so county court proceedings allowed to continue).

[381]   S.Is. 1997/1853 (applications), 1997/1854 (procedure), 1997/1965 (appeals).

[382]   S.I. 1997/1852 (fees); maximum £500 or £150 for challenges to insurance premiums; all are waived for those on benefit. There is an appeal *Bell* v. *Oakins* [2000] R.V.R. 207.

[383]   L.T.A. 1985 s.20C (as replaced by H.A. 1996 s.83(4)); on the earlier version see *Iperion Investments Corporation Ltd.* v. *Broadwalk House Resident Ltd.* [1995] 2 E.G.L.R. 47 C.A.; *Laimond Property Investment Co. Ltd.* v. *Arlington Park Mansions Ltd.* [1989] 1 E.G.L.R. 208 C.A.; *Morgan* v. *Stainer* [1993] 2 E.G.L.R. 73 Ch.D.; *Cymru Investments Ltd.* v. *Watkins* [1997] 37 R.V.R. 171 L.Tr.

[384]   *Sella Holdings Ltd.* v. *Mears* (1989) 21 H.L.R. 147; *Embassy Court Residents' Ass.* v. *Lipman* [1984] 2 E.G.L.R. 60 C.A.; *Holding & Management Ltd.* v. *Property Holding & Investment Trust plc.* [1989] 1 W.L.R. 1313 C.A.

[385]   *Re Sarum Property Ltd.'s Application* [1999] 2 E.G.L.R. 131 L.Tr.

charges to the Tribunal. Procedure is simpler than that adopted in court,[381] the fees are fixed,[382] and landlords are unable to recover their costs. There is power to deny the landlord recovery of costs in proceedings which are brought unreasonably,[383] in which case the sum will not be relevant costs and should not be added to the service charge.[384] A former leaseholder may apply even after selling the flat to which the dispute relates.[385]

2. Management code of practice

Ministerial approval can be given to a code of management practice for residential property.[386] This is helpful in proof of the standard of work which is reasonable.

3. Service charge notices

When a landlord demands service charge in relation to a dwelling, the demand must include the name and address of the landlord, and no payments are due until this information has been given.[387] Particular care is required where the company is registered overseas. An address for service must also be given, though not necessarily in the service charge demand.[388]

4. Control of amount of service charge

Service charges affecting dwellings[389] are subject to legislative controls, which apply to any sum, additional to rent, which relates directly or indirectly to services,[390] repairs, maintenance, insurance, or management costs,[391] including also overheads, actual bills, and estimated sums to meet future costs.[392]

The leaseholder has improved rights to challenge work before it is carried out. Where works are to be undertaken costing more than £1,000[393] two estimates must be obtained

---

[386] L.R.H.U.D.A. 1993 s.87; S.Is. 1996/2839, 1998/106.

[387] L.T.A. 1987 ss.46–47; *Drew-Morgan* v. *Hamed-Zadeh* [1999] 2 E.G.L.R. 13 C.A.

[388] L.T.A. 1987 ss.48–49; *Dallhold Estates (U.K.) Property Ltd.* v. *Lindsey Trust Properties Ltd.* [1994] 1 E.G.L.R. 93 C.A.; *Rogan* v. *Woodfield Building Services Ltd.* [1995] 1 E.G.L.R. 72 C.A.; *Marath* v. *MacGillivray* (1996) 28 H.L.R. 484 C.A.; see above p. 367.

[389] L.T.A. 1985 ss.18–30 as amended by L.T.A. 1987 ss.41–45. Short term public sector tenants are not protected: L.T.A. 1985 s.26.

[390] *I.V.S. Enterprises Ltd.* v. *Chelsea Cloisters Management Ltd.* [1994] E.G.C.S. 14 C.A. (excessive charges for satellite tv services disallowed).

[391] L.T.A. 1985 s.18.

[392] s.19(2) (limits).

[393] s.30(3); S.I. 1988/1285 (or £50 for each dwelling if greater); *Martin* v. *Maryland Estates Ltd.* [1998] 2 E.G.L.R. 81 C.A.

[394] L.T.A. 1985 new s.20(3)–(4). Information should be provided through a recognised tenant's association: subs.(5). Grants must be deducted: s.20A.

[395] One month is provided for tenants to comment, and the ground landlord must have regard to the observations.

[396] *Wilson* v. *Stone* [1998] 2 E.G.L.R. 155 L.V.T.; *Wandsworth L.B.C.* v. *Griffin* [2000] 26 E.G. 147 L.Tr.; *Hoggett* v. *Knox* [2000] 05 C.L. 434 C.Ct.

[397] L.T.A. 1985 s.19(2A) inserted by H.A. 1996 s.83.

[398] H.A. 1996 s.84.

[399] L.T.A. 1985 s.20B.

and provided to each leaseholder,[394] and a consultation process must be followed.[395] Dispensation will be allowed in emergencies.[396] Application can be made to a Tribunal for a ruling that proposed work would be within the terms of the service charge provision.[397] Recognised tenants' associations have the right to appoint a surveyor to advise on any matter relating to service charge.[398] Notice of costs must be given within 18 months of the work, and otherwise contributions are not recoverable.[399] The leaseholder may require a summary of costs in writing.[400] A trust is imposed on the leaseholders contributions.[401]

Leaseholders are also protected against excessive demands. Services charges are limited to costs reasonably incurred and on services of a reasonable standard,[402] matters on which the terms of the lease cannot pre-empt the decision,[403] which is now one over which the Leasehold Valuation Tribunal has exclusive jurisdiction.[404] After the work has been carried out the leaseholder can challenge liability to pay for it if the cost turns out to be twice that indicated in the notice,[405] and it will be common to limit what is recoverable to a part of the claimed cost.[406]

5. Restrictions on forfeiture for non-payment of service charge

The threat of forfeiture is removed until the service charge is agreed or adjudicated. Forfeiture for non-payment of a service charge cannot occur unless the amount is agreed, admitted, or fixed in proceedings[407]—now by a Leasehold Valuation Tribunal—though it is obviously sufficient to obtain a judgment in default of defence.[408] Notices warning of forfeiture must alert the leaseholder to his entitlement to claim these rights.[409]

6. Possible restriction of no set off clause

The unfair contract terms legislation does not apply to land,[410] though it is arguable that the European based regulations do[411]; if so this may have an impact on the validity of a no set off clause. In other words, the leaseholder may, whatever the lease says, be able to withhold service charge payments to cover damages for failures by the management company to carry out its functions.

---

[400] ss.21–25; *Taber* v. *Macdonald* (1999) 31 H.L.R. 73 Div.Ct.; *R.* v. *Marylebone Magistrates Ct. ex parte Westminster C.C.* (2000) 32 H.L.R. 266.

[401] L.T.A. 1987 s.42; the trust is to defray costs and otherwise to hold for contributing leaseholders: subs.(3); S.I. 1988/1284 (authorised investments); [1990] *N.L.J.* 785.

[402] L.T.A. 1985 s.19(1); D. Gilder [1997] 32 *E.G.* 79.

[403] L.T.A. 1985 s.19(3).

[404] s.19(2A) inserted by H.A. 1996 s.83; see above p. 459.

[405] *Martin* v. *Maryland Estates Ltd.* [1998] 2 E.G.L.R. 81 C.A.; *R.* v. *London L.V.T.* [2000] Times October 20th.

[406] *Yorkbrook Investments Ltd.* v. *Batten* [1985] 2 E.G.L.R. 100 C.A.; *Gordon* v. *Selico & Co. Ltd.* [1986] 1 E.G.L.R. 71 C.A.; *Wandsworth L.B.C.* v. *Griffin* (2000) 26 E.G. 147 L.Tr.

[407] H.A. 1996 s.81; in force September 24th 1996.

[408] *Southwark L.B.C.* v. *Tornaritis* [1999] 07 C.L. 330 C.Ct.

[409] H.A. 1996 s.82; there appears to be no prescribed form.

[410] *Unchained Growth III plc.* v. *Granby Village (Manchester) Management Co. Ltd.* [1999] Times November 4th C.A.

[411] See above pp. 198–199.

[412] L.T.A. 1985 s.30B; *R.* v. *London R.A.P. ex parte Henry Smith's Charity Trustees* [1988] 1 E.G.L.R. 34; C.P. Rodgers [1988] *Conv.* 363.

7.   Consultation and participation in decisions about service charges

Recognised tenants' associations have the right to be consulted about the appointment of managing agents.[412] There are as yet no professional qualifications required of managing agents, though this is a matter on which consultation is under way. Qualifying leaseholders have a right to appoint an auditor, with power to demand information from the landlord in order to carry out a management audit and so determine to what extent the landlord is carrying out his obligations in an efficient and effective manner.[413] This right is now supplemented by power to appoint a surveyor and his right to insist on access to the common parts in the course of the audit.[414]

L.   SERVICE CHARGE: REFORM PROPOSALS

1.   Service charge—proposals to extend controls to improvements

Existing controls of domestic service charges to recover the cost of repairs do not extend to the cost of improvements, but the Government now proposes to make good this defect.[415] The most important change will be to increase the scope of the definition of the power of Leasehold Valuation Tribunals to control the reasonableness of service charges,[416] but corresponding changes will be made in a number of the provisions about management control[417] and in the provisions to enable a former public sector tenant to take out a loan to cover service charge demands after a right to buy purchase.[418] There will be a general power to make regulations altering the definitions of service charges, management, and management functions further.[419]

2.   Ongoing contracts—new consultation requirement

It is proposed to replace the existing provision which requires consultation with the service charge payers before the entry into contracts with a completely new rewording. This will require consultation before any ground landlord enters into any arrangement relating to service charge costs where the agreement has a duration of twelve months, providing protection in the frequent cases where ground landlords place long-term management contracts.[420] Costs shall not be taken into account in determining the

---

[413]   L.R.H.U.D.A. 1993 ss.76–84.

[414]   H.A. 1996 s.84.

[415]   Commonhold and L.Ref. Bill 2000 cl.138 and sch.9; White Paper Part II paras.2.18, 3.V.14.

[416]   L.T.A. 1985 ss.18(1)(a) (definition), 19 (L.V.T. jurisdiction); *Stapel* v. *Bellshore* [2000] 08 C.L. 477.

[417]   Commonhold and L.Ref. Bill 2000 cl.146 imposes control on Crown Estates.

[418]   Commonhold and L.Ref. Bill 2000 sch.9 paras.1–6, amending H.A. 1985 s.450A, 450B, 458, s.459, s.621A; White Paper Part II para.3.V.18.

[419]   Commonhold and L.Ref. Bill 2000 sch.9 para.13; White Paper Part II paras.3.V.13–14.

[420]   White Paper Part II paras.3.V.21–22; *Consultation 1998* paras.4.9–4.13; *Analysis* para.57; *Way Forward* para.17.

[421]   L.T.A. 1987 s.20(6)–(7) (as it will be amended by Commonhold and L.Ref. Bill 2000 cl.139) will allow the following requirements: to provide details of the proposed works to the leaseholders or a recognised tenants' association; to obtain estimates; to invite leaseholders or their association to obtain other estimates; to have regard to any observations; and to give reasons in prescribed cases; see White Paper Part II paras.3.V.23–25.

[422]   Commonhold and L.Ref. Bill 2000 cl.139 substitutes a new L.T.A. 1985 s.20.

[423]   White Paper Part II paras.3.V.19–20.

amount of any service charge unless proper consultation, following prescribed require-ments[421] took place. The Leasehold Valuation Tribunal may grant a dispensation from the need for consultation where it is satisfied that the landlord has acted reasonably.[422] The same provisions apply to the costs of works exceeding a prescribed amount, in which case the excess is irrecoverable under the service charge. At present[423] there is a fixed figure irrespective of the size of the block, but it is more likely in future that it will be based on work which exceeds a specified percentage of the total annual cost.

The existing jurisdiction of the Leasehold Valuation Tribunal will be extended to include determination of whether a particular sum is payable on the terms of the lease, and to decide whether consultation requirements have been met,[424] though implemen-tation of this reform will depend upon future legislation to rationalise all the jurisdic-tions of those tribunals.

3. Additional controls of forfeiture

These are described above.[425]

4. Accounting for leaseholders' monies

The Government is concerned that leaseholders[426] should receive clear and transparent information about how their service charge money is held and how it is to be spent. A number of possible changes to accounting requirements imposed on ground land-lords[427] are being considered and consulted upon, though this issue is not included in the Bill introduced in December 2000.[428] It is undoubtedly difficult to strengthen the machinery against fraud, and to enable leaseholders to determine whether they are receiving good value for money, without placing undue burdens on reputable ground landlords.

One issue is how to protect money paid into service charge accounts and sinking funds. The current law requires that service charge payments should be held in a trust account,[429] which provides protection against insolvency. However it is often impossible to discover details of what sums are held where sums are held in a general client account. Hence it is likely that a separate designated account will be required for each property or group of properties.[430] There will be a cost in reduced interest receipts, but this should be modest in comparison with the benefit of ensuring greater transparency. Consideration is being given to the likely costs and about how to define a group of service charge payers.

Another likely outcome is a requirement to supply a summary of the calculation of the service charge in a prescribed form annually with a right for leaseholders to with-hold payments until proper information is provided. The basic change is that this

---

[424] Commonhold and L.Ref. Bill 2000 cl.140 inserting L.T.A. 1985 s.27A.
[425] See above pp. 375–376.
[426] White Paper Part II para.4.1.69 seeks views on its application to short term rack renting residential tenants.
[427] White Paper Part II paras.4.1.64–68 seek views about the application of the proposals to local authorities, registered social landlords, residential management companies, and managers employed by ground landlords.
[428] White Paper Part II 2.2.2–3, 4.1.1–15.
[429] L.T.A. 1987 s.42.
[430] White Paper Part II paras.4.1.16–20 (offence with level 4 fine proposed).

information would have to be supplied without the leaseholders having to ask. Under the current law leaseholders find it difficult to obtain even most basic financial information from the ground landlord, many leaseholders are unaware of their rights to financial information, and those who are clued up may still encounter difficulties in enforcing their rights. Ground landlords and leaseholders would all benefit from a requirement to provide detailed information. So it is proposed that a ground landlord should have to give leaseholders an annual service charge statement, showing costs incurred (with large items according to percentage of total stated separately), income and the balance at the end of the year.[431] A statement should be provided annually. The existing six-month time limit would apply.[432] Detailed rules about the form of balance sheets and the provision of greater freedom for the ground landlord of small blocks will be set out in regulations after appropriate consultation.[433] There is also an issue about how much information one leaseholder is entitled to about the service charge arrears of a neighbour.[434] A further proposal to assist in the reconciliation of accounts is that leaseholders should have a right of access to the statement of account at the bank and other supporting documentation including insurance details.[435] Rights to documentation should be exercisable at any time on 21 days notice, and not just (as at present) immediately after receiving a summary. Access to insurance policies could be required without a prior request for information about the cover.[436] There would be a right to a photocopy and to check this against the original document.[437] Criminal sanctions will be imposed,[438] but a more serious threat may be the removal of the right to enforce service charge payments until proper information has been provided.

Clarification of the responsibilities of auditors is required. Certificates of information requested by a leaseholder must currently be given by a qualified accountant (except in the case of small blocks), and this requirement of certification would be maintained for the new service charge statements. This does not, and will not, involve a rigorous audit, particularly as there is a separate right to a thorough audit. Leaseholders are often unaware of the limits of this procedure, and it is proposed that the certificate signed by the accountant should include a statement of the limits of the certification process.[439]

M. ADMINISTRATION CHARGES: PROPOSED CONTROLS

The Government proposes a new power to control administration charges payable by residential tenants.[440] An administration charge will be an amount payable by a tenant

---

[431] Replacement of L.T.A. 1985 ss,21–28 is proposed by White Paper Part II paras.4.1.21–23.

[432] White Paper Part II paras.4.1.47–50.

[433] White Paper Part II paras.4.1.31–36.

[434] White Paper Part II paras.4.1.51–54.

[435] White Paper Part II paras.4.1.24–37.

[436] White Paper Part II paras.4.1.55–56.

[437] White Paper Part II paras.4.1.57–58.

[438] White Paper Part II paras.4.1.59–4.1.63

[439] White Paper Part II paras.4.1.38–46.

[440] Commonhold and L.Ref. Bill 2000 cl.141 and sch.10; White Paper Part II paras.3.V.15–17. For previous consultation see *Analysis* para.57. Landlords and leases affected will be widely defined.

[441] Commonhold and L.Ref. Bill 2000 sch.10 para.1(4).

[442] A subsequent agreement cannot determine how to determine this.

of a dwelling as part of or in addition to the rent directly or indirectly for grants of approvals, the provision of information or documents, or the failure to make a payment by a due date. There will be power to amend this definition by regulations.[441] The proposed controls will apply where the sum is in the discretion of the landlord or a reasonable sum, but controls will not apply if the sum is specified in the lease[442] or is calculated in accordance with a formula specified in the lease. Nor will the statutory procedure negate an arbitration agreement or other provision for determination by an arbitral tribunal. A sum will only payable to the extent that it is reasonable and the tribunal also has power to determine whether the sum is due under the lease.[443] It will be open to a leaseholder, or short-term residential tenant,[444] to refer a charge which cannot be agreed[445] to a Leasehold Valuation Tribunal for a determination of its reasonableness. A number of consequential amendments are needed to other statutory schemes so that they refer to administration charges—levying an unreasonable administration charge will be a ground for the appointment of a manager,[446] information requirements currently applying to rent demands will be amended to include administration charges[447] and the provision of an address for service of notices.[448]

N. INSURANCE RENTS

All buildings need insurance, and in communal blocks it is normal for the landlord to insure the entire block, with individual leaseholders reimbursing their share of the premium. Common law principles provided very little control: landlords had no implied obligation to shop around for the cheapest quote,[449] and indeed many landlords made a profit from the commission paid by insurers.[450] However the landlord's choice may not provide the best value or adequate cover and leaseholders have a right of challenge before the court or a Leasehold Valuation Tribunal.[451] Leaseholders have a number of rights such as to request a summary of the cover, to inspect the original insurance policy, and to require notification of possible claims.[452]

The most important right is the leaseholders' right to challenge the ground landlord's choice of insurer. The wording inserted in 1987[453] proved to be defective and *Berrycroft Management Co. Ltd.* v. *Sinclair Gardens Investments (Kensington) Ltd.*[454] identified a

---

[443] Commonhold and L.Ref. Bill 2000 sch.10 paras.2–3.
[444] Including a statutory tenant.
[445] Payment will not count as an admission.
[446] L.T.A. 1987 s.24(2)(ab), 24(2B), s.46(3).
[447] L.T.A. 1987 s.47.
[448] L.T.A. 1987 s.48.
[449] *Berrycroft Management Co. Ltd.* v. *Sinclair Gardens Investments (Kensington) Ltd.* [1997] 1 E.G.L.R. 47 C.A. (obiter); *Bandar Property Holdings Ltd.* v. *J.S. Darwen (Successors) Ltd.* [1968] 2 All E.R. 305; *Havenridge* v. *Boston Dyers Ltd.* [1994] 2 E.G.L.R. 73 C.A.
[450] But see *Williams* v. *Southwark L.B.C.* [2000] Times April 5th, Lightman J. (loyalty bonus had to be passed on, but not payment to landlord for administering claims).
[451] L.T.A. 1985 s.30A and sch., inserted by L.T.A. 1987 s.43(1).
[452] L.T.A. 1985 sch. paras.2–7.
[453] L.T.A. 1987 sch. para.8.
[454] [1997] 1 E.G.L.R. 47, 49–52, Beldam L.J.; N. Roberts [2000] *Conv.* 307.
[455] L.T.A. 1985 sch. para.8 as amended by H.A. 1996 s.83(2).

number of the drafting defects in the original provisions. A redraft operates as from September 1997[455] to improve the legislation. The power applies where the leaseholder is required to insure the dwelling with an insurer nominated by the landlord. Powers arose where the insurance was unsatisfactory in any respect or the premiums were excessive. Jurisdiction is now shared by the court and a Leasehold Valuation Tribunal. A ground landlord can be required to nominate another insurer. However neither can act in relation to a premium which is agreed or admitted, is subject to an arbitration agreement, or after a determination by a court or arbitral tribunal. Unfortunately defects remain: it is arguable that the schedule does not cover the ground landlord's power to approve the tenant's choice nor where a *management company* effects insurance rather than the landlord.[456] There is also power to vary leases to ensure that there are adequate insurance provisions.[457]

Proposals to improve rights to information are considered above.[458]

[456] L.T.A. 1985 sch. para.4 applies to insurance effected by a superior landlord; para.9 provides some exceptions in the public sector.

[457] See above p. 454.

[458] See above pp. 463–464.

17

COMMONHOLD

Reform proposals. Sites for commonhold developments. Registration of commonholds. Rectification. Applicants, consents and documentation. Registration of a commonhold. Developments and conversions. Commonhold units. Communal management structures. Commonhold associations. Documentary constitution. Variations. Common parts and communal management. Finances. Commonhold assessments. Insolvency. Termination.

A. REFORM PROPOSALS

Commonhold is proposed[1] as a means of reconciling the freehold ownership of parts of land with common arrangements for the management of the whole. Although it could be used for commercial blocks or industrial estates,[2] the primary aim of the reform is to improve the position of residential leaseholders in blocks of flats. The main advance lies in the tenurial reform which will allow for the creation of freehold flats, but this will be associated with the management potential of positive covenants[3] and a commonhold association providing a more cohesive corporate management vehicle.[4] There is a broad consensus about the need for reform, which is, indeed, self-evident.

1. Strata titles abroad

England and Wales are the only countries retaining leasehold schemes for flats. Proposals to provide a tailor-made scheme can be traced back to the Wilberforce Committee on positive covenants affecting land,[5] which recommended an optional system similar to the strata title legislation of New South Wales. Similar schemes operate throughout Australasia,[6] Asia, South Africa and (as condominium laws) in North America.[7] France[8] has a regime of copropiété to regulate buildings in communal ownership, the basic characteristic of which is that the scheme is imposed on the owners of

---

[1] Commonhold and Leasehold Reform Bill 2000; *Commonhold and Leasehold Reform—Draft Bill and C.P.* (Cm 4843, August 2000), hereafter "White Paper". Copies are available electronically at <www.housing. detr.gov.uk/information/consult/cm4843/index.htm> and on the Lord Chancellor's Department website <www.open.gov.uk/lcd>

[2] White Paper Part I para.1.3.1.

[3] White Paper Part I paras.1.2.1–4.

[4] See below pp. 481–484.

[5] Cmnd 2719, 1965.

[6] A.H. Walstab [1986] *Conv.* 222 (Victoria).

[7] J.E. Cribbet (1962) 61 *Mich.L.R.* 1207, 1217; see also L. Charlebois [1997] *Conv.* 169.

[8] J. Hill [1985] *Conv.* 537; L.N. Brown (1963) 60 *L.S.G.* 35; J. Bell, S. Boyron & S. Whittaker, *Principles of French Law* (Oxford U.P., 1998) 296–298.

parts of any building sub-divided into independent units. Many other civilian systems have adopted a similar regime. The English tradition has been to allow the commercial market to drive development practice and so commonhold is to be based on the common law precedents favouring a voluntary scheme.

This is unfortunate because the market has so signally failed to work adequately, and it would be better to impose a legal regime in the French fashion. Scotland is already far in advance of our property law, so the proposals of the Commonhold and Leasehold Reform Bill 2000 are restricted to England and Wales.[9]

2. Commonhold proposals for England and Wales

New Labour arrived in office in 1997 with a manifesto commitment:

> "to introduce 'Commonhold', a new form of tenure for blocks of flats and other multi-unit properties, under which occupiers would own their own units individually and, through an association, own and manage common parts collectively. For new developments, this will provide a complete answer to many of the problems which have plagued flat-owners over the decades."[10]

Conversion of existing leasehold properties to commonhold will require the agreement of all interested parties. So there will be many unable or unwilling to convert to commonhold. The radical reforms to the leasehold scheme (radical at least to those drafting the Manifesto) contained in Part II of the 2000 Bill and described in the previous chapter of this book, are intended as a supplement to the commonhold scheme for the protection of such existing and future leaseholders. Considerable political momentum has been injected into the reform process by the emphasis being placed by the Government on auditing the fulfilment of its manifesto commitments, and this gives cause to hope for an end to the long-standing failure to commit Parliamentary time to this important topic.

Many past reports have been shelved after abortive consultations. After the report of Lord Wilberforce[11] the term "commonhold" emerged from an inter-departmental working group chaired by the then Law Commissioner, Trevor Aldridge[12]; this report was followed under the Thatcher and Major administrations by three rounds of consultation on details—in 1987,[13] 1990,[14] and again in July 1996. That last round consisted of a Consultation Paper on *Commonhold* issued by the Lord Chancellor's Department with a draft Bill,[15] though the proposals proved too controversial[16] to secure enactment before the 1997 election.

[9] Commonhold and L.Ref. Bill 2000 cl.156. The Crown will be bound: cl.60.

[10] White Paper, Ministerial Foreword, v.

[11] See above n. 5.

[12] *Commonhold* Cm 179 (1987) ("the Aldridge Report"); T. Aldridge [1986] *Conv.* 361.

[13] *Commonhold—a C.P.*, Cm 79 (1987); C. Owen [1988] 18 *L.S.G.* 25; C. Bell (1988) 132 *S.J.* 285.

[14] *Commonhold* Cm 1345 (1990); H.W. Wilkinson [1991] *Conv.* 70, 170; A. Stewart (1992) 136 *S.J.* 826; C. Owen [1991] 45 *L.S.G.* 26; S. Bright [1994] *Conv.* 211, 221; D.W. Williams [1996] 37 *E.G.* 128.

[15] *Commonhold C.P.* (July 1996).

[16] Opposition came e.g. from the Church Commissioners: R. Hudson [1992] *N.L.J.* 1616.

3. Commonhold and Leasehold Reform Bill 2000

If the proposals published in August 2000 were over-hyped as "the biggest overhaul of English and Welsh property law for more than a century",[17] they nevertheless represent the fruits of careful and protracted consultation extending throughout the period since New Labour came to office in 1997.[18] As the Ministerial foreword puts it, the provisions "take account of pioneering work over the years by the Law Commission and of more recent detailed discussion with leaseholders, landlords, property professionals and academics."[19] After consultation, aimed at fine-tuning of details, the Bill itself reached the House of Lords at the end of 2000, with intention that it should become law by spring 2001.[20]

B. SITES FOR COMMONHOLD DEVELOPMENT

1. Freehold basis of the block

Commonhold will be a collective form of the familiar freehold tenure, with its essence being the acquisition by unit-holders of titles unlimited in time, so that the developer who constructs the site must originally hold a perpetual freehold estate. When a commonhold is registered the title must be absolute.[21] Another restriction which follows is that it will not be possible to develop leasehold land as a commonhold.[22] However, the policy reasons against long leasehold homes do not necessarily apply to businesses, and so consideration is being given to the desirability of a special regime for commercial leaseholds in common with a provision for the scheme to terminate on the fixed date when the underlying leasehold estate is due to end.[23] Whatever the commercial attractions of this form of development, it would adulterate the conceptual purity of the commonhold.

2. Consents from those interested in the land

Registration will only be possible of a complete parcel of land including all subsidiary interests, so that registration will subsume the entire estate in fee simple absolute in possession free from incumbrances. The registered proprietors of the freehold estate will apply for the commonhold registration.[24] Consents will be needed from all other parties interested in the land,[25] including in particular a registered proprietor of an estate in any part of the development site, any person with an interest in the land or any part of it, the registered proprietor of any charge, any cautioner, and any other person falling

---

[17] Independent, August 22nd 2000.
[18] *Leasehold Reform: The Way Forward* (D.E.T.R., December 1999) para.1.1.
[19] White Paper, Ministerial Foreword, v.
[20] December 20th 2000.
[21] Commonhold and L.Ref. Bill 2000 cl.2(3); White Paper Part I para.2.3.2.
[22] White Paper Part I para.2.3. Any existing lease will terminate.
[23] White Paper Part I paras.2.3.3–7.
[24] Commonhold and L.Ref. Bill 2000 cl.2; see further below pp. 471–472.
[25] Commonhold and L.Ref. Bill 2000 cl.3.

within prescribed classes. Regulations will also provide for many other aspects of a consent—the form, its effect, its proprietary effect, procedures for its withdrawal and its
eventual irrevocability. In some circumstances there will be a deemed consent, and in
others power for the court to dispense with a consent and to make ancillary orders.[26]

3.   Prohibition on commonhold with defeasible title

Defeasible titles will not support a commonhold registration (unless the person contin-
gently entitled consents to the registration) and this will rule out any conversion of
Victorian school sites[27] or any other land held with a contingent title.[28] Quite why this
should be is not clear. Surely land subject to a determinable fee simple is land in which
the person entitled on exercise of the right of reverter is a person interested in this land,
and it would be sufficient to provide that a person with a right of reverter is a person
who must consent to a commonhold registration.

4.   Avoidance of flying freeholds

In a simple case, the site for a commonhold development will be isolated from its neighbours, so that no part of it lies above or below non-commonhold land. For example a
block of flats often stands in its own grounds, with parking spaces and communal gardens. The whole point of a commonhold is to create a universe in which all obligations
are reciprocal. Relationships with neighbouring land can be dealt with by easements and
restrictive covenants. The requirement of the 1996 scheme that a commonhold should
relate to the division of a building has been dropped,[29] and there is to be no objection
to the inclusion of non-contiguous parcels of land.[30]

Conveyancing problems begin where there are flying freeholds, that is any part of
freehold land above another part. Positive covenants cannot run with freehold land.[31]
For this reason it is intended that no part of the commonhold should be over or under
any non-commonhold part of the development.[32] The Aldridge Committee scheme was
limited to a building with a suitable degree of structural independence based on a rule
of vertical division.[33] Current proposals are not neatly drafted, even allowing for the
difficulty of framing in words a precise test for a concept which is easy to explain. The
present draft states the test in this way: if any of the land is raised above ground level, all
of the land from ground level upwards must be subject to the same application.
However if the lower land is commonhold, higher parts can be added to it, provided that

---

[26] Commonhold and L.Ref. Bill 2000 cl.3(2)–(3). Jurisdiction is conferred by the High Court or any county
court by cl.63; but this may be subject to an allocation order.
[27] The School Sites Act 1841 provides for the site to be held under a determinable title with a reverter if the
school shuts; since the Reverter of Sites Act 1987, the reverter is equitable; see Sparkes, *N.L.L.* 68–70.
[28] Commonhold and L.Ref. Bill 2000 sch.2 para.3. White Paper Part I para.2.1.
[29] Draft Commonhold Bill 1996 cl.3(2); this was defined by cl.53 to include any form of structure.
[30] Draft Commonhold Bill 1996 cl.3(1); Commonhold and L.Ref. Bill 2000 cl.55.
[31] Sparkes *N.L.L.* 622–628.
[32] Associated commonholds will be allowed to exist in defiance of this rule; see below p. 471.
[33] Draft Commonhold Bill 1996 cl.3(3); this means detached or with a vertical division for adjoining property:
Draft Commonhold Bill 1996 cl.3(5).

the end result is that all land from ground level to the raised land is included.[34] As it stands the draft appears to be seriously defective as a statement of principle. Presumably the reference to ground level is to ensure that a reservation of mineral rights does not affect commonhold status, but what of a block built on a subterranean shopping precinct like Centre Point in London?

5.   Master and servant commonholds

The aim must be that a single commonhold association has control of a natural unit of communal management, but it may be a tricky problem to translate that simple principle into a tightly defined test applying to complex multi-purpose developments. Ticklish problems will arise where a single development includes both residential and commercial parts—flats and shops.[35] Each will have conflicting needs, but there has to be some stable basis for managing relations between the two parts, if only to deal with shared use of an access road and parking. After consultation it seems that the Government is content to rely on general property law to provide adequate rights of way and easements.[36]

C.   REGISTRATION OF A COMMONHOLD

The commonhold schemes of 1996[37] and 2000[38] are designed to make use of compulsory registration. Clause 1(1) of the 2000 Bill provides for registration of a freehold as an estate in commonhold land. It will remain commonhold so long as it is subject to a commonhold registration, and this in turn requires that there is a commonhold association and a commonhold community statement.[39] These various elements must now be explained.

1.   Applicants for registration

The commonhold association will be registered at the land registry. An application for a commonhold registration may be made by the registered proprietor of the freehold estate holding with an absolute title.[40] It could also be made by a person who has applied to be registered and has shown the right to absolute freehold title.[41] A commonhold registration may be made collectively by two or more people who each own part of the land provided that when their individual plots are added together they own collectively all

---

[34] Commonhold and L.Ref. Bill 2000, sch.2 para.1; White Paper Part I para.2.1.
[35] White Paper Part I para.3.3.
[36] White Paper Part I paras.3.3.4–6.
[37] Draft Commonhold Bill 1996 cl.1(6).
[38] Commonhold and L.Ref. Bill 2000 cls.2–10; White Paper Part I paras.1.3.2–3.
[39] Commonhold and L.Ref. Bill 2000 cl.1(1).
[40] Commonhold and L.Ref. Bill 2000 cl.1. This includes joint tenants, who are deemed to be a single owner: cl.55(3)–(4).
[41] Commonhold and L.Ref. Bill 2000 cl.2(3)(b).

the land with no one else interested in it. Registration will be refused if any part of the land is already included in a commonhold.[42]

2.   Consents to registration

As explained above[43] it will be necessary to obtain the consent of every person other than the registered proprietor with an interest in the land,[44] including in particular a registered proprietor of an estate in part of the land, any person interested in the land or any part of it, the registered proprietor of any charge, and any cautioner, along with any other person within prescribed classes. Indeed regulations will be made providing for many aspects of a consent—the required form, its effect, for binding successors, for withdrawal and irrevocability; in some circumstances there will be a deemed consent or power for the court to dispense with a consent and to make ancillary orders.[45] Where a consent is overlooked, the rights of that person will be a matter of competing priorities—the third party will usually lose his rights for failure to protect his interest by registration unless, that is, he has an overriding interest or he establishes a reason to rectify the register.[46]

3.   Constitution

The commonhold association must be formed before registration of the commonhold, since the applicant for registration must produce the certificate of incorporation of the commonhold association (with any alteration of it), and also its memorandum and articles of association.[47] The collective management of the development will be governed by a commonhold community statement, which must be prepared and executed in advance.

4.   Certification of compliance

The commonhold association must certify compliance with the requirements of the Bill[48] by:

> The memorandum and articles of association[49];
> The commonhold community statement; and
> The character of the land i.e. that it is not land which may not be a commonhold,[50] with the following categories of exclusions proposed at present:
> > Flying freeholds;[51]

---

[42] Draft Commonhold and L.Ref. Bill 2000 cl.2.
[43] See above p. 469.
[44] Commonhold and L.Ref. Bill 2000 cl.3; existing leases terminate: cls. 7(4), 9(3), (4). A leased tenant who ends his lease by consenting may be liable to any sub-tenant whose interest is lost: cl.10.
[45] Commonhold and L.Ref. Bill 2000 cl.3(2). Jurisdiction is conferred by the High court or any county court by cl.63; but this may be subject to an allocation order.
[46] White Paper Part I para.4.2.3; see further below pp. 473–474.
[47] Commonhold and L.Ref. Bill 2000 cl.2(2), sch.1 paras.2–4.
[48] Commonhold and L.Ref. Bill 2000 sch.1 para.7.
[49] Commonhold and L.Ref. Bill 2000 sch.3 para.2.
[50] Rectification could not cure a problem: White Paper Part I para.4.2.4.
[51] See above pp. 470–471.

Agricultural land—as defined by the Agriculture Act 1947 or within an agricultural holding or farm business tenancy;[52] and

School sites and other land with a defeasible title.[53]

If the certificate happens to be inaccurate the court would have power to rule on the effect of failure to comply with the statutory requirements.[54]

5. Registration

It may be convenient to list the documents required by the land registry[55]:

The prescribed application form;

The certificate of incorporation of the commonhold association (and any altered certificate);

The memorandum and articles of association of the commonhold association;

A commonhold community statement;

Any necessary consents; and

A certificate by the commonhold association.

After registration as a commonhold, the land registry will maintain a register, including the following prescribed details and copy documents[56]:

Details of the commonhold association;

Proprietors of the commonhold units;

Commonhold community statement;

Memorandum and articles of association; and

Any other documents which are filed.

Land registration rules will flesh out the details, both for registrations and for cancellations, and provide for fees.[57]

Registrations of variations to and the termination of a commonhold are considered below.[58]

6. Defective commonhold registration

Errors in a commonhold constitution or the application documents might invalidate a commonhold registration, but since it is important to limit the possibility of technical errors bringing down a commonhold the Government proposals contain extensive discussion of rectification,[59] and the stated policy is to ensure that the commonhold continues wherever this is possible. There will be power to apply to the court for an order rectifying the constitution of a commonhold—the memorandum and articles of

[52] Commonhold and L.Ref. Bill 2000 sch.2 para.2; Draft Commonhold Bill 1996 cl.2(3)–(4).
[53] Commonhold and L.Ref. Bill 2000 sch.2 para.3.
[54] Commonhold and L.Ref. Bill 2000 cl.6; White Paper Part I para.4.3.
[55] Commonhold and L.Ref. Bill 2000 cl.2(2), sch.1.
[56] Commonhold and L.Ref. Bill 2000 cl.5.
[57] Commonhold and L.Ref. Bill 2000 cl.62.
[58] See below p.484.
[59] White Paper Part I paras.4.1.1–9.

association of the commonhold association and the commonhold community state-ment[60]—but only on the ground that the documentation does not comply with the legal requirements. Only in the last resort of irreconcilable conflict with the statutory require-ments would the court order that the commonhold registration should not have occurred, in which case it could make consequential orders or award compensation.[61] There does not appear to be any power to vary documentation which makes defective provision for necessary matters such as service charges,[62] though surely such a power will prove to be essential? Reference should be made to the Consultation Paper for expla-nation of a range of issues associated with rectification.[63]

D. COMMONHOLD DEVELOPMENTS

1. Development mechanics

Any new flat development has three phases—(1) planning and construction, (2) the period after the sale of the first flat, when construction of other parts of the development may well be continuing (called "the transitional period") and (3) when all flats are sold and the development is handed over to the leaseholders. The current commonhold pro-posals are better tailored to this natural cycle of development than the 1996 draft Bill, which had adopted the Aldridge "built rule"—that a commonhold could only be set in place when the development on the ground had reached a viable stage of structural completion.[64] Registration of a commonhold would have established strata titles in the flats immediately though they would initially have been registered in the name of the developer/promoter.[65]

This model has been refined by the consultation process. The Parliamentary Bill pro-vides for a *transitional period* during which the land is registered as a commonhold, but without unit holders. [66] Initial registration of a new development would normally occur in this form,[67] when the transitional phase would last during the construction of the building condominium and until the first unit is sold. During this transitional period the developer will appear as registered proprietor but without any details of the propri-etors of commonhold units. A commonhold community statement will be necessary to secure commonhold registration and to show prospective purchasers of flats how com-munal management will be effected, but during the transitional period it will not be effective.[68] Prescribed aspects of the statutory scheme and of the memorandum and

---

[60] Commonhold and L.Ref. Bill 2000 cl.39; White Paper Part I para.4.2.

[61] Commonhold and L.Ref. Bill 2000 cl.6. The Registrar could not rectify of his own motion. In such a case there would be a liquidation under cl.53.

[62] Compare flat schemes; see above p. 454.

[63] White Paper Part I para.4.4.10.

[64] Draft Commonhold Bill 1996 cl.3(3); this would be defined by regulations.

[65] Draft Commonhold Bill 1996 cl.12.

[66] Commonhold and L.Ref. Bill 2000 cls.7–8.

[67] Commonhold and L.Ref. Bill 2000 cl.7(1); an immediate full registration will only occur if a request under cl.9(1)(b).

[68] Commonhold and L.Ref. Bill 2000 cl.7(2)(b).

articles of association of a commonhold association will also be frozen during this transitional period.[69]

The developer will be allowed to withdraw during this transitional period with the consent of all proprietors and of all others interested in the land.[70] Where development land has been pooled, but one or more of the developers wishes to withdraw unilaterally during the development process, the provisional view[71] is that the general termination procedure will have to be followed, with a termination statement providing for how the land is to be dealt with; it might reflect terms agreed between the developers or standard terms of the commonhold community statement, or a negotiated exit package; otherwise the court would have power to impose suitable terms.

2. The end of the transitional period

The commonhold will come into full operation when the first unit is sold and the unit-holder is registered as proprietor. The commonhold association will be registered without any application being necessary and the developer will be registered as proprietor of the unsold units. A second (unnamed) period lasts until all units have been sold, and during this period the developer has special rights to complete the development and to market unsold units. Development business is defined[72] to mean the completion or execution of works on the commonhold land and land which is or may be added to it or removed from it, the marketing of commonhold units, and the variation of the geographical scope of the commonhold, variation of the commonhold community statement, and the appointment and removal of directors of the commonhold association.[73] The rights will attach to the original developer and any successor, during the transitional period until the sale of the first unit and afterwards so long as he is registered as proprietor of any unit.[74] It will be permissible to include terms in the commonhold community statement requiring co-operation by the commonhold association and individual unit-holders for specified purposes.[75] The rights can be surrendered by notice given by the developer to the land registry,[76] and this should presumably be done when the completed development is "handed over" to the commonholders after the sale of the last unit.

3. Inaccurate construction

It is standard practice for builders to construct buildings that do not match the plans of their housing estate or leasehold flat development, and the same practice may be

---

[69] Commonhold and L.Ref. Bill 2000 cl.8(2), (3); i.e. those who consented to the application for registration.
[70] Commonhold and L.Ref. Bill 2000 cl.8(4), (5).
[71] Commonhold and L.Ref. Bill 2000 cls.41–46; White Paper Part I paras.3.4.1–8.
[72] Commonhold and L.Ref. Bill 2000 sch.4. There seems to be nothing (at least in the Bill) to prevent the inclusion of terms about matters not falling within this definition, though such additional terms would not be proprietary in character. However regulations may restrict the rights: cl.56(5).
[73] Commonhold and L.Ref. Bill 2000 cl.56.
[74] Commonhold and L.Ref. Bill 2000 cl.57.
[75] In the case of appointment and removal of directors, this is subject to the memorandum and articles of association of the company.
[76] Commonhold and L.Ref. Bill 2000 cl.56(6).

expected to continue with commonholds. In such cases, the estate documentation will have to be made to correspond to the physical construction by rectification of the register, or after application to the court[77] to authorise changes to the Commonhold Community Statement (if these cannot be agreed); there will be a presumption in favour of continuation of the commonhold.[78]

E.   CONVERSION TO COMMONHOLD

1.   Entitlement to convert

Existing leasehold schemes may be converted to a commonhold, though the scheme will be voluntary and conversion may be difficult in practice.

There will be nothing to prevent the indefinite continuation of existing leasehold schemes or indeed the creation of new ones. Hence professional reaction and the attitude of developers is critical to the success of the scheme, but some commentators feel they may be hostile. Will the cachet of freehold ownership give commonhold developments an edge in the market?

Consent to a conversion must be obtained from 100 per cent of the existing leaseholders and/or other owners of what would become units in the commonhold. Consent would also be needed from the freeholder and any one else interested in the land. So the sort of flat scheme suitable for conversion is one in which the freehold is vested in a flat management company representing the leaseholders collectively and all the leaseholders hold very long (999-year) leases. Here no purchase costs are involved so the conversion requires the goodwill of all concerned and preparedness to meet professional costs. Application will be made by the development company with the consent of all the leaseholders.[79]

In other cases the conversion will involve conversion costs. Suppose that the freehold is held by a ground landlord who collects ground rent and controls management and there is a mix of very long (999-year) and shorter (50 year) leases. This freehold has a value which resides outside the collective group of leaseholders. The leaseholders with very long leases are likely to want to convert to freehold ownership under a commonhold scheme since the cost to them will be very small, but those with shorter leases will have to pay a substantial premium to reach the equivalent of freehold ownership. Compulsory or negotiated enfranchisement will be a first step. Conversion cannot occur without the consent of the ground landlord, as freehold estate owner, and this will involve the acquisition of his rights. Thus conversion will require collective enfranchisement or purchase of the freehold by agreement.[80] There will be no power to dispense with any consent. This very high hurdle is justified, despite the fact that it will prevent many conversions, to maintain the principle that all unit-holders should be members of the commonhold association with mutual rights and duties.[81] The 1996

---

[77] White Paper Part I para.4.4.8.
[78] White Paper Part I paras.4.4.3–8.
[79] White Paper Part I paras.2.2.1–5. See also the Explanatory Notes to the 2000 Bill.
[80] White Paper Part I paras.1.3.5–7.
[81] White Paper Part I paras.2.2.1–3; para.2.2.4 refers to the problems arising from hybrid commonholds.

scheme was also based on the consent of those interested in the land, but if some consents were not forthcoming, the court would have had power to override the refusal of consent of up to 20 per cent of potential unit holders, provided that it is fair and reasonable to issue a dispensation. [82] Removal of this power from the 2000 draft suggests that the reactionary forces of the development lobby have once again succeeded.

Many of the difficulties of conversion could be reduced if the strict freehold basis of a commonhold was watered down for pre-existing schemes, though no doubt it is right to insist on freehold ownership of units for the future.

2.   Commercial conversions

Commercial leaseholders will have no special right to convert to commonhold so consent from all parties (including the landlord) will be essential. It is not intended that commercial leaseholders or rack renters would have rights to convert, except that short term residential tenants may benefit from collective pre-emption if they can meet the asking price.[83]

3.   Procedure for conversion

Conversion from an existing flat scheme may involve considerable adaption of the flat management company to turn it into a qualified commonhold association. Fewer changes should be needed as a development progresses from a right to manage, through collective enfranchisement to commonhold, since the corporate structures are broadly comparable but changes of membership will be required: the members of a right to manage company will be the participating leaseholders and the ground landlord, in an enfranchisement company the leaseholders participating in the purchase, and in a commonhold association all unit-holders. Where an existing scheme is converted, registration should proceed to a full commonhold with a request that there should be no transitional period.[84] From the moment of registration the leasehold interests will cease, the commonhold association will take control and the Commonhold Community Statement will regulate the management of the block.[85]

F.   COMMONHOLD UNITS

Commonhold is a new form of tenure for blocks of flats and other multi-unit properties, under which occupiers would own their own units individually whilst owning and managing common parts collectively through an association. Consideration of the individual aspect will precede that of the collective aspect.

1.   Nature of a unit

A commonhold must consist of at least two units. [86] This neutral term could describe flats in a block, houses on an estate, shops, or light industrial units on a commercial

---

[82] Draft Commonhold Bill 1996 cls.10–11.
[83] White Paper Part I para.2.3.6.
[84] Commonhold and L.Ref. Bill 2000 cl.9(1)(b). It is necessary to list all original unit-holders.
[85] White Paper Part I para.1.3.7.
[86] Commonhold and L.Ref. Bill 2000 cl.11(2).

estate.[87] A unit could be residential or commercial, but agricultural land will be excluded.[88] Division within a commonhold could be vertical (terraced houses) or horizontal (flats and maisonettes) or the units could be free-standing (detached houses or units on an industrial park). No doubt blocks of flats will be the most common type: each unit will consist of a flat in individual ownership probably including physically separate areas such as a garage or a small plot of individual garden. [89]

2.   Definition of the units

Individual units will be described and defined in extent by a commonhold community statement,[90] a document described in the superseded 1996 scheme as a commonhold declaration.[91] The statement (or "C.C.S.") lays down the internal constitution of the commonhold and, as has been explained,[92] this needs to be in place before the land can be registered as commonhold. One important function will be to specify the number of units and to define the geographical extent of each one. There will need to be a verbal description, which may for example define the flat as a given area but exclude particular walls or structures, or communal apparatus and appurtenances.[93] It will also be essential to use a plan of a prescribed type.

Many aspects of the commonhold community statement will be subject to variation, but clearly the basic integrity of the unit has to be protected against variations at the behest of the other flat owners. No one would buy a flat if the master bedroom could be commandeered by his neighbours. Just as important is the consideration that a potential buyer would not be able to find a lender prepared to accept the security of a unit that could be made to disappear by a vote of the other owners in the block. So the geographical integrity of the units laid down in the commonhold community statement is guaranteed by the provision that a unanimous vote would be required for any reduction in the size of a unit (including therefore the vote of the unit-holder affected).[94] In order to protect a lender, any change to a commonhold community statement which redefines the extent of a unit may not be made unless the lender (that is the registered proprietor of a legal charge secured on that unit) consents, in writing and in advance, to the change. There would be power for the court to rule that a variation should be allowed without that consent. When a change is authorised, the charge will be enlarged or reduced automatically to match the extent of the redefined unit. [95]

3.   Units during the development process

Where a new development is built, the site will be registered at some stage during the

---

[87] White Paper Part I para.1.3.1. For earlier proposals see Draft Commonhold Bill 1996 cl.1.

[88] Commonhold and L.Ref. Bill 2000 sch.2 para.2; Draft Commonhold Bill 1996 cl.2(3)–(4).

[89] Commonhold and L.Ref. Bill 2000 cl.11(3)(d); White Paper Part I para.1.3.4. However, it is not necessary for a unit to form part of a building at all: cl.11(4).

[90] Commonhold and L.Ref. Bill 2000 cl.11(2), (3).

[91] Draft Commonhold Bill 1996 cl.1(6). The form would be prescribed and the registrar required to check that formalities were satisfied.

[92] See above p. 472.

[93] Commonhold and L.Ref. Bill 2000 cl.11(3)(b)–(c); White Paper Part I para.1.3.8.

[94] See further below p. 486.

[95] Commonhold and L.Ref. Bill 2000 cl.22–23.

construction as a commonhold under the proprietorship of the developer, but without at that stage having any separate units. This is described as the transitional phase. When construction work is completed to a sufficient degree, the developer will sell the first unit and the first buyer's title to that unit will be registered, bringing to an end the transitional period. All the units will be registered at that time, though at first the developer will continue to hold most of them, and it is only when a majority of the units have been sold that the unit-holders collectively will be able to dominate the management of the commonhold.[96]

4.   Freehold basis of unit-holding

The person registered as proprietor of an individual flat is described as a unit-holder.[97] Commonhold will facilitate the freehold ownership of units, since the whole point is that the ownership of the unit-holder will be perpetual. This reform will end the problem of leasehold flats with wasting terms, provided only that developers choose to adopt the commonhold system. Enfranchisement rights will be unnecessary. The scheme of the Bill is to treat both a commonhold and unit as a freehold estate, albeit a special kind of commonhold variant of the common law estate, a scheme which enables the Bill to get by with trivial amendments to the existing legislation.[98]

The year 2000 proposals compare very favourably with the complexity of the 1996 scheme.[99] That proposed to create a new kind of estate called a commonhold, being a freehold with special statutory attributes. Normal property rules would have been amended to preclude dealings with parts of units, adverse possession and prescription in order to preserve the boundaries and rights delineated in the commonhold constitution. The estate was potentially perpetual but the peculiarities of the liquidation regime proposed at the time for commonhold associations would have left the ownership of the unit liable to terminate on the start of the liquidation process—for example when the block had reached the end of its useful life and had to be knocked down—at which time rights in the land would have been replaced by a share in the assets of the association.[100] This scheme has been dropped as a result of the most recent consultation process.

5.   Transactions with units

Free transferability will be inherent in the nature of a commonhold unit and it will not be permissible for the commonhold constitution to impose any restriction on sales, gifts, dealings, or any transmission by law, though dealings must relate to the whole unit and sub-division will not be allowed.[101] Units will be subject to normal compulsory purchase procedures.[102] Transfer of a unit will have implications for the membership of

---

[96] See above pp. 474–475.
[97] Commonhold and L.Ref. Bill 2000 cl.1(3). Entitlement to registration is sufficient: cl.12. Joint owners are provided for by cl.13.
[98] Commonhold and L.Ref. Bill 2000 sch.5; there are minor amendments to prevent dispositions of part of a unit, e.g. by a mortgage-lender. The Bill makes use of property, registration and company law definitions: cl.66(3).
[99] Draft Commonhold Bill 1996 cl.2.
[100] Draft Commonhold Bill 1996 cl.2(6).
[101] Commonhold and L.Ref. Bill 2000 cl.15, 21.
[102] Commonhold and L.Ref. Bill 2000 cl.58. This may relate to part: cl.21(3).

the commonhold association[103] and, therefore, any transfer of a commonhold unit must be notified to the commonhold association by the new unit-holder. Regulations will lay down a time limit, a form of notice, and the consequences of failure to give notice.[104]

There will be a right to create a mortgage or charge of a unit.[105] A lender with a legal security has special rights to object to a change in the commonhold constitution.[106] Any mortgage must relate to a whole unit and not to any part. [107]

Interests other than mortgages may also be created, but only with the consent and participation of the commonhold association.[108]

6. Leases

Unless steps were taken to avoid this danger, a commonhold scheme could easily degenerate into a quasi-leasehold scheme. A developer might, for example, sub-let all the flats to a subsidiary company, which could then grant long sub-leases to individual purchasers. An outright ban on the grant of long leases is needed to prevent leasehold structures re-emerging under the umbrella of a commonhold. A clearly defined interest in participation in the doings of the commonhold association is needed, along with a clear responsibility for the payment of assessments. Sale will be the only means of realisation of the capital value of the unit.[109] Under the 1996 draft Bill, leases were to be limited to 25 years,[110] leaving a unit-holder free to exploit his unit by a short-term, rackrental, letting.

Restrictions on leasing are thus an integral part of the commonhold scheme, though varying according to whether the scheme is residential or non-residential.[111] A term of years absolute in a commonhold unit will only be allowed if it complies with prescribed conditions. Letting of commonhold units will be restricted to short-term lets for a limited period at a rack rent.[112] Full details are not yet available, but in due course regulations will prescribe any special terms that should be incorporated in sub-lettings and also on the maximum duration that will be allowed—surely this should be 21 years in line with the normal definition of a long lease?[113] Terms of excessive length may be cut down to fit within the scheme. Regulations will govern the terms of tenancies, including

---

[103] See below pp. 482–483.

[104] Commonhold and L.Ref. Bill 2000 cl.15(3)–(4).

[105] Commonhold and L.Ref. Bill 2000 cl.20(1); however this is subject to the restriction on leasing, so a legal charge should be used.

[106] See below p. 484.

[107] Commonhold and L.Ref. Bill 2000 cl.31; any sale by a lender is subject to this restriction but compulsory purchase is an exception by cls.17(3), 58.

[108] Commonhold and L.Ref. Bill 2000 cl.16(3)–(5); cl.16(4) requires a unanimous vote in favour of the transaction.

[109] White Paper Part I para.2.4.3. Leases pre-dating the commonhold registration will terminate.

[110] Cls.2(3), 13.

[111] Commonhold and L.Ref. Bill 2000 cl.17. A residential scheme is one where the commonhold community statement requires it to be used only for residential purposes: cl.17(5).

[112] White Paper Part I para.2.4

[113] White Paper Part I para.2.4.4.

providing for the payment of service charges contributions by tenants, and may vary any other provision of landlord and tenant law.[114]

7.   Sub-letting in commercial commonholds

Commercial developments (or more strictly non-residential ones) raise different considerations, since there is no policy reason to oppose long leasehold interests and no enfranchisement rights. A special regime for commercial commonholds will allow the letting of units, and a future possibility is the creation of commonholds of land with leasehold title, with a provision for termination on a fixed date when the underlying leasehold estate ended.[115]

G.   COMMUNAL MANAGEMENT STRUCTURES

Just as a leasehold scheme requires a flat management company, so a corporate vehicle to be called a commonhold association will be required for communal ownership, management, and decision-making within a commonhold.

1.   The 1996 model commonhold association

The commonhold association envisaged by the 1996 draft Bill would not have been a registered company, but a new institutional structure was to be created. On the basis that the association would not be able to trade and would lack private investors, it was argued that streamlined company procedures would be suitable for regulating the relationships of the owners within the block, with only a side glance needed at the interests of outside creditors. It was proposed to establish the commonhold association automatically on registration of a commonhold,[116] with automatic membership, voting rights, and obligations, for every unit-holder,[117] though it would have been necessary to establish the documentary framework of the corporate constitution before seeking registration. The association itself would have maintained a register of members, mortgage-lenders secured on units, and tenants,[118] but some duplication of the land register was inevitable since voting rights would have followed automatically from a registration of a purchase of a unit on the development.[119]

Departure from the Companies Act involved a considerable legislative overhead— including a new commonhold constitution register, ultra-vires rule, and investigations regime.[120] A tailor-made regime of limited liability was also on the agenda: the liability of the commonhold association for debts would have been unlimited, but individual unit holders would not have been liable beyond their proper proportion of the overall debt. Normal execution would have been prohibited,[121] so that a creditor could only

---

[114] Commonhold and L.Ref. Bill 2000 cl.19. By cl.59 this also applies to a spouse with a matrimonial home right.
[115] Commonhold and L.Ref. Bill 2000 cl.18; White Paper Part I paras.2.3.3–7.
[116] Draft Commonhold Bill 1996 cl.12.
[117] Draft Commonhold Bill 1996 cl.1(7).
[118] Draft Commonhold Bill 1996 cl.15(1), sch.5 para.13.
[119] Draft Commonhold Bill 1996 cl.15(4), (5).
[120] Draft Commonhold Bill 1996 respectively cl.16 and sch.3, cl.48, cl.28, and cl.28 and sch.7.
[121] Draft Commonhold Bill 1996 cl.27.

enforce a debt by the appointment of a commonhold administrator.[122] A unique liquidation regime was proposed based on irretrievable insolvency, but this was heavily criticised.[123]

Debate about the merits of the new scheme may well proceed by comparison with the defects of these discarded proposals.

2. The 2000 model commonhold association

The new proposals have opted for a conventional company—the private company limited by guarantee, with a member's guarantee of £1.[124] It will be registered at Companies House in the usual way,[125] and regulations will provide for a distinctive form of name.[126] This is a much more conventional structure involving less legislative regulation. However, as the White Paper says:

> "a commonhold association will be an unusual type of company. It will consist of members who are only members because of their property ownership within the commonhold development. The members will be liable for the sum of the guarantee (expected to be a nominal sum of one pound) on the winding up the company. The object to the company will be to manage the commonhold development, including its maintenance and insurance".[127]

Rules for naming commonhold associations will be prescribed.[128]

A feature of the scheme will be the considerable degree of regulation of the framework of the company, intended to ensure that the vehicle used is suitable in all cases and to facilitate a smooth transition from right to manage company through collective enfranchisement to commonhold association. The association will have a normal set of memorandum and articles of association, but a standard set will be prescribed by the Lord Chancellor with only a limited scope for variation of this model. The constitution of a commonhold association will be regulated partly by its memorandum and articles of association,[129] partly by the commonhold legislation, and partly by regulations prescribing some of the contents.[130] The memorandum and articles will have to be registered when the commonhold is formed[131] and any alterations will also require registration.[132] The company will be formed, or at least adapted, for the purpose of managing commonhold land and its objects will have to include the exercise of the functions of a commonhold association.[133]

---

[122] Draft Commonhold Bill 1996 cls.29–31.
[123] Draft Commonhold Bill 1996 cl.32; L Crabb [1996] *Conv.* 283.
[124] Commonhold and L.Ref. Bill 2000 cl.33.
[125] White Paper Part I para.1.3.1.
[126] Commonhold and L.Ref. Bill 2000 sch.3 para.16.
[127] White Paper Part I para.3.5.4.
[128] Commonhold and L.Ref. Bill 2000 sch.3 para.16.
[129] Normal rules apply by Commonhold and L.Ref. Bill 2000 sch.3 para.4, except for Companies Act 1985 ss.2(6)–(7), 3, 8. If a memorandum is altered by special resolution, the period for challenge must have expired and any challenge must have been resolved before commonhold registration can proceed: Commonhold and L.Ref. Bill 2000 sch.3 para.4(2).
[130] Commonhold and L.Ref. Bill 2000 cl.28, sch.3, paras. 2, 3.
[131] Commonhold and L.Ref. Bill 2000 cl.2(2), sch.1 para.4.
[132] Commonhold and L.Ref. Bill 2000 sch.3 para.3.
[133] Commonhold and L.Ref. Bill 2000 cl.33(1)(a). Objects are defined by cl.66(1).

Membership of the commonhold association will be coincident with the ownership of units: only unit-holders will be allowed to be members and conversely membership will be imposed automatically after acquisition of the ownership of a unit. A buyer of a flat should be entered in the register as soon as practicable after the purchase and the membership of the former owner will cease when he sells his unit, without affecting accrued liabilities. Joint unit-holders should nominate one of their number as a member of the association; otherwise it will be the first named proprietor, though the court will have power to substitute another.[134] These restrictions on membership will apply from the time that the first flat is sold.[135] During the transitional period—between initial registration of the land as commonhold and the sale of the first unit—the developer is the only member, apart from the promoters, and the full link between membership of the association and unit-holding therefore dates from the first sale.

Modern company law allows a commercial company to acquire its own shares, subject to disclosure and investor protection measures, but a commonhold association will not be allowed to own units to prevent a small group of unscrupulous people gaining control of an entire development.[136]

3. Commonhold community statement

This is the document which will lay down the mutual scheme of regulation between the unit-holders, making provision for the rights and duties of a commonhold association and the unit-holders,[137] and replacing the commonhold declaration of the 1996 scheme. A form for it will be prescribed and so will many of the contents,[138] but there also needs to be a degree of flexibility to allow for unique features of a particular development, for example a sheltered housing component.[139] It seems that the articles of association will regulate the corporate structure whereas the commonhold community statement should regulate the property law aspects of the development—in particular the inter-relationship of all the unit-holders. However, the division is artificial and there is no good reason to require three separate documents. Surely the three parts could be included in a single constitution? The likely terms are sketched below.[140]

4. Control by the members

Voting structures and the size of the majorities required will be set out either in the memorandum and articles of association of the company or in the commonhold community statement; the former seems more appropriate.[141]

Very often a vote will be needed to decide upon a particular matter. A "voting provision" is any statutory provision which requires a vote of a commonhold association to

---

[134] Commonhold and L.Ref. Bill 2000 sch.3 para.7–8. A person becomes a unit-holder as soon as he is *entitled* to be registered as proprietor: cl.12.

[135] Commonhold and L.Ref. Bill 2000 sch.3 para.7; rules in Companies Act 1985 s.22 are disapplied.

[137] Commonhold and L.Ref. Bill 2000 cl.30(1)–(3); White Paper Part I para.1.3.2.

[138] Commonhold and L.Ref. Bill 2000 cl.31(4), (9); regulations will be made under c.25.

[139] Commonhold and L.Ref. Bill 2000, sch.3, para. 9; White Paper Part I para.1.3.2.

[140] See below pp. 486–487.

[141] Commonhold and L.Ref. Bill 2000 cl.30(1)–(3); White Paper Part I para.1.3.2.

be passed unanimously[142] or with a specified percentage of members voting in favour. Every member must be given a chance to vote, under relevant provisions in the memorandum and articles of association or the commonhold community statement, possibly in person, by post or by proxy.[143]

5. Directors

Large flat schemes are going to require a mechanism for day-to-day management through a board of directors, though the legislative scheme is not prescriptive in this regard. The 1996 scheme would have required a management committee to be set up for any scheme of six or more units.[144]

6. Variations

Lenders would not advance money on the basis of commonhold units unless the integrity of their unit was guaranteed. For this reason variation of the commonhold scheme will be closely limited. A change to a commonhold community statement which redefines the extent of a unit may not be made unless the registered proprietor of the charge of that unit consents in writing and in advance to the change or the court allows the change. The charge is automatically enlarged or reduced so that its new extent matches the redefined unit. [145]

Other amendments will be less controversial, and a degree of flexibility will be desirable, so a commonhold community statement will have to make provision for its amendment.[146] Any amendment will require registration, and in order to secure this the association will have to certify that it complies with the legislation.[147] The association will be free to acquire additional land,[148] but this will require the unanimous vote of all unit holders voting. Amendments may be needed to the commonhold community statement [149] and also the memorandum of association if the existing commonhold association does not extend to the new land. There will be a procedure for the merger of two commonholds, though only with unanimous consent, with a simplified registration procedure.[150] Special restrictions apply to alterations affecting the extent of the common parts[151] or of any commonhold unit.[152]

---

[142] This means passed by all of those voting: Commonhold and L.Ref. Bill 2000 cl.35 (except for a termination vote under cl.41).

[143] Commonhold and L.Ref. Bill 2000 cl.55.

[144] Draft Commonhold Bill 1996 sch.2 para.3.

[145] Commonhold and L.Ref. Bill 2000 cls.22, 23, 32.

[146] Commonhold and L.Ref. Bill 2000 cl.32.

[147] Commonhold and L.Ref. Bill 2000 cl.32(5).

[148] Commonhold and L.Ref. Bill 2000 cl.40 requires the consent of the holder of a registered charge or a court order. Compare Draft Commonhold Bill 1996 cl.18.

[149] Commonhold and L.Ref. Bill 2000 cl.32(7); the consent of the proprietor of any registered charge over the common parts will be required in accordance with cls.27, 29. Compare Draft Commonhold Bill 1996 c.15.

[150] Commonhold and L.Ref. Bill 2000 cl.40.

[151] Commonhold and L.Ref. Bill 2000 cl.29; a consent or court order is required.

[152] Commonhold and L.Ref. Bill 2000 cl.32(7); a consent of the proprietor of a registered charge or court order is required; see above p. 472.

H. COMMUNAL MANAGEMENT

1. Ownership of common parts

Common parts means every part of commonhold land which is not for the time being[153] a commonhold unit.[154] Any block of flats or other estate will contain common parts, in which unit-holders will have an interest through their membership of the commonhold association which holds the common parts, in addition to their direct interest in their own unit.[155]

These might include the structure of the block, communal services, and parts used in common—such as hallways, staircases, communal gardens and shared parking areas. Common parts will in general be available for common use between all unit-holders, subject to regulation by the commonhold community statement; this might, for example, allocate some areas as gardens, for parking, or other limited uses [156] and exclude unit holders from other parts such as a caretaker's flat.[157]

Legal title to the commonhold parts will be vested in the commonhold association by registration. During the transitional period title to the entire development will be registered in the developer, so the title of the commonhold association to registration accrues on the sale of the first unit.[158] This will be as soon as the commonhold is constituted if there is a conversion or in other cases with no transitional period.[159]

As is the case with the ownership of individual units, the 2000 model of the community association uses a conventional freehold with minor modifications, so that the changes required to conventional property law are minimal. It will be possible to sell common parts[160] or to buy additional land[161]; either transaction will require changes to the commonhold community statement, the consent of any lender secured on the land in issue, and registration.[162]

2. Management of common parts

The commonhold community statement will be required to deal with the use, insurance and repair of the common parts.[163]

Restrictions proposed is on mortgaging the common parts are drawn from the 1996 model[164] but modified in the 2000 version.[165] The association will have power to transfer all or any of the common parts or to create interests in them. Any charge existing over

---

[153] Alteration of a unit can therefore alter the extent of the common parts, but special restrictions apply to such alterations; see above p. 484.
[154] Commonhold and L.Ref. Bill 2000 cls.1(2), 7, 9; similar was Draft Commonhold Bill 1996 cl.4.
[155] White Paper Part I para.1.3.1.
[156] Commonhold and L.Ref. Bill 2000 cl.24.
[157] White Paper Part I para.3.2.3.
[158] Commonhold and L.Ref. Bill 2000 cl.7.
[159] Commonhold and L.Ref. Bill 2000 cl.9.
[160] Commonhold and L.Ref. Bill 2000 cl.26.
[161] Commonhold and L.Ref. Bill 2000 cl.29.
[162] Commonhold and L.Ref. Bill 2000 cls.27, 29.
[163] Commonhold and L.Ref. Bill 2000 cl.25.
[164] Draft Commonhold Bill 1996 cl.2(2).
[165] Commonhold and L.Ref. Bill 2000 cl.27.

the commonhold shall be extinguished at the time that the common parts are vested in the commonhold association[166]: it is quite likely that the developer will have charged the whole development to secure funds to finance the building work, but this charge will shrink when the common parts are removed. However new (post-registration) mortgages will be allowed, provided that they are legal, and provided that they are approved by a resolution of the commonhold association passed unanimously by all those voting in favour.[167]

3. Reciprocal obligations

A commonhold will be a sophisticated form of scheme of development,[168] that is a scheme covering an area of land where all the landowners are affected by a reciprocal[169] scheme of easements and covenants. Terms affecting a commonhold will be laid down in the commonhold community statement,[170] subject to some of the contents being prescribed by regulations.[171] Easements will be needed for a unit-holder to get access to the various parts of his unit—his flat, garage and garden plot—and to make use of communal services—electricity wires, telephone cables, water pipes, drains and so on. Use of the common parts will also require easements. Every right needed by one unit-holder will also be needed by his neighbours, so the easements need to be uniform (if not necessarily identical) and reciprocal. A second form of obligation the commonhold community statement should include is a scheme of restrictions—performing the functions of restrictive covenants in a normal scheme of development. It must regulate the use of units[172] and other restrictions will be to refrain from specified transactions (though freedom of sale and mortgaging is guaranteed[173]), to limit use, to restrict alterations and other work, not to cause a nuisance or annoyance, and to impose other controls on behaviour.[174]

Thus far the scheme is no different from that to be found on any housing estate, but the novel—indeed revolutionary—feature of commonholds is the facility with which positive covenants may be imposed. Existing property law rules do not permit positive covenants to run with freehold land, a rule recently confirmed in *Rhone* v. *Stevens*,[175] and one that has led to a proliferation of estate rentcharges on housing estates. Hence the need for leasehold flat schemes exploiting the more realistic rules for landlord and tenant covenants.[176] Commonholds are designed to secure the reciprocal enforceability of positive obligations. Provision must be made in the commonhold community statement for the insurance of individual units,[177] and also for their repair and maintenance,

---

[166] Commonhold and L.Ref. Bill 2000 cls.27(4); for this reason the consent of any lender will be required.
[167] Commonhold and L.Ref. Bill 2000 cl.28. White Paper Part I paras.3.1, 3.5.13–14.
[168] Sparkes *N.L.L.* 605–607.
[169] White Paper Part I para.1.3.11 and see also Draft Commonhold Bill 1996 sch.1.
[170] Commonhold and L.Ref. Bill 2000 cl.30(1); White Paper Part I para.1.3.2.
[171] Commonhold and L.Ref. Bill 2000 cl.31(4), (9); regulations will be made under cl.31.
[172] Commonhold and L.Ref. Bill 2000 cl.25.
[173] See above p. 479.
[174] Commonhold and L.Ref. Bill 2000 cl.30(3); terms may be prescribed: cls.30(a), 31.
[175] [1994] 2 A.C. 310 H.L.; Sparkes *N.L.L.* 622–625; White Paper Part I para.1.2.
[176] See below Chapter 28.
[177] The association will be required to insure against the negligence of its officers: White Paper Part I para.3.5.12.

though the two latter obligations may be imposed either on individual owners or on the commonhold association.[178] The statement will oblige the commonhold association to insure, to repair and to maintain the common parts.[179] There may be obligations to undertake works, to grant access[180], or to give notices. Much of the cost will fall within the commonhold assessment, and the positive obligation to make contributions will be enforceable against all present and future unit-holders.[181]

The scheme of rights will be created by the commonhold community statement, and this will be effective without further formality to create property interests in the land.[182] The basis of the obligations is that they will be proprietary rather than personal. All terms governing the unit created by the commonhold community statement—whether easements, rights, privileges and duties—will affect a new unit holder in the same way as it affected the former unit-holder,[183] but on a transfer a former unit-holder will be discharged for the future.[184] So there will be no nonsense like the old privity of contract liability of original leaseholders.[185]

4.   Communal management by the commonhold association

The association will exercise its powers so as to permit or facilitate the exercise of each unit-holder's rights and his enjoyment of the estate in his unit.[186] However, it will have to hold the balance between its various members. To this end, the commonhold association will be under a duty to ensure that the unit-holders comply with their obligations: it must use its powers for the purpose of preventing, remedying or curtailing a failure on the part of a unit-holder to comply with a requirement or duty imposed on him, but this will be counter-balanced by a discretion not to act in relation to a particular failure if the association considers that inaction will best establish or maintain harmonious relations within the commonhold.[187] Unit-holders may be given direct rights against other unit-holders,[188] and also where the association[189] fails in its duties including:

Compensation where a right is exercised;
Compensation for failure to comply with a duty;
Recovery of the cost of work which has not been carried out.

[178] Commonhold and L.Ref. Bill 2000 cls.14, 66.
[179] Commonhold and L.Ref. Bill 2000 cl.25.
[180] White Paper Part I para.1.3.11.
[181] Commonhold and L.Ref. Bill 2000 cl.30; White Paper Part I para.1.3.2.
[182] Commonhold and L.Ref. Bill 2000 cl.30(7).
[183] Commonhold and L.Ref. Bill 2000 cl.16. Regulations under cl.19 may provide for enforcement against tenants.
[184] Commonhold and L.Ref. Bill 2000 cl.16(2). This principle cannot be varied by agreement: cl.16(3). The discharge dates from the time of disposal and is not dependent upon registration: cl.16(4).
[185] See below pp. 776–778.
[186] Commonhold and L.Ref. Bill 2000 cl.34(1).
[187] Commonhold and L.Ref. Bill 2000 cl.34(2)–(3). These provisions also cover tenants of units, and by cl.59, also a spouse with a matrimonial home right.
[188] Commonhold and L.Ref. Bill 2000 cl.36.
[189] Commonhold and L.Ref. Bill 2000 cl.36.

5. Dispute resolution

Under 1996 brand commonhold, dispute resolution was left to the courts.[190] The 2000 model includes among the matters to be covered by regulations[191] the possibility of imposing internal dispute resolution, arbitration or other alternative dispute resolution technique, or require recourse to the courts and Leasehold Valuation Tribunals,[192] but there is as yet no indication of what proposals will be made. Superficially many of the controls of residential management discussed in the previous chapter[193] may be needed. It would be surprising if proposals did not emerge for an ombudsman,[194] arbitration,[195] or some specialised tribunal. Consumer protection is a common feature of second-generation commonhold schemes[196]: experience overseas shows the need for measures to protect commonhold owners and for alternative dispute resolution machinery.

I. COMMONHOLD FINANCES

1. Commonhold assessments

Some associations may have assets that can be used to provide a "trade income", but it is anticipated that most associations will depend upon the commonhold assessments levied on the unit holders to provide the income.[197] Provision for this will be one of the central matters to be included in the commonhold community statement.[198] It will provide for the service charge mechanism,[199] or, as it is now called, the "commonhold assessment"—no official explanation is provided for this change of nomenclature. The commonhold association will be required to make an assessment annually, estimating the income required in order to meet the expenses of the association, and it could also make supplementary estimates during the course of a year. Services to be charged for will be defined in the commonhold community statement, including insurance of the block and the units, repair of the block, maintenance of common parts,[200] and other services such as lifts or porterage according to the class of the development. There may in some cases be an obligation to create a reserve or sinking fund to build up a capital sum to meet major expenses in the future.[201]

The global sums will be allocated to individual units in accordance with a scheme contained in the commonhold community statement, perhaps based on floor area or

---

[190] On the unfortunate Australian experience see H.W. Wilkinson [1993] *Conv.* 97.
[191] Commonhold and L.Ref. Bill 2000 cl.36(2). See also White Paper Part I paras.1.3.1–10.
[192] White Paper Part I para.1.3.2.
[193] See above pp. 452–454.
[194] H.W. Wilkinson [1991] *Conv.* 97.
[195] A.J. Hawkins [1986] *Conv.* 12.
[196] L. Charlebois [1997] *Conv.* 169.
[197] White Paper Part I para.3.5.4.
[198] Commonhold and L.Ref. Bill 2000 cl.30(1)–(3); White Paper Part I para.1.3.2.
[199] Commonhold and L.Ref. Bill 2000 cl.37.
[200] Commonhold and L.Ref. Bill 2000 cl.25; compare Draft Commonhold Bill 1996 sch.5.
[201] Commonhold and L.Ref. Bill 2000 cl.38; White Paper Part I para.1.3.9. This will be released by cl.54 on a liquidation without a phoenix association.

council tax bands. Allocation rules must ensure that 100 per cent of the costs are apportioned between the units.[202]

The association will give notice of the amount required from unit-holders—under a prescribed notice procedure. Interest may be added to arrears, though the rate will be limited.[203] Forfeiture for non-payment of assessments will not be allowed.[204] All terms are proprietary as explained above.[205] It has also been explained above how the commonhold association will be under a (qualified) duty to compel unit-holders to comply with their obligations.[206] *Leaseholders* may challenge unreasonable service charge demands, and it may be assumed that the power to make regulations will be used to refer disputes between *commonholders* to a Leasehold Valuation Tribunal.[207]

2.   Accounting rules

Commonhold of the year 2000 model relies on standard accounting requirements of company law.[208]

3.   Insolvency

It is to be hoped that commonhold associations would not often become insolvent. The 1996 scheme had a tailor-made liquidation procedure[209] but this has been dropped under the weight of a barrage of responses[210] and academic criticism[211] in favour of the normal company law winding up procedure.[212]

Normal insolvency procedure will apply,[213] so a commonhold association will be liable to be wound up when it is unable to pay its debts[214] using the normal definition of being "unable to pay its debts".[215] Responsibility for avoiding insolvency must rest with the directors and membership, through assessments, reserve funds, additional levies, and the enforcement of assessments against individual leaseholders. A charging order against a flat would, in the ultimate event, lead to a sale of the flat. The Government concludes that the risk of insolvency of an association should be small.[216] However, in principle any creditor should have the option of starting the winding up procedure for any unpaid bill exceeding the Insolvency Act limit.[217] Standard insolvency regimes will operate, subject to possible rescue mechanisms.[218] The end of the road might, therefore, be dissolution of the commonhold association and the end of the

---

[202] Commonhold and L.Ref. Bill 2000 cl.37(2)(a).
[203] Commonhold and L.Ref. Bill 2000 cl.30(6).
[204] Commonhold and L.Ref. Bill 2000 cl.30(8).
[205] See above pp. 486–487.
[206] See above p. 487.
[207] White Paper Part I para.1.3.2.
[208] White Paper Part I para.3.5.3
[209] Draft Commonhold Bill 1996 cls.32–41.
[210] White Paper Part I para.3.5.3.
[211] L. Crabb [1996] *Conv.* 283.
[212] Commonhold and L.Ref. Bill 2000 cls.41–54.
[213] Commonhold and L.Ref. Bill 2000 cls.47–51.
[214] I.A. 1986 ss.122–125.
[215] I.A. 1986 s.123.
[216] White Paper Part I paras.3.5.5–6.
[217] White Paper Part I para.3.5.6; the limit is currently £750.
[218] White Paper Part I para.3.5.4; I.A. 1986; I.R. 1986.

commonhold.[219] However it is proposed to offer protection to unit holders who have met their individual obligations through the formation of a *phoenix association*,[220] at least in the normal course of events.[221] A new commonhold association would be brought into existence on the final order for winding up the old association, distinguished in its name by the addition of the year of formation or of a number.[222] Its members would consist of all the non-defaulting unit-holders and all new unit holders who had purchased the units of defaulting members from the liquidator. The old company could only be wound up when all defaults had been made good or all units had been sold.[223] Common parts would be transferred to the phoenix association by the winding up order,[224] which would operate a new Commonhold Community Statement, similar to the old one. Insolvency must not be the vehicle for a commonhold association to escape from paying its debts and business generally must have confidence in the commonhold system and the means by which they can obtain payment for their services. Personal guarantees could be demanded as used on some leasehold developments.[225] However, the practical safeguard here is the power to charge and sell individual units, and one wonders whether there needs to be a power to wind up the commonhold association for debt at all.

J.   TERMINATION

Buildings rarely have a useful life exceeding 100 years or so, and a chance accident might destroy any construction at any time.

The *1996 scheme* aimed to terminate the common ownership scheme with what was called a "minimum of complexity".[226] In essence the whole development would have ceased to be a commonhold at the commencement of the winding up, so that the freehold estates in the individual units would be terminated, so that the freehold in the entire site would then have vested in the commonhold association.[227] This would enable the liquidator to realise the redevelopment value by selling the development. Former unit holders would have rights of occupation for the duration of the realisation procedure[228] and entitlement on completion of the winding up process to a handout of capital representing the share of the overall development value to which each is entitled under the commonhold constitution.[229] Fortunately this is not reproduced in the 2000 draft Bill—did we really need a completely new liquidation regime?—though what remains is difficult enough.

[219] Commonhold and L.Ref. Bill 2000 cl.51. Any reserved fund is released: cl.54.
[220] White Paper Part I para.3.5.8; Commonhold and L.Ref. Bill 2000 cls.48–50 ("succession order").
[221] The court would retain power to order a dissolution: White Paper Part I para.3.5.11.
[222] This change of name would require registration.
[223] White Paper Part I para.3.5.9.
[224] Reserve funds and rights of action against original unit-holders would remain with the old association. Under present proposals reserve funds would be protected from creditors unless a particular debt is referable to reserve fund activities, but consultation is under way on this protection: Draft Commonhold and L.Ref. Bill 2000 cl.32(4); White Paper Part I paras.3.6.1–5.
[225] White Paper Part I para.3.5.10.
[226] White Paper Part I para.2.9.
[227] Draft Commonhold Bill 1996 cl.33(1).
[228] Draft Commonhold Bill 1996 cl.35; cls.36–37 and sch.9 provide for tenancies and leases.
[229] Draft Commonhold Bill 1996 cls.5, 24, 33(1)(b).

Under the Commonhold and Leasehold Reform Bill 2000, a commonhold association will be able to make a termination resolution that all the land over which it exercises functions should cease to be commonhold land.[230] It would fail unless it was
passed by at least an 80 per cent majority. If it were to be passed unanimously (meaning
here all unit-holders and not just the ones voting), the association would be free to apply
for termination within six months by sending it to the registrar.[231] If it is passed by 80
per cent of the members voting in favour, the association would be free to apply to the
court to determine the terms on which a termination application ought to be made, and
there would then be three months to secure the approval of more than 50 per cent of the
members of the association to the terms approved by the court.[232] The association
would have to make a termination statement containing its proposals for the transfer of
the former commonhold land and for the distribution of the assets of the association;
the contents would be pre-determined to some extent by the commonhold community
statement,[233] though the court will have overriding powers on the application by any
member.[234] An application to the registrar will include the termination resolution and
termination statement, whereupon it will be noted in the register.[235]

A termination application would lead to a member's voluntary winding up. The liquidator would notify the land registry of his appointment and then, as soon as is reasonably practicable, consider the termination statement and decide whether or not he is
content with it. If so he should notify the land registry. If he is not he should apply to the
court for an order varying it and should submit the order when it is made to the registry.[236] At that time the freehold estate in the units is transferred to the commonhold
association.[237] The liquidator should then proceed to realise the assets of the commonhold association acting in accordance with the termination statement.[238]

---

[230] Commonhold and L.Ref. Bill 2000 cls.41–42.

[231] Commonhold and L.Ref. Bill 2000 cl.41; curiously there is no provision for mortgage-lenders to consent.

[232] Commonhold and L.Ref. Bill 2000 cl.42. As presently drafted cl.35 (voting provisions) applies so it seems that
these are a percentage of those voting, but this is surely not intended and the particular words of cl.42 may override the more general provision.

[233] White Paper Part I para.1.3.12.

[234] Commonhold and L.Ref. Bill 2000 cl.44.

[235] Commonhold and L.Ref. Bill 2000 cl.46. Cl.52 applies if no termination application.

[236] Commonhold and L.Ref. Bill 2000 cl.45(3); the application is made under Insolvency Act 1986 s.112.

[237] Commonhold and L.Ref. Bill 2000 cl.46.

[238] Commonhold and L.Ref. Bill 2000 cl.46(3). Any reserve fund is released by cl.54.

18

RIGHT TO BUY

---

*Public sector landlords. The social sector. Secure tenants. Residential
qualification. Exclusion of employees. Houses. Flats. Dwellings in rural
areas. Price. Notice procedures. Compelling completion. Loss of the right to
buy.*

In England and Wales 1.3 million homes have been sold out of the public sector between
1979[1] and 1998; the peak rate of 200,000 sales in 1982 has now declined to about 40,000
a year.[2] An estimated four million homes remain in public ownership, though many of
these are not attractive propositions. Although the pattern is very uneven, sales have
tended to remove houses from the public sector in the counties and outer London, leaving behind inner city estates, flats and particularly high-rise units.[3]

A. LANDLORDS AND TENANTS

1. Public sector

Secure tenancies are residential leases granted by public sector landlords, defined by reference to the "landlord condition",[4] and embracing local authorities, new town corporations, housing action trusts, urban development corporations, the Development
Board of Rural Wales, and housing co-operatives.[5] Public sector tenants have the right
to buy their dwellings under Part V of the Housing Act 1985,[6] and many have done just
that since 1979. [7] Many councils also run voluntary local sales schemes. However, the
Crown is not compelled to sell.[8]

2. Social sector

Tenants of housing associations and other registered social landlords may have one of
three rights to compel their landlords to sell their homes to them. All these rights are

---

[1] H.A. 1980 part I.

[2] *Secure Tenants' Right to Buy* (D.E.T.R., August 1998) para.9. Green Paper: *Quality and Choice: A Decent Home
for All* (D.E.T.R., April 2000) paras.4.34–4.36. No changes are proposed by the New Labour Government.

[3] *English House Condition Survey 1996* (D.E.T.R., 1998) paras.1.20–1.22.

[4] H.A. 1985 s.80; see above pp. 7–10.

[5] H.A. 1985 sch.4 para.7; s.137 (transfers within the public sector); S.I. 1993/2240 (where public sector landlords
hold a superior interest).

[6] H.A. 1985 ss.118–188; H.W. Wilkinson [1986] *Conv.* 300; Woodfall ch.27; Davey 336–344.

[7] H.A. 1980 part I.

[8] H.A. 1985 sch.5 para.8.

confirmed by the Charters issued to social tenants, and they have the additional charter right to information about their rights.[9] Until early 1989 housing associations fell into the public sector, and a tenant who has continued in occupation since then will continue to be a secure tenant. They continue to enjoy the same *right to buy* as local authority tenants. Many public sector estates have been privatised by transfer to a registered social landlord under a large scale voluntary transfer; normally a transfer to the private sector would cause the loss of the right to buy, but in this case the legislation ensures that the tenant retains his former right, which is described as a *preserved* right to buy.[10]

When social landlords were transferred to the private sector in early 1989, they created assured tenancies[11]; the fact that tenants were not secure tenants meant that new tenants after that date no longer qualified to buy.[12] However, a somewhat similar *right of acquisition* has now been introduced.[13] It applies to housing stock created after April 1st 1997 using public money in the form of social housing grant,[14] whether it is new build, a conversion, or a stock transfer. A discount will be allowed to the tenant so as to reduce the cost, a discount funded by a public grant,[15] and the housing association[16] will be required to use the proceeds from the disposal in the construction of replacement property. Existing housing stock may be brought within a voluntary scheme. Qualifying conditions and discount[17] levels are roughly similar to the public-sector right to buy.[18] Details of the scheme are slightly different from the main scheme for public sector secure tenants.

3.   Secure tenants

The right to buy applies only to secure tenants with "life-long" security of tenure and with a residence qualification. Rules to determine that the tenant is a *secure tenant* are considered elsewhere.[19] Normal exclusions operate, removing the right to buy from tenants of land acquired for development, short-term arrangements, licences during repairs to the tenant's main residence,[20] student lettings, and non-residential lettings.[21]

4.   Residential qualifications and additions

A person seeking to exercise the right to buy must establish qualification by residence over the necessary qualifying period.[22] Continued residence is a condition of holding

---

[9] *Secure Tenant's Charter* and *Assured Tenant's Charter* (Housing Corporation, 1998), section 8.

[10] H.A. 1985 ss.171A–171H, introduced by Housing and Planning Act 1986 s.8, sch.2.; S.I. 1993/2241 as amended by S.I. 1999/1213.

[11] See above pp. 12–13.

[12] *Wood* v. *South Western Co-operative H.Ass. Ltd.* (1982) 44 P. & C.R. 198 C.A.

[13] H.A. 1996 ss.16, 17; S.I. 1997/619; details of the scheme vary from the right to buy.

[14] H.A. 1996 s.16(2); the intention is that this should apply only to property newly built after the 1996 Act comes into force; query if the wording is restricted in this way.

[15] Up to £16,000 a property.

[16] H.A. 1996 s.16; also included are charities, co-operative housing associations and non-funded housing authorities: S.I. 1997/619.

[17] S.Is. 1997/626, 1999/1135, 1999/3028.

[18] H.A. 1996 s.17(1); S.Is. 1997/619, 1999/1135.

[19] H.A. 1985 part IV; see above Chapter 5.

[20] *Tyler* v. *Kensington & Chelsea R.L.B.C.* (1991) 23 H.L.R. 380 C.A.; J.E. Martin [1992] *Conv.* 111.

[21] H.A. 1985 sch.1 paras.8–11.

[22] (1) Residence since 1985: s.119; (2) periods between 1980 and 1985 are included: s.185; (3) period before 1980 does not give qualification: *Kelley* v. *Dundee City D.C.* [1994] S.L.T. 1268.

the status of a secure tenant, and here too it means occupation of the dwelling as his only or principal home.[23] In a straightforward case the secure tenant has occupied the same dwelling which he is seeking to buy for at least two years.[24] As explained below, longer residential periods will increase the discount which the tenant is able to claim.[25] However the necessary qualification period can be achieved in other ways. An individual can add periods for which he has been the secure tenant of another dwelling, whether that previous one was owned by the same landlord or any other authority. If a married couple split up, the spouse who continues to occupy the house can add periods during which the other spouse occupied the home as secure tenant and as his principal or only home. After the death of a spouse, the survivor can add periods of occupation by the deceased provided that they were living together at the death.[26] A child may also add periods of occupation by his parent.[27] Residence in barracks or other accommodation provided for a member of the regular armed forces also qualifies.[28]

In the case of secure tenants who are joint tenants, the right to buy belongs to them jointly,[29] so that *all* of them must initiate the acquisition procedure. Extra purchasers may be added who are not qualifying tenants. This enables other family members to share in ownership of the family home, but is more usually a device to include people with the necessary earning capacity to raise mortgage finance. Addition is a *right* where the person added is the spouse of the tenant living with the tenant throughout the 12 months before purchase. It is *permitted*, with the consent of the landlord, where up to three additional members of the family share the family home. The right to buy belongs to all jointly.[30] Beneficial interests require careful definition, since it is usually correct for the discount to accrue to the benefit of the tenant who qualifies for it.[31]

5. Exclusion of employees

A public-sector employee is not eligible to buy a dwelling from the authority which employs him if the accommodation is provided for him as an employee, he is required to live in it by his contract of employment,[32] and this is for the better performance of his duties.[33] The status of the employee may change to that of a normal secure tenant (who is thus entitled to buy) if the employer takes no action to evict him after his employment

---

[23] H.A. 1985 sch.4 para.9; *Bruce* v. *Worthing B.C.* (1993) 26 H.L.R. 223 C.A. (loss of right where living elsewhere).

[24] sch.4 para.1.

[25] See below pp. 498–499.

[26] sch.4 para.2.

[27] sch.4 para.4 (the child must have occupied as his principal home at the time of death and have continued in occupation afterwards—either as successor to the same tenancy or under a new tenancy).

[28] sch.4 para.5.

[29] H.A. 1985 s.118. It is only necessary that one of them occupies as his only or principal home and the longest qualifying period may be taken.

[30] s.123.

[31] *Burrows* v. *Sharp* (1989) 23 H.L.R. 82 C.A.; *Savill* v. *Goodall* (1993) 25 H.L.R. 588 C.A.; *Evans* v. *Hayward* [1995] 2 F.L.R. 511 C.A.; *Costello* v. *Costello* (1995) 27 H.L.R. 12 C.A. (right for parents to occupy for life = life interest).

[32] This cannot generally be implied, but should be an express term: *Greenwich L.B.C.* v. *Hughes* [1994] 1 A.C. 170 H.L. (headmaster had right to buy the headmaster's house); A. Phang [1994] *J.B.L.* 255; *Elvidge* v. *Coventry C.C.* [1994] Q.B. 241 C.A. (successful variation at time of promotion of a water bailiff to remove the right to buy).

[33] H.A. 1985 sch.1 para.2(1); see above Chapter 7.

ends.[34] Property within the curtilage of the employer's business cannot be acquired,[35] so that the existence of a separate curtilage is essential, for example where a cottage at the edge of an agricultural college had its own fenced off garden,[36] or where a fireman lived on a small estate built for firemen to be near to the fire station but physically separated from it.[37]

B. DWELLINGS

1. Houses and flats

The estate in the dwelling which can be acquired under the right to buy varies according to whether the dwelling is a house or a flat. A house[38] is defined to be a structure which contains no horizontal divisions so that no material part lies above or below the remainder of the building containing the dwelling. Vertical divisions do not prevent a building qualifying as a house, so that terraced houses are included. If the secure tenant occupies a house, he will usually be entitled to insist on acquiring the freehold estate— in the house and land let with it[39]—unless the landlord's title is leasehold.[40] A dwelling which is not a house is a flat. A secure tenant holding a flat can require the landlord to grant a sub-lease for 125 years at a rent not exceeding £10 a year.[41]

Special provisions apply to dwellings adapted for the disabled or elderly. Under the initial legislation these classes of public sector dwelling were completely outside the right to buy scheme,[42] but most have subsequently been brought within it.[43] However, exemptions continue for sheltered housing in groups normally let together which is used for disabled persons, those suffering from mental disorder, or those over 60[44] in wardened housing.[45] Almshouses are also exempt.[46]

---

[34] *South Glamorgan C.C.* v. *Griffiths* (1992) 24 H.L.R. 334 C.A.; *Greenfield* v. *Berkshire C.C.* (1996) 28 H.L.R. 691 C.A.

[35] H.A. 1985 sch.5 para.1. Different exemptions are provided for the social sector right to acquire: S.I. 1997/619.

[36] *Dyer* v. *Dorset C.C.* [1989] Q.B. 346 C.A.

[37] *Barwick* v. *Kent C.C.* (1992) 24 H.L.R. 341 C.A.

[38] H.A. 1985 s.183.

[39] H.A. 1985 s.184.

[40] There is no right to buy a house where the interest of the landlord is for less than 21 years, but the duty cannot be avoided by artificial creation of a 20 year sub-lease: *R.* v. *Plymouth C.C. ex parte Freeman* (1987) 19 H.L.R. 328 C.A. (Edgcumbe Estate). If a lease for less than 21 years is granted by agreement, it is enfranchisable: H.A. 1985 ss.174, 175.

[41] The period will be reduced if the head-lease is for less than 125 years, but if it is below 50 years, the right to buy is excluded completely: H.A. 1985 sch.5 para.4.

[42] H.A. 1980 sch.1 part I as amended.

[43] H.A. 1985 sch.5 para.10.

[44] L.R.H.U.D.A. 1993 s.106 ensures that there is a single rule (age 60+) for both sexes; this removes the less favourable treatment of men (who receive pensions at 65) under pre-1993 law.

[45] Decided by the local authority, subject to an appeal to the S.S.: H.A. 1985 sch.5 as amended by L.G.H.A. 1989 s.164; previously a ministerial certificate was required. Decisions are subject to public law control: *R.* v. *S.S. for the Environment ex parte West Oxfordshire D.C.* (1993) 26 H.L.R. 417.

[46] H.A. 1985 sch.1 para.12; *Gray* v. *Taylor* [1998] 1 W.L.R. 1093 C.A.; *Stanley* v. *Compton* [1951] 1 All E.R. 859 C.A.; see above p. 172.

2.   Rural areas—restricting onwards sales

Local communities in rural areas are concerned to see to it that dwellings sold from the public sector do not fall into the hands of second home owners and outsiders. Restrictions apply to houses situated in National Parks, Areas of Outstanding Natural Beauty, parts of Wales,[47] and other designated rural areas.[48] Similar restrictions apply to sales by social landlords.[49] On sale, a covenant is imposed restricting the right of resale unless the later buyer is connected by work or residence to the local district. When selling a dwelling, the authority may also impose a right of pre-emption, that is a requirement that if the buyer wishes to sell on the home within 10 years he must first offer to sell it back to the authority.[50] Imposition of a right of pre-emption reduces the value of the house and also the price payable under the right to buy.

C.   PRICE

1.   Assessing the price

The price to be paid is the market value reduced by the amount of the discount.[51] The average in 1997–8 was £43,000 before discount, and £21,000 taking discount into account.[52] Valuation of the dwelling is as at the time that the tenant serves a notice indicating his desire to buy, on the basis of a sale in the open market by a willing seller. Houses are to be sold freehold, and flats on a lease for 125 years at a ground rent not exceeding £10 a year. Valuation is based on the actual terms of the transfer or lease, with the assumption that vacant possession is given, but ignoring the tenant and his family as potential buyers,[53] and disregarding improvements carried out by the tenant.[54] An appeal lies to the District Valuer.[55]

2.   Defects

The landlord must disclose any *known* defects when giving notice of the price.[56] In the past many seriously defective homes were sold and a special rescue package was required,[57] so that the council which had sold the dwelling was obliged to repurchase it

---

[47] S.I. 1997/685.

[48] H.A. 1985 s.157; S.I. 1999/1307. Separate consent may also be required under the green belt legislation: *R. v. S.S. for the Environment ex parte Enfield B.C.* (1988) 86 L.G.R. 549, McNeill J.; *R. v. S.S. for the Environment ex parte O'Byrne* [2000] Times May 25th.

[49] H.A. 1996 s.13; S.I. 1997/619 (right of acquisition which applies in National Parks).

[50] H.A. 1985 ss.157, 159 ("purchasers" and "disposals"), 160–163 ("exempt disposals"). The pre-emption right needs registration as a local land charge, and a restriction should also appear on the land register; s.15 (right to acquire).

[51] H.A. 1985 s.126.

[52] *Secure Tenants' Right to Buy* (D.E.T.R., August 1998) paras.9–11.

[53] ss.127, 128 (figure to be determined by the District Valuer).

[54] ss.127, 125. They should appear separately on the landlord's notice: *Dickinson* v. *Enfield L.B.C.* (1997) 27 H.L.R. 465 C.A.

[55] This appellate function does not prevent the district valuer fixing the initial price appealed from: *R. v. S.S. for the Environment ex parte Norwich C.C.* [1982] Q.B. 808 C.A.

[56] H.A. 1985 s.125(4A).

[57] H.A. 1985 ss.527–577; sch. 20 (repurchase); H.A. 1996 s.138–139; S.Is. 1986/797, 1988/884, 1992/446; H.W. Wilkinson (1988) 138 *N.L.J.* 161, 186.

with state funding, but the time limit for claims has now expired. The council is under no common law duty of care, and it follows that it has no liability for inherent defects of which it was not actually aware at the time of sale.[58] Tenants faced with such defects—which have often rendered homes bought under the right to buy scheme completely unsaleable—are forced to rely on a common law claim in negligence against surveyors who have produced excessive valuations, though the case law does not encourage tenants to expect an easy ride to success.[59]

3. Discount

The person exercising the right to buy is entitled to a discount of a percentage of the value. As Roch L.J. explained in *Bater* v. *Bater*[60]:

> "A person who has been the tenant of a local authority or of certain housing trusts acquires an entitlement to a discount in the price of a property owned by such a public sector landlord which increases the longer he or she has been a secure tenant of such a landlord. The entitlement to discount can be accumulated and carried from one secure tenancy to another, but the right to buy can only exist as an ancillary to a secure tenancy."

The details of the discount, ascertained according to the qualification period,[61] are as follows:

> for a house, 30 per cent plus 1 per cent for each complete year of qualification (meaning that the minimum is 32 per cent) subject to a maximum of 60 per cent;
> for a flat, 40 per cent plus 2 per cent a year (the minimum is thus 44 per cent) to a maximum of 70 per cent.

However, all discounts are capped in two ways: the price must not be reduced below the costs incurred on the dwelling within the last eight years and the total figure is cash limited. In the past this cash limit was £50,000,[62] but the Labour Government considered this to be too generous given that it exceeded the average value (£42,000) of the homes being sold, and that the average discount (£21,000) was much lower. So a new system is based on the average price of houses by region, with a maximum discount set between £22,000 and £38,000 according to region.[63] Any given individual is only entitled to discount once, so any previous purchase will be taken into account when calculating the appropriate reduction from the current purchase price.[64]

Similar principles apply to the right to acquire from social landlords. Discount levels are capped by region and also to a maximum of 50 per cent of the market value of the dwelling.[65]

---

[58] *Payne* v. *Barnet L.B.C.* (1998) 30 H.L.R. 295 C.A. An appeal is pending in *Rushton* v. *Worcester C.C.* [2000] unreported C.Ct.

[59] *Blake* v. *Barking & Dagenham L.B.C.* (1998) 30 H.L.R. 963.

[60] [1999] 4 All E.R. 944, 948b–d, Roch L.J.

[61] H.A. 1985 s.129; as amended by Housing and Planning Act 1986 s.2(1). The qualification period is ascertained by H.A. 1985 sch.4; *Kelley* v. *Dundee City D.C.* [1994] S.L.T. 1268 (succession before 1980 ignored).

[62] H.A. 1985 s.131; S.I. 1989/513.

[63] S.I. 1998/2997; S.I. 1999/292 (maximum £24,000 in Wales).

[64] H.A. 1985 s.130; S.I. 1992/1703 as amended by S.I. 1996/2651.

[65] S.Is. 1997/626, 1999/1135, 1999/3028 (England), 1997/569 (Wales).

4. Protecting the discount

The bonus represented by the sale of public sector housing at a discounted price should be restricted to the sitting tenant. The authority which sells the house is quite entitled to protect the discount so as to ensure that no one else can take advantage of it. If the property is sold within three years of the completion of the transfer under the right to buy,[66] a proportion of the discount will have to be repaid.[67] "Relevant disposals"[68] which call for this repayment include any conveyance of the freehold, any assignment of a lease, and the grant of a lease for 21 years or more at a premium (excluding therefore a lease at a rack rent). "Excluded conveyances" which are allowed without repayment of the discount include those to members of the family, vesting on death, property adjustments orders, and inheritance orders; however liability will arise if a relevant disposal follows the exempt disposal. Transfers under any form of family order are exempt.[69] Compulsory disposals and disposals of ancillary land are totally exempt, the new owner taking free of all liability to repay discount.

If an onwards sale occurs within the first year, the whole discount has to be repaid, but the amount repayable is reduced by one third with each complete year that elapses. Repayment is guaranteed by a covenant taken from the secure tenant when he buys, extension of that covenant to bind successors in title, and by securing the amount repayable as a charge on the premises.[70] Alternatively private finance can be obtained. Taxation will be based on the market value of the house minus any liability to repay the discount.[71]

5. Mortgages

There is no longer a right to a mortgage,[72] but almost all tenants who exercise the right to buy will require a mortgage, and they will often obtain it from the authority which is selling to them. Otherwise, they should apply to an approved lending institution, since mortgages by these lenders have priority over the covenant to repay the discount.[73]

Rent to mortgage schemes[74] are available to a tenant who is not able to afford an outright purchase, provided that he is not reliant on housing benefit.[75] The tenant pays a deposit, but leaves the remainder of the price outstanding. Regular payments are made which act as mortgage instalments,[76] since the outstanding sum is secured on mortgage,

---

[66] H.A. 1985 s.155(2).

[67] s.155 as amended by L.R.H.U.D.A. 1993 s.120.

[68] H.A. 1985 ss.159, 160.

[69] s.160(1)(c), (3). This was inserted by H.A. 1996 sch.18 para.15 in order to reverse *R.* v. *Rushmoor B.C. ex parte Barrett* [1989] Q.B. 60 C.A.; A. Samuels [1992] *L.G.R.* 1000.

[70] H.A. 1985 s.156. Detail is amended by L.R.H.U.D.A. 1993 s.120(3)(4). The charge should be registered at the land registry as a land charge: L.R.A. 1925 s.59(2).

[71] *Alexander* v. *Inland Revenue Commissioners* (1991) 23 H.L.R. 236 C.A.

[72] L.R.H.U.D.A. 1993 s.107.

[73] H.A. 1985 s.36(2); L.R.H.U.D.A. 1993 s.133; there are numerous S.Is.

[74] H.A. 1985 s.143–151B introduced by L.R.H.U.D.A. 1993 ss.108–120.

[75] H.A. 1985 s.143A.

[76] Payments must exceed the rent: s.143B. L.R.H.U.D.A. 1993 s.107 abolished the earlier right to a shared ownership lease.

a mortgage which can be redeemed on notice,[77] or repaid with any discount due on a subsequent sale.

D. PROCEDURE TO EXERCISE THE RIGHT TO BUY

1. Notice procedure

The tenant must initiate the procedure[78] by serving a notice on the landlord of his desire to exercise the right to buy. For the purposes of the subsequent timetable periods run from the service of the notice.[79] A response by the landlord must normally be served within four weeks,[80] either admitting or denying the right to buy. Reasons must be given for a refusal, which can be challenged. Where the tenant's right to buy is established,[81] the landlord serves a notice setting out the terms on which acquisition is accepted, including the property, the price,[82] the provisions proposed for the conveyance, details of the service charge, and so forth. Known defects must be disclosed. By notice of intention served within 12 weeks the tenant indicates whether he intends to proceed or to withdraw.[83] The matter may then proceed to completion.

2. Completion and registration

The detailed terms of the conveyancing documentation are laid down. Houses should be transferred freehold,[84] with a full title guarantee, subject to existing tenant's incumbrances and burdens. New covenants may also be imposed, for example not to build on the garden; in one case the council demanded 90 per cent of the development value for releasing this covenant, but this was held to be unlawful.[85] In another case reported in the press the council has used the covenant to keep the property fit for resale to prevent a man burying the remains of his wife in the garden of his council house in Dover.[86]

Flats[87] are usually "sold" by the grant of a lease for a term of 125 years at a rent which is not to exceed £10 a year. Covenants are set out in detail. In essence the landlord covenants to maintain the block and common facilities, to provide services, and to rebuild after fire. A service charge may be levied to cover the cost of communal services, though not the cost of repair of the block.[88] A fixed charge is also acceptable.[89] Challenges to the level of service charge are a separate issue to be resolved after execu-

---

[77] H.A. 1985 s.151A, sch.6A.

[78] J.E. Adams [1981] *Conv.* 171.

[79] H.A. 1985 ss.176 (notices), 177 (errors); S.Is. 1986/2194 as amended (Form RTB 1), 1994/2932 (Welsh language equivalents).

[80] H.A. 1985 s.124; S.I. 1986/2194 (form RTB 2); S.I. 1988/1265 (Welsh forms).

[81] H.A. 1985 s.125.

[82] s.125(5) as amended (the value less any discount). No duty of care is owed to the tenant: *Blake* v. *Barking & Dagenham L.B.C.* (1998) 30 H.L.R. 963 Q.B.D.

[83] ss.125D, 125E (landlord's notice in default).

[84] sch.6 parts I, II.

[85] *R.* v. *Braintree D.C. ex parte Halls* [2000] Times March 1st C.A., reversing [1999] Times July 21st Jackson J.

[86] Independent February 15th 2000.

[87] sch.6 parts I, III.

[88] sch.6 para.18(1)(a).

[89] *Coventry C.C.* v. *Cole* [1994] 1 W.L.R. 398 C.A.

tion of the conveyancing documents.[90] The tenant covenants to repair the interior of the flat. Alterations require consent, for which no charges may be levied. Easements and covenants are needed to regulate relationships with neighbouring owners.[91] Estate management schemes can be used even after the sale of some or all of the houses on the estate.[92] Terms should be agreed if possible, but otherwise disputes have to be determined by a County Court.[93]

Registration of title has been compulsory ever since the first introduction of compulsory right to buy provisions. The authority which is selling provides a certificate of its title, stating any incumbrances, so that sale and registration proceeds on the basis of that certificate.[94]

E.   COMPELLING COMPLETION AND LOSS OF THE RIGHT

1.   Landlord's notice to complete

The mechanism by which a landlord can force a tenant to proceed is by completion notice: a first notice to complete[95] is followed by a second notice, and 56 days later there is a presumption that the application to buy has been withdrawn.[96] However a notice can be waived or the time stated can be extended by the council, which means that it is possible for the effect of a notice to be destroyed by estoppel. This occurred on the facts of *Milne-Berry* v. *Tower Hamlets L.B.C.*[97] where completion was delayed as a result of disputes about repairs, but the tenant was reassured by the council that his application would be treated as continuing. Deferral rights have been withdrawn.[98]

2.   Compelling completion by injunction

The procedure for claiming the right to buy is complicated by the legislative assumption—which was originally only too well justified by events—that many authorities would be hostile to the exercise of the right to buy, and the consequent inclusion of powers of compulsion[99] and prohibition of contracting out.[100] Particular tenants may compel their landlord to complete a sale.

English legislation (in contrast to the Scottish[101]) does not provide for the transaction to have contractual force at any stage, so that the tenant does not acquire any equitable

[90]   *Sheffield C.C.* v. *Jackson* [1998] 1 W.L.R. 1591 C.A.

[91]   A. Samuels [1992] *L.G.R.* 61.

[92]   See above pp. 417–419.

[93]   *Guinan* v. *Enfield L.B.C.* (1997) 27 H.L.R. 456 C.A. (unreasonable terms can be excised).

[94]   H.A. 1985 s.154; A. Samuels (1991) 155 *L.G.R.* 147.

[95]   H.A. 1985 s.140. In *Bater* v. *Bater* [1999] 4 All E.R. 944 C.A. a completion notice was served after a notice to quit which removed the tenant's right to buy; the completion notice was a mistake and no point is taken in relation to it.

[96]   s.141.

[97]   (1998) 30 H.L.R. 229 C.A.

[98]   H.A. 1985 s.153A; H.A. 1988 s.124; L.R.H.U.D.A. 1993 sch.21 para.13, sch.22.

[99]   H.A. 1985 ss.164–170; *R.* v. *S.S. for the Environment ex parte Norwich C.C.* [1982] Q.B. 808 C.A.; s.82 gives power to override local Acts.

[100]   H.A. 1985 s.179.

[101]   *Bristol C.C.* v. *Lovell* [1998] 1 W.L.R. 446, 456–457, Lord Hope, citing *Cooper Executors* v. *Edinburgh City D.C.* (1991) 23 H.L.R. 349 H.L.

interest in the home in advance of completion. Rather the principle is that the tenant remains a secure tenant until the moment of legal completion, when the tenancy comes to an end and the former tenant becomes owner of his home.[102] However the landlord is under an obligation to proceed[103] as soon as all matters in relation to the transfer and mortgage are agreed or determined, provided that rent is up to date, the price is paid, and any mortgage is executed. This duty to complete can be enforced by injunction, a remedy which fulfils the normal function of specific performance.[104] Issue of an injunction is not discretionary in the normal equitable sense, since the tenant has a right to the remedy once the statutory conditions are fulfilled.[105]

3. Dependence upon continuance of secure tenancy

Bater v. *Bater*[106] confirms that the right to buy is not an independent property right, because it lacks the four *Ainsworth* characteristics[107] of being definable, identifiable by third parties, capable of assumption by third parties and having some degree of permanence or stability. Rather it is analogous to a personal equity: there is no right to transfer the right to buy separately from the tenancy to which it belongs. The fact that the right to buy is dependent upon the continuing existence of a secure tenancy to which it is incident from the moment of its exercise until completion of the purchase[108] creates a substantial period of vulnerability,[109] which must now be explored.

4. Grounds for repossession

A secure tenant is an individual occupying the property in question as his only or principal home. This status must be retained until completion of the acquisition, a principle which is particularly important where completion is deferred over a substantial period for financial reasons.[110]

After a *breach of covenant*, the right to buy is removed if the authority obtains a possession order against the tenant because of his breach of covenant[111] or bankruptcy.[112] This penalty applies only if the misconduct is such that a ground for possession is made out, so that racial harassment or anti-social behaviour which falls short of being a ground for possession does not remove the right to buy.[113] Termination of the tenant's

---

[102] H.A. 1985 s.139(2); sub-tenancies are preserved by L.P.A. 1925 s.139.

[103] H.A. 1985 s.138.

[104] *Bristol C.C.* v. *Lovell* [1998] 1 W.L.R. 446 H.L.; previous cases overruled or explained are: *Dance* v. *Welwyn Hatfield D.C.* [1990] 1 W.L.R. 1097 C.A.; *Taylor* v. *Newham L.B.C.* [1993] 1 W.L.R. 444 C.A.; *Dickinson* v. *Enfield L.B.C.* [1996] 2 E.G.L.R. 88 C.A.

[105] *Lovell* at 453H, Lord Hoffmann.

[106] [1999] 4 All E.R. 944, 953e–g, Roch L.J.; also at 952e, Thorpe L.J; *Bradford M.B.C.* v. *McMahon* [1994] 1 W.L.R. 52, 60–62.

[107] *National Provincial Bank Ltd.* v. *Ainsworth* [1965] A.C. 1175 H.L.

[108] *Sutton L.B.C.* v. *Swann* (1985) 18 H.L.R. 140 C.A.; *Jennings* v. *Epping Forest D.C.* (1991) 25 H.L.R. 241 C.A.; *Bradford M.B.C.* v. *McMahon* [1994] 1 W.L.R. 52 C.A.; *Bater* v. *Bater* [1999] 4 All E.R. 944, 947h, Thorpe L.J.

[109] *Bater* at 952f, Thorpe L.J.

[110] e.g. *Harrow L.B.C.* v. *Tonge* (1992) 25 H.L.R. 99 C.A.

[111] H.A. 1985 s.121; *Dance* v. *Welwyn Hatfield D.C.* [1990] 1 W.L.R. 1097 C.A.; *Wansbeck D.C.* v. *Charlton* (1981) 79 L.G.R. 523 C.A.; *Enfield L.B.C.* v. *McKeon* [1986] 2 All E.R. 730 C.A.

[112] H.A. 1985 s.121; also if there is a composition or arrangement with creditors whose terms have not been fulfilled.

[113] *Taylor* v. *Newham L.B.C.* [1993] 1 W.L.R. 444 C.A. (no discretion); *Bristol C.C.* v. *Lovell* [1998] 1 W.L.R. 446, 453A, Lord Hoffmann (drug dealing).

right occurs only at the stage of the possession order and not merely when the authority has issued a notice to recover possession.[114]

The House of Lords had to resolve a conflict between the timing of a tenant's application for an injunction to enforce his right to buy and the local authority's application for a possession order in *Bristol C.C.* v. *Lovell.*[115] Lovell rented a house on the Southmead Estate in Bristol which he was proposing to buy for cash. It had steel grilles over the doors, closed circuit television to monitor visitors, and electronic counter-surveillance equipment, facts which the authority thought were suggestive of its use for the supply of drugs. Lovell applied for an injunction to compel completion and then, in an order to frustrate the hearing of repossession proceedings, an interlocutory application for the injunction. Giving the leading judgment, Lord Hoffmann confirmed that there was no discretion to refuse a right to buy injunction, but this principle did not affect the general discretion of the County Court to determine the order in which applications were heard.[116] Otherwise the right to buy would have been a game of chance, turning upon which application was put in first. On the facts it was clearly right to decide the possession proceedings based on nuisance or annoyance of neighbours first, and only to allow the right to buy to proceed if possession was refused. Later cases have adopted this order of hearings.[117]

5. Losing qualification before completion

If the secure tenant *moves out* before completion, he loses his residential qualification and with it the right to buy. This may be fair enough if he sub-lets the property before completion,[118] but the same principle may work outrageously unfairly if, for example, he moves out to receive residential care.[119]

Death before completion is usually a bar to the right to buy, since the right is personal to the secure tenant and cannot vest in the personal representatives of a deceased secure tenant.[120] Where a tenant died before final completion of the Scottish conveyancing formalities his executors were held to have no right to enforce the contract.[121] However, if a relative has lived with the deceased tenant in the home as his main residence, the succession rights which apply to the tenancy[122] also extend to the right to buy, and to the accrued entitlement to discount.[123] Where a joint purchase was started before the death of the tenant who was not qualified, the right to buy will survive the death: the non-qualified person who has been joined as joint tenant is deemed for these purposes to be a joint secure tenant, so as to enable the right to buy to pass by survivorship.[124]

---

[114] *Camden L.B.C.* v. *Sale* [1997] C.L.Y 2718.

[115] [1998] 1 W.L.R. 446 H.L.

[116] C.C.R. Order 13; now C.P.R. 3.1.

[117] *Tandridge D.C.* v. *Bicker* [1998] 3 E.G.L.R. 31 C.A.

[118] *Muir Group Housing Association Ltd.* v. *Thornley* (1992) 25 H.L.R. 89 C.A.; *Sutton L.B.C.* v. *Swann* (1985) 18 H.L.R. 140 C.A.

[119] *Jennings* v. *Epping Forest D.C.* (1991) 25 H.L.R. 241 C.A.

[120] *Bradford M.C.C.* v. *McMahon* [1994] 1 W.L.R. 52 C.A.; A.R. Brierley [1995] Conv. 114, 224.

[121] *Cooper* v. *Edinburgh D.C.* (1991) 23 H.L.R. 349 H.L.

[122] See above pp. 115–123.

[123] *McIntyre* v. *Merthyr Tydfil B.C.* (1989) 21 H.L.R. 320 C.A.

[124] H.A. 1985 s.123; *Harrow L.B.C.* v. *Tonge* (1992) 25 H.L.R. 99 C.A.

6.   Destruction of a joint tenancy by a *Monk* notice

It will be recalled from previous discussion that where a tenancy is vested in a couple as joint tenants, one of them is able to terminate the tenancy by giving notice to quit to the landlord without reference to the other joint tenant.[125] This is usually done after the breakdown of the relationship between them. Notice may be given while the remaining tenant is in the process of pursuing his right to buy, though it has no effect once the purchase is completed. Its effect is to terminate the secure tenancy and so remove the qualification to buy. In *Bater* v. *Bater*[126] the court held, somewhat reluctantly, that the effect of this doctrine was that it had no power to stop the service of a notice to end the periodic tenancy even if it is done to extinguish the right to buy. The jurisdiction under the Matrimonial Causes Act 1973[127] was of no assistance since the notice was not a disposition of the tenancy, though Thorpe L.J. said[128] that an injunction could be issued to restrain service of a notice if this was done in advance: practitioners should take this step to protect the joint tenancy.

---

[125] *Hammersmith & Fulham L.B.C.* v. *Monk* [1992] 1 A.C. 478 H.L.; see above pp. 124–130.
[126] [1999] 4 All E.R. 944 C.A.
[127] s.37.
[128] At 952–953, Roch L.J. and Lord Lloyd offered no opinion on para.(a); Thorpe L.J.'s opinion might seem to the contrary to House of Lords opinions.

19

COMMERCIAL GRANTS

Legal leases. Registrable leases. Leases as overriding interests. Mid term leases. Short tenancies. Fixed contractual terms. Periodic tenancies. Certainty of termination. Repugnancy. Commencement of leases. Commencement of contracts. Contracts for leases. Walsh v. Lonsdale. Defective leases as contracts. Equitable leases. Basis in specific performance, onset, termination. Perpetual renewal. Options.

A. LEGAL LEASES

For many purposes all that matters is that there is a valid lease of some kind, and this is particularly true of the security of tenure regimes. No distinction needs to be drawn between leases and sub-leases, between fixed and periodic terms, between formal leases by deed and short oral leases, and between legal leases and agreements operating only in equity.[1] What is essential is that the initial grant is made with sufficient formality to create some kind of lease. However in terms of conveyancing treatment leases fall into five categories.[2]

1. Registered and registrable leases

Grandest, and attracting the greatest formality, are leases with more than 21 years outstanding. Registered leases are those substantively registered with their own title number, so that there is a property register, a proprietorship register showing the current legal tenant, and a charges register in which mortgages and other burdens affecting the title can be entered. Registration of one estate is independent of any other in the same land, so that a registered freehold and registered sub-lease may sandwich an unregistered intermediate lease. Registrability of the lease does not depend upon the landlord's title being registered. The simplified scheme introduced in 1986[3] applies substantive registration to any *legal*[4] lease with a term exceeding 21 years remaining unexpired at the time of registration.[5] This applies to (1) a grant of a new lease by a landlord whose title is registered, when the case is one of dealing; (2) a grant of a new lease by a landlord with

---

[1] Statutory definitions include all these: L.T.A. 1954 s.69(1).
[2] Woodfall ch.5; Bright & Gilbert 212–222; Davey 22–31; Evans & Smith (5th) ch.4; Garner (2nd) ch.3. Tenancies by estoppel (where the landlord does not have title to the land) are considered below, pp. 565–566.
[3] L.R.A. 1986; in force January 1st 1987, following Law Com. No.125 (1983).
[4] L.R.A. 1925 s.2; see below p. 508.
[5] L.R.A. 1925 s.8(1)(b) as amended by L.R.A. 1986 s.2.

an unregistered title, when it is a case for first registration[6] or (3) any assignment (that is a transfer) of an unregistered lease with at least 21 years of the term unexpired at the time that it passes.[7]

Today all long leases that are not already registered are registrable after any dealing: all parts of the country are compulsory areas[8] and the dealings which trigger first registration include sales, assignments without value, gifts, devolutions on death and first mortgages, with second mortgages being the only common exception.[9] Procedure is described in *A New Land Law*.[10]

Long residential leases[11] are registrable but some business leases may also fall into this category. Traditional leases of offices and shops were for 25 years and just scraped in (though shorter leases are now conventional) but this category also includes many non-renewable leases, such as a head lease of an entire office block intended for reletting in parts.

2.   Overriding interests

The law remains unsatisfactory despite the greater coherence introduced by the Land Registration Act 1986.[12] Clearly it would be neither practicable nor desirable to keep a complete register of all short-term occupancies of shops: an inaccurate register is worse than none at all. As a result most leases that are incapable of substantive registration are treated as overriding.

Section 70(1) of the Land Registration Act 1925 defines the *paragraph (k)*[13] *overriding interest* as:

"leases granted for a term not exceeding 21 years".

Almost all leases that are not substantively registrable take effect and bind purchasers off the register. However, the force of the word "granted" needs careful appreciation since this innocuous looking word is interpreted so as to restrict this class of overriding interests to legal leases. *City Permanent B.S.* v. *Miller*[14] held that an oral agreement to create a lease for three years and then from week to week (that is for a minimum term of three years and one week) was not a legal lease, and so was not a paragraph (k) overriding interest. A lease by deed is "granted", and it seems to follow from the course of discussion in *Miller* that an informal short lease[15] is also granted. It now makes no difference whether the lease is at a rack rent, reserves a fine, or is purely gratuitous.[16] Protection adheres to a paragraph (k) tenant without any requirement that the tenant be in occu-

---

[6] L.R.A. 1925 s.123, also as amended; the 21 years are measured from the grant, not the later date of the application for registration: s.8(1A) as inserted in 1986.

[7] L.R.A. 1925 ss.8(1) and subs.(1A), as amended as above.

[8] For pre-1990 leases see above p. 384.

[9] s.123 as amended by L.R.A. 1997 s.1.

[10] Sparkes *N.L.L.* chs.1, 4.

[11] See above pp. 382–385.

[12] In force January 1st 1987, following Law Com. No.125 (1983).

[13] As amended by L.R.A. 1986 s.4 from the beginning of 1987.

[14] [1952] Ch. 840 C.A.

[15] L.P.A. 1925 s.54(2).

[16] Amendments by L.R.A. 1986 s.4.

pation, so that the lease can be a totally undiscoverable incumbrance.[17] The initial date for existence of paragraph (k) protection is the date of registration of a later dealing.[18] One important consequence of coming within paragraph (k) is that the grant of the lease is deemed to be by way of registered disposition,[19] so as to enable the tenant to defeat unprotected minor interests, though he is bound by register entries and pre-existing overriding interests.[20]

A tenant who fails to secure protection under paragraph (k) will often have an overriding interest under paragraph (g) by virtue of actual occupation or through receipt of net rents where a sub-tenant is in occupation.[21] This may also provide a second layer of protection for a paragraph (k) tenant, giving fortuitous protection to options and future leases if the person entitled happens to be in occupation under some other right. Protection is lost, of course, under the express terms of paragraph (g) if enquiry is made of the occupier and the lease is not disclosed, and also if the tenant is not in occupation at the time of the completion of some later transaction.[22]

Some leases may be protected against the landlord's title by a protective entry—a notice or caution—in which case the lease is a minor interest, entry of a notice warning all later buyers of the existence of the lease.[23] Protection by notice requires the consent of the landlord or else a court order, but a caution is available be used for non-consensual entries. Entries will be refused if the lease is substantively registered or if it is both overriding and obvious.[24] This means that a protective notice is essential for a strictly limited range of leases:

(1) certain pre-1987 leases: leases for 21 years or less at a fine; leases for 21 years or less without any rent; and any lease made before 1986[25] with an absolute prohibition on assignment;
(2) agreements for leases[26]; and
(3) future leases.

3. Legal leases of mid length (3 to 21 years)

Leases are one of the forms of "conveyances of land or of any interest therein" for which section 52(1) of the Law of Property Act 1925[27] requires a deed. Traditionally a deed could be distinguished from less potent documents by the presence of a seal, but after

---

[17] The same is of course true of a lease by deed of unregistered land, but here the lease should appear with the title deeds.

[18] *Pourdanay* v. *Barclays Bank plc.* [1997] Ch. 321 Ch.D. (also known as *Zaroovabli*).

[19] L.R.A. 1925 s.19(2).

[20] *Freer* v. *Unwins Ltd.* [1976] Ch. 288.

[21] L.R.A. 1925 s.70(1)(g).

[22] *Abbey National B.S.* v. *Cann* [1991] 1 A.C. 56 H.L.

[23] L.R.A. 1925 s.48(1). New forms are provided for cancellations by L.R.R. 1999 S.I. 1999/128, substituting L.R.R. 1925 r.201.

[24] L.R.A. 1925 ss.19(2)(a), 22(2)(a); L.R.R. 1925 r.199.

[25] L.R.A. 1986 s.3; Law Com. No.125 (1983).

[26] *Clark* v. *Chief Land Registrar* [1994] Ch. 370 C.A.; *Chancery* v. *Ketteringham* (1995) 69 P. & C.R. 426 Ch.D.; A.K.R. Kiralfy (1952) 16 *Conv. (N.S.)* 38; J.E. Adams [1994] *Conv.* 265.

[27] Replacing Statute of Frauds 1677 (writing) and Real Property Act 1845 s.3 (upgrade to deed).

the reforms of 1989[28] the test is whether the document is described as, or executed as, a deed. Stamp duty will be payable.[29]

Formality is required for the creation of new leases, with the exception of short leases, and also for the assignment of any existing lease, whether it is long or short.[30] An informal lease is "void for the purpose of conveying or creating a legal estate", so that a lease for five years is *not* good for the first three at law, though it may have a much wider effect in equity.[31]

Next are leases exceeding three years and up to 21 years remaining, which require a deed to be legal but which operate as overriding interests off the register. Today most renewable business leases fall into this category.

4. Informal short-term leases

Leases are generally "void for the purpose of conveying or creating a legal estate" unless made by deed.[32] Short leases have been exempted from the need for full formality in creation since 1677,[33] and although there has been some amendment of detail, the exemption now appears in section 54(2) of the Law of Property Act 1925. The three requirements are: (1) a tenancy taking effect in possession, (2) a term not exceeding three years, whether or not the lessee is given power to extend the term, and (3) the best rent which can reasonably be obtained without taking a fine. A contract can also be created informally.[34] An excepted short lease can be created purely orally[35] and protected without any further actions as a paragraph (k) overriding interest,[36] though full formality is required for a transfer of any existing lease.[37] Residential tenancies fall into the category of short lease for three years or less, which can be created informally and override the register, but it could also include some short-term business arrangements. It is vitally important to consider whether a short-term business letting falls into the exemption from business renewal rights.[38] However it would be very uncommon for any lease to be created in the commercial sector without some written evidence of the terms.

5. Contracts and equitable leases

There are many leases for more than three years where contract formalities have been used but not the deed necessary for a legal grant. Usually what has happened is that the parties have negotiated a conditional contract, but when the conditions are satisfied they carry on without bothering to execute a legal lease by deed, so that the tenant under the contract begins to act as if he were a legal tenant. Such leases need to secure

---

[28] L.P.(M.P.) A. 1989 s.1, in force July 31st, 1990.

[29] See above pp. 380–382.

[30] *Botting* v. *Martin* (1808) 1 Camp. 317; *Crago* v. *Julian* [1992] 1 W.L.R. 372 C.A.; P. Sparkes [1992] *Conv.* 375.

[31] *Walsh* v. *Lonsdale* (1882) 21 Ch. D. 9 C.A.; see below pp. 521–522.

[32] Sparkes *N.L.L.* 216–222.

[33] Statute of Frauds 1677 s.2.

[34] L.P.A. 1925 s.52(1).

[35] P. Sparkes [1992] *Conv.* 252, 337. An oral lease may suffer certain disadvantages as suggested by *Rye* v. *Rye* [1962] A.C. 496 H.L.

[36] As amended by L.R.A. 1986 s.4 from the beginning of 1987.

[37] *Botting* v. *Martin* (1808) 1 Camp. 317, 170 E.R. 970; *Crago* v. *Julian* [1992] 1 W.L.R. 372 C.A.

[38] See below pp. 552–555.

priority—by protective registration or occupation—if they are to be safe against a sale of the reversion. Once this is secured they should operate as equitable leases under the doctrine of *Walsh* v. *Lonsdale*,[39] and in fact the position of the parties will be very similar to that under a legal lease. This book argues for an even closer correlation between legal and equitable leases than conventional theory allows.

B. CONTRACTUAL TERMS

The duration of time for which a tenant is given exclusive possession of his landlord's property is called the term of the lease whereas the terms on which it is held are called the covenants! After 1925 any lease must be a term of years absolute,[40] which is either a fixed term or a periodic tenancy.

1. Fixed terms

This is the archetypal form of lease.[41] Rights to exclusive possession[42] must be given for a maximum duration in years that is ascertained at the outset.[43] Usually, that duration is fixed in the lease, but it might also be fixed by reference to an event which is then certain, or fixed as a certain period before the lease takes actual effect.[44] A freehold estate, by way of contrast, is a period of uncertain duration, measured originally in periods of lives and now[45] being perpetual. In order to maintain the conceptual distinction between the two types of estate, a lease cannot be created for uncertain periods, nor in perpetuity.[46]

English law is remarkable for the flexibility it allows in the creation of a lease. Provided that a maximum duration is specified, the law imposes no limit on how long or short it may be. Leases for 999 years are common.[47] A lease of that length with a nominal rent effectively passes all the value in the land to the tenant, and reduces the value of the landlord's reversion virtually to zero. Mortgages of freehold land used to employ the device of a 3,000-year lease.[48] Renewable business leases of shops and offices occupied by business are generally for relatively short periods—up to 25 years. An important cut-off point is 21 years, for a legal lease longer than that is registrable.[49] Much longer leases are common as investment vehicles in building leases and for institutional leases of large scale commercial premises, such as an office block or an industrial park. These

---

[39] (1882) 21 Ch.D. 9 C.A.

[40] L.P.A. 1925 s.1(1)(b) (legal); an equitable lease is a contract for the grant of a term of years absolute.

[41] L.P.A. 1925 s.205(1)(xxvii) including "a term of years . . . ."; Woodfall 6.012–6.031; Evans & Smith (5th) 122–126; Garner (2nd) ch.1.

[42] See below pp. 551–552.

[43] See below pp. 510–511.

[44] *Bishop of Bath's* case (1605) 6 Co. Rep. 34b, 35b, 77 E.R. 303; *Re Midland Railway Co.'s Agreement* [1971] Ch. 725, 731H, Russell L.J.

[45] L.P.A. 1925 s.1(1)(a).

[46] *Sevenoaks Maidstone & Tunbridge Rly Co.* v. *London Chatham & Dover Rly Co.* (1879) 11 Ch.D. 625, 635, Jessel M.R.

[47] J.T. Farrand [1982] *Conv.* 95: "supposed to last—like the Third Reich—for a 1000 years or so".

[48] L.P.A. 1925 s.85; most are now legal charges under s.87.

[49] See above pp. 507–508.

leases are not renewable so the investor has to rely on contractual negotiation of a lease for a fixed period of time.

Very short terms are recognised just the same. The definition of the term of years absolute recognises the possibility of a "term for less than a year or for a year or years and a fraction of a year . . .".[50] Most residential tenancies are weekly or monthly. A lease of a timeshare may be for one week,[51] and why not a lease for one day to watch a Royal procession or a concert?[52] As is explained later, a very short fixed term will not attract business security of tenure.[53]

2.   Certain and determinable terms

Section 1(1) of the Law of Property Act 1925 restricts legal status to two estates—the fee simple absolute in possession and the term of years absolute. "Absolute" has different meanings depending upon whether the estate is freehold or leasehold. As applied to a fee simple, "absolute" means that the interest is not liable to early determination, so that there must be no condition or provision for determination. When applied to a leasehold term, it means that the *maximum* duration must be fixed in years, and provided that is so, legal status is not removed from the lease because it may be cut short. Leases with a term which is fixed rigidly in advance (called a term "certain") are extremely unusual.

A term of years is absolute despite being:

"liable to determination by notice, re-entry, operation of law, or by a provision for cesser on redemption, or in any other event (other than the dropping of a life or the determination of a determinable life interest) . . .".[54]

Almost all leases have affixed maximum duration but with a provision for earlier termination in stated circumstances. The lease may continue until the period of years reserved by the lease has run out, when it will end by effluxion of time, but it may also end early. Expressly contemplated by the statutory definition are methods of termination agreed in the original lease and which derogate from the full length of the term agreed. A lease may—and except in the case of a *very* short term always does—provide for forfeiture if the tenant fails to comply with his obligations: termination of the lease is not automatic, but if a breach of covenant is sufficiently serious the landlord can break the term of the lease.[55] The lease is legal even though it cannot be known for sure how long it will last. Another common provision is a break clause, enabling the term to be brought to an end by the service of notice.[56] Finally a term of years absolute may be liable to determination on the occurrence of a determining event. Thus a lease *to T for 10 years or until the next general election if sooner* is a valid term of years absolute.[57]

---

[50] L.P.A. 1925 s.205(1)(xxvii).
[51] *Cottage Holiday Associates* v. *Customs & Excise Commissioners* [1983] Q.B. 735; M. Haley (1995) 24 *Anglo-American* 236.
[52] Licences have generally been used: *Krell* v. *Henry* [1903] 2 Q.B. 740 C.A.
[53] See below pp. 551–555.
[54] L.P.A. 1925 s.205(1)(xxvii). For leases for life, see above pp. 363–365.
[55] See below Chapter 29.
[56] *Metropolitan Police District Receiver* v. *Palacegate Properties Ltd.* [2000] 13 E.G. 187 C.A. See below pp. 579–583.
[57] *Eton College* v. *Bard* [1983] Ch. 321 C.A. (until the lease shall cease to be vested in a member of the association).

Any lease, even one described as "certain", is liable to destruction by consensual surrender if the landlord agrees to take back the property let to the tenant.[58]

3. Leases for life

It would be unusual to grant a business lease for life, but if there is such a creature it falls outside the statutory concept of the term of years absolute which explicitly excludes any lease determinable on "the dropping of a life or the determination of a determinable life interest".[59] As already explained in the chapter on long residential leases[60] section 149(6) of the Law of Property Act 1925 effects a statutory conversion of any lease for life that is at rent or fine into a term of 90 years.

4. Periodic tenancies

Many leases are periodic. The term of years absolute is defined[61] to include a term "from year to year", or alternatively called a yearly tenancy. Initially for one year, such a tenancy continues to grow by one year at a time, indefinitely,[62] though it can always be brought to an end by a proper notice.[63] Older authorities treated a year as the archetypal period, no doubt because that was normal for agricultural tenancies, but monthly or quarterly tenancies of business property are common, and any longer or shorter period could be used.

Landlord and tenant are free to create a periodic tenancy by *express* agreement, and of any period, though any business dealing should be recorded in writing. Most periodic tenancies are *implied* because a tenant occupies land to the exclusion of the landlord and rent is paid and accepted. The two sub-heads of the general process have already been studied in the domestic context,[64] but they operate rather differently in the business context. Firstly,[65] where a tenant enters and pays rent, contractual relations are normally created in the form of a periodic tenancy, giving a gateway to rights of renewal of the business lease, but since a tenancy at will is outside the business lease provisions, the courts allow a landlord to take rent from a potential tenant with whom negotiations are proceeding without creating a tenancy and without conceding any security. Secondly,[66] where a tenant continues to hold over after a fixed term has expired, there is usually a contractual renewal through the creation of a periodic tenancy; however a renewable business lease is automatically continued by statute until a notice procedure has been gone through to bring it to an end, so payment of rent is attributable to the statute and cannot act as a novation of the contract.

---

[58] See below pp. 599–603.

[59] L.P.A. 1925 s.205(1)(xxvii).

[60] See above pp. 363–365.

[61] L.P.A. 1925 s.205(1)(xxvii); Woodfall 6.032–6.077; Davey 17–21; Garner (2nd) ch.1.

[62] Hence the odd rule that a yearly tenant can create a valid sub-lease for 99 years: *Pennell* v. *Payne* [1995] Q.B. 192 C.A.; query whether this is logical, since the tenancy is only for one year when looked at prospectively.

[63] Contrast a lease for a year and so on from year to year, which is for a minimum duration of two years: a fixed term of one year, followed by at least one year of a periodic tenancy.

[64] See above pp. 21–23.

[65] See below pp. 551–553.

[66] See below p. 559.

A periodic tenancy will arise where a lease fails for want of formality or for uncertainty, but the tenant enters and rent is paid and accepted. *Prudential Assurance Co. Ltd.* v. *London Residuary Body* concerned a lease of a strip of land granted in 1930 until the strip was required for road widening, a term which was void for uncertainty; however both parties conceded that a yearly tenancy had been created by payment and acceptance of a yearly rent.[67]

The period of the tenancy follows the method by which the rent is calculated.[68] Notice to quit is used to terminate a periodic tenancy; special rules apply to contractual termination of business leases[69] and to agricultural leases.[70]

C. CERTAINTY: TERMINATION AND REPUGNANCY

1. Fixed terms

A lease must obviously be certain in retrospect. When the time comes for the lease to end, this fact must be clear. But quite apart from that rule, and additional to it, the law has always insisted that the duration of a lease must be fixed with prospective certainty, that is in advance. Actually it is the maximum duration that is critical; for example in *Joseph* v. *Joseph* a lease providing for the tenant to give up occupation "by July 31st 1960" was held to be a valid lease.[71] As Lord Greene M.R. said in *Lace* v. *Chantler*:

> "A term created by a leasehold tenancy agreement must be expressed either with certainty . . . or by reference to something which can, at the time when the lease takes effect, be looked to as a certain ascertainment of what the term is meant to be."[72]

The House of Lords has now unanimously approved this same approach in *Prudential Assurance Co. Ltd.* v. *London Residuary Body*. A lease to continue until land was required for widening Walworth Road in South London was held to be uncertain and void. This rule has been traced back to the decision in *Say* v. *Smith* in 1530[73] and has rarely been questioned since.[74]

In *Lace* v. *Chantler*, a tenancy "furnished for duration"—that is for the duration of the Second World War—was held to be uncertain and void.[75] Validation of leases created during that particular war[76] left in place the general principle of the case. When the lease was granted, say in 1940, the difficulty was to know for how many years the war would

---

[67] [1992] 2 A.C. 386 H.L.; Blackstone's *Commentaries* (1st ed. 1766) vol.2, 147.

[68] See above p. 511.

[69] See below Chapter 21.

[70] See below Chapter 22.

[71] [1967] Ch. 78, 86D–G.

[72] [1944] K.B. 368, 370.

[73] (1530) 1 Plowd. 269, 75 E.R. 410; *Prudential Assurance Co. Ltd.* v. *London Residuary Body* [1992] 2 A.C. 386, 390F, Lord Templeman; *Bishop of Bath's* case (1605) 6 Co. Rep. 34b, 35b, 77 E.R. 303; *E.W.P. Ltd.* v. *Moore* [1992] Q.B. 460, 471G, Nolan L.J.

[74] Coke on *Littleton*, para.45b; Blackstone's *Commentaries*, vol.2 (1st ed., 1766) 143; T. Platt, *Law of Leases* (1847) vol.1, 22.

[75] [1944] K.B. 368; (1944) 60 L.Q.R. 219; J.D.G.J. (1945) 9 C.L.J. 121. First instance decisions impliedly overruled were: *Pocock* v. *Carter* [1912] 1 Ch. 663; *Swift* v. *Macbean* [1942] 1 K.B. 375; and *Eker* v. *Becker* [1946] 1 All E.R. 721.

[76] Validation of War Time Leases Act 1944 s.1.

last. At the time of the litigation in 1944 the war was still on with no end in sight, though as we know with the benefit of hindsight the tide had long since turned.

In subsequent cases doubt was cast on the prospective test of certainty. At first, a different rule was laid down for periodic tenancies,[77] and later this relaxation was extended to allow a fixed term tenancy with no period. Thus in *Ashburn Anstalt* v. *Arnold & Co.*[78] the Court of Appeal accepted a lease to last until the landlord served notice that it was ready to begin development of a site, saying that it was sufficient, when the time came to end the lease, that it was clear whether or not the determining event had occurred and that the site could now be redeveloped.[79] Following that, in *Canadian Imperial Bank of Commerce* v. *Bello*,[80] a term to last until a builder had been paid for building work was also held to be certain. Each of these leases was uncertain in prospect, and represented erroneous applications of the *Lace* v. *Chantler* test of prospective certainty, so that each of these cases has now been overruled.[81]

Doctrinal order has been restored by the decision of the House of Lords in *Prudential Assurance Co. Ltd.* v. *London Residuary Body*.[82] This confirms the traditional learning, that the *Lace* test of prospective certainty applies to all leases and to all forms of tenancy. A lease granted in 1930 of land fronting Walworth Road in London was to continue until the land was required for road widening. The House of Lords struck down the validity of the lease, which was to be for a single uncertain term. If road-widening did occur, the terminating event would be certain in retrospect. By 1992 it was in fact extremely unlikely that this would ever happen, and to have allowed the lease to stand would have been to confer a perpetual right of possession at a fixed rent of £30 a year. That injustice was avoided by the decision that the term was unenforceable. A tenancy at will arose, converted to a periodic tenancy by payment and acceptance of rent,[83] but this was terminable and the rent could be increased. So *Prudential Assurance* reconfirmed the *Lace* v. *Chantler* test for a valid term of years, that a lease should be for a period of years which can be ascertained with certainty at the outset. A lease until road widening fails that test.

2.   Reworking an uncertain term as a long determinable term

One escape from uncertainty would be to treat the lease as a term of long duration determinable on the occurrence of the event which limited the original term.[84] In *Great Northern Railway Co.* v. *Arnold*,[85] Rowlatt J. interpreted a lease for the duration of the Great War as a lease for 999 years terminable on the cessation of that war. However, *Lace*

[77] *Re Midland Railway Co.'s Agreement* [1971] Ch. 725 C.A.; see below pp. 514–515.
[78] [1989] Ch. 1 C.A.
[79] The two tests were confused at [1989] Ch. 1, 12E, Fox L.J.
[80] (1991) 24 H.L.R. 155 C.A.
[81] *Prudential* expressly overruled *Midland Railway*, *Ashburn Anstalt*, and *Prudential* in the C.A., and by implication also *Bello*.
[82] [1992] 2 A.C. 386 H.L.; P. Sparkes (1993) 109 *L.Q.R.* 93; P.F. Smith [1993] *Conv.* 461; S. Bridge [1993] *C.L.J.* 26; S. Bright (1993) 13 *L.S.* 38; D. Wilde (1994) 57 *M.L.R.* 117; M. Biles [1994] *N.L.J.* 156; M. Haley (1995) 24 *Anglo-American* 236.
[83] See above p. 511.
[84] Is a term of nine years, terminable after 3 or 6 years, for 3 or 9 years? The court in *Goodright d. Hall* v. *Richardson* (1789) 3 Term Rep. 462, 100 E.R. 678 was divided.
[85] (1916) 33 T.L.R. 114; *Siew Soon Wah* v. *Yong Tong Hong* [1973] A.C. 836, 844 ("this lease shall be permanent" held to create a lease for 30 years, the maximum permitted duration under Malaysian law).

v. *Chantler* reveals some unease about this decision,[86] because the selection of 999 years was artificial; why not 99 years, 90 years taken by statute to cover an adult life,[87] or the more optimistic period of 10 years adopted by statute towards the end of the Second War?[88] Many events are quite uncertain. How long *until Scotland wins the World Cup?*[89] or even until it *reaches the second phase?* Whatever term was fixed, the rent would be fixed for that period, with no guideline about what is a fair period.

3.   Certainty of periodic tenancies

Uncertainty is inherent in the very nature of a periodic tenancy. Initially for only one period, it will roll on from period to period until one or other of the parties takes action to bring it to an end by notice. Looked at in retrospect a monthly tenancy may have lasted for 50 years, but for the future it is for one month only. Hence "the simple statement of the law that the maximum duration of a term must be certainly known in advance of its taking effect cannot therefore have direct reference to periodic tenancies".[90] Nevertheless an element of certainty can be discovered in the fact that the maximum commitment of either party can be fixed at any moment by the service of notice. As Professor Gray has said:

> "the periodic tenancy passes the test of certain maximum duration in the sense that each occupational unit of time, as it is added to the preceding unit of time, is itself of strictly defined duration."[91]

Hence a periodic tenancy was perfectly valid at common law and continues to be so in modern law.

Prudential Assurance[92] has swept away any doubts expressed in *Re Midland Railway Co.'s Agreement*[93] about the need for certainty of a periodic term. Prospective certainty applies equally to both, subject only to the qualification that a periodic tenancy is sufficiently certain if it is capable of being rendered certain. In the *Midland Railway* case, a periodic tenancy of some railway land granted in 1920 contained a term that prevented the landlord from serving notice unless the land was required for the purposes of the railway. When that might be was quite unknown in 1920, and in fact no need had arisen by the time of the dispute in 1971. The tenant very likely had a right to continue in occupation at a fixed rent indefinitely. Even for the mere 100 square yards of land in issue, the rent of £1 fixed in 1920 had become completely unrealistic. In fact it was not a valid tenancy, since *Midland Railway* has since been overruled. Prospective certainty was,[94]

---

[86] [1944] K.B. 368, 371, Lord Greene M.R., 372, MacKinnon L.J.

[87] L.P.A. 1925 s.149(6).

[88] Validation of War Time Leases Act 1944; *Prudential* [1992] 2 A.C. 386, 391G–392A Lord Templeman.

[89] Compare [1992] 1 E.G.L.R. 47, 51A, Scott L.J. (until England wins the Davis Cup, an example happily less striking eight years on).

[90] *Re Midland Railway Co.'s Agreement* [1971] Ch. 725, 732F–G.

[91] *Elements of Land Law* (Butterworths, 1987) 437; *Hammersmith and Fulham L.B.C.* v. *Monk* [1992] 1 A.C. 478, 484E, Lord Bridge; *Bacon's Abridgment* (7th ed.) vol.4, 839.

[92] [1992] 2 A.C. 386, 395G, Lord Templeman.

[93] [1971] Ch. 725 C.A.; D. Macintyre [1971] *C.L.J.* 198; (1973) 89 *L.Q.R.* 457.

[94] *Cheshire Lines Committee* v. *Lewis & Co.* (1880) 50 L.J.Q.B. 121, 138 Brett L.J.; *Doe d. Warner* v. *Browne* (1807) 8 East. 165, 103 E.R. 305; the common law result was approved in Chancery under the name *Browne* v. *Warner* (1808) 14 Ves. 156, 409 (see at 158 Lord Eldon), 33 E.R. 480, 578.

is,[95] and always will be, a requirement for periodic tenancies. Thus in *Prudential Assurance Co. Ltd.* v. *London Residuary Body* a single term to endure until land was required for road widening was held to be uncertain. A tenant who entered under that void tenancy, paid rent yearly, and had this rent accepted, became a yearly tenant. This was terminable by half a year's notice in the normal way because, as the Lords held, it was not permissible to imply a provision restraining termination until the land was required for the purposes of road widening.[96] Rather the implied yearly tenancy could be terminated by a half year's notice at the end of *any* period of the tenancy.

4. Repugnancy in periodic tenancies

A particular term may be rejected because of an inconsistency with the nature of the periodic tenancy of which the term forms a part, whether the term is express or implied. At first no term could relate to a time after the end of the very first period of the tenancy. Thus in a yearly tenancy, a covenant to paint every three years,[97] or to give two years' notice to quit,[98] or to do substantial repairs,[99] was held to be invalid. However a relaxation established that this was only true in prospect, when looking forward at the beginning of the periodic tenancy. After the lease had lasted for a number of years, terms could be enforced if they applied to the time when the tenant had actually been in occupation, and hence to all terms at the end of the lease.[100] Notice provisions are forward-looking, so that the old law (even with this relaxation) invalidated a term requiring a longer period of notice than the period of the tenancy.[101] But even this wisdom was doubted in *Breams Property Investment Co. Ltd.* v. *Stroulger*,[102] where a provision restricting service of notice was permitted, even though it was for a period that was longer than the basic period of the lease. Similarly in *Re Midland Railway Co.'s Agreement*[103] the pre-nationalisation Midland Railway had granted Clay a lease from half year to half year until terminated by three months' notice, with a provision that the railway agreed not to serve notice until it required the land (adjoining Derby station) for use in its business. This last clause was not repugnant.[104] Lord Templeman accepted this novelty in *Prudential Assurance*, for he said[105] that a lease can be made from year to year subject to a fetter on the right of the landlord to determine the lease before the expiry of five years unless the War ends, the effect being a determinable term of five years. The clause becomes repugnant if the landlord can never terminate the lease.[106]

---

[95] *Prudential Assurance* [1992] 2 A.C. 386, 394F, Lord Templeman; *Onyx (U.K.) Ltd.* v. *Beard* [1996] E.G.C.S. 55 Ch.D.

[96] [1992] 1 E.G.L.R. 47 C.A. reversed by H.L. [1992] 2 A.C. 386, 394H. This seems more satisfactory in principle than the alternative strand of authority which treats the tenant as a trespasser or licensee: *St Giles Hotel Ltd.* v. *Microworld Technology Ltd.* [1997] 2 E.G.L.R. 105 C.A.

[97] *Tooker* v. *Smith* (1857) 1 H. & N. 732, 156 E.R. 1396.

[98] *Pinero* v. *Judson* (1829) 6 Bing. 206, 130 E.R. 1259.

[99] *Doe d. Thomson* v. *Amey* (1840) 22 Ad. & El. 476, 479, 113 E.R. 892.

[100] *Pistor* v. *Cater* (1842) 9 M. & W. 315, 152 E.R. 134; *Adams* v. *Clutterbuck* (1883) 10 Q.B.D. 403, 406.

[101] *Tooker* v. *Smith* (1857) 1 H. & N. 732, 156 E.R. 1396.

[102] [1948] 2 K.B. 1 (restriction on service of notice for a fixed term of 3 years); D.C. Potter (1948) 11 *M.L.R.* 342.

[103] Also called *Clay* v. *British Railways Board* [1971] 1 Ch. 725 C.A.; [1971] *C.L.J.* 198.

[104] Though it is uncertain: [1992] 2 A.C. 386, 395A.

[105] [1992] 2 A.C. 386, 395A.

[106] *Centaploy* v. *Matlodge* [1974] Ch 1, Whitford J.; *Midland Railway* [1971] Ch. 725, 733F, Russell L.J.

5. Certainty in equitable leases, contracts for legal leases and licences

Most equitable leases take the form of a contract to create a legal lease, and therefore (after 1925) as a contract to create a term of years absolute. Hence the requirement for a certain term is exactly the same in equity as it is at common law. Lord Denning M.R. recanted in *Harvey* v. *Pratt*,[107] having only lapsed into the heresy of believing that equity could directly rescue an uncertain term on one earlier occasion.[108] Specific performance of an agreement to create an uncertain term would create an invalid lease of uncertain duration,[109] and could not resolve an issue of uncertainty because the same question of repugnancy arose after performance of the contract. Nothing could be clearer given that one persistent tenant failed for uncertainty in the common law courts,[110] transferred to equity, tried again, and failed for uncertainty a second time.[111]

Equity might, however, be able to reinterpret an agreement so as to save it from creating an uncertain right. For example a grant for an unspecified term might be interpreted as a lease for life if made by a freeholder[112] or a sub-lease for the remainder of the landlord's leasehold term.[113] The position under the fused jurisdiction was considered in *Zimbler* v. *Abrahams*.[114] A house was let at weekly rental, but with an agreement by the landlord that:

> "I agree not to raise Mr A any rent as long as he lives in the house and pays rent regular. I shall not give him notice to quit. . .".

Vaughan Williams L.J. treated this as an agreement to create a lease for life, which after 1925 would act as a grant for 90 years.[115]

A *licence* may be created for an uncertain period.[116]

6. Is reform required?

Lord Browne-Wilkinson characterised the result of *Prudential Assurance Co. Ltd.* v. *London Residuary Body* as unsatisfactory,[117] but Lord Templeman appeared perfectly at ease with the result to which his technical analysis directed him. Academic opinion is divided.[118]

When a business lease ends, statute will prolong its duration and the tenant may well be able to renew it. Superficially it seems odd to insist on initial certainty of a term that will be continued indefinitely, but in fact there are two good reasons to require certainty: the rent is fixed for any contractual period, and the grounds on which the landlord can

---

[107] [1965] 1 W.L.R. 1025, 1026E, citing *Marshall* v. *Berridge* (1881) 19 Ch. D. 233, 245, Lush L.J.

[108] *Wallis* v. *Semark* (1951) 2 T.L.R. 222, 226.

[109] *Cheshire Lines Committee* v. *Lewis & Co.* (1880) 50 L.J.Q.B. 121, 129, Brett L.J.

[110] *Doe d. Warner* v. *Browne* (1807) 8 East 165, 103 E.R. 305.

[111] *Browne* v. *Warner* (1808) 14 Ves. 156, 33 E.R. 480.

[112] *Browne* v. *Warner* as above; *Re King's Leasehold Estates* (1873) L.R. 16 Eq. 521, 527, Malins V.C; *Cheshire Lines* at 121, 126, Lush J., 129, Brett L.J.; *Wood* v. *Beard* (1876) 2 Ex.D. 30, 36, Cleasby B.

[113] Further proceedings in *Browne* v. *Warner* (1808) 14 Ves. 409, 33 E.R. 578.

[114] [1903] 1 K.B. 577 C.A.; *Binions* v. *Evans* [1972] Ch 359 367E–H, Lord Denning M.R.

[115] L.P.A. 1925 s.149(6); see above pp. 363–365.

[116] P. Sparkes (1993) 109 *L.Q.R.* 93, 107–110.

[117] [1992] 2 A.C. 386, 396G.

[118] Contrast P. Sparkes (1993) 109 *L.Q.R.* 93, 110–113; and S. Bright (1993) 13 *L.S.* 38.

recover possession are severely limited. The rent should not be fixed at a very low level for ever unless the parties clearly intend this, especially as business tenants will usually have renewal rights.

D. COMMENCEMENT OF LEASES

A perfect lease requires a certain beginning as well as a certain ending.[119] No difficulty exists if the right to possession coincides with the grant of a legal lease, but there are a number of variations requiring detailed analysis.

1. The commencement date

Odd as it may seem, the long established general rule[120] is that if a lease runs "from" a stated day, that day is excluded from the term. Thus in *Whelton Sinclair* v. *Hyland*[121] a lease to run from June 27th 1976 for 10 years did not include that June the 27th. Greater clarity can be achieved by stating that the term is "beginning on" or "from and including", and the general rule could also be excluded by showing that the lease follows on from an earlier one,[122] or by stating the termination date as well.[123]

2. Starting the term from an earlier date

There is no objection to measuring the length of the term from a date before the grant of the lease to the tenant, though clear wording will be needed to overcome the presumption against operating the term retrospectively. At first sight it appears odd that a tenant would wish to take such a lease, because part of the period for which he is taking the land is lost unavoidably before the right to possession accrues on the grant of the lease, but reflection reveals its purpose. In a large leasehold development with a number of units sold on similar long leases, it is good management practice to start all the terms on the same date, so that the terms also expire together. Thus a number of 99-year leases may be granted so that the term of each starts on the same day in 2000, with the result that they will all expire together in 2099. When the last units on the estate are sold, there will be slightly less than 99 years remaining. Obviously rent should not accrue before the tenant has the use of the land. Leases limited to commence at a date before the grant of the lease are also useful where a tenant holds over at the end of a previous lease, so that the two terms link seamlessly, even if the new terms are not agreed until later. *Bradshaw* v. *Pawley* was just such a case.[124] A tenant of business premises held over from 1974 for four years, but when the terms of the new lease were agreed it was backdated to run from

---

[119] *Marshall* v. *Berridge* (1881) 19 Ch.D. 233, 245, Lush L.J.; *Say* v. *Smith* (1530) 1 Plowd. 269, 75 E.R. 410; Blackstone's *Commentaries* (2nd ed. 1766) vol.2, 143; *Prudential Assurance* [1992] 2 A.C. 386, 390, Lord Templeman.

[120] Hill & Redman, *Landlord and Tenant* (18th ed.) para.A[219].

[121] [1992] 2 E.G.L.R. 158 C.A.; E. Cooke [1993] *Conv.* 206. On "from" see below pp. 581–582.

[122] *Whelton Sinclair* as above.

[123] *Meadfield Properties Ltd.* v. *S.S. for the Environment* [1995] 1 E.G.L.R. 39 Ch.D. (term from June 24th 1984 until December 24th 2003); *Associated London Properties Ltd.* v. *Sheridan* [1946] 1 All E.R. 20; *Gardner* v. *Ingram* (1889) 61 L.T. 729.

[124] [1980] 1 W.L.R. 10.

1974, and the higher rent reserved by the 1978 lease was held to be payable from 1974 onwards.

For many purposes the actual length of the tenant's enjoyment of the land should be taken.[125]

3. Future leases

A legal lease may operate immediately from its grant or it may entitle the tenant to possession of the land only in the future. A future lease[126] must be created by deed if it is to operate at law.[127] The main provision regulating future leases is section 149(3) of the Law of Property Act 1925, which states, for any lease granted after 1925, that:

> "A term, at a rent or granted in consideration of a fine . . . to take effect more than 21 years from the date of the instrument purporting to create it shall be void. . . ."[128]

A lease in 1998 to confer possession in 2018 is valid, but if possession were deferred until 2025 it would be void. The basic thrust of this provision is obviously to prevent the irremovable incumbrance created by a legal lease looming over the land for too long a period. A leasehold term should therefore start within 21 years of the execution of the lease. Closer examination reveals one puzzling feature.[129] The provision applies only to commercial leases—granted at a rent or fine—but the incumbrance on the landlord's title is far more serious if the land is tied up without income. Why aren't gratuitous leases included?

4. Terms to commence on a contingency

What if the starting date is an uncertain future contingency? Despite the greatly increased difficulties, such a lease appears to be valid. *Swift* v. *Macbean*[130] decided at first instance that a tenancy to commence on the outbreak of war was a valid legal lease, and earlier cases tended towards the same conclusion.[131] Control is imposed by requiring the contingency to be fulfilled within a perpetuity period.[132]

---

[125] *Roberts* v. *Church Commissioners for England* [1972] 1 Q.B. 278 C.A. (enfranchisement tests are measured from the possession date rather than the notional commencement of the term).

[126] This is better than "reversionary lease", which is also used to mean a lease inserted between an existing landlord and his tenant; see below pp. 742–743.

[127] It is outside the short lease exemption: L.P.A. 1925 s.54(2); though it could qualify as a contract for a short lease: L.P.(M.P.)A. 1989 s.2(5)(a).

[128] Exceptions are leases under settlements, leases created out of equitable interests, and those created under an equitable power for mortgage, indemnity, and like purposes; see *Long* v. *Tower Hamlets L.B.C.* [1998] Ch. 197, James Munby Q.C.

[129] Sparkes *N.L.L.* 394.

[130] [1942] 1 K.B. 375; R.E. Megarry (1941) 57 *L.Q.R.* 158. The tenant was to hold until the termination of hostilities, but this is contrary to *Lace* v. *Chantler* [1944] K.B. 368 C.A., a fact which may cast doubt on the worth of the case.

[131] *Bishop of Bath's case* (1605) 6 Co. Rep. 34b, 35b, 77 E.R. 303; *Ex parte Voisey* (1882) 21 Ch.D. 442 C.A.

[132] It is open to question whether the period should be 21 years, or a full period including lives in being as well as the 21 years.

5. Commencement of contracts

A contract for a legal lease involves three dates, A when the contract is entered into, B when the legal lease is granted, and C when the term of the lease is to commence. Three restrictions are imposed: (1) the date B must be agreed, (2) the period A–B is regulated by the rule against perpetuities, and (3) B–C is regulated by the future lease provisions.

A valid contract for a lease must state a commencement date for the term. It cannot be implied that a lease is to commence after a reasonable time or at the date of the agreement, and indeed there is no concluded contract if the time has never been specified or agreed.[133] However, taking occupation may supply the intended commencement date.

The rule against perpetuities is concerned with the moment at which a legal leasehold estate is vested in the tenant. Vesting occurs when any uncertainty about the entitlement of the tenant to the lease is removed because any precondition to entitlement is removed. Under pre-1926 law, most future leases escaped the rule against perpetuities, because the future tenant immediately acquired an *interesse termini*.[134] Abolition of this rule[135] suggests that the rule against perpetuities should now be applied so as to require the fulfilment of any pre-condition within a defined period.

Contracts for future leases are regulated by section 149(6) of the Law of Property Act 1925, which applies to contracts as well as legal leases.[136] Any contract is void if it is to create "a term, at a rent or granted in consideration of a fine . . . to take effect more than 21 years from the date of the instrument purporting to create it". As with legal leases, the legislation focuses on the gap between execution of the lease and its taking effect in possession, that is dates B and C. Once it takes effect in possession, the lease could be for a very long period. Curious anomalies result.

> Examples.
> 1. A contract (A) in 1998 for a commercial lease to be granted (B) in 1999 for 40 years from (C) 2024. The contract is void.
> 2. A contract (A) in 1998 for a commercial lease to be granted (B) in 2016 for a 40 year term from (C) 2024. The contract is valid.
> The vital interval is between grant of the lease (B) and the lease taking effect in possession (C). This is from 1998 to 2024 in example 1 but only from 2016 to 2024 in example 2.

E. CONTRACTS FOR LEASES

1. Contracts

Formalities are essential for the creation of any contract affecting land. All expressly agreed terms should be recorded in signed writing,[137] and this must include details of the landlord and the tenant, the property, and the price (that is the agreed rent and any

---

[133] *Harvey* v. *Pratt* [1965] 1 W.L.R. 1025, 1027E, Lord Denning M.R.
[134] C. Sweet (1914) 30 *L.Q.R.* 66.
[135] L.P.A. 1925 s.149(1).
[136] See above pp. 363–365.
[137] L.P.(M.P.) A. 1989 s.2; Sparkes *N.L.L.* ch.9; there is a short lease exemption: s.2(5)(a).

premium). It is also essential to agree and record the intended commencement date of the term of the lease; absence of this last term will frequently negate the possibility of conversion of a defective legal lease.[138] Indeed the tougher formality provisions introduced in 1990 make it much more likely that a lease will fail completely. Proprietary estoppel may come into play to create entitlement to a lease if contract formalities are not present but there is an expectation of contractual entitlement that is supported by acts of detrimental reliance.[139]

Contracts require protection. A potential tenant is adequately protected once he has taken occupation if title is registered, but before that time protection is required by an appropriate notice, caution, or land charges registration.

2. Merger and rectification

When the deed granting the legal lease is executed, the rights of the parties must thenceforth be determined by the terms of that deed, the preceding contract merging into the completed transaction[140] and *Walsh* v. *Lonsdale* ceasing to apply. This is subject to the possibility of rectification, by which the court orders a completed lease to be corrected so that it complies with the contractual terms on which it ought to have been granted. A number of recent cases need to be added to those discussed in *A New Land Law*.[141] In *Templiss Properties Ltd.* v. *Hyams*[142] a lease was corrected to remove the landlord's liability to non-domestic rates, since a covenant to pay them had not been agreed in advance and the tenant who had failed to draw attention to this change had knowingly taken advantage of the landlord's error. Similarly, a break clause was removed from a lease in *Coles* v. *William Hill Organisation Ltd.*[143] but a guarantor's covenant was added in *Eason* v. *Brewster*.[144] Unless the tenant is in possession of registered land, rectification rights are easily defeated by a "purchaser", which concept includes a person who pays a nominal £1 consideration but who also agrees to take on the tenant's liabilities under the lease.[145]

3. Defective legal leases as contracts

An attempted legal lease that is defective for want of formalities will operate as a contract for a lease. The Real Property Act 1845[146] provided that a lease over three years was void at law unless by deed. *Parker* v. *Taswell*[147] soon raised the question of the effect of the 1845 provision in equity. Lord Chelmsford L.C. pointed out that it said "void at law"

---

[138] *Harvey* v. *Pratt* [1965] 1 W.L.R. 1025; the difficulty ends on taking possession; see below pp. 529–530.

[139] Sparkes *N.L.L.* ch.11; *Orgee* v. *Orgee* [1997] E.G.C.S. 152 C.A.; M. Pawlowski (1998) 114 *L.Q.R.* 351; *Pridean Ltd.* v. *Forest Taverns Ltd.* (1998) 75 P. & C.R. 447 C.A.

[140] *Carrington Manufacturing Company Ltd.* v. *Saldin* (1925) 133 L.T. 432.

[141] Sparkes *N.L.L.* 182–184, 236–237.

[142] [1999] E.G.C.S. 60. Where a single solicitor acts for both parties and makes a mistake, this shows a common intention, which is a ground for rectification: *Mace* v. *Rutland House Textiles Ltd.* [2000] Times January 11th Ch.D.; Q. Smye [1999] 49 *E.G.* 92.

[143] [1999] L.T.R. 14 Ch.D.

[144] [1997] 1 C.L.Y 1978.

[145] *D.B. Ramsden & Co. Ltd.* v. *Nurdin & Peacock plc. (No.1)* [1999] 1 E.G.L.R. 119, Neuberger J.

[146] s.3, now L.P.A. 1925 s.52; *Tottenham Hotspur Football & Athletic Club Ltd.* v. *Princegrove Publishers Ltd.* [1974] 1 W.L.R. 113, 121, Lawson J.

[147] (1858) 2 De G. & J. 559, 44 E.R. 1106.

as opposed to "void to all intents and purposes",[148] so that a defective lease could be reinterpreted as an agreement enforceable in equity.[149] Though the decision neutralises the 1845 Act,[150] it is now settled even at common law.[151] The next principle to be discussed—the doctrine of *Walsh* v. *Lonsdale*[152]—can then be applied to convert the contract to an equitable term. Conversion of a defective lease to a contract is dependent upon the presence of the contract formalities just discussed.

F. EQUITABLE LEASES

1. Doctrine of Walsh v. Lonsdale

A person with a contractual right to an interest in land can obtain a decree of specific performance, enabling him to get at the land itself, and conferring an immediate equitable interest in the land. Most fully developed in relation to contracts for leases, this doctrine is named after its exemplar, *Walsh* v. *Lonsdale*.[153]

Lonsdale as landlord agreed by an unsealed writing to grant a lease of a mill to Walsh for seven years. The rent varied, but was a minimum of £810 a year. Possession was taken in 1879 and rent paid quarterly in arrears for three years. In March 1882 the landlord served notice on the tenant, as he was entitled to do under the contract, requiring a year's rent in advance from that date and waited only two days before putting in a distress for that rent—that is he seized goods belonging to the tenant. He (Walsh) in turn sued the landlord, Lonsdale, for damages for illegal distress. Had the lease been granted by deed, Lonsdale's right to levy a distress for arrears of rent would have been clear. What took it out of the mundane run of the mill (!) case was the fact that possession was held under a written agreement for a lease for seven years. Specific performance in equity could compel completion of the legal lease, and the right to that remedy was conceded. No doubt the case was unusual in that both parties had the same interest in securing a legal lease: Lonsdale to secure the right to distrain and Walsh to secure the security of occupation throughout the seven year term. The Court of Appeal reached its decision on an interim stage in the proceedings: the tenant made an interlocutory application to get back his goods taken by distress; in order to pursue this claim for trespass to his goods the tenant was required to lodge security for the amount of the rent, the implication being that rent was owing. Hence it was effectively a ruling that the distress had been lawful. If so, the court recognised distress as a legitimate remedy not only under a legal lease but also under an agreement for a lease. Walsh was an equitable tenant for seven years holding under the terms of his agreement.

The principle is general, and can, for example, be applied to a contract for a lease for life.[154]

---

[148] At 570.

[149] *Browne* v. *Warner* (1807) 14 Ves. 156, 33 E.R. 480; (1808) 14 Ves. 409, 33 E.R. 578.

[150] *Zimbler* v. *Abrahams* [1903] 1 K.B. 577, 581, Vaughan Williams L.J.

[151] *Bond* v. *Rosling* (1861) 1 B.& S. 371, 121 E.R. 753; *Tidey* v. *Mollett* (1864) 16 C.B. N.S. 298, 143 E.R. 1143; *Industrial Properties (Barton Hill) Ltd.* v. *Associated Electrical Industries Ltd.* [1977] Q.B. 580 C.A.

[152] See below pp. 521–534.

[153] (1882) 21 Ch.D. 9 C.A.

[154] L.P.A. 1925 s.149(6); *Kingswood Estates Co. Ltd.* v. *Anderson* [1963] 2 Q.B. 169.

2.   The conflict between law and equity

Orthodox analysis assumes that Walsh was liable to pay rent quarterly in arrears at common law and to pay a year's rent in advance, on demand, in equity. Hence there was a conflict between the rule at common law and the rule in equity. Under the fused system, equity prevails. This was an understandable simplification by Maitland when lecturing to students at Cambridge,[155] but in fact rent probably was owing at law—because the provision for rent to be demanded in advance was implied into the periodic tenancy—and all that the Court of Appeal decided was that the common law position was irrelevant.[156]

Equity's approach was founded on the availability of specific performance to implement the contract. This is an order directing the landlord to execute the deed granting the lease and directing the tenant to execute a counterpart lease. Compliance can be secured by the threat of imprisonment or by authorising a Chancery master to execute the lease on behalf of the defaulting party. In the final analysis equity could compel the execution of the legal lease. *Walsh* v. *Lonsdale* governs the effect of a contract in the interim period after a contract has been entered into, but before any court application to compel specific performance. The novelty was to apply to that interregnum the maxim that *equity treats as done that which ought to be done*. As between the original parties, who are contractually bound to grant and to take a lease, the effect of a contract is the same as if a legal lease had been granted—that is the lease is backdated to the time of its contractual creation.[157] The tenant (Walsh) was obliged to execute a legal lease that would enable the landlord, Lonsdale, to demand rent in advance according to the terms of this agreement. Distress was held to be available as a remedy. It is this last point that is totally novel.[158]

3.   Fusion of law and equity

Before 1876 the common law was administered in the three common law courts, Queen's Bench, Common Pleas and Exchequer, while equitable suits went to the Court of Chancery.[159] Litigants might therefore be required to journey between the common law courts and Chancery, possibly several times, in order to achieve a complete resolution of a single dispute. That equity would ultimately prevail was established when James I settled a dispute between the common law courts and Chancery in favour of the Lord Chancellor,[160] the mechanism being a common injunction ordering a litigant not to enforce a common law judgment.

Fusion in the *High Court* was effected by the (Supreme Court of) Judicature Act 1873,[161] operating from November 1875. A single Supreme Court was established, amalgamating the jurisdiction of the old common law courts as well as the Court of

---

[155] Maitland's *Equity* (2nd ed.) 157.

[156] P. Sparkes (1988) 8 *O.J.L.S.* 350, 351–355.

[157] *Trane* v. *Provident Mutual Life Assurance* [1995] 1 E.G.L.R. 33.

[158] P. Sparkes (1988) 8 *O.J.L.S.* 350, 354.

[159] Common Law Procedure Act 1852 effected minor reforms.

[160] *Earl of Oxford's* case (1615) 1 Ch.Rep. 1, 21 E.R. 485.

[161] 36 & 37 Vict. c.66. Amendments in 1875 did not affect the fusion provisions: 38 & 39 Vict. c.77.

Chancery and providing a uniform system of appeal to the Court of Appeal. Procedural fusion was coupled with a provision to resolve substantive conflicts between law and equity, but, unfortunately, *Walsh* v. *Lonsdale* can be explained in either way as will be seen.

Limits apply to the powers of the *county courts,* a principle which appears to create an "Inferior Fusion".[162] A county court which has concurrent jurisdiction both at common law and in equity, may apply *Walsh* v. *Lonsdale* doctrine and so should treat a contract for a lease as an equitable lease.[163] However, the position is different if a case falls within the common law jurisdiction of a county court but outside its power to order specific performance. In the circumstances, *Foster* v. *Reeves* decided that a county court could not apply *Walsh* v. *Lonsdale* equities,[164] the county court being equivalent to a common law court in backward states—such as New York—in which there is no fusion.[165] This devastating conclusion has had relatively little impact in practice, for a number of reasons. First, the decision applies only to *claims* based upon the equitable jurisdiction, since there is full power to deal with defences, counter-claims and set-offs.[166] Secondly, full powers are given by the security of tenure and business tenancies legislation.[167] Thirdly, jurisdictional limits can be increased with the consent of both parties. Fourthly, the ancillary jurisdiction of the county courts includes the power to grant an injunction or declaration in respect of land,[168] so that equitable enforcement may be possible even when specific performance is not. Surely a county court faced with an inability to do full justice because of a limitation on its jurisdiction should transfer the case to the High Court to permit a full remedy?

4. *Walsh* v. *Lonsdale* as an example of procedural fusion

Before 1876 some litigation could only be resolved completely by action both at law and a suit in equity. Fusion brought the courts together and ensured that a result could be achieved in one set of proceedings. Section 24 of the 1873 Act[169] provided for the fusion of High Court procedure—with a new unified form of pleading, a combined procedure, full remedies, and no circuity of action.[170] Conventional theory suggests that this provision created no substantive change in the outcome of litigation, a view which, taken to extremes, would mean that nothing at all was changed by the Judicature Act. This is both orthodox and wrong. As Maitland's analysis of *Walsh* v. *Lonsdale* concluded:

---

[162] P. Sparkes (1987) 6 *C.J.Q.* 304.

[163] *Holland & Andrews* v. *Dowle* (1897) 102 L.T.Jo. 347, Judge Stonor; *Re Young ex parte Vitale* (1882) 47 L.T. 480; *Rickett* v. *Green* [1910] 1 K.B. 253; *Gilbey* v. *Cossey* (1912) 106 L.T. 607.

[164] [1892] 2 Q.B. 255 C.A. (no rent due at law; court not entitled to take agreement into account). This ignored the Judicature Act 1873 s.89.

[165] J.H. Beale (1921) 1 *C.L.J.* 21.

[166] *Cornish* v. *Brook Green Laundry Ltd.* [1959] 1 Q.B. 394 C.A. (obiter); *Kingswood Estate Co. Ltd.* v. *Anderson* [1963] 2 Q.B. 169 (ratio); S. Gardner (1987) 7 *O.J.L.S.* 60, 69–70.

[167] R.A. 1977 s.141; R.(Ag.) A. 1976 s.26; H.A. 1985 s.110; L.Ref.A. 1967 s.20; L.T.A. 1954 s.63.

[168] County Courts Act 1984 s.22.

[169] Now Supreme Court Act 1981 s.49(2).

[170] *Salt* v. *Cooper* (188) 16 Ch.D. 544, 552, Jessel M.R.

"the Court of Appeal in deciding that under the Judicature Acts L[onsdale] could distrain did but give effect to the net result of the previously existing rules of law and equity".[171]

According to Maitland the litigation in *Walsh* v. *Lonsdale* would have proceeded before 1875 something like this. Walsh, the tenant, would have sued for the trespass arising from an improper distress in the common law courts. Lonsdale had no answer to this action at common law, because there were no arrears to justify a distress, so he had to respond by seeking specific performance of the agreement to grant a lease. Before 1876 that entailed halting the common law proceedings, trailing off to equity, and obtaining a decree of specific performance of the contract. He could then return to the common law court, exhibit the legal lease obtained by specific performance and prove that rent was owing under the agreement. After 1875 this same result followed in the one High Court.

In fact the decision to allow distress without a legal lease at the moment of the distress was novel. Rent had to be sued for in common law courts, this being a case where equity followed the law, by insisting that distress should be justified on the basis of some legal relationship.[172] Jessel M.R. said that after the Judicature Act 1873, Walsh:

"being a lessee in equity cannot complain of the exercise of the right of distress merely because the actual parchment has not been signed and sealed."[173]

So the Court of Appeal applied a legal remedy to an equitable right, a change caused by, and attributed to, the 1873 Act.[174]

Reining in of *Walsh* v. *Lonsdale* doctrine occurred during the tenure of Lord Esher M.R., starting with *Coatsworth* v. *Johnson*.[175] Emphasis was placed on the availability of specific performance and it was said that common law rights would be enforceable unless the court would exercise its discretion to award specific performance. Legal and equitable streams remain unmixed in a single riverbed. This proceduralist theory has been applied in a number of later cases,[176] though many turn out to involve conditional contracts giving no immediate right to possession of the land.[177]

5.   *Walsh* v. *Lonsdale* as an example of the conflict provision

Section 25 of the Judicature Act 1873[178] resolved a number of detailed conflicts of rule between the two systems and then specified, more generally, that the rules of equity were

---

[171] Maitland's *Equity* (2nd ed.) 157; Holdsworth's *History* vol.XV 134; R. Evershed (1954) 70 *L.Q.R.* 326; P.V. Baker (1977) 93 *L.Q.R.* 529; J.E. Martin [1994] *Conv.* 13.

[172] *Vincent* v. *Godson* (1853) 1 Sm. & G. 384, 390, 65 E.R. 168, Stuart V.C.; on appeal (1854) 4 De G.M. & G. 546, 554, 43 E.R. 620, Lord Cranworth L.C.; *Jolly* v. *Arbuthnot* (1859) 4 De G & J 224, 242, 45 E.R. 87, Lord Chelmsford L.C.; *Walters* v. *Northern Coal Mining* (1855) 5 De G M & G 629, 43 E.R. 1015, Lord Cranworth L.C.; P. Sparkes (1988) 8 *O.J.L.S.* 350.

[173] (1882) 21 Ch.D. 9, 15.

[174] *Re Young ex parte Vitale* (1882) 47 L.T. 480; *Crump* v. *Temple* (1890) 7 T.L.R. 120; *Murgatroyd* v. *Silkstone & Dodsworth Coal & Iron ex parte Charlesworth* (1895) 65 L.J.Ch. 111; *Manchester Brewery Co.* v. *Coombs* [1901] 2 Ch. 608; *Rickett* v. *Green* [1910] 1 K.B. 253.

[175] (1886) 55 L.J. Q.B. 220.

[176] *Swain* v. *Ayres* (1888) 21 Q.B.D. 289; *Foster* v. *Reeves* [1892] 2 Q.B. 255; *Manchester Brewery Company* v. *Coombs* [1901] 2 Ch. 608; *Gray* v. *Spyer* [1922] 2 Ch. 22; *City Permanent B.S.* v. *Miller* [1952] Ch. 840; *Warmington* v. *Miller* [1973] Q.B. 877 C.A.

[177] e.g. *Cornish* v. *Brook Green Laundry Ltd.* [1959] 1 Q.B. 394 C.A.; see below p. 530.

[178] Now Supreme Court Act 1981 s.49(1).

to prevail over the common law rules in any residual case. Admittedly open conflict was rare. But deep down the whole justification for equity was that it reformed the law, in some cases completely nullifying common law rights,[179] and the legislative intention in 1873 was to *amend* the law.[180]

Often the conflict provision operates at an almost trivial level,[181] but when it does its effect is analysed in terms of a conflict of *rules*. *Walsh* v. *Lonsdale* was certainly an example, the conflict being between the common law (where Walsh held under an implied periodic tenancy) and equity (where it was under the agreement), with the equitable rule being vindicated. That Jessel M.R. applied the conflict provision is shown by this passage[182]:

> "There are not two estates as there were formerly, one estate at common law by reason of the payment of the rent from year to year and an estate in equity under the agreement. There is only one Court and the rules of equity prevail in it. The tenant holds under an agreement for a lease."

Legal rights are simply irrelevant, and there is no legal periodic tenancy[183] so long as there is a contract that is inherently open to specific performance. Hence if distress was justified by legal rights but nullified by equitable rights there could be no distress.[184]

Of the two streams of authority, that which favours a true fusion—a mingling of the waters—springs from *Walsh* v. *Lonsdale* itself and flows most strongly since it has been followed in most cases truly raising the issue.[185] *Walsh* v. *Lonsdale* itself says, and requires, that only one estate is created, the equitable term of years created under the agreement for a lease.

True fusion means that there is no difference between a lease by deed and a lease created by a written agreement, provided only that the agreement has priority—for example by registration of a notice of the estate contract or through occupation. Most modern statutes recognise that fact by including within the definition of a lease agreements under which a tenant has become entitled to have his lease granted. For example it was held by Carnwath J. in *R.* v. *Tower Hamlets L.B.C. ex parte Von Goetz*[186] that a 10-year assured shorthold in writing but not by deed was a valid equitable lease, and one that entitled the tenant to apply for a renovation grant. Some older statutes were more

---

[179] W.N. Hohfeld (1913) 11 *Mich.L.R.* 533; J. Tiley, *A Casebook on Equity* (Stevens, 1968) 5.

[180] Preamble to Judicature Act 1873 s.25 (emphasis supplied).

[181] *Job* v. *Job* (1877) 6 Ch.D. 562; *Lowe* v. *Dixon* (1885) 16 Q.B.D. 455; *Steeds* v. *Steeds* (1889) 12 Q.B.D. 531; *Vibart* v. *Coles* (1890) 24 Q.B.D. 364; *Berry* v. *Berry* [1929] 2 K.B. 316; *Mitas* v. *Hyams* [1951] 2 T.L.R. 1215; *Australian Blue Metal* v. *Hughes* [1963] A.C. 74, 102.

[182] (1882) 21 Ch.D. 9, 14.

[183] *Cardiothoracic Institute* v. *Shrewdcrest Ltd.* [1986] 1 W.L.R. 368, 378B, Knox J.; *Tinsley* v. *Milligan* [1994] 1 A.C. 340, 371A–B, Lord Browne-Wilkinson.

[184] *Murgatroyd* v. *Silkstone & Dodsworth Coal & Iron Co Ltd. ex parte Charlesworth* (1895) 65 L.J.Ch. 111, 112, Chitty J.; *Ellis* v. *Wright* (1897) 76 L.T. 522, Chitty J.; *Zimbler* v. *Abrahams* [1903] 1 K.B. 577 C.A.

[185] *Walsh* v. *Lonsdale* (1882) 21 Ch.D. 9; *Allhusen* v. *Brooking* (1884) 26 Ch.D. 559; *Re Maugham* (1885) 14 Q.B.D. 956; *Lowther* v. *Heaver* (1889) 41 Ch.D. 248; *Crump* v. *Temple* (1890) 7 T.L.R. 120; *Murgatroyd* v. *Silkstone & Dodsworth Coal & Iron Co Ltd. ex parte Charlesworth* (1895) 65 L.J. Ch. 111; *Zimbler* v. *Abrahams* [1903] 1 K.B. 577; *Kingswood Estates Ltd.* v. *Anderson* [1963] 2 Q.B. 169; *Tottenham Hotspur Football & Athletic Club Ltd.* v. *Princegrove Publishers Ltd.* [1974] 1 W.L.R. 113; *Rushton* v. *Smith* [1976] Q.B. 480; *Industrial Properties (Barton Hill) Ltd.* v. *Associated Electrical Industries Ltd.* [1977] Q.B. 580 C.A.

[186] [1999] Q.B. 1019 C.A.

restrictively worded and made available statutory rights to legal tenants that were denied to equitable tenants.[187] There is a strong case for a legislative tidying up operation.

G. *WALSH* v. *LONSDALE*: BASIS IN SPECIFIC PERFORMANCE

1. Proprietary riddle

Browne-Wilkinson J. showed in *Swiss Bank Corporation* v. *Lloyds Bank Ltd.*[188] how a personal jurisdiction could operate to create a proprietary right in land, based on the right to an equitable remedy and the operation of the maxim that "Equity treats as done that which ought to be done". Rights in the plaintiff founded upon the ability of the court to make an order against the defendant personally became an (equitable[189]) interest in the property itself.[190] If specific performance is theoretically available, the *Walsh* v. *Lonsdale* equity might be applied in litigation directed towards other equitable remedies, such as an injunction,[191] declaration,[192] or damages in lieu of specific performance. It is the fact that specific performance is usually granted automatically of a contract relating to land[193] which explains why stable property rights can be based on entitlement to a discretionary remedy.[194] Enforcement is virtually automatic after the tenant has taken possession.

2. Conclusive bars

Specific performance of contracts is prevented by certain circumstances called conclusive bars. Equitable leases are dependent upon the existence of a valid contract[195] meaning that *Walsh* v. *Lonsdale* cannot be applied in the absence of consideration, writing,[196] agreement on the terms,[197] agreement on the commencement date,[198] or capacity. Equitable enforcement may also be barred by misrepresentation,[199] other misconduct giving an entitlement to terminate the contract,[200] or oppressiveness of the contract.[201]

---

[187] *Borman* v. *Griffith* [1930] 1 Ch. 493; K.K.L. [1930] 4 C.L.J. 219 (L.P.A. 1925 s.62); *City Permanent B.S.* v. *Miller* [1952] Ch. 840 C.A. (L.R.A. 1925 s.70(1)(k)); *Re Rycroft's Settlement* [1962] Ch. 263. *Friary Holroyd & Healey's Breweries Ltd.* v. *Singleton* [1899] 1 Ch. 86 (reversed on other grounds [1899] 2 Ch. 261 C.A.) (equitable assignee of lease not entitled to benefit of option to purchase in lease); *Swain* v. *Ayres* (1888) 21 Q.B.D. 289, 295, Lindley L.J.; *Borman* v. *Griffith* [1930] Ch. 493, 497–498 (equitable lease is not a conveyance); *City Permanent B.S.* v. *Miller* [1952] Ch. 840 C.A.; S. Gardner (1987) 7 *O.J.L.S.* 60, 63.
[188] [1979] Ch. 548, 565; reversed, but the statement of principle approved: [1982] A.C. 584, 613, Lord Wilberforce.
[189] *Vincent* v. *Godson* (1854) 4 De G.M. & G. 546, 548, 43 E.R. 620, Lord Cranworth L.C.
[190] At 565F.
[191] *James Jones & Sons Ltd.* v. *Tankerville* [1909] 2 Ch. 440; *Mason* v. *Clarke* [1955] A.C. 778 H.L.
[192] *Collin* v. *Duke of Westminster* [1985] Q.B. 581, 603H, Oliver L.J.; *Bass Holdings Ltd.* v. *Morton Music Ltd.* [1988] Ch. 493 C.A.
[193] *Leech* v. *Schweder* (1874) L.R. 9 Ch.App. 463, 467n; *Hall* v. *Warren* (1804) 9 Ves. 605, 608, Grant M.R.
[194] S. Gardner (1987) 7 *O.J.L.S.* 60.
[195] *Lysaght* v. *Edwards* (1876) 2 Ch.D. 499, Jessel M.R.
[196] *Singh* v. *Beggs* (1996) 71 P. & C.R. 120 C.A.
[197] *Abrol* v. *Kenny* [1996] E.G.C.S. 93.
[198] *Harvey* v. *Pratt* [1965] 1 W.L.R. 1025.
[199] *Rose* v. *Watson* (1864) 10 H.L.C. 672, 11 E.R. 1187.
[200] *Tabor* v. *Ginns* [1995] E.G.C.S. 183 C.A.
[201] *Talbot* v. *Ford* (1842) 13 Sim. 173, 60 E.R. 66.

Less conclusive bars are defective titles,[202] non-disclosure by the vendor, or mistake, since the tenant is often given the option of specific performance shorn of the offending term.[203]

3. Purely executory contracts

Entitlement to specific performance was conceded by both parties in *Walsh v. Lonsdale*,[204] so it is possible to limit the doctrine by focusing on discretionary bars to the availability[205] of specific performance. Lord Esher M.R. said in *Swain v. Ayres*[206] that *Walsh v. Lonsdale* could only be applied "where there is such a state of things that a court of Equity would compel specific performance".[207] Even hardship suffered after the contract was entered into was considered in *Patel v. Ali*.[208] True, the defendant suffered illness, pregnancy at the time of the contract, amputation of a leg, the imprisonment of her husband, birth of her third child, and increased dependency on relatives living near to her existing home, but there were no grounds to refuse specific performance. The better view is that *Walsh v. Lonsdale* should be applied to any contract which is inherently suitable for specific performance.[209] Professor Petit concluded that actual decisions support the view that

> "in deciding whether or not there is conversion the only question is whether there is a valid contract, the availability of the remedy of specific performance being irrelevant".[210]

4. Executed contracts

A contract is said to be "executed" once it has been fully carried out, and in normal circumstances specific performance will follow automatically. Full performance of a contract for sale of a freehold by paying the price and taking possession creates a bare trust, with equitable intervention being limited to an automatic order to perfect the legal title. So if A contracts to sell to B who enters and pays the price, A is ordered to transfer to B. A *Walsh v. Lonsdale* contract is partially executed since creation of the equitable term[211] still leaves things to be done in future, but even this partial execution of a contract inevitably removes most potential bars to specific performance, such as

---

[202] *Jones v. Watts* (1890) 43 Ch. D. 574 C.A.

[203] *Chappell v. Gregory* (1863) 34 Beav. 250, 55 E.R. 631; *Ailion v. Spiekerman* [1976] Ch. 158.

[204] (1882) 21 Ch.D. 9, 14.

[205] *Manchester Brewery Company v. Coombs* [1901] 2 Ch. 608, 617, Farwell J.; *Mason v. Clarke* [1955] A.C. 778 H.L.

[206] (1888) 21 Q.B.D. 289 C.A.; *Coatsworth v. Johnson* (1886) 55 L.J.Q.B. 220 C.A.; *Foster v. Reeves* [1892] 2 Q.B. 255 C.A.; *Gray v. Spyer* [1922] 2 Ch. 22 C.A.

[207] At 293; *Holroyd v. Marshall* (1862) 10 H.L.C. 191, 11 E.R. 999 H.L.; *Rose v. Watson* (1864) 10 H.L.C. 672, 11 E.R. 1187 H.L.; *Howard v. Miller* [1915] A.C. 318, 326, Lord Parker; *Cornwall v. Henson* [1899] 2 Ch. 710, 714, Cozens-Hardy J.; *Ridout v. Fowler* [1904] 1 Ch. 658; on appeal [1904] 2 Ch. 93 C.A.; *Plews v. Samuel* [1904] 1 Ch. 464, 468, Kekewich J.; *Central Trust & Safe Deposit Co. v. Snider* [1916] 1 A.C. 266 H.L.

[208] [1984] Ch. 283 C.A.; *Ashburn Anstalt v. Arnold* [1989] Ch. 1, 28.

[209] *Tailby v. Official Receiver* (1888) 13 App. Cas. 523, 547, Lord Macnaghten; *Lysaght v. Edwards* (1876) 2 Ch.D. 499.

[210] (1960) 24 *Conv (N.S.)* 47, 66.

[211] *Allhusen v. Brooking* (1884) 26 Ch.D. 559; *Re Maugham ex parte Monkhouse* (1885) 14 Q.B.D. 956; *Inland Revenue Commisisoners v. Earl of Derby* [1914] 3 K.B. 1186.

non-mutuality,[212] delay (called laches in the technical vocabulary of equity),[213] and insolvency.[214] After outsiders have become involved, it often becomes impossible to return to square one, especially with building agreements.[215]

H. *WALSH* v. *LONSDALE* AND OUTSIDERS

Maitland, in his Lectures on *Equity* stressed that different considerations had to be applied when *Walsh* v. *Lonsdale* doctrine affected third parties:

> "An agreement for a lease is not equal to a lease. . . . [B]etween the contracting parties an agreement for a lease may be as good as a lease. . . . But introduce the third party and then you see the difference."[216]

His emphasis on the personal character of equitable rights is not generally accepted today. Although equitable remedies are directed *in personam*, the defendant could be someone other than the original contracting party,[217] and indeed could be anyone in the world over whom the contract has priority, a sufficiently wide array of potential defendants to make the right proprietary.

The proprietary interest in the land differs from a legal lease only in being equitable, making it essential to secure priority if the equitable lease is to equate precisely to a legal lease. Priority is best preserved by a protective registration as a land charge C(iv) registration, or by entry of a notice or caution, as appropriate.[218]

Most tenants will qualify for protection under paragraph (g) by virtue of actual occupation or by the receipt of net rents if a sub-tenant is in occupation.[219] Since paragraph (k) does not apply, this is a stand-alone protection for an equitable tenant in possession. Fortuitous protection is provided for a person with an option for a future lease who happens to be in occupation under some other right. Protection is lost under the express terms of paragraph (g) if enquiry is made of the occupier and the lease is not disclosed or if the tenant is out of occupation on the completion of some later transaction.[220]

Given a guaranteed priority, an equitable lease should be exactly equivalent to a legal one. A slight glitch is the result of the older statutes governing the running of leasehold covenants to legal tenants[221] but such failures of statutory definition are the sole explanation of the inferior position of equitable tenants with protected priority. Apparently

---

[212] *Price* v. *Strange* [1978] Ch. 337 C.A.

[213] *Williams* v. *Greatrex* [1957] 1 W.L.R. 31 C.A.. Delay is a problem while the contract is executory: *Southcomb* v. *Bishop of Exeter* (1847) 6 Hare 213, 67 E.R. 1145 (January 1842 to August 1843 treated as laches); *M.E.P.C. Ltd.* v. *Christian-Edwards* [1981] A.C. 205 H.L. (contract dated 1912 was abandoned in 1936 so no specific performance in 1981). A more flexible approach to laches is signalled by *Frawley* v. *Neill* [1999] Times April 5th C.A.

[214] *Amec Properties Ltd.* v. *Planning Research & Systems Ltd.* [1992] 1 E.G.L.R. 70.

[215] See below p. 530.

[216] Maitland's *Equity* (2nd ed.) 158.

[217] The benefit is assignable: *Tolhurst* v. *Associated Portland Cement Manufacturers (1900) Ltd.* [1903] A.C. 414 H.L.; *Industrial Properties (Barton Hill) Ltd.* v. *Associated Electrical Industries Ltd.* [1977] Q.B. 580 C.A.; P. Jackson (1977) 40 *M.L.R.* 718.

[218] J.E. Adams [1994] *Conv.* 265.

[219] L.R.A. 1925 s.70(1)(g).

[220] *Abbey National B.S.* v. *Cann* [1991] 1 A.C. 56 H.L.

[221] See below pp. 755–757.

equitable leases are incapable of substantive registration with a separate title. This at any rate is how the legislation is interpreted though it is a *curiosum* of the Land Registration Act 1925[222] that it refers to a lease "capable of subsisting as a legal estate" which phraseology surely ought to include any term of years absolute whatever the formality used to create it?

I.   *WALSH* v. *LONSDALE*: ONSET OF THE EQUITY

1.   Before the time for legal completion

A contract for a lease envisages that a further step should be taken, which is the execution of the legal lease, so it is essential to state the date on which that further step is to be taken.[223] A writ for specific performance may be issued before the date specified in the contract,[224] but Lord Tucker thought it obvious that the court would not "compel a party to perform his contract before the contract date arrives . . .". [225] Neither party is bound to partake in the execution of the lease before the completion date, so equity should not treat them as having done so. If L contracts on January 1st to grant a lease to T on July 1st, *Walsh* v. *Lonsdale* will not apply to the intervening six months. Where the completion date is left open-ended, a conversion arises immediately,[226] however illogical this rule may be.

2.   Taking possession

After the date for completion of the legal lease, an equitable lease arises without the tenant having to take physical occupation, *Walsh* v. *Lonsdale* itself was applied to an agreement under which possession had been given,[227] and indeed before 1926 a lease could only be fully effective once the tenant had taken possession. Until that moment the tenant had an *interesse termini* (as opposed to a lease), both at law[228] and in equity.[229] Abolition of the doctrine of *interesse termini* in 1925 covered both law and equity,[230] so that equitable leases are no longer dependent upon entry into possession, despite some loose dicta,[231] but what is important is the existence of a contractual right to immediate possession.[232]

---

[222] L.R.A. 1925 s.2.

[223] *Harvey* v. *Pratt* [1965] 1 W.L.R. 1025.

[224] *Oakacre Ltd.* v. *Claire Cleaners (Holdings) Ltd.* [1982] Ch. 197; *Marks* v. *Lilley* [1959] 1 W.L.R. 749; *Hasham* v. *Zenab* [1960] A.C. 316; R.E. Megarry (1960) 76 *L.Q.R.* 200.

[225] At 330.

[226] *Lysaght* v. *Edwards* (1876) 2 Ch.D. 499; R.E. Megarry (1960) 76 *L.Q.R.* 200.

[227] (1882) 21 Ch.D. 9, 14, Jessel M.R.; *Swain* v. *Ayres* (1888) 21 Q.B.D. 289, 295; *Borman* v. *Griffith* [1930] 1 Ch. 493, 497–498, Maugham J. (the agreement was dated 1923); *Coatsworth* v. *Johnson* (1886) 55 L.J.Q.B. 220, 221, Murphy Q.C. in argument.

[228] Megarry & Wade (6th ed.) 784–785; *Hyde* v. *Warden* (1877) 3 Ex.D. 72, 84; *Joyner* v. *Weeks* [1891] 2 Q.B. 31, 47, Fry L.J.; *Ecclesiastical Commissioners* v. *Treemer* [1893] 1 Ch. 166; *Long* v. *Tower Hamlets L.B.C.* [1998] Ch. 197, 205F, James Munby Q.C.

[229] *Lewis* v. *Baker* [1905] 1 Ch. 46, 51.

[230] L.P.A. 1925 s.149(2).

[231] *City Permanent B.S.* v. *Miller* [1952] Ch. 840, 848, Evershed M.R.; *Tottenham Hotspur Football & Athletic Club Ltd.* v. *Princegrove Publishers Ltd.* [1974] 1 W.L.R. 113, 121G, Lawson J.

[232] *William Skelton & Son Ltd.* v. *Harrison & Pinder Ltd.* [1975] Q.B. 361.

Possession remains relevant for other reasons—to ensure that a right to specific performance is not barred by laches,[233] to preserve the enforceability of a building agreement,[234] as part performance of pre-1989 Act oral contracts,[235] and to ensure priority as an overriding interest[236]—and it is also possible in this way to remove many discretionary bars to specific performance.

3. Conditional contracts

Payment of the consideration is not a precondition for the existence of the contract, so that the landlord can enforce a contract for a lease even if the tenant has not paid a contractual deposit or premium.[237] But where there is a genuine precondition, specific performance is not available until the condition is satisfied, and the *Walsh* v. *Lonsdale* equity only arises at that time. In *Lowther* v. *Heaver*,[238] a building agreement provided for the builder (Rowe) to be granted a lease for 99 years of each house on the estate, a lease to be granted as soon as the roof of a particular house was completed. Lowther had bought the benefit of the agreement relating to four houses that Rowe had roofed, and this created equitable leases of these houses. Suspension of building work did not affect those leases, but it did terminate the building agreement so far as it related to uncompleted houses. Possession was held under the leases as soon as the precondition had been satisfied. Conversely where the precondition has not been fulfilled, there is no equitable lease.[239]

Options for renewal of leases often impose a precondition that all covenants under the previous lease have been fulfilled.[240] *Cornish* v. *Brook Green Laundry Ltd.*[241] demonstrates that *Walsh* v. *Lonsdale* could not apply to an agreement for a lease (or any other estate contract[242]) while it was subject to an unperformed, and unwaived, condition precedent.[243] Pending fulfilment the parties are left "on tenterhooks"[244] to see whether or not the contract is to be enforceable.

---

[233] *Williams* v. *Greatrex* [1957] 1 W.L.R. 31 C.A.

[234] *Wolverhampton Corporation* v. *Emmon* [1901] 1 K.B. 515.

[235] Megarry & Wade (6th ed.) 650–651.

[236] L.P.A. 1925 s.70(1)(g); above pp. 506–507.

[237] *Millichamp* v. *Jones* [1982] 1 W.L.R. 1422; *John Wilmott Homes Ltd.* v. *Read* (1986) 51 P. & C.R. 90 (deposit); *Joel* v. *Montgomery & Taylor Ltd.* [1967] Ch. 272 (premium); *Property and Bloodstock Ltd.* v. *Emerton* [1968] Ch. 94 C.A. (requirement of consent of the landlord not a precondition).

[238] (1889) 41 Ch.D. 248 C.A.

[239] *Re Northumberland Avenue Hotel Company Ltd., Sully's case* (1885) 54 L.T. 76, 79; *Inland Revenue Commissioners* v. *Earl of Derby* [1914] 3 K.B. 1186.

[240] *Bass Holdings Ltd.* v. *Morton Music Ltd.* [1988] Ch. 493 C.A.

[241] [1959] 1 Q.B. 394 C.A. (the reasoning of the county court judge was more convincing); J.W.A. Thorneley [1959] *C.L.J.* 171; *Warmington* v. *Miller* [1973] Q.B. 877 C.A.

[242] *Shelley* v. *United Artists Corporation Ltd.* [1990] 1 E.G.L.R. 103 C.A.; *Howard* v. *Miller* [1915] A.C. 318 H.L.; *Greville* v. *Parker* [1910] A.C. 335 P.C.; *Gordon Hill Trust* v. *Segall* [1941] 2 All E.R. 379. C.A.; *Aberfoyle Plantations Ltd.* v. *Cheng* [1960] A.C. 115 P.C.

[243] *J. Sainsbury plc.* v. *O'Connor* [1991] 1 W.L.R. 963, 978–979D, Nourse L.J.; *Chattey Holdings Inc.* v. *Farndale* [1997] 1 E.G.L.R. 153; *Michaels* v. *Harley House (Marylebone) Ltd.* [1997] 1 W.L.R. 967, Lloyd J., on appeal [2000] Ch. 104 C.A.; *Rosen* v. *Camden Charities Trustees* [1999] 2 E.G.L.R. 213, 216–217 L.Tr.

[244] J.T. Farrand, *Contract and Conveyance* (Oyez Longman, 4th ed., 1983) 30.

J.   *WALSH* v. *LONSDALE*: TERMINATION OF THE EQUITY

1.   Forfeiture of equitable leases

In *Coatsworth* v. *Johnson*[245] the Court of Appeal decided that a breach of the terms of the agreement will cause the tenant to lose all his equitable rights. He who comes to equity must come with clean hands. Treating an agreement as an equitable lease is dependent upon the availability of specific performance, a right which is lost if the tenant must admit his own breach of covenant. As the Court of Appeal said in *Sport International Bussum B.V.* v. *Inter-Footwear Ltd.*[246]:

> "the plaintiff in a specific performance action must aver that he is, and has at all material times been, ready, able and willing to perform his part of the contract".

Coatsworth concerned a proposed lease for 21 years of a farm in Kent where the tenant was in breach of the covenant for good husbandry, and since he had broken those terms, the Court of Appeal considered only the common law rights of the parties. For several reasons, *Coatsworth* does not represent the law and should not now be followed.[247]

Firstly, it was not a correct application of the pre-fusion Chancery practice. In *Parker* v. *Taswell*[248] the landlord under an agreement to grant a lease obtained specific performance of the agreement even though the landlord was in breach of his obligation to provide stone for a new building. Lord Chelmsford L.C. analysed the effect of the breach as if a legal lease was already in existence. If the breach would forfeit a legal lease, specific performance would be refused,[249] but if a forfeiture was not clear, it would be granted,[250] leaving disputed forfeitures to be resolved at law.[251] *Secondly*, there is the acid test provided by a contract for a lease that omits a forfeiture clause. What happens where there is a breach that entitles the landlord to terminate the contract but not to forfeit the lease? Litmus exists in the shape of *Lowther* v. *Heaver* (discussed immediately above) in which specific performance was ordered since the breach of the agreement (delay) was not a ground for forfeiture of the resultant leases. In any event breaches might be waived.[252] Once an equitable lease always an equitable lease until validly forfeited. As Sir George Jessel M.R. said in *Walsh* v. *Lonsdale* itself,[253] a tenant holding under an agreement for a lease:

---

[245] (1886) 55 L.J.Q.B. 220; *Swain* v. *Ayres* (1888) 21 Q.B.D. 289 (rent paid so common law periodic tenancy); *Bell Street Investments Ltd* v. *Wood* (1970) 216 E.G. 585, O'Connor J.; Megarry & Wade (6th ed.) 775–776.

[246] [1984] 1 All E.R. 376, 385, Oliver L.J.

[247] P. Sparkes (1987) 16 *Anglo-American* 160.

[248] (1858) 2 De G. & J. 559, 44 E.R. 1106.

[249] *Hill* v. *Barclay* (1811) 18 Ves. 56, 34 E.R. 238; *Nunn* v. *Truscott* (1849) 3 De G. & Sm. 304, 64 E.R. 490; *Lewis* v. *Bond* (1853) 18 Beav. 85, 52 E.R. 34; *Pain* v. *Coombs* (1857) 1 De G. & J. 34, 44 E.R. 634, Lord Cranworth.

[250] *Williams* v. *Cheney* (1796) 3 Ves. 59, 30 E.R. 893; *Jones* v. *Jones* (1803) 12 Ves. 186, 33 E.R. 71; *Peacock* v. *Penson* (1848) 11 Beav. 355, 50 E.R. 854; *Paxton* v. *Newton* (1854) 2 Sm. & G. 437, 440, 65 E.R. 470; *Helling* v. *Lumley* (1858) 3 De G. & J. 493, 44 E.R. 1358.

[251] *Pain* v. *Coombs* (1857) 1 De G. & J. 34, 44 E.R. 634; *Parker* v. *Taswell* (1858) 2 De G. & J. 204, 44 E.R. 1106; *Lillie* v. *Legh* (1858) 3 De G. & J. 204, 44 E.R. 1247; *Poyntz* v. *Fortune* (1859) 27 Beav. 393, 54 E.R. 154; *Rankin* v. *Lay* (1860) 2 De G. F. & J. 65, 45 E.R. 546.

[252] *Evans* v. *Davis* (1878) 10 Ch. D. 747, 762–763; also *Strong* v. *Stringer* (1889) 61 L.T. 470; *Cardiothoracic Institute* v. *Shrewdcrest Ltd.* [1986] 1 W.L.R. 368, 380F, Knox J.; *Coatsworth* v. *Johnson* (1886) 55 L.J.Q.B. 220, 221, is wrong.

[253] At 14, Jessel M.R.

"is protected in the same way as if a lease had been granted; he cannot be turned out by six months' notice as a tenant from year to year. He has a right to say, 'I have a lease in equity, and you can only re-enter if I have committed such a breach of covenant as would if a lease had been granted have entitled you to re-enter according to the terms of a proper proviso for re-entry'".

Finally, Coatsworth v. *Johnson* has been reversed by statute. A pre-forfeiture notice has to be served before a landlord can forfeit a lease for any reason other than non-payment of rent.[254] At the time of *Coatsworth*,[255] section 14 of the Conveyancing Act 1881 applied to a "lease", wording which was held to exclude an agreement for a lease. In 1892 the statutory definition of a lease was extended to add "an agreement for a lease where the lessee has become entitled to have his lease granted".[256] This will not apply to a breach of a precondition since there the tenant has never become entitled to his lease,[257] but it will apply to a breach of covenant in a subsisting lease; Oliver L.J. recognised in *Sport International Bussum B.V.* v. *Inter-Footwear Ltd.*[258] that this reversed *Coatsworth* v. *Johnson.* So an equitable tenant now has the same right to resist a forfeiture as a legal tenant.

2.   Equitable leases created in breach of covenant

A contract cannot act as an equitable lease if a lease could only be created in breach of a covenant against sub-letting. The landlord can use his own breach of covenant as a defence to action for specific performance by the intended sub-tenant. *Wilmott* v. *Barber,*[259] better known for the estoppel *probanda,* concerned an agreement by a tenant of three acres to assign his interest at any time within five years. This option was unenforceable, because the lease contained a covenant not to assign any part without the consent of the landlord, who in fact withheld his consent. A forfeiture would follow automatically[260] from the decision by the landlord to refuse consent, so why grant specific performance. In *Warmington* v. *Miller*[261] the Court of Appeal went further by refusing specific performance of an agreement for a sub-lease, where the head landlord has not refused consent, but his attitude to the sub-letting was simply unknown. In modern law, the sub-lease should have been valid until the head landlord chose to forfeit by serving a section 146 notice and it was wrong to assume that the landlord would refuse consent.

Where a covenant against dealings is qualified, the sub-lease is lawful if consent of the head landlord is sought, a respectable and responsible tenant is proposed, and the head landlord unreasonably refuses consent.[262] It is otherwise if consent is reasonably

---

[254] L.P.A. 1925 s.146; P. Pettit (1960) 24 *Conv. (N.S.)* 125.
[255] (1886) 55 L.J.Q.B. 220; affirmed *Swain* v. *Ayres* (1888) 21 Q.B.D. 289, 293.
[256] 55 & 56 Vict. c.13; now L.P.A. 1925 s.146(5)(a)–(c).
[257] *Greville* v. *Parker* [1910] A.C. 335 P.C.; *Re Good's Lease* [1954] 1 All E.R. 275.
[258] [1984] 1 All E.R. 376, 385e; S. Gardner (1987) 7 *O.J.L.S.* 60, 63, 98; C. Harpum (1984) 100 *L.Q.R.* 369, 372–375; *Re Olympia & York Canary Wharf Ltd. (No.2)* [1993] B.C.C. 159, Morritt J.
[259] (1880) 15 Ch.D. 96; *Weatherall* v. *Geering* (1806) 12 Ves. 504, 33 E.R. 191.
[260] See below pp. 799–800.
[261] [1973] Q.B. 877 C.A.
[262] *White* v. *Hay* (1895) 72 L.T. 281.

withheld.[263] An equitable tenant can claim the procedural protections of the Landlord and Tenant Act 1988.[264]

3. Backdating specific performance

Walsh v. *Lonsdale* treats the parties to a specifically performable agreement as if the agreement had been performed, even before the decree of specific performance is issued, applying the principle that "Equity treats as done that which ought to be done".[265] Specific performance will not usually be obtained until some time after the date specified in the contract for the execution of the legal lease. So by implication its effect is backdated.[266]

Antedating was clearly not the general nineteenth century practice, but some cases did permit it. In one group of cases, a tenant under a contract for a lease now sought specific performance, but there was a dispute as to whether the tenant was entitled to specific performance or whether a forfeiture had occurred.[267] If the breaches of covenant were arguable, or had possibly been waived, then the lease was backdated so that the forfeiture could be tested at law. A second isolated exception was where specific performance was awarded after the end of the lease, contrary to the general rule,[268] in order to achieve justice between the parties. In *Mundy* v. *Joliffe*[269] proceedings for specific performance of a contract for a lease were commenced near the end of the 14-year term of the proposed lease, so that by the time of the decree the term had expired. Lord Cottenham permitted the lease to be backdated. Only the parties to the contract should have been estopped and a stranger to the contract could insist on the correct date[270] if those proceedings required the backing of the legal title. When title is in issue as opposed to obligation or liability, the real date of the execution of the lease must be taken at law.[271] However, in *Walters* v. *Northern Coal Mining Co.*,[272] Lord Cranworth L.C. said in the latter case that it would have to be a very special case that would induce Chancery to decree specific performance of an agreement for a lease after the expiration of the stipulated term. So although the court had power to backdate specific performance, the later practice was to require action at law.[273]

Historically, specific performance of a short-term lease was not obtainable, because the term would inevitably be finished by the time that Chancery could pronounce a

---

[263] *Goldstein* v. *Sanders* [1915] 1 Ch. 549.

[264] s.5(1).

[265] (1882) 21 Ch.D. 9, 14, Jessel M.R.; but see *Coatsworth* v. *Johnson* (1886) 55 L.J.Q.B. 220, 223, Lindley L.J.

[266] P. Sparkes [1989] *J.L.H.* 29.

[267] *Pain* v. *Coombs* (1857) 1 De G. & J. 34, 44 E.R. 634; *Parker* v. *Taswell* (1858) 2 De G. & J. 559, 573, 44 E.R. 1106; *Lillie* v. *Legh* (1858) 3 De G. & J. 204, 44 E.R. 1247; *Rankin* v. *Lay* (1860) 2 De G. F. & J. 65, 45 E.R. 546; *Poyntz* v. *Fortune* (1859) 27 Beav. 393, 54 E.R. 154.

[268] *Western* v. *Pim* (1814) 3 Ves. & B. 197, 35 E.R. 453; *Nesbitt* v. *Meyer* (1818) 1 Swanst. 223, 226, 36 E.R. 366 (4 years between bill and hearings by which time the term had expired); *De Brassac* v. *Martyn* (1863) 9 L.T. 287.

[269] (1839) 9 L.J.Ch. 95, 97–98 (not reported in 5 My. & Cr. 167); S. Gardner (1987) 7 *O.J.L.S.* 60, 82–83; *Turner* v. *Clowes* (1869) 20 L.T. 214, 216, Malins V.C.

[270] *Moreland Timber Co. Pty. Ltd.* v. *Reid* [1946] V.L.R. 237, 240, Herring C.J.; *Cowell* v. *Rosehill Racecourse Co. Ltd.* [1937] 56 C.L.R. 605, 629. Hence the distress in *Walsh* v. *Lonsdale* (1882) 21 Ch. D. 9 C.A. could not have been justified by back dating.

[271] *Bradshaw* v. *Pawley* [1980] 1 W.L.R. 10, 15B, Megarry V.C.

[272] (1855) 5 De G. M. & G. 629, 638–639, 43 E.R. 1015; *Cox* v. *Bishop* (1857) 8 De G.M. & G. 815, 44 E.R. 665.

[273] *Oakeley* v. *Ramsay* (1872) 27 L.T. 745; *Turner* v. *Clowes* (1869) 20 L.T. 214.

decree.[274] But today *Walsh* v. *Lonsdale* is freely applied after the expiration of the agreed term. In the *Tottenham Hotspur* case,[275] the tenant held under a court order for renewal of a business tenancy, on the terms that further security of tenure was excluded.[276] At the end of that renewed lease, the court held that the tenant must be treated as holding on the terms of the court order, and so subject to the provision excluding security of tenure. Similarly in the *Industrial Properties* case[277] the doctrine was applied to a succession of contracts, again after the termination of the term of the agreed lease. *Walsh* v. *Lonsdale* can be applied provided that the contracts were specifically performable during the term. It is very doubtful whether procedure could achieve this result before 1875, but the unfair restriction has been abandoned.[278]

4. Termination by contract

As well as recognising the creation of the relationship of landlord and tenant between the parties, *Walsh* v. *Lonsdale* should also operate when they are varied or end. Thus an agreement for value to surrender to the immediate reversioner will terminate a legal lease,[279] at least between the parties.[280] Equally an agreement to grant a new lease will operate to surrender an existing legal lease.[281]

K. PERPETUAL RENEWAL

Statute defines this concept to be a lease of which the tenant can enforce the perpetual renewal, whether with or without conditions.[282] The one unrepealed part of the Law of Property Act *1922* contains provisions which operate to convert such leases to a single, non-renewable term of 2000 years.[283] The tenant is able to terminate that long lease by giving notice, but the landlord is not able to effect a break. All other provisions of the 1922 Act were repealed and consolidated in 1925, but the perpetually renewable lease sections were left in force, as they are today, a history which suggests that the provision was directed to leases already in existence in 1926, but even if that was the intention there is nothing to prevent the creation of a perpetually renewable lease today.

Many leases provide an option for the tenant to renew the lease. Frequently there is some condition to be fulfilled, such as compliance with the tenant's covenants under the lease, or payment of a fine on renewal. The inclusion of a covenant for renewal makes it renewable on one occasion rather than perpetually, but what transforms it is a provision

---

[274] *Nesbitt* v. *Meyer* (1818) 1 Swanst 223, 36 E.R. 366.

[275] *Tottenham Hotspur Football & Athletic Co. Ltd.* v. *Princegrove Publishers Ltd.* [1974] 1 W.L.R. 113.

[276] L.P.A. 1969 s.5.

[277] *Industrial Properties (Barton Hill) Ltd.* v. *Associated Electrical Industries Ltd.* [1977] Q.B. 580.

[278] *Verrall* v. *Great Yarmouth B.C.* [1981] Q.B. 202, 215D–F, Lord Denning M.R.

[279] Assumed in *Wallace* v. *Pattern* (1846) 12 Cl. & Fin. 491, 8 E.R. 1501 H.L.; this would not be true in a common law court: *Badeley* v. *Vigurs* (1854) 4 E.& B. 71, 119 E.R. 28.

[280] Megarry & Wade (5th ed.) 684, not in 6th ed. at 846–850.

[281] *Ex parte Vitale, re Young* (1883) 47 L.T. 480.

[282] L.P.A. 1922 s.190; Woodfall 18.013–18.018; Davey 17–21.

[283] L.P.A. 1922 s.145, sch.15; S.R. & O. 1925/857. Special terms of the lease are as follows:

(1) assignments must be registered with the landlord;

(2) the original tenant is not liable on covenants after sale; and

(3) a fine reserved by a pre-1926 lease was converted in 1925 to extra rent but a fine reserved in a post-1925 lease is lost.

that the renewed lease is itself renewable, since this gives the term an indefinite poten-tial. In one case,[284] the landlord covenanted to renew a three year tenancy on the request of the tenant, the renewal to be "on same terms, including the present covenant for renewal". The initial three-year tenancy was converted by the 1922 Act to a 2,000-year term. As counsel observed, the covenant for renewal "sowed the seeds of its own repro-duction". An obligation to renew "on identical terms" also creates a perpetually renew-able lease.[285] But a covenant to grant a new lease "at a rent to be agreed"[286] with a like covenant for renewal provides for only one guaranteed renewal, and is not perpetual.[287]

A typical case[288] concerns a three-year lease. Before 1926 the tenant had to remember to initiate the process for renewal towards the end of each three year period, usually by serving a trigger notice within a given time limit. The 1922 Act in a sense merely reverses the burden. The 2,000 year lease will continue, without the need for the tenant to apply for continuous renewals, but he may choose to terminate the extended term by 10 days before one of the old renewal dates. The landlord has most to lose since he grants away his land for a 2,000 year term, and loses the sporting chance that the tenant will forget to initiate a review. Unless there is special provision, the rent will not be reviewable, a risk present before 1926 but greatly magnified by the 1922 Act. Most perpetually renew-able leases are probably created unintentionally, since if the parties wanted to create a fixed rent lease for 2,000 years they could do so. It would be better to leave a perpetually renewable lease unconverted, and to allow enforcement of the covenant for renewal only within a perpetuity period of 21 years.

In formality terms, the validity at law of a perpetually renewable lease should be deter-mined according to the initial grant. Thus a lease for two years with a covenant for per-petual renewal can operate at law informally, being converted to a legal term of 2,000 years without a deed.[289] On the other hand a lease for four years which is perpetually renewable must be by deed, so that if informal writing is used it is converted to an equitable term of 2,000 years.[290] A lease to take effect in the future requires a deed to operate at law or writ-ten contract formalities if it is to operate as an agreement for 2,000 years.[291]

L. LEASEHOLD OPTIONS

1. Nature

Leases often contain options to renew and options to purchase the landlord's rever-sion.[292] From the point of view of the potential buyer, an option is a contractual right to

---

[284] *Parkus* v. *Greenwood* [1950] 1 Ch. 644 C.A.; R.E. Megarry (1950) 66 *L.Q.R.* 22, 162; *Re Hopkin's Lease* [1972] 1 W.L.R. 372 C.A. (leaving open the possibility of challenge in the H.L.); (1972) 88 *L.Q.R.* 177.

[285] *Northchurch Estates Ltd.* v. *Daniels* [1947] 1 Ch. 117; R.E. Megarry (1947) 63 *L.Q.R.* 20; A.C.T (1945) 9 *C.L.J.* 379.

[286] Contrast a lease subject to the performance of future covenants which is renewable. L.P.A. 1925 s.190(iii).

[287] *Marjorie Burnett* v. *Barclay* [1980] Times December 19th; *Plumrose Ltd.* v. *Real and Leasehold Estates Investment Society Ltd.* [1970] 1 W.L.R. 52.

[288] *Parkus* above.

[289] L.P.A. 1922 s.145 and sch.15 para.1(1); *Parkus* v. *Greenwood* [1950] Ch. 644.

[290] L.P.A. 1922 sch.15 para.7(1).

[291] L.P.(M.P.)A. 1989 s.2; *Northchurch Estates Ltd.* v. *Daniels* [1947] Ch. 117.

[292] Woodfall ch.18; Evans & Smith (5th) 133; Garner (2nd) 77–80.

accept or reject a continuing offer within a prescribed period.[293] His rights are unilateral until exercise of option creates a binding contract. But from the point of view of the seller, the option is a conditional contract which binds him to sell if the potential buyer chooses to exercise his right.[294]

2. Contractual validity

It is important that the landlord has power to grant the option.[295] Options contained in leases almost inevitably comply with contractual formalities, though formality may be an issue with freestanding options.[296] There must be a full agreement on all essential terms, including the length of the new lease,[297] the rent and any premium, along with conveyancing details such as the extent of the property,[298] its title, incumbrances, completion, and conditions. Once the option has been partially executed the courts may construe it more liberally so as to avoid the consequences of uncertainty,[299] but while it remains executory, agreement on all vital terms is essential. The price (that is the rent and premium) may be fixed, but with a lease to be granted in the future it will almost inevitably be at a rent to be determined in the future. An option at a rent to be agreed is void as an agreement to agree.[300] So it is essential to provide a formula for determining the rent (usually by way of a modified rent review provision) and preferably a machinery as well. In *Sudbrooke Trading Estate Ltd.* v. *Eggleton*[301] a tenant's option to purchase the freehold reversion was valid when the price was stated to be not less than £12,000 or what may be agreed between two valuers. Options are generally exercisable at market value.[302]

An option invariably lays down a procedure and timetable for its exercise,[303] and makes exercise of an option conditional—for example in *Tomlinson* v. *Millins*[304] on the property not having been destroyed by fire.

3. Perpetuity

An option to *renew* a lease is exercisable at some time in the future, but only at the end of the existing lease. For this reason it is free from control by the rule against perpetu-

---

[293] *Helby* v. *Matthews* [1895] A.C. 471 H.L.; *J. Sainsbury plc.* v. *O'Connor* [1990] S.T.C. 516, Millett J.; *Spiro* v. *Glencrown Properties Ltd.* [1991] Ch. 537, 542–544.

[294] *London & South Western Rly Co.* v. *Gomm* (1882) 20 Ch.D. 562, 581; *Helby* v. *Matthews* [1895] A.C. 471, 482, Lord Macnaughten; *Re Mulholland's W.T.* [1949] 1 All E.R. 460; *Griffith* v. *Pelton* [1958] Ch. 205, 225, Jenkins L.J.

[295] *Stretch* v. *West Dorset D.C.* [1998] 3 E.G.L.R. 342 C.A. (local authority had no power to grant a commercial option over land designated for housing).

[296] L.P. (M.P.) A. 1989 s.2; *Spiro* v. *Glencrown Properties Ltd.* [1991] Ch. 537, Hoffmann J. Pre-1990 options fell within L.P.A. 1925 s.40; *Weeding* v. *Weeding* (1861) 1 J. & H. 424, 70 E.R. 812; *Richards* v. *Creighton Griffiths (Investments) Ltd.* (1972) 225 E.G. 2104, Plowman J.

[297] If the option is for x years, renewal for a shorter period exhausts the option: *Plumrose Ltd.* v. *Real & Leasehold Estates Investment Society Ltd.* [1970] 1 W.L.R. 52.

[298] *Freeguard* v. *Rogers* [1998] E.G.C.S. 145 C.A. (use of external evidence to identify property).

[299] *National Deposit Friendly Society Trustees* v. *Beatties of London Ltd.* [1985] 2 E.G.L.R. 59, Goulding J.

[300] *King's Motors Ltd.* v. *Lax* [1969] 3 All E.R. 665.

[301] [1983] A.C. 444 H.L.; *Corson* v. *Rhuddlan B.C.* [1990] 1 E.G.L.R. 255.

[302] *Griffiths* v. *W.E. & D.T. Cave Ltd.* [1998] 48 L.S.G. 30 C.A. (market value "by reference to the existing agricultural use" included any increase attributable to development potential).

[303] *Parry* v. *Geldard* (1999) 77 P. & C.R. 440 C.A. (whether exercised out of time).

[304] [1998] E.G.C.S. 178 Ch.D.

ities[305] even if the terms are varied,[306] and also from the rules restricting reversionary contracts.[307] The only restriction is that an option or contract to renew a lease for a term exceeding 60 years from the termination of an existing lease is void.[308] Options are usually conditional on compliance with covenants, in which case strict compliance at the date of exercise is required[309]—especially if one particular covenant is referred to[310]—but spent or remedied breaches may be ignored.[311] Beneficial ownership only passes when the condition is fulfilled.[312] Care is needed to avoid creating a perpetually renewable lease.[313]

An option to *purchase the reversion* is valid if it is contained within the lease, is exercisable only by the current tenant, and is exercisable within one year of the end of the lease.[314] Any other option is subject to the usual perpetuity rule[315] which requires it to be restricted so that it is only exercisable within 21 years.[316] The statutory wait and see rule[317] applies for 21 years if the option was granted after mid-1964, so the vital question is whether exercise actually occurs in time. It would be much rarer for a lease to include a right of pre-emption, that is a right of first refusal.[318]

4. Transfer of the benefit

If the lease is transferred, so too is the benefit of any option granted to an original tenant. Express assignment may occur either with the land or by separate later assignment, but formal assignment may be unnecessary. In *Griffith* v. *Pelton*[319] it was held that an option to purchase the freehold made in favour of a tenant and his assigns would pass automatically on a transfer of the lease,[320] though doubts have been expressed about this decision,[321] and it is wise to transfer the benefit of the option expressly when the lease is transferred. No difficulty arises if the lease was created after 1995.[322] If it is intended to

---

[305] *Woodall* v. *Clifton* [1905] 2 Ch. 257 C.A. (obiter since the case concerned an option to purchase the reversion).

[306] *Rider* v. *Ford* [1923] 1 Ch. 541.

[307] L.P.A. 1922 s.149(3); *Re Strand & Savoy Properties Ltd.* [1960] Ch. 582; R.E. Megarry (1960) 76 *L.Q.R.* 352; J.A. Andrews (1960) *24 Conv. (N.S.)* 462; *Weg Motors Ltd.* v. *Hales* [1966] 1 Ch. 49 C.A.

[308] L.P.A. 1922 sch.15 para.7(2); R.E. Megarry (1947) 63 *L.Q.R.* 280.

[309] *West Country Cleaners (Falmouth) Ltd.* v. *Saly* [1966] 1 W.L.R. 1485 C.A.

[310] *Bairstow Eves (Securities) Ltd.* v. *Ripley* (1992) 65 P. & C.R. 230.

[311] *Bass Holdings Ltd.* v. *Morton Music Ltd.* [1988] Ch. 493 C.A.; *West Middlesex Golf Club Ltd.* v. *Ealing L.B.C.* (1995) 68 P. & C.R. 461 Ch.D.

[312] *J. Sainsbury plc.* v. *O'Connor* [1991] 1 W.L.R. 963 C.A.; *Michaels* v. *Haley House (Marylebone) Ltd.* [1998] E.G.C.S. 159 C.A.; *Shelley* v. *United Artists Corporation Ltd.* [1990] 1 E.G.L.R. 103 C.A.

[313] L.P.A. 1922 s.145; see above pp. 534–535.

[314] Perpetuities and Accumulations Act 1964 s.9(1).

[315] *Muller* v. *Trafford* [1901] 1 Ch. 54; *Woodall* v. *Clifton* [1905] 2 Ch. 257; *Re Hunter's Lease* [1942] Ch. 124; *Coronation Street Industrial Properties Ltd.* v. *Ingall Industries plc.* [1989] 1 W.L.R. 304, 307–308, Lord Templeman.

[316] Perpetuities and Accumulations Act 1964 s.9(2).

[317] s.3.

[318] Not an interest in land and not registrable: *Pritchard* v. *Briggs* [1980] Ch. 338 C.A.

[319] [1958] Ch. 205 C.A.; W.J. Mowbray (1958) 74 *L.Q.R.* 242; H.W.R. Wade [1957] *C.L.J.* 148; *Coastplace Ltd.* v. *Hartley Ltd.* [1987] Q.B. 948, French J.

[320] *Re Adams & Kensington Vestry* (1883) 24 Ch.D. 199, affirmed (1884) 27 Ch.D. 394 C.A.; *Friary Holroyd & Healey's Breweries Ltd.* v. *Singleton* [1899] 2 Ch. 261 C.A. (successful if legal assignment); *Batchelor* v. *Murphy* [1920] A.C. 63 H.L.

[321] *Kumar* v. *Dunning* [1989] 1 Q.B. 193, 207, Browne-Wilkinson V.C.

[322] L.T. (Covenants) A. 1995 passes the benefit of all rights in the lease; see below pp. 747–749.

restrict the rights to the original tenant, it should be expressed to be personal.[323] The original tenant no longer[324] bears the risk that contractual liability might continue throughout the extended term created by the option.[325]

5.   Passage of the burden

An option creates an equitable interest in the land which it affects which, since it is a form of estate contract, requires registration. If the landlord's title is unregistered a land charge of class C(iv) must be registered, and non-registration is fatal once the landlord's reversion has been sold.[326] If the option is void for non-registration at the time of first registration of title, it is not revivified by later inaccurate inclusion on the registered title.[327] With registered title, the method of protection is by notice or caution, but the tenant will often be able to claim an overriding interest through occupation.

The need to register an option to purchase the reversion has always been recognised, but it is only recently that it has been made clear at appellate level that an option to renew is also registrable.[328] This judicial clarification greatly reduces the significance of the earlier dispute about whether or not options (and a right of pre-emption[329]) touched and concerned the land.[330]

[323] *London & South Western Rly.* v. *Gomm* (1882) 20 Ch.D. 562; *Re Button's Lease* [1964] Ch. 263; D. Macintyre [1964] *C.L.J.* 31.

[324] L.T. (Covenants) A. 1995 abolishes privity of contract.

[325] *Baker* v. *Merckel* [1960] 1 Q.B. 657.

[326] e.g. *Taylor's Fashions Ltd.* v. *Liverpool Victoria Trustees Co. Ltd.* [1982] Q.B. 133, Oliver J.

[327] *Kitney* v. *M.E.P.C. Ltd.* [1977] 1 W.L.R. 981 C.A.; D.J. Hayton [1978] *C.L.J.* 13.

[328] *Phillips* v. *Mobil Oil Co. Ltd.* [1989] 1 W.L.R. 888 C.A.; J. Howell [1990] *Conv.* 168, 250; *Beesly* v. *Hallwood Estates Ltd.* [1960] 1 W.L.R. 549; *Taylor's Fashions Ltd.* v. *Liverpool Victoria Trustees Co. Ltd.* [1982] Q.B. 133, Oliver J.

[329] *Collison* v. *Lettsom* (1815) 6 Taunt. 224, 128 E.R. 1020; *Charles Frodsham* v. *Morris* (1972) 229 E.G. 961.

[330] *Woodall* v. *Clifton* [1905] 2 Ch. 257.

20

RENEWABLE BUSINESS LEASES

Nature of business. Business occupation. Business use of dwellings. Mixed lettings. Renewable leases. Short term and temporary arrangements. Exclusion by court order. Renewal procedure by notice. The landlord. Terms of the renewed lease. Defences to business renewal. Compensation for disturbance. Court procedure for renewals.

A. BUSINESS RENEWAL RIGHTS

1. Policy

Some 60 per cent of businesses rent their properties, primarily because leasehold tenure confers flexibility. Landlord and tenant law must provide a code suited to the needs of businesses trading from rented premises. Whilst Western systems of land holding agree that domestic tenants require protection, there is much less uniformity about the regulation of business tenancies. When a limited measure of protection was first introduced in England and Wales in 1927, statutory schemes were already in place in some parts of Europe, including Ireland and France,[1] whereas even today there is almost no protection for the hardy business tenants of Scotland.[2] No doubt the basic principle should be that the commercial market is left to set the terms of business leases, with a presumption in favour of common law rights unless there is a clear legislative derogation,[3] but a modern tenant also enjoys a valuable non-contractual bonus represented by renewal rights deriving from his status as a tenant in occupation of business premises.[4] Legislation is needed to correct the effect of goodwill that might otherwise create a substantial distortion to the market to the detriment of sitting tenants. Many businesses trade from the same premises over a long period of time, their reason for doing so being that their existing customers know where they can be found, so that they could lose a significant number of their customers and their trading income if they could be forced to move every time an existing lease expired. The value attached to the business in its current trading position over and above the value of its business assets is called its goodwill. This explains why, when rents are left to open market forces, a sitting tenant tends to end up paying more for his existing property than an incoming tenant.

---

[1] M. Haley [1999] 19 *L.S.* 207. Letting practices in various countries are described in A Hurndale, *Property in Europe: Law and Practice* (Butterworths, 1998).

[2] [1999] 18 *E.G.* 153.

[3] *East Coast Amusement Co.* v. *British Transport Board* [1965] A.C. 58, 71G, Viscount Simonds; *Clift* v. *Taylor* [1948] 2 K.B. 394 C.A.

[4] *O'May* v. *City of London Real Property Co. Ltd.* [1983] 2 A.C. 726, 739D, Lord Hailsham L.C.

Hence the basic nature of the business tenancies legislation in England and Wales with its underpinning principle that the landlord should not benefit from the goodwill attached to his tenant's premises.[5] Michael Haley[6] has recently traced the history of the Parliamentary struggle to implement the Report of the Committee on Town Holdings (1889) and a Select Committee Report on Business Premises (1920) as Part I of the Landlord and Tenant Act 1927. Business tenants were not given security of tenure at that time, the basis of the 1927 Act being a scheme to compensate for the value of any good-will attaching at the end of the tenancy. Haley stigmatises this first scheme as timid, defective, and ill thought out,[7] but there matters rested until well after the Second World War.

Modern protection for business tenants operates under Part II of the Landlord and Tenant Act 1954.[8] Perhaps this timing can be attributed to the fact that wartime bombing had depleted the stock of commercial premises at a time when new building was not feasible,[9] creating a swing of the market pendulum too far in favour of the landlord. Legislation was delayed by divergences between Lord Utthwatt's *Interim Report*[10]— which proposed a very strongly tenant-centred regime—and a more cautious final report under Jenkins L.J.[11]; the Government White Paper that laid out the bones of the current legislation does not precisely support either school,[12] though it is perhaps closest in format to the *Interim Report*. This makes it radical enough, since its foundation is the replacement of compensation rights with renewal rights, as must now be explained.

2.   Current legislation

This book adopts Trevor Aldridge's terminology of the "renewable business lease",[13] a descriptor far more comprehensible than that preferred by Parliament—"business tenancies"—and far less misleading since most commercial leases start as formal, fixed term, leases. However it starts off, a business tenant is usually able to compel a renewal when the existing lease expires. A successful business builds up goodwill attached to its existing location, so that in a truly open market the sitting tenant would have to pay over the odds to retain his trading position. The renewal rights given by Part II of the Landlord and Tenant Act 1954 prevent exploitation of sitting tenants. As Trevor Aldridge summarises:

> "An expiring lease is automatically extended until one party or the other operates the statutory procedure under which the tenant can obtain a new lease".[14]

---

[5]   *Stuchbery* v. *General Accident Fire & Life Assurance Corporation Ltd.* [1949] 2 K.B. 256, 264.
[6]   (1999) 19 *L.S.* 207; Bright & Gilbert 269–274.
[7]   At 215.
[8]   L.T.A. 1954 part II; D. Macintyre [1955] *C.L.J.* 42; A. Brammall (1954) 18 *Conv. (N.S.)* 437; J. Montgomerie (1955) 18 *M.L.R.* 49; L.A. Blundell & V.G. Wellings (1956) 20 *Conv. (N.S.)* 92, 273, 453; (1957) 21 *Conv. (N.S.)* 404.
[9]   M. Haley (1999) 19 *L.S.* 207, 217.
[10] Cmnd. 7706 (1949).
[11] Cmnd. 7982 (1950).
[12] *Government Policy on Leasehold Property in England & Wales,* Cmnd 8713 (1953).
[13] *Leasehold Law* (Oyez,1989).
[14] T.M. Aldridge, *Leasehold Law* (Oyez,1989) para. 1.088; Woodfall ch.22; Bright & Gilbert 269–296; Davey 379–401; Evans & Smith (5th) 449–504; Garner (2nd) ch.21.

These rights can be extremely valuable[15] even though rents are determined by market forces, because the value of the goodwill built up by the tenant has to be ignored, thus counteracting the negotiating lever otherwise available to a commercial landlord. Occasionally the landlord may be able to establish a ground for possession, but compensation will have to be paid if this is for the landlord's convenience, as opposed to being a result of misconduct by the tenant.[16]

3. Reform

There is general acceptance of the principle that a business tenant should be compensated for the loss of renewal rights and a recognition that the current legislation is an effective implementation of that policy. There has been some fine-tuning as a result of Law Commission reports; their first review led to legislation in 1969 to provide for interim rents, the inclusion of rent review clauses in renewed leases, and contracting out of business security by consent.[17] A further review has concluded that only minimal changes are needed, though the complexity of the procedure is a negligence trap for solicitors and major reforms are proposed of the existing notice procedures.[18]

B. BUSINESS

Most business premises will be offices, retail shops, factories, industrial premises, or units on business parks. Leases are renewable if the premises are used for business purposes and the tenant is in occupation.[19] Despite the reference in the Act to use of the land "for the purposes of *a* business" it need not, in fact, be one single business and the phrase really means "for the purposes of business".[20] Renewal rights do exist where a business use is mixed with other purposes.[21]

1. Breadth of concept of business

Trades and professions can be recognised instantly: a manufacturer makes things in a factory, a shopkeeper carries on the retail business of selling goods, and a distributor has a warehouse in which he stores goods he has bought wholesale from manufacturers before reselling them and distributing them to retailers. A solicitor or accountant carries on a profession of advising clients. The landlord and tenant legislation embraces any "trade, profession or employment".[22]

---

[15] See below n. 283.

[16] See below pp. 573–574.

[17] L.P.A. 1969 part I; Law Com. No.17 (1969); D. Macintyre (1970) 34 *Conv.* (N.S.) 17; see below pp. 667–668, 555–558, respectively.

[18] Law Com. No.208 (1992); M. Haley [1993] *Conv.* 334; H. Lewis [1992] *N.L.J.* 1624; D.W. Williams [1988] 48 *E.G.* 61. Main topics are: (1) abolition of s.25 notice procedure, (2) changes to interim rents, and (3) easier contracting out; see below pp. 564–565, 668, 557, respectively; E. Cavanagh [2000] 29 *E.G.* 114.

[19] L.T.A. 1954 s.23(1).

[20] *Town Investments Ltd.* v. *Department of the Environment* [1978] A.C. 359, 402E, Lord Kilbrandon (the same definition in the counter-inflation legislation).

[21] L.T.A. 1954 s.23(1).

[22] s.23(2).

Non-commercial activities are also included, since the definition of business is artificially extended to include any collective activity carried on by an incorporated company or by an unincorporated body of persons.[23] Profit is not essential, so a charitable girls' home would clearly qualify for protection, as would a National Health Service Hospital,[24] offices occupied by civil servants,[25] and a tennis club,[26] though not a Sunday school.[27] A lease to a local authority of a park may be renewed, since maintenance of the flower borders is an activity.[28]

Individuals who conduct non-commercial "activities" do not have renewal rights, though some may possibly qualify within the word "employment", in the sense of a business conducted by an individual.[29] Lindley L.J. said in *Rolls* v. *Miller* that a business could be:

"almost anything which is an occupation as distinguished from a pleasure, anything which is an occupation or duty which requires attention is a business".[30]

Lord Diplock described the term in *Town Investments Ltd.* v. *Department of the Environment* as an "etymological chameleon", capable of assuming different colours when considered against different backgrounds[31]; so when the definition of "business" was lifted wholesale from the business tenancies legislation and transplanted into the counter-inflationary legislation the meaning might have been changed. Offices used to house civil servants working for the Secretary of State for the Environment were held to be occupied by the government for the purposes of a business,[32] a decision reached on the primary definition of "business" without the need to rely on the inclusion of corporate activities.

Where business premises are to be put to multiple uses, the test of use for business purposes also determines which parts qualify for renewal, since business security only applies to the parts actually used for business.[33]

2.   Use in breach of covenant

If a lease contains a covenant prohibiting all[34] business use, no business renewal rights arise.[35] Attention is concentrated by this rule on the purposes for which the lease was granted shown by the use covenants. Actual use in breach of covenant is considered in only two cases, that is either (1) where the immediate landlord has *acquiesced* in the use;

---

[23] s.23(2).

[24] *Hills (Patents) Ltd.* v. *University College Hospital Board of Governors* [1956] 1 Q.B. 90 C.A.; *Willis* v. *Association of Universities of the British Commonwealth* [1965] 1 Q.B. 140 C.A.

[25] *Town Investments Ltd.* v. *Department of the Environment* [1978] A.C. 359 H.L.

[26] *Addiscombe Garden Estates Ltd.* v. *Crabbe* [1958] 1 Q.B. 513 C.A.

[27] *Abernethie* v. *A.M. & J. Kleinman Ltd.* [1970] Q.B. 10 C.A.

[28] *Wandsworth L.B.C.* v. *Singh* (1991) 62 P. & C.R. 216 C.A.

[29] *Town Investments Ltd.* v. *Department of the Environment* [1978] A.C. 359, 384, Lord Diplock.

[30] *Rolls* v. *Miller* (1884) 27 Ch.D. 71, 88, Lindley L.J. (restrictive covenant).

[31] [1978] A.C. 359, 383C.

[32] Lord Morris dissented because he thought that the occupiers were the US Navy.

[33] See below p. 567.

[34] i.e. where the covenant says (1) "no business" or "no trade" or "no profession" as opposed to (2) "no butcher" or "no solicitor": L.T.A. 1954 s.23(5). Breaches of type (2) might give rise to a forfeiture or be a ground for opposing renewal.

[35] *Jones* v. *Christy* (1963) 107 S.J. 374, 374, Lord Denning M.R.

or (2) where the predecessor in title of the current landlord has *consented*. In *Bell* v. *Alfred Franks & Bartlett Co. Ltd.*[36] a landlord let a garage to a tenant company on the basis that it should be used only as a garage for two private cars, whereas in fact the company actually stored cartons and garaged business vehicles there. The original landlord knew of this use, and by failing to object he had certainly acquiesced, but the tenant company failed to prove (as it needed to do) a positive consent. The current landlord was unaware of the tenant's use of the garage, a fact which precluded any finding of acquiescence against him. No renewal rights arose from business use in breach of covenant.[37]

An unlawful sub-tenant can usually be prevented from acquiring security by forfeiting the head lease; however if the superior tenancy is allowed to expire by the effluxion of time it is too late to forfeit the head tenancy, so the unlawful sub-tenancy may then attract protection.[38]

3. Licensed premises

The Landlord and Tenant (Licensed Premises) Act 1990 confers renewal rights on all tenants of licensed premises,[39] for new grants after mid-1989[40] and for earlier leases as from mid 1992.[41] Pubs and other licensed premises were brought into the business tenancies legislation,[42] from which they had previously been excluded, though protection always applied to off-licences, hotels and restaurants,[43] theatres, and refreshment rooms at railway stations.

4. Miscellaneous exclusions

Exemptions from business protection cover leases for certain public purposes,[44] renewal rights removed in the public interest,[45] mining leases,[46] and service occupancies by employees.[47]

5. Agriculture

Leases for agricultural purposes are excluded,[48] and so are mixed lettings where agriculture predominates.[49] Forestry is neither business nor agriculture, and so leases for

---

[36] [1980] 1 W.L.R. 340 C.A.

[37] *Wolfe* v. *Hogan* [1949] 2 K.B. 194 C.A.; *Court* v. *Robinson* [1951] 2 K.B. 60, 74, Denning L.J.; *Methodist Secondary School Trustees* v. *O'Leary* [1993] 1 E.G.L.R. 105 C.A.

[38] *D'Silva* v. *Lister House Developments Ltd.* [1971] Ch. 17, Buckley J.

[39] By repealing L.T.A. 1954 s.43(1)(d).

[40] July 11th 1989 or any earlier contract.

[41] July 11th 1992. Notices served earlier on the assumption that protection would accrue on that date were valid.

[42] L.T.A. 1954 s.43(1)(d).

[43] *Grant* v. *Gresham* [1979] 2 E.G.L.R. 60 C.A.; *Ye Old Cheshire Cheese* v. *Daily Telegraph* [1988] 1 W.L.R. 1173, Browne-Wilkinson V.C.; *Taylor* v. *Courage Ltd.* [1993] 2 E.G.L.R. 127 C.A.; M. Haley [1994] *Conv.* 72.

[44] Atomic installations, railways, prisons, schools and the army.

[45] L.T.A. 1954 ss.57–60B and sch.8.

[46] s.43(1)(b), s.46 (definition); L.T.A. 1927 s.25(1).

[47] s.43(2); many are licences and so outside protection in any event.

[48] *E.W.P. Ltd.* v. *Moore* [1992] Q.B. 460 C.A.

[49] L.T.A. 1954 s.43(1)(a); A.T.A. 1995 sch., para.10.

that purpose fall outside all protection and are governed exclusively by common law principles.

C. BUSINESS OCCUPATION

Entitlement to renewal depends upon occupation by the tenant of at least part of the property let to him for the purposes of a business carried on by him.[50] If a property is in multiple use, renewal rights will be restricted to the part used for business. Renewal of business leases is a recognition of the comparatively weak bargaining position of the sitting tenant requiring renewal of a business tenancy,[51] but there is no policy reason for protecting the commercial interests of investors, nor of intermediate tenants who are not themselves trading from the premises. Hence the emphasis on qualifying occupation.

1. Occupation

"Occupation" is almost a synonym for "use", but the difference emerges from a consideration of an incorporeal thing such as an easement; although this could certainly be used, it may not be occupied and no renewal rights attach,[52] unless it is appurtenant to a renewable lease.[53] Some abstract property can be occupied, one example being a gallops for racehorses.[54]

Lord Nicholls made clear in *Graysim Holdings Ltd.* v. *P. & O. Property Holdings Ltd.*[55] that protection depends upon *some* physical use of the property by the tenant for the purposes of his business. A lease of additional storage space taken for use with a shop may be renewed only if there is proof that something has actually been stored there.[56] The degree of use required varies with the circumstances.[57] Acts preparatory to the commencement of business may suffice.[58] Use must be in furtherance of the business rather than merely for convenience: on this ground renewal was refused of a lease of a cottage occupied by staff at a nearby hotel, so this letting was residential rather than commercial.[59] Use must be a substantial and primary activity, as opposed to being trivial or ancillary,[60] and must amount to occupation rather than just passive presence.[61]

Renewal of a business lease is dependent upon a *"thread of continuity"*[62] stretching from the grant of the lease to the application for renewal. This is broken where a house

[50] L.T.A. 1954 s.23(1); P. Birkett (1999) 22 *P.L.J.* 2.

[51] *O'May* v. *City of London Real Property Co.* [1983] 2 A.C. 726, 739E, Lord Hailsham L.C.; see above pp. 539–541.

[52] *Land Reclamation Co. Ltd.* v. *Basildon D.C.* [1979] 1 W.L.R. 767 C.A.

[53] L.T.A. 1954 s.32(3); where the reversion is physically divided see: *Neville Long & Co. (Boards) Ltd.* v. *Firmenich & Co.* [1983] 2 E.G.L.R. 76 C.A.

[54] *Bracey* v. *Read* [1963] Ch. 88.

[55] [1996] A.C. 329 H.L.; see below p. 545–546.

[56] *Latif* v. *Hillside Estates (Swansea) Ltd.* [1992] E.G.C.S. 75 C.A.

[57] *Lee Verhulst (Investments) Ltd.* v. *Harwood Trust* [1973] Q.B. 204, 213G, Sachs L.J.

[58] *Hillil Property & Investment Co. Ltd.* v. *Naraine Pharmacy Ltd.* (1979) 39 P. & C.R. 67 C.A.

[59] *Chapman* v. *Freeman* [1978] 1 W.L.R. 1298 C.A.

[60] Contrast two cases reported at [1978] 1 W.L.R. 1329 C.A.: in *Cheryl Investments Ltd.* v. *Saldanha* conduct of a business by telephone from a flat was substantial; in *Royal Life Saving Society* v. *Page* use of a flat once or twice for doctors consultations but only in emergencies was ancillary to its residential use.

[61] *Wandsworth L.B.C.* v. *Singh* (1991) 62 P. & C.R. 219 C.A.

[62] *Teasdale* v. *Walker* [1958] 1 W.L.R. 1076, 1086, Pearce L.J.; *I. & H. Caplan Ltd.* v. *Caplan (No. 2)* [1963] 1 W.L.R. 1247, 1260–1261, Cross J.

is uninhabitable for eight years leading to the suspension of the business of sub-letting rooms,[63] where a tenant had abandoned a petrol station allowing the landlord to resume possession,[64] or where the gaming licence for a casino is surrendered irrespective of any intention to reopen in the future.[65] Although the thread is fragile, it may survive non-use in some cases, for example where the premises have been destroyed by fire and the tenant asserts his intention to resume occupation when reconstruction is complete.[66] In *Flairline Properties Ltd.* v. *Hassan*[67] the restaurant run by the tenant in Baker Street— just along from Sherlock Holmes at No. 20A—was destroyed by fire in 1995. Although he had moved further along the same street and reopened at No. 79, he retained the intention to return to the original restaurant when the fire damage was repaired and so he was held to have remained in occupation of No. 20A for business purposes. A business tenant has to prove less to preserve his security than a landlord has to show if he seeks to displace his tenant in order to take up occupation himself.[68] Continuity of occupation also survived in the common circumstances considered in *Bacchiocchi* v. *Academic Agency Ltd.*[69] The tenant had been told the date on which he was obliged to vacate at the end of his lease incorrectly by his solicitor and so he moved out 12 days before the actual termination date. Was he in occupation at the end of the lease so as to qualify to claim compensation? Yes, held the Court of Appeal, because closure to clean the property and hand it back to the landlord was still occupation by the tenant, so long as no-one else had moved into the property.

A good illustration of the need to be occupying the premises for business purposes when applying for a renewal is *Re Blenheim Leisure (Restaurants) Ltd.*[70] A company was dissolved because it failed to file accounts, causing a sub-lease of a club claimed by the company to pass to the Crown as *bona vacantia*. By service of a notice to quit on the Treasury Solicitor as representative of the Crown, the landlord ended this sub-tenancy: the Crown was not in occupation and the supposed sub-tenant was no longer the tenant. The issue was whether the landlord could object to the tenant company's attempt to be restored to the register, since this might revive the company's renewal rights.[71]

2. Commercial sub-letting

Occupation of land can only be held by one business at any one time so as to qualify for business lease protection. In *Graysim Holdings Ltd.* v. *P. & O. Property Holdings Ltd.*[72] the House of Lords had to decide whether the company operating Wallasey market (Graysim) was in "occupation" of the market hall. It had sub-let self-contained retail

---

[63] *Demetriou* v. *Poolaction Ltd.* [1991] 1 E.G.L.R. 100 C.A.

[64] *Domer* v. *Gulf Oil (G.B.) Ltd.* (1975) 119 S.J. 392, Megarry J.

[65] *Aspinall Finance Ltd.* v. *Viscount Chelsea* [1989] 1 E.G.L.R. 103.

[66] *Morrisons Holdings Ltd.* v. *Manders Property (Wolverhampton) Ltd.* [1976] 1 W.L.R. 533 C.A.; *Teasdale* v. *Walker* [1958] 1 W.L.R. 1076 C.A. (lease during summers only).

[67] [1999] 1 E.G.L.R. 138; an appeal is pending: [1999] 22 *E.G.* 140.

[68] i.e. under L.T.A. 1954 s.30(1)(f); see below pp. 571–573.

[69] [1998] 1 W.L.R. 1313 C.A.; P.F. Smith (1998) 18 *R.R.L.R.* 345; *Department of the Environment* v. *Royal Insurance plc.* [1987] 1 E.G.L.R. 83 disapproved; for contrasting cases see below p. 574.

[70] [1999] Times August 13th C.A.

[71] See below p. 775.

[72] [1996] A.C. 329 H.L.; S. Bridge [1996] *C.L.J.* 197; M. Haley [1997] *Conv.* 139; reversing [1994] 1 W.L.R. 992 C.A.; M. Haley [1993] *J.B.L.* 478; M. Haley [1994] *Conv.* 470.

stalls to 35 separate traders, and there was little doubt that those 35 traders were in occupation, and were entitled to renew the leases of the individual units. Graysim, on the other hand, was receiving investment income from sub-lettings. Lord Nicholls posed the question of principle, whether it is possible for both landlord and tenant to occupy the same property for the purpose of securing renewal rights at the same time, but decided that this was impossible. Since the property was occupied by market traders,[73] it followed that Graysim could not at the same time occupy it for the purposes of its business. Intermediate landlords are not in "occupation", since the intention is to protect business operations rather than investment income. Where two or more businesses exercise rights over land, it is a question of degree which of them is in occupation.[74] In one case a firm of solicitors that granted a licence to occupy its office suite to a printing company were not in occupation through the retention of use of the wine cellar and holding occasional staff lunches.[75] On the other hand supervision by the intermediate landlord of a series of outbuildings converted to form 11 light industrial units, taking up one hour each morning, did constitute occupation for business purposes.[76] Occupation cannot be split. Sub-letting of residential units is considered below.[77]

3.   Occupation through agents

Statutory preconditions to the existence of renewal rights are that the property should be occupied "by the tenant" and for the purposes of a business carried on "by him".[78] Borderline cases revolve around a correct identification of the tenant. In *Town Investments Ltd.* v. *Department of the Environment*[79] an office block had been let for use by civil servants and so, the House of Lords held, the tenant was the government acting through the Secretary of State for the Environment. Use by government servants constituted occupation by the Crown, meaning that the occupier was the legal tenant of the premises. *Town Investments* is just one example of the common situation of a business tenant occupying the premises through his *employees*. A local authority can occupy a park maintained as an open space through the presence of its gardeners.[80] Occupation by a company director can be treated as the presence of the company.[81] However, artificial arrangements will be ignored where, for example, an assignment of a lease is dressed up as a management contract involving occupation by an employment.[82] A single test is applied to determine whether occupation under a service tenancy is necessary for the performance of the duties of the employment—which removes residential security of

---

[73]   *Ross Auto Wash Ltd.* v. *Herbert* [1979] 1 E.G.L.R. 95, Fox J.; *Aireps Ltd.* v. *Bradford City M.C.* [1985] 2 E.G.L.R. 143 C.A. (airline desk); J.E. Martin [1986] *Conv.* 122; *Simonite* v. *Sheffield C.C.* [1992] 1 E.G.L.R. 105.

[74]   *Bassari* v. *Camden L.B.C.* [1998] E.G.C.S. 27 C.A.; M. Pawlowski [1998] R.R.L.R. 239.

[75]   *Hancock & Willis* v. *G.M.S. Syndicate Ltd.* [1983] 1 E.G.L.R. 76 C.A.; J.E. Martin [1983] *Conv.* 245; *Trans-Britannia Properties Ltd.* v. *Darby Properties Ltd.* [1986] 1 E.G.L.R. 151 C.A. (garages occupied by sub-tenants rather than tenants).

[76]   *William Boyes & Sons Ltd.* v. *Adams* (1975) 32 P. & C.R. 89, 92–93, Templeman J.

[77]   See below pp. 549–551.

[78]   L.T.A. 1954 s.23(1).

[79]   [1978] A.C. 359 H.L. Lord Morris, dissenting, thought that the U.S. Navy was the occupier.

[80]   *Wandsworth L.B.C.* v. *Singh* (1991) 62 P. & C.R. 216 C.A.; earlier cases are reviewed by M. Pawlowski [1988] 40 *E.G.* 20.

[81]   *Lee Verhulst*, as above.

[82]   *Teasdale* v. *Walker* [1958] 1 W.L.R. 1076 C.A.: *Wang* v. *Wei* (1975) 119 S.J. 492 (sham).

tenure from the employee—and to determine whether the employer is in occupation for business purposes.[83]

Special provision is made for *corporations, partnerships and trusts*, since it is all too likely that the legal vehicle adopted for conducting the business will prevent personal occupation by the actual tenant. Under a trust, occupation by any beneficiary for business purposes is treated as occupation by the trustees.[84] In the case of partnerships, a distinction is drawn between business partners—who must qualify for renewal by occupation—and sitting partners whose contribution is financial investment and so would not be expected to occupy the premises personally.[85] Within a group of companies, occupation by any constituent company counts as occupation by the tenant company. One gap remains; this is where a lease is held in the name of an individual tenant who conducts a business through the vehicle of a company[86] even one that is wholly owned by the tenant.[87]

A periodic review by the Law Commission[88] proposes minor *reforms and improvements*, by drawing a clear equation between an individual and his company, and also by treating all companies within a group as a single unit. Landlords will also benefit from the enactment of these same latitudes when opposing renewal of a tenant's lease.

4.   Occupation defines the holding

The central concept of the business tenancies legislation is the "holding", defined to mean the property included in a lease that "is or includes premises which are occupied by the tenant . . . for the purposes of a business".[89] The holding defines the property for which renewal can be sought, to which compensation rights attach, and the scope of the property which the landlord must intend to occupy in order to oppose a renewal.[90] On renewal the tenant is not allowed to extend his holding, but he is entitled to a new lease of the premises included in the original tenancy without any exclusion.[91] Renewal rights do not apply to parts of the property which are unoccupied, or occupied for non-business purposes, or which are sub-let or licensed to others,[92] a series of points all well illustrated by *Narcissi v. Wolfe*.[93] The tenant of a five-storey building ran a restaurant on the ground floor. He used the basement for storage of food in vermin proof containers—its only permitted use—and the first floor partly for occasional overnight stays and partly to store food. This last use was admittedly designed to secure renewal rights, but it was

---

[83] *Chapman* v. *Freeman* [1978] 1 W.L.R. 1298 C.A. This case is close to the line: at 1301H, Geoffrey Lane L.J.

[84] L.T.A. 1954 s.41(1).

[85] s.41A inserted by L.P.A. 1969 s.9; this reversed *Jacobs* v. *Chaudhuri* [1968] 2 Q.B. 470 C.A.

[86] *Christina* v. *Seear* [1985] 2 E.G.L.R. 128 C.A.; *J.E. Martin* [1986] *Conv.* 122.

[87] *Nozari-Zadeh* v. *Pearl Assurance plc.* [1987] 2 E.G.L.R. 91 C.A.

[88] Law Com. No.208 (1992) paras. 2.7–2.21, draft Bill cl.2.

[89] L.T.A. 1954 s.23(1).

[90] *Nursey* v. *P. Currie (Dartford) Ltd.* [1959] 1 W.L.R. 273 C.A.; *Fernandez* v. *Walding* [1968] 2 Q.B. 606 C.A.; *I. & H. Caplan Ltd.* v. *Caplan (No.2)* [1963] 1 W.L.R. 1247, 1254–1255, Cross J.

[91] *Poster* v. *Slough Estates Ltd.* [1964] 1 Ch. 495, Cross J. (landlord not entitled to remove the mill buildings at the end of the term as this would diminish the tenant's holding).

[92] Or a person employed by the tenant: L.T.A. 1954 s.23(3). Query on this point *Stretch* v. *West Dorset D.C.* [1998] 3 E.G.L.R. 62 C.A.

[93] [1959] 3 All E.R. 71.

sufficient to include the first floor within the premises for which the lease was renewed. Since the second and third floors had been sub-let, the renewed lease excluded them.

D. BUSINESS OCCUPATION OF RESIDENTIAL PROPERTY

A lease of residential accommodation may qualify for business renewal if the tenant conducts a business.

1. Property used to house employee

Business protection attaches to a property used by an employer to accommodate an employee if the housing is necessary for his employment. For example in *Methodist Secondary School Trustees* v. *O'Leary*[94] a school which installed its caretaker in the adjoining house was occupying that house for business purposes; unfortunately for them it was in breach of covenant and so renewal was refused.

2. Sub-letting residential units

Hotels are obviously commercial, and so are boarding houses. Guests obviously have no security in individual rooms, since the trade of hotel keeper requires management of the whole building: the lease of the entire hotel is renewable under the business legislation. Similar principles apply where a block of flats is let to a business for sub-letting to residential occupiers, a point amply demonstrated by the facts of *St Catherine's College Cambridge* v. *Dorling*.[95] The owner of a furnished house granted a lease of it to the College, which in turn sub-let five individual rooms to undergraduates.[96] Residential security attaches only where a single house is let, and let as a separate dwelling.[97] The College's house was undoubtedly residential in character but the fact that it included five units of accommodation meant that the appropriate security regime was commercial rather than residential, and St Catherine's College enjoyed business renewal rights through its business occupation.

3. Business occupation of sub-let residential property

A sub-tenant of a dwelling falls within the residential codes, but his landlord may be in the business of providing residential accommodation for sub-letting and so entitled to claim renewal as a business tenant. Sub-letting is not by itself a business purpose,[98] so a landlord can only qualify by providing services of a kind that require access to and control over the properties. Provision of hot water is not sufficient[99] but tending a hot water boiler may be when coupled with control of cooking and supervision of cleaning

---

[94] [1993] 1 E.G.L.R. 105 C.A.
[95] [1980] 1 W.L.R. 66 C.A.; *Horford Investments Ltd.* v. *Lambert* [1976] Ch. 39 C.A.; *Wright* v. *Howell* (1947) 204 L.T.Jo. 299 C.A.
[96] Sharing the kitchen did not prevent the accommodation being self-contained.
[97] See above pp. 13–15.
[98] *Horford Investments Ltd.* v. *Lambert* [1976] Ch. 39 C.A.; *Anspach* v. *Charlton Steam Shipping Co. Ltd.* [1955] 2 Q.B. 21, 27, Denning L.J. The issue in these cases was whether the head lease was excluded from residential protection.
[99] *Bagettes Ltd.* v. *G.P. Estates Ltd.* [1956] Ch. 290 C.A.

maids.[100] So business tenancies protection of a sub-landlord may co-exist with residential security of tenure for the sub-tenants, and taking in individual lodgers could also be a business purpose if it is conducted on a sufficiently extensive scale.[101]

If only part is sub-let, protection will be restricted to the parts retained for business occupation by the tenant.[102] *Graysim* seems to preclude a decision that the sub-landlord is in occupation of a part in the physical occupation of a sub-tenant.[103]

E. MIXED LETTINGS: BUSINESS AND RESIDENTIAL

Residential security of tenure can apply to a lease only if the business renewal provisions do not[104] and agricultural leases form a third discrete sector; there are three mutually exclusive sets.[105] Mixed use is most likely where a building is used partly as a shop and partly as a dwelling. The test is whether there is a dwelling house used partly as a shop or a shop used partly as a dwelling. The Court of Appeal in *Wellcome Trust Ltd.* v. *Hamad*[106] reviewed the history of the legislation and made clear that the present regime dates from 1965 when existing properties were decontrolled and modern Rent Act protection was applied.[107] Michael Haley[108] has shown why: mixed lettings were included in the first Rent Act in 1915[109] because of pressure from small shopkeepers; even though this protection lapsed in 1921 the first business tenancies legislation (the Landlord and Tenant Act 1927) was based on the earlier proposals of the Select Committee on Business Premises (1920)[110] so mixed lettings remained outside. Since the modern scheme was introduced in 1965, mixed lettings have fallen within the business tenancies legislation.

1. Incidental and substantial business use

If there is only a slight commercial use of a dwelling, the tenancy falls within the residential scheme. Thus in the *Wellcome case*[111] the Court of Appeal held that each of the three properties before the court was a dwelling. Other cases have applied residential rather than business protection to a flat used in one or two emergencies as a doctor's

---

[100] *Lee Verhulst (Investments) Ltd.* v. *Harwood Trust* [1973] Q.B. 204 C.A.; *Linden* v. *Department of Health and Social Security* [1986] 1 W.L.R. 164, Scott J.; J.E. Martin [1986] *Conv.* 122; *Groveside Properties Ltd.* v. *Westminster Medical School* [1983] 2 E.G.L.R. 68 C.A. (house let to medical school who granted occupation to 4 students; substantial control, and provision to foster collegiate spirit).

[101] *Lewis* v. *Weldcrest Ltd.* [1978] 1 W.L.R. 1107 C.A.

[102] *J. Reid (D. & K.) Co. Ltd.* v. *Burdell Engineering Co. Ltd.* (1958) 171 E.G. 281 C.A. (actual occupation by licensees.)

[103] See above pp. 544–545; query now the decision in *Jones* v. *Christy* (1963) 107 S.J. 374 C.A.

[104] R.A. 1977 s.24(3); H.A. 1988 sch.1 paras.4, 5 (assured). The legislation dates from 1957.

[105] J.E. Martin [1983] *Conv.* 390.

[106] [1998] Q.B. 638 C.A.

[107] R.A. 1965 s.1(3), sch.1 paras.1,15; a small residue of tenancies at a very low rateable value were not decontrolled until 1980.

[108] [1999] 19 *L.S.* 207.

[109] Increase of Rent and Mortgage Interest (War Restriction) Act 1915.

[110] *Reports from Committees* (1920) vol.5.

[111] [1998] Q.B. 638 C.A.

consulting rooms,[112] to a flat used by an art historian to conduct his research,[113] and to a house in which dog breeding is a sideline.[114]

Substantial business use moves the tenancy into the business sector, since Part II applies where the property "is or includes premises" occupied by the tenant for business purposes, and particularly where use is for "the purposes of a business carried on by him . . . and other purposes".[115] Thus a lease of a shop with a flat above occupied by the tenant as a whole forms a single holding for the purposes of business renewal, with no residential protection.[116] In *Kent Coast Property Investments Ltd.* v. *Ward*[117] there was a conflict of evidence about whether a corner shop had been used to run a business, but once it was decided that this was the case it followed that the tenant could not claim residential security of tenure for the flat above. In fact he fell between two stools because he had also forfeited his renewal right. A sub-lease of the flat alone may attract residential security, but the head landlord is only bound if the sub-letting is authorised.[118]

What is a substantial business use? In *Cheryl Investments Ltd.* v. *Saldanha*[119] an import business was run from a flat, which removed it from the Rent Acts. So too in the public sector: *Webb* v. *Barnet L.B.C.*[120] concerned a mixed letting by a local authority of a commercial garage with residential accommodation. Termination of the car repair business ended the right to a business renewal, but no residential security accrued since the property had not been let as separate dwelling, and the letting was predominantly commercial.

2. Use covenants

Tenancies are not allocated between security regimes according to the physical use made of premises, but rather according to the object of the letting, as determined from the use covenants contained in the lease. Residential protection follows from letting property *as a separate dwelling*. Thus in *Andrews* v. *Brewer*[121] a tenancy of a guesthouse in Newquay was residential since it included a term that it was to be used only as a private dwelling. In the leading case, *Wolfe* v. *Hogan*,[122] premises were let for use as a shop only, a fact decisive against the award of residential protection, any partial residential occupation occurring without the knowledge or acceptance of the landlord. A similar decision was made in *Wagle* v. *Henry Smith's Charity Kensington Estate Trustees*[123] after unauthorised

---

[112] *Royal Life Saving Society* v. *Page* [1978] 1 W.L.R. 1329 C.A. (reported with *Cheryl Investments Ltd.* v. *Saldanha* which provides a factual contrast).

[113] *Wright* v. *Mortimer* (1996) 28 H.L.R. 719 C.A.

[114] *Gurton* v. *Parrott* [1991] 1 E.G.L.R. 98 C.A.

[115] L.T.A. 1954 s.23(1).

[116] *Pulleng* v. *Curran* (1980) 44 P. & C.R. 58 C.A.; *Alexander Cowan & Sons Ltd.* v. *Acton* [1952] S.L.T. 122 (dentist's waiting room in house); (1952) 68 *L.Q.R.* 323.

[117] [1990] 2 E.G.L.R. 86 C.A.

[118] A Government scheme announced in 1995 was designed to free more vacant flats above shops for letting, particularly by providing Government grants for renovation.

[119] [1978] 1 W.L.R. 1329 C.A.

[120] [1989] 1 E.G.L.R. 49 C.A.; J.E. Martin [1989] *Conv.* 125.

[121] (1998) 30 H.L.R. 203 C.A.; *Russell* v. *Booker* [1982] 2 E.G.L.R. 86, 89–90 Slade L.J.

[122] [1949] 2 K.B. 194 C.A.; *Court* v. *Robinson* [1951] 2 K.B. 60, 74, Denning L.J. (covenant to use only as a working men's club.); *Pulleng* v. *Curran* (1980) 44 P. & C.R. 58 C.A.

[123] [1990] 1 Q.B. 42 C.A.; J.E. Martin [1989] *Conv.* 125.

residential use of a flat, which had been let to a professional artist as a studio and subject to a covenant not to use it for any other purpose. Unauthorised residential use had probably also cost the tenant his right to a business renewal.[124] Property let for commercial purposes does not fall into the residential sector simply because business use ceases and mixed use is physically possible.

F. BASE LETTING

1. Lease

Business renewal rights depend upon the initial grant of a contractual tenancy. Renewal rights attach to all forms of leases and tenancies, defined to include a head lease, a sub-lease, a formal lease by deed, an agreement for a lease and a tenancy agreement.[125] The position of a sub-tenant is often precarious: although the sub-tenancy may be a renewable business lease even though it is granted in breach of the terms of the lease,[126] the landlord is able to terminate the rights of the sub-tenant by forfeiture.[127] Also included are cases where a tenant holds over after the end of a renewable business lease.[128] So what must be shown is a base letting that confers occupation for a leasehold term.

2. Commercial licences

In *London & Associated Investment Trust Ltd.* v. *Calow*, Judge Paul Baker said that[129]:

"Self-contained business offices stand in just the same case as do residential premises".[130]

He was referring to the test of exclusive possession enunciated in *Street* v. *Mountford*,[131] which, if it is satisfied, means that the owner has granted a lease to his commercial tenant.[132] The lease/licence distinction is applied in the same way despite the different structure of the business tenancies legislation and the possibility of contracting out of protection, since the same underlying rule applies security where premises have been *let.*

As with pretences in the residential sphere,[133] false labels and false terms are rejected. A "licence agreement" in *Addiscombe Garden Estates Ltd.* v. *Crabbe*[134] that granted

---

[124] Business use is probably required at the time that the property is let: *Cheryl Investments Ltd.* v. *Saldanha* [1978] 1 W.L.R. 1329 C.A.; *Pulleng* v. *Curren* (1980) 44 P. & C.R. 58 C.A.

[125] L.T.A. 1954 ss.23(1), 69(1) (definition). Leasehold terms in old fashioned mortgages and attornments by a borrower to his lender are excluded; so too are tenancies at will, with consequences explored below, pp. 552–553.

[126] *D'Silva* v. *Lister House Developments Ltd.* [1971] 1 Ch. 17; *Parc (Battersea) Ltd.* v. *Hutchinson* [1999] 2 E.G.L.R. 33, Moore-Bick J.

[127] For tenancies by estoppel, see below pp. 565–566.

[128] *Cornish* v. *Brook Green Laundry Ltd.* [1959] 1 Q.B. 394 C.A.; *Bowes-Lyon* v. *Green* [1963] A.C. 420 H.L.

[129] (1987) 53 P.&C.R. 340, 352; S. Bridge [1987] *Conv.* 137; *Dresden Estates Ltd.* v. *Collinson* [1987] 1 E.G.L.R. 45 C.A.; P.F. Smith [1987] *Conv.* 220; S. Bridge (1987) 50 *M.L.R.* 655.

[130] *University of Reading* v. *Johnson-Houghton* [1985] 2 E.G.L.R. 113; C.P. Rodgers [1986] *Conv.* 275 (gallops); *Delneed* v. *Chin* (1987) 53 P. & C.R. 172; S. Bridge [1987] *Conv.* 298; *Vandersteen* v. *Agius* (1992) 65 P. & C.R. 266 C.A. (two rooms used as surgery for osteopathy practice); *Cricket Ltd.* v. *Shaftesbury plc.* [1999] 3 All E.R. 283, Neuberger J.; J. Morgan [2000] *J.B.L.* 332; *Bassari* v. *Camden L.B.C.* [1998] E.G.C.S. 27 C.A.

[131] [1985] A.C. 809 H.L.; *Woodfall* 1.020–1.033; *Bright & Gilbert* 126–154; *Davey* 1–16; *Evans & Smith* (5th) ch.3; *Garner* (2nd) ch.2.

[132] *Southampton Community Health Services N.H.S. Trust* v. *Crown Estate Commissioners* [1997] E.G.C.S. 155.

[133] See above pp. 152–153.

[134] [1958] 1 Q.B. 513 C.A.; *Bracey* v. *Read* [1963] Ch. 88, Cross J. (exclusive use of gallops for racehorses).

exclusive rights to use some tennis courts in fact created a renewable lease despite the misleading description of the document. *Ashburn Anstalt* v. *Arnold*[135] resolved the true nature of a complex series of arrangements relating to the redevelopment of shop premises in Kensington including a sale and lease-back. Clause 5 of the contract by which Mr Arnold agreed in 1973 to sell leasehold land to Matlodge provided that:

> "from and after 29 September 1973, Arnold & Co shall be entitled as licensee to remain at the property and trade therefrom [rent-free] save that it can be required by Matlodge to give possession on not less than one quarter's notice in writing upon Matlodge certifying that it is ready at the expiration of such notice forthwith to proceed with the development . . .".

The registered leasehold title was transferred, ultimately, to the plaintiffs, Ashburn Anstalt, so Arnold & Co. had to show that its rights constituted an overriding interest. This was so: clause 5 was held to have created a lease of the property, which was protected by Arnold's actual occupation. Although Arnold & Co. was stated to occupy as a licensee, the true nature of the agreement to give exclusive possession was that the company was a tenant.

3. Rent-free arrangements

Ashburn Anstalt v. *Arnold* is also important for Fox L.J.'s decision that the reservation of a rent is not in fact a necessary requirement for a tenancy,[136] despite its inclusion in *Street* v. *Mountford*[137] among Lord Templeman's three indicators of the existence of a tenancy.[138] Lord Templeman in *Street* really meant that many rent-free arrangements will create licences for other reasons. Fox L.J. was undoubtedly correct, but the results can be catastrophic: rent-free occupation of a shop in Kensington was given until planning permission for redevelopment was obtained so that, had permission been refused, there might have been a right to occupy rent-free for ever. In *Birrell* v. *Carey*[139] a tenant company that had been given an agreement lasting for so long as it remained trading, actually obtained exclusive occupation of two workshops rent-free for 12 years.

G. EXCLUSION: SHORT-TERM AND TEMPORARY ARRANGEMENTS

There are three cases to consider: tenancies at will, licences, and short term leases; however sharing of office suites is so common that it may be best to differentiate licences to share business premises from licences recognised for other reasons.

1. Exclusion of tenancies at will

Tenants at will do not enjoy renewal rights.[140] This is an important difference from the residential regimes, which needs to be considered in cases of entry into business

---

[135] [1989] Ch. 1 C.A.; P. Sparkes (1988) 104 *L.Q.R.* 175; A.J. Oakley [1988] *C.L.J.* 353; M.P. Thompson [1988] *Conv.* 201; J. Hill (1988) 51 *M.L.R.* 226.

[136] [1989] Ch. 1, 10B.

[137] [1985] A.C. 809, 816F.

[138] *Onyx (U.K.) Ltd.* v. *Beard* [1996] E.G.C.S. 55 Ch.D.

[139] (1989) 58 P. & C.R. 184 C.A.

[140] Woodfall 6.062–6.074; Davey 17–211; nor do tenancies at sufferance: Woodfall 6.075–6.077.

premises during negotiations for a new lease and in cases of holding over. The question of a tenancy at will can arise only when the original business tenancy expires. It must be remembered[141] that statute continues a renewable business tenancy automatically until a notice procedure has been used to end the statutory continuation—and during that period rent payments are attributable to the old continued lease and cannot themselves operate to create a new tenancy. Holding over and holding over pending a negotiation were said to be classic examples of an implied[142] tenancy at will by Scarman L.J. in *Hagee (London) Ltd.* v. *A. B. Erikson & Larson.*[143] Rent payments will normally operate to create a new or renewed periodic tenancy and one stream of authority applies this common law presumption.[144]

However, other cases have held that rent payments are consistent with the continuation of the occupier's status as a tenant at will. One case ignored a computer-generated rent demand, which was issued in error after possession proceedings had been commenced.[145] That case seems fair enough, but other cases go much further in allowing rent payments from a tenant at will over an extended period, because of an agreement between the parties that business security is not conceded. Thus in *Cardiothoracic Institute* v. *Shrewdcrest Ltd.*[146] a renewal had been agreed subject to an application to the court to allow contracting out, and it was held that in the interim occupation was as a tenant at will. A similar result ensues where a person enters as an express tenant at will,[147] or a potential tenant pays a quarterly rent pending negotiations for a new lease which ultimately prove to be abortive,[148] or a person holds over while negotiating for a new lease.[149] The only requirement is that the tenancy at will should be genuine.[150]

2. Genuine business licences: shared premises

A licensee has a shared or limited right to possession of property and any genuine licence will escape the clutches of the business tenancies legislation. Thus if the owner can enter the property at will or can require the occupier to share with another person, there can only be a licence and not a lease. *Taylor* v. *Caldwell*[151] an early frustration case, concerned an agreement for the use of the Surrey Gardens and Concert Hall on four separate days. The evidence showed that the management was to retain control and only use was to be given, so, although intended as a lease, the arrangement was actually held to

---

[141] See below p. 559.

[142] *Wheeler* v. *Mercer* [1957] A.C. 416 H.L.; D. Macintyre [1956] *C.L.J.* 30.

[143] [1976] Q.B. 209, 217.

[144] *Longrigg Burrough & Trounson* v. *Smith* [1979] 2 E.G.L.R. 42; *Bennett Properties Ltd.* v. *H. & S. Engineering Ltd.* [1998] 2 C.L.Y. 3683 (invoice for the first rent was paid).

[145] *Dreamgate Properties Ltd.* v. *Arnot* (1998) 76 P. & C.R. 25 C.A.

[146] [1986] 1 W.L.R. 368; *London & Associated Investment Trust plc.* v. *Calow* (1987) 53 P. & C.R. 340 (prospective tenant allowed into occupation pending an application to the Court for an order excluding security).

[147] *Hagee (London) Ltd* v. *A. B. Erikson & Larson* [1976] Q.B. 209 C.A.; R.A. Weidberg (1976) 39 *M.L.R.* 337; *Manfield & Sons Ltd.* v. *Botchin* [1970] 2 Q.B. 612; *British Railways Board* v. *Bodywright* (1971) 220 E.G. 651.

[148] *Javad* v. *Aqil* [1991] 1 All E.R. 243 C.A.; *Mattey Securities Ltd.* v. *Ervin* [1998] 2 E.G.L.R. 66 C.A. On potential purchases see *Sparkes* v. *Smart* [1990] 2 E.G.L.R. 245 C.A.

[149] *Cricket Ltd.* v. *Shaftesbury plc.* [1999] 3 All E.R. 283, Neuberger J.; J. Morgan [2000] *J.B.L.* 332. When assessing the 12 month short letting exemption (see below p. 555), any period of holding as a tenant at will does not count.

[150] *Hagee* at 217, Scarman L.J.

[151] (1863) 3 B.& S. 826, 122 E.R. 309.

create a licence. In *Smith* v. *Overseers of St Michael, Cambridge*[152] the distributor of stamps in Cambridge "let" five rooms and a closet to the Inland Revenue's collector of taxes, but he was in fact only a licensee (and so able to escape rating[153]) since the owner reserved access to the rooms to carry out cleaning. An owner with a genuine need to enter the property to provide services is quite entitled to grant occupational licences. Similar are an arrangement by the freehold owner of a garage to appoint a manager while retaining the right to exploit the commercial value of the site[154] and many other arrangements to share business premises.[155]

Serviced accommodation is widely available, and for many small businesses a licence is the best option because of the innate flexibility.[156] Commonly a small business has a small office but with shared facilities for fax, photocopying, and switchboard. Legal fees are low, there are no repairing obligations to worry about, and the occupier can move easily if the terms are monthly or quarterly with only a small deposit. Local authority subsidies are often available to encourage business start ups.

3.   Licences: limited and temporary occupation rights

Exclusive possession, given for a specific, limited, purpose short of full use, creates only a licence.[157] Examples would be rights to erect an advertising hoarding, to hold a car boot sale,[158] to put pleasure boats on a canal,[159] to moor a hulk in the Thames,[160] or to tip waste.[161]

Licences can also be created by limiting the rights of the occupier so that they fall short of a grant of exclusive possession. A person may be in undisturbed occupation for a number of years, and yet not have the right to undisturbed possession. In *Shell-Mex & B.P. Ltd.* v. *Manchester Garages Ltd.*[162] Shell allowed a company to occupy a filling station so that it was in fact undisturbed for four years, an occupation that was covered by a document described as a licence and which was held indeed to be a licence. It provided, crucially, that the garage company would not impede Shell's rights of possession and control, but would promote Shell's products. There was no right to continuation of its undisturbed possession and therefore the garage company was merely a licensee. As Templeman L.J. said there was no grant of exclusive possession. Similarly in *Onyx (U.K.)*

---

[152] (1860) 3 El. & El. 383, 121 E.R. 486.

[153] This is still true today: *Croydon L.B.C.* v. *Maxon Systems Inc. (London) Ltd.* [1999] E.G.C.S. 68, Jowitt J.

[154] *Shell-Mex & B.P. Ltd.* v. *Manchester Garages Ltd.* [1971] 1 W.L.R. 612 C.A.; *Esso Petroleum Ltd.* v. *Fumegrange* (1994) 68 P. & C.R. D15 C.A. (partnership licence and shop franchise); *Davis* v. *Elf Oil U.K. Properties Ltd.* [1995] E.G.C.S. 196.

[155] *Smith* v. *Northside Developments Ltd.* (1988) 55 P. & C.R. 164 C.A. (shared stall in Camden Lock market); J.E. Martin [1989] *Conv.* 55; *Manchester C.C.* v. *National Car Parks Ltd.* [1982] 1 E.G.L.R. 94; *Essex Plan Ltd.* v. *Broadminster* [1988] 2 E.G.L.R. 73 Ch.D.; J.E. Martin [1989] *Conv.* 55; *Clark* v. *Banks* [1996] 2 C.L.Y. 3785 C.A.; *Venus Investments Ltd.* v. *Stocktop Ltd.* (1997) 74 P.& C.R. D23 C.A.

[156] D. Joseph [2000] 07 *E.G.* 122.

[157] *Addiscombe Garden Estates Ltd.* v. *Crabbe* [1958] 1 Q.B. 513 C.A.

[158] *Bedford* v. *A. & C. Properties Ltd.* [1997] E.G.C.S. 108, Lindsay J.

[159] *Hill* v. *Tupper* (1863) 2 H. & C. 121, 159 E.R. 51.

[160] *Watkins* v. *Milton-next-Gravesend Overseers* (1868) L.R. 3 Q.B. 350.

[161] *Hunts Refuse Disposals Ltd.* v. *Norfolk Environmental Waste Services Ltd.* [1997] 1 E.G.L.R. 16 C.A.

[162] [1971] 1 W.L.R. 612 C.A.; *Re Hampstead Garden Suburb Institute* (1995) 93 L.G.R. 470, Carnwath J. (school 1912–93); T. Kerbel [1996] *Conv.* 63, [1996] C.L.J. 229.

Ltd. v. *Beard*[163] undisturbed occupation of club premises from 1957 to 1996 took place under a licence.

Creation of a licence may result from a limitation on the authority of the landlord's negotiating agent.[164]

4. Short term leases

A lease granted for a term certain (that is a fixed term) not exceeding six months is a business tenancy, but one lacking renewal rights. Care is needed by landlords since periodic tenancies are caught, however short the period.[165] A succession of short-term tenancies may each be excluded from protection, but again care is needed because renewal rights accrue after the tenant has been in occupation for a total of 12 months.[166] Calculation of the 12 months takes into account any period during which any predecessor carried on the same business. In *Cricket Ltd.* v. *Shaftesbury plc.*[167] S allowed C to occupy from November 26th 1997 to April 30th 1998 and again from May 1st 1998 to September 30th 1998. Afterwards C held over during negotiations for a longer term lease, which eventually broke down. Even if the licence agreement was reformed as a lease, so the total period was less than 12 months, the period of holding over as a tenant at will not counting. Hence the short lease provision is of most use with a new or temporary business tenant.

H. EXCLUSION: BY COUNTY COURT APPLICATION

1. Exclusion applications

This is the best method of ensuring that business security is excluded.[168] The original 1954 legislation provided that any agreement between landlord and tenant to exclude the protection of the Act was invalid. Power for the court to authorise exclusion was conferred only by a 1969 amendment.[169] The intending landlord and intending tenant must make a joint application to the court for an order permitting them to exclude the security provisions of the Act.[170] Though a reason has to be given in the application, and the original intention was that there would have to be a positive decision to permit contracting out,[171] in practice the courts simply rubber stamp exclusion applications.[172] Nevertheless, Michael Haley[173] has discovered that in 1992 more than one fifth of applications were refused.

---

[163] [1996] E.G.C.S. 55 Ch.D.

[164] *Evans* v. *Cynon Valley B.C.* [1992] E.G.C.S. 3 C.A.; P.H. Pettit [1980] *Conv.* 112. Note however *Bruton,* above pp. 170–179.

[165] L.T.A. 1954 s.43(3) as amended; there must be no provision for renewal or extension beyond six months.

[166] L.T.A. 1954 s.43(3)(b); A. Dowling (1990) 41 *N.I.L.Q.* 176.

[167] [1999] 3 All E.R. 283, Neuberger J.; J. Morgan [2000] *J.B.L.* 332.

[168] Woodfall 22.039–22.040; Bright & Gilbert 311–312; Evans & Smith (5th) 459–460; L. Ahmed [1999] 42 *E.G.* 132.

[169] L.T.A. 1954 s.38(4) inserted by L.P.A. 1969 s.5; it is significantly different from the Law Commission proposals Law. Com. No.17 (1969) para.17.

[170] The county court has unlimited jurisdiction; but see N. Ham [1997] 14 *E.G.* 123.

[171] Law Com. No.17 (1969) para.33.

[172] *Hagee (London) Ltd.* v. *A. B. Erikson & Larson* [1976] Q.B. 209, 215, Lord Denning M.R.

[173] (1999) 19 *L.S.* 207, 226, n.61 (5,000 refusals out of 24,000 applications).

One vital requirement is that the parties must intend to enter into a fixed term tenancy. Exclusion is not allowed in the case of periodic tenancies[174] even where there is an initial fixed period only followed afterwards by a tenancy from year to year.[175] A second requirement is that the court order must be obtained *in advance of* the grant of the lease. Section 38(4) of the Landlord and Tenant Act 1954 provides a jurisdiction on the joint application of the persons "*who will be*" parties to a lease "*to be granted*" which "*will be*" a renewable business lease. The correct conveyancing procedure is thus to enter into the agreement for the lease, next to apply to the court,[176] and only then—after the order— to complete the deed of lease. The parties in *Essexcrest Ltd.* v. *Evenlex Ltd.*[177] departed from this procedure by reversing the second and third stages. The under lease was executed on December 29th 1982, when the sub-tenants took possession, two weeks before the court application and four weeks before the court order. Only at the end of the lease three years later did it become apparent that the attempted exclusion was nugatory and that the tenant was in fact entitled to renew the lease.[178] An order is valid if no objection is taken to jurisdiction.[179]

The instrument creating the tenancy should contain or have endorsed on it (a memorandum of) the agreement to apply for exclusion.[180] It is usual to draft the lease with recitals referring in blank to the future court order; the recitals are then completed after the court order has been obtained, at which stage the lease can be executed. Endorsement of a memorandum on the back of the lease is another possibility. Curiously, if the lease is never executed the exclusion of renewal rights will be effective.[181]

Problems arise where the final lease is executed in a form different from the draft approved provisionally by the court, problems which were ventilated in *Metropolitan Police District Receiver* v. *Palacegate Properties Ltd.*[182] Here the Court authorised version provided for rent to be paid annually in arrears, whereas the actual grant was changed to reflect the mutual intention of the parties that rent should be payable quarterly in advance. The Court of Appeal held that a valid exclusion order occurred only if there was substantial similarity, with any change material to the need for protection invalidating the exclusion order. Pill L.J. also cast doubt on the conventional wisdom that the court should rubber stamp exclusion applications, though he emphasised that the court could not investigate the fairness of the proposed terms or direct the parties what terms ought to be agreed.

Sub-tenants and mortgage-lenders are warned by the recital or memorandum that the normal security of tenure is excluded. Thus in *Parc (Battersea) Ltd.* v. *Hutchinson*[183]

---

[174] *Re Land and Premises at Liss* [1971] Ch. 986.

[175] *Nicholls* v. *Kinsey* [1994] Q.B. 600 C.A.

[176] Urgent applications can be accorded priority: Chancery Division Practice Statement [1973] 1 All E.R. 796; C.P.R. 29.5.

[177] [1988] 1 E.G.L.R. 69 C.A.; P. Sparkes [1988] *Conv.* 445.

[178] The problem could have been avoided by a subsequent memorandum signed by *both* parties.

[179] *St Giles Hotels Ltd.* v. *Microworld Technology Ltd.* [1997] 2 E.G.L.R. 105 C.A.; see below pp. 563–564.

[180] L.T.A. 1954 s.38(4).

[181] *Tottenham Hotspur Football & Athletic Co. Ltd.* v. *Princegrove Publishers Ltd.* [1974] 1 W.L.R. 113.

[182] [2000] 13 E.G. 187 C.A.; N. Dowden [2000] 45 *P.L.J.* 2; M. Haley [2000] *J.B.L.* 341.

[183] [1999] 2 E.G.L.R. 33, Moore-Bick J.

Parc granted a lease to Monarchum Ltd. which excluded business security. Part was sub-let to Hutchinson, but since business security was excluded from the head lease no security could attach to the sub-lease and Hutchinson received an unprotected lease.

2. Exclusion of business tenancy renewal rights

Applications to exclude business security[184] are largely unchanged by Woolf,[185] although they must now be brought by part 8 claim form, amended to allow for the joint application by landlord and tenant and allowing space for both to sign a statement of truth.[186] General rules about venue apply, but it is thought to be very unusual to apply to the High Court[187] and an application to a county court is invariable[188]; it should be the county court for the district where the land is or in the defendant's home court.[189] Very often the landlord's solicitors will commence proceedings in their local court[190] and rely on the power to continue proceedings in the "wrong" court.[191] A pre-Woolf case in which this occurred was *St Giles Hotel Ltd.* v. *Microworld Technology Ltd.,*[192] where application was to the Mayor's and City of London Court—though for the 7' by 7' booth in a shop in Tottenham Court Road the correct court was actually the Central London County Court. This irregularity was validated, since there was deemed to have been a court order to continue in the court where the application was commenced,[193] and Court Service guidance is that this will continue to apply in the post-Woolf courts. Procedure after the application is little changed by Woolf.[194]

3. Reform of exclusion procedure

The latest Law Commission review of the business tenancies legislation[195] proposes a change to the rules about contracting out, since court application has proved to be an ineffective filter. If enacted, exclusion of business security would be allowed by agreement between the parties; subject to some procedural protections the agreement would have to be contained in or endorsed on the lease and give a warning of the tenant's rights on the lease; the tenant would be protected by a requirement to sign a statement that he had read the agreement and understood it.

---

[184] L.T.A. 1954 s.38(4).

[185] M. Walker [1999] 37 *L.S.G.* 42; Simmons & Simmons [1999] 7 *Comm. L.J.* 5; J.E. Adams [1999] *Conv.* 459; S. Thompson-Copsey [1999] 13 *Comm. Leases* 205; D. Cox & M. Davies [1999] 44 *E.G.* 140; S. Hasan [1999] 43 *L.S.G.* 36; Atkin's *Court Forms, Civil Procedure Part 3,* (Butterworths, 1999) 216–225, Form 1; D. Cox & M. Davies [2000] 41 *P.L.J.* 4; P. Francis [1999] *R.R.L.R.* 237.

[186] P.D.8B Table 2 (reference to C.P.R. sch.2 C.C.R. Order 43 r.20(1)); P.D.4 Table 1 (Form N393 is discarded by the 4th update in May 1999 despite initial indications to the contrary); S. Gold [1999] *N.L.J.* 718, [1999] *N.L.J.* 933; J. Frenkel [1999] 18 *L.S.G.* 36; M. Walker [1999] 37 *L.S.G.* 42.

[187] C.P.R. sch.1 R.S.C. Order 97 r.6A(1); P.D. 8B.A Table 1.

[188] C.P.R. sch.2 C.C.R. Order 43 r.9; P.D. 8B.B Table 2.

[189] P.D. 8B.B.6; also C.P.R. sch.2 C.C.R. Order 4 r.8.

[190] M. Walker [1999] 37 *L.S.G.* 42; [1999] 15 *E.G.* 123.

[191] C.P.R. 30.2(2)–(3); M. Walker [1999] 37 *L.S.G.* 42.

[192] [1997] 2 E.G.L.R. 105 C.A.

[193] At 384, Millett L.J.

[194] P.D. 8B.B is based on the old originating application procedure under C.C.R. Order 3 r.4 which applied to C.C.R. Order 43; now amended by C.P.R. sch.2; J. Frenkel [2000] 20 *L.S.G.* 49.

[195] Law Com. No.208 (1992) paras 2.19–2.20, draft bill cl.8; M. Haley [1993] *Conv.* 334; H. Lewis [1992] *N.L.J.* 1624; D.W. Williams [1988] 48 *E.G.* 61.

4.   Ineffective attempts to exclude business security

Protection for a business tenant is normally automatic, and any direct exclusion or agreement to exclude part II renewal rights is ineffective.[196] As usual, an anti-avoidance provision is widely drafted to thwart evasion. It applies whether the agreement is a term of the lease or is outside it, and whether the agreement is to forego renewal rights or to surrender or terminate the lease.[197]

Agreements to surrender business tenancies are the most common victims of the anti-avoidance provision. Nothing prevents a valid surrender that is complete[198]: the target is *agreements* for future surrenders.[199] Any provision requiring a surrender prior to grant of a new lease is void. Thus in *Allnatt London Properties Ltd.* v. *Newton* a business lease provided that the tenant who desired to assign the lease had first to offer to surrender it to the landlord in consideration of its net premium value,[200] an agreement that was void since it purported to remove the tenant's renewal rights.[201] If the normal term date was (say) in 1966, an agreement to surrender it on an earlier assignment attempted to remove the renewal rights that ought to accrue in 1966.[202]

Unfortunately, tenant protection was greatly diluted in *Bocardo* v. *S. & M. Hotels Ltd.*[203] Recognising that the agreement to surrender was void, the Court of Appeal nevertheless allowed validity to a covenant barring assignment without a prior offer of a surrender. The case was decided in the context of a residential lease of a flat, but if it can be carried over to business tenancies, force is given unwontedly to an agreement to surrender.

I.   RENEWAL PROCEDURE

The renewal procedure is complex[204] and reform is required.

1.   Contractual security

Business leases are usually granted for relatively short fixed periods[205] since the need for long-term leases is diminished by tenants' rights of renewal. Any tenant has guaranteed security for the fixed contractual term,[206] which is in no way dependent on the business

---

[196] L.T.A. 1954 s.38(1); *Nicholls* v. *Kinsey* [1994] Q.B. 600 C.A.

[197] *Manfield & Sons Ltd.* v. *Botchin* [1970] 2 Q.B. 612, Cooke J.; *Stevenson & Rush (Holdings) Ltd.* v. *Langdon* (1979) 38 P. & C.R. 208 C.A. (term providing for payment by tenant of landlord's costs.)

[198] *Tarjomani* v. *Panther Securities Ltd.* (1983) 46 P. & C.R. 32, Gibson J.; J.E. Martin [1984] *Conv.* 309 points out there is no policy reason for requiring a *formal* surrender.

[199] L.T.A. 1954 s.38(4); the Law Commission propose to remove this restriction: Law Com. No.208 (1992) para.2.21, Draft Bill cl.11(2).

[200] The tenant should obviously not agree to surrender a valuable lease without payment.

[201] [1984] 1 All E.R. 423 C.A.; C. Blake [1983] *Conv.* 158; *Adler* v. *Upper Grosvenor Street Investment Ltd.* [1957] 1 W.L.R. 227, Hilbery J.; (1957) 73 *L.Q.R.* 157.

[202] *Joseph* v. *Joseph* [1967] Ch. 78 C.A.; *Re Hennessey's Agreement* [1975] Ch. 252, Plowman V.C. (option to purchase residue of term).

[203] [1980] 1 W.L.R. 17 C.A.

[204] Woodfall 22.070–22.155; Evans & Smith (5th) 476–496.

[205] Some 55% are currently (1999) for 5 years or less.

[206] Subject to any break clause.

tenancies legislation and does not require continued occupation.[207] Many commercial tenants also negotiate options to confer contractual renewal rights.[208]

2. Statutory continuation

At the end of the contractual period when the agreed term runs out, a renewable business lease will not expire, since it is continued in force automatically by way of statutory continuation of the contractual tenancy.[209] This precludes adverse possession by a former business tenant,[210] and also means that a tenant cannot leave as soon as his business tenancy reaches its term date.[211] Statutory extension is dependent upon there being a renewable business lease,[212] that is a lease of property occupied by the tenant for a business carried on by the tenant.

Legislation governing renewable business leases does not create a new statutory tenancy—as the Rent Acts did—but rather it acts by way of statutory extension of the existing tenancy. The statutory wording does not extend the original tenant's liability on privity of contract,[213] though express contractual drafting could do so; fortunately this is a dead issue for the future in which privity of contract has been abolished. Another difference from the old residential scheme is that the right of renewal is proprietary in character: it can be transferred to a new tenant simply by assigning the lease.[214]

3. Termination

The use of the renewal procedures to end a business lease is considered in the next chapter.[215]

4. Landlord's trigger notice

Stalemate ensues at the end of a contractual term, since the tenant has no lease but the landlord cannot evict him. Landlords usually make the first move by instigating a termination, either to increase the rent, or because a particular landlord believes that he has grounds to obtain possession by opposing a renewal.

Renewal procedure is triggered when the landlord serves a section 25 notice[216] in the prescribed form.[217] A variant form applies if the tenant might possibly have enfranchisement rights.[218] If the lease is periodic, the notice must also operate as a valid common law notice to quit. In the past the test of validity of the notice was whether it was in

---

[207] For termination see below Chapter 21.

[208] Even an unenforceable agreement to renew removes the statutory right to renewal: *Watney* v. *Boardley* [1975] 1 W.L.R. 857, Goulding J.; *R.J. Stratton Ltd.* v. *Wallis Tomlin & Co. Ltd.* [1986] 1 E.G.L.R. 104 C.A.

[209] L.T.A. 1954 ss.24, 65; *Scholl Manufacturing Co. Ltd.* v. *Clifton (Slim-Line) Ltd.* [1967] Ch. 41, 51, Diplock L.J.; R.E. Megarry (1966) 82 *L.Q.R.* 460; *Willison* v. *Cheverell Estates Ltd.* [1996] 1 E.G.L.R. 116, 117F–G, Balcombe L.J. (could not operate rent review clause during statutory extension).

[210] *Long* v. *Tower Hamlets L.B.C.* [1998] Ch. 197 Ch.D.; S. Higgins [1997] *Conv.* 119.

[211] See below p. 587.

[212] For non-renewable leases see below p. 588.

[213] *City of London Corporation* v. *Fell* [1994] 1 A.C. 458 H.L.

[214] *Cheryl Investments Ltd.* v. *Saldanha* [1998] 1 W.L.R. 1329, 1335, Lord Denning M.R.

[215] See below pp. 586–588.

[216] L.T.A. 1954 s.25; M. Haley [1996] *J.B.L.* 576; H.W. Wilkinson [1999] *N.L.J.* 1489.

[217] S.I. 1983/133, as amended by S.Is. 1989/1548, 1991/724.

[218] *John Lyon's Free Grammar School* v. *Mayhew* [1997] 1 E.G.L.R. 88 C.A.

substantially the same form as the prescribed form,[219] but this has been swept aside by the wider *Mannai* principle that a notice must be judged according to whether it is clear to a reasonable recipient.[220] However even this relaxation in the law cannot remedy such serious defects as a failure to mention storage space and parking rights held with a 9th floor office suite,[221] or reference to the wrong landlord.[222] Powers to allow alterations after the date of the original notice are very limited.[223] Each lease requires a separate statutory trigger notice relating to the whole land contained in it,[224] but a single sheet of paper may be read as two separate notices,[225] and it is also possible to shear off parts not being used for business purposes by serving a notice to quit (which need not be in the statutory form) relating to that part.[226]

Notices take the form of a notice to quit, but this is softened by the requirement that the tenant must be asked whether or not he is willing to give up possession.[227] Tenants are warned of their rights if the prescribed form of notice is used, and a landlord's notice is ineffective if this is omitted.[228] By exercising these rights and responding to the trigger notice, the tenant is able to turn what appears to be a notice to quit the property into a request for a renewal, and it is vital to respond if the tenant wishes to stay since this is a necessary precursor to court proceedings for renewal of the lease.[229] An informal letter may be used,[230] but it must make clear that the tenant is seeking to renew or, rather, that he is not willing to give up possession.[231] A tenant cannot overcome a failure to give a timely response to his landlord's notice by himself serving a notice requesting a new lease.[232]

All joint tenants must join in giving notice, so if one of the joint tenants does not wish to pursue a renewal, the others are unable to proceed alone.[233] However if all the joint tenants are willing to participate *Hackney African Organisation* v. *Hackney L.B.C.*[234]

---

[219] *Sun Alliance & London Assurance Co. Ltd.* v. *Hayman* [1975] 1 All E.R. 248 C.A.; *Snook* v. *Schofield* [1975] 1 E.G.L.R. 69 C.A.; *Tegerdine* v. *Brooks* (1978) 36 P. & C.R. 261 C.A. (reviews earlier cases); *British Railways Board* v. *A.J.A. Smith Transport Ltd.* [1981] 2 E.G.L.R. 69; *Baglarbasi* v. *Deedmethod Ltd.* [1991] 2 E.G.L.R. 71.

[220] See below pp. 579–581.

[221] *Herongrove Ltd.* v. *Wates City of London Properties plc.* [1988] 1 E.G.L.R. 82.

[222] *Morrow* v. *Nadeem* [1986] 1 W.L.R. 1381 C.A.; *Pearson* v. *Alyo* [1990] 1 E.G.L.R. 114 C.A.; *Yamaha-Kemble Music (U.K.) Ltd.* v. *Arc Properties Ltd.* [1990] 1 E.G.L.R. 261, Aldous J.; *Teltscher Bros.* v. *London & India Dock Investments Ltd.* [1989] 1 W.L.R. 770. Errors can be corrected with a new notice: *Smith* v. *Draper* (1990) 60 P. & C.R. 252 C.A.

[223] *Harris* v. *Monro* (1972) 225 E.G. 1551 C.A. (landlord had died!).

[224] *Southport Old Links Ltd.* v. *Naylor* [1985] 1 E.G.L.R. 66 C.A.; J.E. Martin [1989] *Conv.* 58; *Dodson Bull Carpet Co. Ltd.* v. *City of London Corp.* [1975] 1 W.L.R. 781, Goff J.; *M. & P. Enterprises (London) Ltd.* v. *Norfolk Square Hotels Ltd.* [1994] 1 E.G.L.R. 129 (five buildings used as a hotel from four landlords; single lease).

[225] *Moss* v. *Mobil Oil Co. Ltd.* [1988] 1 E.G.L.R. 71 C.A.; J.E. Martin [1989] *Conv.* 57.

[226] L.P.A. 1925 s.140; *William Skelton & Son Ltd.* v. *Harrison & Pinder Ltd.* [1975] Q.B. 361 Ch.D.; *Neville Long & Co. (Boards) Ltd.* v. *Firemanaich* [1983] 2 E.G.L.R. 76 C.A.; J.E. Martin [1982] *Conv.* 224.

[227] S.I. 1991/724, reversing *Bridgers* v. *Stanford* [1991] 2 E.G.L.R. 265 C.A.

[228] *Sabella Ltd.* v. *Montgomery* [1999] 1 E.G.L.R. 65 C.A.; M. Haley [1998] *Conv.* 489.

[229] L.T.A. 1954 s.29(2).

[230] Invalid if it is lost in the post: *Chiswell* v. *Griffon Land & Estates Ltd.* [1975] 1 W.L.R. 1181 C.A.

[231] L.T.A. 1954 s.29(2); *Lewington* v. *Society for Protection of Ancient Buildings Trustees* (1983) 45 P. & C.R. 336 C.A.; *Mehmet* v. *Dawson* [1984] 1 E.G.L.R. 74 C.A. (letter offering to buy freehold insufficient).

[232] L.T.A. 1954 s.26(4); *G. Orlik (Meat Products) Ltd.* v. *Hastings & Thanet B.S.* (1974) 29 P. & C.R. 126 C.A.; *Bar* v. *Pathwood Investments Ltd.* [1987] 1 E.G.L.R. 90 C.A.

[233] *Jacobs* v. *Chaudhuri* [1968] 2 Q.B. 470 C.A.

[234] [1998] E.G.C.S. 139.

makes clear that a request for a new tenancy signed by only one of the tenants will be valid, though it is best to make clear that he is acting for all.

Most notices served by landlords under the business tenancies legislation are designed to lead to renewal, the landlord's objective being to increase the rent, but in a proportion of cases the landlord wishes to repossess the property, to relet it, for the landlord to take over business himself, or to sell the premises with vacant possession. Repossession requires the landlord to establish a ground for possession. Bad tenants can be removed without compensation, but compensation will have to be paid if repossession is based on the landlord's intended use of the property.[235] The way must be paved for repossession right at the beginning of the statutory process, by stating in the trigger notice that the landlord will oppose a renewal and by setting out the grounds on which he intends to rely[236]; it is not necessary to match the precise wording of the statutory ground provided that the notice is not deceptive.[237] If no grounds are stated, a "notice to quit" is an invitation to renew at a renegotiated rent.

5.   Tenant's request for new tenancy

A tenant will not take the initiative in seeking termination and renewal in a rising market, since this will accelerate a rent increase. A request may be useful to forestall a forfeiture,[238] or to overcome the landlord's use of a break clause. A tenant is not allowed to change his mind and ask for a new tenancy after he has once given a statutory notice to terminate the lease.[239] A similar principle has also be applied (with much less justice) to prevent the use of a contractual break clause to end an existing lease at a higher rent so as to obtain a new tenancy at a lower rent[240]: it is open to doubt whether this decision is a correct interpretation of the statutory wording.

A section 26 request can only be made by a tenant who started with a lease conferring at least one year's contractual security through either a fixed term or a yearly tenancy.[241] The tenant must use the form current at the time it is given,[242] which states the rent and terms he proposes.[243] An absolutely vital element of a valid notice[244] is a commencement date for the new lease, which must be at least six months distant (with a maximum of 12 months). Since this will also be the termination date for the existing lease, it must be on or after[245] the term date of an existing fixed term lease,[246] or sufficiently distant to act as a common law notice to quit an existing periodic tenancy.[247]

---

[235] L.T.A. 1954 s.30; see below pp. 573–574.

[236] s.25(6).

[237] *Philipson-Stow* v. *Trevor Square Ltd.* [1981] 1 E.G.L.R. 56, Goulding J. (redecoration).

[238] *Meadows* v. *Clerical Medical & General Life Assurance Society* [1981] Ch. 70, Megarry V.C.

[239] s.27. A notice is invalid if the tenant does not wish to renew: *Sun Life Ass.* v. *Racal Tracs* [2000] 1 E.G.L.R. 138.

[240] *Garston* v. *Scottish Widows' Fund & Life Assurance Society* [1996] 4 All E.R. 282, Rattee J., reversed on the facts [1998] 1 W.L.R. 1583 C.A.

[241] L.T.A. 1954 s.26(1); H.W. Wilkinson [1999] *N.L.J.* 1521.

[242] *Sun Alliance & London Assurance Co. Ltd.* v. *Hayman* [1975] 1 All E.R. 248 C.A.

[243] L.T.A. 1954 s.26(3); S.I. 1983/133, as amended by S.Is. 1989/1548, 1991/724.

[244] *Bristol Cars Ltd.* v. *R.K.H. (Hotels) Ltd.* (1979) 38 P. & C.R. 411 C.A. (no date; but defect waived).

[245] Not before: *Garston* as above.

[246] L.T.A. 1954 s.26(1), (4).

[247] s.26(5).

If the landlord takes no action, the tenant's response acts as an unopposed request for a renewal of the tenancy, and the tenant should proceed to a court application.[248] Failure to do so destroys the tenant's renewal rights. Thus in *Railtrack plc. v. Gojra*[249] a tenant gave a section 26 request in 1994, which had not been followed by a court application. Although this notice was not addressed to the current landlord but to a former landlord British Railways Board, legislation governing the privatisation of the railways provided that it was given to the current landlord. A further application in 1995 was followed by a timely court application, but this was to no avail; the tenancy had ended under the 1994 notice and the second notice was inoperative. Alternatively the landlord has two months in which to give notice of opposition to an application for a new tenancy and to state a ground of opposition.[250]

6. Court application by tenant

Renewal occurs through a court application[251] made by the tenant, usually to a county court.[252] The application should contain details of the existing lease[253] and of the new terms proposed by the tenant. Agreement on the terms of a renewal is desirable,[254] but the hope of reaching a negotiated settlement must not lead the tenant into a state of tor-por: it is vital to serve the court application in time in case negotiations fall through. Failure to comply with the time limit severely prejudices the tenant, since the landlord cannot be compelled to accept the validity of proceedings taken out of time.[255] Information necessary to take proceedings can be obtained by advance notice[256] or by disclosure once proceedings have commenced.[257]

The tenant is free to withdraw the application for renewal,[258] in which case the existing lease will terminate three months after the withdrawal take effect; this cannot be backdated so as to terminate liability to pay rent sooner.[259]

7. Timetable

A *landlord's trigger notice* must specify a date on which the lease is to end, which must be after the contractual term date,[260] and at least six months after the date of the notice.[261] The period of notice should not exceed 12 months.[262] The *tenant's response* to

---

[248] *Stile Hall Properties Ltd. v. Gooch* [1980] 1 W.L.R. 62 C.A.; *Polyviou v. Seeley* [1980] 1 W.L.R. 55 C.A.

[249] [1998] 1 E.G.L.R. 63.

[250] L.T.A. 1954 s.30; see above pp. 268–273.

[251] s.29(1).

[252] See below pp. 575–576.

[253] *Re Nos. 55/57 Holmes Road, Kentish Town* [1959] Ch. 298; R.E. Megarry (1958) 74 *L.Q.R.* 346 (no rectification of summons in wrong name).

[254] L.T.A. 1954 s.28; the existing lease ends on the date specified in the agreement and is outside part II.

[255] s.29(3); subject to the possibility of estoppel.

[256] s.40(1), (2).

[257] C.P.R. 31; on the old law of discovery see *Wine Shippers (London) Ltd. v. Bath House Syndicate Ltd.* [1960] 1 W.L.R. 613, Buckley J.; P.V. Baker (1960) 76 *L.Q.R.* 354.

[258] L.T.A. 1954 s.36(2) (possible penalty in costs).

[259] *Covell Matthews & Partners v. French Wools Ltd.* [1978] 1 W.L.R. 1477 C.A.

[260] *Lewis v. M.T.C. (Cars) Ltd.* [1975] 1 W.L.R. 457 C.A.; *Whelton Sinclair v. Hyland* [1992] 1 E.G.L.R. 158 C.A.; J. Hewitt (1993) 137 *S.J.* 154 (notice ended on last day of contractual term and so valid).

[261] L.T.A. 1954 s.25(2).

[262] s.25(2); the length of the notice is extended if more than 6 months' notice is needed to terminate a periodic tenancy: subs.(3).

the landlord's trigger notice must be given within two months, indicating whether or not he is willing to give up possession.[263] Strict compliance is essential, as otherwise the court has no power to consider an application for renewal.[264]

A *tenant's request for a new tenancy* must be made not earlier than the end of the contractual tenancy, so as to commence between six to 12 months from the request.[265] It is essential that the date stated for commencement of the new tenancy is a valid date.[266] Notices can be amended by the court to correct formal defects, and this can occur after the time limit has expired provided that the defective notice was served in time.[267] Two months are allowed for the landlord to seek possession by giving notice of a section 30 ground of opposition.

Court applications by the tenant for renewal of a lease are also subject to strict time limits. Application must be made not less than two nor more than four months after the landlord's trigger notice[268]; this window means that a tenant may fail by being either too early[269] or too late. Time available for service[270] is a skimpy two months,[271] and this period will only be extended in very exceptional cases.[272] Provided that proceedings have been served in time there is less objection to late amendments,[273] in particular to allow the correction of the names of the parties.[274]

Months are measured according to the corresponding date rule laid down in *Dodds* v. *Walker*[275]: a period of months is calculated by taking the same numerical date in a later month, so that if the landlord served notice on September 30th 1978, an application by the tenant on January 31st 1979 would be outside the four month time limit.[276]

8. Estoppel

Existing procedure is unsatisfactory in that it makes no provision for consensual extensions of the time limits nor for acceptance of informal notices. However, as the House of Lords held in the leading case of *Kammins Ballrooms Co. Ltd.* v. *Zenith Investments*

---

[263] s.25(2).

[264] s.29(2).

[265] s.26(1), (4); if periodic, when the current tenancy ends at common law: s.26(5).

[266] See above p. 562.

[267] *G. Orlik (Meat Products) Ltd.* v. *Hastings & Thanet B.S.* (1974) 29 P. & C.R. 126 C.A.; *Bar* v. *Pathwood Investments Ltd.* [1987] 1 E.G.L.R. 90 C.A.

[268] L.T.A. 1954 s.29(3); if the tenant has requested a new tenancy the period runs from the s.26 request; J. Frenkel [2000] 20 *L.S.G.* 49.

[269] *Kammins Ballrooms Co. Ltd.* v. *Zenith Investments (Torquay) Ltd.* [1971] A.C. 850 H.L. (waiver on facts); P.V. Baker (1970) 86 *L.Q.R.* 438.

[270] For methods of service see: *Italica Holdings S.A.* v. *Bayadea* [1985] 1 E.G.L.R. 70, French J. (notice sent to business premises validly served); *Lex Services Ltd.* v. *Johns* [1990] 1 E.G.L.R. 92 C.A. (post).

[271] *Joan Barrie Ltd.* v. *Gus Property Management Ltd.* [1981] 2 E.G.L.R. 65 C.A.

[272] *Robert Baxendale Ltd.* v. *Davstone (Holdings) Ltd.* [1982] 3 All E.R. 496 C.A.; J.E. Martin [1983] *Conv.* 245; *Ward-Lee* v. *Lineham* [1993] 2 All E.R. 1006 C.A. (failure by *court* to effect service unknown to the tenant).

[273] *Williams* v. *Hillcroft Garage Ltd.* (1971) 22 P. & C.R. 402 C.A.; *Signet Group plc.* v. *Hammerson U.K. Properties Ltd.* (1998) 75 P. & C.R. D33 C.A.

[274] *Evans Construction Ltd.* v. *Charrington & Co.* [1983] Q.B. 810 (2:1 amendment allowed); J.E. Martin [1983] *Conv.* 247.

[275] [1981] 1 W.L.R. 1027 H.L.; *E.J. Riley Investments Ltd.* v. *Eurostile Holdings Ltd.* [1985] 1 W.L.R. 1139 C.A.

[276] *Hogg Bullimore & Co.* v. *Co-Operative Insurance Society Ltd.* (1985) 50 P. & C.R. 105, Whitford J. (notice on April 2nd to end on October 2nd 1984 valid); *Schnabel* v. *Allard* [1967] 1 Q.B. 627 C.A.; see below p. 581. Dates when the courts are closed are ignored.

(Torquay) Ltd.,[277] procedural defects may be waived, a procedure which removes much potential injustice. Waiver requires knowledge of the defect, but estoppel can come to the rescue where a party seeks to overcome a defect that is unknown to the other party provided that an expectation has been induced.[278] If both parties act on the assumption that the procedure is correct an estoppel by convention should arise, and should bind both parties.[279] Where the landlord states his intention to grant a new lease, this statement could found the basis for a proprietary estoppel—creating the lease despite the absence of formality or even of a concluded agreement[280] but detrimental reliance is an essential ingredient.[281]

9. Proposed procedural changes

Early optimistic forecasts that the renewal procedure was reasonably simple[282] have proved to be wide of the mark, as witnessed by the voluminous negligence claims spawned by business lease renewals.[283] The Law Commission[284] has now recommended radical change—or at least a radical evolution—encompassing the abolition of the section 25 notice procedure. A landlord who simply wants to initiate a renewal of the lease will be able to serve a notice proposing the terms of a new tenancy directly, and court proceedings will be needed (within the time limit of the notice) only if the tenant is unhappy with the terms proposed. Alternatively the tenant would have power to apply directly for a renewal. A landlord who sought possession would serve a notice stating his grounds and could apply to the court for a termination order or leave it to the tenant to apply for a new tenancy before the notice expired. If the ground for possession is made out, the court will order possession, but otherwise the court will order a renewal. Proceedings could only be withdrawn with the permission of the court.

Major changes proposed are that the tenant could issue a claim for a new tenancy immediately after the landlord's trigger notice[285] (whereas at present he must wait two months from the date of the landlord's notice). More fundamental still is the proposal to allow the parties to agree an extension of the time limit for taking proceedings between themselves, thus removing the need for prophylactic court applications where

---

[277] [1971] A.C. 850 H.L. (premature application for new tenancy); P.V. Baker (1970) 86 *L.Q.R.* 438.

[278] *Watkins* v. *Elmslie* [1982] 1 E.G.L.R. 81 C.A. (no estoppel); J.E. Martin [1983] *Conv.* 245; *Stevens & Cutting* v. *Anderson* [1990] 1 E.G.L.R. 95 C.A. (obiter).

[279] *Bristol Cars Ltd.* v. *R.K.H. (Hotels) Ltd.* (1979) 38 P. & C.R. 411 C.A. (application for interim rent waived defect in tenant's notice); *Litre Garages (Green Park) Ltd.* v. *Mobil Oil Co. Ltd.* [1985] unreported; C. Whippman [1985] *J.B.L.* 472; *John Lyon's Free Grammar School* v. *Mayhew* [1997] 1 E.G.L.R. 88 C.A. (tenant estopped from reliance on landlord's defective notice of termination).

[280] Sparkes *N.L.L.* ch. 11; *J.T. Developments Ltd.* v. *Quinn* [1991] 2 E.G.L.R. 257 C.A.; *Saloman* v. *Akiens* [1993] 1 E.G.L.R. 101 C.A. (not if "subject to lease").

[281] *Wroe* v. *Exmos Cover Ltd.* [2000] 15 E.G. 155 C.A. (licensee had not relied on landlord's letter stating he would be treated as a tenant).

[282] J. Montgomerie (1955) 18 *M.L.R.* 49, 57.

[283] *Rumsey* v. *Owen White & Catlin* [1976] 1 E.G.L.R. 99 C.A.; *Hodge* v. *Clifford Cowling & Co.* [1990] 2 E.G.L.R. 89 C.A.; *Robins* v. *Meadows & Moran* [1991] 2 E.G.L.R. 137 (4 notices, all defective); *Herbie Frogg Ltd.* v. *Lee Barnett Needleman* [1997] 2 C.L.Y. 3267 C.A.

[284] Law Com. No.208 (1992) paras.2.26–2.60; M. Haley [1993] *Conv.* 334; H. Lewis [1992] *N.L.J.* 1624; D.W. Williams [1988] 48 *E.G.* 61.

[285] If the tenant initiated the procedure by a request for a new tenancy, he would be obliged to wait until the landlord's time for giving a counter-notice had elapsed before going to court.

a renewal is proceeding by consent. These proposals merit an immediate allocation of Parliamentary time, since when enacted they will remove most of the unnecessary traps from the business tenancies legislation.

J.   RENEWAL: THE LANDLORD

1.   Competent landlord

Where a business tenancy is a head lease, it is clear that the freeholder is the competent landlord to undertake the renewal of the lease. Otherwise, it will normally be the immediate landlord, but this is dependent upon the landlord holding a sufficiently long term to be able to grant a renewed lease of the length sought by the tenant.[286] His interest must be a freehold or a leasehold estate not terminating or terminable within 14 months.[287] This excludes a landlord holding over after the end of his contractual term, and one on whom the head landlord has served a section 25 trigger notice,[288] but reversionary leases are ignored.[289]

The next immediate landlord who retains a reversion for 14 months qualifies. If there is a mesne landlord with less than a 14-month reversion, the competent landlord can effectively bind the inferior landlord's interest without consultation, though it is best to allow the mesne landlord to participate in the renewal negotiations to ensure that no compensation rights arise. If the competent landlord has only a short term it will be necessary to join the superior landlord who will be needed to grant the appropriate length of renewed tenancy: unless he consents he can be compelled to grant a lease only by being joined as a defendant to the tenant's renewal application.

2.   Tenancy by estoppel

The principle is that a tenant cannot dispute that his landlord has title to grant the lease and the landlord is also bound[290]; no estoppel arises against a third party who does not claim under the tenant.[291] If the lease is by deed it is a true estoppel, but exactly the same principle applies to a less formal lease. A business tenant who accepts possession from his landlord is bound by the terms of the business tenancies legislation and so—as was decided in *Bell* v. *General Accident Fire & Life Assurance Corporation Ltd.*[292]—liable to pay an interim rent increase at the time of a renewal application. The principle applies to a landlord without title,[293] and also as the House of Lords has recently decided to a

---

[286] L.T.A. 1954 ss.44, 65, 69, sch.6; Woodfall 22.156–22.167; a mortgage-lender in possession may act as landlord: s.67; see generally Woodfall 22.156–22.167.

[287] L.T.A. 1954 s.65 (end of reversion).

[288] *Piper* v. *Muggleton* [1956] 2 Q.B. 569 C.A.; *Rene Claro (Haute Coiffure) Ltd.* v. *Hallé Concerts Society* [1969] 1 W.L.R. 909 C.A.; *Shelley* v. *United Artists Corp.* [1990] 1 E.G.L.R. 103 C.A. (consider effect of option).

[289] *Bowes-Lyon* v. *Green* [1963] A.C. 420 H.L., explaining *Cornish* v. *Brook Green Laundry Ltd.* [1959] 1 Q.B. 394.

[290] *E.H. Lewis & Son Ltd.* v. *Morelli* [1948] 2 All E.R. 1021, 1024–1025, Harman J. in C.A.; Woodfall 1.034–1.045.

[291] *Tadman* v. *Henman* [1893] 2 Q.B. 168.

[292] [1998] 1 E.G.L.R. 69 C.A.; J. Morgan [1999] *J.B.L.* 274 (welcome); M. Pawlowski (1998) 142 *S.J.* 248.

[293] Though not one who holds the legal estate: *St. Giles Hotel Ltd.* v. *Microworld Technology Ltd.* (1998) 75 P.& C.R. 380, 383, Millett L.J.

landlord known to be without title.[294] It also protects a tenant holding from a limited owner who does own the land but who lacks the power to grant a lease.[295]

The estoppel terminates when the landlord's title ends.[296] Thus a sub-tenant has no obligation to pay rent to his landlord after the head lease ends.[297] It was once said that the estoppel was lifted as soon as the tenant goes out of possession.[298] But this principle appears erroneous[299] as illustrated in *Industrial Properties (Barton Hill) Ltd.* v. *Associated Electrical Industries Ltd.*[300] A tenant who had given up an industrial unit in disrepair at the end of his lease was held liable on the repairing covenant, and was not excused when he found that his landlord did not in fact hold the legal freehold title to the land. The true principle is that the estoppel would end if the tenant were evicted by a title paramount.

K. RENEWAL: TERMS OF THE LEASE

A tenant has the right to a renewal if the landlord serves a renewal notice, does not oppose renewal, the tenant has replied, and then applies to the court in time.[301] It is then necessary to settle the terms of the lease following statutory guidelines.[302] Agreement is desirable,[303] and it should be formalised despite the theoretical possibility of estoppel.[304] Disputed cases require a court order.

1. Rent

The court will set a market rent,[305] usually on the basis that the lease will include a rent review provision[306] and provisions for guarantors if the tenant is a partnership.[307] Evidence will be required of comparables, and the rent will necessarily be affected by the permitted use. Three factors should be ignored: (1) the effect of occupation by the tenant and any predecessors; (2) goodwill; and (3) improvements for 21 years after they are made, but only if made when the tenant has no obligation to make them. After the court fixes the new rent, the tenant has 14 days in which to indicate that he will not accept a new lease at the rent decided upon. Rent awards can be backdated, taking into account

---

[294] *Bruton* v. *London & Quadrant Housing Trust* [2000] A.C. 406 H.L.

[295] J.E. Martin (1978) 42 *Conv. (N.S.)* 137. Statutory provisions to validate leases may also help: L.P.A. 1925 s.152; *Pawson* v. *Revell* [1958] 2 Q.B. 360.

[296] *Sarjeant* v. *Nash Field & Co.* [1903] 2 K.B. 304, 312, Collins M.R.

[297] *National Westminster Bank Ltd.* v. *Hart* [1983] Q.B. 773 C.A.; J. Price [1984] *Conv.* 64.

[298] *Harrison* v. *Wells* [1967] 1 Q.B. 263 C.A.; P.V Baker (1967) 83 *L.Q.R.* 19.

[299] *Cuthbertson* v. *Irving* (1859) 4 H. & N. 742, 157 E.R. 1034.

[300] [1977] Q.B. 580 C.A.

[301] While negotiations are proceeding timely court application is essential.

[302] L.T.A. 1954 ss.29, 32–36, 43A; Woodfall 22.140–22.155; Evans & Smith (5th) 489–496; M. Haley (1993) 13 L.S. 225 makes a case for major changes.

[303] s.28; V. King [1997] 1 *L.T. Rev.* 103.

[304] See above pp. 170–179.

[305] L.T.A. 1954 s.34; see below pp. 655–656.

[306] L.T.A. 1954 s.34(3); L.P.A. 1969 s.2; Law Com No 17 (1969); M Haley (1999) 19 *L.S.* 207, 225–226; *Northern Electric plc.* v. *Addis* [1997] 2 E.G.L.R. 111 C.A. (judge has a discretion to exclude a rent review provision).

[307] L.T.A. 1954 s.41A(6) inserted by L.P.A. 1969 s.9.

any interim rent that has been set.[308] Pending proceedings the landlord will generally apply for the award of an interim rent.[309]

2. Duration of new lease

This is a matter for the judge, balancing the inconvenience to the landlord against the business effect on the tenant,[310] but with a maximum of 14 years.[311] A tenant with a track record of occupation built up over a period of years can expect progressively longer renewals. Conversely a landlord may be allowed to safeguard future development rights by including a break clause exercisable in the event of redevelopment.[312] Landlords can legitimately object to a request for a very short lease since this is likely to diminish the value of the reversion.[313] Renewal will take effect three months from final disposal of the litigation, including any appeal, but given the uncertainty of this date when the judge makes his order at first instance, the preferred practice is to order a lease to last until a stated termination date a fixed period (say five years) distant from the date of the court order.[314]

3. Property

Renewal rights are restricted to the "holding",[315] that is that part of the property comprised within the lease that is actually occupied by the tenant.[316] An option to buy the reversion should not be included, since the object is not to create a new saleable asset,[317] nor should it extend the holding by granting additional easements[318] though existing ancillary rights are generally included.[319]

4. Other terms

Rent apart, renewal is presumed to occur on the same terms as the existing lease,[320] so a sound reason must be demonstrated before the structure of the existing covenants can be changed. A covenant that prevents change of use without the consent of the landlord (which depresses the rent) may be altered so as to provide that the landlord should not

---

[308] *Bradshaw* v. *Pawley* [1980] 1 W.L.R. 10.

[309] L.T.A. 1954 s.24A; see below pp. 667–668.

[310] L.T.A. 1954 s.33; *Chipperfield* v. *Shell U.K. Ltd.* [1981] 1 E.G.L.R. 51 C.A. (3 years correct on facts); D.W. Williams [1994] 49 E.G. 102.

[311] L.T.A. 1954 s.33; Law Com. No.208 (1992) para.2.79 (proposed increase to 15 years).

[312] *Amika Motors Ltd.* v. *Colebrook Holdings Ltd.* [1981] 2 E.G.L.R. 62 C.A.; *J.H. Edwards & Sons Ltd.* v. *Central London Commercial Estates Ltd.* [1984] 2 E.G.L.R. 103 C.A.; *National Car Parks Ltd.* v. *Paternoster Consortium Ltd.* [1990] 1 E.G.L.R. 99, Browne-Wilkinson V.C.; *Becker* v. *Hill Street Properties Ltd.* [1990] 2 E.G.L.R. 78 C.A. See also *Coppen* v. *Bruce Smith* (1999) 77 P. & C.R. 239 C.A. (10 year term to allow for future development of tennis courts).

[313] *C.B.S. United Kingdom Ltd.* v. *London Scottish Properties Ltd.* [1985] 2 E.G.L.R. 125 (obiter); J.E. Martin [1986] *Conv.* 122.

[314] *Turone* v. *Howard de Walden Estates Ltd. (No. 2)* [1983] 2 E.G.L.R. 65 C.A.; *Re 88 High Road, Kilburn* [1959] 1 W.L.R. 279; R.E. Megarry (1959) 75 L.Q.R. 180.

[315] L.T.A. 1954 s.23(3).

[316] s.32; the landlord may elect to include the whole of his property: subs.(2).

[317] *Kirkwood* v. *Johnson* (1979) 38 P. & C.R. 392 C.A.; *Derby & Co.* v. *I.T.C. Pension Trust Ltd.* [1977] 2 All E.R. 890, Oliver J.

[318] *G. Orlik (Meat Products) Ltd.* v. *Hastings & Thanet B.S.* (1974) 29 P. & C.R. 126 C.A.

[319] L.T.A. 1954 s.32(3).

[320] s.35.

unreasonably refuse consent,[321] and it may be quite reasonable to require the tenant to provide a guarantee.[322] Deeper-rooted changes may well be required as a result of the new scheme for the running of leasehold covenants introduced by the Landlord and Tenant (Covenants) Act 1995.[323]

An onus lies on the party who wishes for an alteration to show why it should be allowed. In the leading case, *O'May* v. *City of London Real Property Co.*,[324] the landlord tried to shift all repairing obligations onto the tenant, so that the landlord secured a clear lease—that is one giving a pure income profit with no deduction for outgoings. Had this been allowed the lease would have been much more valuable, so much so that the landlord offered to forego 10 per cent of the rent in order to secure it. Still it was held that the tenant had the right to refuse a change.[325] Alterations must be fair and reasonable and should not exploit the relatively weak bargaining position of the tenant seeking renewal.[326]

5.   Costs of renewal

The Costs of Leases Act 1958 applies, so that each party must pay its own costs.[327]

L.   DEFENCES TO BUSINESS RENEWAL

Grounds for opposition to a renewal are set out in section 30.[328]

1.   Misconduct by the tenant

Business security is naturally dependent upon compliance by the tenant with the terms of the lease, since his lease may be terminated by forfeiture if he breaks the terms on which he holds. During a contractual period—before the term date—the lease is ended without any renewal right, and sub-tenants are also vulnerable.

Once the contractual period has ended, the landlord may terminate the holding over by giving the tenant a section 24 trigger notice stating that he will oppose a renewal on the grounds of breach of covenant. There is no policy reason to protect poor tenants[329] and no entitlement to compensation. Available grounds include ground (a) for disrepair, ground (b) for rent arrears[330] and ground (c) for unauthorised changes of use and other miscellaneous breaches of covenant.[331] If the tenant gives a counter-notice and

---

[321] *Charles Clements (London) Ltd.* v. *Rank City Wall Ltd.* [1978] 1 E.G.L.R. 47, Goulding J. Absolute covenant against dealings: *St Giles Hotel Ltd.* v. *Microworld Technology Ltd.* (1998) 75 P. & C.R. 380 C.A.

[322] L.T.A. 1954 s.41A(6) (partners); *Cairnplace Ltd.* v. *C.B.L. (Property Investment) Co. Ltd.* [1984] 1 W.L.R. 696 C.A.; J.E. Martin [1984] *Conv.* 170.

[323] L.T.A. 1954 s.35(2) added by L.T. (Covenants) Act 1995 sch.1 para.4; R. Bruce & P. Williams [1996] 15 *E.G.* 96.

[324] [1983] 2 A.C. 726 H.L.; *Northern Electric plc* v. *Addison* [1997] 2 E.G.L.R. 111 C.A.

[325] Increase in value of reversion of £1–2 million.

[326] At 746A–D, Lord Hailsham L.C.

[327] *Stevenson & Rush (Holdings) Ltd.* v. *Langdon* (1978) 28 P. & C.R. 208.

[328] L.T.A. 1954 s.30 as amended by L.P.A. 1969 s.6; Woodfall 22.099–22.139; Evans & Smith (5th) 476–488.

[329] Bright & Gilbert 269–274.

[330] *Rawashdeh* v. *Lane* [1988] 2 E.G.L.R. 109 C.A.

[331] *Turner & Bell* v. *Searles (Stanford-le-Hope) Ltd.* (1977) 33 P. & C.R. 208 C.A. (breach of a planning enforcement notice); *Gloucester C.C.* v. *Williams* (1990) 88 L.G.R. 853 C.A. (sale of fruit and vegetable rather than high class salads).

follows it up with a court application for renewal this will force the case into court for a decision on whether a ground for possession has been made out. The landlord is restricted to the grounds stated in the notice, but possession is discretionary[332] and evidence of other complaints may sway the exercise of discretion.[333]

2.   Alternative accommodation

The landlord can specify ground (d)[334] in his trigger notice if an offer of satisfactory alternative accommodation has been made to the tenant. Factors that are obviously relevant are the extent of the accommodation, its location, and the time at which it would be available.[335] Since the object of allowing renewal of business tenancies is to protect the goodwill attached to a particular trading position, it will often be difficult to show that an alternative is adequate, and there is no reported case law. No compensation is available.

3.   Uneconomic sub-letting

Ground (e) is little used.[336] If the landlord let a whole unit to a tenant and it has been sub-let in parts the landlord may secure possession of the property in the sub-lease if he wishes to sell or let the whole of the property in the head lease. Possession should be ordered if the rents received on the parts are substantially less than the value of the property in the head lease as a whole. Landlords usually protect themselves by covenants against economic dissipation, and again there is no reported decision.

4.   Intention to demolish or reconstruct

Ground (f)[337] enables the landlord to recover possession where the landlord intends to demolish or reconstruct the premises, or to carry out substantial work of construction to the holding. This ground is irrelevant once the tenant has vacated and reconstruction has occurred.[338] Termination is possible at the end of any contractual period, and within it if there is a break clause agreed in order to preserve the landlord's redevelopment potential.[339] Success for landlords is variable, but many try.

Development work covered by ground (f) is very widely defined. Usually, work affects a building, in which case the vital matter is to distinguish between reconstruction[340] on the one hand and refurbishment —consisting of work such as rewiring and renewal of central heating—on the other.[341] Work on open land such as tearing down a City Farm

---

[332] *Beard* v. *Williams* [1986] 1 E.G.L.R. 148 C.A.; *Hurstfell* v. *Leicester Square Property Co. Ltd.* [1988] 2 E.G.L.R. 105 C.A.

[333] *Hutchinson* v. *Lambeth* [1984] 1 E.G.L.R. 75 C.A. (noise from disco).

[334] L.T.A. 1954 s.30(1)(d).

[335] s.31(2) allows an order to be made where alternative accommodation will be available within a year.

[336] s.31(2) applies as above.

[337] s.30(1)(f).

[338] *Aireps Ltd.* v. *Bradford City M.C.* [1985] 2 E.G.L.R. 143 C.A.; J.E. Martin [1986] *Conv.* 122.

[339] *Aberdeen Steak House plc.* v. *Crown Estate Commissioners* [1997] 2 E.G.L.R. 107 C.A.

[340] *Romulus Trading Co. Ltd.* v. *Henry Smith's Charity Trustees* [1990] 2 E.G.L.R. 75 C.A.

[341] *Barth* v. *Pritchard* [1990] 1 E.G.L.R. 109 C.A. (whole is not construction if each item is not); P.F. Smith [1989] *Conv.* 455.

and converting it to a school car park would justify repossession,[342] but not just infill-ing;[343] and digging up a tennis court is not demolition and is not covered.[344] The work may relate to part only: demolition or reconstruction must affect a substantial part, but construction might affect any part since the test of substantiality is applied to the work itself.

The landlord faces two hurdles. First, he must show a *requirement for possession*: a landlord should be entitled to terminate the tenant's holding only where he could not reasonably carry out the work without obtaining possession of the holding.[345] The land-lord's counter-notice should ideally state this fact, but remains valid without it.[346] In the leading case, demolition and reconstruction of a dangerous wall would last up to nine months, but could be carried out without possession of the holding, so possession was refused.[347] If a need for the property is demonstrated, a second hurdle comes into play in the shape of section 31A.[348] The tenant can avoid conceding possession by giving the landlord access to the property which enables the work to be carried out without sub-stantial interference in time or extent,[349] though clearly not in a case of total demoli-tion.[350] Alternatively a tenant may be able to identify a part of the holding that is economically separable so that he can claim a new tenancy of that part leaving the land-lord to take possession of (or as the case may be have access to) the other parts.[351] The tenant may be encouraged to accede to a possession order by an offer of an option for a new lease of the reconstructed premises.[352]

Proof of intention on the part of the competent landlord[353] must relate to his inten-tion to carry out major work on the premises let to the tenant. It must be established as at the date of termination of the current lease (and continuing to the date of the hear-ing[354]) or, alternatively, where the intention will be present within one year.[355] A rede-velopment defence is not satisfied by an intention to sell,[356] but this difficulty is easily

---

[342] *Turner* v. *Wandsworth L.B.C.* [1994] 1 E.G.L.R. 134 C.A.; *Hunt* v. *Decca Navigator Co. Ltd.* (1972) 222 E.G. 625. (conversion of open site to use as car park); *Hounsleys Ltd.* v. *Bloomer-Holt Ltd.* [1966] 1 W.L.R. 1244 (garage and wall); R.E. Megarry (1966) 82 L.Q.R. 462.

[343] *Botterill* v. *Bedfordshire C.C.* [1985] 1 E.G.L.R. 82 C.A.

[344] *Coppen* v. *Bruce Smith* (1999) 77 P. & C.R. 239 C.A.

[345] L.T.A. 1954 s.30(1)(f).

[346] *Bolton's (House Farms) Ltd.* v. *Oppenheim* [1959] 1 W.L.R. 913; R.E. Megarry (1960) 76 L.Q.R. 13.

[347] *Heath* v. *Drown* [1973] A.C. 498 H.L. (by 3:2).

[348] L.T.A. 1954 s.31A introduced by L.P.A. 1969 s.7. On the old law see *Decca Navigator Co. Ltd.* v. *Greater London C.* [1974] 1 W.L.R. 748 C.A.

[349] subs.(1)(a); *Cerex Jewels Ltd.* v. *Peachey Property Corporation plc.* [1986] 2 E.G.L.R. 65 C.A. (work for 2 weeks on 4% of holding insubstantial).

[350] *Mularczyk* v. *Azralnare Investments Ltd.* [1985] 2 E.G.L.R. 141 C.A.; *Leathwoods Ltd.* v. *Total Oil G.B. Ltd.* [1985] 2 E.G.L.R. 237 C.A.; *Blackburn* v. *Hussain* [1988] 1 E.G.L.R. 77, 78M, Parker L.J.

[351] L.T.A. 1954 s.34A(1)(b), (2); para.(b) is relevant only if para.(a) fails the tenant: *Romulus Trading Co. Ltd.* v. *Henry Smith's Charity Trustees (No.2)* [1991] 1 E.G.L.R. 95. However the landlord can in turn object on the basis that the rental return on the separate parts would be less than on a letting of the entire unit.

[352] *National Deposit Friendly Society Trustees* v. *Beatties of London Ltd.* [1985] 2 E.G.L.R. 59, Goulding J.

[353] Proof of intention of a company: *H.L. Bolton (Engineering) Co. Ltd.* v. *T.J. Graham & Sons Ltd.* [1957] 1 Q.B. 159 C.A.; R.E. Megarry (1957) 77 L.Q.R. 15.

[354] *Betty's Cafés Ltd.* v. *Phillips Furnishing Stores Ltd.* [1959] A.C. 20 H.L.; R.E. Megarry (1958) 74 L.Q.R. 344.

[355] L.T.A. 1954 s.31(2).

[356] *P.F. Ahern & Sons Ltd.* v. *Hunt* [1988] 1 E.G.L.R. 74 C.A.

avoided by granting a building lease.[357] Motive is irrelevant[358] provided the landlord's intention is genuine, and reconstruction is a primary purpose.[359] Much more important is that the intention is settled[360] as opposed to being a vague idea.[361] Leaving the zone of contemplation—where ideas are tentative, provisional, or exploratory[362]—the landlord must show that he has entered the valley of decision, where there are reasonable prospects of successful development without too many hurdles ahead.[363] Outline[364] planning permission and finance should be in place, with a contractor selected.[365]

5. Landlord's own accommodation

The landlord may be able to deny renewal of a business lease on ground (g)[366] that the landlord requires occupation of the property for his own accommodation, either for the purposes of a business to be carried on by him at his premises or as his residence.[367] Once this is proved, possession must be ordered.[368]

The *business* subhead is the more commonly used. However if conversion of the property to business use involves substantial changes to the property, the application should be made under both paragraphs (f) and (g).[369] The landlord may intend to set up a new business or to extend an existing business from his current premises into the tenant's neighbouring holding.[370] Eviction of a sitting tenant is not permitted simply in order to replace him with a different commercial tenant[371] or to sell; in order to gain possession the landlord must show that he, the landlord, will run a business at the property. The business may be operated via an agent or manager[372] or relative,[373] but the existing

[357] *Gilmour Caterers Ltd.* v. *St Bartholomew's Hospital Governors* [1956] 1 Q.B. 387 C.A.; *Spook Erection Ltd.* v. *British Railways Board* [1988] 1 E.G.L.R. 76 C.A.; *Turner* v. *Wandsworth L.B.C.* [1994] 1 E.G.L.R. 134 C.A.; M. Haley [1994] *N.L.J.* 1699.

[358] *Houseleys Ltd.* v. *Bloomer-Holt Ltd.* [1966] 1 W.L.R. 1244 C.A.; *Betty's Cafés Ltd.* v. *Phillips Furnishing Stores Ltd.* [1959] A.C. 20 H.L.

[359] *J.W. Smart (Modern Shoe Repairs) Ltd.* v. *Hinkley & Leicester B.S.* [1952] 2 All E.R. 846 C.A.; *Atkinson* v. *Bettison* [1955] 1 W.L.R. 1127 C.A.; R.E. Megarry (1956) 72 *L.Q.R.* 21.

[360] *Cunliffe* v. *Goodman* [1950] 1 All E.R. 720, 724A–E, Asquith L.J.; *Cadogan* v. *McCarthy & Stone Developments Ltd.* [1996] E.G.C.S. 94, Saville L.J.; *Coppen* v. *Bruce Smith* (1999) 77 P. & C.R. 239 C.A.; V.M. King [1999] 3 R.R.L.R. 158.

[361] *Fisher* v. *Taylors Furnishings Ltd.* [1956] 2 Q.B. 78 C.A.; *Reohorn* v. *Barry Corporation* [1956] 1 W.L.R. 845 C.A.

[362] *Lightcliffe & District Cricket & Lawn Tennis Club* v. *Walton* [1978] 1 E.G.L.R. 35 C.A.

[363] *Cunliffe* v. *Goodman* [1950] 1 All E.R. 720, 724A–E, Asquith L.J.; *DAF Motoring Centre (Gosport) Ltd.* v. *Hutfield & Wheeler Ltd.* [1982] 2 E.G.L.R. 59 C.A.; *Palisade Entertainments Ltd.* v. *Collin Estates Ltd.* [1992] 2 E.G.L.R. 94 C.A.; *Cadogan* v. *McCarthy & Stone (Developments) Ltd.* [1996] E.G.C.S. 94 C.A.

[364] *Capocci* v. *Goble* [1987] 2 E.G.L.R. 102 C.A.; *Peter Goddard & Sons Ltd.* v. *Hounslow L.B.C.* [1992] 1 E.G.L.R. 281 C.A.

[365] *Edwards* v. *Thompson* [1990] 2 E.G.L.R. 71 C.A. (no developer selected and estimates not complete).

[366] L.T.A. 1954 s.30(1)(g).

[367] Or part each: *Cox* v. *Binfield* [1989] 1 E.G.L.R. 97 C.A.

[368] *Skeet* v. *Powell-Sheddon* [1988] 2 E.G.L.R. 112 C.A.

[369] *Cam Gears Ltd.* v. *Cunningham* [1981] 1 W.L.R. 1011 C.A.; *Leathwoods Ltd.* v. *Total Oil (G.B.) Ltd.* (1985) 51 P. & C.R. 20 C.A.; *J.W. Thornton* v. *Blacks Leisure Group Ltd.* (1987) 53 P. & CR. 223 C.A.

[370] *Nursey* v. *P. Currie (Dartford) Ltd.* [1959] 1 W.L.R. 273 C.A.; *Cam Gears Ltd.* v. *Cunningham* [1981] 1 W.L.R. 1011 C.A.; *J.W. Thornton Ltd.* v. *Blacks Leisure Group plc.* (1987) 53 P. & C.R. 223 C.A.; *London Hilton Jewellers Ltd.* v. *Hilton International Hotels Ltd.* [1990] 1 E.G.L.R. 112 C.A.

[371] *Hodson* v. *Cashmore* (1972) 226 E.G. 1203, Brightman J. (architect to be replaced by barristers' chambers).

[372] *Teeside Indoor Bowls Ltd.* v. *Stockton-on-Tees B.C.* [1990] 2 E.G.L.R. 87; *Parkes* v. *Westminster R.C. Diocese Trust* [1978] 2 E.G.L.R. 50 C.A.

tenant is entitled to continue if he is to be replaced by a new tenant distinct from the landlord.[374]

Extensions have now been made for *corporate vehicles*. A landlord may oppose renewal of an existing lease to enable a business to be run by a company,[375] in which he has a controlling interest.[376] Where the landlord's interest is held *in trust*,[377] the business could be run by the trustees as landlords or by the beneficiaries,[378] in which case the beneficiary can claim possession, provided that he occupies under the terms of the trust[379]; but if two beneficiaries are entitled under a will, a desire by one to buy out the other to run a business does not meet the terms of the possession ground.[380] Ground (g) is not available for five years after a *purchase* of the property by the landlord,[381] unless there is an intervening contractual renewal of the tenancy.[382]

Proof of intention is based on case law that largely overlaps that on ground (f), since what is required here is a firm and settled intention, the following test being reaffirmed recently by the Court of Appeal in *Dolgellau Golf Club* v. *Hett*[383]:

> Within a reasonable time after the termination of the tenancy has the landlord a reasonable prospect of achieving his genuine intention of occupying the demised premises for the purposes of conducting the proposed business?

In other words what is assessed is the landlord's state of mind and not the likelihood of his success. Relevant factors are proof of business plans,[384] necessary consents from the head landlord,[385] and planning permission. If permission is needed, ground (g) may be established by proof that it is likely to be forthcoming: in *Westminster C.C.* v. *British Waterways Board*[386] the Board recovered possession of a street cleaning depot adjoining its canal, because once it was in possession there was every prospect of a successful planning application. *Dolgellau Golf Club* v. *Hett*[387] shows that the absence of planning or

---

[373] *Skeet* v. *Powell-Sheddon* [1988] 2 E.G.L.R. 112 C.A.

[374] *Willis* v. *British Commonwealth Universities' Association* [1965] 1 Q.B. 140 C.A. (obiter); P.V. Baker (1964) 80 *L.Q.R.* 325.

[375] *Tunstall* v. *Steigmann* [1962] 2 Q.B. 593 C.A.; (1962) 78 *L.Q.R.* 315.

[376] L.T.A. 1954 s.30(3). Ideally the notice should state this. Landlords within the same group of companies are also protected: s.42(3).

[377] *Re Crowhurst Park Ltd.* [1974] 1 All E.R. 991, Goulding J. (problems arising from proof of will only in Jersey).

[378] L.T.A. 1954 s.41(2); *Morar* v. *Chauhan* [1985] 1 W.L.R. 1263 C.A. (obiter because purchase within 5 years).

[379] *Meyer* v. *Riddick* [1990] 1 E.G.L.R. 107 C.A.; *Frish Ltd.* v. *Barclays Bank Ltd.* [1955] 2 Q.B. 541 C.A.

[380] *Carshalton Beeches Bowling Club* v. *Cameron* [1979] 1 E.G.L.R. 80 C.A.

[381] Or the landlord's interest is created by grant or merger: *Morar* v. *Chauhan* [1985] 1 W.L.R. 1263 C.A. (transfer from trustees to beneficiary was not a bar to repossession by the former beneficiary). On the problems arising from rail privatisation see *V.C.S. Car Park Management Ltd.* v. *Regional Railways North East Ltd.* [2000] 1 All E.R. 403 C.A.

[382] L.T.A. 1954 s.30(2); *Fisher* v. *Taylors Furnishing Stores Ltd.* [1956] 2 Q.B. 78 C.A.; R.E. Megarry (1956) 72 *L.Q.R.* 341; *Jones* v. *Jenkins* [1986] 1 E.G.L.R. 113 C.A.; J.E. Martin [1987] *Conv.* 53.

[383] [1998] 2 E.G.L.R. 75 C.A.; H. Toole (1998) 17 *P.L.J.* 3.

[384] *Europark (Midlands) Ltd.* v. *Town Centre Securities plc.* [1985] 1 E.G.L.R. 88, Warner J.; *Cox* v. *Binfield* [1989] 1 E.G.L.R. 97 C.A. (business likely to fail, but genuine); *Chez Gerard Ltd.* v. *Greene Ltd.* [1983] 2 E.G.L.R. 79 C.A. (undertaking accepted in borderline case); *Mirza* v. *Nicola* [1990] 2 E.G.L.R. 73 C.A.

[385] *Wates Estate Agency Services Ltd.* v. *Bartleys Ltd.* [1989] 2 E.G.L.R. 87 C.A.

[386] [1985] A.C. 676 H.L.; *Cadogan* v. *McCarthy & Stone Developments Ltd.* [1996] E.G.C.S. 94 C.A.

[387] [1998] 2 E.G.L.R. 75 C.A.; J. Morgan [1999] *J.B.L.* 269; H. Toole [1998] 17 *P.L.J.* 3; H.W. Wilkinson [1998] *N.L.J.* 1644.

licensing is not decisive. Hett wanted to repossess part of a golf course in order to develop his own course, and he succeeded, even though his application did not demonstrate the detail and practicality of his intentions. This was because of his long-standing interest in the project, the fact that he had spent large sums on preliminary work, he had the necessary practical skills, and a clear determination. The test is no longer whether it was more likely than not but rather whether there was a realistic prospect that the landlord will bring it about. Thus in *Gatwick Parking Service Ltd.* v. *Sargent*[388] possession was ordered of off-site parking at Gatwick airport, even though the planning permission was personal to the tenant and permission had been refused to the landlord, since the landlord showed a determination to pursue an appeal against the refusal and had some prospect of success. His chances do not have to be odds on. Thus there is an important shift of principle underway, which significantly and unfairly reduces the tenant's security.

M. COMPENSATION FOR DISTURBANCE

Compensation for improvements is considered as an aspect of repair.[389] The subject under discussion here is the compensation that a business tenant may obtain when he is forced to quit a holding on a no-fault ground.

A tenant will be allowed compensation for disturbance where renewal of the tenant's lease is refused on any of the no-fault grounds in section 30(1), that is ground (e) uneconomic sub-letting, ground (f) landlord's intention to demolish or reconstruct, or ground (g) where the landlord intends to occupy himself for the purposes of a business or residence.[390] Extra compensation was payable for a short transitional period where tenants of public houses were displaced by their landlords.[391] The Law Commission proposes to allow compensation in every case where the landlord objects successfully to a renewal.[392]

Entitlement to compensation rights cannot be excluded in advance, though it is possible to quantify compensation in advance by agreement.[393] At first it was necessary for the tenant to pursue proceedings to the point where possession was ordered after the landlord established a defence to renewal in order to preserve the tenant's right to compensation,[394] but later amendments to the legislation preserve compensation rights where termination occurs without proceedings if the landlord pursues only no-fault grounds.[395] If the tenant starts proceedings and later wishes to withdraw, the court

---

[388] [2000] E.G.C.S. 11 C.A.; M. Haley [2000] *Conv.* 456.

[389] See below pp. 649–695.

[390] L.T.A. 1954 s.37(1); Woodfall 22.170–22.177. Compensation is also available where a landlord obtains possession by misrepresentation (s.55) or where property is required for national purposes (s.59).

[391] L.T. (Licensed Premises) No.2 A. 1990 (July 11th 1989 to July 11th 1992).

[392] Law Com. No.208 (1992) paras.2.81–2.87, draft Bill cls.6, 7; other changes would relate to calculation of compensation for parts and compensation where a landlord obtains possession by a misrepresentation.

[393] L.T.A. 1954 s.38(2).

[394] s.37(4); if the court makes an order on no-fault grounds, this must be certified in the order, so entitling the tenant to make a claim.

[395] s.37(1) as amended by L.P.A. 1969 s.11. A tenants request for a new tenancy is invalid if the only aim is to claim compensation: *Sunlife Ass.* v. *Racal Tracs* [2000] 1 E.G.L.R. 138.

should leave the tenant free to claim compensation if he chooses to do so.[396] Occupation is required at the termination date, but this rule should not be applied so as to deny compensation to tenants who move out a few days early. In *Bacchiocchi* v. *Academic Agency Ltd.*[397] the tenant moved out 12 days early because he had been told the wrong date by his solicitor, but it was held that the tenant retained occupation during the cleaning up period. So, provided the tenant has a valid business reason to move out and no one else has moved in, his compensation rights are not prejudiced. However the tenant in *Sight & Sound Educational Ltd.* v. *Books etc. Ltd.*[398] who moved out in September 1997, many months before the end of the term in February 1998, lost all entitlement to compensation at double the rateable value: the tenant must not vacate before the date for termination in the landlord's section 25 notice.

Quantum is assessed at the termination date,[399] which is when the tenant is required to quit rather than the date of the court order.[400] The normal basis of compensation is a multiplier (currently 1!)[401] of the rateable value of the property.[402] Rating revaluations tend to have a major impact on business compensation, and it may be anticipated that this will recur with the 2000 revaluation.[403] This applies if the tenant has been in occupation for less than 14 years.[404] Where the tenant (including previous owners of the same business) has chalked up longer than that,[405] the compensation is doubled.[406] Abolition of domestic rating potentially reduced compensation claims significantly where the holding was of mixed business and residential property. An alternative basis of claim was introduced to overcome this problem,[407] which (after some initial doubt) has been held to apply only to a mixed holding[408]: compensation is then based on eight (or 16) times the rateable value. Compensation is derived from the legislation on business leases, rather than from the lease, and so is not assessable to capital gains tax.[409]

---

[396] *Lloyds Bank Ltd.* v. *City of London Corporation* [1983] Ch. 192 C.A; J.E. Martin [1982] *Conv.* 384; *Ove Arup Inc.* v. *Howland Property Investment Co. Ltd.* [1982] 1 E.G.L.R. 62.

[397] [1998] 1 W.L.R. 1313 C.A.; J. Morgan [1999] *J.B.L.* 264; P.F. Smith [1998] 18 *R.R.L.R.* 345; *Department of the Environment* v. *Royal Insurance plc.* [1987] 1 E.G.L.R. 83 disapproved.

[398] [1999] 3 E.G.L.R. 45 Ch.D.; S. Murdoch [1998] 48 *E.G.* 146; J. Morgan [2000] *J.B.L.* 336; contrast *Webb* v. *Sundown Sports Club Ltd.* [2000] E.G.C.S. 13, Arden J.

[399] L.T.A. 1954 s.25 (termination date stated in landlord's notice); s.26 (date for commencement of new term in tenant's request).

[400] *Cardshops Ltd.* v. *John Lewis Properties Ltd.* [1983] Q.B. 161 C.A.; J.E. Martin [1982] *Conv.* 85; *International Military Services Ltd.* v. *Capital & Counties plc.* [1982] 1 W.L.R. 575, Slade J.; J.E. Martin [1982] *Conv.* 225.

[401] S.I. 1990/363; previously it was 3; the rating revaluation in 1990 increased the compensation payable (despite the reduction in multiplier) by a factor of 8/3.

[402] S.I. 1954/1255 lays down a procedure for resolving disputes about the rateable value.

[403] T. McDermott [1999] *P.L.J.* 2.

[404] L.T.A. 1954 s.37(2)(b).

[405] s.37(2)(a),(3).

[406] *Edicron Ltd.* v. *William Whitely Ltd.* [1984] 1 W.L.R. 59 C.A.; J.E. Martin [1984] *Conv.* 58 (part); *Department of Environment* v. *Royal Insurance plc.* [1987] 1 E.G.L.R. 83, Falconer J. (occupation one day short of 14 years; reduced compensation by £162,000); J.E. Martin [1989] *Conv.* 58.

[407] L.T.A. 1954 s.37 subss.(5A)–(5D) as amended by Local Government and Housing Act 1989 s.149, sch.7 paras.3, 4 (the higher sum is payable after 14 years' occupation).

[408] *Busby* v. *Co-operative Insurance Society Ltd.* [1994] 1 E.G.L.R. 136; H. Lewis [1993] *N.L.J.* 140; M. Spencer & S. Fogel [1990] 32 *L.S.G.* 17 (now to be read subject to *Busby*).

[409] *Drummond* v. *Austin Brown* [1986] Ch. 52 C.A.

N. BUSINESS RENEWAL PROCEDURE

There are now a number of helpful guides to the Woolf procedures applying specifically to business lease renewal and exclusion applications.[410]

1. Venue

Business renewal may also occur in the High Court or a county court.[411] If a county court is chosen, it should be the tenant's home court (that is the one for the district where he lives or carries on business) or where the subject matter is situated.[412] In the High Court a claim form issued out of the Chancery Division or out of the District Registry covering the area where the land is situated should be used to begin proceedings.[413]

2. High Court

Part 8 procedure is used for claims under many of the landlord and tenant statutes in the High Court, including business renewal,[414] applications to fix an interim rent[415] and claims for compensation for improvements.[416] The Part 8 claim form (N208) should be used.[417] In many cases there are specific procedural rules,[418] but general Woolf provisions cover such matters as service.

3. County court

Litigation about business tenancies usually takes place in the county court, following the re-enacted County Court Rules.[419] Cases allocated to this procedure include business renewal,[420] applications to fix an interim rent[421] and claims for compensation for improvements,[422] as well as any proceedings under the Landlord and Tenant Acts 1954, 1985 or 1987.[423] Procedure is laid down by Section B of the Part 8B Practice Direction (itself a modified form of Part 8 procedure[424]), though this can be overridden by the

---

[410] Simmons & Simmons [1999] 7 *Comm. L.J.* 5; J.E. Adams [1999] *Conv.* 459; S. Thompson-Copsey [1999] 13 *Comm. Leases* 205; D. Cox & M. Davies [1999] 44 *E.G.* 140; S. Hasan [1999] 43 *L.S.G.* 36; Atkin's *Court Forms, Civil Procedure Part 3* (Butterworths, 1999) 216–225, Form 1; P. Francis [1999] *R.R.L.R.* 237; D. Cox & M. Davies [2000] 41 *P.L.J.* 4; J. Frenkel [2000] 20 *L.S.G.* 49.

[411] L.T.A. 1954 s.63; H.C.C.C.J.O. 1991 art.2(1)(d); transfers are provided for by s.63(4).

[412] P.D. 8B.B.6–7. Previously application could be made to any county court: *Sharma* v. *Knight* [1986] 1 W.L.R. 757 C.A.

[413] C.P.R. sch.1 R.S.C. Order 97 r.2; S. Hasan [1999] 43 *L.S.G.* 36.

[414] C.P.R. 8.1(6); C.P.R. sch.1 R.S.C. Order 97 r.6(1).; P.D. 8B.A. 1–3 and Table 1.

[415] L.T.A. 1954 s.38; C.P.R. sch.1 R.S.C. Order 97 r.9A(1); P.D. 8B.A Table 1.

[416] L.T.A. 1927 Part I; C.P.R. sch.1 R.S.C. Order 97 r.5; P.D. 8B.A Table 1.

[417] P.D. 8B.A.3; P.D. 4 Table 1. N208A gives notes for the claimant, N208C notes for the defendant, N209 a notice of issue and N210 an acknowledgement of service. For the text of claim forms see: D.R. Perkins & M. Madden [1999] 3 *L.T. Rev.* 129; Atkin's *Court Forms, Civil Procedure Part 3*, (Butterworths, 1999), 216, Form 141.

[418] P.D. 8B.A.1–3, Table 1.

[419] C.P.R. sch.2 C.C.R. Order 43; P.D. 8B.B.2; [1999] 14 *E.G.* 147.

[420] L.T.A. 1954 s.24; C.P.R.sch.2 C.C.R. Order 43 rr.6–8; P.D. 8B.B Table 2; claim form N397; for exclusion see above p. 557.

[421] L.T.A. 1954 s.24; C.P.R. sch.2 C.C.R. Order 43 r.9; P.D. 8B.B Table 2.

[422] L.T.A. 1927 Part I; C.P.R. sch.2 C.C.R. Order 43 r.4; P.D. 8B.B Table 2; (claim forms N394–N396).

[423] C.P.R. sch.2 C.C.R. Order 43 r.2(1); P.D. 8B.B Table 2.

[424] P.D. 8.2.1; P.D. 8B.B.5; J. Frenkel [2000] 20 *L.S.G.* 49.

terms of the re-enacted County Court Rules in specific cases.[425] On issue of the claim form, the court fixes a date for a hearing. Notice has to be given to each party at least 10 days before the hearing date.[426] Section B varies part 8 procedure even further by dispensing with the requirement for an acknowledgement of service, though it is wise to file one if a claim is disputed, since this enables the defendant to put in written evidence. When the hearing date arrives, the court may determine the case or may give case management directions—a defended case will have to be allocated to a track at this stage.[427]

4.   Claim forms

Writs, summonses, originating applications and sundry other methods of starting actions under the old procedure are all replaced by a single type of claim form. A knock-on effect of the shift to claim forms is the replacement of the familiar "plaintiff" with a "claimant", though defendants emerge from the reforms unscathed.[428] A claim form is one type of statement of case (the modern version of a pleading), which requires the inclusion of a "statement of truth".[429] This is best signed by the landlord or tenant in person, but if a solicitor signs for a party it is important to ensure that he has authority to commit his client to the truth of what is stated in the claim form. A Practice Direction provides for statements of truth to be made on behalf of a company, a partnership, or trustees, but the landlord's managing agent is not included among those authorised to give a statement of truth.[430]

5.   Service

As explained elsewhere,[431] the court usually serves the claim form by first class post, and after an acknowledgement of service, subsequent documents are usually served between the parties' solicitors.

6.   Defended cases

Lease renewals turn into fully blown defended cases if the landlord opposes renewal either on the basis of the tenant's misconduct or because of the landlord's proposed use of the property—usually for redevelopment or to take over the business himself.[432] The ground will be set out in the landlord's initial notice or the landlord's response to a tenant's request for a new tenancy. So it will be clear from the earliest stage that the case is likely to be defended. The general practice is to split off any dispute about the right to renew at the stage of the answer and treat this as a preliminary issue.[433] Initial allocation is to the multi-track[434] and in response to the allocation questionnaire the court should

---

[425] P.D. 8B.B.2–3.

[426] P.D. 8B.B.9–10.

[427] P.D. 8B.B.13.

[428] C.P.R. 2.3.

[429] C.P.R. 22; S. Hasan [1999] 43 *L.S.G.* 36; M. Walker [1999] 37 *L.S.G.* 42.

[430] C.P.R.22; P.D. 22.3.11; M. Walker [1999] 26 *L.S.G.* 32; M. James [1999] *N.L.J.* 937. S. Gerlis [1999] 34 *L.S.G.* 38.

[431] See below pp. 593–594.

[432] See above pp. 563–568.

[433] A. Hindle [2000] 03 *E.G.* 124.

[434] C.P.R. 8.9(c).

order the trial of the preliminary issue, ordering standard disclosure and issuing a timetable for case management. An innovation of the Woolf reforms is that *either* party may apply for summary judgment where there is no reasonable prospect for success; it has always been possible to cut off a defence in this way but the power to forestall a claim to possession is new.[435] Otherwise the preliminary issue must be tried to establish whether the landlord has succeeded in raising a ground for possession—for example a proved intention to redevelop the property—in which case the court will order possession.

7. Cases where the terms of renewal are disputed

There is an inherent tension between the active case management, which lies at the heart of the Woolf reforms of civil procedure, and the practice in business renewal.[436] A tenant is compelled by the legislative timetable[437] to make a timely application to the court for renewal of his tenancy, as otherwise he is barred from all security rights. After that, proceedings often go to sleep while the parties negotiate the terms of renewal, and it is desirable that the proceedings should be held in suspended animation so that litigation costs are not added to the conveyancing costs.

However the Woolf reforms envisage a strict timetable of procedural steps. After the filing of an acknowledgement of service or defence, the court will allocate the case to the fast or multi-track and give allocation directions: like features are a date for service of an answer, standard disclosure, a date for the delivery of a draft lease, and a timetable for amendments to it. The case will then proceed to trial if the terms of the new lease cannot be agreed within the Woolf timetable. There must be many cases in the system that were issued pre-Woolf and left dormant pending negotiations, but these are now subject to active case management[438] and an automatic stay if pre-Woolf proceedings have not come before a judge before April 26th 2000.[439] Tenants will therefore be forced to reactivate cases to prevent the loss of their renewal rights even if negotiations of new terms are under way.

Reform is desirable, either to remove the Woolf-based active case management of business tenancy renewals or (better still) to remove the need to litigate unless and until there is a genuine dispute.[440]

---

[435] C.P.R. 24.2.

[436] A. Hindle [2000] 03 *E.G.* 124.

[437] See above pp. 561–563.

[438] R. Hastie [1999] 13 *Comm. Leases* 254; R. Hastie [1999] 41 *E.G.* 155; S. Hasan [1999] 43 *L.S.G.* 36; J. Frenkel [2000] 20 *L.S.G.* 49 (can now seek stay).

[439] P.D. 51.19.

[440] As proposed by the Law Commission, see above pp. 564–565.

21

TERMINATION WITHOUT RENEWAL

Notices. The reasonable recipient principle. Measuring time. Break clauses.
Notices to quit. Warning notices. Notices to terminate business leases. Form.
Rent and service charge notices. Service of notices. Service of proceedings.
Union of lease and reversion. Leases to oneself. Merger. Express surrender.
Implied surrender. Preservation of derivative interests.

The main subject of this chapter is unilateral, hostile, termination by notice[1]; that is where one party or the other can break the natural duration of the lease by service of notice on the other party.[2] Some reference is also made to statutory warning notices and notices relating to claims to security of tenure. Later parts of the chapter consider rules about the form and length of notice required and how notices must be served.

A. THE REASONABLE RECIPIENT PRINCIPLE

As Nourse L.J. has said:

"The reasonable recipient [is] a formidable addition to the imagery of our law."[3]

It was badly needed. The older law required strict literal compliance with the lease and any statutory requirements,[4] meaning that the many defective notices were so much waste paper. Negotiations between landlord and tenant were turned into a hair-splitting search for flaws in the drafting skills of their legal advisers. A completely fresh and much more modern approach was introduced by the House of Lords[5] in *Mannai Investment Co. Ltd.* v. *Eagle Star Life Assurance Co. Ltd.*[6] in which a bare majority of the Lords

---

[1] Woodfall 17.285–17.312, Davey 119–123.

[2] There are numerous methods of ending leases. Others discussed elsewhere are: statutory extension, enfranchisement, forfeiture, disclaimer after insolvency, and frustration.

[3] *Garston* v. *Scottish Widows Fund & Life Assurance Society* [1998] 3 All E.R. 596, 598a, Nourse L.J.

[4] *Hankey* v. *Clavering* [1942] 2 K.B. 326 C.A.; R.E. Megarry (1943) 59 L.Q.R. 17 (criticism); *Chiltern Court (Baker Street) Residents Ltd.* v. *Wallabrook Property Co. Ltd.* [1989] 2 E.G.L.R. 207 C.A.; *Mannai* [1995] 1 W.L.R. 1508 C.A.; *Garston* v. *Scottish Widows' Fund & Life Assurance Society* [1996] 4 All E.R. 282, Rattee J.; *Aylward* v. *Fawaz* (1997) 29 H.L.R. 408 C.A.

[5] Lords Steyn, Hoffmann and Clyde, with Lords Goff and Jauncey dissenting.

[6] [1997] A.C. 749, H.L.; D.R. Perks (1997) 1 L.T.R. 120; L. Tee [1998] C.L.J. 29; P.F. Smith [1998] Conv. 326; M. Biles, "The Shift Towards the Commercial Interpretation of Leases—Hunting for Allegories on the Banks of the Nile", in P. Jackson & D.C. Wilde (eds.), *Contemporary Property Law* (Ashgate, Dartmouth, 1999).

approved the test for validity of any unilateral notice stated by Goulding J. in *Carradine Properties Ltd.* v. *Aslam*[7]:

> "Is the notice quite clear to a reasonable tenant reading it? Is it plain that he cannot be misled by it?"

Hence trivial and obvious defects in a notice can be overlooked if the meaning would be clear to a reasonable recipient of the notice. However, a flaw in a notice which leaves a genuine ambiguity is still destructive of the validity of the notice. What counts as a trivial defect and what as an ambiguity is not based on the subjective interpretation of the notice, but rather on an objective reading of it, alongside the terms of the lease. If the notice is designed to end the lease, the notice must unambiguously communicate this intention and indicate the right of determination being exercised, whether under a break clause, a notice to quit, a notice to determine a licence or a notice of intention to quit.[8] Similar principles apply to other types of warning notice required by the law of landlord and tenant, and the courts are also taking a more relaxed view of the use of out-of-date forms.[9]

The facts of *Mannai* were as follows. A lease of offices in Jermyn Street was to run for 10 years commencing from and including[10] January 13th 1992. A break clause permitted termination by notice expiring on the third anniversary of the term commencement date. This was actually January 13th 1995, but the tenant's letter purported to terminate it one day early on January 12th.[11] The House of Lords held that this minor misdescription did not mar the validity of the notice. The only objective was to convey the tenant's decision to terminate and that would be quite clear to a reasonable person reading the notice.[12]

Plainly erroneous dates can be ignored.[13] In *Carradine* an impossible date (1973 to end a lease in a notice dated 1974) was read as if it said the correct date (1975).[14] In *Micrografix* v. *Woking 8 Ltd.*[15] the tenant's letter and the actual notice stated two different, but equally erroneous, dates, but the notice was held to refer to the correct date that would be obvious to the landlord reading the lease. Many cases now provide specific illustrations of the kind of trivial defects overcome by *Mannai*. In *Garston* v. *Scottish Widows Fund & Life Assurance Society*[16] a tenant who was exercising a break clause muddled the tenth anniversary of the commencement of the term (June 24th 1995) and the anniversary of the date of the execution of the lease (July 9th 1995); the error in the date

---

[7] [1976] 1 W.L.R. 442, 444, Goulding J.; approved in *Germax Securities Ltd.* v. *Spiegal* (1978) 37 P. & C.R. 204, 206 C.A.; *Morrow* v. *Nadeem* [1986] 1 W.L.R. 237 C.A.

[8] *Mannai* [1997] A.C. 749,768F–H, Lord Steyn.

[9] *Tadema Holdings Ltd.* v. *Ferguson* [1999] Times November 25th, Peter Gibson L.J.

[10] J.E. Adams [1986] *Conv.* 306.

[11] *Oliver Ashworth (Holdings) Ltd.* v. *Ballard (Kent) Ltd.* [2000] Ch. 12 C.A. (notice to break on September 25th 1996 should have said 24th; valid under *Mannai*): *Fox & Widley* v. *Gurham* [1998] 1 E.G.L.R. 91, Clarke J. (May 25th for 23rd was a typographical error).

[12] *Doe d. Bedford* v. *Knightley* (1796) 7 Term. Rep. 63, 101 E.R. 856.

[13] A possible date is not lightly to be ignored: at 379g, Lord Hoffmann.

[14] [1976] 1 W.L.R. 442, Goulding J.

[15] [1995] 2 E.G.L.R. 32, Jacob J.; T. Coyne [1996] 23 *L.S.G.* 38; approved in *Mannai* [1997] A.C. 749, 771C, Lord Steyn, 780F, Lord Hoffmann, 783C, Lord Clyde.

[16] [1998] 3 All E.R. 596 C.A.

he gave would be clear to the landlord who was bound by the notice. In *Havant International Holdings Ltd. v. Lionsgate (H.) Investment Ltd.*[17] the tenant (H.I.H.L.) had a break clause, but an associated company (H.I.L.) actually occupied the land, and it was a director of H.I.L. who signed the notice seeking to exercise the break clause. A reasonable recipient would assume that this was an error so the notice was valid, though if the two companies were not associated a reasonable recipient would not be able to dismiss the possibility that an assignment had occurred.[18] A doubt about the physical extent of the property may also be overcome.[19]

B. MEASURING TIME

1. Corresponding date rule

Months measured from (say) January 20th, expire on the 20th day of February, March, April and so on. The number of days in a particular month is irrelevant, so that if notice is required of so many months duration it may expire on the corresponding date of any later month. In *Dodds v. Walker*[20] a business tenant had four months for application to court for a renewal of his lease, a period which ran from the date of the landlord's notice on September 30th 1978. The date of service (September 30th) was excluded, so the notice expired on the corresponding day (January 30th 1979), meaning that court application on January 31st 1979 was out of time.[21]

The corresponding date rule applies to years, weeks,[22] and other periods. A month is a calendar month.[23] For quarters, measured from a day which is not itself a quarter day, two quarters are equal to six months,[24] but where measurement starts on one of the traditional agricultural quarter days,[25] one quarter's notice runs until the next quarter day.

2. From

Where a period is measured "from" a particular date, the rule in *Sidebotham v. Holland*[26] operates to exclude that date. So a term from September 20th, actually begins on the 21st; and ends at midnight[27] on the 20th in a later month.[28] Notice to quit at noon is

---

[17] [1999] 47 L.S.G. 34, Hart J.

[18] *Lemmerbell Ltd. v. Britannia I.A.S. Ltd.* [199] 3 E.G.L.R. 67 C.A.

[19] *Safeway Food Stores Ltd. v. Morris* [1980] 1 E.G.L.R. 59; but contrast *Herongrove Ltd. v. Wates City of London Properties plc.* [1988] 1 E.G.L.R. 82.

[20] [1981] 1 W.L.R. 1027 H.L.; J.T. Farrand [1981] *Conv.* 321; (1980) 96 *L.Q.R.* 485 C.A.

[21] *E.J. Riley Investments Ltd. v. Eurostile Holdings Ltd.* [1985] 1 W.L.R. 1139 C.A. (notice March 23 1983; tenant's application May 23rd 1983); (1986) 102 *L.Q.R.* 3.

[22] *Thompson v. Stimson* [1961] 1 Q.B. 195 Div.Ct.; R.E. Megarry (1961) 77 *L.Q.R.* 23.

[23] L.P.A. 1925 s.61(a).

[24] *Samuel Properties (Developments) Ltd. v. Hayek* [1972] 1 W.L.R. 1296 C.A.; (1972) 88 *L.Q.R.* 459.

[25] March 25th, June 24th, September 29th, December 25th. This is usually because the lease is agricultural.

[26] [1895] 1 Q.B. 378 C.A.

[27] Contrast where the notice is to expire at midnight, so the notice could state either the day before or the one after: *Sidebotham v. Holland* [1895] 1 Q.B. 378 C.A.; *Crate v. Miller* [1947] K.B. 946 C.A.; R.E. Megarry (1947) 63 *L.Q.R.* 417.

[28] *Yeandle v. Reigate & Banstead B.C.* [1996] 1 E.G.L.R. 20 (term began September 29th 1968; notice to quit served on July 27th 1992 to give possession on September 28th 1993 was held valid, since this implied termination at the end of the 28th or beginning of the 29th).

invalid.[29] The rule is counter-intuitive, and easily excluded.[30] The simplest technique is to state that the term runs from and including[31] a particular day, as was done in *Mannai* itself.[32]

It is very common for the commencement date of a term to be backdated so that when the lease is executed a short period of the term has already expired. When measuring a period from a particular date, it is important to know which of these two dates is the base date. In *Garston* v. *Scottish Widows Fund & Life Assurance Society*,[33] for example, a lease was executed on July 9th, but the 20-year term started a few days earlier on June 24th. Mannai resolved the confusion in this particular case, but in general it remains important to use the correct date as a base for calculating the duration of notices.

C. BREAK CLAUSES

1. Break clauses exercisable by landlord

A lease may provide for the landlord to terminate the contractual term, but often this is of limited value, since it merely brings into play the tenant's security of tenure.[34] Leases often restrict a landlord's right to serve notice to a case where he can demonstrate an intention to redevelop.[35] A notice to break a renewable business lease is not fully effective unless it also complies with the statutory requirements for such leases: exercise of a break clause will end the original contractual term, but there will be a statutory continuation of the tenancy, and a tenant who qualifies (through business occupation) will be entitled to seek a renewal.[36]

2. Break clauses exercisable by the tenant

A tenant may have a right to terminate a lease by notice. This enables the introduction of considerable flexibility, for example in a lease to a quarry it may give the right for the tenant to stop rent running when all the minerals are exhausted.[37] Leases to partnerships often contain a retirement clause allowing an individual partner to remove himself as a tenant when he retires from the partnership, though this cannot be used to terminate the lease by a mass resignation.[38]

---

[29] *Bathavon R.D.C.* v. *Carlile* [1958] 1 Q.B. 461 C.A. "Within" a particular time includes the expiry of that time: *Manorlike Ltd.* v. *Le Vitas Travel Agency & Consultancy Services Ltd.* [1986] 1 All E.R. 573 C.A.

[30] *Ladyman* v. *Wirral Estates Ltd.* [1968] 2 All E.R. 197; *Meadfield Properties Ltd.* v. *S.S. for the Environment* [1995] 1 E.G.L.R. 39.

[31] J.E. Adams [1986] Conv. 306.

[32] [1997] A.C. 749 H.L.

[33] [1998] 3 All E.R. 596 C.A.

[34] One notice may exercise the break clause and act as a notice to end the business lease under L.T.A. 1954 s.25: *Keith Bayley Rogers & Co.* v. *Cubes* (1975) 31 P. & C.R. 412.

[35] The ground for repossession under L.T.A. 1954 s.30(1)(f) (see above pp. 569–571) must be proved, but one notice will satisfy both the break clause and s.30(1)(f): *Aberdeen Steak Houses Group Ltd.* v. *Crown Estate Commissioners* [1997] 2 E.G.L.R. 107 C.A.

[36] *Scholl Manufacturing Ltd.* v. *Clifton (Slim-line) Ltd.* [1967] 1 Ch. 41, 51E–G, Diplock L.J.; *Safeway Food Stores Ltd.* v. *Morris* [1980] 1 E.G.L.R. 59, Walton J.

[37] *Nocton Ltd.* v. *Walter Hall Group plc.* [1997] E.G.C.S. 97 Ch.D.

[38] *Axa Equity & Law Life Assurance Society plc.* v. *Wootton* [1997] E.G.C.S. 30.

Until recently exercise of break clauses was rare, since any commercial value could be realised by sale of the lease. However the recession of the early 1990s led to a slump in market rentals, and an old lease with a high rental could become unsaleable, or indeed have a negative value. Break clauses were of immense value since the tenant could end an onerous lease at a high rent and take a cheaper lease elsewhere. Many tenants negotiated for a right to break a lease rather than submit to a massive rent increase at the time of a rent review. Notice to break a renewable business lease must also comply with the statutory requirements for such leases.[39]

The notice exercising a break clause must purport to be a break notice and must be an unambiguous exercise of it.[40] Careful compliance is required with the terms of the lease about when to serve notice and how long it should be, though—as already explained at the start of this chapter—the House of Lords has recently mitigated the rigour of the law. It may be very difficult to tell whether a break clause is personal to the original tenant[41] or is proprietary, so that it is incapable of passing to future tenants. The current tenant must give notice, and notice by the wrong tenant is ineffective[42]; but the state of play is assessed (curiously) from the state of the legal title, so that before registration of a transfer it is the seller who can break the lease.[43]

Tenants should not be able to evade liability on repairing covenants by breaking the lease. So exercise of a break clause is usually *conditional on compliance with all covenants* up to the moment of termination. Breaches of covenant that subsist at the time of the break notice will prevent termination of the lease,[44] with triviality of the breach being no defence.[45] However it is common for the terms of the break clause to require only reasonable compliance with the covenant,[46] and the law has been liberalised so that generally no account is taken of breaches which are spent or which have been remedied.[47] Landlords may, of course, be estopped from insisting on full compliance.[48]

---

[39] See below pp. 586–587.

[40] *Aylward* v. *Fawaz* (1997) 29 H.L.R. 408 C.A., distinguishing *Hankey* v. *Clavering* [1942] 2 K.B. 326.

[41] *Max Factor Ltd.* v. *Wesleyan Assurance Society* [1996] 2 E.G.L.R. 210 C.A. (if T0 assigns and then rebuys, a personal break clause is lost); *Olympia & York Canary Wharf Ltd.* v. *Oil Property Investments Ltd.* [1994] 2 E.G.L.R. 48 C.A. (good reason to refuse consent to assignment if T0 could exercise break clause).

[42] *Dun & Bradstreet Software Services (England) Ltd.* v. *Provident Mutual Life Assurance Association* [1998] 2 E.G.L.R. 175 C.A.

[43] *Brown & Root Technology Ltd.* v. *Sun Alliance & London Assurance Co. Ltd.* [1997] 1 E.G.L.R. 39 C.A. relying on the unsatisfactory decision in *Gentle* v. *Faulkner* [1900] 2 Q.B. 267 C.A.

[44] *West Country Cleaners (Falmouth) Ltd.* v. *Saly* [1966] 3 All E.R. 210 C.A.; *Bass Holdings Ltd.* v. *Morton Music Ltd.* [1988] Ch. 493, 518B, Kerr L.J.; *A. & J. Mucklow (Birmingham) Ltd.* v. *Metro-Cammell Weymann* [1994] E.G.C.S. 64; *Trane (U.K.) Ltd.* v. *Provident Mutual Life Assurance* [1995] 1 E.G.L.R. 33; N. Cheffings & J. Richards [1994] 31 *E.G.* 143.

[45] *Bairstow Eves (Securities) Ltd.* v. *Ripley* [1992] 2 E.G.L.R. 47 C.A.; *Burch* v. *Farrows Bank Ltd.* [1917] 1 Ch. 606; *Simons* v. *Associated Furnishers Ltd.* [1931] 1 Ch. 379.

[46] *Reed Personnel Services plc.* v. *American Express Ltd.* [1997] 1 E.G.L.R. 229, Jacob J.; H.W. Wilkinson [1997] *N.L.J.* 499. Earlier cases are: *Starkey* v. *Barton* [1909] 1 Ch. 284; *Gardner* v. *Blaxhill* [1960] 1 W.L.R. 752; *Bassett* v. *Whiteley* (1982) 45 P. & C.R. 87.

[47] *Bass Holdings Ltd.* v. *Morton Music Ltd.* [1988] Ch. 493 C.A. (whether positive or negative but possibly excluding persistent breaches).

[48] *William Hill (Southern) Ltd.* v. *Waller* [1991] 1 E.G.L.R. 271 C.A.; M. Shelton [1999] 16 *E.G.* 150 (procedural advice); *HB Property Developments Ltd.* v. *S.S. for the Environment* (1999) 78 P. & C.R. 108 C.A. (no waiver on facts because he did not know of rights).

D. NOTICES TO QUIT PERIODIC TENANCIES

1. Nature of notice to quit

A periodic tenancy has no set length when it is created, since it can be allowed to run on indefinitely, the parties being content to start on the basis that either of them may end the tenancy by notice at any time in the future.[49] If the landlord gives notice it is called a notice to quit. It ends the periodic tenancy at the time set out in the notice. Sometimes the landlord genuinely wants possession, but at other times the notice to quit is simply a vehicle to secure a rent increase or a variation in the terms, so there is no objection to a notice to quit containing an offer of a new tenancy.[50] Very frequently a landlord's notice will not be effective to end the lease because it will trigger statutory security of tenure. If the tenant wishes to leave, he may give a notice of his intention to quit.

Periodic tenancies can be terminated in many other ways—for example by forfeiture for non-payment of rent or consensual surrender—but the ease with which short periodic tenancies can be ended by notice reduces the significance of these other means, except perhaps in the case of a yearly tenancy.

2. Length of notice

Express agreement. Every periodic tenancy must be terminable by notice. The length of notice is decided, first, by any express provision in the tenancy agreement. The notice need not be of the same length as the period of the tenancy. *Re Midland Railway Co.'s Agreement* concerning a six-monthly tenancy terminable by three months' notice demonstrates that it may be shorter.[51] Express agreement can also require a longer period of notice, despite theoretical problems with repugnancy, so long as the period of notice is of certain duration.[52]

Implication from period of tenancy. Failing an express agreement, the length of notice required to terminate a periodic tenancy is determined by rules of law. A yearly tenancy can be terminated by half a year's notice which must expire on an anniversary date of the commencement of the tenancy.[53] A yearly tenancy arising by implication from payment of rent on October 10th could be terminated at the end of the October 9th in any subsequent year; the notice would have to be served on or before May 9th in the year of termination.[54] Otherwise, if the law required a full year's notice, termination might be delayed for up to two years if the decision to terminate was taken at the worst moment in the cycle.

With periods other than a full year, the length of notice required is one full period of the tenancy. Thus to terminate a monthly tenancy requires a whole month's notice,[55]

---

[49] Woodfall 17.196–17.269, Davey 127–134, Evans & Smith (5th) 232–236, Garner (2nd) 136–139.

[50] *Ahearn* v. *Bellman* (1879) 4 Ex.D. 201 C.A.

[51] [1971] Ch. 725 C.A.

[52] *Breams Property Investment Ltd.* v. *Stroulger* [1948] 2 K.B. 1 C.A. (quarterly tenancy terminable by three years' notice); D.C. Potter (1948) 11 *M.L.R.* 342; *Prudential Assurance Co. Ltd.* v. *London Residuary Body* [1992] 2 A.C. 386 H.L. accepts this result.

[53] *Bennett Properties Ltd.* v. *H. & S. Engineering Ltd.* [1998] 2 C.L.Y. 3683 Q.B.D.

[54] If the tenancy was created on a traditional quarter day (December 25th, March 25th, June 24th and September 29th) two quarters' notice is required, but otherwise the corresponding date rule is applied; see above p. 581.

[55] But see E. Cooke [1992] *Conv.* 263.

and for a weekly tenancy it is one week's notice. Notice must still terminate at the end of a full period of the tenancy.[56] A monthly tenancy created on the 15th July can be terminated by notice expiring on the 14th of August,[57] September, October, or any subsequent month. Thus in *Calcott* v. *J.S. Bloor (Measham) Ltd.* [1998] 1 W.L.R. 1490 C.A. an agricultural tenancy was converted to a yearly basis as soon as it was created, and a notice had to expire on an anniversary date of the original agreement. Notice relating to an inhabited house (whichever side gives it) must be of at least 28 days or four weeks a time that runs immediately from the date of the notice irrespective of the period of the tenancy.[58] A notice to quit in the alternative is of doubtful validity,[59] but uncertainties can be smoothed over by a notice to quit "on or before" a given date.[60]

Withdrawal. Service of a notice to quit by the landlord is a binding election to terminate, rather like a decision to forfeit, and the notice cannot be withdrawn unilaterally.[61] It should be remembered that if the notice to quit expires but the tenant remains and the landlord accepts rent from him, this usually acts as an implied creation of a new periodic tenancy.

3.   Notices served in advance

There may be an implied requirement that a notice cannot be served too far in advance.[62]

4.   Termination of joint periodic tenancies

Any one of joint periodic tenants can give a valid notice to quit—the rule in *Hammersmith & Fulham L.B.C.* v. *Monk* that has been considered in the residential context.[63]

5.   Notices to end sub-tenancies

These are discussed below.[64]

E.   WARNING NOTICES

Many hostile steps that a business[65] landlord may wish to take against his tenant have to be preceded by a warning notice. Forfeiture terminates a lease (usually commercial or a

---

[56] It is possible to contract out of this rule: *Harler* v. *Calder* [1989] 1 E.G.L.R. 88 C.A. Where the creation date of the tenancy is unknown, the term date may be assumed to be the date on which rent is paid.

[57] Notice before the lease began is bad in the case of an agricultural holding, since it undermines the security of tenure legislation: *Lower* v. *Sorrell* [1963] 1 Q.B. 959 C.A.; R.E. Megarry (1963) 79 L.Q.R. 178.

[58] Protection from Eviction Act 1977 s.5.

[59] *Bridgers* v. *Stanford* [1991] 2 E.G.L.R. 265 C.A.; *Addis* v. *Burrows* [1948] 1 K.B. 444; *P. Phipps & Co. (Northampton & Towcester Brewers) Ltd.* v. *Rogers* [1925] 1 K.B. 14 C.A. (Atkin L.J. at 29 said that the notice was "short, simple and wrong").

[60] *Dagger* v. *Shepherd* [1946] K.B. 215 C.A.

[61] *Lower* v. *Sorrell* [1963] 1 Q.B. 959 C.A.; R.E. Megarry (1963) 79 L.Q.R. 178; D.G. Barnsley (1963) 27 *Conv. (N.S.)* 335; A. Dowling [1994] *Conv.* 437 (prefers the Irish view which permits withdrawal).

[62] Contrast *Multon* v. *Cardell* [1986] 1 E.G.L.R. 44, with *Biondi* v. *Kirklington & Piccadilly Estates Ltd.* [1947] 2 All E.R. 59, Roxburgh J.

[63] [1992] 1 A.C. 478 H.L.; J. Dewar (1992) 108 *L.Q.R.* 375; L. Tee [1992] *C.L.J.* 218; see above pp. 124–130.

[64] See below pp. 618–620.

[65] For residential notices see above pp. 45–49 (old law for shortholds), 318–319 (notice warning of claim to repossession).

long lease of a flat or house) following a breach of covenant by the tenant, but a section 146 notice is required before termination proceeds for disrepair or any other ground apart from than non-payment of rent; this is the subject of a later chapter.[66] This is the best method of hostile termination of a renewable business lease during the contractual term of the lease.

F.   NOTICES TO TERMINATE BUSINESS LEASES

1.   Statutory continuation of renewable business leases

At the end of the contractual period when the agreed term runs out, a renewable business lease will not expire as it would at common law[67] since it is continued in force automatically by way of statutory continuation of the contractual tenancy.[68] This means that a tenant cannot leave as soon as his business tenancy reaches its term date.[69] Statutory extension is dependent upon the premises being occupied by the tenant for a business carried on by him. If so, there is no statutory tenancy created as a separate entity—as occurred with the Rent Acts—but rather a statutory extension of the existing tenancy. Liability under the contract ends: this is shown by the fact that the original tenant is no longer liable for privity of contract[70] unless clear contractual words were used to extend this burden; fortunately this issue is now dead since privity of contract has been abolished. Nevertheless the liability of the current tenant to rent is extended.

2.   Landlord's trigger notice

A landlord who wishes to evict the tenant must take the initiative by serving a section 25 notice in the prescribed form,[71] asking the tenant whether he is willing to give up possession, and indicating any ground for repossession the landlord intends to rely upon. This will only terminate the lease if the tenant chooses to accept it as a termination by indicating that he is willing to leave, or by declining to seek a renewal.

During the contractual term of a renewable lease, the landlord must rely upon an agreed surrender[72] or a breach of covenant justifying a forfeiture. So a section 25 trigger notice must specify a date on which the lease is to end that is on or after the contractual term date,[73] and at least six months after the date of the notice.[74] If the lease is periodic, the notice must also be long enough to act as a common law notice to quit. The period of notice should not exceed 12 months.[75] The procedure, the strict timetable for

---

[66] See below Chapter 27.

[67] Woodfall 17.002–17.007.

[68] L.T.A. 1954 ss.24, 65; *Scholl Manufacturing Co. Ltd.* v. *Clifton (Slim-Line) Ltd.* [1967] Ch. 41, 51, Diplock L.J.; R.E. Megarry (1966) 82 L.Q.R. 460; *Willison* v. *Cheverell Estates Ltd.* [1996] 1 E.G.L.R. 116, 117F–G, Balcombe L.J. (could not operate rent review clause during statutory extension).

[69] See below pp. 586–587.

[70] *City of London Corporation* v. *Fell* [1994] 1 A.C. 458 H.L.; see above p. 559.

[71] L.T.A. 1954 s.25; see above pp. 559–560.

[72] See below pp. 592–603.

[73] *Lewis* v. *M.T.C. (Cars) Ltd.* [1975] 1 W.L.R. 457 C.A.; *Whelton Sinclair* v. *Hyland* [1992] 1 E.G.L.R. 158 C.A.; J. Hewitt (1993) 137 S.J. 154 (notice ended on last day of contractual term and so valid).

[74] L.T.A. 1954 s.25(2).

[75] s.25(2); the length of the notice is extended if more than 6 months' notice is needed to terminate a periodic tenancy: subs.(3).

renewal, and the proposed procedural changes have all been considered in the last chapter.[76] Usually a landlord's notice will merely trigger the renewal process, but if the tenant wishes to leave he can do so, either by giving notice of his intention to leave or simply by ignoring his landlord's notice.[77]

Since there is a statutory continuation of a renewable business lease, the tenant will be bound to continue paying rent until the date stated by the landlord for expiration of his section 25 notice.[78] If the tenant decides to renew at first but then changes his mind and withdraws his court claim for a new lease, rent is due until three months after the withdrawal with no jurisdiction to terminate liability to rent sooner.[79]

3.   Tenant's termination notice

In a declining market or when he is in business difficulties, it may be in the tenant's interest to take the initiative in seeking to leave the property. He is bound for the length of any contractual term, but he can leave at the end of the term or earlier if he is able to take advantage of a break clause. A non-statutory form of notice may effectively end a contractual periodic tenancy, but it will still leave in place its statutory continuation. If he decides to end the lease—whether using a statutory notice[80] or a contractual break clause[81]—a tenant cannot afterwards request a new tenancy: a business tenant is not allowed to secure a rent reduction by breaking an existing lease and then using the business tenancies legislation to request a new tenancy.

Unilateral termination by the tenant of any renewable business lease (where the tenant is in business occupation) must employ the section 27 notice mechanism in order to end the statutory continuation of the tenancy. Notice may be served at any time during the contractual term[82] but it must last six months and expire on or after the term date; the expiry date must be either the contractual term date[83] or some later date.[84] A statutory notice is essential to end liability to rent. Thus in *Provident Mutual Life Assurance Association* v. *Greater London Employers Association*[85] a tenant notified his landlord that he was leaving in April 1994 but, even though he quit in May and his contractual term ended in June, his liability for rent continued until the section 27 notice expired towards the end of September.

---

[76] See above pp. 558–565.

[77] *Kammins Ballrooms Co. Ltd.* v. *Zenith Investments (Torquay) Ltd.* [1971] A.C. 850 H.L.; *Artoc Bank & Trust Ltd.* v. *Prudential Assurance Co. Ltd.* [1984] 1 W.L.R. 1181; *Lloyds Bank Ltd.* v. *City of London Corporation* [1983] Ch. 192; *Young Austen & Young* v. *British Medical Association* [1977] 1 W.L.R. 881.

[78] *Long Acre Securities Ltd.* v. *Electro Acoustic Industries Ltd.* [1990] 1 E.G.L.R. 91 C.A.

[79] *Covell Matthews & Partners* v. *French Wools Ltd.* [1978] 1 W.L.R. 1477 C.A.; also in cases where the court rules against the tenant in a dispute about whether the landlord has a ground to oppose a renewal.

[80] s.27.

[81] *Garston* v. *Scottish Widows' Fund & Life Assurance Society* [1996] 4 All E.R. 282, Rattee J.; E. Slessenger & R. Ballaster [1994] 46 E.G. 196 (reversed on the facts [1998] 3 All E.R. 596, 598a).

[82] *Weinbergs Weatherproofs Ltd.* v. *Radcliffe Paper Mill Co. Ltd.* [1958] Ch. 437, Harman J.; R.E. Megarry (1958) 74 L.Q.R. 184.

[83] *Long Acre Securities Ltd.* v. *Electro Acoustic Industries Ltd.* [1990] 1 E.G.L.R. 91 C.A.

[84] L.T.A. 1954 s.27; S. Murdoch [1990] 06 E.G. 117. Notice cannot be served before the tenant has been in occupation for 1 month.

[85] [1996] 1 E.G.L.R. 106, Lightman J.

4.   Non-renewable business leases

A lease is not renewable if the tenant is not in occupation of the premises for the purpose of carrying on a business,[86] and there is no statutory continuation of it: it ends at the end of the contractual period.[87] Parts can be sheared off if they are not being used for business purposes or have been sub-let, the notice to quit that part not needing to be in the statutory form.[88]

The term of a non-renewable lease may be ended by effluxion of time on its term date, by notice to quit or of intention to quit a periodic tenancy, or by exercise of a break clause. *Esselte A.B.* v. *Pearl Assurance plc.*[89] provides a definitive statement of the law about termination in the particular context of an office block in Peterborough. The contractual term ran for five years from 1988, but the block was left empty after December 1992. Rent payments were halted as soon as the contractual term expired on February 14th 1993. The Court of Appeal held that the lease expired on that term date, with no statutory continuation, since business use had ceased during the contractual term. A "tenancy to which this Act applies" excludes one to which it had applied in the past if it no longer does so.[90] A non-renewable business lease ends on the term date without notice. A landlord who is unsure whether or not a tenant is in occupation should serve a statutory notice to quit and institute proceedings for a declaration that the tenant has no entitlement to seek renewal. It is, no doubt, odd that a tenant can curtail his liability to rent by moving out, but no doubt in many cases there will be a covenant to maintain continuity of occupation.

G.   FORM OF NOTICE

1.   Form

Notice to terminate a lease must follow any contractual arrangement reached in the lease, at least if the terms are mandatory.[91] A (masculine) lease might, for example, require a notice to be served on blue paper, in which case it would be no good serving it on (feminine) pink paper.[92]

Most notices relating to land must be in writing.[93] Section 196 of the Law of Property Act 1925[94] states the formality needed, unless the contrary appears, when a notice is

---

[86] L.T.A. 1954 s.23(1); if it is partly occupied by the tenant and partly sub-let, the landlord can serve a notice to sever the reversion and so exclude the parts not occupied.

[87] Even if it subsequently becomes a renewable business lease during the notice: L.T.A. 1954 s.24(3)(b). If it is renewable when the contractual term runs out but ceases to be so while it is being continued, it can be terminated by notice of a duration between 3 and 6 months: s.24(3)(a).

[88] L.P.A. 1925 s.140; *William Skelton & Son Ltd.* v. *Harrison & Pinder Ltd.* [1975] Q.B. 361 Ch.D.; *Neville Long & Co. (Boards) Ltd.* v. *Firemanaich* [1983] 2 E.G.L.R. 76 C.A.; J.E. Martin [1982] *Conv.* 224.

[89] [1997] 2 All E.R. 41 C.A.; H.W. Wilkinson [1996] *N.L.J.* 885; S. Higgins [1997] *Conv.* 119; M. Haley [1998] *Conv.* 218; *Hancock & Willis* v. *G.M.S. Syndicate Ltd.* [1983] 1 E.G.L.R. 70; *Demetriou* v. *Robert Andrews (Estate Agencies) Ltd.* (1990) 62 P. & C.R. 536. A number of earlier cases were said to have been decided *per incuriam*.

[90] The tenant's s.27 notice of termination was spurious.

[91] An offer can specify the method of acceptance, but some terms are merely directory: *Yates Building Co. Ltd.* v. *R.J. Pulleyn & Sons (York) Ltd.* [1976] 1 E.G.L.R,. 157 C.A.

[92] *Mannai Investment Co. Ltd.* v. *Eagle Star Life Assurance Co. Ltd.* [1997] A.C. 749, 776B, Lord Hoffmann.

[93] L.P.A. 1925 s.196(1); *New Hart Builders Ltd.* v. *Brindley* [1975] Ch. 342,, Goulding J.; L.T.A. 1927 s.23(1).

[94] Derived from the Conveyancing Act 1881 s.67; J.E. Adams [1980] *Conv.* 246, 323. It does not apply to court proceedings: s.196(6).

required by 1925 Act[95] or by any post-1925 document affecting property.[96] Unfortunately no form is laid down for notices to end a periodic tenancy where the term about the length of the notice to quit is merely implied from the payment and acceptance of rent.[97]

2. Parties

Validity of a notice depends upon service by the correct landlord on the correct tenant. Notices must be served on the current tenant, landlords being held to strict compliance.[98] Some cases suggest that it is also important to purport to act as a party to the lease: a solicitor who also happens to be the landlord (for example when acting as personal representatives) must make clear when he is acting as landlord.[99] Thus in *Fuller* v. *Judy Properties Ltd.*[100] the first section 146 notice was ineffective because it was not served on the current tenant, an error not made good by sending to the current tenant's solicitors a copy of the notice made out in the name of the previous tenant. It is the buyer who is entitled to receive notice after an assignment, even one in breach of covenant since the estate is validly passed.[101] Difficulties arise where the property is empty.[102] If the lease is vested in the Public Trustee after a death intestate, notice must be served on the Public Trustee.[103] However if the reversion is sold after service of the notice, the benefit of it should pass as an appurtenance to the land.[104] Doubts about the identity of the tenant may be resolved by service on the tenant and "all others whom it may concern".[105]

Errors by tenants most commonly occur with a co-owned lease, since notice must be served on, or by, all of the legal joint tenants. A formal notice like a landlord's section 25 notice must be given by all joint parties. If one is opposed, the notice is not valid[106] but a notice signed by one may be valid if it is clear from the circumstances that he is acting for all, though it is better to make this mandate clear.[107]

[95] L.T.A. 1927 s.23 applies to notices under landlord and tenant legislation, including business renewal: *Italica Holdings S.A.* v. *Bayadea* [1985] 1 E.G.L.R. 70 Q.B.D.

[96] *Re 88 Berkeley Road N.W. 9* [1971] Ch. 648, Plowman J. (notice of severance); *New Hart Builders Ltd.* v. *Brindley* [1975] Ch. 342, Goulding J. (exercise of an option to renew).

[97] *Wandsworth L.B.C.* v. *Atwell* [1995] 1 W.L.R. 95 C.A.; J.E. Adams [1995] *Conv.* 186; J. Montgomerie (1952) 16 *Conv.* (N.S.) 98, 107.

[98] *Jones* v. *Lewis* (1973) 25 P. & C.R. 375 C.A.; *Blewett* v. *Blewett* [1936] 2 All E.R. 188 C.A.

[99] *Divall* v. *Harrison* [1992] 2 E.G.L.R. 64 C.A.; *Prichard* v. *Bishop* (1975) 31 P. & C.R. 108 C.A. A person serving notice is not allowed to produce evidence that he is acting for an undisclosed principal: *Stock Gayland Estate Co.* v. *Rendell* [2000] 02 C.L. 374.

[100] [1992] 1 E.G.L.R. 75 C.A.

[101] *Old Grovebury Manor Farm Ltd.* v. *W. Seymour Plant Sales & Hire Ltd. (No. 2)* [1979] 1 W.L.R. 1379 C.A.; following *Kanda* v. *Church Commissioners for England* [1958 1 Q.B. 332; *Church Commissioners for England* v. *Ve-Ri-Best Manufacturing Co. Ltd.* [1957] 1 Q.B. 238; *Cusack-Smith* v. *Gold* [1958] 1 W.L.R. 611; *Dudley & District B.B.S.* v. *Emerson* [1949] Ch. 707.

[102] *Re Cannon Brewery Co. Ltd.* (1928) 139 L.T. 384 (left with person on property good); *Henry Smith's Charity Trustees* v. *Kyriakou* [1989] 2 E.G.L.R. 110 C.A. (letter box at entrance to building containing bedsits).

[103] L.P. (M.P.) A. 1995 ss.14–18. It appears that service on a tenant who is bankrupt (rather than his trustee in bankruptcy) is effective: *Stock Gayland Estate Co.* v. *Rendell* [2000] 02 C.L. 374.

[104] *Marks* v. *British Waterways Board* [1963] 1 W.L.R. 1008 C.A. (sale; new landlord could rely on s.30(1)(f) ground stated by old landlord).

[105] *Cronin* v. *Rogers* (1884) Cab. & El. 348.

[106] *Jacobs* v. *Chaudhuri* [1968] 2 Q.B. 470 C.A.

[107] *Hackney African Organisation* v. *Hackney L.B.C.* [1998] E.G.C.S. 139 (four trustees of a charitable unincorporated association).

Can the *Mannai* principle of the reasonable recipient[108] overcome defects in notices about the names of the giver or recipient? A confusion of names between Havant International Holdings Ltd. and Havant International Ltd. was overcome in this way in one case since the confusion would have been obvious to a reasonable recipient,[109] but the opposite conclusion was reached in another case involving two companies associated within a group since a reasonable recipient could not dismiss the possibility of an assignment and in that case a break notice served in the name of the wrong company was a nullity.[110] If there happens to be an agency between the recipient of the notice and the proper addressee this may be used to cure deficiencies in notices, as for example in the case of the statutory deemed agency between the recipient of the notice (British Railways Board) and the landlord (Railtrack)[111]; however there is not usually any agency between one company and another within the same group so the utility of the agency principle is severely circumscribed.[112]

3.   Honesty of statements

A landlord has a common law duty of honesty, so that if a landlord is required to state particular facts in his notice—for example that rent is in arrears—the notice is void if the landlord knows of the falsity of the statements.[113]

H.   RENT AND SERVICE CHARGE NOTICES

A special rule was introduced in 1987 to deal with absentee landlords who do not leave an address for contact in relation to complaints, especially about service charges,[114] though the duties are not particularly onerous.[115] A landlord must furnish his tenant with an address for the service of notices relating to rent and service charge,[116] and, until he complies, no rent or service charge falls due. Notice must be in writing but there is no prescribed form. Thus in *Dallhold Estates (U.K.) Property Ltd.* v. *Lindsey Trust Properties Ltd.*[117] an agricultural and "sporting" estate consisting of an Elizabethan mansion with 940 acres and cottages was let at a rent of £50,000 a year. Notice to quit was served after rent went unpaid for five quarters, but the tenant successfully defended the action on the basis of failure by the landlord to give an address for service. Liability

---

[108] See above pp. 579–581.

[109] *Havant International Holdings Ltd.* v. *Lionsgate (H.) Investment Ltd.* [1999] 47 L.S.G. 34, Hart J.

[110] *Lemmerbell Ltd.* v. *Britannia I.A.S. Direct Ltd.* [1999] 3 E.G.L.R. 67 C.A.

[111] *Railtrack plc.* v. *Gojra* [1998] 1 E.G.L.R. 63 C.A.

[112] *Dun & Bradstreet Software Services (England) Ltd.* v. *Provident Mutual Life Assurance Association* [1998] 2 E.G.L.R. 175 C.A.

[113] *Rous* v. *Mitchell* [1991] 1 W.L.R. 469 C.A.; *Lazarus Estates Ltd.* v. *Beasley* [1956] 1 Q.B. 702 C.A.; see above p. 27.

[114] L.T.A. 1987 s.48, amending L.P.A. 1925 s.196; in force on February 1st 1988 and applying to existing leases: *Hussain* v. *Singh* [1993] 2 E.G.L.R. 70 C.A.

[115] *Drew-Morgan* v. *Hamid-Zadek* [1999] 2 E.G.L.R. 13, 14H, Judge L.J.

[116] In *Leeds* v. *Islington L.B.C.* [1998] Env. L.R. 655 a notice under the Environmental Protection Act 1995 s.106 complaining of Pharaoh ant infestation was not properly served at the address given for complaints about rent; however *Hall* v. *Kingston upon Hull C.C.* [1999] 2 All E.R. 609 Div. Ct. takes a more lenient line; see above pp. 269–270.

[117] [1994] 1 E.G.L.R. 93 C.A.; M. Haley [1994] *Conv.* 325; *Marath* v. *MacGillivray* (1996) 28 H.L.R. 484 C.A.

is suspended rather than extinguished: when a proper notice is served the past rent becomes due.[118]

The initially frightening aspects of this decision have been watered down. Sufficient statements include the address of the landlord's registered office in a Rent Act tenancy,[119] an entry in a rent book, or a shorthold notice[120]; both *Dallhold* and *Drew-Morgan* v. *Hamid-Zadek*[121] show it to be unnecessary for the address to be mentioned as one at which notices could be served,[122] though more precision is needed in a notice served after entry into the lease. A notice giving two addresses causes no confusion and is valid.[123] It is odd that the provision in the lease in *Dallhold Estates*[124] for payment of the rent to a firm of London solicitors was not sufficient,[125] since the address can be that of an agent. It is notable that the case concerned a lease between a Panama company as landlord and an Australian company as tenant, and severe applications of the statute may be limited to foreign landlords.[126]

I. SERVICE

1. Notices

Service is the delivery of a document to a particular person.[127] Notices relating to property are regulated by section 196 of the Law of Property Act 1925,[128] where the notice is required by that Act or by any post-1925 document affecting property.[129] Unfortunately this wording excludes periodic tenancies with no express terms about the length of a notice to quit.[130] Similar provisions appear in the landlord and tenant legislation,[131] including business renewal,[132] and notices giving reasons for refusing consent to an assignment.[133] Most statutory regimes have their own provisions.[134] Due service need

---

[118] Also *Marath* v. *MacGillivray* (1996) 28 H.L.R. 484 C.A.

[119] *Rogan* v. *Woodfield Building Services Ltd.* [1995] 1 E.G.L.R. 72 C.A.; M. Haley [1995] *Conv.* 78; C. Barker [1994] 42 *L.S.G.* 23.

[120] *Marath* v. *MacGillivray* (1996) 28 H.L.R. 484 C.A.

[121] [1999] 2 E.G.L.R. 13 C.A.; S. Murdoch [1999] 31 *E.G.* 84.

[122] *Drew-Morgan* v. *Hamid-Zadek* [1999] 2 E.G.L.R. 13,14K Judge L.J.

[123] *Rogan* [1995] 1 E.G.L.R. 72, 76A, Ralph Gibson L.J.; *Marath* v. *MacGillivray* (1996) 28 H.L.R. 484 C.A.

[124] [1994] 1 E.G.L.R. 93 C.A.; M. Haley [1994] *Conv.* 325.

[125] *Drew-Hamid* at 158, Judge L.J.

[126] The address must be in England and Wales: *Drew-Morgan* at 14J–K, Judge L.J.

[127] *Tadema Holdings Ltd.* v. *Ferguson* [1999] Times November 25th, Peter Gibson L.J. The case shows that a mental patient can be served in the same way as any other person.

[128] Derived from Conveyancing Act 1881 s.67; J.E. Adams [1980] *Conv.* 246, 323. It does not apply to court proceedings (s.196(6)), nor a notice (under s.54) to terminate a derelict tenancy, where no one has been in occupation for 6 months and no rent has been paid.

[129] Including a notice of severance: *Re 88 Berkeley Road N.W. 9* [1971] Ch. 648, Plowman J.; also the exercise of an option to renew: *New Hart Builders Ltd.* v. *Brindley* [1975] Ch. 342, Goulding J.

[130] *Wandsworth L.B.C.* v. *Atwell* [1995] 1 W.L.R. 95 C.A.; J.E. Adams [1995] *Conv.* 186; J. Montgomerie (1952) 16 *Conv. (N.S.)* 98, 107.

[131] L.T.A. 1927 s.23.

[132] *Italica Holdings S.A.* v. *Bayadea* [1985] 1 E.G.L.R. 70 Q.B.D.

[133] L.T.A. 1988 s.5(2).

[134] L.T.A. 1927 s.18(2); R.A. 1977 s.151; A.H.A. 1986 s.93; A.T.A. 1995 s.36.

not be pleaded, since this is an inherent requirement of a valid notice.[135] Commonly these provisions yield to contrary terms of the lease.

Personal service. Due service need not be pleaded, since this is an inherent requirement of a valid notice. Notice is valid even if the recipient is absent, under a disability, unborn or unascertained.[136] It can be directed to "the tenant" or to "persons interested" without naming them.[137] At common law it was sufficient to give notice to the tenant's wife.[138] A notice pushed under the tenant's door and supposed lying hidden under the lino for five months was validly served, since the landlord had done what a reasonably minded person seeking to reach the person addressed would have done.[139] Statute provides that service may occur by leaving the notice at the last place of abode or business, or by fixing it to the property itself.[140]

Service by post. Postal service of notices is more common and more convenient.[141] Notices can be sent by registered post, and for statutory notices recorded delivery is an alternative,[142] but ordinary post will not do.[143] A letter must be addressed to a named recipient at his last known address, service occurring when a letter would arrive in the ordinary course of post,[144] provided that the letter is not returned undelivered.[145] Service is validly made where someone other than the intended recipient signs for the letter[146] but not where the person takes the letter in and destroys it so the tenant never receives it.[147] Hi-tech messages are valid methods of giving notices,[148] though they do not benefit from the statutory presumptions described above. Notices served under landlord and tenant legislation enjoy a special provision relating to service of notices on the tenant's agent[149] and requiring notification of a sale of the reversion.[150] The question of non-receipt was discussed in *Commercial Union Life Assurance Co. Ltd.* v. *Moustafa*[151]: was a

---

[135] *Gates* v. *W.A. & R.J. Jacobs Ltd.* [1920] 1 Ch. 567; but *Michaels* v. *Harley House (Marylebone) Ltd.* [1997] 3 All E.R. 446, Lloyd J. (no proof of valid service), on appeal [2000] Ch. 104 C.A.

[136] *Van Haarlam* v. *Kasner* [1992] 2 E.G.L.R. 59, Harman J. (service even though in prison for spying and unlikely to receive the notice); J.E. Martin [1993] *Conv.* 296; *Tadema Holdings Ltd.* v. *Ferguson* [1999] Times November 25th C.A. (patient).

[137] L.P.A. 1925 s.196(2). Conversely it is sufficient to identify a person: *Re Oliver & Son Ltd.* [1999] S.L.T. 1039; C. Connal [2000] 02 *E.G.* 115.

[138] *Tanham* v. *Nicholson* (1872) L.R. 5 H.L. 561 H.L.

[139] *Newborough* v. *Jones* [1975] Ch. 90 C.A.

[140] L.P.A. 1925 s.196(3); L.T.A. 1927 s.23(1); *Henry Smith's Charity Trustees* v. *Kyriakou* [1989] 2 E.G.L.R. 110 C.A.

[141] L.P.A. 1925 s.196(4); L.T.A. 1927 s.23(1)

[142] Recorded Delivery Service Act 1962 s.1; this does not apply to ordinary documents.

[143] *Holwell Securities Ltd.* v. *Hughes* [1973] 1 W.L.R. 757, Templeman J. (option not exercised). Contrast *Yates Building Society Co. Ltd.* v. *R.J. Pulleyn & Sons (York) Ltd.* [1976] 1 E.G.L.R. 157 C.A.

[144] *Carne* v. *De Bono* [1988] 1 W.L.R. 1107 C.A. (presumed 48 hours after posting; could prove actual service earlier); *Holwell Securities* as above (postal acceptance rule displaced); *Lex Services plc.* v. *Johns* [1990] 1 E.G.L.R. 92 C.A. (on L.T.A. 1927 s.23; illegible signature, but tenant had not proved it was not him).

[145] *Stephenson & Son* v. *Orca Properties Ltd.* [1989] 2 E.G.L.R. 129; J.E. Martin [1990] *Conv.* 147.

[146] *New Hart Builders Ltd.* v. *Brindley* [1975] Ch. 342, Goulding J.

[147] *Kinch* v. *Bullard* [1998] 4 All E.R. 650; M. Percival [1999] *Conv.* 60.

[148] *Hastie & Jenkerson* v. *McMahon* [1990] 1 W.L.R. 1575 C.A. (fax).

[149] L.T.A. 1927 s.23(1); *Galinski* v. *McHugh* [1989] 1 E.G.L.R. 109 C.A. (agency of solicitor proved).

[150] L.T.A. 1927 s.23(2).

[151] [1999] 2 E.G.L.R. 44, Smedley J.; S. Murdoch [1999] 32 *E.G.* 88; J. Brown & R. Duddridge [1999] 1 *R.R.L.R.* 3; B. Naftalin [1999] 30 *P.L.J.* 7.

default notice[152] served on an original tenant liable under privity of contract properly served by a letter sent to his last known abode by recorded delivery but returned? Smedley J. entered judgment for the rent. Many cases showed that a notice was validly served despite non-receipt,[153] the one case that was out of line being rejected as *per incuriam*.[154]

Special rules for repairing covenants. Forfeiture for breach of a repairing covenant may occur only if it is proved that the fact of service of the pre-forfeiture notice is known to one of the following: the tenant, or any sub-tenant where the tenant has only a nominal reversion, or the person who last paid rent; in addition a reasonable time must be allowed to elapse after service to enable repairs to be carried out.[155] Notice by registered post is deemed to have come to knowledge in the ordinary course of post, unless the contrary is proved.

2. Service of proceedings

Standard procedures govern service of proceedings,[156] except to the extent of any specific statute, procedural rule, practice direction, or court order in the particular case.

Claim forms to initiate proceedings are normally served by the court, the standard procedure being to use first class post, this Woolf-induced liberalisation allowing the courts to catch up with the outside world. If the letter is not returned, first class post is deemed to be an effective on the second day after posting.[157] If, however it is returned, the court will give the claimant notice of the non-service and send the documents to him for service.[158] It will usually be because the court's attempt at postal service has failed that the claimant effects service himself, but it is open to the claimant to choose to take service out of the hands of the court at the outset. The time allowed is four months after issue of proceedings (or six months where service is abroad[159]) and there is now a procedure by which a defendant may compel the claimant to effect service.[160] In some cases, notice of service must be filed with the court within seven days with a copy of the documents served.[161]

Service of documents apart from court orders is left to the parties.[162] This is not as daunting as it sounds: a claim form will usually include particulars of a solicitor who is willing to accept service of document, and an acknowledgement of service enables a

---

[152] L.T. (Covenants) A. 1995 s.17. s.27 applies L.T.A. 1927 s.23, which in turn applies the Recorded Delivery Act 1962 s.1.

[153] *Chiswell* v. *Griffon Land & Estates Ltd.* [1975] 1 W.L.R. 1181 C.A.; *Italica Holdings S.A.* v. *Bayadea* [1985] 1 E.G.L.R. 70, French J.; *Galinski* v. *McHugh* [1989] 1 E.G.L.R. 109 C.A.; *Railtrack plc.* v. *Gojra* [1998] 1 E.G.L.R. 63 C.A.

[154] *Lex Services plc.* v. *Johns* [1990] 1 E.G.L.R. 92 C.A. (*Galinski* not cited).

[155] L.T.A. 1927 s.18(2). Previously it was common to provide that the obligation to repair arose only after notice, as e.g. in *Cove* v. *Smith* (1886) 2 T.L.R. 778.

[156] C.P.R. 6; these are amended by C.P.Am.R. 2000 r4, sch.1.

[157] C.P.R. 6.7(1); T. Lancaster [1999] 29 *L.S.G.* 34.

[158] In the case of the accelerated procedures, the landlord may request bailiff service: C.P.R. sch.2 C.C.R. Order 25 r.3(3A)–(3D), inserted by C.P.Am.R. 2000 r.32.

[159] P.D. 7.6.1(2). Service out of the jurisdiction is covered by C.P.R. 6.17–6.31 (inserted in 2000). Claim forms and other documents cannot be served on unsociable days (such as Christmas Day): C.P. Amendment R. 2000 r4.

[160] C.P.R. 7.7.

[161] C.P.R. 6.10. Documents may be filed by fax, but not documents requiring a fee: P.D. 5 (revised in May 2000).

[162] C.P.R. 6.3.

defendant to give corresponding particulars of his solicitor. Afterwards service should generally be effected on the solicitor.[163] Service by first class post is normal. However the parties can agree to use document exchange by giving a DX box number or fax by giving a fax number or e-mail.[164] Personal service is possible (except where solicitors are instructed) by leaving with an individual, a partner, or senior officer of a company.[165] Special rules apply to children and patients.[166] It is also possible to leave the document to be served at a place.[167]

Alternative methods are allowed under court authority, but evidence of service will be required.[168] One set of alternatives is used in *county court* actions for the recovery of land where normal methods are impracticable.[169] Papers can be handed to a spouse or heterosexual cohabitee,[170] or to a person present at the premises who appears to have authority and who lives there, conducts business, manages the premises, receives rents or profits, or pays outgoings; also a person who safeguards or deals with the premises.[171] If a property is vacant (apart from any furniture or goods) a claim for repossession may be served by affixing it to a conspicuous part of the property,[172] but this is not usually a valid service of any associated money claim.[173] The old wording describes these procedures as restricted to cases where a claim for the recovery of land is to be served by the bailiff, whereas under the Civil Procedure Rules there is no longer any provision for bailiff service. A *High Court* claim for the repossession of land that is not in the possession of any person may be effected by affixing a copy to some conspicuous part of the land; permission of the court must be obtained, though it may be retrospective.[174]

Application can be made to the court for leave to dispense with service; the grounds for doing so must be verified with a statement of truth. [175]

J.   UNION OF LEASE AND REVERSION

A lease can be destroyed if both the reversion and the leasehold estate are passed to a single person. Merger occurs where a tenant acquires the reversion, or where both interests are transferred to one outside person. Surrender occurs where the lease is given up to the landlord. Termination is not automatic but depends upon the intention of the parties. This section also considers the related question of granting a lease to oneself.

---

[163] C.P.R.6.4; service is deemed to occur on the second day after posting by C.P.R. 6.7.
[164] P.D. 6.2, 6.3; the date of deemed service is given by C.P.R. 6.7; faxes received after 4 p.m. are deemed to be delivered on the next working day: P.D. 5.
[165] C.P.R. 6.4. A business or residential address in the U.K. must be given for this purpose; C.P.R. 6.5(2)(3). C.P.R. 6.5(6) gives a table of places for service of initial proceedings before an address for service is given.
[166] C.P.R. 6.6.
[167] C.P.R. 6.5.
[168] C.P.R. 6.8.
[169] C.P.R. sch.2 C.C.R. Order 7 r.15.
[170] r.15(2)–(3).
[171] r.15(2).
[172] r.15(4).
[173] r.15(4).
[174] C.P.R. sch.1 R.S.C. Order 10 r.4..
[175] C.P.R. 6.6.9; T. Lancaster [1999] 29 *L.S.G.* 34. This should be stated explicitly in the court order, but otherwise it may be implicit; *Bass Holdings Ltd.* v. *Brodie* [1998] 1 E.G.L.R. 51 Q.B.D.

K. LEASE TO ONESELF

It is now possible to convey land to oneself,[176] a facility that is especially useful where a personal representative wishes to assent to himself as a beneficiary, but *Rye v. Rye*[177] decides that one cannot grant an oral lease to oneself. Lord Denning's stated reasoning[178]—that a lease requires a contract between two parties able to contract—seems to apply logically to a formal lease as well.

If an owner cannot let land to himself as tenant, the problem can easily be avoided by granting the lease *to a nominee*. The legality of this dodge was doubted in the Scottish case *Clydesdale Bank plc. v. Davidson*,[179] which held that *pro indiviso* heritable proprietors (what we would call tenants in common) could not create a lease over their own property in favour of one of their own number. The owners were Davidson (with a 1/2 share) and his parents (with 1/4 each). They purported to let to Davidson alone for three years at £4,000 a year, but he was held to occupy as a co-owner and not as a tenant. The smaller right was absorbed into the greater. However the House of Lords has now made clear that a lease by a landlord to his nominee is valid. Lady Ingram, the appellant in *Ingram v. I.R.C.*,[180] wanted in her old age to give her house to her children but to retain the right to live in the house. Three transactions took place on successive days. On the first, she conveyed the house to her solicitor; on the second the solicitor granted her a lease rent-free for 20 years, and on the third the freehold was conveyed to trustees for her family. The House decided that for taxation purposes the value of the property transferred to the family trustees was to be valued on the basis of the freehold estate subject to the lease. In other words, the House of Lords held that the lease granted by the solicitor (as nominee for Lady Ingram) to Lady Ingram was valid. Although the speeches concentrate on the taxation issue—now a dead duck since the inheritance tax loophole exploited by Lady Ingram has since been closed[181]—it seems that the Lords affirmed Millett L.J.'s dissent in the Court of Appeal on the property issues.[182] It is possible to vest a freehold estate in a nominee, so why not also a lease?

L. MERGER

Merger[183] describes a dealing with a lease that terminates the lease because the leasehold estate and reversion pass into a single ownership—either the tenant or some outside party—an event that sometimes causes the two estates to fuse. This is in contrast to a surrender by which the tenant gives up his lease to his landlord.

---

[176] L.P.A. 1925 ss.72, 82 (covenants); previously one could transfer only from A to A and B: L.P. Amendment A. 1859 s.21 (personalty); Conveyancing Act 1881 s.50 (freehold land).

[177] [1962] A.C. 496 H.L.; P.V. Baker (1962) 78 *L.Q.R.* 175; J.C. Hall [1962] *C.L.J.* 34; D.G. Valentine (1962) 25 *M.L.R.* 466.

[178] At 514 cited in *Ingram v. I.R.C.* [1997] 4 All E.R. 395, 401a–c Nourse L.J.

[179] [1998] S.C. 51 H.L.; contrast *Pinkerton v. Pinkerton* [1986] S.L.T. 672 H.L.

[180] [2000] A.C. 293 H.L.; J. Woolf [2000] *N.L.J.* 468.

[181] Finance Act 1986 s.102A, inserted by Finance Act 1999 s.104.

[182] *Ingram v. I.R.C.* [1997] 4 All E.R. 395 C.A.

[183] Woodfall 17.196–17.269, Evans & Smith (5th) 239–240.

Merger usually occurs where the lease and the immediate reversion become vested in the same person[184] in the same right.[185] For example, the tenant may buy out the landlord's interest, or a third person may buy both interests. Successive leases do not merge,[186] but a longer sub-lease could merge into a shorter head-lease. A contract to purchase the reversion effects a provisional merger, which holds good so long as the contract remains enforceable, but which will be suspended if the contract is later rescinded.[187] Since it is usually advantageous to the buyer for a merger to occur, for example to end liability on the covenants in the lease,[188] it was once automatic.[189] However, it may be undesirable to allow merger for taxation reasons, or to preserve a longer sub-lease[190] the security of a mortgage,[191] an easement,[192] or security of tenure.[193] So modern law has come to see merger as dependent upon intention.[194] This intention may be evidenced by a declaration in the conveyancing documents that merger is not to occur,[195] or by acts showing an intention not to allow merger,[196] or it may be inferred from the fact that merger is not, for once, beneficial.[197] Land Registry practice is to assume that a lease does merge once both reversion and lease pass to the same person, but the title is cancelled only after a request is made by letter.[198]

M. EXPRESS SURRENDER

Surrender occurs when the tenant agrees to give up his lease (or part of it[199]) to the landlord,[200] and the landlord accepts it.[201]

---

[184] *Southampton Community Health Services N.H.S. Trust* v. *Crown Estate Commissioners* [1997] E.G.C.S. 155 Ch.D.

[185] *Chambers* v. *Kingham* (1878) 10 Ch. D. 743 (freehold held as administrator, the lease beneficially); *Brandon* v. *Brandon* (1862) 31 L.J.Ch. 47; *Re Coole* [1920] 2 Ch. 536.

[186] *Hyde* v. *Warden* (1877) 3 Ex.D. 72 C.A. (doctrine of interesse termini now abolished); *Doe d. Rawling* v. *Walker* (1826) 5 B. & C. 111, 108 E.R. 41; *Ingle* v. *Vaughan Jenkins* [1900] 2 Ch. 368, Farwell J.

[187] *Matthews* v. *Sawell* (1818) 8 Taunt. 270, 129 E.R. 387; *Ellis* v. *Wright* (1897) 76 L.T. 522 C.A.; *Nightingale* v. *Courtney* [1954] 1 Q.B. 399 C.A.

[188] *Webb* v. *Russell* (1789) 3 Term. Rep. 393, 100 E.R. 639; *Dynevor* v. *Tennant* (1888) 13 App. Cas. 279 H.L.; *Golden Lion Hotel (Hunstanton) Ltd.* v. *Carter* [1965] 1 W.L.R. 1189; P. Fairest [1965] *C.L.J.* 36; *Watney* v. *Boardley* [1975] 1 W.L.R. 857; *International Press Centre* v. *Norwich Union* (1986) 36 Build. L.R. 130.

[189] *Stephens* v. *Bridges* (1821) 6 Madd. 66, 56 E.R. 1015; *Gunter* v. *Gunter* (1857) 23 Beav. 571, 53 E.R. 225.

[190] *Hughes* v. *Robotham* (1593) Cro. Eliz. 302, 78 E.R. 554.

[191] *Capital & Counties Bank Ltd.* v. *Rhodes* [1903] 1 Ch. 631 C.A.; *Ingle* v. *Vaughan Jenkins* [1900] 2 Ch. 368, Farwell J.

[192] J.T. Farrand [1983] *Conv.* 89.

[193] *Nightingale* v. *Courtney* [1954] 1 Q.B. 399 C.A.; *Doe d. Gray* v. *Stanion* (1836) 1 M. & W. 695, 150 E.R. 614; *Leek & Moorlands B.S.* v. *Clark* [1952] 2 Q.B. 788.

[194] L.P.A. 1925 s.185; *Ingle* v. *Vaughan Jenkins* [1900] 2 Ch. 368, 370, Farwell J.; *Westwood* v. *Heywood* [1921] 2 Ch. 130, 140, Astbury J.

[195] *Re Fletcher* [1917] 1 Ch. 339 C.A.; *Belaney* v. *Belaney* (1867) L.R. 2 Ch. App. 138; *International Press Centre Ltd.* v. *Norwich Union Insurance Co.* (1986) 36 Build. L.R. 130 (absence of term may imply merger).

[196] *Thellusson* v. *Liddard* [1900] 2 Ch. 635.

[197] *Lea* v. *Thursby* [1904] 2 Ch. 57, obiter.

[198] L.R.R. 1925 r.206; L.R. Practice Leaflet 21.

[199] *Bayton* v. *Morgan* (1888) 22 Q.B.D. 74 C.A.; *Allen* v. *Rochdale B.C.* [1999] 3 All E.R. 443 C.A. (school playing field).

[200] If the reversion is mortgaged, a borrower in possession can accept a surrender only with the concurrence of the lender: L.P.A. 1925 s.100, re-enacting Conveyancing Act 1881 s.3; *Robbins* v. *Whyte* [1906] 1 K.B. 125; *Turner* v. *Watts* (1928) 97 L.J.K.B. 403.

[201] Woodfall 17.008–17.048, Davey 123–126, Evans & Smith (5th) 236–239.

1. Formal surrender

At law a deed is required. No particular words are needed, but both parties must show an intention to end the lease now rather than at some time in the future. One old case held that the wording "We hereby renounce and disclaim and also surrender and yield up" was sufficient to effect a surrender.[202] It should be the current tenant who effects a surrender,[203] or exercises a break clause in order to surrender,[204] while the leasehold estate is vested in him. All joint tenants should participate.[205] If title is registered, the deed of surrender must be executed by all interested and the legal surrender is only completed only when the leasehold title is deleted from the register.[206] Surrender terminates liability under the lease for the future[207] but existing breaches live on,[208] as does liability under a rent review that has not been settled at the date of the termination.[209]

2. Informal surrender

A contract to give up a lease is effective in equity[210] if there are formalities[211] and consideration.[212] *Camden L.B.C.* v. *Alexandrou (No.2)*[213] considered the effect of this letter to a local authority landlord:

> "I the undersigned to hereby state that he above flat is no longer my responsibility as I am unable to pay for the upkeep [Mr Alexandrou]."

Although too informal to amount to a legal assignment, this letter was good as a surrender, leaving the local authority free to grant a new tenancy to Alexandrou's wife. This case, like many others reported, is based on the old contract formalities at a time, though even then a purely oral agreement was ineffective. In *Take Harvest Ltd.* v. *Liu*[214] a tenant indicated to his landlord orally that he wished to give up his lease, and he moved out on

---

[202] *Doe d. Wyatt* v. *Stagg* (1839) 5 Bing. N.C. 564, 132 E.R, 1217; *Weddell* v. *Capes* (1836) 1 M. & W. 50, 150 E.R. 341.

[203] *Re A.B.C. Coupler & Engineering Co. Ltd. (No.3)* [1970] 1 All E.R. 656; *Cadle* v. *Moody* (1861) 30 L.J. Ex. 385; *Barclays Bank Ltd.* v. *Stasell* [1956] 3 All E.R. 439.

[204] *Seaward* v. *Drew* (1898) 67 L.J.Q.B. 322; *Stait* v. *Fenner* [1912] 2 Ch. 504.

[205] *Leek & Moorlands B.S.* v. *Clarke* [1952] 2 Q.B. 788; *Featherstone* v. *Staples* [1986] 1 W.L.R. 861 C.A.; *Burton* v. *Camden L.B.C.* [1998] 1 F.L.R. 681 C.A. (now reversed on other points by the H.L.). Contrast a notice to quit a joint periodic tenancy; see above pp. 124–130.

[206] L.R.R. 1925 r.200 applies if the reversion is not registered; where the reversion is registered but the lease is unregistered Form 92 is used.

[207] Rent must be apportioned: Apportionment Act 1870 s.3; *William Hill (Football) Ltd.* v. *Willen Key & Hardware Ltd.* (1964) 108 S.J. 482; *Shaw* v. *Lomas* (1888) 59 L.T. 477 (arrears).

[208] *Torminster Properties Ltd.* v. *Green* [1983] 1 W.L.R. 676, 683A–C; *William Hill* v. *Willen Key* as above; *Re Fussell ex parte Allen* (1882) 20 Ch.D. 341; *Dalton* v. *Pickard* [1920] 2 K.B. 545n C.A.; *Richmond* v. *Savill* [1926] 2 K.B. 530 C.A.

[209] *Torminster* at 682H; *Walker's case* (1587) 3 Co. Rep. 22a, 76 E.R. 676; *A.G.* v. *Cox* (1850) 3 H.L.C. 240, 10 E.R. 893; *Shaw* v. *Lomas* (1888) 59 L.T. 477.

[210] *Smith* v. *Smith* (1636) 1 Rep. Ch. 108, 21 E.R. 521; *Torminster* as above.

[211] *Doe d. Read* v. *Ridout* (1814) 5 Taunt. 519, 128 E.R. 792; *Roe d. Berkeley* v. *York* (1805) 6 East. 86, 102 E.R. 1219.

[212] *Wallace* v. *Patton* (1846) 12 Cl. & Fin. 491, 8 E.R. 1501 H.L.; *Baddeley* v. *Vigurs* (1854) 4 E. & B. 71, 119 E.R. 28.

[213] (1998) 30 H.L.R. 534 C.A.

[214] [1993] A.C. 552 P.C.; *Barakat* v. *Ealing L.B.C.* (1996) 36 R.V.R. 138 Q.B.D. (letter spelling out terms of surrender not a surrender).

December 10th, confirmed by a fax to the landlord the next day. The tenant was held liable for rent until the following February 11th when the landlord re-entered, long after the alleged oral agreement to surrender.[215] What was required to overcome the formality problems[216] was an act of part performance. Today a contract must be by writing signed by both parties,[217] so that the role of relaxing the law to allow informal transactions has now passed to estoppel.

3. Future surrender

Since a surrender must take effect immediately, one to operate at a future date must take the form of a contract.[218] Neither party can be forced to surrender against his will. Many leases have a monetary value, which the tenant should not agree to give up without a payment from the landlord. Other leases are onerous—because the rent is above the market level or because of serious disrepair—in which case the tenant may be glad to hand it back to the landlord, and may be prepared to pay a large sum to settle the liabilities under a very burdensome lease.

Some commercial leases contain an agreement to surrender in certain circumstances, perhaps every third year.[219] There is no objection to a clause requiring the landlord to accept a surrender but a tenant cannot be bound in advance to surrender without destroying the protection of security of tenure legislation, so all legislative schemes attack agreements to surrender[220] (as opposed to actually completed surrenders[221]). Commercial tenants are free, during the contractual term of a renewable business lease, to stop rent running by a consensual surrender that is accepted by the landlord: this avoids the statutory continuation of the tenancy while a notice to leave takes effect.[222] What is not allowed is to agree in advance not to execute a surrender in the future.[223] Indeed to avoid undue pressure being brought to bear on the tenant a tenancy cannot be terminated until the tenant has been in occupation for at least one month.[224]

N. IMPLIED SURRENDER

Surrender of an existing lease may be implied where landlord and tenant conduct themselves in a manner inconsistent with continuation of the lease. This long established principle[225] is based on an estoppel,[226] requiring some change of circumstances or

---

[215] Since Hong Kong law was similar to L.P.A. 1925 s.40, the question remitted to the trial judge was whether there were acts of part performance.

[216] *Lyon* v. *Reed* (1844) 13 M. & W. 285, 306, 153 E.R. 118, Parke B.; *Wallis* v. *Hands* [1893] 2 Ch. 75, Chitty J.

[217] L.P. (M.P.) A. 1989 s.2; Sparkes *N.L.L.* ch.9.

[218] *Doe d. Murrell* v. *Milward* (1838) 3 M. & W. 328, 150 E.R. 1170.

[219] *Bacon* v. *Waller* (1616) 3 Bulst. 203, 81 E.R. 171; *Burton* v. *Barclay* (1831) 7 Bing. 745, 131 E.R. 288.

[220] *Re Hennesey's Agreement* [1975] Ch. 252 (L.T.A. 1927 part I); *J.W. Childers W.T.* v. *Anker* [1996] 1 E.G.L.R. 1 C.A. (agricultural).

[221] *Foster* v. *Robinson* [1951] 1 K.B. 149 C.A.; *Collins* v. *Claughton* [1959] 1 W.L.R. 145 C.A. (Rent Act); *R.* v. *Croydon L.B.C. ex. parte Toth* (1988) 20 H.L.R. 576 C.A. (secure).

[222] See above pp. 586–588.

[223] L.T.A. 1954 s.38(4).

[224] L.T.A. 1954 s.24(2)(a)–(b).

[225] *Wrotesley* v. *Adams* (1560) 1 Plowd. 189, 75 E.R. 290; and many later cases.

[226] *Camden L.B.C.* v. *Alexandrou (No.2)* (1998) 30 H.L.R. 534, 540, Aldous L.J.

detriment,[227] and sometimes operating unjustly and contrary to the subjective intentions of the parties.[228] A surrender will be implemented on the register on production to the land registry of sufficient evidence of an implied surrender.[229]

1.   Implied surrender: reletting

When a surrender is implied it is almost always because of grant of a new lease[230] of the property. The new lease sits in place of old one,[231] which is impliedly ended[232] even if it is shorter.[233] This doctrine can work arbitrarily, but the court should not invent a new lease simply to promote a just solution.[234] Illogical it may be, since an oral agreement to surrender is ineffective, but an oral lease is able to bring about a surrender by operation of law.[235]

Surrender of the lease is not inferred from an agreement for *variation of an existing lease* or its terms, for example an agreed rent increase,[236] an extension of the contractual term,[237] or even a change in the identity of the tenants.[238] The existing lease is subject to a proprietary variation, binding future parties, for example in relation to rent review.[239] Informal variation is allowed, even if the lease is by deed.[240] However, it is possible for the terms to suffer such catastrophic change that the only presumption is of a new lease,[241] for example by changing the physical identity of the property let.[242]

An new lease that is *invalid* will not cause a surrender, for example because the terms remain in negotiation,[243] or the agreement is not open to specific performance,[244] because the new grant is void,[245] and also (according to a preponderance of a massive

---

[227] *Jenkin R. Lewis & Son Ltd. v. Kerman* [1971] Ch. 477, 496, Russell L.J.; *Foster v. Robinson* [1951] 1 K.B. 149 C.A.

[228] *Lyon v. Reed* (1844) 13 M. & W. 285, 153 E.R. 118.

[229] L.R. Practice Leaflet 21.

[230] Not the execution of a legal lease under an existing contract: *Pole-Carew v. Western Counties & General Manure Co. Ltd.* [1920] 2 Ch. 97, 122, Warrington L.J.

[231] Another possibility is two leases to sit side by side: *J.W. Childers W.T. v. Anker* [1996] 1 E.G.L.R. 1 C.A.

[232] *Foster v. Robinson* [1951] 1 K.B. 149 C.A.; *Corpus Christi College v. Rogers* (1879) 49 L.J.Q.B. 4 C.A.

[233] *Ive's case* (1597) 5 Co. Rep. 11a, 77 E.R. 64; *Belfield v. Adams* (1615) 3 Bulst. 80, 81 E.R. 69.

[234] *Sidebotham v. Holland* [1895] 1 Q.B. 378.

[235] *Fenner v. Blake* [1900] 1 Q.B. 426.

[236] *Donellan v. Read* (1832) 3 B. & Ad. 899, 110 E.R. 330; *Crowley v. Vitty* (1852) 7 Exch. 319, 155 E.R. 968; *Re Young ex parte Vitale* (1882) 47 L.T. 480; *Gable Construction Co. Ltd. v. I.R.C.* [1968] 2 All E.R. 968; *Jenkin R. Lewis & Son Ltd. v. Keman* [1971] Ch. 477, 497, Russell L.J.; P.V. Baker (1970) 86 *L.Q.R.* 305; *Smirk v. Lyndale Developments Ltd.* [1975] Ch. 317.

[237] *Re Savile S.E.* [1931] 2 Ch. 210; *Re Arkwright's S.* [1945] Ch. 195; *Baker v. Merckel* [1960] 1 Q.B. 657 C.A.; however the land registry view is that a term cannot be extended: R.L. Practice Leaflet 21.; this is supported by *Goodaston Ltd. v. F.H. Burgess plc.* [1999] L.T.R. 46, Jacob J.

[238] *Saunders Trustees v. Ralph* [1993] 2 E.G.L.R. 1, Jowitt J.; A. Dowling [1995] *Conv.* 124; *Collins v. Claughton* [1959] 1 W.L.R. 145 C.A.

[239] *Jaskel v. Sophie Nursery Products Ltd.* [1993] E.G.C.S. 42 C.A.; J.E. Adams [1993] *Conv.* 254; E. Cooke [1993] *Conv.* 387.

[240] *Mitas v. Hyams* [1951] 2 T.L.R. 1215; *Plymouth Corporation v. Harvey* [1971] 1 W.L.R. 549, Plowman J.

[241] *Joseph v. Joseph* [1967] Ch. 78 C.A. (partnership deed).

[242] *Jones v. Bridgman* (1878) 39 L.T. 500; *Giles v. Spencer* (1857) 3 C.B.N.S. 244, 140 E.R. 734.

[243] *Take Harvest Ltd. v. Liu* [1993] A.C. 552 P.C.; *Dreamgate Properties Ltd. v. Arnot* [1997] E.G.C.S. 121 C.A.

[244] *Inland Revenue Commissioners v. Derby* [1914] 3 K.B. 1186.

[245] *Canterbury Corporation v. Cooper* (1908) 99 L.T. 612, 100 L.T. 597 C.A.

case law) if it is voidable.[246] Conditional grants only effect a surrender when the condition is satisfied.[247] However, an express agreement to surrender can still operate even if the lease containing it is void.[248]

2.   Implied surrender: lease to another party

Acceptance by the landlord of a new tenant may be a surrender,[249] but the new tenant will have to take possession.[250] In *E.S. Schwab & Co. Ltd.* v. *McCarthy*[251] an agreement to return keys followed by reletting to a weekly tenant was held to create an equitable surrender. Giving a lease to a completely different tenant may also surrender the existing lease, but it will be necessary to show that the existing tenant gives up possession or agrees in some other way.[252] If an assignee enters during negotiations about the terms of an assignment and pays rent, the acceptance of rent by the landlord is not necessarily inconsistent with the continuation of the old lease and is not alone proof of a surrender of it.[253]

3.   Implied surrender: other acts

Surrenders are based on mutual agreement. Unilateral acts by the tenant that are irrelevant include abandonment of the lease,[254] moving out,[255] vacating a property after fire damage,[256] handing back the keys without their being accepted by the landlord,[257] and giving notice to the landlord to leave. So are acts by the landlord if the tenant has not given up possession.[258] Inactivity will not cause a surrender.[259]

Mutual acts may form a surrender. Acts short of reletting may suffice if the change of possession is clearly accepted. Examples of actions by the landlord are accepting the tenant's letter of surrender of an agreement for a lease,[260] attempting to relet,[261] advertis-

---

[246] *Doe d. Egremont* v. *Courtenay* (1848) 11 Q.B. 702, 116 E.R. 636; *Canterbury Corporation* v. *Cooper* (1909) 100 L.T. 597 C.A.; *Knight* v. *Williams* [1901] 1 Ch. 256.

[247] *Coupland* v. *Maynard* (1810) 12 East. 134, 104 E.R. 53; *Longman* v. *Viscount Chelsea* [1989] 2 E.G.L.R. 242 C.A. ("subject to formal surrender").

[248] *Rhyl U.D.C.* v. *Rhyl Amusements Ltd.* [1959] 1 W.L.R. 465, Harman J.; *Barclays Bank Ltd.* v. *Stasek* [1957] Ch. 28, Danckwerts J.; R.E. Megarry (1957) 73 *L.Q.R.* 14.

[249] *Thomas* v. *Cook* (1818) 2 B. & Ald. 119, 106 E.R. 310; but see *Mathews* v. *Sawell* (1818) 8 Taunt. 270, 129 E.R. 387.

[250] *Doe d. Huddleton* v. *Johnston* (1825) M'Cle. & Yo. 141, 148 E.R. 359; *Tower Hamlets L.B.C.* v. *Ayinde* (1994) 26 H.L.R. 631 C.A.

[251] (1975) 31 P. & C.R. 196, Oliver J.

[252] *Wallis* v. *Hands* [1893] 2 Ch. 75; *Walker* v. *Richardson* (1837) 2 M. & W. 882, 150 E.R. 1616; *Davison* v. *Gent* (1857) 1 H. & N. 744, 156 E.R. 1400; *Metcalfe* v. *Boyce* [1927] 1 K.B. 758 Div.Ct.

[253] *Mattey Securities Ltd.* v. *Ervin* [1998] 2 E.G.L.R. 66 C.A.; the court applied *Lyon* v. *Read* (1844) 13 M. & W. 285, 153 E.R. 118.

[254] *McDougall's Catering Foods Ltd.* v. *B.S.E. Trading Ltd.* (1998) 76 P. & C.R. 312 C.A.

[255] *Preston B.C.* v. *Fairclough* (1983) 8 H.L.R. 70; *Chamberlain* v. *Scalley* (1994) 26 H.L.R. 26 C.A. (possessions left).

[256] *Bhogal* v. *Cheema* [1998] 2 E.G.L.R. 50, Vinelott J.

[257] *Proudreed Ltd.* v. *Microgen Holdings plc.* [1996] 1 E.G.L.R. 89 C.A.; *Oastler* v. *Henderson* (1877) 2 Q.B.D. 575 C.A.

[258] *Zionmor* v. *Islington L.B.C.* (1998) 30 H.L.R. 822 C.A.

[259] *Westminster C.C.* v. *Basson* (1990) 23 H.L.R. 225.

[260] *Inntrepreneur Pub Co. (C.P.C.) Ltd.* v. *Deans* [1999] B.P.I.R. 361, David Steel J.

[261] *Nickells* v. *Atherstone* (1847) 10 Q.B.D. 944, 116 E.R. 358.

ing for a new tenant,[262] taking possession at the tenant's request,[263] accepting the tenant's return of the key,[264] or taking back possession and carrying out major repair work.[265] Very unusual circumstances arose in *Lansdowne Tutors Ltd.* v. *Younger*[266] in which the landlord and tenant were companies controlled by the same individual; it was held that a surrender had occurred when the landlord sued for possession, the tenant admitted the claim, and rent payments had stopped.

A surrender requires a complete delivery of possession. In *Hoggett* v. *Hoggett*[267] a husband who was a weekly tenant purported to surrender the tenancy of the matrimonial home while his wife was in hospital and got the landlord to grant a new lease to his girlfriend, Miss Wallis. The surrender was not a sham, because the landlord was not a party to the deceit. But, the court held, the lease had not been surrendered because possession had not been delivered so long as the wife of the old tenant retained occupation.[268] Since the old lease continued, the wife was able to claim a matrimonial home right. This case must be contrasted with *Sanctuary Housing Association* v. *Campbell*[269] in which a woman left a secure weekly tenancy because of her husband's violence and returned the keys, which the authority accepted as terminating her rent liability. Her husband moved back in and changed the locks so that the landlord did not secure possession; it was held that a surrender had occurred between the wife and the landlord, and this prevented the husband claming a matrimonial home right. On these facts, and in the case of a secure tenancy, a surrender had occurred without a delivery of possession. The last case distorts conventional doctrine to promote a just solution and must be suspect in property law terms. Land registry practice is to require evidence both of the new lease and of possession being taken under it.[270]

O. PRESERVATION OF DERIVATIVE INTERESTS

1. Effect of hostile termination

Termination of a head lease by the unilateral and hostile act of the landlord ends the sub-lease. All derivative interests end if a head lease ends by forfeiture,[271] by effluxion, or by break instigated by the landlord. This list must now be extended as a result of the

---

[262] *Phene* v. *Popplewell* (1862) 12 C.B.N.S. 334, 142 E.R. 1171; *Oastler* v. *Henderson* (1877) 2 Q.B.D. 575; *Re Panther Lead Co.* (1896) 65 L.J.Ch. 499.

[263] *Moss* v. *James* (1878) 38 L.T. 595 C.A.; *Smith* v. *Blackmore* (1885) 1 T.L.R. 267; *Relvok* v. *Dixon* (1972) 25 P. & C.R. 1; *Re Edward's W.T.* [1982] Ch. 30 C.A.; *R.* v. *Croydon L.B.C. ex p. Toth* (1988) 20 H.L.R. 576 C.A. However not from taking possession to keep the property safe from squatters: *McDougall's Catering Foods Ltd.* v. *B.S.E. Trading Ltd.* [1997] 2 E.G.L.R. 65 C.A.

[264] *Dodd* v. *Acklom* (1843) 6 Man. & G. 672, 134 E.R. 1063; *Barakat* v. *Ealing L.B.C.* [1996] E.G.C.S. 67, Brooke J.; *Filering Ltd.* v. *Taylor Commercial Ltd.* [1996] E.G.C.S. 95 C.A.; C. Majowski-Gavrikou [2000] 43 *P.L.J.* 7.

[265] *Smith* v. *Roberts* (1892) 9 T.L.R. 77 C.A.; *Bessell* v. *Landesbery* (1845) 7 Q.B. 638, 115 E.R. 630.

[266] [2000] 04 L.S.G. 34 C.A.

[267] (1979) 39 P. & C.R. 121; *Old Gate Estates Ltd.* v. *Alexander* [1950] 1 K.B. 311 C.A.; *Middleton* v. *Baldock* [1950] 1 K.B. 657 C.A.

[268] Contrast *Bolnore Props Ltd.* v. *Cobb* (1997) 29 H.L.R. 202 C.A.

[269] [1999] 3 All E.R. 460 C.A.

[270] L.R. Practice Leaflet 21.

[271] *Great Western Rly. Co.* v. *Smith* (1876) 2 Ch.D. 235 C.A., affirmed (1877) 3 App. Cas. 165 H.L. Surrender leaves the sub-tenancy unaffected even if it is liable to forfeiture.

decision of the House of Lords in *Barrett* v. *Morgan*[272] to include a notice to quit given by the tenant. In that case head landlords had granted a periodic tenancy to head tenants, both parties being members of the Eldon family, and they were able by arrangement between them to give a notice of intention to quit to end the head tenancy. The effect was to bring to an end the agricultural security of tenure of a periodic sub-tenant. This confirms the earlier strand of Court of Appeal decisions culminating in *Pennell* v. *Payne*.[273] It disapproves an alternative strand of authority—including *Sparkes* v. *Smart*[274]—that denied effect to a collusive notice to quit. As a result of *Barrett* v. *Morgan* we now know that a notice to quit or of intention to quit a head tenancy will always destroy any sub-tenancy.

2.   Effect of consensual termination

A sub-tenancy can be surrendered to the tenant,[275] but a complete surrender obviously requires the participation of both tenant and sub-tenant.[276] This is because surrender and merger[277] do not affect derivative interests. Common law logic apparently required all estates to end with the ending of the superior estate, though Lord Coke's *Commentary on Littleton*[278] took the opposite view that the sub-lease "hath in consideration of law a continuance"; statute has long ago adopted Coke's view.[279] All parties with derivative interests are put in the same position as if no surrender had occurred.[280] Usually this protects sub-tenants or lenders, and it causes the next interest moves up to form the reversion.[281]

The common law was very inconvenient when the tenant wanted to renew his lease, since all sub-tenants had to participate, but the modern statutory law facilitates contractual extensions, rent reviews, variations of terms, and regrants. *Ecclesiastical Commissioners for England* v. *Treemer*[282] is a good illustration: a surrender and regrant acted as one continuous lease, meaning that the tenant had a sufficiently long interest to grant a sub-lease. Similarly in *Plummer & John* v. *David*[283] the validity of a notice to quit served on a sub-tenant was not affected when the sub landlord surrendered his lease and accepted a new tenancy from the head landlord.

[272] [2000] 1 All E.R. 481 H.L., reversing [1998] 4 All E.R. 179 C.A.; see below pp. 618–620.

[273] [1995] Q.B. 192 C.A.; K. Stepien (1995) 139 S.J. 122, 222; *Brown* v. *Wilson* (1949) 208 L.T.Jo. 144, Hilbery J., was overruled.

[274] [1990] 2 E.G.L.R. 245 C.A.; *Elsden* v. *Pick* [1980] 1 W.L.R. 898 C.A.

[275] *Hughes* v. *Rowbotham* (1593) Cro. Eliz. 302, 78 E.R. 554; *Southwell* v. *Scotter* (1880) 49 L.J.Q.B. 356 C.A.

[276] *Paramour* v. *Yardley* (1579) 2 Plowd. 539, 75 E.R. 794.

[277] *Fairweather* v. *St Marylebone Property Co. Ltd.* [1963] A.C. 510 H.L.; but see L.P.A. 1925 ss.139, 150.

[278] Coke on *Littleton* 338a; cited in *Fairweather* as above at 546, Lord Denning; H.W.R. Wade (1962) 78 *L.Q.R.* 541.

[279] Landlord and Tenant Act 1730 s.6; now L.P.A. 1925 s.150; *Ecclesiastical Commissioners for England* v. *Treemer* [1893] 1 Ch. 166, 172, Chitty J.

[280] *Doe d. Palk* v. *Marchetti* (1831) 1 B. & Ad. 715, 109 E.R. 953.

[281] L.P.A. 1925 s.139; Real Property Act 1845 s.9; *London Regional Transport* v. *Brandt* (1997) 29 H.L.R. 193 C.A.

[282] [1893] 1 Ch. 166, Chitty J.; *Slough Picture Hall Co. Ltd.* v. *Wade* (1916) 32 T.L.R. 542; *Re Grosvenor's S.E.* [1932] 1 Ch. 232, 241, Maugham J.; *Cousins* v. *Phillips* (1865) 3 H. & C. 892, 159 E.R. 786.

[283] [1920] 1 K.B. 326.

Usually the rule protects sub-tenants,[284] possibly creating new public sector residential security of tenure,[285] but other interests protected include mortgages, restrictive covenants[286] and rights to remove fixtures.[287] A surrender should therefore be analysed as a transfer of the lease (that is as an assignment) rather than as a termination of it.[288] If title is registered, a surrender will operate subject to the rights of the holders of existing interests (for example registered mortgages) unless their consent is proved. It will be necessary to apply to expunge the title or note of the lease and outright cancellation will only be allowed if all necessary consents are forthcoming.[289]

[284] *Pleasant d. Hayton* v. *Benson* (1811) 14 East. 234, 104 E.R. 590 (notice had to be in tenant's name!); *Doe d. Beadon* v. *Pyke* (1816) 5 M. & S. 146, 105 E.R. 1005; *Mellor* v. *Watkins* (1874) L.R. 9 Q.B. 400; *Parker* v. *Jones* [1910] 2 K.B. 32 (even if sub-tenancy unlawful). Contrast *Twogate Properties Ltd.* v. *Birmingham Midshires B.S.* (1998) 75 P. & C.R. 386 C.A. where it had already been terminated by forfeiture before surrender of the head lease.

[285] *Basingstoke & Deane B.C.* v. *Paice* [1995] 2 E.G.L.R. 9 C.A.

[286] *Piggott* v. *Stratton* (1859) 1 De G.F. & J. 33, 45 E.R. 271; *Wilkes* v. *Spooner* [1911] 2 K.B. 473 C.A.

[287] *New Zealand Government Property Corp.* v. *H.M. & S. Ltd.* [1982] Q.B. 1145 C.A.

[288] N. Hopkins [1996] *Conv.* 284.

[289] L.R. Practice Note 21.

22

AGRICULTURAL LEASES

Protective codes. Agricultural holdings. Farm business tenancies. Agricultural uses. Mixes with business and residence. Yearly basis of farm business tenancies. Yearly basis of agricultural holdings. Agricultural holdings security of tenure. Agricultural sub-tenancies. Succession rights. Loss of security. Agricultural rents. Agricultural compensation.

A. PROTECTIVE CODES

1. Autumn 1995

Agricultural tenants are vitally affected by one date—September 1st 1995—when the Agricultural Tenancies Act 1995[1] came into force. Fresh agricultural leases granted on or after that date will be *farm business tenancies*[2]—they are subject to market forces,[3] and with greatly reduced protection for tenants.

Agricultural leases created before that date will generally be *agricultural holdings*,[4] and if so they will continue indefinitely to be within the protection of the Agricultural Holdings Act 1986.[5] Tenants within the scope of this Act are favoured with much greater security—usually for life—supplemented in the case of leases granted up to midsummer 1984 by succession rights for family members on the tenant's death.[6] Certain leases granted after the autumn 1995 watershed also continue to be agricultural holdings: these are later leases granted under earlier binding contracts, variations of old tenancies, and tenancies created under succession rights on the death of the tenant of an agricultural holding.[7] Full security dates from 1947,[8] soon afterwards consolidated in the Agricultural Holdings Act 1948,[9] and although the legislation was applied retrospectively to then existing tenants transitional provisions continue to apply to older tenancies.[10] Nothing prevents the tenant agreeing to surrender his agricultural holding and

---

[1] Woodfall 21.360–21.388; Bright & Gilbert 721–729; Evans & Smith (5th) 545–562; W.D.W. Barr (1994) 138 *S.J.* 175; S. Bright [1995] *Conv.* 445; S. McNulty & D. Evans [1995] 30 *E.G.* 82; R. Yates [1995] *N.L.J.* 1372; C.P. Rodgers [1996] *Conv.* 164; J.M. Bishop [1996] *Conv.* 243.

[2] A.T.A. 1995 ss.2, 3.

[3] See below pp. 627–628.

[4] Woodfall 21.001–21.359; Evans & Smith (5th) 505–545.

[5] The consolidation follows Law Com. No.153 (1985); C.P. Rodgers [1987] *Conv.* 177.

[6] See below pp. 620–621.

[7] A.T.A. 1995 ss.2, 3.

[8] Agriculture Act 1947 part III.

[9] J. Muir Watt (1948) 12 *Conv.* (*N.S.*) 15, 890; H. Potter (1948) 12 *Conv.* (*N.S.*) 459.

[10] A.H.A. 1986 sch.12 (on or after March 1st 1948).

taking a regrant of the same farm as a farm business tenancy; there is not even a warning of the dangers of doing so.[11]

2. Policy

Governments have always intervened in agriculture; even Norman law recognised a special peace for farmers. [12] Farming by tenants was always common, especially when landed families owned much of the land within large strict settlements, so that before the First World War some 90 per cent of agricultural land was rented. Legislative intervention began in the 1880s.[13] Lord Salmon has said that it was experience during the Second World War that reinforced the need for measures to encourage and promote efficiency in agriculture,[14] though agricultural security of tenure was really another successful aspect of the social policy of the under-regarded Attlee Labour Government.

Nevertheless, the agricultural holdings legislation failed to arrest the decline of the rented sector, the proportion of tenant farmers declining during the latter half of the twentieth century to a figure below 40 per cent. This is not necessarily a failure of the security legislation, since it may merely indicate that more farmers are owner-occupiers, and there has been an obvious trend towards large corporate farming operations. Full security depreciated the landlord's interest by up to 50 per cent and discouraged a supply of farm land to rent, the reasoning behind the Conservative deregulation brought about by the Agricultural Tenancies Act 1995.[15] Relatively few tenant farmers enjoyed full protection and the impact of the security of tenure legislation had been to withdraw much farmland from the letting market. The terms of agricultural leases are now left to be agreed between the parties in an open market, with only minimal security to tenant farmers.

B. AGRICULTURAL USES

The category of agricultural leases first delineated in 1947 is still applied to agricultural holdings (created before autumn 1995),[16] and in a more concise form for farm business tenancies (granted after that date).

1. Agriculture

Farming is obviously agricultural, including by the express words of the definition dairy farming, livestock breeding and livestock keeping,[17] and by self-evident extension also growing corn,[18] cutting hay, and grazing farm animals.[19] Other protected uses are hor-

---

[11] A. Sydenham [1996] 11 *Farm T.B.* 6.
[12] F.W. Maitland, *Forms of Action* (Cambridge U.P., 1936) 29.
[13] *Johnson* v. *Moreton* [1980] A.C. 37, 59, Lord Hailsham L.C.
[14] At 52, Lord Salmon.
[15] Following the Northfield Committee on the *Acquisition and Occupancy of Agricultural Land*, Cmnd. 7599 (1979).
[16] September 1st 1995.
[17] A.H.A. 1986 s.96(1); A.T.A. 1995 s.38(1). The R.(Ag.)A. 1976 s.1 (applied to tied cottages) has a slightly different definition, discussed e.g. in *Normanton* v. *Giles* [1980] 1 W.L.R. 28 H.L. (which illuminates the meaning of livestock and other defined expressions).
[18] *McClinton* v. *McFall* (1974) 232 E.G. 707 C.A.
[19] See also below p. 614.

ticulture, fruit growing, seed growing, the cultivation of osier, and the use of ancillary woodland.[20] Security schemes bite only if the tenant is a commercial farmer and do not assist those engaged in leisure activities, such as fishing[21] and raising game birds for what is sometimes called "sport".[22] *Allotments* are usually gardened for recreational purposes, but could qualify for security if used commercially.[23] Legislation provides for the acquisition of land for allotments,[24] protects sites against sale,[25] and gives a very limited guarantee of security by requiring 12 months notice to quit.

2. Business

Statutory security applies to agricultural leases that are commercial in character. Agricultural holdings (granted before autumn 1995) must be occupied for the purposes of a trade or business,[26] and the same rule is restated even more forcibly in the Agricultural Tenancies Act 1995 since a farm business tenancy must satisfy a business condition.[27]

Businesses with an agricultural flavour have to be allocated to either the agricultural or the business codes,[28] two mutually exclusive schemes so that any particular lease must be assigned to one category or the other. Agricultural character is tested by reference to the use made of the land as opposed to the character of the business,[29] a distinction of particular importance with "horsey" businesses. Breeding racehorses is not agricultural,[30] so that land let for that purposes falls under the business tenancies legislation, as would land let for use as a riding school.[31] On the other hand grazing horses *is* agricultural, so that a five-acre field used to pasture the horses of a riding school business is an agricultural holding.[32] Market gardens and nursery grounds are agricultural.[33] A lease of a garden centre may fall within either code, but it will be agricultural if most of the plants are raised at the centre.[34]

Forestry leases fall between all stools and have no protection.

---

[20] A.H.A. 1986 s.96(1); A.T.A. 1995 s.38(1).

[21] *Glendyne* v. *Rapley* [1978] 1 W.L.R. 601, approved in *Normanton* v. *Giles.*

[22] *Normanton* v. *Giles* [1980] 1 W.L.R. 28 H.L.; *Wetherall* v. *Smith* [1980] 1 W.L.R. 1290 (recreational jumping in paddock).

[23] *Stevens* v. *Sedgeman* [1951] 2 K.B. 434 (potatoes cultivated for sale).

[24] Allotments Acts 1908–1950; only 18,000 acres remained in 1997.

[25] Consent of the Secretary of State is required: *R.* v. *S.S. for the Environment ex parte Gosforth Allotments & Gardens Association Ltd.* [1996] 2 E.G.L.R. 117 C.A. (suitability of a replacement depends upon needs, not upon existing provision).

[26] A.H.A. 1986 s.1(2),(4).

[27] A.T.A. 1995 s.1(2).

[28] L.T.A. 1954 s.43(1)(a); A.T.A. 1995 sch., para 10; C.P. Rodgers [1988] *Conv.* 430; *E.W.P. Ltd.* v. *Moore* [1992] Q.B. 460 C.A.

[29] *Rutherford* v. *Maurer* [1962] 1 Q.B. 16; *McClinton* v. *McFall* (1974) 232 E.G. 707 C.A. (stud farm).

[30] *Re Joel's Lease* [1930] 2 Ch. 359 (on 1923 Act).

[31] *Weatherall* v. *Smith* [1980] 1 W.L.R. 1290.

[32] *Rutherford* v. *Maurer* [1962] 1 Q.B. 16.

[33] A.H.A. 1986 s.96(1); A.T.A. 1995 s.38(1).

[34] *Short* v. *Greeves* [1988] 1 E.G.L.R. 1 C.A.

3. Changes of use: agricultural holdings (before late 1995)

The agricultural character of the tenancy is determined mainly from the purposes for which the land is let.[35] Consideration is given to the terms of the tenancy interpreted in the light of the actual or contemplated use of the land at the time of conclusion of the contract of tenancy, along with any other circumstances.[36] Subsequent use of the land is a factor, but changes of use *towards* agriculture are taken into account only if they are authorised—they must be permitted by the use covenants in the lease or made in circumstances in which the landlord is deemed to have concurred through his permission, consent, or acquiescence.[37] So holdings cannot acquire protection from a unilateral and unauthorised change of use towards farming.

A reverse migration away from protection occurs if an existing agricultural use is ended. Use must be tested qualitatively at the time that a tenant claims the protection of the legislation.[38] Protection is lost if agricultural activity has been abandoned, completely or substantially, since the whole object of the legislation is to maintain continuity in the conduct of farming and horticultural operations.[39] If a business use is started in breach of covenant the fact that this change is unauthorised may well deny the protection of the business code, and the same applies to unauthorised residential use.

4. Changes of use: farm business tenancies (since late 1995)

The old law is reproduced more concisely. The business condition states that all or part of the land must be farmed for the purposes of a trade or business,[40] and at all times since the beginning of the tenancy; if this is true at the time of a dispute, there is a rebuttable presumption that it has been true at all earlier times.[41] The agriculture condition requires that the use is primarily agricultural, having regard to the terms of the tenancy, the use, and the nature of the commercial activities.[42] As an alternative, a lease may be agricultural if the notice condition is satisfied: this is that notice is given that the lease is intended to create a farm business tenancy and at that time the use is primarily agricultural.[43] Changes of use of land (whether the commencement or cessation of a particular use) are disregarded if they are in breach of covenant.[44]

---

[35] That is the primary purpose; there is no objection to subsidiary purposes e.g. keeping horses for pleasure: *Brown* v. *Tiernan* [1993] 1 E.G.L.R. 11.

[36] A.H.A. 1986 s.1(2).

[37] *Godfrey* v. *Waite* (1951) 157 E.G. 582 (consent of owner).

[38] *Weatherall* v. *Smith* [1980] 1 W.L.R. 1290 C.A.

[39] At 1299F, Sir David Cairns; *Hickson & Welch Ltd.* v. *Cann* (1977) 40 P. & C.R. 218 C.A. (cessation for two years ended protection); *Russell* v. *Booker* [1982] 2 E.G.L.R. 86 C.A.

[40] A.T.A. 1995 s.1(2).

[41] s.1(7).

[42] s.1(3); this may encourage a wider diversification.

[43] s.1(4). An existing notice continues in force after a surrender and regrant where the term date is shortened: s.3.

[44] s.1(8).

5. Exclusion of business security

A lease that is agricultural in character, within the above definition, is excluded from business security, the test being the dominant character of the use.[45] There is either/or protection.

C. AGRICULTURE USES: RESIDENTIAL MIXES

Many leases include a dwelling along with some agricultural land. Indeed a typical farm contains a farmhouse surrounded by land to be cultivated or grazed, and this is obviously agricultural in character.[46] Borderline cases must be allocated either to the residential or to the agricultural codes, since the protection offered is mutually exclusive.[47] Tenants of tied cottages have special protection, discussed elsewhere.[48]

1. Dwelling let with land

A lease falls within the residential sector where a dwelling is let with a small area of agricultural land.[49] The land is deemed to be let with the dwelling,[50] a test applied at the time that security comes into question (that is on repossession) rather than at the time of the initial letting.[51]

2. Agricultural holdings (before late 1995)

The basic unit is the land let by an individual lease.[52] Agriculture need not be the sole purpose of the tenancy but it must be the main one. If so, protection attaches to the entire holding—that is the "aggregate of land comprised in a contract of tenancy"—so that some land that is not agricultural may be included.[53] The test is applied to the whole of the land comprised in the contract, "subject to such exceptions as do not substantially affect the character of the tenancy".[54] Case law shows how these rules operate to allocate leases of mixed holdings. In *Dunn* v. *Fidoe* a lease of a pub together with 12 acres of fields for crops and grazing was held to be agricultural.[55] So too was a lease of seven acres of

---

[45] L.T.A. 1954 s.43(1)(a); A.T.A. 1995 sch., para.10; *E.W.P. Ltd.* v. *Moore* [1992] Q.B. 460 C.A.

[46] *National Trust* v. *Knipe* [1998] 1 W.L.R. 230, 243F–G, Judge L.J.; C.P. Rodgers [1998] *J.H.L.* 123, 138.

[47] R.A. 1977 s.10 (as amended); H.A. 1988 sch.1 paras.6, 7 (as amended); A.T.A. 1995 sch. paras.10, 27, 33–34.

[48] See above Chapter 7.

[49] However a lease of a dwelling may be agricultural without any land, for example where a cottage is let to a farmer for sub-letting to an employee: *Blackmore* v. *Butler* [1954] 2 Q.B. 171.

[50] R.A. 1977 s.6 dwelling let with other land not protected; but s.26 includes agricultural land not exceeding 2 acres in extent with the dwelling-house; H.A. 1988 s.2; sch.1 paras.6–7 (assured); H.A. 1985 s.112 (secure).

[51] *Mann* v. *Merrill* [1945] 1 All E.R. 708 (2 acres added to smallholding of 3.5 acres; held agricultural not residential); *Whitty* v. *Scott-Russell* [1950] 2 K.B. 32, 39–40, Asquith L.J.; R.E. Megarry (1950) 66 *L.Q.R.* 304.

[52] A.H.A. 1986 s.1(5); *Darby* v. *Williams* (1974) 232 E.G. 579 (separate leases of farm land and cottages); *Avon C.C.* v. *Clothier* [1977] 1 E.G.L.R. 4 C.A. (grazing land and stabling separate).

[53] A.H.A. 1986 s.1(1). Small plots were protected in *Stevens* v. *Sedgeman* [1951] 2 K.B. 434 and *Craddock* v. *Hampshire C.C.* [1958] 1 W.L.R. 202.

[54] A.H.A. 1986 s.1(2); H.W. Wilkinson (1988) 138 *N.L.J.* 329.

[55] [1950] 2 All E.R. 685.

farm land, in *Howkins* v. *Jardine* even though it contained three cottages that were sub-let to non-employees.[56]

Severance is not generally possible: a lease is either wholly agricultural or it has no agricultural protection.[57] However, security can be restricted to the agricultural parts if the landlord transfers the reversion in non-agricultural parts to a nominee; the effect is to split the holding, and that nominee can then terminate the unprotected tenancy of the non-agricultural parts.[58]

Changes of use made in breach of covenant must be ignored in assessing the character of the tenancy.[59] Conversion of agricultural land to residential use will not attract residential security, since a precondition for the operation of the residential security codes is that the property was originally let as a dwelling, and subsequent changes of use can be taken into account only if the landlord consents. In *Russell* v. *Booker*[60] a farmhouse had been converted to a bed and breakfast operation without permission, but this unilateral and unauthorised change of use was irrelevant, so the letting of a farmhouse with two acres of land and an orchard was an agricultural holding. Similarly in *Lester* v. *Ridd*[61] the severance of a house from the agricultural land with which the house had been let without the landlord's permission did not create a residential tenancy, and conferred no enfranchisement rights.

3.   Farm business tenancies (since late 1995)

At least part of the land must be farmed for agricultural purposes,[62] and the character of the whole tenancy must be primarily agricultural. This is assessed having regard to the terms of the tenancy, actual use, commercial activities, and other relevant circumstances. If a notice is given in advance that there is to be a Farm Business Tenancy the test is applied at the beginning, regard being had to the terms of the tenancy and other relevant circumstances.[63]

4.   Protection from eviction

Most holdings include a farmhouse in which the tenant lives. Is he entitled to the benefit of the Protection from Eviction Act 1977? This question was considered by the Court of Appeal in *National Trust* v. *Knipe*.[64] Agricultural tenants are protected against arbitrary eviction like any other residential tenant, so the rule in section 3 (that court proceedings are required before a person is removed from their home) does protect a farmer. That far the 1977 Act applies, but no further. Section 5 prescribes detailed rules

---

[56] [1951] 1 K.B. 614 (severance is not possible); *Manson* v. *Bond* [1954] 1 W.L.R. 1321 (no protection where sale of flowers and shrubs grown on holding only 10% of turnover of shop).

[57] *Godfrey* v. *Waite* (1951) 157 E.G. 582; R.E. Megarry (1954) 70 *L.Q.R.* 311 (lease of half a farmhouse not agricultural).

[58] *Persey* v. *Bazley* [1984] 2 E.G.L.R. 3 C.A.; *John* v. *George* [1996] 1 E.G.L.R. 7 C.A.; see below p. 627.

[59] A.H.A. 1986 s.1(3).

[60] [1982] 2 E.G.L.R. 86 C.A.

[61] [1990] 2 Q.B. 430 C.A.; J.E. Martin [1989] *Conv.* 126.

[62] A.T.A. 1995 s.1(2)(a)–(b).

[63] A.T.A. 1995 s.1(3), (4).

[64] [1998] 1 W.L.R. 230 C.A.; C.P. Rodgers [1998] *J.H.L.* 123, 138. Leave to appeal was refused: [1998] 1 W.L.R. 696 H.L.

about the length of a notice to quit a dwelling and about the warning notices and information to the tenant to be included in a notice to quit. *Knipe* held that rules about residential notices to quit are inappropriate and irrelevant, so that a notice to quit has only to comply with the appropriate agricultural code in order to end the tenant's right to live in the farmhouse along with his right to farm the land.

D. YEARLY BASIS

Crops take a long time to bring to fruition: the land must be prepared, seed sown, the plants nurtured and protected against disease, until they are ready to be harvested. The soil has then to prepared for the next crop. Farming has to be planned over a long period, a cycle liable to be interrupted in the case of a tenant farmer by termination of his lease. The common law developed a rough and ready solution to this problem in the shape of emblements,[65] the right for a tenant whose estate in the land has ended to go back to the land to harvest what he has planted. A more complete solution is to preserve the leasehold estate in the land for a sufficient period to enable the agricultural cycle to be brought to an end. Since most farming involves a yearly cycle of activities, a landlord should not be allowed to terminate an agricultural letting at will,[66] or even by the common law notice of two quarters to end a yearly tenancy. The minimum needed to do justice is that he should give his tenant at least a year's notice to enable him to harvest his crops, to reap his profits, and to plan how to wind down his operations. Statute allows a tenant to hold over at the end of an agricultural lease on a yearly tenancy, and recasts agricultural leases on a yearly basis.

1.   Yearly basis of farm business tenancies

For initial grants made after autumn 1995, tenant farmers can only protect themselves by contractual negotiation of a fixed leasehold term.[67] The best protection is to negotiate a fixed term that exceeds two years, since when the fixed term is up the tenant will be continued automatically from year to year.[68] Holding over can be avoided by giving written notice of the intention to terminate; to do this the tenant must be given at least 12 months before the contractual term date (though not more than 24 months). Once a holding over has occurred, the lease may be ended on the first anniversary[69] or in any later year.[70] Exercise of a break clause also requires this same period of notice, the one point where the 1995 Act[71] is markedly less generous that its 1986 predecessor. If a farm business tenancy is granted as a tenancy *from year to year*, written notice is required to terminate and it must again be of least 12 months (but not more than 24 months) and must expire at the end of a year of the tenancy.[72] Common law rules about the length of

---

[65]   Megarry & Wade (5th ed.) 98–101, more briefly in the 6th ed. at 86.

[66]   *Johnson* v. *Moreton* [1980] A.C. 37, 52F, Lord Salmon.

[67]   A.T.A. 1995 s.38(1); all forms of tenancy are covered including sub-tenancies and agreements; for tenancies at will see below n. 92.

[68]   s.5.

[69]   s.6(2).

[70]   s.6(1).

[71]   s.7.

[72]   s.6.

notice are overridden. A tenant wishing to quit is bound just as much as a landlord seeking repossession.[73] In short the fundamental protection provided by the Agricultural Tenancies Act is that a tenant with an initial fixed term of two years or a yearly tenancy is entitled to at least one year's notice to quit the holding.

2.   Tenancies not converted to the yearly basis as farm business tenancies

No protection applies to a tenant at will[74] or a licensee: the owner of a farm can grant a right to occupy it pending negotiations for a lease or a limited right such as a grazing licence that does not confer exclusive possession without conceding a yearly based occupation.

Possession can be granted without conceding the right to a year's notice by creating a periodic tenancy with a period that is weekly, monthly or quarterly (as opposed to being annual) or by granting a term for a fixed period of up to two years.[75] If the tenant is allowed to hold over after the short fixed term it will often be as a yearly tenant, and this will bring into play the yearly basis of notice. However a gap in the legislation exists where a holding over is on a period that is less than annual. Much of the bite can be removed from the Act by granting a contractual tenancy for less than two years[76] with rent payable quarterly, so that holding over is also on quarterly terms; however long he occupies, it seems that the farmer will never pass onto the yearly notice basis.

3.   Yearly basis of agricultural holdings

The Agricultural Holdings Act 1986 protects tenants of farms etc. under leases created before the autumn of 1995, applying the yearly basis of holding in four cases.

Fixed term of two years or more. Agricultural tenants have always been able to secure continuity in their farming by agreeing a fixed contractual term, during which time the tenant can rely on his contractual rights[77]—whether under a legal lease by deed or an equitable lease by agreement.[78] The legislation refers specifically to a fixed term of years, so full security is dependent upon an initial grant having been made for a fixed term of two years or more. Safely included, of course, is any lease for life since any lease reserving a rent will be converted to a lease for 90 years.[79] A fixed term lease may be ended on its term date, but to do so notice must be served at least one year before the lease is to end, and there is usually little point in a landlord doing so, given that statutory security will always be claimed and this will negate the effect of the notice. [80]

Yearly grants. Tenancies from year to year are the archetype of the agricultural holding. Any fixed term lease for two years or more will run on as a tenancy from year to year until terminated.[81] Initial grants were often on yearly terms, since this form of tenure

---

[73] Except by s.6(3) where the tenant responds to a severance of the reversion by terminating the whole lease.
[74] s.38(1).
[75] s.5; there is no Crown exemption: s.37.
[76] i.e. outside s.5.
[77] A.H.A. 1986 s.1(1).
[78] *Land Settlement (Association) Ltd.* v. *Carr* [1944] K.B. 657; *Re Land and Premises at Liss* [1971] Ch. 986 (on business code); *Re Lancaster & Macnamara* [1918] 2 K.B. 472 (on the 1908 Act); M. Cardwell [1993] *Conv.* 138.
[79] L.P.A. 1925 s.149(6); A.H.A. 1986 s.3(3); see above pp. 363–365.
[80] A.H.A. 1986 s.3(2).
[81] A.H.A. 1986 s.3; *Harrison* v. *Wing* [1988] 2 E.G.L.R. 4 C.A. (express anyway).

naturally suits the annual character of much farming.[82] The yearly basis of holding is established by the rule requiring one full year's notice of termination, that notice being required to expire at the end of a year of the tenancy. To this bare minimum, most tenants of (pre-autumn 1995) agricultural holdings are entitled to long-term security of tenure, and indeed this is often life-long.[83]

Tenancies for less than a year. A letting for an interest less than from year to year was transformed by the agricultural holdings scheme into a tenancy with a period of a year, that conversion being applied to weekly, monthly, or quarterly tenancies, and also to a fixed term tenancy for part of a single year.[84] The precise stage at which this statutory conversion affects a fixed grant for six months was considered by the Court of Appeal in *Calcott* v. *J.S. Bloor (Measham) Ltd.*[85] It was clear that a notice to quit was required, that it had to be given before an anniversary date, and so as to expire one year later on the next anniversary date of the granting of the original lease. Were the anniversary dates computed from the beginning or the end of the six-month contractual period? It was decided that the statutory conversion occurs as soon as the grant is made, and therefore anniversary dates have to be computed from the beginning.

The residential principle of *Street* v. *Mountford*[86] to ensure that any licence conferring exclusive possession of agricultural land is reformed as a lease.[87] But even if there is such a thing as an exclusive licensee, this is of no assistance to the landlord since full security is provided to *exclusive licensees*: the statutory metamorphosis to the yearly basis affects any exclusive licence[88] to occupy land commercially for the purposes of agriculture.[89] One example is where a potential purchaser is allowed to occupy a farm before completion of his contract.[90] Non-exclusive licences remain true licences and do not attract security.[91] Apparently, a tenant at will remains unprotected.[92] Conversion to a yearly tenancy takes effect subject to any necessary modifications, but only if the arrangement is capable of taking effect in that way while remaining recognisably the same agreement.[93]

---

[82] *Midgley* v. *Scott* [1977] 2 E.G.L.R. 6 C.A.

[83] See below pp. 615–617.

[84] A.H.A. 1986 s.2(1)(a). An attornment clause in a mortgage does not create an agricultural holding: *Steyning & Littlehampton B.S.* v. *Wilson* [1951] Ch. 1018. Conversion does not occur if the landlord's interest is too short to support it: s.2(3)(b). Disputes are referred by s.2(4) to arbitration.

[85] [1998] 1 W.L.R. 1490 C.A.

[86] [1985] A.C. 809 H.L.

[87] *Gisbourne* v. *Burton* [1989] Ch. 390 C.A.; *Harrison* v. *Wing* [1988] 2 E.G.L.R. 4 C.A.; also *Collier* v. *Hollinshead* [1984] 2 E.G.L.R. 14, Scott J. (full protection even though rent below market rate).

[88] *Avon C.C.* v. *Clothier* [1977] 1 E.G.L.R. 4 C.A. (stabling horses); *James* v. *Lock* [1978] 1 E.G.L.R. 1 C.A.; *Mitton* v. *Farrow* [1980] 2 E.G.L.R. 1 C.A.; *Lampard* v. *Barker* [1984] 2 E.G.L.R. 11 C.A.; *Padbury* v. *York* [1990] 2 E.G.L.R. 3.

[89] *S.S. for Social Services* v. *Beavington* [1981] 1 E.G.L.R. 13 (licence for 364 days not used for grazing or mowing).

[90] *Walters* v. *Roberts* (1980) 41 P. & C.R. 210; *Goldsack* v. *Shore* [1950] 1 K.B. 708; *Verrall* v. *Farnes* [1966] 1 W.L.R. 1254; *Mitton* v. *Farrow* [1980] 2 E.G.L.R. 1 C.A.; *Dockerill* v. *Fitzpatrick* [1989] 1 E.G.L.R. 1 C.A.; *Gold* v. *Jacques Amand Ltd.* (1992) 63 P. & C.R. 1, Browne-Wilkinson V.C.

[91] See below pp. 614–615.

[92] *Goldsack* v. *Shore* [1950] 1 K.B. 708, 713, Evershed M.R.; contrast *Epps* v. *Ledger* (1972) 225 E.G. 1373.

[93] A.H.A. 1986 s.2(1); Woodfall 1.020–1.033; *Goldsack* at 713, Evershed M.R.; but see *Bahamas International Trust Co. Ltd.* v. *Threadgold* [1974] 1 W.L.R. 1514, 1521B, Megaw L.J., a point Lord Diplock left open in the H.L.

4.   Tenancies not converted to a yearly basis as agricultural holdings

Fixed term tenancies of between one and two years. No protection is provided for a fixed term tenancy of this intermediate duration.[94] Security of tenure is excluded, though the tenant does have rights to agricultural compensation, with the result that such a lease also fails to make it as a renewable business tenancy. Time is calculated from the actual grant, rather than any earlier date from which the term is calculated, meaning that the two years are computed according to the time for which the land is actually available for use by the tenant.[95] Short-term agreements were so common that before the 1995 legislative upheaval up to 50 per cent of all tenanted agricultural land was held on non-security deals.[96]

Seasonal mowing and grazing agreements. These also missed the protection of the Agricultural Holdings Acts. The purpose had to be exclusively for grazing or mowing (or both[97]), determined according to the purpose of the letting, rather than the actual use made of the land; unauthorised use for general farming never created full agricultural security.[98] What is seasonal? The 1986 Act refers to a licence for a specified period of the year,[99] so that it is arguable that full security was given to a straight six-month term,[100] though the majority of cases regard any period of less than a full year as being seasonal,[101] and regular use was in fact made of licences for 364 days.[102] One day longer would have brought full protection.[103] Care was needed to eschew provisions for crop rotation or other terms, which implied occupation throughout the year.[104] Provided each agreement qualified in isolation, grazing arrangements could be renewed over a long period of years without attracting security,[105] though it was possibly wiser to leave a short gap between lets.

Non-exclusive licences had no protection, a rule which disqualified any non-exclusive care-taking arrangement by which the landlord retains access to the property.[106] Service agreements confer no security whether they are non-exclusive[107] or exclusive, where the right of occupation is given for the duration that any person continues in an office,

---

[94] *Gladstone* v. *Bowers* [1960] 2 Q.B. 384 C.A. (18 months); *Short Bros. (Plant) Ltd.* v. *Edwards* [1979] 1 E.G.L.R. 5 C.A.; *Cox* v. *Husk* [1976] 2 E.G.L.R. 1, Griffiths J.; *E.W.P. Ltd.* v. *Moore* [1992] Q.B. 460, 464–465, Nolan L.J.

[95] *Keen* v. *Holland* [1984] 1 W.L.R. 251 (agreement in October 1979 for term of 14 months from September 1978; i.e. a letting for two weeks; took effect as tenancy from year to year); C.P. Rodgers [1984] *Conv.* 315.

[96] M. Cardwell [1993] *Conv.* 138, 148.

[97] A.H.A. 1986 s.2(3)(a).

[98] *Boyce* v. *Rendells* [1983] 2 E.G.L.R. 146 C.A.; *Avon C.C.* v. *Clothier* [1977] 1 E.G.L.R. 4 C.A.

[99] A.H.A. 1986 s.2(3)(a), (4) (arbitration).

[100] *Rutherford* v. *Maurer* [1962] 1 Q.B. 16.

[101] *Scene Estates Ltd.* v. *Amos* [1957] 2 Q.B. 205 (4 × 6 months held exempt); *Watts* v. *Yeend* [1987] 1 W.L.R. 323 C.A.; *Chaloner* v. *Bower* [1984] 1 E.G.L.R. 4 C.A.

[102] *Reid* v. *Dawson* [1955] 1 Q.B. 214; R.E. Megarry (1955) 71 *L.Q.R.* 19; *South West Water Authority* v. *Palmer* [1983] 2 E.G.L.R. 5; J.E. Martin [1982] *Conv.* 442.

[103] *Brown* v. *Tiernan* [1993] 1 E.G.L.R. 1; M. Welstead [1993] *Conv.* 170.

[104] *Lory* v. *Brent L.B.C.* [1971] 1 W.L.R. 823.

[105] *Short Bros. (Plant) Ltd.* v. *Edwards* [1979] 1 E.G.L.R. 5 C.A.; *Stone* v. *Whitcombe* (1980) 40 P. & C.R. 296; *Luton* v. *Tinsey* [1979] 1 E.G.L.R. 1 C.A.

[106] *Harrison-Broadley* v. *Smith* [1964] 1 W.L.R. 456; *Bahamas International Trust Co. Ltd.* v. *Threadgold* [1974] 1 W.L.R. 1514, 1527H, Lord Diplock; *Evans* v. *Tomkins* [1993] 2 E.G.L.R. 6 C.A.

[107] *Bahamas International Trust Co. Ltd.* v. *Threadgold* [1974] 1 W.L.R. 1514 H.L.

appointment or employment held from the landlord.[108] A particular form of non-exclusive licence arose with share farming, an arrangement to divide the profits of farming between landlord and farmer; since the person conducting farming operations does not have exclusive possession of the land, he is not a tenant.[109]

Protection for agricultural holdings could be excluded by *ministerial certificate*.[110] Although the most elaborate provision was made for a fixed term of between two and five years,[111] almost all reported cases relate to short leases and licences.[112] Both provisions insisted upon a joint application to the minister, and it was essential that his approval was obtained before entry into the lease. Full security was attracted if the landlord jumped the gun, or if an excluded lease was renewed without a renewed ministerial exclusion.[113] The lease had to be in writing and contain a statement of the exclusion from protection.[114]

E. AGRICULTURAL HOLDINGS: SECURITY OF TENURE

There is nothing to be said in this section about farm business tenancies since the whole object of the Agricultural Tenancies Act 1995 is to restrict the farmer to his contractual rights, and long-term security depends upon negotiation of a fixed term grant. However a lease initially granted before autumn 1995 will be an agricultural holding, and "life-long" security of tenure continues to operate.

1.   Security of tenure

Fertility is not built up over six months but takes years of toil and investment.[115] There in a nutshell is the case for ensuring continuity in farming operations through the agricultural holdings legislation. Security of tenure is provided by negativing the effect of a notice to quit,[116] thus extending the contractual duration or yearly holding over. Repossession is limited to those cases in which a landlord can issue a valid notice to quit and otherwise the tenant's holding will be extended indefinitely—for life and even beyond to his successors.[117]

A first requirement is to wait for the expiration of any fixed contractual period. The tenancy can be ended by a notice served in advance to expire on the term date, but otherwise the yearly basis of the tenancy kicks in.[118] The common law rule accepting a half

---

[108] A.H.A. 1986 s.1(1); *Verrall* v. *Farnes* [1966] 1 W.L.R. 1254, 1269D, Cross J. (new tenant could be tried out by employment as a bailiff).

[109] *Wallace* v. *C. Brian Barratt & Son Ltd.* [1997] 2 E.G.L.R. 1 C.A.; H.W. Wilkinson [1986] *Conv.* 65; C.P. Rodgers [1991] *Conv.* 58; M. Slatter [1991] *Conv.* 207.

[110] It could cover all lettings by a named Government department: *Finbow* v. *Air Ministry* [1963] 1 W.L.R. 697.

[111] A.H.A. 1986 s.5.

[112] A.H.A. 1986 s.2(1); (1984) 128 *S.J.* 536; *Epsom & Ewell B.C.* v. *C. Bell (Tadworth) Ltd.* [1983] 1 W.L.R. 379; *Pahl* v. *Trevor* [1992] 1 E.G.L.R. 22 C.A.; *Jones* v. *Owen* [1997] 2 E.G.L.R. 5; A. Sydenham [1997] 40 *E.G.* 138.

[113] *Bedfordshire C.C.* v. *Clarke* (1974) 230 E.G. 1587; *S.S. for Social Services* v. *Beavington* [1981] 1 E.G.L.R. 13; *Ashdale Land & Co. Ltd.* v. *Manners* [1992] 2 E.G.L.R. 5.

[114] A.H.A. 1986 s.5(3).

[115] *Johnson* v. *Moreton* [1980] A.C. 37, 59B, Lord Hailsham.

[116] A.H.A. 1986 s.25; Woodfall 21.086–21.152.

[117] *Rugby Joint Water Board* v. *Foottit* [1973] A.C. 202, 221C, Lord Simon dissenting.

[118] A.H.A. 1986 s.25; also s.30 and sch.5 (notices to servicemen).

year's notice to end a yearly tenancy is reversed in order to accommodate the yearly cycle of agriculture, so that the notice must last a full year and expire on an anniversary date of the lease at least one year distant.[119] This is also so to exercise a break clause[120] or if the tenant wishes to quit.[121] In some circumstances the notice can be shorter than a year, and no minimum period is specified; these are[122]: (a) insolvency of the tenant; (b) a notice to resume possession not for agriculture; (c) notice by a tenant to sub-tenant; and (d) notice to terminate a lease for life. Although a lease cannot provide in advance for notice to be longer or shorter than a year, it is open to the parties to agree a surrender at any time, so one side may accept a short notice from the other.[123]

Full security beyond the year's notice period is obtained by a *counter-notice* mechanism, under which the tenant has one month in which to write claiming the protection of the Act,[124] a right which cannot be excluded.[125] After the counter-notice, the landlord's notice to quit is invalidated unless a ground for possession is shown,[126] and most tenants will be entitled to remain. Unusually, and regrettably, the agricultural security legislation prescribed no form for a landlord's notice to quit an agricultural holding and the courts have refused to imply any requirement that the tenant be given a warning of his right to serve a counter-notice. Hence many agricultural tenants will lose security of tenure through being unaware of their rights.[127] In most cases in which a tenant is removed, the landlord has already applied to the Agricultural Land Tribunal for a certificate before he has served a notice to quit on the tenant. If the Tribunal issues a certificate (say) of bad husbandry,[128] the tenant will have no defence to a notice to quit, so the dispute is resolved before the notice to quit is served.

What happens if a landlord wishes to dispute the existence of an agricultural holding but just in case to make use of the Tribunal machinery? The answer is[129] that he may serve notices and even arbitrate "without prejudice", so as to protect his position pending the outcome of the dispute about the tenancy. Mance L.J. has described the three possible courses for an arbitrator: to state a case for the county court, to decide that there is no lease and that he has no jurisdiction, or to make an award and leave it to be challenged on appeal. Arbitration could and should be stayed while court proceedings are resolved.

2.   Contractual terms where security operates

Statutory continuation of a tenancy may require rearrangement of the contractual terms. The Act provides a right to claim a written tenancy agreement[130] and for arbi-

---

[119]   *Yeandle* v. *Reigate & Banstead B.C.* [1996] 1 E.G.L.R. 20 (yearly tenancy commencing September 29th 1968 could be terminated by notice in July 1992 to end on September 28th (or 29th) 1993).

[120]   *Edell* v. *Dulieu* [1924] A.C. 38 H.L.

[121]   A.H.A. 1986 s.25(1); *Flather* v. *Hood* (1928) 44 T.L.R. 698, Charles J. (on earlier Act). After a rent increase the tenant can terminate by six months' notice.

[122]   s.25(2).

[123]   s.25(1), (5); *Elsden* v. *Pick* [1980] 1 W.L.R. 898; *Knapdale* v. *Donald* [2000] Times August 22nd.

[124]   s.26; *Mountford* v. *Hodkinson* [1956] 1 W.L.R. 422 C.A. (counter-notice should refer to what is now s.26).

[125]   *Johnson* v. *Moreton* [1980] A.C. 37 H.L.

[126]   See below pp.621–627.

[127]   *Crawford* v. *Elliott* [1991] 1 E.G.L.R. 13.

[128]   The legislation ignores the need for gender neutrality of language.

[129]   *Grammer* v. *Lane* [1999] Times December 2nd C.A.

[130]   A.H.A. 1986 s.6; sch.1 (detailed contents).

tration to determine whether discrepancies between the agreed terms and model clauses should be allowed to stand.[131] Rent can be increased by arbitration.[132]

3. Contracting out of protection void

Agreements to contract out of protection are not permitted; there are some express provisions[133] but the wider and more general rule is simply implicit in the whole security of tenure scheme, and the fact that it is designed to protect the public as well as individual tenant farmers.[134] Any attempt to interfere with the tenant's right to respond to his landlord's notice to quit by serving a counter-notice claiming the benefit of the Act is void.[135] A condition stating that no counter-notice could be served without the consent of L. Ltd was held in *Featherstone* v. *Staples*[136] to be contrary to the public interest and void. The right to protection cannot be renounced[137] or surrendered[138] in advance. Equally if the landlord is one of the tenants, the remaining tenants are able to claim security,[139] and collusive schemes to remove sub-tenants are void.[140]

4. Joint tenants

Strict co-ownership principles are generally applied, so that all landlords must serve notice on all tenants[141] in order to end an agricultural lease, though this is subject to the rule in *Monk*[142] that one joint tenant can end a periodic tenancy[143]—a rule even more unfortunate when applied to agricultural tenants; it seems that the trust existing between co-owners cannot be used to compel the service of a counter-notice.[144] Unfortunately this appeared to open the way for evasion of agricultural security with this scheme. When the landlord is in a position to end the lease, for example by notice to quit a periodic tenancy, it is up to the tenant to take the initiative and refer the landlord's notice to the Tribunal. If the tenant does so this will usually lead to invalidation of the notice, and so to security of tenure. A landlord could prevent this by becoming a party to the lease as a joint tenant and refusing to participate in reference of the notice to quit to the Tribunal.[145] This procedure flouted the intention of the legislation governing agricultural leases, and was disallowed in *Gisbourne* v. *Burton*.[146]

---

[131] s.7.
[132] See below pp. 627–629.
[133] A.H.A. 1986 ss.5 (conversion of fixed term tenancies under s.3), 25(1) (length of notice to quit).
[134] *Johnson* v. *Moreton* [1980] A.C. 37, 51E, Lord Salmon; (1979) 95 *L.Q.R.* 4; N.D.M. Parry [1980] *Conv.* 117.
[135] *Parry* v. *Million Pigs Ltd.* [1981] 2 E.G.L.R. 1, Ewbank J. (forfeiture clause).
[136] [1986] 1 W.L.R. 861 C.A.
[137] *Johnson* at 51E, Lord Salmon.
[138] *Trustees of Saunders* v. *Ralph* (1993) 66 P. & C.R 335, Jowitt J.
[139] *Featherstone* v. *Staples* [1986] 1 W.L.R. 861 C.A.
[140] But see *Barrett* v. *Morgan* [2000] 1 All E.R. 481 H.L.; see below pp. 619–620.
[141] *Newman* v. *Keedwell* (1977) 35 P. & C.R. 393; *Jones* v. *Lewis* (1973) 25 P. & C.R. 375 C.A.
[142] *Hammersmith & Fulham R.L.B.C.* v. *Monk* [1992] 1 A.C. 478 H.L.
[143] *Parsons* v. *Parsons* [1983] 1 W.L.R. 1390.
[144] *Sykes* v. *Land* [1984] 2 E.G.L.R. 8 C.A.; *Cork* v. *Cork* [1997] 1 E.G.L.R. 5, Knox J.; see the *Monk* cases cited above at pp. 124–130.
[145] *Re J.E. Cade & Son Ltd.* [1992] B.C.L.C. 213, Warner J.
[146] [1989] Q.B. 390 C.A.

F. AGRICULTURAL SUB-HOLDINGS

1. Unauthorised sub-lettings

These are common. Landlords naturally wish to retain control of the selection of the farmer tenant, and for this reason it is normal for an agricultural tenancy to restrict sub-letting. In such a case the head lease will be liable to termination for breach of covenant. The security provisions are inapplicable to termination for an irremediable breach of covenant. Mandatory case E applies and the notice to quit ends the head tenancy without the need for consent from the Agricultural Land Tribunal. The sub-tenancy will be destroyed when the head tenancy is ended.

2. Authorised sub-letting

If a tenant of an agricultural holding sub-lets it lawfully,[147] both the head lease and the sub-lease will be protected by the agricultural holdings legislation. The sub-tenant acquires the same rights as a tenant under the Act.

3. Position of a sub-tenant on a surrender of the head tenancy

A surrender is simply an assurance by which a lease or tenancy is given up before its expiration. If a tenant surrenders his tenancy to an immediate landlord, and he accepts it, the tenancy is absorbed by the landlord's reversion and is extinguished by operation of law. It ends prematurely, in a way not provided by the terms of the tenancy agreement and hence the consent of the landlord is essential.[148] A sub-tenant cannot be prejudiced by a surrender. This was already clear at the time of Lord Coke's commentary on *Littleton*,[149] and statute has progressively reformed the law[150] so that today the sub-tenant becomes a direct tenant of the head landlord and retains the security of tenure he had at the time of the surrender.

4. Notice to quit

The position is different where the head lease is terminated by notice to quit: a notice to quit ends the superior tenancy and so brings to an end all derivative interests—including an agricultural sub-tenancy. Proper termination of the head lease will also terminate the sub-lease,[151] and it will not be necessary to given a year's notice.[152] This is now made absolutely clear by the decision of the Lords in *Barrett* v. *Morgan*.[153] The freeholders and head tenants were all members of the Scott family—descendants of the great Lord Chancellor, Lord Eldon. The family now decided that it wished to sell some farmland in Northumberland with vacant possession as building land. The problem it faced was that it had been sub-let to Morgan for over 18 years. In order to end his rights, the freeholders

---

[147] *Rous* v. *Mitchell* [1991] 1 W.L.R. 469 C.A. (consent given to sub-letting other than for holiday lets).

[148] *Barrett* v. *Morgan* [2000] 1 All E.R. 481, 485b.

[149] Coke on *Littleton* 338.

[150] L.T.A. 1730 s.6 (now L.P.A. 1925 s.150) and Real Property Act 1845 s.9 (now L.P.A. 1925 s.139). Case law is considered above at pp. 299–301.

[151] *Sherwood* v. *Moody* [1952] 1 All E.R. 389; also *Bell* v. *McCubbin* [1990] 1 Q.B. 976 C.A.

[152] A.H.A. 1986 s.25(2)(c).

[153] [2000] 1 All E.R. 481 H.L.

served notice to quit upon that the head tenants, under an informal arrangement that no counter-notice would be served, so that there would be no claim to the benefit of the agricultural holdings legislation. This ended the head tenancy at the expiration of the notice to quit, and the House of Lords held that it also terminated the sub-tenancy.

A periodic tenancy comes to an end by effluxion of time on the expiration of a notice to quit served by the landlord on the tenants or by the tenants on the landlord.

> "By granting and accepting a periodic tenancy with provision, expressed or implied, for its determination by notice to quit, the parties have agreed at the outset on the manner of determination. The parties and their successors in title, including those who derive title under them, are bound by their agreement."[154]

So the sub-tenant's derivative title is always precarious, and it cannot survive the natural termination of the head tenancy.

5. Upwards notices and collusive agreements

Why did the head tenants in *Barrett* v. *Morgan* not serve a notice to quit on the head landlords? It is now clear that they could in fact have done so—the House of Lords ruled that there was no difference between a downwards notice served by the freeholder on his immediate tenant, and upwards notice given to the freeholder. It also treated in the same way a collusive agreement between the freeholder and the head tenant for one to serve a notice and the other to accept it. However these last two cases require more discussion given the divergent authorities on downwards notices and collusive agreements.

In the past it could be argued that an upwards notice was the same as an offer to surrender the tenancy.[155] This is particularly so as the tenant seems to derogate from his own grant to his sub-tenant if he acts to bring a premature end to both holdings. However, in *Pennell* v. *Payne*[156] the Court of Appeal allowed an upwards notice to quit by a tenant to end a lawful sub-tenancy. Lord Millett reached the same conclusion in *Barrett*, the difference in principle being that an offer to surrender requires acceptance by the landlord before it takes effect, where as a notice to quit is unilateral and non consensual.[157]

It was also open to argument (in the past) that a consensual agreement for the head landlord to serve a notice to quit on his head tenant and an agreement by him not to serve a counter-notice the same as a surrender. In *Gisborne* v. *Burton*[158] the tenant was the landlord's wife, who sub-let to Burton (the real tenant). After the landlord's death, his personal representatives served notice to quit on his widow, who served no counter-notice. By a majority, it was held that termination of the wife's head lease destroyed Burton's security. Against that must be set Ralph Gibson L.J.'s dissent in *Gisbourne* on the basis that a collusive lease and sub-lease should not have been allowed to destroy security of tenure is much more convincing. So too in *Sparkes* v. *Smart*[159] a collusive

---

[154] At 485a, Lord Millett.
[155] *Mellor* v. *Watkins* (1874) L.R. 9 Q.B. 400, 405, Blackburne J.; *Phipos* v. *Callegari* (1910) 54 S.J. 635, Warrington J.
[156] [1995] Q.B. 192 C.A.; A.S. Price (1995) 46 *N.I.L.Q.* 215; P. Luxton & M. Wilkie [1995] *Conv.* 263.
[157] At 488b; *Pennell* v. *Payne* [1995] Q.B. 192 C.A.
[158] [1989] Q.B. 390 C.A.
[159] [1990] 2 E.G.L.R. 245 C.A.; J.E. Adams [1992] *Conv.* 63.

agreement between a tenant and his son-in-law (who had become landlord by purchase of the reversion) ended the head tenancy since the tenant did not serve a counter-notice claiming arbitration. But this was held not to destroy the sub-tenancy of the tenant's youngest son, who became a direct tenant of the freeholder when the head lease was ended. In other words the collusive agreement acted as a surrender. The Court of Appeal followed this line in *Barrett* v. *Morgan*.[160]

When this tangle reached the Lords in *Barrett*,[161] Lord Millett overruled *Sparkes* v. *Smart*, and also reversed the decision under appeal. Hence a collusive agreement between head landlord and head tenant is effective to wipe out the agricultural security of a sub-tenant. Lord Millett took the view that an agreement between the parties could not deprive a notice to quit of the effectiveness that it would have had without their consent or collusion.

The decision is sad. It is inherent in security schemes that the court must be astute to root out apparent agreements that are a pretence. The failure to follow this principle of residential tenancy law in the agricultural context threatens the security of many farmers. Landlord and tenant law is so horribly complex because landlords are not required to observe the spirit of the security legislation while following its letter.

G. AGRICULTURAL HOLDINGS: SUCCESSION RIGHTS

This section applies only to agricultural holdings—there are no succession rights to a farm business tenancy. Succession rights may arise on the death of the sole tenant of an agricultural holding. Survivorship will occur on the death of any of the joint tenants until the tenants are reduced to a single survivor, and on his death a succession may occur.

1. Tenancies granted up to 1984

If an agricultural holding was granted before mid 1984,[162] a relative of the deceased tenant who has worked on the farm may have the very valuable[163] right to claim a succession to the tenancy. If a tenancy qualifies by the date of its initial[164] grant, a succession to the tenancy is possible on the death of the first tenant, followed by a second succession on the new tenant's death, but a line is drawn to prevent a third devolution.[165] Hence a landlord conceded possession for a maximum of three generations.

Eligibility depends upon two things. First, the successor must show a close family relationship to the deceased tenant.[166] Second, he must show an economic interest in the tenancy before the death, shown by two separate sub-requirements: (1) the occupancy condition requires that the successor has been employed on the holding for five

---

[160] [1998] 4 All E.R. 179 C.A.

[161] [2000] 1 All E.R. 481 H.L.

[162] See below n. 171.

[163] *Layzell* v. *Smith Morton & Long* [1992] 1 E.G.L.R. 169.

[164] Succession rights are preserved on renewal of a pre-1984 tenancy.

[165] A.H.A. 1986 s.37; C.P. Rodgers [1984] *Conv.* 207; Woodfall 21.159–21.216. This consolidates Ag.(M.P.)A. 1976 which was retrospective. See also J.F. Mackeson (1972) 36 *Conv. (N.S.)* 229.

[166] Defined in s.35(2) to include spouse, brother, sister, child, or child of the family.

of the previous seven years[167]; and (2) the livelihood condition requires that the successor does not already occupy a commercial unit of agricultural land.[168] Qualification has to be established in front of the Agricultural Land Tribunal.[169] There is a broadly comparable procedure enabling a tenant farmer to retire at 65, with the intention of passing the tenancy on to a designated and qualifying successor.[170]

2. Grants between mid-1984 and autumn 1995

Succession rights to agricultural holdings were effectively removed for initial grants made after the Agricultural Holdings Act 1984 came into force in mid 1984: succession rights were conferred only if the tenancy expressly said so.[171] A fixed term tenancy exceeding two years will be terminated by the death itself if the death occurs more than one year before the term date.[172] If death occurs in the last year of a fixed term, it will continue for one year, but will expire on the first anniversary of the term date without attracting security of tenure.[173] Yearly tenancies granted after mid 1984 will not terminate automatically, but the tenancy can be ended by notice to quit.[174] A tenant who wishes to retire must give notice to quit and leave.[175]

3. Notice to quit where no succession

If a death occurs and there is no succession, a mandatory ground for possession arises under Case G.[176] The landlord has three months from receipt of a written notice of the tenant's death in which to serve notice to quit,[177] a notice to which there is no defence, and upon which no compensation rights accrue.

H. AGRICULTURAL HOLDINGS: REMOVAL OF SECURITY

The agricultural holdings legislation created a statutory system designed to protect agricultural tenants from unreasonable, oppressive and precipitate notices to quit,[178] by allowing the tenancy to continue except in a few exceptional cases in which a valid notice to quit is allowed. Of course, this section is not relevant to a farm business tenant who

---

[167] For a slight relaxation see *Littlewood* v. *Rolfe* [1981] 2 All E.R. 51; J.E. Martin [1982] *Conv.* 442.

[168] A.H.A. 1986 sch.6; annual Units of Production Orders, for 2000–2001 it is S.I. 2000/1984. The new tenant may have been farming at a loss: *Welby* v. *Casswell* [1995] 2 E.G.L.R. 1 C.A.

[169] s.39; S.I. 1984/1301; the time limit is 3 months from the day after the death; terms are fixed by arbitration: ss.47, 48.

[170] ss.49–58.

[171] s.34, as from July 12th 1984; C.P. Rodgers [1985] *Conv.* 111.

[172] s.4(2)(a).

[173] s.4(2)(b), subs.(3) preserves (compensation rights).

[174] As to leases for life, see s.25(2)(d).

[175] A mandatory ground for possession (case A) is available where the holding is a smallholding let after 1984 by a smallholdings authority where the tenant reaches retirement age, providing suitable alternative residential accommodation is provided: sch.3 part II paras 2–7.

[176] Any application for succession rights must be determined first: s.43.

[177] sch.3 para.12; *Lees* v. *Tatchell* [1990] 1 E.G.L.R. 10 (landlord's presence at tenant's funeral not notice in writing!; nor was receipt of rent cheque from executor); J.E. Martin [1991] *Conv.* 456.

[178] *National Trust* v. *Knipe* [1998] 1 W.L.R. 230, 237H, Judge L.J.

has no security. As Glidewell L.J. explained in *Rous* v. *Mitchell*[179] the procedure falls into two heads, and the initial notice must choose one or the other.

If the landlord intends to rely on a *discretionary ground* he does not need to spell out the ground in his initial notice. However, the tenant has the right to require the matter to be referred to the Agricultural Land Tribunal by serving a counter notice. No warning has to be given to the tenant, since notification of his rights is neither a statutory requirement nor one that can be implied.[180] The discretionary ground relied upon must be stated by the landlord when applying to the Tribunal for consent.[181] A number of specific grounds are stated[182] along with a more general ground of greater hardship.[183] Possession remains discretionary even if a ground is proved, since the Tribunal shall withhold its consent if "in all the circumstances it appears to them that a fair and reasonable landlord would not insist on possession".[184] Notice is of no effect unless the Agricultural Land Tribunal consents to it,[185] and this is not easy to obtain. Refusals are commonplace.

Eight *mandatory grounds* for possession are provided in which the consent of the Tribunal is not required[186]—these are discussed in the succeeding parts of this chapter. Title to possession is based on a precise statement of the exact ground relied upon in the notice.[187] Tenants may dispute that the alleged ground for possession actually exists, though only by arbitration,[188] and a notice is virtually conclusive in the absence of a request for arbitration. However the court retains a residual power to reject a notice that is based on fraudulent statements—meaning any made without honest belief in their truth. In *Rous* v. *Mitchell*[189] a notice was served on the basis of unlawful sub-lettings, but it was successfully challenged in court when it was shown that the landlord had in fact given permission for sub-letting other than for holiday lets, so that the statement that there had been unlawful sub-letting was known by the landlord to be untrue.

If a notice to quit is served and expires the lease ends, which means that if the tenant is allowed to continue in occupation and pay rent a new , tenancy is created.[190]

1.   Non-payment of rent

Case D(a) provides for possession where there is a remediable breach of covenant, including rent arrears. Possession is based on a demand notice, setting out the precise

---

[179] [1991] 1 W.L.R. 469, 475; *Cowan* v. *Wrayford* [1953] 1 W.L.R. 1340; *Mills* v. *Edward* [1971] 1 Q.B. 379 C.A.

[180] *Crawford* v. *Elliott* [1991] 1 E.G.L.R. 13 C.A.

[181] A.H.A. 1986 s.27(1).

[182] s.27(3): (a) good husbandry; (b) sound estate management; (c) agricultural research; (d) provision of allotments; (f) use for purposes other than for agriculture (where mandatory case B cannot be used).

[183] s.27(3)(e); *R.* v. *Agricultural Land Tribunal ex parte Parslow* [1979] 2 E.G.L.R. 1 Div.Ct. (desire to leave by will not hardship).

[184] s.27(2); the Tribunal may impose conditions by subss.(4)–(6).

[185] s.26; S.I. 1996/337 (fees).

[186] sch.3 part I.

[187] *Rous* v. *Mitchell* [1991] 1 W.L.R. 469 C.A.

[188] A.H. (Arbitration on Notices) O. 1987, S.I. 1987/710.

[189] [1991] 1 W.L.R. 469 C.A. Unsuccessful allegations of fraud were *Luttenberger* v. *N. Thoresby Farms Ltd.* [1992] 1 E.G.L.R. 261 C.A.; and *Omnivale* v. *Boldan* [1994] E.G.C.S. 63 C.A. (landlord genuinely believed statement of extent of land was correct).

[190] *Lower* v. *Sorrell* [1963] 1 Q.B. 959.

arrears, requiring payment of those arrears, and allowing at least two months for pay-ment.[191] Payment is not made by an unsigned cheque[192] or one that bounces.[193] Termination can follow immediately after the permitted two months expire,[194] there being no equity to extend the time.[195] Within that time the tenant may challenge the notice by arbitration (and only by arbitration[196]) on the basis that the rent is not due perhaps because of failure to serve the statutory notice giving details of the landlord's address for service,[197] or that a set off should be allowed for the landlord's disrepair.[198] Failure to demand arbitration or to pay what is properly demanded results in a manda-tory ground for possession.

2. Other misconduct by the tenant

Bad husbandry is a ground for possession. Agricultural tenants are required to comply fully with the rules of good husbandry, ignoring any trivial complaints.[199] Landlords have two grounds for attack on the tenant's methods. The best is to apply to the Agricultural Land Tribunal for a certificate that the tenant has not been farming in accordance with the rules of good husbandry, after which notice to quit is given within six months from the certificate and Case C provides a mandatory ground for posses-sion.[200] Failure of good husbandry also provides a discretionary ground for possession if the landlord can show that termination is in the interests of good husbandry respect-ing the land treated as a separate unit.[201] Here the landlord serves notice first, and the tenant serves a counter-notice, which refers the case to the Agricultural Land Tribunal, and denies the allegations of bad husbandry. Consent to the operation of the notice to quit should be refused by the Tribunal if a fair and reasonable landlord would not insist on possession.

Remediable breach of covenant is dealt with by a notice procedure reminiscent of that used to forfeit a lease for disrepair. The landlord is required to serve a notice in advance on the tenant specifying what breach has occurred, requiring remedy of the breach,[202] and allowing at least six months and possibly longer if remedial work requires even more time.[203] The tenant may refer a notice alleging a failure to do work to the Tribunal

---

[191] S.I. 1987/711 (forms); *Dickinson* v. *Boucher* [1984] 1 E.G.L.R. 12 C.A. (notice invalid when it stated £650 instead of the correct figure £625).

[192] *Luttenberger* v. *N. Thoresby Farms Ltd.* [1993] 1 E.G.L.R. 3, Ferris J.; W.D.W. Barr (1994) 138 *S.J.* 175.

[193] *Hannaford* v. *Smallacombe* [1994] 1 E.G.L.R. 9 C.A.; M. Haley [1994] *J.B.L.* 302.

[194] *Stoneman* v. *Brown* [1973] 1 W.L.R. 459 C.A. (cheque posted before but received after expiration of land-lord's notice); *Beevers* v. *Mason* [1978] 2 E.G.L.R. 3 C.A. (notice expired December 22nd; cheque received on December 24th was on facts a valid discharge).

[195] *Stoneman* v. *Brown* as above, taking Cairns L.J.'s view in preference to that of Lord Denning M.R.

[196] *Magdalene College, Oxford* v. *Heritage* [1974] 1 W.L.R. 441.

[197] L.T.A. 1987 s.48; *Dallhold Estates (U.K.) Pty. Ltd.* v. *Lindsey Trading Properties Ltd.* [1994] 1 E.G.L.R. 93 C.A.; see above pp. 590–591.

[198] *Burton* v. *Timmis* [1987] 1 E.G.L.R. 1 C.A. (argument failed on facts); *Barribal* v. *Everett* [1994] E.G.C.S. 62 C.A. (rates set off only after payment); see below p. 647.

[199] *Price* v. *Romilly* [1960] 1 W.L.R. 1360, Diplock J.

[200] A.H.A. 1986 sch.3.

[201] s.27(3)(a).

[202] S.I. 1987/711 (forms).

[203] *Shepherd* v. *Lomas* [1963] 1 W.L.R. 962 (failure by landlord to provide materials for repair); *Wykes* v. *Davis* [1975] Q.B. 843 C.A. (7 months insufficient).

by counter-notice, in which case the landlord's notice only stands if the Tribunal consents to it.[204] Refusal prevents a further notice for one year unless there is a change of circumstances.[205] Possession is mandatory if the notice is not challenged by arbitration[206] once the time for remedial work has expired.

Repairing obligations are generally derived from Model Forms applicable to agricultural holdings,[207] though these may be overridden by express terms of the lease,[208] though the obligation to follow the rules of good husbandry is itself overriding. A notice and counter-notice procedure applies, with the notice being final if there is no response,[209] and any disputes resolved by arbitration.[210] Any sum recoverable each year is limited.[211] A landlord who has an obligation to repair can be compelled to do so by notice. At the end of the three month notice period[212] the tenant can take over the work and sue for the costs.

Irremediable breach of covenant falls within mandatory Case E where the breach materially prejudices the interest of the landlord.[213] However, where the tenant was sentenced to prison, and so broke a residence condition in the lease, it was held that the breach was remediable.[214]

It is likely that clauses about genetically engineered crops will become increasingly important.[215]

3. Death and insolvency

Following the *death* of a tenant, the landlord can usually serve notice to quit, that is unless it is a pre-1984 Act tenancy with a right to succession enforced.[216] A mandatory ground for possession arises under Case G. The landlord has three months from receipt of a written notice of the tenant's death[217] in which to serve notice to quit.[218] In *Lees* v. *Tatchell*[219] the requirement of *written* notice to the landlord to start time running in the favour of the tenant's personal representatives was applied over-literally, so that a landlord who had attended the tenant's funeral and had received rent from the tenant's executor was held not to have notice of his death! The notice to quit is short (less than a

---

[204] A.H.A. 1986 s.28.

[205] sch.3 para.10(1)(b).

[206] *Harding* v. *Marshall* [1983] 2 E.G.L.R. 1 C.A.; *Parrish* v. *Kinsey* [1983] 2 E.G.L.R. 13 C.A.

[207] A.H.A. 1986 s.7; S.I. 1973/1473 as amended by S.I. 1988/281.

[208] *Roper* v. *Prudential Assurance Co. Ltd.* [1992] 1 E.G.L.R. 5 Q.B.D.

[209] *Hammond* v. *Allen* [1994] 1 All E.R. 307, Owen J.

[210] *Tustian* v. *Johnston* [1993] 2 E.G.L.R. 8 C.A.

[211] *Grayless* v. *Watkinson* [1990] 1 E.G.L.R. 6 C.A.

[212] *Hammond* v. *Allen* [1994] 1 All E.R. 307, Owen J.

[213] Cases D and E are mutually exclusive: *Budge* v. *Hicks* [1951] 2 K.B. 335 C.A.

[214] *Sumnall* v. *Statt* [1984] 2 E.G.L.R. 4 C.A.

[215] R. Ramage [1998] *N.L.J.* 1524.

[216] Case G is not available until any application for succession rights is determined: s.43.

[217] On intestacy it has been held that the 3 month period does not run until administrators are appointed, so that case G is not relevant while title remains vested in the President of the Family Division (or now the Public Trustee): *B.S.C. Pension Fund Trustees* v. *Downing* [1990] 1 E.G.L.R. 4; J.E. Martin [1991] *Conv.* 456.

[218] A.H.A. 1986 sch.3 para.12; *Land* v. *Sykes* [1992] 1 E.G.L.R. 1 C.A.; J.E. Martin [1991] *Conv.* 456 (no implied grant of new tenancy from acceptance of rent after death of tenant); *Crawford* v. *Elliott* [1991] 1 E.G.L.R. 13 C.A. (form of notice).

[219] [1990] 1 E.G.L.R. 10.

year), there is no right for the tenant's personal representative to serve a counter-notice, consent from the Agricultural Land Tribunal is not required, any unauthorised assignee can be removed, and no compensation rights accrue.

Insolvency gives rise to a mandatory ground for possession (case F)[220] where the tenant was a bankrupt at the date of giving notice to quit. Short notice (that it less than a full year) is acceptable.[221]

4. Sub-letting

Unauthorised sub-lettings are common.[222] Landlords naturally wish to retain control of the selection of the tenant farmer and for this reason it is normal for an agricultural tenancy to restrict sub-letting. In such a case the head lease will be liable to termination for breach of covenant. The security provisions are inapplicable to termination for an irremediable breach of covenant. Mandatory case E applies and the notice to quit ends the head tenancy without the need for consent from the Agricultural Land Tribunal.

Authorised sub-tenancies are immune from action by the freeholder so long as the head tenant honours the rights of his sub-tenants but, as discussed above,[223] the sub-tenant is vulnerable if they collude together. This enables the freeholder and the head tenant to share the profits from development of the land without giving anything to the sub-tenant.

5. Use of property by landlord for agriculture

It is a discretionary ground for possession to show that the landlord requires it in the interests of *sound estate management*,[224] meaning management of the farm in the physical sense as opposed to by the landlord's financial interests.[225] Usually the landlord will own adjoining land but this is not essential.[226] Since the ground is discretionary it is necessary to weigh the interests of the two parties by considering whether a fair and reasonable landlord would insist on possession.[227]

Proposed use of the land for *agricultural schemes* is another discretionary ground for possession, if it can be shown to be desirable in the interests of good husbandry, sound management of the estate, research, or an allotment scheme. The Agricultural Land Tribunal must consent to the operation of the notice to quit,[228] and this will not be forthcoming if a fair and reasonable landlord would not insist on possession. Special rules apply where the minister requires the holding for amalgamation or reconstruction of holdings, when the tenant was warned of this possibility in advance.[229]

---

[220] A.H.A. 1986 sch.3 part I.
[221] s.25(2)(a).
[222] The position on an authorised sub-letting is considered above p. 618.
[223] See above at p. 618 n. 147.
[224] A.H.A. 1986 s.27(3)(a); *Evans* v. *Roper* [1960] 1 W.L.R. 814.
[225] *National Coal Board* v. *Naylor* [1972] 1 W.L.R. 908 C.A. (uneconomic term to provide electricity).
[226] *Greaves* v. *Mitchell* (1971) 222 E.G. 1395.
[227] A.H.A. 1986 s.27(2); *Evans* v. *Roper* [1960] 1 W.L.R. 814; *Purser* v. *Bailey* [1967] 2 Q.B. 500 C.A. (greater hardship to landlord's estate proved after his death).
[228] A.H.A. 1986 s.27(3)(a).
[229] sch.3 part I, case H.

6.   Use of the property by the landlord for non-agricultural purposes

Much use is made by landlords of the facility provided by the mandatory case B[230] to insist on recovering possession of an agricultural holding for some non-agricultural use. Case B applies after an express grant of planning permission, a statutory permission, or where the Crown has an exemption from the requirement of planning permission. *Bell* v. *McCubbin*[231] extended these cases in 1990 to a landlord with a deemed permission under a general development order, and to any other circumstance in which he would have the right to reuse the land for non-agricultural purposes. On the particular facts, a landlord obtained possession of a farmhouse under case B in order to sub-let the house himself. On that basis a tenant would never have the right to use any part of his holding for non-agricultural purposes, and so it proved necessary to tighten the wording of case B by amending legislation later in 1990.[232] The new wording ensures that express planning permission must be obtained—meaning a fresh permission[233]—before the landlord is entitled to take advantage of the mandatory ground to end the tenancy. Tight controls to the change of use of agricultural land make permission difficult to obtain. A lease was terminated to allow the landlord to use the land for mineral extraction under a planning permission in *Floyer-Acland* v. *Osmond*[234]; the Court of Appeal established that it was not necessary to establish a new planning use for the land, and it was sufficient that agricultural use would be excluded for the foreseeable future. The Crown continues its wider right to take land back into hand, for example for the purpose of afforestation of sheep walks in Wales.[235]

Once planning permission has been obtained, the notice to terminate the tenancy need not be a full year,[236] and a break clause to terminate a fixed term in these circumstances became a standard feature of most fixed term agricultural holdings.[237] The validity of the notice can be disputed through the arbitration process[238] and even if the notice is technically valid an estoppel may prevent the landlord from relying on it in order to claim possession. In a leading case, *John* v. *George*,[239] the tenant did not object to planning permission to reconstruct a fire damaged farmhouse because he believed that there was an agreement that the proceeds from selling the ruins would be used to build a new bungalow for the tenant. If the court rules that a lease has been properly terminated, for example by exercise of a break clause, there is no other avenue open for a challenge and it becomes an abuse of process to seek an injunction to require the land

---

[230] sch.3 part I as altered by A.H. (Amendment) Act 1990.

[231] [1990] 1 Q.B. 976 C.A.; C.P. Rodgers [1990] *Conv.* 217; to the contrary was *Minister of Agriculture, Fisheries and Food* v. *Jenkins* [1963] 2 Q.B. 317, 324, Lord Denning M.R.

[232] A.H. (Amendment) A. 1990 s.1.

[233] *Paddock Investments Ltd.* v. *Lory* [1975] 2 E.G.L.R. 5 C.A.

[234] [2000] E.G.C.S. 53 C.A.

[235] *Minister of Agriculture Fisheries and Food* v. *Jenkins* [1963] 2 Q.B. 317 C.A.

[236] A.H.A. 1986 s.25(2)(b); *Re Disraeli* [1939] Ch. 382; *Coates* v. *Diment* [1951] 1 All E.R. 890.

[237] *Rugby Joint Water Board* v. *Foottit* [1973] A.C. 202 H.L. (break clause did not cover compulsory purchase by the water board).

[238] A.H. (Arbitration on Notices) O. 1987, S.I. 1987/710; *Jones* v. *Gates* [1954] 1 W.L.R. 222 C.A.; *Cawley* v. *Pratt* [1988] 2 E.G.L.R. 6 C.A.

[239] [1996] 1 E.G.L.R. 7 C.A.

registry to enter a notice reflecting the existence of the lease.[240] Where a case falls outside case B, there is still a discretionary power for the Agricultural Land Tribunal to allow possession to enable the landlord to adopt a use other than for agriculture, but the Tribunal should allow the notice to stand only if a fair and reasonable landlord would insist on possession.[241]

It is generally possible to sever physical *parts* of a holding[242] and so remove from an agricultural lease any part for which planning permission is obtained for a non-agricultural use.[243] In fact this is usually essential since the mandatory ground is limited to the extent of the land included within the express planning permission.[244] However it is arguable that an artificial severance to a nominee merely in order to facilitate service of a notice to quit should be ignored.[245]

I.   AGRICULTURAL RENTS

Agricultural rents are determined by arbitration.[246]

1.   Agricultural holdings (grants before autumn 1995)

While a tenant exercises security of tenure, his landlord may well wish to increase the rent to ensure that he receives a proper return for his land, but the tenant should be protected against excessive rent increases. The parties to an agricultural holding can agree a new rent at any time, but otherwise either party may require arbitration.[247] Review may be upwards or downwards. For this reason, a landlord who makes a request for arbitration cannot withdraw it unilaterally.[248] The rent fixed should be the letting value on the terms of the existing tenancy taking into account any increases or decreases caused by the tenant, other than those required by the tenancy.[249] A notice procedure enables the rent to be increased to reflect landlord's improvements.[250] Changes made in 1984 omitted reference to the value on the open market and also instructed the arbitrator to ignore the scarcity of agricultural land.[251] Relevant issues include designation as an S.S.S.I., management agreements, and accrued compensation rights, and also the vital issue of milk quotas.[252] During any fixed contractual period, the rent can only be reviewed under a contractual review clause,[253] so the statutory machinery is restricted to a time

---

[240] *McLean Homes (North London) Ltd.* v. *Dace* [1997] E.G.C.S. 120, Blackburne J.

[241] A.H.A. 1986 s.27(2).

[242] L.P.A. 1925 s.140.

[243] A.H.A. 1986 ss.31–33.

[244] *Omnivale* v. *Boldan* [1994] E.G.C.S. 63 C.A.

[245] *Persey* v. *Bazley* [1983] 2 E.G.L.R. 3 C.A.; see also *Stiles* v. *Farrow* [1977] 1 E.G.L.R. 5.

[246] Woodfall 21.073–21.086 (agricultural holdings), 21.362–21.366 (farm business tenancies).

[247] A.H.A. 1986 s.12(3); the arbitrator must be appointed before the termination date: *Robinson* v. *Moody* [1994] 2 E.G.L.R. 16 C.A.

[248] *Buckinghamshire C.C.* v. *Gordon* [1986] 2 E.G.L.R. 8.

[249] A.H.A. 1986 s.12, sch.2 para.1.

[250] s.13; *Tummon* v. *Barclays Bank Trust Co. Ltd.* (1979) 39 P. & C.R. 300 (conversion of part to caravan site).

[251] A.H.A. 1986 s.12; *J.W. Childers Trustees* v. *Anker* [1996] 1 E.G.L.R. 1 C.A.; R. Gibbard (1996) 16 R.R.L.R. 22.

[252] Agriculture Act 1986 s.15.

[253] *J.W. Childers* as above.

when there is a periodic tenancy, any review operating from a termination date.[254] The rent is fixed for the first three years of the term,[255] and for three years from the last review under the same tenancy.[256]

2. Farm business tenancies

The Agricultural Tenancies Act 1995 more or less leaves the existing machinery in place. Initial rents are fixed by the market. Landlord and tenant are free to adopt any mechanical formula provided that the rent can move downwards as well as upwards, or can decide that it shall remain fixed.[257] However, a normal rent review clause (which is upwards only) fails this statutory test, meaning that either party may opt at any time to revert to the statutory basis for any later review.[258] A statutory review is triggered by a review notice, given at least 12 months before the rent is to be changed (though no longer than 24 months in advance).[259] Agreed review dates are respected, but otherwise the review date must fall at the end of a period of a periodic tenancy.[260] Ideally the identity of the arbitrator will be agreed, but otherwise there is a procedure to compel an appointment in the six-month period leading up to the review date.[261]

The rent is what is "properly payable under the holding" assessed as at the review date.[262] This may be more or less, or the existing rent may be confirmed as it is. It should be the rent at which the holding might reasonably be let on the open market between willing parties,[263] disregarding the tenant's occupation.[264] Terms of the tenancy that purport to define how the rent should be assessed on a statutory review are ignored,[265] but all other relevant factors are considered. Tenant's improvements are disregarded to the extent that they are made under contractual obligation, or are paid for or compensated by the landlord[266] and conversely the rent is not depreciated by tenant's disrepair.[267]

J. AGRICULTURAL COMPENSATION

Customary rights of agricultural tenants to compensation that were given statutory force in 1947, and continue in force for tenants of agricultural holdings. Rights of farm business tenants are much less extensive.[268] All are subject to arbitration.[269]

---

[254] A.H.A. 1986 s.12(1); *University College, Oxford* v. *Durdy* [1982] Ch. 413 C.A. (notice of increase in 1979 led to review from February 2nd 1981).

[255] Unless the lease contains a rent review procedure.

[256] *Mann* v. *Gardner* (1991) 61 P. & C.R. 1 C.A. (surrender of part and rent adjustment 1985; rent could not be increased until 1988 when 3 years would have passed).

[257] A.T.A. 1995 s.9.

[258] s.9.

[259] s.10.

[260] ss.10(5), 14, 11 (reversion divided).

[261] s.12.

[262] s.13(1).

[263] s.13(2).

[264] s.13(3).

[265] s.13(2).

[266] ss.13(3)–(5), 34.

[267] s.13(4).

[268] Woodfall 21.238–21.328 (agricultural holdings), 21.367–21.382 (farm business tenancies). Compensation is not liable to capital gains tax: *Davis* v. *Powell* [1977] 1 All E.R. 471.

[269] A.H.A. 1986 s.83; A.T.A. 1995 ss.28–30 (subject to agreement of some other method of dispute resolution).

1. Disturbance

This claim is available to tenants of agricultural holdings (grants up to autumn 1995), but not to farm business tenants. Compensatable disturbance occurs where a tenant under an agricultural holding is forced to leave by a notice to quit,[270] for example where the landlord obtains planning permission for a non-agricultural use, no compensation is payable if possession has been ordered as a result of the tenant's default.[271] The basic level of one year's rent can be increased to up to two year's worth if actual loss can be proved to that amount; additional compensation is added at a rate of four times the annual rent.[272] Compensation levels are increased where the landlord seeks possession for non-agricultural purposes.[273]

2. Improvements—agricultural holdings

On the termination of an agricultural holding, the tenant may obtain compensation for certain improvements.[274] Long-term improvements require consent, sometimes from the landlord (as with irrigation), but if he refuses or the work is of other kinds from the Tribunal.[275] Work with only short-term effects, such as application of fertiliser, may not require any consent.[276] No compensation rights accrue from compliance with statutory or customary requirements.[277] Essentially the measure of compensation is the increase in value of the holding, and the right to it can be rolled forward through successor tenancies.[278] Compensation rights cannot be excluded.[279]

Special provision was made for *milk quotas* attached to agricultural holdings. A milk quota[280] is a valuable asset which can be transferred with ownership of the farm,[281] held in trust and mortgaged,[282] even if it not strictly a property right and will not pass to a lender as an incident of a mortgage.[283] Compensation is payable[284] on variation in the holding—such as a partial surrender[285]—on termination,[286] or on termination of the farming partnership which is entitled to the quota.[287]

---

[270] ss.60(1), 60(6) (notice within last month of the tenancy), 63 (supplementary), 74 (parts), 75 (division of the reversion).

[271] s.61 referring to sch.3 part I.

[272] s.60(2)–(5).

[273] s.62.

[274] s.64.

[275] s.67, sch.7; *E.D. & A.D. Cooke Bourne (Farms) Ltd.* v. *Mellows* [1982] 2 All E.R. 208 C.A. (claim for £75,000 in respect of barn).

[276] sch.8 (notice is required by s.68); sch.9 (pre-1948 improvements).

[277] s.77.

[278] s.69.

[279] ss.78, 74–75 (parts).

[280] S.I. 1986/1530.

[281] *R.* v. *Ministry of Agriculture, Fisheries and Food ex parte Cox* [1993] 1 E.G.L.R. 17 Q.B.D.

[282] *Swift* v. *Dairywise Farms Ltd.* [2000] 1 All E.R. 320, Jacob J.

[283] *Harries* v. *Barclays Bank plc.* [1997] 2 E.G.L.R. 15 C.A.

[284] Agriculture Act 1986 s.13, sch.1; *Walker* v. *Crocker* [1992]] 1 E.G.L.R. 29 (letter sufficient); *Carson* v. *Cornwall C.C.* [1993] 1 E.G.L.R. 21 (valuation).

[285] *Holdcroft* v. *Staffordshire C.C.* [1994] E.G.C.S. 56 C.A.

[286] *Creear* v. *Fearon* [1994] 2 E.G.L.R. 12 C.A.

[287] *Faulks* v. *Faulks* [1992] 1 E.G.L.R. 9, Chadwick J.

3.   Improvements—farm business tenancies

Limited compensation rights are given to tenants under tenancies granted after autumn 1995 (in place of the scheme just described for agricultural holdings) both for improvements and for physical and intangible advantages such as planning permissions and milk quotas.[288] They cannot be excluded by agreement.[289] Consent from the landlord must be obtained in advance,[290] though refusals can be challenged by arbitration.[291] Compensation is based on the increase in value attributable to the improvement.[292] Rights to compensation have proprietary effect and are divided on physical division of the land.[293]

4.   Miscellaneous compensation rights restricted to agricultural holdings

Compensation is available for *tenant right,* such as the volume of growing crops,[294] planted seeds, pasturing, residual fertility value, and special farming systems.[295] *Damage caused by game* to agricultural holdings gives the tenant compensation rights if he has no right to kill the game that has caused the damage because "sporting" rights are reserved to the landlord. Animals covered include deer, pheasants, partridges, grouse, and black game, but not hares or rabbits.[296]

5.   Right to fixtures (old and new law)

Similar rights exist under both schemes, though the new law is rather stronger. A tenant of an agricultural holding has a statutory right to remove fixtures and buildings he has erected for two months after termination of his tenancy.[297] Contracting out of the compensation provisions was permitted.[298] Statutory compensation can be displaced by any contractual entitlement,[299] and is excluded for any item that the tenant is obliged to provide by the terms of his tenancy. Removal must cause no avoidable damage, and all damage caused must be made good. Removal by the tenants of an agricultural holding (that is under the old law) is dependent upon the rent being paid and covenants being performed. At least one month's notice must be given to the landlord who may elect to buy the fixture[300] and failure to give notice destroys both the right of removal and the compensation rights. Both of these requirements are dropped from the new law, but farm business tenancies may not exclude compensation rights.[301]

---

[288] A.T.A. 1995 ss.15, 16.

[289] s.26.

[290] ss.17, 18.

[291] ss.19, 22, 28–30.

[292] ss.20, 21 (planning permissions).

[293] ss.16 (must be attached to holding), 23 (successive tenancies), 24–25 (parts).

[294] The common law attempted to provide some protection through the law of emblements, which ensured that a tenant had the right to come back onto the land at the end of a lease and reap crops which he had sown.

[295] A.H.A. 1986 ss.65, 70, sch.8 part II.

[296] s.20; there is no corresponding provision for farm business tenants.

[297] s.10.

[298] *Premier Dairies Ltd.* v. *Garlick* [1920] 2 Ch. 17.

[299] *Mears* v. *Callander* [1901] 2 Ch. 388 (glass houses erected without consent and so not compensatable).

[300] *Re Harvey & Mann* (1920) 89 L.J.K.B. 687 C.A.

[301] A.T.A. 1995 s.8(6)–(7).

23

FREEDOM OF BUSINESS CONTRACT

Express terms. Implied terms. Standardisation of terms. Statutory protection.
Law Commission reform. Substantive protection.

It is a fundamental tenet of the law of landlord and tenant that the terms of leases are left for negotiation in a free market, and it is also commonly said that no protection is needed for tenants who are themselves in business. This chapter explores this concept of the sanctity of contracts and the underlying assumption that the market provides a sufficient control on the activities of bad commercial landlords.

A. TERMS

1. Express terms

Most leases contain detailed terms regulating the interrelationship of landlord and tenant in the form of covenants—promises by deed each side makes to the other—or corresponding equitable or contractual obligations in informal leases. Given that it has priority, an informal agreement is just as good as a formal covenant by deed.[1]

Traditional leases followed a common format: the habendum (the creation of the term for a particular period) was followed by the parcels (a description of the land let), the reddendum (the reservation of the rent), landlords' covenants and tenants' covenants. Leases were characterised by archaic language, and comprehension was severely impeded by the division of obligations between landlord and tenant. Plain English has greatly improved modern drafting: subjects are grouped into topics making them much easier for non-lawyers to understand. To take one example (admittedly little used in practice) the Law Society's Standard Business Lease covers in turn such matters as rent, rates and taxes, use, access, the condition of the property, transfer, control by the landlord, rent review, damage to the property, quiet enjoyment, insurance, forfeiture, and return of the property at the end of the lease.

2. Implication in leases—business efficacy

Terms may be implied into leases under contractual rules, but only on the basis of necessity. This test is much too restrictive: very often commercial leases are defectively drafted simply because of the complexity of the issues, and it would be much better if terms could be implied when it was reasonable to do so. The exhaustive style of drafting

---

[1] *System Floors Ltd. v. Ruralpride Ltd.* [1995] 1 E.G.L.R. 48 C.A.

necessitated by our current law is an attempt to provide for every contingency, but the more that is said the more likely it is that there are hidden gaps.

Implication is limited to terms that are necessary to give business efficacy to the lease. In *Liverpool City Council* v. *Irwin*[2] the House of Lords highlighted both the possibility of implying terms relating to common parts of a building outside the control of individual tenants, and the possible inadequacy of those terms. The case concerned the Piggeries, a notorious block of high-rise flats in Liverpool. Tenants signed tenancy agreements relating to individual flats, which impose obligations on the tenants but not on landlords, so that there was scope for implying terms against the landlords. They provided communal lifts and garbage disposal units. Since the tenancy agreements made no reference to any communal facilities, it was necessary to imply rights in the nature of easements to make use of them, a necessity not contested in view of the height of the tower blocks. Realistically the flats were not habitable if the tenants had to use the stairs. More pressing was the question whether the landlord was under an obligation to maintain the facilities. A duty was implied, but it was limited to doing what was reasonable in the circumstances. Since damage to the lifts was attributable to repeated vandalism, which was beyond the control of the council landlords, there was no breach of duty on the facts of the case. The flats remained useless, and ultimately it became necessary to blow up the block. The result would have been radically different if a full repairing covenant could have been implied, since in that case the landlord would have been obliged to keep the lifts in working order irrespective of the reason for the disrepair.

Numerous other cases on repair,[3] the provision of facilities,[4] and insurance[5] demonstrate the inadequate scope of contractual implication.

3.   Contracts

It is not necessary to enter into any formal agreement before executing a lease, and if the terms are all agreed in advance and the tenant is to take up occupation immediately the practice may well be to dispense with the earlier stage. However contracts[6] are essential if there are conditions to be fulfilled before the terms of the lease come into force (for example because the landlord agrees to do some repair work) or if the tenant is to take possession at some future time, and they will also be usual where there is a substantial premium paid for the right to the lease.[7] The only safe course is to agree the precise terms of the lease and to refer to them in the contract.

4.   Implication in contracts—usual covenants

Terms for a lease can be agreed simply by settling upon the property, the rent, the parties, and the commencement date. Specific performance is then granted on terms

---

[2] [1977] A.C. 239 H.L.; D. McIntyre [1977] *C.L.J.* 15; these issues are discussed fully in contract texts.

[3] *Sleafer* v. *Lambeth M.B.C.* [1960] 1 Q.B. 43 C.A.; J.C. Hall [1960] *C.L.J.* 40; *Barrett* v. *Lounova (1982) Ltd.* [1990] 1 Q.B. 348 C.A.; *Duke of Westminster* v. *Guild* [1985] Q.B. 668 C.A.; *Hafton Properties Ltd.* v. *Camp* [1994] 1 E.G.L.R. 67.

[4] *Chorley B.C.* v. *Ribble Motor Services Ltd.* (1997) 74 P. & C.R. 182 C.A. (no implied obligation to provide toilets in lease of bus station).

[5] See below pp. 685–690.

[6] Woodfall 16.008–16.038; also ch.4.

[7] A protective registration is essential; see above p. 520.

settled by counsel. Traditionally there was a list of recognised covenants that were "usual" in a technical sense that would be included. Examples were not to cause an inconvenience to neighbours, to permit re-entry on breach of covenant,[8] not to assign without consent,[9] and to pay all costs in the grant of the lease.[10] However the list was very deficient since covenants that are universal in modern practice did not figure. Flexibility has been restored by a decision in 1981,[11] which held that usual covenants are those commonly met with in practice. Argument is best avoided by providing a formula for determining what covenants to include—perhaps all other covenants reasonably required by the landlord[12]—or better still to spell out the proposed terms in as much detail as in the formal lease which follows.

5.   Rectification

A lease may be rectified to ensure that it reflects the preceding agreement accurately.[13]

B.   STANDARDISATION OF TERMS

1.   Institutional lease

Landlords will not be able to demand more than a market rent or impose particularly harsh terms, without causing their property to stand empty. Indeed during the 1990s one did see the market actively at work. At its start there was a common form of lease acceptable to institutional investors. The editor of the *Encyclopaedia of Forms and Precedents*[14] identifies the terms agreed before the recession of the 1990s as these: a 25 year term, five yearly upwards only rent reviews, rent quarterly in advance, all repairs, services and insurance to be paid for the tenant, tight control of use, a qualified right to assign, sureties, original tenant liability, and the right of termination on breach of any covenant or insolvency. The recession led to shorter terms, agreement to allow rent review in a downward direction. It was also common to draft the privity of contract liability so that it ended on an assignment, though this last point has in any event fallen by the wayside as a result of the legislative reforms in 1995[15]; institutional investors now insist that a tenant offer an Authorised Guarantee Agreement before being allowed to assign. The industry has also developed standards for other forms of commercial lease such as building agreements and development agreements.[16]

---

[8]   *Flexman* v. *Corbett* [1930] 1 Ch. 672 (the first is usual only on a large estate).

[9]   *Hampshire* v. *Wickens* (1878) 7 Ch.D. 555.

[10]   *Allen* v. *Smith* [1924] 2 Ch. 308; Costs of Leases Act 1958.

[11]   *Chester* v. *Buckingham Travel Ltd.* [1981] 1 W.L.R. 96; G. Woodman (1981) 97 *L.Q.R.* 381; J.E. Adams [1980] *Conv.* 92; *Flexman* v. *Corbett* [1930] 1 Ch. 672; L. Crabb [1992] *Conv.* 18 (older cases).

[12]   This was held to be sufficiently certain in *Sweet & Maxwell Ltd.* v. *Universal News Services Ltd.* [1964] 2 Q.B. 699 C.A.; D. Macintyre [1965] *C.L.J.* 41.

[13]   Sparkes *N.L.L.* 236–237.

[14]   Vol.22(1) para.172.

[15]   See below Chapter 28.

[16]   J. Vivian & B. Dear [1999] 36 *P.L.J.* 19.

2.   Law Commission

Early in the life of the Law Commission, considerable emphasis was placed on the programme to rationalise the law of landlord and tenant with a view to making leases
shorter and more comprehensible.[17] Statutory obligations and overriding terms (such
as quiet enjoyment and non-derogation from grant) were envisaged, coupled with a
series of defaults that would operate as the terms of the agreement unless the parties
exercised their freedom. A sharp division would have been created between commercial
and residential leases since contracting out would have been severely restricted in the
domestic sector, whereas most terms of commercial leases would remain open to negotiation with an irreducible core of standard covenants. Later work[18] added the suggestion of key words, which would trigger the implication of a standard term, though it was
recognised that any scheme for commercial tenants would be voluntary, since landlords
would not accept compulsion.[19] It also suggested action against misleading terms and
defective leases.[20] However, few of these very sensible proposals have been implemented,
and the thrust of the reform programme has shifted to basic land law and trusts, so that
any legislative standardisation of leasehold covenants is left as a distant prospect.

3.   Standard business leases

The Law Society has published standard forms of lease[21] for use in simple business situations, for example a shop with flat above or a single unit in a parade of shops or shopping arcade. The clauses must be incorporated in full, but with space for the insertion
of variable details (such as the parties, rent, review dates, length of the term and permitted use) and with the possibility of variation of the clauses. The standard clauses have
not been widely adopted, perhaps because landlords traditionally draft business leases,
and they see the Standard Business Lease as too fairly balanced between the interests of
the landlord and tenant. The British Property Federation has recently published a rival
set of forms for a short-term commercial lease, which is good enough to meet with the
approval of Professor Martin.[22] Negotiations should proceed under the Department of
the Environment Code of Practice.[23]

4.   Europe

Membership of the European Union has no direct impact on property law within the
Member States, but clearly participation in a common economic market will have some
impact on the commercial leasing practices of large commercial organisations. At
present there seem to be significant differences within the Union, with shorter leases

---

[17] Law Com. No.67 (1975).

[18] Law Com. No.162 (1987).

[19] Para. 3.16.

[20] Paras.3.19–3.21.

[21] S. Fogel & J. Ellison [1991] 38 *L.S.G.* 24; J. Adams (1991) 135 *S.J.* 826. M. Ansley & P. Freedman [1991] 24
L.S.G. 27; J.E. Martin [1991] 26 *E.G.* 78. The second edition (1996) is set out in Butterworth's *Encyclopaedia of
Forms and Precedents*, vol.22(1).

[22] J. Martin [1999] 18 *E.G.* 156; [1999] 16 *L.S.G.* 9; [1999] 29 *P.L.J.* 16.

[23] (1995); Butterworth's *Encyclopaedia of Forms and Precedents*, vol. 22(1); J.E. Adams [1996] *Conv.* 241. This is
not working well: J.E. Adams [2000] *Conv.* 372.

common in some states because rent review practice is less refined.[24] One might expect the emergence of a common standard for a lease of a supermarket or petrol station wherever it happens to be in Europe.

C. STATUTORY PROTECTION

Many old statutes continue in force, all of them having the fundamental objective of curbing the power of landlords.[25]

1. Distress

Legislative intervention is wide ranging, the object in all cases being to protect tenants and those outside the lease from abuses by the landlord.[26]

2. Forfeiture

There has been a consistent thread of Parliamentary intervention in forfeitures, essentially because of the potential for unjust enrichment of a landlord who terminates a lease with a significant capital value in response to a trivial default by the tenant. Georgian and Victorian legislation concentrated on abusive forfeitures arising from rent arrears, the Law of Property Act 1925 dealt with procedural protection is in relation to disrepair, and substantive protection against unfair dilapidation claims was introduced in 1938.[27] As explained below, activity is current in this field.[28]

3. Substantive nature of leases

The Birkenhead property legislation dealt with future leases, leases for life, perpetual renewal, defective leases, and the general scheme of estate ownership.[29]

4. Assignment

Legislative intervention in covenants to assign has aimed to ensure that landlords do not exploit their rights for financial gain,[30] that they act with substantive justice towards their tenants,[31] and more recently that substantive rights are not affected by procedural inertia, this last being an exemplar of what the Law Commission can achieve.[32]

5. Renewal rights

This is the main area of statutory intervention in business leases, the two successive waves of reform in 1927 and 1954 being explained elsewhere, as is Law Commission

---

[24] D. Ryland [1992] 26 *E.G.* 110; T. Thornton [1999] 10 *E.G.* 173; A. Hurndale, *Property in Europe: Law and Practice* (Butterworths, 1999).

[25] Law Com. No.162 (1987) paras.2.5–2.7.

[26] See below pp. 650–653.

[27] See below Chapter 23. L.T.A. 1927 s. 18 applies corresponding protection in relation to damages.

[28] See below Chapter 29.

[29] L.P.A. 1922 s.145; L.P.A. 1925 ss.139–154.

[30] L.P.A. 1925 s.144.

[31] L.T.A. 1927 s.19.

[32] LTA 1988; see below Chapter 27.

involvement in tidying up the legislation.[33] General recognition exists of the need to protect business tenants in their occupation of a particular trading position, a protection that is quite inconsistent with the perception that business agreements are sacrosanct.

6. Agricultural tenure

The former protection for agricultural holdings, and much reduced protection for farm business tendencies, is explained elsewhere.[34]

7. Running of covenants

First introduced by statute in 1540, and progressively refined, these rules were originally designed to benefit landlords. Eventually, however, it became clear that they were worked very strongly against the interests of tenants, primarily because the original tenant (T0) remained liable on privity of contract throughout the duration of the lease. Law Commission proposals led to the enactment of the Landlord and Tenant (Covenants) Act 1995 to remove this on-going liability; this remains the most notable success for the Law Commission in the field of landlord and tenant law.

8. Conclusion

This brief review shows how Parliament has consistently intervened in commercial leases to redress the inherent imbalance that exists between a landlord who commands a scarce resource of land and a tenant who seeks access to it. There are many areas where Parliamentary intervention would greatly facilitate the operation of a smooth market; examples are ratchet rent review clauses,[35] banning abusive negotiating practices and unfair terms in commercial contracts, dealing with extortionate service charges, and providing a remedy for the many defectively drafted commercial leases.[36]

D. LAW COMMISSION

Item VIII of the First Programme of Reform proposed by the Law Commission was the Codification of the Law of Landlord and Tenant. Admittedly codification was a distant prospect even then—not an objective and not immediately attainable. In 1971 it was still thought likely that a code could be produced within four years.[37] Enactment was bound to fall short of that high goal, but it is questionable whether it should have been expected to fall so far short.

Undoubtedly the most successful area for Commission activity has been in consolidation, particularly in relation to security of tenure schemes.

---

[33] See above pp. 564–565.
[34] See below Chapter 22.
[35] See below pp. 658–660.
[36] Protection in all these cases is limited to residential leases; see below p. 638.
[37] Law Com. No. 162 (1987) para.1.8.

1. Tabulation of Law Commission work on security of tenure.

Law Com. Report	W.P. or C.P.	Topic consolidated or amended	Result
17 (1969)	W.P. 7 (1967)	Renewable business leases	L.P.A. 1969
81 (1977)		Rent Bill	R.A. 1977
144 (1985)		Housing Acts	H.A. 1985 etc.
153 (1985)		Agricultural Holdings	A.H.A. 1986
208 (1992)	W.P. 111 (1988)	Renewable business leases	

Work on substantive reform has been less impressive as the following table shows.

2. Tabulation of Law Commission work on business property (excluding security of tenure)

Law Com No.	Law Com W.P./C.P.	Topic	Implementation
5 (1966)		Distress for rent (interim)	
67 (1975)	W.P. 8 (1967)	Obligations of landlord and tenant	
141 (1985)	W.P. 25 (1970)	Restrictions on Dispositions, Alterations and Change of Use	L.T.A. 1988
142 (1985)	W.P. 16 (1968)	Forfeiture of tenancies	
161 (1987)		Leasehold Conveyancing	L.T.A. 1988
162 (1987)		Reform of the law	
174 (1988)	W.P. 95 (1986)	Privity of contract and estate	L.T. (Covenants) A. 1995
178 (1989)		Compensation for Tenant's Improvements	
194 (1991)	W.P. 97 (1986)	Distress for rent	
221 (1992)		Termination of Tenancies Bill	
238 (1996)	W.P. 123 (1992)	Responsibility for the State and Condition of Property	

It appears that the work on forfeiture is nearing fruition, so that, according to the 33rd Annual Report[38] spring 2000 should see the publication of a second bill (now retaining peaceable re-entry). However, there is no sign of any consensus about what reform is desirable in relation to repairing covenants or the general terms of commercial leases and no Consultation Paper has been published since 1992. Some Law Commission projects have been subsumed into wider reviews—for example forfeiture as an aspect of the enforcement of civil judgments, and fitness standards as a part of a wider review of housing law.[39] However the innate restriction of the Commission to non-contentious reform makes it an unsuitable vehicle to tackle the commercial property lobby. Political

[38] Law Com. No.258 (1999) paras.5.5–5.6.
[39] 33rd *Annual Report,* Law Com. No. 258 (1999) paras.1.20–1.21.

momentum must be injected if there is to be any headway. It can only be a surprise that so little pressure for reform is exerted on behalf of commercial tenants.

E. SUBSTANTIVE PROTECTION

1. Oppression

Equity can protect against oppressive contracts,[40] but it is very hard to prove that businesses have been subject to oppression,[41] and there is no general intervention in hard dealings.[42] Stronger protections are needed against misleading and harsh terms.[43]

2. Unfair terms

It is uncertain whether the unfair terms provisions can operate to invalidate terms of leases. The statutory regime introduced in 1977 does not apply to land,[44] but it is open to argument whether the European-based[45] Unfair Terms in Consumer Contracts Regulations 1999 do apply to some transactions with land,[46] but only if the tenant is a consumer, defined as a natural person who is acting for purposes that are outside his business. Leases to companies and all other commercial leases certainly fall outside the Regulations.

3. Fundamental rights

Rights are laid down in the European Convention on Human Rights and, although many of them are available exclusively to humans, the right to property[47] is available to any legal person—including companies and building societies,[48] as well as individuals. The right to a home under Article 8 has been held to apply to business premises.[49] So sole traders may well be able to take advantage of a number of the Convention rights. It seems likely that many commercial sector cases will turn on challenges to the fairness of a hearing,[50] and in this connection it has been suggested that peaceable re-entry and distress may be open to challenge.[51]

---

[40] Snell's *Equity* (Sweet & Maxwell, 30th ed. by J. McGhee, 2000) ch.38.

[41] *Multiservice Bookbinding Ltd.* v. *Marden* [1979] Ch. 84.

[42] *Lloyds Bank Ltd.* v. *Bundy* [1975] Q.B. 326, 339, Lord Denning M.R., is not generally accepted, though protection is desirable: M. Halliwell (1999) 14 *L.S.* 15; A. Phang [1995] *J.B.L.* 352; D. Capper (1998) 114 *L.Q.R.* 479.

[43] Law Com. No.162 (1987) paras.3.19–3.21.

[44] Unfair Contract Terms Act 1977 sch.1 para.1(6); *Electricity Supply Nominees Ltd.* v. *I.A.F. Group plc.* [1993] 1 W.L.R. 1059; *Havenridge* v. *Boston Dyers Ltd.* [1994] 2 E.G.L.R. 73 C.A.; *Star Rider Ltd.* v. *Inntrepreneur Pub Co. Ltd.* [1998] 1 E.G.L.R. 53.

[45] Dir.93/13 [1993] O.J. L95/29.

[46] S.I. 1999/2083.

[47] Art. 1 of Protocol 1; see above pp. 200–208.

[48] *National & Provincial B.S.* v. *U.K.* (1998) 25 E.H.R.R. 127.

[49] *Niemietz* v. *Germany* (1992) 16 E.H.R.R. 97.

[50] S. Gerlis [2000] 23 *L.S.G.* 51; see above p. 205.

[51] *Langborger* v. *Sweden* (1989) 12 E.H.R.R. 416; A. Bruce [2000] *N.L.J.* 462.

24

BUSINESS RENTS

Rent obligations. Quantum. Payment of rent. Defences and deductions. Action for rent. Distress. Recovery of overpayments. Suspension. Determining business rents. Rent review clauses. Open market rents. Crude forms of review. Interim rents. Rates and taxes.

Rent[1] is the dominant fact of commercial life. Some 60 per cent of business premises are rented. This allows flexibility in business planning, easing the move to larger or more central premises when the business succeeds and retrenchment when business is poor. Businesses have therefore to balance the need to find property that is affordable with the fact that prime trading sites will always command a scarcity premium.

Commercial landlords are primarily involved in the market as investors, putting money into buying a freehold estate or leasehold reversion, intending to obtain a secure rental stream in the future, and also hoping that the capital value of the land will increase. Historically commercial property has been a good investment—indeed, perhaps the best—since along with the income yield, there has also been an inexorable growth in the capital value of prime commercial sites. The planning system in force since the Second World War limited the land suitable for business use and so has inevitably pushed up the value of what is available. The market reached a new high in 1998 with a maximum rental in the City of £52.50 a square foot.[2]

Modern practice is to create a full repairing lease that imposes all obligations of repair and insurance on the tenant, called a "clear lease", meaning that the rent is received by the landlord as a pure profit. The only deduction is income or corporation tax. The guarantee this provides against any fluctuation in the landlord's income yield is of great value, and one that substantially increases the capital value of the reversion.[3]

A. RENT OBLIGATIONS

Lord Diplock stated the modern understanding of the nature of rent obligations when he stated in *United Scientific Holdings Ltd.* v. *Burnley B.C.*[4] that:

---

[1] Woodfall chs.7–10, 12, 19; Bright & Gilbert 417–489; Davey 36–37, chs.6, 9, 10; Evans & Smith (5th) ch.8; Garner (2nd) 60–66.

[2] i.e £565 a square metre; [1999] 23 *E.G.* 43.

[3] *O.May* v. *City of London Real Property Co.* [1983] 2 A.C. 726 H.L.

[4] [1978] A.C. 904, 935A.

"The medieval concept of rent as a service rendered by the tenant to the landlord has been displaced by the modern concept of a payment which a tenant is bound by his contract to pay to the landlord for the use of his land."

That compensation may be payable to a landlord either in contract or in restitution.

1. Contractual obligations

Landlords invariably agree with their tenants what rent is to be paid for a property. Most business leases are created by deed, and if so the promise to pay the rent will take the form of a covenant.[5] A formal reservation of rent (traditionally called a reddendum) has the same effect, the traditional phrase "yielding and paying" being equal to an express covenant. Informal short term legal leases (for three years or less) and equitable leases are not by deed and so the rent obligation is not technically a covenant, but the corresponding contractual obligation has much the same effect. An equitable lease is valid only if the rent to be paid is agreed, since this term is one essential of the validity of a contract for a lease,[6] but if the agreement is valid it will create what is effectively an equitable rent.[7] Until the Judicature Act 1873 there was a fundamental distinction between a rent created by deed and recognised by the common law—which was enforceable by the common law action for covenant—and a purely contractual obligation. However, since the abolition of the forms of action in 1875 all rent has to be pursued in contract, and there is no longer any merit in maintaining a distinction between common law rents and equitable rents. [8] This consideration is the dominant force in the move to see leases as contractual entities rather than as estates in the land.

It is a fundamental of the law of landlord and tenant that entitlement to rent ends when the duration of the lease ends, subject to any statutory extension. Whether rent is due in the future depends upon whether either party is able to terminate the lease and so stop rent running. As Lord Millett observed in *Re Park Air Services plc.*:

"[R]ent is not a simple debt. It is the consideration for the right to remain in possession . . .. Its existence depends upon future events. Rent in respect of a future rental period may never become payable at all. Rent payable in future under a subsisting lease cannot be treated as a series of future debts making up a pure income stream."[9]

One unusual illustration of this principle arose in *Oliver Ashworth (Holdings) Ltd.* v. *Ballard (Kent) Ltd.*[10] The landlord claimed double rent because (it said) the tenant was holding over after the tenant had served a break notice to end the lease, a claim which the tenant defended on the basis that the landlord had also sued for rent, and so had elected not claim double rent. The Court of Appeal ruled that this was not a case of elective waiver: no rent was due under the agreement since the contractual claim had in fact

---

[5] *Royton Industries Ltd.* v. *Lawrence* [1994] 1 E.G.L.R. 110, Aldous J.
[6] See above p. 520 n. 138.
[7] *Walsh* v. *Lonsdale* (1882) 21 Ch.D. 9 C.A.
[8] Also *Walsh* v. *Lonsdale*.
[9] [1999] 1 All E.R. 673, 682g, Lord Millett.
[10] [2000] Ch.12 C.A.; S. Murdoch [1999] 23 *E.G.* 142; [1998] 3 E.G.L.R. 60 Ch.D. reversed.

been ended by the break clause. As Laws L.J. observed since the break clause was valid the landlord had no right to continuing rent.[11]

2.   Compensation for use

A person may become a tenant at a time when there is no contractual agreement to pay rent. This is likely to occur in only two situations: where the potential tenant enters property with a view to taking a lease of it at a time when negotiations are continuing, or where an existing tenant holds over with his landlord's permission during negotiations for a new lease. In these two cases if the licensee passes over the threshold and becomes a tenant, there is an obligation to pay reasonable compensation for use and occupation. This may be assessed on the letting value [12] but any agreement about the rent may be used as evidence.[13] A tenant may also be liable where a sub-tenant retains occupation,[14] though not where the sub-tenant has security of tenure.[15]

The action for compensation for use and occupation is restitutionary in character. Until recently this was expressed as a quasi-contract,[16] but developments in restitution law mean that it is now based on the unjust enrichment of the tenant that occurs if he occupies property belonging to the landlord without providing reasonable compensation for his occupation of it.[17] No agreement is required, though the action is quasi-contractual in a negative sense since it can be excluded by a clear agreement that occupation is to be rent-free; a rent is not an essential ingredient of a valid lease.[18] A statutory remedy is also available.[19]

3.   Rent and double rent after termination of the lease

If a former tenant continues in occupation after *hostile* termination of his lease—by forfeiture or after a notice to quit has expired—he is in the same position as any other trespasser and so liable to compensate the owner for *mesne profits*.[20] A previous rack rent[21] is usually a good estimate of the level of mesne profits.

A penalty of *double rent* is imposed by the Distress for Rent Act 1737[22] provides that a tenant holding over against the wishes of his landlord is liable to compensate the landlord with double rent. This might arise, for example, where the landlord serves a notice to quit that has expired in circumstances in which the tenant has no renewal rights. Unusual facts arose in *Oliver Ashworth (Holdings) Ltd. v. Ballard (Kent) Ltd.*[23] The tenant served a notice under a break clause to terminate his lease, but the landlord disputed its validity and the tenant remained in occupation. That the notice was valid became

---

[11] Nevertheless the claim to double rent failed for reasons explained below.
[12] Woodfall ch.10; *Lewisham L.B.C.* v. *Masterson* [2000] 1 E.G.L.R. 134 C.A.
[13] *Canterbury Cathedral Dean & Chapter* v. *Whitbread plc.* [1995] 1 E.G.L.R. 82.
[14] *Ibbs* v. *Richardson* (1839) 9 Ad. & El. 849, 112 E.R. 1436.
[15] *Watson* v. *Saunders-Roe Ltd.* [1947] K.B. 437 C.A.
[16] *Thetford* v. *Tyler* (1845) 8 Q.B. 95, 1020, 115 E.R. 810.
[17] A. Burrows, *The Law of Restitution* (Butterworths, 1993).
[18] *Ashburn Anstalt* v. *Arnold* [1989] Ch. 1, 9E–10C, Fox L.J.
[19] Distress for Rent Act 1737 s.14.
[20] See below pp. 806–807.
[21] This is obviously not so with a ground rent.
[22] s.18; Woodfall 19.011–19.029; Evans & Smith (5th) 261–264.
[23] [2000] Ch. 12 C.A.; S. Murdoch [1999] 23 *E.G.* 142; [1998] 3 E.G.L.R. 60 Ch.D. reversed.

clear as a result of the House of Lords decision in *Mannai*,[24] and so the landlord changed tack and claimed double rent on the basis of the holding over after the termination of the tenant's lease. The Court of Appeal ruled that this was not a case for double rent. The statutory wording did not cover a case where the tenant held over only because his landlord asserted that the lease was continuing. The penalty attached only if the landlord treated an ex-tenant as a trespasser, that is the tenant had received a notice to quit which had expired and he was wilfully holding over against the wishes of his landlord.

B.   QUANTUM

1.   Sum

A rent is a periodical payment for the use of land. Broadly speaking there are two methods by which a landlord can be compensated for giving up the physical use of his land. Short leases tend to reserve a rack rent, that is a rent reflecting the full periodic value of the land,[25] which is usual for short residential tenancies, but is also very common for renewable leases of shops and offices. Normally the lease has no inherent value, because the full economic value of the land is paid periodically to the landlord, but it is possible for a rack rental lease to attract a positive value if the rent is slightly below market levels or a negative value if the market rents fall so that the rent payable under the lease is expensive.

Leases for longer terms are usually bought with an initial capital payment (a premium), the tenant paying a much smaller annual ground rent.[26] This kind of arrangement is usual for the ownership of houses and flats, and is also common for some kinds of commercial arrangements. Building leases are one example where a developer pays a landowner for the right to develop his land, being granted a lease of the finished building that he can exploit by granting sub-leases. An investor may buy a long-term lease of an entire office block, which he will not be able to renew because he is not in occupation of it, but which he will be able to exploit by granting sub-leases of individual suites of offices. Indeed some rents are purely nominal, the tradition being to reserve a symbolic single peppercorn, payable only if demanded. It is important that the tenant should be able to realise his capital investment either by sale or by sub-letting.

2.   Value Added Tax

This tax was imposed on commercial rents[27] after *European Commission* v. *United Kingdom*[28] held that zero rating of the construction and disposal of commercial buildings infringed European law. Under the new scheme a landlord may elect whether or not to charge V.A.T. Rent-free periods allowed at the start of a lease were originally

---

[24] See above pp. 571–573.

[25] *Compton Group Ltd.* v. *Estates Gazette Ltd.* (1977) 36 P. & C.R. 148.

[26] Ground rents may or may not be reviewable. Contrast a rentcharge where freehold land was (before the Rentcharges Act 1977 took effect in early 1978) sold subject to an annual rent.

[27] Value Added Tax Act 1994 sch.10.

[28] *Case 416/85* [1988] S.T.C. 456.

exempt,[29] but it is now the policy to charge for them.[30] Sureties may also be liable.[31] Normally the liability of rent to V.A.T. is a matter of small moment to a tenant who is trading, since the tax paid on rent may be deducted from the V.A.T. due on sales, but special action is required if the tenant is exempt from V.A.T. [32] A recent case shows a problem when the property is sold: a landlord who has made a V.A.T. election on a property must charge V.A.T. on the sale price unless a written election not to do so was lodged with the Customs & Excise Commission before the date of the transfer—the crucial date is not when the sale is completed but when a deposit is paid to the seller (as opposed to a stakeholder) or on exchange of contracts.[33] To add insult to injury, stamp duty is chargeable on the V.A.T., though an infinite spiral is prevented by the rule that V.A.T. is not chargeable on that stamp duty.[34] Reserving the V.A.T. as additional rent can save money.

3. Variable rents

Rent must be certain, but this is necessarily so only when it is payable, since at that moment the tenant must know what he is required to do to discharge his obligations. There is nothing to prevent the rent varying over the duration of the lease, and in fact almost all commercial rents can be altered. Perhaps the best-known case law illustration is *Walsh* v. *Lonsdale,* in which a contract for a lease of a cotton mill provided for the rent to change according to the number of looms being run.[35] Rents can even be varied by a notice given by the landlord, a standard provision in tenancies of public-sector homes.[36] This was only workable because of the public law controls on what councils can charge their tenants, and no commercial tenant would ever agree to pay whatever his landlord demanded, unless perhaps there was an immediate right to terminate the lease in response to a rent increase notice.

Commercial leases generally provide for rent review, which adapts the rent payable under a particular lease to take account of increases in market rentals. The reason is obvious. Commercial leases are often granted for 25 year terms, but if one looks back now to 1975, one can appreciate the enormous increase in property values and rentals likely to occur over that time scale. So any lease at a rack rental is likely to include a provision for review of the rent—commonly every five years—which provides a mechanism for lifting the rental level to the market level at the review date. Rents are fixed in business leases only if the duration is very short.[37]

---

[29] *Neville Russell* v. *Customs & Excise* [1987] V.A.T.T.R. 194.
[30] M. Hynes [1993] *B.T.R.* 479; K. Stepien (1994) 138 *S.J.* 241.
[31] *Knighton Estates Ltd.* v. *Gallic Management Co. Ltd.* (1999) 78 P. & C.R. 52 C.A.
[32] M. Ross & T. Johnson [1990] 50 *L.S.G.* 17.
[33] *Higher Education Statistics Agency* v. *Customs & Excise Commissioners* [2000] 25 *L.S.G.* 8.
[34] R.S. Nock & C. Jamieson [1991] 35 *L.S.G.* 24; I. Marsh [1991] 42 *E.G.* 94. On stamp duties generally see above pp. 380–382.
[35] *Walsh* v. *Lonsdale* (1882) 21 Ch.D. 9 C.A. Mining leases commonly reserved a fixed element (a dead rent) and a share of profits (a royalty).
[36] *Greater London C.* v. *Connolly* [1970] 2 Q.B. 100 C.A.
[37] See below pp. 656–657.

4.   Foreign currencies

Rents of properties in England and Wales are usually paid in pounds sterling. Payment could take any other agreed form, historically including rabbits, bottles of wine or red roses,[38] and now more likely gold or a foreign currency. The old common law took a jingoistic view of foreign currency arrangements, as was natural in the post-War period of exchange control, but money now flows freely between countries in a global market, and French landlords of commercial premises in London could quite legitimately demand rent in pounds or francs or euros,[39] the only issue being an assessment of the exchange rate risk; there is no legal reason why this risk should not be passed to a commercial tenant. Hence the historical preference for the pound has bowed to the commercial realities of the modern world.

5.   Service charges etc

If the tenant takes only a part of the landlord's holding,[40] the landlord will probably agree to carry out some of the obligations commonly imposed on tenants, such as to repair and to insure, but with the cost of these services being paid by the tenant. Sums payable as service charges or insurance rents are not strictly rent—since they are not payments for the use of the land itself—but they are commonly reserved as if they were rent, a device which opens up for the landlord the possibility of distress and the rent only procedure for forfeiture.[41]

C.   PAYMENT OF RENT

1.   Tender

This is of enormous practical significance, since a proper tender of what is owed is an answer to an action for rent; the amount of the rent is still owed, but the costs of an action will not be allowed to a landlord who has rejected a valid tender. The lease will not be liable to forfeiture and any distress will be unlawful. Tender occurs where the full amount of the rent is offered, in the correct form, by the correct person as tenant, and to the correct landlord. Technically, perhaps, rent should be offered in legal tender but an agreement to accept a cheque is often implied.[42] Leases are often drafted by landlords so as to require payment in a specific way, for example by direct debit. Generally only the tenant can make an effective tender, and people other than the tenant have no right to preserve the lease by tendering the rent.[43]

---

[38] *Treseder-Griffin* v. *Co-Operative Insurance Ltd.* [1956] 2 Q.B. 127; (1956) 72 *L.Q.R.* 311; D.E.C. Yale [1956] *C.L.J.* 169; F.A. Mann (1957) 73 *L.Q.R.* 181. B. Hargrave (1957) 21 *Conv. (N.S.)* 265.

[39] T. Thornton [1999] 10 *E.G.* 173.

[40] See below Chapter 26.

[41] See below pp. 795–796.

[42] *Official Solicitor* v. *Thomas* [1986] 2 E.G.L.R. 1 C.A.; C.P. Rodgers [1987] *Conv.* 301; *D'Jan* v. *Bond Street Estates Ltd.* [1993] E.G.C.S. 43 C.A. (tender of £1528 by cheque valid, so distress for that sum illegal).

[43] *Presson Plus plc.* v. *Lancaster* [1997] E.G.C.S. 42 C.A. (cohabitee). The matrimonial home right will not be relevant in the case of commercial property.

2. Deduction of tax

Landlords are liable to pay income tax on their rent receipts, or corporation tax in the case of a corporate landlord. Usually this is only of concern to the landlord, the tenant being obliged to pay the rent in full, but the one exception is where the landlord is an overseas company: the tenant must be careful in that case to make only a net payment to the landlord, deducting the tax and accounting for it to the Revenue.[44]

3. Due date

A lease will specify with precision how and when rent should be paid. The presumption is that payments will be annual,[45] but a rack rent is generally paid quarterly or monthly, in which case the lease needs to define the exact days on which payment is required; a choice of traditional quarter days has implications for the length of notices.[46] Early payment is not advisable since a new landlord who buys the reversion can sue for the same rent again,[47] and early payment gives no right to a discount except on a disclaimer of an onerous lease after insolvency.[48]

Rent is payable in arrears unless the lease provides otherwise.[49] This old common law principle does not accord with the general practice of landlords, who not unreasonably want to see the colour of the tenant's money before allowing him into possession. Almost all leases, therefore, require rent to be paid in advance, that is at the start of the period for which rent is paid. A breach of covenant occurs if the rent is not paid on the stated date and action can be taken; for example a lease can be forfeited during the quarter for which the rent was payable.[50]

4. Interest

Commercial leases generally impose interest on late payments of rent as well as service charge and insurance premiums.[51] Tenants may try to negotiate a reduced rate of interest, a period of grace before interest begins to run, a requirement for the landlord to put the tenant on notice. However care is needed to ensure that the interest rate is not so high that it falls foul of the jurisdiction to protect against penalties. Statutory interest will not run under the Late Payment of Commercial Debts (Interest) Act 1998, since this is restricted to contracts affecting goods as defined in the Sale of Goods Act 1979,[52] but interest will be added to rent (without any provision in the lease) once a judgment has been obtained.

---

[44] Income and Corporation Taxes Act 1988 s.42A inserted by Finance Act 1995 s.40; *Tenbry Investments Ltd.* v. *Peugeot Talbot Motor Co. Ltd.* [1992] S.T.C. 791 Ch.D.

[45] *Turner* v. *Allday* (1836) Tyr. & Cr. 819; *Metropolitan Police District Receiver* v. *Palacegate Properties Ltd.* [2000] 13 E.G. 187 C.A.

[46] See above p. 584 n. 54.

[47] *De Nicholls* v. *Sanders* (1870) L.R. 5 C.P. 589.

[48] See below pp. 772–775.

[49] *Metropolitan Police District Receiver* v. *Palacegate Properties Ltd.* [2000] 13 E.G. 187 C.A.

[50] *City & Capital Holdings Ltd.* v. *Dean Warburg Ltd.* [1989] 1 E.G.L.R. 90 C.A.

[51] *Encyclopaedia of Forms and Precedents* (5th ed.) vol.23 para.[32].

[52] s.2(7), referring to s.61 of the 1979 Act.

5. Apportionment

If payment is made in advance, it is necessary to effect an apportionment when the lease is sold,[53] or on a surrender,[54] so that the new tenant reimburses the outgoing tenant for part of the rent which he has already paid.[55] Liability for arrears naturally continues.[56]

D. DEFENCES AND DEDUCTIONS

1. Legal defences

The common law had a limited range of defences to an action for rent including, for example, a receipt or other proof that the rent demanded has already been paid. Legal defences include limitation. Arrears can only be recovered if action is taken within six years.[57] However limitation is rarely destructive of the lease itself: a squatter may destroy an oral lease by taking adverse possession for 12 years without paying rent, but a landlord with a written lease cannot lose his estate by adverse possession before the date for its natural termination.[58] Even if the action is properly struck out on limitation principles, the tenant may still be allowed to pursue a set off.[59]

2. Duty to mitigate

If the tenant quits the property, can he stop future rent accruing by insisting that the landlord mitigate his loss by seeking to relet the property? English law asserts the absolute character of the rent action so that mitigation is not required. This was re-emphasised recently in *Bhogal* v. *Cheema*[60] where a tenant in financial difficulties abandoned the property. A surety was sued for rent but argued that there had been a surrender and that the landlord was obliged to mitigate the tenant's loss by retaking the property and attempting to relet it. Sir John Vinelott described this argument as misconceived.[61] In *Re Park Air Services plc.*[62] the House of Lords held that a landlord seeking to claim compensation on the disclaimer of a lease by the tenant's liquidator had to claim compensation assessed on a contractual basis, discounted for the early receipt, and presumably also the possibility of reletting; however this was on the basis that the tenant had a right to terminate the lease (by disclaimer) and did not directly affect the case where the tenant left the property in breach of contract and without the right of termination. So it seems that English law retains the no-mitigation principle. However, in

---

[53] *Laimond Property Investment Co. Ltd.* v. *Arlington Park Mansions Ltd.* [1989] 1 E.G.L.R. 208 C.A. (sale of a freehold reversion by landlord to tenant.)
[54] Apportionment Act 1870; *William Hill (Football) Ltd.* v. *Willen Key & Hardware Ltd.* (1964) 108 S.J. 482.
[55] P. Freedman [1990] 35 *L.S.G.* 25; S. Marks [2000] 28 *E.G.* 141.
[56] *Shaw* v. *Lomas* (1888) 59 L.T. 477.
[57] Limitation Act 1980 s.19; Woodfall 19.134–19.148; Sparkes *N.L.L.* ch.25.
[58] sch.1 paras.4–5.
[59] *Filross Securities Ltd.* v. *Midgeley* [1999] 3 E.G.L.R. 43 C.A.; *The Brede* [1974] Q.B. 233, 245, Lord Denning M.R.; *Westdeutsche Landesbank Girozentrale* v. *Islington L.B.C.* [1994] 4 All E.R. 890, 945, Hobhouse J.
[60] [1998] 2 E.G.L.R. 50, Sir John Vinelott.
[61] At 52E–G.
[62] [1999] 1 All E.R. 673 H.L.

Australia a duty to mitigate is recognised.[63] In England a shift to contractual assessment of damages for non-payment of rent should logically follow from the shift that has occurred from estate-based to contractual analysis of leases.[64]

3. Counterclaims

The common law duty to pay rent was absolute, being based on the covenant contained in the lease that was independent of any other actions. If the tenant wished to complain about disrepair or allege that the landlord had promised informally to reduce his rent or raise any other defence, he had to take separate proceedings, usually in equity. The Judicature Act 1873 effected a radical shift in power, because it provides that counterclaims are to be dealt with in the same way as more traditional defences to legal actions, equitable arguments based on promissory estoppel[65] or a set-off provided that it is sufficiently connected to the main action.[66] Indeed the changes in 1875 seem to have altered the concept of rent itself, since a set off is even allowed as a defence to a distress.[67]

Set off has been studied in the context of the residential tenant's rent strike as a response to his landlord's failure to keep his property in repair, but it applies generally to any commercial contract.[68] *British Anzani (Felixstowe) Ltd.* v. *International Marine Management (U.K.) Ltd.*,[69] the leading disrepair case, concerned industrial warehouses at Felixstowe with defective floors costing £1 million to rectify, a claim that was held to be a complete defence on the facts to the action for arrears of rent.[70] Commercial leases of single units usually impose the repairing obligation on the tenant, and of course a tenant who has no legitimate cause of action has no case for a set off against the landlord: rent cannot be withheld because of the alleged unfitness of the premises for their intended commercial use[71] or on account of the wrongs of a former landlord.[72]

---

[63] *Vickers* v. *Stichtenoth Investments Pty. Ltd.* (1989) 52 S.A.S.R. 90, Bollen J.; *Progressive Mailing House Pty.* v. *Tabali Pty.* (1985) 157 C.L.R. 17, Mason J.; *Highway Properties Ltd.* v. *Kelly Douglas & Co. Ltd.* (1971) 17 D.L.R. (3d) 710.

[64] The three most obvious examples are forfeiture (see below Chapter 29) repudiation (see below p. 691) and grants by non-owners (see above pp. 178–179).

[65] *Central London Property Trust Ltd.* v. *High Trees House Ltd.* ("High Trees") [1947] K.B. 130, Denning J.; *Dorkins* v. *Wright* [1983] C.L.Y. 1364; *Central Street Properties Ltd.* v. *Mansbrook Rudd & Co. Ltd.* [1986] 2 E.G.L.R. 33; *Smith* v. *Lawson* (1998) 75 P. & C.R. 466 C.A.

[66] Supreme Court Act 1981 s.49(2); *B.O.C. Group plc.* v. *Centeon LLC* [1999] 1 All E.R. (Comm.) 970 C.A. (connection not sufficiently explicit); *Courage Ltd.* v. *Crehan* [1999] 2 E.G.L.R. 145 C.A. (claim for damages for infringing European competition law not sufficiently close to rent to allow set off); *Khan* v. *Islington L.B.C.* [1999] E.G.C.S. 87 C.A. (landlord could set off rent arrears before making home loss payment); *Yankwood Ltd.* v. *Havering L.B.C.* [1999] E.G.C.S. 75, Neuberger J. (death of horses as a result of the use of weedkiller); see also the domestic cases discussed above at pp. 256–258.

[67] *Lee-Parker* v. *Izzet* [1971] 1 W.L.R. 1688, 1692–1693, Goff J.

[68] Woodfall 7.097–7.118; *Gilbert Ash (Northern) Ltd.* v. *Modern Engineering (Bristol) Ltd.* [1974] A.C. 689; I.N. Duncan Wallace (1974) 90 L.Q.R. 21; this overrules *Dawnrays Ltd.* v. *F.G. Minter Ltd.* [1971] 1 W.L.R. 1205 C.A. (only liquidated sums or admitted due).

[69] [1980] Q.B. 137, Forbes J.

[70] *Bankes* v. *Jarvis* [1903] 1 K.B. 549 applied; *Televantos* v. *McCulloch* [1991] 1 E.G.L.R. 123 C.A. (arrears of rent £2,274 but damages under landlord's statutory repairing covenant £2,700; counterclaim held to be a complete defence).

[71] *Dailworth Ltd.* v. *T.G. Organsiation (Europe) Ltd.* (1998) 75 P. & C.R. 147 C.A.

[72] *Kemra Management Ltd.* v. *Lewis* [1999] 10 C.L. 489, Recorder Hayton; but see R. Derham (1991) 107 L.Q.R. 126.

4.   No deduction clauses

Whatever the old law was,[73] it is now settled that set off can be excluded in a commercial context by a sufficiently clear contractual provision.[74] A requirement to pay rent without "any deduction" is ambiguous, since it is arguable that the rent has been paid in an alternative way (for example by paying the cost of repairs), so this phraseology operates to leave in place the tenant's normal set off.[75] Better worded was the contract that provided for payment of $5 million "free and clear of any right of set off or counterclaim or any withholding or deduction whatsoever . . ."[76]; this belt and braces job did compel a gross payment. Identical principles apply to rent claimed by action and on distress.[77]

In a domestic lease it is conceivable that the clause might be vulnerable to attack as an unfair contract term,[78] but commercial clauses have withstood attack on this ground.[79]

E.   REMEDIES

"Whereas the remedy for recovering rents . . . are tedious and difficult."[80]

Whatever remedy is adopted today, the recoverable rent should be the same, since no distinction is drawn by the modern law between distrainable rent and rent recoverable by action: what is recoverable is what has been agreed.

1.   Action for rent

Arrears of rent are often recovered by a personal action through the courts, in a county court if the sum claimed is less than £25,000, and in the High Court if it is above £50,000, or in either court between these figures.[81] The procedure is described in the chapter on business repossessions.[82] Action is much more common than a distress.

---

[73] *Lechmere* v. *Hawkins* (1798) 2 Esp. 626, 627, 170 E.R. 477, Lord Kenyon; *Taylor* v. *Okey* (1806) 13 Ves. 180, 33 E.R. 263, Lord Erskine L.C.; *Quadrant Visual Communications Ltd.* v. *Hutchison Telephone (U.K.) Ltd.* [1993] B.C.L.C. 442 C.A. (cannot fetter right to grant specific performance).

[74] *Halesowen Presswork & Assemblies Ltd.* v. *National Westminster Bank Ltd.* [1971] 1 Q.B. 1; on appeal [1972] A.C. 785, 804, 808; *Melville* v. *Grapelodge Developments Ltd.* (1978) 39 P. & C.R. 179; *Hong Kong & Shanghai Banking Corporation* v. *Kloeckner & Co. A.G.* [1990] 2 Q.B. 514, Hirst J.

[75] *Connaught Restaurants Ltd.* v. *Indoor Leisure Ltd.* [1994] 1 W.L.R. 501 C.A.; J.E. Adams [1993] *Conv.* 183; *Quadrant Visual Communications Ltd.* v. *Hutchinson Telephone (U.K.) Ltd.* [1993] B.C.L.C. 442 C.A. ("free of any equity" did not remove discretion to order specific performance).

[76] *Coca-Cola Financial Corporation* v. *Finsat International Ltd.* [1998] Q.B. 43 C.A.; *Surzar Overseas Ltd.* v. *Ocean Reliance Shipping Co. Ltd.* [1997] 1 C.L.Y. 906, Toulson J.; *John Dee Group Ltd.* v. *W.M.H. (21) Ltd.* [1997] B.C.C. 578 Ch.D; also Standard Business Lease (1996 edition) cl.1.6(a).

[77] J.E. Adams [1991] *Conv.* 79; A. Dowling (1988) 39 *N.I.L.Q.* 258; *Eller* v. *Grovecest Investments Ltd.* [1995] Q.B. 272 C.A.; J. Adams (1994) 57 *M.L.R.* 960; J.E. Adams [1993] *Conv.* 183.

[78] Unfair Terms in Consumer Contracts Regulations 1999, S.I. 1999/2083; see above p. 638.

[79] *Hong Kong & Shanghai Banking Corporation* v. *Kloeckner & Co. A.G.* [1990] 2 Q.B. 514; *Electricity Supply Nominees Ltd.* v. *I.A.F. Group plc.* [1993] 1 W.L.R. 1059; J.E Adams [1993] *Conv.* 109; [1993] *Conv.* 457; *Overland Shoes Ltd.* v. *Shenkers Ltd.* [1998] 1 Lloyd's Rep. 498 C.A.; *Star Rider Ltd.* v. *Inntrepreneur Pub Co. Ltd.* [1998] 1 E.G.L.R. 53 Ch.D.; *Unchained Growth III plc* v. *Granby Village (Manchester) Management Co. Ltd.* [1999] Times November 4th C.A. (same principle for payments to a management company).

[80] L.T.A. 1730 s.8.

[81] H.C.C.C.J.O. 1991, S.I. 1991/724, para.7.

[82] See below pp. 832–836.

Until 1875 an action in covenant was available for rent payable under a lease by deed, but different actions were required under written and oral leases. The Judicature Act 1873, which took effect in that year, removed the forms of action, and substituted a single action for contractually agreed rent, whether there was an express covenant in a deed, an express but informal agreement, or any implied agreement. This change provided for the impetus towards the recognition of leases as primarily contractual in nature.[83]

2. Forfeiture

An action for arrears leaves in place the lease for the future, with the inconvenience that the tenant may again fail to pay the rent. For this reason, all properly drawn leases contain a provision for forfeiture in the event of non-payment, which enables the landlord to terminate the lease if the rent is unpaid—usually after default for 14 days; so much so that termination on a non-payment is a usual covenant that will be implied into a contract,[84] and if the tenant enters under the contract itself, the equitable lease will also be terminable in the same events.[85]

Forfeiture is not an effective threat unless the landlord is genuinely happy to remove the tenant. If market rents have declined and the tenant is left with an expensive lease on his hands, he may jump at the chance to end the lease and so end his liability to the rent, since the lease will not be assignable in these circumstances. However, most tenants are anxious to avoid eviction from their business premises, in which case the threat of forfeiture is a very effective lever since the tenant must make good his defaults in order to lift the threat of eviction. Forfeiture may occur either through a possession action—a procedure explained in a later chapter[86]—or by peaceable re-entry, that is by changing the locks.

3. Rent diversion notice

If the rent of a tenant is in arrears the head landlord may divert the rent payable by a sub-tenant or lodger, the mechanism being a notice requiring future payments of rent to be made direct to the head landlord.[87] A conflict of priority arose in *Rhodes* v. *Allied Dunbar Pension Services Ltd*.[88] A lease to a tenant company was subject both to a floating charge and also to a sub-lease of part. The head landlord was entitled to serve a rent diversion notice on the sub-tenant, since the bank's entitlement to the floating charge did not give it possession and so it had no right to receive rent from the sub-tenant. Even appointment of a receiver would have made no difference, since the receiver would act as an agent of the tenant.

---

[83] See above n. 64.

[84] See below p. 796.

[85] See above pp. 531–532.

[86] See below Chapter 29.

[87] Law of Distress Amendment Act 1908 s.6; *Lawrence Chemical Co. Ltd.* v. *Rubinstein* [1982] 1 W.L.R. 284 C.A. (notice may be signed by the landlord's solicitors).

[88] [1989] 1 W.L.R. 800 C.A.; F. Oditah [1990] *J.B.L.* 431; J.E. Adams [1993] *Conv.* 11.

F. DISTRESS

In one of its earlier reviews, the Law Commission[89] described distress as the process of seizing goods belonging to a debtor as a means of securing satisfaction of a demand, including rent due from a tenant[90] under a lease. The process of carrying out the seizure is called a distraint. Modern landlords do not rely on a purely passive right of retention since there is a power to sell the goods which are seized,[91] and to put the proceeds of sale from the goods towards the discharge of the arrears of rent.

1.   Judicial control

Given the protection of residential tenants,[92] distress is most often targeted against business,[93] agricultural[94] and other non-residential tenants, since landlords of these premises may distrain for rent due without any judicial intervention. It will be interesting to see whether there is any challenge based on the right to a fair hearing given by Article 6 of the European Convention on Human Rights.[95] As it stands, the commercial landlord has a self-help remedy which enables him to secure priority over other creditors of the tenant, especially since distress falls outside the moratorium on legal processes imposed by insolvency or administration.[96] A few years ago the remedy appeared to be dying a natural death, but lack of judicial supervision has encouraged an unfortunate revival. Control by the courts can only be applied, retrospectively, in an action by the tenant alleging that an unlawful distress has resulted in a trespass to the tenant's goods.

2.   Rent owing

Distress is most commonly used today to recover arrears of local taxation[97] and duties,[98] but its use for non-payment of rent is more ancient. Today rent means the contractual money payment made by a tenant to his landlord in consideration of the use of the latter's land, and the contractual rent should equal the distrainable rent.[99] Assessed costs will be added.[100] Distress is available under any form of lease, it making no difference whether it was a legal fixed term, a periodic tenancy, a tenancy at will or, apparently, an

---

[89] Law Com. No.5 (1966) para.3; see generally Woodfall ch.9.

[90] Not a licensee: *Rendell* v. *Roman* (1839) 9 T.L.R. 192.

[91] Distress for Rent Act 1689, 2 W. & M. c.5.

[92] H.A. 1988 s.19 (assured); R.A. 1977 s.147 (Rent Act protected tenants); R.(Ag.)A. 1976 s.8; see above p. 103. Restrictions also apply to distress against a serving member of the armed forces.

[93] *Khazanchi* v. *Faircharm Investments Ltd.* (1999) 77 P. & C.R. 29 C.A.; J. Kruse (1998) 17 *C.J.Q.* 41, (1999) 18 *C.J.Q.* 58.

[94] Under agricultural holdings (granted before 1996) distress is limited to one year's arrears: A.H.A. 1986 s.16(1); there is no limit for newer farm business tenancies.

[95] J. Karas & J. Maurici [1999] 17 *E.G.* 126; this is a human right so a corporate tenant will not be protected; see above p. 205.

[96] I.A. 1986 ss.11, 252(6); *McMullen & Sons Ltd.* v. *Cerrone* [1994] 1 E.G.L.R. 99 Ch.D.

[97] Rules for rent discussed below do not necessarily apply: *Potts* v. *Hickman* [1941] A.C. 212, 241, Lord Wright; *Quinlan* v. *Hammersmith & Fulham L.B.C.* [1989] R.A. 43 C.A.

[98] S.I. 1997/1431.

[99] *United Scientific Holdings Ltd.* v. *Burnley B.C.* [1978] A.C. 904, 947C–D, Lord Simon.

[100] S.I.s 1999/2360, 1999/2564.

equitable lease.[101] The remedy is only available for a precise sum of rent that is actually owing (no right where interim rent not yet ascertained by court).[102]

Very often a tenant will argue that a distress is unlawful because no rent was due under the lease, for example after rejection of a proper tender,[103] or because of a set off for any counterclaim. In *Eller* v. *Grovecrest Investments Ltd.*[104] the tenant withheld rent because of acts of nuisance by the landlord, and distraint for the amount of rent withheld was held to be a trespass. The set off must arise from the same action, and usually under the same lease.[105] It is discretionary, and might, for example, be disallowed where the effect would be that music albums recovered after a wrongful distress would be swallowed up by the legal aid fund charge.[106]

3. Procedural requirements

Distress is an archaic procedure with archaic rules requiring, for example, that it should occur in daylight and not on Sunday. The Statute of Marlborough 1267,[107] which applies to any distress for rent, prohibits distraint on public highways or away from the land, and also prohibits driving the goods taken out of the county: these rules may prevent seizure of a car parked outside on the road,[108] though it must be remembered that the tenant usually owns the land to the mid point of the road, which may give a sufficient title to support a distress.[109]

Distress must be carried out by a certificated bailiff. New rules were introduced in 1999[110] to require a new form of application, an examination on oath at a designated county court, and the provision of a bond before a certificate is issued.

The bailiff's function is to effect an *entry and impoundment*. In *Evans* v. *South Ribble B.C.*[111] Simon Brown J. identified three stages essential to a complete distress: entry on the premises, seizure of goods, and their impoundment. In the case, the bailiff, Evans, posted a notice of distress through the letterbox, but it was held that this act was not sufficient to complete the distress. Initial entry must be peaceable, but after these stages are complete, the bailiff may, according to *Khazanchi* v. *Faircharm Investments Ltd.*,[112] use force to seize the good and secure them for impounding. Once entry has been accomplished minor acts are sufficient to maintain an impoundment: commonly the tenant signs a walking possession agreement, which leaves listed goods on the premises[113] and

---

[101] *Walsh* v. *Lonsdale* (1882) 21 Ch.D. 9 C.A.; but see P. Sparkes (1988) 8 *O.J.L.S.* 350, 354.

[102] *Eren* v. *Tranmac Ltd.* [1997] 2 E.G.L.R. 211 C.A.; M. Codd (1994) 138 *S.J.* 524.

[103] *D'Jan* v. *Bond Street Estates Ltd.* [1993] E.G.C.S. 43 C.A.

[104] [1995] Q.B. 272 C.A.; M. Codd (1994) 138 *S.J.* 524.

[105] *Eller* as above; *Hanak* v. *Green* [1958] 2 Q.B. 9 C.A.; *British Anzani (Felixstowe) Ltd.* v. *International Marine Management (U.K.) Ltd.* [1980] Q.B. 137, Forbes J.

[106] *Brookes* v. *Harris* [1995] 1 W.L.R. 918, Ferris J.

[107] Also called the Distress Act 1267.

[108] *Quinlan* v. *Hammersmith & Fulham B.C.* [1989] R.A. 43 C.A. (obiter).

[109] *Hodges* v. *Lawrence* (1854) 18 J.P. 347.

[110] Law of Distress Amendment Act 1888 s.7; Law of Distress Amendment Act 1895 ss.1–3; S.I. 1988/2050, as amended by S.I.s 1999/2360, 1999/2564.

[111] [1992] Q.B. 757 (community charge); J. Kruse [1995] *N.L.J.* 1337; *Wilson* v. *S. Kesteven D.C.* [2000] 4 All E.R. 577 C.A.

[112] (1999) 77 P. & C.R. 29 C.A.; J. Kruse (1998) 17 *C.J.Q.* 41, (1999) 18 *C.J.Q.* 58.

[113] Distress for Rent Act 1737 s.10; S.I. 1953/1702.

in the possession of the tenant,[114] but on the terms that he is barred from removing or selling them.[115] Distress is complete as soon as the goods are impounded, after which it is a trespass for the tenant to interfere with them, but this stage had not been reached in *Evans.* However it is not a breach of the custody of the law to retake goods, if the tenant is unaware that the person seizing his goods was a bailiff.[116]

Seizure confers a special property in the goods and priority on insolvency.[117] If the tenant removes impounded goods, the landlord may follow them and seize them.[118] A magistrate's court may direct restoration of improperly seized goods, or payment of their value,[119] but a more common solution today would be an action for trespass to goods in the county court. A power of sale is conferred by the Distress for Rent Act 1689. The tenant has five clear days to replevy, that is to take proceedings for recovery of the goods by paying the rent, though this period can be extended by notice to 15 days.[120] Crops can be protected by payment of the arrears at any time before they are cut.[121] Irregularity in sale is a trespass, but it will not invalidate the earlier seizure.[122]

4.   Property exempt from distraint

Certain property is exempt from distress, at least for rent arrears,[123] including personal items such as clothes and bedding and tools of the trade.[124] This last exemption was held in *Brookes* v. *Harris,*[125] to include a collection of records, tapes and disks, made by a disk jockey for use when presenting radio and television programmes. Many perishables are exempt. Distress does not authorise the removal of fixtures and fittings, nor taking things in actual use. Bailiffs will be most interested in high value items which are easily saleable, so that a tenant faced with a visit from the bailiff should turn on his television, hi fi, and vacuum.

5.   Property not belonging to the tenant

Goods distrained must belong to the tenant liable for the rent,[126] so that action may be taken in trespass to protect the goods of *former tenants*. Items belonging to *strangers* may be vulnerable to distraint, on account of the rule that allows a landlord to take all goods on the property that appear to be in the reputed ownership of the tenant. However in

---

[114] *Re a Debtor No.10 of 1992* [1995] B.C.C. 525 Ch.D.; *Re Dalton* [1963] Ch. 336; *Davies* v. *Property & Reversionary Co. Ltd.* [1929] 2 K.B. 222 (inventory not required).

[115] *Lumsden* v. *Burnett* [1892] 2 Q.B. 197 C.A.; *Tennant* v. *Field* (1857) 8 E. & B. 336, 120 E.R. 125; *Jones* v. *Bernstein* [1900] 2 Q.B. 100 C.A.; *Lavell & Co. Ltd.* v. *O'Leary* [1933] 2 K.B. 200 C.A.; *Abingdon R.D.C.* v. *O'Gorman* [1968] 2 Q.B. 881 C.A.

[116] *Khazanchi* v. *Faircharm Investments Ltd.* (1999) 77 P. & C.R. 29 C.A.; J. Kruse (1998) 17 *C.J.Q.* 41, (1999) 18 *C.J.Q.* 58.

[117] *Re Davies ex parte Williams* (1872) L.R. 7 Ch.App. 314; *Re A Debtor* [1995] B.C.C. 525 Ch.D.

[118] Distress for Rent Act 1737 ss.1–7 (criminal offences and protection for innocent buyers).

[119] Law of Distress Amendment Act 1895 s.4. Before impoundment, improperly taken goods may be rescued.

[120] Law of Distress Amendment Act 1888 s.6.

[121] s.9.

[122] Distress for Rent Act 1737 s.19.

[123] *Hutchins* v. *Chambers* (1758) 1 Burr. 579, 588, 97 E.R. 458, Lord Mansfield (local taxation different).

[124] Law of Distress Amendment Act 1888; County Courts Act 1984 s.89.

[125] [1995] 1 W.L.R. 918, Ferris J.

[126] *Wharfland* v. *S. London Co-operative Building Co. Ltd.* [1995] 2 E.G.L.R. 21 Q.B.D. (rent due before the assignment).

Salford Van Hire (Contracts) Ltd. v. *Bocholt Developments Ltd.*[127] it was held that a 7.5 ton Mercedes truck on hire from Salford Van Hire was not in the reputed ownership of the tenant, since any landlord should know that businesses often hire trucks and can easily check ownership of a vehicle.[128] The landlord in fact sold Salford's van, but was afterwards liable to them for its value.

Strangers whose goods happen to be at the tenant's property may protect themselves against seizure of their goods by serving a notice,[129] with special provisions for finance companies to protect goods sold on hire purchase.[130] Protection for a (lawful) sub-tenant or lodger is dependent on paying rent direct to the landlord.[131] Spouses, beneficiaries, business partners and company officers are not protected.[132]

6. Proposed abolition

Distress is a self-help remedy, which means that it is not subject to direct judicial control. Most self-help remedies have fallen out of favour in recent years, because of the danger that exercise of such a remedy may provoke violence. Frequently the amount of rent owing is a matter of dispute, and there is no possibility of weighing discretionary factors, such as the tenant's ability to pay. In 1991 the Law Commission recommended that the whole procedure should be consigned to history,[133] a move supported by the judiciary,[134] and work on this proposal is to continue.[135] However, it should not be discarded without an appreciation of its effectiveness as a remedy: 90 per cent of cases lead to payment and goods are moved in only 3 per cent of cases. It appears that distress is now to be considered as wider aspect of enforcement procedures for civil judgments.[136]

G. RECOVERY OF OVERPAYMENTS

Mistake of law is no longer a defence to a claim for restitution.[137] So a tenant who pays an excessive rent demand will normally be able to recover it. Neuberger J. gave full effect to this new principle in *Nurdin & Peacock plc.* v. *D.B. Ramsden & Co. Ltd.*[138] Tenants liable for a quarterly rent of £51,000 made several payments of £66,000, after mistaken advice from their legal advisers (under the law as it was then understood) that they would be able to recover any overpayments. This was a mistake of law, and but for it they would not have made the payment. On the facts, there was a direct connection between the mistake and the payment, but this may not have been a strict requirement

---

[127] [1995] 2 E.G.L.R. 50 C.A.; *Interoven Stove Co. Ltd.* v. *Hibbard & Painter* [1936] 1 All E.R. 263, Hibery J.
[128] *Re Fox* [1948] Ch. 407 Div.Ct.; *Ex parte Watkins* (1873) L.R. 8 Ch.App. 520; *Re Watson* [1904] 2 K.B. 753.
[129] Law of Distress Amendment Act 1908 s.1(c).
[130] s.4A.
[131] s.1(a),(b).
[132] s.4.
[133] Law Com. No.194 (1991); H.W. Wilkinson [1991] *Conv.* 246; R.G. Lee [1991] *J.S.W.L.* 310; I. Loveland (1990) 17 *J.L.S.* 363.
[134] *Salford Van Hire (Contracts) Ltd.* v. *Bocholt Developments Ltd.* [1995] 2 E.G.L.R. 50, 54M, Sir Ralph Gibson.
[135] J.E. Adams [1998] *Conv.* 349.
[136] Law Com. No.258 (1999) para.1.21.
[137] *Kleinwort Benson Ltd.* v. *Lincoln C.C.* [1999] A.C. 349 H.L.
[138] [1999] 2 E.G.L.R. 15; A. Bruce [1999] *N.L.J.* 1053; W. Miller & J. Pickston [1998] 51 *E.G.* 76; C. Lamont [1999] 3 *L.T.Rev.* 12.

for recovery. The landlord had been unjustly enriched to the amount of the overpayment and would be required to make restitution to the tenant. Possible defences are a change of position by the landlord after receipt of the overpayment and proof that the payment was a genuine compromise of a dispute about the correct amount.

H. SUSPENSION OF RENT

The tenant must continue to pay the rent throughout the lease, even after complete destruction of the property by fire even if reconstruction of the property is prevented by planning or building restrictions. The same applies to destruction by a hostile bomb—or, indeed, one that is friendly.[139] Rent also continues on requisition,[140] the tenant being obliged to seek compensation from the military authorities. Potential unfairness can be avoided by providing for a *suspension of rent* while the property is unfit for use or by enabling the tenant to break the lease by notice. It is important to deal with insurance premiums and service charge separately if these items are also to be suspended, since this is not implied.[141]

Rent is suspended after *eviction* either *by title paramount* or by the landlord. It is a fundamental term of a lease that the landlord should allow the tenant to take possession, and interference with his possession stops the right to rent, an exception that is obvious even if its source is concealed. Only if the events amount to a frustration[142]—for example in the case of supervening illegality or destruction by an earthquake—will the lease end along with the liability to rent.

I.   DETERMINING BUSINESS RENTS

Commercial rents are usually fixed initially by contractual negotiation between landlord and tenant. Most commercial leases and some long domestic leases contain rent review provisions that enable the rent to be increased in line with inflation. Sometimes rents have to be fixed by a court, for example when a lease is granted under a binding option to a sitting tenant, or where a business tenant exercises his statutory right to renew his lease.

1.   The initial rent

Determination of the initial rent charged to a commercial sector tenant is left to negotiation between landlords and tenants. It will be determined both by the intrinsic value of the property being let and also by the terms agreed between the parties. Rentals are usually quoted on the basis of floor area, which must, since March 1995[143] be quoted in

---

[139] This depends on whether it is dropped from an enemy aircraft or by one's own side.

[140] *Crown Lands Commissioners* v. *Page* [1960] 2 Q.B. 274 C.A.; H.W.R. Wade [1961] *C.L.J.* 34; *Matthey* v. *Curling* [1922] 2 A.C. 180 H.L.; *Eyre* v. *Johnson* [1946] K.B. 481.

[141] *P. & O. Property Holdings Ltd.* v. *International Computers Ltd.* [1999] 2 E.G.L.R. 17, Neuberger J.; J.E. Adams [1999] *Conv.* 284.

[142] See below pp. 713–716.

[143] S.I. 1995/1804.

metric terms. In a recession, rents drop and landlords will have to give way on the terms,[144] but in a buoyant letting market landlords can dictate their own terms.

2. Rent review

Traditional commercial leases endured for 25 years,[145] over which time rental levels could fluctuate dramatically, possibly downwards but more likely upwards. Landlords obviously stood to lose from fixed rents, but responded to the effects of inflation by incorporating rent review provisions in long-term commercial leases. Such clauses were uncommon before the 1960s.[146] Tenants are benefited as well since the initial rent demanded by the landlord is lower if he knows that it can be increased later.[147] The industry standard form of rent review[148] provides for the appointment of an arbitrator or expert to determine the open market rent for the property as at the review date. However, this standard form has never been universal, has not been updated since 1985, and would now require some amendment to take account of developments in relation to disregards.[149] From slight beginnings,[150] the case law has burgeoned.[151]

Reviews will certainly occur every five years,[152] and quite possible more frequently. Agreement on the frequency of reviews is one of the critical aspects of any commercial lease negotiation. Unfortunately it is all to easy to say what is not meant: one lease for 71 years provided for annual index-linked rises for five years and then for the rent to be fixed by arbitration, leaving a one-off review to fix the rent for the last 66 years.[153] Careful definition is required of the review date and review period,[154] particularly where land is sub-let leaving the possibility of confusion about whether dates refer to the term of the head lease or of the sub-lease.[155]

3. Business lease renewal

Business tenants usually have the right to renewal of their lease when it expires. Tenants who build up goodwill from trading in a particular location are protected against being manoeuvred into paying more than the market rate to retain possession of their existing trading position. Renewal is usually triggered by a notice from the landlord followed by a tenant's counter-notice and a court application by the tenant for an order granting a new lease.[156] The parties may reach an agreement for the renewal of the

[144] L. Lawrence & S. Petley [1992] 48 *E.G.* 54; R. Abbey [1993] 02 *L.S.G.* 20; H.W. Wilkinson [1993] *Conv.* 326; J.E. Adams [1994] *Conv.* 97.

[145] During the recession of the early 1990s leases became shorter: J.E. Adams [1995] *Conv.* 102 says 72% were for 5 years, 46% had break clauses, and only 1.5% were for the traditional 25 years.

[146] Law Com. No.162 (1987) para.3.17.

[147] *United Scientific Holdings Ltd.* v. *Burnley B.C.* [1978] A.C. 904, 918C, Lord Salmon.

[148] Issued jointly by the Law Society and the Royal Institution of Chartered Surveyors Model Forms (1985 edition) (Surveyors Publications); (1985) 82 *L.S.G.* 3664; also Standard Business Lease (1996 edition) cl.8.

[149] J.E. Adams [1999] *Conv.* 284.

[150] P.F. Smith (1979) 43 *Conv. (N.S.)* 10.

[151] Woodfall ch.8; see also the bibliography above.

[152] *United Scientific Holdings Ltd.* v. *Burnley B.C.* [1978] A.C. 904, 918C.

[153] *Stedman* v. *Midland Bank plc.* [1990] 1 E.G.L.R. 146 C.A.; *Northern Electric plc.* v. *Addison* [1997] 2 E.G.L.R. 111 C.A.

[154] Law Society/R.I.C.S. Model Forms cl.1.

[155] *F.L.C. Management Ltd.* v. *Ganton House Investments Ltd.* [1991] E.G.L.R. 132 C.A.

[156] See above Chapter 20.

lease,[157] thus removing the necessity to pursue court proceedings, but often the parties cannot agree the rent to be charged so that a court hearing is needed to set the new rent. After the court fixes the terms, the tenant has 14 days in which to indicate that he will not accept a new lease at the determined rent.[158]

Rent apart, the other terms of the renewed lease are presumed to reproduce the terms of the lease being renewed.[159] The onus is on the party who wishes to alter other terms to show why they should be amended. In the leading case, *O'May* v. *City of London Real Property Co.,*[160] the landlord tried to shift all repairing obligations onto the tenant, so that the landlord secured a "clean lease", giving a pure income profit with no deduction for outgoings. A clean lease was much more valuable in the market as it had developed—the particular reversion being increased in value by between £1 and £2 million—a prize for which the landlord was prepared to forego 10 per cent of the rent. Nevertheless the tenant thought that it was in his interest to stand out against this change, and it was held that he was entitled to do so. Changes must be proved to be fair and reasonable, having regard to the relatively weak bargaining position of the tenant seeking renewal.[161]

4. Options

Some landlords prefer to grant relatively short leases, but to give the tenant the opportunity to extend the holding by exercising an option to take a new lease. It is necessary to define at the outset the rent to be charged when the option is exercised; it will almost always be the open market rental at that time.[162] An option for a lease is valid if the rent is to be agreed at a figure not exceeding the current rent.[163] When the option is exercised the rent has to be fixed by a process which is in many ways similar to a review.

J.   RENT REVIEW

1. Contractual basis

Rent review is based on contractual arrangement between landlord and tenant and so is limited to the original contractual term.[164] It is a standard part of commercial letting practice, but is also becoming more common in long leases of residential property.[165] Unfortunately the contractual basis of review procedures has proved to be totally inadequate, because complex drafting is required to deal satisfactorily with all future possibilities, and many clauses are sloppily drafted. Estoppel by convention smoothes over some of the difficulties, since it ensures that an understanding between the parties about

---

[157] Determined by offer and acceptance: *Lovely & Orchard Services Ltd.* v. *Daejean Investments (Grove Hall) Ltd.* [1977] 1 E.G.L.R. 44.

[158] For interim rents see below pp. 668–669.

[159] Changes are allowed to reflect the change from the old to the new system for the running of covenants: L.T.A. 1954 ss.34(4), 35(2), both inserted by L.T (Covenants) A. 1995 sch.1.

[160] [1983] 2 A.C. 726 H.L.; J. Gaunt [1982] *Conv.* 385.

[161] At 740H, Lord Hailsham L.C.

[162] *A.R.C. Ltd.* v. *Schofield* [1990] 2 E.G.L.R., 52 Millett J.

[163] *Carson* v. *Rhuddlan B.C.* (1990) 59 P. & C.R. 185 C.A.; see above p. 536.

[164] *Willison* v. *Cheverell Estates Ltd.* [1996] 1 E.G.L.R. 116 C.A.

[165] D. Clarke [1989] *Conv.* 111.

how to operate the clause becomes a conventional and binding meaning of their agreement.[166] Issue estoppel prevents the parties reopening issues that have already been litigated.[167] Rectification proceedings may be needed where the clause as drafted does not represent what was agreed.[168] These partial solutions cannot deal with clearly expressed and agreed contractual wording. Landlords have been known to insert extortionate clauses, and in commercial bargains the court has very limited powers to intervene. One well known clause provided for the rent for the next period to be the previous rent (say £10,000) and *in addition* the market rent (say £15,000), leading to an excessive new rent (£25,000) with the potential for exponential increase in the future.[169] Tortious remedies may be available against a landlord who has deliberately attempted to mislead the tenant.[170]

2. Review: automatic or triggered?

The modern tendency to provide for an *automatic* review, that is to provide that on the rent review date the rent will rise to the market rent then prevailing, with a default procedure for ascertaining what that rent is.[171] For example the Model Forms provide that the rent is the market rent agreed on the review date, as agreed at any time between the parties or as determined by an arbiter not earlier than the review date. An advantage is that time is *not* of the essence,[172] so that if the landlord's advisers omit to serve the trigger notice on time, the landlord can still demand the rent increase later. Lenders also need to be able to trigger the review in order to be able to protect their interests.[173] Even if a whole cycle is skipped the landlord can still insist upon a retrospective determination of the old rent.[174]

Older leases[175] provided for a review to be set in motion by a *trigger notice*, the giving of which was a precondition to the occurrence of any review, though a "subject to contract" notice just scraped by.[176] Usually the landlord was required to propose a new rent and failure to quantify the rent sought invalidated the notice.[177] No doubt minor discrepancies could be ignored if they would not mislead the tenant.[178] Naturally it was

[166] *Troop* v. *Gibson* [1986] 1 E.G.L.R. 1 C.A.

[167] *Arnold* v. *National Westminster Bank plc.* [1991] 2 A.C. 93 H.L. (no issue estoppel after change in law); *National Westminster Bank plc.* v. *Arthur Young McClelland Moores (No.2)* [1990] 2 E.G.L.R. 141 (Walton J.'s judgment on first review stands).

[168] *Kemp* v. *Neptune Concrete Ltd.* [1988] 2 E.G.L.R. 87 C.A.; *Brimican Investments Ltd.* v. *Blue Circle Heating Ltd.* [1995] E.G.C.S. 18, Chadwick J.; *Stavrides* v. *Manku* [1997] E.G.C.S. 58 Ch.D.

[169] Tenants can often pass on liability to their solicitors, who are negligent if they fail to advise on the risks inherent in unusual forms of rent review clause: *County Personnel (Employment Agency) Ltd.* v. *Alan R. Pulver & Co.* [1987] 1 W.L.R. 916 C.A.

[170] *Whyfe* v. *Michael Cullen & Partners* [1993] E.G.C.S. 193 C.A.

[171] *United Scientific Holdings Ltd.* v. *Burnley B.C.* [1978] A.C. 904 H.L.; S.D. Corke [1990] 42 *L.S.G.* 17.

[172] *United Scientific Holdings Ltd.* v. *Burnley B.C.* [1978] A.C. 904 H.L.; *Bickenhall Engineering Co. Ltd.* v. *Grandmet Restaurants Ltd.* [1995] 1 E.G.L.R. 110 C.A.

[173] J.E. Adams [1992] *Conv.* 16.

[174] *Wakefield (Tower Hill Trinity Square) Trust* v. *Janson Green Properties Ltd.* [1998] E.G.C.S. 95 Ch.D.

[175] *Cheapside Land Development Co. Ltd.* v. *Messels Service Co.* [1978] A.C. 904 H.L.; *Samuel Properties (Developments) Ltd.* v. *Hayek* [1972] 1 W.L.R. 1296 C.A.

[176] *Royal Life Insurance Ltd.* v. *Phillips* [1990] 2 E.G.L.R. 135 Q.B.D.

[177] *Commission for New Towns* v. *R. Levy & Co.* [1990] 2 E.G.L.R. 121 Ch.D.; *Addin Investments Ltd.* v. *S.S. for the Environment* [1997] 1 E.G.L.R. 99, Jacob J.

[178] *Durham City Estates Ltd.* v. *Felicetti* [1990] 1 E.G.L.R. 143 C.A.

much easier to go wrong under the older type of procedure, a fact that explains the shift to more automatic systems of review. Older leases very often made time of the essence for initiating a review; if the landlord missed the date for service of a trigger notice, he was deprived of rent for the whole review period.[179] This was so if, for example, notice was required six months before the start of the period for which the new rent was to be paid.[180] Many landlords were caught out,[181] and so were many professional advisers of landlords.[182]

Old style notice procedures required the tenant to respond to the landlord's trigger notice, and though a response could usually be informal,[183] it was certainly essential.[184] Again it was possible (and again dangerous) to make time of the essence for service of the tenant's counter-notice. One specimen lease provided that "the rack rent shall be conclusively fixed at the amount in the lessor's notice" unless a counter-notice was served within two months.[185] The only defence for the tenant was to show that the landlord's trigger notice was itself so defective that it did not count as a proper notice. Service of a response notice leads to an opportunity to negotiate the new rent, but negotiations often stall, in which case it will usually be the landlord who has the greatest interest in insisting on the appointment of an arbiter to resolve the dispute. It was even more dangerous to insist on time being of the essence of arbitral procedures.[186] Very often a break clause is associated with an upwards review.[187]

3. Upwards only or upwards/downwards

Review is directed to increasing the rent to reflect the impact of inflation. What happens if rents *fall*? Broadly two possibilities exist, the course adopted depending entirely upon the state of the market.

Most rent review provisions only operate in an *upwards* direction.[188] This is assumed if it is only the landlord who can initiate a review.[189] A further refinement insisted upon by landlords in a buoyant market is a *ratchet*, which ensures that each time the rent is increased on review the higher rent provides a new base-line below which the rent

---

[179] *Samuel Properties (Developments) Ltd.* v. *Hayek* [1972] 1 W.L.R. 1296 C.A.; (1973) 89 *L.Q.R.* 8; *Darlington B.C.* v. *Waring & Gillow (Holdings) Ltd.* [1988] 2 E.G.L.R. 159 Ch.D.; *Richurst* v. *Pimenta* [1993] 1 W.L.R. 159 C.A.; M. Haley [1993] *Conv.* 382.

[180] *Maraday* v. *Sturt Properties Ltd.* [1988] 2 E.G.L.R. 163 Ch.D.; *Bailey* v. *Supasnaps Ltd.* (1995) 70 P. & C.R. 450 C.A. ("at the *expiration* of the 10th year" means at the *last* moment).

[181] [1978] A.C. 904, 947G, Lord Salmon.

[182] *Knight* v. *Lawrence* [1991] 1 E.G.L.R. 143 Ch.D.

[183] *Prudential Property Services Ltd.* v. *Capital Land Holdings Ltd.* [1993] 1 E.G.L.R. 128 Ch.D.; *Glofield Properties Ltd.* v. *Morley* [1988] 1 E.G.L.R. 113, *(No.2)* [1989] 2 E.G.L.R. 118 C.A.; *Barrett Estate Services Ltd.* v. *David Greig (Retail) Ltd.* [1991] 2 E.G.L.R. 123 Q.B.D.

[184] *Patel* v. *Peel Investments (South) Ltd.* [1992] 2 E.G.L.R. 116, Morritt J.

[185] *Mammoth Greeting Cards Ltd.* v. *Agra Ltd.* [1990] 2 E.G.L.R. 124, Mummery J.; *Fox & Widley* v. *Gurham* [1998] 1 E.G.L.R. 91, Clarke J. obiter.

[186] *Darlington B.C.* v. *Waring & Gillow (Holdings) Ltd.* [1988] 2 E.G.L.R. 159 Ch.D.

[187] See below at p. 659.

[188] Law Society/ R.I.C.S. Model Forms cl.2 "whichever be the greater". Cases are: *S.S. for the Environment* v. *Associated News Holdings Ltd.* [1995] E.G.C.S. 166 C.A.; *Brimican Investments Ltd.* v. *Blue Circle Heating Ltd.* [1995] E.G.C.S. 18, Chadwick J.

[189] *Standard Life Assurance Co. Ltd.* v. *Unipath Ltd.* [1997] 2 E.G.L.R. 121 C.A.

cannot drop,[190] so that on a fifth review the rent cannot fall below that set on the fourth review. The prevalence of ratchet clauses has had a disastrous effect on the business community; many tenants were forced out of business during the recession of the early 1990s because they were locked into properties at rents which were way above the market rent at the time and ratchet clauses delayed the necessary self-adjustment of the market. The Commercial Letting Code suggests that clauses should not automatically be upwards only,[191] but legislation to ban ratchet clauses failed.[192] Even if it is theoretically possible for the rent to fall, this is only helpful to a tenant who can compel his landlord to trigger a review, a matter that is not implied.[193] Business lease renewals under part II of the Landlord and Tenant Act 1954 usually provide for upwards only review[194] though the position is less settled where the court fixes the terms of a lease under an option or agreement.[195]

A more realistic protection for the tenant is to couple a *ratchet clause with a break clause*. Suppose that a rent is fixed at £100,000 when market levels have fallen to half this, but a ratchet clause operates to leave the rent at £100,000, far above the current market rental. If the tenant has a break clause when he hears the result of the review he will be able to end the lease and rent alternative premises elsewhere. Fairness to tenants is achieved, and businesses are not locked into uneconomic buildings,[196] but the fact is that a commercial landlord will only agree to this essential balance where the letting market is weak.[197] Where the tenant has an opportunity to break the lease, it is essential for the rent review to be conducted promptly, and it will be implied that time is of the essence to the review,[198] because the tenant must know what the new rent is to be when deciding whether or not to end the lease. Morritt L.J. provided the leading judgment in *Central Estates Ltd. v. S.S. for the Environment*[199] in which he identified three particular cases of linkage where time became of the essence: (1) where the rent review was upward only with a set period for the tenant to decide to terminate[200] or some other ultimatum procedure,[201] (2) where the break clause was exercisable up to the last day for review,[202]

---

[190] *Addin Investments Ltd. v. S.S. for the Environment* [1997] 1 E.G.L.R. 99.

[191] R. Castle and A. McFarquahar [1995] *N.L.J.* 1166; J.E. Adams [1996] *Conv.* 9; P.H. Kenny [1996] *Conv.* 83; see also Law Com. No.162 (1987) paras.4.60–4.61.

[192] Upwards-only Rent Review Clauses (Abolition) Bill 1993; R. Hudson [1993] *N.L.J.* 782; J.E. Adams [1993] *Conv.* 423, [1997] *Conv.* 252.

[193] *Sunflower Services Ltd. v. Unisys N.Z. Ltd.* (1997) 74 P. & C.R. 112. The P.C. approved *Harben Style Ltd. v. Rhodes Trust* [1995] 1 E.G.L.R. 118 Ch.D. in preference to *Royal Bank of Scotland plc. v. Jennings* [1996] 1 E.G.L.R. 101 C.A.; J.E. Adams [1997] *Conv.* 252; *Standard Life Assurance Co. Ltd. v. Unipath Ltd.* [1997] 2 E.G.L.R. 121 C.A.

[194] *Boots the Chemist Ltd. v. Pinkland Ltd.* [1992] 2 E.G.L.R. 98; *Blythewood Plant Hire Ltd. v. Spiers* [1992] 2 E.G.L.R. 103; *Theodore Goddard v. Fletcher King Services Ltd.* [1997] 2 E.G.L.R. 131 Q.B.D.

[195] Contrast: *Norwich Union Life Insurance Society v. A.G.* [1995] E.G.C.S. 85 P.C.; and *Melanesian Mission Trust Board v. Australia Mutual Provident Society* [1997] 2 E.G.L.R. 128 P.C.

[196] M. Southern [1991] 27 *L.S.G.* 25.

[197] J.E. Adams [1995] *Conv.* 102 says that in 1995 46% of commercial leases incorporated a break clause.

[198] *United Scientific Holdings Ltd. v. Burnley B.C.* [1978] A.C. 904, 946C, Lord Simon.

[199] [1997] 1 E.G.L.R. 239, 240–241.

[200] *Coventry C.C. v. J. Hepworth & Son Ltd.* [1983] 1 E.G.L.R. 119 C.A.

[201] *Banks v. Kokkinos* [1998] E.G.C.S. 187 Ch.D., preferring *Visionhire Ltd. v. Britel Fund Trustees* [1992] 1 E.G.L.R. 128 C.S. (Inner House) to *Phipps-Faire Ltd. v. Malbern Construction Ltd.* [1987] 1 E.G.L.R. 129, Warner J.; see also *Henry Smith's Charity Trustee v. Awada Trading and Promotion Services Ltd.* [1984] 1 E.G.L.R. 116 C.A.

[202] *Legal & General Assurance (Pension Management) Ltd. v. Cheshire C.C.* [1984] 1 E.G.L.R. 102 C.A.

and (3) where the review was up or down but only the tenant had power to terminate the lease.[203]

4.   The arbiter

Large sums are at stake in review procedures, so that the desirability of an agreement is often cast aside as a review develops into a bitter dispute requiring resolution by an outside valuer. Three variant procedures are available, where the surveyor acts as an arbitrator, or as an expert, or where the choice is left to the landlord.[204] An expert is likely to reach a decision more cheaply and more quickly. This is good for small cases. Arbitration is probably safer, with better argument and a clearer appeal procedure, and is the desirable choice if much money is at stake or if the review clause is of an unusual type.[205] Option agreements also require a mechanism for resolving disputes.

An *arbitrator* can be appointed to act under the Arbitration Act 1996, but only by consent or under a written agreement.[206] So, the review clause must provide a procedure for appointment of an arbitrator if the parties are unable to agree, usually a person nominated by the President of the Royal Institution of Chartered Surveyors under a procedure regulated by the R.I.C.S. rulebook,[207] with replacements under the Arbitration Act 1996.[208] It may be slightly easier to find someone to act as arbitrator, given the immunity from negligence liability which is not extended to an expert. Arbitration is a judicial function, the arbitrator being required to act on the basis of the evidence submitted and to follow a statutory procedure. An award can be enforced as if it is a court judgment. Costs can be awarded against the unsuccessful party.

Experts are invariably valuers, but operating less formally than they do as arbitrators, and with no immunity from negligence liability. The review clause must provide a procedure for appointment.[209] Procedure is non-statutory and so the review clause may need to lay down details of matters such as the evidence to be permitted. Costs are not awarded so each side bears its own costs.[210]

So much is at stake that many rent review awards are subject to an *appeal.* The arbiter (whether an arbitrator or expert) will invariably be empowered to make a conclusive determination of facts, and to fix the rent with regard to comparables, and no appeal is possible against these factual decisions unless they are so grossly wrong as to be erroneous in law. Unfortunately there is always ample scope for disagreements about the correct interpretation of the review provision, which raise points of law capable of challenge in court; very often arbitral procedures have to be delayed while preliminary legal challenges are resolved[211]; whether a pre-emptive challenge is allowed must be deter-

---

[203] *Metrolands Investments Ltd.* v. *J.H. Dewhurst Ltd.* [1986] 1 E.G.L.R. 125 C.A.
[204] Model Forms, variations A, B, and C.
[205] H. Hughes [1991] 30 *E.G.* 50; J. Ody & R. Butler [1994] 10 *E.G.* 99.
[206] s.5.
[207] Model Forms cl.3; *Staines Warehousing Co. Ltd.* v. *Montague Executor and Trustee Co.* (1987) 54 P. & C.R. 302 C.A.
[208] s.12.
[209] Model Forms cl.4 (agreement or nomination by President of the R.I.C.S.); replacement is contractual.
[210] Model Forms cl.4(A)(i).
[211] *PosTel Properties Ltd.* v. *Greenwell* [1992] 2 E.G.L.R. 130 Ch.D.

mined by construction of the wording of the lease.[212] A clear route to appeal is provided against the *arbitrator's* decision on legal points, that is on interpretation of the review clause,[213] and this can also be used to obtain an initial ruling on a point of law. Many cases are litigated simply because vast sums are at stake, though this alone is not a reason for allowing court action or referring a case to the Court of Appeal.[214] Appeal from an *expert* can only occur if reasons are given, and they are obviously wrong.

5. Memorandum

Review between the current landlord and tenant binds future parties, such as future purchasers of the lease and sureties. Hence the result of the review should be recorded by an executed memorandum placed on the lease stating the amount of the reviewed rent and the date from which it is operational and executed by all parties bound by it.

K. OPEN MARKET RENTS

1. Date for fixing rent

Rental levels rise and fall,[215] and it is essential to specify the date on which quantification is to occur. In rent review clauses this should be the review date from which the new rent is payable, but sloppy drafting may lead to its being the date of the landlord's trigger notice[216] or—to the disadvantage of the tenant—the actual date of the determination.[217] In the case of a business lease renewal it is three months after final disposal of the tenant's application for renewal.[218]

2. Market rent

Quantification of the rent on a business lease renewal will occur under the Landlord and Tenant Act 1954,[219] with longer leases often providing for review.[220] Most rent reviews proceed on the terms of the Model Forms of the Law Society and Royal Institution of Chartered Surveyors,[221] though commonly with modifications. Leases created under option agreements follow the terms of that agreement. Broadly each envisages a similar method of quantification. One imagines a notional lease[222] of the property granted on

---

[212] *National Grid Co. plc.* v. *M25 Group Ltd.* [1999] 1 E.G.L.R. 65 C.A.; S. Fulford [1998] 18 *P.L.J.* 6; *Mercury Communications Ltd.* v. *Director General of Telecommuniations* [1996] 1 W.L.R. 48; *British Shipbuilding plc.* v. *V.S.E.L. Consortium plc.* [1997] 1 Lloyd's Rep. 106, Lightman J.

[213] *British Railways Board* v. *Ringbest Ltd.* [1996] 2 E.G.L.R. 82, Scott V.C.; *Euripides* v. *Gascoyne Holdings Ltd.* (1996) 72 P. & C.R. 301 C.A.

[214] *Prudential Assurance Co. Ltd.* v. *99 Bishopsgate Ltd.* [1992] 1 E.G.L.R. 119 Ch.D.; *Henry Boot Construction (U.K.) Ltd.* v. *Malmaison Hotel (Manchester) Ltd.* [2000] N.L.J. 86 C.A. (refusal of judge to give certificate cannot be challenged in C.A.).

[215] S. Morley [1995] 03 *E.G.* 110, 112, fig.3.

[216] *Parkside Knightsbridge Ltd.* v. *German Food Centre Ltd.* [1990] 2 E.G.L.R. 265 Ch.D.

[217] *Prudential Assurance Co Ltd* v. *Gray* [1987] 2 E.G.L.R. 134; *Glofield Properties Ltd.* v. *Morley (No 2)* [1989] 2 E.G.L.R. 118 C.A.; this works unfairly to the landlord's advantage if rental levels rise and the determination is delayed.

[218] L.T.A. 1954 s.64; but the landlord may seek an interim rent, see below pp. 668–669.

[219] s.34, as amended by L.P.A. 1969 s.2.

[220] L.T.A. 1954 s.34(3); subs.(4) was added by L.T. (Covenants) A. 1995 sch.1.

[221] (1985) 82 *L.S.G.* 3664.

[222] A response to *Ponsford* v. *H.M.S. Aerosols Ltd.* [1979] A.C. 63 H.L., discussed below.

the review date, and determines the market rent payable under that lease, but certain factors are disregarded to try to ensure that the rent is what this particular tenant should be asked to pay.

The industry standard model forms[223] require determination of the yearly rent at which the demised premises might reasonably be expected to be let, the assumption being that the demised premises are available for letting in the open market without a fine or premium with vacant possession[224] with willing parties.[225] Some variant of this form of open market rent figured in all the early cases.[226] Slightly variant methods of expression—for example a rack rental[227]—have little impact on the actual rent to be set. Where a reference is made to a "reasonable"[228] or "fair and reasonable"[229] rent, it is more arguable that subjective factors affecting this particular tenant should be taken into account, though in fact the House of Lords has held that the rent is an objective rent determined by the market.[230]

Both on review[231] and on business lease renewal,[232] valuation in a genuine market[233] is based on *comparables*, that is evidence of rents achieved on actual lettings of similar property on similar terms,[234] provided that they were made *before* the review date.[235] The weight to be attached to a particular comparable is entirely a matter for the arbitrator.[236] Many landlords impose confidentiality clauses to conceal concessions such as rent-free fitting out periods made to individual tenants and so to create false comparables, but this practice is to be deprecated.[237] Where evidence from similar lettings is not available, a last resort is to split the proposals of landlord and tenant.[238]

Market rents are elusive for *specialised property* of a type for which there is no market and hence no true comparables. Rental levels may have to fixed as a proportion of profits, whether on review or on a business lease renewal.[239] Usually rents are fixed on the basis of market expectations of profitability[240] but if it is based on the actual profits of

---

[223] Model Forms cl.3.

[224] *Northern Electric plc. v. Addison* [1997] 2 E.G.L.R. 111 C.A.

[225] *Dennis & Robinson Ltd. v. Kiossos Establishment Ltd.* [1987] 1 E.G.L.R. 133 C.A.; *Northern Electric plc. v. Addison* [1999] 2 E.G.L.R. 111, Potter L.J. (this precludes any ransom element).

[226] [1979] A.C. 63, 79D–E, Lord Salmon dissenting.

[227] *Leigh v. Certibilt Investments Ltd.* [1988] 1 E.G.L.R 116; *G.R.E. Compass v. Draper's Co.* [1994] E.G.C.S. 97, Lindsay J.; *Ashworth Frazer Ltd. v. Gloucester C.C.* [1997] 1 E.G.L.R. 104 C.A.

[228] *Ponsford v. H.M.S. Aerosols Ltd.* [1979] A.C. 63 H.L.; (1978) 94 L.Q.R. 481.

[229] *A.R.C. Ltd. v. Schofield* [1990] 2 E.G.L.R. 52 Ch.D.

[230] *Ponsford* as above; the dissenting opinions are more convincing.

[231] *British Railways Board v. Mobil Oil Co. Ltd.* [1994] 1 E.G.L.R. 146 C.A.

[232] *Newey & Eyre v. J. Curtis & Son Ltd.* [1984] 2 E.G.L.R. 105 Ch.D.; *Janes (Gowns) Ltd. v. Harlow Development Corporation* [1979] 1 E.G.L.R. 52 Ch.D.

[233] *Baptist v. Gray's Inn* [1993] 2 E.G.L.R. 136 C.Ct.

[234] *Fine Fare Ltd. v. Kenmore Investments Ltd.* [1989] 1 E.G.L.R. 143 Ch.D.

[235] *Khalique v. Law Land plc.* [1989] 1 E.G.L.R. 105 C.A.

[236] *Living Waters Christian Centres Ltd. v. Conwy B.C.* [1999] 3 E.G.L.R. 1 C.A.; dicta of Colman J. on the use of comparables approved.

[237] *Commercial Letting Code* (1995); R. Castle & A. McFarquhar [1995] *N.L.J.* 1166; J.E. Adams [1996] *Conv.* 9; P.H. Kenny [1996] *Conv.* 83.

[238] *Halberstam v. Tandalco Corp. N.V.* [1985] 1 E.G.L.R. 90 C.A.

[239] *W.J. Barton Ltd. v. Long Acre Securities Ltd.* [1982] 1 W.L.R. 398 C.A.; (1982) 98 L.Q.R. 341; J.E. Martin [1982] *Conv.* 227 (petrol station).

[240] *Electricity Supply Nominees Ltd. v. London Clubs Ltd.* [1988] 2 E.G.L.R. 152 Ch.D.

the tenant's business it will be necessary to ensure both that the landlord has access to the tenant's books and that confidentiality is observed.[241]

3. Notional lease

The need for an artificial lease to eliminate market distortions is illustrated by *Ponsford* v. *H.M.S. Aerosols Ltd.*[242] The tenant had reinstated the factory after fire damage incorporating £32,000 worth of improvements, but when the rent was reviewed it was held that the rent had to be increased to reflect the improved state of the property. This monstrous result has led to an enormous increase in complexity of review procedures because, in order to avoid it, it has become necessary to assume a notional lease of the actual property on similar terms to the actual lease, making artificial assumptions to avoid unfair results. The specific decision is avoided by the general practice of disregarding the effect of improvements.

The industry has developed a standard form for regards and disregards which is common to rent review provisions,[243] business lease renewals,[244] and option agreements. Terms of the artificially assumed lease are, in general, imported from the actual lease,[245] subject to stated exceptions (that is to disregards). Experience suggests that the terms should be as similar as possible to the real lease—a presumption of reality first stated by Hoffmann J.[246]—since unprincipled divergences may lead to radical errors,[247] and judges are becoming more sympathetic to the need to find commercial solutions.[248]

4. Assumptions and disregards

Review provisions require a *disregard of the existing rent*, but balance is only obtained if it is assumed that the imaginary lease will contain a rent review provision.[249] If this is not stated explicitly—as it should be[250]—it will in any event be assumed that disregard of the rent leaves in place the review provision,[251] though this result was achieved only after voluminous litigation and judicial prevarication.[252]

In a real commercial letting it is common to allow a *rent-free period*—perhaps for as long as six months—for fitting out a shop or office block. Benefit flows to the landlord because liability to rates is transferred to the tenant. However following this practice

---

[241] J.E. Adams [1993] *Conv.* 190.

[242] [1979] A.C. 63 H.L.; (1978) 94 *L.Q.R.* 481; F. Jenkins [1996] 07 *L.S.G.* 24.

[243] Standard Business Lease (1996 ed.) cl.8.2.

[244] L.T.A. 1954 s.34.

[245] *Jaskel* v. *Sophie Nursery Products Ltd.* [1993] E.G.C.S. 42 C.A.; E. Cooke [1993] *Conv.* 387; A. Dowling [1995] *Conv.* 124; *Commercial Union Life Assurance Co. Ltd.* v. *Woolworths plc.* [1994] 1 E.G.L.R. 237.

[246] *Norwich Union Life Insurance Society* v. *Trustee Savings Banks Central Board* [1986] 1 E.G.L.R. 136, 137G.

[247] Divergence was justified in *Brown* v. *Gloucester C.C.* [1998] 1 E.G.L.R. 95 C.A.

[248] *Law Land Co. Ltd.* v. *Consumers' Association Ltd.* [1980] 2 E.G.L.R. 109, 112, Brightman L.J.; *Dukeminster (Ebbgate House One) Ltd.* v. *Somerfield Property Co. Ltd.* [1997] 2 E.G.L.R. 125 C.A.

[249] Otherwise the initial rent might be higher by 10–20%: J.E. Adams [1986] *Conv.* 75.

[250] Standard Business Lease (1996) cl.8.2. is unclear, but the Model Forms said explicitly "save for this proviso".

[251] *British Gas Corporation* v. *Universities Superannuation Scheme Ltd.* [1986] 1 W.L.R. 398, Browne-Wilkinson V.C.; *Arnold* v. *National Westminster Bank plc* [1991] 2 A.C. 93 H.L. (issue estoppel); *Prudential Assurance Co. Ltd.* v. *Salisbury Handbags Ltd.* [1993] 1 E.G.L.R. 153, Chadwick J.

[252] *National Westminster Bank plc.* v. *Arthur Young McLelland Moores* [1985] 1 E.G.L.R. 61, Walton J., on appeal [1985] 2 E.G.L.R. 13 C.A.

on the notional (rent review) letting would reduce the rent yield, so drafting aims to eliminate this effect by assuming that any rent-free period has expired.[253]

Practice diverges sharply on the *length of term* to be assumed for the notional letting. It is unwise to leave this crucial matter undefined.[254] Normally it is what the actual tenant has left[255] including any reversionary lease,[256] and taking into account any break clause.[257] If the assumed lease is the same length as the real lease, the presumption of reality requires that it should be treated as starting from the real commencement date of the term and not from the review date, thus giving the tenant the same term remaining for review purposes as he has in real life.[258]

The Standard Business Lease[259] provides for a notional term for the duration of the unexpired residue of the real term. The possibility of business renewal is a legitimate consideration when considering the term of the notional letting,[260] but otherwise the position of the current tenant should be disregarded as an obstruction in the search for an objectively correct market rent,[261] including his goodwill,[262] marriage prospects, and business tenancies protection.[263]

5. Assumptions about the condition of the property

Rents of commercial buildings should be reviewed on the basis of a notional lease (usually a single letting) of the *buildings*[264] as opposed to the bare site,[265] except that is in the case of a building lease which should be restricted to the cleared site.[266]

---

[253] *99 Bishopsgate Ltd. v. Prudential Assurance Co. Ltd.* [1985] 1 E.G.L.R. 72; *City Offices plc. v. Bryanston Insurance Co. Ltd.* [1993] 1 E.G.L.R. 126, Aldous J.; *London & Leeds Estates Ltd. v. Paribas Ltd.* [1993] 2 E.G.L.R. 149 C.A.; *Co-operative Wholesale Society Ltd. v. National Westminster Bank plc.* (1994) 68 P. & C.R. 256 C.A.; *Broadgate Square plc. v. Lehman Brothers Ltd.* [1995] 2 E.G.L.R. 97 C.A., *(No.2)* [1995] 2 E.G.L.R. 5 Ch.D.; *Scottish Amicable Life Assurance Society v. Middleton Potts Godfrey & West* (1995) 69 P. & C.R. 475, Arden J.

[254] *Prudential Assurance Co. Ltd. v. Salisbury Handbags Ltd.* [1992] 1 E.G.L.R. 153 Ch.D.; *Lynnthorpe Enterprises Ltd. v. Sidney Smith (Chelsea) Ltd.* [1990] 2 E.G.L.R. 131 C.A.; *Brown v. Gloucester C.C.* [1998] 1 E.G.L.R. 95 C.A.

[255] *British Gas plc. v. Dollar Land Holdings Ltd.* [1992] 1 E.G.L.R. 135, Knox J.; *St Martin's Property Investments Ltd. v. Citycorp Investment Bank Properties Ltd.* [1998] E.G.C.S. 161 C.A. (sub-lease linked to head lease); *Westside Nominees Ltd. v. Bolton M.B.C.* [2000] E.G.C.S. 20, Neuberger J.

[256] *Stylo Barratt Properties Ltd. v. Legal & General Assurance Society Ltd.* [1989] 2 E.G.L.R. 116 Ch.D.

[257] *Commercial Union Life Assurance Co. Ltd. v. Woolworths plc.* [1994] 1 E.G.L.R. 237.

[258] *St Martins Property Investment Ltd. v. Citycorp Investment Bank Properties Ltd.* [1998] E.G.C.S. 161 C.A.; P.F. Smith [1999] *Conv.* 346.

[259] (1996 ed.) cl.8.2.

[260] *Pivot Properties Ltd. v. S.S. for the Environment* (1979) 39 P. & C.R. 386, Phillips J., on appeal [1980] 2 E.G.L.R. 126 C.A.

[261] L.T.A. 1954 s.34(1).

[262] *Prudential Assurance Co. Ltd. v. Grand Metropolitan Estate Ltd.* [1993] 2 E.G.L.R. 153 C.A.

[263] *Toyota (GB) Ltd. v. Legal & General Assurance (Pensions Management) Ltd.* [1989] 2 E.G.L.R. 123 C.A.; *Brett v. Brett Essex Golf Club Ltd.* [1986] 1 E.G.L.R. 154 C.A.; J.E. Adams [1991] 08 *E.G.* 72.

[264] *Goh Eng Wah v. Yap Phooi Yin* [1988] 2 E.G.L.R. 148 P.C.; *Ravenseft Properties Ltd. v. Park* [1988] 2 E.G.L.R. 164; *Laura Investments Co. Ltd. v. Havering L.B.C.* [1992] 1 E.G.L.R. 155, Hoffmann J., *(No.2)* [1993] 1 E.G.L.R. 124 Ch.D.

[265] *Worcester C.C. v. A.S. Clarke (Worcester) Ltd.* [1994] E.G.C.S. 31; *Guildford B.C. v. Cobb* [1994] 1 E.G.L.R. 156; *Braid v. Walsall M.B.C.* (1999) 78 P. & C.R. 94 C.A.

[266] *British Airways plc v. Heathrow Airport Ltd.* [1992] 1 E.G.L.R. 141, Mummery J.; *Ipswich Town F.C. Co. Ltd. v. Ipswich B.C.* [1988] 2 E.G.L.R. 141, Browne-Wilkinson V.C.; J.E. Martin [1988] *Conv.* 437; *Sheerness Steel Co. plc. v. Medway Ports Authority* [1992] 1 E.G.L.R. 133 C.A.; *Braid v. Walsall M.B.C.* (1999) 78 P. & C.R. 94 C.A. (building lease differentiated land and future buildings).

Quantification of a rent to be fixed on a review must be based on the assumption that the tenant's obligations with regard to *repair* in the real world lease have been carried out, any fire damage restored, and that the rental value has not been diminished by the tenant's acts. Otherwise the tenant will be able to depress the rent obtainable on review by his own failings. The standard of repair must be drawn from the actual lease,[267] but it should be remembered that an onerous repairing covenant—perhaps obliging the tenant to reconstruct the building[268]—may severely depreciate the rent payable on review. If a building fails to meet statutory standards for matters such as access for the disabled, this may reduce the rent which a tenant would be willing to pay for it, and hence the rent obtainable on review.[269]

Unless special provision is made in the lease, the tenant's rent will be increased by *improvements.*[270] This result is grossly inequitable and courts strive to prevent unfairness by refusing to rentalise work carried out at a tenant's expense. This is done under a standard term that provides a disregard for actual[271] authorised[272] improvements and trade fixtures,[273] meaning that these items are not taken into account on review.[274] Inclusion of this clause renders irrelevant the question of reinstatement.[275] Where works are carried out by someone other than the tenant, the tenant should get credit for the work if he identifies the work to be done, finances it or supervises it[276]; however, the position is open where it is a sub-tenant or licensee who has carried out the work.

6. Use

Generally the *use covenant* is transferred from the actual lease to the notional lease used to quantify rent reviews. Tight restriction of permitted uses is penalised by a severe diminution in the rent achievable.[277] Rental yield from commercial property is best preserved by allowing any use within a given planning law use class,[278] though review provisions have difficulty in coping with changes in the legislative classes.[279] Rent review should take into account the potentiality for wider uses, particularly after planning permission has been granted, so much so that it may be beneficial for the landlord to seek

---

[267] *Ladbroke Hotels Ltd.* v. *Sandhu* [1995] 2 E.G.L.R. 92, Robert Walker J. (the remaining commercial life of the property is irrelevant).

[268] *Norwich Union Life Insurance Society* v. *British Railways Board* [1987] 2 E.G.L.R. 137.

[269] V. King & T. Phillips [1999] 04 *E.G.* 150.

[270] *Ponsford* v. *H.M.S. (Aerosols) Ltd.* [1978] A.C. 63 H.L.; (1978) 94 *L.Q.R.* 481; J.E. Martin [1988] *Conv.* 437. Apparently the tenant had to buy the reversion to avoid the consequences: J.E. Adams [1993] *Conv.* 423.

[271] *Iceland Frozen Foods plc* v. *Starlight Investments Ltd.* [1992] 1 E.G.L.R. 126 C.A.

[272] Unauthorised improvements will increase the rent increased: *Historic Houses Hotels Ltd.* v. *Cadogan Estates Ltd.* [1995] 1 E.G.L.R. 117 C.A.; *Euston Centre Properties Ltd.* v. *H.& J. Wilson Ltd.* [1982] 1 E.G.L.R. 57, Cantley J. (work prior to grant).

[273] *Ocean Accident & Guarantee Corporation* v. *Next plc.* [1996] 2 E.G.L.R. 84 Ch.D.

[274] L.T.A. 1954 s.34(1); Standard Business Lease (1996 ed.) cl.8.2.

[275] *Pleasurama Properties* v. *Leisure Investments (West End) Ltd.* [1986] 1 E.G.L.R. 145 C.A.; *Orchid Lodge (U.K.) Ltd.* v. *Extel Computing Ltd.* [1991] 2 E.G.L.R. 116 C.A.

[276] *Durley House Ltd.* v. *Cadogan* [2000] 09 *E.G.* 183 C.A.; R. Cohen [2000] 12 *E.G.* 142.

[277] *Plinth Property Investment Co. Ltd.* v. *Mott, Hay & Anderson* [1979] 1 E.G.L.R. 17 (rent as consulting engineers £89,000, whereas with any use it was £130,000).

[278] *SI Pension Trustees Ltd.* v. *Peru* [1988] 1 E.G.L.R. 119; *PosTel Properties Ltd.* v. *Greenwell* [1992] 2 E.G.L.R. 130 Ch.D.

[279] *Brewers' Co.* v. *Viewplan plc.* [1989] 2 E.G.L.R. 133 Ch.D. (change from 1972 to 1987 Orders); see below pp. 708–709.

additional planning permissions before instigating a review procedure.[280] If the permitted uses are varied, this should be done formally so that future reviews will assess the rent on the basis of the new use.[281]

Particular difficulty is caused by use rights that are personal to the tenant. Restricting use to a single named company[282] might severely depress the rent, but it is generally to be assumed that the hypothetical tenant company will be a permitted user.[283] Assignment rights that are personal to the current tenant might depress the rent by more than 5 per cent.[284] Existing management agreements[285] and gaming licences[286] can be assumed to be available to the notional tenant. Removal of an "anchor" tenant, such as a major supermarket in a shopping centre, should reduce the rent that other tenants pay.[287]

L. CRUDE FORMS OF REVIEW

1. General

Full blown review provisions are sometimes inappropriate and it may be possible to get by with something cruder. Some leases may provide for fixed increases set out in advance, or linkage of rent rises to the retail prices index,[288] or to turnover,[289] or setting the rent on a sub-lease as a percentage of the rent payable under the head-lease.[290] However, despite the saving in cost, crude machinery often breaks down when it becomes necessary to rely on arbitration to iron out dislocations.[291]

2. Turnover rents

This American concept has been adopted with increasing frequency in this country since the early 1990s. It is particularly useful to a landlord with a marginal shopping centre in which units are hard to let. Tenants may well feel that landlords will take more care about the selection of other tenants and achieving a satisfactory letting mix. Rents are linked to the sales made in a financial year, so that tenants pay more in good times

---

[280] *Tea Trade Properties Ltd.* v. *C.I.N. Properties Ltd.* [1990] 1 E.G.L.R. 155, Hoffmann J.

[281] *Lynnthorpe Enterprises Ltd.* v. *Sidney Smith (Chelsea) Ltd.* [1990] 2 E.G.L.R. 131 C.A.

[282] *James* v. *British Crafts Centre* [1987] 1 E.G.L.R. 139 C.A.

[283] *Orchid Lodge (U.K.) Ltd.* v. *Extel Computing Ltd.* [1991] 2 E.G.L.R. 116 C.A.; *Law Land Co. Ltd.* v. *Consumers' Association Ltd.* [1980] 2 E.G.L.R. 109; *Post Office Counters Ltd.* v. *Harlow D.C.* [1991] 2 E.G.L.R. 121 (post office).

[284] *Fiveways Properties Ltd.* v. *S.S. for the Environment* [1990] 2 E.G.L.R. 126.

[285] *J.W. Childers Trustees* v. *Anker* [1996] 1 E.G.L.R. 1 C.A.

[286] *Ritz Hotel (London) Ltd.* v. *Ritz Casino Ltd.* [1989] 2 E.G.L.R. 135 Ch.D.; *Parkside Clubs (Nottingham) Ltd.* v. *Armgrade Ltd.* [1995] 2 E.G.L.R. 96 C.A.

[287] *French* v. *Commercial Union Assurance Co. plc.* [1993] 1 E.G.L.R. 113 C.A.; *Dukeminster (Ebbgate House One) Ltd.* v. *Somerfield Property Co. Ltd.* [1997] 2 E.G.L.R. 125 C.A.; A. Oswald [1999] 37 E.G. 161.

[288] *Cumshaw Ltd.* v. *Bowen* [1987] 1 E.G.L.R. 30 (changes in basis of R.P.I.); M. Dockray (1979) 43 *Conv. (N.S.)* 258; [1999] 35 *P.L.J.* 19 (stamp duty).

[289] *Heathrow Airport Ltd.* v. *Forte (U.K.) Ltd.* [1998] E.G.C.S. 13; H. Willett [1997] 1 *L.T.Rev.* 90; F. Jenkins & S. Cullen [1999] 45 *E.G.* 174 (problems on assignment).

[290] *R. & A. Milletts (Shops) Ltd.* v. *Leon Allan International Fashions Ltd.* [1989] 1 E.G.L.R. 138 C.A. (surrender); *Ashworth Frazer Ltd.* v. *Gloucester C.C.* [1997] 1 E.G.L.R. 104 C.A. (rents based on non-existent sub-letting); R. Cooper & W. Killick [1999] 13 *E.G.* 109 (link to ground rental); *Standard Life Co. Ltd.* v. *Greycoat Devonshire Square Ltd.* [2000] E.G.C.S. 40.

[291] *Wyndham Investments Ltd.* v. *Motorway Tyres & Accessories Ltd.* [1991] 2 E.G.L.R. 114 C.A.

but less during a lean period. Variants of pure turnover which provide more protection for the landlord are to take 75 per cent of the market rental, with a top up based on turnover or to impose a ratchet so that the profit base will never fall below (say) 90 per cent of the takings in the most successful year. Problems are that the landlord needs to ensure that the tenant trades seriously and on every available day, transfer of such a tenancy is more complicated than a rack rental lease,[292] and careful drafting is needed to cope with regrants and variations of the tenant's lease.[293]

M. INTERIM BUSINESS RENTS

1. Business lease renewal

Tenants with an established right to renewal have an incentive to defer proceedings in order to delay the operation of a rent increase. Landlords respond by making application to secure an interim rent, permitted at any time after service of the landlord's trigger notice[294] or after a tenant's request for a new tenancy.[295] If a tenant responds to the landlord's notice requesting a new lease, he is estopped from disputing the right to an interim rent.[296] Even a landlord with no title can claim an interim rent on the basis of the estoppel that exists between landlord and tenant.[297] Landlords will normally be entitled to an award of an interim rent.[298] An award is backdated (for up to six years)[299] to the date of the application[300] when the summons is issued,[301] provided that the summons is served in due time.[302] Interim rent should *quantified* on the basis of what it is reasonable for the tenant to pay,[303] but there is a statutory requirement to have regard to the previously agreed rent.[304] Usually (though not necessarily[305]) this leads to a cushion, to protect the tenant against the shock of a big rent rise,[306] amounting to a deduction of about 10 per cent from the market rent,[307] ranging upwards to as much as 50 per

---

[292] F. Jenkins and S. Cullen [1999] 45 *E.G.* 174; A. Wernham [2000] 30 *E.G.* 110 (e-commerce).

[293] *Berthon Boat Co. Ltd.* v. *Hood Sailmaker Ltd.* [2000] 08 E.G. 175 Q.B.D.

[294] L.T.A. 1954 s.24A(1).

[295] s.26; assignment of the reversion makes no difference: *Bloomfield* v. *Ashwright Ltd.* [1983] 1 E.G.L.R. 82 C.A.

[296] *Benedictus* v. *Jalaram Ltd.* [1989] 1 E.G.L.R. 251.

[297] *Bell* v. *General Accident Fire & Life Assurance Corp. Ltd.* [1998] 1 E.G.L.R. 69 C.A.; J. Morgan [1999] *J.B.L.* 274.

[298] *English Exporters (London) Ltd.* v. *Eldonwall Ltd.* [1973] Ch. 415, Megarry J.

[299] *Morris* v. *Royel Properties Ltd.* [1995] C.L.Y. 2963.

[300] L.T.A. 1954 s.24A(2); *Steam Properties Ltd.* v. *Davis* [1972] 1 W.L.R. 645, Pennycuick V.C.; *Bailey Organisation* v. *U.K. Temperance & General Provident Institution* [1975] 1 E.G.L.R. 61 C.A.

[301] *Victor Blake (Menswear) Ltd.* v. *Westminster C.C.* (1979) 38 P. & C.R. 448; *Coates Bros. plc.* v. *General Accident Life Assurance Ltd.* [1991] 1 W.L.R. 712, Millett J. (procedure); *Thomas* v. *Hammond-Lawrence* [1986] 1 W.L.R. 456 C.A. (in the landlord's answer to the tenant's request for a new tenancy).

[302] *Texaco Ltd.* v. *Benton & Bowles Holdings Ltd.* [1983] 2 E.G.L.R. 62, Falconer J.; *R.* v. *Gravesend C.C. ex parte Patchett* [1993] 2 E.G.L.R. 125.

[303] L.T.A. 1954 s.24A(1).

[304] s.24A(3); *Fawke* v. *Viscount Chelsea* [1980] Q.B. 441 C.A. (lack of repair relevant when fixing interim rent).

[305] *Department of the Environment* v. *Allied Freehold Property Trust Ltd.* [1992] 2 E.G.L.R. 100 C.Ct.

[306] *Charles Follett Ltd.* v. *Cabtell Investments Ltd.* [1987] 2 E.G.L.R. 88 C.A. (50% and fix for almost 3 years too much).

[307] *U.D.S. Tailoring Ltd.* v. *B.L. Holdings Ltd.* [1982] 1 E.G.L.R. 61 C.A.; *Amarjee* v. *Barrowfen Properties Ltd.* [1993] 2 E.G.L.R. 133; *French* v. *Commercial Union Assurance Co. Ltd.* [1993] 1 E.G.L.R. 113 C.A.; M. Haley [1993] *Conv.* 228.

cent in quite exceptional cases.[308] Landlords can guard against this judicial cushion by stipulating for a rent review to occur on the last day of the contractual term.

The tenant may *discontinue* his proceedings for a new lease, without permission from the court,[309] but if he does any *existing* application by the landlord for an interim rent continues as a counterclaim.[310] It is vital that the landlord should seek his interim rent before the tenant discontinues his renewal application.[311]

The *Law Commission*[312] propose that the interim rent should be the market rent, but fixed on the last day of the contractual term rather than date of hearing. Tenants should have a new right to make an application that would bring forward the date on which the rent was reduced after market levels had fallen.

2. Rent review

Most reviews are delayed while the rent to be fixed is subject to a dispute. Once the rent is fixed, it is payable retrospectively back to the review date.[313] However a landlord should require either an interim rent or interest to be paid on the arrears of rent emerging when the determination is made.

N. RATES AND TAXES

Numerous charges are imposed by statute on the occupiers of land so that, as between landlord and tenant, most fall on the tenant. If this primary statutory responsibility is to be changed, a lease must contain a covenant by the landlord in clear language.[314]

As the name Non-domestic rating (N.D.R.) suggests, rates now apply only to business and commercial property.[315] The rates for a particular office or shop are based on the rateable value entered on the valuation list. This is determined by the notional rent that could be charged for it. Before 1988 premises were valued on the assumption that they were in a reasonable state of repair unless any disrepair was so extensive that repairs would be uneconomic, and this principle has been applied by an amending Act, both to the 2000 revaluation[316] and retrospectively to the 1990 and 1995 valuation lists.[317] Valuation lists are compiled every five years, the most recent revaluation taking effect in April 2000. Large increases were anticipated in some parts of the country, given that the

---

[308] *Simonite* v. *Sheffield C.C.* [1992] 1 E.G.L.R. 105 (25% allowed); but see *Charles Follett Ltd.* v. *Cabtell Investments Ltd.* [1987] 2 E.G.L.R. 88 C.A. (50% too much as was fix for almost 3 years); *Conway* v. *Arthur* [1988] 2 E.G.L.R. 113 C.A. (retrial where cushion of 15%).

[309] *Artoc Bank Trust Ltd.* v. *Prudential Assurance Co. Ltd.* [1984] 1 W.L.R. 1181, Falconer J.

[310] *Michael Kramer & Co. Ltd.* v. *Airways Pension Fund Trustees Ltd.* [1978] 1 E.G.L.R. 49 C.A.; *Fawke* v. *Viscount Chelsea* [1980] Q.B. 441 C.A.; *Ratners (Jewellers) Ltd.* v. *Lemnoll Ltd.* [1980] 2 E.G.L.R. 65, Dillon J.; *Artoc* as above.

[311] *R.* v. *Gravesend C.C. ex parte Patchett* [1993] 2 E.G.L.R. 125.

[312] Law Com. No.208 (1992) paras.2.063–2.260, draft Bill cl.3; M. Haley (1993) 22 *Anglo-American* 97; M. Haley [1993] *Conv.* 334; H. Lewis [1992] *N.L.J.* 1624; D.W. Williams [1988] 48 *E.G.* 61.

[313] *United Scientific Holdings Ltd.* v. *Burnley B.C.* [1978] A.C. 904 H.L.; *C.H. Bailey Ltd.* v. *Memorial Enterprises Ltd.* [1974] 1 W.L.R. 728 C.A.

[314] *Stockdale* v. *Ascherberg* [1904] 1 K.B. 447 C.A.; there are many cases considering the meaning of particular words such as rates, taxes, assessments, duties, and burdens; Woodfall ch.12.

[315] Local Government Finance Act 1988. Council tax will be charged on the domestic element of a mixed hereditament, for example a flat above a shop; see above pp. 214–218.

[316] sch.6 para.2(1)(b) as amended by Rating Revaluation Act 1999.

[317] *Benjamin* v. *Anston Properties Ltd.* [1998] R.A. 53 reversed.

previous valuation list was based on the depressed market operating in 1993. Transitional relief will phase in the impact of large rises in rates.[318] The rate payable is determined by applying a multiplier fixed nationally each year to the rateable value for the particular business premises. Rates are payable by the occupier, meaning the tenant in possession,[319] but the local authority has a default power to collect rates from the landlord. Protection against this eventuality takes the form of a covenant by the tenant to pay these statutory charges and to reimburse the landlord if he is called upon, but no doubt there would in any event be a liability to make restitution.[320]

Tenants also need to consider water and sewerage charges.

---

[318] Details announced in January 2000 are that increases will be limited as follows: (1) small businesses: 5% in 2000/2001 and 7.5% for each of the next four years; (2) larger businesses: 12.5% in 2000/2001, 15% in 2001/2002, and 17.5% in each of the next three years.

[319] But not a licensee: *Croydon L.B.C.* v. *Maxon Systems Inc. (London) Ltd.* [1999] E.G.C.S. 68, Jowitt J. (receivership of landlord).

[320] P. Birks, *An Introduction to the Law of Restitution* (Clarendon, 1985) 185–203; A. Burrows, *The Law of Restitution* (Butterworths, 1993) 205–230.

25

REPAIRS TO BUSINESS PREMISES

Repairing obligations. Tenants' express covenants. Waste. Landlords' covenants. The standard of repair. Major work. Landlord's damages. Specific performance. Insurance. Fitness for commercial purpose. Improvements. Statutory requirements. Fixtures.

A. REPAIRING COVENANTS

Commercial leases almost always require the tenant to repair the property.[1]

1. Express covenants

Liability under a commercial letting rests solely on repairing covenants[2]; so express covenants are universal.[3] Express duties are imposed on the tenant in order that the landlord does not need to rely on the arcane law of waste. Most commercial leases are full repairing leases, which allocate all duties to repair to the tenant, enabling the landlord to treat rent receipts as pure income.[4] Covenants are frequently drafted so as to overlap.[5]

Tenant's repairing obligations may require work at a stated time such as painting every three years,[6] or after a stated condition is fulfilled,[7] or only after notice from the landlord.[8] But it is more common to require repair work to be carried out as and when it becomes necessary. Even if this form of covenant is adopted, forfeiture can occur only after the tenant has been given a warning notice stating what work needs to be done.[9]

2. Obligation not to cause injury

Denning L.J. thought it obvious that a tenant must not damage the land and must rectify any damage he does cause.[10] Historically this obligation arose from the fact that

---

[1] Woodfall ch.13; Bright & Gilbert 313–385; Davey 45–78; Evans & Smith (5th) ch.9; Garner (2nd) ch.7.
[2] *Demetriou* v. *Poolaction Ltd.* [1991] 1 E.G.L.R. 100 C.A.
[3] *Mancetter Developments Ltd.* v. *Garmanson Ltd.* [1986] Q.B. 1212 C.A.
[4] *O'May* v. *City of London Real Property Co. Ltd.* [1983] 2 A.C. 726 H.L.
[5] *Lurcott* v. *Wakeley* [1911] 1 K.B. 905, 915, Fletcher Moulton L.J.
[6] *Kirklinton* v. *Wood* [1917] 1 K.B. 332; *Dickinson* v. *St Aubyn* [1944] K.B. 454.
[7] *Westacott* v. *Hahn* [1918] 1 K.B. 495 C.A.; *Thomas* v. *Cadawallader* (1744) Willes. 496, 125 E.R. 1286.
[8] *Lister* v. *Lane* [1893] 2 Q.B. 212; *Torrens* v. *Walker* [1906] 2 Ch. 166; *Lurcott* v. *Wakely* [1911] 1 K.B. 905, 921–923, Fletcher Moulton L.J.
[9] L.P.A. 1925 s.146; see below pp. 796–801.
[10] *Warren* v. *Keen* [1954] 1 Q.B. 15, 20.

tenants were automatically[11] liable for voluntary waste[12] a concept embracing damage arising from the tenant's own acts.[13] Cases of deliberate damage have included glass breakages,[14] pulling down walls, doors, windows, and fixtures,[15] removing a shelf,[16] and—with a suitable period flavour—destruction of a dovecote.[17] Damage caused by the tenant's negligence also has to be reinstated, though at least one case has allowed a tenant to escape the consequences of frozen pipes.[18] The duty not to cause damage is distinct from repair,[19] since liability for voluntary waste did not arise from omissions[20] nor from any proper use of the property.[21]

3. Waste

This archaic[22] subject becomes relevant only if a particular item is not covered by the repairing covenants in the lease. Any spoil or destruction or injury to the reversion amounts to waste,[23] but the variant called permissive waste is equivalent to repair, since it arises where the tenant suffers the condition of the property to worsen—that is he allows the property to fall into disrepair.[24]

Liability for waste attached only to estates created by operation of law according to the very early medieval law, but liability was extended by the Statute of Marlborough 1267[25] to "fermors". This term was interpreted by Lush J.[26] to mean all who held by a lease for *lives* or for *years*,[27] with or without a deed. So fixed term tenants are liable to repair by statute. *Dayani* v. *Bromley L.B.C.*[28] applied the 1267 Act to a lease of three houses used by a local authority to house homeless people, each for a term of three years; the authority was held liable on vacating for allowing the state of the properties to decline. On modern construction techniques it was arguable that fixed terms were not covered by the Statute of Marlborough 1267 but the court interpreted the statute as it was understood when it was passed: if land is let for a period of years the tenant is liable for per-

---

[11] *Walgrave* v. *Somerset* (1587) Goulds. 72, 75 E.R. 1002; *Gibson* v. *Wells* (1805) B. & P. (N.R.) 290, 127 E.R. 473 (tenant at will).

[12] *Edge* v. *Pemberton* (1843) 12 M. & W. 187, 152 E.R. 1164.

[13] *Mancetter Developments Ltd.* v. *Garmanson Ltd.* [1986] Q.B. 1212, 1218, Dillon L.J.

[14] *Irvine* v. *Moran* (1991) 24 H.L.R. 1.

[15] *Marsden* v. *Edward Heyes Ltd.* [1927] 2 K.B. 1 C.A.

[16] *Pyot* v. *St John* (1613) Cro. Jac. 329, 79 E.R. 281.

[17] *Kimpton* v. *Eve* (1813) 2 Ves. & B. 349, 35 E.R. 352, Eldon L.C.

[18] *Wycombe Health Area* v. *Barnett* [1982] 2 E.G.L.R. 35 C.A.

[19] *Regis Property Co. Ltd.* v. *Dudley* [1959] A.C. 370 H.L.; *Haskell* v. *Marlow* [1928] 2 K.B. 45, Talbot J.

[20] *Mancetter Developments Ltd.* v. *Garmanson Ltd.* [1986] Q.B. 1212, 1218, Dillon L.J.

[21] *Saner* v. *Bilton* (1878) 7 Ch.D. 815.

[22] *Mancetter Developments Ltd.* v. *Garmanson Ltd.* [1986] Q.B. 1212, 1223D, Kerr L.J.; see generally Woodfall 13.108–13.130, 13.124.

[23] At 1218, Dillon L.J.

[24] *Davies* v. *Davies* (1888) 38 Ch.D. 499, 504.

[25] 52 Hen.3 c.23 (still in force).

[26] *Woodhouse* v. *Walker* (1880) 5 Q.B.D. 404, 406, Lush J.

[27] *Harnett* v. *Maitland* (1847) 16 M. & W. 257, 153 E.R. 1184; *Greene* v. *Cole* (1672) 2 Wms. Saunds. 252, 85 E.R. 1037, n.7; *Yellowly* v. *Gower* (1855) 11 Exch. 274, 156 E.R. 833.

[28] [1999] 3 E.G.L.R. 144 Q.B.D.; T. Weekes [2000] 43 *P.L.J.* 5.

missive waste, though the standard required is limited to the condition of the property at the time of the lease.[29]

Actions on express repairing covenants are taken in contract.[30] However, if the lease omits an express covenant, so that reliance has to be placed on the law of waste, the action is in tort, the old writ of waste having been superseded centuries ago by an action on the case.[31] Long after the forms of action were buried, a decision was required on the precise nature of the action in 1986. In *Mancetter Developments Ltd.* v. *Garmanson Ltd.*[32] a tenant of industrial premises cut holes in an outside wall to accommodate manufacturing plant. The lease was sold, thus destroying any pure contractual action. Subsequently, when the new tenant quit the premises, fixtures and pipes were removed, leaving gaping holes in the walls. A majority of the Court of Appeal imposed an obligation to make good the damage, actionable in tort, meaning that the cost fell on the person who removed the pipes.

4.   Short term tenancies

A tenant *from year to year* fell outside the Statute of Marlborough 1267 and so was not liable for waste.[33] Coleridge J. once observed that the absence of authority for imposing liability on a landlord was conclusive against it. Hence neither landlord nor tenant is liable to repair,[34] though it is possible that the tenant is obliged to keep a building wind and watertight.[35] Tenants under short periodic tenants should obviously also escape. In *Warren* v. *Keen*[36] the local authority required a landlord to repair the roof of a tenanted property, and the landlord then sought to pass on the cost to his weekly tenant. It was absurd that a tenant with such a short-term interest should have an obligation to repair, or even be obliged to keep the property wind and water tight.[37] The case is even more obvious if a person enters initially as a tenant at will,[38] but where a tenant holds over at the end of a contractual term the terms of the previous tenancy may be extended to cover the period of holding over.[39]

---

[29] *Pomfret* v. *Ricroft* (1671) 1 Wms. Saunds. 321, 323, 85 E.R. 462 note (7); unless the property was ruinous at the time of the lease: Coke on *Littleton* 54b.

[30] *Yellowly* v. *Gower* (1855) 11 Exch. 274, 156 E.R. 833; *Jones* v. *Hill* (1817) Taunt. 392, 129 E.R. 156 (assumpsit not case).

[31] *Pomfret* v. *Ricroft* (1671) 1 Wms. Saunds. 321, 323, 85 E.R. 462 note 7; *Greene* v. *Cole* (1672) 2 Wms. Saunds 252, 85 E.R. 1037, 1037–1038 note (7) (damages only but superior procedure).

[32] [1986] Q.B. 1212 C.A.

[33] The statement to the contrary in Coke on *Littleton* 54b was not followed in *Horsefall* v. *Mather* (1815) Holt 7, 171 E.R. 141; *Auworth* v. *Johnson* (1832) 5 C. & P. 239, 172 E.R. 955; *Torriano* v. *Young* (1833) 6 C. & P. 8, 172 E.R. 1123; *Martin* v. *Gilham* (1837) 7 Ad. & El. 540, 112 E.R. 574; *Pomfret* v. *Ricroft* as above nn. (7) and (x).

[34] *Gott* v. *Gany* (1853) 2 E. & B. 845, 118 E.R. 984.

[35] *Leach* v. *Thomas* (1835) 7 C. & P. 327, 173 E.R. 125; *Wedd* v. *Porter* [1916] 2 K.B. 91 C.A.

[36] [1954] 1 Q.B. 15 C.A.; R.E. Megarry (1954) 70 *L.Q.R.* 9; H.W.R. Wade [1954] *C.L.J.* 71; J.D.B. Mitchell (1954) 17 *M.L.R.* 81.

[37] At 18, Somervell L.J., 20, Denning L.J., 21, Romer L.J.; *Wedd* v. *Porter* [1916] 2 K.B. 91, 100, Swinfen Eady L.J. Short term tenants of houses are discussed above at pp. 261–264.

[38] *Shrewsbury's case* (1600) 5 Co. Rep. 13b, 77 E.R. 68; *Gibson* v. *Wells* (1805) B. & P. (N.R.) 290, 127 E.R. 473; *Harnett* v. *Maitland* (1847) 16 M. & W. 257, 153 E.R. 1184; *Blackmore* v. *White* [1899] 1 Q.B. 293, 299–300.

[39] *Wedd* v. *Porter* [1916] 2 K.B. 91 C.A. (tenant from year to year); *Burchell* v. *Hornsby* (1808) 1 Camp. 360, 170 E.R. 985; *Beale* v. *Sanders* (1837) 3 Bing. N.C. 850, 132 E.R. 638 (void lease); *Torriano* v. *Young* (1833) 6 C. & P. 8, 172 E.R. 1123 (tenant at will).

5.   Landlord's repairing obligations

A commercial lease of part of the landlord's total property—for example a unit in a shopping centre or industrial estate—the landlord often accepts the responsibility for maintenance on the basis that the tenant is required to pay a service charge to cover the cost; such arrangements are discussed in a subsequent chapter.[40] Such cases almost always involve a division between the structural responsibilities of the landlord and the internal responsibilities of the tenant. It is vitally important that the express covenants deal with every part, and leave nothing unallocated.

The landlord is under no implied obligation to repair commercial property.[41] Hence if the tenant covenants to pay £x to the landlord towards the cost of repairs, there is no duty on the landlord to make up the shortfall: he has to spend that £x on repairs but no more.[42] In *Adami v. Lincoln Grange Management Ltd.*[43] long leases of flats placed the responsibility for internal repair of the flats on the tenants, but it was held that there was no reason to impose responsibility for the maintenance of the structure and exterior on the management company irrespective of the cause of the problem. Landlords are usually only liable for disrepair arising in their own time.[44] Any repairing duty imposed on the landlord is qualified by the tenant's obligation to use the property in a *tenant-like manner,* and the qualification is usually expressed. Small jobs have to be carried out by all tenants—whether holding for a fixed term, yearly or under a tenancy of some other period[45]—under the principle that has already been explained in the domestic context.[46] However, the landlord remains liable if it is unreasonable to expect the tenant to carry out particular work.[47]

6.   Reform

The Law Commission's report on the *Responsibility for the State and Condition of Property*[48] proposes to continue to leave the general concept of repair to case-law development. Apart from structural work to dwellings under short residential leases, the parties would remain free to settle the liability for repair by negotiation, but a new covenant would be implied to impose the responsibility on the landlord unless some other arrangement was made.[49] A second implied covenant would relate to what the report

---

[40] See below Chapter 26.

[41] *Gott v. Gandy* (1853) 2 E. & B. 845, 118 E.R. 984; *Arden v. Pullen* (1842) 10 M. & W. 321, 152 E.R. 492; *Cockburn v. Smith* [1924] 2 K.B. 119; *Duke of Westminster v. Guild* [1985] Q.B. 688; P. Jackson [1985] *Conv.* 66; *Alton House Holdings Ltd. v. Calflane (Management) Ltd.* [1987] 2 E.G.L.R. 52, John Mowbray Q.C.; *Tennant Radiant Heat Ltd. v. Warrington Development Corporation* [1988] 1 E.G.L.R. 41 C.A.; *Chorley B.C. v. Ribble Motor Services Ltd.* (1996) 74 P. & C.R. 182 C.A.

[42] *Alton House Holdings Ltd. v. Calflane (Management) Ltd.* [1987] 2 E.G.L.R. 52, John Mowbray Q.C.

[43] [1998] 1 E.G.L.R. 58 C.A.; *Yankwood Ltd. v. Havering L.B.C.* [1999] E.G.C.S. 75, Neuberger J.

[44] *Kemra (Management) Ltd. v. Lewis* [1999] 10 C.L. 489, Prof David Hayton sitting as a recorder.

[45] *Marsden v. Edward Heyes Ltd.* [1927] 2 K.B. 1 C.A. Earlier cases are: *Powley v. Walker* (1793) 5 T.R. 373, 101 E.R. 208; *Ferguson v. Anon* (1797) 2 Esp. 590, 170 E.R. 465; *Horsefall v. Mather* (1815) Holt. 7, 171 E.R. 141. *Auworth v. Johnson* (1832) 5 C. & P. 241, 172 E.R. 955; *Torriano v. Young* (1833) 6 C. & P. 8, 172 E.R. 1123.

[46] *Warren v. Keen* [1954] 1 Q.B. 15, 20, Denning L.J.; see above pp. 261–264.

[47] *Sturloson & Co. v. Mauroux* (1988) 20 H.L.R. 332, 338, Glidewell L.J.

[48] Law Com. No.238 (1996); S. Bridge [1996] *Conv.* 342; Law Com. C.P. No.123 (1992); P.F. Smith [1994] *Conv.* 186. Earlier proposals were in Law Com. No.67 (1975) paras.108–157; D. Hughes [1984] *J.S.W.L.* 137.

[49] para.7.10; draft Bill cls.1, 2.

describes as "associated premises", that is common parts, which the landlord would be obliged to keep in repair unless there was some other agreement.[50] All of these proposals would only apply to new tenancies after the implementation of the new legislation.

The law of waste and the duty to use in a tenant-like manner would be abolished and replaced by an obligation to take proper care of property, avoiding negligence, wilful damage and unauthorised alterations.[51] The Commission also propose improvements to the legislation governing specific performance of covenants relating to repairs and similar obligations,[52] so that this remedy should always be available to either party, though it should remain in the discretion of the court. All these improvements in the law are welcome, though further work is required before legislative implementation.[53]

B. STANDARD OF REPAIR

1. The standard of repair

The rule in *Proudfoot* v. *Hart*[54] is that an ordinary covenant to repair (or actually to maintain in "good tenantable repair") imposes an obligation to carry out such repair, having regard to the age, character and locality of the house, as would make it reasonably fit for the occupation of a tenant of the class who would be likely to take it.[55] A higher standard is expected of a new house than of one that is 200 years old,[56] but the objective standard has to be met irrespective of the remaining commercial life of the building.[57] Location is relevant, a higher standard being expected of a house in Grosvenor Square than in Spitalfields,[58] at least as those two areas stood in the late Victorian period.

The *Proudfoot* v. *Hart* standard can be altered by contract. One example is that "tenantable" repair means keeping habitable,[59] and so excludes painting (unless the structure would otherwise decay), decorating and repapering.[60] "Necessary" adds nothing[61] but a "thorough repair" is of a higher standard.[62]

---

[50] paras.7.26–7.29; draft Bill cls.1(2)–(5), 2(2)–(5).

[51] paras.10.35–10.37; draft Bill cls.9–11; the parties would be free to modify the terms implied.

[52] paras.9.32–9.33; draft bill cl.13; no changes are proposed to damages for disrepair.

[53] Further work is proposed by the Labour Government: Law Com. No.258 (1999) para.1.20; DETR Press Release (February 1998).

[54] (1890) 25 Q.B.D. 42 C.A.

[55] At 55, Lopes L.J.

[56] At 52, Lord Esher M.R.; *Harris* v. *Jones* (1832) 1 Mood. & R. 173, 174 E.R. 59; *Stanley* v. *Towgood* (1836) 3 Bing N.C. 4, 132 E.R. 310; *Gutteridge* v. *Munyard* (1834) 7 C. & P. 129, 173 E.R. 57.

[57] *Ladbroke Hotels Ltd.* v. *Sandhu* [1995] 2 E.G.L.R. 92; H.W. Wilkinson [1997] *N.L.J.* 420.

[58] At 55, Lopes L.J., 52–53, Lord Esher M.R.; *Mantz* v. *Goring* (1838) 4 Bing. N.C. 451, 132 E.R. 861; *Stanley* v. *Towgood* (1836) 3 Bing. N.C. 4, 132 E.R. 310.

[59] *Payne* v. *Haine* (1847) 16 M. & W. 541, 153 E.R. 1304.

[60] *Proudfoot* v. *Hart* (1890) 25 Q.B.D. 42; this states the effect of *Crawford* v. *Newton* (1886) 36 W.R. 54 C.A.; now doubtful is *Monk* v. *Noyes* (1824) 1 C. & P. 265, 171 E.R. 1189.

[61] *Truscott* v. *Diamond Rock Boring Co.* (1882) 20 Ch.D. 251 C.A.

[62] *Lurcott* v. *Wakely* [1911] 1 K.B. 905, 918, Fletcher Moulton L.J.

2.   Maintenance of existing standard or improvement?

Whether a covenant requires an improvement in standard depends upon the particular wording. If the covenant is *to repair* without further qualification[63] it is necessary to maintain the standard set at the time of the lease, neither more[64] nor less.[65] Factual evidence of the general condition at the time is allowed.[66] Different leases of the same property could require different standards of repair simply because they are granted at different times.[67] The landlord is entitled to insist on the maintenance of the initial standard, irrespective of the length of commercial life left in the building at the time that he enforces the covenant,[68] though bad workmanship by a previous landlord may be a defence for a tenant under a repairing covenant.[69] Literal performance is not required.[70]

A covenant to *put into repair*, discussed in *Proudfoot v. Hart,*[71] involves improvement in the standard of the property. Here the obligation is to raise the standard of the property so that it comes into a state of repair. The age and class of the property at the time of the letting can be considered.[72] If it is *to keep in repair*, this implies two distinct duties, first to put it in repair and then to keep it in repair.[73] Thus a landlord who has covenanted to keep in good and tenantable repair was obliged to repair leaking stone cladding, which had never been in a satisfactory condition.[74] This interpretation has been acted upon in hundreds of cases.[75] A final variant is to covenant *to leave in good condition,* which involves more than just repair, since it is necessary to do all that is necessary to keep it in good condition.[76]

The Law Society's standard form for commercial letting imposes an obligation to maintain, that is to conserve the standard existing at the date of the lease, rather than to repair.[77] Hence the reason the property does not meet that standard is irrelevant.

3.   Renewal of parts contrasted with improvement of whole

In essence, to repair is to make good damage that has occurred so as to leave the property as if no damage had occurred,[78] that is renewal and replacement of what was there before.[79]

---

[63] *Coward* v. *Gregory* (1866) L.R. 2 C.P. 153.

[64] *Shaw* v. *Kay* (1847) 1 Exch. 42, 154 E.R. 175.

[65] *Re London Corporation* [1910] 2 Ch. 314, Eve J. (a railway station).

[66] *Burdett* v. *Whithers* (1837) 7 Ad. & El. 136, 112 E.R. 422; *Mantz* v. *Goring* (1838) 4 Bing. N.C. 451, 132 E.R. 861.

[67] *Walker* v. *Hatton* (1842) 2 Dowl. N.S. 263, 152 E.R. 462 (query the result on the facts, since the covenant was to put in repair).

[68] *Ladbroke Hotels Ltd.* v. *Sandhu* [1995] 2 E.G.L.R. 92; H.W. Wilkinson [1997] *N.L.J.* 420.

[69] *Optilon Ltd.* v. *Commission for New Towns* [1993] 2 E.G.L.R. 89.

[70] *Harris* v. *Jones* (1832) 1 Mood. & R. 173, 174 E.R. 59.

[71] (1890) 25 Q.B.D. 42 C.A.

[72] *Paine* v. *Haine* (1847) 16 M. & W. 541, 153 E.R. 1304, Parke B.; *Woolcock* v. *Dew* (1858) 1 F. & F. 337, 175 E.R. 753.

[73] *Proudfoot* v. *Hart* (1890) 25 Q.B.D. 42, 50, Lord Esher M.R.; *Paine* v. *Haine* as above; *Luxmore* v. *Robson* (1818) 1 B. & Ald. 584, 106 E.R. 215.

[74] *Crédit Suisse* v. *Beegas Nominees Ltd.* [1994] 4 All E.R. 803, Lindsay J.; H.W. Wilkinson [1995] *N.L.J.* 718.

[75] At 821d, Lindsay J.

[76] *Lurcott* v. *Wakely* [1911] 1 K.B. 905, 915, Fletcher Moulton L.J.

[77] Standard Business Lease cl.5.1.

[78] *Lurcott* v. *Wakely* [1911] 1 K.B. 905 C.A.; *Anstruther-Gough-Calthorpe* v. *McOscar* [1924] 1 K.B. 716, 734, Atkin L.J.; H.W. Wilkinson [2000] *N.L.J.* 892.

[79] Reversal of Cave J.'s decision by the C.A. in *Proudfoot* v. *Hart* (1890) 25 Q.B.D. 42; *Lurcott* at 920, Fletcher Moulton L.J.

The leading case, *Lurcott* v. *Wakeley*,[80] decided that repair may include demolition and reconstruction of a subsidiary part of a building, if this is what is necessary to put the whole house in repair. At a trivial level this is obvious. If a pipe is cracked, the best way to repair it will be to install a replacement pipe.[81] If something cannot be patched up, it must be replaced. The application to the particular facts of the case is more startling. The London County Council had served a notice on the landlord of a house requiring the demolition and reconstruction of the front wall of the house that was unsafe and, after the landlord had paid for the work, he successfully passed on the cost to the tenant under the tenant's express repairing covenant. The wall was a subsidiary part, which had to be renewed completely if the whole house was to be in repair.[82] Other cases have involved electrical rewiring[83] and the complete replacement of a worn-out roof.[84] In *Minja Properties Ltd.* v. *Cussins Property Group Ltd.*[85] it was held that replacing single-glazed windows with double-glazing was a repair, since the existing windows were rusted out of repair and repair included the replacement of worn out parts. Similarly in *Creska Ltd.* v. *Hammersmith & Fulham L.B.C.*[86] when the underfloor heating broke down, the tenant wanted to install heaters rather than repairing the central heating system as he had covenanted to. The tenant was held to his repairing covenant despite the expense of the work and the element of improvement involved.

Work that involves a change in the character of the property let[87] is a rebuilding, and is excluded from a repairing covenant by the principle that a tenant is not required to substitute new for old.[88] An example was work to replace the entire "eggshell" round an office[89]—at a cost of £3,500 against an estimated cost of £10,000 for complete rebuilding—work which lay just over the borderline beyond repair.[90]

4. Fair wear and tear excepted

The Statute of Marlborough 1267 excluded liability for inevitable accident,[91] a principle reproduced in modern repairing obligations by the exclusion of liability for fair wear and tear.[92] In *Regis Property Co. Ltd.* v. *Dudley*[93] the House of Lords had to determine the rent for a residential letting, the rent being determined according to the extent of the tenant's obligations to repair the interior, from which fair wear and tear and fire were

[80] [1911] 1 K.B. 905 C.A.; W. Strachan (1911) 27 *L.Q.R.* 433.
[81] At 912, Cozens-Hardy M.R.
[82] At 919, Fletcher Moulton L.J.
[83] *Roper* v. *Prudential Assurance Co. Ltd.* [1992] 1 E.G.L.R. 5 Q.B.D.
[84] *New England Properties Ltd.* v. *Portsmouth New Shops Ltd.* [1993] 1 E.G.L.R. 84; *Elite Investments Ltd.* v. *T.I. Bainbridge Silencers Ltd.* [1986] 2 E.G.L.R. 43.
[85] [1998] 2 E.G.L.R. 52.
[86] [1998] 3 E.G.L.R. 35 C.A.
[87] At 914.
[88] *Lister* v. *Lane* [1893] 2 Q.B. 212; *Torrens* v. *Walker* [1906] 2 Ch. 166; *Lurcott* v. *Wakeley* [1911] 1 K.B. 905 C.A.
[89] *City Offices (Regent Street) Ltd.* v. *Europa Acceptance Group Ltd.* [1990] 1 E.G.L.R. 63 C.A.
[90] *Halliard Property Co. Ltd.* v. *Nicholas Clarke Investments Ltd.* [1984] 1 E.G.L.R. 45 (jerry-built shed to proper building was improvement); J.E. Martin [1985] *Conv.* 285.
[91] *Paradine* v. *Jane* (1647) Aleyn 26, 82 E.R. 897; *Carstairs* v. *Taylor* (1871) L.R. 6 Ex. 217 (rat eating water pipe could not be guarded against).
[92] L.A. Blundell (1937) 2 *Conv.* (N.S.) 1; *Brown* v. *Davies* [1958] 1 Q.B. 117 C.A.; R.E. Megarry (1958) 74 *L.Q.R.* 33. The onus lies on the tenant to prove an item falls within fair wear and tear: *Haskell* v. *Marlow* [1928] 2 K.B. 45.
[93] [1959] A.C. 370 H.L.; A.L. Diamond (1959) 22 *M.L.R.* 323.

excepted. The rent fixed[94] shows that the House regarded the exemption as relatively minor, and that the tenant was left with an onerous repairing obligation. Fair wear and tear excused damage to minor things that wear out in the course of time, following reasonable use by the tenant under the ordinary operation of natural forces. Grubby decorations can be left.[95] Even if the work itself is covered by the fair wear and tear exception, the tenant may be liable for consequential damage.[96]

C. MAJOR WORK

1. Reconstruction

In *Lurcott* v. *Wakely*[97] the Court of Appeal indicated that replacement or renewal of the whole goes beyond what counts as a "repair". This constriction of the concept of repair represents a reasonable compromise, at least for business premises, leaving the tenant responsible for fairly extensive works but stopping short of requiring the tenant to hand back completely new property to the landlord. Even in 1893 the courts were predisposed to find some limitation, as Lord Esher M.R. revealed in *Lister* v. *Lane*[98] when he said that:

> "However large the words of the covenant may be, a covenant to repair a house is not a covenant to give a different thing from that which the tenant took when he entered into the covenant."

Thus after a flank wall had tilted as its weight collapsed into a drain in *Brew Brothers Ltd.* v. *Snax (Ross) Ltd.*,[99] the cost of the remedial work which was equal to the cost of a new building was work which a majority [100] held went far beyond what any reasonable person would call repair. Exemption of improvements from V.A.T. may be a small consolation to a person required by an express covenant to carry out work that is so extensive that it exceeds the bounds of maintenance.[101]

Apart from short-term domestic leases, the tenant may be placed under a duty to reconstruct the property by clear and explicit language of an express covenant. If good drafting practice is followed, two covenants will be used in order to make clear that reconstruction is additional to repair.[102] Liability should only be made to bite once all

---

[94] 5/3rds of Rateable Value, where 4/3rds was appropriate if the tenant was liable for *all* repairs.

[95] *Citron* v. *Cohen* (1920) 36 T.L.R. 560 (tenant not liable for bursting of frozen pipe); *Terrell* v. *Murray* (1901) 17 T.L.R. 570. Div.Ct. (tenant not liable for repointing, painting outside, and the repair of a kitchen floor with dry rot; these items were caused by the friction of air, exposure, and ordinary use).

[96] *Regis Property Co. Ltd.* v. *Dudley* [1959] A.C. 370, 393–394 approving *Haskell* v. *Marlow* [1928] 2 K.B. 45, Talbot J., rather than *Taylor* v. *Webb* [1937] 2 K.B. 283 C.A.

[97] [1911] 1 K.B. 905, 923–924, Buckley L.J.; H.W. Wilkinson [2000] *N.L.J.* 892.

[98] [1893] 2 Q.B. 212, 217.

[99] [1970] 1 Q.B. 612 C.A.

[100] At 640, Sachs L.J., 640, Phillimore L.J.: Harman L.J.'s dissent (at 631F) that this was a risk which the tenant ought to discover by survey is more convincing; *Adami* v. *Lincoln Grange Management Ltd.* [1998] 1 E.G.L.R. 58 C.A.

[101] *A.C.T. Construction Ltd.* v. *Customs & Excise Commissioners* [1981] 1 W.L.R. 49 C.A. (work to remedy subsidence); P.F. Smith [1983] *Conv.* 231. Landlord and tenant cases are not decisive for all taxation purposes.

[102] *London* v. *Nash* (1747) 3 Atk. 512, 26 E.R. 1095. Specific performance is available: *Lucas* v. *Commerford* (1790) 3 Bro. C.C. 166, 29 E.R. 469.

necessary permissions have been obtained.[103] The extra covenant is unusual and onerous and may lead to a very substantial reduction in the rental yield.[104]

2. Inherent defects

A commercial tenant is usually obliged to repair, that is to make good damage caused by the natural effects of time, and to renew subsidiary parts. This does not require design faults to be corrected. If a building is of such kind that by its own inherent nature it will in course of time fall down, correcting that effect is not within a covenant to repair: why should a landlord get new work?[105] Neither is the landlord liable.[106]

The leading modern case which reveals how tenants can escape from liability on a repairing covenant because the root problem is a design defect is *Post Office* v. *Aquarius Properties Ltd.*[107] Porous concrete used in the construction of a 1960s office block in the City of London led to the basement being ankle deep in water when the water table was high. The tenant's duty to repair did not extend to providing a remedy for this inherent defect. Ralph Gibson L.J. found it startling, at first, that a basement ankle deep in water was not in disrepair, but that is so if the property has always suffered from the defect.[108] Water damage cause by design problems has therefore to be differentiated from damage caused by damaged rendering.[109]

The same rule has been applied, with less justice, to limit the landlord's obligation to provide proper dwellings. If inherent defects had to be remedied, the landlord would be forced to replace the existing house with something superior. In *Quick* v. *Taff Ely B.C.*[110] houses were uninhabitable[111] as a result of design defects that led to excessive condensation. Alleviation of this problem required replacement of the metal windows, but the existing windows and lintels were sound. A thing is not in disrepair simply because it is inherently inefficient for living in or provides unsatisfactory living conditions. Similarly in *McDougall* v. *Easington D.C.*[112] the tenant failed because the work needed to rectify an inherent design defect, and so prevent water penetration, involved such major work—replacement of the front and rear elevations, a new roof and new windows—that it exceeded a mere repair.

Remedying disrepair might necessarily involve some element of improvement,[113] a point confirmed in *Post Office* v. *Aquarius Properties Ltd.* by the Court of Appeal.[114] This

---

[103] *M.E.P.C. plc.* v. *Grosvenor (Mayfair) Estates Ltd.* (1991) 64 P. & C.R. 41, Morritt J. (absolute or dependent on planning permission); *John Lewis Properties Ltd.* v. *Viscount Chelsea* [1993] 2 E.G.L.R. 77, Mummery J. (listing).

[104] *Norwich Union Life Insurance Society* v. *British Railways Board* [1987] 2 E.G.L.R. 137, Hoffmann J. (rent on review reduced by 27.5%).

[105] *Lister* v. *Lane* [1893] 2 Q.B. 212, 217, Esher M.R.; *Harris* v. *Jones* (1832) 1 Mood. 7, 174 E.R. 59; *Gutteridge* v. *Munyard* (1834) 7 C. & P. 129, 173 E.R. 57; *Wright* v. *Lawson* (1903) 19 T.L.R. 510, 510, Vaughan Williams L.J.

[106] *Strathford East Kilbride Ltd.* v. *Film Design Ltd.* [1997] S.C.L.R. 877.

[107] [1987] 1 All E.R. 1055 C.A.; P.F. Smith [1987] *Conv.* 224; S. Murdoch [1987] *J.B.L.* 383.

[108] At 1063c; also at 1065c, Slade L.J.

[109] *Fincar S.R.L.* v. *Mount St Management Co. Ltd.* [1998] E.G.C.S. 173.

[110] [1986] Q.B. 809 C.A.; *Palmer* v. *Sandwell M.B.C.* [1987] 2 E.G.L.R. 79 C.A.

[111] At 323H, Dillon L.J.

[112] (1989) 58 P. & C.R. 201 C.A.; P.F. Smith [1990] *Conv.* 335.

[113] *Elmcroft Developments Ltd.* v. *Tankerley-Sawyer* [1984] 1 E.G.L.R. 47 C.A. (new d.p.c.); *Wainwright* v. *Leeds C.C.* [1984] 1 E.G.L.R. 67 C.A. (absence of damp proof course to cure rising damp not repair; not new and different thing).

[114] [1987] 1 All E.R. 1055, 1066, Forbes J.

in turn confirmed the decision of Forbes J. in *Ravenseft Properties Ltd.* v. *Davstone Ltd.*[115] Camden Hill Towers, a modern flat block, was made of concrete with external stone cladding. Since the design omitted expansion joints, stone bowed away from the surface of the building and was in danger of falling off. Remedial work was carried out by the landlords but they successfully passed on the cost to the owner-tenants under the terms of their repairing covenants. Inclusion of expansion joints in the redesign of the building was a trivial part of the whole work, which shows that work to rectify inherent defects might be a repair if the degree of improvement required is not too great. This particular block could only be repaired by improving it. *Elmcroft Developments Ltd.* v. *Tankersley-Sawyer*[116] involved a defective damp course in a Victorian mansion block which consisted of a layer of slates below ground level, it being uncertain whether the defects arose from poor design, construction faults or poor workmanship. Curing the resultant rising damp was held to fall within a landlord's repairing covenant.[117] Similarly in *Stent* v. *Monmouth D.C.*[118] the council was required to stop water running in under the front door of a house. The problem arose because there was no sill to stop rain seeping in. Since the original door had rotted and had to be repaired, fitting special aluminium self-sealing doors was a repair. Here it was cheaper to do the job properly. Very extensive work would not count as a repair.[119] The distinction is very often important in relation to service charges.[120]

Sometimes faults arising from poor design may be covered by insurance, but if not a tenant should seek an *express covenant* by the landlord to remedy the defect.[121] However this is a term to which a commercial landlord is unlikely to agree, and it is more realistic to press for the inclusion of a clause that terminates the tenant's obligation to pay rent if the property becomes unusable (a cesser of rent provision).[122]

3. Statutory (non)-protection

Protective legislation often assumes that the tenant will be under an obligation to repair, but that reconstruction and the remedy of inherent defects will exceed the scope of the tenant's obligations. Problems in business contexts arise in relation to the restriction of damages recoverable for non-repair by the tenant,[123] and the procedural safeguards against abusive forfeitures.[124]

---

[115] [1980] Q.B. 12, Forbes J.; P.F. Smith [1979] *Conv.* 429.

[116] [1984] 1 E.G.L.R. 47, 48G, Ackner L.J., approving *Ravenseft.*

[117] On d.p.c.s contrast *Pembery* v. *Lamdin* [1940] 2 All E.R. 434 and *Sotheby* v. *Grundy* [1947] 2 All E.R. 761.

[118] [1987] 1 E.G.L.R. 59 C.A.; H.W. Wilkinson (1988) 138 *N.L.J.* 161, 186.

[119] No decision was possible on the known facts in *Plough Investments Ltd.* v. *Manchester C.C.* [1989] 1 E.G.L.R. 244.

[120] *Scottish Mutual Assurance plc.* v. *Jardine Public Relations Ltd.* [1999] E.G.C.S. 43 Q.B.D.; see below p. 703.

[121] P. Sparkes (1990) 10 *R.R.L.R.* 218.

[122] *Smedley* v. *Chumley & Hawke Ltd.* (1982) 44 P.& C.R. 50.

[123] L.T.A. 1927 s.18.

[124] Leasehold Property (Repairs) Act 1938; see below pp. 801–804.

D. LANDLORD'S DAMAGES

Damages payable to a landlord for disrepair are capped by the Landlord and Tenant Act 1927,[125] though it may be that the Act merely restates common law principles.[126] It applies only to damages for disrepair and not, for example, to a covenant to spend £500 a year on the property.[127]

1. End of lease—demolition or alteration

This case is simplest given the specific provisions of the 1927 Act and the fact that this is the mischief at which the Act was targeted. No damages at all are to be awarded if the premises would be pulled down shortly after the end of the lease, nor if alterations will be so expensive that the repairs are irrelevant.[128] Consider what is supposed to have been a regular practice of landlords in the early 1920s, that is terminating leases of soldiers returned from the First World War, suing the displaced tenants for failing to deliver up the property in good repair, and promptly demolishing the houses in question. Landlords were able to secure a double profit, from full damages for disrepair[129] and from the redevelopment, even though the state of repair or disrepair was a matter of complete indifference to a landlord. The 1927 Act strips out the double profit by ensuring that the landlord will be unable to claim any damages at all.[130]

Proof is required of a firm decision on the part of the landlord which has moved beyond the realm of contemplation—that which is tentative, provisional and exploratory—into the valley of decision.[131] The question is: when performance was properly due, was it inevitable that the property would be pulled down or altered because of a settled intention on the part of the landlord or some extraneous reason?[132] If the cap is once fitted, but the landlord then changes his mind, damages are not recoverable,[133] but conversely the landlord may still be capped if he decides upon demolition at some later date.[134]

[125] s.18(1); J. O'Connor (1928) 44 *L.Q.R.* 209; A.M. Tettenborn (1978) 42 *Conv. (N.S.)* 366; D.N. Clarke (1988) 104 *L.Q.R.* 372.

[126] Law Com. No.238 (1996) para.9.36; *Portman* v. *Lattan* [1942] W.N. 97; *Lansdowne Rodway Estates Ltd.* v. *Portman Ltd.* [1984] 2 E.G.L.R. 80.

[127] *Moss Empires Ltd.* v. *Olympia (Liverpool) Ltd.* [1939] A.C. 544 H.L.; *Plummer* v. *Ramsey* (1934) 78 S.J. 175.

[128] L.T.A. 1927 s.18(1) proviso; [2000] 31 *L.S.G.* 8 (protocol).

[129] *Joyner* v. *Weeks* [1891] 2 Q.B. 31 C.A.; *Rawlings* v. *Morgan* (1865) 18 C.B.N.S. 776, 144 E.R. 650; *Inderwick* v. *Leech* (1885) 1 T.L.R. 484 C.A.

[130] *Salisbury* v. *Gilmore* [1942] 2 K.B. 38 C.A.; *Re King* [1963] Ch. 459 C.A.

[131] *Cunliffe* v. *Goodman* [1950] 2 K.B. 237 C.A.; (1950) 66 L.Q.R. 429; *Culworth Estates Ltd.* v. *Licensed Victuallers Society* [1991] 2 E.G.L.R. 54 C.A.

[132] *Shortlands Investments Ltd.* v. *Cargill plc.* [1995] 1 E.G.L.R. 51, 57D Off.Rec. A local authority tenant cannot take advantage of its own disrepair in order to acquire the property in disrepair more cheaply though compulsory purchase: *Hibernian Property Co. Ltd.* v. *Liverpool Corporation* [1973] 1 W.L.R. 751, Caulfield J.; *London County Freehold & Leasehold Properties Ltd.* v. *Wallis-Whiddett* [1950] W.N. 180.

[133] *Keats* v. *Graham* [1960] 1 W.L.R. 30 C.A.

[134] *Salisbury* v. *Gilmore* [1942] 2 K.B. 38 C.A.; *Keats* v. *Graham* [1960] 1 W.L.R. 30 C.A.

2. End of lease—repairs to be carried out

The principles discussed here apply whether the lease ends through forfeiture[135] or by expiration of the term of the lease.[136] Damages should be measured by the common law standard, but capped by section 18(1)[137] so as not to exceed the diminution in value of the reversion attributable to the disrepair.

Damages for disrepair are intended to put the landlord in the position in which he would have been if the tenant had fulfilled his contractual promise to repair. So if the work is to be carried out the appropriate measure is usually the *cost* of the necessary work,[138] along with Value Added Tax,[139] and any consequential damage. A *cap* has then to be applied to limit the damages to the *loss in value of reversion*, that is the actual change in the value of the landlord's interest. For example if the reduction in the selling value is £5,000 and the cost of the repairs is £10,000 the damages are limited to £5,000. It makes no difference that the reversion has a negative value.[140] If the value is not diminished, there are no damages.[141] The length of the remaining term is relevant to assessment, and should be pleaded.[142] After all if the landlord holds only a nominal reversion, the damage to it is likely to be nominal,[143] unless there are special reasons to award substantial damages.[144]

The cost of repairs may also be a useful guide in some analogous cases. One is where work must be carried out because the landlord is obliged to do so by the terms of a head-lease.[145] Another is if the property is sold at a price devalued by the cost of the repairs.[146] A third case is where the landlord relets the property in its dilapidated condition, and any incoming tenant would use the disrepair as a bargaining counter.[147]

3. Action during lease

Permission to sue may be required under the Leasehold Property (Repairs) Act 1938 before bringing a claim for damages for disrepair.[148] In order to obtain leave, it will be

---

[135] *Hanson* v. *Newman* [1934] Ch. 298 C.A.; *Associated Deliveries Ltd.* v. *Harrison* [1984] 2 E.G.L.R. 76 C.A.; J.E. Martin [1985] *Conv.* 285.

[136] *Jaquin* v. *Holland* [1960] 1 W.L.R. 258 C.A.; *Sun Life* v. *Racal Tracs* [2000] 1 E.G.L.R. 138.

[137] L.T.A. 1927 s.18(1).

[138] *Joyner* v. *Weeks* [1891] 2 Q.B. 31, 43, Lord Esher M.R.; *Landeau* v. *Marchbank* [1949] All E.R. 172, 175, Lynskey J.; *Smiley* v. *Townshend* [1950] 2 K.B. 311, 319, Denning L.J., 323–324, Singleton L.J.; *Jones* v. *Herxheimer* [1950] 2 K.B. 106, 117, Jenkins L.J.; *Crewe Services & Investment Corporation* v. *Silk* [1998] 2 E.G.L.R. 1 C.A.

[139] *Elite Investments Ltd.* v. *T.I. Bainbridge Silencers Ltd. (No.2)* [1987] 2 E.G.L.R. 50; P.F. Smith [1987] *Conv.* 140; *Sun Life* v. *Racal Tracs* as above.

[140] *Shortlands Investments Ltd.* v. *Cargill plc.* [1995] 1 E.G.L.R. 51 Off.Rec.

[141] *Mather* v. *Barclays Bank Ltd.* [1987] 2 E.G.L.R. 254; D.N. Clarke (1988) 104 *L.Q.R.* 372; J.E. Martin [1988] *Conv.* 437.

[142] *Turner* v. *Lamb* (1845) 14 M. & W. 412, 153 E.R. 535.

[143] *Espir* v. *Basil Street Hotel Ltd.* [1936] 3 All E.R. 91 C.A.; *Terroni & Necchi* v. *Corsini* [1931] 1 Ch. 515, Maugham J. (later grant of reversionary lease irrelevant).

[144] *Lloyds Bank Ltd.* v. *Lake* [1961] 1 W.L.R. 884 (*Espir* distinguished); *Hanson* v. *Newman* [1934] Ch. 298 C.A.

[145] *Conquest* v. *Ebbetts* [1896] A.C. 490, 493, Lord Herschell.

[146] *Culworth Estates Ltd.* v. *Society of Licensed Victuallers* [1991] 2 E.G.L.R. 54 C.A. (no cap where cost of repairs exceeds loss in value of the reversion).

[147] *Shortlands Investments Ltd.* v. *Cargill plc.* [1995] 1 E.G.L.R. 51 Off.Rec.; *Cunliffe* v. *Goodman* [1950] 2 K.B. 237; *Haviland* v. *Long* [1952] 2 Q.B. 80.

[148] s.1, as amended by L.T.A. 1954 s.51.

necessary to show why immediate recovery is required,[149] for example because the disrepair is very serious, the reversion is reduced in value, or the compensation obtainable on compulsory purchase is reduced.[150] Permission is usually refused.[151]

However where the landlord carries out the work under a power of entry and then seeks to *recover the cost*, the claim is to a debt rather than for disrepair, and specific performance falls outside the 1938 Act.[152] This route depends upon the landlord having power to enter to effect repairs.[153] The court may make an order permitting access but at the pre-trial phase this will be ordered only if the right is very clear.[154] Where the landlord has carried out work, leave is not required to take action to recover the cost.

It is not fair to award the cost of repairs as the *measure of damages* for disrepair if the lease has a long time left to run,[155] and in particular where the landlord has no intention of using the award to carry out repair work.[156] In such a case there is no reason to add Value Added Tax to the award.[157] The 1927 Act imposes a cap at the diminution in value of the reversion.[158] Damages are not necessarily nominal since the reversion may well be reduced in value by disrepair.[159] Disrepair is a continuing breach of covenant so that, theoretically, a landlord could take multiple actions for disrepair, but the damages awarded on a second occasion must be reduced by the amount of the first award.[160]

Damages will be limited if the head lease ends leaving a business sub-tenant in possession who intends to seek a business renewal. In this case it is assumed that the landlord is adequately compensated by the higher rent he can receive from the sub-tenant, since this is calculated ignoring the disrepair of the property. Hence the damages against the head tenant are reduced.[161] The reduction is not necessarily to zero, because loss may arise from any non-correspondence between the repairing covenants in the sub-lease and the head-lease.[162]

---

[149] s.1(5) sets out five overlapping grounds (a)–(e); see below p. 802.

[150] *Phillips* v. *Price* [1959] Ch. 181.

[151] *Sidnell* v. *Wilson* [1966] 2 Q.B. 67, 77E, Lord Denning M.R.

[152] *Jervis* v. *Harris* [1996] Ch. 195 C.A.; R. Hewitson [1997] *Conv.* 299; *Hamilton* v. *Martell Securities Ltd.* [1984] Ch. 266, Vinelott J.; J.E. Martin [1984] *Conv.* 229.

[153] H.A. 1988 s.16 (assured tenancy; right of access implied).

[154] *Ford Sellar Morris Developments Ltd.* v. *Grant Seward Ltd.* [1989] 2 E.G.L.R. 40, Hoffmann J.; *Hi-Lift Elevator Services Ltd.* v. *Temple* (1995) 70 P. & C.R. 620 C.A. (injunction to prevent work).

[155] *Doe d. Worcester* v. *Rowlands* (1841) 9 C. & P. 734, 173 E.R. 1030, Coleridge J.; *Conquest* v. *Ebbetts* [1896] A.C. 490, 493, Lord Herschell.

[156] *Joyner* v. *Weeks* [1891] 2 Q.B. 31, 43, Lord Esher M.R.; *Tito* v. *Waddell (No.2)* [1977] Ch. 106, 333–334, Megarry V.C.; *Smiley* v. *Townshend* [1950] 2 K.B. 311, 322, Denning L.J.; *Crewe Services and Investment Corporation* v. *Silk* [1998] 2 E.G.L.R. 1 C.A.

[157] *Elite Investments Ltd.* v. *T.I. Bainbridge Silencers Ltd. (No.2)* [1987] 2 E.G.L.R. 50.

[158] *Crown Estate Commissioners* v. *Town Investments Ltd.* [1992] 1 E.G.L.R. 61, 63H; *Ultraworth Ltd.* v. *General Accident Fire & Life Assurance Corporation plc.* [2000] E.G.C.S. 19 (aged heating system).

[159] *Sturcke* v. *S.W. Edwards Ltd.* (1971) 23 P. & C.R. 185, Goff J.; *Dodd Properties (Kent) Ltd.* v. *Canterbury C.C.* [1980] 1 W.L.R. 433, 456G–457A, Donaldson L.J.; *Culworth Estates Ltd.* v. *Society of Licensed Victuallers* [1991] 2 E.G.L.R. 54, 56D–F, Dillon L.J.; *Crewe Services* as above (cost £16,000, damages £3,000).

[160] *Henderson* v. *Thorn* [1893] 2 Q.B. 164.

[161] *Family Management* v. *Gray* [1980] 1 E.G.L.R. 46 C.A.

[162] *Crown Estate Commissioners* v. *Town Investments Ltd.* [1992] 1 E.G.L.R. 61 Off.Rec.

4. Alterations

The 1927 Act cap has no application to a covenant to restore alterations at the end of the lease. No damages arise from improvements such as replacing an old shop front with a modern one since there is no loss,[163] but harmful alterations will give rise to an entitlement to the full cost of restoration.[164]

E. SPECIFIC PERFORMANCE

It was long thought that a tenant would not be compelled to carry out a repairing obligation by a grant of specific performance.[165] Reasons given were the lack of mutuality, the problem of adequate definition of the works required and the need for constant supervision by the court. However this conventional learning was rejected by Laurence Collins Q.C. in *Rainbow Estates Ltd.* v. *Tokenhold Ltd.*[166] A grade II listed mansion block in Essex was let on long residential leases with tenant's repairing covenants, but the tenants had failed to carry out the necessary works. So much so that work costing £300,000 was required, and the Epping Forest D.C. had served statutory dilapidations notices. A strange facet of the leases was that they omitted the usual forfeiture provision, so that the landlord could not terminate the leases as a result of the disrepair.

Lack of mutuality had long been a reason for refusing to aid a landlord since an order could not be made against a tenant, but the deputy judge held that this was a discretionary matter.[167] The need for precise statement of what exactly has to be performed is a long established and important factor,[168] but the House of Lords had recently held that it was not decisive.[169] Constant supervision was another dubious objection since the court is able to examine the end result of the repair to see whether it meets the required standard.[170]

Specific performance is reserved for those cases where damages are inadequate as a remedy. On the particular facts of *Tokenhold* specific performance was the only possible remedy, since there was no right of re-entry[171] and the property was deteriorating rapidly.[172] There is clearly a danger of using specific performance to circumvent the statutory restriction on damages[173] or the use of actions to secure damages during the term since the Leasehold Property (Repairs) Act 1938 does not apply but the court would seek to avoid oppression of a tenant.[174] Nevertheless the irony remains, as

---

[163] *James* v. *Hutton* [1950] 1 K.B. 9 C.A.

[164] *Eyre* v. *Rea* [1947] K.B. 567, Atkinson J.

[165] *Hill* v. *Barclay* (1810) 16 Ves. Jun. 402, 33 E.R. 1037.

[166] [1999] Ch. 64 Ch.D.; P. Luxton [1998] *J.B.L.* 564; P.H. Kenny [1998] *Conv.* 163; M. Pawlowski & J. Brown [1998] *Conv.* 495; S. Bridge [1999] *C.L.J.* 283; O. Breen (1999) 50 *N.I.L.Q.* 102.

[167] *Price* v. *Strange* [1978] Ch. 337, 357, Goff J.

[168] *Rayner* v. *Stone* (1762) 2 Eden 128, 28 E.R. 845.

[169] *Co-operative Insurance Society Ltd.* v. *Argyll Stores (Holdings) Ltd.* [1998] A.C. 1, 12–16, Lord Hoffmann.

[170] *Argyll* at 12–16, Lord Hoffmann; *Wolverhampton Corporation* v. *Emmons* [1901] 1 K.B. 515; *Jeune* v. *Queen's Cross Properties Ltd.* [1974] Ch. 97; *Francis* v. *Cowcliffe Ltd.* [1976] 2 E.G.L.R. 54; *Posner* v. *Scott-Lewis* [1987] Ch. 25; *Gordon* v. *Selico Co. Ltd.* [1986] 1 E.G.L.R. 71.

[171] For forfeiture see below Chapter 29.

[172] At 74.

[173] L.T.A. 1927 s.18.

[174] At 72.

Peter Luxton points out,[175] that specific performance is more readily awarded because statute imposes restrictions on claims to damages.

The court may also enforce by a mandatory injunction,[176] even making such an order at a pre-trial stage,[177] though exceptional circumstances have to be shown to justify such an order. It follows that there is also an equitable jurisdiction to award damages in lieu of an equitable remedy.[178]

F. INSURANCE

Insurance[179] protects both landlord and tenant against destruction of the property by fire and other risks. An insurance company agrees to bear the risk in return for the payment of a premium. Insurance obligations arise from express covenants,[180] so it is necessary for the lease to define the insured risks, to ensure that premiums are paid, and to deal with reinstatement of the property after fire damage.

1. Defining the form of insurance

Leases generally specify the company with which insurance is to be effected, the risks to be insured against, and the insured value. Tenants often want the cheapest possible insurance, but landlords should ensure that the insurance company is reputable, perhaps by naming a particular company, by allowing the landlord to nominate a company,[181] by requiring insurance with an approved company,[182] or by describing the type of insurance company to be used.[183]

Fire is always an insured risk, unless caused by war[184] or nuclear damage. An insurance company may legitimately object to meeting damage that occurs before the commencement of the insurance policy.[185] It is usual to insure to the full repairing cost of the building, a figure that should be assessed as at the time that reinstatement is to occur,[186] taking into account professional fees and other expenses. If a fire does occur and the insurance does not raise sufficient to rebuild the property, the tenant will be left to top up the insurance payout, but excessive insurance is wasteful, and surplus premiums are not recoverable.[187]

---

[175] [1998] *J.B.L.* 564, 572–573; S. Bridge [1999] *C.L.J.* 283.

[176] *Hemingway Securities Ltd.* v. *Dunraven Ltd.* [1995] 1 E.G.L.R. 61 Ch.D.; P. Luxton & M. Wilkie [1995] *Conv.* 416.

[177] *Chelsea* v. *Muscatt* [1990] 2 E.G.L.R. 48 C.A.; *Minja Properties Ltd.* v. *Cussins Property Group plc.* [1998] 2 E.G.L.R. 52; C.P.R. Part 25.

[178] *Hindley* v. *Emery* (1865) L.R. 1 Eq. 52.

[179] Woodfall 11.089–11.090; Evans & Smith (5th) 114–115. On drafting see A. Mitchell [1999] 30 *P.L.J.* 2; I. Lynch [1999] 41 *E.G.* 147.

[180] There is an implied obligation to insure agricultural property: S.I. 1973/1473 reg.3 and sch. para.2; fire insurance was a usual covenant: *Kendall* v. *Hill* (1860) 2 L.T. 717.

[181] The tenant has no obligation until a nomination: *Crane* v. *Batten* (1854) 2 C.L.R. 1696.

[182] The landlord has an absolute discretion: *Tredegar* v. *Harwood* [1929] A.C. 72 H.L.

[183] *Doe d. Pitt* v. *Shewin* (1811) 3 Camp. 134, 170 E.R. 1331 (some sufficient insurance office).

[184] *Upjohn* v. *Hitchens* [1918] 2 K.B. 48 C.A. (enemy action properly excluded).

[185] *Kelly* v. *Norwich Union Fire Insurance Soc. Ltd.* [1990] 1 W.L.R. 139 C.A.

[186] *Gleniffer Finance Co.* v. *Bamar Wood & Products Ltd.* (1978) 37 P. & C.R. 208.

[187] *Leather Cloth Co.* v. *Bressey* (1862) 3 Giff. 474, 66 E.R. 496.

Many factors affect the premiums and all defects must be disclosed.[188] Leases usually include provisions designed to stabilise premiums, for example by requiring the tenant not to increase the risk of fire, and the landlord should enter into equivalent covenants in relation to his retained land and any land that has been let to other tenants.[189]

2. Who insures?

Simple leases of a complete building may provide for the tenant to effect insurance of a quality defined by the lease. There is no problem about the tenant paying to protect land belonging to the landlord since the tenant has an insurable interest up to the full value of the land.[190] However, the landlord has most to lose, and there is often a practical difficulty in compelling a tenant to carry out his obligations, given that the onus is on the landlord to prove a breach.[191] At the least, the landlord must have a right to insist on the production of proof of the insurance—a term which is not implied[192]—and default powers to effect the insurance and to recoup the cost from the tenant. Failure to insure will give rise to a forfeiture,[193] the breach being continuous in character so that even acceptance of rent will not act as a waiver to protect the tenant.[194] Despite the seriousness of leaving a property uninsured, the breach is nevertheless remediable, a forfeiture notice has to allow time for the tenant to make good the breach,[195] and relief may be available.[196] Insurance obligations pass to later tenants.[197]

Landlords generally insure at their own cost property let on short residential leases,[198] but otherwise this is most unusual.

Many leases provide for the *landlord* to effect insurance (giving control over the cover) but at the *cost* of the tenant. With a lease of a single building, the insurance premium is usually reserved as an additional rent ("an insurance rent"), enabling the landlord to forfeit if the rent is not paid. Insurance premiums for a block of flats are apportioned between the units in a block and then added to the service charge,[199] the obligation to pay the proportion allocated to each tenant being backed up by a forfeiture proviso. Since the tenant can take action if the landlord fails to insure,[200] it is usual to provide that the landlord's obligations arise only after the tenant has paid his share.

[188] *Aldridge Estates Investment Co. Ltd.* v. *McCarthy* [1996] E.G.C.S. 167.

[189] *O'Cedar Ltd.* v. *Slough Trading Co. Ltd.* [1927] 2 K.B. 123; *Bandar Property Holdings Ltd.* v. *J.S. Darwen (Successors) Ltd.* [1968] 2 All E.R. 305.

[190] *Re King* [1963] Ch. 459, 498–500, Diplock L.J.; *Lonsdale & Thompson Ltd.* v. *Black Arrow Group plc.* [1993] Ch. 361.

[191] *Doe d. Bridger* v. *Whitehead* (1838) 8 Ad. & El. 571, 112 E.R. 955; *Price* v. *Worwood* (1859) 4 H. & N. 512, 157 E.R. 941.

[192] *Chaplin* v. *Reid* (1858) 1 F. & F. 315, 175 E.R. 743.

[193] *Penniall* v. *Harborne* (1848) 11 Q.B. 368, 116 E.R. 514

[194] *Penniall*, as above, and many other cases.

[195] *Cardigan Properties Ltd.* v. *Consolidated Property Investments Ltd.* [1991] 1 E.G.L.R. 64 Ch.D.; *John Lyon's Charity* v. *Haysport Properties Ltd.* [1995] E.G.C.S. 171, Carnwath J. J.E. Adams [1997] *Conv.* 12.

[196] L.P.A. 1925 s.146(2), introduced by L.P.Am.A. 1859 c.35 s.4; *Page* v. *Bennett* (1860) 2 Giff. 117 66 E.R. 50.

[197] *Vernon* v. *Smith* (1821) 5 B. & Ald. 1, 106 E.R. 1094 (pre 1995 law); all covenants pass under L.T. (Covenants) A. 1995; see below pp. 765, 768.

[198] *Lambert* v. *Keymood Ltd.* [1997] 2 E.G.L.R. 70 (implied).

[199] See below p. 703.

[200] *Fleetwood* v. *Engineering Construction Industry Training Board* [1996] 2 C.L.Y. 3786, May J.

The tenant can protect himself against the landlord's failure to insure by effecting the insurance and recouping the cost from the rent.[201]

If the same property is insured with two companies, the payment is apportioned between them, so that surplus premiums are wasted, and sums paid out under policy 1 may be partially diminished by payments under policy 2. Covenants should be framed so as to avoid wasteful *double insurance*.[202] It is, for example, a breach of covenant justifying a forfeiture, to add the tenant's name to an insurance policy when the covenant is to insure in the landlord's name.[203] Similarly it is a breach to insure in the sole name of the tenant as opposed to joint names, even if landlord professes himself to be happy with the arrangements made.[204]

3.   Tenant's control of landlord's insurance policy

All buildings need insurance, and in communal blocks it is normal for insurance to be carried out by the landlord for the entire block. Individual tenants reimburse their share of the premium. Common law principles provided tenants with very little control over what went on. As explained below, there is some control in the case of long residential leases.[205]

4.   Reinstatement

The lease should direct what form of reinstatement should occur. In *Vural Ltd.* v. *Security Archives Ltd.*[206] fire destroyed the beechwood floor of the factory in which the tenant had been making clothes for Burberrys, following their strict requirements about the necessary working conditions. The tenant requested reinstatement of the wooden floor in order to meet these terms, but the landlord delayed hoping to push the tenant out and finally proposed an unsuitable heavy linoleum floor. Knox J. decided[207] that the tenant was justified in rejecting the linoleum floor. Slavish reconstitution was not required, but a substitute was not adequate if the original was materially more effective. The case shows the need to describe what form reinstatement should take.[208]

5.   Right to require reinstatement.

Most modern leases under which the landlord insures contain an *express covenant* that the proceeds of the insurance will be spent on rebuilding. Thee is no implied requirement that the landlord should top up the proceeds from the insurance.[209]

Otherwise there may be a *statutory right* to require reinstatement under the Fires Prevention (Metropolis) Act 1774, which defies its name by extending across the whole country.[210] When stripped of its Georgian verbiage, section 83 provides that:

---

[201] *Naumann* v. *Ford* [1985] 2 E.G.L.R. 70; J.E. Martin [1985] *Conv.* 285.

[202] *Portavon Cinema Co. Ltd.* v. *Price & Century Insurance Co. Ltd.* [1939] 4 All E.R. 601.

[203] *Penniall* v. *Harborne* (1848) 11 Q.B. 368, 116 E.R. 514.

[204] *Doe d. Muston* v. *Gladwin* (1845) 6 Q.B. 953, 115 E.R. 359; *Havens* v. *Middleton* (1853) 10 Hare 641, 68 E.R. 1085; *Nokes* v. *Gibbon* (1856) 26 L.J.Ch. 433.

[205] L.Ref.A. 1967 s.15(3); L.T.A. 1954 s.10(1).

[206] (1990) 60 P. & C.R. 258; P. Sparkes [1991] *Conv.* 294.

[207] At 273–277.

[208] *Reynolds* v. *Phoenix Assurance Co. Ltd.* [1978] 2 Lloyd's Rep. 440.

[209] *Adami* v. *Lincoln Grange Management Ltd.* [1998] 1 E.G.L.R. 58 C.A.

[210] *Sinnott* v. *Bowden* [1912] 2 Ch. 414; W.D. Ainger [1994] *Conv.* 166.

"[D]irectors of . . . insurance offices for insuring . . . buildings against loss by fire . . . are . . . required, upon the request [211] of any person or persons interested in . . . any . . . buildings which may . . . be burnt down, . . . to cause the insurance money to be laid out . . . towards rebuilding . . .".

The insurance company must participate in the reinstatement, unless the party entitled to receipt of the insurance money provides sufficient security for the work to be undertaken within 60 days of the claim being adjusted.[212] A tenant is a person interested, with a right to apply directly to the insurance company for policy monies to be laid out in reinstatement,[213] but operation of the 1774 Act can be impliedly excluded by a clause that insurance money is to belong to the landlord if reinstatement is prevented.[214] Further restrictions are that the Act extends only to insurance against *fire*, and ceases to have effect once the insurers have settled with the insured.[215] For these reasons it is unwise to rely on the statutory provision.

Implied rights to insist on reinstatement are limited. For example the right is not implied simply because the lease lacks a provision suspending the rent after a fire.[216] It is necessary to show that the tenant is interested in the land, a condition best satisfied by ensuring that both landlord and tenant are parties to the insurance policy.[217] Otherwise the tenant's interest should be noted on the policy, but a right is implied from paying the premiums.[218] Effectiveness can only be ensured if the landlord is required to submit an insurance claim, a duty that may be implied,[219] but is better expressed. An obligation to reinstate may also arise simply because the tenant has covenanted to meet the cost of the insurance premiums. In *Mumford Hotels Ltd.* v. *Wheler*[220] this obligation was based on a proprietary right, arising from payment of the premiums.[221]

6. Pending reinstatement

A landlord may be obliged to effect *emergency repairs* in order to make a property secure after a fire, for example by replacing a damaged door.[222] After serious damage the tenant will be forced to move out. This throws into doubt the continuation of the tenant's *business security of tenure*, for which continued occupation is a requirement. In *Morrisons Holdings Ltd.* v. *Manders Property (Wolverhampton) Ltd.*[223] it was held that a

---

[211] A distinct request must be proved: *Simpson* v. *Scottish Union Insurance Co.* (1863) 32 L.J. Ch. 329.

[212] *Sun Insurance Office* v. *Galinsky* [1914] 2 K.B. 545.

[213] At 272. *Lonsdale & Thompson Ltd.* v. *Black Arrow Group plc.* [1993] Ch. 361 (tenant where landlord insure).

[214] *Penniall* v. *Harborne* (1848) 11 Q.B. 368, 116 E.R. 514.

[215] At 376–377, Lord Denman C.J.

[216] *Bullock* v. *Domitt* (1796) 6 Term Rep. 650, 101 E.R. 752; *Leeds* v. *Cheetham* (1827) 1 Sim. 146, 57 E.R. 533.

[217] *Mark Rowlands Ltd.* v. *Berni Inns Ltd.* [1986] Q.B. 211 C.A.; J. Birds (1986) 6 *O.J.L.S.* 305; *Lambert* v. *Keymood Ltd.* [1997] 2 E.G.L.R. 70, Laws J.; but distinguished in *Sadlers* v. *Clements* [1995] E.G.C.S. 197.

[218] *Cleveland Shoe Co. Ltd.* v. *Murray's Book Sales (King's Cross) Ltd.* (1973) 227 E.G. 987, reversed on appeal (1973) 229 E.G. 1465 C.A.; *Hamer* v. *Drummond* (1939) 187 L.T.Jo. 156.

[219] *Vural Ltd.* v. *Security Archives Ltd.* (1990) 60 P. & C.R. 258.

[220] [1964] Ch. 117 Ch.D.

[221] Harman L.J. (sitting in the Ch.D.) seemed to prefer Lord Denning M.R.'s dissent in *Re King* [1963] Ch. 459 to the view of the majority of the C.A.; (1964) 28 *Conv.* (*N.S.*) 305, 306; also *Beacon Carpets Ltd.* v. *Kirby* [1985] Q.B. 755.

[222] *Morris* v. *Liverpool C.C.* [1988] 1 E.G.L.R. 47 C.A. (no unreasonable delay); J.E. Martin [1988] *Conv.* 437.

[223] [1976] 1 W.L.R. 533 C.A.; (1976) 92 *L.Q.R.* 323.

tenant could be in occupation of property despite its total destruction by fire and was therefore entitled to request a business renewal. Residential security of tenure may also survive[224] but usually a residential tenant needs another home and will be content to give notice to quit and move elsewhere after a fire.[225]

At common law, *liability on a repairing covenant* was absolute, so that the tenant was obliged both to repair and to continue to pay rent, even after a total destruction by lightning or enemy action.[226] Statute reversed this rule, removing liability on a repairing covenant after destruction by an *accidental* fire,[227] though obviously an action is allowed after a *deliberate* fire.[228] Express covenants often reimpose liability after accidental fire damage,[229] though the tenant may be able to avoid an action for disrepair by exercising an option to purchase.[230] If the property was insured in the full value and was sold at a reduced price when fire damaged, the landlord can require the full insurance money to compensate for the reduction in the sale price caused by the fire damage.[231]

7. Suspension of rent and termination

A tenant's liability to rent continues despite destruction of the property by fire,[232] so it is essential for the tenant's protection that the lease should contain a *suspension of rent provision* until rebuilding is finished.[233] This is not a situation in which equity will intervene to prevent a landlord from suing for rent before he has completed the reinstatement of the building.[234] Care is needed when drafting a suspension clause to make clear whether service charge provisions are also suspended, since this is not implied.[235] Some leases provide for termination in the event that reinstatement proves to be impossible. *Tomlinson v. Millins*[236] demonstrates that it is important to define in what circumstances the right to terminate should arise; in that case the landlord had the right to end the lease if reinstatement proved to be impracticable during the term of lease. The tenant was unable to exercise an option to buy the reversion exercisable during the term of the lease, even though reinstatement might prove to be practicable at some later time.

---

[224] See above pp. 107–109.

[225] L.T.A. 1985 s.28 and sch. para.7.

[226] *Paradine v. Jane* (1647) Aleyn 26, 82 E.R. 897.

[227] *Bayne v. Walker* (1815) 3 Dow. 233, 3 E.R. 1049 H.L.

[228] *Ehlmer v. Hall* [1993] 1 E.G.L.R. 137 C.A.; *Jeremy v. Lowgar* (1594?) Cro. Eliz. 461, 78 E.R. 714.

[229] *Sharp v. Milligan* (1857) 23 Beav. 419, 53 E.R. 165; *Matthey v. Curling* [1922] 2 A.C. 180 H.L.; *Redmond v. Dainton* [1920] 2 K.B. 256; *Chesterfield v. Bolton* (1739) 2 Com. 627, 92 E.R. 1241; *Pym v. Blackburn* (1796) 3 Ves. 34, 30 E.R. 878; *Gregg v. Coates* (1856) 23 Beav. 33, 53 E.R. 13.

[230] *Reynard v. Arnold* (1875) L.R. 10 Ch. App. 386 C.A.; *Edwards v. West* (1878) 7 Ch.D 858.

[231] *Lonsdale & Thompson Ltd. v. Black Arrow Group plc.* [1993] Ch. 361; M. Haley [1993] *Conv.* 472.

[232] *Chesterfield v. Bolton* (1739) 2 Com. 627, 92 E.R. 1241; *Pym v. Blackburn* (1796) 3 Ves. 34, 30 E.R. 878; *Hare v. Groves* (1796) 3 Anst. 687, 145 E.R. 1007; *Gregg v. Coates* (1856) 23 Beav. 33, 53 E.R. 13; *Redmond v. Dainton* [1920] 2 K.B. 256; *Matthey v. Curling* [1922] 2 A.C. 180 H.L.

[233] *Saner v. Bilton* (1878) 7 Ch.D. 815 (not disrepair); *Manchester Bonded Warehouse Co. v. Carr* (1880) 5 C.P.D. 507; Law Society's Standard Business Lease cl.9.1.

[234] *Leeds v. Cheetham* (1827) 1 Sim. 146, 57 E.R. 533; *Lofft v. Dennis* (1859) 1 E. & E. 474, 120 E.R. 987; *Mumford Hotels Ltd. v. Wheeler* [1964] Ch. 117; *Mark Rowlands v. Berni Inns Ltd.* [1985] Q.B. 211 C.A.

[235] *P. & O. Property Holdings Ltd. v. International Computers plc.* [1999] 2 E.G.L.R. 17, Neuberger J.; J.E. Adams [1999] *Conv.* 284.

[236] [1998] E.G.C.S. 178 Ch.D.

8.   Ownership of insurance money where reinstatement impossible

In *Re King*[237] a fire occurred at a time when reinstatement was impossible because of wartime restrictions. So in 1945 the policy money was invested in the joint names of landlord and tenant, the money being held on the terms of an agreement contained in a solicitor's letter. Subsequently, compulsory purchase of the ruins prevented reinstatement. It was held by a majority that the insurance money belonged to the tenant when reinstatement proved impossible, ownership resulting to the person who had paid the premiums. Although insurance was to be in joint names, Upjohn L.J.[238] interpreted this as an arrangement to ensure that a joint receipt was given, thus ensuring that the landlord could insist on reinstatement and did not affect the resulting trust imposed on the insurance money. Lord Denning M.R.'s dissenting opinion[239] that the money ought to have been divided between landlord and tenant according to their proportionate interests in the deposit account was more convincing.[240]

G.   FITNESS ETC

1.   Fitness for commercial purpose

A builder who grants a long lease may be liable to the tenant for defects in construction,[241] but one builder employed by an outside landlord is not liable to the tenant.[242] There is no obligation to ensure that commercial property is fit for the purpose for which it is let,[243] so an attempt to require a landlord to ensure fitness of an office for its commercial use was struck out as bound to fail, and commercial tenants are not entitled to withhold rent on this ground.[244] It might just be arguable in a lease of a spa that there is an implied obligation on the landlord to supply water fit for consumption.[245]

2.   Quiet enjoyment

In the soundproofing case, *Southwark L.B.C.* v. *Mills*,[246] the House of Lords made clear that the landlord's obligation of quiet enjoyment cannot impose a repairing obligation and certainly not an obligation to make improvements. The conventional understanding is "Caveat lessee" (let the tenant beware).

---

[237] [1963] Ch. 459 C.A.

[238] At 492–494, 498–500, Diplock L.J.

[239] At 484–486; *Beacon Carpets Ltd.* v. *Kirby* [1985] Q.B. 755 C.A. (insurance money owned in the same proportions as the building at the time of the fire).

[240] *Mark Rowlands Ltd.* v. *Berni Inns Ltd.* [1986] Q.B. 211 C.A.; J. Birds (1986) 6 *O.J.L.S.* 304.

[241] *Rimmer* v. *Webster* [1902] 2 Ch. 163; *Perry* v. *Sharon Development Co. Ltd.* [1937] 4 All E.R. 390 C.A.; *Targett* v. *Torfaen B.C.* [1992] 1 E.G.L.R. 275 C.A.

[242] *Strathford East Kilbride Ltd.* v. *Film Design Ltd.* [1997] Times December 1st (Scottish law follows English).

[243] *Sutton* v. *Temple* (1843) 12 M. & W. 52, 152 E.R. 1108 (grazing); *Manchester Bonded Warehouse Co.* v. *Carr* (1880) 5 C.P.D. 507 (warehouse); *Westropp* v. *Elligott* (1884) 9 App. Cas. 815, 826–827, Lord Blackburn; *Hill* v. *Harris* [1965] 2 Q.B. 601 (no promise that use is lawful).

[244] *Dailworth Ltd.* v. *T.G. Organisation (Europe) Ltd.* (1998) 75 P. & C.R. 147 C.A.

[245] *Phillips* v. *Radnor D.C.* [1998] E.G.C.S. 30.

[246] [1999] 4 All E.R. 449 H.L.; D. Rook [2000] *Conv.* 161; P. Saunders (2000) 144 S.J. 348; see above Chapter 9.

"It would be inconsistent with this basic understanding if quiet enjoyment was construed so as to create liability for the condition of the property."[247]

In *Guild* v. *Duke of Westminster*[248] the tenant failed to impose liability on his landlord to repair a drain on the landlord's property; no obligation to make the land suitable for use by the tenant arose. Quiet enjoyment was not an appropriate vehicle for the imposition of any obligation about the state and condition of property.[249]

3.   Repudiation of the lease

Is a tenant entitled to terminate his lease and so end his liability to rent because of the poor condition of the property?[250] Clearly a breach has to be very serious to justify repudiation. If so, it appears that a tenant may be entitled to repudiate a lease after a breach by the landlord of a fundamental term of the lease. The decision to recognise a right of repudiation occurred in the case of a private sector shorthold in *Hussein* v. *Mehlman*.[251] A grant for three years proved worthless when it became apparent that the landlord would not maintain the property and the tenant returned the key. The collapse of the ceiling was itself sufficient to vitiate the tenancy agreement. Sedley Q.C. relied on nineteenth century authority[252] and treated an adverse Court of Appeal decision[253] as impliedly overruled by recent developments in frustration law. The brilliant reasoning of this judgment represents a further step towards recognition of a contractual basis to leasehold law and is now fully accepted.[254] In principle a commercial lease can be repudiated. In *Chartered Trust plc.* v. *Davies*[255] a tenant was allowed to end his lease of a unit in a shopping mall because the landlord had let the next shop to a pawnbroker, whose queue of customers caused a nuisance and interfered with the tenant's light. It was held that the landlord had failed in his duty to prevent the nuisance and hence the tenant could repudiate his lease. However *Nynehead Developments Ltd.* v. *R.H. Fibreboard Containers Ltd.*[256] makes clear that breaches of covenant will rarely be so serious as to allow a commercial tenant to walk away; it is mainly up to the tenant to negotiate for express rights of termination and to incorporate appropriate contractual provisions.

---

[247] At 456h–j, Lord Hoffmann; *Anderson* v. *Oppenheimer* (1880) 5 Q.B.D. 602; *Sanderson* v. *Berwick upon Tweed Corp.* (1884) 13 Q.B.D. 547 C.A.

[248] [1985] Q.B. 668 C.A.; *Bennett Properties Ltd.* v. *H. & S. Engineering* [1998] 2 C.L.Y. 3683 Q.B.D.; *Mills* [1999] 4 All E.R. 449, 458g, Lord Hoffmann, 469j, Lord Millett.

[249] At 470a, Lord Millett.

[250] Woodfall 17.313–17.315; Evans & Smith 229–231; W. Barr, "Repudiation of Leases—a Fool's Paradise" in P. Jackson & D.C. Wilde (eds.), *Contemporary Property Law* (Ashgate Dartmouth, 1999) ch.14.

[251] [1992] 2 E.G.L.R. 87, Stephen Sedley Q.C.; C. Harpum [1993] *C.L.J.* 212; S. Bright [1992] *Conv.* 71; J.W. Carter [1985] *Conv.* 289; J.W. Carter & J. Hill [1986] *Conv.* 262.

[252] *Edwards* v. *Etherington* (1825) Ry. & M. 268, 171 E.R. 1016; *Collins* v. *Barrow* (1831) 1 M. & Rob. 112, 174 E.R. 38; *Izon* v. *Gorton* (1839) 5 Bing. (N.C.) 501, 132 E.R. 1193; *Arden* v. *Pullen* (1842) 10 M. & W. 321, 152 E.R. 492; *Smith* v. *Marrable* (1843) 11 M. & W. 5, 152 E.R. 693; *Wilson* v. *Finch-Hatton* (1877) 2 Ex.D. 336.

[253] *Total Oil Great Britain Ltd.* v. *Thompson Garages (Biggin Hill) Ltd.* [1972] 1 Q.B. 318.

[254] *Olympia & York Canary Wharf Ltd.* v. *Oil Property Investments Ltd. (No.2)* [1994] 2 E.G.L.R. 48 C.A.; *Kingston on Thames R.L.B.C.* v. *Marlow* [1996] 1 E.G.L.R. 101, 102K–L.

[255] [1997] 2 E.G.L.R. 83 C.A.

[256] [1999] 1 E.G.L.R. 7 Ch.D.; M. Pawlowski & J. Brown [1999] *Conv.* 150; P. Luxton [1999] *J.B.L.* 471.

4. Administrative controls

Environmental Protection Act 1990 powers over statutory nuisances are available for commercial premises[257] and offices and similar premises are also subject to control under the Health and Safety at Work etc. Act 1974.[258]

H. IMPROVEMENTS

1. Nature of improvement

An improvement is a change for the better made to the structure of the property let to the tenant. Who judges what is better? A tenant is only likely to make changes that he thinks are of benefit to his holding, but from the landlord's perspective an alteration may not look like an improvement. In the leading case, *F.W. Woolworth & Co. Ltd.* v. *Lambert*[259] the tenant wanted to knock away the back wall of a shop in the Square at Bournemouth so that it communicated with the neighbouring shop held by the same tenant from another landlord. The tenant got a larger shop with a tasteful Assyrian facade,[260] but the landlord got a shop without a wall and lacking a staircase and toilets. The majority held that improvements had to be considered from the point of view of the tenant[261] so that, on the facts, the proposed work could be judged an improvement, taking into account the tenant's adjoining building.[262]

2. Improvements under the old law of waste

It is natural for a landlord to wish to control changes to his property. Any active[263] change in the property fell within the common law definition of waste: a tenant was not permitted to dump spoil all over the land to a depth of 10 feet,[264] nor to turn a meadow into an orchard, nor wood into pasture,[265] nor waste land to arable,[266] and it followed that it was waste to build a new house.[267] However waste was actionable only if it caused significant damage to the reversion,[268] the medieval exemption for waste causing only trivial damage was defined by Blackstone to mean damage worth less than 12 pence in 1189.[269] If no damage to the reversion is proved, waste is not action-

---

[257] See above pp. 266–272.

[258] *Westminster C.C.* v. *Select Managements Ltd.* [1985] 1 E.G.L.R. 245 C.A.; J.E. Martin [1986] *Conv.* 45.

[259] *(No.1)* [1937] Ch. 37 C.A.; *(No.2)* [1938] Ch. 883 C.A.; the shop is the one now (2000) occupied by Boots.

[260] *(No.2)* at 907, Slesser L.J.; R.E. Megarry, *Miscellany at Law* (Stevens, 1955) 30–31.

[261] *(No.1)* at 49, Lord Wright M.R.; *Balls Brothers Ltd.* v. *Sinclair* [1931] 2 Ch. 325, Luxmore J.; Greene L.J.'s dissent is more convincing. The decision in *(No.1)* is technically obiter according to *(No.2)*, Slesser & MacKinnon L.JJ., with Greer L.J. dissenting.

[262] At 49, Lord Wright M.R.

[263] Not leaving land uncultivated: *Hutton* v. *Warren* (1836) 1 M. & W. 466, 472, 150 E.R. 517.

[264] *West Ham Central Charity Board.* v. *East London Waterworks Ltd.* [1900] 1 Ch. 624.

[265] *Darcy* v. *Askwith* (1618) Hob. 234, 80 E.R. 380.

[266] *Queen's College Oxford* v. *Hallett* (1811) 14 East. 489, 104 E.R. 689.

[267] Coke on *Littleton* 53a; *Queen's College Oxford* v. *Hallett* (1811) 14 East. 489, 104 E.R. 689.

[268] *Jones* v. *Chappell* (1875) L.R. 20 Eq. 539, Jessel M.R.

[269] *Doherty* v. *Allman* (1878) 3 App. Cas. 709 H.L.; *Harrow School Governors* v. *Alderton* (1800) 2 Bos. & P. 86. 126 E.R. 1170 (award of one farthing); *Green* v. *Cole* (1672) 2 Wms. Saunds. 252, 85 E.R. 1037 n.(o); *Barret* v. *Barret* (1627) Het. 35, 124 E.R. 321, Richardson C.J.

able.[270] Taking down the railing from in front of a chapel in the course of its conversion to a cinema gave no cause for complaint.[271] Even stronger is the case of "ameliorating waste" which increases the value of the reversion, which is a good defence to an action[272]: examples are the conversion of a farm to a more profitable market garden[273] or of artillery barracks to houses.[274]

3. Covenants against alterations

The old law of waste has been superseded by covenants against alterations or additions,[275] especially for agricultural leases.[276] Landlords commonly impose an *absolute* restriction on making alterations, meaning that any change requires the landlord's agreement.[277] What is prohibited depends upon the wording used in the covenant. In *Bent v. High Cliff Developments Ltd.*[278] a covenant in a 999-year lease of a penthouse apartment not to make *structural* alterations did not affect the replacement of windows and external doors given the careful definition of the structure in the lease. The statutory rules discussed immediately below do not apply to a covenant that imposed an absolute prohibition.[279]

Usually the tenant has some right to make improvements, but only with the prior consent of the landlord, that is there is a *qualified covenant*, which strikes a fairer balance between the interests of the two parties. Statute implies a proviso that the consent of the landlord is not to be unreasonably withheld.[280] The tenant cannot contract away this protection, though the rule is easily evaded by imposing an absolute bar. A similar proviso may be implied by the common law into a covenant to secure approval to building plans.[281] If consent is sought and unreasonably withheld, the tenant cannot proceed without more but should apply for a declaration.[282] Factors entitling the landlord to refuse consent are the short duration of the tenancy,[283] or that the work would involve trespass on the landlord's property,[284] but it is reasonable to require the payment of legal expenses and compensation for the loss in value of the reversion.[285] In *F.W. Woolworth & Co. Ltd. v. Lambert*[286] a store in Bournemouth was to be improved by combining two

---

[270] *Young* v. *Spencer* (1829) 10 B. & C. 145, 109 E.R. 405 (pulling down barn); *Doe d. Grubb* v. *Burlington* (1833) 5 B. & Ad. 507, 110 E.R. 878.

[271] *Hyman* v. *Rose* [1912] A.C. 623 H.L.

[272] *Simmons* v. *Norton* (1831) 7 Bing. 640, 131 E.R. 247.

[273] *Meux* v. *Cobley* [1892] 2 Ch. 253, Kekewich J.

[274] *Doherty* v. *Allman* (1878) 3 App. Cas. 709 H.L.

[275] *Balls Brothers Ltd.* v. *Sinclair* [1931] 2 Ch. 325, Luxmoore J.; *Lilley & Skinner Ltd.* v. *Crump* (1929) 73 S.J. 366, Rowlatt J.; Woodfall 11.254–11.263; Evans & Smith (5th) 126–130.

[276] *Meux* v. *Cobley* [1892] 2 Ch. 253, Kekewich J.; see above pp. 629–630.

[277] e.g. the covenant not to maim the main walls in *Lilley & Skinner Ltd.* v. *Crump* (1929) 73 S.J. 366, Rowlatt J.

[278] [1999] 34 L.S.G. 35.

[279] *F.W. Woolworth & Co. Ltd.* v. *Lambert* [1937] Ch. 37.

[280] L.T.A. 1927 s.19(2); *Woolworth* as above at 53, Romer L.J; L.T.A. 1954 s.83 (county courts have jurisdiction).

[281] *Cryer* v. *Scott Bros. (Sunbury) Ltd.* (1988) 55 P. & C.R. 183 C.A.; J.E. Adams [1988] *Conv.* 172.

[282] *Balls Brothers Ltd.* v. *Sinclair* [1931] 2 Ch. 325, Luxmoore J.

[283] *Tideway Investment & Property Holdings Ltd.* v. *Wellwood* [1952] Ch. 791 C.A.

[284] At 801, Harman J. (on appeal on different points); *Davies* v. *Yadegar* [1990] 1 E.G.L.R. 70 C.A.; *Harries* v. *Florensa* [1990] 1 E.G.L.R. 73 C.A. (airspace).

[285] Fines are not allowed for improvements, but are permissible in relation to alterations: L. Crabb [1993] *Conv.* 215, 220–221.

[286] *(No.1)* [1937] Ch. 37 C.A.; *(No.2)* [1938] Ch. 883 C.A.

blocks, removing the back wall and placing the staircase in the extension. Given that these were held to be improvements, the question was whether it was reasonable for the landlord to demand £7,000 as his price for granting permission for the change. In the first round, the tenant failed to prove its case, but in the second round it won by showing that the landlord's condition was unreasonable.[287] A consent granted "subject to licence" is immediately valid.[288]

4. Preventing work and forcing reinstatement

An injunction can be obtained to stop work that is not authorised,[289] in a clear case even by a mandatory injunction granted pre-trial.[290] Unauthorised alterations may also justify termination of the lease by forfeiture.[291] The classic example of how not to proceed was *Billson* v. *Residential Apartments Ltd.*[292] in which work was commenced to convert a block into 24 bedsits, which greatly increased the value of the blocks, but work commenced without the landlord's permission, continued after service of a forfeiture notice, and proceeded once the tenant had forced his way back in after a peaceable re-entry and recommenced work. Forfeiture proceedings succeeded.[293]

The tenant may be required to reinstate the property to the condition it was in before the work.[294] In this way statute has improved a landlord's remedies, since common law damages were limited to the loss in value of the reversion, excluding the cost of reinstatement.[295]

5. Compensation for improvements

Statute[296] provides an *entitlement* to compensation for improvements and goodwill on the termination of business tenancies.[297] It is important to notice that what is defined here are business tenancies as opposed to renewable business tenancies; the wider net for compensation purposes includes some tenancies where there is security under the Landlord and Tenant Act 1954, for example where the tenant lacks the business occupation to support a claim for a new lease. What should be compensated is the erection of a building[298] or any other improvement on the holding, excluding any trade fixture that the tenant is entitled to remove. Compensation is payable whether the improvement was made by the current tenant or by any predecessor in title, such as a sub-

---

[287] *Alleyn's Estate Governors* v. *Williams* (1995) 70 P. & C.R. 67, Nicholls V.C.

[288] *Prudential Assurance Co. Ltd.* v. *Mount Eden Land Ltd.* [1997] 1 E.G.L.R. 37 C.A.

[289] *Bonnett* v. *Sadler* (1808) 14 Ves. 526, 33 E.R. 622; *British Empire Mutual Life Insurance Co.* v. *Cooper* (1888) 4 T.L.R. 362.

[290] *Viscount Chelsea* v. *Muscatt* [1990] 2 E.G.L.R. 48 C.A.

[291] *St Marylebone Property Co. Ltd.* v. *Tesco Stores Ltd.* [1988] 2 E.G.L.R. 40, Hoffmann J.; *Duke of Westminster* v. *Swinton* [1948] 1 W.L.R. 524, Denning J.

[292] [1992] 1 A.C. 494 H.L.

[293] *Billson (No.3)* [1993] E.G.C.S. 55.

[294] This is unaffected by L.T.A. 1927 s.19(1).

[295] *James* v. *Hutton* [1950] K.B. 9 C.A. (better shop front).

[296] L.T.A. 1927 part I, as amended by L.T.A. 1954 part III; R. Anyamere [1999] 26 *E.G.* 148.

[297] L.T.A. 1927 s.17; Woodfall 22.196–22.228; Evans & Smith (5th) 497–504.

[298] *National Electric Theatres Ltd.* v. *Hudgell* [1939] Ch. 553, Morton J. (demolition and rebuilding could be improvement).

tenant who has assigned to the current tenant.[299] *Quantification* of compensation falls to the county court.[300] The principle is that the landlord has to pay the increase in value of the holding: compensation is not to exceed the net additional value, though reduced by any extra liability to rates,[301] and capped at the reasonable cost of carrying out the improvement, regard being had to the intended use.[302]

Compensation is *excluded* where the improvement occurred before 1927, under a statutory obligation between 1927 and 1954,[303] under a contractual obligation reflected in the rent,[304] or within three years of termination of the tenancy, and also where renewal of a business lease is offered and rejected.[305] Contracting out can occur only if the landlord provides adequate consideration.[306] Since compensation rights can be excluded by agreement, the Law Commission propose that rights should be withdrawn after a 25-year transitional period.[307]

Rights to compensation accrue only where the tenant obtained *prior approval*, notifying the landlord[308] in advance,[309] and so giving the landlord an opportunity to object to the improvement. Refusal is a veto unless the county court overrides it by a certificate that it is a proper improvement, on the ground that it is calculated to add to the letting value at the end of the lease, is reasonable and suitable, and will not diminish the value of the holding.[310] This certificate must be obtained before work of improvement starts[311]: in *Hogarth Health Club Ltd.* v. *Westbourne Investments Ltd.*[312] improvements had been completed in late 1981, seven long years before the county court action for approval of them was struck out for inordinate and inexcusable delay. There is no power to grant retrospective permission.

The right to compensation accrues to the tenant at the end of a tenancy on quitting.[313] The basic *time limit* for a claim is three months,[314] usually measured from the time that the landlord serves a notice under the business tenancies legislation to end the tenancy.[315]

---

[299] *Pelosi* v. *Newcastle Arms Brewery (Nottingham) Ltd.* [1981] 2 E.G.L.R. 36 C.A.; see also on rent review *Durley House Ltd.* v. *Cadogan* [2000] 09 E.G. 183 C.A.; see above p. 665.

[300] L.T.A. 1927 s.21; L.T.A. 1954 s.63.

[301] L.T.A. 1927 s.16; also any claim can be set off: s.11.

[302] s.1(1)(a)–(b). Allowance is made for any necessary repair.

[303] s.2(1)(b) was repealed by L.T.A. 1954 s.48.

[304] s.2(1)(a); *Owen Owen Estate Ltd.* v. *Livett* [1956] Ch. 1 (L contracted with ST to make improvement; L had no claim against HL).

[305] s.2(1)(d).

[306] s.9 as amended by L.T.A. 1954 s.49.

[307] Law Com. No.268 (1992).

[308] s.8 applies where there are several landlords.

[309] By letter: *Deerfield Travel Services Ltd.* v. *Leatherseller's Company* [1982] 2 E.G.L.R. 39 C.A.

[310] *Land Securities plc.* v. *Metropolitan Police District Receiver* [1983] 1 W.L.R. 439, Megarry V.C.

[311] L.T.A. 1927 s.3(5).

[312] [1990] 1 E.G.L.R. 89 C.A.; *Deerfield Travel Services Ltd.* v. *Leathersellers Society* (1983) 46 P. & C.R. 132 C.A.

[313] L.T.A. 1927 s.1.

[314] L.T.A. 1954 s.47.

[315] s.25; other possibilities are: when the landlord could give notice in response to a tenant's request under s.26; between 6 and 3 months from the end of a lease by effluxion of time; 3 months after the time for possession under an order for forfeiture; and 3 months after a physical re-entry.

6.   Statutory requirements

Standards required of commercial buildings constantly change. It is common to require the tenant to carry out work needed to comply with new regulations, work for which compensation rights are excluded. The most recent example is the Disability Discrimination Act 1995. An employer with more than 20 employees[316] has a duty to prevent physical features of workplace placing any disabled person[317] at a disadvantage.[318] Leasehold covenants are amended[319] so that a tenant may ask the landlord for consent to carry out necessary work and the landlord cannot withhold consent or attach unreasonable conditions. The Act also affects commercial leases of shops, theatres, and other services, since it becomes illegal to discriminate in relation to the provision of goods, facilities and services,[320] for example by denying access to disabled persons, though the expenses of compliance is restricted.[321] New buildings will have to comply with more extensive building regulations, requiring, for example, the provision of ramped access to public buildings.

I.   FIXTURES

1.   Fixtures between landlord and tenant

A tenant is entitled to fixtures during the term, but at the end of the lease they pass to the landlord[322]; however tenants have customary or statutory rights to remove many fixtures at the end of a lease

2.   Physical parts of the land

Things that form part of the land are owned with it.[323] *Elitestone Ltd.* v. *Morris*[324] concerned one of the plots on Holtsfield, a 14 acre site on the Gower Peninsula containing 27 chalets and a community of almost 80 people. Morris paid an annual licence fee and was undoubtedly a tenant of the *land* comprised in his plot, but he also needed to show that his *chalet* was included in his lease[325] in order to claim Rent Act 1977 security of tenure. It had been built in 1945 without any physical connection to the land, since

---

[316] s.7; the total for the firm rather than the particular workplace.

[317] Defined by s.1, sch.1.

[318] s.6; s.8 provides for enforcement.

[319] s.16; sch.4 part I.

[320] Part III in force December 2nd 1996; ss.19, 20 (discrimination), 21 (duty to make adjustments), 22 (premises), 23 (exception for small dwellings), 24 (meaning of discrimination), 25 (enforcement), 27 (alteration covenants).

[321] Max 10% of rateable value.

[322] *Never-Stop Rly (Wembley) Ltd.* v. *British Empire Exhibition (1924) Inc.* [1926] Ch. 877; *Webb* v. *Frank Bevis Ltd.* [1940] 1 All E.R. 247 C.A.; *Elitestone Ltd.* v. *Morris* [1997] 1 W.L.R. 687, 694H–696C, Lord Clyde.

[323] [1997] 1 W.L.R. 687, 691G, Lord Lloyd; Woodfall 13.131.

[324] [1997] 1 W.L.R. 687 H.L.; H.W. Wilkinson [1997] *N.L.J.* 1031; S. Bridge [1997] *C.L.J.* 498; H. Conway [1998] *Conv.* 418; reversing (1997) 73 P. & C.R. 259 C.A. and restoring the county court judgment. *Chelsea Yacht & Boat Club Ltd.* v. *Pope* [2000] Times June 7th C.A. (houseboat) is discussed at the end of Chapter 6.

[325] This implied that the rent would be regulated; the site owner had increased the annual licence fee from £85 to £1,000.

when it had rested under its own weight on a separate base.[326] Old cases permitting the removal of wooden buildings resting on their own weight were doubted.[327] Morris' chalet was unlike a Portakabin or mobile home, because it was so constructed that it could only be enjoyed *in situ* and removal would involve its total destruction. So, it had become a part of the land, was included in the lease, and Morris did enjoy security of tenure.

A building starts off as a pile of breeze blocks, bricks, and tiles, which are brought on to the building site as chattels. Incorporation into the building causes them to lose their character as individual bricks, and become incorporated in the wall as a part of the land. So do the component parts of a dry stone wall on a moorland farm.[328] The same principle applies to a conservatory,[329] doors,[330] windows,[331] central heating boilers, and radiators.[332]

3. Fixtures

Objects that are removable without overwhelming damage to the fabric of the land are fixtures if they have become part of the land by being affixed to it.[333] Identification becomes an issue when ownership of the land is divided between competing claimants, as it is under a lease.[334] Whether an item remains a chattel is determined objectively from two factors[335]:

(1) the degree of annexation; and
(2) the object of annexation.

4. Degree of annexation

Objects firmly annexed to land are more likely to be fixtures than those lying on top of the land, so that the greater the amount of damage done in removing an item the more likely that annexation has occurred.[336] "Mere juxtaposition" does not usually make an object a fixture. Something lying on land under its own weight is not a fixture,[337] even if it is a printing machine weighing several tons,[338] or a free-standing statue.[339] Light

---

[326] At 694E–F, Lord Clyde.

[327] At 692B–C, Lord Lloyd, 697G–698G, Lord Clyde; *Reid* v. *Smith* (1905) 3 C.L.R. 656.

[328] *Holland* v. *Hodgson* (1872) L.R. 7 C.P. 328, 335, Blackburn J.

[329] *Buckland* v. *Butterfield* (1820) 2 Brod. & Bing. 54, 129 E.R. 878; *Montague* v. *Long* (1972) 24 P. & C.R. 240 (bridge).

[330] *Cooke's case* (1582) Moore K.B. 177, 72 E.R. 515; *Climie* v. *Wood* (1869) L.R. 4 Exch. 328; *Phillips* v. *Lamdin* [1949] 2 K.B. 33, 41.

[331] *Boswell* v. *Crucible Steel Co.* [1925] 1 K.B. 119, 123, Atkin L.J.

[332] *Holiday Fellowship Ltd.* v. *Hereford* [1959] 1 W.L.R. 211; *Elitestone* [1997] 1 W.L.R. 687, 690G, Lord Lloyd.

[333] Woodfall 13.131–13.168; Evans & Smith (5th) ch.15; *Bradshaw* v. *Davey* [1952] 1 All E.R. 350 (rateable value includes fixtures).

[334] Other cases are considered in Sparkes, *N.L.L.* ch.20.

[335] *Leigh* v. *Taylor* [1902] A.C. 157, 161, Lord Halsbury L.C. (fact); *Berkley* v. *Poulett* [1977] 1 E.G.L.R. 86, 88K, Scarman L.J. (fact); but *Reynolds* v. *Ashby Son* [1904] A.C. 466 (law).

[336] *Spyer* v. *Phillipson* [1931] 2 Ch. 183, 209, 210, Romer L.J.

[337] *Bain* v. *Brand* (1876) 1 App.Cas. 762 H.L.; *Deen* v. *Andrews* [1986] 1 E.G.L.R. 262, 264G, Hirst J.

[338] *Hulme* v. *Brigham* [1943] K.B. 152. Movable parts follow the character of the machine: *Mather* v. *Fraser* (1856) 2 K. & J. 536, 69 E.R. 895.

[339] *Berkley* v. *Poulett* [1977] 1 E.G.L.R. 86 C.A.

fittings are fixtures, but not the bulbs.[340] A carpet may not be a fixture even if nailed down,[341] Greenhouses may or may not count as fixtures depending upon whether they are attached to a mortared foundation and walls,[342] or (as most now are) free-standing.[343] The defendant in *Botham v. TSB Bank plc.*[344] bought a flat in London as a shell for £130,000 and proceeded to furnish it lavishly at a total cost of £60,000. After repossession, the Court of Appeal allowed the lenders to keep the bathroom and kitchen units and recessed ceiling lights as fixtures, but the borrower (Botham) retained ownership of light fittings, carpets, curtains and blinds, gas fires and kitchen white goods.

Physical annexation is not decisive either way, but it does raise a rebuttable presumption for the thing being a fixture. Even nailing machines to wooden plugs in the floor to keep them steady during use[345] has shifted the presumption towards them being fixtures. Failure of annexation raises a rebuttable presumption that the item retains its status as a chattel belonging to the tenant.

5. Object of annexation

Modern law takes this to be the primary rule. A chattel is not a fixture if the object of attaching it was to improve its convenience of use as a chattel.[346] *Leigh v. Taylor*[347] involved a valuable tapestry displayed by its owner in the drawing room of Luton Hoo, which she occupied as tenant for life. Strips of wood were nailed to the walls, canvas stretched between them, and the tapestry was fastened to the canvas with tacks, but it had not become a fixture. The court found it unnecessary to investigate the length of the screws![348] Other examples are oak panelling and a chimney piece,[349] picture frames screwed into recesses in the dining room panelling and a half-ton statue of a Greek athlete,[350] and cinema seats,[351] but objects forming part of the overall architectural composition of the house are fixtures.[352]

No one can make a thing real or personal merely by wishing it so.[353] Sufficient fixing makes it a part of the land irrespective of intention. Contracts to retain ownership of fixtures are invalid. *Melluish v. B.M.S. (No.3) Ltd.*[354] concerned central heating equipment

---

[340] *Sewell v. Angerstein* (1868) 18 L.T. 300 (gasoliers); *British Economical Lamp Co. Ltd. v. Empire, Mile End, Ltd.* (1913) 29 T.L.R. 386.

[341] *Hellawell v. Eastwood* (1851) 6 Exch. 295, 155 E.R. 554.

[342] *Jenkins v. Gething* (1862) 2 John. & H. 520, 70 E.R. 1165.

[343] *Deen v. Andrews* [1986] 1 E.G.L.R. 262; *H.E. Dibble Ltd. v. Moore* [1970] 2 Q.B. 181; P.V. Baker (1970) 86 L.Q.R. 19.

[344] (1997) 73 P. & C.R. D1 C.A.

[345] *Holland v. Hodgson* (1872) L.R. 7 C.P. 328.

[346] [1997] 1 W.L.R. 687, 692C–693H, Lord Lloyd.

[347] [1902] A.C. 157 H.L.

[348] *Re De Falbe* (the same case in the C.A.) [1901] 1 Ch. 523, 531, Rigby L.J.

[349] *Spyer v. Phillipson* [1931] 2 Ch. 183.

[350] *Berkley v. Poulett* [1977] 1 E.G.L.R. 86 C.A.

[351] *Vaudeville Electric Cinema Ltd. v. Muriset* [1923] 2 Ch. 74; *Lyon & Co. v. London City & Midland Bank* [1903] 2 K.B. 135.

[352] *D'Eyncourt v. Gregory* (1866) L.R. 3 Eq. 382 (Baroque fittings at Harlaxton, Lincolnshire); but see *Re De Falbe* [1901] 1 Ch. 523, 531, 532.

[353] *Dixon v. Fisher* (1843) 5 D. 775, 793, Lord Cockburn; *Elitestone* [1997] 1 W.L.R. 687, 698H, Lord Clyde.

[354] [1996] A.C. 454 H.L.; *Aircool Installations v. British Telecommunications* [1995] C.L.Y. 821; *Stokes v. Costain Property Investments Ltd.* [1983] 1 W.L.R. 907, Harman J. Tax rules have been tightened.

supplied to a local authority for installation in 180 of its houses, on terms providing for ownership to be retained by the hiring company. Also in issue were plant for swimming pools, alarm systems for sheltered housing, lifts for car parks and cremators. The equipment belonged to the local authority for the duration of the time that it was annexed to the authority's land, so that the only relevant intention was that deduced from the degree and purpose of annexation.[355]

6. Covenant to repair fixtures

Such a covenant applies to removable items, but not to structural parts of a house[356] nor to separate buildings.[357] A covenant by the tenant to repair fixtures does not affect his right of removal when the lease ends.[358] The covenant runs with the land so as to bind future tenants and benefit future landlords.[359]

7. Removable fixtures

Three classes of fixture can be removed by tenants—ornamental and domestic fixtures, trade fixtures, and agricultural fixtures. No ownership is conferred in advance of removal.[360]

Ornamental and domestic fixtures obviously belong to the tenant, whose short-term interest in the land means that he does not decorate for the benefit of the landlord. Panelling was once an essential attribute of a fashionable house, but few tenants now install or remove panelling,[361] or move with chimney glasses, stoves, grates, ranges and ovens. Items of decoration may not be fixtures at all according to the House of Lords' view of the tapestry case, *Leigh v. Taylor*. The Court of Appeal considered it was a fixture, but one which the tenant for life could remove.[362]

Trade fixtures are those that the tenant himself has fixed to the premises for the purposes of his trade.[363] This ancient exception to encourage trade[364] was formalised by *Poole's case*,[365] which allowed a soap boiler to remove his vats and coppers. Examples from Her Majesty's Theatre, Haymarket included seats bolted to the ground, brackets for wall lights, and electric transformers.[366] The same applies to the fittings of a pub[367]

[355] At 473B, Lord Browne-Wilkinson; *Elitestone* [1997] 1 W.L.R. 687, 690E, Lord Lloyd.

[356] *Boswell v. Crucible Steel Co.* [1925] 1 K.B. 119 C.A.

[357] *Pole-Carew v. Western Counties & General Manure Co. Ltd.* [1920] 2 Ch. 97; *Jordan v. May* [1947] K.B. 427 C.A. (batteries not fixture).

[358] *New Zealand Government Property Corp. v. H.M. & S. Ltd.* [1982] Q.B. 1145 C.A.

[359] *Williams v. Earle* (1868) L.R. 3 Q.B. 739.

[360] *Melluish v. B.M.S. (No.3) Ltd.* [1996] A.C. 454 H.L. Removal rights may be overridden if a sculpture is listed as part of the building; there is an unreported C.A. case (1999) concerning the Time Life Building in London.

[361] *Spyer v. Phillipson* [1931] 2 Ch. 183.

[362] *Re de Falbe* [1901] 1 Ch. 523 C.A.; *Spyer v. Phillipson* [1931] 2 Ch. 183, 205, Lord Hanworth M.R. (very substantial fixing).

[363] *New Zealand Government Property Corporation v. H.M.& S. Ltd.* [1982] Q.B. 1145, 1157A–B, Lord Denning M.R.

[364] *Penton v. Robart* (1801) 2 East. 88, 90, 102 E.R. 302, Kenyon C.J. (glass houses).

[365] (1703) 1 Salk. 368, 91 E.R. 320; *Mansfield v. Blackburne* (1840) 6 Bing. N.C. 426, 133 E.R. 165.

[366] [1982] Q.B. 1145, 1157A–B.

[367] *Elliott v. Bishop* (1845) 10 Exch. 496, 156 E.R. 534.

and to petrol pumps,[368] but not to major plant used for the manufacture of sulphuric acid.[369]

Agricultural fixtures were not regarded as trade fixtures.[370] Statutory regimes have achieved justice for agricultural tenants who attach fixtures to the holding or erect buildings.[371] Items that are not removable are replacements of landlord's fixtures and those the tenant has contracted to provide. A notice procedure applies when a tenancy ends, giving the landlord a right to require the tenant to leave a fixture, by offering its fair value in compensation.[372]

8.   Exercise of right to remove

A contractual right to remove chattels gives an equitable right of entry which binds a buyer,[373] except one without notice. Removal is bound to cause some damage, but there must be no material damage to freehold.[374] Any damage caused either by installation *or* by removal must be remedied.[375] Removal rights continue throughout the lease, during renewals,[376] and perhaps for a short period afterwards.[377] However on a surrender it is wise to preserve the right of removal expressly.

---

[368] *Smith* v. *City Petroleum Co.* [1940] 1 All E.R. 260.

[369] *Pole-Carew* v. *Western Counties & General Manure Co.* [1920] 2 Ch. 97.

[370] *Elwes* v. *Maw* (1802) 3 East 38, 102 E.R. 510 (animal house, carpenter's sheds, fuel shed, wagon-house, fold yard).

[371] A.T.A. 1995 s.8 (post-1995 tenancies); A.H.A. 1986 s.10 (earlier tenancies). The old Acts were subject to contracting out: *Premier Dairies Ltd* v. *Garlick* [1920] 2 Ch. 17. Under the 1995 Act, this requires advance agreement and compensation will be payable.

[372] A.H.A. 1986 s.10(4).

[373] *Re Morrison Jones & Taylor Ltd.* [1914] 1 Ch. 50, 58; *Poster* v. *Slough Estates Ltd.* [1968] 1 W.L.R. 1515, 1520G, 1521C; A.G. Guest & J. Lever (1963) 27 *Conv. (N.S.)* 30.

[374] *Buckland* v. *Butterfield* (1820) 2 Brod. & B. 54, 129 E.R. 878 (conservatory); *Gibson* v. *Hammersmith & City Ry Co.* (1863) 2 Drew & Sm. 603, 62 E.R. 748, Kindersley V.-C.

[375] *Mancetter Developments Ltd.* v. *Garmenson Ltd.* [1986] Q.B. 1212 C.A.

[376] *New Zealand Government Property Corporation* v *H.M. & S. Ltd.* [1982] Q.B. 1145 C.A.; (1982) 98 L.Q.R. 342; H.W. Wilkinson (1982) 132 *N.L.J.* 786; G. Kodilinye [1987] *Conv.* 253.

[377] *Penton* v. *Robart* (1801) 2 East. 88, 102 E.R. 302; *Weeton* v. *Woodcock* (1840) 7 M. & W. 14, 151 E.R. 659 (rights lost on forfeiture).

26

BUSINESS LEASES OF PART

Commercial service charges. Units and common parts. Repairs and services. Disputes. Allocation between units. Tenants' right to compel work covered by the service charge. Use covenants. Planning use classes. Absolute and qualified use covenants. Anchor tenants. Trading restrictions. Frustration. Interference by the landlord. Interference by neighbouring tenants.

A. NEED FOR COMMERCIAL SERVICE CHARGES

1. Leases not requiring a service charge

Many commercial tenants take only a part of the property held by the landlord, but sometimes the part let is not structurally dependent upon its neighbour so that the value of it is not dependent upon the maintenance of the nearby units, the classic example being a lease of a single shop in a parade of shops. After all one could sell such a shop freehold without the need for communal management arrangements, so it can be let without a service charge provision. The only concessions to the fact that the property let is only part of the landlord's estate are the precision needed in defining the part let, the inclusion of easements and covenants (as one would in a freehold sale of part),[1] and strict control of permitted uses. The basis of commercial letting practice is the full repairing lease, which imposes all liability to repair on the tenant so that the landlord receives the rent as pure income without deduction. However, it is common for the landlord to insure and to reserve the cost of premiums (or a proportion of the premium for the whole block in the case of a flat) as an additional insurance rent.

2. Leases requiring a service charge

Positive covenants to repair or to pay money are not enforceable when they are imposed on freehold land.[2] So estate management of communally occupied property has to be based on the creation of leases and the payment for repairs and communal facilities through a service charge, since there are no conceptual problems to prevent the running of covenants with leasehold land.[3] Leases are granted of the individual units and the fact that these leases are subject to the payment of a service charge creates no problem, since the covenant to pay the service charge will run with the land.

---

[1] Sparkes *N.L.L.* chs.20–23. A letting scheme may be created if an estate of neighbouring properties are all let on the same terms; Sparkes pp.605–607.

[2] *Rhone* v. *Stephens* [1994] 2 A.C. 310 H.L.; Sparkes *N.L.L.* 622–624.

[3] See below Chapter 28.

Special machinery is required where the landlord's property consists of an estate of interdependent parts, each reliant upon its neighbours for its structural integrity. Examples of properties for which a service charge scheme is essential are office blocks, shopping arcades, and industrial estates.[4] Management companies are uncommon for commercial developments, so that it is likely that the landlord himself will take on the responsibility for the structural and exterior work. The principle of full repairing leases is maintained because the tenant is required to maintain the parts within his exclusive use—that is the interior of the units—and to pay a proportion of the money spent by the landlord as a service charge. Commercial landlords will also provide some communal services at the expense of the tenants—such as porterage, lifts, and landscaping. Contractual principles operate and the legislative controls governing residential leases are not in play.

3. Commonhold proposals

When the proposals are enacted,[5] the widest use of commonhold is likely to be for flat developments, but it will also be available to commercial developers with warehouse developments or office blocks.

B. COMMERCIAL SERVICE CHARGES

1. Units and common parts

Service charge schemes are based on a division between units and common parts. It is essential to state with precision the extent of the property which is let ("the demised premises"), and also to define precisely the remaining property of the landlord ("the common parts") over which rights are granted, and for which maintenance costs fall within the service charge. In a building this generally includes hallways, stairs and lifts, and, outside, the grounds. Particular attention is needed to the definition of the ownership of the roof space[6] and also to such matters as walls, ceilings, and floors. In *London Underground Ltd.* v. *Shell International Petroleum Co. Ltd.*[7] the underside of the first floor was the upper limit of the ground floor unit, and disrepair of the girders supporting the first floor was not the responsibility of the tenant of the ground floor. It is also important to consider windows and external doors.[8]

The landlord generally retains the structural and load-bearing walls of a building—which will be maintained via the service charge—leaving internal walls within the

---

[4] Law Society Business Lease (Part of a Building) (Law Society, 1996) cls.3, 13; Woodfall 7.162–7.231; Davey 345–353; Evans & Smith (5th) 416–422; Garner (2nd) ch.17. See generally M. Pawlowski & J. Brown [2000] *R.R.L.R.* 21.

[5] See above Chapter 17.

[6] *Devonshire Reid Properties Ltd.* v. *Trenaman* [1997] 1 E.G.L.R. 45 (precise number of flats in scheme so new flat in roof space infringed the scheme); *Hannon* v. *169 Queen's Gate Ltd.* [2000] 09 E.G. 179 Ch.D. (new flats in roof space were permitted by letting scheme); there are many earlier cases.

[7] [1998] E.G.C.S. 97 Ch.D.

[8] *Bent* v. *High Cliff Developments Ltd.* [1999] 34 L.S.G. 35 (excluded on facts); also *Pearlman* v. *Harrow School Governors* [1979] Q.B. 56 C.A.; *Irvine* v. *Moran* [1991] 1 E.G.L.R. 261.

domain of the owner of each unit. The estate documentation must ensure that the two parts mesh perfectly so that nothing is included twice and nothing is left out.[9]

2. Repair and maintenance

Maintenance of common parts is the responsibility of the landlord or management company, the cost being recovered through a service charge. Individual units must be repaired by each owner, with a covenant forcing him to keep up the standard of repair, and with reserve powers for the landlord or management company to enter and carry out the necessary work at the cost of the defaulting tenant.[10] No terms can be implied.[11]

Work which is authorised may cover repairs only, in which case it may be important to determine whether work such as installation of a new window is an improvement as opposed to repair,[12] though repair is not restricted just to first aid.[13] This limitation is irrelevant if the service charge covers work of improvement,[14] though no doubt tenants will insist upon some definition of the types of improvement for which they will be liable to pay. Frequently the landlord will have to produce plans of proposed work and there will be some procedure for tenants to object to over-lavish work.[15]

3. Services within the charge

Estates require maintenance and management, and so landlords will generally contract to provide certain facilities and services at the expense of their tenants. Services will be differentiated into core functions which the landlord must provide and others which he (or his managing agent) has a discretion to provide should he choose to do so. It is common to include a catch-all provision for "other beneficial services" but, wide as this is, it does not justify a charge for major external repairs.[16] Disputes may arise about whether particular work is necessary,[17] and when it should be included, since this may affect which tenant has to bear the costs.

Other sums included are V.A.T.,[18] interest (the right to which is implied if not expressed[19]) and the costs of employing managing agents if there is a clear contractual provision.[20] If the service charge is limited to sums "expended", the landlord can recover

---

[9] *Graystone Property Investments Ltd.* v. *Margulies* [1984] 1 E.G.L.R. 27 C.A.; J.E. Adams [1984] *Conv.* 171; D. Williams [1988] 01 *L.S.G.* 14.

[10] Law Society Business Lease (Part of a Building) (Law Society, 1996) cls.4, 5.

[11] *Hafton Properties Ltd.* v. *Camp* [1994] 1 E.G.L.R. 67 (landlord not liable for failure of management company to maintain).

[12] *Mullaney* v. *Maybourne Grange (Croydon) Management Co. Ltd.* [1986] 1 E.G.L.R. 70 (new window not repair).

[13] *Manor House Drive Ltd.* v. *Shahbazian* (1965) 195 E.G. 283.

[14] *Mullaney* v. *Maybourne Grange (Croydon) Management Co. Ltd.* [1986] 1 E.G.L.R. 70; *Reston Ltd.* v. *Hudson* [1990] 2 E.G.L.R. 51; *Holding & Management Ltd.* v. *Property Holding & Investment Trust plc.* [1989] 1 W.L.R. 1313 C.A.; *New England Properties plc.* v. *Portsmouth News Shops Ltd.* [1993] 1 E.G.L.R. 84.

[15] *Northway Flats Management Co. (Camden) Ltd.* v. *Wimpey Pension Trustees Ltd.* [1992] 2 E.G.L.R. 42 C.A.

[16] *Lloyds Bank plc.* v. *Bowker Orford* [1992] 2 E.G.L.R. 44 Ch.D.

[17] *Postel Properties Ltd.* v. *Boots the Chemist Ltd.* [1996] 2 E.G.L.R. 60, Ian Kennedy J. (reasonable to repair roof before it failed).

[18] *Nell Gwynn House Maintenance Fund* v. *Commissioners of Customs & Excise* (1996) 72 P. & C.R. 522 C.A.

[19] *Skilleter* v. *Charles* [1992] 1 E.G.L.R. 73 C.A.; *Boldmark Ltd.* v. *Cohen* [1986] 1 E.G.L.R. 47 C.A.

[20] *Embassy Court Residents Association Ltd.* v. *Lipman* [1984] 2 E.G.L.R. 60 C.A.; *Woodtrek Ltd.* v. *Jezek* [1982] 1 E.G.L.R. 45 (cost of rent collection).

money only after it has actually been spent.[21] However many leases provide for the creation of a sinking fund, that is a fund built up to provide for future work or to cover the cost of deprecation of machinery; previous taxation problems[22] are now reduced.[23] It is the tenant current when the charge is levied who is liable to contribute, even if the work is not done until long after he has sold.[24]

4. Disputes

The ground landlord's managing agent is required to certify the sums chargeable to the service charge that have been spent and also the proportions to be allocated to each tenant. Leases generally provide that the certificate is to be conclusive. In one case a copy of the letter stating the amount was sent to a lender which incorrectly filed the letter with the deeds rather than ensuring that the borrower made payment, and this letter was held to be a proper certificate in writing of the amount of the service charge.[25] However, the certificate cannot be conclusive against errors of interpretation of the lease or erroneous calculation of the proportions because rateable values have been applied wrongly.[26] In *Universities Superannuation Scheme Ltd.* v. *Marks & Spencer plc.* the lease of a store in Telford town centre provided for payment of a proportion of the costs as calculated in accordance with a schedule to the lease, but the landlords made an error in the method of calculation. It was held in these circumstances that the tenant could legitimately dispute the demand, since the liability was based on the terms of the lease itself, and the certificate was irrelevant when determining liability.

Leaseholders often complain about *excessive work*. Landlords should recover only what was fair and reasonable, this being an implied limitation at common law, so the landlord has no power to adopt the highest possible cost.[27] Charges should be based on the actual cost of providing services, with no profit element.[28] Another problem is work of *defective quality*: a court may disallow any part that is not within the service charge provision,[29] and the leaseholder may be justified in refusing to pay a demand.[30]

5. Costs

Until recently tenants were caught on a particularly nasty variant of Morton's fork.[31] If the tenant disputed the service charge levied by the landlord and won, the court would

---

[21] *Capital & Counties Freehold Equity Trust Ltd.* v. *B.L. plc.* [1987] 2 E.G.L.R. 49 Ch.D.; *Finchbourne* v. *Rodrigues* [1976] 3 All E.R. 581 C.A.; *Frobisher (Second Investments) Ltd.* v. *Kiloran Trust* [1980] 1 All E.R. 488.

[22] P. Spencer [1990] 31 *L.S.G.* 24; J. Carter [1994] 08 *E.G.* 111.

[23] The Inland Revenue has announced that it will treat sinking funds as investment trusts with effect from March 31st 1998: F.A. 1998 s.38, sch.5.

[24] *S.S. for the Environment* v. *Possfund (North West) Ltd.* [1997] 2 E.G.L.R. 56 C.A. However on sale midway through a service charge period, the charge has to be apportioned: G. Sheriff [1991] *N.L.J.* 1148.

[25] *Rexhaven Ltd.* v. *Nurse* (1996) 28 H.L.R. 241.

[26] *Universities Superannuation Scheme Ltd.* v. *Marks and Spencer plc.* [1999] 1 E.G.L.R. 13 C.A.; S. Murdoch [1999] 10 *E.G.* 182.

[27] *Finchbourne Ltd.* v. *Rodrigues* [1976] 3 All E.R. 581 C.A.

[28] *Jollybird Ltd.* v. *Fairzone Ltd.* [1990] 2 E.G.L.R. 55 C.A.

[29] *Yorkbrook Investments Ltd.* v. *Batten* [1985] 2 E.G.L.R. 100 C.A.

[30] *Gordon* v. *Selico Co. Ltd.* [1986] 1 E.G.L.R. 71 C.A.

[31] Henry VII's Chancellor levied forced loans from rich men; those who displayed their wealth ostentatiously were deemed to be able to afford it, whereas those who lived frugally were deemed to have sufficient savings.

be likely to order costs against the landlord who had lost the litigation; but the landlord would then have a contractual right to add the costs to the service charge under the contractual provisions of the lease. This problem can be solved by insisting on an assessment of costs to exclude money spent on an unsuccessful challenge by the landlord.[32]

6. Allocation between units

Leases may adopt any agreed method of allocation but in practice the system is laid down by the developer when the block is first sold, and is difficult to alter afterwards. It may be equal division between units or set proportions for particular units, according to floor area or rateable value[33] or according to the rent paid on a head lease.[34] If the formula depends upon, say, the measurement of floor areas, the managing agent usually has to certify the proportions. A certificate should be given by an agent who is independent of the landlord[35] since the determination is arbitral in character.[36] Certificates are often stated to be conclusive, but in fact it is not possible to exclude the jurisdiction of the court over errors of calculation and the determination of what items are properly included.[37]

In essence a service charge mechanism is very simple. Costs of repair and providing services incurred by a manager are aggregated and then allocated to individual units according to some pre-agreed formula. But in practice the simple procedure rarely works satisfactorily, and no amount of legislation can secure fruitful collaboration between neighbours.

C. TENANTS' RIGHTS TO COMPEL WORK COVERED BY A SERVICE CHARGE

This passage considers the extent to which a tenant who is liable to contribute to the cost of repairs to the structure or common parts under a service charge can take action to ensure that the landlord carries out those repairs.

1. Specific performance

Lord Eldon laid down in *Hill* v. *Barclay*[38] the historical restriction of the remedy based on the refusal of the court to make an order that would require constant supervision. The statutory jurisdiction applying to a dwelling[39] will not assist commercial tenants. However specific performance can now be ordered of a repairing covenant relating to common parts under Pennycuick V.C.'s decision in *Jeune* v. *Queen's Cross Properties*

---

[32] *Primeridge Ltd.* v. *Jean Muir Ltd.* [1992] 1 E.G.L.R. 273; *Morgan* v. *Stainer* [1993] 2 E.G.L.R. 73 Ch.D.

[33] The landlord cannot then reopen the service charge if rateable values are subsequently changed: *Universities Superannuation Scheme Ltd.* v. *Marks & Spencer plc.* [1999] 1 E.G.L.R. 13 C.A.

[34] But note the problems if the head lease ends: *Electricity Supply Nominees Ltd.* v. *Thorn E.M.I. Retail Ltd.* [1991] 2 E.G.L.R. 46 C.A.

[35] *Finchbourne Ltd.* v. *Rodrigues* [1976] 3 All E.R. 581 C.A. (wholly owned company).

[36] J.E. Adams [1983] *Conv.* 94.

[37] *Re Davstone Estate Ltd.'s Lease* [1969] 2 All E.R. 849; *Dean* v. *Prince* [1954] 1 All E.R. 749.

[38] (1810) 16 Ves. 402, 33 E.R. 1037, Lord Eldon L.C.

[39] See above pp. 255–256.

Ltd.[40] This was based on Snell's three requirements,[41] which may conveniently be treated in the reverse order. Specific performance should related to land of which the landlord is in possession, meaning in other words the *common parts* of the development. Second, the tenant must show a substantial interest in the performance of the covenant, which he can do if the value of his unit is affected by the disrepair of the common part. Finally, the work must be sufficiently defined, so that the court does not have to engage in continuous supervision but can apply a one-off judgment at the end of the work about whether it meets the terms of the order. A mandatory injunction has the advantage that a penal notice can be added, making it a contempt of court to fail to carry out the work.[42]

2.   Damages

A tenant forced to carry out work for which the landlord is responsible will certainly be entitled to recover the *cost* of the work. *Consequential damages* are available to compensate for injuries caused by disrepair and for damage to the tenant's property or furnishings.[43] Where a tenant is forced out, the proper measure of damages is the diminution in the price or rent, which could be a notional reduction in the rent, a global sum for discomfort, or both.[44]

3.   Repair and deduct

Commercial tenants may be able to go on a rent strike in order to secure the payment of arrears of rent. Indeed, the leading case—*British Anzani (Felixstowe) Ltd.* v. *International Marine Management (U.K.) Ltd.*[45]—concerned two warehouses built on land reclaimed from the sea at Felixstowe. However, it is very common to provide that service charge should be paid without any deduction—thus ensuring that payment is made in full even if there are complaints about the standard of some of the services or repairs. The unfair contract terms legislation has no impact on leases of land, especially those to commercial tenants.[46]

4.   Notice to repair

A landlord's duty to repair under an express covenant[47] arises only when the tenant has given notice of the need for repair and has allowed access to carry out the work.

---

[40] [1974] Ch. 97, 99–100; applied in *Francis* v. *Cowlcliff Ltd.* [1976] 2 E.G.L.R. 54 Ch.D.

[41] Snell's *Equity* (Sweet & Maxwell, 30th ed. by P. McGhee, 2000) 658–659.

[42] *R.* v. *Wandsworth C.Ct. ex parte Munn* (1994) 26 H.L.R. 697, Sedley J.; *Hackney L.B.C.* v. *Mullen* (1997) 29 H.L.R. 592 C.A.

[43] *Calabar Properties Ltd.* v. *Stitcher* [1984] 1 W.L.R. 287 C.A.; Woodfall 13.075–13.094; F. Jenkins and J. Woodman [1999] 03 *E.G.* 133.

[44] *Wallace* v. *Manchester C.C.* [1998] 3 E.G.L.R. 38 C.A.; *Electricity Supply Nominees Ltd.* v. *National Magazine Co. Ltd.* [1999] 32 E.G. 84 (failure to maintain lifts/air conditioning); *Larksworth Investments Ltd.* v. *Temple House Ltd. (No.2)* [1999] B.L.R. 297 C.A.; see above in the domestic context pp. 259–260.

[45] [1980] Q.B. 137, Forbes J.; see the detailed discussion above at pp. 256–258.

[46] *Unchained Growth III plc.* v. *Granby Village (Manchester) Management Co. Ltd.* [1999] Times November 4th C.A.; see above p. 638.

[47] *Makin* v. *Watkinson* (1870) L.R. 6 Ex. 25 (2:1); *Torrens* v. *Walker* [1906] 2 Ch. 166, Warrington J.; *Hugall* v. *M'Lean* (1885) 53 L.T. 94 C.A.

Landlords are not in breach until a reasonable time has elapsed after notice,[48] so that the landlord may not be liable for an injury that occurs before or shortly after notice, unless the property is unsafe.[49] The landlord's duty arises immediately on breach, without any need to allow a reasonable period to provide a remedy, if the property requiring repair is under the control of the landlord,[50] as for example in the case of a common part. *British Telecommunications plc.* v. *Sun Life Assurance Society plc.*[51] concerned a bulge in the external cladding of an office block in Croydon which appeared at fifth floor level, one floor below the office suite occupied by the plaintiff tenant. Notice was not required from the tenant, since the defect was in a part of the building under the landlord's control.

5. Access to repair

Repairing covenants that impose duties on the landlord usually include an express right to enter to carry out the work[52] and otherwise this may be implied.[53] The leading authority is *Jervis* v. *Harris*[54] in which it was held that the claim to the cost of work done was a debt, so the landlord was not subject to the restrictions on enforcing repairing covenants in section 1 of the Leasehold Property (Repairs) Act 1938.[55]

D. USE COVENANTS

1. Allocation to security codes

The primary function of use covenants is to allocate a lease to one of the three main security regimes—residential, business, or agricultural.[56] Renewal rights arise where land is let to a business tenant—though business is widely defined and renewal rights are confined to tenants in occupation for the purposes of their business. A property let as a home or for agriculture does not usually become a business lease simply because the tenant uses it for business, where the change of use occurs in a breach of covenant. Where the landlord consents to a change of use he needs to be conscious of the possibility that this may switch the tenant between security codes, but a landlord will not be prejudiced unless he has consented to or has at least acquiesced in the change. For this reason a commercial tenant must be precluded from switching to a residential use and vice versa. Landlords need to maintain strict control of sub-lettings to prevent sub-tenants acquiring security of tenure.

---

[48] *Morris* v. *Liverpool C.C.* [1988] 1 E.G.L.R. 47; *Calabar Properties Ltd.* v. *Stitcher* [1984] 1 W.L.R. 287, 298, Griffiths L.J.

[49] *Griffin* v. *Pillet* [1926] 1 K.B. 17.

[50] *Murphy* v. *Hurly* [1922] 1 A.C. 369, 389 (sea wall on neighbouring property); *Bishop* v. *Consolidated London Properties Ltd.* (1933) 102 L.J. K.B. 257 (roof under landlord's control); *Melles & Co.* v. *Holme* [1918] 2 K.B. 100 Div.Ct.; *Ladsky* v. *T.S.B. Bank plc.* (1997) 74 P. & C.R. 372 C.A. (simple disrepair was breach of mortgage).

[51] [1995] 4 All E.R. 44 C.A.; *Passley* v. *Wandsworth L.B.C.* (1996) 30 H.L.R. 165 C.A. (roof); P.F. Smith [1997] *Conv.* 59 (query whether notice is required where the covenant is "to repair" as opposed to "to keep in repair").

[52] *Saner* v. *Bilton* (1878) 7 Ch.D. 815, Fry J.

[53] *Mint* v. *Good* [1951] 1 K.B. 517 C.A.; also under R.A. 1977 s.148.

[54] [1996] Ch. 195 C.A.; R. Hewitson [1997] *Conv.* 299; P.G. Taylor [1998] 2 *L.T. Rev.* 11.

[55] See below pp. 801–803.

[56] See above pp. 13–15, 541–544, 606–609.

2.   Estate management

Use covenants are essential to preserve control of estate management, since new tenants will pay more rent for a local monopoly than they will to compete with an established trader, and established traders will want protection from new competitors.[57] However, it is sensible for landlords to allow the greatest possible width of uses, since this increases the potential market of the lease, and hence the rent which can be expected from a rent review.[58] A use covenant is a restriction on the tenant rather than a warranty by the landlord that any particular use will be permitted,[59] since many changes would require planning permission.

3.   Form

Use covenants[60] sometimes specify a particular trade that the tenant is or is not to carry out. Apart from the voluminous case law on residential restrictive covenants, recent cases have concerned a jeweller's shop,[61] sales of car spares,[62] and a covenant to sell high class salads—a trade distinct from selling fruit and veg[63]—as well as conversion to a deli/diner in breach of a covenant not to open a restaurant.[64] It is usual today to allow any use within one of the planning law Use Classes,[65] though a problem with this form of clause arises on changes in the statutory format.[66] The onus is on the landlord to prove a breach.[67]

4.   Planning use classes

Material change of use is a form of development for which planning permission is required.[68] Use is any activity done on land which does not interfere with its physical characteristics,[69] and for planning purposes this is assessed against the planning unit— a single unit of occupation. Business and commercial purposes are classified into use classes, specified by the Town and Country Planning (Use Classes) Order 1987.[70] These classes are often referred to in an express planning permission,[71] though implied per-

---

[57] A use covenant in a head lease may apply to a sub-tenant as a restrictive covenant, but this is a matter of construction: *Bristol & West B.S.* v. *Marks and Spencer plc.* [1991] 2 E.G.L.R. 57, Hoffmann J.

[58] See above p. 212.

[59] *Hill* v. *Harris* [1965] 2 Q.B. 601 C.A.; R.E. Megarry (1965) 81 *L.Q.R.* 334.

[60] Woodfall 11.179–11.253; Bright & Gilbert 390–395; Evans & Smith (5th) 130–133; Garner (2nd) 68–70.

[61] *Montross Associated Investments S.A.* v. *Mousaieff* [1992] 1 E.G.L.R. 55 C.A.

[62] *Atwal* v. *Courts Garages Ltd.* [1989] 1 E.G.L.R. 63.

[63] *Gloucester C.C.* v. *Williams* (1990) 88 L.G.R. 853 C.A.

[64] *Walker* v. *Arkay Caterers Ltd.* [1997] E.G.C.S. 107.

[65] *International Drilling Fluids Ltd.* v. *Louisville Investments (Uxbridge) Ltd.* [1986] Ch. 513 C.A.

[66] *Brewer's Co.* v. *Viewplan plc.* [1989] 2 E.G.L.R. 133 (the lease referred to the 1972 Order and was not amended when the 1987 Order came into force).

[67] *Basildon Development Corporation* v. *Mactro Ltd.* [1986] 1 E.G.L.R. 137 C.A.

[68] T.C.P.A. 1990 ss.55, 57(2)–(4) subject to sch.4.

[69] *Parkes* v. *S.S. for the Environment* [1978] 1 W.L.R. 1308, 1311, Lord Denning M.R.; *Thames Heliport Ltd.* v. *Tower Hamlets L.B.C.* (1997) 74 P. & C.R. 164 C.A.

[70] S.I. 1987/764 (in force June 1st 1987) as amended. Alterations between versions create difficulties with the drafting of leases: R.E. Megarry (1960) 76 *L.Q.R.* 489; J.E. Adams [1987] *Conv.* 243, [1990] *Conv.* 247.

[71] T.C.P.A. 1990 s.75(2).

mission exists for use for the purpose for which a new building was designed.[72] A change of use within the same use class does not require planning permission.[73] Current classes are:

Class A1	Shops etc.
Class A2	Financial and professional services.[74]
Class A3	Sale of food or drink for consumption on the premises or of hot food for consumption off the premises.
Class B1	General business purposes e.g. offices.
Class B2	General industrial.
Class B8	Storage or distribution.
Class C1	Hotels.
Class C2	Residential institutions e.g. care homes.
Class C3	Dwelling house.
Class D1	Non-residential institutions.
Class D2	Assembly and leisure e.g. cinemas.

There are some individual uses not included in any class.

5. Permitted changes between use classes

Generally a change between use classes is a material change requiring express permission.[75] However the Town and Country Planning (General Permitted Development) Order 1995[76] provides deemed permission for certain changes of use:

Shops:	A3 to A1; sale of motor vehicles to A1; A3 to A2; A2 to A1 (shop which has a display window); shop to shop and flat, and vice versa.
Commercial:	B2 to B1; B8 to B1; B1 to B8; B2 to B8.

Most of the permitted changes are unidirectional. In *Cynon Valley B.C.* v. *Secretary of State for Wales and Oi Mee Lan*[77] a change from a fish and chip shop (A3) to an antique shop (A1) resulted in the loss of the right to use it as a fish and chip shop.

6. Absolute and qualified covenants

A lease may impose an absolute restriction on changes of use, but most provide that use cannot be changed without the landlord's consent. A statutory proviso prevents any fine being charged for the consent; however the landlord can make a reasonable charge for any diminution in value of the landlord's reversion. Once the court has fixed what is reasonable, the landlord must grant a licence.[78] Physical alterations must be licensed

---

[72] s.75(3).

[73] s.55(2)(f); S.I. 1987/764 art.3(1); subject to any express condition.

[74] Possibly including a solicitor's office: *Kalra* v. *S.S. for the Environment* (1996) 72 P. & C.R. 423 C.A.

[75] *Young* v. *S.S. for the Environment* [1983] 2 A.C. 662 H.L.; *Cynon Valley B.C.* v. *S.S. for Wales* (1987) 53 P. & C.R. 68 C.A.

[76] S.I. 1995/418.

[77] (1987) 53 P. & C.R. 68 C.A.; *J.L. Engineering* v. *S.S. for the Environment* (1994) 67 P. & C.R. 354 Div. Ct. (industrial to agriculture and back); *Young* v. *S.S for the Environment* [1983] 2 A.C. 662 H.L. (no lawful use left).

[78] L.T.A. 1927 s.19(3).

separately. Of course the landlord may be estopped from objecting to a change of use,[79] and an ambiguous decision may be construed as a consent, even if this puts him in breach of his covenants to other tenants.[80]

The leading authority on qualified covenants is *International Drilling Fluids Ltd.* v. *Louisville Investments (Uxbridge) Ltd.*[81] The covenant protects the landlord from undesirable uses, but objections based on matters extraneous to the relationship of landlord and tenant are not allowed. The landlord need prove no more than that the conclusions might have been reached by a reasonable person, and anyway the onus is on the tenant.[82] The court might overrule the landlord if the detriment to the tenant far outweighs the loss to the landlord. The particular lease allowed uses within Class II of the Use Classes Order. A buyer of the lease proposed to use the building to provide serviced offices, a use within class II, but one which the landlord said would affect the value of the reversion. The refusal was unreasonable because the detriment was minimal compared to the detriment to the tenant. In *Sportoffer Ltd.* v. *Erewash B.C.*[83] a lease of a squash club provided that consent to a change of use could not be unreasonably withheld. The tenant wished to increase the gymnastic element of the activities, but permission was refused because this would compete with two fitness centres operated by the landlord. He was held to be acting within his rights under *Louisville* since any reasonable landlord would fear competition and the landlord could consider his own interests unless the tenant's loss was wholly disproportionate.

In particular the landlord is entitled to consider tenant mix as a factor in estate management. Three recent cases demonstrate the importance of this factor. In *Crown Estate Commissioners* v. *Signet Group plc.*[84] the Crown was entitled to refuse to allow a jewellers in Regent Street to be changed to a bureau de change and ticket agency, given its management strategy of moving the street up market. In *Chelsfield M.H. Investments Ltd.* v. *British Gas plc.*[85] a landlord successfully prevented the conversion of a gas showroom to a mix of gas and electricity goods, since there was an existing electricity showroom directly opposite. In *Moss Bros Group plc.* v. *C.S.C. Properties Ltd.*[86] a unit in the fashion section of the Metro Centre at Gateshead could not be converted to selling computer games given the difference in the likely clientele. The conclusion must be[87] create a policy, put it in writing, make it known, and enforce it consistently.

7. Enforcement between landlord and tenant

A lease will always include a use covenant, by which the tenant agrees to use the property for particular purposes and not to use it for other purposes. One important function of this use covenant is to allocate the lease to one or other of the sectors of the landlord and tenant legislation, but it also has a different function in a lease of part—

---

[79] *Wates Estate Agency Services Ltd.* v. *Bartleys Ltd.* [1989] 2 E.G.L.R. 87 C.A.
[80] *Rose* v. *Stavrou* [1999] 23 L.S.G. 29, Neuberger J.
[81] [1986] Ch. 513 C.A.
[82] *Tollbench Ltd.* v. *Plymouth C.C.* [1988] 1 E.G.L.R. 79 C.A.; J.E. Martin [1989] *Conv.* 124.
[83] [1999] E.G.C.S. 37, Lloyd J.
[84] [1996] 2 E.G.L.R. 200; L. Crabb (1999) 115 *L.Q.R.* 191.
[85] [1995] N.P.C. 169.
[86] [1999] E.G.C.S. 47.
[87] C. Carvalho & E. Slessenger [1999] 33 *E.G.* 74; G. Lloyd-Brunt (2000) 144 *S.J.* 244.

such as one shop in a terrace, one unit on an industrial estate, or one suite of offices in a block. Here the landlord uses the covenant to control estate management, that is it allocates particular business uses to particular units, perhaps designating one shop as a fast food outlet and the adjacent one as a convenience store. Individual tenants can be kept to the agreed use by action by the landlord, since the use covenant will be enforceable between the current parties as a leasehold covenant.[88] Where the lease was granted after 1995, the covenant affects the land demised to the tenant and can be enforced as a tenant's covenant by the current landlord.[89] For pre-1996 leases, the old amalgam of common law rules and statutory additions continues to operate, the covenant must touch and concern the lease, and numerous cases[90] establish that covenants regulating the use of the land by the tenant are part of the core of the leasehold relationship. All touch and concern, and all will run.

8. Enforcement between neighbouring tenants—new law

The position where one tenant of a post-1995 lease tries to enforce the covenant against *another tenant* of the same landlord was considered in *Oceanic Village Ltd.* v. *United Attractions Ltd.*[91] After County Hall in London had been converted to private use by a Japanese company, a part was let to Oceanic Village (tenant A) for 20 years from 1998. It was intended that it would be used as a gift shop associated with the London Aquarium. The lease included a covenant by the landlord not to permit any other unit in the building to be used as a gift shop. Another part was let to United Attractions (tenant B) for use as a Football Hall of Fame, but this second lease had no restriction on the sale of football kit or other gifts. Tenant A's application for an injunction against tenant B failed. An action on the covenant as a leasehold covenant failed, because the defendant was not a successor to the landlord as holder of a part of the land let by the lease (lease A) containing the covenant. Tenant B held another part of the building. Hence one tenant can only enforce a use covenant against another tenant as a restrictive covenant. For this to be possible, the covenant must touch and concern the unit benefited as well as the one that is burdened. Restrictive covenants are in principle enforceable against any subsequent owner with notice of the covenant (here the tenant of unit B when he took a lease from the landlord), but traditional notice doctrine was superseded in 1925 by the requirement of registration.[92] On the particular facts Tenant A had not registered the covenant against the landlord's registered title, and so failed in its claim against the tenant of unit B.

9. Enforcement between neighbours—old law

For leases granted before 1996, the same principle must operate since there is no privity of estate between two neighbouring tenants of the same landlord[93] and there is the

---

[88] See below Chapter 26.

[89] L.T. (Covenants) A. 1995 ss.2, 3(1)–(3), 24, 28.

[90] *Congleton Corporation* v. *Pattison* (1810) 10 East 130, 138, 103 E.R. 725, Bayley J.; *Gibson* v. *Doeg* (1857) 2 H. & N. 615, 157 E.R. 253; *Eccles* v. *Mills* [1898] A.C. 360 P.C.; *Chapman* v. *Smith* [1907] 2 Ch. 97; *Barnes* v. *City of London Real Property* [1918] 2 Ch. 18.

[91] [2000] Ch. 234, Neuberger J.

[92] Sparkes *N.L.L.* 602–603.

[93] This might be overcome by using L.P.A. 1925 s.56; see Sparkes *N.L.L.* 608–609.

additional problem that a use covenant will not touch and concern the neighbouring land[94]—the requirement laid down in *Spencer's case*[95] before a covenant could run. So the decision in *Oceanic Village* does not alter the law.[96]

E.   ANCHOR TENANTS

Many large shopping malls have an anchor tenant, that is one shop—often a major supermarket—which will attract customers to the entire development. Landlords seek to entrench such tenants by imposing a covenant that the tenant must continue to trade in a particular shop. If the shop is closed, however, the only remedy is damages. In *Co-operative Insurance Services Ltd.* v. *Argyll Stores (Holdings) Ltd.*[97] Safeways had entered into an anchor tenant covenant at the Hillsborough Shopping Centre. When it was discovered that the supermarket was running at a loss of £70,000 a year, the store was shut and stripped, to such an extent that reopening it would have cost £1 million. The House of Lords refused to order specific performance of the covenant to keep the shop open.[98] Settled practice in common law jurisdictions[99] is that the court will not make an order requiring continued supervision, and although a covenant to build is enforceable,[100] a covenant to keep open a shop is not. Tenants cannot be compelled to carry on bad businesses. An injunction could not be framed with precision, and anyway the landlord would be unjustly enriched if he could compel his tenant to trade at a loss, so the landlord must be content with damages.[101] These could be very substantial if other tenants on the estate were able to negotiate rents downwards as a result of their loss of trade.[102] It is helpful for the landlord to reserve the right to maintain a window display in the shop after it is closed, since the development will look less run down than it is.[103]

F.   TRADING RESTRICTIONS

A specialised form of use covenant is one which ties the tenant to trading with the landlord, for example a tied house clause by which a publican agrees to take beer only from his brewer landlord. Although the point was arguable, it has long since been recognised

---

[94]   *Thomas* v. *Hayward* (1869) L.R. 4 Ex. 311; *Kumar* v. *Dunning* [1989] Q.B. 193, 205, Browne-Wilkinson V.C.; *Dewar* v. *Goodman* [1908] 1 K.B. 94, 104, Alverstone L.C.J.; see below pp. 770–771.

[95]   (1583) 5 Co. Rep. 16a, 77 E.R. 72; *Oceanic Village* [2000] Ch. 234, 243G, Neuberger J.

[96]   At 247D, Neuberger J.

[97]   [1998] A.C. 1 H.L.; H.W. Wilkinson [1997] *N.L.J.* 1281; D. Brogden [1997] 1 *L.T. Rev.* 110; A. Tettenborn [1998] *Conv.* 23; H.Y. Yeo [1998] J.B.L. 254; P. Luxton [1998] *Conv.* 396.

[98]   Approving *A.G.* v. *Colchester Corporation* [1955] 2 Q.B. 207, 217, Lord Goddard C.J.; *F.W. Woolworth plc.* v. *Charlwood Alliance Properties Ltd.* [1987] 1 E.G.L.R. 53 C.A.; *Braddon Towers Ltd.* v. *International Stores Ltd.* [1987] 1 E.G.L.R. 209, 213, Slade J.; *Chorley B.C.* v. *Ribble Motor Services Ltd.* (1997) 74 P. & C.R. 182 C.A. (no implied obligation to keep toilets open).

[99]   Contrast Scotland: *Retail Parks Investments Ltd.* v. *Royal Bank of Scotland* [1995] S.L.T. 1156.

[100]   *Shiloh Spinners Ltd.* v. *Harding* [1973] A.C. 691, 724, Lord Wilberforce.

[101]   P. Luxton [1998] *Conv.* 396 suggests increasing the rent if trading ends or a pre-agreement on damages, though care is needed to avoid creating a penalty.

[102]   *Transworld Land Co. Ltd.* v. *J. Sainsbury plc.* [1990] 2 E.G.L.R. 255 (£100,000 plus); *Costain Developments Ltd.* v. *Finlay & Co. Ltd.* [1989] 1 E.G.L.R. 237. Anchor tenants should ensure that other tenants have no action against the landlord.

[103]   *Charville Estates Ltd.* v. *Unipart Group Ltd.* [1997] E.G.C.S. 36; P. Luxton [1998] *Conv.* 396.

that this could create a land obligation, binding the pub whoever bought the lease, whether the pub was freehold or leasehold.[104] However these clauses may be vulnerable to reform under competition law including the common law doctrine of unlawful restraint of trade, under the special legislation governing tied pubs,[105] and as an infringement of the free trading provisions of European law.[106] If a tied house clause is void, other parts of the same lease may be severable, and the rent covenant is unaffected,[107] and it is possible that a tie that was once illegal may become valid if the landlord is changed.[108]

G. FRUSTRATION

1. Frustration; contractual doctrine

Frustration[109] was defined by Viscount Simon L.C. in *Cricklewood Property & Investment Ltd.* v. *Leighton's Investment Trust Ltd.*[110] as:

> "the premature determination of an agreement between the parties, lawfully entered into and in course of operation at the time of its premature determination, owing to the occurrence of an intervening event or change in circumstances so fundamental as to be regarded by the law both a striking at the root of the agreement and as entirely beyond what was contemplated by the parties when they entered into the agreement."

Historically, before the development of frustration, the contractual obligations of the parties were absolute, it being left to the parties to provide for changed circumstances if they so desired. Thus in *Paradine* v. *Jane*[111] a tenant was held to be liable to pay rent even after eviction by Royalist forces during the Civil War.

A shift in contractual analysis can be traced to *Taylor* v. *Caldwell*.[112] Decided in 1863 and allowing an unforeseen event to terminate a contract, it is ironic that the case dates from the time when sanctity of contract was reaching its zenith. A contract to allow the use of a concert hall was frustrated when the hall was burnt down, so that both parties were excused performance. That case concerned a short-term licence for the use of a hall rather than a lease. Contractual payments were terminated by physical destruction of the building in issue. For a long time it appeared that the same relaxation would not be extended to leases, with *Paradine* v. *Jane* remaining authority for the absolute character of rent. Unequivocal expansion to embrace leases dates only from the later part of the twentieth century, and its application to other land contracts remains conjectural.

---

[104] See below p. 769.

[105] S.I. 1989/2390; *Plummer* v. *Tibsco Ltd.* [1999] 47 L.S.G. 32, Neuberger J.; *Courage Ltd.* v. *Crehan* [1999] 2 E.G.L.R. 145 C.A. (any damages cannot be set off against rent).

[106] *Holteran* v. *Daniel Thwaites plc.* [1989] 2 C.M.L.R. 917, Peter Gibson J.

[107] *Inntrepeneur Estates (G.L.) Ltd.* v. *Boyes* [1993] 2 E.G.L.R. 112 C.A.; *Greenalls Management Ltd.* v. *Canavan (No.1)* [1997] Times May 19th C.A.; *(No.2)* [1997] Times August 20th C.A.

[108] *Passmore* v. *Morland plc.* [1999] 1 E.G.L.R. 51 C.A.; *Inntrepreneur Pub Co. (C.P.C.) Ltd.* v. *Price* [1998] Times December 4th, Neuberger J.

[109] Woodfall 7.138–7.149.

[110] [1945] A.C. 221, 228.

[111] (1647) Aleyn 26, 82 E.R. 897.

[112] (1863) 3 B. & S. 826, 122 E.R. 309.

To some extent, the scope of frustration must depend upon the theoretical justification for the doctrine. Three theories need to be tested. (1) Termination may be ascribed to the intention of the parties at the time the contract is made, unexpressed, but introduced to the contract in the shape of an implied term. This was the basis accepted in *Taylor* v. *Caldwell*, and is realistic for a term that was readily in the contemplation of the parties, like the destruction of a concert hall by fire. But frustration is needed more where the event is unforeseen and unforeseeable, where it is difficult to ascribe any intention to the parties.[113] (2) Frustration has sometimes been ascribed to total failure of consideration. If so leases could not be frustrated, since the tenant did receive a legal estate in the land even if it was one that has been rendered useless by unforeseen events. Frustration is now applied after partial performance of the contract, so this reason for precluding the frustration of leases falls to the ground. (3) Today the dominant theory is that frustration is a solution applied independently of contractual acceptance by the parties, which is used to secure escape from injustice. Variant formulations refer to cases where the contract has become totally different from that agreed between the parties,[114] or where it is applied as a doctrine of abstract justice.[115] If this dominant tradition is accepted, there is every reason to apply frustration to tenants, since they may suffer injustice just as much as any other contracting party. So this theoretical explanation for the doctrine facilitates its spread into land law.

2.   Leases

Frustration does apply to leases. Doubts had arisen after the decision of the House of Lords in *Cricklewood Property & Investment Trust Ltd.* v. *Leighton's Investment Trust Ltd.*[116] The case concerned building leases for shops, the ground rent being one peppercorn until the landlord obtained planning permission, and thereafter £35 a year. Planning permission was obtained but the tenant was prevented from implementing it because of wartime building restrictions. No frustration arose on the facts—that much was clear—but there was an equal division of opinion about whether the doctrine could ever apply to leases on more favourable facts. These doubts are now resolved by dicta in *National Carriers Ltd.* v. *Panalpina (Northern) Ltd.*[117] Commercial premises in Hull were let for 10 years with a covenant by the tenant to use them only as a warehouse. The only access from a public street was blocked during construction work for an estimated period of 20 months, for which time the building became useless for warehousing. Again the Lords decided unanimously that no frustration arose on those facts, but a majority of four to one indicated that a lease could be ended by frustration if the circumstances were sufficiently exceptional.

Arguments against extension were fourfold. (1) Frustration usually applies where the commercial venture of the contract has been frustrated, and it could be argued that the grant of the leasehold estate was the venture. In most cases execution of the lease will

---

[113] *Denny Mott & Dickson Ltd.* v. *James B. Fraser & Co. Ltd.* [1944] A.C. 265 H.L.

[114] *National Carriers Ltd.* v. *Panalpina (Northern) Ltd.* [1981] A.C. 675, 717D, Lord Roskill.

[115] *Panalpina* at 701C, Lord Simon.

[116] [1945] A.C. 221 H.L.; (1945) 61 *L.Q.R.* 111; (1946) 62 *L.Q.R.* 320.

[117] [1981] A.C. 675 H.L.; (1981) 97 *L.Q.R.* 193; K. Hodkinson [1981] *Conv.* 227; S. Tromans [1981] *C.L.J.* 217; B. Dickson (1981) 32 *N.I.L.Q.* 162.

give the tenant what is bargained for, that is a legal estate in the land. Thus in *London & Northern Estates Co. Ltd.* v. *Schlesinger*[118] a flat was leased to an Austrian who was prohibited from occupying it when he was classified as an enemy alien during the Great War. Frustration was rejected on the basis that the Austrian had received the term for which he had bargained. However, receipt of the estate is not really a consideration if the land is unusable and the *Panalpina* case shows a lease may encapsulate a distinct frustratable commercial venture.[119]

(2) It is said that estates in land present particular problems of termination, because of the regularity with which lenders and other outsiders are involved, though the same problems can arise with personal contracts.[120] (3) A better argument is that risk passes on a conveyance of the legal estate. If for example a house is swallowed up in an earthquake, the current owner loses the value of the land and cannot take action against the person who sold him the house, arguing that the risk of loss survives completion of the sale. That is axiomatic. A lease for 999 years at a nominal ground rent is so like a freehold that it ought not usually to be frustrated. The same argument is less convincing when applied to a shorter lease, since the whole object is to allocate risks in a continuing relationship, and the only question is where to place the risk. A short commercial lease can in fact be rendered totally worthless if the intended use becomes impossible.[121] (4) Finally the floodgates argument was advanced, but the absence of any successful case since *Panalpina* in 1981 suggests that this is scarcely an issue.[122]

The House felt that the opponents of extension had not met the onus that lay on them to explain why frustration should not apply to leases. Arguments in favour of extension are that it avoids unnecessary compartmentalisation, that it merely adds one further method of termination to an existing array, and that it has been recognised in other common law jurisdictions.[123]

3. Frustrating events

When can a lease be frustrated? The answer must remain very rarely indeed. Lord Hailsham echoed W.S. Gilbert when he expressed the liberalising effect of *Panalpina* as the difference between "never" and "hardly ever".[124] Frustration should not normally apply to a simple lease at a rent where the tenant is free to use the property as he wants.[125] One possible frustrating event is where the lease is granted with a specific commercial opportunity in mind which collapses, or where the lease is merely one part of a larger venture. A second frustrating event is physical destruction. Viscount Simon L.C. spoke in *Cricklewood*[126] of the possibility of frustration when there is some vast convulsion of nature. There seems to be no point in maintaining the existence of a lease after

---

[118] [1916] 1 K.B. 20; [1981] A.C. 675, 694; *Whitehall Court Ltd.* v. *Ettlinger* [1920] 1 K.B. 680.
[119] *Panalpina* at 694, Lord Wilberforce.
[120] *Cricklewood* at 229–230, Viscount Simon L.C.
[121] *Panalpina* at 691E, Lord Hailsham L.C.
[122] *Panalpina* at 697A, Lord Wilberforce.
[123] Especially for leases of bars in America at the time of prohibition: *Highway Properties Ltd.* v. *Kelly Douglas & Co. Ltd.* (1971) 17 D.L.R. (3d) 710, Laski J.
[124] At 688H.
[125] *Cricklewood* at 229, Viscount Simon L.C.
[126] At 229.

the land has fallen into the sea.[127] And frustration is the most convenient way of dealing with physical destruction of a block of flats, since it would be inconvenient to maintain notional leases of bits of airspace following the collapse of the building.[128]

Frustration often derives from legal interference with property rights. Contractual cases identify the outbreak of war, government interference, and supervening illegality as frustrating events. Frustration will not be triggered by requisition[129] nor by destruction by a hostile bomb.[130] However a building lease might be ended by building restrictions, or by dedication of the land as an open space,[131] and a lease of a holiday cottage by restrictions on the use of second homes.[132]

4. Effect of frustration

The term of the lease will be ended automatically for the future by a frustrating event. At common law loss was left to fall where it lay at that time, but the Law Reform (Frustrated Contracts) Act 1943 allows the recovery of prepayments of money even if there is no total failure of consideration, and also allowing compensation for part performance. Developments in restitutionary remedies also need to be kept in mind. The court is therefore enabled to achieve a fair break in the contractual relationship. Contract and restitution texts provide more detail.

When it applies, frustration may terminate a lease completely, in which case a claim by the tenant to frustration will result in the termination of his occupation right. However, it is also possible for it to strike at an individual covenant while leaving the remainder of the lease in force. *John Lewis Properties Ltd.* v. *Viscount Chelsea*[133] concerned the Peter Jones store in Sloane Square. A lease of the store provided for its demolition and reconstruction, but this became impossible after its listing prevented demolition. That particular covenant was frustrated. Individual covenants may also be suspended by the implication of a contractual qualification to adapt the express wording to unforeseen circumstances. In *Bailly* v. *de Crespigny*[134] a covenant not to build on land was held to be terminated by compulsory acquisition of the land for a station. This tenant escaped paying damages, and was presumably safe from forfeiture.[135] Full suspension of the tenant's covenants occurs only on eviction by title paramount or by the landlord, which is not a frustration but rather a temporary suspension of liability until the eviction is lifted.

H. INTERFERENCE BY THE LANDLORD

A landlord must grant exclusive possession of property to his tenant for the duration of the term, and must allow him to use it for the purpose for which it has been let to

[127] *Panalpina* at 691C, Lord Hailsham L.C.
[128] Commonhold will resolve this problem; see above Chapter 17.
[129] *Whitehall Court Ltd.* v. *Ettlinger* [1920] 1 K.B. 680; tenants receive statutory compensation.
[130] *Denman* v. *Brise* [1949] 1 K.B. 22 C.A.
[131] *Cricklewood* at 229, Viscount Simon L.C.
[132] *Swift* v. *Macbean* [1942] 1 K.B. 375, Birkett J.; *Cricklewood* [1943] K.B. 493, Asquith J. at first instance.
[133] [1993] 2 E.G.L.R. 77, Mummery J.; J. Morgan [1995] *Conv.* 74.
[134] (1869) L.R. 4 Q.B. 180.
[135] *Brewster* v. *Kitchell* (1698) 1 Salk. 198, 91 E.R. 177; *Cricklewood* [1945] A.C. 221, 234–235, Lord Russell.

him. A variety of remedies are available to deal with unauthorised intrusions by the landlord.

1.   Trespass

Physical entry by the landlord on the property which is let to the tenant without lawful authority will lead to an action in trespass. For example in *Lawson* v. *Hartley-Brown*[136] a landlord redeveloped the property which he had let, by erecting scaffolding outside the tenant's existing shop and building two storeys on top. Since the lease of the shop included the air space above it this new building was a trespass to that air space, for which the tenant obtained damages of £8,000, even though he was unable to prove any damage to his trade. Physical trespass is often also an interference with quiet enjoyment or a derogation from grant, but these additional heads of action will not increase the recoverable damages. An act is not a trespass if the lease permits a particular intrusion, for example because the tenant had covenanted to permit the landlord to enter to view the state of repair. In one case, the tenant had covenanted to maintain a window display. When the tenant failed to do so the landlord entered and put the display to rights—this is important to create a good impression in a shopping arcade—but the landlord's entry was neither a trespass nor a breach of the covenant for quiet enjoyment.[137] If the lease has been ended by forfeiture for breach of covenant, the tenant no longer has the right to keep the landlord out and he cannot recover damages for re-entry under the possession order, even if the forfeiture is later reversed on appeal.[138]

2.   Quiet enjoyment

The obligation to allow quiet enjoyment[139] usually appears as an express covenant in the lease, but is implied anyway,[140] for a tenant has the right to be put into occupation and to be free from physical interference by his landlord.[141] It is not, of course, limited to freedom from noise.[142] The major obligation of a landlord is to allow the tenant to take physical possession of the property leased to him and to allow him to continue in undisturbed occupation. It reproduces trespass in so far as it guards against physical encroachment, but quiet enjoyment[143] is much wider, in that it also covers physical use of the landlord's property that has a direct impact on the tenant's property. Enjoyment is interrupted if a landlord erects scaffolding obstructing access to the tenant's shop for two weeks[144] or if a workman's foot comes through the ceiling of a flat.[145] The tenant may obtain damages[146] or an injunction.

[136] (1996) 71 P. & C.R. 242 C.A.; M. Haley [1997] *Conv.* 304.
[137] *Charville Estates Ltd.* v. *Unipart Group Ltd.* [1997] E.G.C.S. 36.
[138] *Hillgate House Ltd.* v. *Expert Clothing Services & Sales Ltd.* [1987] 1 E.G.L.R. 65; J.E. Martin [1987] *Conv.* 366.
[139] Woodfall 11.266–11.313; Davey 37–44; Evans and Smith (5th) 101–105, 113; Garner (2nd) ch.5 and p.66.
[140] *Kenny* v. *Preen* [1963] 1 Q.B. 499; R.E. Megarry (1963) 79 *L.Q.R.* 21; T. Platt, *Covenants* (Maxwell, 1829) 313.
[141] *Browne* v. *Flower* [1911] 1 Ch. 219, 228, Parker J.; *Perera* v. *Vandiyar* [1953] 1 W.L.R. 672 C.A.; (1953) 69 *L.Q.R.* 295.
[142] *Mills* at 454j, Lord Hoffmann, 466g, Lord Millett; *Jenkins* v. *Jackson* (1888) 40 Ch.D. 71, 74, Kekewich J.
[143] H.W. Wilkinson [1990] *N.L.J.* 1158.
[144] *Owen* v. *Gadd* [1956] 2 Q.B. 99 C.A. (award of £2 damages upheld on appeal(!)).
[145] *Mira* v. *Aylmer Square Investments Ltd.* (1990) 22 H.L.R. 182 H.L.
[146] Including profits from lost sub-lettings: *Mira* v. *Aylmer Square Investments Ltd.* (1990) 22 H.L.R. 182 C.A.; H.W. Wilkinson [1990] *N.L.J.* 1159; *Molyneux-Child* v. *Coe* [1996] 2 C.L.Y. 3722.

Commercial tenants do not enjoy the statutory protection from harassment enjoyed by domestic tenants.[147]

3. Non-derogation from grant

Landlords must not derogate from their grants, an obligation that is implied if it is not for once expressed.[148] The basic concept is common sense. If the landlord lets property to a tenant for a particular purpose, the landlord is prevented from using his adjoining land[149] so as to interfere with the purpose for which the premises were let to the tenant. A classic illustration is provided by the lease of an explosives store discussed in *Harmer (Nigeria) Tin Areas Ltd.* v. *Jumbil.*[150] The ability of the tenant to obtain a licence to keep explosives depending upon the restriction of the use of the adjoining land (also owned by the landlord).[151] The landlord granted a mining lease of the adjoining land, and the tenant of the mine started to erect pithead buildings. Since the explosives licence might be revoked, the erection of the pithead buildings was restrained by injunction.[152] A much more recent illustration concerned a lease of an equestrian centre, diminished in value when the council landlord permitted its surrounding land to be used for flying model aeroplanes.[153] Derogation cannot arise from a use of the adjoining land that was contemplated at the time of the lease.[154]

However there are many unsuccessful cases. Opening a competing shop so as to make the tenant's business less profitable is not a derogation,[155] nor is a change of use[156] or the imposition of a restrictive covenant.[157] It is not a derogation to obstruct the flow of air to the tenant's timber drying sheds,[158] to remove privacy from the tenant's flat[159] or to let neighbouring premises for a dangerous trade which increases the fire risk and hence the insurance premiums.[160] Wide statements of principle[161] are doubtful in the land law context.

---

[147] See above Chapter 12.

[148] D.W. Elliott (1964) 80 *L.Q.R.* 244.

[149] Including possibly land acquired after the tenant's lease: *Johnston & Sons Ltd.* v. *Holland* [1988] 1 E.G.L.R. 264.

[150] [1921] 1 Ch. 200 C.A.

[151] There could be no public access within 134 yards, no building within 355 yards, and no Royal Palace within 4¾ miles.

[152] *Johnston & Sons Ltd.* v. *Holland* [1988] 1 E.G.L.R. 264 (erection of wall was derogation from grant of right to advertising hoarding).

[153] *Yankwood Ltd.* v. *Havering L.B.C.* [1998] E.G.C.S. 75.

[154] *Lyttleton Times Co. Ltd.* v. *Warners Ltd.* [1907] A.C. 476 H.L.; *Southwark L.B.C.* v. *Mills* [1999] 4 All E.R. 449, 456d, Lord Hoffmann; contrast *Pwllbach Colliery Co. Ltd.* v. *Woodman* [1915] A.C. 634 H.L.

[155] *Port* v. *Griffith* [1938] 1 All E.R. 295 C.A. (wool shop); *Romulus Trading Ltd.* v. *Comet Properties Ltd.* [1996] 2 E.G.L.R. 70, Garland J. (two bank safe deposits).

[156] *Kelly* v. *Battershell* [1949] 2 All E.R. 830 C.A. (flat block converted to hotel).

[157] *Re Beechwood Homes Ltd.'s Application* (1992) 64 P. & C.R. 535, 547.

[158] *Aldin* v. *Latimer Clark Muirhead & Co.* [1894] 2 Ch. 437.

[159] *Browne* v. *Flower* [1911] 1 Ch. 219.

[160] *O'Cedar Ltd.* v. *Slough Trading Co. Ltd.* [1927] 2 Ch. 123.

[161] *British Leyland Motor Corporation Ltd.* v. *Armstrong Patents Co. Ltd.* [1986] A.C. 577 H.L.; *Molton Builders Ltd.* v. *Westminster C.C.* (1975) 30 P. & C.R. 182, 186, Lord Denning M.R.

I.   INTERFERENCE BY NEIGHBOURING TENANTS

One tenant of a landlord may be able to complain about the conduct of neighbouring tenants—either by taking action against the landlord or by direct action against the tenant.

1.   Tort

If a neighbouring tenant causes problems, the most likely remedy is in tort. Liability is delineated to some extent by the lease, since it describes the exact physical extent of each property, grants easements, and may reserve the right to commit what would otherwise be a nuisance, but otherwise interference with the tenant's land can be tortious under ordinary common law principles. Encroachments can be repelled by action in trespass. The neighbour will be liable if he uses his land to interfere with the tenant's use of his land, if he commits a nuisance in the technical sense, giving the right to an injunction, damages, or abatement action. In extreme cases, the landlord's failure to prevent nuisances may be a ground on which the tenant is entitled to repudiate the lease.[162] Occupier's liability may arise if the tenant is injured by the neighbour's failure to repair his property correctly. If a neighbour is committing a *statutory nuisance*—for example, and particularly, noise[163]—the tenant can ask the local authority to take action to abate that nuisance.[164]

2.   Obligation to enforce covenants in neighbour's lease

Some leasehold estate schemes require the landlord to take action to enforce covenants against tenants elsewhere on the estate, so that the tenant can himself take action if the landlord fails to do so, or even repudiate the lease.[165] This may be so under a scheme of development which creates a reciprocal letting scheme.[166] Otherwise a landlord is not responsible for a nuisance caused by others and an action should be struck out.[167]

3.   Quiet enjoyment—acts of neighbouring tenants

It is possible for the covenant for quiet enjoyment to create rights binding both the landlord and future tenants. However, this possibility is severely reduced by the principle on which the House of Lords decided *Southwark L.B.C. v. Mills.*[168] A tenant of Southwark L.B.C. complained that he could hear all the normal living activities as his neighbour used his flat, but the council was held not liable to provide sound-proofing. This was because the obligation was only prospective—to avoid interfering with a tenant after his

---

[162] *Nynehead Developments Ltd.* v. *R.H. Fibreboard Containers Ltd.* [1999] 1 E.G.L.R. 7 Ch.D.

[163] Noise and Statutory Nuisance Act 1993; F.R. McManus (1994) 39 *J.L.S.* 86.

[164] Environmental Protection Act 1990 part III; *Aitken* v. *South Hams D.C.* [1995] 1 A.C. 262 H.L.; *Network H.Ass.* v. *Westminster C.C.* (1995) 27 H.L.R. 189 Q.B.D.

[165] *Chartered Trust plc.* v. *Davies* [1997] 2 E.G.L.R. 83 C.A.; H.W. Wilkinson [1998] *N.L.J.* 57; M. Heighton [1997] 38 *E.G.* 140.

[166] Sparkes *N.L.L.* pp.605–607.

[167] *Hussain* v. *Lancaster C.C.* (1999) 31 H.L.R. 164; K. Bretherton [1998] *J.H.L.* 143.

[168] [1999] 4 All E.R. 449 H.L.

lease is granted[169]—meaning that a tenant must accept the condition of the property at the time of the grant. Obligations to improve a property can arise only from a clear agreement.[170]

If a problem did exist at the time of the tenant's lease, the obligation to prevent interference will bind the landlord for his own acts, and also for the acts of those deriving title through him, though only if the landlord is responsible for the act and it falls within the covenant.[171] It is rare to encounter an absolute obligation,[172] since the covenant is invariably qualified, so that the landlord is only liable for himself and the lawful[173] acts of those claiming under him. In *Sanderson* v. *Berwick-on-Tweed B.C.*,[174] after the council had let one farm to Sanderson and two adjoining farms to other tenants, use of the drains by the tenant of the other farms damaged the land farmed by Sanderson. In one case the landlord council was held liable, since the drains were properly used, damage arising from the fact that the drains were defective, a matter within the landlord's sphere of responsibility. In the other case, concerning sound drains excessively used, the landlord escaped, since the tortious act of the other tenant did not make the landlord liable.[175] Another aspect of the qualification is demonstrated by *Celsteel Ltd.* v. *Alton House Holdings Ltd. (No.2)*.[176] Flats were let, each with a garage and a right of way to get to it. Another part of the development was let to a petrol company to build a filling station, but unfortunately the car wash intruded onto the driveway used by the tenants to gain access to their garages. The petrol company had no claim against the freeholder for breach of the covenant for quiet enjoyment because the tenants did not claim under the landlord but relied on their existing leases.[177] The landlord is not generally responsible for the acts of superior landlords[178] but of course an express covenant can extend liability to cover their acts,[179] or indeed those of any other person.

4.   Derogation from grant

If the landlord lets property to a tenant for a particular purpose, the *landlord* is prevented from using his adjoining land[180] so as to interfere with the purpose for which the premises were let to the tenant, and this obligation may extend to bind neighbours, and to enable action against landlords for the acts of subsequent tenants. In many ways this

---

[169] At 455h, Lord Hoffmann, 467g, Lord Millett; *Spoor* v. *Green* (1874) L.R. 9 Exch. 99 (subsidence); *Anderson* v. *Oppenheim* (1880) 5 Q.B.D. 602 C.A. (water cistern); *Lyttleton Times Co. Ltd.* v. *Warners Ltd.* [1907] A.C. 476 P.C. (noise of printing press).

[170] At 470a, Lord Millett.

[171] M.J. Russell (1976) 40 *Conv. (N.S.)* 427.

[172] *Young* v. *Raincock* (1849) 7 C.B. 310, 137 E.R. 124.

[173] Not alterations for which the head landlord had refused consent: *Matania* v. *National Provincial Bank Ltd.* [1936] 2 All E.R. 633 C.A.

[174] (1884) 13 Q.B.D. 547 C.A.; *Queensway Marketing Ltd.* v. *Associated Restaurants Ltd.* [1988] 2 E.G.L.R. 49 C.A.; *Mills* [1999] 4 All E.R. 449, 457e, Lord Hoffmann, 467h, Lord Millett.

[175] *Rickards* v. *Lothian* [1913] A.C. 263 P.C. (not liable for the malicious act of an unknown person).

[176] [1987] 1 W.L.R. 291 C.A.; J.E. Martin [1987] *Conv.* 366.

[177] The decision highlights the need for a guarantee of title; see Sparkes *N.L.L.* 718–721.

[178] *Jones* v. *Lavington* [1903] 1 K.B. 253.

[179] *Queensway Marketing Ltd.* v. *Associated Restaurants Ltd.* [1988] 2 E.G.L.R. 49 C.A.

[180] Including possibly land acquired after the tenant's lease: *Johnston & Sons Ltd.* v. *Holland* [1988] 1 E.G.L.R. 264.

overlaps with quiet enjoyment.[181] Derogation creates an obligation that is effectively a proprietary right, enforceable not only against the landlord's neighbouring land but also against subsequent buyers and tenants of that neighbouring land. So it was that in *Harmer (Nigeria) Tin Areas Ltd.* v. *Jumbil*[182] an injunction was granted against the *tenant* under the mining lease, who had taken a lease from the common landlord, since the landlord had been obliged not to derogate from his own prior lease of the explosives magazine to the plaintiff. If the lease is legal this right is also legal,[183] and so binds the world, including later tenants of the same landlord, despite its undiscoverability. As already noted,[184] there are many unsuccessful cases.

[181] *Mills* at 467f, Lord Millett.
[182] [1921] 1 Ch. 200 C.A.
[183] Despite its absence from L.P.A. 1925 s.1(2); otherwise it is equitable.
[184] See above p. 717.

27

DEALINGS

Forms of dealing. Assignment. Sub-letting. Mortgages. Devolutions. Parts. Absolute and qualified covenants. Procedural requirements under qualified covenants. Reasonable grounds. Express terms and conditions. Buyer and seller. Dealings with the landlord's reversion.

The basic subject matter of this chapter is dealings with a lease where the current tenant deals with an outside person—a new tenant intending to take a transfer of the lease, a lender, or a potential sub-tenant—where the landlord is not directly involved in the transaction. Hence the issue arises whether the landlord is willing to accept the new party or, if not, the tenant is able to force the landlord to accept him under the terms of the lease. Business leases almost always allow a tenant to deal with the lease, but require the tenant to obtain his landlord's consent before the transaction occurs. In this case statute imposes an obligation on the landlord to act reasonably when reaching his decision, and also imposes procedural requirements, such as a duty to act promptly and to give reasons in writing. Total prohibitions are likely on some forms of transaction—particularly physical division of a lease. The chapter concludes with a discussion of the methods of dealing with the landlord's reversion.

A. ASSIGNMENT (TRANSFER OF A LEASE)

1. Nature

Transfer of a leasehold estate is usually described as an assignment[1]—made by a person traditionally described as an assignor in favour of an assignee—but functionally this is simply a transfer of the lease, and it is often described in that way in this book. Leases are presumed to be freely transferable, so that a tenant who holds a lease free of any express restriction on dealings is free to transfer his estate as he wishes. This untrammelled freedom is appropriate for long leases in which all the economic value of the land resides with the tenant and the landlord receives only a ground rent; a person who has bought a flat by making a substantial capital payment would not accept any restriction on realising the value by resale. Freedom of sale is central to the success of a tenure that equates to leasehold ownership. At the other extreme lie residential tenants with short tenure and subject to a rack rental, where dealings with the tenancy are inevitably restricted, since no landlord would rent out residential accommodation on the terms

---

[1] Woodfall 16.001–16.007, 16.041–16.080.

that the tenant could choose who was to succeed him in occupation. Commercial leases fall between these two, since it is in the best interests of both parties to allow transfer, but landlords generally wish to ensure the financial stability of a new tenancy by requiring that their consent is obtained before a transfer proceeds: this best balances control over unsuitable tenants and the preservation of rights on a rent review.[2] Where a rack rental lease is transferred it usually has little value and so the new tenant will not pay a large premium, although there may be a small positive or negative value according to whether the rent is above or below market values and the state of repair. If a new tenant takes over the lease for a consideration of £1 and the acceptance of the liabilities under the lease he will be treated for priority purposes as a "purchaser".[3]

2.   Legal formality

An assignment of a lease creates no new landlord and tenant relationship, but rather it transfers the existing leasehold estate to a new tenant, who takes in substitution for the previous tenant. A deed is required for it to operate at law,[4] even for a short tenancy orally created.[5]   Landlords are commonly estopped from disputing that an assignment has occurred, for example because they have accepted rent from the new tenant.[6]

3.   Equitable assignment

A contract for value to assign the lease will operate as an equitable assignment if contractual formalities are complied with.[7] Covenants against assignment have to deal separately with legal and equitable transactions: *Gentle* v. *Faulkner*[8] held that a covenant against assignment prevented only legal assignment, so that a transfer that was valid only in equity was not caught. The decision is based upon an outdated and misguided view of the fusion of law and equity, and has undesirable consequences, but while its authority stands, it remains necessary to trap equitable transfers separately, for example by a covenant against parting with possession.[9]

B.   SUB-LETTING

1.   Nature

A grant of a head lease arises where a freehold owner creates a lease of his land when it is devoid of any letting. A sub-lease[10] is created, using normal leasehold formalities,[11]

---

[2] See above pp. 663–666.

[3] *Nurdin & Peacock plc.* v. *D.B. Ramsden & Co. Ltd.* [1999] 1 E.G.L.R. 119, Neuberger J.

[4] L.P.A. 1925 s.52(1).

[5] *Botting* v. *Martin* (1808) 1 Camp. 317, 319, 170 E.R. 970, Sir A. M'Donald C.B.; *Crago* v. *Julian* [1992] 1 W.L.R. 372 C.A.; *Camden L.B.C.* v. *Alexandrou* (1998) 30 H.L.R. 534 C.A.; *Parc (Battersea) Ltd.* v. *Hutchinson* [1999] 2 E.G.L.R. 33, Moore-Bick J.; see above pp. 293–294.

[6] *Rodenhurst Estates Ltd.* v. *W.H. Barnes Ltd.* [1936] 2 All E.R. 3; *Official Trustee of Charities* v. *Ferriman Trust Ltd.* [1937] 3 All E.R. 85.

[7] See above pp. 293–294.

[8] [1900] 2 Q.B. 267 C.A.

[9] See below p. 728.

[10] Woodfall 16.081–16.087.

[11] See above pp. 505–509.

where the person granting the lease is a leasehold estate owner rather than a freeholder. Assuming that exclusive possession of the land (or any part of it) has been given, there is a sub-tenancy,[12] creating two separate leasehold relationships. The person creating the lease can be seen to occupy a dual position, as tenant under the head lease and as land-lord under the sub-lease,[13] the freeholder being referred to as a head landlord, and the ultimate tenant as the sub-tenant.[14] Since two leases are created, there is no direct rela-tionship—that is no privity of estate[15]—between the head landlord and the sub-tenant. Sub-letting can be repeated to create chains of three[16] or more leases, and the process is theoretically infinite, but there are practical restraints on the manageable number of relationships.

2. Sub-lease which disposes of entire term

A sub-lease must reserve a reversion to the sub-landlord, so that there is some period when the property can revert to his possession. To put it another way, a sub-lease must be shorter than the head lease from which it is created, so if a tenant attempts to create a sub-lease for the entire term remaining to him, the lack of a reversion means that it cannot in fact operate as a sub-lease but must instead operate as an assignment.[17] *Milmo* v. *Carreras* [18] concerned a tenant who had 13 months of his lease remaining, and at that time purported to grant a sub-lease for one year and then from quarter to quarter— meaning that the minimum period of the sub-lease would be 15 months. This pur-ported sub-lease was in fact held to be an assignment of the 13-month term. A more recent illustration is *Parc (Battersea) Ltd.* v. *Hutchinson.*[19] In December 1997 Parc granted a lease over some land to Monarum for a fixed term expiring on March 31st 1998 from which business rights were excluded by agreement. In breach of covenant, Monarum sub-let a part to Hutchinson on a monthly tenancy, before vacating when its interest as tenant expired. The sub-tenant was left in possession and claimed the right to business security, but his claim failed. An oral grant of a sub-tenancy for a period that exceeded the tenant's term acted as an assignment of the head lease, so Hutchinson had in fact taken an assignment of Monarum's lease, from which business tenancies protec-tion had been excluded. The principle does not apply where advance calculation is impossible, for example because the superior lease is a periodic tenancy,[20] a business tenancy extension[21] or a lease for life.[22]

Superficially formality is a problem, since a short sub-lease may be oral whereas a deed is required for an assignment, but in fact it has been held repeatedly that an oral

---

[12] *Brent L.B.C.* v. *Cronin* (1998) 30 H.L.R. 43 C.A.
[13] i.e. as head tenant and sub-landlord.
[14] The older terminology was head-lessor, head-lessee, sub-lessor and sub-lessee respectively.
[15] See below pp. 749–753.
[16] That is a sub-sub-tenant or a sub-under-tenant.
[17] *Bryant* v. *Hancock & Co.* [1898] 1 K.B. 716, 719, Smith L.J. on appeal [1899] A.C. 442 H.L.
[18] [1946] K.B. 306 C.A.; (1946) 62 L.Q.R. 212.
[19] [1999] 2 E.G.L.R. 33, 36–37, Moore-Bick J.; S. Murdoch [1999] 24 *E.G.* 154; *Stretch* v. *West Dorset D.C.* [1998] 3 E.G.L.R. 62 C.A.
[20] *Pike* v. *Eyre* (1829) 9 B. & C. 909, 109 E.R. 338; *Curtis* v. *Wheeler* (1830) Moo. & M. 493, 173 E.R. 1235; *Oxley* v. *James* (1844) 13 M. & W. 209, 153 E.R. 87; *Pennell* v. *Payne* [1995] Q.B. 192 C.A.
[21] *William Skelton & Son Ltd.* v. *Harrison & Pinder Ltd.* [1975] Q.B. 361.
[22] *Bruerton* v. *Rainsford* (1583) Cro. Eliz. 15, 78 E.R. 28.

sub-lease is effective as an assignment of the term[23]: however paradoxical this may seem, it is a logical working out of the statute.[24] Despite glitches characteristic of old case-law principles[25] the authorities reveal a remarkable unanimity about the effect of a sub-lease longer than the head lease.[26] Rent cannot be distrained,[27] a notice to quit served on the "sub-tenant" is waste paper,[28] and privity of estate is ended.[29] Strangely it is possible to impose a forfeiture clause[30] and it is arguable that rent may be recoverable in contract.[31]

3. Control of sub-letting

Authority is inconsistent about the extent to which a covenant against sub-letting is needed as distinct from a covenant against transfer. Apparently a covenant against assignment may catch sub-letting[32] but the converse is not true: a covenant against sub-letting does not catch assignment.[33] Whatever the exact case-law position it is essential in practice to employ two distinct covenants, particularly as many leases permit transfer with consent but place an absolute bar on sub-letting, and dealings with parts.

Two refinements are needed. (1) *Not to commute rent.* Some of the value can be extracted from the land by a tenant granting a sub-lease at a premium or by a later agreement to commute (that is reduce) the rent in return for a capital payment. Therefore, tenants are commonly required not to sub-let on these terms. However a way round this covenant was found in one case in which the tenant accepted a capital payment of £130,000 to accept a surrender of the sub-lease: this was not a breach of a covenant against commuting the rent.[34] (2) *Parting with possession.*[35] Allowing a licensee to take possession is not caught by a straightforward covenant against assignment,[36] so that a separate covenant is required to prevent the grant of exclusive licences,[37] and agreements to shared occupation require separate treatment.[38] Whether a *tenant* is in breach

---

[23] At 310, 312, Lord Greene M.R., 314, Morton L.J.

[24] *Preece* v. *Corrie* (1828) 5 Bing. 24, 130 E.R. 968.

[25] *Hicks* v. *Downing* (1696) 1 Ld. Raym. 99, 91 E.R. 962 (already settled); *Palmer* v. *Edwards* (1783) 1 Doug. 187, 99 E.R. 122n; Platt, *Leases* vol.1 devoted pages 9–19 to older authorities; *Grosvenor Estates Belgravia* v. *Cochran* [1991] 2 E.G.L.R. 83 C.A.; P.F. Smith [1991] *Conv.* 393.

[26] *Wollaston* v. *Hakewill* (1841) 3 Man. & G. 297, 133 E.R. 1154; *Pluck* v. *Digges* (1831) 5 Bli. N.S. 31, 5 E.R. 219 H.L.

[27] *Parmenter* v. *Webber* (1818) 8 Taunt. 593, 129 E.R. 515; *Pascoe* v. *Pascoe* (1837 3 Bing. N.C. 898, 132 E.R. 656; *Lewis* v. *Baker* [1905] 1 Ch. 46.

[28] *Milmo* v. *Carreras* [1946] K.B. 306 C.A.

[29] *Thorn* v. *Woollcombe* (1832) 3 B. & Ad. 586, 110 E.R. 213.

[30] *Shiloh Spinners Ltd.* v. *Harding* [1973] A.C. 691 H.L.; *Doe d. Freeman* v. *Bateman* (1818) 2 B. & Ald. 168, 106 E.R. 328; *Williams* v. *Hayward* (1859) 1 E. & E. 1040, 120 E.R. 1200.

[31] P. Jackson (1967) *31 Conv. (N.S.)* 159, 161–164; but *Poultney* v. *Holmes* (1720) 1 Strange 405, 93 E.R. 596 (true rent), was overruled by *Palmer* v. *Edwards* as above.

[32] *Re Town Investments Ltd.'s Underlease* [1954] Ch. 301, Danckwerts J.

[33] *Greenaway* v. *Adams* (1806) 12 Ves. 395, 33 E.R. 149; the point is treated as doubtful by Megarry & Wade (6th) 905 n.41.

[34] *Associated Newspaper Properties Ltd.* v. *Drapers Co.* [1997] 1 E.G.L.R. 88 C.A.

[35] D.G. Barnsley (1963) 27 *Conv. (N.S.)* 159, 170–175.

[36] *Horsey Estate Ltd.* v. *Steiger* [1899] 2 Q.B. 79 C.A.; *Wallace* v. *C. Brian Barratt & Son Ltd.* [1997] 2 E.G.L.R. 1 C.A. (since a company could never farm personally it was no breach of the lease to allow a partnership to farm).

[37] Assignments are also caught: *Marks* v. *Warren* [1979] 1 All E.R. 29 Browne-Wilkinson J.

[38] *Gian Singh & Co.* v. *Naher* [1965] 1 W.L.R. 412 (partnership); *Edwardes* v. *Barrington* (1901) 85 L.T. 650 H.L.; *Chaplin* v. *Smith* [1926] 1 K.B. 198 C.A.; *Stening* v. *Abrahams* [1931] 1 Ch. 470.

when a sub-tenant allows another person possession depends on the wording of the particular covenants; it is certainly no breach if the sub-lease permits assignment.[39]

4. Physical division by sub-letting parts

Commercial leases commonly impose an absolute prohibition on physical division of the holding by sub-leases of parts.[40]

C. OTHER DEALINGS

Covenants against dealings need to be drawn comprehensively so as to bar all possible forms of transaction, and in clear terms, since a covenant will be construed against the landlord.[41] The Landlord and Tenant Act 1988[42] covers covenants by tenants not to enter into any of the following transactions affecting the property let:

assigning:
underletting,
charging, or
parting with possession.

1. Mortgages

Regulation of mortgages is desirable, because if the tenant fails to pay what is due under the mortgage the lender has the right to take possession of the land and sell the lease to a buyer over whose identity the landlord will have no control, unless he imposes control over the initial creation of a mortgage. Mortgages in the technical sense are sub-leases,[43] whereas the more common legal charge is not[44]; so a covenant should deal separately wth mortgages, legal charges, declarations of trust in favour of lenders,[45] and informal equitable mortgages.[46]

2. Devolutions

Involuntary dealings such as the devolutions[47] that occur on death or insolvency cannot be prevented.[48] Property vests automatically in a tenant's personal representatives on death,[49] or in his trustee in bankruptcy on insolvency.[50] Other forms of involuntary

---

[39] *Storehouse Properties Ltd.* v. *Ocobase Ltd.* [1998] Times April 3rd, Rimer J.
[40] See below pp. 728–729.
[41] *Contra proferentem: Crusoe d. Blencowe* v. *Bugby* (1771) 2 W. Bl. 766, 96 E.R. 448.
[42] ss.1(1)(a), 5(1) (agreement or condition); L.T.A. 1927 s.19 is similar.
[43] L.P.A. 1925 ss.85–86.
[44] *Sarjeant* v. *Nash Field & Co.* [1903] 2 K.B. 304 C.A.
[45] *Gentle* v. *Faulkner* [1900] 2 Q.B. 267 C.A.
[46] *Doe d. Pitt* v. *Hogg* (1824) 4 Dow. & Ry. 226 (query the decision that covenant not to part *with the lease* does not catch equitable mortgages by deposit, but this is now of historical interest only).
[47] Woodfall 16.101–16.156.
[48] *Crosbie* v. *Tooke* (1833) 1 My. & K. 431, 434, 39 E.R. 745, Brougham L.C.; *Crusoe d. Blencowe* v. *Bugby* (1771) 3 Wils. 234, 237, 95 E.R. 1030; *Re Birkbeck Permanent Benefit B.S.* [1913] 2 Ch. 34.
[49] A.E.A. 1925 s.1.
[50] *Re Riggs* [1901] 2 K.B. 16 (voluntary petition).

transfers occur under compulsory purchase orders,[51] court orders[52] and executions.[53] In all cases, the real question is whether a covenant can prevent the *next* dealing. Yes, so it appears, but it requires clear wording to compel a trustee in bankruptcy[54] or a liquidator[55] to obtain the landlord's consent before selling the lease. Consent is not required on a gift by will,[56] neither is it generally required for the subsequent assent— by which the personal representatives give effect to the will by passing the lease to a beneficiary,[57] though a comprehensively worded covenant could catch this transaction.[58]

3.   Parting with possession

It is usual to supplement a covenant against sub-letting by adding a covenant not to part with possession; the benefit is this catches a licence arrangement without the need to prove what form of legal transaction has occurred. However an action on such a covenant failed in *Gondal* v. *Dillon Newsagents Ltd.*,[59] where a potential purchaser of a sub post office began to run the business, but the landlord was unable to prove that the original tenant had given up possession without the landlord's consent.

4.   Dealings with parts

A lease that contains no explicit prohibition will permit physical division, either by sale or subletting. However leases commonly impose an outright bar, ensuring that the landlord has to deal with only one tenant. Before the Landlord and Tenant (Covenants) Act 1995, physical division of the holding was rare, because if a tenant of part A breached a covenant, the tenant of part B would generally also be liable to the landlord. It was also difficult to create a binding apportionment (that is a division) of the rent. A major objective of the 1995 reforms was to create a safe method of division, both for tenants' holdings and for landlords' reversions, and to resolve problems in the law of forfeiture.[60] Neither the Standard Property Conditions nor the Standard Commercial Property Conditions (1999)[61] deal with sales of part, so express conditions will be required.

A covenant against sub-letting is not broken by a dealing with part,[62] though a covenant against dealing with parts may include the whole. Landlords are frequently anxious to prevent division, a result best achieved by two separate covenants, an *absolute* prohibition on dealings with *part* and a *qualified* covenant against dealings with the *whole*.[63] Whatever the intention, express and explicit wording is desirable.

---

[51] *Slipper* v. *Tottenham & Hampstead Junction Rly.* (1867) L.R. 4 Eq. 112.
[52] *Marsh* v. *Gilbert* [1980] 2 E.G.L.R. 44.
[53] *Doe d. Mitchinson* v. *Carter* (1798–9) 8 Term. Rep. 57, 300, 101 E.R. 1264, 1400.
[54] *Re Wright* [1949] Ch. 729.
[55] *Re Farrow's Bank Ltd.* [1921] 2 Ch. 164 C.A.
[56] *Fox* v. *Swann* (1655) Sty. 482, 82 E.R. 881; D.G. Barnsley (1963) 27 *Conv. (N.S.)* 159 (after 1925 the will operates only in equity).
[57] *Roe d. Gregson* v. *Harrison* (1788) 2 Term. Rep. 425; D.G. Barnsley (1963) 27 *Conv. (N.S.)* 159.
[58] *Doe d. Goodbehere* v. *Bevan* (1815) 3 M. & S. 353, 105 E.R. 644; *Re Birkbeck Permanent Benefit B.S.* [1913] 2 Ch. 34, 38, Neville J.; *Re Farrow's Bank Ltd.* [1921] 2 Ch. 164 C.A.
[59] [1998] N.P.C. 127 C.A.
[60] See below pp. 757–759.
[61] J. Martin [1999] 21 *E.G.* 132.
[62] *Church* v. *Brown* (1808) 15 Ves. 258, 265, 33 E.R. 752; *Cook* v. *Shoesmith* [1951] 1 K.B. 752 C.A.; *Esdaile* v. *Lewis* [1956] 1 W.L.R. 709 C.A.; R.E. Megarry (1956) 72 *L.Q.R.* 325 (unfortunate decision).
[63] *Re Cooper's Lease* (1968) 19 P. & C.R. 541, Cross J.

5. Destructive dealings: merger and surrender

Passing both the reversion and the leasehold estate to a single person can destroy a lease. Merger occurs where a tenant acquires the reversion, or where both interests are transferred to one outside person. Surrender occurs where the lease is given up to the landlord. Termination is not automatic but depends upon the intention of the parties. Given that, the landlord is necessarily involved in these forms of destructive dealing, they have been treated as an aspect of termination.[64]

D. METHODS OF CONTROLLING DEALINGS

Freedom to deal with freehold land cannot generally be restricted. But a landlord has a genuine reason to want to restrict transfer of the lease, since he will be anxious to ensure that any incoming tenant will be able to pay the rent and carry out the tenant's obligations in the lease. There is also the fear that a tenant may extract value from the land by taking a premium when he grants a sub-lease, leaving nothing for the head landlord except a rent below the market rate. Another problem is damage caused to the landlord's adjoining estate by activities on the tenant's property. In recognition of these concerns,[65] the law has always allowed restrictions on the freedom of a tenant to deal with his lease,[66] provided that any restriction must be express.[67] Very few business tenants enjoy untrammelled freedom to deal with their land.

Any covenant against dealings should be buttressed by a forfeiture provision. A transfer in breach of covenant is effective to pass the leasehold estate, but the landlord is protected by the fact that forfeiture is virtually automatic against the purchaser.[68]

1. Freedom to deal

A tenant may transfer his lease freely, if it contains no restriction, and this includes the power to grant sub-leases, to create mortgages, and to enter into any other transaction.[69]

2. Registration of transfers

Some landlords are not unduly concerned about who owns the lease. If a house or a flat is let for 999 years, the tenant is the real owner, and the landlord is concerned only to keep track of the identity of the current tenant, so as to be able to demand the ground rent. Successive tenants have to register a transfer with the landlord within a set period of time after it has occurred, and to pay a registration fee.[70]

---

[64] See above pp. 596–603.

[65] Lord Eldon L.C. said in *Church* v. *Brown* (1808) 15 Ves. 258, 264, 33 E.R. 752 that it was as old as *Dumpor's case* (1603) 4 Co. Rep. 119b, 76 E.R. 1110.

[66] Woodfall 11.113–11.178; Bright & Gilbert 417–489; Davey 79–95; Evans & Smith (5th) 115–126; Garner (2nd) 72–77.

[67] However a restriction can be implied into a lease if it is contained in the rent book: *R. C. Glaze Properties Ltd.* v. *Alabdinboni* (1992) 25 H.L.R. 150 C.A.

[68] See below pp. 820–821.

[69] *Doe d. Mitchinson* v. *Carter* (1798) 8 Term. Rep. 57, 60, 101 E.R. 1264, Kenyon C.J.; *Keeves* v. *Dean* [1924] 1 K.B. 685, 691, Bankes L.J.; *Houlder Brothers & Co. Ltd.* v. *Gibbs* [1925] Ch. 575, 583, Pollock M.R.

[70] Generally this is not liable to V.A.T.: [1990] 26 *L.S.G.* 14.

One particular example of this type of arrangement is a building lease, that is a lease granted for more than 40 years at a price that includes the erection or improvement of buildings. Consent to dealings is not required during most of the years of the lease, provided that the tenant gives notice in writing of the dealing to the landlord within six months.[71] Any term of the lease requiring consent is overridden. However repairing obligations are more onerous in the last seven years of the term, so a requirement to obtain consent is permitted during that last phase of the lease. Landlords who wish to control dealings can easily evade the statutory provisions by taking a covenant to offer a surrender of the lease before any dealing proceeds.[72]

3. Absolute covenants

An absolute prohibition restricts dealing by the tenant completely. No tenant who holds under a long lease should accept an absolute prohibition, since who can tell when circumstances will alter and it will become necessary to sell what one owns? Restrictions on dealings are also detrimental to the landlord's interest, since they adversely affect the market rental obtainable when the lease is granted, and again when it is reviewed, though they are, of course, normal in short leases and particularly for residential tenants.[73] Any apparent severity is tempered by the fact that the landlord may waive the restriction, so that an absolute covenant against dealings really operates as a covenant not to deal without obtaining the landlord's permission to the particular dealing. But there is an enormous difference between a tenant who has a *right* to transfer, and one who has to go cap in hand to the landlord to beg for permission.[74] Apart from the statutory prohibition of sexually and racially discriminatory covenants, there is no Parliamentary intervention in absolute covenants, so the landlord can act in his own interest without being required to act reasonably.[75] It is perfectly proper to impose absolute restrictions on physical divisions by dealings with part of the land or sub-letting. Estate management becomes much more difficult if the number of properties is multiplied by subdivision, and it is reasonable and common to provide against the substantial risk that sub-tenants may acquire security of tenure.

4. Qualified covenants

Most covenants against dealings are qualified, which means that the landlord's consent must be obtained. A good balance is obtained, for the landlord has scope to object to a buyer on the basis of his unsatisfactory financial status, while the tenant is free to sell his lease if he needs to do so. A fundamental statutory protection is given by section 19(1) of the Landlord and Tenant Act 1927: a proviso is implied that the landlord's consent is

---

[71] L.T.A. 1927 s.19(1)(b). Certain public landlords are excepted. The deemed consent is withdrawn for commercial leases by L.T.A. 1927 s.19(1D), which was inserted by L.T. (Covenants) A. 1995 s.22.

[72] *Vaux Group Ltd.* v. *Lilley* [1991] 1 E.G.L.R. 60; P. Sparkes [1991] *J.B.L.* 494; J.E. Adams [1990] *Conv.* 332; see above p. 558.

[73] See above Chapter 11.

[74] *F.W. Woolworth & Co. Ltd.* v. *Lambert (No.1)* [1937] Ch. 37, 58–59, Romer L.J.

[75] *Property & Bloodstock Ltd.* v. *Emerton* [1968] Ch. 94, 119G–120A, Danckwerts L.J., has not been followed: *Bocardo S.A.* v. *S. & M. Hotels Ltd.* [1980] 1 W.L.R. 17, 22, Megaw L.J., 26G, Browne L.J.; *Guardian Assurance Co. Ltd.* v. *Gants Hill Holdings Ltd.* [1983] 2 E.G.L.R. 36, 37B, Mervyn Davies J.; *Vaux Group Ltd.* v. *Lilley* [1991] 1 E.G.L.R. 60, Knox J.

not to be unreasonably withheld. This term is implied into any lease[76] containing a qualified covenant against dealings and is of enormous practical significance. If the tenant has the right to deal with his landlord's permission he also has the right to insist that the landlord should act reasonably, since any express provision to the contrary is overridden. In fact the operation of the statute is usually anticipated by express provision.[77] However, as will be explained below, the parties to a business lease are now allowed to reach a binding agreement about what is reasonable.[78]

5. Forms of dealings

Covenants against dealings need to be drawn comprehensively to cover all possible forms of transaction, especially since any covenant will be construed against the landlord.[79] One statutory definition refers to a qualified covenant against any of the following transactions affecting the property let: that is assigning, underletting, charging or parting with possession of the premises comprised in the tenancy.[80] It may also be desirable to try to restrict the automatic devolutions that occur on death and bankruptcy. *Gentle* v. *Faulkner* merits re-emphasis: it was held that a covenant against assignment prevented only legal assignment, so that a separate provision is needed to block transfers valid only in equity; commercial leases generally prohibit tenants from parting with possession of any part of the land.[81]

E. PROCEDURAL REQUIREMENTS AFFECTING QUALIFIED COVENANTS

Before 1988, many a tenant was treated unjustly by his landlord's failure to consider an application for consent to a dealing promptly. Delay very often killed a sale.[82] Outright refusals were difficult to challenge, and remedies were poor. The Landlord and Tenant Act 1988[83] implements Law Commission proposals[84] to remedy these deficiencies for applications for consent made since late 1988.[85] The Act applies only to qualified covenants against dealings,[86] that is where consent is not to be unreasonably withheld.[87] Its procedural requirements are also imposed on head landlords who have power to control the dealings of their sub-tenants where the requirement to act reasonably is imposed

---

[76] Widely defined in L.T.A. 1927 s.25(1) to include e.g. an underlease, tenancy or agreement for a lease, and to include pre-1927 leases. Agricultural holdings are excluded: s.19(4). The 1927 Act does not apply to covenants by head landlords with sub-tenants, but L.T.A. 1988.

[77] Law Com. No.141 (1985) paras.4.61–4.71 proposes that all covenants should be fully qualified in this way.

[78] See below p. 741.

[79] i.e *contra proferentem: Crusoe d. Blencowe* v. *Bugby* (1771) 2 W. Bl. 766, 96 E.R. 448.

[80] L.T.A. 1988 s.1(1)(a) (procedure); L.T.A. 1927 s.19 is similar.

[81] [1900] 2 Q.B. 267 C.A.; see above p. 728.

[82] *City Hotels Group Ltd.* v. *Total Property Investments Ltd.* [1985] 1 E.G.L.R. 253, Judge Paul Baker Q.C.

[83] J. Gaunt (1987) 284 *E.G.* 1371; R. Shuttleworth (1987) 284 *E.G.* 1480; R. Cullum (1987) 284 *E.G.* 1580; J.E. Adams [1988] 32 *E.G.* 35.

[84] Law Com. No.141 (1985); A.J. Waite [1986] *Conv.* 240; H.W. Wilkinson [1988] *Conv.* 1.

[85] On or after September 29th 1988: L.T.A. 1988 ss.5(4), 7(2).

[86] "Covenant" includes condition or agreement: s.5(1); "lease" is also widely defined by s.5, though secure (public sector residential) tenancies are excluded.

[87] The qualification may be: (1) express, or (2) implied under L.T.A. 1927 s.19.

expressly. Landlords have no requirement of procedural efficiency under absolute covenants. Where procedural duties are imposed on the landlord, the first is to inform the tenant of the decision within a reasonable time and the second is not to behave unreasonably when withholding consent.

1.   The need to ask for consent

In order to bring into play the landlord's duties, the tenant must serve a written request for permission to assign.[88] This has always been essential. As *Hendry* v. *Chartsearch Ltd.* has recently reconfirmed,[89] there is a breach of covenant if the tenant does not ask, even if the circumstances are such that the landlord would be bound to grant consent.[90] If the tenant proceeds to sell without requesting consent, the landlord can forfeit the lease.[91]

2.   Duty on landlord to give prompt decision

After a tenant[92] serves a written application for consent, the landlord owes a duty to the tenant to serve[93] a written notice of decision on the tenant within a reasonable time.[94] The landlord is entitled to ask for information required in the decision making process,[95] such as details of the proposed new tenant, but not the terms of the assignment to him.[96] If notice is served on the wrong person the landlord has a duty to pass it on promptly.[97] An onus rests on the landlord to show that matters were dealt with within a reasonable time.

Practical operation of the Act is illustrated by *Midland Bank plc.* v. *Chart Enterprises Inc.*[98] The letter asking for consent was sent on February 15th, 1989. After a bare acknowledgement, there was no written response until May 5th, 1989. Since the Act required the landlord to respond in writing,[99] this was the first relevant communication and by the time it was received the delay was already unreasonable. In the event the decision letter contained an unreasonable condition, so that the landlord still had not given a valid consent, and the delay was compounded by further desultory correspondence lasting until July. On a summons taken out in August, the court granted a declaration that consent was unreasonably refused and awarded damages. Harold Wilkinson

---

[88] L.T.A. 1988 s.1(3).

[89] [1998] Times September 16th.

[90] *Barrow* v. *Isaacs & Son* [1891] 1 Q.B. 417 C.A.; *Eastern Telegraphic Co.* v. *Dent* [1899] 1 Q.B. 835 C.A.; *Cohen* v. *Popular Restaurants Ltd.* [1917] 1 K.B. 480; *Creery* v. *Summerskell* [1949] Ch. 751; *Marks* v. *Warren* [1979] 1 All E.R. 29.

[91] See below p. 799.

[92] Or lender exercising the power of sale: s.5.

[93] L.T.A. 1988 s.5(2), using methods provided by the tenancy or by L.T.A. 1927 s.2.

[94] L.T.A. 1988 s.1(3); the duty is imposed by subs.(2) on the landlord, any superior landlord or mortgage-lender, those included in the s.5 definition, and the Crown (s.6).

[95] *Norwich Union Life Insurance Society* v. *Shopmoor Ltd.* [1997] 2 All E.R. 32, Scott V.C. (no reason to refuse consent on facts); P.H. Kenny [1998] *Conv.* 346.

[96] *Kened Ltd.* v. *Connie Investments Ltd.* [1997] 1 E.G.L.R. 21 C.A.

[97] L.T.A. 1988 s.2.

[98] [1990] 2 E.G.L.R. 59, Popplewell J.; *Fischer* v. *Toumazos* [1991] 2 E.G.L.R. 204 (landlord stalling to try to secure surrender); L. Crabb [1992] *Conv.* 213.

[99] L.T.A. 1988 s.1(3)(b); *Footwear Corporation Ltd.* v. *Amplight Properties Ltd.* [1998] 2 All E.R. 52, Neuberger J. (9 weeks unreasonable); P.H. Kenny [1998] *Conv.* 340.

concludes[100] that the cases to date "indicate that the courts are likely to require such requests to be treated by landlords with a good deal of urgency". However, it would be churlish of a tenant to complain that the landlord had acted too swiftly, and a complaint on this ground was rejected in *Moss Bros. Group plc.* v. *C.S.C. Properties Ltd.*[101]; if the landlord acts in a pre-emptory fashion it is necessary to challenge the substantive reasons given for refusal.

3. Duty on landlord to state reasons

The landlord is under a duty to give consent unless it is reasonable not to do so.[102] A written notice of decision must be given to the tenant within a reasonable time. Before 1988 writing was required only if the lease said so,[103] but the landlord will often be estopped from denying the validity of an oral licence.[104] Reasons must be given[105] for refusal of permission or for attaching any condition to a grant of consent—since conditions must themselves be reasonable.[106]

There was no clear[107] duty to state reasons before the Act. Thus the landlord could rely on other grounds; not perhaps on appeal,[108] but certainly ones that have been properly pleaded.[109] The 1988 Act changes all this. A landlord is restricted to circumstances known at the time of giving consent, and cannot introduce evidence discovered later.[110] One other important change in the common law is the shift in the onus on to the landlord,[111] so that it is now up to him to demonstrate that any conditions were reasonable or that refusal was reasonable. The test of what is reasonable is not altered.[112] Neuberger J. deduced the obligation to give reasons from the fact that a decision (and the reasons for it) must be communicated in writing in *Footwear Corporation Ltd.* v. *Amplight Properties Ltd.*[113]; a refusal to allow a change of use to a pet shop by sub-letting was ineffective because the refusal occurred only in a telephone conversation, and an additional reason relating to the financial accounts of the proposed sub-tenant was not reduced to writing.

---

[100] [1999] *N.L.J.* 1039, 1040.

[101] [1999] E.G.C.S. 47, Neuberger J.

[102] L.T.A. 1988 s.1(3)(a).

[103] *Roe d. Gregson* v. *Harrison* (1788) 2 Term. Rep. 425, 100 E.R. 229; *Bellamy's case* (1605) 6 Co. Rep. 38a, 77 E.R. 309.

[104] *Richardson* v. *Evans* (1818) 3 Madd. 218, 56 E.R. 490; *Bader Properties Ltd.* v. *Linley Property Investments Ltd.* (1968) 19 P. & C.R. 620.

[105] L.T.A. 1988 s.1(3)(b).

[106] *Dong Bang Minerva (U.K.) Ltd.* v. *Davina* [1996] 2 E.G.L.R. 31 C.A.; K. Stepien (1994) 138 *S.J.* 910 (costs of rent review).

[107] Despite *Young* v. *Ashley Gardens Property Investment Ltd.* [1903] 2 Ch. 112, 115, Vaughan Williams L.J.

[108] *Lovelock* v. *Margo* [1963] 2 Q.B. 786 C.A.; R.E. Megarry (1963) 79 *L.Q.R.* 479.

[109] *Bromley Property Garden Estates Ltd.* v. *Moss* [1982] 1 W.L.R. 1019 C.A.; L. Crabb [1983] *Conv.* 140; and several earlier cases.

[110] *C.I.N. Properties Ltd.* v. *Gill* [1993] 2 E.G.L.R. 97; L. Crabb [1994] *Conv.* 314; *Kened Ltd.* v. *Connie Investments Ltd.* [1997] 1 E.G.L.R. 21 C.A.; *Blockbuster Entertainments Ltd.* v. *Leakcliff Properties Ltd.* [1997] 1 E.G.L.R. 28, Neuberger J.

[111] *International Drilling Fluids Ltd.* v. *Louisville Investments (Uxbridge) Ltd.* [1986] Ch. 513, 520, Balcombe L.J., and many earlier cases.

[112] *Midland Bank plc.* v. *Chart Enterprises Inc.* [1990] 2 E.G.L.R. 59, 60C, Popplewell J.; *Air India* v. *Balabel* [1993] 2 E.G.L.R. 66, 69, Stuart Smith L.J.

[113] [1998] 2 E.G.L.R. 38 Ch.D.; *Norwich Union Life Insurance Society* v. *Shopmoor Ltd.* [1998] 3 All E.R. 32, Scott V.C.

4.   Remedies

Undoubtedly tenants would be helped most by giving deemed consent to a dealing after the landlord had exceeded a reasonable time for responding to the tenant's request for consent. However, the Law Commission shied away from this radical and, it felt, unworkable change.[114] Instead the Act continues the existing right to take action in tort for breach of duty,[115] the usual remedy being an injunction.[116] There is a new right to damages, which were not available at common law[117] unless there was a positive covenant to give consent,[118] and which are still withheld from the owners of mobile homes.[119] Tortious damages aim to put the tenant in the position in which he would have been if the landlord had observed the correct procedure, including losses reasonably foreseeable at the time of the breach, and compensation for loss of bargain. The deterrent effect has been strong.[120]

If the landlord refuses consent unreasonably *after being asked for permission* the tenant may proceed anyway[121] but it is most unlikely that a buyer will accept the risk involved: in practice it is necessary to obtain a declaration from the court that consent is being unreasonably withheld, or an injunction requiring the landlord to comply with his statutory duty.[122]

F.   REASONABLE AND UNREASONABLE GROUNDS

The landlord must act reasonably, both if refusing consent and when attaching conditions to a consent.[123] Reasonableness is assessed in the same way when considering express provisos,[124] the 1927 Act implied proviso that the landlord must act reasonably,[125] and the 1988 Act procedural duties.[126]

Although the test is objective[127]—so that if a head landlord acts unreasonably so too does the immediate landlord[128]—it remains difficult to provide consistent results when

---

[114] Law Com. No.141 (1985) para.8.106.

[115] L.T.A. 1988 s.4.

[116] *Hemingway Securities Ltd.* v. *Dunraven Ltd.* [1995] 1 E.G.L.R. 61, Jacob J.

[117] *Treloar* v. *Bigge* (1874) L.R. 9 Ex. 151; *Sear* v. *House Property & Investment Society* (1880) 16 Ch.D. 387, Hall V.C.

[118] *Ideal Film Renting Co. Ltd.* v. *Nielsen* [1921] 1 Ch. 575.

[119] *Berkeley Leisure Group Ltd.* v. *Lee* (1997) 29 H.L.R. 663 C.A.

[120] Law Com. No.141 (1985) para.1.108.

[121] *Treloar* v. *Bigge* (1874) L.R. 9 Ex. 151; *Sear* v. *House Property & Investment Society* (1880) 16 Ch.D. 387; *Re Winfrey & Chatterton's Agreement* [1921] 2 Ch. 7; *Fuller's Theatres & Vaudeville Co. Ltd.* v. *Rofe* [1923] A.C. 435 P.C.; *Lewis & Allenby (1909) Ltd.* v. *Pegge* [1914] 1 Ch. 782, 785, Neville J.

[122] *Hemingway Securities Ltd.* v. *Dunraven Ltd.* [1995] 1 E.G.L.R. 61, Jacob J.

[123] L.T.A. 1988 s.1(3)(a); *Jaison Property Development Co. Ltd.* v. *Roux Restaurants Ltd.* (1997) 74 P. & C.R. 357 C.A.

[124] G. Kodilinye [1988] *Conv.* 45.

[125] L.T.A. 1927 s.19(1).

[126] L.T.A. 1988 s.1(5); T. Aldridge (1989) 133 *S.J.* 1277; *Air India* v. *Balabel* [1993] 2 E.G.L.R. 66 C.A.; *Footwear Corporation Ltd.* v. *Amplight Properties Ltd.* [1998] 2 All E.R. 52, Neuberger J.; P.H. Kenny [1998] *Conv.* 340.

[127] *Louisville Investments* [1986] Ch. 513, 520C, Balcombe L.J., citing *Pimms Ltd.* v. *Tallow Chandlers Co.* [1964] 2 Q.B. 547.

[128] *Vieniet Ltd.* v. *W. Williams & Sons (Bread St.) Ltd.* [1958] 1 W.L.R. 1267.

the matter is always a question of fact.[129] In *Bickel* v. *Westminster*[130] Lord Denning M.R. argued for a broad-brush approach unconstrained by authorities—typically enough, though atypically this would have favoured the landlord on the facts rather than the tenant—but later English courts have been less than enthusiastic about this suggestion.[131]

Broadly speaking the landlord may act on four grounds: (1) undesirability of the proposed new tenant; (2) control of use; (3) damage to the landlord's reversion; and (4) the interests of estate management.

1. Undesirability of new tenant

Balcombe L.J. reiterated in *International Drilling Fluids Ltd.* v. *Louisville Investments (Uxbridge) Ltd.*, the leading case, that the main purpose of the covenant was to protect the landlord from having his premises pass to an undesirable sub-tenant or assignee, though also to control the use after the assignment has occurred.[132]

Landlords will obviously worry about the *financial stability* of proposed new tenants. It is reasonable to ask for references, and to refuse consent if the references give rise to doubts about the proposed tenant's ability to meet his financial obligations under the lease.[133] Previous personal experience of the new tenant is relevant.[134] However there are many cases where a refusal has been held not to be justified, for example where a landlord wished to hang on to an existing tenant who was cash rich.[135] The landlord was held to have acted unreasonably in *Storehouse Properties Ltd.* v. *Ocobase Ltd.*,[136] where a parent company asked for permission to assign to a subsidiary. Although the paid-up share capital of the subsidiary was only £2, the net assets were £38 million, and it was held that the landlord's fears were unfounded; hence the requirement that the parent company should guarantee future rent payments was unreasonable. Express covenants often restrict the landlord exclusively to objections based on the financial status of the new tenant.[137]

Serious *breaches of covenant by the tenant* justify withholding consent to a sale until they are rectified,[138] though trivial breaches do not.[139] Fears that the new tenant will breach the covenants will often not be a legitimate ground for refusal; consent will be

---

[129] *International Drilling Fluids Ltd.* v. *Louisville Investments (Uxbridge) Ltd.* [1986] Ch. 513, 521D, Balcombe L.J.; *Houlder Brothers. & Co. Ltd.* v. *Gibbs* [1925] Ch. 575, 584, Warrington L.J.; *Deverall* v. *Wyndham* [1989] 1 E.G.L.R. 57.

[130] [1977] Q.B. 517, 524D, Lord Denning M.R.

[131] G. Kodilinye [1988] *Conv.* 45.

[132] [1986] Ch. 513, 519H; *Bates* v. *Donaldson* [1896] 2 Q.B. 241, 247; *Houlder Brothers & Co. Ltd.* v. *Gibbs* [1925] Ch. 575 C.A.

[133] *Shanly* v. *Ward* (1913) 29 T.L.R. 714 C.A.; *Ross* v. *Hestdrive Ltd.* [1985] 1 E.G.L.R. 50; *British Bakeries (Midlands) Ltd.* v. *Michael Testler & Co. Ltd.* [1986] 1 E.G.L.R. 64, Peter Gibson J.; *Ponderosa International Development Inc.* v. *Pengap Securities (Bristol) Ltd.* [1986] 1 E.G.L.R. 66, Warner J. (sufficient if market would have doubts).

[134] *Air India* v. *Balabel* [1993] 2 E.G.L.R. 66 C.A.

[135] *Louisville Investments* [1986] Ch. 513 C.A.

[136] [1998] Times April 3rd, Rimer J.; *Venetian Glass Gallery Ltd.* v. *Next Properties Ltd.* [1989] 2 E.G.L.R. 42, 46, Harman J. obiter.

[137] *Moat* v. *Martin* [1950] 1 K.B. 175 C.A.

[138] *Goldstein* v. *Sanders* [1915] 1 Ch. 549, Eve J.; *Orlando Investments Ltd.* v. *Grosvenor Estate Belgravia* (1990) 59 P. & C.R. 21 C.A.; P. Luxton [1991] *J.B.L.* 57.

[139] *Farr* v. *Ginnings* (1928) 44 T.L.R. 249; *Beale* v. *Worth* [1993] E.G.C.S. 135 C.A.; L. Crabb [1994] *Conv.* 316.

given and the landlord will be left to pursue the new tenant if and when a breach of covenant occurs.[140]

Refusals on grounds of sex are prohibited by statute.[141] Race is another improper factor to consider, though the legislation[142] exempts a landlord of small premises if he or a near relative is sharing any accommodation. In *Parker* v. *Boggon*[143] it was held to be unreasonable to refuse consent to an assignment to a Turkish diplomat, but this decision is unsatisfactory since Macnaghten J. stated no reasons, and surely diplomatic immunity from action for the rent was a genuine concern? Refusal is not justified simply because the new tenant is thought to be awkward.[144]

2. Control of use

Balcombe L.J. made clear in *International Drilling Fluids Ltd.* v. *Louisville Investments (Uxbridge) Ltd.* that it is legitimate for a landlord to control dealings with the lease in order to exert control over the proposed use to be made of the property.[145] In principle both parties will be bound by the use covenants in the lease[146]: while tenants obviously cannot insist on changing to a use which is expressly prohibited,[147] landlords are not allowed to restrict the permitted uses at the time of a transfer of a lease so as to maximise the rental value of adjoining property.[148] However, if the use covenant is very wide, the landlord may have some scope to restrict the use to which a buyer may put the property.[149] Any restriction has to be agreed when the lease is granted or negotiated freely at a later time. In *Ashworth Frazer Ltd.* v. *Gloucester City Council*[150] the council's actions as planning authority in permitting the use of a site for metal recycling did not affect its position as landlord. However, it was not entitled to refuse consent to the assignment of a lease of the site for that use merely because it feared that the buyer would breach the use covenants in the lease. In *International Drilling* itself the tenant could insist on transferring the lease to a new tenant who intended to change the use from offices to serviced offices, since both uses were permitted.[151] The landlord's objection that parking problems would be magnified was overruled, since on the facts the landlord's attitude would have forced the tenant to leave the property vacant. This demonstrates that a tightly drawn use covenant cannot be tightened further at the time of a dealing. It is equally unacceptable to link a grant of consent to a change in the terms of the lease,[152] for exam-

---

[140] *Granada TV Network Ltd.* v. *Great Universal Stores Ltd.* (1966) 187 E.G. 391; *Killick* v. *Second Covent Garden Property Co. Ltd.* [1973] 1 W.L.R. 658 C.A.

[141] Sex Discrimination Act 1975 s.31.

[142] Race Relations Act 1976 s.24.

[143] [1947] K.B. 346; (1947) 63 L.Q.R. 147.

[144] A. Samuels [1982] *Conv.* 6.

[145] [1986] Ch. 513, 520D, Balcombe L.J.; *Warren* v. *Marketing Exchange for Africa* [1988] 2 E.G.L.R. 247.

[146] *Rayburn* v. *Wolf* (1985) 18 H.L.R. 1 C.A. (sub-letting).

[147] *Killick* v. *Second Covent Garden Property Co. Ltd.* [1973] 1 W.L.R. 658 C.A.

[148] *Anglia B.S.* v. *Sheffield C.C.* [1982] 1 E.G.L.R. 57 C.A.

[149] *Bridewell Hospital Governors* v. *Fawkner* (1892) 8 T.L.R. 637; *Sonnethal* v. *Newton* (1965) 109 S.J. 333 C.A.; *Whiteminster Estates Ltd.* v. *Hodges Menswear Ltd.* (1974) 232 E.G. 715.

[150] [2000] 12 E.G. 149 C.A.; L. Hutton (2000) 144 S.J. 374.

[151] [1986] Ch. 513, 522–523, doubting *Premier Confectionery (London) Ltd.* v. *London Commercial Sale Rooms Ltd.* [1933] Ch. 904.

[152] *Young* v. *Ashley Gardens Property Investments Ltd.* [1903] 2 Ch. 112; *Mills* v. *Cannon Brewery Co. Ltd.* [1920] 2 Ch. 38, P.O. Lawrence J.; *Balfour* v. *Kensington Gardens Mansions Ltd.* (1932) 49 T.L.R. 29.

ple by insisting on a change to a full repairing lease,[153] or insisting on the eviction of a lawful sub-tenant.[154]

Once a landlord has granted consent to a change of use, he cannot backtrack simply because his grant of consent is a breach of covenant to other tenants.[155]

3.   Financial interests of the landlord

Assessment of what is reasonable behaviour by a landlord is based primarily on the motives and convenience of the landlord[156] since a landlord is not required to be fair to the tenants,[157] nor to demonstrate public law reasonableness.[158] A landlord is not bound to balance his own interests against those of the tenant, and may stick to his guns even if he secures a trivial benefit that is far outweighed by the loss to the tenant.[159]

The landlord is entitled to control the letting scheme on an estate to preserve the *value of his reversion*. Thus it was held in *B.R.S. Northern Ltd.* v. *Templeheights Ltd.* that a landlord who was a development partner of the Sainsburys chain of supermarkets was entitled to object to an assignment to a rival chain, Safeways, which intended to obtain planning permission to spoil the Sainsburys bid.[160] Objection can be taken to transactions that drain value from the land. Sub-letting at a substantial premium is one transaction that removes much of the capital value from the land for the future, and a head landlord could quite properly object to it.[161] The effect is similar if a sub-lease is granted at a low rent, since the landlord is left with less than the market yield from the property.[162]

Overwhelmingly the most important consideration for a landlord is to ensure that a dealing does not attract unwelcome *security of tenure* or *enfranchisement rights* for the new tenant. Control of dealings is the best defence mechanism available to the landlord, and it is reasonable to object to a dealing that causes the value of the reversion to be reduced. The courts have given up the attempt to differentiate between "normal" and "abnormal" dealings.[163]

Enfranchisement legislation is an obvious concern: a landlord may refuse consent to a transaction passing the land from one tenant who could not enfranchise[164] to another

---

[153] *Roux Restaurants Ltd.* v. *Jaison Property Development Co. Ltd.* (1997) 74 P. & C.R. 357 C.A.
[154] *Midland Bank plc.* v. *Chart Enterprises Inc.* [1990] 2 E.G.L.R. 59, Popplewell J.
[155] *Rose v. Stavrou* [1999] 23 L.S.G. 29, Neuberger J.
[156] *Tredegar* v. *Harwood* [1929] A.C. 72, 81–82, Lord Phillimore.
[157] *Marsh* v. *Gilbert* [1980] 2 E.G.L.R. 44, 46K, Nourse J.
[158] *Plymouth C.C.* v. *Tollbench Ltd.* (1988) 152 L.G.R. 809.
[159] *Tredegar* v. *Harwood* [1929] A.C. 72, 78, Viscount Dunedin; *West Layton Ltd.* v. *Ford* [1979] Q.B. 593, 605; *Bromley Park Garden Estates Ltd.* v. *Moss* [1982] 1 W.L.R. 1019, 1027; *Louisville Investments* [1986] Ch. 513, 520D–521E, Balcombe L.J.; *Orlando Investments Ltd.* v. *Grosvenor Estate Belgravia* (1990) 59 P. & C.R. 21 C.A.
[160] [1998] 2 E.G.L.R. 182, Neuberger J.
[161] *Re Town Investments Ltd.'s Underlease* [1954] Ch. 301, 315, Danckwerts J.
[162] *Straudley Investments Ltd.* v. *Mount Eden Land Ltd.* (1997) 74 P. & C.R. 306 C.A.; *Blockbuster Entertainments Ltd.* v. *Leakcliff Properties Ltd.* [1997] 1 E.G.L.R. 28, Neuberger J. obiter.
[163] *West Layton Ltd.* v. *Ford* [1979] Q.B. 593 C.A.; *Brann* v. *Westminster Anglo-Continental Investment Co. Ltd.* [1976] 2 E.G.L.R. 72 C.A.
[164] This reasoning does not apply if one potential enfranchisee transfers to another: *Marsh* v. *Gilbert* [1980] 2 E.G.L.R. 44, 46L–M, Nourse J.

who could.[165] Otherwise the landlord may be compelled to sell the freehold below its market value. Legislation enacted after the date of the lease can be taken into account.[166] The landlord can also object to transactions which confer new residential security of tenure directly[167] or indirectly,[168] or which might do so.[169] A company, which cannot enjoy statutory protection, can be prevented from transferring a tenancy to an individual director who can,[170] and the landlord can also prevent transfers of staff accommodation from employees to outsiders.[171] Conversely the landlord may object to assignment to a tenant who will be able to *break* an onerous lease.[172] Where attracting security is not a risk the landlord cannot refuse just because the property is residential.[173] There is no legitimate objection to a sub-lease that is envisaged by the lease,[174] nor to a shorthold with minimal security.[175]

However, a landlord must not seek to achieve a *collateral purpose*. A decision must be reached on grounds connected with the landlord–tenant relationship, and not on collateral grounds.[176] Landlords must not manoeuvre to improve their own position, perhaps by securing occupation for themselves[177] or to seek joint control over deposits paid by sub-tenants.[178] A policy of requiring the surrender of residential flats rather than allowing transfers is therefore unacceptable.[179] In *Houlder Brothers & Co. Ltd.* v. *Gibbs* it was held to be unreasonable to refuse consent because the buyer would give up another property, which would be difficult to relet.[180] This decision feels right. Critical dicta in the House of Lords[181] are both obiter and doubtful.[182] Preservation of the rental level on adjoining properties is an equally unacceptable motive.[183]

---

[165] *Welch* v. *Birrane* (1974) 29 P. & C.R. 102, Lawton J.; *Norfolk Capital Group Ltd.* v. *Kitway Ltd.* [1977] Q.B. 506 C.A.; *Bickel* v. *Duke of Westminster* [1977] Q.B. 517 C.A.

[166] *Leeward Securities Ltd.* v. *Lillyheath Properties Ltd.* [1984] 2 E.G.L.R. 54 C.A.

[167] *West Layton Ltd.* v. *Ford* [1979] Q.B. 593, 605, Roskill L.J.

[168] *Brann* v. *Westminster Anglo-Continental Investment Co. Ltd.* [1976] 2 E.G.L.R. 72, 74, Cairns L.J.

[169] *Pimms Ltd.* v. *Tallow Chandlers Co.* [1964] 2 Q.B. 547; *Bickel* v. *Duke of Westminster* [1977] Q.B. 517, 528F, Waller L.J.

[170] *Lee* v. *K. Carter Ltd.* [1949] 1 K.B. 85 C.A.; R.E. Megarry (1948) 63 *L.Q.R.* 453; *Swanson* v. *Forton* [1949] Ch. 143 C.A.

[171] *West Layton Ltd.* v. *Ford* [1979] Q.B. 593 C.A.

[172] *Re Olympia & York Canary Wharf (No.2)* [1994] 2 E.G.L.R. 48 C.A.; L. Crabb [1994] *Conv.* 316.

[173] *Louisville Investments* [1986] Ch. 513, 520.

[174] *Rayburn* v. *Wolf* (1985) H.L.R. 1 C.A.; *Deverall* v. *Wyndham* [1989] 1 E.G.L.R. 57 Div.Ct. (loss of value of reversion of £600,000).

[175] *Leeward Securities Ltd.* v. *Lillyheath Properties Ltd.* [1984] 2 E.G.L.R. 54 C.A.

[176] *Louisville Investments* [1986] Ch. 513, 520B, Balcombe L.J.; *Rayburn* v. *Wolf* (1985) 18 H.L.R. 1 C.A.

[177] *Bates* v. *Donaldson* [1896] 2 Q.B. 241, 247, A.L. Smith L.J.; *Lehmann* v. *McArthur* (1867) L.R. 3 Eq. 746; contrast the dubious decision in *Pimms Ltd.* v. *Tallow Chandler Co.* [1964] 2 Q.B. 547.

[178] *Mount Eden Land Ltd.* v. *Straudley Investments Ltd.* (1997) 74 P. & C.R. 306 C.A.

[179] *Bromley Park Garden Estates Ltd.* v. *Moss* [1982] 1 W.L.R. 1019.

[180] [1925] Ch. 575 C.A.

[181] *Tredegar* v. *Harwood* [1929] A.C. 72, 78, Viscount Dunedin, 80, Lord Shaw, 82, Lord Phillimore; G. Kodilinye [1988] *Conv.* 45, 46–49.

[182] *Bromley Park Gardens Estates Ltd.* v. *Moss* [1982] 1 W.L.R. 1019, 1031B, Cumming-Bruce L.J.

[183] *Norwich Union Life Insurance Society* v. *Shopmoor Ltd.* [1998] 2 All E.R. 32, Scott V.C.; *Blockbuster Estates Ltd.* v. *Leakcliff Properties Ltd.* [1997] 1 E.G.L.R. 28 Ch.D.

4. Estate management

Many landlords own an estate of neighbouring properties, and they are entitled to man-age the estate as a whole.[184] Pollock M.R. in *Houlder Brothers & Co. Ltd.* v. *Gibbs* recog-nised the validity of such concerns,[185] an extension supported by subsequent Court of Appeal decisions,[186] and also by the House of Lords in *Tredegar* v. *Harwood*. In a case concerning fire insurance on a large estate of houses, members of the House indicated, obiter, that a landlord was entitled to refuse consent to sales of houses which might threaten uniformity across the estate.[187] A landlord may also consider the impact of the transaction on the letting potential of other units[188] and the landlord's own redevelop-ment proposals.[189]

G. EXPRESS TERMS AND CONDITIONS

1. Express terms restricting the landlord's discretion

If a covenant is qualified, statute[190] requires that consent must not be unreasonably withheld, but extra control can be imposed on the landlord's behaviour. Some leases, for example, provide that consent should not be refused in the case of a respectable and responsible assignee.[191] The statutory requirement to act reasonably has superimposed upon it the contractual requirement and the landlord must observe both. This result is preserved by the 1988 Act in most obscure language: a landlord acts reasonably in refus-ing consent to a proposed transaction only if the tenant would be in breach of covenant if he proceeded with the transaction without consent.[192] In other words, a transaction must be allowed if permission for it is given by the express terms of the lease.[193]

2. Express terms restricting the tenant's right to insist on reasonableness

Under the general law *express terms limiting a tenant* are ignored, because the statutory requirement to act reasonably applies "notwithstanding anything to the contrary" in the lease.[194] According to *Creery* v. *Summersell*[195] this overrides any contractual agreement

---

[184] *Bridewell Hospital Governors* v. *Fawkner* (1892) 8 T.L.R. 637 (General Booth of the Salvation Army); *Crown Estate Commissioners* v. *Signet Group plc.* [1996] 2 E.G.L.R. 200; G. Lloyd-Brunt (2000) 144 *S.J.* 244.

[185] [1925] Ch. 575, 582–583, Pollock M.R.; G. Kodilinye [1988] *Conv.* 45.

[186] *Bickel* v. *Duke of Westminster* [1977] Q.B. 517, 523H, 524C–G, Lord Denning M.R.; *Louisville Investments* [1986] 1 Ch. 513, 519–521, Balcombe L.J.; *Re Town Investments Underlease* [1954] Ch. 301, 315, Danckwerts L.J.; L. Crabb [1987] *Conv.* 381, 385.

[187] [1929] A.C. 72, 78, Viscount Dunedin, 80, Lord Shaw.

[188] *Premier Confectionery (London) Co. Ltd.* v. *London Commercial Sale Rooms Ltd.* [1933] Ch. 904 was criticised in *Louisville* [1986] Ch. 513, 522–523; *F.W. Woolworth plc.* v. *Charlwood Alliance Properties Ltd.* [1987] 1 E.G.L.R. 53 (Manchester Arndale Centre); L. Crabb [1987] *Conv.* 381; *West Layton Ltd.* v. *Ford* [1979] Q.B. 593 C.A.

[189] *Pimms Ltd.* v. *Tallow Chandlers Co.* [1964] 2 Q.B. 547.

[190] L.T.A. 1927 s.19.

[191] *Moat* v. *Martin* [1950] 1 K.B. 175, 181, Denning L.J.; *De Soysa* v. *De Pless Pol* [1912] A.C. 194 H.L.; *Re Greater London Property Ltd.'s Lease* [1959] 1 W.L.R. 503; (1959) 75 *L.Q.R.* 306.

[192] L.T.A. 1988 s.1(5).

[193] T. Aldridge (1989) 133 *S.J.* 1277; Law Com. No.161 (1987), 9.

[194] L.T.A. 1927 s.19(1).

[195] [1949] Ch. 751, 759–760, Harman J.; *Houlder Brothers & Co. Ltd.* v. *Gibbs* [1925] Ch. 575, 585, Warrington L.J.; *Willson* v. *Fynn* [1948] 2 All E.R. 40, 43B, Denning J.; G. Kodilinye [1988] *Conv.* 45.

about what is reasonable, and it also strikes down a clause requiring an offer to surrender the lease before being allowed to sell it.[196]

3. Conditions imposed by the landlord

A lease may, and usually will, require the payment of the landlord's reasonable legal expense, the normal wording covering both successful and unsuccessful applications for consent.[197] But granting consents should not be a source of profit[198]: without an express provision[199] the landlord is not allowed to ask for a *fine* for the granting of consent,[200] a concept which includes indirect profits like a tied house clause,[201] but not entry into a surety or indemnity covenant. Payment is not illegal, so the "very unfortunate"[202] rule is that a fine that has been paid cannot be recovered,[203] but the tenant is free to assign if the landlord makes an improper demand.[204] The landlord can impose reasonable *conditions*, provided they are set out in the written notice of decision,[205] perhaps requiring sureties[206] or entry into direct covenants.[207] This last is not a "fine".[208] If an attempt is made to impose unreasonable conditions, consent is deemed to be given free of conditions.[209]

4. Licence to assign

Landlords generally give consent by means of a licence to assign. Since the new tenant is usually required to enter into a express covenant to observe the terms of the lease, it is usual to join the new tenant as a party, along with any new surety. If outright consent to assign has been given, attaching a condition that the consent is "subject to formal licence" is meaningless, and the consent is valid.[210] A concluded licence to assign is not revocable,[211] unless it is voidable on account of its having been obtained by fraud, and

---

[196] *Re Smith's Lease* [1951] 1 All E.R. 346, Roxburgh J.; E.O. Walford (1950) 14 *Conv. (N.S.)* 303; *Bocardo S.A.* v. *S. & M. Hotels Ltd.* [1980] 1 W.L.R. 17 C.A.; R. Sheldon & M. Friend (1982) 98 *L.Q.R.* 14; C.G. Blake [1980] *Conv.* 14.

[197] On a solicitor's undertaking to pay see: *Goldman* v. *Abbott* [1989] 2 E.G.L.R. 78 C.A.; *Dong Bang Minerva (U.K.) Ltd.* v. *Davina Ltd.* [1996] 2 E.G.L.R. 31 C.A.; K. Stepien (1994) 138 *S.J.* 910.

[198] *Waite* v. *Jennings* [1906] 2 K.B. 11, 17, Fletcher Moulton L.J.

[199] L.P.A. 1925 s.144, replacing Conveyancing Act 1892 s.3; *F.W. Woolworth & Co. Ltd.* v. *Lambert (No.1)* [1937] Ch. 37 C.A.

[200] L.P.A. 1925 s.205(1)(xxiii).

[201] *Gardner & Co. Ltd.* v. *Cone* [1928] Ch. 955, Maugham J.; *Jenkins* v. *Price* [1907] 2 Ch. 229, Swinfen Eady J.; *Comber* v. *Fleet Electrics Ltd.* [1955] 1 W.L.R. 566, Vaisey J.

[202] *Comber* v. *Fleet Electrics Ltd.* [1955] 1 W.L.R. 566, 571, Vaisey J.

[203] *Waite* v. *Jennings* [1906] 2 K.B. 11, 16, Stirling L.J.; *Andrew* v. *Bridgman* [1908] 1 K.B. 596.

[204] *West* v. *Gwynne* [1911] 2 Ch. 1 C.A.

[205] L.T.A. 1988 s.1(3).

[206] *Vaux Group Ltd.* v. *Lilley* [1991] 1 E.G.L.R. 60, Knox J.; P. Sparkes [1991] *J.B.L.* 494; *Kened Ltd.* v. *Connie Investments Ltd.* [1997] 1 E.G.L.R. 21 C.A.

[207] *Orlando Investments Ltd.* v. *Grosvenor Estate Belgravia* (1990) 59 P. & C.R. 21 C.A.; P. Luxton [1991] *J.B.L.* 57; P.F. Smith [1989] *Conv.* 371 (direct covenant); *Evans* v. *Levy* [1910] 1 Ch. 452 (surety covenant); B.T.D. (1964) 108 *S.J.* 47.

[208] *Waite* v. *Jennings* [1906] 2 K.B. 11, 18 C.A.; *Orlando Investments Ltd.* v. *Grosvenor Estate Belgravia* (1990) 59 P. & C.R. 21 C.A.; P. Luxton [1991] *J.B.L.* 57, 58–59.

[209] L.T.A. 1988 s.1(4); *Re Spark's Lease* [1905] 1 Ch. 456, Swinfen Eady J.

[210] *Venetian Glass Gallery Ltd.* v. *Next Property Ltd.* [1989] 2 E.G.L.R. 42; P. Luxton [1990] *J.B.L.* 246; *Prudential Assurance Co. Ltd.* v. *Mount Eden Land Ltd.* [1997] 1 E.G.L.R. 37 C.A.; *Rutter* v. *Michael John Ltd.* (1966) 201 E.G. 299; *Glynn* v. *Mackay* [1998] 2 C.L.Y. 3649 C.Ct.

[211] *Mitten* v. *Fagg* [1978] 2 E.G.L.R. 40, Goulding J.

even this will not necessarily permit the rescission of a completed assignment of the lease.[212]

5. Business leases under the 1995 Act

The Landlord and Tenant (Covenants) Act 1995[213] inserts a new subsection[214] into the Landlord and Tenant Act 1927 governing qualified covenants so as to give a landlord of business property much greater control. Residential and agricultural leases are unaffected, but business leases are caught whether granted before or after the commencement of the 1995 Act—this is one of the few parts of the 1995 Act which applies to leases granted before its commencement at the beginning of 1996.

Landlord and tenant may agree the circumstances in which the landlord is entitled to withhold his licence to a transfer and also the conditions which may be attached to any grant of consent. This agreement may be contained in the lease or in any later document,[215] but if it is to affect a particular dealing it must be made before an application is made for consent to that dealing. The landlord acts reasonably in withholding consent to an assignment while following the agreed terms.[216] Where any factor is left for determination by the landlord, there must either be a requirement that the landlord act reasonably *or* a right to require an independent review of the landlord's decision.[217] Previously there was no right to insist on a guarantee,[218] but clearly an agreement to require sureties as a condition of consent to a sale would now be valid, and so is a requirement that the assigning tenant should enter into an authorised guarantee agreement.[219]

H. BUYER AND SELLER

When a lease is sold, it is the seller's obligation to obtain the landlord's licence,[220] with damages available if the seller does not use his best endeavours to obtain permission or if a refusal is induced by the seller.[221] The buyer is obliged to co-operate—for example by proffering satisfactory referees when requested.[222] Once consent is obtained, the seller is in a position to serve a completion notice.[223] If the landlord refuses consent, the

---

[212] *Sanctuary H.Ass.* v. *Baker* [1998] 1 E.G.L.R. 42 C.A.

[213] s.27. Creation of a sub-lease is not affected (s.28(1)) though this is normally prevented by an absolute covenant.

[214] L.T.A. 1927 s.19(1A).

[215] s.19(1B).

[216] s.19(1D). On the burden of proof see L. Crabb [2000] *J.B.L.* 182.

[217] s.19(1C); examples of the former might be to enter into an A.G.A. or to assign to a company with a specified capitalisation or to require a director's guarantee. Examples of the latter may be to provide an acceptable guarantor or to conduct an appropriate trade.

[218] *Pakwood Transport Ltd.* v. *15 Beauchamp Place Ltd.* (1978) 36 P. & C.R. 112 C.A.

[219] See below pp. 779–780.

[220] S.C.S. (3rd ed.) cond. 8.3.2; *Lloyd* v. *Crispe* (1813) 5 Taunt. 249, 128 E.R. 685.

[221] *Day* v. *Singleton* [1899] 2 Ch. 320; *Glynn* v. *Mackay* [1998] 2 C.L.Y 3649 C.Ct. (breach of S.C.S. to query P's reference).

[222] S.C.S. (3rd ed.) cond. 8.3.2; *Shires* v. *Brock* [1978] 2 E.G.L.R. 153 C.A.; *Scheggia* v. *Gradwell* [1963] 1 W.L.R. 1049, 1062.

[223] *Frost* v. *Walker* [1994] N.P.C. 60 C.A. (20 days reasonable).

contract falls since the title is then doubtful[224] (even if the refusal is unreasonable), and there is usually a contractual right to rescind.[225] The Standard Conditions of Sale provide that the contract can be rescinded if no licence is available three days before the contractual completion date,[226] irrespective of whether or not the landlord is acting unreasonably. However, these conditions are inadequate, and the Standard Commercial Property Conditions (1999) are much more comprehensive[227]: completion may be deferred for up to four months while consent is obtained and express reference is made to the Landlord and Tenant (Covenants) Act 1995, though express conditions are required if the new tenant is to be allowed to occupy before completion.

I.   DEALINGS WITH THE LANDLORD'S REVERSION

1.   Transfer (assignment of the reversion)

Where the landlord's interest is sold subject to a lease, it is traditional to refer to an "assignment" of the reversion[228] though in this book it is referred to as a transfer (or usually a sale) of the reversion. A deed is required for a legal transfer,[229] as well as land registration formalities where appropriate; if title is unregistered a transfer will often trigger first registration.[230] The tenant cannot generally control the identity of his landlord (except in the case of the right of pre-emption for tenants of a residential block of flats[231]) but the landlord who is selling needs to implement the statutory procedure described below to free himself of liability on the covenants after the sale has been completed.[232]

2.   Transfer of part

Landlords who have a simple method of splitting the reversion so as to create two separate leases simply by selling part of the land,[233] possibly by transferring to a nominee for themselves. Unfortunately the statutory provisions are open to abuse, since a landlord can artificially divide his holding into parts in an attempt to remove security of tenure.[234]

3.   Lease of the reversion

A landlord may create a lease that sits between the reversion and the existing lease,[235] using normal formalities.[236] This is called a concurrent lease or a lease of the rever-

---

[224]   *White* v. *Hay* (1895) 72 L.T. 281.

[225]   *Barings Securities Ltd.* v. *D.G. Durham Group plc.* [1993] E.G.C.S. 192, Ferris J.

[226]   S.C.S. (3rd ed.) cond. 8.3.4.

[227]   J. Martin [1999] 21 *E.G.* 132.

[228]   Woodfall 16.037–16.040; parties are the assignor (seller) and assignee (buyer).

[229]   *Brawley* v. *Wade* (1824) M'Clel. 664, 148 E.R. 278, Hullock B.

[230]   That is if the reversion is freehold or a legal lease with 21 years outstanding.

[231]   See above pp. 426–432.

[232]   See below pp. 748–749.

[233]   L.P.A. 1925 s.140(3) applies generally, but not to a pre-1882 lease, severed before 1926, a shortcoming of the Conveyancing Act 1881 s.12; B. Rudden (1961) 25 *Conv.(N.S.)* 384.

[234]   See below p. 760.

[235]   *Neale* v. *Mackenzie* (1836) 1 M. & W. 747, 150 E.R. 635.

[236]   Must be by deed: L.P.A. 1925 s.52; query whether an oral lease is possible if for less than 3 years: *Brawley* v. *Wade* (1824) M'Clel. 664, 148 E.R. 278.

sion.[237] It could be longer or shorter than the existing lease.[238] For its contractual duration it separates the pre-existing lease and the pre-existing reversion,[239] giving the right
to collect rent from the original tenant.[240] Problems may arise in interpretation of the
original lease, since it may be drafted on the assumption that it will continue to be held
directly from the landlord who granted it.[241]

[237] Before the development of legal charges, this was the normal method of creating second mortgages: *Re Moore
& Hulm's C.* [1912] 2 Ch. 105; L.P.A. 1925 ss.85, 86.

[238] *Stephens* v. *Bridges* (1821) 6 Madd. 66, 56 E.R. 1015; *Burton* v. *Barclay* (1831) 7 Bing. 745, 131 E.R. 288; *Horn*
v. *Beard* [1912] 3 K.B. 181; *Cole* v. *Kelly* [1920] 2 K.B. 106.

[239] *Wright* v. *Burroughes* (1846) 3 C.B. 685, 136 E.R. 274; *Harmer* v. *Bean* (1853) 3 C. & K. 307, 175 E.R. 566;
Wordsley Brewery Co. v. *Halford* (1903) 90 L.T. 89; *Cole* v. *Kelly* [1920] 2 K.B. 106.

[240] This will not occur where the new lease *follows* an existing lease: *Smith* v. *Day* (1837) 2 M. & W. 684, 150 E.R.
931; *Hyde* v. *Warden* (1877) 3 Ex. D. 72 C.A.; *Lewis* v. *Baker* [1905] 1 Ch. 46.

[241] *Adelphi (Estates) Ltd.* v. *Christie* (1983) 47 P. & C.R. 650 C.A.

28

RUNNING OF COVENANTS

New and old law. Estate-based liability under new law. Privity of estate.
Existing breaches. Informal leases. People not liable as estate owners.
Proprietary effect of forfeiture. Covenants not running. Core covenants
(touching and concerning). Tenants unable to pay. Substitutes. Privity of
contract. Sureties. Passing the benefit. Arrears notices. Ending liability.
Reimbursement and indemnity.

This chapter considers the enforcement of the terms of a lease after dealings with it. After an introduction to the major change enacted in 1995, the discussion is grouped into three sections. The first of these considers estate-based liability (or in older language privity of estate), that is enforcement of the terms of the lease between the parties who currently hold the leasehold estate in the land and the reversion. This is followed by a consideration of the package of covenants—those that pass and also those that are treated as peripheral and so incapable of passing to later parties. The final section considers substitute liabilities where the current tenant is unable or unwilling to pay, including the liability of former tenants under either privity of contract or authorised guarantee agreements and also the position of sureties.

A. NEW AND OLD LEASES

The Law Commission prompted a radical reform of the law of the running of covenants.[1] However the original scheme was substantially distorted before it ever reached the statute book as the Landlord and Tenant (Covenants) Act 1995[2] by pressure brought to bear by the commercial landlords' lobby during the passage of the Bill through Parliament. Almost all of its provisions apply only to those leases (inelegantly referred to as "new tenancies") that have been granted after the Act came into force on January 1st 1996.[3] In this book these are called post-1995 leases.[4] The old law[5] continues in force for "old tenancies", that is pre-1996 leases but also including leases granted

---

[1] *Privity of Contract and Estate*, Law Com. No.174 (1988); Law Com. W.P. No. 95 (1986); D. Gordon [1987] *Conv.* 103; T.M. Aldridge (1986) 130 *S.J.* 435; G.L. Leigh (1983) 127 *S.J.* 832; H.W. Wilkinson [1989] *Conv.* 145; H.W. Wilkinson [1992] *Conv.* 393; J. Male [1994] 02 *L.S.G.* 28; S. Shaw [1989] *N.L.J.* 1277.

[2] P. Luxton [1996] *J.B.L.* 388; S. Bridge [1996] *C.L.J.* 313; P.H. Kenny [1996] *Conv.* 3, 81, 237; S. Williams (1996) 11 *J.I.B.F.L.* 230; M. Davey (1996) 59 *M.L.R.* 78; J. Richards [1996] *R.R.L.R.* 22; T. Francourt [1997] *L.T. Rev.* 61.

[3] S.I. 1995/2963; *Oceanic Village Ltd.* v. *United Attractions Ltd.* [2000] Ch. 234, 242F–G, Neuberger J.

[4] Woodfall 11.075A-11.075P; Evans & Smith (5th) 88–99.

[5] Woodfall 11.048A-11.075; Evans & Smith (5th) 77–88; Garner (2nd) 112–129.

after 1995 under old contracts,[6] which means that the dual system will continue in force for generations and centuries to come.

This point is so fundamental and its effect so important that it must be stressed and re-stressed. In any matter concerning the running of covenants between landlord and tenant, the very first issue is to determine whether the lease falls into the old or new world. The crucial date is the grant of the original lease. If that date is in 1996, or any subsequent year, the 1995 Act normally applies, but it remains necessary to check the lease to see whether it states that it was granted under an earlier contractual obligation.

Many business leases are now for relatively short terms, and on renewal they will fall into the new scheme, an adjustment to the terms of the new lease being required to reflect this shift.[7] A lease is also moved to the new system where there is a deemed surrender of an old lease and a regrant as a new lease, for example on a variation of the land which is let or of the length of the leasehold term.[8]

B. ESTATE-BASED LIABILITY

Parties are so confusing that a standard terminology is required. The following diagram indicates the usage adopted here:

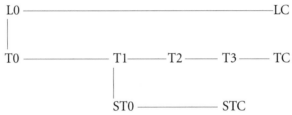

Key:
L = landlord, T = tenant, ST = sub-tenants.
0 = original party; C = current party; 1,2,3 etc = intermediate parties.

After a tenant has bought a lease, he is required for the future to pay the rent for the use of the land and to carry out the other covenants in the lease. Similarly, any promise made by the original landlord—for quiet enjoyment, repair, and so forth—must be honoured by the landlord for the time being. Actions to enforce covenants in a lease are normally taken on the basis of the estate that exists between the current landlord and the current tenant, and these actions (by LC against TC, or TC against LC) form the subject for discussion in the early parts of this chapter. "Privity of estate" was the description applied to this liability under the pre-1996 law, but the phrase is a shorthand, and one which has not been strictly accurate for many years. Privity is not used as a descriptor by the 1995 Act, but the estate-based liability imposed under post-1995 leases is in fact very similar to what went before. Two main differences must be noted: under the old law only

---

[6] s.1 (contracts, court orders and options).
[7] P.H. Kenny [1996] *Conv.* 3.
[8] *Friends Provident Life Office* v. *British Railways Board* [1996] 1 All E.R. 336 C.A.; F. Jenkins [1996] 07 *L.S.G.* 24.

covenants that touched and concerned the land passed, and a distinction was drawn between legal and equitable leases. The new law is all-embracing, treated the whole bundle of covenants in a lease as a single package, and all leases are treated alike. All this, and more, must now be described.

Joint tenants are joint debtors, who owe the same primary liability to the landlord, and are usually (subject to any express contractual terms) jointly and severally liable.[9] Thus if there are two tenants[10] the landlord may sue A, or B, or A and B collectively, but if A is targeted, B is liable to contribute one half to A.[11] Care must be taken not to lose contribution rights, as may occur if one tenant reaches an agreement with the landlord behind the back of the potential contributor.[12]

C. NEW ESTATE-BASED LIABILITY

1. Liability of current estate owners

Clearly leases can only be transferred satisfactorily if both the benefit and the burden of the covenants in the lease are able to run,[13] so that the current tenant pays the rent, and the current landlord collects it. The Landlord and Tenant (Covenants) Act 1995 ensures that this is indeed the case for fresh leases granted after 1995, always excluding contractual replacements for old leases.[14] All covenants do indeed pass with the leasehold term and with the reversion, so as to be enforceable between the current parties to the lease.[15] The current tenant (TC) is liable to the current landlord (LC) on all covenants in the lease for the duration of his ownership, and when the whole lease is disposed of, this passes the benefit and burden of all covenants to the new tenant, binding him immediately.[16] Existing arrears will not pass, but may be assigned separately.[17] In the same way, covenants are annexed and incident to the reversion, so that a new landlord is bound by the terms of the lease, and also entitled immediately to the benefit of the tenant's covenants.[18] It makes no difference whether the covenant relates to existing buildings or to future additions.[19]

2. The single package

A fundamental reform of the 1995 Act code is that it applies to *all* covenants in new leases, the lease forming a single package. It is no longer necessary to differentiate

---

[9] s.28(4); the same is true of the old law.

[10] s.13(2).

[11] Civil Liability (Contribution) Act 1978 as amended by L.T. (Covenants) A. 1995 s.13(3); *Morris* v. *Wentworth-Stanley* [1999] 2 W.L.R. 470 C.A.; *Stimpson* v. *Smith* [1999] N.L.J. 414 C.A.; *Co-operative Retail Services Ltd.* v. *Taylor Young Partnerships Ltd.* [2000] Independent July 14th; *Howkins & Harrison* v. *Tyler* [2000] Times August 8th C.A.

[12] *B.S.E. Trading Ltd.* v. *Hands* [1996] 2 E.G.L.R. 214 C.A.

[13] *City of London Corporation* v. *Fell* [1994] 1 A.C. 458, 464G, Lord Templeman.

[14] L.T. (Covenants) A. 1995 s.1; L.P.A. 1925 ss.78–79 and 141–142 are repealed.

[15] L.T. (Covenants) A. 1995 s.2; *Oceanic Village Ltd.* v. *United Attractions Ltd.* [2000] Ch. 234, 242–247, Neuberger J. (enforcement between neighbouring tenants).

[16] L.T. (Covenants) A. 1995 s.3(2); a personal waiver or release is disregarded: s.3(4).

[17] s.23(2); contrast the old law; see below pp. 753–755.

[18] ss.3(3), 24. On the definition of landlords' covenants in s.28 see *Oceanic Village Ltd.* v. *United Attractions Ltd.* [2000] Ch. 234, 242–247, Neuberger J.

[19] s.3(7) confirming that the old *in esse* rule is irrelevant.

between peripheral and core covenants, express and implied covenants,[20] or the terms of the lease and those of collateral agreements.[21] Burdens will *not* pass to a current estate owner if the covenant is expressed to be personal, or if it is an option that is void for non-registration; also on a physical division if the covenant solely affects another part of the land, and certain covenants imposed under the right to buy scheme.[22]

3. Release of previous tenants

Authorised assignments are ones that are permitted, either by the terms of the lease or by a consent given by the landlord in the particular case, meaning that the assignment is not a breach of covenant and that there is no right of forfeiture after it has occurred. An unauthorised transfer of a post-1995 lease releases the former tenant from liability for all covenants, including any that are personal. Full release is dependent upon a sale of the whole premises, whereas if only a part is sold, the release relates solely to that part.[23] Previous tenants cannot be liable for the defaults of current tenants directly (as opposed to accepting a substitute liability to guarantee their performance under an Authorised Guarantee Agreement), so indemnity covenants are no longer required.[24] Releases operate prospectively from the date of the sale, leaving existing arrears and defaults unaffected.[25]

No release occurs on an "excluded assignment" a concept that takes two forms[26]: *first* any transmission by operation of law such as that which occurs on death to the personal representatives or on bankruptcy to the trustee in bankruptcy and *second* any assignment in breach of covenant. Any tenant who parts with the lease must take care to ensure that the terms of any covenant against assignment are complied with, so that the transaction is authorised and he is able to secure his release. Liability is attached to the new tenant by an unauthorised sale, but the former tenant is not released; both will be freed, prospectively,[27] after the next non-excluded assignment.[28]

4. Release of previous landlords

Release is not automatic on a sale or gift of the *reversion*, the reason for the difference in rule being that a tenant is unable to vet his new landlord. Rather, a reversioner must apply to be released, again for the future only,[29] and only for the part sold, when he assigns the premises.[30] It is up to the old landlord to initiate a release by giving a notice to the tenant,[31] either before, or up to four weeks after, the transfer. This should be done as a matter of automatic practice. Release follows four weeks after receipt of the notice

---

[20] s.2(1).

[21] s.28(1).

[22] s.2(1); see below p. 765.

[23] s.5(2)–(4), respectively the whole, parts, and previous divisions.

[24] s.14 repeals L.P.A. 1925 s.77(1)(c)–(d) and L.R.A. 1925 s.24(1)(b)–(c); for A.G.A.s see below pp. 790–791.

[25] L.T. (Covenants) A. 1995 s.24(1).

[26] s.11(1); the "or" should read "and".

[27] s.24(3).

[28] s.11(2).

[29] s.24(1).

[30] s.6; F. Jenkins [1999] 20 *P.L.J.* 22.

[31] S.I. 1995/2964 form 3 (current landlord of whole); form 4 (part), form 5 (former landlord), form 6 (former landlord, part); see also L.T.A. 1985 s.3(3A).

by the tenant if he has not by then objected. Tenants will be likely to object only if the financial solvency of the new landlord is doubtful. Disputes are resolved by an application by the landlord for a court declaration.[32] Four weeks after completion of a dealing with the reversion the old landlord loses his ability to apply for a release, and, although it is true that another chance occurs on the next sale,[33] how is the former owner to know that this second opportunity has presented itself? No release occurs on a transmission of the reversion by operation of law,[34] at least until the next authorised assignment when both transmitter and receiver will be discharged.

5. Existing breaches

The 1995 Act ensures that estate-based liability arises between the parties to a post-1995 lease who are privy to the estate at the time of the breach.[35] Liability for arrears does not pass on an assignment. Unfortunately, as explained below, this is not the rule for old leases.[36]

6. Informal leases

The Landlord and Tenant (Covenants) Act 1995 applies whether leases are legal or equitable and whether assignments are formal or informal. This is a considerable change, but just how radical it is must be considered below.[37]

D. OLD PRIVITY OF ESTATE

Medieval common law did not allow any stranger to take advantage of the benefit of a covenant according to the preamble to the Grantees of Reversions Act 1540.[38] So, the lease was essentially a private contract and not at all proprietary in character.

The motivating force behind the Grantees of Reversions Act 1540 was Henry VIII's wish to off-load monastic land, much of which was let, after it had been forfeited at the time of the Reformation, though the statute also affected leases by common citizens.[39] Legislation was essential to enable buyers to enforce the covenants in a lease: running of express leasehold covenants is based solely on statute, and this is probably also true of terms that are implied.[40] Section 1 allowed the benefit of the tenant's obligations to run between landlords, referring specifically to rights of forfeiture, remedies by action and other conditions, covenants, or agreements and section 2 is a

---

[32] L.T. (Covenants) A. 1995 s.8.

[33] s.8; the time limits are the same.

[34] s.11(3), (4), (7).

[35] ss.23–24.

[36] See below pp. 753–755.

[37] s.28, definitions of "tenancy" and "assignment"; see below pp. 755–757.

[38] *Spencer's case* (1583) 5 Co. Rep. 16a, 77 E.R. 72; Holdsworth's *History*, vol.7, 287; *Re King* [1963] Ch. 459, 479, Lord Denning M.R.

[39] *Hill* v. *Grange* (1556) 2 Dyer 130b, 73 E.R. 284; *Re King* at 479, Lord Denning M.R.

[40] *Wedd* v. *Porter* [1910] 2 K.B. 91, 100–101, Swinfen Eady L.J.; *Cole* v. *Kelly* [1920] 2 K.B. 106 C.A.; *Re King* at 479, Lord Denning M.R.

corresponding provision for burdens. The 1540 Act and 1881 amendments[41] were consolidated in 1925.[42]

1. Passing the benefit between landlords after 1925

A current landlord is enabled to enforce the core obligations of the lease[43] since statute passes the benefit between landlords. Express mention is given to rights of forfeiture, rent, and the benefit of every other covenant having reference to the subject matter of the lease; these are "annexed and incident to, and shall go with, the reversionary estate".[44] It is not possible to separate the rent from the reversion, or to create a new rent when assigning a lease, except, that is, by the device of a reversionary lease.[45] Action is brought by the person who can show title to the immediate reversionary estate—for example by transfer,[46] under an Act,[47] or by estoppel.[48]

2. Original landlord against current tenant

This is the archetypal case in which the original landlord seeks to sue the current tenant (L0 v. TC).

L0
|
T0 ——————— TC

Henry VIII was only concerned to deal with the successors to the original monastic landlords,[49] so the 1540 Act left a gap, plugged by the Elizabethan decision in *Spencer's case*.[50] Spencer and his wife (together being L0) had leased land to S (T0) who had assigned to J (T1), who in turn assigned to Clarke (TC). When the Spencers sought to enforce a covenant to erect a wall, they failed, but only because the covenant was worded so as to be personal to the original tenant. Coke's report contains scant reference to the

---

[41] Conveyancing Act 1881 s.10 as amended by Conveyancing Act 1911 s.2 (provision for severance of the reversion and extension to informal leases).

[42] L.P.A. 1925 ss.141–142.

[43] *Darrell* v. *Wybone* (1561) 2 Dyer 206b, 73 E.R. 455; *Matures* v. *Westwood* (1598) Cro. Eliz. 599, 78 E.R. 842; *Thursby* v. *Plant* (1669) 1 Saund. 230, 85 E.R. 254; *Martyn* v. *Williams* (1857) 1 H. & N. 817, 156 E.R. 1430; *Stuart* v. *Joy* [1904] 1 K.B. 362.

[44] L.P.A. 1925 s.141(1) for all leases whenever made; subs.(4) applies where severance of the reversion occurred before 1882.

[45] See below p. 760.

[46] *Davis* v. *James* (1884) 26 Ch.D. 778; *Pledge & Sons* v. *Pomfret* (1905) 74 L.J.Ch. 357; *Harris* v. *Beavan* (1828) 4 Bing. 646, 130 E.R. 918.

[47] *Sutherland Orphan Asylum* v. *River Wear Commissioners* [1912] 1 Ch. 191; *Halifax* v. *Coal Commissioners* [1945] Ch. 253.

[48] *Cuthbertson* v. *Irving* (1860) 6 H. & N. 135, 158 E.R. 56.

[49] L0 was covered only if he was a grantee of the Crown.

[50] (1583) 5 Co. Rep. 16a, 77 E.R. 72.

Act, and this meant that the rules for the running of covenants between tenants became established as a common law rule, operating outside the statute.[51] But this was erroneous. Careful reading of the last words of Coke's report shows that the case was decided by Wray C.J. on the 1540 Act:

> "See the statute of 32 Henry 8 [1540] c.24 which Act *was resolved to* extend to covenants which touch or concern the thing demised and not to collateral covenants."[52]

So the case was decided on the equity of the 1540 Statute.[53] As reported, the case focuses on whether or not the particular covenant was collateral.

The Conveyancing Act 1881 did not cover the action L0–TC, but sat on top of the 1540 Act amending it in detail. Unfortunately the 1925 legislators misunderstood this legislative structure and clumsy consolidation opened an enormous chasm in the modern statutory provisions: the 1540 Act was repealed, leaving the consolidated form of the 1881 Act as a stand-alone provision, with no wording to cover the commonplace L0–TC action. Leases created between 1925 and 1996 operate without any legislative support for the passage of covenants between tenants.[54] The authority of *Spencer's case* for the common law action against the current tenant rests on a repealed Act.

It is the current tenant who can be sued under *Spencer's case* in an action taken by the current landlord who takes the benefit under section 141. The defendant may be the original tenant if he retains the lease, a later tenant who takes by assignment, or a tenant of any part. Liability rests on holding the legal estate. Adverse possession does not effect a transfer of the lease to the squatter, who cannot, therefore, be sued on a repairing covenant.[55] It is all too easy for a tenant to plead an assignment to attempt to get out of the landlord's way. Even a transfer in breach of covenant suffices,[56] though the landlord can insist on liability being imposed after a fraudulent transfer, for example because the old tenant retains possession after the sale.[57] A buyer who secures a licence to assign from the landlord may become liable by estoppel, especially after taking possession,[58] though not simply by paying rent.[59]

3.   Enforcement between current parties

This is an archetypal case, in which the current landlord takes action against the current tenant (LC v. TC):

---

[51] *Williams* v. *Earle* (1868) L.R. 3 Q.B. 739, Blackburn J.; *Muller* v. *Trafford* [1901] 1 Ch. 54, 61–62, Farwell J.

[52] At 18a.

[53] *Hill* v. *Grange* (1556) 2 Dyer 130b, 73 E.R. 284; *Hyde* v. *Windsor* (1597) Cro. Eliz. 457, 552, 78 E.R. 710, 798 (Dean and Chapter of Windsor (L0) could sue TC under 1540 Act).

[54] G.D. Muggeridge (1934) 50 *L.Q.R.* 66.

[55] *Tichborne* v. *Weir* (1892) 67 L.T. 735 C.A.; *Re Nisbet & Potts' C.* [1905] 1 Ch. 391; *Taylor* v. *Twinberrow* [1930] 2 K.B. 16; *Fairweather* v. *St Marylebone Property Co. Ltd.* [1963] A.C. 510 H.L.

[56] *Paul* v. *Nurse* (1828) 8 B. & C. 486, 108 E.R. 1123. This would render the lease liable to forfeiture.

[57] *Knight* v. *Peachee* (1679) Freem. K.B. 465, 89 E.R. 347; *Doe d. Hemmings* v. *Durnford* (1832) 2 Cr. & J. 667, 149 E.R. 286; *Beale* v. *Sanders* (1837) 3 Bing. N.C. 850, 132 E.R. 638; *Williams* v. *Heales* (1874) L.R. 9 C.P. 177 (receipt of rent from sub-tenant); *Stratford on Avon C.* v. *Parker* [1914] 2 K.B. 562.

[58] *Rodenhurst Estates Ltd.* v. *Barnes Ltd.* [1936] 2 All E.R. 3 C.A.

[59] *Official Trustee of Charity Lands* v. *Ferriman Trust Ltd.* [1937] 3 All E.R. 85.

This action was expressly covered by the Grantees of Reversions Act 1540,[60] but it slipped out of the legislation by mistake at the time of the 1925 consolidation. The benefit passes between landlords (L0 to L1 to L2 etc.) by statute, but it is necessary to call in aid the "common law" rule in *Spencer's case* to explain how the burden runs between tenants (T0 to T1 to T2 etc.). This unfortunate mistake has destroyed the symmetry of the old law, left the 1881 amendments free standing, and means that pre-1881 cases are an unreliable guide to modern law.[61] Estate-based liability has survived the Parliamentary fumbling,[62] but by mistake the burden of informal and equitable leases is prevented from running.[63]

4. Passing the burden between landlords

Commercial leases make landlords (collectively) responsible for quiet enjoyment and possibly for some aspects of repair. Enforcement is fully catered for by section 142 of the Law of Property Act 1925.[64] The obligation under a condition or core covenant entered into by a landlord shall be annexed to and go with that reversionary estate. Liability is naturally restricted to the extent that the landlord has power to bind successive owners. The obligation may be taken advantage of by, and enforced against, any person entitled from time to time to the reversionary estate. If the landlord's interest has been split after 1881 the burden attaches to the divided parts of the reversionary estate.[65] Informality has made no difference since 1925.[66]

The rules vindicate an action taken by the current tenant against the current landlord (TC v. LC). Section 142 provides that the covenant can be taken advantage of by any person holding the leasehold term from time to time, irrespective of how the lease came to be vested in him.[67] So section 142 follows the 1540 Act in passing both the burden between landlords and the benefit of landlord's covenants between tenants.[68] Thus:

[60] s.1.

[61] *Re King* [1963] Ch. 459, 483, 490, 494.

[62] *Moss Empires Ltd.* v. *Olympia (Liverpool) Ltd.* [1939] A.C. 544 H.L.

[63] See below pp. 755–757.

[64] Restating the effect of Grantees of Reversions Act 1540 s.2 and Conveyancing Act 1881 s.11, and applying to any lease whenever made.

[65] L.P.A. 1925 s.142(2).

[66] *Breams Property Investments Ltd.* v. *Stroulger* [1948] 2 K.B. 1, 7–8, Scott L.J.

[67] E.g. by conveyance, devolution of law or otherwise. There is no equivalent to s.141(2) which allows a person entitled to the income from the reversionary estate to sue the tenant on tenant's covenants: *Duncliffe* v. *Caerfelin Properties Ltd.* [1989] 2 E.G.L.R. 38, 39J, Garland J.

[68] *Muller* v. *Trafford* [1901] 1 Ch. 54, 61, Farwell J., is misleading.

Section 142 therefore justifies the action against the original landlord if he still holds the reversion (L0),[69] or against the current holder of the reversion (LC) if it has been sold.[70]

5. Special problems

Two matters which are resolved simply enough by the post-1995 law are much more complex for leases which continue to operate under the old law and will require extended treatment in the two succeeding sections; these are the effect of an assignment on existing breaches and the effect of equitable leases and assignments.

E. EXISTING BREACHES (OLD LAW)

The Landlord and Tenant (Covenants) Act 1995 ensures that estate-based liability under leases to which it applies can be pursued between the parties privity to the estate at the time of the breach.[71] Unfortunately this is not the rule for older leases.

1. Breaches by tenants

Pre-1881 law was much like post-1995 law. The benefit of an existing breach of covenant did not pass on an assignment of the reversion. A new landlord could not sue the tenant for arrears due before he became landlord,[72] without a separate assignment of the arrears,[73] and this was also true for implied covenants.[74] If there was a continuing breach of covenant (as, for example, when the property was in disrepair) the right to sue did pass.[75]

A different rule applied for a pre-1996 lease, if the sale of the reversion occurred after 1881.[76] The property involved in *Re King decd.*[77] burnt down and remained in a derelict condition when the tenant died, after which the freehold was compulsorily purchased by the London County Council. The Council's right to sue for damages was nominal (since it intended to knock down the ruined factory) but the original landlord was also held to have no no claim since, according to a majority of the Court of Appeal,[78] their right to sue passed along with the land when it was compulsorily purchased. The right of action is not an independent chose in action, but an integral part of the land. Upjohn L.J. laid emphasis on the central words of section 141, that the benefit of the covenant "is annexed to and incident to and goes with the reversionary estate", which he interpreted as meaning that there is an automatic transfer. The decision was extended in

---

[69] *Webb* v. *Russell* (1789) 3 Term Rep. 393, 401–402, 100 E.R. 639, Kenyon C.J.

[70] *Baylye* v. *Hughes* (1628) Cro. Car. 137, 79 E.R. 720 (1540 Act); *Ricketts* v. *Enfield Churchwardens* [1909] 1 Ch. 544 (Conveyancing Act 1881 s.11).

[71] L.T. (Covenants) Act 1995 ss.23–24.

[72] *Flight* v. *Bentley* (1835) 7 Sim. 149, 58 E.R. 793 is representative of many; *Re Lyne-Stephens & Scott-Miller's C.* [1920] 1 Ch. 472 C.A.

[73] *Ellis* v. *Torrington* [1920] 1 K.B. 399.

[74] *Wedd* v. *Porter* [1916] 2 K.B. 91, 100–101, Swinfen Eady L.J.

[75] *Re King* [1963] Ch. 459, 479, Lord Denning M.R.

[76] L.P.A. 1925 s.141, re-enacting Conveyancing Act 1881 s.10.

[77] [1963] Ch. 459 C.A.

[78] At 488, Upjohn L.J., supported by Diplock L.J.; Lord Denning's dissent is more convincing: R. Thornton (1991) 11 *L.S.* 47, 51.

London & County (A. & D.) Ltd. v. *Wilfred Sportsman Ltd.*[79] to existing arrears *of rent*. Hence it is clear, at least to the level of the Court of Appeal, that the benefit of an existing breach does pass on a sale of the reversion.

2. Forfeiture

As with the new law, a right to forfeit is not waived by a sale of the landlord's reversion, so that the buyer of the landlord's interest can sue for forfeiture for breaches occurring during his predecessor's time. Section 141(3) provides that:

> "Where that person becomes entitled by conveyance . . . such provision [for forfeiture] may be . . . taken advantage of by him notwithstanding that he becomes entitled after the condition of re-entry or forfeiture has become enforceable."

This was always the case for continuing breaches,[80] but for single breaches it represented a reform of the law,[81] the change occurring in 1911.[82] Thus in modern law, if there is (1) an existing right to forfeit, and (2) a sale of the reversion subject to the forfeitable lease, the right to forfeit survives the sale. Protection of the right to forfeit applies to any dealing with the reversion, including for example the grant of a reversionary lease.[83] In *Kataria* v. *Safeland plc*.[84] the current landlord was not personally owed any rent because, when he bought the reversion, he had assigned existing arrears to the previous landlord who sold to him. Nevertheless the new landlord was entitled to forfeit the lease for the breach of covenant involved in non-payment of rent to the previous landlord.

3. Breaches by landlords

The statute that passes benefits between tenants[85] does not pass the right to sue for breaches of covenant committed by a previous landlord. In *City and Metropolitan Properties Ltd.* v. *Greycroft Ltd*.[86] T0 could sue for damages for disrepair after he had sold the lease to TC at profit. This is because of a notable absence from section 142; there is no suggestion that the burden of a landlord's covenant is to be "annexed to and go with" the reversion.[87] One unfortunate consequence is that two possible plaintiffs—both TC and TC–1—can pursue a continuing breach.

So far as *burdens* passing between landlords are concerned, a landlord is liable only for a breach in his own time. In *Duncliffe* v. *Caerfelin Properties Ltd*.[88] it was held that a landlord who bought the reversion was liable for the state of disrepair at the time of acquisition, since this was a continuing breach. But he was not liable for consequential

---

[79] [1971] Ch. 764 C.A.

[80] *Rickett* v. *Green* [1910] 1 K.B. 253.

[81] *Fenn d. Matthews* v. *Smart* (1810) 12 East. 444, 104 E.R. 173; *Flight* v. *Bentley* (1835) 7 Sim. 149, 151, 58 E.R. 793; *Cohen* v. *Tannar* [1900] 2 Q.B. 609 C.A.

[82] Conveyancing Act 1911 s.2, now L.P.A. 1925 s.141(3); *Atkin* v. *Rose* [1923] 1 Ch. 522.

[83] *London & County (A. & D.) Ltd.* v. *Wilfred Sportsman Ltd.* [1971] Ch. 764 C.A.; *Davenport* v. *Smith* [1921] 2 Ch. 270 doubted.

[84] [1998] 1 E.G.L.R. 39 C.A.

[85] L.P.A. 1925 s.142.

[86] [1987] 1 W.L.R. 1085; P.F. Smith [1987] *Conv.* 374; *Pettiward Estates Ltd.* v. *Shephard* [1986] C.L.Y. 1861.

[87] See above p. 753.

[88] [1989] 2 E.G.L.R. 38, Garland J.; P.F. Smith [1990] *Conv.* 335, 345; J.E. Martin [1990] *Conv.* 126; *Oakley* v. *Martin* [1993] 06 E.G. 113 L.Tr.

loss which the tenant incurred before the new landlord came on the scene. Action to recover that damage could only be pursued against the previous landlord who had actually caused the damage.

F.   INFORMAL LEASES (OLD LAW)

The Landlord and Tenant (Covenants) Act 1995 applies whether leases are legal or equitable and whether assignments are formal or informal.[89] This is a change from the old law, which requires much lengthier study.

1.   Between landlords

The Grantees of Reversions Act 1540 referred to "covenants comprised in the Indentures of their said leases, demises and grants", so that the scope of the Act was limited strictly to leases by deed.[90] Extensions were made[91] to include written leases in 1881,[92] and oral leases in 1925.[93]

2.   Between tenants

The statutory rules just described between landlords do not apply between tenants. *Spencer's case*,[94] which governed the running of covenants between tenants, was restricted by analogy by the 1540 Act—certainly to legal leases and possibly even more tightly to those by deed. Later statutory extensions to written leases and oral tenancies did not apply as between tenants. So the basic principle of orthodox dogma is that the burden of the covenants in an equitable lease does not run between tenants.

Relevant principles are simply stated; it is just a question of how to knit them together. (1) The terms of the agreement can be enforced between the original parties as decided in the classic case of *Walsh* v. *Lonsdale*,[95] even after the expiration of the term of the agreement.[96] (2) The benefit of a contract is assignable, allowing LC to sue T0.[97] (3) The burden of a contract cannot be assigned in contract law. (4) As just explained, the Grantees of Reversions Act 1540 applied only if the lease was by deed and *Spencer's case* was apparently limited in the same way. (5) Statutory provisions such as those in the Law of Property Act 1925[98] apply to equitable leases, but these operate only to transfers of

---

[89] s.28, definitions of "tenancy" and "assignment".

[90] *Standen* v. *Christmas* (1847) 10 Q.B. 135, 116 E.R. 53; *Bickford* v. *Parson* (1848) 5 C.B. 920, 136 E.R. 1141; *Smith* v. *Eggington* (1874) L.R. 9 C.P. 145; *Allcock* v. *Moorhouse* (1882) 9 Q.B.D. 366 C.A.

[91] *Re King* [1963] Ch. 459, 483, Lord Denning M.R., 487, Upjohn L.J.

[92] Conveyancing Act 1881 s.10; *Rickett* v. *Green* [1910] 1 K.B. 253; *Gilbey* v. *Cossey* (1912) 106 L.T. 607 D.C.; *Cole* v. *Kelly* [1920] 2 K.B. 106 C.A.; *J. Betts & Sons Ltd.* v. *Price* (1924) 40 T.L.R. 589; *Rye* v. *Purcell* [1926] 1 K.B. 446. See now: L.P.A. 1925 s.154 ("lease" includes an underlease or other tenancy); *Breams Property Investment Co. Ltd.* v. *Stroulger* [1948] 2 K.B. 1, 7, Scott L.J.; *Weg Motors Ltd.* v. *Hales* [1962] Ch. 49, 73, Evershed M.R., 76, Donovan L.J.

[93] L.P.A. 1925 ss.205(1)(xxiii), 154. These were not included in 1881: *Blane* v. *Francis* [1917] 1 K.B. 252 C.A.; *Elliott* v. *Johnson* (1868) L.R. 2 Q.B. 120.

[94] (1585) 5 Co. Rep. 16a, 77 E.R. 72.

[95] (1882) 21 Ch.D. 9 C.A.; see above pp. 521–534.

[96] *Gilbey* v. *Cossey* (1912) 106 L.T. 607 Div.Ct.

[97] *Manchester Brewery Co. Ltd.* v. *Coombs* [1901] 2 Ch. 608; *Dowell* v. *Dew* (1843) 12 L.J. Ch. 158 (reverse action by TC against L0 permitted).

[98] ss.141, 142.

the reversion between landlords. (6) A specifically performable contract is treated between the original parties as though it had been specifically performed. (7) An estate contract creates an equitable interest in the land that requires registration as a C(iv) land change a protective notice or caution, or occupation of registered land, but once protected it binds the world.

The combined effect of these principles was to prevent the burden of covenants in an equitable lease running between tenants. Old cases to the contrary[99] were repudiated in the early Victorian era.[100] Rent was a legal action and before the procedural fusion of law and equity an equitable entitlement to a lease was insufficient to found an action for rent. Even after the administration of law and equity was fused in a single set of courts in 1875, it was held in *Purchase* v. *Lichfield Brewery Co.*[101] that the position remained unchanged. An agreement for a lease between L0 and T0 was assigned by deed to TC, but since there was neither privity of contract nor of estate between the current parties the landlord was unable to recover rent.[102] If rent had been paid and accepted a common law periodic tenancy arose between LC and TC to justify the rent action. Denning L.J. challenged this view head on in *Boyer* v. *Warbey*, holding that covenants could run under an informal legal tenancy for less than three years and indicating obiter that the same was true of informal contractual arrangements for more than three years. However, his attribution of this last change to the operation of the Judicature Act 1873[103] cannot be correct given *Purchase*. Before 1875 the landlord could resolve his difficulty, at the expense of additional litigation costs, by going to Chancery for an order for specific performance. If *Walsh* v. *Lonsdale*[104] is accepted, this decree was back-dated.[105] With that the landlord could return to the common law court, produce the legal lease and insist on judgment for the rent. Fusion in 1875 would short-circuit the need for these multiple proceedings. However, it seems that the tenant would always have the option of giving up possession and refusing to submit to an action for specific performance by the tenant, since there is nothing to make the burden of the contract run so as to bind him as an outsider to it. If a tenant does submit to specific performance, he becomes liable on the covenants on the agreement, retrospectively so it seems.

3. Informal assignments

An assignment of a leasehold term must be by deed if it is to take effect at law. Otherwise it is only contractual, that is an equitable assignment, and (under the old law) this did not cause the new tenant to become liable on the covenants in the lease. The old law[106]

---

[99] *Lucas* v. *Commerford* (1790) 3 Bro.C.C. 166, 29 E.R. 469, Thurlow L.C.; *Flight* v. *Bentley* (1835) 7 Sim. 149, 58 E.R. 793.

[100] *Moores* v. *Choat* (1839) 8 Sim. 508, 59 E.R. 202; *Moore* v. *Greg* (1848) 2 Ph. 717, 41 E.R. 1120, Lord Cottenham L.C.; *Cox* v. *Bishop* (1857) 8 De G.M. & G. 815, 44 E.R. 604; *Whitton* v. *Peacock* (1836) 2 Bing. (N.C.) 411, 132 E.R. 161 (LC v. TC before L.P.A. 1925 s.141).

[101] [1915] 1 K.B. 184 Div.Ct.; *Friary Holroyd & Healey's Brewery Ltd.* v. *Singelton* [1899] 1 Ch. 86, Romer J., obiter and reversed on the facts: [1899] 2 Ch. 261 C.A.

[102] R.J. Smith [1978] *C.L.J.* 95.

[103] [1953] 1 Q.B. 234, 245, Denning L.J.

[104] (1882) 21 Ch.D. 9 C.A.

[105] P. Sparkes [1989] *J.L.H.* 29.

[106] Contrast L.T. (Covenants) A. 1995 s.28.

dates from the Grantees of Reversions Act 1540, and nothing in *Spencer's case*[107] or the 1925 statutes[108] affects it as between tenants. Thus, in *Cox* v. *Bishop*,[109] it was held that taking possession under an agreement for an assignment was not sufficient to enable a landlord to sue on the covenants in the lease. However, a tenant who conducts himself so as to lead the landlord to believe that it is a legal assignee may become bound by an estoppel.[110] Further, a new tenant might be pressured to accept specific performance of the contract for assignment if he wants to keep his lease. A potential tenant who submits to specific performance will retrospectively become bound by the lease.

G. PHYSICAL DIVISION

1. New law

A major objective of the 1995 reforms was to introduce a safe method of physical division of a lease. Where only a part is sold, whether it is the lease or the reversion, the liabilities under the lease are apportioned, and so is the possibility of forfeiture; similar principles apply to a partial disclaimer. If a covenant "falls to be complied with" in relation to a specific part,[111] the tenant of that part is obviously bound, but the tenant of the other part takes free of any covenant which has no impact on his part.[112] Hence if a tenant of part commits a breach entitling the landlord to forfeit the lease, he will only be able to forfeit that part, and the "innocent" tenant of the other part will be unaffected.[113] If the covenant affects both parts, liability is apportioned: owners of both parts are bound, but they can reach an agreement about how to apportion liability, including a total exclusion of liability for one part[114]; that agreement can be made binding on the other party—for example a landlord—by a notice and counter-notice[115] procedure.[116]

In short the 1995 reforms enable sub-division of the holding to take place by physical division rather than by sub-letting, a safe title being created by an assignment of a part subject to a binding apportionment. Control of estate management can be retained by the inclusion of an absolute covenant against dealing with parts, which means that any division is an "excluded assignment".[117]

---

[107] An equitable tenant for life was not liable: *Arkwright* v. *Colt* (1842) 2 Y. & C. Ch. Cas. 4, 63 E.R. 2.

[108] *Rickett* v. *Green* [1910] 1 K.B. 253 (on the Conveyancing Act 1881); to the contrary is *Manchester Brewery Co. Ltd.* v. *Coombs* [1901] 2 Ch. 608, 619, Farwell J.

[109] (1857) 8 De G.M. & G. 815, 44 E.R. 604.

[110] *Rodenhurst Estates Ltd.* v. *Barnes Ltd.* [1936] 2 All E.R. 3 C.A.

[111] L.T. (Covenants) A. 1995 s.28(2).

[112] s.3(2) (lease), (3) (reversion). *Oceanic Village Ltd.* v. *United Attractions Ltd.* [2000] Ch. 234, 242F–G, Neuberger J., shows that the same is true of landlords' covenants.

[113] ss.4, 21.

[114] s.9.

[115] S.I. 1995/2964 forms 7 and 8; P.H. Kenny [1996] *Conv.* 324.

[116] s.10; s.26(3) preserves other statutory procedures for apportionment, e.g. under the Inclosure Acts.

[117] s.11; see above p. 748.

2. Division of landlord's reversion—old law

So long as one concerns oneself with leases split after 1925,[118] the law is simple. The holder of the reversion in any part can enforce the covenants or forfeit the lease against the tenant of any part.[119]

The 1540 Act did, after some discussion, extend to buyers of part,[120] and this is now made clear by the 1925 legislation.[121] Difficulties caused by landlords holding as tenants in common[122] have been cured by the 1925 reforms of co-ownership.[123] A buyer of part of the reversion could compel apportionment of the rent[124] so that, on an equal division, each new landlord is entitled to half the rent, with the benefit annexed to each part of the reversionary estate in the land.

3. Severance to avoid security of tenure legislation

Section 140 of the Law of Property Act 1925 permits the severance of a holding into its several parts. Thus in *Land* v. *Sykes*,[125] the landlord of a farm conveyed a strip of land to Crittendens, and was afterwards able to serve a valid[126] notice to quit the farm, excluding the strip already sold. The lease operates after a severance as if only the current part was originally comprised in lease, meaning that a notice to quit can be served affecting each individual part.[127] A landlord is able to sever off parts of the property which will not in isolation attract security of tenure and shave these of the tenant's protected holding. For example the landlord of a renewable lease can split off parts not occupied by the tenant for the purposes of his business, and after a notice to end the tenancy of this part the tenant will have no renewal rights.[128] Success has varied according to the exact wording of individual legislation and case law reveals many unsuccessful ruses by landlords. Artificial divisions, for example by transferring part to a bare trustee for the landlord— have not been successful to defeat agricultural security of tenure.[129] In *Jelley* v. *Buckman*[130] the landlord severed the reversionary title to a house, with residential security of tenure, from the adjoining land. The new owner of the adjoining land claimed possession of it, but it was held to be "let together" with the house so that the whole unit

---

[118] L.P.A. 1925 s.140(3) applies generally, but not to pre-1882 leases severed before 1926 (since the Conveyancing Act 1881 s.12 did not apply).

[119] B. Rudden (1961) 25 *Conv.(N.S.)* 384.

[120] *Twynam* v. *Pickard* (1818) 2 B. & Ald. 105, 106 E.R. 305. *Badeley* v. *Vigurs* (1854) 4 E. & B. 71, 119 E.R. 28 (2 out of 3 tenants in common).

[121] L.P.A. 1925 s.141; *Swansea Corporation* v. *Thomas* (1882) 10 Q.B.D. 48, Pollock B.

[122] *Twynam* v. *Pickard* (1818) 2 B. & Ald. 105, 106 E.R. 305; *Swansea Corporation* v. *Thomas* (1882) 10 Q.B.D. 48 (privity of contract case); *Roberts* v. *Holland* [1893] 1 Q.B. 665.

[123] L.P.A. 1925 s.36.

[124] *Walter* v. *Maunde* (1820) 1 Jac. & W. 181, 37 E.R. 344.

[125] [1992] 1 E.G.L.R. 1 C.A.

[126] The tenant omitted to take proper steps to claim agricultural security of tenure.

[127] Previously a notice to quit part was bad: *Price* v. *Evans* (1874) 29 L.T. 835; *Re Bebington's T.* [1921] 1 Ch. 559. The last case is overruled by subs.(2): *Smith* v. *Kinsey* [1936] 3 All E.R. 73.

[128] *William Skelton & Son Ltd.* v. *Harrison & Pinder* [1975] Q.B. 361.

[129] *Persey* v. *Bazley* [1983] 2 E.G.L.R. 3 C.A.; J.E. Martin [1985] *Conv.* 292.

[130] [1974] Q.B. 488 C.A.; *Neville Long & Co. (Boards) Ltd.* v. *Firemanaich* [1983] 2 E.G.L.R. 76 C.A. (business premises and easement); *Dodson Bull Carpet Co.* v. *City of London Corporation* [1975] 1 W.L.R. 781, Goff J.

attracted residential security, a principle that overrode section 140. Tenants may also be protected by estoppel.[131]

Since a landlord is able to end part of a lease by notice, a tenant might be left with an *unusable or undesirable part* of the original holding, in which case the tenant has the right, exercisable within one month of the partial termination, to demand that the landlord also accept the termination of the remainder.[132]

4. Division of lease—old law

Covenants that support and maintain the thing demised followed each part of the lease:

> "Let them go where they will. They stick so fast to the thing on which they wait that they follow every part of it. For if lessee assigns 20 parts to 20 persons he may follow the assignee of every part."[133]

Hence the burden of the tenant's covenants has always been divisible.[134] If part of the land is surrendered, the tenant remains liable on the other part,[135] and must limit his liability to that part by appropriate pleading.[136]

5. Rights of forfeiture

These are also divisible. Either the reversionary estate or the leasehold estate can be severed into parts, causing the burden of any right of forfeiture to be annexed to and enforced against the severed parts. How severance occurs is irrelevant. Pre-1859 law drew a distinction between a severance that occurred by an act of law, which did not split the forfeiture right,[137] and a severance by voluntary act, which destroyed the forfeiture right over both parts.[138] This was all very inconvenient, but is rarely a practical problem today.[139]

The fundamental problem with the old law was that the landlord could forfeit the whole lease for a breach of covenant occurring on another part, admittedly with a claim to relief by the tenant of the innocent part. There was no procedure to compel a landlord to accept an apportionment of liability agreed between the tenants on the division of the parts. Buyers rarely accepted this title and insisted that sub-division should occur by a sub-lease. Hopefully the simpler procedures under the 1995 Act will ensure that leases are readily divisible.

---

[131] *John* v. *George* [1996] 1 E.G.L.R. 7 C.A.

[132] L.P.A. 1925 s.140(2); *Liddy* v. *Kennedy* (1871) L.R. 5 H.L. 134 H.L. (Irish Act).

[133] *Bally* v. *Wells* (1769) Wilm. 341, 346, 97 E.R. 130.

[134] *United Dairies Ltd.* v. *Public Trustee* [1923] 1 K.B. 469, 473, Greer J. lists older authorities. See also *Stevenson* v. *Lambard* (1802) 2 East. 575, 102 E.R. 480, Ellenborough C.J.; *Norval* v. *Pascoe* (1864) 34 L.J. Ch. 82.

[135] *Baynton* v. *Morgan* (1888) 22 Q.B.D. 74 C.A.

[136] *Merceron* v. *Dowson* (1826) 5 B. & C. 479, 108 E.R. 179.

[137] *Winter's case* (1572) 3 Dyer 308b, 73 E.R. 697; *Piggott* v. *Middlesex C.C.* [1909] 1 Ch. 134 (c.p.o.).

[138] *Knight's case* (1588) 5 Co. Rep. 54b, 77 E.R. 137; *Hyde* v. *Warden* (1877) 3 Ex.D. 72 C.A. (no problem if part vested in tenant himself). Total destruction of the forfeiture clause was also occasioned by any partial waiver of any breach: *Dumpor's case* (1603) 4 Co. Rep. 119b, 76 E.R. 1110; *Wright* v. *Burroughes* (1846) 3 C.B. 685, 136 E.R. 274.

[139] L.P.A. 1925 s.143, replacing L.P. Am.A. 1859 s.1; *G.M.S. Syndicate Ltd.* v. *Gary Elliott Ltd.* [1982] Ch. 1; R. Griffith [1981] *Conv.* 381.

H. PEOPLE NOT LIABLE AS ESTATE OWNERS

1. Sub-tenants

Privity of estate does not exist unless the person holding the land is the immediate ten-ant of the landlord.[140] There is no privity between head landlord and a sub-tenant,[141] a rule which precludes the sub-tenant from enforcing landlord's covenants contained in the head-lease,[142] and which also prevents action against the sub-tenant. This does not mean that a sub-tenant can flout the covenants affecting the head lease for many reasons: there is always the possibility of forfeiture, the head landlord applies pressure to his tenant (the sub-landlord) to enforce the covenant against the sub-tenant, restric-tive covenants may be enforced against anyone with notice,[143] and it is possible for covenants in a sub-lease to be worded in such a way that the head-landlord secures the benefit of covenants in the sub-lease between T and ST.[144] A sub-tenant can be made liable to pay rent by a rent diversion notice.[145] Otherwise the sub-tenant must be wary of paying rent to the head landlord, since the rent under the two leases are different debts, and there will usually be no restitutionary reimbursement.[146]

2. Original parties after the grant of a reversionary leases

The landlord can give the right to the rents for a fixed period by a reversionary lease,[147] even orally.[148] Once this has been done there is no direct privity of estate between the original landlord and the original tenant since the reversionary lease is inserted between the old landlord and the original tenant, who becomes a sub-tenant holding from the tenant under the reversionary lease. An existing landlord can exploit this device in order to curtail his liability to an existing tenant.

3. Intermediate tenants

Liability of an intermediate tenant begins and ends with his character as estate holder.[149] Having passed on the lease they are exempt from action. Thus in *Granada Theatres Ltd. v. Freehold Investment (Leytonstone) Ltd.*[150] the current tenant was not liable for past breaches of a repairing covenant committed by his predecessor, though clearly an intermediate tenant might become liable at the time of his acquisition of a lease, subject to a continuing duty to see that the property is kept in repair. The exemption of inter-

---

[140] L.T. (Covenants) A. 1995 s.3 applies to *assignment.*
[141] *Hall* v. *Ewin* (1887) 37 Ch.D. 74 C.A. (covenant still enforceable as a restrictive covenant).
[142] *South of England Dairies Ltd.* v. *Baker* [1906] 2 Ch. 631, Joyce J.
[143] L.T. (Covenants) A. 1995 s.3(5).
[144] L.P.A. 1925 s.56; *Amsprop Trading Ltd.* v. *Harris Distribution Ltd.* [1997] 1 W.L.R. 1025, Neuberger J.; Sparkes *N.L.L.* 608–609; similar results can now be achieved by the Contracts (Rights of Third Parties) Act 1999; M. Shelton [2000] *R.R.L.R.* 89.
[145] See above p. 649.
[146] See below pp. 788–790.
[147] *London & County (A. & D.) Ltd.* v. *Wilfred Sportsman Ltd.* [1971] Ch. 764 C.A.
[148] *Plummer & John* v. *David* [1920] 1 K.B. 326, Lush J.
[149] *Onslow* v. *Corrie* (1817) 2 Madd. 330, 56 E.R. 357; *Gooch* v. *Clutterbuck* [1899] 2 Q.B. 148 C.A.
[150] [1959] Ch. 592 C.A.

mediate tenants was settled very early.[151] After he has sold on, he is still liable to be sued, but only for breaches occurring while he was tenant.[152] Leases could be sold to a poor person to curtail liability and, indeed, trustees in bankruptcy were once advised to do just this.[153] Landlords often overcame this limitation by taking an express covenant from a new tenant.[154]

4. Beneficiaries

Rent is a legal obligation that affects the trustees rather than the beneficiaries under a trust of the lease.[155]

5. Enforcement against a lender secured by a mortgage of the lease

Creditors secured by a mortgage of a lease commonly wish to blow hot and cold, avoiding liability on the lease themselves but having the right to pursue the tenant for rent and disrepair. So long as the borrower is left in possession of the land, the lender is not a party to the leasehold estate and cannot be sued on the landlord's covenants. However, the law is not quite as comfortable for lenders as it used to be, since the covenants are enforceable against a lender who takes possession from the tenant, a liability that can no longer be avoided.[156] This is a change in the law.

Lenders secured on a leasehold estate naturally wish to be able to pursue the tenant for rent without themselves becoming liable to the tenant on the landlord's covenants in the lease. The old law was rather too cosy for lenders. In the eighteenth century mortgages were made by assignment of the estate being mortgaged, so legal lenders became the legal tenant and as such liable to the landlord on the covenants in the lease.[157] This unwelcome liability was avoided by developing the practice of taking a mortgage by sub-demise so that as a sub-tenant the lender could not be liable to the landlord.[158] After 1925 a lease may only be mortgaged by sub-demise[159] and a legal charge acts in the same way.[160] Hence lenders are not generally liable on the covenants in pre-1996 leases, and taking possession makes no difference.

---

[151] *Overton* v. *Sydal* (1597) Cro. Eliz. 555, 78 E.R. 801; *Marrow* v. *Turpin* (1599) Cro. Eliz. 715, 78 E.R. 949; *Pitcher* v. *Tovey* (1692) 4 Mod. Rep. 71, 87 E.R. 268; *City of London* v. *Richmond* (1701) 2 Vern. 421, 23 E.R. 870, on appeal (1702) 1 Bro. Parl. Cas. 516, 1 E.R. 727 H.L.

[152] *Harley* v. *King* (1835) 2 Cr. M. & R. 18, 150 E.R. 8, Abinger C.B.

[153] *Onslow* v. *Corrie* (1817) 2 Madd. 330, 56 E.R. 357, Plumer V.C.; *Hopkinson* v. *Lovering* (1883) 11 Q.B.D. 92, Denman J. (review of earlier cases).

[154] See below pp. 778–790.

[155] *Walters* v. *Northern Coal Mining Co.* (1855) 5 De G.M. & G. 628, 43 E.R. 1015; *Cox* v. *Bishop* (1857) 8 De G.M. & G. 815, 44 E.R. 604; *Ramage* v. *Womack* [1900] 1 Q.B. 116, Wright J.; *Schalit* v. *Joseph Nadler Ltd.* [1933] 2 K.B 79 (bare trust); H. Potter (1933) 49 *L.Q.R.* 486; D.H. Parry (1934) 50 *L.Q.R.* 158; H. Potter (1934) 50 *L.Q.R.* 320. Payment of rent to a beneficiary could be a defence to an action by the landlord: *Bankes* v. *Jarvis* [1903] 1 K.B. 549.

[156] L.T. (Covenants) A. 1995 s.15(3), (4); F. Jenkins [1996] 07 *L.S.G.* 24.

[157] *Williams* v. *Bosanquet* (1819) 1 Brod. & Bing. 238, 129 E.R. 714.

[158] *Hand* v. *Blow* [1901] 2 Ch. 721; *Re J.W. Abbott & Co. Ltd.* (1913) 30 T.L.R. 13.

[159] L.P.A. 1925 s.86.

[160] s.87.

6.   Enforcement by a lender secured by a mortgage of the reversion

A major departure from "privity of estate" is the rule that landlord's covenants are enforceable *against* a tenant by any lender,[161] even though the lender has no direct estate-based relationship with the tenant. This rule for post-1995 leases reproduces the effect of the old law.

Lenders secured by a mortgage of the landlord's reversion have a different problem. They wish to be able to collect the rent from the tenant without being held liable to the tenant for breach of any repairing covenants in the lease. Before 1881 legal title in the borrower precluded action by the lender[162] unless there was a direct covenant. After 1881,[163] any tenant's covenant can be enforced by any person entitled to the income of the land leased. Literally this seems to allow both parties to a mortgage of the landlord's reversion to sue,[164] but the courts have interpreted it as an either/or provision that allocates the right of action to the borrower while in possession,[165] but passes it to the lender if he takes possession of the rents.[166] The ability of a lender to sue when he is not privy to the leasehold estate between landlord and tenant shows that "privity of estate" has not been a strictly accurate delineation of the entitlement to enforce leasehold covenants since 1881.

I.   PROPRIETARY EFFECT OF FORFEITURE

A landlord may use the threat of forfeiture as a means to secure payment of rent, since to avoid termination of the lease the tenant is obliged to pay all arrears of rent with interest. This threat is effective where a lease has value, for example because the rent is below market value, or because the tenant paid a premium for a lease, and some of the value of the premium remains. If the lease is onerous—because the rental level exceeds market value or as a result of heavy repairing obligations—a threat of forfeiture is unwise since it will give the tenant an opportunity to bolt.

The *burden* of the landlord's right to re-enter the tenant's land and to terminate the lease where the tenant breaks a covenant with an associated proviso for forfeiture is a right that is proprietary in character. It binds not only the original tenant but also anyone deriving title from him. If it is a legal right—that is if it is contained in a legal lease[167]—it binds any subsequent derivative title. If contained in an equitable lease or imposed on assignment of a legal lease,[168] the right to forfeit is equitable, in which case enforceability against an unregistered title is based on the doctrine of notice[169]; if title is registered, protection is by notice, caution, or occupation.

---

[161] L.T. (Covenants) A. 1995 s.15(1), (2).

[162] *Webb* v. *Russell* (1789) 3 Term. Rep. 393, 100 E.R. 639; *Matthews* v. *Usher* [1900] 2 Q.B. 535 C.A.

[163] L.P.A. 1925 s.141(2) re-enacting Conveyancing Act 1881 s.10(1).

[164] Wolstenholme & Cherry, *Conveyancing Statutes* (13th ed. by J.T. Farrand, Oyez, 1972) i, 258.

[165] *Turner* v. *Walsh* [1909] 2 K.B. 484 C.A.

[166] *Re Ind Coope & Co. Ltd.* [1911] 2 Ch. 223.

[167] L.P.A. 1925 s.1(2), (3); right of re-entry = right of forfeiture.

[168] *Doe d. Freeman* v. *Bateman* (1818) 2 B. & Ald. 168, 106 E.R. 328; *Hyde* v. *Warden* (1877) 3 Ex. D. 72, 84; *Shiloh Spinners Ltd.* v. *Harding* [1973] A.C. 691, 717, Lord Wilberforce.

[169] *Shiloh Spinners Ltd.* at 718C, 721, Lord Wilberforce.

Forfeiture therefore affects a buyer of the lease, or of any part of the property let, a sub-tenant, or any mortgage-lender. All derivative interests fall.[170] True, this is subject to the possibility of a sub-tenant seeking relief from forfeiture, but this will usually only be available if the breach of the terms of the head lease is remedied.[171]

Thus:

Before   L0 ——————— LC   After   LC
          | |
          T0 —————— TC   Claims to relief
                   | from forfeiture
                   ST0 ———————————— STC   by TC/ST/Lender
                                    |
                                 Lender.

The Landlord and Tenant (Covenants) Act 1995 makes specific provision for the transmission of the *benefit* of rights of entry for post-1995 leases. Forfeiture rights are annexed and incident to the reversion, and so pass on a sale. If the reversion[172] or lease[173] is divided, the right of forfeiture is divided appropriately. Sale does not affect the right of re-entry, unless a waiver occurs.[174]

For *old leases*, section 141 of the Law of Property Act 1925[175] carries forward the *benefit* of forfeiture provisions which, are "annexed and incident to and shall go with the reversionary estate", including all core covenants such as rent and repairing obligations, and apparently also peripheral covenants.[176] Since any right of forfeiture is an independent property right, separate from the lease, it should pass automatically as a vested right with the landlords' reversion. If the reversion or lease is divided the right to forfeit passes with each part.[177]

J. THE PACKAGE: COVENANTS WHICH DO NOT RUN

New and old laws are considered together.

1. Personal covenants

Under the *new law* any covenant can be excluded from the single package created by the covenants in a post-1995 lease and so excluded from the automatic transfer of the benefit and burden of covenants on any transfer, by qualifying the wording of the covenant

---

[170] *Hall* v. *Griffin* [1987] 1 E.G.L.R. 81 C.A.
[171] At least for the part occupied by the sub-tenant; see below pp. 812–815.
[172] s.4(b).
[173] s.21.
[174] s.23.
[175] The earlier statutes were: Grantees of Reversions Act 1540 s.1; Conveyancing Act 1881 s.10 as amended by the Conveyancing Act 1911 s.2. The question of existing breaches is discussed above at p. 754.
[176] *Shiloh Spinners* [1973] A.C. 691, 717H–718A, Lord Wilberforce.
[177] L.P.A. 1925 s.141.

so as to make it personal.[178] If this is done, liability will remain between the original parties.[179]

The *old law* was elucidated by Lord Oliver in *P. & A. Swift Investments* v. *Combined English Stores Group plc.*,[180] who stated that a covenant could not touch and concern the land if it was expressed to be personal, so that it was given only to a specific reversioner or in respect of the obligations of a specific tenant. No doubt Lord Oliver recognised the possibility of a covenant being personal on one side (say to the original tenant) but proprietary on the other side. Ordinarily, leasehold covenants will be presumed to be proprietary without any need to mention assigns[181]—as for example in the case of a covenant against assignment of a petrol station.[182] The contractual scope of the covenant has to be restricted if it is intended to give it only a personal effect,[183] preferably by an express declaration.[184] In many cases this has to be gathered from construction of the contract. If a landlord covenants not to give notice to quit to a tenant "so long as you desire to continue *my* tenant", the italicised word makes it clear that the covenant is personal.[185] A personal restriction was also implied in *Hua Chiao Commercial Bank Ltd.* v. *Chiaphua Industries Ltd.*,[186] where one party was defined to include successors but the other is not, which implied that the correct construction was that the covenant was assignable on one side but not on the other,[187] and in *Re Royal Victoria Pavilion, Ramsgate,*[188] where a covenant to procure that the Royal Victoria Pavilion should only be used for performances by live actors was held to be personal, given the use of words of personal obligation.

2.   Options void for non-registration

Leasehold options require registration[189] and so can lose priority through a failure of registration, particularly where title is unregistered. Covenants are not binding on a new tenant if the previous tenant who is assigning was not bound, and here, no doubt, the new Act[190] reproduces the old law.

---

[178] L.T. (Covenants) A. 1995 s.15.

[179] Unless the benefit is assignable.

[180] [1989] A.C. 632, 642F.

[181] *Spencer's case* (1583) 5 Co. Rep. 16a, 77 E.R. 72; the problem of covenants relating to a thing not in existence (not *in esse*) under the second resolution is now solved by L.P.A. 1925 s.79(1).

[182] *Caerns Motor Services Ltd.* v. *Texaco Ltd.* [1994] 1 W.L.R. 1249.

[183] *Kumar* v. *Dunning* [1989] Q.B. 193, 197, Browne-Wilkinson V.C.

[184] *Eccles* v. *Mills* [1898] A.C. 360 P.C.

[185] *Roberts* v. *Tregaskis* (1878) 38 L.T. 176; *Muller* v. *Trafford* [1901] 1 Ch. 54, Farwell J. ("in case the said David Austin shall obtain" personal).

[186] [1987] A.C. 99 P.C.

[187] *Re Robert Stephenson & Co.* [1915] 1 Ch. 802; *Federated Homes Ltd.* v. *Mill Lodge Ltd.* [1980] 1 W.L.R. 594 C.A.

[188] [1961] Ch. 581 (excluded by implication); *Morrells of Oxford Ltd.* v. *Oxford United F.C. Ltd.* [2000] Times August 15th C.A. (personal).

[189] Sparkes *N.L.L.* 179–180. The same is true of restrictive covenants as between neighbouring tenants: *Oceanic Village Ltd.* v. *United Attractions Ltd.* [2000] Ch. 234, Neuberger J.; see above p. ***.

[190] L.T. (Covenants) A. 1995 s.3(6)(b).

3.   Right to buy discounts

When a public sector flat is sold on a long lease under the right to buy scheme, covenants may be imposed to repay a discount on a sale or to require redemption of the landlord's share.[191] Both types are personal.

4.   Core covenants (covenants which touch and concern/have reference)

The reforms effected by the *Landlord and Tenant (Covenants) Act 1995* have an enormous theoretical impact, even if the practical effect of the change is likely to be minimal. New leases form a package, under which all the terms agreed between original landlord and tenant pass, a package including also covenants with outside parties such as management companies.[192] Hence it is no longer necessary to separate covenants which are central from those which are merely peripheral, except perhaps for the one advantage that a covenant which touches and concerns is exempt from the effects of the perpetuity rule.[193] The reform follows that suggested by some American commentators[194] who questioned the wisdom of attempting to identify central covenants, but it remains to be seen whether eccentric or over-zealous landlords will begin to abuse their new found freedom. Only core covenants were capable of running under the *old law*, that is for pre-1996 leases; their identity is considered immediately below.

K.   CORE COVENANTS

Where the pre-1996 law applies to a lease, covenants run only if they form one of the core obligations of the lease. Unfortunately there are two ways to describe this concept: *Spencer's case* (1583) used the phrase "touch and concern" to identify covenants which pass with leasehold land as between tenants,[195] whereas between landlords the statutory rules require that a covenant should "have reference to the subject matter of the lease".[196] The two expressions are exact equivalents, and the change in wording has not altered the class of covenants defined.[197]

Cheshire's test for covenants that touch and concern the land, which is often used today, is:

> "Does it affect the landlord in his normal capacity as landlord or the tenant in his normal capacity as tenant?"[198]

---

[191] s.2(1).

[192] ss.3(6)(b), 12.

[193] *Muller* v. *Trafford* [1901] 1 Ch. 54, 60–61, Farwell J.; *Coronation Street Industrial Properties Ltd.* v. *Ingall Industries plc* [1989] 1 W.L.R. 304, 307H–308A, Lord Templeman.

[194] Summarised by Gray's *Elements* (2nd ed.) 860–861.

[195] Lord Loreburn in *Dewar* v. *Goodman* [1909] A.C. 72, 75 said touch *or* concern, but *Spencer's case* (1583) 5 Co. Rep. 16a, 16b, 77 E.R. 72, uses the negative phraseology "doth not touch or concern", which suggests that "and" is correct in the positive formulation; H.A. Bigelow (1914) 30 *L.Q.R.* 319; Holdsworth's *History*, vii, 287–292.

[196] L.P.A. 1925 ss.141–142.

[197] *Davis* v. *Town Properties Investment Corporation Ltd.* [1903] 1 Ch. 797, 805, Cozens-Hardy L.J.; *Breams Property Investment Co. Ltd.* v. *Stroulger* [1948] 2 K.B. 1, 7, Scott L.J., 9, Asquith L.J.

[198] Cheshire & Burn, *Modern Law of Real Property* (15th ed.) 446; *Hua Chiao Commercial Bank Ltd.* v. *Chiaphua Industries Ltd.* [1987] A.C. 99, 107, Lord Oliver.

The more precise test stated by Bayley J. in *Congleton Corporation* v. *Pattison*[199] is definitive of the law[200] after judicial approval in the highest courts[201]:

"The covenant must either: (1) affect the land itself during the term, or (2) be such as by itself, and not merely from collateral circumstances, affects the value of the land."

Despite its apparent simplicity, the authorities applying this test were notoriously lacking in principle: Romer L.J. once said that the question whether a covenant touched and concerned the land was identical to the question whether there was authority for it,[202] but a spate of appellate decisions late in the twentieth century has introduced some coherence.[203] Most covenants usually agreed between landlord and tenant are in fact treated as part of the core, though one peripheral covenant which surely ought to run is a covenant to repay a deposit to a tenant at the end of the lease.[204] The remainder of this section considers what covenants form the core.

1. Money payments

Rent is at the heart of every lease—especially from the landlord's point of view—and no covenant can be more central to the relationship of landlord and tenant than the covenant to pay rent. So naturally it runs,[205] a point settled even before *Spencer's case.*[206]

Service charge payments, water charges,[207] and similar sums can be *reserved as rent.* When, in *Vyvyan* v. *Arthur*,[208] a tenant of agricultural land covenanted to grind all corn grown on the land let to him at the landlord's mill, this was held to be a core covenant that could run. Perhaps the best explanation is that the landlord's milling fees were an additional profit in the nature of rent.[209] However some logical limit has to be imposed, to prevent every collateral payment being made to run simply by reservation as an additional rent.[210]

Surety covenants are covenants to pay rent or other liabilities if the tenant defaults. The House of Lords held in *P. & A. Swift Investments* v. *Combined English Stores plc.*[211] that the covenant by a surety does touch and concern the land. This decision extirpated

---

[199] (1810) 10 East. 130, 103 E.R. 725.

[200] *Keppell* v. *Bailey* (1834) 2 My. & K. 517, 538, 39 E.R. 1042, Lord Brougham L.C.; *Horsey Estate Ltd.* v. *Steiger* [1899] 2 Q.B. 79, 89, Russell L.C.J.; *Forster* v. *Elvet Colliery Co. Ltd.* [1908] 1 K.B. 629, 640, Farwell L.J.; *Kumar* v. *Dunning* [1989] Q.B. 193, 200D, Browne-Wilkinson V.C.

[201] *Hua Ciao Bank Ltd.* v. *Chiaphua Industries Ltd.* [1987] A.C. 99, 107, Lord Oliver; *P. & A. Swift Investments* v. *Combined English Stores Group plc.* [1989] A.C. 632, 640, Lord Oliver.

[202] *Grant* v. *Edmondson* [1931] 1 Ch. 1, 28; *P. & A. Swift Investments* v. *Combined English Stores Group plc.* [1989] A.C. 632, 640, Lord Oliver.

[203] C. Harpum [1988] *C.L.J.* 180, 182.

[204] *Hua Chiao Commercial Bank Ltd.* v. *Chiaphua Industries Ltd.* [1987] A.C. 99 P.C.; R. Thornton (1991) 11 *L.S.* 47, 63.

[205] *Parker* v. *Webb* (1693) 3 Salk. 5, 91 E.R. 656; *Kumar* v. *Dunning* [1989] 1 Q.B. 193, 199H, Browne-Wilkinson V.C.

[206] *Walker's case* (1587) 3 Co. Rep. 22b, 76 E.R. 676; Holdsworth's *History*, vii, 287.

[207] *Lambeth L.B.C.* v. *Thomas* (1998) 30 H.L.R. 89 C.A.

[208] (1823) 1 B. & C. 410, 107 E.R. 152. Compare *Uxbridge* v. *Staveland* (1747) 1 Ves. Sen. 56, 27 E.R. 888.

[209] Despite criticism in *Keppell* v. *Bailey* (1834) 2 My. & K. 517, 538, 39 E.R. 1042, Lord Brougham L.C., *Vyvyan* has been cited in many modern cases, e.g. *Swift* [1989] A.C. 632, 640; and *Kumar* v. *Dunning* [1989] Q.B. 193, 204.

[210] *Gower* v. *Postmaster General* (1887) 57 L.T. 527.

[211] [1989] A.C. 632 H.L.; J.E. Adams [1989] 47 *E.G.* 24; see below pp. 780–781.

the heretical view that was common before *Swift* that all money covenants apart from rent were automatically precluded from running. Whereas a tenant promises to do a thing (such as, for example, to repair the property), the surety promises to pay damages if it is not done.[212] Whether a surety covenant can touch and concern the land depends upon whether the obligation guaranteed is part of the core of the lease. Browne-Wilkinson V.C. observed in *Kumar v. Dunning*[213] that a surety covenant is given as a support or buttress to core covenants given by a tenant to a landlord, and so is itself a covenant affecting the nature, quality, or mode of use of the land.[214] *Coronation Street Industrial Properties Ltd. v. Ingall Industries plc.* extended the principle in *Swift* to a covenant by a surety to accept a lease if the tenant was in liquidation.[215]

A controversial and borderline decision[216] denied core status to a covenant to repay a tenant's deposit. In *Hua Chiao Commercial Bank Ltd. v. Chiaphua Industries Ltd.*[217] a tenant provided a deposit equivalent to two months' rent at the outset of the tenancy, the landlord promising to return it when the lease ended if no default had occurred. Characterisation of this covenant as personal by the Privy Council meant that a buyer of the reversion escaped having to return the deposit to his tenant. Lord Oliver said that it was a once and for all money payment, with only an oblique relation to the rent. With due respect to the eminence of the panel that decided the case, it is a difficult decision to accept[218]: a deposit to guarantee performance of the core covenant of paying the rent is surely closely analogous to a surety covenant.

Spencer's case makes clear that a covenant to make *collateral payments* to the landlord does not touch and concern the land.[219] Examples are to pay the landlord's taxes on other land,[220] to pay fees under a building licence, to pay extra rent if the landlord increased the size of the house, to account for profit on wine sold on the land, to pay an annual sum to churchwardens, to repay an unsecured loan and to provide a box in a theatre free of charge.[221]

2. Repair and insurance

A covenant to *repair* clearly touches and concerns the property which is let, a point decided by the sixth resolution of *Spencer's case*, and followed ever since.[222] Covenants to pay money to cover the cost of repairs are also core covenants because, as already

---

[212] At 642.

[213] [1989] 1 Q.B. 193, 199H; C. Harpum [1988] *C.L.J.* 180, 180 ("remarkable and bold"); J.E. Martin [1987] *Conv.* 288; P. Luxton [1987] *J.B.L.* 299.

[214] *Swift* [1989] A.C. 632, 642B–D, Lord Oliver; compare *Kumar v. Dunning* [1989] Q.B. 193, 201H, Browne-Wilkinson V.C.

[215] [1989] 1 W.L.R. 304 H.L.

[216] *Kumar v. Dunning* [1989] Q.B. 193, 206B–F, Browne-Wilkinson V.C.

[217] [1987] A.C. 99 P.C.; *Eden Park Estates Ltd. v. Longman*, noted by P.H. Kenny [1982] *Conv.* 239.

[218] Compensation paid by a landlord to an outgoing tenant does run: *Mansel v. Norton* (1883) 22 Ch.D. 769 C.A.; *Re Hunter's Lease* [1942] Ch. 124; R.E. Megarry (1941) 57 *L.Q.R.* 307; J.S. (1942) 8 *C.L.J.* 99.

[219] (1583) 5 Co. Rep. 16a, 16b (resolution 2), 77 E.R. 72.

[220] *Gower v. Postmaster General* (1887) 57 L.T. 527.

[221] *Camden v. Batterbury* (1860) 7 C.B.N.S. 864, 141 E.R. 1055.

[222] (1583) 5 Co. Rep. 16a, 77 E.R. 72; *Matures v. Westwood* (1598) Cro. Eliz. 599; *Martyn v. Clue* (1852) 18 Q.B. 661, Campbell C.J.; *Williams v. Earle* (1868) L.R. 3 Q.B. 739 (also covenant to repair tenant's fixtures); *Martyn v. Williams* (1857) 1 H. & N. 817, 156 E.R. 1430 (to deliver up in repair).

explained,[223] a money payment touches and concerns if it is a buttress to a covenant which itself touches and concerns. This included the covenant in *Moss Empires Ltd.* v. *Olympia (Liverpool) Ltd.*[224] to expend £500 a year on decoration and repairs and to make up any shortfall,[225] since the money covenant was so inextricably bound up with the repairing covenant that it was impossible to sever the two.[226] Similarly in *Boyer* v. *Warbey*[227] a covenant by a tenant to pay his landlord £40 towards redecoration on quitting the premises did touch and concern the land.

A covenant to *build* on the land that has been let to the tenant affects the nature of the occupation of that land, and so does touch and concern it. Until 1925 covenants were treated less favourably if they did not relate to a thing *in esse*—for example the new wall that was the subject of the litigation in *Spencer's case*; covenants relating to things not yet in existence has to include the word "assigns" if they were to bind future tenants.[228] However modern law has abolished this need for special treatment of building covenants.[229]

A covenant to *insure* against fire was held in *Vernon* v. *Smith*[230] to run with the land. Statute required that if the particular building in that case was burnt down, the insurance money received had to be used in rebuilding. This obligation to reinstate the land showed that the covenant to insure was not merely financial but actually related to the land. Without an obligation to reinstate the case is less strong,[231] but the agreement qualifies for the core because it adds value to the land insured.

3. Use

Covenants regulating the use of the land by the tenant, or the services to be provided by the landlord,[232] are part of the core of the leasehold relationship. The form of covenant will depend up on the type of lease. Commercial leases may prevent use for a particular trade, or preclude use as a shop.[233] Agricultural leases will regulate the method of farming.[234] Residential leases may require personal residence or the keeping of a housekeeper.[235] All touch and concern.

---

[223] See above pp. 766–767.

[224] [1939] A.C. 544 H.L.; *De Walden* v. *Barber* (1903) 19 T.L.R. 183 (covenant to pay damages for breach of restrictive covenant).

[225] This is difficult to reconcile with the main decision that the sum was a debt rather than damages for breach of a repairing covenant.

[226] At 551, Lord Atkin, 560, Lord Porter.

[227] [1953] 1 Q.B. 234 C.A.

[228] *Spencer's case* second resolution; *Keppell* v. *Bailey* (1834) 2 My. & K. 517, 39 E.R. 1042, Lord Brougham L.C.; *Minshull* v. *Oakes* (1858) 2 H. & N. 793, 157 E.R. 327 (heavily qualifying the principle).

[229] L.P.A. 1925 s.79(1); L.T. (Covenants) Act 1995 s.3(7).

[230] (1823) 5 B. & Ald. 1, 106 E.R. 1094.

[231] Platt on *Leases* (1847) ii, 403.

[232] *Jourdain* v. *Wilson* (1821) 4 B. & Ald. 266, 106 E.R. 935 (supply of water).

[233] *Congleton Corporation* v. *Pattison* (1810) 10 East 130, 138, 103 E.R. 725, Bayley J.; *Gibson* v. *Doeg* (1857) 2 H. & N. 615, 157 E.R. 253.

[234] *Sale* v. *Kitchingham* (1713) 10 Mod. 158, 88 E.R. 673; *Cockson* v. *Cock* (1607) Cro. Jac. 125, 79 E.R. 109 (covenant not to plough); *Eccles* v. *Mills* [1898] A.C. 360 P.C. (covenant by landlord to finish laying down 1,000 acres in good English grass; obiter); *Chapman* v. *Smith* [1907] 2 Ch. 97 (to manure).

[235] *Tatem* v. *Chaplin* (1793) 2 H.Bl. 133, 126 E.R. 470; *Barnes* v. *City of London Real Property* [1918] 2 Ch. 18.

Commercial landlords will very commonly want to create a market for their products. A clause compelling the tenant of a pub to sell the landlord's beer is called a *tied house clause*. In *Keppell* v. *Bailey*[236] Lord Brougham inveighed against the running of such covenants, but later in the nineteenth century their proprietary character was firmly established, the tide turning with *Clegg* v. *Hands*.[237] A clause tying the tenant to the original landlord's beer was enforceable by Cain who bought out the landlord's interest. If the landlord owned neighbouring land it was enforceable as a restrictive covenant, but if he held only the reversion, it was enforceable as a leasehold covenant. A pub is not just bricks and mortar, but a business property with associated goodwill and a duty on the tenant to maintain it. The way in which business property is used is of vital concern to the landlord: one example of a core covenant is that a named person (S) is not to be involved in any business on the property.[238] Competition law invalidates many such covenants, but those that survive scrutiny will form part of the core of the lease.[239]

4. Assignment and termination

Who holds the lease is very material to the interest of landlord, and so a covenant by the tenant not to assign,[240] or not to assign without consent,[241] does touch and concern. Termination is cognate, for example in proviso for forfeiture in the event of liquidation of the tenant company,[242] break clauses,[243] and a covenant by the landlord not to serve notice to quit.[244] However, a covenant to pay a premium by instalments does not touch and concern the lease, since it relates to he acquisition of the estate in the land rather than being an incident of a lease.[245]

5. Landlord's covenants affecting the land let

The *Congleton Corporation* principle should apply to landlords just as much as tenants, as illustrated by the landlord's covenant for quiet enjoyment.[246] Covenants to maintain what is let do follow the reversion, examples being a covenant to prevent destruction of

---

[236] (1834) 2 My. & K. 517, 39 E.R. 1042 (limestone from Trevill Quarry).
[237] (1890) 44 Ch.D. 503 C.A.; *White* v. *Southend Hotel Co.* [1897] 1 Ch. 767; *Manchester Brewery Co. Ltd.* v. *Coombs* [1901] 2 Ch. 608, Farwell J.; *Regent Oil Ltd.* v. *J.A. Gregory (Hatch End) Ltd.* [1966] Ch. 402 C.A. (solus agreement for petrol).
[238] *Lewin* v. *American & Colonial Distributors Ltd.* [1945] Ch. 225, 237, Scott L.J.; H.J.A.A. (1945) 9 *C.L.J.* 245.
[239] See above pp. 712–713.
[240] *Williams* v. *Earle* (1868) L.R. 3 Q.B. 739, Blackburn J.; *Re Stephenson Poole & Co. Ltd.* [1915] 1 Ch. 802, Sargant J.; *Caerns Motor Services Ltd.* v. *Texaco Ltd.* [1994] 1 W.L.R. 1249.
[241] *Goldstein* v. *Sanders* [1915] 1 Ch. 549, Eve J.; *Cohen* v. *Popular Restaurants Ltd.* [1917] 1 K.B. 480, 482, Rowlatt J.; *Hemingway Securities Ltd.* v. *Dunraven Ltd.* (1996) 71 P. & C.R. 30, 33, Jacob J. obiter.
[242] *Horsey Estate Ltd.* v. *Steiger* [1899] 2 Q.B. 79, Russell L.J.
[243] *Roe d. Bamford* v. *Hayley* (1810) 12 East. 464, 469, 104 E.R. 181, Ellenborough C.J.; *Liddy* v. *Kennedy* (1871) L.R. 5 H.L. 134 H.L.
[244] *Breams Property Investment Co. Ltd.* v. *Stroulger* [1948] 2 K.B. 1 C.A.; *Prudential Assurance Co. Ltd.* v. *London Residuary Body* [1992] 2 A.C. 386 H.L.
[245] *Hill* v. *Booth* [1930] 1 K.B. 381 C.A.; *Regor Estates Ltd.* v. *Wright* [1951] 1 K.B. 689, 697–698, Cohen L.J.; *Manson* v. *Duke of Westminster* [1981] Q.B. 323 C.A. Reasoning in each of these cases is technical and open to objection.
[246] *Middlemore* v. *Goodale* (1638) Cro. Car. 503, 79 E.R. 1033; *Campbell* v. *Lewis* (1820) 3 Barn. & Ald. 392, 106 E.R. 706; compare *Davis* v. *Town Properties Investment Corporation Ltd.* [1903] 1 Ch. 797 C.A.

incorporeal rights by unity of possession,[247] and a covenant to conduct the business of a public house so as not to cause the suspension of the drinks licence.[248] Surely a covenant by an intermediate landlord to observe the covenants in his head-lease should exemplify this principle? In *Dewar* v. *Goodman*, a covenant by the landlord of one house to observe the terms on which he held the entire estate of 210 houses (that is to repair the other 209 houses) was held not to touch and concern the underlease,[249] but that decision must be wrong.[250]

6. Covenants affecting neighbouring land

Spencer's case required that covenants affect a parcel of the demise, that is the land let to the tenant. *Tenants' covenants* to build a house on other land are collateral,[251] and so (as was just noted) are covenants to pay the landlord's taxes on other land.[252] Only two authorities permit a covenant affecting neighbouring land to touch and concern the land demised.[253] In *Vyvyan* v. *Arthur*[254] a tenant covenanted to grind all corn grown on the land let to him at the landlord's mill. In *Easterby* v. *Sampson*[255] a covenant to build a new smelting mill ran with the reversion, since it tended to the support and maintenance of the thing demised. The latter case in particular is difficult to reconcile with principle.

It is common for a landlord to own neighbouring property, and it is inconvenient that *landlord's covenants* relating to that neighbouring land will usually not touch and concern the tenant's land. Examples are a covenant for quiet enjoyment,[256] a covenant to allow advertisements,[257] and an option to purchase.[258] A covenant restricting the use of the landlord's adjoining land does not touch and concern,[259] but the rule is harsh and the leading decision is borderline.[260] Arguably the *Congleton* test was misunderstood,[261] but in any case such covenants should be enforceable as restrictive covenants.[262]

---

[247] *Bally* v. *Wells* (1769) Wilm. 341, 97 E.R. 130 (tithe); *Vernon* v. *Smith* (1821) 5 B. & Ald. 1, 106 E.R. 1094.

[248] *Fleetwood* v. *Hull* (1889) 23 Q.B.D. 35.

[249] [1909] A.C. 72 H.L.; *Doughty* v. *Bowman* (1848) 11 Q.B. 444, 116 E.R. 543 Ex. Ch.; but that case assumed that an indemnity covenant cannot touch and concern (see Pattison J. at 448) which is inconsistent with *Swift*.

[250] *Dewar* v. *Goodman* as impliedly overruled by *Dyson* v. *Forster* [1909] A.C. 98 H.L.; *Kumar* v. *Dunning* [1989] Q.B. 193, 205G, Browne-Wilkinson V.C.

[251] *Spencer's case* (1583) 5 Co. Rep. 16a (resolution 2), 77 E.R. 72.

[252] *Gower* v. *Postmaster General* (1887) 57 L.T. 527, Kay J.

[253] *Dewar* v. *Goodman* [1909] A.C. 72, 77, Lord Collins; *Ricketts* v. *Enfield Churchwardens* [1909] 1 Ch. 544, 554, Neville J.

[254] (1823) 1 B. & C. 410, 107 E.R. 152.

[255] (1830) 6 Bing. 644, 130 E.R. 1429.

[256] *Davis* v. *Town Properties Investment Corporation Ltd.* [1903] 1 Ch. 797 C.A.

[257] *Re No. 1 Albermarle St.* [1959] Ch. 531.

[258] *Collinson* v. *Lettsom* (1815) 6 Taunt. 224, 128 E.R. 1020.

[259] *Thomas* v. *Hayward* (1869) L.R. 4 Ex. 311 (not to sell spirits or beer on his neighbouring land within half a mile).

[260] *Kumar* v. *Dunning* [1989] Q.B. 193, 205, Browne-Wilkinson V.C.; *Dewar* v. *Goodman* [1908] 1 K.B. 94, 104, Alverstone L.C.J.

[261] Bramwell B. said (at 311) that it does not touch the thing itself even though it touches the beneficial occupation of the thing (which ought to be within the *Congleton Corporation* test).

[262] It could benefit the value of the tenant's leasehold property *as neighbouring land*; *Oceanic Village Ltd.* v. *United Attractions Ltd.* [2000] Ch. 234, Neuberger J.; above pp. 711–712.

A covenant should be treated as central to a lease if it requires work on neighbouring land, in circumstances where the work has a direct impact on the property let to the tenant. An example is a covenant to repair an adjacent sea wall so as to preserve the land that is let is enforceable by a purchaser of the lease.[263] Leasehold schemes are used for developments of houses on a building estate[264] and for blocks of flats, and it is quite clear that a covenant to repair the common parts must touch and concern the individual units: the whole point of using leasehold schemes is to make these positive covenants run.[265]

Covenants *restricting the use of neighbouring land* present problems, because they have a dual character as leasehold *and* restrictive covenants. The same test for touching and concerning is applied in all contexts, including for example the passing of the benefit of a positive covenant at common law, and restrictive covenants. But with freehold land, it is applied in relation to land of the person with the benefit of the covenant (usually neighbouring land) rather than in relation to the land burdened by the covenant (the land let to a tenant). Application of the same test[266] in these different contexts can lead to divergent decisions about the same covenant.[267] The point is often ignored,[268] but illumination floods from *Dyson* v. *Forster*.[269] A lease of mining rights granted by the owner of minerals (who did not own the surface) contained a covenant by the tenant of the mine to pay compensation to the owner of the surface. The surface owner was brought within the benefit of the covenant only[270] if the covenant touched and concerned some land of the person to whom the promise is made, that is of the surface owner.[271] The decision was that it did, since it prevented subsidence and so enhanced the value of the surface land.

7.   Covenants affecting the value of the landlord's reversion

A covenant that does not affect the method of occupation of the land let to the tenant must fall into the second head of *Congleton Corporation* v. *Pattison*,[272] by affecting the value of the land *per se* and not through collateral circumstances.

According to Browne-Wilkinson V.C., approving the rule stated by Best J. in *Vyvyan* v. *Arthur*,[273] the *acid test* is whether the covenant is of value to the landowner from time to time and to no other person.[274] This test has been applied repeatedly. In *Vernon* v.

---

[263] *Lyle* v. *Smith* [1909] 2 I.R. 58; *Morland* v. *Cook* (1868) L.R. 6 Eq. 252.

[264] *Ricketts* v. *Enfield Churchwardens* [1909] 1 Ch. 544 (building line); *Wheeler* v. *Birmingham Chamber of Commerce Pension Funds & Trustees Co.* [1954] C.L.Y. 1803 C.Ct. (covenant to make up road).

[265] For post-1995 leases, the point is covered by L.T. (Covenants) A. 1995 s.12.

[266] *Rogers* v. *Hosegood* [1900] 2 Ch. 388 C.A.; C. Harpum [1988] *C.L.J.* 180, 182. For the new law see *Oceanic Village Ltd.* v. *United Attractions Ltd.* [2000] Ch. 234, Neuberger J.

[267] *Rogers* v. *Hosegood* [1900] 2 Ch. 388, 395, Farwell J.

[268] *P. & A. Swift Investments* v. *Combined English Stores Group plc.* [1989] A.C. 632, 640, Lord Oliver.

[269] [1909] A.C. 98 H.L., on appeal from *Forster* v. *Elvet Colliery Co. Ltd.* [1908] 1 K.B. 629 C.A.

[270] Real Property Act 1845 s.5; but L.P.A. 1925 s.56 is wider.

[271] Under the 1845 Act the covenant had to be "respecting *any* land or tenements" which is not the same as whether it touches and concerns *the* land let to a tenant.

[272] (1808) 10 East. 130, 103 E.R. 725.

[273] (1823) 1 B. & C. 410, 107 E.R. 152 (covenant to grind corn grown on tenant's land at landlord's neighbouring mill).

[274] *Kumar* v. *Dunning* [1989] Q.B. 193, 204, approved in *Swift* [1989] A.C. 632, 640–641, Lord Oliver. Despite *Keppell* v. *Bailey* (1834) 2 My. & K. 517, 538, 39 E.R. 1042, Lord Brougham L.C.

Smith[275] a covenant to insure could only benefit the owner of the estate as owner, so it did touch and concern. Similarly in *Forster* v. *Elvet Colliery Co. Ltd.*[276] a covenant by the tenant of minerals with the owner of the surface to pay compensation for any damage caused by mining benefited only the surface owner and so did touch and concern the surface. In *Kumar* v. *Dunning* it was held that a surety covenant qualified as a covenant touching and concerning the land under this head.[277]

A *collateral effect on the value* of the land to the landlord is not sufficient to make a covenant part of the core of the lease. In *Congleton Corporation* v. *Pattison* itself,[278] a lease of Byflatt Silk Mill contained a covenant not to employ workers from outside the parish. This was designed to limit claims for poor relief and so keep down the poor rate in the parish, but this link was held to be too tenuous to allow the covenant to touch and concern the reversion.

L. TENANTS UNABLE TO PAY

1. Insolvent tenants

Insolvency is not technically a defence to an action for rent,[279] but in practice it prevents recovery since the tenant does not have enough money to pay. The landlord is required to prove for rent in the tenant's insolvency, claiming either against an individual's trustee in bankruptcy or the liquidator of a corporate tenant. A liquidator or trustee in bankruptcy can become personally liable for rent, for example by taking steps to sell the lease.[280] Usually however the landlord is restricted to a claim against the assets left over at the time of insolvency. The court has a discretion to treat rent as a liquidation expense.[281] Insolvency means that only a proportion of the debts can be paid and the rent will abate proportionately. If the available assets match only half the debts, only half the arrears of rent can be obtained.

Substitutes will be exposed to the extent that sums are not collected through the insolvency process. If actual payments are made, the landlord may appropriate them to future rent payments, leaving the whole of the arrears untouched, and so leaving sureties to cover any arrears.[282] Indeed landlords are not bound to prove at all, but often prefer to proceed directly against a substitute, leaving him to prove in the tenant's liquidation by subrogation.

Sometimes a moratorium is put in place to try to give an opportunity for the company to recover from its debts, perhaps by an *administration order*[283] or a *voluntary*

---

[275] (1821) 5 B. & Ald. 1, 9, 10, 11, 106 E.R. 1094, Best J. A covenant to stock land with game can only benefit the current owner of the reversion: *Hooper* v. *Clark* (1867) L.R. 2 Q.B. 200.

[276] [1909] A.C. 72 H.L.

[277] [1989] Q.B. 193 C.A.; query after *Swift* which appears to hold that it falls into the first head of *Congleton*.

[278] (1808) 10 East. 130, 103 E.R. 725; *Walsh* v. *Fussell* (1829) 6 Bing. 163, 130 E.R. 1243.

[279] *St Thomas' Hospital* v. *Richardson* [1910] 1 K.B. 271.

[280] *Re Page* (1884) 14 Q.B.D. 401; *Re A.B.C. Coupler & Engineering Co. Ltd. (No.3)* [1970] 1 W.L.R. 702, 709, Plowman J.; *Re Downer Enterprises Ltd.* [1974] 1 W.L.R. 1460, Pennycuick V.C.

[281] *Re Oaks Pits Colliery Co.* (1882) 21 Ch.D. 322, 330, Lindley L.J.

[282] *Milverton Group Ltd.* v. *Warner World Ltd.* [1995] 2 E.G.L.R. 28 C.A.; M. Haley [1995] *J.B.L.* 181.

[283] I.A. 1986 part II; *Re Atlantic Computer Systems plc.* [1992] Ch. 505, 541G–544H; *Re Lomax Leisure Ltd.* [1999] 2 E.G.L.R. 37, Neuberger J.

arrangement made out of court between the tenant and his creditors. These procedures are designed to give a breathing space during which creditors agree not to enforce their debts and so give the tenant a chance to ward off his insolvency. The register has been improved.[284] The particular arrangement may or may not preclude action by the landlord for future rent,[285] but substitutes will certainly be exposed to action.[286]

2. Overcoming the risk of an insolvent tenant

Commercial leases usually provide for *forfeiture* on insolvency or incipient insolvency, leaving the landlord free to terminate the lease and so to be free to relet the property.[287] Procedure is explained elsewhere, but if the lease is valuable the trustee in bankruptcy or liquidator can generally obtain relief provided that they sell the property within one year.[288]

3. Disclaimer

Running of rent can be prevented for the future by a disclaimer of the lease, either on corporate liquidation or personal bankruptcy.[289] The right to disclaim the lease continues even if the liquidator or trustee in bankruptcy has entered into possession, has endeavoured to sell, or has carried out other acts of ownership.[290]

Any onerous property can be disclaimed by giving a prescribed notice[291]; this includes any unprofitable contract,[292] any property that is unsaleable or not readily saleable, and any property that may give rise to any liability.[293] Commercial[294] leases become onerous either because of high rents (especially if the market has fallen), large repairing obligations, or terms preventing assignment.[295] In *M.E.P.C. plc. v. Scottish Amicable Life Assurance Society*[296] a lease was successfully ended by disclaiming all interest under the licence to assign it to the bankrupt, since this could only have been an indirect way of referring to the lease itself. Court application is no longer needed to effect a disclaimer, nor is it limited to 12 months from the insolvency.[297]

---

[284] I.Am.R. 1999 S.I. 1999/359.

[285] *McMullen & Sons Ltd.* v. *Cerone* [1994] 1 E.G.L.R. 99; *Cazaly Irving Holdings Ltd.* v. *Cancol Ltd.* [1995] E.G.C.S. 146, Knox J.; *Burford Midland Properties Ltd.* v. *Marley Extrusions Ltd.* [1995] 2 E.G.L.R. 15; *Doorbar* v. *Alltime Securities Ltd.* [1996] 2 E.G.L.R. 33 C.A.; *Johnson* v. *Davies* [1999] Ch. 117 C.A.

[286] *R.A. Securities Ltd.* v. *Mercantile Current* [1995] 3 All E.R. 581, Jacob J.; *Mytre Investments Ltd.* v. *Reynolds* [1995] 3 All E.R. 588.

[287] See below pp. 829–831.

[288] See below p. 831.

[289] I.A. 1986 ss. 178–182 (companies), 315–321 (bankruptcy); Woodfall 17.271–17.276; Bright & Gilbert 641–642; Davey 126–127.

[290] I.A. 1986 ss.178(1), 315(1); *Re Lister* [1926] Ch. 149.

[291] I.A. 1986 ss.178(1), 315(1); S.I. 1986/1925 rr.4.187–4.189, r.6.178, as amended by S.I. 1987/1919.

[292] *Re Gough* (1927) 96 L.J.Ch. 233 (contract for sub-sale); *Official Receiver* v. *Environment Agency* [1999] 3 E.G.L.R. 21 C.A. (waste management licence).

[293] I.A. 1986 ss.178(3), 315(2).

[294] As to residential tenancies see above Chapter 14.

[295] *Eyre* v. *Hall* [1986] 2 E.G.L.R. 95 C.A. (terms very stringent).

[296] [1993] 2 E.G.L.R. 93 C.A.

[297] Companies Act 1985.ss.618–620.

Disclaimer destroys the leasehold estate in the land,[298] and ends future liability on the covenants, but all benefits are also lost.[299] The person suffering loss—*the landlord*—is a creditor who can claim in the insolvency,[300] who has 14 days to object to the disclaimer[301] and can force the liquidator or trustee in bankruptcy to decide whether or not he will disclaim.[302] The landlord will usually look to sureties in this situation[303]; termination does not affect the position of any other party.[304] In *Re Park Air Services plc.*,[305] the House of Lords had to decide whether the landlord could prove for the whole of the aggregate rents due for the remainder of the term, or whether a discount had to be allowed to reflect the fact that payments were accelerated by the tenant's insolvency. In the particular case the liquidators of the tenant company had disclaimed the lease. The decision was that a discount had to be applied, though even so the landlord was awarded £1 million. Lord Millett observed that the right to rent was ended by the disclaimer to be substituted by a claim for compensation by a person suffering loss as a result of a disclaimer, who is deemed to be a creditor of the company and so is entitled to prove "for the loss or damage".[306] Damages should be assessed as if there was a contract that had been wrongfully terminated, and accordingly the landlord had to allow credit for rents that he would obtain from reletting the property and also a discount for early receipt of the rent. The Court of Appeal[307] had reached the opposite conclusion—that proofs could relate to the aggregate of rents due for the remainder of the term (less rents obtainable from a reletting)—on the basis that the landlord's right to forfeit the lease on a disclaimer was a security interest, but Lord Millett demolished this reasoning. The landlord could not sell the lease and on disclaimer the right to end the lease had gone, a right that could not be described as a security.[308] The decision would not necessarily have been the same had the contract provided for sums to become immediately payable on breach, nor if the question had been of entitlement to prove in an insolvency (as opposed to on a disclaimer).[309]

Protection is also provided for those with any *derivative interest* that might be affected by a disclaimer; before leasehold property can be disclaimed notice must be served on all known sub-tenants and mortgage-lenders.[310] In the case of a dwelling disclaimed by a trustee in bankruptcy, notice must be given to all people interested in the house and all occupiers.[311] All these interested are ended if there is a disclaimer and no application

---

[298] *M.E.P.C. plc.* v. *Scottish Amicable Life Assurance Society* [1993] 2 E.G.L.R. 93 C.A.; *Re Bastable* [1901] 2 K.B. 518; *Re Hyams* (1923) 93 L.J.Ch. 184 C.A.

[299] *Re Wadsley* (1925) 94 L.J.Ch. 215.

[300] I.A. 1986 ss.178(6), 315(5).

[301] ss.179, 317.

[302] s.178(5), 316; A. Waltham & P. Cane [1992] 25 *E.G.* 19.

[303] See below p. 780.

[304] I.A. 1986 ss.178(4), 315(5).

[305] [1999] 1 All E.R. 673 H.L.

[306] I.A. 1986 s.178(6).

[307] [1997] 3 All E.R. 193 C.A.; *Re Hide* (1871) L.R. 7 Ch.App. 28.

[308] *Re Lomax Leisure Ltd.* [1999] 2 E.G.L.R. 37, Neuberger J.

[309] I.R. 1986 r.11.13 was subjected to strong criticism by Lord Millett.

[310] I.A. 1986 ss.179(1), 317. Relief for a lender may be conditional on surplus proceeds being paid to the tenant's trustee in bankruptcy: *Lee* v. *Lee* [1999] Times September 22nd C.A.

[311] I.A. 1986 s.318.

for relief.[312] It follows that it is not permissible to grant relief to a tenant subject to a sub-tenancy where the sub-tenant does not seek relief.[313] It also follows that anyone prejudicially affected should consider applying to the court, which has power to make whatever order is just.[314] Sub-tenants are usually offered the grant of a new lease[315] with liability to the extent of an assignee.[316] Even forfeiture by peaceable re-entry after the disclaimer will not remove a lender's right to relief.[317]

4. Dissolution of a company without liquidation

Similar principles apply where a company is struck off the register of companies, usually because of default in filing company returns. Any property, including any lease, will vest in the Crown, and may be sold if it is valuable, or disclaimed if it is onerous.[318] Commercial leases invariably provide that dissolution of the tenant company is a termination event entitling the landlord to forfeit the lease; however if he chooses to do so, he must retake possession from whoever is trading there.[319] Very often the directors of the tenant company continue to trade as if nothing has happened, and later apply to restore the company to the register. This may prejudice the landlord, who may well lose the right to end the lease. This is demonstrated by the facts of *Re Blenheim Leisure (Restaurants) Ltd.*[320]; the landlord had successfully served notice on the Crown, which held the lease as *bona vacantia* after the dissolution of the tenant company, but which had no renewal rights since it was not in business occupation. When the directors of the company applied for it to be restored, it was held that the landlord should be entitled to join in the proceedings to oppose the application since he was directly affected by the proceedings. In other cases it may be the landlord who wishes to apply to the court for an order restoring the company to the register, a procedure that is useful if the landlord wishes to institute a rent review,[321] or to restore the right to sue sureties for rent arrears.[322]

M. SUBSTITUTES: PREVIOUS TENANTS

Tenants often fail to pay rent or pay for repairs. Though the usefulness of substitutes is not confined to such cases, substitutes are particularly important when a tenant becomes insolvent. Landlords generally seek to protect themselves by ensuring that they have the right to terminate the lease for the future when the tenant becomes insolvent,

---

[312] *Sterling Estates Ltd.* v. *Pickard U.K. Ltd.* [1997] 2 E.G.L.R. 33 Ch.D.; *Re Cock ex p. Shilston* (1887) 20 Q.B.D. 343; *Hackney L.B.C.* v. *Crown Estate Commissioners* (1996) 72 P. & C.R. 233 (effect on a local land charge).

[313] *Re I.T.M. Corporation Ltd.* [1997] 2 E.G.L.R. 33.

[314] I.A. 1986 ss.181, 320.

[315] s.320; *Re Vedmay* (1995) 69 P. & C.R. 247; *Beegas Nominees Ltd.* v. *B.H.P. Petroleum Ltd.* [1998] 2 E.G.L.R. 57 C.A.

[316] I.A. 1986 ss.182, 321.

[317] *Barclays Bank plc.* v. *Prudential Assurance Co. Ltd.* [1998] 1 E.G.L.R. 44 Ch.D.

[318] Companies Act 1985 s.656.

[319] *Cromwell Developments Ltd.* v. *Godfrey* [1998] 2 E.G.L.R. 62 C.A.

[320] [1999] Times August 13th C.A.

[321] *Re Priceland Ltd.* [1996] E.G.C.S. 188 Ch.D.

[322] *Allied Dunbar Assurance plc.* v. *Fowle* [1994] 1 E.G.L.R. 122, Garland J.; *Stanhope Pension Trust Ltd.* v. *Registrar of Companies* (1995) 69 P. & C.R. 238 C.A.; A. Belcher [1995] *Conv.* 199.

and by securing contractual guarantees so that there are others beyond the current tenant who are liable to meet any payment that becomes due under the terms of the lease. Substitutes described in this chapter fall into three main classes. First, there are original contracting tenants who remain liable throughout the contractual term on the basis of privity of contract under pre-1996 leases. Second, there are tenants liable under authorised guarantee agreements (A.G.A.s) under the scheme of the Landlord and Tenant (Covenants) Act 1995. Finally there are contractual sureties, who agree to guarantee what the tenant has contracted to do; most landlords will not grant or allow the transfer of a commercial lease until the tenant has provided sureties. These three groups of unfortunates form the subject of study in the remainder of this chapter.

1.   Privity of contract (pre-1996 leases)

Until the 1995 reforms, English landlords[323] enjoyed two alternative remedies for rent, one founded on privity of estate and the other on privity of contract, this last exposing the original tenant throughout the original contractual duration.[324] During the recession of the early 1990s many landlords enforced this most unfair liability.[325]

When the Grantees of Reversions Act 1540 made it possible for the burden of a lease to pass to the current tenant, the Act left an ambiguity about the fate of the older privity of contract. *Walker's case* (1587)[326] settled that the original tenant remained liable on privity of contract after the assignment of the lease and later cases showed that this continued after acceptance of the assignee by the landlord.[327] Liability was never afterwards disputed, and is made clear by modern statute law.[328] Hence the original tenant (or original landlord as the case may be) remains liable on the covenants throughout the term of the lease. This is in addition to the estate-based liability of the current party. Kenyon C.J. explained the reason for allowing this double action in *Auriol* v. *Mills*[329]:

> "[W]hen a landlord grants a lease, he selects his tenant; he trusts to the skill and responsibility of that tenant; and it cannot be endured that he should afterwards be deprived of his action on the covenant to which he trusted by an act to which he cannot object, as in the case of an execution. . . . The assignees are bound to sell the term and perhaps they may assign to a person in whom the lessor has no confidence."

The possibility of multiple actions had been recognised immediately after 1540.[330] Lord Templeman added in *City of London Corporation* v. *Fell* that[331]:

> "The common law did not release the original tenant from liability for breaches of covenant committed after an assignment because of the sacred character of covenant in English law.

---

[323]   *City of London Corporation* v. *Fell* [1994] 1 A.C. 458, 465F, Lord Templeman.
[324]   L.P.A. 1925 s.141(1), s.142(2); *Re King* [1963] Ch. 459, 481, Lord Denning M.R.; Woodfall 11.048A–11.075P; Evans & Smith (5th) 77–99; Garner (2nd) 112–129.
[325]   *City of London Corporation Ltd.* v. *Fell* [1993] Q.B. 589, 603H, 604D, Nourse L.J.
[326]   (1587) 3 Co. Rep. 22a, 76 E.R. 676.
[327]   *Baynton* v. *Morgan* (1888) 22 Q.B.D. 74, 82, Lopes L.J.
[328]   L.P.A. 1925 ss.141(1), 142(2); *Friends' Provident Life Office* v. *British Railways Board* [1996] 1 All E.R. 336, 351a, Sir Christopher Slade.
[329]   (1790) 4 Term. Rep. 94, 99, 100 E.R. 912.
[330]   *Anon* (1533) Bro. N.C. 18, 73 E.R. 854 (query whether the date is really pre-1540); *Brett* v. *Cumberland* (1619) Cro. Jac. 521, 79 E.R. 446.
[331]   [1994] 1 A.C. 458, 465F.

This only means that the fortunate English landlord has two remedies after an assignment, namely his remedy against an assignee and his remedy against the original tenant."

Where a covenant in a pre-1996 lease has reference to the subject matter of the lease, the position is straightforward. The landlord's choice[332] lay between the original tenant (T0)[333] and the current tenant (TC). Thus:

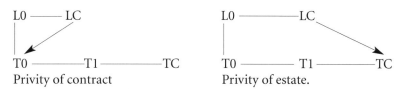

Privity of contract   Privity of estate.

Contractual liability can always be excluded[334] or qualified, for example by limiting the tenant's responsibility to his personal acts.[335] However, commercial landlords usually held the whip hand and used it to insist that the original tenant should accept liability for the rent throughout the term.

An original contracting party remains liable for the duration of the term of the (pre-1996) lease for which he contracted,[336] but no longer. A continued power to ensure compliance with the covenant is not necessary, since the original tenant usually remains liable for the acts of his successors.[337] If an extension of the term of the lease is agreed in advance, this will usually fall within the covenant to pay rent.[338] But the original tenant is exonerated once the original term ends and the current tenant holds over, for example under the business tenancies legislation.[339] In *City of London Corporation* v. *Fell* a suite of offices in the City was taken by Wilde Sapte (T0), a prominent firm of City solicitors, under a 10-year lease. They sold the lease to Grovebell Group Ltd. and those tenants (TC) remained in occupation when the lease expired in 1986, holding over under the business tenancies legislation. By the time the tenant vacated, the company was in arrears with the rent and was insolvent. The landlord pursued the original tenants, Wilde Sapte, for the unpaid rent, but failed at first instance,[340] in the Court of Appeal[341] and in the Lords.[342]

[332] It is the current landlord (LC) who can enforce the contractual action; a point explained below at pp. 781–782.

[333] *Moule* v. *Garrett* [1872] L.R. 7 Exch. 101; *Johnsey Estates Ltd.* v. *Lewis & Manley (Engineering) Ltd.* [1987] 2 E.G.L.R. 69 C.A.

[334] *Eccles* v. *Mills* [1898] A.C. 360 P.C.

[335] E.g. "not to suffer or permit": *Bryant* v. *Hancock & Co. Ltd.* [1898] 1 Q.B. 716 C.A., appealed on other grounds; *Wilson* v. *Twamley* [1904] 2 K.B. 99 C.A.; *Villiers* v. *Oldcorn* [1903] 20 T.L.R. 11.

[336] E.g. a surrender: *Matthews* v. *Sawell* (1818) 8 Taunt. 270, 129 E.R. 387; but it survives forfeiture: *Weaver* v. *Mogford* [1988] 2 E.G.L.R. 48 C.A. (disrepair).

[337] L.P.A. 1925 s.79; *Mumford* v. *Walker* (1901) 71 L.J.K.B. 19; *Holloway Bros. Ltd.* v. *Hill* [1902] 2 Ch. 612; *Palethorpe* v. *Home Brewery Co.* [1906] 2 K.B. 5; *Thames Manufacturing Co. Ltd.* v. *Perrotts (Nichol & Peyton) Ltd.* (1985) 50 P. & C.R. 1, 6, Scott J.

[338] *Baker* v. *Merckel* [1960] 1 Q.B. 657 C.A.

[339] See above Chapter 20.

[340] [1993] Q.B. 589 at 591, Desmond Perrett Q.C.; P. Luxton [1992] *J.B.L.* 507.

[341] [1993] Q.B. 589 C.A.; P.F. Smith [1993] *Conv.* 164; D. Evans [1992] *Conv.* 67.

[342] [1994] 1 A.C. 458 H.L.; M. Haley [1993] *J.B.L.* 473; P.F. Smith [1993] *Conv.* 164; S. Bridge [1994] *C.L.J.* 28; M. Haley [1994] *Conv.* 247; N. Osborn (1994) 138 *S.J.* 849.

Contractual liability was limited to the 10-year term of the lease, and the House found nothing in the business tenancies legislation to impose continuing liability. Argument for the landlords was based on the proposition that if the current tenants were liable on the covenants, then the original covenanting party must also be liable, but the logic of this argument was firmly denied by Lord Templeman. "Covenants are introduced on the creation of a lease, but are not necessary to sustain a lease."[343] Wilde Sapte should not be compelled to pay a sum that they never covenanted to pay in respect of an estate that they never enjoyed. Clear wording could always extend contractual liability.[344]

2.   Intermediate tenants

Estate-based liability ends when an intermediate tenant (T1, T2, etc.) sells the lease, and he was not a party to the contract so as to attract privity of contract liability. However landlords commonly sought to reinforce their position by insisting that a tenant who wished to divest himself of the lease should enter into the licence for assignment[345] in order to provide a guarantee.[346] The liability was usually drafted to extend to the whole of the remaining term of the lease.[347] Obligations to indemnify the original tenant are unaffected by a direct covenant.[348]

3.   Abolition of privity of contract for post-1995 leases

Privity of contract was an unwarranted trap for tenants who might be caught many years after having parted with the land, especially during a recession. Law Commission research revealed widespread public ignorance of the potential liability.[349] Inflation greatly increases the danger since, after the rent has been reviewed, the original tenant may find himself liable for sums much larger than he ever had to pay as a tenant. Total abolition was the solution, though the Law Commission proposals were watered down before enactment as the Landlord and Tenant (Covenants) Act 1995, and abolition applies only to "new tenancies". Sadly, privity of contract liability will continue for pre-1996 leases, and later ones made under pre-1996 contractual arrangements, for generations to come.

The mechanism of abolition, which has already been studied, is that a tenant obtains a release from liability on the covenants when he assigns the lease.[350] This is supplemented by an anti-avoidance provision, rendering void any agreement purporting to exclude, directly or indirectly, the right to a release.[351] Original tenants must inevitably

---

[343] At 465H.

[344] *Herbert Duncan Ltd.* v. *Clutton* [1993] Q.B. 589, 605–608 (liability did extend to the period of holding over but not to an increased rent awarded under the business tenancies legislation).

[345] If an assignment must be registered with the landlord, liability on the covenants cannot be avoided by failing to register the assignment: *Cerium Investments Ltd.* v. *Evans* [1991] 1 E.G.L.R. 80 C.A.

[346] *Friends' Provident Life Office* v. *British Railways Board* [1996] 1 All E.R. 336 C.A.

[347] *Estates Gazette Ltd.* v. *Benjamin Restaurants Ltd.* [1995] 1 All E.R. 129 C.A.; R. Castle (1991) 135 S.J. 1087; *J. Lyons & Co. Ltd.* v. *Knowles* [1943] 1 K.B. 366 C.A.

[348] *Becton Dickinson U.K. Ltd.* v. *Zwebner* [1989] Q.B. 208 McNeill J.; P. McLoughlin [1989] *Conv.* 292; *Re a Debtor (No. 21 of 1995)* [1996] C.L.Y. 3750.

[349] Law. Com. No.174 (1988) para.3.15; R. Thornton (1991) 11 L.S. 47, 61.

[350] L.T. (Covenants) A. 1995 s.5; see above p. 748.

[351] s.25.

be discharged on a sale of the lease. In the interim this may be a small comfort, for he is likely to be required to enter into an authorised guarantee agreement, but a full release will occur after a second sale.

4. Authorised guarantee agreements: former tenants under post-1995 leases

Where a tenant assigns a new lease and is granted a release from liability on a covenant, he—the old tenant disposing of the lease—may enter into an authorised guarantee agreement (or A.G.A.).[352] Clearly this extra liability will not be volunteered, so the important question is when a landlord will be able to insist upon it. This is so where assignment of the lease is restricted, so that entry into an A.G.A. is a condition of giving consent to a sale, in particular if[353]: (1) the landlord has an absolute right to refuse consent to a sale, or (2) the landlord must not unreasonably withhold consent to a sale, but entry into an A.G.A. is on the particular facts a reasonable condition, or (3) where entry into an A.G.A. is a reasonable condition because of a prior agreement[354] to accept this condition between landlord and tenant. The Landlord and Tenant Act 1927 was amended in 1995[355] to give commercial[356] landlords much greater control over assignment,[357] a concept widely defined but only so as to embrace transfers of the tenant's estate and this does not impose additional controls on the creation of a sub-lease.[358]

Landlord and tenant may reach a written agreement—it must be made before the current application for consent to assign[359]—about the circumstances in which the landlord may reasonably withhold his licence, and any conditions that may be attached to a grant of consent. Typically this agreement will be contained in the lease itself and will provide that the assigning tenant must offer to enter into an A.G.A. on specific terms before being allowed to assign the lease. The landlord will act reasonably if he withholds consent to an assignment following the agreed terms.[360] If any factor is left for the landlord to determine—for example what is a suitable surety—there must either be a requirement for the landlord to act reasonably *or* a right to an independent review of the landlord's decision.[361]

An authorised guarantee agreement will provide for the previous tenant to guarantee the obligations of the current tenant, usually as a principal debtor, and commonly also with an obligation to take a new lease on a default by the current tenant.[362] The law of guarantees applies.[363] In a normal case the A.G.A. is provided by the immediate past

---

[352] ss.16, 28 (definition); Woodfall 11.075A–11.075P; Evans & Smith (5th) 88–99; M.C.E. Wright [1997] *L.T. Rev.* 52; A.G. Walker [1998] 2 *L.T. Rev.* 124.

[353] L.T. (Covenants) A. 1995 s.16(3).

[354] L.T.A. 1927 s.19(1A); see above p. 741.

[355] s.19(1A)–(1E).

[356] Building leases are included by s.19(1D), but residential or agricultural tenancies are excluded by s.19(1E).

[357] This was part of a package deal by which the landlords lobby offered restrictions on tenant's secondary liability: M. Davey (1996) 57 *M.L.R.* 78, 89–91; typically the landlords came off best.

[358] L.T.A. 1927 s.19(1E)(b).

[359] s.19(1B).

[360] s.19(1A)

[361] s.19(1C); examples of the former might be to enter into an A.G.A., to assign to a company with a specified capitalisation, or to require a director's guarantee; examples of the latter are to provide an acceptable guarantor or to conduct only appropriate trades.

[362] s.16(7).

[363] s.16(8).

tenant, and when the current tenant in turn sells the lease, all liability of the previous tenant is discharged, since the guarantee must not impose liability beyond the estate-ownership of the assignee.[364] The landlord may also require the former tenant to provide a surety of its A.G.A. obligations,[365] a possibility presumably not intended by the legislators but not clearly excluded. However, since section 16 applies only to a tenant as defined,[366] it is arguable that an additional surety requirement is caught by the anti-avoidance provision as tending to frustrate the release intended by the Act.[367] A previous tenant must obtain a full release from all liability on a second sale, since an authorised guarantee agreement does not guarantee any person other than the assignee or impose any liability after that tenant's release.[368] In the case of an "excluded assignment" (meaning either a transmission or an assignment in breach of covenant), there is no release, and the former tenant remains liable until the next proper sale; at that time the landlord can seek an A.G.A. from any unreleased tenant, not necessarily the most recent one.[369]

N. SUBSTITUTES: SURETIES

This section applies to all leases, new and old. Lord Templeman described a surety in *P. & A. Swift Investments* v. *Combined English Stores Group plc.*[370] as a quasi-tenant who volunteers to be a substitute or twelfth man for the tenant's team, and is subject to the same rules and regulations as the player he replaces. The essence is a primary or ultimate obligation (in TC) and a surety providing a secondary or substitute liability *for the same* obligation. It is very common for the landlord to demand a surety whose function is to guarantee the tenant's performance of the obligations when a new lease is granted, and sureties are also commonly demanded as a condition of permitting an assignment of an existing lease. A contract of guarantee is formed by any special promise to accept liability for the failure of another to perform legal obligations arising from any source.[371] Guarantees are often relatively informal—though writing is required[372]—whereas a surety is usually restricted to a liability accepted under a bond (that is a deed of surety).[373]

Sureties guarantee that the tenant will perform the covenants. If the tenant fails to pay the rent, the landlord can call on his surety to do so, though this is a claim for damages in respect of the failure to pay rent, rather than a rent action as such.[374] The same applies

[364] s.16(4).
[365] J.E. Adams [1996] *Conv.* 161; E. Slessenger & S. Cullen [1998] 30 *E.G.* 102 (parent companies).
[366] s.28(1).
[367] s.25.
[368] s.16(4).
[369] s.16(6). The next sale will effect a release.
[370] [1989] A.C. 632, 638, Lord Templeman.
[371] *Moschi* v. *Lep Air Services Ltd.* [1973] A.C. 331, 347H, Lord Diplock.
[372] Statute of Frauds 1677 s.4; *Deutsche Bank A.G.* v. *Ibrahim* [1991] *Financial Times*, December 13th; *Elpis Maritime Co. Ltd.* v. *Marti Chartering Co. Inc.* [1992] 1 A.C. 21 H.L.; *M.P. Services Ltd.* v. *A Lawyer* (1996) 72 P. & C.R. D49 C.A.; *Goodaston Ltd.* v. *F.H. Burgess plc.* [1999] L.T.R. 46, Jacob J.
[373] Jowitt, *Law Dictionary* (Sweet & Maxwell, 1995).
[374] Hence the limitation period is 6 years: Limitation Act 1980 s.19; *Romain* v. *Scuba T.V.* [1997] Q.B. 887 C.A.; *Collin Estates Ltd.* v. *Buckley* [1992] 2 E.G.L.R. 78 C.A.

to any other covenants within the scope of the guarantee. Surety covenants are primarily contractual, the scope of the guarantee being determined by the words used.[375] Usually the surety covenant will only survive for the original contractual term, ending when the current tenant holds over at the end of his term under the business tenancies legislation,[376] unless clearly and unequivocally extended beyond the end of the original contract.[377] It is also possible to provide for the surety to be discharged after a fixed period of time, perhaps only if the covenants have been complied with to that date.[378] Some tenants are allowed to alter the sureties by notice, though the landlord invariably requires that the alternates are financially satisfactory.[379]

O. SUBSTITUTES: PASSING THE BENEFIT

It will be the current landlord who is able to enforce the liability of tenant substitutes.

1. Extending the contractual scope to future landlords

It is possible to draft a substitute liability in favour of the original landlord so that the contract is itself enforceable by future landlords when they acquire in the reversion. This is possible under the statutory provisions regulating land covenants[380] and for the future under the Contracts (Rights of Third Parties) Act 1999.[381]

2. Privity of contract after a change of parties

After a dealing with the reversion there are two landlords (L0 and LC) to consider, giving rise to a difficult question; there was an ambiguity about whether privity of contract always existed between the original parties to the lease (L0 to T0),[382] or whether privity of contract merely meant the existence of a contractual relationship, which could be assigned, giving an action between LC and T0. Privity of contract was asserted in a personal action, originally in *assumpsit*, based on the assumption by the original contracting party of a personal obligation,[383] analysis that was later re-phrased as an action in contract. As contractual benefits became generally assignable, so too did the benefit of the privity of contract in a lease.

In modern law it clear that a transfer of the reversion also transfers the benefit of the contracts contained in the lease. It is LC who can sue rather than L0. Although other explanations are possible,[384] it is easiest to see this as a function of the Grantees of

---

[375] *Eastern Counties B.S.* v. *Russell* [1947] 1 All E.R. 500, 503C, Hilbery J.; *T.C.B. Ltd.* v. *Gray* [1988] 1 All E.R. 108 C.A. (condition precedent).

[376] *G.M.S. Syndicate Ltd.* v. *Gary Elliott Ltd.* [1982] Ch. 1, Nourse J.; *Junction Estates Ltd.* v. *Cope* (1974) 27 P. & C.R. 482, MacKenna J.; *A. Plesser & Co. Ltd.* v. *Davis* [1983] 2 E.G.L.R. 70, French J.; J.E. Martin [1984] *Conv.* 58; this is implicit in *City of London Corporation* v. *Fell* [1994] 1 A.C. 458 H.L.

[377] *A. Plesser & Co. Ltd.* v. *Davis* [1983] 2 E.G.L.R. 70, French J.

[378] *Knighton Estates Ltd.* v. *Gallic Management Co. Ltd.* (1999) 78 P. & C.R. 52 C.A.

[379] *L.E. Grovewood Ltd.* v. *Lundy Properties Ltd.* (1995) 69 P. & C.R. 507, Parker J.

[380] L.P.A. 1925 s.56; Sparkes *N.L.L.* 608–609.

[381] M. Shelton [2000] *R.R.L.R.* 89; see above p. 760.

[382] *Walker's case* (1587) 3 Co. Rep. 22a, 76 E.R. 676.

[383] *Thursby* v. *Plant* (1669) 1 Lev. 259, 83 E.R. 359 (L1 could sue T0 in London in contract as well as in Lincoln on the covenant).

[384] *Vyvyan* v. *Arthur* (1823) 1 B. & C. 410, 107 E.R. 152.

Reversions Act 1540 since the diversity of opinion noted by Coke[385] was already settled by 1600.[386] Where there was no statutory assignment (because of informality),[387] privity of contract remained between the original parties for ever.[388] In most cases, however, the 1540 Act (and now its 1925 successor) would pass the benefit of the contract as well as the benefit of the covenant. Any other rule would be madness: how could a single tenant be liable to pay the same rent to two different people? And how could an original landlord be allowed to release the tenant's covenants once the reversion had passed?[389]

So privity of contract on the tenant's covenants that have reference to the subject matter of the lease exists between current landlord and original tenant (LC v. T0): the same person can enforce both privity of estate and privity of contract, and there is one benefit even if there are two burdens. *Arlesford Trading Co. Ltd.* v. *Servansingh*[390] concerned three simple transactions in a common sequence. First, there was a lease by L0 to T0, second an assignment of the lease to TC, and third a sale of the landlord's reversion to LC. There was never any moment at which T0 was directly a tenant of LC, but nevertheless an action lay between them in contract. T0 remained liable on his contract throughout the term to the current holder of the reversion (LC) who had the benefit of the contract.

The rules for *landlord's covenants*[391] are a mirror image of those for tenants, unless the covenant is personal in nature.[392] In one case a current tenant (TC) with an award of compensation (for the replacement of milestones!) could recover the cost from the original landlord (L0) just as much as the current landlord (LC).[393]

3. Sureties as against new landlords

For all leases, new and old, the benefit of a surety covenant is transmitted from one landlord to another under common law rules[394]; statutory rules for passing benefits do not apply since a surety is not a tenant.[395] Before a sale of the reversion, the original landlord (L0) has a contractual action against a surety, and afterwards the new landlord (LC) can enforce it. This is because it is now finally settled, after much agitation,[396] that the

---

[385] *Walker's case* (above), reporter's comment at 24B.

[386] *Matures* v. *Westwood* (1598) Cro. Eliz. 617, 78 E.R. 858; *Brett* v. *Cumberland* (1619) Cro. Jac. 521, 79 E.R. 446; *Edwards* v. *Morgan* (1685) 3 Lev. 233, 83 E.R. 666; *Parker* v. *Webb* (1693) 3 Salk. 5, 91 E.R. 656, Holt C.J.

[387] *Boot* v. *Wilson* (1807) 8 East. 311, 103 E.R. 360; *Brydges* v. *Lewis* (1842) 3 Q.B. 603, 114 E.R. 639; *Allcock* v. *Moorhouse* (1882) 9 Q.B.D. 366 C.A. Now L.P.A. 1925 s.141 applies to an informal lease.

[388] Action L0–T0: *Bickford* v. *Parson* (1848) 5 C.B. 920, 136 E.R. 1141; *Allcock* v. *Moorhouse* (1882) 9 Q.B.D. 366 C.A.

[389] *Harper* v. *Bird* (1678) T. Jo. 102, 84 E.R. 1167.

[390] [1971] 1 W.L.R. 1080 C.A.; D. Gordon [1987] *Conv.* 103. The point is assumed in many later cases.

[391] L.P.A. 1925 s.142(2).

[392] Action is then T0–L0: *Eccles* v. *Mills* [1898] A.C. 360 P.C.; *Smith* v. *Eggington* (1874) L.R. 9 C.P. 145; *Muller* v. *Trafford* [1901] 1 Ch. 54, Farwell J.

[393] *Stuart* v. *Joy* [1904] 1 K.B 362, 367, Cozens-Hardy L.J.; *Bath* v. *Bowles* (1905) 93 L.T. 801, 804, Alvestone C.J. (novel doctrine); *Celsteel* v. *Alton House Holdings Ltd. (No.2)* [1986] 1 W.L.R. 666, 672–673, Scott J., affirmed [1987] 1 W.L.R. 291, 296D–E, Fox L.J.; D. Gordon [1987] *Conv.* 103.

[394] K. Reynolds (1984) 81 *L.S.G.* 2214; J.E. Adams & H. Williamson [1989] 47 *E.G.* 24 S. Murdoch [1986] *Conv.* 50.

[395] *Kumar* v. *Dunning* [1989] 1 Q.B. 193, 199H; *P. & A. Swift Investments Ltd.* v. *Combined English Stores plc.* [1989] A.C. 632, 639H, Lord Oliver.

[396] *Kumar* v. *Dunning* [1989] 1 Q.B. 193, 201, Browne-Wilkinson V.C.; C. Harpum [1988] *C.L.J.* 180; H.W. Wilkinson (1987) 137 *N.L.J.* 1083; J.E. Martin [1986] *Conv.* 424.

benefit of the covenant does touch and concern the land and so it does run at common law.[397] In *P. & A. Swift Investments* v. *Combined English Stores Group plc.*[398] Swifts bought the reversion on a lease from the liquidator of the original landlord. They were able to enforce the covenants in the lease against the surety of the original tenant (T0) without any express assignment of the benefit of the guarantee, and exactly the same applies if it was a later tenant.[399]

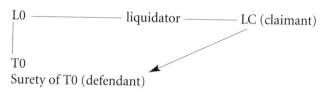

The only real issue was whether the covenant touched and concerned the land.[400] Given that it was, no distinct contractual right could remain in L0 after an assignment to LC.[401]

P. SUBSTITUTES: ARREARS NOTICE

Substitutes often complained that landlords had no incentive to chase the current tenant for rent, when they knew that they had copper-bottomed security in the shape of substitute liabilities. This problem is addressed by sections of the Landlord and Tenant (Covenants) Act 1995 which (contrary to the general scope of the Act) *apply both to old and new leases*; these apply to all forms of substitute liability[402] and all financial claims for rent, service charge, and liquidated sums payable on any default.[403] A default notice in a prescribed form[404] must be served[405] on the substitute within six months of the sum becoming due. This warns the surety that the current tenant has defaulted in his rent payments, and prevents landlords from allowing large arrears to build up without the knowledge of the surety. However, it is no defence for one substitute to argue that no default notice has been served on another substitute who might also have been liable.[406] The sum payable by the substitute is capped at the amount specified in the arrears notice. In *Commercial Union Life Assurance Co. Ltd.* v. *Moustafa*[407] it was held that a default notice that misstated the amount of the arrears was valid to the extent that it did include genuine arrears.

---

[397] *Pinemain Ltd.* v. *Welbeck International Ltd.* [1984] 2 E.G.L.R. 91; S. Murdoch [1986] *Conv.* 50.
[398] [1989] A.C. 632 H.L.
[399] *Kumar* v. *Dunning* [1989] 1 Q.B. 193 C.A.
[400] See above pp. 766–767.
[401] R. Thornton (1991) 11 *L.S.* 47, 55.
[402] Those protected include tenants sued on privity of contract, tenants liable under authorised guarantee agreements and sureties. However a default notice is irrelevant to a reimbursement action between two substitutes: *Fresh (Retail) Ltd.* v. *Emsden* [1999] 5 C.L. 455.
[403] s.17.
[404] S.I. 1995/2964; P.H. Kenny [1996] *Conv.* 324.
[405] *Commercial Union Life Assurance Co. Ltd.* v. *Moustafa* [1999] 2 E.G.L.R. 44, Smedley J.; see above pp. 591–593.
[406] *Cheverell Estates Ltd.* v. *Harris* [1998] 1 E.G.L.R. 27, Geoffrey Brice Q.C.
[407] [1999] 2 E.G.L.R. 44, Smedley J.; S. Murdoch [1999] 32 *E.G.* 88.

The landlord is not required to enforce the substitute liability immediately after the default notice has been served; he has the normal limitation period in which to take legal action, and could sue on several arrears notices at once; arrears may be added as they accumulate.[408] An indemnity claim by a substitute against the ultimate does not require a default notice.[409]

Q. SUBSTITUTES: ENDING THE LIABILITY

It would be unfair to impose extra liabilities on a surety by a variation of a lease agreed between landlord and tenant; variations may terminate the guarantee or they may attract protective measures to ensure that a surety is not prejudiced by a variation.

1. End of the lease

Generally a substitute's liability ends when the contractual duration of the he is guaranteeing ends.[410] This may be because the time runs out, but it might also be as a result of a variation in the terms of a lease that is so fundamental as to amount to a surrender of the existing lease and a regrant of a new one; if this occurs all secondary liabilities under the defunct lease are extinguished.[411]

2. Prejudicial variation of leases

The current parties are free to vary the terms of the lease as to relax the terms or to operate neutrally on substitutes.[412] What they are not allowed to do is to alter the terms of the lease in such a way as to place the burden on the surety.[413] The courts have gone overboard in protecting sureties: any variation which, judged objectively,[414] could conceivably prejudice the surety will discharge the surety completely unless the surety is consulted or the contract provides for variations. In *Holme* v. *Brunskill*[415] a surrender of one field in a lease of a hill farm discharged the surety; although the jury decided that this made no material difference to the burden imposed on the surety a majority of the Court of Appeal decided that the surety ought to have been consulted.[416] Many sureties have escaped by the application of this principle. Other cases have involved landlord's

---

[408] L.T. (Covenants) A. 1995 s.17(4).

[409] *M.W. Kellogg Ltd.* v. *F. Tobin* [1999] L.T.R. 513 Q.B.D.; D. Stevens [1999] 20 *E.G.* 152.

[410] He might of course enter into a new contract of guarantee for a new lease: *Goodaston Ltd.* v. *F.H. Burgess plc.* [1999] L.T.R. 46, Jacob J.

[411] *Friends' Provident Life Office* v. *British Railways Board* [1996] 1 All E.R. 336, 342e–345b, Beldam L.J., 350d–h, Sir Christopher Slade (obiter on facts); M. Davey (1996) 59 *M.L.R.* 78, 82; see generally S. Bright, "Variation of Leases and Tenant Liability" in *The Reform of Property Law* (Ashgate Dartmouth, 1997, eds P. Jackson & D.C. Wilde) ch 5.

[412] *Friends Provident* as above; *Metropolitan Properties (Regis) Co. Ltd.* v. *Bartholomew* [1996] 1 E.G.L.R. 82 C.A.; H.W. Wilkinson [1995] *N.L.J.* 1141; J.E. Adams [1995] *Conv.* 289; *Beegas Nominees Ltd.* v. *B.H.P. Petroleum Ltd.* [1998] 2 E.G.L.R. 57 C.A.

[413] *Friends Provident* at 342e–345b, Beldam L.J., 350d–h, Sir Christopher Slade; M. Davey (1996) 59 *M.L.R.* 78, 82.

[414] *Howard de Walden Estates Ltd.* v. *Pasta Place Ltd.* [1995] 1 E.G.L.R. 79, Morland J.; *Rees* v. *Bennington* (1795) 2 Ves. 540, 30 E.R. 765.

[415] (1877) 3 Q.B.D. 495 C.A.

[416] At 505, Cotton L.J; Brett L.J., dissenting, thought the contractual variation immaterial; surely he was right?

improvements—since rent, insurance premiums, and the tenant's repairing obligations could potentially be increased if the property were improved—and a change of use covenant to include off licence sales of alcohol.[417] Where there is a complete discharge there is no need to rely on the protection provided by the Landlord and Tenant (Covenants) Act 1995.[418]

3. Variations which do not discharge

Substitute liability is not terminated by a non-prejudicial variation, that is one which is obviously immaterial or which is beneficial.[419] A person providing a guarantee should not be liable for a contractual variation agreed between the current parties. In *Friends' Provident Life Office* v. *British Railways Board*,[420] the Court of Appeal held that a rent increase agreed with the current tenant (TC) did not bring to an end the liability for privity of contract (T0) at the original rent, but could not impose the extra rent on T0 acting as substitute.[421]

Discharge will not occur if there is a *contractual term* permitting variation, most commonly because a commercial tenant has agreed to be bound by future rent reviews.[422] In *Selous Street Properties Ltd.* v. *Oronel Fabrics Ltd.*[423] landlord and tenant conducted a rent review taking into account a new toilet, which could have increased the rent. Normally this would have discharged the substitute but a contractual clause prevented the surety claiming that a discharge had occurred. The contractual term must cover the specific variation that occurs and cannot prevent a discharge when a completely new agreement is reached.[424] For example in *Herbert Duncan Ltd.* v. *Cluttons*,[425] the covenant was to pay the rent reserved by the lease during the contractual term and any extension. It was held that the original tenant was liable for rent at the originally agreed rate for the period that the current tenant held over; but he had not agreed to pay an increased interim rent obtained by the landlord under the business tenancies legislation.

Statutory protection is provided by the Landlord and Tenant (Covenants) Act 1995 to limit the liability of former tenants against variations in a lease (new or old).[426] The scope is privity of contract liability under old leases, authorised guarantee agreements under new leases, guarantees given in licences to assign[427] and any other cases where a surety guarantees a former tenant.[428] A former tenant is exempted from liability arising

---

[417] *Howard de Walden* as above; also *Jaskel* v. *Sophie Nursery Products Ltd.* [1993] E.G.C.S. 42 C.A.; *Averbrian* v. *Willmalight* [1994] C.L.Y. 2799.

[418] s.18(3); see below nn. 426–430.

[419] *Metropolitan Properties (Regis) Ltd.* v. *Bartholomew* [1996] 1 E.G.L.R. 82 C.A.; H.W. Wilkinson [1995] *N.L.J.* 1141; J.E. Adams [1995] *Conv.* 289.

[420] [1996] 1 All E.R. 336 C.A.; *Beegas Nominees Ltd.* v. *B.H.P. Petroleum Ltd.* [1998] 2 E.G.L.R. 57 C.A.

[421] At 351e, Sir Christopher Slade.

[422] The best explanation of *Centrovincial Estates plc.* v. *Bulk Storage Ltd.* [1983] 2 E.G.L.R. 45; P. McLoughlin [1984] *Conv.* 443; M. Davey (1996) 59 *M.L.R.* 78, 82; *Friends' Provident Life Office* v. *British Railways Board* [1996] 1 All E.R. 336, 345c–348f, Beldam L.J., 350j–351e, Sir Christopher Slade.

[423] [1984] 1 E.G.L.R. 50, Hutchison J.; subject to [1996] 1 All E.R. 336, 351c, Sir Christopher Slade.

[424] *West Horndon Industrial Park Ltd.* v. *Phoenix Timber Group plc.* [1995] 1 E.G.L.R. 77 Ch.D.

[425] [1993] Q.B. 589, 605–608, Nourse L.J.

[426] s.18.

[427] s.18(1).

[428] s.18(3); for old leases it only applies to variations after 1995: subs.(6).

from any relevant variation[429] being any variation to which the landlord has the right to refuse his agreement.[430]

4.   Release of current tenant releases substitutes

If a landlord releases the current tenant from liability, this acts as a release of liability for all others offering guarantees. In *Deanplan Ltd. v. Mahmoud*[431] Judge Paul Baker Q.C. found a surprising lack of authority.[432] In that case the landlord accepted a surrender of the lease and a distress for £300 in lieu of a claim for arrears of rent of £18,000. By making this settlement with the current tenant (TC), he also gave up his claim against intermediate tenants who had entered into express surety covenants. The decision has commanded considerable support,[433] though *Sun Life Assurance Society plc. v. Tantofex (Engineers) Ltd.*[434] adds that *Deanplan* is subject to the principle that release of one is not a release of others unless there is an accord and satisfaction. On the facts, discharge of an intermediate tenant (T1) did not release an original tenant (T0) from his liability for privity of contract.

5.   Disclaimer

Similar principles apply to voluntary arrangements, after a company has been struck off the register for failing to file returns[435] but then restored,[436] and on forfeiture.[437] If the liquidator of the current tenant disclaims the lease, the current tenant cannot be sued for ongoing rent. Worse for the landlord is the rule that the termination of the contractual duration of the lease will operate to discharge any surety of the current tenant. However a surety is invariably required to covenant that in this situation the landlord may compel the surety to take over the lease or at least accept a new lease. This covenant touches and concerns the land,[438] and should be drafted to cover both disclaimer on liquidation and dissolution of the tenant company for failing to make returns.[439]

The landlord can also pursue other substitutes, who are not discharged by the ending of the liability of the current tenant. This was established in *Hindcastle Ltd. v. Barbara Attenborough Associates Ltd.*[440] The liquidator of the current tenant company disclaimed the lease, ending the lease by a deemed surrender[441] and discharging the

---

[429] s.18(2).

[430] s.18(4).

[431] [1993] Ch. 151; H.W. Wilkinson [1993] *N.L.J.* 28.

[432] He felt himself bound by *Re E.W.A. (A Debtor)* [1901] 2 K.B. 642 C.A.

[433] *Friends' Provident Life Office* v. *British Railways Board* [1996] 1 All E.R. 336, 348h–349, Beldam L.J.; *Mytre Investments Ltd.* v. *Reynolds* [1995] 3 All E.R. 588 Q.B.D.; *B.S.E. Trading Ltd.* v. *Hands* (1998) 75 P. & C.R. 138 C.A. (agreement with one of three sureties); C. Mitchell [1998] *Conv.* 133; *Morris* v. *Wentworth-Stanley* [1999] 2 W.L.R. 470 C.A. (accord with one debtor); *Johnson* v. *Davies* [1999] Ch. 117 C.A. (no release on facts).

[434] [1999] 2 E.G.L.R. 135 Ch.D.; G. Baker [1999] 34 *P.L.J.* 18.

[435] *Re Yarmarine* [1992] B.C.L.C. 276.

[436] *Allied Dunbar Assurance plc.* v. *Fowle* [1994] 1 E.G.L.R. 122, Garland J.; *Stanhope Pension Trust Ltd.* v. *Registrar of Companies* (1995) 69 P. & C.R. 238 C.A.; A. Belcher [1995] *Conv.* 199.

[437] *Ivory Gate Ltd.* v. *Spetale* [1998] 2 E.G.L.R. 43 C.A.

[438] *Coronation Street Industrial Properties Ltd.* v. *Ingall Industries plc.* [1989] 1 W.L.R. 304 H.L.; *Xey S.A.* v. *Abbey Life Assurance Co. Ltd.* [1994] E.G.C.S. 190; *Re Spirit Motorsport Ltd.* [1996] 1 B.C.L.C. 684, Laddie J.

[439] *Re Yarmarine* [1992] B.C.L.C. 276, Millett J.

[440] [1997] A.C. 70 H.L.; S. Bridge [1995] *C.L.J.* 253; J. Tayleur [1997] *Conv.* 24.

[441] *Hill* v. *East & West India Dock Co.* (1884) 9 App.Cas. 448 H.L.; *Stacey* v. *Hill* [1901] 1 Q.B. 660 C.A.

current tenant from liability for future rent.[442] However the landlord was then allowed to pursue substitutes, and indeed the whole object of taking sureties is to protect the landlord against the insolvency of the current tenant. On the facts of *Hindcastle*, three different forms of substitutes were sued: the original tenant,[443] an intermediate tenant under a direct covenant, and his surety. Other possibilities are a surety of the original tenant[444] and a surety of a later assignee.[445]

6.   Overriding leases

Conversely the Landlord and Tenant (Covenants) Act 1995 gives a surety or a tenant who is compelled to make payments[446] under an arrears notice issued under a relevant lease (whether new or old) the right to claim an overriding lease.[447] This is a reversionary lease, identified as such, three days longer than the relevant lease under which the default has occurred.[448] This will not usually be a sensible thing for a substitute to do. It is unlikely that much use will be made of this procedure, but if there do happen to be several claims, a tenant is preferred to a guarantor, and an earlier claim has priority over a later one. The landlord is deemed to consent to the grant of the lease, which is not a breach of covenant against assignment.

R.   SUBSTITUTES: REIMBURSEMENT AND INDEMNITY

If a substitute is target by a landlord and compelled to make a payment, the substitute may seek reimbursement from the current tenant with ultimate liability[449] or some intermediate party with a liability which is higher than the person claiming reimbursement.

---

[442] Not for existing arrears: *Re No.1 London Ltd.* [1991] B.C.L.C. 501, Hoffmann J., a good point despite the reliance on *Stacey* v. *Hill*.

[443] *Warnford Investments Ltd.* v. *Duckworth* [1979] Ch. 127, Megarry V.C.; *W.H. Smith Ltd.* v. *Wyndham Investments Ltd.* (1995) 70 P. & C.R. 21.

[444] *Kumar* v. *Dunning* [1989] 1 Q.B. 193 C.A.; *P & A. Swift Investments* v. *Combined English Stores Group plc.* [1989] A.C. 632 H.L.; *M.E.P.C. Ltd.* v. *Scottish Amicable Life Assurance Society* [1993] 2 E.G.L.R. 93 C.A.

[445] *Barclays Bank plc.* v. *Prudential Assurance Co. Ltd.* [1998] 1 E.G.L.R. 44 Ch.D.

[446] s.17.

[447] ss.19, 20; S. Elvidge & P. Williams [1996] 47 *E.G.* 132; E. Slessenger (2000) 144 *S.J.* 725.

[448] s.20(2); S.I. 1995/3154 (prescribed form of statement); the terms are the same as the previous lease unless otherwise agreed.

[449] *Re Downer's Enterprises Ltd.* [1974] 1 W.L.R. 1460, 1470D, Pennycuick V.C.; *Kumar* v. *Dunning* [1989] Q.B. 193, 201, Browne-Wilkinson V.C.; *Becton Dickinson U.K. Ltd.* v. *Zwebner* [1989] Q.B. 208, McNeill J.

Reimbursement may occur contractually or in restitution. A default notice is not required.[450]

1.   Dual liability

Landlords have at least two tenants as potential defendants in any action for rent against an assignee, and commonly the landlord's position is further strengthened by a multiplicity of sureties. Liability is dual, or in other words concurrent.[451] The landlord can chose the plumpest target for his writ. Thus if the landlord charges rent without V.A.T. from his tenant, he may nevertheless pursue the surety for the unpaid V.A.T.[452] Satisfaction of any given debt can only be obtained once, though there could be multiple actions and multiple executions.[453] A receipt issued against one will discharge all others.[454] It is no defence to say that the landlord was careless in accepting a financially risky tenant, and no defence to say that another defendant should have been pursued first.[455] However, this is not a joint liability (as it is if two tenants hold a lease jointly[456]) because the order of liability is ranked into one primary or ultimate liability and the other a substitute, so that if the substitute is forced to pay he has a right of reimbursement from the person with ultimate liability.[457]

2.   Restitutionary claims for reimbursement

Where there is no direct contractual relationship between the plaintiff seeking reimbursement and the defendant who must pay, the reimbursement may be described as a quasi-contractual indemnity, but it is really a freestanding obligation in restitution. A duty on A to make restitution to B arises where A is unjustly enriched at B's expense, and that includes the current tenant who allows a substitute to be sued on covenants for which he is liable. Restitution and contractual indemnity provide independent heads of liability so that, apparently, express exclusion of the right to contractual indemnity will not affect liability in restitution.[458]

One well-recognised head of restitutionary claim arises where another person's debt is paid under legal compulsion. Cockburn C.J. stated generally in *Moule* v. *Garrett*[459] that:

---

[450] *M.W. Kellogg Ltd.* v. *F. Tobin* [1999] L.T.R. 513 Q.B.D.; D. Stevens [1999] 20 *E.G.* 152; *Fresh (Retail) Ltd.* v. *Emsden* [1999] 5 C.L. 455 (no requirement for s.17 notice between ST0 and ST2).

[451] *Allied London Investments Ltd.* v. *Hambro Life Assurance plc.* (1985) 50 P. & C.R. 207, 210, Ackner L.J.

[452] *Knighton Estates Ltd.* v. *Gallic Management Co. Ltd.* (1999) 78 P. & C.R. 52 C.A.

[453] *House Property & Investment Co. Ltd.* v. *Bernardout* [1948] 1 K.B. 314, Singleton J., explaining *Brett* v. *Cumberland* (1619) Cro. Jac. 521, 79 E.R. 446.

[454] *March* v. *Brace* (1614) 2 Bulst. 151, 153, 80 E.R. 1025 (T1 paid rent; L0 could not sue T0); *Orgill* v. *Kemshead* (1812) 4 Taunt. 642, 128 E.R. 407; *Sturgess* v. *Farrington* (1812) 4 Taunt. 614, 128 E.R. 471 (defence rejected only because of defect in pleading).

[455] *Norwich Union Life Insurance Society* v. *Low Profile Fashions Ltd.* [1992] 1 E.G.L.R. 86 C.A.; S. Bridge [1992] *C.L.J.* 425.

[456] See above p. 747 n. 11.

[457] Not if payment is volunteered: *Crantrave Ltd.* v. *Lloyds Bank plc.* [2000] 4 All E.R. 473 C.A.

[458] *Re Healing Research Trustee Co. Ltd.* [1992] 2 All E.R. 481, Harman J.

[459] (1872) L.R. 7 Exch. 101 Exch. Ch., affirming (1870) L.R. 5 Exch. 132.

"where one person is compelled to pay damages on the legal default of another, he is entitled to recover from the person by whose default the damage was occasioned for the sum so paid."[460]

Assignment of leases provides a major application of this restitutionary reimbursement principle.[461]

Goff and Jones state three requirements: (1) that the plaintiff was compelled or at least compellable to discharge another's debt; (2) that he did not officiously expose himself to liability; and (3) that the payment discharged a liability of the defendant.[462] *Moule* v. *Garrett* illustrates all three. The original tenant was required to pay damages for disrepair in an action brought by the executors of the original landlord. It was held that he was entitled to obtain an indemnity direct from the current tenant, despite the presence of express contractual indemnities in the intermediate assignments.

At one time it was said that it made no difference whether the indemnity rested on an implied contract or was an obligation imposed by law. Restitution was then less firmly based and there was a tendency to seek a contractual basis for indemnity.[463] However if there are intermediate assignments, there is no negotiating relationship between the parties and no occasion to imply contractual bargains.[464] It is now clearly best to view this as an obligation based on the moral and legal duty to restore what has been obtained unjustly.

Goff and Jones' third requirement is that payment discharged a liability of the defendant, so (since the plaintiff must be compellable) the claimant must demonstrate that he is a substitute.[465] Action is permitted by the original tenant to enforce the ultimate liability of the current tenant.[466] Other legitimate examples of reimbursement are between tenants of parts,[467] and against an intermediate tenant for a breach occurring while he was tenant,[468] and possibly also against an equitable assignee.[469] A sub-tenant is not normally liable on the same obligation as the head tenant,[470] but if ultimate responsibility for a service charge falls on a sub-tenant, there is no reason why a tenant cannot claim reimbursement from the sub-tenant.[471]

In *Selous Street Properties Ltd.* v. *Oronel Fabrics Ltd.*[472] action was allowed both by the original tenant (T0) sued on privity of contract and his surety (S0) for reimbursement

---

[460] This is based on contribution principle: *Bonner* v. *Tottenham & Edmonton P.I.B.S.* [1899] 1 Q.B. 161, 172–173, Vaughan Williams L.J.

[461] Goff & Jones, *The Law of Restitution* (Sweet & Maxwell, 4th ed., 1993) 347–349. On relief from distress see: *Exall* v. *Partridge* (1799) 8 Term.Rep. 308, 101 E.R. 1405; *Groom* v. *Bluck* (1841) 2 Man. & G. 567, 133 E.R. 873.

[462] At 344; see n. 457 above.

[463] (1870) L.R. 5 Ex. 132, 138, Channell B.

[464] *Re Healing Research Trustee Co. Ltd.* [1992] 2 All E.R. 481, Harman J.; P. Luxton [1992] *J.B.L.* 178.

[465] *Duncan Fox & Co.* v. *N. & S. Wales Bank* (1860) 6 App.Cas. 1, 10, Selborne L.C.; *Re Downer Enterprises Ltd.* [1974] 1 W.L.R. 1460, 1468, Pennycuick J.

[466] *Moule* v. *Garrett* (1872) L.R. 7 Ex. 101 Ex. Ch.; *Humble* v. *Langston* (1841) &. M. & W. 517, 151 E.R. 871.

[467] *Whitham* v. *Bullock* [1939] 2 K.B. 81 C.A.

[468] *Burnett* v. *Lynch* (1826) 5 B. & C. 589, 108 E.R. 220; *Walker* v. *Bartlett* (1856) 18 C.B. 845, 139 E.R. 1004; *Humble* v. *Langston* (1841) 7 M. & W. 517, 530, 151 E.R. 871, Parke B., distinguished.

[469] *Close* v. *Wilberforce* (1838) 1 Beav. 112, 48 E.R. 881, Landgale M.R.

[470] *Bonner* v. *Tottenham & Edmonton P.I.B.S.* [1899] 2 Q.B. 161 C.A.

[471] *Electricity Supply Nominees Ltd.* v. *Thorn E.M.I. Retail Ltd.* [1991] 2 E.G.L.R. 46 C.A.; P. Luxton [1992] *J.B.L.* 178.

[472] [1984] 1 E.G.L.R. 50, 61–62, Hutchison J.; C. Whippman & C. Green [1984] *J.B.L.* 419; P. McLoughlin [1984] *Conv.* 443.

from an intermediate assignee (T2),[473] and against the surety of the current tenant (SC).[474] These actions where the defendant is not the ultimate are more contentious and the reliance on subrogation theory[475] may be defective; all three claims were novel and the liabilities of those obliged were not genuinely secondary to those whom they reimbursed.[476]

3. Contractual indemnity

A contract to reimburse another for loss suffered as a result of the conduct of that other is called an indemnity. These are redundant for *post-1995 leases*. Liability of a previous tenant cannot now survive sale of a lease so indemnity covenants are never required.[477] For *pre-1996 leases* statute implied an indemnity covenant into every assignment of a pre-1996 lease for valuable consideration.[478] This statutory covenant applies to any covenant, whether or not it touches and concerns the land. No indemnity covenant is implied in a pure gift, so that a gift requires either an express contractual indemnity or the payment of a nominal price to secure the implication of the statutory indemnity covenant.[479] Express covenants are also essential following transmissions on death. The covenant implied by statute is an indemnity covenant.[480] No promise is made by the buyer of the lease to observe the covenants, so that the seller has no right to enforce the covenants directly.[481] Nor can the courts make a general declaration of a future duty to indemnify.[482] An indemnity merely provides reimbursement to the seller for any damages paid out to the landlord or earlier tenants, plus costs.[483]

Contractual indemnity relies on a chain of indemnity. The present purchaser promises that he will indemnify for all future breaches even after he has sold on.[484] This requires a whole sequence of actions, or rather one mammoth cause of action into which all parties are drawn by third party notices.[485] A good example is *Smith* v. *Howell*[486]:

[473] Contrast *Wolveridge* v. *Steward* (1833) 1 Cr. & M. 644, 149 E.R. 557; *Smith* v. *Peat* (1853) 9 Exch.161, 156 E.R. 69 (question of fact). The rule was not settled at the time of the early case *Anon* (1577) 4 Leon. 17, 74 E.R. 698 (tenant can choose whom to sue, immediate assignee or later one).

[474] *Cale* v. *Assuidoman K.P.S. (Harrow) Ltd.* [1996] B.P.I.R. 245 (T0 v SC).

[475] *Banque Financière de la Cité* v. *Parc (Battersea) Ltd.* [1999] A.C. 229 H.L.; D. Wright [1999] *Conv.* 113; C. Mitchell [1998] *Rest.L.R.* 144; *B.S.E. Trading Ltd.* v. *Hands* (1998) 75 P. & C.R. 138 C.A.; C. Mitchell [1998] *Conv.* 133 (cannot subrogate S to L to give right to forfeit).

[476] P. Sparkes, "Reimbursement of Tenant Substitutes" in P. Jackson and D.C. Wilde (eds.), *Contemporary Property Law* (Ashgate Dartmouth, 1999).

[477] L.T. (Covenants) A. 1995 s.14; S.I. 1995/3153.

[478] L.P.A. 1925 s.77(1)(c) (unregistered); L.R.A. 1925 s.24(1)(b) (registered); *Re Healing Research Trustee Co. Ltd.* [1992] 2 All E.R. 481, Harman J. (transfer lost).

[479] *Johnsey Estates Ltd.* v. *Lewis & Manley (Engineering) Ltd.* [1987] 2 E.G.L.R. 69 C.A. (consideration of £1 is value); *Re Lawley* [1911] 2 Ch. 530 (payment to the assignee is not value).

[480] *Re Poole & Clarke's C.* [1904] 2 Ch. 173.

[481] *Butler Estates Co.* v. *Bean* [1942] 1 K.B. 1 C.A.; *Ayling* v. *Wade* [1961] 2 Q.B. 228; R.E. Megarry (1961) 77 L.Q.R. 316; *Yorkbrook Investments Ltd.* v. *Batten* [1985] 2 E.G.L.R. 100. On pre-1926 express indemnities see: *Harris* v. *Boots the Cash Chemists (Southern) Ltd.* [1904] 2 Ch. 376; *Reckitt* v. *Cody* [1920] 2 Ch. 452.

[482] *Lloyd* v. *Dimmack* (1877) 7 Ch.D. 398.

[483] *Smith* v. *Howell* (1851) 6 Ex. 730, 155 E.R. 739, Pollock J.; *Howard* v. *Lovegrove* (1870) L.R. 6 Ex. 43; *Re Russell* (1885) 29 Ch.D. 254.

[484] *Crossfield* v. *Morrison* (1849) 7 C.B. 286, 137 E.R. 114; *Short* v. *Kalloway* (1839) 11 Ad. & El. 28, 113 E.R. 322.

[485] *Baker* v. *Merckel* [1960] 1 Q.B. 657 C.A. (L sued T0, who brought in T1, who brought in T2).

[486] (1851) 6 Exch. 730, 155 E.R. 739.

Previous cases had held T0 liable to L0 and had allowed T0 to reimburse himself from T1, so the reported action (T1 v TC) was the third in the sequence.

Insolvency or death may break the chain. In *Warnford Investments Ltd.* v. *Duckworth*[487] there were successive assignments to T3, who became bankrupt. As Megarry V.C. pointed out the landlord will prefer to claim against the original, solvent, tenant, rather than the current bankrupt one. And T0 will prefer his contractual indemnity claim to a claim to a dividend in T3's bankruptcy. The liability can be passed down by successive indemnity claims from T0 to T1, from T1 to T2; T2 will then be compelled to prove in T3's bankruptcy. It is justice, of a sort, to place the greatest burden on the party who has sold to the person who becomes bankrupt.

The benefit of a contractual indemnity can be assigned, and this enables action to be taken between parties who are not neighbours in the chain. Thus in *Fresh (Retail) Ltd.* v. *Emsden*[488] the original sub-tenant (ST0) took an assignment of the benefit of the contractual indemnity ST2 gave to ST1. This assignment to ST0 occurred after ST1's bankruptcy, and in this way ST0 was enabled to sue ST2 directly. However this all depends upon the ability to secure an assignment (which will have to be bought). The collapse of the Mirror Group empire of Robert Maxwell gave rise to the litigation in *R.P.H. Ltd.* v. *Mirror Group Newspapers Ltd.*[489] The landlord (itself ironically a Mirror Group company) sought £1.5 million rent from the current tenant which was unable to pay. It therefore sued Reed, the original tenant, who sought to pass on liability to successive assignees that were all members of the Mirror Group. Mirror Group Holdings, the first tenant down the chain, was insolvent and so was unable to pay, thus blocking action further down the chain. Nicholls V.C. refused to order the liquidator of T1 to assign to T0 the benefit of its covenant against T2. If the lease is sold at a time when there is a breach of covenant,[490] the seller may sue for an indemnity from the buyer,[491] but the buyer may have an equal and correlative action on the covenants for title[492]; this impasse achieves the right result, since the party responsible for the breach must carry the can for it. It is better to modify the contractual indemnity covenant to limit it to breaches occurring after the sale.[493]

---

[487] [1979] 1 Ch. 127, 140–141, Megarry V.C.
[488] [1999] 5 C.L. 455.
[489] (1992) 65 P. & C.R. 252,; A. Belcher [1995] *Conv.* 199. Nicholls V.C. followed *Re Perkins* [1898] 2 Ch. 182 C.A.; *British Union & National Insurance Co.* v. *Rawson* [1916] 2 Ch. 476; *Re Harrington Motor Co.* [1928] Ch. 105.
[490] The breach may be a defence to an action for specific performance: *Rellie* v. *Pyke* [1936] 1 All E.R. 345.
[491] *Gooch* v. *Clutterbuck* [1899] 2 Q.B. 148 C.A.
[492] *Cator Art Services Ltd.* v. *Kenneth Bieber Photography Ltd.* [1969] 1 W.L.R. 1226 C.A.
[493] *Hawkins* v. *Sherman* (1828) 3 C. & P. 459, 172 E.R. 500.

29

FORFEITURE

Leases affected. Reservation of right. Arrears of rent. Notice procedure. Disrepair and arrears of service charge. Reform. Re-entry by proceedings. Physical re-entry. Waiver. Reform. Relief from non-payment of rent. Relief from other breaches. Relief after physical re-entry. Procedure and reletting. Reform. Relief for derivative holders. Insolvency. Denial of title. Court procedure. Land registry practice.

Forfeiture is the right of a landlord to terminate a lease as a result of the tenant's breach of covenant.[1] The picture to be presented is one of the least coherent of any aspect of the law of property. Part of the problem arises from the fact that strict common law rules are overlaid by equity and various statutory rules, in an inconsistent pattern. More fundamental is the fact that piecemeal development has created two distinct procedures, one where forfeiture arises from non-payment of rent and another where any other covenant is broken. Equitable intervention has led to too great an indulgence to indolent tenants, and the law of waiver is a positive trap for landlords. The Law Commission has reported in favour of a comprehensive statutory code stated in modern terms,[2] and has proposed clauses for a Termination of Tenancies Bill.[3] Some rejigging is now required to allow for the retention of physical re-entry,[4] but it is intended to publish a second draft bill in the year 2000,[5] and it must be hoped that legislative time will be made available for the enactment of this badly needed reform.

A. LEASES AFFECTED

Forfeiture is the right of the landlord to re-enter the premises that he had let to the tenant because of the tenant's breach of covenant, and to terminate the lease on account of that breach. Its greatest use is for flats and commercial premises. The threat of forfeiture is the main weapon available against the leaseholder of the long lease of a house or flat to ensure that he complies with his covenants. If the leaseholder fails to repair his flat as he has promised, the landlord can threaten to terminate the lease, knowing that any

---

[1] Woodfall 17.057–17.195, 19.030–19.133; Bright & Gilbert 558–570; Davey 134–155; Evans & Smith (5th ed.) 241–260; Garner (2nd ed.) ch.11.

[2] Law Com. No.142 (1985); S. Tromans [1986] *Conv.* 187; P.F. Smith [1986] *Conv.* 165.

[3] Law Com. No.221 (1994); H.W. Wilkinson [1994] *Conv.* 177; J.E. Adams [1994] *Conv.* 184; M. Codd & T. Bayley [1994] *N.L.J.* 1420, 1456; C. Peete [1994] 26 *E.G.* 133. Clause numbers in this chapter are from this draft.

[4] See below p. 811.

[5] Law Com. *Press Release*, June 30th 1999, para.1; Law Com. No.258 (1999) para.5.6.

sensible owner of a valuable leasehold estate will choose to carry out repairs rather than lose the investment represented by his estate. Forfeiture of business and agricultural property is also common. Most business tenants pay a market rent for their premises, meaning that termination of the lease is a less effective threat. Its value as a sanction is that termination of a business lease removes the goodwill attaching to the existing trading location. Nevertheless many tenants are looking for an opportunity to walk away from a property, perhaps because the repairing covenants are very onerous, because the tenant is insolvent or nearly so, or because the rent was set at a high level in a period of prosperity and has become unrealistically high in a period of recession. A tenant may view a decision to forfeit in such situations as a godsend.

A tenancy which is periodic and with a short period—weekly or monthly—does not require any forfeiture provision, since the tenancy is soon ended by notice to quit. The right to serve notice may be made dependent upon a breach of covenant.[6] This is still a notice to quit and not a true forfeiture, so the tenant has no right to remain by remedying the breach of covenant. Tenancies with a longer period may need a provision for termination on breach of covenant.

In any event, a short residential tenancy within the security of tenure schemes will not be ended by forfeiture, but rather under a statutory ground for repossession.[7] This point was determined in relation to assured tenancies—that is private sector residential tenancies granted after early 1989—but the same result must flow for earlier Rent Act tenancies and public sector secure tenancies. In *Artesian Residential Developments Ltd.* v. *Beck*[8] a 10-year lease of a dwelling in Bridgnorth contained a right for the landlord to re-enter if rent was 14 days in arrears. Since the tenant occupied the property as his principal home this was an assured tenancy.[9] The landlord gave notice on the statutory ground of major rent arrears, which meant that a possession order was mandatory. Having paid the arrears within three days of the possession order, the tenant then sought to continue in occupation. His argument was that he came within the contractual protection of the 10-year term, that this contractual protection could only be ended by forfeiture, and that therefore he had a right to relief by paying what owing.[10] The Court of Appeal rejected this argument: the assured tenancies legislation[11] made clear that a possession order ended the tenancy and that this was by virtue of the court order and not under the terms of the forfeiture provision. A clause providing for termination on breach is needed to end the contractual protection, but exercise of it is a repossession rather than a forfeiture.

B. TERMINATION EVENTS: RESERVATION OF THE RIGHT

The right of the landlord to re-enter the premises on account of the tenant's breach of covenant must be reserved by the terms of the lease, apart, that is, for one rare case.[12] In

---

[6] *Clays Lane Housing Co-Operative* v. *Patrick* (1985) 49 P. & C.R. 72 C.A.; J.E. Martin [1986] *Conv.* 44.
[7] See also above Chapter 13.
[8] [1999] 3 All E.R. 113 C.A.
[9] See above pp. 104–105.
[10] The particular relief claimed was under the County Courts Act 1984 s.138; see below p. 816.
[11] H.A. 1988 ss.5(1), 7(3), 45(4).
[12] For denial of the landlord's title, see below pp. 835–836.

all other cases, existence of this remedy is dependent upon the terms of the lease. Leases can be made conditional on the performance of particular covenants, but this is rare in modern practice. Usually covenants are set out as straightforward promises between landlord and tenant,[13] the right of termination taking the form of a separate proviso—beginning in old leases with the words "provided always that"—which gives the right of the landlord when a particular covenant is breached. If a lease requires payment of rent on the 1st of each month, with a proviso for forfeiture in the event of non-payment for 21 days, there is a breach of covenant at any time after the 1st, but the right of termination only arises on the 23rd. Provisos are generally drafted so as to allow forfeiture for breach of *any* covenant, but it is perfectly possible to create two classes of breach, some of which are and some which are not termination events.

C. TERMINATION EVENTS: ARREARS OF RENT

1. No notice requirement

Notice is not required before the landlord forfeits a lease for non-payment of rent.[14] Leases generally provide for termination when rent is left unpaid for a stated period, and after that period the landlord may elect to forfeit, probably by suing for possession. While proceedings are pending or after judgment, the landlord may be compelled to allow relief to a tenant who stumps up the money. Contrast the notice procedure adopted for other breaches,[15] by which the tenant is given time right at the beginning to rectify the breach, can claim relief during court proceedings, but has lost all rights once the judgment for possession is enforced. The notice procedure works better.

Division of forfeiture procedures implies a borderline and the need to allocate cases to one procedure or another. Rent means any periodical sum for which distress is available,[16] which certainly includes payment for the use of land, but could also include other payments, such as service charges and insurance premiums. *Escalus Properties Ltd.* v. *Robinson*[17] concerned four leases of houses and flats in South London, each subject to service charges. In two cases[18] the service charge was deemed to be additional rent, so the Court of Appeal held that the rent procedure applied. Another lease lacked this provision, so that the service charge was not directly reserved as rent,[19] meaning that the section 146 notice procedure applied. The later Court of Appeal which decided *Khar* v. *Delmounty Ltd.*[20] confirmed that *Escalus* was a binding decision, so that the terms of the lease are decisive: the rent procedure does not apply unless the service charge is either mentioned in the reddendum—the technical part of the lease beginning "reserving"

---

[13] On forfeiture of equitable leases, see: P. Sparkes (1987) 16 *Anglo-American* 160; *Dream Factory Ltd.* v. *Crown Estate Commissioners* [1998] Times October 22nd Ch.D.; and above pp. 531–532.

[14] L.P.A. 1925 s.146(11). For proposals for ground rent demands, see above p. 376.

[15] See below pp. 796–804. As to service charges see above Chapter 16.

[16] [1996] Q.B. 231, 243H, Nourse L.J. Query this definition since earlier cases had distinguished contractual rent and distrainable rent.

[17] [1996] Q.B. 231 C.A.

[18] *Robinson* and *Cooper-Smith*; the case of *Walsh* concerned arrears of rent exclusively; all the cases are reported together.

[19] *Dennis* (also reported with *Robinson*); this may now be subject to H.A. 1996.

[20] (1998) 75 P. & C.R. 232 C.A.

which creates the rent—or is deemed to be recoverable as rent. A tenant whose breach is "rent-only" may be entitled to an automatic stay of the proceedings by paying what is due into court,[21] whereas in other cases relief is discretionary.

2. Entitlement to forfeit

The landlord must show that the rent is owing[22] and that the terms of the forfeiture provision are satisfied. Leases commonly allow for forfeiture if rent is unpaid for 21 days, but this period is contracted even further in modern commercial leases to 14 (or even seven) days.[23] Special provisions apply to service charges.[24]

Formal demand for the rent was essential at common law. The landlord had to attend at the property and request the rent owing from the tenant, appearing a sufficient period before sunset to allow the money to be counted out in daylight. An alternative[25] is to rely upon an old statute that abolished the requirement of formal demand where rent is six months in arrears, though a disadvantage of this is that the landlord must show that there is no sufficient distress on the premises. In practice landlords are prepared neither to waste money on an abortive distress nor to wait six months. These inconveniences are best avoided by providing for forfeiture on non-payment of rent "whether formally demanded or not".

Totally novel, but of exceptional difficulty and interest, is the point raised in *Kataria* v. *Safeland plc*.[26] The tenant of a walk-in kiosk on Kingsway in London owed £10,000 rent. When the freehold was sold to Safeland it was on the terms that the arrears would be recoverable by the previous landlord. Two days after acquiring the freehold, Safeland re-entered the property and forfeited the lease on the grounds of arrears of rent. This was so, even though no rent was owing to the new landlord company at that time. Brooke L.J. held that it was entitled to forfeit since the proprietary right to re-enter was distinct from the personal right to take action on the covenant. Under the present law, Safeland was entitled to behave as it had done.

D. TERMINATION EVENTS: NOTICE PROCEDURE

1. Requirement of notice

Breaches other than arrears of rent[27] entitle a landlord to forfeit (whether by court proceedings or by peaceable re-entry) only after service of a notice on the current tenant[28] under section 146 of the Law of Property Act 1925.[29] The right to a notice cannot be

---

[21] See below p. 816.

[22] It may be subject to a set-off: *Old Grovebury Manor Farm Ltd.* v. *W. Seymour Plant Sales & Hire Ltd.* [1979] 1 W.L.R. 263 C.A.

[23] Rent is usually payable in advance, meaning that the landlord can forfeit before the end of the period for which rent is due: *Capital & City Holdings Ltd.* v. *Dean Warburg Ltd.* [1989] 1 E.G.L.R. 90 C.A.

[24] See below p. 804.

[25] Common Law Procedure Act 1852 s.210, re-enacting L.T.A. 1730 s.2.

[26] [1998] 1 E.G.L.R. 39 C.A.

[27] L.P.A. 1925 s.146(11).

[28] *Fuller* v. *Judy Properties Ltd.* [1992] 1 E.G.L.R. 75 C.A.

[29] Re-enacting Conveyancing Act 1881 s.14, as amended by Conveyancing Act 1892 s.4.

excluded, directly or indirectly,[30] and it is not permissible to make a lease determinable when a breach occurs.[31] Forfeiture without service of a notice is a trespass.[32]

A section 146 notice is intended to inform the tenant what is wrong and so give him an opportunity to rectify any breach if this is possible. Before 1881, when the notice procedure was first enacted, landlords often forfeited before the tenant had an opportunity to meet the complaint, and even before he was aware of the allegation that a breach had occurred.[33] The tenant must be given an opportunity to consider his position, and to decide whether to admit the breach, whether it is capable of remedy, how much compensation to offer, and whether or not to apply for relief.[34] Hence the three (almost) essential contents of a pre-forfeiture notice: (1) it must specify the particular breach complained of; (2) it must require the tenant to remedy the breach, assuming that it is capable of remedy; and (3) it must require the tenant to make compensation in money for the breach. Additional requirements apply to notices alleging disrepair or non-payment of service charge.[35]

2. Specification of the breach

The whole point of a notice is to alert the tenant to the fact that particular remedial work is required. Precise compliance with covenants is always an impossibility.[36] Literally there is a breach whether the roof is about to collapse or there is one missing roof tile. Re-entry out of court could scarcely be avoided, since no property can be kept constantly in a perfect state of repair. Section 146 notices prevent this. The landlord is obliged to specify "the particular breach complained of",[37] ensuring that the tenant is forewarned both that he is alleged to be in breach and what that breach is, and is also given a chance to put matters right.

A general notice stating that "You have broken the covenants for repairing the inside and the outside of the house" is insufficient.[38] But provided the breach is particularised, there is no requirement to spell out precisely what it is that the tenant is being required to do.[39] The leading modern case, *Adagio Properties Ltd.* v. *Ansari*,[40] concerned a notice that specified the breach as "making alterations so as to divide the flat without permission". The Court of Appeal held that this was sufficiently explicit to tell the tenant what needed doing, and so was valid. Each statement in a section 146 notice is separate[41]: hence the notice is valid provided that it includes some genuine breaches, despite the addition of other

[30] L.P.A. 1925 s.146(12).
[31] s.146(7); *Plymouth Corporation* v. *Harvey* [1971] 1 W.L.R. 549 (undated surrender).
[32] *Charville Estates Ltd.* v. *Unipart Group Ltd.* [1997] E.G.C.S. 36.
[33] *Fox* v. *Jolly* [1916] 1 A.C. 1, 7–8, Lord Buckmaster L.C.
[34] *Horsey Estates Ltd.* v. *Steiger* [1899] 2 Q.B. 79, 91, Lord Russell C.J.
[35] See below pp. 801–805.
[36] *Bass Holdings Ltd.* v. *Morton Music Ltd.* [1988] Ch. 493, 528C, Nicholls L.J.
[37] L.P.A. 1925 s.146(1).
[38] *Fletcher* v. *Nokes* [1897] 1 Ch. 271, North J.; *Re Serle* [1898] 1 Ch. 652, Kekewich J.; *Fox* v. *Jolly* [1916] 1 A.C. 1 H.L.
[39] *Fox* v. *Jolly* [1916] A.C. 1, 11, Lord Buckmaster L.C.; *Cardigan Properties Ltd.* v. *Consolidated Property Investments Ltd.* [1991] 1 E.G.L.R. 64, 67E, P.J. Cox Q.C.; J.E. Martin [1991] *Conv.* 222.
[40] [1998] 2 E.G.L.R. 69 C.A.
[41] *Fox* v. *Jolly* [1916] 1 A.C. 1, 18, Lord Atkinson; also at 12–13.

inaccurate complaints.[42] In theory the landlord could still undertake a nit-picking inspection and serve a draconian dilapidations notice requiring expensive but trivial work, but this is largely prevented by allowing relief from forfeiture and by additional restrictions on notices relating to repairs.[43] As explained below[44] acceptance of rent after service of a notice will often waive the right to forfeit, but repair is a continuing breach and no new notice is required, particularly if further deterioration occurs after the date of the notice.[45]

3.   Reasonable time for remedy

A section 146 notice must require that the breach specified in it should be remedied. Hence a notice cannot be served after the remedial work has been completed.[46] A solitary case that upheld a notice served after re-entry for an irremediable breach is thought to be doubtful, since there is still a right to apply for relief.[47]

A reasonable time must elapse between service of the pre-forfeiture warning notice and the commencement of proceedings,[48] though curiously there is no requirement for the notice to state what that reasonable time is.[49] The time to be allowed is determined by the court that hears any challenge to the validity of the forfeiture notice. Two days have been held to be too short a time to effect a repair.[50] As much as four weeks have been allowed to effect insurance,[51] though this last decision seems over generous. In *Expert Clothing Service & Sales Ltd.* v. *Hillgate House Ltd.*,[52] the tenants had agreed to reconstruct a property ready for occupation by September 1982, and 15 more months had elapsed by the time that the landlord sought to forfeit, but further time had to be allowed by the section 146 notice. Breaches of a positive covenant are generally capable of remedy.[53]

The landlord may be prevented by injunction from proceeding to forfeit before a reasonable period of time for remedial work has elapsed.[54] After that time, the landlord will usually claim possession by court proceedings—in which case the tenant can seek relief by way of defence to the proceedings. An alternative is physical re-entry, after which the tenant is entitled to claim relief in separate proceedings.[55]

---

[42] *Lock* v. *Pearce* [1893] 2 Ch. 271, Lord Esher M.R.; *Fletcher* v. *Nokes* [1897] 1 Ch. 271, North J.; *Pannell* v. *City of London Brewery Co.* [1900] 1 Ch. 496; *Guillemard* v. *Silverthorne* (1908) 99 L.T. 584, Ridley J.; *Silvester* v. *Ostrowska* [1959] 1 W.L.R. 1060; *Blewett* v. *Blewett* [1936] 2 All E.R. 188 C.A.

[43] See below pp 801–803.

[44] See below pp. 812–815.

[45] *Greenwich L.B.C.* v. *Discreet Selling Estates Ltd.* [1990] 1 E.G.L.R. 65 C.A., following *Penton* v. *Barrett* [1898] 1 Q.B. 276 C.A.

[46] *Horsey Estates Ltd.* v. *Steiger* [1899] 2 Q.B. 79, 91, Lord Russell C.J.; *S.E.D.A.C. Investments Ltd.* v. *Tanner* [1982] 1 W.L.R. 1342.

[47] *Fuller* v. *Judy Properties Ltd.* [1992] 1 E.G.L.R. 75 C.A.

[48] L.P.A. 1925 s.146(1).

[49] J.E. Adams [1991] *Conv.* 325.

[50] *Horsey Estate Ltd.* v. *Steiger* [1899] 2 Q.B. 79 C.A.

[51] *Cardigan Properties Ltd.* v. *Consolidated Property Investments Ltd.* [1991] 1 E.G.L.R. 64, P.J. Cox Q.C. (10 days too short); *John Lyon's Charity Trustees* v. *Haysport Properties Ltd.* [1995] E.G.C.S. 171, Carnwath J.

[52] [1986] Ch. 340 C.A.

[53] *Bhojwami* v. *Kingsley Investments Trust Ltd.* [1992] 2 E.G.L.R. 70; J.E. Martin [1993] *Conv.* 296 (2 months to remedy disrepair is adequate).

[54] *Associated Electrical Industries Ltd.* v. *Central Shops Ltd.* (1974) 230 E.G. 1123, Plowman J. (injunction unnecessary on the facts).

[55] See below pp. 821–822.

4. Breaches incapable of remedy

Since a pre-forfeiture notice needs to require the tenant to remedy the breach only "if it is capable of remedy",[56] it is implicit that some breaches are incapable of remedy. If so it is necessary only to specify the breach, require compensation where appropriate, and give a short period to quit[57]: two days are inadequate, but 14 days have been held to be sufficient.[58] Eviction of the tenant will not follow automatically since, strange as it may seem, the court has power to grant relief from forfeiture even after an irremediable breach.

Breaches of a covenant against *assignment* were brought within the section 146 notice procedure only in 1925.[59] A dealing is valid even if it is made in breach of covenant, so the landlord must pursue forfeiture against the buyer.[60] This is permitted after completion of a transaction made without asking for the landlord's permission,[61] or after consent has been asked for but refused by the landlord on reasonable grounds. A landlord's refusal is a defence to a forfeiture action if it is unreasonable,[62] but no buyer should accept a title made without a court declaration that the landlord has acted improperly. Assignment in breach of covenant is treated as an irremediable breach, so that the section 146 notice merely gives a short period of notice to quit. *Scala House & District Property Co. Ltd.* v. *Forbes*[63] held that 14 days' notice was sufficient. Even sub-letting cannot (apparently) be remedied by removal of the sub-tenant. The draconian nature of these rules about forfeiture is softened by the frequency with which waiver of the breach will occur where the landlord recognises the existence of the lease or sub-lease after receiving knowledge of the dealing.[64] A person who buys in breach of covenant becomes safe once the landlord has accepted rent from him. Irremediability of the breach does not prevent the court from acting, cautiously and sparingly, to grant relief from forfeiture[65] to a buyer who is blameless.[66] A buyer who deliberately broke the assignment covenant will be evicted,[67] as will one who failed to check the title.[68]

---

[56] L.P.A. 1925 s.146(1)(b).

[57] *Civil Service Co-operative Society Ltd.* v. *McGrigor's Trustees* [1923] 2 Ch. 347, 356, Russell J.

[58] *Scala House & District Property Co. Ltd.* v. *Forbes* [1974] Q.B. 575 C.A.

[59] L.P.A. 1925 s.146(8)(i), reversing Conveyancing Act 1881 s.14(6)(i); *Barrow* v. *Isaacs & Son* [1891] 1 Q.B. 417 C.A.; *Abrahams* v. *MacFisheries Ltd.* [1925] 2 K.B. 18 (parting with possession was always covered); *Scala House* [1974] Q.B. 575, 584–585.

[60] *Old Grovebury Manor Farm Ltd.* v. *W. Seymour Plant Sales & Hire Ltd. (No. 2)* [1979] 1 W.L.R. 1397, 400, Lord Russell C.J.

[61] *Fox* v. *Whitchcocke* (1616) 2 Bulst. 290, 80 E.R. 1129, Coke C.J.; *Doe d. Henniker* v. *Watt* (1828) 8 B. & C. 308, 108 E.R. 1057; D.G. Barnsley (1963) 27 *Conv.* (*N.S.*) 159, 175–177.

[62] *Pakwood Transport Ltd.* v. *15 Beauchamp Place Ltd.* (1978) P. & C.R. 112 C.A. The landlord loses the right to impose conditions that might have been reasonable: *Treloar* v. *Bigge* (1874) L.R. 9 Exch. 151.

[63] [1974] Q.B. 575 C.A.; P.V. Baker (1973) 89 L.Q.R. 460, D.J. Hayton [1974] *C.L.J.* 54; *Savva* v. *Houssein* [1996] 2 E.G.L.R. 65, 66G, Staughton L.J.

[64] *Welch* v. *Birrane* (1974) 29 P. & C.R. 102, Lawton J.

[65] *Savva* v. *Houssen* [1996] 2 E.G.L.R. 65, 66H, Staughton L.J.; *House Property & Investment Co. Ltd.* v. *James Walker, Goldsmith & Silversmith, Ltd.* [1948] 1 K.B. 257, Lord Goddard C.J. (*Barrow* v. *Isaacs & Son* [1891] 1 Q.B. 417 explained as a pre-1925 case); *Creery* v. *Summersell* [1949] Ch. 751.

[66] *Imray* v. *Oakshette* [1897] 2 Q.B. 218, 225, Lopes L.J.

[67] *Boxbusher Properties Ltd.* v. *Graham* [1976] 2 E.G.L.R. 58 Q.B.D.; *Ellis* v. *Allen* [1914] 1 Ch. 904, 909, Sargant J.

[68] *Imray* v. *Oakshette* [1897] 2 Q.B. 218 C.A.

A large clutch of cases arises from the *immoral stigma* that attaches to a property after it has been used for prostitution. Sexual immorality is invariably stated to be a termination event.[69] The stigma devalues the property itself, and so the breach is not remedied by cessation of the prostitute's trade.[70] In many cases the immoral use is by sub-tenants, who will certainly be evicted. The position of the tenant presents more difficulty. If wholly innocent of involvement with the prostitutes, he may not even be in breach of the terms of the lease,[71] but where the tenant does know of them, immediate steps to remedy the breach by evicting the sub-tenants may be sufficient to escape eviction,[72] especially if the stigma is minor or short-lived.[73] A tenant guilty of encouraging prostitution or standing by will have to prove exceptional hardship to stand any chance of relief from forfeiture.[74] No general relaxation is occurring in stigma cases.[75]

Scala House & District Property Co. Ltd. v. *Forbes*[76] suggested that any breach of *any negative covenant* is incapable of remedy: on this view one occurrence of something which is prohibited breaks the covenant for all time. However this draconian view did not take account of the fact that termination of an offending use is often an adequate remedy.[77] So the Court of Appeal held in *Savva* v. *Houssein*[78] that it is possible to remedy breaches of some negative covenants. Advertising signs were erected in breach of covenant, a problem solved simply by removing them. Similarly, unauthorised alterations can be removed to restore the landlord to the position in which he was before the breach. So a notice period often ought to be allowed to give time for the tenant to restore the property to its original condition. This chimes with the well-established rule that an option for renewal of a lease that is dependent upon compliance with the covenants in the existing lease is enforceable despite spent breaches.[79] Even if the particular breach cannot be remedied, waiver often occurs and there is the possibility of discretionary relief from the consequences of the breach.

5. Compensation

A pre-forfeiture notice should ask for compensation, at least if the landlord requires it,[80] and a reasonable time must then be allowed for payment of adequate compensation.[81]

---

[69] *Burfort Financial Investments Ltd.* v. *Chotard* [1976] 2 E.G.L.R. 53, Foster J. (the facts are racy).

[70] *Rugby School* v. *Tannahill* [1935] 1 K.B. 87 C.A. (the school were landlords!); L.G.C. (1933) 5 *C.L.J.* 396; *Borthwick-Norton* v. *Romney Warwick Estates Ltd.* [1950] 1 All E.R. 798 C.A.

[71] If it is not to *suffer* use for prostitution: *Egerton* v. *Esplanade Hotels London Ltd.* [1947] 2 All E.R. 88, Morris J.; (1947) 63 *L.Q.R.* 415.

[72] *Glass* v. *Kencakes Ltd.* [1966] 1 Q.B. 611, Paull J.; D. Macintyre [1965] *C.L.J.* 213.

[73] *Hoffmann* v. *Fineberg* [1949] Ch. 245, Harman J.; (1948) 63 *L.Q.R.* 312; *Ropemaker Properties Ltd.* v. *Noonhaven Ltd.* [1989] 2 E.G.L.R. 56, Millett J.

[74] *Central Estates (Belgravia) Ltd.* v. *Woolgar (No.2)* [1972] 1 W.L.R. 1048 C.A.

[75] *British Petroleum Pension Trust Ltd.* v. *Behrendt* [1985] 2 E.G.L.R. 97, 99G, Purchas L.J.

[76] [1974] Q.B. 575, 588B, Russell L.J.; P.V. Baker (1977) 89 *L.Q.R.* 460; *Rugby School* v. *Tannahill* [1934] 1 K.B. 695, 700–701, Mackinnon J. at first instance; *Billson* v. *Residential Apartments Ltd.* (1990) 60 P. & C.R. 392, 406, Mummery J.

[77] *St Marylebone Property Co.* v. *Tesco Stores Ltd.* [1988] 2 E.G.L.R. 40, Hoffmann J.

[78] [1996] 2 E.G.L.R. 65 C.A.; J. Harcup (1996) 140 *S.J.* 898. Doubts had been expressed: *Rugby School* v. *Tannahill* [1935] 1 K.B. 87, 92, Maugham L.J.; *Hoffmann* v. *Fineberg* [1949] Ch. 245, Harman J.

[79] *Bass Holdings Ltd.* v. *Morton Music Ltd.* [1988] Ch. 493.

[80] *Rugby School* v. *Tannahill* [1935] 1 K.B. 87 C.A. This followed *Lock* v. *Pearce* [1893] 2 Ch. 271, 276, Lord Esher M.R., and *Fox* v. *Jolly* [1916] 1 A.C. 1, 8, Lord Buckmaster L.C.

[81] L.P.A. 1925 s.146(1).

The amount which can be claimed under a section 146 notice does not include the cost of the notice itself, which means that a landlord cannot claim the costs of an abortive forfeiture: but leases invariably include an express covenant by the tenant to pay such costs.[82] If this clause is absent, and the case proceeds to the point of a court application by the tenant for relief, the costs of preparing a forfeiture notice are almost always allowed as a condition of allowing the tenant to claim relief,[83] even if the court technically retains power to refuse the landlord his full costs.[84]

6.   Special cases

Separate consideration is given to forfeiture on insolvency and for denial of the landlord's title.[85]

E.   TERMINATION EVENTS: DISREPAIR AND ARREARS OF SERVICE CHARGE

This section discusses the special requirements relating to notices alleging these two forms of breach.

1.   Proof of receipt of notice

If a notice relates to repair, the landlord must show that the tenant knew of it, and that a reasonable period of time has elapsed since it came to his attention.[86]

2.   Internal decorative repair

A pre-forfeiture notice relating to internal decorative repair must be shown to be reasonable.[87] This prevents excessive fussiness about standards of painting and wallpapering but, amazingly, there appear to be no reported cases which discuss what is reasonable.

3.   Unfair disrepair claims

Before the Second World War[88] unscrupulous people would buy up leases and then put pressure on tenants by producing exaggerated lists of dilapidations.[89] Many tenants lost their leases rather than face the expense of defending a forfeiture action.[90] The *Leasehold Property (Repairs) Act 1938* relieves this pressure, since the landlord must obtain

---

[82] *Bader Properties Ltd.* v. *Linley Property Investments Ltd.* (1968) 19 P. & C.R. 621; *Middlegate Properties Ltd.* v. *Gridlow-Jackson* (1977) 34 P. & C.R. 4 C.A.; *Pertemps Group Ltd.* v. *Crosher & James* [1999] 07 C.L. 325 (incidental costs include those incurred *after* the service of the notice).

[83] L.P.A. 1925 s.146(3); *Skinners Co.* v. *Knight* [1891] Q.B. 542 C.A.; *Nind* v. *Nineteenth Century B.S.* [1894] Q.B. 226 C.A.

[84] *Billson* v. *Residential Apartments Ltd.* [1992] 1 A.C. 494, 541, Lord Templeman (costs not on an indemnity basis).

[85] See below pp. 829–832.

[86] L.T.A. 1927 s.18(2).

[87] L.P.A. 1925 s.147.

[88] L.A. Blundell (1938) *Conv.* (N.S.) 10; (1938) 2 *M.L.R.* 160.

[89] *Sidnell* v. *Wilson* [1966] 2 Q.B. 67, 76E, Lord Denning M.R.; *Middlegate Properties Ltd.* v. *Messiemris* [1973] 1 W.L.R. 168, Lord Denning M.R.

[90] [1990] 2 A.C. 703, 709B, Lord Templeman.

permission from the court before proceeding to forfeit the lease. Five grounds are set out and, if none of them can be established, the action is blocked. In essence the requirement is for the landlord to demonstrate why immediate enforcement is important.

In *Associated British Ports* v. *C.H. Bailey plc.*[91] the landlords had granted a lease of Barry Docks. The premises included a commercial dry dock, which changes in boat repairing practice gradually rendered obsolete, so that it was not used after 1983 and gradually fell into disrepair. Four years later the landlords served a section 146 notice requiring remedial work costing £600,000. The tenant demonstrated that the dry dock would have been worn out by the end of the term in 2049, that changes in working practices rendered it obsolete, and that the landlord's loss amounted to no more than £3,500. Compare this with the £600,000 the tenants were being asked to spend to no good purpose, and it can be seen that the landlord's real intention was to force Baileys out of Barry, so that the landlord would take all the profits from residential redevelopment. Happily, the landlord lost.

Virtuous landlords are inevitably sometimes caught in the net laid for the sinner.[92]

The 1938 Act bites only if five years or more of the term remain outstanding when the section 146 notice is served.[93] Protection extends to houses and also any commercial premises.[94] Repairing covenants are affected, but the Act has no impact on covenants to rebuild after fire,[95] use covenants,[96] and covenants to permit the landlord to view the state of repair.[97] Mixed breaches are best handled by issuing two notices, so that only the one dealing with disrepair needs to meet the 1938 Act requirements.[98]

Five grounds are laid down as *filters*, one or more of which must be satisfied before the landlord has any chance of proceeding with his forfeiture action. They are[99]:

(a) immediate remedy is required to prevent substantial diminution in the value of the reversion;

(b) immediate remedy is required to meet a legal obligation;

(c) immediate remedy is required in the interests of the occupier;

(d) immediate remedy would cost little compared to the cost occasioned by postponement; or

(e) special circumstances make it just and equitable to give permission for forfeiture.

Until *Associated British Ports* v. *C.H. Bailey*, it was thought that the landlord should be required to establish only a *prima facie* case,[100] a principle which led the Court of

---

[91] [1990] 2 A.C. 703 H.L.; P.F. Smith [1990] *Conv.* 305; S. Bridge [1990] *C.L.J.* 401.

[92] *Sidnell* v. *Wilson* [1966] 2 Q.B. 67, 79, Harman L.J.

[93] Leasehold Property (Repairs) Act 1938 s.1(1); *Baker* v. *Sims* [1959] 1 Q.B. 114 C.A.; *Starrokate Ltd.* v. *Burry* [1983] 1 E.G.L.R. 56, 57G, May L.J.

[94] s.1(1); L.T.A. 1954 s.51; *Associated British Ports* v. *C.H. Bailey plc.* [1990] 2 A.C. 703, 709D, Lord Templeman.

[95] *Farimani* v. *Gates* [1984] 2 E.G.L.R. 66 C.A.

[96] *Starrokate* as above.

[97] *Jervis* v. *Harris* [1996] Ch. 195 C.A.

[98] *Starrokate* as above.

[99] s.1(5); *Phillips* v. *Price* [1959] Ch. 181. Cases overlap: *Sidnell* v. *Wilson* [1966] 2 Q.B. 67 C.A.; *Land Securities plc.* v. *Metropolitan Police District Receiver* [1983] 1 W.L.R. 439, Megarry V.C.

[100] *Phillips* v. *Price* [1959] Ch. 181, Harman J.; *Sidnell* v. *Wilson* [1966] 2 Q.B. 67 C.A.; *Land Securities plc.* v. *Metropolitan Police District Receiver* [1983] 1 W.L.R. 439, Megarry V.C.

Appeal to give permission to the landlord to forfeit.[101] But the House of Lords[102] held that this was too lenient, and that the landlord should be required to prove one of the grounds (a) to (e) on the balance of probabilities.[103] The case was remitted for further hearing, at which Associated British Ports could have an opportunity to adduce further evidence.

Once the landlord passes any one of the five filters (a) to (e), the court still retains a *discretion* whether or not to allow the landlord's repossession action to proceed, and to impose conditions.[104] In the great majority of cases permission is refused because the value of the landlord's reversion is not immediately threatened,[105] and it might also be refused if the issue between the parties would be better settled under other procedures.[106]

The 1938 Act relies on a clumsy *notice and counter-notice procedure*, which is triggered where a landlord serves on a tenant a pre-forfeiture notice relating to disrepair. The tenant must claim the right to the benefit of the Act, but in order to be given an opportunity to do so he must be alerted to his rights. A section 146 pre-forfeiture notice must state, in characters no less conspicuous than the rest of the notice, (1) that the tenant has the right to serve a counter-notice, (2) what time limits apply, and (3) an address for service on the landlord.[107] Precise compliance is required since tenants will not often be found to have waived these requirements.[108] Service is required only on the tenant in possession.[109] The tenant has 28 days from the service of this 1938 Act notice to serve his counter-notice claiming the benefit of the Act.[110] If he does so, peaceable re-entry,[111] and any forfeiture action, is prevented until permission is obtained from the court. It is always correct for a tenant to claim the benefit of the Act, but this procedure means that a tenant can avoid court costs by deciding not to oppose the forfeiture.

4.   Damages for disrepair

The 1938 Act, where it applies, also extends to claims for damages for disrepair,[112] and actions to obtain reimbursement of the cost of work which the landlord has carried out[113]: a pre-forfeiture notice in the 1938 Act form is essential before the landlord starts work, even in the most urgent cases![114]

[101]   [1989] 2 E.G.L.R. 83 C.A.; affirming [1989] 1 E.G.L.R. 69, Harman J.

[102]   [1990] 2 A.C. 703 H.L.; P.F. Smith [1990] *Conv.* 305; S. Bridge [1990] *C.L.J.* 401.

[103]   [1990] 2 A.C. 703, 713D.

[104]   s.1(6).

[105]   *Sidnell* v. *Wilson* [1966] 2 Q.B. 67, 77E, Lord Denning M.R.

[106]   *Land Securities Ltd.* v. *Metropolitan Police District Receiver* [1983] 1 W.L.R. 439, Megarry V.C. (legitimacy of improvements); P.F. Smith [1983] *Conv.* 323.

[107]   s.1(4). It should be possible to remedy a defect by issuing a second notice: P.F. Smith [1986] *Conv.* 85.

[108]   *B.L. Holdings Ltd.* v. *Marcolt Investments Ltd.* [1979] 1 E.G.L.R. 97 C.A.; trivial defects will however be ignored: *Middlegate Properties Ltd.* v. *Messimeris* [1973] 1 W.L.R. 168 C.A.

[109]   *Church Commissioners for England* v. *Ve-Ri-Best Manufacturing Co. Ltd.* [1957] 1 Q.B. 238, Lord Goddard C.J. (mortgage lender under legal charge); *Kanda* v. *Church Commissioners for England* [1958] 1 Q.B. 332 C.A.; *Cusack-Smith* v. *Gold* [1958] 1 W.L.R. 611, Pilcher J. (sub-tenant).

[110]   s.1(1).

[111]   *Target Home Loans Ltd.* v. *Iza Ltd.* [2000] 02 E.G. 117 C.Ct.

[112]   But not a covenant to pay the costs of a s.146 notice: *Middlegate Properties Ltd.* v. *Gridlow-Jackson* (1977) 34 P. & C.R. 4 C.A.

[113]   *Hamilton* v. *Martell Securities Ltd.* [1984] Ch. 266, Vinelott J.; (1984) 100 L.Q.R. 338.

[114]   *S.E.D.A.C. Investments Ltd.* v. *Tanner* [1982] 1 W.L.R. 1342, Michael Wheeler Q.C.; P.F. Smith [1983] *Conv.* 54; J.E. Martin [1983] *Conv.* 71.

5. Service charge

The Housing Act 1996 introduces special restrictions on forfeiture of the lease of a dwelling[115] on the ground of non-payment of service charge.[116] Forfeiture cannot proceed[117] until the amount payable has been agreed, admitted, settled by arbitration, or determined by a leasehold valuation tribunal.[118] After adjudication 14 days must be allowed for payment before proceedings are commenced, but forfeiture can proceed despite any appeal. The rent procedure will apply if service charge is reserved as rent,[119] but otherwise it is necessary to serve a preliminary section 146 notice.[120] Notice can be served before the amount of the charge is adjudicated,[121] though the notice must be in a prescribed form warning the tenant of his rights,[122] and it cannot be acted on until 14 days after the adjudication.

F. TERMINATION EVENTS: REFORM

The Law Commission Report on *Termination of Tenancies*[123] and its draft *Termination of Tenancies Bill*[124] propose the creation of a single unified procedure, with the differences between rent and other covenants removed.[125] Failure to pay rent will be a termination order event, after 21 days unless the lease specifies some other length of time, and with no requirement to make a formal demand.[126] The special insolvency regime would be repealed. The rule that certain breaches are incapable of remedy is unfair and should be reformed. Notice would be required only for disrepair[127] but in other cases it would be necessary in practice to give a notice to protect the landlord against the risk of the court awarding costs against him. The special protection against unfair dilapidations notices would continue: after the landlord's notice the tenant would have 28 days to serve a counter notice requiring the landlord to obtain permission from the court to proceed.[128]

---

[115] The definition of a "dwelling" in L.T.A. 1985 s.18 is adopted: H.A. 1996 s.81(5); business and agricultural lettings are excluded: s.81(4). For further reform proposals see above p. 372.

[116] H.A. 1996 s.81(6).

[117] s.81(1).

[118] ss.81(2), 83; S.I. 1997/1854 (form and contents of applications). But the L.V.T. can only determine the reasonableness of the service charge and where there are other issues it may be convenient to allow county court procedures to continue: *Aylesbond Estates Ltd.* v. *MacMillan* (2000) 32 H.L.R. 1 C.A.

[119] *Escalus Properties Ltd.* v. *Robinson* [1996] Q.B. 231 C.A.; *Khar* v. *Delmounty Ltd.* (1998) 75 P. & C.R. 232 C.A.; but see L.P.A. 1925 s.205(1)(xxiii) (any annual or periodical payment).

[120] *Abbey National B.S.* v. *Maybeech* [1985] Ch. 190, Nicholls J.; *Rexhaven Ltd.* v. *Nurse* (1996) 28 H.L.R. 241, Colyer J.

[121] H.A. 1996 s.81.

[122] s.82(3), (4); the warning must be at least as conspicuous as the operative parts.

[123] Law Com. No.142 (1985).

[124] Law Com. No.221 (1994). A further draft Bill is expected.

[125] cl.5(3).

[126] cl.5.

[127] cl.12 which would replace L.P.A. 1925 s.146 and the 1938 Act.

[128] cl.12(5) closely follows the 1938 Act: it would not apply to agricultural tenancies, nor within the last 3 years of the term, but the existing requirement for a 7-year term would be removed.

A time limit would be introduced to prevent the landlord relying on a stale breaches of covenant.[129] This would be 6 months[130] from the time that the event first comes to the knowledge of the landlord or his agents, unless the landlord preserves his rights by notice.[131] Time-barred breaches would remain relevant when the court was considering how to exercise its discretion. The pre-forfeiture notice served within a six-month period would: (1) give particulars of the breach; (2) specify what corrective action was required; and (3) state an allowance of time for remedial work. If no time was stated in the notice, six months would be taken.

G. RE-ENTRY: PROCEEDINGS

1. The landlord's election

Breach of covenant by a tenant is much the same as any other contractual repudiation[132] in that it gives an option whether or not to treat the lease as forfeited. The lease is voidable rather than void, the landlord making the choice, so a tenant cannot excuse himself from future rent payments by his past arrears of rent. A collective management scheme for a block of flats may contain covenants that compel the landlord to try to forfeit on the request of the other tenants in the block. This can be used to ensure, for example, that service charge for an entire block is collected.[133] The landlord makes his election by re-entering the premises, either by suing for possession or by retaking actual possession, but notice of the landlord's intention to enter is not sufficient by itself.[134] Once he has decided, he must adhere strictly to the theory that he has made a binding, once and for all, election to terminate the lease.

2. Proceedings

Re-entry is usually effected by making a claim for possession through the courts,[135] which is equivalent to a physical re-entry,[136] and this is the only lawful method for occupied dwellings. Even if the tenant is insolvent, no prior permission is required from the court before issuing a claim.[137] A claim to forfeit should be protected as a pending land action.[138] The Woolf reforms of civil procedure are considered at the end of this chapter.[139]

---

[129] cl.10.

[130] In the case of a continuing breach, this would be the date when it was last continuing.

[131] cl.10(2)–(6).

[132] *Kingston-on-Thames R.L.B.C.* v. *Marlow* [1996] 1 E.G.L.R. 101, 102K–L.

[133] *Britel Corporation N.V.* v. *Orbach* (1997) 27 H.L.R. 883 C.A.

[134] *Warner* v. *Sampson* [1959] 1 Q.B. 297, 320–321, Hodson L.J.

[135] Woodfall 19.047–19.133.

[136] *Evans* v. *Davis* (1878) 10 Ch.D. 747, 763, Fry J.

[137] I.A. 1986 s.383(2); *Razzaq* v. *Pala* [1997] 1 W.L.R. 1336, Lightman J.

[138] *Selim* v. *Bickenhall Engineering Ltd.* [1981] 1 W.L.R. 1318 (caution to protect preliminary application for permission to forfeit valid).

[139] See below pp. 832–836.

3.   Progress of a re-entry

Once the landlord seeks forfeiture he is committed,[140] and the lease will end if the tenant does not apply for relief.[141] The landlord must treat the tenant as an ex-tenant from that moment forward. The crucial moment is the service of the claim form[142] seeking forfeiture.[143] Damages for disrepair are assessed at this date,[144] and the landlord becomes liable for rates.[145] It is important to claim mesne profits rather than rent.[146] Strict compliance with this logic is essential: the landlord must eschew alternative claims made on the assumption that the lease continues, remain alert to the danger of waiving the right of forfeiture by acts recognising the continued existence of the lease, and must not accept rent from sub-tenants or licensees.[147]

From the point of view of the tenant, the lease remains on foot until an order for possession is made so that he may, for example, apply to the Lands Tribunal to modify restrictive covenants in the lease.[148] The continued existence of the lease is demonstrated by *Ivory Gate Ltd.* v. *Spetale*.[149] Proceedings for forfeiture of a lease after the appointment of a receiver were compromised by an agreement that the tenant would surrender the lease to the landlord. Sureties argued that they were not liable for rent accruing after the issue of the landlord's claim for possession since they said that the forfeiture proceedings ended the lease. The Court of Appeal rejected this argument: service of a claim for possession is an election to terminate the lease but does not by itself end the lease. On the facts, the lease had not been ended until an agreed surrender and the surety remained liable for rent until that moment. On the other hand, the tenant may treat the lease as still in existence while forfeiture proceedings are pending, and may, for example, serve a notice under the renewable business leases provision,[150] or seek to enfranchise.[151]

4.   Mesne profits

As from the date of the election to forfeit,[152] the landlord is no longer entitled to rent—for the lease has terminated—but must claim mesne profits for trespass. Mesne profits

---

[140]   *G.S. Fashions Ltd.* v. *B. & Q. plc.* [1995] 1 E.G.L.R. 62 Ch.D.; M. Haley [1995] *Conv.* 161.

[141]   Despite later changes of mind: *Silverman* v. *AFCO (U.K.) Ltd.* [1988] 1 E.G.L.R. 51 C.A.

[142]   Not its issue by the court: *Dendy* v. *Evans* [1910] 1 K.B. 263, 267, Cozens Hardy M.R.

[143]   *Borzak* v. *Ahmed* [1965] 2 Q.B. 320, Fenton Atkinson J., citing *Driscoll* v. *Church Commissioners of England* [1957] 1 Q.B. 330; D.G. Barnsley (1964) 29 *Conv. (N.S.)* 267.

[144]   *Associated Deliveries Ltd.* v. *Harrison* [1984] 2 E.G.L.R. 76 C.A.

[145]   *Kingston on Thames R.L.B.C.* v. *Marlow* [1996] 1 E.G.L.R. 101 Q.B.D.

[146]   See below pp. 806–807.

[147]   *Cromwell Developments Ltd.* v. *Godfrey* [1998] 2 E.G.L.R. 62 C.A. (dissolution of tenant company, but related company remaining in possession and paying rent).

[148]   *Driscoll* v. *Church Commissioners for England* [1957] 1 Q.B. 330 C.A.; *Pips (Leisure Productions) Ltd.* v. *Walton* [1981] 2 E.G.L.R. 172; J.E. Martin [1982] *Conv.* 248; *Peninsular Maritime Ltd.* v. *Padseal* [1981] 2 E.G.L.R. 43 C.A.; J.E. Martin [1982] *Conv.* 155.

[149]   [1998] 2 E.G.L.R. 43 C.A.; the confusion arose from a dictum in *Billson* v. *Residential Apartments Ltd.* [1992] 1 A.C. 494, 535G, Lord Templeman.

[150]   *Baglarbasi* v. *Deedmethod Ltd.* [1991] 2 E.G.L.R. 71 Ch.D. (notice under L.T.A. 1954 s.25 to end lease and so curtail liability to rent).

[151]   *Hynes* v. *Twinsectra Ltd.* [1995] 2 E.G.L.R. 69 C.A.; M. Pawlowski [1996] *Conv.* 55.

[152]   *Associated Deliveries Ltd.* v. *Harrison* [1984] 2 E.G.L.R. 76 C.A.

run from the date of the breach[153] or, if rent is paid in advance from the next rent day, until the actual recovery of possession.[154] Sub-tenancies end, so rent cannot be collected from sub-tenants.[155]

The measure of damages for trespass is often identical to the previous rent,[156] but only where there is a rack rental. With a lease subject to a ground rent, mesne profits are based on a market (rack) rental,[157] though proof of value is required if the landlord claims more than the actual rent. A landlord may secure an undeserved profit through a forfeiture. *Escalus Properties Ltd.* v. *Robinson*[158] concerned flats held on long leases subject to ground rents. Claims by mortgage-lenders for relief would normally be prospective only, entitling the landlord to charge the lenders for mesne profits, and so exposing the lenders to a large increase in the outgoings until relief was finalised. This would obviously be wrong.[159] Fortunately, the Court was able to find a means of giving retrospective relief,[160] thus ensuring that the old leases continued, leaving the lenders liable only for the ground rent. Recent cases have suggested a restitutionary basis for damages, though this is believed to be heretical. It is very important for the landlord to make a claim for damages for trespass and not for rent, and is required to name the correct parties.[161]

5. Deserted tenements

There is a statutory procedure for retaking possession where a tenant pays a rack rent, if he runs away leaving his tenement deserted and owing arrears exceeding six months.[162] The procedure involves application to the magistrates' court.

6. Reform

The Law Commission draft Termination of Tenancies Bill[163] proposes that the doctrine of re-entry should be abolished, meaning that a lease would continue until a court ordered that it should end. Any breach of covenant will be a termination event entitling the landlord to apply to the court for termination. A proposal for tenants to have a matching right to terminate his lease after a landlord's breach has now been dropped.[164]

New legislation would cover the procedure for obtaining a termination order. The court would be given a general jurisdiction to order termination of the lease or to require remedy of a breach. No relief and stigma cases would be abolished, with the

[153] *Elliott* v. *Boynton* [1924] 1 Ch. 236 C.A.; A.T. Denning (1927) 43 *L.Q.R.* 53.
[154] Common Law Procedure Act 1852 s.214; *Elliott* v. *Boynton* [1924] 1 Ch. 236.
[155] *Viscount Chelsea* v. *Hutchinson* (1997) 28 H.L.R. 17 C.A.
[156] *Swordheath Properties Ltd.* v. *Tabet* [1979] 1 W.L.R. 285 C.A.; *Viscount Chelsea* v. *Hutchinson* [1994] 2 E.G.L.R. 61 C.A.
[157] *Ministry of Defence* v. *Ashman* [1993] 2 E.G.L.R. 102 C.A. (special case: between market rent and concessionary licence fee); *Ministry of Defence* v. *Thompson* [1993] 2 E.G.L.R. 107 C.A.; E. Cooke (1994) 110 *L.Q.R.* 420.
[158] [1996] Q.B. 231 C.A.; [1998] *P.L.J.* 14.
[159] At 251F, Nourse L.J.
[160] See below pp. 825–826.
[161] A receiver collecting rent is not liable for mesne profits at a higher rate: *Official Custodian of Charities* v. *Mackey (No.2)* [1985] 1 W.L.R. 1308.
[162] Distress for Rent Act 1737 s.16; Deserted Tenements Act 1817.
[163] Law Com. No.221 (1994).
[164] J.E. Adams [1994] *Conv.* 184.

court always having a full discretion.[165] An absolute order would only be made if the tenant was so unsatisfactory that he ought not to remain.[166] The landlord would have to show a breach during the tenure of the present tenant, and could consider all the circumstances, including time-barred breaches. Absolute orders might be appropriate for unauthorised assignments, on insolvency, and where the tenant is unwilling to comply with remedial order. The effect would be to end the lease on a stated day. Normally the court would be expected to make a remedial order,[167] so that the lease would end only if the tenant failed to put matters right, thus giving the tenant an opportunity to continue as tenant by taking specified remedial action within a set time limit. The tenant might to be ordered to end a use or act, find a suitable surety, or pay rent arrears, damages, costs and expenses. Either party could seek to vary the terms.[168]

H. RE-ENTRY: PHYSICAL REPOSSESSION

1.   Residential property

A landlord cannot terminate the lease of a dwelling that is occupied simply by changing the locks but has, for 40 years, been required to obtain a court order before re-entering.[169] Forfeiture can occur only in court,[170] it is an offence to use force in a repossession,[171] and an offence to forfeit against a residential occupier who is opposed to the repossession.[172] None of this applies after the tenant has abandoned the property, when repossession out of court is allowed.[173]

2.   Commercial property

The right of a landlord to repossess business and agricultural property out of court is undisputed.[174] Usually, in practice, the landlord arranges for the locks of the property to be changed.

The right has been exercised in a large number of recent cases, including the leading decision of the House of Lords, *Billson* v. *Residential Apartments Ltd.*[175] Tenants undertook a major alteration of a property on the Gunton Estate in South Kensington without the landlord's permission. This was a clear deliberate breach of covenant, to which the landlords responded by serving a section 146 notice, and barging in at 6 a.m. one morning. The lease was undoubtedly terminated by the landlord's action, and remained terminated even when the tenant forced his way back in four hours later and recom-

---

[165] cl.2(1).
[166] cls.13–15.
[167] cl.15(2); definition in cl.4(3).
[168] cls.16 (tenant), 20 (landlord).
[169] *Kataria* v. *Safeland plc.* [1998] 1 E.G.L.R. 39, 41M, Brooke L.J.
[170] Protection from Eviction Act 1977 s.2.
[171] s.3.
[172] Criminal Law Act 1977 s.6.
[173] *Betterkey* v. *Joseph* [1991] Independent November 1st (forfeiture because windows not cleaned); relief would now be available after a physical re-entry.
[174] Woodfall 19.030–19.046.
[175] [1992] 1 A.C. 494 H.L.; P.F. Smith [1992] *Conv.* 273; S. Bridge [1992] *N.L.J.* 216; S. Payne [1992] *N.L.J.* 22.

menced work! The issue in the litigation was whether the tenants were in time to claim relief, a matter which requires detailed discussion below.[176] In *Kataria* v. *Safeland plc.*[177] a landlord bought the reversion on a walk-in kiosk on Kingsway in London and two days later changed the locks because the tenant owed £10,000 in rent to the previous landlord. When holding that they had acted lawfully, Brooke L.J.[178] differentiated the proprietary right to re-enter from the personal right to take action on the covenant. Law Commission proposals that commercial landlords should also require a court order[179] had not been implemented and would not be implemented until there was a fast-track procedure for landlords to obtain possession in clear and obvious cases. Under the present law, Safeland was entitled to behave as it had done. In *Bland* v. *Ingrams Estates Ltd.*[180] physical re-entry occurred after the tenant had allowed charging orders to be made against the leasehold estate.

3. Actual re-entry

Re-entry occurs by the landlord retaking control of the property, usually by changing the locks. In marginal cases the landlord's belief may be important in determining that a re-entry has indeed occurred.[181] *Abandoned land* can be retaken using a special statutory procedure made available against a tenant who has vacated the property.[182]

4. Constructive re-entry

Where a landlord relets the property, this is treated as a re-entry since it shows that the previous lease has been ended. This had not happened on the facts of *Cromwell Developments Ltd.* v. *Godfrey.*[183] The tenant company (C.B.L.) had been struck off the Companies Register for failure to file returns at a time when the lease in question was still vested in the company at that time, so that this vested in the Crown as *bona vacantia*. The landlords accepted rent from a related company (C.B.T.S.) but only at a time when they were unaware of the dissolution of the tenant company. The Court of Appeal had to decide whether this constituted a re-entry. If a re-entry had occurred the lease had ended, and the landlord could not pursue the original tenant on its privity of contract liability and under an express covenant. Re-entry may be constructive, where the landlord relets the property to a new tenant, but any other intention on the part of the landlord cannot act as a forfeiture.[184] On the particular facts the rent had actually been accepted from Cole, the controller of the two companies, and it was not clearly shown that the landlord (who was unaware of the dissolution of the tenant company) had intended to accept a related company as tenant. No forfeiture had occurred and it remained open to the landlord to pursue substitute liabilities against the original tenant.

[176] See below p. 822.
[177] [1998] 1 E.G.L.R. 39 C.A.
[178] At 41M.
[179] Law Com. No.142 (1985); Law Com. No.221 (1984).
[180] [1999] 2 E.G.L.R. 49 Ch.D.; *Target Home Loans Ltd.* v. *Iza Ltd.* [2000] 02 E.E. 117 C.Ct. (ground rent and service charge on flat).
[181] *Eaton Square Properties Ltd.* v. *Beveridge* [1993] E.G.C.S. 91 C.A.
[182] L.T.A. 1954 s.54.
[183] [1998] 2 E.G.L.R. 62 C.A.
[184] *London & County (A. & D.) Ltd.* v. *Wilfred Sportsman Ltd.* [1971] Ch. 764 C.A.

5. Rent and notice procedures

No protection exists against physical re-entry for *rent* arrears.[185] If the lease says that a right of re-entry arises 14 days after rent is due, the landlord can immediately take back the property if the rent is unpaid. No warning need be given. The lease is ended so that, for example, the tenant will lose his fixtures unless the lease contains a express provision giving the right of removal on termination.[186] Relief is potentially available.[187]

Breaches of *other covenants* entitle a landlord to forfeit by peaceable re-entry only after service of a notice under section 146 of the Law of Property Act 1925, a right of the tenant which cannot be excluded, directly or indirectly.[188] The notice must warn the tenant what breach has occurred and re-entry is lawful only after a reasonable time for the necessary remedial work has passed. The landlord may be prevented by injunction from proceeding to forfeit before a reasonable period of time for remedial work has elapsed.[189] If a landlord proceeds without a notice, the re-entry will be a trespass.[190] When serving a notice, he must be careful to ensure that his notice states a valid termination event. In *Gondal* v. *Dillon Newsagents Ltd.*[191] a sub-postmaster had been suspended from office after a post office audit and so he arranged for someone else to carry on the business. The landlord treated this as a breach of the covenant against giving up possession to a third party, but the court held that possession had not been given up, there was no breach, and the landlord had committed a trespass. No doubt the tenant could have taken proceedings to challenge the validity of the notice before re-entry occurred.

Despite *Fuller* v. *Judy Properties Ltd.*,[192] it is believed that a notice should not be accepted as valid if it is served only after re-entry for an irremediable breach. The decision to accept such a notice does not chime with those authorities that suggest that a notice cannot be validly served after remedial work has been completed.[193]

Tenants are well protected against re-entry for disrepair in those circumstances in which the *Leasehold Property (Repairs) Act 1938* applies.[194] The tenant has 28 days after service of a section 146 notice to serve a counter-notice claiming its benefit,[195] which he should always do. Permission is then required from the court before proceeding with a physical repossession. This will not be given unless the landlord establishes one of the five statutory grounds in section 1(5) in which immediate enforcement is important, and even then the grant of permission remains discretionary.[196]

---

[185] L.P.A. 1925 s.146(11); *Twogate Properties Ltd.* v. *Birmingham Midshires B.S. (1998)* 75 P. & C.R. 386 C.A.

[186] *Re Palmeiro* [1999] 3 E.G.L.R. 27; S. Murdoch [1999] 44 *E.G.* 142.

[187] See below pp. 821–822.

[188] L.P.A. 1925 s.146(12).

[189] *Associated Electrical Industries Ltd.* v. *Central Shops Ltd.* (1974) 230 E.G. 1123, Plowman J. (injunction refused on facts).

[190] *Fuller* v. *Judy Properties Ltd.* [1992] 1 E.G.L.R. 75 C.A.; *Charville Estates Ltd.* v. *Unipart Group Ltd.* [1997] E.G.C.S. 36.

[191] [1998] N.P.C. 127 C.A.

[192] [1992] 1 E.G.L.R. 75 C.A.

[193] *Horsey Estates Ltd.* v. *Steiger* [1899] 2 Q.B. 79, 91, Lord Russell C.J.; *S.E.D.A.C. Investments Ltd.* v. *Tanner* [1982] 1 W.L.R. 1342.

[194] See above pp. 801–803.

[195] s.1(1).

[196] s.1(5), (6).

Insolvency is often followed by peaceable re-entry without the need for prior permission from the insolvency court.[197]

6. Relief

After a physical re-entry, tenants[198] and sub-tenants[199] are entitled to claim relief in separate proceedings.

7. Reform

Proposals about termination of leases out of court have undergone a radical rethink. The initial Law Commission proposals were that forfeiture should always occur through court proceedings, except after abandonment. Hence peaceable re-entry would have been abolished where the tenant retained possession of the property. However, the commercial landlords' lobby was concerned about the removal of the right of physical re-entry, and this seems to have been the primary reason why the government did not accept the Law Commission proposals on termination of tenancies. This led to a further round of consultation in January 1998,[200] which revealed overwhelming support for the retention of a right of physical re-entry as a commonly used and effective management tool for commercial property. A press announcement[201] reveals that the peaceable re-entry will be retained, and put on a statutory basis, with a draft bill promised for the year 2000. Peaceable re-entry is now seen to be useful in cases of clear breaches that are unlikely to be rectified, and to require a court order for possession might greatly increase the workload of the courts. It is intended to incorporate safeguards for the legitimate interests of tenants. Residential tenants will be safe from physical re-entry and the commission propose to exclude all leases with more than 25 years outstanding. These tend to have a substantial capital value, so it is surely right for judicial consideration of such cases before termination is ordered. This would leave physical re-entry available for all normal business leases. Physical re-entry will not effect an immediate termination, but rather will trigger a period during which the tenant or others interested could apply to the court for relief, the period being limited to one month. A pre-forfeiture warning notice will be required, though limited to seven days in the case of non-payment of rent or irremediable breach of covenant. Repairs (and by extension service charge disputes) will be subject to the right of a tenant to serve a counter notice referring the dispute to the court. However if the property had been abandoned the landlord would be able to relet immediately.

However it is possible that the self-help remedy of forfeiture out of court may infringe the human rights of the tenant,[202] so the Convention may achieve what the Law Commission cannot.

---

[197] See below pp. 829–831.
[198] See below pp. 821–822.
[199] See below p. 826.
[200] *Termination of Tenancies by Physical Re-entry*, Law Com. Consultation Document (January 1998); J. Adams [1998] *Conv.* 165; L. Hutchinson [1998] 08 *E.G.* 149; M. Pawlowski [1998] 2 *L.T. Rev.* 24.
[201] June 30th 1999.
[202] See above p. 205.

I. WAIVER

Landlords are not entitled to blow hot and cold. Tenants need to know that they will not for ever be vulnerable to old claims for forfeiture and a purchaser needs to know the slate will be wiped clean. Waiver is a very substantial qualification on the landlord's right to terminate the lease. However necessary the principle is, English law does not operate satisfactorily, since it is weighted too heavily in favour of tenants and often acts as a trap for a landlord who extends temporary generosity to a tenant.

1. Nature

Exercising a right of forfeiture, for example by suing for possession, acts as an irrevocable decision to end the lease. The landlord must see this logic through, and avoid any act that recognises its continued existence. Such an act will operate as a waiver, that is an election to continue the lease rather than to end it,[203] which estops the landlord from alleging that the lease has been forfeited. He can be restrained from proceeding by injunction,[204] and must wait until another termination event comes along.

At least in modern law, waiver applies only to the particular breach, so that a future breach of the same covenant will give rise to a right to forfeit.[205] Some breaches of covenant are one-off breaches, where waiver wipes the slate clean for ever.[206] One common example is sub-letting in breach of covenant.[207] Waiver is less of a trap to the landlord when it relates to a continuing breach of covenant,[208] such as a prohibited use[209] since waiver on day one still leaves a breach on day two and a renewed opportunity to decide to forfeit. In relation to disrepair it has been held that a new section 146 notice is not necessary if the breach worsens,[210] but query if the waiver should not be held to have destroyed the previous notice.

2. Elements of an implied waiver

Although waiver may be express,[211] it is much more commonly implied, where the landlord[212]:

---

[203] *Kammins Ballrooms Co. Ltd.* v. *Zenith Investments (Torquay) Ltd.* [1971] A.C. 850, 882–883, Lord Diplock; *Peyman* v. *Lanjani* [1985] Ch. 457; S. Anderson [1985] *Conv.* 408; J.F. Clerk (1921) 37 *L.Q.R.* 203 (notice to quit); *Storehouse Properties Ltd.* v. *Ocobase Ltd.* [1998] Times April 3rd, Rimer J.; *Oliver Ashworth (Holdings) Ltd.* v. *Ballard (Kent) Ltd.* [1999] 2 All E.R. 791, 801–802, Robert Walker L.J.

[204] *Iperion Investments Corporation Ltd.* v. *Broadwalk House Residents Ltd.* [1992] 2 E.G.L.R. 235.

[205] L.P.A. 1925 s.143, re-enacting L.P. Amendment A. 1860 s.6; this reversed *Dumpor's case* (1603) 4 Co. Rep. 119b, 76 E.R. 1110.

[206] *Platt* v. *Parker* (1886) 2 T.L.R. 786 C.A. (late completion of building agreement); *Jacob* v. *Down* [1900] 2 Ch. 156, Stirling J.; *Expert Clothing Service & Sales Ltd.* v. *Hillgate House Ltd.* [1986] Ch. 340, 358–362, Slade L.J.

[207] *Walrond* v. *Hawkins* (1875) L.R. 10 C.P. 342.

[208] An important factor is power to discontinue: *Downie* v. *Turner* [1951] 2 K.B. 112 C.A.; distinguished in *Dobbs* v. *Linford* [1952] 1 Q.B. 48.

[209] *Cooper* v. *Henderson* [1982] 2 E.G.L.R. 42 C.A.

[210] *Greenwich L.B.C.* v. *Discreet Selling Estates Ltd.* [1990] 2 E.G.L.R. 65 C.A.; P. Luxton [1991] *J.B.L.* 342; P. Walter (1988) 132 *S.J.* 1166.

[211] *Ward* v. *Day* (1864) 5 B. & S. 359, 122 E.R. 865; *Weaver* v. *Mogford* [1988] 2 E.G.L.R. 48 C.A. (unsuccessful).

[212] *Matthews* v. *Smallwood* [1910] 1 Ch. 777, 786 Parker J.; *Fuller's Theatres & Vaudeville Co. Ltd.* v. *Rofe* [1923] A.C. 435 P.C.; *Kammins Ballrooms Co. Ltd.* v. *Zenith Investments (Torquay) Ltd.* [1971] A.C. 850 H.L.; *Cornillie* v. *Saha* (1996) 28 H.L.R. 561, 569–570, Aldous L.J.

(1) is aware of the acts or omissions of the tenant which make the lease liable to forfeiture, but

(2) does some unequivocal act recognising its continued existence.

Both elements are essential to raise an estoppel.

3. Knowledge

Landlords derive some protection from the fact that they cannot waive a breach of which they have no knowledge: only an informed landlord can be said to acquiesce.[213] There is no duty of inquiry, so constructive notice is irrelevant. Official publication of notice of the tenant's liquidation does not result in the landlord waiving the breach of covenant arising on insolvency.[214] *Cornillie* v. *Saha*[215] demonstrates a trap: gathering information to permit an action for forfeiture may give the knowledge necessary to sue, and hence the knowledge to support a waiver. However, mere suspicion that a breach has occurred causes no waiver, since the landlord's failure to take action can be explained by his uncertainty about whether the tenant's explanation would be accepted in court.[216]

4. Unequivocal acts

Intention to waive a breach is deduced only from the unequivocal acts of the landlord in the interim period between his becoming aware of the breach and actual re-entry.[217] Waiver of breaches of covenants other than rent arrears is certainly possible by accepting rent after service of the statutory notice that is a precursor to forfeiture,[218] but apparently not before,[219] though service of the notice cannot itself waive a breach.[220]

The most likely acts relate to *rent*. *Creery* v. *Summersell*[221] provides some weak support for allowing forfeiture even after routine issue of a rent demand in ignorance of matters giving rise to a right of forfeiture, but most authority is against this prejudicing the landlord. Waiver occurs if the landlord (knowing of the breach) demands,[222] sues for,[223]

---

[213] *Boxbusher Properties Ltd.* v. *Graham* [1975] 2 E.G.L.R. 58 (no sub-letting on facts).

[214] *Official Custodian of Charities* v. *Parway Estate Developments Ltd.* [1985] Ch. 151; *Pakwood Transport Ltd.* v. *15 Beauchamp Place Ltd.* (1977) 36 P. & C.R. 112.

[215] (1996) 28 H.L.R. 561 C.A.

[216] *Chrisdell* v. *Johnson* (1987) 54 P. & C.R. 257 C.A.; J.E. Martin [1988] *Conv.* 18.

[217] *Doe d. Morecraft* v. *Meux* (1824) 1 C. & P. 346, 171 E.R. 1225; *Windmill Investments (London) Ltd.* v. *Milano Restaurants Ltd.* [1962] Q.B. 373, Megaw J.; *David Blackstone Ltd.* v. *Burnetts (West End) Ltd.* [1973] 1 W.L.R. 1487; *Farimani* v. *Gates* [1984] 2 E.G.L.R. 66.

[218] *Guillemard* v. *Silverthorne* (1908) 99 L.T. 584.

[219] *Billson* v. *Residential Apartments Ltd.* (1990) 60 P. & C.R. 392; query this point.

[220] *Church Commissioners for England* v. *Nodjoumi* (1986) 51 P. & C.R. 155, Hirst J.; *Few* v. *Perkins* (1867) L.R. 2 Exch. 92; *Penton* v. *Barnett* [1898] 1 Q.B. 276 C.A.; *Greenwich L.B.C.* v. *Discreet Selling Estates Ltd.* [1990] 2 E.G.L.R. 65 C.A.

[221] [1949] Ch. 751; *Legal & General Assurance Society Ltd.* v. *General Metal Agencies Ltd.* (1969) 20 P. & C.R. 953 (creation of a new lease rather than waiver); H.W. Wilkinson (1988) 138 *N.L.J.* 95.

[222] *Davis Blackstone Ltd.* v. *Burnetts (West End) Ltd.* [1973] 1 W.L.R. 1487, Swanwick J.; *Welch* v. *Birrane* (1974) 29 P. & C.R. 102, Lawson J. Unless vague: *Yorkshire Metropolitan Properties Ltd.* v. *Co-operative Retail Services Ltd.* [1997] E.G.C.S. 57; *Chatterton* v. *Terrell* [1923] A.C. 578 H.L.

[223] *Dendy* v. *Nicholl* (1858) 4 C.B.N.S. 376, 140 E.R. 1130; *Oliver Ashworth (Holdings) Ltd.* v. *Ballard (Kent) Ltd.* [1999] 2 All E.R. 791, 800–801, Robert Walker L.J.

distrains for,[224] or accepts[225]—even "without prejudice"[226]—rent due after the breach.[227] Mechanical issue of a rent demand may lead to waiver even though there is no conscious decision by the landlord to demand rent when aware of the right to forfeit.[228] Hence forfeiture may occur, and indeed perhaps usually does occur, by accident.[229] This represents a considerable trap for a landlord, which may also snare his bank manager[230] or managing agent.[231]

Many acts relating to rent do not waive a breach. Suing for arrears of rent that had already accrued before the breach causing the forfeiture does not recognise the continued future existence of the lease.[232] Neither does entry into negotiations,[233] offering time for payment,[234] accepting rent offered by the tenant without any demand,[235] taking out rent paid into court[236] nor accepting payments from a guarantor.[237] Waiver cannot occur during the statutory phase of a Rent Act tenancy.[238]

Many *other acts,* other that is than demanding rent, may act as a waiver. These include suing for specific performance,[239] effecting insurance,[240] advancing money under a building agreement,[241] or seeking access to view the state of the property.[242] Dealing with the reversion, for example by granting a reversionary lease, is not a waiver.[243]

Inaction will not generally be a waiver, since an election can only be made by an act, and even lengthy passivity will not be a recognition that the lease continues.[244] Acquiescence might perhaps be implied over a very lengthy period.[245] Estoppel usually involves active inducement, for example leading a tenant to believe that a forfeiture will

---

[224] *Green's case* (1582) Cro. Eliz. 3, 78 E.R. 269.

[225] *Jones* v. *Carter* (1846) 15 M. & W. 718, 153 E.R. 1040.

[226] *Davenport* v. *R.* (1877) 3 App.Cas. 115 P.C.; *Croft* v. *Lumley* (1858) 6 H.L.C. 672, 10 E.R. 1459.

[227] Or settling a claim for damages for other beach of covenant: *Pellatt* v. *Boosey* (1862) 31 L.J. C.P. 281.

[228] *Central Estates (Belgravia) Ltd.* v. *Woolgar (No.2)* [1972] 1 W.L.R. 1048 C.A.; *Henry Smith's Charity Trustees* v. *Willson* [1983] Q.B 316 C.A.; J.E. Martin [1983] *Conv.* 248; *Dreamgate Properties Ltd.* v. *Arnot* (1998) 76 P. & C.R. 25 C.A.

[229] *Greenwich L.B.C.* v. *Discreet Selling Estates Ltd.* [1990] 2 E.G.L.R. 65, 67B, Staughton L.J.

[230] *Pierson* v. *Harvey* (1888) 1 T.L.R. 430; *The Laconia* [1977] A.C. 850 H.L.; *John Lewis Properties Ltd.* v. *Viscount Chelsea* [1993] 2 E.G.L.R. 77; J.E. Adams [1993] *Conv.* 332.

[231] S. Murdoch (1988) 284 *E.G.* 791; S. Copland [1992] 39 *L.S.G.* 19.

[232] *Re Debtor No.13A–I.O.–1995* [1995] 1 W.L.R. 1127, Rattee J.; *Civil Service Co-operative Society Ltd.* v. *McGrigor's Trustees* [1923] 2 Ch. 347, Russell J.

[233] *Re National Jazz Centre* [1988] 2 E.G.L.R. 57 Ch.D.

[234] *Doe d. Rankin* v. *Brindley* (1832) 4 B. & Ad. 84, 110 E.R. 387; *Doe d. De Rutzen* v. *Lewis* (1836) 5 Ad. & El. 277, 111 E.R. 1170.

[235] *John Lewis Properties Ltd.* v. *Viscount Chelsea* [1993] 2 E.G.L.R. 77, Mummery J.; J.E. Adams [1993] *Conv.* 332.

[236] *Toleman* v. *Portbury* (1872) L.R. 7 Q.B. 344 Exch.Ch.

[237] *London & County (A. & D.) Ltd.* v. *Wilfred Sportsman Ltd.* [1971] Ch. 764 C.A.

[238] *Henry Smith's Charity Trustees* v. *Willson* [1983] Q.B. 316 C.A.

[239] *Evans* v. *Davis* (1878) 10 Ch.D. 747, Fry J.; *Moore* v. *Ullcoats Mining Co.* [1908] 1 Ch. 575.

[240] *Mills* v. *Griffiths* (1876) 45 L.J. Q.B. 771; *Cardigan Properties Ltd.* v. *Consolidated Property Investments Ltd.* [1991] 1 E.G.L.R. 64, 68F–68M.

[241] *Re Garrud ex parte Newitt* (1881) 16 Ch.D. 522 C.A.

[242] *Cornillie* v. *Saha* (1996) 28 H.L.R. 561 C.A.; H.W. Wilkinson [1996] *N.L.J.* 1545.

[243] *London & County (A. & D.) Ltd.* v. *Wilfred Sportsman Ltd.* [1971] Ch. 764 C.A.

[244] *Doe d. Sheppard* v. *Allen* (1810) 3 Taunt. 78, 128 E.R. 32 (trading for 6 years); *Perry* v. *Davis* (1858) 3 C.B. (N.S.) 769, 140 E.R. 945 (not objecting to alterations).

[245] *Hepworth* v. *Pickles* [1900] 1 Ch. 108 (24 years' use); *Re Summerson* [1900] 1 Ch. 112n (30 years' use); *Gibbon* v. *Payne* (1905) 22 T.L.R. 54 (coach-house not built & rent paid for 40 years).

not be enforced,[246] and purely passive inducement is only possible if the restrictive *Willmott* v. *Barber* probanda are met.[247] Relaxation of general estoppel doctrine[248] does not appear to have had any direct effect on waiver of forfeiture. Laches is the doctrine that delay removes the right to seek an equitable remedy, including relief from a forfeiture. A new approach to laches is signalled by *Frawley* v. *Neill*[249] in which the Court of Appeal discarded the earlier case law in favour of a single broad principle: would it be unconscionable for the claimant to assert his beneficial rights?

5. Contractual provisions against waiver

Many leases attempt to modify the doctrine of waiver, for example by stating that demand for or acceptance of rent shall not be deemed to be a waiver. The validity of such provisions must be doubted since the Privy Council has refused to enforce a clause that any waiver had to be in writing.[250]

6. Reform

The Law Commission draft Termination of Tenancies Bill[251] would modify waiver doctrine, so as to apply only if the tenant believed that the landlord would not seek a termination order; mere acceptance of rent would no longer be a waiver.[252] There would be a subjective test (what this tenant believed) and an objective test (what a reasonable tenant would believe).

J. RELIEF: NON-PAYMENT OF RENT

At common law, if a lease said that it ended when the tenant fell into arrears for a specified number of days, the landlord acquired a vested right to possession and if he elected to take advantage of this right, the tenant had no defence to the action for possession. This left plenty of scope for oppressive behaviour by landlords. Long ago statute provided an equitable claim for relief. Unfortunately the precise jurisdiction depends upon whether forfeiture occurs in or out of court, the level of the court in which proceedings take place, and the amount of rent owing. It is strongly arguable that the law is too favourable to tenants.

A tenant can apply for relief either by way of defence to a landlord's possession or by making a separate claim for relief. Relief is not available to a residential tenant against whom a statutory ground for possession has been made out.[253] Procedure is described below.[254]

---

[246] *Hughes* v. *Metropolitan Rly. Co.* (1877) 2 App. Cas. 439 H.L.; *Doe d. Knight* v. *Rowe* (1826) 2 C. & P. 246, 172 E.R. 111; *Doe d. Pittman* v. *Sutton* (1841) 9 C. & P. 706, 173 E.R. 1019.

[247] (1880) 15 Ch.D. 96; *Kammins Ballrooms Co. Ltd.* v. *Zenith Investments (Torquay) Ltd.* [1971] A.C. 850, 883, Lord Diplock.

[248] See Sparkes *N.L.L.* ch.11.

[249] [1999] Times April 5th C.A. (specific performance of an agreement to sell land).

[250] *R.* v. *Paulson* [1921] 1 A.C. 271 P.C.

[251] Law Com. No.221 (1994).

[252] cl.11.

[253] *Artesian Residential Developments Ltd.* v. *Beck* [1999] 3 All E.R. 113 C.A. (assured tenancy; ground 8 mandatory repossession for major rent arrears); see above p.***

[254] See below pp. 833–835.

1.   Non-payment of rent: automatic stay

In some cases the tenant has an automatic right to stay proceedings by paying what is owed in terms of arrears of rent and costs before proceedings come to court. Entitlement to an automatic stay is restricted to rent-only actions,[255] so the right is removed even by adding a claim for the costs of the forfeiture action.[256]

There are two distinct jurisdictions. *High Court* powers to grant relief, introduced by equity, subjected to statutory regulation in 1730,[257] and re-enacted in 1852,[258] are now heavily dated. All proceedings are stayed if the tenant pays all outstanding arrears and costs into court before trial.[259] Curiously the provisions are drafted in such a way that the court's automatic powers are restricted to cases where the arrears amount to more than six months[260]: relief is technically discretionary if the arrears are smaller. In a *county court* relief is governed by the County Courts Act 1984 where a landlord is claiming re-entry for non-payment of rent.[261] A tenant has the right to stay proceedings by paying all arrears and costs into court five clear days before the return date in the action.

The Court of Appeal in *Maryland Estates Ltd.* v. *Joseph*[262] had to determine the meaning of the phrase "all the rent in arrear". Did this mean all arrears at the time of the issue of proceedings (now by claim form), or did it include arrears accruing up to the time of the payment into court? Common sense suggests the latter. To find that this is indeed so, the Court of Appeal traced the jurisdiction back to the County Courts Amendment Act 1856, a provision clearly modelled on the High Court jurisdiction in the Common Law Procedure Act 1852,[263] though the power to stay proceedings in the county courts stood alone for many years until a discretionary power to grant relief was finally introduced in 1934.[264] Reference to this history showed Beldam L.J. that a stay could only be obtained by paying in to court all arrears owing at the time of payment. Relief is automatic in rent-only cases once this payment has been made.[265]

2.   Non-payment of rent—discretionary relief in proceedings

A tenant who misses the chance of an automatic stay will often be entitled to discretionary relief from forfeiture. In the *High Court* there are three cases. First *before trial where small arrears:* where arrears amount to less than six months there is no statutory entitlement to an automatic stay of proceedings, but the tenant may seek discretionary relief. [266] Second in a *rent only case after judgment:* equitable relief can be sought by

---

[255] *Escalus Properties Ltd.* v. *Robinson* [1996] Q.B. 231 C.A. (the *Robinson* case).

[256] *Longmint Ltd.* v. *Akinlade & Gibbons* [1997] 2 C.L.Y. 3292 C.Ct.

[257] L.T.A. 1730 ss.2–4.

[258] Common Law Procedure Act 1852 ss.210–212.

[259] s.212.

[260] *Standard Pattern Co. Ltd.* v. *Ivey* [1962] Ch. 432, Wilberforce J.; R.E. Megarry (1962) 78 *L.Q.R.* 168.

[261] s.138(1), as amended by Administration of Justice Act 1985 s.55, sch.8; the court has ancillary powers of the High Court: subs.(10).

[262] [1999] 1 W.L.R. 83 C.A.

[263] s.212.

[264] County Courts Act 1934 s.180.

[265] *Escalus Properties Ltd.* v. *Robinson* [1996] Q.B. 231 C.A. (the *Robinson* case); *United Dominions Trust* v. *Shellpoint* [1993] 4 All E.R. 310 C.A.; N.P. Gravells (1994) 110 *L.Q.R.* 15; P. Luxton [1994] *J.B.L.* 37.

[266] *Standard Pattern Co. Ltd.* v. *Ivey* [1962] Ch. 432, Wilberforce J.; R.E. Megarry (1962) 78 *L.Q.R.* 168.

application within 6 months of execution of the judgment for possession,[267] although it is a condition of being allowed to seek relief that all arrears and costs are paid in within 40 days of the application.[268] Third there are some *residual cases*. In any action in the High Court for forfeiture of a lease for non-payment of rent, there is power to grant relief against forfeiture in a summary manner,[269] subject to such terms and conditions as to payment of rent, costs or otherwise, as could have been imposed under earlier practice. Relief is normal if all[270] arrears are paid, unless the circumstances are wholly exceptional.[271]

Different legislation[272] applies where a landlord is proceeding on the grounds of arrears of rent by action in a *county court*. If rent is not paid in five clear days before the return date in the action the right to an automatic stay is lost, but discretionary relief may be available. The court must proceed to enter judgment and order possession. Possession must be suspended for at least four weeks, and the tenant can avoid repossession during any suspension by paying in the arrears and costs[273]; in those circumstances the right to relief may technically remain discretionary, but a grant of relief is virtually automatic.[274] The tenant may apply for an extension of time permitted under the court order or for suspension of a warrant for possession.[275] Nevertheless, under the original drafting of the county court legislation, the tenant had a much less ample allowance of time than if the landlord pursued forfeiture in the High Court.[276] Amendment in 1985 [277] equalises the time limits, so as to give the tenant six months after execution of any judgment for possession in which to apply for relief, thus aligning the procedure in all civil courts. Late relief is discretionary but, if it is ordered, its effect is to revivify the original lease. [278]

Tenants must seek relief within the *time limit*. In the High Court where there are six months' arrears of rent[279] and in the county court[280] irrespective of the size of the arrears, the time limit is six months from the execution of the judgment.[281] After that the tenant is barred from all relief, and the landlord holds discharged from the lease, subject only to the possibility of a successful appeal. Where the arrears are small the time

---

[267] Common Law Procedure Act 1852 s.210.

[268] s.211; this reverses *Bowser* v. *Colby* (1841) 1 Hare 109, 66 E.R. 969.

[269] Supreme Court Act 1981 s.38(1); *Escalus Properties Ltd.* v. *Robinson* [1996] Q.B. 231 (*Cooper-Smith* case); *Standard Pattern Co. Ltd.* v. *Ivey* [1962] Ch. 432, Wilberforce J. The most recent predecessor was the Supreme Court of Judicature (Consolidation) Act 1925 s.46.

[270] Not just 6 months: *Barratt* v. *Richardson* [1930] 1 K.B. 686.

[271] *Gill* v. *Lewis* [1956] 2 Q.B. 1 C.A.

[272] County Courts Act 1984 s.138(1) as amended by Administration of Justice Act 1985 s.55, sch.8.

[273] subs.(3); the tenant can apply for an extension of time under subs.(4); *Narndean Estates Ltd.* v. *Buckland* (1967) 111 S.J. 684 C.A. (18 months); M. Wonnacott [1994] *N.L.J.* 296.

[274] subs.(5); *Target Home Loans Ltd.* v. *Iza Ltd.* [2000] 02 E.G. 117, C.Ct.

[275] subss.(8), (9).

[276] County Courts Act 1984 s.138; *Di Palma* v. *Victoria Square Property Co. Ltd.* [1986] Fam. 150 C.A.

[277] Administration of Justice Act 1985 s.55.

[278] subss.(9A), (9B); *Escalus Properties Ltd.* v. *Robinson* [1996] Q.B. 231 C.A. (the *Walsh* case); for those interested in the lease see below pp. 823–827.

[279] Common Law Procedure Act 1852 s.210.

[280] County Courts Act 1984 s.138(9A).

[281] *Stanhope* v. *Haworth* (1886) 3 T.L.R. 34 C.A. (application just before end of 6 months; this was a factor to consider).

limit is not applied rigidly, for "equity will not boggle at a matter of days", so relief is possible even outside the six-month time limit.[282]

3.   Exercise of the discretion where rent arrears

Relief is discretionary unless there is a right to an automatic stay of proceedings.[283] However, there is a consistent practice in rent cases to grant relief on payment of what is due with costs, unless the circumstances are exceptional.[284] This same principle applies to arrears of service charge, whether it is reserved as rent or the section 146 notice procedure applies. In *Khar* v. *Delmounty Ltd.* Lord Woolf M.R. said that the same principle apply to liquidated sums of money, whether technically rent or not.[285] Equity treats the right to forfeit as a mere security for the payment of rent, and is generally prepared to allow relief from forfeiture where the tenant pays up to date what is owing to the landlord,[286] disregarding any previous history of rent arrears.[287] Invariably the tenant will be required to pay in all arrears and costs as a condition of granting relief,[288] the courts refusing to take account of speculative and unproven claims for damages[289]: future collateral claims did not show that arrears would be paid within a reasonable time. If there are complaints other than rent arrears,[290] there is a separate discretion to grant relief under the section 146 notice procedure. Other conduct can be considered, even if it does not amount to a breach of covenant, but in a leading case the court was prepared to ignore a conviction for an indecent assault that occurred on the property itself.[291] An appellate court can exercise a fresh discretion if circumstances have changed.[292]

After a High Court order for possession has been made, relief occurs by the grant of a new lease,[293] but in a county court the original term is always restored.[294] Rent reviews should be preserved.[295]

---

[282]   *Thatcher* v. *C.H. Pearce & Sons (Contractors) Ltd.* [1968] 1 W.L.R. 748, Simon P. (6 months and 4 days). Note the highly special facts: the tenant was in Parkhurst and unable to communicate with his solicitor.

[283]   See above p. 816.

[284]   *Gill* v. *Lewis* [1986] 2 Q.B 1, 13, Jenkins L.J.

[285]   (1998) 75 P. & C.R. 232, 239.

[286]   *Hill* v. *Barclay* (1810) 16 Ves. 402, 33 E.R. 1037, where Lord Eldon L.C. suggests (at 405) that equity was too lax and contradicted everyday experience.

[287]   *Newbolt* v. *Bingham* (1895) 72 L.T. 852, 853, Lord Esher M.R., 854, Rigby L.J.

[288]   *Bowser* v. *Colby* (1841) 1 Hare 109, 66 E.R. 969.

[289]   *Inntrepreneur Pub Co. (C.P.C.) Ltd.* v. *Langton* [1999] 08 E.G. 169, Arden J. (damages for breach of European competition law).

[290]   *Bowser* v. *Colby* (1841) 1 Hare 109, 66 E.R. 969 (insolvency; trial at law to determine whether breach).

[291]   *Gill* v. *Lewis* [1986] 2 Q.B. 1, 13G, Jenkins L.J.

[292]   *Darlington B.C.* v. *Denmark Chemists Ltd.* [1993] 1 E.G.L.R. 62 C.A.; *Quilter* v. *Mapleson* (1882) 9 Q.B.D. 672 C.A. But it should not upset a consent order: *Ropac* v. *Inntrepreneur Pub Co. Ltd.* [2000] June 7th, Neuberger J.

[293]   *Dendy* v. *Evans* [1910] 1 K.B. 263, 266–267 Cozens Hardy M.R. Before judgment the court grants an injunction to restrain action at common law.

[294]   County Courts Act 1984 s.138(9B).

[295]   *Soteri* v. *Pyslides* [1991] 1 E.G.L.R. 138 C.A.

K. RELIEF: BREACHES OTHER THAN RENT ARREARS

1. Relief after notice and proceedings

Where the termination event is some breach of covenant other than rent arrears, re-entry must be preceded by a section 146 notice, which must allow a reasonable time for remedy of any breach. Relief may be needed if the period allowed by the notice for remedy has expired, or where the breach is irremediable so that no time has to be allowed. Section 146(2) permits relief "where a tenant is proceeding, by action . . . to enforce such a right of . . . forfeiture." So relief must be sought during the currency of the proceedings and not after the landlord has actually re-entered under an order,[296] a rule now forming settled law.[297] Relief is available while the tenant is proceeding, not where he has proceeded. Procedure is considered later.[298]

2.   Exercise of discretion

When granting relief to a tenant under section 146(2) of the Law of Property Act 1925, the court has a very wide discretion indeed.[299] The large cash bonus which may accrue to the landlord is not necessarily an unjust enrichment nor in itself a reason to grant relief.[300]

   Relief is usual if the breach of covenant has been rectified completely,[301] though subject to the problem of stigma, which is discussed below. Innocent parties who are prepared to do necessary work should therefore be relieved,[302] late performance being excused.[303] Proper[304] costs must be paid,[305] and other terms may be imposed, subject to any later relaxation.[306] It would be wrong to insist upon a surrender of the lease.[307] Early equity may have insisted on a complete remedy[308] and no doubt this is usually a requirement today,[309] but there are cases where it is unjust to insist on full performance of the leasehold covenants. Obvious examples are where the covenant cannot be carried out because of wartime restrictions,[310] or where listed building controls have made

---

[296] *Quilter* v. *Mapleson* (1882) 9 Q.B.D. 672, 677, Bowen L.J.; *Rogers* v. *Rice* [1892] 2 Ch. 170, 171–172, Coleridge C.J.; *Lock* v. *Pearce* [1893] 2 Ch. 271, 274 C.A.

[297] *Billson* v. *Residential Apartments Ltd.* [1992] 1 A.C. 494, 538, Lord Templeman; *Pakwood Transport Ltd.* v. *15 Beauchamp Place Ltd.* (1977) 36 P. & C.R. 112 C.A. is overruled.

[298] See below pp. 832–834.

[299] *Hyman* v. *Rose* [1912] A.C. 623, 631, Earl of Loreburn L.C.; this was cited in *Associated British Ports* v. *C.H. Bailey plc.* [1990] 2 A.C. 703, 708, Lord Templeman.

[300] *Darlington B.C.* v. *Denmark Chemists Ltd.* [1993] 1 E.G.L.R. 62 C.A.

[301] *Rugby School* v. *Tannahill* [1935] 1 K.B. 87 C.A.

[302] *Duke of Westminster* v. *Swinton* [1948] 1 K.B. 524, Denning J.; *Capital & Counties Property Co. Ltd.* v. *Mills* [1966] E.G.D. 96 (error by solicitor, no damage to landlord, and breach brought to an end).

[303] *Expert Clothing Service & Sales Ltd.* v. *Hillgate House Ltd.* [1986] Ch. 340 C.A. J.E. Martin [1986] *Conv.* 44; *Jacob* v. *Down* [1900] 2 Ch. 156, Stirling J. (willingness to build was valid defence).

[304] *Geen* v. *Herring* [1905] 1 K.B. 152 C.A.

[305] *Hartley* v. *Larkin* (1950) 66 (1) T.L.R. 896; *Skinners Co.* v. *Knight* [1891] 2 Q.B. 542 C.A.; *Bridge* v. *Quick* (1892) 67 L.T. 54; *Page* v. *Bennett* (1860) 2 Giff. 117, 66 E.R. 50.

[306] *Gaze* v. *London Drapery* (1900) 44 S.J. 722, Farwell J.

[307] *Fuller* v. *Judy Properties Ltd.* [1992] 1 E.G.L.R. 75 C.A.

[308] *Barrow* v. *Isaacs & Son* [1891] 1 Q.B. 417 C.A.

[309] *West* v. *Rogers* (1888) 4 T.L.R. 229 Div.Ct.

[310] *Westminster* v. *Swinton* [1948] 1 K.B. 524, Denning J.

demolition illegal.[311] A tenant should be protected from unreasonably strict landlords, for example in relation to the standard of a repair.

3. Reasons for refusing relief

Poor conduct by the tenant can be penalised by refusing relief, or by granting it subject to the payment of the landlord's costs on an indemnity basis.[312]

It is not the job of the court to turn a wrong into a right,[313] so that relief may be refused after any *flagrant breach,* that is a deliberate flouting of the landlord's rights.[314] Perhaps the most blatant was *Billson* v. *Residential Apartments Ltd.* in which a major series of alterations was begun without the landlord's consent and continued despite a peaceable re-entry. Although the House of Lords left the matter open,[315] the subsequent decision that relief should be withheld seems beyond question.[316] Breaches of negative covenants, such as unauthorised assignments[317] or changes of use,[318] often lead to the refusal of relief on this ground rather than irremediability.[319] However, a residual discretion remains even with wilful breaches,[320] so that relief was granted in *Mount Cook Land Ltd.* v. *Hartley*[321] even after the tenant had persisted in a sloppy practice of subletting without the landlord's consent.

Relief is less likely if breaches are *longstanding,* promises of Pauline conversion being viewed with natural suspicion.[322]

Certain breaches attach a *stigma* to the property that is not cleansed by cessation of the offending use, in particular use for prostitution.[323] There remains a discretion to grant relief even in stigma cases, though it is only exercised on grounds of exceptional hardship,[324] and no relaxation is occurring in the majority of stigma cases.[325] Immoral

[311] *John Lewis Properties Ltd.* v. *Viscount Chelsea* [1993] 2 E.G.L.R. 77, Mummery J.

[312] *Billson* v. *Residential Apartments Ltd. (No.3)* [1993] E.G.C.S. 55 (tenant's conduct poor, but not so bad as to justify indemnity basis).

[313] *Lock* v. *Pearce* [1893] 2 Ch. 271, 279, Lord Esher M.R.; *Batson* v. *London School Board* (1904) 69 J.P. 9; *Eyre* v. *Rea* [1948] K.B. 567, 570, Atkinson J.

[314] *Shiloh Spinners Ltd.* v. *Harding* [1973] A.C. 691, 725, Lord Wilberforce; *St Marylebone Property Co. Ltd.* v. *Tesco Stores Ltd.* [1988] 2 E.G.L.R. 40, Hoffmann J.; S. Fitzgerald & J. Aldridge (2000) 54 *P.L.J.* 8.

[315] [1992] 1 A.C. 494 H.L.; *Van Haarlam* v. *Kasner* [1992] 2 E.G.L.R. 59, Harman J. (spying).

[316] *Billson (No.2)* [1993] E.G.C.S. 150; see also *Crawford* v. *Clarke* [2000] E.G.C.S. 33 C.A. (two six-month periods, but then outright possession).

[317] *Clifford* v. *Johnson P.Rs.* [1979] 2 E.G.L.R. 41 C.A.

[318] *Tulapam Properties Ltd.* v. *De Almeida* [1981] 2 E.G.L.R. 55 Q.B.D.; *St Marylebone Property Co. Ltd.* v. *Tesco Stores Ltd.* [1988] 2 E.G.L.R. 40, Hoffmann J. (trade in breach); *Sood* v. *Barker* [1991] 1 E.G.L.R. 87 C.A.; *Darlington B.C.* v. *Denmark Chemists Ltd.* [1993] 1 E.G.L.R. 62 C.A. (shop); *Davis* v. *Elf Oil U.K. Properties Ltd.* [1995] E.G.C.S.196 (petrol tie).

[319] *Savva* v. *Hussein* [1996] 2 E.G.L.R. 65 C.A.

[320] *Cremin* v. *Barjack Properties Ltd.* [1985] 1 E.G.L.R. 30 C.A.; *Southern Depot Co. Ltd.* v. *British Railways Board* [1990] 2 E.G.L.R. 39, Morritt J.

[321] [2000] E.G.C.S. 08 Ch.D.

[322] *Darlington B.C.* v. *Denmark Chemists Ltd.* [1993] 1 E.G.L.R. 62 C.A. (pharmacy run in breach of a covenant not to open a shop).

[323] *Rugby School* v. *Tannahill* [1935] 1 K.B. 87 C.A. (the school were landlords!); L.G.C. (1933) 5 *C.L.J.* 396; *Borthwick-Norton* v. *Romney Warwick Estates Ltd.* [1950] 1 All E.R. 798 C.A.; *Burfort Financial Investments Ltd.* v. *Chotard* [1976] 2 E.G.L.R. 53, Foster J.

[324] *Central Estates (Belgravia) Ltd.* v. *Woolgar (No.2)* [1972] 1 W.L.R. 1048 C.A. (homosexual brothel, elderly tenant, and potential for large gain by landlord; relief was allowed by Lord Denning M.R. and Cairns L.J., despite the doubts of Buckley L.J.).

[325] *British Petroleum Pension Trust Ltd.* v. *Behrendt* [1985] 2 E.G.L.R. 97, 99G, Purchas L.J.

use by *sub-tenants* may not be a breach at all by an innocent *tenant*, since the usual covenant is not to suffer prostitution[326]; where the tenant does know, immediate steps to remedy the breach by evicting the sub-tenants may be sufficient to escape eviction[327] especially after minor or short-lived use.[328]

4. Effect of relief to tenants

After re-entry, the lease enters a trance-like state.[329] The effect of a grant of relief is that the old lease is restored, and it is as if the lease was never forfeited. The tenant holds under the original lease,[330] so that no new grant is necessary.[331] Rent is due for the period between issue of the claim to forfeit and the order for relief.[332] Thus in *Dendy v. Evans*,[333] the tenant was able, after obtaining relief, to take action against a sub-tenant for arrears of rent, since both leases were automatically revivified. The lease had not been destroyed, and did not have to be recalled to life.[334] The importance of this rule emerges from *Escalus Properties Ltd.* v. *Robinson*,[335] which concerned four leases of flats held on long leases at low rents. The landlord argued that relief could only be prospective from the date of the court order for relief, thus entitling them to mesne profits equal to the (much higher) market rent. But this would have been grossly unfair, and Nourse L.J.[336] was able to give retrospective relief in all four cases.

L.   RELIEF: AFTER PHYSICAL RE-ENTRY

Where a landlord forfeits a lease of commercial property or property that is vacant by physical re-entry, the tenant is entitled to claim relief in separate proceedings.

1. Non-payment of rent

Power to seek relief in the High Court after a peaceable forfeiture for non-payment of rent is equitable.[337] The statutory time limit which applies to court proceedings for rent arrears exceeding six months is applied by analogy, but not rigidly so: "equity will not boggle at a matter of days" and so relief is possible even outside the six-month time

---

[326] *Egerton v. Esplanade Hotels London Ltd.* [1947] 2 All E.R. 88, Morris J.; (1947) 63 *L.Q.R.* 415.

[327] *Glass v. Kencakes Ltd.* [1966] 1 Q.B. 611, Paull J.; D. Macintyre [1965] *C.L.J.* 213.

[328] *Hoffmann v. Fineberg* [1949] Ch. 245, Harman J.; (1948) 63 *L.Q.R.* 312; *Ropemaker Properties Ltd.* v. *Noonhaven Ltd.* [1989] 2 E.G.L.R. 56, Millett J.

[329] *Meadows v. Clerical Medical & General Life Assurance Society* [1981] Ch. 70, 75, Megarry V.C.; *Liverpool Properties Ltd.* v. *Oldbridge Investments Ltd.* [1985] 2 E.G.L.R. 111, 112.

[330] Supreme Court Act 1981 s.38 (whether in or out of court); *Church Commissioners for England* v. *Nodjoumi* (1986) 51 P. & C.R. 155, Hirst J.

[331] Supreme Court Act 1981 s.38(2); Common Law Procedure Act 1852 s.212 (after stay by payment in before trial); County Courts Act 1984 s.138(5); *Hynes* v. *Twinsectra Ltd.* [1995] 2 E.G.L.R. 69 C.A. (enfranchisement claim can proceed); M. Pawlowski [1996] *Conv.* 55.

[332] *Hill v. Griffin* [1987] 1 E.G.L.R. 81 C.A.

[333] [1910] 1 K.B. 263 C.A.

[334] At 270–271, Farwell L.J. Contrast and query *Hammersmith & Fulham L.B.C.* v. *Tops Shop Centres Ltd.* [1990] Ch. 237, Scott J.

[335] [1996] Q.B. 231 C.A.

[336] At 251F.

[337] *Thatcher v. C.H. Pearce & Sons (Contractors) Ltd.* [1968] 1 W.L.R. 748, 774-775, Simon P.; despite *Lovelock v. Margo* [1963] 2 Q.B. 786 C.A.

limit.[338] The statutory right to apply to a county court is limited to claims for relief made within six months.[339]

2.   After a section 146 notice

Where the landlord forfeits out of court, the tenant has a right to apply to the court for relief. After the landlord has served a section 146 notice but before he has actually re-entered, the landlord is still "proceeding" and the right to relief is clear in subsection (2). Much more difficult is the question whether a landlord can be said to be "proceeding" where he has actually re-entered and has changed the locks. Whatever the literal meaning of the subsection, relief is allowed following physical re-entry under the decision of the House of Lords in *Billson* v. *Residential Apartments Ltd.*[340] Tenants undertook a major alteration of a property on the Gunton Estate in South Kensington without the landlord's permission. This was a clear deliberate breach of covenant, to which the landlords responded by serving a section 146 notice, and barging in at 6 a.m. one morning. The issue in the litigation was whether the tenants were now allowed to claim relief.

The Court of Appeal[341] thought that the phrase "is proceeding" in subsection (2) precluded an application for relief made after the landlord has completed a peaceable re-entry. The House of Lords unanimously reversed this judgment, Lord Oliver saying that it was wrong to equiparate a peaceable re-entry with an executed judgment.[342] A landlord "is proceeding" if he is taking the necessary steps.[343] To have decided otherwise would have meant that tenants were forced to institute litigation as soon as they received a section 146 notice and would have left the non-litigious at the mercy of aggressive landlords. Rights to relief end if the landlord secures possession under a final and unassailable court judgment,[344] if he sells,[345] and (probably) if the tenant allows a period of six months to elapse from the date of the re-entry without claiming relief.[346]

A similar problem arises where a lease is disclaimed on the insolvency of the original tenant, but again the courts have found a means to allow relief to third parties.[347]

3.   Principles of granting relief

These are the same as in applications for relief made in a forfeiture by court action.[348]

---

[338] *Thatcher* as above (6 months and 4 days). Note the special facts: the tenant was in Parkhurst and out of communication with his solicitor.

[339] County Courts Act 1984 s.139(2).

[340] [1992] 1 A.C. 494 H.L.; P.F. Smith [1992] *Conv.* 273; S. Bridge [1992] *N.L.J.* 216; S. Payne [1992] *N.L.J.* 22.

[341] At 501 C.A.; S. Bridge [1991] *C.L.J.* 401; S. Goulding [1991 *Conv.* 380; P.F. Smith [1992] *Conv.* 32; *Bristol & West B.S.* v. *Turner* [1991] 2 E.G.L.R. 52, Mummery J.

[342] At 544B, Lord Oliver.

[343] At 538H–539B, Lord Templeman, 544B, Lord Oliver.

[344] At 542.

[345] *Bhojwani* v. *Kingsley Investment Trust Ltd.* [1992] 2 E.G.L.R. 70.

[346] By analogy with the statutory time-limit; see above pp. 817–818.

[347] *Barclays Bank plc.* v. *Prudential Assurance Co. Ltd.* [1998] 1 E.G.L.R. 44 Ch.D.

[348] See above pp. 815–821.

M. RELIEF: DERIVATIVE INTERESTS

1. Proprietary effect

A right to forfeit a legal lease is an independent legal interest[349] in which case it affects all derivative interests and is enforceable by the current landlord against all current parties. If the reversion is divided the right to forfeit passes with each part[350] and it affects the tenant of each part of the lease. A defect of the law applying to leases granted before 1997 is that the tenant of part A risked forfeiture for a breach occurring on part B; for new leases under the Landlord and Tenant (Covenants) Act 1995 the forfeiture only terminates the lease of the part affected by the particular breach.[351]

It is essential that the landlord terminate all derivative interests[352]: an arrangement to end the head lease while leaving sub-leases in place is not a forfeiture.[353] If the tenant obtains relief, it is as if the forfeiture had never occurred and derivative interests are unaffected. However, it is common for the holders of derivative interests to have to apply for relief independently of the tenant.

2. Relief for the holders of derivative interests

Sub-tenants and mortgage-lenders usually seek relief under the tailor-made provisions of section 146(4) of the Law of Property Act 1925. Unlike the rest of section 146, this subsection applies where the lease is forfeited for non-payment of rent.[354] Introduction of the statutory power in 1892[355] superseded the old equitable power to relieve lenders.[356] Holders of derivative interests will most often need to claim relief where the tenant is disqualified,[357] or regards the lease as onerous.

Potential applicants include *sub-tenants,*[358] a term which incorporates a person claiming a derivative interest through a sub-tenant,[359] equitable tenants,[360] equitable sub-tenants and assignees,[361] and those holding over under a renewable business lease.[362] Acquisition of new rights to security of tenure will not by itself preclude

---

[349] L.P.A. 1925 s.1(2)(e); otherwise it is equitable but unregistrable.

[350] L.P.A. 1925 s.141; L.T. (Covenants) A. 1995 s.4.

[351] s.21; see above p. 759.

[352] *Hall* v. *Griffin* [1987] 1 E.G.L.R. 81 C.A.; *Viscount Chelsea* v. *Hutchinson* [1994] 2 E.G.L.R. 61 C.A.

[353] *Ashton* v. *Sobelman* [1987] 1 All E.R. 755; *Baylis* v. *Le Gros* (1858) 4 C.B.N.S. 537, 140 E.R. 1201. *Hammersmith & Fulham L.B.C.* v. *Tops Shop Centres Ltd.* [1990] Ch. 237, Scott J., is surely doubtful.

[354] *Belgravia Investments Co. Ltd.* v. *Meah* [1964] 1 Q.B. 436, 448, Russell L.J.; *Abbey National B.S.* v. *Maybeech Ltd.* [1985] Ch. 190, 198A, Nicholls L.J.

[355] Conveyancing Act 1892 s.4; *Gray* v. *Bonsall* [1904] 1 K.B. 601 C.A.

[356] *Webber* v. *Smith* (1689) 2 Vern. 103, 23 E.R. 676; *Doe d. Whitfield* v. *Roe* (1811) 3 Taunt. 402, 128 E.R. 160; *Hare* v. *Elms* [1893] 1 Q.B. 604.

[357] E.g. more than one year after a liquidation: L.P. (Amendment) A. 1929 s.1 disapplies L.P.A. 1925 s.146 subss.(8)–(10) to permit relief to a sub-tenant etc.

[358] *Great Western Rly Co.* v. *Smith* (1876) 2 Ch.D. 235; on appeal (1877) 3 App. Cas. 165 H.L.; *Cholmeley's School* v. *Sewell* [1893] 2 Q.B. 254; *Pascall* v. *Galinski* [1970] 1 Q.B. 38 C.A.; S. Tromans [1986] *Conv.* 187.

[359] s.146(5)(e).

[360] *Coatsworth* v. *Johnson* (1886) 55 L.J.Q.B. 220 C.A.; *Swain* v. *Ayres* (1888) 21 Q.B.D. 289 C.A.; *Strong* v. *Stringer* (1889) 61 L.T. 470; *Foster* v. *Reeves* [1892] 2 Q.B. 255; *Gray* v. *Spyer* [1922] 2 Ch. 22; P. Sparkes (1987) 16 *Anglo-American* 160.

[361] *High Street Investments Ltd.* v. *Bellshare Property Investments Ltd.* [1996] 2 E.G.L.R. 40 C.A.

[362] *Cadogan* v. *Dimovic* [1984] 1 W.L.R. 609 C.A.; J.E. Adams [1992] *Conv.* 405.

relief[363] but it is a factor that weighs against it.[364] Essentially this includes anyone with a proprietary interest in the lease, but not squatters and not the wife of a deceased tenant who is not an assignee.[365] *Lenders* with any form of security are able to claim relief,[366] including those with a sub-demise,[367] a legal charge,[368] and any equitable security.[369] A majority of the Court of Appeal in *Croydon (Unique) Ltd.* v. *Wright* decided that a creditor holding a charging order over a lease was entitled to join the proceedings to assert his rights against the landlord.[370] Butler Sloss L.J. thought it would be astonishing if the chargee could not be heard, although Pill L.J. dissented because an equitable charge conferred no right of sale. In the particular case the creditor had by far the largest interest, given that his debt was £233,888, whereas the arrears were £653; the charging orders were made against a lease worth £70,000. Since the creditor was a party entitled to seek relief and had not been notified of the proceedings, the possession order was set aside. A lease granted by way of relief to the lender is redeemable by the borrower/tenant.[371]

3. Claiming relief

The procedure for claiming relief as a sub-tenant is described below.[372] So too is the statutory requirement to claim while the landlord "is proceeding, by action or otherwise" to forfeit[373] and the equitable relief available to a sub-tenant after the landlord had concluded the termination of the tenant's interest.[374]

4. Exercise of the discretion

Cases emphasise the width of the discretion when dealing with sub-tenants and lenders.[375] Relief will usually be conditional on making good earlier breaches,[376] but will usually be granted if that is done,[377] particularly if the applicant is himself innocent of

---

[363] *John Lyon's Free Grammar School Governors* v. *James* [1995] 4 All E.R. 740 C.A.

[364] *Clifford* v. *Johnson's P.R.s* [1979] 2 E.G.L.R. 41 C.A.

[365] *Tickner* v. *Buzzacott* [1965] Ch. 426, Plowman J.; F.L.A. 1996 s.30(3)–(5).

[366] J.E. Adams [1992] *Conv.* 405. Only a lender in possession is entitled to serve a counter-notice to claim the benefit of the Leasehold Reform (Repairs) Act 1938: *Target Home Loans Ltd.* v. *Iza Ltd.* [2000] 02 E.G. 117, C.Ct.

[367] *Sinclair Gardens Investments (Kensington) Ltd.* v. *Walsh* [1996] 2 E.G.L.R. 23 C.A.; *Escalus Properties Ltd.* v. *Robinson* [1996] Q.B. 231 C.A.; *Rexhaven Ltd.* v. *Nurse* (1996) 28 H.L.R. 241, Colyer J.

[368] *Grand Junction Co. Ltd.* v. *Bates* [1954] 2 Q.B. 160, Upjohn J.; *Belgravia Investments Co. Ltd.* v. *Meah* [1964] 1 Q.B. 436 C.A.; *Abbey National B.S.* v. *Maybeech Ltd.* [1985] Ch. 190, 198d, Nicholls J.; *Chelsea Estates Investments Trust Co. Ltd.* v. *Marche* [1955] Ch. 328, Upjohn J.; *Barclays Bank plc.* v. *Prudential Assurance Co. Ltd.* [1998] 1 E.G.L.R. 44 Ch.D.

[369] *Jacques* v. *Harrison* (1884) 12 Q.B.D. 165 (mortgage); *Ladup* v. *Williams & Glyn's Bank Ltd.* [1985] 1 W.L.R. 851 (charge); *Re Good's Lease* [1954] 1 W.L.R. 309, Harman J. (guarantor with right to call for legal charge).

[370] [1999] 3 E.G.L.R. 28 C.A.; S. Hasan [1999] 40 L.S.G. 45; S. Murdoch [1999] 45 E.G. 178; this confirms *Bland* v. *Ingram Estates Ltd.* [1999] 2 E.G.L.R. 49, Peter Leaver Q.C.

[371] *Chelsea Estates Investment Trust Co. Ltd.* v. *Marche* [1955] Ch. 328.

[372] See below pp. 833–834.

[373] L.P.A. 1925 s.146(2).

[374] See below p. 834.

[375] *Ewart* v. *Fryer* [1901] 1 Ch. 499, 515–516, Romer L.J.; on appeal as *Fryer* v. *Ewart* [1902] A.C. 187 H.L.

[376] *Hill* v. *Griffin* [1987] 1 E.G.L.R. 81 C.A.

[377] *Belgravia Investments Co. Ltd.* v. *Meah* [1964] 1 Q.B. 436, 446, Lord Denning M.R.; citing *Bowser* v. *Colby* (1841) 1 Hare 109, 134, 66 E.R. 969, Wigram V.C.; *Newbolt* v. *Bingham* (1895) 72 L.T. 852; *Gill* v. *Lewis* [1956] 2 Q.B. 1, 17, Hodson L.J.

fault.[378] But landlords are not absolutely entitled to insist on meticulous compliance with the terms of the lease and relief remains discretionary.[379] Accrual of new security of tenure is a factor weighing against relief, but it is not decisive.[380] Costs are almost invariably awarded.[381]

Relief to a sub-tenant granted under sub-section (4)—as opposed to relief granted to a tenant under sub-section (2)—does not occur by restoration of the original lease. A new lease is created and vested in the applicant on such terms as the court thinks fit. The term may not be longer than the remaining residue of the head lease that has been forfeited.[382] Relief is possible if the term of the sub-lease has ended but the sub-tenant is a protected business tenant.[383] Being new, the lease cannot have retrospective effect, and the reversioner is entitled to mesne profits (as opposed to rent) between the date of the forfeiture and the order for relief to the sub-tenant.[384] The landlord is entitled to any net balance held by the receiver but not to gross receipts, nor to mesne profits at a higher rate.[385]

Jurisdiction to grant relief to a person interested in *part* was conferred in 1892[386] and this is now commonly exercised in favour of sub-tenants of part, for example allowing a new lease of a part used as a cinema but denying it for another part used as a restaurant.[387]

5. Claiming relief for derivative owners as "tenants"

Relief for derivative interests suffers from one fundamental disadvantage, that the relief is prospective only, since it operates through the grant of a new lease, and so only from the date that the court makes an order. This was very inconvenient on the facts of *Escalus Properties Ltd. v. Robinson*[388] since the landlord was entitled to mesne profits equal to the rack rental value of the land, even though the property was let on long leases at low rents. The lender ought only to have been made to pay the relatively low ground rents that the tenant had omitted to pay. A procedural means of achieving this was discovered in *Escalus*. The lenders succeeded in bringing themselves within the extended statutory definition of "tenants" and so were able to claim retrospective relief, which operated as if the original lease had never gone away.[389] Nourse L.J. found that this procedural

---

[378] *Abbey National B.S. v. Maybeech Ltd.* [1985] Ch. 190, 205.

[379] *Egerton v. Jones* [1939] 2 Q.B. 702 C.A.

[380] *Factors (Sundries) Ltd. v. Millers* [1952] 2 All E.R. 630.

[381] *Egerton v. Jones* [1939] 2 Q.B. 702 C.A.; *Factors* as above; *Abbey National B.S. v. Maybeech Ltd.* [1985] Ch. 190, 205.

[382] *Ewart v. Fryer* [1901] 1 Ch. 499, 516, Romer L.J.; on appeal *Fryer v. Ewart* [1902] A.C. 187 H.L.; *Factors (Sundries) Ltd. v. Millers* [1952] 2 All E.R. 630; *Hill v. Griffin* [1987] 1 E.G.L.R. 81 C.A.

[383] *Cadogan v. Dimovic* [1984] 1 W.L.R. 609 C.A.

[384] *Official Custodian of Charities v. Mackey* [1985] Ch. 168, Scott J.; *City of Westminster Assurance Co. v. Ainis* (1975) 29 P. & C.R. 469 C.A.; *Meadows v. Clerical Medical & General Life Assurance Society* [1981] Ch. 70, Megarry V.C.

[385] *Official Custodian for Charities v. Mackey (No. 2)* [1985] 1 W.L.R. 1308, Nourse J.

[386] Conveyancing Act 1892 s.4, reversing *Burt v. Gray* [1891] 2 Q.B. 98; now L.P.A. 1925 s.146(4).

[387] *Chatham Empire Theatre (1955) Ltd. v. Ultrans* [1961] 1 W.L.R. 817, Salmon J.; P.V. Baker (1961) 77 *L.Q.R.* 318; *London Bridge v. Thompson* (1903) 89 L.T. 50 not followed.

[388] [1996] Q.B. 231 C.A.

[389] See above p. 818 n. 294.

dodge was available for rent-only cases whether in the High Court[390] or the county court,[391] and also (with more difficulty) for breaches of other covenants.[392]

6.   Relief for sub-tenants after peaceable re-entry

A *sub-tenant* is entitled to apply for relief subject to the same condition as a tenant, which is that the landlord "is proceeding" to enforce a right of re-entry.[393] The decision in *Billson v. Residential Apartments Ltd.*[394] to allow a tenant a reasonable period after a peaceable re-entry for relief made it unnecessary to consider the position of those with derivative interests, but by implication the Lords[395] must have intended to protect the more deserving sub-tenants and lenders. Relief is now allowed in the lower courts.[396] The need for liberality towards derivative interests is best illustrated by the facts of *Abbey National B.S. v. Maybeech.*[397] A landlord forfeited a lease of a flat without informing the building society that held a mortgage of the flat. The omission was deliberate,[398] the lender becoming aware of the forfeiture only when the land registry wrote proposing to close the leasehold title. The decision to deny relief would no longer be followed after *Billson.*

In any event landlords may waive the time limit by failing to enforce forfeiture for four years, and may be estopped if they lead the tenant to believe that they will not be evicted.[399]

7.   Reletting

If the landlord relets the property, the new tenant may or may not secure priority,[400] but if he does the old tenant has necessarily lost his right to recover his lease.

What happens if the landlord has relet the property? There is merit in the view that the *tenant* should be barred by a reletting,[401] and in many cases this has been so. Where relief was claimed only near the end of the six-month time limit and the landlord had arranged to relet, the discretion may be exercised so as to refuse relief.[402] Even two weeks after the hearing may be too late to offer rent, if the original proceedings are not

---

[390]   *Newbolt* v. *Bingham* (1895) 72 L.T. 852.

[391]   County Courts Act 1984 s.138 as extended by ss.138(9C), (10), 140. The time limit is 6 months: *United Dominions Trust* v. *Shellpoint Trustees* [1993] 4 All E.R. 310 C.A.

[392]   [1996] Q.B. 231 (*Dennis* case); *Nind* v. *Nineteenth Century B.S.* [1894] 2 Q.B. 226 not followed.

[393]   L.P.A. 1925 s.146(4).

[394]   [1992] 1 A.C. 494 H.L.

[395]   Overruling *Billson* v. *Residential Apartments Ltd.* [1992] 1 A.C. 501 C.A. Nicholls L.J. dissented, and this dissent now represents the law.

[396]   *Cardigan Properties Ltd.* v. *Consolidated Property Investments Ltd.* [1991] 1 E.G.L.R. 64 Q.B.D.; *Barclays Bank plc.* v. *Prudential Assurance Co. Ltd.* [1998] 1 E.G.L.R. 44 Ch.D. (disclaimer).

[397]   [1985] Ch. 190 C.A.; contrast Nicholls J. at first instance.

[398]   There is in any event a residual power to allow relief in cases of fraud, surprise and mistake: *Barrow* v. *Isaacs & Son* [1891] 1 Q.B. 417; *Billson* [1992] 1 A.C. 494, 540E, Lord Templeman; *British Telecommunications plc.* v. *Department of Environment* [1996] unreported.

[399]   *Hammersmith & Fulham L.B.C.* v *Tops Shop Centres Ltd.* [1990] Ch. 237, Scott J.

[400]   See the personal property case *On Demand Information plc.* v. *Michael Gerson (Finance) plc.* [1999] 2 All E.R. 811.

[401]   *Re A.G.B. Research Ltd.* [1995] B.C.C. 1091, Vinelott J.; *Redleaf Investments Ltd.* v. *Talbot* [1994] Times May 5th, Vinelott J.

[402]   *Stanhope* v. *Haworth* (1886) 3 T.L.R. 34.

defended and the landlord has already executed a new lease.[403] A tenant may be estopped from claiming relief if he has earlier indicated that he will not do so.[404] However it appears that a *tenant's* right to relief could survive,[405] and in many cases justice will require that *derivative interests* are relieved. Priority can be preserved by registering an application for relief as a pending action.[406] If this is not done, the new tenant may become a bona fide purchaser beyond the reach of the power to grant relief.[407] The lease will be binding if relief is granted irrespective of notice.[408] The solution adopted in one case was to make the original tenant's lease reversionary on the reletting,[409] but this is likely to prove unsatisfactory to the displaced tenant. There is much room for improvement in procedure here.

N. RELIEF: REFORM

1. Law Commission proposals for reform

The Law Commission in its Report on Forfeiture[410] and its draft Termination of Tenancies Bill[411] proposes reform of the law of relief, which would effect a great simplification without much practical change. The court would be given a general jurisdiction to order termination or the remedy of a breach, with no relief cases based on stigma abolished. Normally the court will make a remedial order, which will give the tenant a chance to correct the breach,[412] and so to continue as tenant. Either party[413] could vary either the time limit or the conditions attached to relief.[414] Sub-tenancies and mortgages will still end automatically as under current law, but the landlord would have a new right to preserve derivative interests by notice.[415] The power for sub-tenants and lenders to apply for relief would be much like the current law,[416] though with stronger rights for the landlord to obtain an indemnity from the tenant and with power to grant a new lease to the landlord to preserve the mortgage.

---

[403] Subject to the original tenants having priority, e.g. by registration of a pending action.
[404] *Silverman* v. *A.F.C.O. (U.K.) Ltd.* [1988] 1 E.G.L.R. 51 C.A.; J.E. Martin [1988] *Conv.* 138.
[405] *Bank of Ireland Homes Mortgages Ltd.* v. *South Lodge Developments Ltd.* [1996] 1 E.G.L.R. 91 Ch.D. The landlord can be prevented from selling pending an application for relief: *Bristol & West B.S.* v. *Turner* [1991] 2 E.G.L.R. 52, Mummery J.
[406] *Selim Ltd.* v. *Bickenhall Engineering Ltd.* [1981] 3 All E.R. 210, Megarry V.C.
[407] *Bland* v. *Ingrams Estates Ltd.* [1999] 2 E.G.L.R. 49 Ch.D.
[408] *Bhojwani* v. *Kingsley Investment Trust Ltd.* [1992] 2 E.G.L.R. 70, T. Morison Q.C.; J.E. Martin [1993] *Conv.* 296.
[409] *Fuller* v. *Judy Properties Ltd.* [1992] 1 E.G.L.R. 75 C.A.; J.E. Martin [1992] *Conv.* 343; this was also agreed in *Bank of Ireland Homes Mortgages Ltd.* v. *South Lodge Developments Ltd.* [1996] 1 E.G.L.R. 91 Ch.D.
[410] Law Com. No.142 (1985); S. Tromans [1986] *Conv.* 187; P.F. Smith [1986] *Conv.* 165.
[411] Law Com. No.221 (1994); M. Codd & T. Bayley [1994] *N.L.J.* 1420, 1456; C. Peete [1994] 26 E.G. 133; H.W. Wilkinson [1994] *Conv.* 177; J.E. Adams [1994] *Conv.* 184; N. Hopkins (1995) 58 *M.L.R.* 547. A further Bill is expected late in 2000.
[412] cls.15(2), 4(3) (definition).
[413] cl.16 (tenant); cl.20 (landlord).
[414] e.g. ending action; finding suitable surety; payment rent arrears; damages; costs/expenses.
[415] cl.26; the effect would be like a surrender.
[416] cl.28.

2. Removing the unjust enrichment of landlords

Landlord and tenant law displays a schizophrenia about the extent to which the landlord should be allowed to profit from the tenant's breach of covenant. Applying the literal terms of the lease, once the covenant has been broken the condition on which the land is held is no longer fulfilled and the tenant's right to possession has ended. Such a literal interpretation would lead to great hardship to tenants and great opportunities for unmerited profits for landlords. As St Mark foretold:

"The man who has will be given more, and the man who has not will forfeit even what he has."[417]

In one case[418] a lease of a flat provided that the lease should be forfeited unless the windows were cleaned regularly. By allowing the landlord to re-enter the property, the court handed the capital value of the flat to the landlord for a trivial breach of a trivial covenant. Conventionally this has been righted in equity by allowing relief from onerous conditions though, as has been seen,[419] greater flexibility has been allowed to tenants in arrears with their rent than those in breach of other obligations.

This overlay of common law and equity explains the impotence of the law of restitution. Profits are stripped from a person who has been unjustly enriched at the expense of another. Landlords who succeed in forfeiting are often substantially richer, which is why forfeiture proceedings are so common, but the enrichment is not "unjust". In *Dollar Land (Cumbernauld) Ltd.* v. *C.I.N. Properties Ltd.*[420] the development corporation of a Scottish new town had granted a building lease of a of site to C.I.N. It built a shopping centre that was leased back to the development corporation in order that it could grant sub-leases, the arrangement being to share rents between the development corporation and the developer. Dollar Land bought the lease but later failed to pay the rent. The head landlord, C.I.N., raised an action for a declarator of irritancy and removing—the Scots procedure for forfeiting the lease—in which it succeeded. After the eviction of Dollar Land it sued for compensation for the unjust enrichment that the landlord had obtained. The action failed. There was indeed an enrichment, but the retention of this profit was not unjust. Dollar Land was entitled to participate in the profits derived from sub-letting only by ensuring the continued existence of the head lease, from which C.I.N. now benefited according to the agreed contractual terms.

In other words the common law action for restitution was so crude that it could only look at the common law rights and wrongs of the situation.

A possible way forward is suggested by *Khar* v. *Delmounty Ltd.*[421] A lease of a flat was forfeited for non-payment of service charge, but the parties agreed that the court should make an order for sale of the property. This enabled the landlord to recover the arrears

---

[417] ch.4 v.25.
[418] *Betterkey* v. *Joseph* [1991] Independent November 1st.
[419] See above pp. 815–821.
[420] [1998] 3 E.G.L.R. 79 H.L. From *Crawford* v. *Clarke* [2000] E.G.C.S. 33 C.A., it appears that the windfall that accrues to the landlord is a relevant factor when considering whether to order relief; it was also considered in *Mount Cook Land Ltd.* v. *Hartley* [2000] E.G.C.S. 08 Ch.D.
[421] (1998) 75 P. & C.R. 232, 239, Lord Woolf M.R.

of service charge while returning the net value of the flat to the tenant-owners. The presence of a shorthold sub-tenant led to a deferral of sale until the shorthold could be terminated, meaning that the full vacant possession value could be obtained on sale. Forfeiture of leases with a capital value[422] can never work happily. Sale should replace forfeiture just as judicial sale replaced the foreclosure of mortgages; only in this way can be lack of virility in the law of restitution be overcome.

O. SPECIAL CASES: INSOLVENCY AND DENIAL OF TITLE

1. As a termination event

Most leases provide for forfeiture on insolvency.[423] Landlords find difficulty in collecting rent after the insolvency of the tenant, an eventuality against which they protect themselves by taking sureties and reserving the right to forfeit the lease. To catch all cases where they might be prejudiced, a landlord will generally insist upon a widely drawn forfeiture provision, covering individual bankruptcy, compulsory liquidation of a corporate tenant, voluntary liquidation excepting reconstructions for the purposes of amalgamation,[424] corporate dissolution after failure to file company returns,[425] voluntary arrangements,[426] making of an administration order,[427] other insolvency procedures, and the bankruptcy of a surety.[428] Since 1892,[429] a pre-forfeiture warning notice (a section 146 notice) has been necessary in relation to liquidation or bankruptcy.[430]

Permission is needed to enforce a security interest after an insolvency. In *Re Park Air Services plc.*[431] Lord Millett analysed whether a right of forfeiture is a security interest and decided that it is not. On insolvency a secured creditor must realise or surrender his security, but this analysis . This is completely inappropriate to the landlord's right of re-entry, which is not a security, cannot be realised, has no value and is incapable of surrender. Forfeiture does not secure the performance of the tenant's liability to pay rent, which remains after termination of the lease as it was before. As Lord Millett said, it would be a curious security that evaporated just when it was needed. Hence permission is not required from the court before issuing a claim for possession based on a forfeiture,[432]

---

[422] e.g. *Target Home Loans Ltd.* v. *Iza Ltd.* [2000] 02 E.G. 117, C.Ct.

[423] In the case of a short residential tenancy a term for termination on insolvency becomes a term of a statutory tenancy: *Cadogan Estates Ltd.* v. *MacMahon* (2000) Times November 1st H.L.

[424] *Fryer* v. *Ewart* [1902] A.C. 187 H.L., approving *Horsey Estate Ltd.* v. *Steiger* [1899] 2 Q.B. 79 C.A.

[425] *Cromwell Developments Ltd.* v. *Godfrey* [1998] 2 E.G.L.R. 62 C.A.

[426] *Re Nadeem* [1990] 1 W.L.R. 48 (interim order would forfeit): *Exchange Travel Agency Ltd.* v. *Triton Property Trust Ltd.* [1991] 2 E.G.L.R. 50; D. Brown [1991] *Conv.* 465.

[427] *Re Lomax Leisure Ltd.* [1999] 2 E.G.L.R. 37, Neuberger J. (permission of the court not required); D. Brown [1999] *Conv.* 255; S. Murdoch [1999] 26 *E.G.* 150.

[428] *Halliard Property Co. Ltd.* v. *Jack Segal Ltd.* [1978] 1 W.L.R. 377, Goulding J.

[429] Conveyancing Act 1892 s.2(2); *Horsey Estate Ltd.* v. *Steiger* [1899] 2 Q.B. 79, 91, Lord Russell C.J.; *Halliard Property Co. Ltd.* v. *Jack Segal Ltd.* [1978] 1 W.L.R. 377, Goulding J.

[430] *Re Riggs* [1901] 2 K.B. 16, Wright J.

[431] [1999] 1 All E.R. 673, 681e.

[432] I.A. 1986 s.383(2); *Razzaq* v. *Pala* [1997] 1 W.L.R. 1336, Lightman J.

[433] I.A. 1985 s.212(3); *Ezekiel* v. *Orakpo* [1977] Q.B. 260 C.A.; *Re Debtor No. 13A–IO–1995* [1995] 1 W.L.R. 1127, Rattee J.; *Olympia & York Canary Wharf Ltd.* v. *Oil Property Investments Ltd.* [1994] 2 E.G.L.R. 48 C.A.; *Razzaq* v. *Pala* [1997] 1 W.L.R. 1336.

physical re-entry[433] after any insolvency procedure, or while an administration order is in force.[434]

The claim to forfeit should be protected as a pending land action.[435]

2. Insolvency: protecting creditors

Although the landlord has a natural interest in ensuring that the rent can be paid it must also be considered that the lease is an asset of the insolvent person or company which the creditors will wish to have sold. Section 146 seeks to strike a balance between these competing demands, listing cases in which forfeiture is automatic with no possibility of relief, but permitting limited relief in other cases.

Section 146 is *excluded altogether,* so that no relief is possible, for forfeiture occurring on insolvency in leases of agricultural land, mines, pubs, and furnished houses.[436] So too if the personal qualifications of the tenant are important,[437] thus excluding claims for relief from a foreigner barred from entry to the country[438] and a tenant arrested under the Official Secrets Act.[439] The only protection for a tenant is the law of waiver.[440]

Section 146 *applies for 1 year* from the date of the forfeiture in all other cases, and relief is usual.[441] For example, in a compulsory winding up, the crucial date is the making of the winding up order by the court.[442] Relief may be available after entry into a voluntary arrangement.[443] This enables the trustee in bankruptcy or liquidator to realise the lease, by sale within one year. If sale occurs within that year,[444] protection in favour of the purchaser is indefinite.[445]

The potential inadequacy of these provisions was illustrated during the first phase of the long-running *Parway Estates* litigation: since there is no requirement that the year runs from service of the section 146 notice implementing forfeiture, it is possible that parties may be unaware of the need to sell. In *Official Custodian of Charities* v. *Parway Estates Developments Ltd.*[446] a building lease created in 1961 provided for its termination on the liquidation of the tenant company. Winding up was ordered on the Revenue's petition in 1979 and notified in the London Gazette. However, the landlord company did

---

[434] I.A. 1986 s.11(3); *Re Lomax Leisure Ltd.* [1999] 2 E.G.L.R. 37, Neuberger J., relying on *Re Park Air Services plc.* [1999] 1 All E.R. 673 H.L.; *Clarence Café Ltd.* v. *Colchester Properties Ltd.* [1999] 11 C.L. 331. This reverses the earlier understanding in e.g. *Re Atlantic Computer Systems plc.* [1992] Ch. 505 C.A.

[435] *Selim* v. *Bickenhall Engineering Ltd.* [1981] 1 W.L.R. 1318 (caution to protect preliminary application for permission to forfeit valid).

[436] L.P.A. 1925 s.146(9).

[437] s.146(9)(e).

[438] An archetypal case (giving ample scope for display of Lord Denning's jingoism) is *Bathurst* v. *Fine* [1974] 1 W.L.R. 905 C.A. (American tenant banned from re-entry); (1974) 90 L.Q.R. 441; *Hockley Engineering Co. Ltd.* v. *V. & P. Midlands Ltd.* [1993] 1 E.G.L.R. 76, Judge Micklem (para.(e) not applied on the facts).

[439] *Van Haarlam* v. *Kasner* [1992] 2 E.G.L.R. 59, Harman J.

[440] *Davenport* v. *Smith* [1921] 2 Ch. 270, Astbury J. (conveyance of reversion subject to and with benefit of lease).

[441] *Re Blue Jeans Sales Ltd.* [1979] 1 W.L.R. 362, Oliver J.; *Re Brompton Securities Ltd. (No.2)* [1988] 3 All E.R. 677, Vinelott J.

[442] *General Share and Trust Co. Ltd.* v. *Wetley Brick Pottery Co. Ltd.* (1882) 20 Ch.D. 260 C.A. The year probably runs from the date of an adjudication in bankruptcy.

[443] *Exchange Travel AgencyLtd.* v. *Triton Property Trust Ltd.* [1991] 2 E.G.L.R. 50; D. Brown [1991] *Conv.* 465; *Barclays Bank plc.* v. *Prudential Assurance Co. Ltd.* [1998] 1 E.G.L.R. 44 Ch.D.

[444] *Pearson* v. *Gee* [1934] A.C. 272 H.L. (despite delay in hearing).

[445] L.P.A. 1925 s.146(10); *Re Brompton Securities Ltd. (No.2)* [1988] 3 All E.R. 677, Vinelott J.

[446] [1985] Ch. 157 C.A. The case was cited to the H.L. in *Billson* but its current status is hard to judge.

not become aware of the forfeiture until it received a company search in July 1981, at which stage it refused to accept further rent, and served a section 146 notice. Relief for the tenant was no longer possible because more than a year had elapsed since the liquidation. The statutory provision for relief was exhaustive and precluded any equitable jurisdiction. It is essential therefore for a liquidator to seek relief immediately the liquidation gets under way, without waiting for the landlord to initiate a forfeiture.[447]

3. Insolvency: derivative interests and sureties.

Relief is available to sub-tenants and lenders[448] following insolvency irrespective of the circumstances, and continues even one year after the insolvency.[449] Sureties are not relieved by forfeiture of the lease: the whole object of taking sureties is to protect the landlord against the insolvency of the tenant, so that liability survives the forfeiture that occurs on bankruptcy or liquidation.[450]

4. Denial of the landlord's title

Landlords may not deny the validity of the lease,[451] but an even greater restriction placed on tenants is the rule that they may not deny that their landlord is owner of the property without risking a forfeiture,[452] and one that is automatic.[453] *W.G. Clark (Properties) Ltd.* v. *Dupre Properties Ltd.*[454] shows this to resemble a unilateral repudiation by the tenant, which the landlord is free to accept or reject. Coke mentioned that forfeiture arose by (1) sale, (2) claiming a greater title than the lease, or (3) affirming the title of a stranger to the reversion.[455] This appears to be a curious relic of the old feudal law of fealty by which a tenant owed a personal obligation of loyalty to his lord. This is now redundant as it refers to freehold land, and, since there was no case affecting a leasehold estate for 345 years after 1590 it appeared to have become obsolete. Its revival in 1935[456] creates a most inconvenient feudal relic.[457] Hence the restrictive decision in *Warner* v. *Sampson*[458] that a general denial in pleadings in litigation did not involve setting up an adverse title, and is insufficient to work a forfeiture. Similarly disclaimer of part is not a forfeiture of the whole.[459] There are a number of circumstances that end the estoppel, leaving the tenant free to question the superior title.[460]

---

[447] On the facts, the head lease by itself was valueless. For follow on see *Hammersmith & Fulham L.B.C.* v. *Tops Shop Centres Ltd.* [1989] 2 All E.R. 655, Warner J.

[448] L.P.A. 1925 s.146(4).

[449] L.P. (Amendment) A. 1929 s.1 disapplies L.P.A. 1925 s.146 subss.(8)-(10).

[450] See above pp. 780–781.

[451] *E.H. Lewis & Son Ltd.* v. *Morelli* (1949) 65 T.L.R. 56 C.A.; (1949) 65 *L.Q.R.* 293.

[452] Woodfall 17.302–17.312.

[453] L.P.A. 1925 s.146 does not apply: *Warner* v. *Sampson* [1958] 1 Q.B. 404, 424-425, Ashworth J. at first instance; query this opinion.

[454] [1991] 2 E.G.L.R. 59 Ch.D.; J.E. Martin [1993] *Conv.* 296.

[455] Coke on *Littleton* ii, 251b; this was cited at [1959] 1 Q.B. 297, 315, Lord Denning M.R.

[456] *Pelham's case* (1590) 1 Co.Rep. 14b, 76 E.R. 31; *Kisch* v. *Hawes Brothers Ltd.* [1935] Ch. 102, Farwell J.

[457] *Warner* v. *Sampson* [1959] 1 Q.B. 297, 315–316, Lord Denning M.R.

[458] [1959] 1 Q.B. 297 C.A.; H.W.R. Wade [1959] *C.L.J.* 47; P.V. Baker (1959) 75 *L.Q.R.* 310; the C.A. reversed *Kisch* v. *Hawes Brothers Ltd.* [1935] Ch. 102 and Ashworth J.'s decision at [1958] 1 Q.B. 404.

[459] *G.M.S. Syndicate Ltd.* v. *Gary Elliott Ltd.* [1982] Ch. 1, Nourse J.; *W.G. Clark (Properties) Ltd.* v. *Dupre Properties Ltd.* [1991] 2 E.G.L.R. 59, 62K-L; doubting *Doe d. Phipps* v. *Gower* (1837) 1 Jur. 794.

[460] C.J.W. Allen (1968) 32 *Conv. (N.S.)* 249.

There is, apparently, no power to allow relief from a forfeiture arising on the basis of denial of the landlord's title.[461]

P. FORFEITURE PROCEDURE

Forfeiture, like most other actions affecting land, is hardly affected by the Woolf reforms.[462]

1. High Court

Proceedings in the High Court must be commenced in the local District Registry for the district where the property is situated.[463] It may be appropriate to use the High Court because of the financial value of the land, the complexity of the facts, or the importance of the case to the public.[464] Most forfeitures are pursued at common law in the Queen's Bench Division. Action is taken in trespass. Forfeiture is the process of repossessing land because the tenant has broken the terms on which he holds the land, the lease being ended by the breach of covenant, and the landlord asserts that the former tenant remains in occupation as a trespasser.[465] Expedited procedures used against squatters are not apposite against a tenant who entered as a lawful occupier,[466] so full proceedings are essential. However, an equitable claim in the Chancery Division is also permissible.[467]

Actions for recovery of land fall within the alternative procedure of Part 8.[468] The landlord is described as the "claimant" (as opposed to a plaintiff), though the tenant continues to be described as a defendant.[469] In the High Court, forfeitures[470] are commenced using the standard. Part 8 claim form (Form N208),[471] stating that the landlord wishes to re-enter for the breach of a term of the lease.[472] It is usual to include particulars of claim, verified by a statement of truth, in which case the claimant may rely on the matters set out in evidence.[473]

2. County court

Proceedings brought in a county court must be commenced in the local court for the district where the property is situated.[474] Action at common law is most common, though an equitable claim is permissible provided that it is within the equity jurisdic-

---

[461] According to *Warner* v. *Sampson* [1958] 1 Q.B. 404, 424–425, Ashworth J. at first instance, but query Ashworth J.'s view.

[462] Simmons & Simmons [1999] 7 *Comm. L.J.* 5; J.E. Adams [1999] *Conv.* 459; S. Thompson-Copsey [1999] 13 *Comm. Leases* 205; D. Cox & M. Davies [1999] 44 *E.G.* 140.

[463] C.P.R. sch.1 R.S.C. Order 97; S. Hasan [1999] 43 *L.S.G.* 36.

[464] C.P.R. 30.2.

[465] *Commissioners for Work* v. *Hull* [1922] 1 K.B. 205.

[466] C.P.R. sch.1 R.S.C. Order 113.

[467] Supreme Court Act 1981 sch.1 para.1.

[468] C.P.R. 8.1(2); P.D. 8.1.4(5).

[469] C.P.R. 2.3.

[470] P.D. 8.A.

[471] P.D. 4 Table 1; P.D. 8.2.2.

[472] C.P.R. 8.2; any representative capacity must be stated.

[473] C.P.R. 8.5(7).

[474] C.P.R. sch.2 C.C.R. Order 4 r.3; P.D. 8B.B.7.

tion of a county court[475]; the claim form should be marked "Chancery business". Procedure follows Part 8, but in a modified form laid down by a Practice Direction.[476] The claim form uses the old form of summons (Form N6), which is retained at this stage of the Woolf Reforms.[477] The form has a jurat (as in a pre-Woolf affidavit) so a statement of truth is not required in addition.[478]

3. Particulars of claim

These should be served with the claim form and in forfeiture cases are usually incorporated within it. County court repossessions have always required extensive particulars, and it seems that these are now also mandatory in the High Court. Particulars required when forfeiting commercial premises [479] are:

(1) identification of the land;

(2) proof of the landlord's title, such as office copies of a registered title;

(3) a statement that no dwelling-house is included—extra particulars are required where one is; [480]

(4) details of any agreement or tenancy under which the land was held—stating when it commenced and the amount of rent or licence fee payable;

(5) the daily rate at which rent is in arrear is to be calculated where forfeiture is for non-payment of rent in a county court; and

(6) the statutory or other ground on which possession is claimed.

Any written evidence to be used by the claimant should be served with the claim form, to obviate the need to obtain permission from the court to make use of additional evidence.[481]

Holders of derivative interests have the right to be joined in order to claim relief, as explained below, and particulars of the names and addresses of any known to the claimant must be included in the particulars.[482]

Claims are usually served by the court by first class post whereas subsequent documents can be served between the solicitors to the parties. Alternative procedures may have to be followed where the land is vacant.[483]

4. Defence

Procedure in forfeiture actions is characterised by applications by the tenant for relief from the forfeiture. The tenant should file an acknowledgement of service within 14 days of the service of proceedings, with a copy for the claimant and any other party.[484] Form PF 210 may be used, but an informal letter also suffices. An acknowledgement is

---

[475] County Courts Act 1984 s.23.

[476] P.D. 8B.B.

[477] P.D. 4 Table 3; P.D. 8B Table 3; other forms are: N11 (reply form), N.27 (judgment for forfeiture).

[478] C.P.R. 22.1.6 (inserted by update 7); S. Gerlis [1999] 34 L.S.G. 38.

[479] C.P.R. sch.2 C.C.R. Order 6 r.3; P.D. 8B.B.4; A. Myers [1999] 12 E.G. 160.

[480] C.P.R. sch.2 C.C.R. Order 6 r.3(3).

[481] C.P.R. 8.5.1. Oral evidence is in the discretion of the court.

[482] See below pp. 835–836.

[483] See above p. 594.

[484] C.P.R. 8.3; P.D. 8.3.

essential if the defendant wishes to contest the claim, to take part in the subsequent court hearing, and to have the right to put in evidence. It can also to be used to challenge the court's jurisdiction or the use of Part 8.[485] A date for a hearing will be set either when the acknowledgement is filed or when the time for an acknowledgement has passed.[486]

Strictly speaking a defendant to Part 8 proceedings does not need to serve a defence, and does not risk a default judgment by failing to do so. A knock-on effect is the disapplication of the provisions for obtaining judgment in default of a defence,[487] though this scarcely matters since it is possible for either party (including under Woolf the defendant) to apply for summary judgment where there is no reasonable prospect of success of a claim or a defence.[488] Landlords will not usually obtain a summary judgment for possession since it would be a rare case where the tenant could not at least argue the case for relief.[489]

However this is largely hypothetical since almost all tenants wish to claim relief, and a defence is an appropriate way to make this application. Commercial forfeitures are often contested bitterly. Most tenants wish to avoid repossession, and it is open to the defendant to file a defence.[490] All joint tenants must apply.[491] However, in *Bassett Road H.A.* v. *Gough*[492] it was apparently held that a single beneficial co-owner could apply as a person interested in the lease (in the same way as a sub-tenant or secured lender). A common method of defence is to issue a counterclaim for relief, but while the claim remains under Part 8[493] this requires court permission.[494] Relief could also be granted on an informal basis at trial.[495]

5. Separate claims for relief

It is open to the tenant to make a claim to relief from forfeiture where a landlord has taken repossession proceedings.[496] Pre-Woolf this was treated as an equitable counterclaim inextricably linked up with the claim to forfeiture,[497] and no doubt it still is. A separate claim is essential after a peaceable re-entry.

---

[485] C.P.R. 8.1–8.5; P.D. 8.5.3; C.P.R. 8.4; otherwise court permission is required P.D. 8.3.6; by written statement accompanying the acknowledgement P.D. 8.4.1–2.

[486] P.D. 8.4.1–2.

[487] C.P.R. 14.4–14.7; P.D. 8.3.5.

[488] C.P.R. 24.

[489] *Sambrin Investments Ltd.* v. *Tabourn* [1990] 1 E.G.L.R. 61, Peter Gibson J. (old R.S.C. Order 14; now C.P.R. 12; note the amendments by C.P.Am.R. 2000 r.6).

[490] C.P.R. 7.8.

[491] *T.M. Fairclough & Sons Ltd.* v. *Berliner* [1931] 1 Ch. 60; *Jacobs* v. *Chaudhuri* [1968] 2 Q.B. 470 C.A.; *Newman* v. *Keedwell* (1977) 35 P. & C.R. 393; *Lloyd* v. *Sadler* [1978] Q.B. 774 C.A.

[492] [1998] 2 C.L.Y. 3653.

[493] Transfer to Part 7 is a possibility: C.P.R. 8.1.

[494] C.P.R. 8.7.

[495] *Lam Kee Ying Sdn Bhd* v. *Lam She Tong* [1975] A.C. 247 P.C.

[496] *High Street Investments Ltd.* v. *Bellshare Property Investments Ltd.* [1996] 2 E.G.L.R. 40 C.A.

[497] *Morgan & Son Ltd.* v. *S. Martin Johnson & Co. Ltd.* [1949] 1 K.B. 107 C.A.; *Sambrin Investments Ltd.* v. *Taborn* [1990] 1 E.G.L.R. 61, 62L, Peter Gibson J.

6. Hearing date

After the filing of an acknowledgement of service or when the time for doing so expires,[498] the court fixes a date for a hearing—at least 21 days after service, which may be used for a final hearing of a case if no acknowledgement of service is filed by the defendant and there are no known third party claims to relief. However in most cases there will be an arguable claim for relief in play, in which case the hearing will be used to give case management directions,[499] and to lay out the timetable for procedural steps leading to a full hearing.[500] Forfeitures are allocated to the multi-track[501] and will therefore continue as conventional proceedings under an open-ended timetable with traditional costs based on the work done,[502] but an alternative is a switch to the fast track. It will be best to agree directions and to ask the District Judge to dispense with allocation questionnaire.[503] Repossession hearings in county courts are now private.

7. Terms for relief

The terms on which relief is granted have already been considered in this chapter; in a rent action, for example, the tenant is required to pay all arrears and costs within the time scale laid down for such payments. Arden J. held in *Inntrepreneur Pub Co. (C.P.C.) Ltd.* v. *Langton*[504] that the overriding principles of the Woolf reforms[505] have had no impact on the established principles on which relief was granted, the old discretion continuing to be exercised on well-settled principles. The court has wide powers to modify the terms of an order[506]; pre-Woolf procedure required a tenant to apply to be heard on a suspension application.[507]

8. Additional parties

Where the claimant knows of any persons entitled to claim relief as a sub-tenant or mortgage lender,[508] the particulars must name each such person, with an address, and extra copies of the claim bundle must be filed for service on each person named. In the *Parway* litigation[509] there were over 500 potential claimants, and so it was inevitable that some would be missed.

---

[498] P.D. 8.4.4; S. Hasan [1999] 43 *L.S.G.* 36.

[499] P.D. 8B.B.9.

[500] C.P.R. 3 (as amended by C.P.Am.R. 2000 r.3), 26–29, 30 (transfer between courts and tracks), 34–39 (stages leading up to trial).

[501] C.P.R. 8.9(c); S. Hasan [1999] 43 *L.S.G.* 36.

[502] *Mount Cook Land Ltd.* v. *Hartley* [2000] E.G.C.S. 08 Ch.D. (no costs after rejection of C.P.R. Part 36 offer).

[503] J. Frenkel [1999] 18 *L.S.G.* 36.

[504] [1999] 08 E.G. 169, Arden J.

[505] C.P.R. 1.3(6) (equality).

[506] *Starside Properties Ltd.* v. *Mustapha* [1974] 1 W.L.R. 816 C.A.

[507] *Fleet Mortgage & Investment Co. Ltd.* v. *Lower Maisonette 46 Eaton Place Ltd.* [1972] 1 W.L.R. 765.

[508] L.P.A. 1925 s.146(4); C.C.A. 1984 s.138(9C); C.P.R. sch.2 C.C.R. Order 6 r.3(2); for the old law see S.I. 1986/1187 r.2.

[509] *Official Custodian of Charities* v. *Mackey* [1985] Ch. 168, Scott J. This remedies a defect apparent from *Egerton* v. *Jones* [1939] 2 Q.B. 702 C.A. and *Abbey National B.S.* v. *Maybeech Ltd.* [1985] Ch. 190, Nicholls J.

Croydon (Unique) Ltd. v. *Wright* demonstrates that a possession order is voidable, and may be set aside, if a party entitled to relief was not notified of proceedings.[510] Any person interested in the lease (such as sub-tenants) may claim relief by applying to be added as parties[511] to the landlord's forfeiture action against the tenant, and relief is also possible by separate claim—for example if the landlord forfeits out of court or the sub-tenant becomes aware of the proceedings only after execution of a judgment for possession.

9. Dormant cases

It was previously common to issue the case and leave it dormant for several years, but all cases are now subject to active case management.[512] A stay will have been imposed automatically if proceedings begun before Woolf did not come before a judge within the first year, that is before April 26th 2000.[513]

Q. LAND REGISTRY PROCEDURE

Procedure in applications to reflect forfeitures on the land register has recently changed.[514] Where the leasehold title is registered, the application is to close the title[515]; otherwise it will be to delete a notice of the lease as a burden against the landlord's title.[516] Apart from the fee, it is necessary to lodge the lease and any sub-leases, the land certificates and consent of the landlord's lender.

Application is not allowed during forfeiture proceedings, but it is allowed at any time after actual re-entry under an order for possession. The registry will require a copy of the claim form and the order for possession, and also the sheriff's return or a statutory declaration proving actual re-entry. Peaceable re-entry must also be proved by a statutory declaration. All forfeitures are now treated alike, and it is no longer necessary to wait six months before deleting the lease after a forfeiture for arrears of rent. Proof will be required that peaceable re-entry has not been practised on an occupied dwelling and that the service charge provisions have been complied with.

The registry gives notice to anyone who seems to be interested in lease; after time allowed deal with the application. *Croydon (Unique) Ltd.* v. *Wright*[517] is just one example of many where land registry notification is the first a lender knows of a forfeiture, so an application for relief may well be provoked at this stage. An application for relief should be protected by caution as a pending land action, and if the title has already been closed, it will be necessary to apply for its revival. If the court orders the grant of a new lease in order to give relief to a sub-tenant or lender, a first registration will be required.

---

[510] [1999] 3 E.G.L.R. 28 C.A.; S. Hasan [1999] 40 *L.S.G.* 45.
[511] C.P.R. 19 (as amended by C.P.Am.R. 2000 sch.2).
[512] S. Hasan [1999] 43 *L.S.G.* 36.
[513] C.P.R. 51.2; P.D. 51.19; M. Walker [1999] 14 *L.S.G.* 32; S. Hasan [1999] 43 *L.S.G.* 36.
[514] O. Christopherson [1999] 37 *L.S.G.* 34, [1999] 39 *L.S.G.* 37.
[515] Form AP1 (closure of title—forfeiture). The landlord's title must be proved if it is not registered.
[516] Form CN1.
[517] [1999] 3 E.G.L.R. 28 189 C.A.; S. Hasan [1999] 40 *L.S.G.* 45; S. Murdoch [1999] 45 *E.G.* 178; this confirms *Bland* v. *Ingram Estates Ltd.* [1999] 2 E.G.L.R. 49 Ch.D.

INDEX